Literature Criticism from 1400 to 1800

Guide to Gale Literary Criticism Series

For criticism on	Consult these Gale series
Authors now living or who died after December 31, 1999	*CONTEMPORARY LITERARY CRITICISM (CLC)*
Authors who died between 1900 and 1999	*TWENTIETH-CENTURY LITERARY CRITICISM (TCLC)*
Authors who died between 1800 and 1899	*NINETEENTH-CENTURY LITERATURE CRITICISM (NCLC)*
Authors who died between 1400 and 1799	*LITERATURE CRITICISM FROM 1400 TO 1800 (LC)* *SHAKESPEAREAN CRITICISM (SC)*
Authors who died before 1400	*CLASSICAL AND MEDIEVAL LITERATURE CRITICISM (CMLC)*
Authors of books for children and young adults	*CHILDREN'S LITERATURE REVIEW (CLR)*
Dramatists	*DRAMA CRITICISM (DC)*
Poets	*POETRY CRITICISM (PC)*
Short story writers	*SHORT STORY CRITICISM (SSC)*
Black writers of the past two hundred years	*BLACK LITERATURE CRITICISM (BLC)* *BLACK LITERATURE CRITICISM SUPPLEMENT (BLCS)*
Hispanic writers of the late nineteenth and twentieth centuries	*HISPANIC LITERATURE CRITICISM (HLC)* *HISPANIC LITERATURE CRITICISM SUPPLEMENT (HLCS)*
Native North American writers and orators of the eighteenth, nineteenth, and twentieth centuries	*NATIVE NORTH AMERICAN LITERATURE (NNAL)*
Major authors from the Renaissance to the present	*WORLD LITERATURE CRITICISM, 1500 TO THE PRESENT (WLC)* *WORLD LITERATURE CRITICISM SUPPLEMENT (WLCS)*

ISSN 0740-2880

Volume 59

TOPICS VOLUME

Literature Criticism from 1400 to 1800

Critical Discussion of the Works
of Fifteenth-, Sixteenth-, Seventeenth-, and
Eighteenth-Century Novelists, Poets, Playwrights,
Philosophers, and Other Creative Writers

Lawrence J. Trudeau
Editor

GALE GROUP

Detroit
New York
San Francisco
London
Boston
Woodbridge, CT

Library of Congress Catalog Card Number 94-29718
ISBN 0-7876-3274-0
ISSN 0740-2880
Printed in the United States of America

10 9 8 7 6 5 4 3 2 1

Contents

Preface vii

Acknowledgments xi

Preface

Literature Criticism from 1400 to 1800 (LC) presents critical discussion of world literature from the fifteenth through the eighteenth centuries. The literature of this period is especially vital: the years 1400 to 1800 saw the rise of modern European drama, the birth of the novel and personal essay forms, the emergence of newspapers and periodicals, and major achievements in poetry and philosophy. LC provides valuable insight into the art, life, thought, and cultural transformations that took place during these centuries.

Scope of the Series

LC provides an introduction to the great poets, dramatists, novelists, essayists, and philosophers of the fifteenth through eighteenth centuries, and to the most significant interpretations of these authors' works. Because criticism of this literature spans nearly six hundred years, an overwhelming amount of scholarship confronts the student. LC organizes this material concisely and logically. Every attempt is made to reprint the most noteworthy, relevant, and educationally valuable essays available.

A separate Gale reference series, Shakespearean Criticism, is devoted exclusively to Shakespearean studies. Although properly belonging to the period covered in LC, William Shakespeare has inspired such a tremendous and ever-growing body of secondary material that a separate series was deemed essential.

Each entry in LC presents a representative selection of critical response to an author, a literary topic, or to a single important work of literature. Early commentary is offered to indicate initial responses, later selections document changes in literary reputations, and retrospective analyses provide the reader with modern views. The size of each author entry is a relative reflection of the scope of the criticism available in English. Every attempt has been made to identify and include the seminal essays on each author's work and to include recent commentary providing modern perspectives.

Volumes 1 through 12 of the series feature author entries arranged alphabetically by author. Volumes 13-47 of the series feature a thematic arrangement. Each volume includes an entry devoted to the general study of a specific literary or philosophical movement, writings surrounding important political and historical events, the philosophy and art associated with eras of cultural transformation, or the literature of specific social or ethnic groups. Each of these volumes also includes several author entries devoted to major representatives of the featured period, genre, or national literature. With volume 48, the series returns to a standard author approach, with occasional entries devoted to a single important work of world literature. One volume annually is devoted wholly to literary topics.

Organization of the Book

An LC entry consists of the following elements:

- The **Author Heading** cites the name under which the author most commonly wrote, followed by birth and death dates. Also located here are any name variations under which an author wrote, including transliterated forms for authors whose native languages use nonroman alphabets. If the author wrote consistently under a pseudonym, the pseudonym will be listed in the author heading and the author's actual name given in parenthesis on the first line of the biographical and critical information. Uncertain birth or death dates are indicated by question marks. Topic entries are preceded by a **Thematic Heading,** which simply states the subject of the entry. Single-work entries are preceded by the title of the work and its date of publication.

- The **Introduction** contains background information that introduces the reader to the author, work, or topic that is the subject of the entry.

- A **Portrait of the Author** is included when available.

- The list of **Principal Works** is ordered chronologically by date of first publication and lists the most important works by the author. The genre and publication date of each work is given. In the case of foreign authors whose works have been translated into English, the title and date (if available) of the first English-language edition is given in brackets following the original title. Unless otherwise indicated, dramas are dated by first performance, not first publication. Lists of **Representative Works** by different authors appear with topic entries.

- Reprinted **Criticism** is arranged chronologically in each entry to provide a useful perspective on changes in critical evaluation over time. The critic's name and the date of composition or publication of the critical work are given at the beginning of each piece of criticism. Unsigned criticism is preceded by the title of the source in which it appeared. All titles by the author featured in the text are printed in boldface type. Footnotes are reprinted at the end of each essay or excerpt. In the case of excerpted criticism, only those footnotes that pertain to the excerpted texts are included. Criticism in topic entries is arranged chronologically under a variety of subheadings to facilitate the study of different aspects of the topic.

- Critical essays are prefaced by brief **Annotations** explicating each piece.

- A complete **Bibliographical Citation** of the original essay or book precedes each piece of criticism.

- An annotated bibliography of **Further Reading** appears at the end of each entry and suggests resources for additional study. In some cases, significant essays for which the editors could not obtain reprint rights are included here. Boxed material following the further reading list provides references to other biographical and critical sources on the author in series published by Gale.

Cumulative Indexes

A **Cumulative Author Index** lists all of the authors that appear in a wide variety of reference sources published by the Gale Group, including *LC*. A complete list of these sources is found facing the first page of the Author Index. The index also includes birth and death dates and cross references between pseudonyms and actual names.

A **Cumulative Nationality Index** lists all authors featured in *LC* by nationality, followed by the number of the *LC* volume in which their entry appears.

A **Cumulative Topic Index** lists the literary themes and topics treated in the series as well as in *Nineteenth-Century Literature Criticism, Twentieth-Century Literary Criticism,* and the *Contemporary Literature Criticism* Yearbook, which was discontinued in 1998.

A **Cumulative Title Index** included in all volumes, with the exception of Topics volumes lists in alphabetical order all of the works discussed in the series. Each title listing includes the corresponding volume and page numbers where criticism may be located. Foreign-language titles that have been translated into English are followed by the titles of the translation— for example, *El ingenioso hidalgo Don Quixote de la Mancha* (*Don Quixote*). Page numbers following these translated titles refer to all pages on which any form of the titles, either foreign-language or translated, appear. Titles of novels, dramas, nonfiction books, and poetry, short story, or essay collections are printed in italics, while individual poems, short stories, and essays are printed in roman type within quotation marks.

Citing *Literature Criticism from 1400 to 1800*

When writing papers, students who quote directly from any volume in the Literary Criticism Series may use the following general format to footnote reprinted criticism. The first example pertains to material drawn from periodicals, the second to material reprinted from books.

Eileen Reeves, "Daniel 5 and the *Assayer*: Galileo Reads the Handwriting on the Wall, " *The Journal of Medieval and Renaissance Studies,* 21, no. 1 (Spring 1991): 1-27; reprinted in *Literature Criticism from 1400 to 1800,* vol. 45, ed. Jelena Krstovi and Marie Lazzari (Farmington Hills, Mich.: The Gale Group, 1999), 297-310.

Margaret Anne Doody, *A Natural Passion: A Study of the Novels of Samuel Richardson* (Oxford University Press, 1974), 17-22, 132-35; excerpted and reprinted in *Literature Criticism from 1400 to 1800,* vol. 46, ed. Jelena Krstovi and Marie Lazzari (Farmington Hills, Mich.: The Gale Group, 1999), 20-2.

Suggestions are Welcome

Readers who wish to suggest new features, topics, or authors to appear in future volumes, or who have other suggestions or comments are cordially invited to call, write, or fax the Managing Editor:

Managing Editor, Literary Criticism Series
The Gale Group
27500 Drake Road
Farmington Hills, MI 48331-3535
1-800-347-4253 (GALE)
Fax: 248-699-8054

Acknowledgments

The editors wish to thank the copyright holders of the excerpted criticism included in this volume and the permissions managers of many book and magazine publishing companies for assisting us in securing reproduction rights. We are also grateful to the staffs of the Detroit Public Library, the Library of Congress, the University of Detroit Mercy Library, Wayne State University Purdy/Kresge Library Complex, and the University of Michigan Libraries for making their resources available to us. Following is a list of the copyright holders who have granted us permission to reproduce material in this volume of *LC*. Every effort has been made to trace copyright, but if omissions have been made, please let us know.

COPYRIGHTED EXCERPTS IN *LC*, VOLUME 59, WERE REPRODUCED FROM THE FOLLOWING PERIODICALS:

Black American Literature Forum, v. 19, Summer, 1985. © 1985 Indiana State University. Reproduced by permission.—*ELH*, v. 23, 1968; v. 50,1983; v. 53, 1986; v. 60,1993; v. 61,1994; v. 66, 1999. © 1968 Johns Hopkins University Press. Reproduced by permission.—*Genre*, v. VII, June, 1974. Reproduced by permission.—*Journal of the History of Ideas*, v.22, April-June, 1961; v. 34, April-June, 1973. Copyright © Journal of the History of Ideas, Inc. Reprinted by permission.—*New Literary History*, v. 30, 1999. Copyright © 1999 by New Literary History, The University of Virginia. All rights reserved. Reproduced by permission. —*Shakespeare Quarterly*, v. 14, Autumn, 1963. © 1963 Folger Shakespeare Library. Reproduced by permission.

COPYRIGHTED EXCERPTS IN *LC*, VOLUME 59, WERE REPRODUCED FROM THE FOLLOWING BOOKS:

Barrell, John, and John Bull. From *The Penguin Book of English Pastoral Verse*. Edited by John Barrell and John Bull. Allen Lane, 1974. Copyright © John Barrell and John Bull 1974. All rights reserved. Reproduced by permission.—Bell, Bernard W. From "African-American Writers" in *American Literature 1764-1789: The Revolutionary Years*. Edited by Everett Emerson. The University of Wisconsin Press, 1977. Copyright © 1977 The Regents of the University of Wisconsin System. All rights reserved. Reproduced by permission.—Benito, Jesus, and Ana Manzanas. From "The (De-)Construction of the 'Other' in 'The Interesting Narrative of the Life of Olaudah Equiano" in *Black Imagination and the Middle Passage*. Edited by Maria Diedrich, Henry Louis Gates, Jr., and Carl Pedersen, Oxford University Press, 1999. Copyright © 1999 by Oxford University Press, Inc. Reproduced by permission.—Bowden, Martha F. From an introduction to *The Reform'd Coquet: Or Memoirs of Amoranda; Familiar Letters Betwixt a Gentleman and a Lady; and The Accomplish'd Rake: Or Modern Fine Gentleman*. By Mary Davys, edited by Martha F. Bowden. University of Kentucky Press, 1999. Copyright © 1999 by The University of Kentucky Press. All rights reserved. Reproduced by permission.—Cook, Elizabeth Heckendorn. From *Epistolary Bodies: Gender and Genre in the Eighteenth- Century Republic of Letters*. Stanford University press, 1996. Copyright © 1996 by the Board of Trustees of the LeLand Stanford Junior University.—Day, Robert Adams. From an introduction to *Olinda's Adventures: Or the Amours of a Young Lady*. By Anonymous. William Andrews Clark Memorial Library, University of California, Los Angeles, 1969. Reproduced by permission.—Dugaw, Dianne. From *Warrior Women and Popular Balladry, 1650-1850*. Cambridge University Press, 1989. © Cambridge University Press 1989. Reproduced by permission.—Empson, William. From *Some Versions of Pastoral*. Copyright © 1974 by New Directions Publishing Corp. Reprinted by permission of New Directions Publishing Corp.—Fabre, Genevieve. From "The Slave Ship Dance" in *Black Imagination and the Passage*. Edited by Maria Diedrich, Henry Louis Gates, Jr., and Carl Pedersen. Oxford University Press, 1999. Copyright © 1999 by Oxford University Press, Inc. All rights reserved. Reproduced by permission.—Fogarty, Ann. From "Looks That Kill: Violence and Representation in Aphra Behn's 'Oroonoko'" in *The Discourse of Slavery: Aphra Behn to Toni Morrison*. Edited by Carl Plasa and Betty J. Ring. Routledge, 1994. Collection © 1994 Carl Plasa and Betty J. Ring. All rights reserved. Reproduced by permission.—Frye, Northrop. From "Literature as Context: Milton's 'Lycidas'" in *20th Century Literary Criticism*. Edited by David Lodge. Longmans, 1972. Reproduced by permission.—Grieder, Josephine. From an introduction to *Letters from the Marchioness de M*** to the Count de R***. By Claude Prosper Jolyot de Crebillon. Garland Publishing, 1972. Introduction © 1972, by Garland Publishing, Inc. All rights reserved. Reproduced by permission.—Hillard, Stephen S. From *The Singularity of Thomas Nashe*. University of Nebraska Press, 1986. Copyright 1986 by the University of Nebraska Press. All rights reserved. Reproduced by permission.—Hodgart, M. J. C. From *The Ballads*. W. W. Norton & Company, Inc., 1962. Copyright © 1962 by M. J. C. Hod-

British Ephemeral Literature

INTRODUCTION

Ephemeral literature refers to published writing not intended to have any lasting significance; rather, such works were produced to address topical issues, narrow interests, or particular needs. British ephemeral literature comprises printed materials marketed primarily to less-educated readers, such as broadside ballads, chapbooks, abridged classics and legends, almanacs, jestbooks, and early versions of newspapers. These documents are studied today for their historical, social, and cultural interest. As records of "popular culture" from earlier periods, they provide invaluable insight into the lives and tastes of common English folk that may not be gleaned from works of "high" literary art.

During the Middle Ages the reproduction of books and other printed materials had been a time-consuming process of rewriting entire volumes by hand, page by page. Only the most valuable or useful texts, which were almost exclusively religious in nature, were copied. Few people could afford to buy books, and even fewer were literate. The introduction of the printing press in Britain in the 1470s had an enormous impact on the way people read. As printing became more common, the number of printed materials exploded. The concurrent increase in the availability of elementary education also began to create a more literate society. It is difficult to determine exactly what percentage of the population could read by the end of the fifteenth century, but certainly most English boys and some girls had at least a few years of schooling, and thus the majority of people were at least partially literate. Publishers soon began to produce and distribute reading material specially targeted to these members of society. Commoners, including rural peasants and urban laborers, who could not afford—or, indeed, understand—the leather-bound volumes of high culture, began purchasing for their entertainment cheaply produced and simply written works, including broadsheets with ballad lyrics, chapbooks, and small books containing, for example, bawdy jokes, prophesies, children's verse, and tales of heroic exploits. This ephemeral or "street" literature offers some of the greatest insights into the culture and mindset of middle- and lower-class English people in the sixteenth, seventeenth, and eighteenth centuries, insights that are not available in the works of gentleman-poets and landed nobility of the same period.

The first popular printed materials were broadsides. These were single-sheet printed documents issued in response to specific popular or newsworthy events or were otherwise designed for short-lived purposes. Broadsides could be handbills, royal proclamations, advertisements, and so forth, but they were most widely used to print songs or ballads. Early broadsides were printed in black letter print, so are often called black-letter broadsides. The broadside sheets, often adorned with wood engravings or woodcuts, were sold in stalls or by travelling peddlers or singer-sellers. People pasted the sheets on walls to learn the lyrics, and discarded or pasted over them when the song was familiar. The earliest broadsides of popular tunes appeared in the 1500s and covered a variety of subjects. There were bawdy ballads such as "The Babes in the Wood," those about female warriors such as "Mary Ambree," and hundreds of other songs dealing with every topic from love and courtship to political events. The broadside ballad gave expression, in simple and clear terms, to the everyday human experience of the lower and middle classes to whom it was mainly directed. However, it is also likely that it was not only the lower classes who were reading these texts, but the gentry and the literary-minded as well. William Shakespeare knew street ballads intimately, and in his plays seem to both delight in them and revel in denouncing their authors as hacks. In the late eighteenth century, however, the Romantic poets took an interest in the ballad form and transformed it into respectable, "high" art.

In the seventeenth century readers turned away from reading broadsides in favor of chapbooks. One of the reasons for the movement toward these longer, more complex works may have been that the proliferation of pamphlet literature during the English Civil War gave readers a taste for more substantial works. In terms of its physical characteristics, the chapbook was a single sheet of paper that was printed on both sides and then folded so as to make a book of twelve leaves or twenty-four pages. It often contained engravings or woodcuts and, like most ephemeral literature, was fragile and printed on paper of inferior quality. The derivation of the word "chapbook" is unclear. It may be a corruption of the word "cheap" or a derivation of the old English word "ceap," which means trade. These small books, which were also called "penny histories," were sold by peddlers, or chapmen, who traveled between towns with their wares. As with broadsides, chapbooks covered a wide array of subjects. There were tales of murder and intrigue, children's stories, fairy tales, folktales, medieval romances, and retellings of classics such as the Faust legend. Few chapbooks contained original material, and stories appeared in various permutations in different books. Some of the most popular chapbooks were those that told of the exploits of Guy of Warwick, a hero who displayed during his many adventures a particular brand of English virtue. Collections of songs and ballads in chapbooks were known as "garlands." Samuel Pepys, a devoted collector of ephemera of various sorts, collected a number of chapbooks, including many that were compilations of ballads. Chapbooks remained popular throughout the 1700s and continued to flourish into the next century.

The styles and types of British ephemeral literature are not limited to broadside ballads and chapbooks, although those seem to have been the two most popular forms between the early 1500s and 1800. Other examples of the many forms of popular ephemeral literature include the "Penny Dreadfuls," jestbooks, and popular books on religion. The Penny Dreadfuls were novelettes, short stories, and serial novels—again cheaply printed and usually read once and discarded by their readers—that featured gruesome stories, gallows tales, and adventures in foreign lands. There were special stories for women included in these books. Jestbooks were usually concerned with sex, music, and scatological jokes while small religious books often emphasized fear of death and the wrath of God. These and the many popular publications that are not generally examined by scholars of English literature offer the contemporary reader a glimpse into a world that looks much different from that portrayed by acknowledged "literary masters." As literary continue to widen the literary canon to include works of artists representing a greater range of human social and cultural experience, ephemeral literature will likely be examined in greater depth. Those scholars who have already begun to explore these texts point out that they can promote a better understanding of the development of English literature and that they offer insights into aesthetic values and beliefs held by common citizens.

REPRESENTATIVE WORKS

Anonymous
"The Babes in the Wood" (ballad) original date unknown

Anonymous
"Francis' New Jig" (song) 1595

Anonymous
Guy of Warwick (chapbook) date unknown

Anonymous
"Mary Ambree" (ballad) 1590?

Anonymous
Robyn Hood (chapbook) date unknown

Anonymous
Valentine and Orson (chapbook) date unknown

Robert Armin
A Nest of Ninnies (jestbook) 1608

Archee Armstrong
A Banquet of Jests (jestbook) 1633

Thomas Deloney
The Queenes visiting of the Campe at Tilsburie with her entertainment there (journalism) 1588

Robert Greene
Greene's Groats-worth of Wit (pamphlet) 1592

Richard Johnson
The Seven Champions of Christendom (chapbook) 1608

Thomas Nashe
Pierce Penniless His Supplication to the Devil (pamphlet) 1592

Samuel Pepys
The Diary of Samuel Pepys (diary) 1667
Penny Merriments (collection of chapbooks by various authors) date unknown

Thomas Percy
Reliques of Ancient Poetry (collection of ballads by various authors) 1765

George Wilkins and Thomas Dekker
Jests to Make You Merry (jestbook) 1607

OVERVIEWS AND GENERAL STUDIES

Hyder E. Rollins (essay date 1922)

SOURCE: Preface to *A Pepsyian Garland: Black Letter Broadside Ballads of the Years 1595-1639, Chiefly from the Collection of Samuel Pepys,* edited by Hyder E. Rollins, Cambridge University Press, 1922, pp. vii-xxiii.

[*In the following excerpt, Rollins explains that a great many sixteenth- and seventeenth-century broadsides, ballads, and jigs served not only as popular entertainments but as journalism and social commentary as well.*]

Perhaps the most important of all the treasures—apart from the inimitable *Diary*—in the library bequeathed by Samuel Pepys to Magdalene College, Cambridge, is his collection of broadside ballads. These were grouped loosely according to subject-matter and provided with title-pages and descriptive headings in Pepys's own hand before being bound into five large folio volumes. The first title-page runs:

> My Collection of Ballads. Vol. I. Begun by Mr Selden; Improv'd by ye addition of many Pieces elder thereto in Time; and the whole continued to the year 1700. When the Form, till then peculiar thereto, vizt. of the Black Letter with Picturs, seems (for cheapness sake) wholly laid aside, for that of the White Letter without Pictures.

Nearly every broadside in the first four volumes is printed in black-letter type, while in the fifth volume appear only broadsides in roman and italic type. Ballads of a comparatively early date—almost none later than 1640—are found in the first volume, those in the other volumes being, for the most part, printed during the years 1660-1700. It seems likely that the majority of the older ballads came from John Selden's collection. A careful study of the old numbering on the separate sheets and of Pepys's new pagination would no doubt partially reveal the extent of the Selden nucleus on which the collection was built.

A manuscript catalogue of the collection shows 1797 entries of first lines. This number, however, not only includes printed duplicates as well as manuscript ballads that Pepys copied but also fails to indicate when more than one ballad is printed on a single sheet. J. W. Ebsworth[1], after a painstaking examination of the collection, stated that it contains 1738 individual printed sheets, 67 of which are duplicates, and that of the 1671 distinct ballads in the five volumes 964 are unique.

No edition of Pepysian ballads has hitherto been published: for the present edition students are indebted to the good offices of Mr Stephen Gaselee and Mr O. F. Morshead, past and present Librarians of the Bibliotheca Pepysiana. The Ballad Society, founded by Dr Furnivall in 1868, announced its intention of printing the Pepys collection as an initial effort, but, failing to obtain the necessary authorization, turned instead to the huge collections in the British Museum. The Roxburghe and Bagford collections, have, as a result, long been accessible in the eleven volumes published by the Ballad Society under the titles of the *Roxburghe Ballads* (1871-1891) and the *Bagford Ballads* (1878). Among the eight volumes of these publications that appeared under his riotous, if learned, editorship, Ebsworth[2] estimated that he had reprinted, in one form or another, at least five hundred ballads that occur in Pepys's collection. From the collection, too, long before Ebsworth's time, distinguished students had drawn heavily. Bishop Percy made a thorough study of it before beginning the publication of his epoch-making *Reliques of Ancient English Poetry* (1765), in that work reproduced a number of Pepysian ballads, and had many others copied for him. These copies, by the way, are now preserved in the Percy Papers owned by the Harvard College Library. Others were reprinted by Thomas Evans and R. H. Evans in various editions of their *Old Ballads, Historical and Narrative* (1777-1810). Macaulay gleaned from the ballads some picturesque facts for his *History of England;* and within the last few years many other broadsides from the collection have been here and there reprinted[3], often in unexpected places. Many of Pepys's ballads, then, are accessible if one searches diligently. The bulk of the collection, however, is still generally unknown, and is likely to remain so until a trustworthy printed catalogue is published. Such a catalogue I hope to make some day. Meanwhile, this *Garland* reprints the most interesting seventeenth century ballads in Pepys's first volume, none of a later date

than 1639, and to them adds from other sources six or seven early ballads in which Pepys himself would have revelled.

Undeniably the golden age of the ballad, like the golden age of the theatre, ended with the outbreak of the Great Rebellion. During the Commonwealth period (1649-1659) ballad-singing was prohibited by law, and offending street singers were flogged out of the trade. To be sure, ballads continued to be printed, but in not so large numbers as in the years before 1642 and after 1660. For this decay repressive laws were but partly to blame: more important is the fact that the chief writers turned from ballads to chapbooks and news-pamphlets. Martin Parker, the greatest of them all, is known to have written many pamphlets but only five or six ballads after 1642, and with his death in 1652 the best part of balladry came to an end. Laurence Price, almost the last of the distinguished line of balladwriters that began in 1559 with William Elderton (or in 1512 with John Skelton), wrote for only a brief time after the Restoration. In authorship, in typography, and in subject-matter, Restoration ballads can seldom compare in interest with those of the reigns of the Tudors and early Stuarts.

It may be well to explain the use of the word *ballad.* Modern critics very often think of a ballad only as a traditional song that, like "Sir Patrick Spens," "Barbara Allen," or "Johnny Armstrong," has decided merits as poetry. This unhistoric restriction of the term to the English and Scottish "popular" ballads is a development of the nineteenth century. To quarrel with it would be out of place; but at least readers may be reminded that to Shakespeare, Jonson, Beaumont, Fletcher, Dryden, and Pepys the word *ballad* had in general one meaning only: namely, a song (usually written by a hack-poet) that was printed on a broadside and sold in the streets by professional singers. If "Johnny Armstrong," "Chevy Chase," or Sir Edward Dyer's "My Mind to Me a Kingdom Is" got into the hands of the John Trundles of London, it, too, became a ballad. Elizabethans and Jacobeans recognized no difference whatever in type between what are now called traditional (or popular) ballads and broadside (or stall) ballads: some of them no doubt thought "Chevy Chase" a better ballad than, say, "The Famous Rat-catcher" (No. 10). But, if so, they were judging each by its manner and matter, not discriminating between traditional and stall songs. In this book the word *ballad,* when otherwise unqualified, refers to the printed broadside type only.

To judge the ballad as poetry is altogether unfair. A few ballads, to be sure, do appear in *Tottel's Miscellany,* the *Paradise of Dainty Devises,* and the *Gorgeous Gallery of Gallant Inventions* without reeking of their humble origin; while the *Handfull of Pleasant Delights* (1584), which contains nothing but ballads, has been absurdly overpraised by critics (who, apparently, do not know that all of its songs had before collection been printed as broadside ballads) as "a work of considerable merit, containing some notable songs," or as "one of the most prized of the poetical book gems of the Elizabethan period," or as "lyric po-ems[4]." If such criticism of the *Handfull* were sound, an editor need have no fear in introducing the eighty ballads in this book as a very notable collection indeed of Elizabethan and Stuart lyrics. But sound it is not.

Ballads worthy to be called real poetry can almost be counted on the fingers of both hands. Among them might be placed the old ballad of "Love Will Find Out the Way," which Palgrave included in his *Golden Treasury* and which Thomas Hardy and Alfred Noyes quote with evident gusto; or "A Farewell to Love," from Thomas Deloney's *Garland of Good Will,* that is also included in the *Passionate Pilgrim* as the work of Shakespeare; or "Mary Ambree," a stirring song beloved by literary men from Ben Jonson to George Meredith; or, possibly, "The Babes in the Woods," so highly praised in Wordsworth's preface to the *Lyrical Ballads.*

From the point of view of sheer melody and rhythm, ballads often answer more than fairly to the test. It is a fact too often forgotten that, whatever their subject, ballads were written to be sung to certain definite and well-known tunes. Hence it often happens that the most doleful subject-matter is embodied in a measure that is decidedly musical and attractive. Cases in point are the refrains to the lugubrious ditty of Mrs Francis (No. 52) and the history of Jonah (No. 11). The matter and the diction of ballads are often contemptible while the measure is very good indeed. For this reason, or simply from the fact that a naïve news-story is told, ballads may at times pardonably be described as "remarkable" or "splendid" or even "delicious."

Ballads were not written for poetry. They were, in the main, the equivalent of modern newspapers, and it cannot well be denied that customarily they performed their function as creditably in verse as the average newspaper does in prose. Journalistic ballads outnumbered all other types. Others were sermons, or romances, or ditties of love and jealousy, of tricks and "jests," comparable to the ragtime, or music hall, songs of the present time. As such they may be beyond praise, however woefully lacking in high seriousness and criticism of life. The ballad has interest and value quite independent of its defects or its merits as poetry; and many of the most delightful and most valuable ballads are those which as poetry are worthless or even contemptible. Written for the common people by professional rhymesters—journalists of the earth earthy—ballads made no claims to poetry and art. They have always interested educated men, not as poems but as popular songs or as mirrors held up to the life of the people. In them are clearly reflected the lives and thoughts, the hopes and fears, the beliefs and amusements, of sixteenth and seventeenth century Englishmen. In them history becomes animated.

Shakespeare knew dozens of ballads by heart: he and his fellow-dramatists quote from ballads in nearly every play; and if occasionally they quote in ridicule, then their ridicule applies also to "John Dory," "George Aloe," "Little

Musgrave," and "Mussleborough Field,"—traditional ballads now enshrined in Professor Child's *English and Scottish Popular Ballads.* The great Elizabethans did not dream of judging ballads as poetry—though indisputably they enjoyed reading and singing them—and lost no opportunity of denouncing their authors. Ben Jonson, for example, flatly declared that "a poet should detest a ballad-maker," echoing Thomas Nashe's grave remark that if a man would "love good poets he must not countenance ballad-makers." The Parkers and Prices of balladry were butts of never-ceasing ridicule: their very names were odious to poets, though many of their ballads rang pleasingly on the ear, sounded trippingly on the tongue. Nothing else brings one so close to the mass of people for whom Shakespeare wrote as do these songs of the street. Produced solely for the common people, in them are presented topics often of real value and interest. It is doubtful if a more remarkable group of ballads has ever been brought together in one volume than those here reprinted; but he would be a bold man who should characterize them as poetry.

The *Pepysian Garland* contains eighty ballads. Seventy-three of them come from the Pepys collection, six from the Wood and Rawlinson collections at the Bodleian Library, and one from the Manchester Free Reference Library. The earliest is dated 1595, the latest (except for No. 26, which is included only to illustrate another ballad) 1639. For obvious reasons a chronological arrangement has been adopted, with the result that great variety of subjects greets the eye of a reader as he turns through the pages,—a variety characteristic of the wares offered daily in the streets of seventeenth century London. A ballad-monger, said Thomas Middleton, never lacked "a subject to write of: one hangs himself today, another drowns himself tomorrow, a sergeant, stabbed next day; here a pettifogger a' the pillory; a bawd in the cart's nose, and a pander in the tail; *hic mulier, haec vir,* fashions, fictions, felonies, fooleries;—a hundred havens has the ballad-monger to traffic at, and new ones still daily discovered[5]." Middleton's comment reads like a description of the *Pepysian Gerland!*

Among the eighty ballads are historical accounts, more or less trustworthy,—a few derived from news-books, others from actual observation,—of the assassination of Henry IV of France, the execution of Sir Walter Raleigh, the activities of three Northamptonshire witches against the Earl of Rutland, the fall of Oldenbarneveldt and of Sir Francis Michell, prodigies above Cork and the burning of that city in 1622, the Amboyna Massacre, the murder of Dr John Lamb, and a battle between the Dutch and Spanish fleets in 1639. Journalistic, too, are the "hanging ballads" and doleful "good-nights" of criminals who atoned for their crimes at the stake or on the gallows—illustrating a curiosity for news, often mistakenly called morbid, that is quite as eager to-day as then. As journalism some of these ballads are admirable.

Sermonizing ballads full of dire warnings and moralizing also have a place, and we are asked to shudder at a "passing bell" that tolled from heaven in 1582, at Caleb Shillock's prophecies for the year 1607, and at a prophecy of the Judgment Day found in France in 1618. In a curiously modern tone "The Goodfellow's Complaint" and "The Back's Complaint" present the woes attendant on drunkeness and plead for total abstinence; while for the edification of the unread other ballads paraphrase the Biblical account of Solomon's judgment and of Jonah.

A number deal with marvellous events or persons,—with the "admirable" teeth and stomach of Nicholas Wood, with a "monstrous strange" fish caught in Cheshire, with a sprightly "pig-faced gentlewoman" who was called Miss Tannakin Skinker, or with the too severely punished Lamenting Lady who bore 365 children at one burden. Fewer demands on one's credulity are made by the romances of Hero and Leander, of a conventionally cruel Western Knight and a Bristol maid, of a Wiltshire Cressid and a doting old dad. Pictures of manners and customs as valuable as those in the comedies of Dekker and Middleton,— coming as they do from another angle of observation,— are given in "Whipping Cheer," "The Rat-catcher," "A Banquet for Sovereign Husbands," and "Turner's Dish of Lenten Stuff." Satires of the foibles of the people abound. Lovers and their ladies are laughed at in "Ten Shillings for a Kiss," "A Proverb Old," and "The Wiving Age"; husbands are depicted as "He-Devils," wives as incorrigible scolds; and all trades and professions are held up to scorn for their dishonest actions. In contrast to these tirades, however, are a number of pleasing ballads written to glorify certain low trades and honest manual labour.

The most important single ballad in the volume is "Francis' New Jig" (No. 1), of the date 1595. This is apparently the only printed Elizabethan jig that has been preserved. Of hardly less interest is the "Country New Jig between Simon and Susan" (No. 21), and there are at least two other ballads (Nos. 29, 36; cf. also No. 38) that perhaps were jigs. A jig may be defined as a miniature comedy or farce, written in ballad-measure, which, at the end of a play, was sung and danced on the stage to ballad-tunes. Thanks to the mystifications of J. P. Collier[6] the jig has received scanty and inadequate treatment from historians of the English drama. A number of other genuine jigs are extant. First in importance is that preserved in MS. Rawlinson Poet. 185 under the title of "A proper new ballett, intituled Rowland's god-sonne. To the tune of *Loth to departe.*" There is a reference to this jig in the prologue to Nashe's play *Summer's Last Will,* and a two-part moralization was registered on April 28 and 29, 1592[7]. Almost as interesting is an unnamed jig preserved among the Henslowe papers at Dulwich College, which Collier misled scholars into believing to be a fragment of a play by Christopher Marlowe[8]. Still other jigs occur among the *Roxburghe Ballads*[9], in Robert Cox's drolls[10], and, from lost originals, in German translations[11].

By 1590 jigs were thoroughly established in London theatres as the usual conclusions to plays. In his *Pierce Penilesse* (1592) Thomas Nashe sneered at

the queint comedians of our time,
That when their Play is donne do fal to ryme[12];

and he threatened Gabriel Harvey that "Comedie vpon Comedie he shall haue, a Morall, a Historie, a Tragedie, or what hee will . . . with a Iigge at the latter ende in English Hexameters of *O neighbour Gabriell, and his wooing of Kate Cotton*[13]." Comparatively few jigs were registered at Stationers' Hall, all during the years 1591-1595. The reason for the small number lies, no doubt, in the unwillingness of the dramatic companies to have their jigs "staled" by the press: they protected the jigs in their repertory more successfully than their plays. Uncertainty about printers' rights to the copies caused the Clerk of the Stationers' Company to license, in December, 1591, two jigs with the proviso, so often met with in entries of plays, "so that they appertain not to any other[14]." But jigs did not die out in 1595; far from it.

On December 12, 1597, Philip Henslowe bought two jigs for the use of a company of actors, paying for the two six shillings and eight pence[15],—proof that jigs had received the approval of the box-office. In 1598, Ben Jonson tells us, jigs came "ordinarily after a play[16]." He loathed "the concupiscence of jigs and dances," and believed that they prevented audiences from appreciating plays[17]. "Your only jig-maker," Hamlet calls himself after he has carried on a vulgar dialogue with the bewildered Ophelia. As for Polonius, who is bored by the long tragic speech of the Player, Hamlet sarcastically remarks: "He's for a jig or a tale of bawdry, or he sleeps[18]."

Customarily when a play was finished and the epilogue spoken, the musicians struck up a tune and the comedians came dancing out for the jig. "I haue often seene," wrote Thomas Dekker in 1613, "after the finishing of some worthy Tragedy, or Catastrophe in the open Theaters, that the Sceane after the Epilogue hath beene more blacke (about a nasty bawdy Iigge) then the most horrid Sceane in the Play was[19]." There can be no doubt that some people went to the theatres to see the jig no less than the play. Says Thrift, in Thomas Goffe's *Careless Shepherdess*[20] (about 1620):

> I will hasten to the money Box,
> And take my shilling out again, for now
> I have considered that it is too much;
> I'le go to th' Bull, or Fortune, and there see
> A Play for two pense, with a Jig to boot.

A document of the highest importance,—not quoted, I believe, in any work on the drama,—that shows the attitude both of the common people and of the civil authorities towards jigs is printed in J. C. Jeaffreson's *Middlesex County Records* (II, 83). It is "An Order for suppressinge of Jigges att the ende of Playes" passed at the General Sessions of the Peace on October 1, 1612, which runs as follows:

> Whereas Complaynte have [*sic*] beene made at this last Generall Sessions that by reason of certayne lewde Jigges songes and daunces vsed and accustomed at the

play-house called the Fortune in Gouldinglane divers cutt-purses and other lewde and ill disposed persons in greate multitudes doe resorte thither at th' end of euerye playe many tymes causinge tumultes and outrages . . . Itt was hereuppon expresselye commaunded and ordered by the Justices of the said benche That all Actors of euerye playehouse within this cittye and liberties thereof and in the Countye of Middlesex that they and euerie of them utterlye abolishe all Jigges Rymes and Daunces after their playes And not to tollerate permitt or suffer anye of them to be used vpon payne of ymprisonment and puttinge downe and suppressinge of theire playes, And such further punishment to be inflicted upon them as their offences shall deserve . . .

As a result of this order, the comedian John Shank ceased "to sing his rhymes," as William Turner (cf. p. 35) phrased it: no doubt other jig-dancers suffered a like eclipse; but the effect of the order was temporary, and jigs continued to be sung regularly down to 1642.

At least two characters were required in all jigs for the sake of dialogue, and the number often, perhaps usually, was three or four. Jigs were never improvised: instead they were composed by professional ballad-writers or jig-makers, and were performed with fairly elaborate costumes and stage-properties. "Francis' New Jig" has rôles for two women, both of whom were at times masked, and for two men, whose costumes indicate which was the gentleman, which the farmer. Furthermore, the gentleman was provided with ten pounds in stage money and a ring to give his supposed mistress. One scene in "Rowland's Godson" is represented as taking place in an orchard, where the servant beats his master, who is disguised in a woman's clothes. One of Robert Cox's jigs required a bedroom set and a chest big enough to hold a man. Stage-directions, too, were as explicit as in the majority of plays and, with the action itself, show that jigs were written with the peculiar conventions of the Elizabethan stage in mind. Notice, for example, the principle of alternating scenes and the lapse of an entire night's time in "Francis' New Jig."

There is reason to believe that educated and ignorant people alike delighted in jigs. Good jig-makers invariably aimed at making their work "both witty to the wise, and pleasing to the ignorant[21]." That they succeeded the continual protests of the great dramatists show. Shortly before his death John Fletcher declared with some bitterness that a good play

> Meets oftentimes with the sweet commendation
> Of "Hang't!" "'tis scurvy": when for approbation
> A jig shall be clapt at, and every rhyme
> Prais'd and applauded by a clamorous chime.[22]

In jigs Elizabethan comedians won much of their fame. William Kemp, in particular, gained enormous popularity during the years 1591-1595 with his jigs of "The Broomman," "The Kitchen-Stuff Woman," "A Soldier, a Miser, and Sym the Clown," and the three parts of "Kemp's Jig[23]." That his reputation for jigs had not declined in 1599 is at-

tested by striking allusions to them in the satires of John Marston and Edward Guilpin[24]. Hardly less popular, perhaps, were Augustine Phillips—an actor in Shakespeare's plays—whose "Jig of the Slippers[25]" was licensed in May, 1595; George Attowell, who danced "Francis' New Jig" in 1595; John Shank, who is mentioned in "Turner's Dish" (No. 5); and, much later, Robert Cox.

Of the widespread influence of the jigs a bare mention must suffice. Through the visits of English comedians to the Continent after 1585, a lively imitation of English ballad-tunes and jigs grew up, especially in the Netherlands, Scandinavia, and Germany. A particularly notable result in Germany was the *Singspiele* of Jacob Ayrer and his successors[26]. In England itself, until the closing of the theatres by the Long Parliament, jigs lost none of their popularity. In 1633 Lupton wrote that "most commonly when the play is done, you shal haue a Iige or dance of all trads, they mean to put their legs to it, as well as their tongs[27]." After the severe anti-stage laws of 1642 and 1649, jigs continued to be performed regularly, though the term usually applied to them nowaday is *droll*. "The incomparable Robert Cox, who," as Francis Kirkman[28] wrote, "was not only the principal actor, but also the contriver and author of most of these farces," did not flatter himself on inventing a new type of amusement. He merely substituted jigs for the plays themselves; his performances were called jigs by some of his contemporaries[29]; and in several of them, like "Singing Simpkin," he merely revived old jigs that years before had been carried abroad by English comedians and that survive in Swedish, Dutch, and German versions far earlier than his own[30].

But by an extension of the drolls to include farces in prose as well as comic scenes cut from the plays of Shakespeare, Fletcher, and other playwrights, the jig may have been partially forgotten. After the Restoration, however, it was immediately revived. Typical early examples are "A Dialogue Betwixt Tom and Dick, The former a Countryman, The other a Citizen, Presented to his Excellency and the Council of State, at Drapers-Hall in London, March 28. 1660[31]," and Thomas Jordan's "The Cheaters Cheated. A Representation in four parts to be Sung by Nim, Filcher, Wat, and Moll, made for the Sheriffs of London[32]." Jigs and drolls long survived in the provincial towns after they had been displaced from the London theatres[33]; and possibly their influence can be traced in the farces with which plays even in the first half of the nineteenth century customarily ended. Certainly their influence is seen in the dances and dialogue songs[34] so common in Restoration plays. Few minor forms of literature have had so great an influence, and none has been so neglected by students.

The *Garland* introduces a number of ballad-writers who have for three centuries been forgotten, in spite of the belief they once must have shared with other members of their tribe that

> Who makes a ballad for an ale-house door
> Shall live in future times for evermore![35]

The most important of these old ballad-poets is undoubtedly Thomas Brewer. His ballad of the year 1605 on the Society of Porters, and another, dated 1609, on two monstrous births (cf. No. 2) clearly indicate that he flourished rather in 1605-10 than, as all writers interested in the history of the drama have said, in "1620?" The 1605 ballad is the earliest work of Brewer's yet brought to light. Interesting also is the signature of George Attowell, a well-known Elizabethan actor, though the authenticity of it is open to grave suspicion. William Turner, a figure who has mystified earlier commentators, is the author of No. 5, and is shown to have been actively writing ballads in 1613. Other new ballad-authors, about whom no biographical details are obtainable, are William Meash, T. Platte, Edward Culter, William Cooke, Thomas Dickerson, Ll. Morgan, and T.F.

Many well-known writers, too, are represented here by ballads that have not before been reprinted,—among them John Cart, Richard Climsal, and Robert Guy. Sixteen of the ballads are signed by Martin Parker, most of them new additions to his bibliography. Only one ballad by him now remains in the Pepys collection (I, 410) unreproduced: "The Married-womans Case. Or, Good Counsell to Mayds, to be carefull of hastie Marriage, by the example of other Married-women. To the tune of *The Married-mans Case.*" It was printed by H[enry]. G[osson]. and begins "You Maidens all, that are willing to wed," but almost the entire first column is torn away. Laurence Price is the author of five of the ballads, and one in the Pepys collection (I, 218) still remains to be reprinted: "Oh Gramercy Penny. To the tune of *Its better late thriue then neuer.*"

Notes

1. *Roxburghe Ballads,* VIII, 740.

2. *Roxburghe Ballads,* VIII, 740.

3. Noteworthy are the photographic reproductions in Professor C. H. Firth's six volume illustrated edition of Macaulay's *History.*

4. See a discussion of *A Handfull of Pleasant Delights* by the present writer in the *Journal of English and Germanic Philology,* January, 1919.

5. *The World Tost at Tennis,* 1620 (*Works,* ed. A. H. Bullen, VII, 154).

6. In his *New Facts Regarding the Life of Shakespeare* (1835), pp. 18-20, Collier gave an erroneous definition and a specimen jig from a spurious MS. that have deceived his followers. Fleay (*Biographical Chronicle of the English Drama,* II, 258), Furness (*New Variorum Hamlet,* I, 190), A. W. Ward (*History of English Dramatic Literature,* I, 454, 476), and others accept Collier's definition and his specimen as genuine. W. W. Greg (*Henslowe's Diary,* II, 189) says that "no undoubtedly genuine specimen [of a jig] is extant."

7. Andrew Clark's *Shirburn Ballads,* p. 354; *Herrig's Archiv,* 1904, CXIV, 326 ff.; R. B. McKerrow's *Nashe,* III, 235; Arber's *Transcript of the Stationers' Registers,* II, 609 f.

8. Collier's *Alleyn Papers,* pp. 8-11; G. F. Warner's *Catalogue of the MSS. and Muniments of Alleyn's College at Dulwich,* pp. 60 f.; A. Dyce's *Marlowe,* Appendix.

9. *E.g.* I, 125, 201, 249.

10. *Actaeon and Diana,* etc., 1656.

11. *E.g.* "Roland und Margareth, Ein Lied, von Englischen Comedianten albie gemacht" (F. M. Boehme's *Altdeutsches Liederbuch,* 1877, pp. 174 ff.), which appears to be a translation of the "gigge betwene Rowland and the Sexton" that was licensed on December 16, 1591.

12. R. B. McKerrow's *Nashe,* I, 244.

13. *Ibid.* III, 114.

14. Arber's *Transcript,* II, 600.

15. *Henslowe's Diary,* ed. W. W. Greg, I, 70, 82.

16. *Every Man out of His Humour,* II, i.

17. Induction to *Bartholomew Fair.*

18. *Hamlet,* III, ii, 132; II, ii, 522.

19. *A Strange Horse Race* (*Works,* ed. Grosart, III, 340). Cf. Edmund Gayton's *Pleasant Notes upon Don Quixot,* 1654, pp. 108, 187, 271-272.

20. 1654 ed., sig. B 4ᵛ (*Praeludium*).

21. *Hog Hath Lost His Pearl* (Dodsley-Hazlitt's *Old Plays,* XI, 435).

22. Prologue to *The Fair Maid of the Inn.*

23. Cf. Arber's *Transcript,* II, 297, 600, 669; III, 50.

24. Marston's *Works,* ed. A. H. Bullen, III, 372; Guilpin's *Skialethia,* Satire V.

25. Arber's *Transcript,* II, 298.

26. Cf. J. Bolte's *Die Singspiele der englischen Komoedianten und ihrer Nachfolger in Deutschland, Holland, und Skandinavien,* 1893, and a review by B. Hoenig in *Anzeiger für Deutsches Altertum,* XXII, 296-319.

27. *London and Country Carbonadoed,* p. 81.

28. Preface to *The Wits, or Sport upon Sport,* 1672.

29. Thus *Mercurius Democritus* for June 22-29, 1653, tells of how soldiers raided the Red Bull playhouse and arrested Cox who was performing "a modest and ha[r]mless jigge, calle[d] Swobber"—one of the drolls on which Kirkman lavished praise.

30. See especially Cox's own edition, *Actaeon and Diana,* etc., and cf. the work of Bolte previously cited.

31. Luttrell Collection, II, 63 (British Museum); *The Rump,* 1662, II, 188 ff.

32. Thomas Jordan's *A Royal Arbor of Loyal Poesie,* 1664, pp. 34-55.

33. At Norwich licenses were granted to players of drolls on October 21, 1671, and March 9, 1687 (Walter Rye, *Depositions taken before the Mayor and Aldermen of Norwich,* 1905, pp. 143, 180).

34. Many of them are printed with the music in *Wit and Mirth, or Pills to Purge Melancholy* (*e.g.* 1719 ed., I, 46, 91, 236).

35. *Parnassus Plays,* ed. Macray, p. 83.

Roger Thompson (essay date 1977)

SOURCE: Introduction to *Samuel Pepys' Penny Merriments, Being a Collection of Chapbooks, full of Histories, Jests, Magic, Amorous Tales of Courtship, Marriage and Infidelity, Accounts of Rogues and Fools, together with Comments on the Times,* edited by Roger Thompson, Columbia University Press, 1977, pp. 11-23.

[*In the following excerpt, Thompson argues that Samuel Pepys's collection of seventeenth-century ballads and chapbooks are invaluable aids to understanding the lives and tastes of ordinary English people of the period.*]

Two months before he died in 1703, Samuel Pepys made his will. Being childless, he left his treasured library of three thousand volumes to his nephew John Jackson, with the stipulation that on Jackson's death the books should go either to his old college, Magdalene, or to Trinity College, Cambridge. In 1724, therefore, the *Bibliotheca Pepysiana* came to Magdalene, to be housed in their glass-fronted cases in the finely proportioned first-floor room of the recent building to which Pepys himself had generously contributed.

Among the meticulously arranged and catalogued books, mostly bound in calf and sheepskin leather, are three squat volumes, which Pepys entitled *Penny Merriments.* Beside them is a similar volume of *Penny Godlinesses.* The *Merriments* contain 115 small books, later known as chapbooks. The pages usually measure only 8.5 × 14 cm—a few are even smaller—and books in the first two volumes are sixteen or twenty-four pages long, that is, printed from a single sheet. The third volume contains longer 'histories' and 'romances'. The majority of the chapbooks are printed in black-letter type on very cheap paper, and many are illustrated with crude woodcuts. . . .

These merriments are a vivid and invaluable source of popular culture for historians: a rare window on the minds of ordinary people. Such chapbooks formed a part of that ephemeral 'street literature' of the seventeenth century along with ballads, broadsides, almanacks, political propaganda and news-sheets. They cost a penny, or at most twopence, and were so cheaply and shoddily produced that very few have survived. The more popular titles were printed over and over again, possibly from the same typesetting; certainly the blocks for the crude woodcuts were re-used—sometimes with little or no reference to the text.

The poor quality of the printing and the number of typographical errors suggest that this task was relegated to prentice work. How large editions were is not known, but it is probable that it was a good deal higher than the normal 1,500 copies for more respectable literature. In 1683 it was said that 20,000 copies of William Russell's speech from the scaffold were run off as a broadside. This example of street literature may be a better guide.[1]

Pepys was an inveterate collector. And he had the three personal attributes of a collector: insatiable curiosity, wealth, and a strongly developed acquisitive urge. He gathered books for his library with care and discrimination for over forty years. His collection of ballads is the finest in the world. He also accumulated manuscripts, prints, maps, plans, frontispieces and music. Why he bothered with popular ephemera he never tells us. It could be that as the son of a poor tailor he felt an urge to keep in touch with his humble roots. Or he may like other contemporaries, Thomason, Rawlinson, Luttrell, Wood, for instance, have had the conscious intention of preserving examples of his own culture for later generations. Like John Selden, whose collection of ballads he acquired, he may have felt that 'Though some make slight of Libells; yet you may see by them how the wind sits. . . . More solid Things do not show the complexion of the Times so well as Ballads and Libells.' Their 'simplicity and nakedness of style' probably appealed to him, as it did to other bibliophiles. Or, again, he may have felt an urge similar to Boswell's in 1763, to gain 'a great acquaintance with the humours and traditions of the English common people'. The market for ballads was declining in the last quarter of the seventeenth century, and the broadsheets were being replaced by chapbooks. The *Penny Merriments* may therefore be a reflection of this change in popular taste.

The chapbooks which are, or can be, dated suggest that Pepys was an active collector in the decade of the 1680s, when he rose to the height of his influence as a naval administrator, and then fell after the Glorious Revolution. At this time the lucrative ballad and chapbook market was dominated by two groups of publishers, who jealously guarded their copyrights registered with the Stationers' Company. The Coles-Vere-Wright-Clarke-Thackeray-Passinger-Millet partnership traced its origins back to the 1620s, and specialised in old popular favourites in black-letter type. The other group, including Brooksby, Deacon, Dennisson, Back, Blare, Conyers and Kell, seems to have been less tightly organised, and to have ventured on some more topical material. The two centres of the London chapbook trade were around Pye Corner—the ballad warehouse—and London Bridge. Londoners bought their pennyworths from booksellers' stalls or from hawkers; provincial readers relied on travelling chapmen, who set out like Autolycus in the spring, or booths at country fairs. The publishers of chapbooks were not fly-by-night pedlars, but usually substantial citizens, freemen of the Stationers' Company, and on occasion its masters or wardens.[2]

What was the readership that these experienced and successful stationers aimed at? Though research on seventeenth-century literacy in England is incomplete, there seems little doubt that the ability at least to read was spreading widely down the classes. The enormous expansion of publishing would support this view, and remarks in prefaces of popular books corroborate it.[3] It seems improbable that the poorest classes, cottagers, day-labourers—the frequent butt of chapbook humour—or unskilled workers in the towns would have the time, ability or motivation to read chapbooks. Women—another popular quarry—were similarly probably less literate than men. The most likely audience is the middle classes: the lower echelons, tradesmen, artisans, journeymen, yeomen and substantial husbandmen, for simpler jests, histories, romances and rogueries, the better educated for the subtler humour, the garlands, the satire and the complements. The themes of such tales as Jack of Newbery, Dick Whittington or Aurelius would certainly appeal to the aspiring lower-middle classes, who would likewise identify with many of the characters in other stories. The prevailing tone of merriness and uncorseted ribaldry is again essentially that of the non-puritan bourgeoisie. A typical 'pill to purge melancholy' is 'Chaucer Junior's' *Canterbury Tales*. This 'Choice Banquet of delightful Tales' is dedicated to 'The Bakers, Smiths, Millers and other Readers'. Occasionally one finds a literary reference to chapbook readers; for instance, in Alexander Oldys's sophisticated *The Fair Extravagant* the hero wishes to write a note from a country inn, and calls for pen and paper. The hostess's paper is 'torn from *The Practice of Piety* or *The Famous History of Valentine and Orson*'.[4]

There is not space in this brief introduction to discuss the fascinating and complex question of the sources of these chapbook stories and jests. Many of the indigenous English myths and stories may well have been handed down orally, in their verse form, before they were first printed in the fifteenth, sixteenth and early seventeenth centuries. Other rich treasuries which were pilfered shamelessly by English hack writers were Italian *facetiae* and *novelle*, French *fabliaux* and Spanish and German rogue stories. Many of these, in turn, can be traced even farther back to Arabic origins.[5] Suffice it to say here that very few, if any, of the plots, situations, puns or jests are original to the editions selected here.

Most of the chapbooks were written anonymously. Writers were paid only about £2 for their work, and most of them were probably exploited denizens of Grub Street. Occasionally a popular author is cited, no doubt to boost sales. Thus we have Martin Parker and Lawrence Price, two of the most prolific and successful ballad writers of the early seventeenth century, and Thomas Deloney and Richard Johnson, equally famous as romanciers. Crompton, Crouch, Lanfier and Smithson were also well known to seventeenth-century readers of street literature. William Lilly and Richard Saunders were household words as astrologers and almanac writers. For the rest of the anonymous hacks, survival rather than fame was no doubt their prime consideration.[6] . . .

Hyder Rollins once wrote that after the *Diary*, Pepys' collection of broadside ballads was 'perhaps the greatest treasure in his library'. For the social historian, there is much justice in this apparently perverse relegation of fine and rare editions, important manuscripts and prints to scruffy ephemera of the streets. The great paradox of historical research is that we know most about the few at the peak of the social pyramid, least about the many. Intensive work on parish, county and legal records in recent years has produced many invaluable additions and revisions to our conceptions of 'the inarticulate' in pre-industrial England, but the very nature of the evidence used tends to preclude answers to important questions like 'What made ordinary people laugh?' 'What were their everyday worries?' 'What were their fantasies?' 'What were their popular prejudices?' 'What were their ambitions?' 'How did they organise their day-to-day lives?' 'How did they spend their leisure time? 'What were their ideals?'

Obviously literary evidence of any sort must be handled with great circumspection by historical researchers. Anyone who assumed that Restoration comedy accurately and completely reflected the life and thought of the upper classes in later Stuart England would receive a nasty shock if transported back three hundred years. Nonetheless, the insights into the minds and lives of ordinary people which judicious reading of the *Penny Merriments* affords, places them alongside the five volumes of ballads as veritable treasures of the Pepysian Library.

Notes

1. On this genre, see Leslie Shepard, *History of Street Literature* (1973); on printing, D. F. Mckenzie, 'Printers of the Mind: Some Notes on Bibliographical Theories and Printing-House Practices', *Studies in Bibliography,* XXII (1969), 1-76.

2. This paragraph paraphrases the brilliant bibliographical research of Cyprian Blagden: 'Notes on the Ballad Market in the second half of the Seventeenth Century', *Studies in Bibliography,* VI (1954) 161-180. A chapman is portrayed in Sec. III, *A Country Garland.*

3. Roger Schofield, 'Measurement of Literacy in Pre-industrial England' in Jack Goody, ed., *Literacy in Traditional Societies* (Cambridge, 1968) pp. 311-325; H. S. Bennett, *English Books and Readers 1600-1640* (Cambridge, 1970) pp. 84-85, 180-181.

4. London, 1682; Bunyan's youthful reading of this class of literature is well known.

5. John Wardroper, *Jest Upon Jest* (London, 1970) pp. 1-25; Gershon Legman, *The Horn Book* (New Hyde Park, 1964) *passim;* invaluable reference works are Katharine M. Briggs, *A Dictionary of Folk-Tales,* 4 vols. (London, 1970-1971), and E. C. Brewer, *Dictionary of Phrase and Fable.* See also my source-tracing in the forthcoming Check list in *The Library* (1976).

6. Bennett, *English Books,* p. 229.

BROADSIDE BALLADS

M. J. C. Hodgart (essay date 1962)

SOURCE: "The Ballads and Literature," in *The Ballads*, W. W. Norton and Company, 1962, pp. 140-50.

[*In the following excerpt, Hodgart examines how broadside ballads went from being considered "low art" in the seventeenth century to being a form that was embraced by British literary masters such as William Wordsworth and Samuel Taylor Coleridge by the end of the eighteenth century.*]

The ballads have taken a great deal from learned literature, and . . . many of them show the hand of skilled poets. Throughout Europe there has been a continual movement of *motifs* and forms from the poetry of the *élite* into folk tradition. But there has also been a movement in the opposite direction. The ballads have exerted an influence on learned literature during at least the last four centuries, and they have been important in the history of taste, and above all in the history of Romanticism.

They made their earliest impact on learned literature through the medium of the broadsides. The development of cheap printing at the beginning of the sixteenth century caused a revolution in popular taste. Poems were printed on folio sheets, sometimes in two quarto pages, with the title of a known tune to which they could be sung, and often with a rough wood-cut illustration. Publishers began to produce these sheets in the first decades of the sixteenth century, but it was not until after the middle of the century that they appeared in large numbers. Most of these poems, but not all, were narrative songs, and the majority were written in the quatrain of the traditional ballads. A certain number of the traditional ballads were printed in this way, but the great majority of the broadsides were original compositions. They represent a commercial exploitation of the popular taste for the traditional ballads, and they were the nearest thing that the Elizabethans had to a popular press. A great number are journalistic in subject and as sensationalist as our modern press. Unlike the traditional ballads they are not all anonymous: a few names of the writers have been kept, the most famous being Thomas Deloney (1543?-1600?), whom Nashe calls "the balleting silk-weaver". The printers issued the broadsides to wandering sellers who would sing them at fairs and then sell the sheets to the country people. The trade was evidently profitable and it expanded greatly at the end of the sixteenth century. Broadsides had to be registered, and the records of the Stationers' company show how popular they were.

Shakespeare gives the classic picture of the itinerant ballad seller in *A Winter's Tale*: up-to-date broadsides are part of Autolycus's wares:

> Here's one to a very doleful tune, how a usurer's wife was brought to bed of twenty money bags at a burden; and how she longed to eat adders' heads and toads carbonadoed.

Mopsa: Is it true, think you?

Autolycus: Very true, and but a month old."

And Autolycus has another one about "a fish that appeared upon the coast on Wednesday the fourscore of April". "Is it true too, think you?" "Five justices' hands at it, and witnesses more than my pack will hold."

There is a fine study of the broadsides by Sir Charles Firth,[1] who says: "Shakespeare was as familiar with the English ballads of his time as Burns was with the songs of Scotland", and he points out the large number of references to them in the plays. They show the outlook of the townsman, in that they are topical, and, like other bourgeois art, often indecent. Falstaff threatens Hal that he will have "ballads made on you all and sung to filthy tunes" (*I Henry IV*, II, 2) and Cleopatra tells Iras that if they are led in triumph "scald rhymers" will "ballad us out of tune". But sometimes the broadsides were moralist, and, as Firth says, "discharged the functions of the modern pulpit", or existing ballads were moralized. The topics of the journalistic ballads are much the same as those of the modern cheap press, public calamities, crises, scandals, and victories. Falstaff wants his capture of Colevile immortalized "in a particular ballad with my own picture on the top on't, Colevile kissing my foot" (*II Henry IV*, IV, 3). The surprises at the end of *A Winter's Tale* cause the comment: "Such a deed of wonder is broken out within this hour that the ballad makers cannot be able to express it." A fairly stiff censorship was imposed: for example, no ballad on the death of Essex was allowed until after the death of Elizabeth. The ballad makers were, however, loyal in their sentiments, though they occasionally expressed social criticism like discontent against landlords.

After journalistic subjects, the most popular were stories taken from the Bible (like the ballad referred to in Hamlet's "Jeptha, judge of Israel") and from the classics. One of the oldest ballads is about Troilus, and, as Firth says, there is "nothing absurd in supposing that Elizabethan artisans were familiar with the story of Pyramus". English history was used; the ballad makers ransacked Holinshed and other chroniclers, and they may have contributed details to Shakespeare's History Plays. But it is often difficult to say which came first in Elizabethan literature, the play or the ballad. For example, a ballad on Dr. Faustus antedated Marlowe by eight years, but Kyd's *Spanish Tragedy* was probably the source of the ballad with that title, as is the case with *King Lear*. Shakespeare used the ballads not only as material to work on, but also as a body of common knowledge to which he could make direct or indirect allusions in the certainty that his audience would get the point.

It can be seen that most of the broadsides were very different in origin and content from the traditional ballads. Some of them have great literary merit, showing a highly developed lyrical technique and even great imaginative force, as, for example, "Loving Mad Tom"[2]:

    The moon's my constant mistress
      And the lovely owl my marrow
      The flaming drake
      And the night crow, make
    Me music to my sorrow.

But they lack the peculiar virtues of the traditional ballads. They tell their stories, not with the dramatic compression of the latter, but in the more leisurely manner of the "vulgar ballads". "The Babes in the Wood", most famous of vulgar ballads, is the typical broadside, registered in 1595 as "The Norfolk Gentleman, his Will and Testament and how he committed the keeping of his children to his own brother, who delte most wickedly with them and how God plagued him for it".

It has been suggested that the journalistic broadsides caused a decline in the singing of the traditional ballads, especially in the south of England where the ballad sellers flooded the countryside with their sheets. Gerould attributes the predominance of Scottish versions to the fact that Scotland suffered less in this respect: "It is not a question of a finer development in Scotland than in England, but of an earlier decay in regions nearer London as a result of the infiltration of songs from Grub Street."[3] Modern collectors have, however, shown that many of the traditional ballads in fact survived in areas within the range of Grub Street, and the predominance of Scottish versions in Child comes rather from the fact that most of the early nineteenth-century collectors were Scottish. As for the suggestion that the broadsides brought about a decline in folksong generally, it is certainly possible that the printed sheets had a higher prestige than oral songs among the country people. The insistence on truth in the passages quoted above from *A Winter's Tale* may be significant, and so may Mopsa's other comment on the subject: "I love a ballad in print and life, for then we are sure they are true." But it would be wrong to make too much of this point, for many traditional ballads were, in fact, printed on early broadsides. Over fifty of Child's texts come from this source, including "Fair Margaret and Sweet William" (74 A), "Little Musgrave and Lady Barnard" (81 A), both of which are quoted in Beaumont and Fletcher's *Knight of the Burning Pestle,* and such typical supernatural ballads as "Riddles Wisely Expounded" (1 A), "The Elfin Knight" (2 A), and "The Twa Sisters" (10 A). And again, as I have suggested, the broadsides have had a profound influence on the oral transmission of certain traditional ballads, notably in stabilizing one of the versions of "Lord Thomas and Fair Elinor" (73 D). It would be truer to say that both types of ballad have gone on surviving side by side in the countryside, the journalistic broadsides perhaps more fashionable at the time but also more ephemeral, the traditional ballads despised by Mopsas but more enduring. The distinction between the typical broadside and the typical traditional ballad is an æsthetic one, and it is only quite recently that it has been made at all. Before the nineteenth century, people never spoke of the two types as in any way different.

The first sign of any literary appreciation of the ballads is Sir Philip Sidney's famous remark in his *Apology for Poetry,* presumably about some version of "Chevy Chase": "I never heard the old song of *Percy* and *Douglas* that I found not my heart mooved more than with a trumpet; and yet it is sung but by some blinde Crowder, with no rougher voyce, than rude style." Sidney was partly apologizing for his barbarity and partly asserting that "Chevy Chase" was good poetry because it instructed as well as delighted: it promoted the epic virtue of magnanimity, making it shine throughout all misty fearfulness and foggy desires. But Sidney's praise was exceptional; other Elizabethans speak scornfully of the ballads. Ben Jonson takes off the connoisseur of ballads in *Bartholomew Fair,* where Squire Cokes recalls "the ballads over the nursery chimney at home of my own pasting up".

Nevertheless, the ballads did play an important part in English literary life of the seventeenth century. They were all known by intellectuals and ploughmen alike. One of John Aubrey's anecdotes is about the poet, John Corbet, later a bishop, and a Doctor of Divinity at this time, going to Abingdon on a market day. "The ballad singer complayned, he had no custome, he could not put off his ballades. The Jolly Docter putts off his gowne, and putts on the ballad-singer's leathern-jacket, and being a handsome man, and had a full rare voice, he presently vended a great many, and had a great audience."

A few antiquarians or men of a curious spirit made collections of broadsides. The most famous is Pepys's, finished in 1703, which has over sixteen hundred, a thousand of them unique. Although the broadsides were despised, they became an accepted literary form for burlesque or mock heroic. Many ballads of this kind were produced by literary men of the eighteenth century, including Swift and Cowper; they are sometimes excellent in their own way, but have little in common with folk-literature.

The next major event in the history of ballad criticism, and perhaps the first sign of a genuine appreciation, is Addison's appraisal of "Chevy Chase". In 1711, he published two remarkable *Spectators*[4] on what he called "the favourite Ballad of the people of England". The theory underlying his criticism is not very different from that of Sidney's. According to neo-classical dogma, poetry must instruct and delight: epic poetry is the highest kind of literature because it gives instruction in the best kind of principles. "The greatest modern critics have laid it down as a rule, that an Heroic poem should be founded upon some important precept of Morality, adapted to the constitution of the country in which the Poet writes. *Homer* and *Virgil* have formed their plans in this view." Addison showed great originality and daring when he put "Chevy Chase" on the same plane as the Iliad and the neid. "The Poet before us has not only found out an Hero in his own country, but raises the reputation of it by several beautiful incidents." He quotes the heroic end of Earl Douglas:

    Who never spoke more words than these;
      Fight on my merry men all!
    For why, my life is at an end,
      Lord Percy sees my fall.

and compares it with the death of Turnus in the neid. He begins cautiously in the first article: "Earl Percy's Lamentation over his enemy is generous, beautiful and passionate; I must only caution the reader not to let the simplicity of the style, which one may well pardon in so old a poet, prejudice him against the greatness of the Thought." But he finally warms up to the point of praising the style itself: he compares its simplicity with the simplicity of the Ancients and says that it is not "Gothic", but truly classical. ("Gothic", he applies to what he calls the false wit of the Metaphysical poets.) "Homer, Virgil, or Milton, so far as the language of their poems is understood, will please a reader of plain commonsense, who could neither relish nor comprehend an epigram of Martial or a poem of Cowley. So, on the contrary, an ordinary song or ballad, that is the delight of the common people, cannot fail to please all such readers as are not unqualified for the entertainment by their affectation or ignorance: and the reason is plain, because the same paintings of nature which recommend it to the ordinary reader will appear beautiful to the most refined." Addison was indeed unconventional and far-sighted in these essays, and he was taken to task by his fellow neo-classics. In the first half of the eighteenth century it was fashionable to sneer at this eccentric quirk of taste on the part of an otherwise impeccable critic.

But under the surface of Augustan correctness, a true revolution in taste was beginning. Despite the dominant influence of Pope, writers and critics began to look for poetry that would be simple, sensuous, and passionate. The superiority of "nature" to "art" was not a new concept in eighteenth-century thought; a kind of primitivism had been part of the European climate of thought since the Renaissance. The belief that man was somehow better in a "natural" state can be traced back to Montaigne and was certainly widely held long before Rousseau elaborated his doctrine of the Noble Savage: it is expressed by Pope:

> Can that offend great Nature's God
>   Which Nature's self inspires?

At the beginning of the eighteenth century, primitivism became transferred to nature, in the sense of scenery; that, too, was somehow better in a natural state. This belief lay behind the gardens of Capability Brown and Kent, with their ha-has or invisible fences, their dead trees carefully planted in picturesque situations; even Pope's grotto was a rather contorted product of the "cult" of nature. As Lovejoy points out,[5] it was only a matter of time before this primitivism became extended from philosophy and gardening to literature; someone was bound to say that poetry, too, would be better if it were in a state of nature. Lovejoy gives Warton's poem, "The Enthusiast" (1740), as the first instance:

> What are the lays of artful Addison
>   Coldly correct, to Shakespeare's warblings wild.

But we have already seen a hint of the same doctrine in Addison's own criticism, though certainly not in his lays. Fantastic as it now seems, others besides Warton looked upon Shakespeare as the child of Nature, who had produced his warblings without the help of rules; and the new complex of feeling about nature had something to do with the growing appreciation of Shakespeare in the first half of the eighteenth century. Despite their outward adherence to correctness and neo-classical dogma in poetry, readers were becoming prepared to accept the ballads. A few collections were made in England and Scotland in the first decades of the eighteenth century: *A Collection of Old Ballads* (1724) consisted mainly of broadsides, but Allan Ramsay's *Evergreen* (1724) and *The Tea Table Miscellany* (1724-7) contained some folksongs. The Foulis brothers in Glasgow printed "Gill Nourrice", "Young Waters", and "Edom o Gordon" in 1755. Gray quotes the first of these in a letter to Mason (1757) and showed great critical acumen when he described it as beginning in the fifth act; that was the first attempt to judge ballads on their own grounds. The swing-over in taste had already begun when Percy produced his *Reliques of Ancient Poetry* in 1765, but that work did most to accelerate it. It caused more excitement all over Northern Europe than almost any other book of the period except MacPherson's *Ossian,* a bogus primitive epic which met much the same demands. Percy suffered a conflict between his impulse to reveal the poetry of nature and his anxiety about conforming with current good taste. He felt he could not leave in their crudity the poems from the seventeenth-century folio he had rescued from the house-maids, and so he tricked them out to meet the contemporary requirements of correctness. He added a few contemporary ballad versions sent to him from Scotland, some broadsides, and some mediæval verse. As scholarship, the collection is useless, and it is highly uneven in literary value; it is nevertheless a remarkable achievement.

Largely through the *Reliques,* the ballads influenced many of the poets of the middle eighteenth century. Dr. Johnson resisted to the end what he considered a deplorable deviation from neo-classical standards. In 1777, "he observed that a gentleman of eminence in literature had got into a bad style of poetry of late. . . . Boswell: That is owing his being much versant in Old English Poetry. Johnson: What is that to the purpose, Sir? If I say a man is drunk and you tell me it is owing to his taking much drink, the matter is not mended. No, Sir ——— has taken to an odd mode." (And he then produced his famous parody: "Hermit hoar, in solemn cell".)

Percy's *Reliques* caused an even greater stir in Germany than in England. The younger German writers were looking for poetry that would be natural rather than artificial, popular rather than aristocratic and national rather than cosmopolitan; there were strong political and social influences which made them ready to accept the *Reliques.* Percy's work stimulated them into searching their own folk-tradition. The first result was Bürger's "Lenore" (1773), a combination of a Low German folktale and of "Sweet William's Ghost" from Percy. Bürger presents the international theme of the Dead Rider, who carries off his love to the grave, with some very "Gothic" effects of gallows and coffins, and with some heavy moralizing. Though it is not very like folksong, it is extremely original. In the same year, Herder included a translation of Percy's "Edward" in his *Correspondence of Ossian:*

> Dein Schwert, wie ist's von Blut so rot?
> Edward, Edward!

He included a revised version of this in his *Volkslieder* (1778-9), which is a collection and translation of folksongs from many nations. Many of Goethe's earlier poems were written under the same stimulus; for example, "Erlkönig" (1782) owes something to Herder's translations of the Danish ballads.

The stimulus of Percy's *Reliques* came back from Germany to this country like a boomerang. In the 1790's, Walter Scott translated Bürger's "Lenore" (inaccurately), and Goethe's "Erlkönig", as well as some traditional German ballads. Scott's translations are poor poetry, but mark an important stage in the Romantic Revival. The Germans inspired Scott to collect and to adapt the traditional ballads of his own district, and to write his own poetry in the ballad style. Scott's *Minstrelsy of the Scottish Border* was published in 1802-3, and by that time, a number of collections had been issued, including David Herd's, Ritson's, and Johnson's *Scots Musical Museum* (to which Burns contributed). The ballads had won their status as serious poetry.

In 1798, appeared the most famous book of all to bear their name. Wordsworth, curiously enough, was less influenced by Percy's *Reliques* or the traditional ballads than by the broadsides. This embarrassing fact is proved by the way he quotes in his Preface a stanza from "The Babes in the Wood"; and elsewhere, his remarks on "Goody Blake and Harry Gill" show that he was thinking of the broadsides. They did not do Wordsworth any good but rather encouraged the naïveté of his worst poetry. Coleridge, on the other hand, learned a great deal from the traditional ballads. "The Rime of the Ancient Mariner" was professedly written in imitation of the style as well as the spirit of the elder poets, and Coleridge has taken over and transmuted the rhythm, diction, and atmosphere of the best supernatural ballads.

The ballads then became part of the heritage of the nineteenth-century poets, to be rediscovered and used by each generation in turn. After "The Ancient Mariner", the finest transformation of the ballad form into literature is "La Belle Dame Sans Merci". Matthew Arnold based "The Forsaken Merman" on a Danish ballad story, but not on ballad forms: the result is far removed from folksong. The Pre-Raphaelites' generation took the ballads for their own purposes: William Morris wrote an admirable pastiche called "Two Red Roses across the Moon", and less happily, Rossetti painted Clerk Saunders' portrait. Swinburne was also an enthusiast and came near to reproducing the "ballad note". It is possible that the ballads are now an exhausted vein, that the poets have no more to learn from them for the time being. Yet in the 1930's, one of the

"little reviews" which had a Surrealistic ambience was publishing modern American versions: and with their violent and shocking imagery they did not look out of place beside the last flarings of European Romanticism.

Notes

1. Sir C. H. Firth, "Ballads and Broadsides", *Shakespeare's England,* 1916, ch. xxiv; reprinted in *Essays Historical and Literary,* 1938, pp. 1-33.

2. "Loving Mad Tom", first found in Giles Earle, *Songbook,* 1615.

3. Gerould, *op. cit.,* pp. 243-4.

4. *The Spectator,* numbers 70 and 74.

5. A. O. Lovejoy, "The Discrimination of Romanticisms", *Publications of the Modern Language Society of America,* Vol. XXXIX, 2, June, 1924.

Diane Dugaw (essay date 1989)

SOURCE: "Prologue" and "The fashion for Female Warrior ballads: new 'hits' and old favorites, 1600-1650," in *Warrior Women and Popular Balladry, 1650-1850,* Cambridge University Press, 1989, pp. 1-14; 43-64.

[*In the following excerpts, Dugaw examines the popular appeal of* Mary Ambree, *an early seventeenth-century ballad about a transvestite warrior woman, a story that appeared in various manifestations in chapbooks for over two hundred years.*]

The Anglo-American Female Warrior is a high-mettled heroine of popular ballads who masquerades as a man and ventures off to war for love and for glory. Songs celebrating such women flourished as lower-class "hits" for over 200 years, reaching the zenith of their popularity in the eighteenth century. Indeed, the Female Warrior and masquerading heroines like her were an imaginative preoccupation of the early modern era, appearing not only in popular street ballads but in a host of other genres as well: epic, romance, biography, comedy, tragedy, opera, and ballad opera. But the popular ballad gives us this transvestite heroine in one of her most explicit forms, and in the only form which has carried her right up to our own time. Once a "hit-song" commonplace, the Anglo-American Female Warrior survives today—albeit marginally—in the folksong traditions of Britain and North America. This book will examine the Female Warrior of Anglo-American ballad tradition with particular attention to what she reveals to us about women, gender, and the makeup of heroism in that early modern era in which she flourished.[1]

Female Warrior ballads are success stories. Highly conventionalized, they sing of valiant "Nancys" and "Pollys" who defy oppressive parents, don men's clothing, sail the seas, and fight cruel wars. Inevitably their masquerading heroine—a model of bravery, beauty, and pluck—proves herself deserving in romance, able in war, and rewarded in both. The earliest such ballad in Anglo-American tradition is *Mary Ambree,* a London "hit-song" of about 1600 which remained popular to the 1800s.[2] . . .

Mary Ambree was a spectacular success. Indeed, the ballad remained in print more than two centuries beyond 1609. . . . In the context of my discussion here, the commercial career of the ballad *Mary Ambree* is instructive because it illustrates just how the motivic status and the tremendous popularity of the Female Warrior of balladry developed. To remain popular over a long period of time, a street-song must go through stages, its popularity in each stage won by its being marketed, purchased, sung, shared, and valued for reasons singular to that stage. These stages in a song's popularity can be identified as: (1) emergence as a "new hit" with topical resonance and immediacy; (2) continuing revival as a "golden oldie," a well-known standard whose familiarity keeps on selling; and (3) studied preservation as an "antique," that is, as a curious, moribund, and consequently valuable cultural heirloom.[3] Over the two-century career of the celebrated *Mary Ambree,* fans and publishers pushed this "brave bonny Lasse" and her ballad through all three of these phases of commercial popularity. This chapter and the next will follow the career of *The Valorous Acts of Mary Ambree,* reconstructing as they do the history of the Female Warrior motif in Anglo-American balladry . . .

As we have seen, *Mary Ambree* enjoyed "new hit" status early in the seventeenth century. Luxurio's remarks attest that anyone on a road to London in 1600 would immediately recognize the lines "When Captain couragious whom deeth could not daunt." *Mary Ambree* was the equivalent in her time of *Ain't She Sweet* in the 1920s, *Blowin' in the Wind* in the 1960s. Moreover, as theatrical references make clear, she was controversial. She represented issues that were obviously the focus of heated attention. At this first stage when a new song catches like a brushfire, it is often topical in just this way—controversial in content and perhaps novel in style and form. People notice it because it is new and different, and because it partakes of some pressing event or issue that is commanding their attention. Such was the case with this first Female Warrior.

Mary Ambree was not the only viraginous woman on the minds of Jacobean men and women. In the first decades of the seventeenth century the English at all levels formulated social and ethical controversies in terms of the mannish woman and the womanish man—*hic mulier* and *haec vir,* to quote Middleton's *World Tost at Tennis* (I, i, 32). This attention to dress, gender, and behavior gave *Mary Ambree* an immediacy, a topical resonance, that could only have boosted sales. The ballad both contributed to and partook of this charged preoccupation with dress, gender, and viraginous women. Its success, if noteworthy, is not altogether astonishing. Jacobean England was suddenly preoccupied with just such heroines as Mary Ambree.[4]

After this initial notoriety, *Mary Ambree* continued to flourish into the second stage of commercial popularity,

becoming in the commercial ballad repertoire a revival piece, in our parlance, a "golden oldie." The ballad's belated appearance in the Stationers' Company Register probably signals this second stage of commercial life.[5] By the time the ballad "partenours" registered *Mary Ambree* in 1629, the song had been on the streets for a good generation. It had clearly outlasted a single season. The ballad had moved from being a momentary triumph to being a revival piece—a secure, reliable, and ongoing "best-seller."

Only exceptional ballads reached this second stage of commercial popularity. Indeed, most popular songs are, even today, short-lived phenomena. The fact that both early female transvestite ballads, *Mary Ambree* and *The Merchant's Daughter of Bristol* continued to flourish as standard revival pieces attests to their continuing relevance and import. They were more than idiosyncratic, one-time-only moments in popular song history.[6] By contrast, most broadside songs—the majority of the Female Warrior ballads among them—were fugitive and ephemeral pieces, surfacing for a short time as "new hits" before being displaced on the street-corners by still newer ones.[7]

A ballad like *Mary Ambree* that endures past its season transcends the journalistic particulars that sparked its initial appearance—the immediate situation, issue, event, or moment of fancy which spawned it and to which it refers. As contemporary references make clear, Mary Ambree quickly came to signify a type of heroine. As we shall see, the Female Warrior ballad eventually became a type of song. This process of generalization has two parts. First, a piece—*Mary Ambree,* for example—continues to be revived among singers until its value lies more in its familiarity than in its novelty. It acquires for its audience a *history* of meaning and sentiment—a vertical or diachronic dimension, one might say. Then, there appear new pieces modeled on this ever more familiar old one. This part of the process adds meaning by the cross-referencing of songs one to another—a lateral or synchronic dimension. Thus, the old song in relation to its "progeny" becomes a type, a prefiguring idea. Certainly, the two processes of maintaining old models and imagining new permutations of them intersect. Indeed, new ballads cut from the cloth of old ones actually contribute by their imitation to the revival process. Thus, they reinforce the popularity of their well-known prototypes by assuring people that the "golden oldie" in addition to being a familiar old friend, still has relevance.

The ballad virago Mary Ambree was not alone for long. By the middle of the century when *The Valorous Acts . . . of Mary Ambree* still flourished, a handful of new songs about women donning soldier disguise appeared in print. A ballad of the 1640s, *The Valiant Commander, with his Resolute Lady,* sings—"To A New Northern Tune"—of a feisty loyalist woman who fought in the Civil War.[8] When her commander husband urges her to flee from besieged Chester to loyalist Shrewsbury, this cavalier heroine, amidst protestations of her love, replies stoutly:

> Put me on Mans attire,
>   give me a Souldiers Coat,

I'le make King Charles his foes,
  quickly to change their note.
Cock your match, prime your pan
  let piercing bullets flye,
I do not care a pin
  whether I live or dye.

The ballad then goes on to show her true to her word—quite in keeping with the "dangerous example" of Mary Ambree,

She took a Musquet then,
  and a sword by her side
In disguise like a man
  her valour so she try'd
And with her true-love she,
  march'd forth couragiously,
And made away with speed,
  quite through the Enemy.

Particularizing its story with journalistic dispassion, this ballad probably refers to actual events and persons.[9] *Mary Ambree* seems indeed to have posed an "example."

Soon after, in the 1650s, two Female Warrior ballads appear which likewise manifest a journalistic style. Moreover, they betray the beginnings of motivic coherence both in their textual borrowing and in their conscious heightening of the innuendo left more implicit in *Mary Ambree*. The Female Warrior was emerging as a single coherent idea. *The Famous Woman Drummer* and *The Gallant She-Souldier*—both commendatory but facetious—tell of a valiant, tough, and sturdy woman who accompanied her soldier to war, aggressively carrying out her masquerade as a man until "she was grown so big with child, which made her fellows wonder."[10] So alike are these two ballads, not only in their general narrative and thematic tenor but also in their details, that the author of one ballad probably took the text of the other as a model.[11] Behind both texts—as with *The Valiant Commander*—there seem to be actual persons and events. *The Gallant She-Souldier* ends with the following invitation:

All that are desirous to see the young souldier and his Mother, let them repair to the sign of the Black-Smith's Armes, in East Smithfield, neere unto Towerhill, in London, and inquire for Mr. Clarke, for that was the woman's name.

In these two ballads, *The Famous Woman Drummer* and *The Gallant She-Souldier,* we can observe the topical, journalistic impulse at work in broadside ballads, especially in those of the Cromwellian period. At the same time, however, we see joined to this journalistic topicality the emerging features of the Female Warrior as a type, as a conventional motif. These ballads accentuate the facticity of their stories—their immediacy and actuality, indeed, their particularity.[12] Nonetheless, even amidst the factual and purportedly idiosyncratic details of the Royalist "Wife" of *The Valiant Commander* or the "She-Souldier" mother of *The Famous Woman Drummer,* the outlines of the Female Warrior as a type of heroine and story begin to surface, especially when these ballads are seen next to each other. Thus, in all of them we recognize the conjunction of Love and Glory which shapes the woman's heroism and our appreciation of it. Then, we note in all a commendatory—if sometimes jocular—tone. And finally, we detect the regularizing of events and language in the stories, and even the interdependence of texts.

Ballad Female Warriors multiplied noticeably after the 1660 Restoration of Charles II to the throne and the loosening of restrictions on ballad publishing. At about this time, the publisher Thomas Vere, one of a later group of "ballad partenours," popularized *Constance and Anthony,* which tells of a woman disguised as a sailorboy whose story is conspicuously more sentimental and romantic than the journalistic ballads just discussed. The ballad's opening lines highlight its focus on love:

Of two constant Lovers as I understand,
Were born near Appleby in Westmoreland,
The Lads name Anthony, Constance the Lass,
To sea they went both and great dangers did pass.[13]

Then, a few stanzas later, the ballad summarizes its message:

O see what Love can do,
  at home she will not bide:
With her true Love she'll go,
  let weal or woe betide.

Thus, the ballad unfolds as a saga of true love under trial. "Drest in Mans array," Constance goes aboard ship with her sailor. In her disguise she serves as the ship's cook until a tempest hurls these "constant Lovers" literally into a sea of troubles: a shipwreck casts them into the ocean and separates them; rescued by a Spanish merchant, Constance becomes his serving-boy for two years; captured by English pirates, Anthony becomes a galley slave. Finally, the two lovers are united and freed in "Bilbo" at the conclusion of their romantic adventure.

These early Female Warrior ballads—*Mary Ambree, The Merchants Daughter of Bristol, The Valiant Commander, with His Resolute Lady, The Gallant She-Souldier, The Famous Woman Drummer,* and *Constance and Anthony*—appear at first glance to be more different than alike. Yet, closer scrutiny shows that, their disparities notwithstanding, these ballads do indeed evidence some of the interconnectedness that characterizes a coherent song tradition or type. First, all have thematic and narrative ingredients in common: the heroic conjunction of Love and Glory; the overturning of a threatened separation by the woman's masquerade; various tests of the heroine's love and soldiering; across the board commendation of her success in love and war. Then, there is textual correspondence, probably imitation, between *The Gallant She-Souldier* and Price's *The Famous Woman Drummer.* (As we shall see, a conscious reworking of old texts became quite common among makers of later Female Warrior ballads.) Finally, in addition to serving as textual models, earlier ballads began to supply the tunes for later ones—the tune to *The Valiant Commander, with His Resolute Lady,* for example, being used for *Constance and Anthony.* Thus one instance of the emerging type called to mind another. As more new Female Warrior ballads appeared in print, these connections from one ballad to another increased.

Meanwhile, the earliest of ballad Female Warriors, *Mary Ambree,* continued to turn a profit in the streetsong market. On 1 March 1674/5 inheritors of the ballad stock of Francis Coles—who had entered the ballad in 1629—re-registered it along with 196 other broadside and chapbook titles.[14] Then, in about 1680, these stationers went into a partnership with W. Thackeray of Duck-Lane who continued to print and reprint *Mary Ambree* through the period, listing it on a broadside catalogue of "small Books, Ballads and Histories" which he published around 1689.[15]

While *Mary Ambree* continued in print as a revival piece, the broadside presses of the 1690s turned out Female Warriors regularly.[16] Increasingly, these new ballads took the shape of a coherent and recognizable motif as heroines and stories more and more resembled each other. Songmakers formulated their new pieces, having in mind an imaginative model of the Female Warrior as a type. Moreover, texts of old ballads were reconstituted into new ones. And so, in the century's last decades more than twenty Female Warrior ballads appeared in print. In addition to the revival pieces, *Mary Ambree, The Merchants Daughter of Bristol* and *Constance and Anthony,* there were published *The Mariners Misfortune,*[17] *The Seamans Doleful Farwell,*[18] *The Valiant Virgin,*[19] *The Woman Warrier,*[20] *The Female Souldier,*[21] and *The Maiden Warrier,*[22] to name a handful of titles.

By the eighteenth century the increasingly popular subject of the Female Warrior took on the quiddity of a shaping formula. It became a regularized and coherent motif. The fascination that began with the notorious "Mary Ambree" and her "dangerous examples" was through the Georgian era a manifest preoccupation. Between 1700 and the middle of the nineteenth century some 100 new Female Warrior ballads came into print—most of them conspicuously predictable examples of an idea that had become commonplace and prototypical.

As new Female Warrior ballads multiplied, interest in *Mary Ambree* took a new turn, for the old ballad became the subject of antiquarian study. So began the third stage of its career in print: preservation as an "antique." In 1765, Thomas Percy published his *Reliques of Ancient English Poetry* which contained in its second volume a version of *Mary Ambree.*[23] Percy's three-volume work was a collection of archaic songs and romances—many of them distinctly "lowbrow"—which he claimed to have acquired from an old manuscript—"the greater part of them . . . extracted from an ancient folio manuscript in the editor's possession," as he says.[24] In truth, a significant number of the "reliques" probably came from outdated broadsides and chapbooks which Percy had purchased from the mid-

century mogul of printed street literature, Cluer Dicey.[25] In his remarks, Percy emphasized the antiquity of his ballads and romances, seeing in them "the infancy of genius," a progenitive stage in Britain's literature and history. A presumption of cultural progress is of course implicit in his nostalgia. Thus, he declares in his "Dedication":

> No active or comprehensive mind can forbear some attention to the reliques of antiquity. It is prompted by natural curiosity to survey the progress of life and manners, and to inquire by what gradations barbarity was civilized, grossness refined, and ignorance instructed.[26]

Nonetheless, at base there is a powerful admiration and an imaginative romanticizing as he presents to his polite readers

> the select remains of our ancient English bards and minstrels, an order of men, who were once greatly respected by our ancestors, and contributed to soften the roughness of a martial and unlettered people by their songs and by their music.[27]

Percy's *Reliques* became unquestionably one of the most influential and important books of the late eighteenth century. A harbinger of Romanticism, it marks the point at which an interest in antiquities and in the common people swept literary circles—an interest which has yet to subside.[28] Creating a sensation in the 1760s, Percy's *Reliques* soon went into a second, and then a third edition.[29] Clearly, upper-class readers of all kinds purchased Percy's studious three-volume collection and made fashionable the humble verses which he presented as ancient minstrelsy of the Middle Ages. Among such verses was *The Valorous Acts of Mary Ambree.* Looking for antiquities to celebrate and committed to the belief that he had found some, Percy began the "museum life" of *Mary Ambree.*

At the same time, even as the old ballad was making its appearance in *The Reliques,* whose audience was decidedly above that of the broadsides, eighteenth-century balladsingers continued to want copies of their old favorite, *Mary Ambree.* We find editions of the ballad published early in the century—about 1720—and at its halfway point.[30] Interestingly enough, however, by the middle of the century *Mary Ambree* seems to have acquired the status of an archaic piece even among the streetsong publishers—perhaps by way of their familiarity with upper-class antiquarians such as Percy.[31] Thus, the dominant broadside and chapbook publishers of Georgian England, William and Cluer Dicey, separated their stock in a catalogue of 1754 into new pieces and old, listing *Mary Ambree* and other similarly archaic revival pieces as "Old Ballads" as opposed to "New Sorts coming out daily."[32]

The Vocal Magazine, a monthly "miscellaneous Assemblage of Songs" from the 1770s, shows how Percy's appreciation of ballad antiques translated into the fashionable parlance of song buyers at the polite level. Published in 1778, this "Assemblage" includes—alongside opera pieces, pastoral lyrics, and playhouse songs—a sampling of antique songs, among which we find *Mary Ambree; An Old Ballad*. In describing the contents of this *Vocal Magazine,* the compiler proudly claims to have gathered together "all the English, Scotch, and Irish Songs, Catches, Glees, Cantatas, Airs, Ballads, &c. deemed any way worthy of being transmitted to Posterity."[33] As an antique, *Mary Ambree* was considered so "worthy." The introductory remarks characterize how the compiler—and presumably his audience—regarded such archaic pieces in the collection. They represent, he says,

> another Fund of which I shall avail myself, it's Produce being but little known to the generality of the Public; I mean, the Labours of those old Historians, who, like the famous *Grecian* Bard, though perhaps not quite so successfully, chaunted any memorable Transaction in the rude Poesy of their Times. For . . . I am fully persuaded some of them contain sufficient Beauties to render them well worthy a Place *among* the Productions of more enlightened Days.

(A2ᵛ)

The echoing of Percy in these remarks is unmistakable. Thus, a suddenly fashionable antique of "unenlightened Days," the long-sung *Mary Ambree* inhabited pages in a polite songbook such as *The Vocal Magazine*. There among playhouse and drawing-room songs of a manifestly more genteel provenance, the "Old Ballad" does indeed seem a curiosity.

By the late 1700s, the Female Warrior motif probably had its widest currency in English culture. Not only were Female Warrior ballads current on the streets as "new hits," "golden oldies," and even "antiques," but soldier heroines also appeared in more refined songs of this era that were routinely performed in the theatres and pleasure gardens—Covent Garden and Sadler's Wells, Vauxhall and Ranelagh.[34] Aristocrats and prosperous citizens would not hear from these garden stages the lowly street songs which the broadside publishers of the day busily produced for the lower-classes. Nor would anyone in that context have imagined performing so curious and antique a museum piece as *Mary Ambree*. Rather, writers of polite songs such as the popular Dibdins or James Wrighten wrote of sprightly female soldiers and sailors as stirring examples of love and patriotism.[35]

The Female Warrior thus flourished briefly as a polite fashion of the second half of the eighteenth century when, amidst wars and revolutions in America and France, a patriotic militancy swept the country. Sometime about 1790 Mrs. Wrighten was performing *The Female Captain,* a song written by her husband James Wrighten, prompter to the Theatres Royal of Drury Lane and the Haymarket. Dressed in uniform, she announced to her male listeners: "'Tis your king and your country now calls [*sic*] for your aid," and warns that, should they refuse, she will "the breeches assume."[36] Already in the middle of the century Peg Woffington had similarly delivered *The Female Volunteer: or, an Attempt to make our Men Stand,* an epilogue "intended to be Spoken by Mrs. Woffington in the Habit of

a Volunteer, upon reading the Gazette containing an Account of the late Action at Falkirk." A later stage song by the younger Charles Dibdin called *The Female Volunteer* presented its female singer as "a merry little wag in a scarlet frock" who coyly queried her audience: "When our gallant lads are obliged to roam / Why should women idly stay at home?"[37] With little or no narrative, these stage pieces evidence the widespread fashion for women in soldier regalia and for the image of the Female Warrior. Indeed, so generally popular was the figure of the masquerading Female Warrior in the eighteenth century that the Sadler's Wells Theatre included among its performers one of the many real-life Female Warriors of the day, Hannah Snell. This woman, who fought in the English army and navy under the name of "James Gray," regularly carried out military exercises in uniform as a part of the entertainments.[38] Such upper-class manifestations of the Female Warrior idea show just how widely familiar the heroine was by 1800, and how complex the texture of her popularity in English song traditions had become.

Meanwhile, all through the eighteenth century the lower classes continued their longstanding enthusiasm for the Female Warrior. Broadside publishers in London, the provinces—eventually even in Boston, Providence, and Philadelphia—rolled from their presses new disguise ballads that their songmakers modeled on prototypical "oldies": *The Bristol Bridegroom,*[39] *The Female Sea-Captain,*[40] *The Frolicsome Maid Who Went To Gibralter,*[41] *Jack Monroe,*[42] *The Sailor's Happy Marriage,*[43] *The Female Drummer,*[44] *The Female Tar,*[45] *The Female Champion,*[46] and a host of others. These new songs supplied the broadside- and chapbook-buying public with up-to-date permutations of the long-popular Female Warrior motif that had by then been appearing regularly in street balladry for over a century. Thus, by 1800 we see the Female Warrior idea flourishing in Anglo-American song culture in three ways: (1) The broadside printers continued to turn out Female Warrior ballads, both old and new. (2) A handful of polished and rather idiosyncratic stage songs with theatrical routines brought the Female Warrior as a novelty to a polite audience of playgoers. And (3) *Mary Ambree*—the most "golden oldie" of all the Female Warriors—had taken on a new guise: she had become a museum piece.

These many permutations of the Female Warrior show the textual complexity that a century and a half of commercial popularity had brought about. If there is no question that the Female Warrior was immensely—and primarily—popular among ballad-singing shoemakers and milkmaids, at the same time she was not unknown to their masters, employers, and Members of Parliament. Moreover, the lower-class ballads show themselves to be representatives of a single motif, a single imaginative idea as they take the shape, almost formulaically, of an over-arching thematic and narrative pattern.

The coherence of the Female Warrior ballads as a tradition is evident even at the surface as the trends evident by the middle of the seventeenth century continued. The tunes, for instance, often bespeak the interdependence and "cross-referencing" of ballads one to another. Later ballads set to the tunes of earlier ones include: *Constance and Anthony* to the tune used for *The Valiant Commander,*[47] *The Female Cabin Boy* to *The Female Drummer,*[48] *Young Henry of the Raging Main* to *William of the Royal Waggon Train,*[49] *William and Phillis* to *William and Harriet.*[50] Moreover, some ballads resemble each other so much that one text must have served as the model for the other: *The Gallant She-Souldier* for *The Famous Woman Drummer,*[51] *The Valiant Virgin* for *The Bristol Bridegroom,*[52] and *William of the Royal Waggon Train* for *William of the Man-of-War.*[53]

Eighteenth- and early nineteenth-century balladmakers also came up with new Female Warrior ballads by simply revising the texts of old ones—usually shortening them, sometimes changing their tone or style. For example, a bawdy ballad might be cleaned up for Britons grown more sentimental and priggish than their Restoration forebears. *The Constant Lovers of Worcestershire,* an "excellent New Song" of the eighteenth century, is in fact an abbreviated and sentimentalized revision of the cheeky Restoration ballad, *The Valiant Virgin.*[54] In addition to shortening the original, the revision plays down the impish descriptions and ribald innuendo of the Restoration text, omitting altogether the episode in which the disguised surgeon's-mate "drest and kist" the wof'ul wounded part" after her sweetheart has been shot in the thigh ("oh! that shot came something nigh").[55] Setting the two texts side-by-side, we can see the transforming hand of the revisor:

The Valiant Virgin
To every faithful Lover
that's constant to her dear,
This Ditty doth discover
Affections pure and claere;
Affections and afflictions too
do in this Story move,
Where Youth, and truth,
obtain the Crown of Love.
A Man of mean extraction,
brought up in Worc'ster-shiere,
Was guided by Affection
to love a Lady dear,
Whose eyes did shew like morning dew,
that doth on Lillies lye;
Her face, and grace,
well mixt with Majesty.
She was the only Heiress
unto a Gentleman,
And all her Fathers care is
to marry her to one,
Whose welth & wit, may fairly fit
a Lady of such worth;
But he, that she did Love,
was poore by birth.
A farmers son being handsome,
did catch this Ladies heart
So fast in hold, no ransome,
can free it from the Dart:
The gentleman, when he began
to understand this thing,
Quoth hee, I'le free,

my fond daughter in the spring.
The Spring came, & the Pressing
was every where begun;
Her Fathers fears increasing,
did Press the Farmers Son,
No money could Redeem him,
thought she, if he must go,
I'le ne're, stay here,
But I'le be a Seaman too.

The Second Part,
The Gentleman did Press him,
and sent him to the slaughter,
He thought fit to Press the Man
& would have prest his daughter;
His Wit prevents all her intents,
for on her knees he brought her;
But one, Love gone,
straight the tother follows after.
This Maid with ingenuity
had every Surgeons part,
A Ladies hand, an Eagles eye,
but yet a Lyons heart;
She knew all tents, & instruments
Salves, Oyntments, Oyls & all,
They they imploy
in the fight when Souldiers fall.
In mans Aparil she did
resolve to try her Fate,
and in the Ship where he rid,
she went as Surgons Mate;
Sayes she, my souldier shall not be
destroy'd for want of Cure,
I'le Dress, and Bless,
whatsoever I endure.
Their names Philip and Mary,
who then were both at Sea;
Phil fought like old king Harry,
but from the Enemy
Poore Philip had receiv'd a shot,
through that part of the thigh,
Did joyn to's groin,
oh! that shot came something nigh.
Into the Surgeons Cabbin,
they did convay him straight,
Where first, of all ye wounded men,
the pretty Surgens Mate,
Though in this trim, unknown to him
did bravely shew her Art,
She drest, and kist,
the woful wounded part.
Which she did most mildly dress,
and shed her teares upon't;
He observ'd, but could not guess,
or find the meaning on't,
Although he wou'd in tears & blood
oft times on Mary call,
And pray, she may
be there at his funeral.
Fierce fights at Sea this Couple
did valiantly indure,
As fast as one did aime to kill,
the other striv'd to cure;
The souldier & the Surgens Mate
did both imploy their parts,
That they, each way,

did win all the Seamens hearts.
The Summer being ended,
that they could fight no more,
The ship came to be mended,
and all men went a shore;
Stout Philip lov'd the Surgeons Mate
so much he could not be
An houre, or more,
out of his company.
He often view'd her feature,
and gaz'd on every part;
(Quoth Philip) such a Creature
is Mistress of my heart,
If she be dead, I'le never wed,
but be with thee for ever,
We'l walk, and talk,
Live, Lye, and Dye together.
Poore Mary full of passion,
to hear him prove so kind,
Orejoy'd with this Relation,
could not conceale her mind,
but fondly hangs about his neck,
her tears did trickle down,
Sayes she, I'le be
still thy true Companion.
Since providence hath vanquish'd
The dangers of the Sea,
I'le never marry whilst I live
unless it be with thee;
No womankind, shall ever find
my heart to be so free,
If thou, wilt vow,
to be as true to mee.
E're he could speak, she told him
I am thy dearest dear,
Thy Mary thou hast brought a shore
and now thou holdst here,
This man's attire, I did but hire,
when first I followed thee;
Thy Love, I'le prove,
but no Surgeons Mate am I.
He flung his arms about her
he wondred, kist and wept;
His Mary he did hold so fast,
as if he would have crept
Into her soul and body too;
his eyes in joy did swimm,
And she, as free,
was as fully fond of him.
They both rid towards Worc'ster,
to shew how they had sped;
But upon the Road they heard
her Father he was dead,
Two months at least after he prest
the Farmers son for slaughter;
In tears, appears
the sad duty of a Daughter.
Philip having cheer'd her up,
they rid directly home,
Where after many a bitter cup
the Marriage day was come,
Which they in state did Celebrate
the Gallants that were there,
Were grave, and brave,
all the best in Worc'ster-shire.
Thus may you by this Couple see,

what from true love doth spring
When Men love with fidelity
their Mistriss & their king:
When maids shew men, true love agen
in spight of fortunes frowns,
They'l wive, and thrive,
for such crosses have their crowne.
            FINIS.

The Constant Lovers
A Man of mean Directions
Of late in Worcestershire,
Was guided by Affection,
To Court a Lady fair.
Whose Eyes shin'd like the Morning Dew,
Upon a Lilly bright;
She had Grace in her Face,
Was pleasing to the sight.
She was an only Heir
Unto a Gentleman,
And all her Father's Care,
Was to match her unto one:
But the Farmer's Son being handsome,
To gain the Lady's Heart,
In so far that no Ransome,
Could ease a Lover's Smart.
But when her Father came to hear,
And understand the Thing;
Then said he, I will free,
My fine Daughter in the Spring;
The Spring time being come and gone,
There did a Press begin;
And all her Father's Care,
Was to press the Farmer's Son.
No Money shall be taken,
Said she, if it be so,
For I will never tarry here,
But along with him will go.
on the twenty-third of April,
She writ a Surgeon's Part.
With Bagle and with Instrument,
To all true loyal Heart.
With Bagle and with Instrument,
A Surgeon's Part to try,
Then said she, I will be
Where the Cannon Bullets fly:
On the twenty third of May,
Then did the Fight begin;
In the Forefront of the Battle,
There stood the Farmer's Son.
Who did a Wound receive,
in thick part of this Thigh,
In his Veins near his Reins,
There it pierc'd something nigh;
Then to the Surgeon's care,
He was commanded straight,
The first that he saw there
Was the Surgeon's Mate.
And when that he had seen her,
And view'd her in every part;
then said he, one like thee,
Once was the Mistress of my Heart;
If she be dead, I ne're will wed,
But stay with thee for ever;
And we will love, like a Dove,
And we'll live and die together.

I'll go to thy Commander,
If he'll set thee at large
Ten Guineas I'll surrender,
To purchase thy Discharge;
So they went both together,
And in a little space,
She met with his Commander,
And to him told her Case.
He pleased with the Gold,
Soon set the Farmer free;
And she brought him to England,
Over the raging Sea;
And when she came to her Father's Gate,
And there had knock'd a while,
Then out came her Father,
Who said, here stands my Child.
Which long Time hath been missing,
I thought to see no more;
Then said she, I've been seeking,
For him that you sent o're;
And since that I have found him,
And brought him safe to shore,
I'll spend my Days in England,
And cross the seas no more.
Oh Daughter, I am sorry,
For the thing that I've done;
Oh Daughter I am willing,
That he shall be my Son;
Oh, then they were married,
without any more delay,
And now the Farmer's son,
does enjoy his Lady gay.

That the later text came from the earlier is incontrovertible. Moreover, the later "Lovers" play their story manifestly cleaner and straighter than their progenitors in *The Valiant Virgin*.

With this particular text, the process of recomposition continued into the nineteenth century. On broadsides from about 1800 we find the *London Heiress*, a further abbreviation of the story which has three telling changes: (1) it relocates the hero's wound from his thigh to his breast, carefully side-stepping any hint of the original's cheeky focus on the sailor's groin; (2) it edits out the homoerotic innuendo in the earlier texts by omitting the wounded hero's pledge of loyalty to the surgeon's "boy"; and (3) it betrays throughout an increasing confusion and uneasiness about the heroine's gender disguise.

London Heiress
In London lived an Heiress unto a Gentleman,
And all her Father's care was to wed her to a man;
The farmer's son being handsome, he gain'd the
　lady's heart
They were so close engaged no ranson [sic] could
　them part.
When her Father came to know his daughter's foolish
　mind
He said unto his daughter you must be other ways
　inclin'd
For spring time is drawing near and press time
　coming on
And all the father's care was to press the farmer's son
But when this lady came to know of her father's

cruelty,
She said unto herself, my love, I soon will follow
　thee,
I'll dress myself in man's attire and after him will go,
I'll boldly plough the ocean where the stormy winds
　do blow.
On the Fourth of October, the battle it began,
In the front of the battle they plac'd the farmer's son,
Where he receiv'd a dreadful wound, which pierc'd
　him to the heart,
O! said he, where is she that would ease me of my
　smart.
Unto the Surgeon's cabin they had this lad convey'd,
There was no one to wait on him but the Surgeon's
　serv[ing] maid;
And when she turned herself around, he view'd her
　every part,
O! said he, one like thee, was once mistress of my
　heart.
You are very right young man, she said, your freedom
　I'll enlarge,
Here is fifty guineas for to clear you of your discharge;
then she went before the Captain, & fell upon her
　knees
She bought her love, and brought him safe over the
　raging seas.
When she came to her father's gate, she kneeled there
　awhile
Then her father said unto her now I see my own dear
　child
The child I have been wanting these seven long years
　& more
She said, I have been looking for the lad that you sent
　o'er.
And now since I have found him, all on my native
　shore,
We will live at home in peace and never sunder more.[56]

These three ballads, conscious reworkings of a single text, set before us a fascinating transformation. *The Valiant Virgin*—a humorously ironic text which exploits in all directions the enacted "punning" of the heroine's disguise—becomes the *London Heiress*—a straightforward love song which plays down any hint of innuendo and seems on the verge of doing away with the transvestism altogether. Indeed, this progression in which *The Valiant Virgin* becomes *The Constant Lover of Worcestershire* and then the *London Heiress* provides a revealing case study. As we shall see, an increasing sentimentality and uneasiness with the disguise characterize the later ballads and actually signal the waning of the Female Warrior motif in Balladry.

But such transformations of sentiment were not always the rule as old ballads became new ones. Often balladmakers brought their audiences a new song simply by cropping an old one in ways which left the tone of the original unaltered. For example, a balladmaker of the eighteenth century turned *The Seamans Doleful Farewell*, an eighty-line black-letter ballad from about 1690, into *Billy and Nancy's Kind Parting*, a much shorter "slipsong," which was published in various forms—usually of twenty or twenty-four lines—in the nineteenth century.[57] The shorter song has been widely collected as a folksong among twentieth-century singers in Britain and North America. A glance at the opening lines of a few sample texts testify to the song's lineage. The seventeenth-century ballad opens:

> Farewel my dearest Love now must I leave thee,
>> to the East-Indies my Course I must steer,
> And when I think upon't sore it doth grieve me;
>> let nothing possess thee with doubt or with fear.[58]

Billy and Nancy's Kind Parting appears in James Boswell's collection of mid-eighteenth-century chapbooks and begins almost identically:

> Farewell my dear Nancy, for now I must leave you
>> and to the West Indies my course I must steer,
> I know very well my absence will grieve you,
>> but my dear I'll return in the spring of the year.[59]

And so does *Molly and Johnnie,* which the traditional performer Frank Knox sang for MacEdward Leach at St. Shott's, Newfoundland in the 1960s. Knox's version begins:

> Said Molly to Johnny I'm now going to leave you
> Bound to the West Indies my long course to steer
> Don't let my long absence now grieve you or trouble you
> Oh my darling I'll be back in the spring of the year.[60]

The longstanding folksong strain in the history of the Female Warrior ballads is occasionally evident in eighteenth-century texts.[61] Knox's *Molly and Johnnie* exemplifies the non-commercial song tradition which held onto the Female Warrior long after she and the commercial ballad sheets had disappeared from the streets of Britain and America. But a handful of Female Warrior ballads that happen to survive in manuscripts of the eighteenth century show that already at that time the ballads were vigorously passed around—as one would expect they would be—in non-commercial channels. Manuscripts of this period that contain versions of Female Warrior ballads illustrate this personal level of the heroine's popularity. Among them we find, for example, Percy's famous *Folio Manuscript* of the seventeenth century with its oral version of *Mary Ambree,*[62] a 1745 teenager's diary with a meticulously penned text of *The Loyal Lovers Garland* undoubtedly copied from a broadside;[63] an imprisoned American sailor's journal of the Revolutionary War era with scrawled versions of *The Silk Merchant's Daughter* and *The Maid's Lamentation in Bedlam;*[64] a continental soldier's orderly book with irregularly spelled copies of *Johnny and Molly* and *The Valiant Maiden.*[65]

By 1800 the Female Warrior flourished in a demonstrably longstanding, coherent, complex, and multi-layered tradition. At the apex of her popularity, this originally lower-class heroine was engaging the interest not only of her longstanding broadside- and chapbook-buying public, but that of polite antiquarians and patriotic theatre-goers as well. But this widespread fashion for Female Warriors in ballads, chapbooks, and theatrical entertainments was soon to ebb. . . . Despite its obvious popularity at the outset of the nineteenth century, the Female Warrior did not prevail

for long as a commercial song motif. By the middle of the century female soldiers and sailors were no longer the stuff of "hit" songs. Shortly thereafter they were rarely seen at all anywhere. What explains this shift in popular taste and imagination? To some extent, changes in marketing brought about changes in the style and subject matter of all street ballads as newspapers took on the task of journalism and popular songs became increasingly tied to the music hall.[66] But even more important for the demise of the Female Warrior motif was the marked change in experience and people's view of it. The Female Warrior played her part in a world and worldview that have disappeared. . . . [T]he idealized "Mary Ambrees," "Polly Olivers," and "Wounded Nancys" of balladry slipped out of the popular fancy sometime in the nineteenth century.

Notes

1. I use the term "early modern era" in this study to designate that period of time in Britain (and Anglo America) between the Elizabethan and the Victorian ages. The Anglo-American Female Warrior appeared in printed street ballad tradition around 1600, became a popular convention by the eighteenth century, and remained commercially popular until the nineteenth century. The apex of the ballad heroine's popularity is that long "eighteenth century" to which scholars customarily refer, bounded on the one side by the Restoration of the monarchy in 1660, and on the other by the end of the Georgian era in 1837. My discussion—like the ballad tradition itself—sits astride this long eighteenth century. While my center of focus is this period, my discussion will necessarily extend both back in time from it and forward as the topic warrants.

2. For a text of this ballad, see *Bagford Ballads,* I, 308. . . .

3. While the three phases of popularity outlined here are derived from my study of ballads in the broadside and chapbook era, the same patterns are discernible in popular songs of our own time, though electronic media have considerably quickened the process. D. K. Wilgus has observed the parallels between the broadside song milieu and the radio and recording industry. See his *Anglo-American Folksong Scholarship Since 1898* (New Brunswick: Rutgers University Press, 1959), p. 430, and "An Introduction to the Study of Hillbilly Music," *Journal of American Folklore,* 78 (1965), pp. 196-97. The current terms I use here, "hit songs" and "golden oldies," while anachronistic, are nevertheless functionally appropriate.

4. The ways the ballad Female Warrior reflects the facts and preoccupations of the time which produced her will be examined in chapters 5, 6, and 7. For now, it is enough to observe that at the time that *Mary Ambree* was a controversial success, there was a general preoccupation with women and cross-dressing. For an overview of this early

seventeenth-century controversy see Louis B. Wright, *Middle-Class Culture in Elizabethan England* (Chapel Hill: University of North Carolina Press, 1935), pp. 494-97.

5. See Arber, IV, p. 216 and ii, p. 496, and Rollins, *Analytical Index,* Nos. 2803 and 2804. See also "Tradelist of William Thackeray" in *Bagford Ballads,* I, pp. liv-lxxvi and the 1754 catalogue of Dicey in Thomson, p. 298.

6. *The Merchant's Daughter of Bristol* was consistently re-registered along with *Mary Ambree.* See Rollins, "Analytical Index," pp. 147-49, Nos. 1692, 1707, 1708, and 1709. See also "Tradelist" in *Bagford Ballads,* I, liv-lxxvi and the catalogues of Norris and Brown (1712) and Dicey (1754) in Thomson, pp. 283 and 294.

7. The registration of Female Warrior ballads illustrates the ephemeral character of these songs. The registering of ballads with the Company of Stationers continued from 1557 to 1712. Of thirty Female Warrior ballads published during this early phase, only four were ever registered with the Stationers' Company—two in addition to *Mary Ambree* and *The Merchant's Daughter of Bristol.* See Dugaw Cat., pp. 386 and 471.

8. This ballad was never registered. The lines quoted are from a London version of 1678-80, Harvard, 25242. 67PF, II, no. 193. See Dugaw Cat., p. 481. Events in the ballad took place in February, 1644/45. (See *Roxburghe Ballads,* VI. p. 283.)

9. For actual women soldiers of this period, see Antonia Fraser, *The Weaker Vessel* (New York: Alfred Knopf, 1984), pp. 195-96.

10. For texts of these ballads, see *Roxburghe Ballads,* VII, pp. 728 and 730. See Dugaw Cat., pp. 814 and 818. For the tune to *The Famous Woman Drummer,* see Simpson, p. 775.

11. Price is known to be the author of *The Famous Woman Drummer.* Ebsworth (*Roxburghe Ballads,* VII, p. 729) proposes that he wrote *The Gallant She-Souldier* as well. However, it is unlikely that he wrote two such similar songs. More probably he modeled his ballad on that of a contemporary, or *vice versa.*

12. Both ballads exploit a bawdy use of the word "drum" in seventeenth-century parlance. On the facticity of seventeenth-century street literature, see Lennard Davis, *Factual Fictions: The Origins of the English Novel* (New York: Columbia University Press, 1983). Restrictions on printing during the Puritan Commonwealth encouraged this journalistic mode. See Rollins, "Martin Parker," pp. 129-32, and Leslie Shepard, *The Broadside Ballad: A Study in Origins and Meaning* (London: Herbert Jenkins, 1962; Hatboro, Pennsylvania: Legacy, 1978), p. 56.

13. From a 1680s London broadside entitled *An Admirable New Northern Story,* in *Euing Collection,* No. 8, p. 9. See Dugaw Cat., pp. 507-8. This broadside gives the tune as "I would thou wert in Shrewsbury," probably the "New Northern tune" of *The Valiant Commander.* This ballad, like *Mary Ambree,* remained a revival favorite through the eighteenth century, appearing in both the Stationers' Register and printers' catalogues.

14. Arber, II, p. 496; Rollins, *Analytical Index,* no. 2804. For discussion of this partnership, see Thomson, pp. 70-72.

15. "Thackeray Trade List," *Bagford Ballads,* pp. liv-lxxiv.

16. For a list of ballads dating from the seventeenth century, see Dugaw Cat., pp. 82-83. To this list can be added several more ballads from late in the period.

17. A late seventeenth-century London text (1683-1706) is in *Bagford Ballads,* I, p. 247. See Dugaw Cat., p. 503. For the tune, see Simpson, p. 191.

18. A late seventeenth-century London text (1685-1700) is in the British Library, c. 22, fo. 176. See Dugaw Cat., p. 373. For the tune, see Simpson, p. 683.

19. A late seventeenth-century London text (1664-95) is in *Roxburghe Ballads,* VII, p. 546. See Dugaw Cat., pp. 598-99. For the tune see Simpson, p. 768.

20. An early eighteenth-century London text (1709-12) is in Harvard, 25242.68/pEB-B65H, II, 307r. See Dugaw Cat., p. 828. The tune is from Henry Purcell's 1690 opera, *The Prophetess.* See Simpson, p. 440.

21. A London text of the 1690s is in *Pepys Ballads,* VI, p. 301. See Dugaw Cat., p. 838. The tune is the same Purcell air used for *The Woman Warrier,* Simpson, p. 440.

22. Thomas D'Urfey wrote two stanzas of this ballad in 1689. See his *New Poems Consisting of Satyrs, Elegies, and Odes* (London: J. Bullord and A. Roper, 1690), p. 183. The song quickly appeared in a lenghtened broadside version. See *The Maiden Warrier, Euing Collection,* p. 331. See Dugaw Cat., pp. 475-76. For the tune, see Simpson, pp. 733-34.

23. Percy, II, p. 231.

24. Percy, I, p. 7.

25. Questioning of Percy's sources and his tinkering with texts began already in the 1780s with the acerbic attacks of Joseph Ritson in *Observations on the First Three Volumes of the History of English Poetry* (London: J. Stockdale, 1782), p. 11 and *A Select Collection of English Songs,* 3 vols. (London: J. Johnson, 1783), I, p. x. For discussion of what became a heated controversy, see Sigurd B. Hustvedt, *Ballad Criticism in Scandinavia and Great Britain during the Eighteenth Century* (New York: American Scandinavian Foundation; London: Humphrey Milford, Oxford University Press, 1916),

pp. 157-200; Albert Friedman, *The Ballad Revival* (Chicago and London: University of Chicago Press, 1961), pp. 203-12; Thomson, pp. 113 and 125-27; and Stephen Vartin, "Thomas Percy's *Reliques:* Its Structure and Organization" (Ph.D. dissertation, New York University Press, 1972), pp. 80-94. In 1868 the Folio Manuscript which was Percy's point of departure was published exactly as it survives. See *Bishop Percy's Folio Manuscript,* ed. John W. Hales and Frederick J. Furnivall, 3 vols. (London: N. Trübner, 1867-68).

26. Percy, I, p. 2.

27. Percy, I, p. 7.

28. On Percy's place in this "ballad revival," see Friedman, pp. 185-232. See also Dianne Dugaw, "The Popular Marketing of 'Old Ballads': The Ballad Revival and Eighteenth-Century Antiquarianism Reconsidered," *Eighteenth-Century Studies,* 21 (1987), pp. 71-90.

29. In Percy's lifetime the *Reliques* went into editions in 1765, 1767, and 1775. With his nephew he revised for a fourth edition which came out after his death. For discussion of the work's popularity, see Bertram H. Davis, *Thomas Percy* (Boston: Twayne, 1981), pp. 80-108. See also Friedman, pp. 200-2.

30. See *The Valarous Acts . . . &c.,* printed for Joseph Hinson, Cambridge University, Madden Collection, III, no. 797, p. 199, and *The valarous Acts . . . &c.,* Printed and Sold in Bow-Church-Yard, London, Harvard, pEB75P4128C, no. 250.

31. Dugaw, "Popular Marketing," pp. 80 and 84-85.

32. See Thomson, pp. 288-99, and Dugaw, "Popular Marketing," pp. 75-85.

33. *The Vocal Magazine; or, British Songster's Miscellany . . . Volume the First* (London: J. Harrison, 1778), pp. 156-57. The description of the contents is on sig. A2^r.

34. For discussion of these popular amusement parks, see Warwick Wroth, *The London Pleasure Gardens of the Eighteenth Century* (London: Macmillan, 1896). See also Richard Altick, *The Shows of London* (Cambridge, Massachusetts and London: Harvard University Press, 1978).

35. On the relationship of streetsongs to theatre and music hall, see J. S. Bratton, *The Victorian Popular Ballad* (New York: Macmillan, 1975), pp. 27-28.

36. For a text of this song, see *Roundelay, or the New Syren* (London: W. Lane, n.d.), p. 14. See Dugaw Cat., p. 870. For information on James Wrighten, see *Thespian Dictionary; or, Dramatic Biography of the Eighteenth Century* (London: T. Hurst, 1802). *The Female Captain* was written before 1792 when Mary Ann Matthews Wrighten Pownall left Wrighten and went to America. See *Who Was Who in America. Historical Volume 1607-1896,* rev. edn (Chicago: A. N. Marquis, 1967), p. 493.

37. For a text of this song, see *Songsters Multum in Parvo,* 6 vols. (London: John Fairburn, n.d.), III, pp. 113. It is described as "written by Mr. C. Dibdin, and sung by Mrs. Dibdin, in character, with universal applause, at the aquatic theatre, Sadlers Wells." The piece may have been performed in *The British Amazons,* a revue of 1803 which ended with a chorus of "female volunteers" doing military exercises. See Dennis Arundell, *The Story of Sadler's Wells 1683-1977* (Newton Abbot: David and Charles, 1978), p. 71. See Dugaw Cat., p. 868.

38. See Arundell, *Sadler's Wells,* p. 17. See also *DNB,* vol. XVIII, p. 614. For a recent facsimile of a 1750 edition of Snell's "life and adventures," see *The Female Soldier* (1750) (Los Angeles: William Andrews Clark Memorial Library, 1989).

39. For a text, see *Roxburghe Ballads,* VIII-l, p. 146. See Dugaw Cat., p. 591. For the tune, see Simpson, p. 296.

40. An eighteenth-century text is in *The New Play-House Garland,* Harvard, 25252.6, Garland 55. The title of this chapbook links the ballad to theatrical performances of some kind. See Dugaw Cat., p. 768.

41. A mid-eighteenth-century chapbook text is in Harvard, 25274.2, XXVIII, no. 8. See Dugaw Cat., p. 765.

42. For a late eighteenth-century broadside text, see Harvard, 25242.85F, 21^r. See Dugaw Cat., p. 613.

43. An eighteenth-century broadside text is in Holloway and Black, p. 239. See Dugaw Cat., 638.

44. For a Scottish broadside text of about 1800, see Harvard, 25252.19, ch. 31. See Dugaw Cat., p. 846.

45. For a late eighteenth-century London broadside text, see Harvard, 25274.2, IV, 2. See Dugaw Cat., 406.

46. For a mid-eighteenth-century chapbook text, see Harvard, 25276.43.5. See Dugaw Cat., pp. 623-25. This is N-10 in Laws (p. 207).

47. See n. 11 above.

48. For an 1830s Catnach text of *The Handsome Cabinboy* which identifies the tune, see Huntington, 297337, I. See n. 42 above for a text of *The Female Drummer.* A manuscript book of the poet John Clare contains the earliest tune. It appears in Roy Palmer, *The Rambling Soldier: Military Life through Soldiers' Songs and Writings* (New York: Penguin, 1977), p. 163.

49. See chapter 1, n. 27 above on John Morgan's authorship. For an early nineteenth-century text of *William of the Royal Waggon Train,* see Harvard, 25242.71, 26r. I have found tunes only in recent folksong collections. See Dugaw Cat., 430.

50. An 1830s Catnach text of *William and Phillis* identifies the tune. See UCLA, No. 605. For an 1820s London text of *William and Harriet,* see

Kentucky, V, 15. I have found tunes only in recent folksong collections. See Dugaw Cat., p. 517.

51. See n. 9 above.

52. For a seventeenth-century text of *The Valiant Virgin,* see *Roxburghe Ballads,* VII, p. 546. See Dugaw Cat., pp. 598-99. For the tune, see Simpson, p. 768. For *The Bristol Bridegroom,* see *Roxburghe Ballads,* VIII-l, p. 146. See Dugaw Cat., pp. 591-93. For the tune, see Simpson, p. 296.

53. For *William of the Royal Waggon Train,* see n. 47 above. An 1830s Catnach text of *William of the Man-of-War* is in Huntington, 297337, I. See Dugaw Cat., p. 426.

54. Ebsworth believed that Sterne had this ballad in mind when he wrote *Tristram Shandy.* His remarks posit that the ballad "suggested to [Sterne] a certain incident (and comment of Corporal Trim) concerning the wound received by the immortal Uncle Toby." (*Roxburghe Ballads,* VII, p. 548). For discussion of Uncle Toby's wound, see chapters 21 and 25 of the novel.

55. *The Valiant Virgin* text here is from a late seventeenth-century London broadside in Harvard, 25242.67PF, vol. II, no. 195. For the tune, see Simpson, p. 768. See Dugaw Cat., pp. 598-99. *The Constant Lovers* text is from a mid-eighteenth-century London chapbook in Harvard, 25252.6, G.32. See Dugaw Cat., p. 605. *The Bristol Bridegroom* is probably also a reworking of *The Valiant Virgin.*

56. Harvard, 25242.4, I, 67. See Dugaw Cat., p. 611.

57. For a discussion of the origins of "slipsongs" and the role of the Diceys in popularizing them, see Thomson, p. 112.

58. From a late seventeenth-century London broadside in the British Library, c. 22, fo. 176. See Dugaw Cat., p. 373. For the tune, see Simpson, p. 683.

59. From a mid-eighteenth-century chapbook, Harvard, 25274.2, XXVIII, 30. See Dugaw Cat., pp. 377-78. This ballad is K-14 in Laws (p. 147).

60. Memorial University of Newfoundland Folklore and Language Archive, MacEdward Leach Collection, no. 18. See Dugaw Cat., pp. 377-78.

61. For discussion of this interrelationship of traditional and commercial versions of ballads, see Dianne Dugaw, "Anglo-American Folksong Reconsidered: The Interface of Oral and Written Forms," *Western Folklore,* 43 (1984), pp. 83-103. For discussion of the concept of folksong, see Wilgus, *Anglo-American Folksong Scholarship,* pp. 231ff. For a recent critical reappraisal of the concept, see Dave Harker, *Fakesong: The Manufacture of British "Folksong" 1700 to the Present Day* (Milton Keynes and Philadelphia: Open University Press, 1985).

62. See Hales and Furnivall, I, p. 515. For discussion of Percy's acquisition of the manuscript, see Friedman, pp. 187-88.

63. "Elizabeth Williams, Her Book, 1745," Harvard, 25252.8, p. 63. See Dugaw Cat., pp. 578-79.

64. George Carey, *A Sailor's Songbag: An American Rebel in an English Prison, 1777-79* (Amherst: University of Massachusetts Press, 1976), pp. 69 and 132. See Dugaw Cat., pp. 623 and 469.

65. Library of Congress, Manuscript Division, "Orderly Book of Thomas Cole," Boston, 1778 (Item 64, Handbook, AC966). See Dugaw Cat., pp. 401 and 768.

66. Bratton, *The Victorian Popular Ballad,* pp. 23-26.

Abbreviations

Arber: Edward Arber, *A Transcript of the Registers of the Company of Stationers of London: 1554-1640 AD,* 5 vols. (London and Birmingham: privately printed 1875-94)

Bagford Ballads: The Bagford Ballads, ed. Joseph Woodfall Ebsworth, 2 vols. (Hertford: Stephen Austin and Sons, 1878)

Brown: Brown University, John Hay Library Collections

DNB: The Dictionary of National Biography, ed. Sidney Lee, 2nd edn, 22 vols. (New York: Macmillan, 1906)

Dugaw Cat.: Dianne M. Dugaw, "The Female Warrior Heroine in Anglo-American Popular Balladry" (Ph.D. dissertation, University of California Press, Los Angeles, 1982)

Euing Collection: Euing Collection of Broadside Ballads (Glasgow: University of Glasgow Press, 1971)

Harvard: Harvard University, Houghton Library Collections

Holloway and Black: John Holloway and Joan Black, *Later English Broadside Ballads* (Lincoln: University of Nebraska Press, 1975)

Huntington: Huntington Library Collections

Kentucky: University of Kentucky, Martha I. King Library, Special Collections Department, Broadside Ballads

Laws: G. Malcolm Laws, *American Balladry from British Broadsides: A Guide for Students and Collectors of Traditional Song* (Philadelphia: Publications of the American Folklore Society, Bibliographic and Special Series, vol. 8, 1957)

NYPL: New York Public Library Collections

Pepys Ballads: The Pepys Ballads, ed. Hyder Rollins, 8 vols. (Cambridge, Massachusetts: Harvard University Press, 1929-32)

Percy: Thomas Percy, *Reliques of Ancient English Poetry* (1765), ed. Henry B. Wheatley, 3 vols. (London: Swan Sonneschein, Lebas, and Lowrey, 1886; rpt. New York: Dover, 1966)

Roxburghe Ballads: The Roxburghe Ballads, ed. William Chappell and Joseph Woodfall Ebsworth, 9 vols. (Hertford: Stephen Austin and Sons, 1871-99)

Rollins, *Analytical Index:* "An Analytical Index to the Ballad Entries (1557-1709) in the Registers of the Company of Stationers of London," *Studies in Philology,* 21 (1924), pp. 1-324 (rpt. Chapel Hill: University of North Carolina, 1924; rpt. Hatboro, Pennsylvania: Tradition, 1967)

Simpson: Claude Simpson, *The British Broadside Ballad and Its Music* (New Brunswick: Rutgers University Press, 1966)

Thomson: Robert S. Thomson, "The Development of the Broadside Ballad Trade and its influence upon the Transmission of English Folksongs" (Ph.D. dissertation, University of Cambridge, 1974)

UCLA: University of California at Los Angeles, University Research Library, Special Collections

Wilgus, *Anglo-American Folksong Scholarship:* D. K. Wilgus, *Anglo-American Folksong Scholarship since 1898* (New Brunswick: Rutgers University Press, 1959)

Yale: Yale University, Beinecke Library Collections

Natascha Würzbach (essay date 1990)

SOURCE: "Literary and social conditions for the rise, distribution and textual structure of the street ballad," in *The Rise of the English Street Ballad, 1550-1650,* translated by Gayna Walls, Cambridge University Press, 1990, pp. 1-27.

[*In the following excerpt, Würzbach analyzes the relationship between English ballads, theater, and commerce between 1550 and 1650.*]

1.1 PERFORMANCE AND RENDITION

The text of the street ballad, available to us in broadsides and in edited collections, some of which are annotated, was usually sung and sometimes read to the audience of the time as part of the selling process. Performance and sale were closely linked, and it is only later analyses which artificially separated these two integral aspects of the street ballad.

'Performance' and 'rendition' are extremes of possible textual realization. They denote on the one hand dramatic role-play, which is evidently required in many of the texts, and simple rendition on the other. The latter follows the text and the tune, rendering the ballad without any special gesturing, mime, or varied voice inflection. In practice, the tendency towards simple rendition probably predominated, though a textual rendering in the manner of a performance after Richard Tarlton, as an 'afterpiece' in the theatre or by an ambitions balladmonger, cannot be ruled out. Whatever the case, the performance and rendition of the street ballad had the function of communicating the text in as lively a way as possible and of catching and holding the attention of the audience.

> Starting out with his arms and his pack full of broadsides, the singer would go to the doors of theaters, to markets, fairs, bear baitings, taverns, ale-houses, wakes or any other places where a crowd could gather, and begin his song.
>
> (Rollins [1919a], pp. 308-9)

Such is the list which the street-ballad expert gives of the places where the balladmonger hawked his wares. The performance and distribution of the street ballad took place on the periphery of certain, mainly popular, festivities but was not integrated into them to the same extent as were the songs of the minstrel into court occasions, Lord Mayors' processions, May games, weddings or christenings. It was the printer and the publisher who commissioned the ballad-singer, not a festival organizer. The singer would go along independently to places where crowds were expected, since it was his responsibility to distribute the printed copies he had been commissioned to sell. So the balladmonger, who had only his performance and the copies themselves to attract an audience and potential customers and hold their attention, was dependent on the success of his rendition. He would make use of any possible raised position, a bench or simple stall, for instance, though he could also attract an audience without such aids.[1] Unlike the German *Bänkelsänger,* the balladmonger did not have the use of a series of pictures on a board with a pointing-stick, as both eyecatcher and text illustration. The woodcut on the broadside was of only limited illustrative use as it usually depicted single figures and not scenes, far less a series of scenes. In addition, the illustrations were often hackneyed and had little or no connection with the actual text.[2] Apart from the fact that the balladmonger was his own manager and dependent on his performance of the ballad for success (with the help of the tune), he also had to contend with very fierce competition. There was a large and diverse selection of ballads on offer,[3] especially in London, and this required of him the high degree of persuasive power and skill of a present-day salesman in order to arouse people's interest and attract their attention. The means to do this lie, as we shall see, in the text itself, and only had to be put into practice in the performance. In small towns and rural areas the pedlar[4] selling his wares would often function as ballad-seller and performer as well, or the ballads might be performed as part of the entertainment offered at a fair. The urban performance of ballads had to compete with many other diversions and amusements, however.

The street-ballad texts themselves give some explicit references to the performance situation. The frequent request for attention was meant to keep the passer-by standing at the balladmonger's pitch or, in a public house, to keep the focus of interest solely on the ballad-singer, or again, to beat the showman at the fair at his own game. The exhortation to stop and gather round emphasizes this:

Good people all to me draw neer,
and to my Song a while attend,[5]

I Pray good People all draw near,
and mark these lines that here are pen'd,[6]
Give eare, my loving countrey-men,
    that still desire newes,
Nor passe not while you heare it sung,
    or else the song peruse;
For, ere you heare it, I must tell,
    my newes it is not common;
But Ile unfold a trueth betwixt.[7]

Frequent references to both the oral and written transmission of a ballad text appear juxtaposed in the text itself. This makes quite explicit the duality of text rendition on the one hand, and the sale of copies as back-up to the performance and opportunity for private perusal on the other. The printing of street ballads brought about the transition from purely oral tradition to duplication, distribution of written copies and a consequent fixing of the text. Although this also holds true for the development of book printing, we cannot overlook the close link between the writing of the street ballad and its performance, and the resulting more complex process of initial reception. Terms such as 'written' and 'lines penned' are often interchangeable with 'Ile tell' and 'song', without any distortion of meaning. There is always an invitation to listen implied, whereby the (past tense) allusion to the writing of the ballad often, significantly, referred to the process of writing which preceded the performance, so giving priority to the actual performance itself. This is also seen in the textual procedures which involve direct communication with the audience.

Let no body grudge,
Nor ill of me iudge
    because I haue *pend* this same *ditty.*[8]

O whoe can *wryte with pen,* or yet what *tongue* can showe,
What loue these blessèd men did to their maker owe?[9]

All you which sober minded are,
    come listen and Ile *tell,*
The saddest story Ile declare,
    which in our dayes befell:
Therefore 'tis for example sake,
    the business *written is . . .*[10]

Be silent, therefore, and stand still!
    marke what proceedeth from *my quill;*
I *speake* of tokens good and ill,[11]

Give eare, my loving countrey-men,
    that still desire newes,
Nor passe not while you heare it *sung,*
    or else the *song peruse;*[12]

Round boyes indeed.
    Or
The Shoomakers Holy-day.
Being a very pleasant new Ditty,

To fit both Country, Towne and Citie,
Delightfull to peruse in every degree.[13]

The balladmonger performing and selling his wares was such a common component of everyday life in the seventeenth century that many allusions to this figure can be found. There are several literary depictions of balladmongers, of which the best known is the character Autolycus in Shakespeare's *The Winter's Tale,*[14] although Nightingale's scene in Ben Jonson's *Bartholomew Fair* (1614)[15] is more informative on the subject of performance practices. The balladmonger formed part of the whole pattern of the fair, where ballads, as well as other items from mousetraps to gingerbread, were offered for sale. Nightingale is the same kind of showman as a market-crier, and tries to entice his audience by describing and praising his wares (naming of themes). Although he has difficulty in making himself heard among the visitors to the fair he does find a ballad fan in Cokes, who is immediately ready both to listen and to buy. The rendition is prefaced by an address to the audience and a request to gather round; the fascination thus established is so strong that the pickpocket Edgeworth succeeds in relieving the listener Cokes of his purse while Nightingale is just delivering a warning about such practices. The ballad-monger keeps the interest of the audience constantly on the boil by means of his addresses, explanations, and responses to heckling. His success is confirmed by the sale of copies which then follows.

Similarly, the showmanlike and market-crier aspect of ballad performance is illustrated in *A Song for Autolycus* (c. 1620). The name 'Autolycus' as an allusion to Shakespeare's balladmonger shows the almost proverbial renown of the figure of the balladmonger under that name. Here also, the ballad itself is not given, but instead the typical behaviour of the balladmonger is reproduced. The same goes for a servants' scene in William Cavendish's *The Triumphant Widow* (1677), where the pedlar and balladmonger Footpad offers the rendition of a ballad as the high point of his selection of wares. He skilfully arouses the curiosity of his audience by giving a general description of theme and content, a typical procedure of the balladmonger. The documentary value of this literary treatment of the phenomenon of street-ballad performance and sale lies not only in the portrayal of the typical behaviour of balladmonger and audience. It is also of interest for the fact that knowledge of street-ballad texts and performance practice was taken for granted to such an extent that quoting the ballad texts themselves was found to be unnecessary for an albeit rudimentary portrayal of the process on stage. The mainly negative evaluation of ballad literature and ballad selling is biased, being based on the tenets of 'orthodox' literature.[16]

The musical quality of the ballad rendition was judged inferior by contemporaries.[17] The coarseness of the tunes was deplored,[18] and the untrained croaking or sentimental whining of the singers dismissed with contempt.[19] Here too the decided rejection, already entrenched at the time, by men of letters of ballad literature and its enormous and enviable success was probably instrumental in distorting the reality of the situation. In fact those tunes which have survived, if in some cases altered by time, prove to be of better quality than contemporary commentators would have had us believe (see also Rollins [1919a], p. 312). Rollins accords them higher status than the popular hits of his time,[20] describing them as 'attractive' and clearly distancing himself from seventeenth-century opinion (ibid., p. 314). In any event the tune had an important phatic and mnemonic function, and it was one of the balladmonger's tasks to teach it to those who bought his printed copies (ibid., p. 312).

The transmission and distribution of the street-ballad text is characterized by its public nature, and the personal element in the phatic relationship between balladmonger and audience. This relationship was based partly on economic considerations, but also developed as a result of the showmanship involved in the performance of street ballads, which were instruments of amusement or of instruction. They were hawked and performed in places familiar to the public at which they were aimed: markets, street corners, public houses, and fairs. The absence of any elitist cultural nimbus makes these texts of the lower stratum of the populace particularly accessible. They involve no psychological block in relation to printed texts, no claims on the intellect, and no contact with the unfamiliar. The popular nature of the street ballad is evident in the affinity between audience and text in theme, language, straightforwardness of textual procedure, and ease of reception due to certain communication factors. It becomes even clearer when comparison is made with some analogous aspects of late medieval popular drama. The showmanlike demeanour of the balladmonger, which has its expression in the text itself, has characteristics in common with the presenter in popular drama. The latter stands at the edge of the stage or walks round it, thereby indicating a certain distance between himself and the action, which makes him an ideal go-between and commentator. His position near the audience on the *platea*, that part of the stage reserved for action representing ordinary life and the common people as opposed to the *locus*, confirms his close association with the audience and especially with those of the lower classes (R. Weinmann [1967], pp. 55, 164). This presenter, together with low-class characters only, addresses the audience directly from the *plateau* (ibid., pp. 39-40, 174-5, 181, 249). R. Weimann and H.-J. Diller have shown that the audience relationship as an explicit constituent of the text and dramaturgy is a device limited to popular drama only.[21] It became a distinctive feature of the type of drama which evolved in the vernacular, while liturgical drama contains no genuine address to the audience which would interrupt the solemnity of the closed ritual (see Diller [1973], p. 148, *passim*). The orientation of the ballad performance towards the audience is even more obvious in the street ballad than in popular drama.

1.2 POSITION OF THE STREET BALLAD WITHIN THE CONTEMPORARY SPHERE OF LITERARY ACTIVITY

It is the coupling of the performance of street ballads with the sale of copies that gives this literary form, in very large measure, the character of 'wares'. The institutional reasons for this lie in special features relating to the printing of the street ballad and to its distributors. The position of the street ballad within the literary sphere of the time is of interest to us from the point of view of both social history and literary scholarship. Here also there is reciprocal influence between the social, literary, and economic environments on the one hand, and the form of the text on the other.

1.2.1 PRINTING PRODUCTION, AND STREET BALLADS AS 'WARES'

The position of the street ballad in the contemporary sphere of literary activity, as with other printed matter of the time, can be understood from two main aspects. These are on the one hand trade controls, after the establishing of the Stationers' Company in 1557 from which time entries in the Stationers' Register are to be found, and state decrees on the other. From the outset there are numerous ballad entries to be found (see Rollins [1924]) and as early as 1559 'ballates' are expressly mentioned together with plays and prose works in the *Injunctions given by the Queen's Majesty* against 'publicatyon of vnfrutefull, vayne and infamous bokes and papers . . . nothing therein should be either heretical, seditious, or vnsemely for Christian eares'.[22] Queen Elizabeth was particularly concerned, together with the church, to retain influence over at least the most important and successful printers such as John Day, Richard Tottel, and John Jugge. This was achieved through the use of patronage, the conferring of privileges, and special commissions.[23] Although the role of the street ballad in this system of feudally controlled business competition has not yet been examined, there are indications that owing to certain circumstances the ballad became free from this constraint more rapidly than most of the other printed works of the time.

The business of the literature of entertainment, the cheap chapbooks and the ballads, must have flourished increasingly[24] alongside the bestsellers of the time. These were the Bible, the catechism, the ABC, Foxe's *Martyrs,* Sternhold and Hopkins's *Singing Psalms,* legal works and state proclamations, and they provided the main source of income for the leading printers in the Company. As early as 1557 there was a printer who specialized in the production and distribution of ballads: William Pickering, a founder member of the Stationers' Company, who had a shop at London Bridge (see F. A. Mumby [1956], p. 94). In the last two decades of the sixteenth century, the fierce competition between the printers, together with high printing costs, led to a gradual separation of printing and selling (ibid., p. 69). After that the booksellers, as a separate marketing group, began to gain influence over the printers. The demand for printed works—the needs of a public which also expected to be offered entertainment and moral instruction in an interesting form—in turn influenced the production of printed material. It was therefore possible to achieve success in the business outside the sphere of royal privilege. At the same time, this influence of public taste on what was printed was only possible in a social context where author and seller were dependent solely on financial profit, and not relatively protected from that necessity by membership of a rich and respectable social class, enjoying the patronage that went with it.[25]

When the Stationers' Company became something similar to a joint-stock company in 1603 and was reorganized by James I into five sections, ballad literature was clearly such an important component that as Ballad Stock it was given its own defined area alongside Bible Stock, Irish Stock, Latin Stock, and English Stock.[26] Ballad production was thus drawn into the aegis of the Stationers' Company, whose monopoly position was becoming increasingly established. It can be assumed that the street ballad thus acquired a special financial back-up and a certain literary legitimacy. There are other indications, however, that the producers of street ballads were despised by the higher-status Company printers and tried to leave the monopoly, thus showing a greater willingness to take financial risks.[27]

The broadside should be assigned, bibliographically and institutionally, to the periodical press rather than the book trade. Although it did not appear with an exact date nor in a series published periodically, it was a fly-sheet, like the first newsletters in the second half of the sixteenth century and the later news-sheets of the seventeenth century, and was sold under the same conditions.[28] Those who dealt with the sale of ballads on a large scale were often also involved in the publication of news-sheets and cheap, small-scale popular literature: printers and booksellers such as Bernard Alsop (1617-53?), Francis Coles (1626-81), Henry Gosson (1601-40), Francis Grove (1623-61), Thomas Pavier (1600-25), Thomas Symcock (1619-29), and John Wright (1605-58).[29] This cheap and popular material was not printed by the rich and influential members of the Company but most frequently by printers on the periphery of that institution. We do know of some printers, such as Henry Gosson, John Grismand (1618-38), Thomas Pavier, John Wright, and Edward Wright (1642-48), who were presumably shareholders in the Ballad Stock (see McKerrow [1910], pp. 302-3) and others, like Francis Coles, William Gilbertson (1640-65), and Thomas Vere (1646-80), who had business connections with them. But there seem to be no indications that any ballad-printer ever belonged to the higher echelons of the Company as warden or assistant, able to share in policy decisions. We know that the better-known ballad-printers were accepted as freemen, so they were certainly members. Whether this was as livery-men, with some communal influence on policy, or as mere yeomen, is not clear.[30] A large number of ballad-printers, whose activity can often be established only for a short period, were not members of the Company. These printers would probably dabble only occasionally in ballads and ephemera, dependent as they were on immediate profit.[31]

For any printer, whether a specialist in the genre or only an occasional producer, the ballad trade would, at the very least, have been profitable enough for them to do without privileges (monopoly), patronage, and subsidies.[32] The popularity of the texts,[33] the low price of a broadside, and a comparatively effective distribution, where the product was taken directly to the buyer,[34] resulted in relatively high sales.[35] The price of a ballad copy (one halfpenny) was the same as the cost of half a loaf of bread; standing room in the stalls of the public theatre cost a penny, seats in the gallery tuppence, and comfortable chairs in the stalls threepence (see H. Castrop [1972], p. 120). Popular literature in book form could be had from a penny upwards, but more serious books cost a shilling, which was beyond the means of members of a class earning £10 a year (see E. H. Miller [1959], pp. 41-2).

> Like the newspaper today, the broadside was so cheap that any apprentice could soon accumulate a collection, which had for the Elizabethan somewhat more permanency than present-day papers hold for their readers.
>
> (L. B. Wright [1964], p. 419)

The ballad business was mostly fairly profitable for both printer and author.[36] Indeed it could be lucrative enough to enable a printer to start up on his own. The ballad producers' urge to make a profit even outweighed the fear of censorship and punishment during the Cromwell dictatorship. The large number of broadsides printed at that time was not only due to the need for news and political invective (see Rollins, *CP*, p. 14). Rollins calculated that the ballad-writer sometimes earned more than a playwright.[37]

The importance of street ballads—as shown by the large quantity printed—contrasts with the low status of street-ballad publishers in the guild. At the same time there is a consequent independence of street-ballad publishers as an enterprise, as they were in receipt of absolutely no support through privilege or subsidy. All these are determinant components in the production of street ballads which contribute to the character of this literary form as one of 'wares'. The method of distribution emphasized this aspect which was especially obvious when one considers that copies of a ballad were handed round at a low price like fruit and vegetables, as soon as there was a need for them. The printed copy was highly desirable both as an illustrated reminder of the performance experience and as a means of privately repeating it. The wide circulation of this printed product made it profitable for the printer/publisher and author in spite of its low price; nothing is known of the size of the balladmonger's cut.

The street ballad can be described as an early type of bestseller. Its production and distribution correspond to the increasingly capitalist economic system of the seventeenth century, where the spirit of enterprise and calculated risk held out the promise of success (see A. L. Rowse [1964], pp. 109-12), a motivation which no doubt had its effect in the field of literature. The Company's contempt for the street ballad, in spite of its incorporation in the Stock, is probably based not only on its trivial and ephemeral character but also on a certain competitive envy, which is often evident in other criticism of the ballad (see below, pp. 243-4).

1.2.2 Social and economic status of the ballad writer and singer/seller

The ballad writer stood completely outside the feudal system of patronage. This was a specifically medieval component of cultural life which was already diminishing in importance after 1600.[38] Only one or two authors of recognized serious literature still had noble patrons with whom they were in personal contact and who offered them permanent support and encouragement. In popular literature circles it was customary, even for insignificant hack writers who would not normally have come up to the cultural and aesthetic standards required by noble patrons, to try to establish an apparent connection with and extract money from a rich and socially well-placed gentleman, by means of flattering dedications. The ballad-writer dispensed with this, whether from a sense of financial independence or a realistic assessment of the success of such an attempt. Advancement through patronage or the conferring of public or private offices was similarly closed to him. Most ballad writers probably shared the proverbial poverty of Elizabethan writers,[39] unless writing was not their main source of income. It was the printers and publishers who made the money.

Like the street-ballad trade, which did not belong to a feudalistically organized printing 'guild', the balladmonger was under no corporate or social obligation. A comparison with the actor, with whom he shared the role of performer, makes this quite clear. The actor was a member of a troupe which enjoyed the patronage of a nobleman or the Master of the Revels of the royal court. He had a contract of service and his social status was determined by his rights and obligations. He could be fairly sure that his clothing and keep would be provided, as long as the theatres did not close for any length of time owing to the threat of plague. For its part the troupe had to put on the agreed number of performances, eliminate any subversive or seditious political opinion from the texts of their plays, and take preventive measures against theft or other immoral activities during their performance.[40] In contrast, the balladmonger's activity was merely included in the printing licence which the publisher had to obtain for each new ballad. The balladmonger could sell the ballads wherever and whenever he liked, thus supplementing his income. He needed no licence to trade or perform, and he as an individual was defined only by his ability or inability to perform the text and sell the broadsheets. Thus his value, or lack of it, as a member of society derived primarily from his individual standing and not from a fixed social position. As a result, the author of a ballad could risk expressing subversive opinions through the balladmonger, thereby slipping through the censor's net. Similarly, it was not uncommon for a balladmonger, while performing, to work sucessfully in collusion with a pickpocket.[41]

The financial success[42] of the balladmonger, a certain legitimizing of his performance, and the popularity of his 'wares' also derived from the tradition of the minstrel.[43]

The late medieval figure of the minstrel in his role of entertainer with various functions is certainly similar to that of the balladmonger. In contrast to the minstrel, however, with his diverse talents and functions—musician, actor, acrobat, story-teller, reciter, poet, singer, dancer, and comedian—the balladmonger was a specialist. At its widest, his range included very occasionally textual construction, but for the most part his job was to perform and sell. Performance did imply some acting and musical ability, however, and selling involved a certain amount of showmanship and salesmanship. The diversification of the balladmonger's tasks derived from the relatively large number of possibilities for textual shaping allowed the performer in that genre. We may also assume that wandering minstrels sometimes took over the balladmonger's business,[44] and that itinerant actors, too, would try their hand at the job.[45] We should keep in mind, however, that ballad production was a specifically urban activity which was dependent on the printers in and around London. On the other hand there would be fewer failed actors in London, and the activity of down-at-heel minstrels would be confined to the provinces. Other occasional writers and performers of ballads would probably have been the general unemployed, the work-shy, and cripples (see Rollins [1919a], pp. 306-10). In the provinces the ballads were marketed mainly by itinerant traders, whose assortment of cures, cosmetics, haberdashery, and calendars would sometimes include thin, often loosely bound, chapbooks and broadsides.

The figures of the ballad writer and the balladmonger of Elizabethan and Stuart times are difficult to define clearly. They belonged to the literary *demi-monde* but also to the vague no-man's-land between hack writer, itinerant trader, vagabond, and cony-catcher. If the texts were by more or less professional ballad authors such as William Elderton (d. 1592?), Thomas Deloney (1543?-1600?), Laurence Price (1628-80?), and Martin Parker,[46] and handled by booksellers and proficient balladsingers, one could expect a relatively high quality of ballad and a performance which did justice to the text. The products of occasional writers, and the marketing of them by traders and dubious individuals, tended to result in ballads and performances of inferior quality. The increasing mobility of the lower classes of the populace and especially of the vagabonds, due to social reshuffling and unemployment, made possible a larger-scale distribution of ballads. The author's and balladmonger's lack of social ties stems not least from this circumstance. The relationship between performer and audience can similarly be described as fluctuating. The 'no obligation' element of the performance was matched by the ready availability and ease of transportation of the broadsides, and in general the texts and tunes were simple and easily retained. There is therefore a correspondence between author status, performance and sales methods, reception, bibliographical format, and text construction, which can be summed up as mobility, independence, and availability.

1.2.3 CENSORSHIP AND PUBLIC TASTE

The extent of the ballad producers' and distributors' free hand was limited by two essential factors: censorship and public taste. Both were components of contemporary literary activity which represented links with social reality and could influence textual content and strategy only indirectly. Influence was exerted by means of directives, institutional measures, and sanctions on the one hand, and through the market mechanism of supply and demand on the other. In the case of the ballad, literary criticism as a possible regulator of literary production played only a marginal role. Evidence of the practicalities and functioning of censorship is sparse.[47] Censorship decrees have for the most part survived, but only isolated cases of their enforcement have come down to us.

Censorship was directed against seditious, politically or religiously inopportune, immoral, and obscene publications, and affected therefore in the first instance the content of texts and their vocabulary. The power and effect of censorship in our period of study is difficult to assess, especially as so little research has been done on the subject. The aim and the severity of censorship changed according to the political situation and the circumstances of the day. The strictness or laxity of its enforcement depended not least on the occupancy of the relevant posts, which were in the hands of the state and church. Before 1576 the censor's role was presumably performed by the Master and the wardens of the Stationers' Company, who were not infrequently represented by a clerk who kept the Register. In addition there were the Archbishop of Canterbury and the Bishop of London, who could delegate the job to other clerics,[48] and of course there were censors appointed in their own right.[49] There are very few references to, or records of, rejected publications,[50] although Rollins ([1919a], p. 285) estimates that half of the extant ballads were never recorded in the Register in the first place. Evidence of the punishment of individual printers or authors does not prove anything with regard to the general operation and effectiveness of the censorship system.[51]

From the middle of the sixteenth century onwards there was no lack of government edicts on the licensing and control of printed matter.[52] In 1559 a royal edict decreeds that ballads, together with plays and shorter printed texts, could only be published with a licence from minor officials of the church and state. Control over the publication of more serious books was in the hands of higher-ranking officials (see F. S. Siebert [1952], p. 56). The Star Chamber Decree of 1586 reinforced the compulsory licensing of ballads (ibid., pp. 72-3). We know little of the individual operation of the controls. The issue of licences was mainly the responsibility of the Company, which tended towards a milder enforcement of controls, perhaps because of the infighting over monopolies (ibid., p. 59). E. H. Miller attributes to Elizabethan censorship nominal rather than actual success, surmising on the other hand that pressure of public opinion, which was predominantly loyal to the government and morally conservative, would have exerted a considerable controlling effect. Miller maintains that political criticism was more harshly dealt with than offences of a moral nature. He comes to the conclusion that 'most authors were not seriously affected by the edicts and proclamations' (see E. H. Miller [1959], p. 199).

During the first period of Stuart rule up to 1640, the system of censorship remained the same, but as the power of the crown diminished and political opinion became more differentiated it lost its effectiveness.[53] At the same time business interests, both of the members of the Company and of the journeymen, who were printing in secret, began to outweigh the interests of church and state. Everywhere, ways and means were being found to circumvent censorship controls.[54] Since ballads were checked less stringently than books, a typical ballad title would often serve as cover for the registering of a book (see F. S. Siebert [1952], pp. 143-4). There was generally less risk of being caught and punished for publishing without a licence than in the Elizabethan era, in spite of more stringent government measures (see H. S. Bennett [1970], pp. 45-8). The rapid burgeoning of print production made censorship doubly difficult (ibid., pp. 78-86). H. S. Bennett describes the situation as follows: 'From the evidence available it would seem that the trade took a very liberal view of what it might publish, always remembering that the risks of meddling with matters of Church or State were considerable, so that other kind of business was desirable could it be obtained' (ibid., p. 58).

It is the period 1640-60 which yields most information on censorship and its effectiveness (see Rollins, *CP*, pp. 3-29). Nearly every year Parliament passed new, stricter laws against any form of criticism of its policies, and against itinerant traders and balladmongers. At first the effect was only slight: 'Hawkers and ballad singers flourished in spite of occasional mishaps' (ibid., p. 29). But gradually the number of ballads and prose texts decreased, especially those of a royalist tendency; they were only sold clandestinely. In 1649 ballad-singers and sellers of broadsheets were no longer to be seen in the streets. Royalist newsbooks also disappeared. Ballads continued to be published: secretly in anthologies, in the royalist *drolleries,* and as insertions in prose texts. Between 1643 and 1656 no ballads were recorded in the Stationers' Register. After Cromwell's death in 1658 the censorship of ballads ceased and ballad production started up again with renewed vigour.

It is just as difficult to establish the influence of public taste on ballad production and textual form as it is to assess the effects of censorship. Author and seller were dependent on the profit from the sale of broadsides, the supply was large, and competition fierce.[55] It is tempting to assume here concessions to public taste and a backwash effect of public expectation on textual form. This is difficult to prove, however, as apart from the literary texts we have hardly any evidence of what that taste was. Investigations of the topic have always moved in the methodological circle of literary supply and the public taste which derived from it.[56] For popular literature, especially the street ballad, this is justified in so far as the sales success confirms a certain conformity between literary 'consumer goods' and 'consumer needs'. The question remains, however, as to how far this consumer pattern, which derived from the methods of distribution described above, in turn generated certain public needs which it then proceeded to reinforce. It is only in isolated cases that we can observe a backwash effect of non-literary factors on the text. For the rest, we can only describe the tendencies of public taste in very general terms.

We must first establish the type and composition of the ballad public. If 'public' in this sense is defined as a group of persons characterized by a 'common interest in some specific kind of social behaviour such as music, literature or sport' (see A. Silbermann [1969], p. 11), it is necessary to make the difficult distinction between the regular ballad audience and customers, and occasional listeners. Certainly it can be assumed that there was a large regular public for whom the author wrote and the printer/publisher made his selection, although business interests must have encouraged them to try to extend the range of customers; the wide variation of form and content in the ballads supports this assumption.

The interest shown by the public in the ballad—a very small part of an individual's whole spectrum of behaviour—was not dependent on the nature of the ballad alone. There were certain preconditions which affected public reaction, involving the audience's own experience and cultural background as well as the social origins of the individual.[57] The mass of the ballad public belonged to the urban bourgeoisie—merchants and craftsmen and the servants of their household—and secondly to the urban and agricultural working classes.[58] There are various reasons for assuming this to be the case. For one thing the low price of the street ballad would bring it within the means of the poorer classes. Another important point is that the method of sale—market-crier and showman tactics—would tend to reduce built-in prejudices and inhibitions regarding a 'culture' which ordinarily would have been inaccessible to the common man. The middle-class audience brought with them not only their literacy—acquired in order to cope with the practical demands of business and further their knowledge and understanding of religion and the Bible (see L. B. Wright [1964], pp. 43-80)—but also curiosity, open-mindedness, and a need for information and entertainment, as can be generally deduced from the substantial and diverse selection of printed works on offer (ibid., pp. 81-200).

Since the primary reading interests of such a public were in works which were useful for their practical advice, and given their meagre literary background, very limited leisure and general lack of means, they were likely to have been passive rather than otherwise with regard to purchasing printed texts or influencing their content. It was in these circumstances that the street ballad came into its own, saving the potential customer the journey to the bookstalls near St Paul's[59] and providing short, manageable,

straightforward listening and reading material. The ballad catered for a mainly lower-class, relatively uncultured, practically minded public with simple needs in the way of entertainment.

In the absence of more solid evidence we will assume a broad correspondence between public taste and ballad production. Cautious deductions concerning the needs of the ballad public will emerge during the course of this study when themes and textual procedures in the ballad are investigated. The uncomplicated nature of the entertainment and instruction, combined with strategies for simplifying reception, point to a certain element of audience expectation.

1.3 RELATIONSHIP OF TEXTS TO SOCIAL AND
CULTURAL CONTEXT

Transmission of the street-ballad text was characterized by improvisation—of a given text—by a 'no obligation' situation with the likelihood of interruptions, and a fluctuating audience. It must be assumed that this necessitated special techniques both for attracting and keeping the public's attention and also for ease of reception. Indeed these techniques can be found in the texts in both implicit and explicit form. The predominantly lower-class audiences and the atmosphere surrounding the performance would require an accommodation of both language and topic to the taste of the public. The on-the-spot mercantilism of the street-ballad trade demanded effective advertising strategies, which are similarly incorporated into the text. The balladmonger was under severe pressure from competition, and moreover he had to rely absolutely on his own performance techniques for financial success. He would therefore do his utmost to impress himself, and press his 'wares', as literary products, upon his audience, a factor that is also allowed for in the text. We know little about the actual vocal and mimetic interpretation of the 'textual score'. The accounts we do have of street-ballad performances, although they are polemical in tone, indicate little exploitation of the possibilities inherent in the text. We must merely conjecture about the histrionic shaping of the text on the basis of the theatrical connections. The use of the street ballad as an 'afterpiece' in the theatre, the similarity of the dialogue ballad to the short 'jig'—a play interpolated with songs[60]—which was performed both in the theatre and at popular festivities and dance (see C. R. Baskerville [1929], pp. 32, 35, 164), and the possible coming together of the ballad-singer and unemployed actor in one person, imply an occasional very competent ballad performance which did justice to the text. The possibility of itinerant trader or market-crier doubling as ballad-singer also presupposes at least some mastery of the art of showmanship.

The assumption that textual composition was influenced by literary and social considerations,[61] that is, that the author bore in mind the context of performance and sale at the time of writing, is reinforced by the fact that the ballad writer was paid once, in a lump sum (see Rollins [1919a], pp. 296-300). It was therefore in his interest, if he wanted further commissions from the printer/publisher, to ensure sales by bolstering up the function of the singer as sales-man and producing a performer-friendly text. The effects of these conditioning factors on the nature of the texts per-formed should not be underestimated, especially as the genre, being in an early phase of development, was still fairly flexible.

Notes

1. Most of the references in contemporary documents describe only the ballad-monger's vocal and gestural efforts to attract an audience. There is however also mention of such aids as 'stall', and 'pitch': see B 22. In this connection see also H. E. Rollins (1919a), p. 320; A. B. Friedmann (1961), p. 48.

2. See above, p. 9 and p. 45. For the situation as regards the German street ballad, see K. V. Riedel (1963): 'The presenter stands outside and above the action, directing the attention through his words and pictorial display' (p. 39). L. Petzoldt (1974), pp. 57-8.

3. See H. E. Rollins (1919a), pp. 306-11; also below, pp. 18-21.

4. For the distribution of the street ballads by pedlars, see also documentary references in the appendix: B 3, B 23, B 45, B 68, B 83.

5. *True Wonders, and strange news* (c. 1670-5), *POA*, no. 32, pp. 191-4; v. 1,1-2, p. 192.

6. *The Worlds Wonder* (1677), *POA*, no. 33, pp. 195-9, v. 1,1-1,2, p. 196.

7. *A Pleasant new Ballad you here may behold* (1630), *RB*, II, pp. 366-71, v. 1,1-7, p. 367.

8. *Euery Mans condition* (1627), *PG*, no. 47, pp. 270-5, v. 11,1-3, p. 274. My italics.

9. *A songe of foure Preistes that suffered death at* Lancaster (1601), *OEB*, no. 11, pp. 70-8, v. 14,3-4, p. 74.

10. *Terrible News from* Brainford (1661), *POA*, no. 13, pp. 75-80; v. 1,1-6, p. 77.

11. *Faire fall all good Tokens!* (between 1624 and 1640), *RB*, I, pp. 341-6; v. 1,5-8, p. 342.

12. *A Pleasant new Ballad you here may behold* (1630), *RB*, II, pp. 366-71; v. 1,1-4, p. 367.

13. *PG,* no. 78, pp. 443-8; title, p. 444.

14. First performed c. 1609 or 1610; see appendix B 37 and 38.

15. See appendix B 42-4. The closeness to reality of this scene is confirmed by Robert Greene's earlier (1591/2) description of the teamwork between rogues and balladmongers; see appendix B 22.

16. For more detail see the evaluation of all documentary evidence below, pp. 242-5.

17. See also H. E. Rollins (1919a), p. 310 and W. Chappell (1859), II, p. 484.

18. See appendix B 16, B 60, B 61.

19. See appendix B 33, B 39, B 61.

20. Preface to *PB*, I, p. xiii, see quotation above, p. 5.

21. R. Weimann (1967), p. 20. Where stage play and audience are no longer indivisible in the ritual, an attempt is made to bridge the developing separation with the newly established audience relationship (ibid., pp. 33-47). H.-J. Diller (1973): see esp. '*Die Zuschaueranrede*', pp. 148-216.

22. Quoted after R. B. McKerrow (1910).

23. Day had the privilege of printing the catechism, Tottel, that of printing all legal documents and Jugge printed all the Bibles. See F. A. Mumby (1956), pp. 66-7.

24. 'It is remarkable how soon after its invention the art of printing became an instrument of popular amusement and instruction—an active agent in the development of the mind of the people', remarks the private collector of old MSS and prints, Henry Huth (Introduction, *AB,* xv).

25. See ibid., pp. 76-7 and E. H. Miller (1959), pp. 94-136.

26. F. A. Mumby (1956), p. 90. C. Bladgen (1954) modifies the meaning of 'Ballad Stock' along the lines that this group of printers, in comparison with the other 'Stocks', were not so specialized in what they produced (p. 163).

27. P. M. Handover (1960) shows how the Company's monopoly and financial security stifled initiative in the printing trade (p. 50).

28. For the periodical press, see ibid., p. 98.

29. These dates are derived from McKerrow (1910) and H. R. Plomer (1907); dates given refer to verifiable activity.

30. F. Coles, H. Gosson, J. Grismand, H. Kirkham (1570-93), J. Trundle (1603-26), C. Wright (1613-39), J. Wright. For the hierarchical structure of the Company and conditions for membership, see McKerrow (1910), Introduction, pp. xvii-xxii.

31. W. M. Chappell's list of ballad-printers, *RB*, I, pp. xvii-xxii, contains numerous names not mentioned by McKerrow and Plomer. Such printers are therefore documented only in their inclusion in the Stationers' Register and not through their membership of the Company.

32. See F. A. Mumby (1956), p. 93. A ballad or short published work earned the author the same amount as the translation of a whole book - a few pounds (see H. S. Bennett [1970], p. 229).

33. The popularity of the street ballad is amply confirmed in secondary literature (see V. de Sola Pinto, *CM,* Introduction; H. E. Rollins [1919a], pp.

260-1; and others), and can be discerned in the contemporary comment of actual opponents of this literary form (see below, chapter 6).

34. In contrast to the sale of books, which was stationary and could count on a traditional type of customer.

35. See E. H. Miller (1959), pp. 75-7. H. E. Rollins (1919a) points out the fact that well-known and popular ballad authors at least were highly rated by publishers as commercial successes (pp. 304-5). Interest in the ballad business can be clearly seen in the competition for privileges.

36. P. Sheavyn (1909) talks of a 'large, ready sale for ballads . . . proven by the very large numbers of "ballets" and broadsides registered by the stationers' company' (p. 39).

37. He usually received a single, one-off fee; see H. E. Rollins (1919a), pp. 296-7.

38. See E. H. Miller (1959), pp. 94-136: 'Like the concept of order and the moralistic hostility toward usury, patronage was in conflict with a world moving from an agricultural economy and closed society to a capitalistic system and open society' (p. 94). See also G. A. Thompson (1914), pp. 26-35. For the following period there has to my knowledge been no research undertaken. L. L. Schücking deals with patronage from the aspect of the development of literary taste (1961), pp. 18-21.

39. 'With the notable exception of Shakespeare and Spenser, the lives of Elizabethan authors comprise case histories of poverty' (E. H. Miller [1959], p. 12).

40. See E. K. Chambers (1923), I, pp. 308-18; H. Castrop (1972), pp. 106-12.

41. See Ben Jonson's portrayal, appendix B 44 and B 22.

42. H. E. Rollins (1919a), pp. 318-19, surmises that the balladmonger frequently earned a fair amount, in spite of his minor sales role, through tips.

43. For this see E. K. Chambers (1954), I, pp. 1-88; E. Faral (1910).

44. See E. K. Chambers (1954), I, p. 69.

45. In *The Actors' Remonstrance* (1643) there is an indication that many actors who became destitute through the closing of the theatres went over to the ballad trade (see H. E. Rollins, *CP*, p. 14).

46. First verifiable ballad in 1624/25; last entry in the Stationers' Register in 1660.

47. Even a comprehensive investigation such as that of F. S. Siebert (1952) makes only occasional mention of the street ballad.

48. See W. W. Greg (1956), pp. 45-6 and 51. The Master of the Revels was responsible for the theatre, and after the beginning of the seventeenth century this position was in the gift of the Lord Chamberlain.

49. Captain Francis Bethen, appointed on 13 September 1648 and particularly strict in pursuing prose pieces and ballads, practically succeeded in banning the sale of ballads from the streets (see H. E. Rollins, *CP*, p. 40).

50. E. H. Miller (1959) maintains that there are no sources relating to this (p. 181).

51. See ibid., pp. 171-202. The case of John Stubbes, whose right hand was severed on 27 September 1579, led earlier scholars to overestimate censorship in Elizabethan times.

52. See R. B. McKerrow (1910), pp. x-xix, E. H. Miller (1959), pp. 171-202, W. W. Greg (1956), pp. 41-52, H. E. Rollins, *CP*, pp. 3-74, F. S. Siebert (1952), pp. 21-41.

53. F. S. Siebert (1952), p. 21; R. Fraser (1970) on the other hand maintains that it was precisely owing to the decrease in power that censorship measures became stricter.

54. F. S. Siebert (1952), pp. 143-6; H. S. Bennett (1970), pp. 45-58.

55. See H. E. Rollins (1919a), pp. 292-4; from 1557-1640, ballad titles comprised approximately half of the entries in the Stationers' Register (Rollins [1924], p. 1).

56. See L. B. Wright (1964), pp. 81-118; E. H. Miller (1959), pp. 63-93.

57. In this connection, see literary-sociological investigations by H. N. Fügen (1963), esp. pp. 169-76, and R. Escarpit (1961), esp. p. 83.

58. See H. E. Rollins (1919a), pp. 329-33; he also points out, however, that members of the higher ranks of society also read and listened to ballads. E. H. Miller (1959): 'Ballads were the common man's delight—and sometimes, but of course surreptitiously, the nobleman's too . . . The reasons for their popularity were obvious enough. Ballads were brief, farcically humorous, or sentimentally tragic, frequently bawdy, almost always topical and "new", poetic in the mechanical singsong fashion that the uncultivated admire, and generally set to a popular tune. In addition, they were inexpensive' (pp. 75-6).

59. 'To one person who visited the book-stalls there were of course hundreds who heard ballads sung' (H. E. Rollins [1919a], p. 295).

60. 'Ballad jig', 'farce jig' and 'stage jig' are terms which describe the possible transitions. C. R. Baskervill (1929) gives the following assessment, based on his knowledge of the field: 'a number of other ballads on one score or the other give evidence of dramatic presentation' (p. 164).

61. Rollins (1919a) recognized, at least to a certain extent, that this applied to the street ballad: 'Ballad singing affected ballad writing. Responding quickly

to the exigencies of the trade, writers would insert lines or even whole stanzas, to help the singers, and many of these insertions eventually became part of the ballad-technique. For one thing, all ballads were made to insist upon their newness' (p. 315).

Works Cited

Baskerville, C. R., *The Elizabethan Jig and Related Song Drama* (Chicago, 1929).

Bennett, H. S., *English Books and Readers 1603 to 1640. Being a Study of the History of the Book Trade in the Reign of James I and Charles I* (Cambridge, 1970).

Diller, H.-J., *Redeformen des englischen Misterienspiels* (Munich, 1973).

McKerrow, R. B., *A Dictionary of Printers and Booksellers in England, Scotland and Ireland, and of Foreign Printers of English Books 1557-1640* (London, 1910).

Miller, E. H., *The Professional Writer in Elizabethan England. A Study of Nondramatic Literature* (Cambridge, Mass., 1959).

Mumby, F. A., *Publishing and Bookselling. A History from the Earliest Times to the Present Day* (4th edn, London, 1956).

Rollins, H. E., 'The Black-Letter Broadside Ballad', *PMLA*, 34 (1919a), pp. 258-339.

Rollins, H. E., *An Analytical Index to the Ballad-Entries (1557-1709) in the Register of the Company of Stationers of London* (Chapel Hill, N.C., 1924).

Rollins, H. E., 'Introduction', *Cavalier and Puritan. Ballads and Broadsides Illustrating the Period of the Great Rebellion 1640-1660* (New York, 1923), pp. 3-74.

Siebert, F. S., *Freedom of the Press in England 1476-1776* (Urbana, Ill., 1952).

Silbermann, A. (ed.), *Reader. Massenkommunikation,* vol. I (Beielefeld, 1969).

Weimann, R., *Shakespeare und die Tradition des Volkstheaters. Soziologie. Dramaturgie. Gestaltung* (Berlin, 1987).

Wright, L. B., *Middle Class Culture in Elizabethan England* (London, 1925, 2nd edn, 1964).

Abbreviations

Titles are given in shortened form.

AB:	*Ancient Ballads and Broadsides,* H. Huth, ed. (London 1867)
BB:	*Ballads and Broadsides,* H. L. Collmann, ed. (Oxford 1912)
BBBM:	*The British Broadside Ballad and Its Music,* C. M. Simpson, ed. (New Brunswick 1966)
BBLB:	*Broadside Black-letter Ballads,* J. P. Collier, ed. (published privately, 1868)
CM:	*The Common Muse,* V. de Sola Pinto, ed. (London 1957)
CP:	*Cavalier and Puritan,* H. E. Rollins, ed. (New York 1923)
OB:	*Old Ballads from Early Printed Copies,* J. P. Collier, ed. (London 1840)
OEB:	*Old English Ballads: 1553-1625,* H. E. Rollins, ed. (Cambridge 1920)
POA:	*The Pack of Autolycus,* H. E. Rollins, ed. (Cambridge, Mass. 1927)
PB:	*The Pepys Ballads,* 8 vols., H. E. Rollins, ed. (Cambridge, Mass. 1929-32)
PG:	*A Pepysian Garland,* H. E. Rollins, ed. (Cambridge 1922)
PMO:	*Popular Music of the Olden Time,* 2 vols., W. Chappell, ed. (London 1855-9)
RB:	*The Roxburghe Ballads,* 9 vols., W. Chappell and J. W. Ebsworth, eds. (London, Hertford 1869-99)
SB:	*Songs and Ballads,* T. Wright, ed. (London 1860)
SHB:	*The Shirburn Ballads,* A. Clark, ed. (Oxford 1907)

System of quotation from the above ballad editions: reference to sources in these editions is by abbreviation, the number of the text (in so far as the texts are numbered in the particular edition), volume number in roman numerals (if there is more than one volume), and page number in arabic numerals. For example: *PB,* no. 84, II, pp. 224-8; *PG,* no. 8, pp. 49-53; *RB,* III, pp. 556-9. For reasons of consistency the verse number is given in every case, even if in the edition itself the verses are not numbered (in the case of *RB* the *line* number is also given). Where there is no division into verses, only the line number is given, even if lines are not numbered in the editions. For example: *PG,* no. 44, v. 10, pp. 52-3; ibid. 10, 1-3, p. 52; *RB,* II, vv. 3-5, lines 17-40, p. 263; *AB,* no. 22, lines 10-32, p. 125.

Tessa Watt (essay date 1991)

SOURCE: Introduction to *Cheap Print and Popular Piety,* Cambridge University Press, 1991, pp. 1-8.

[*In the following excerpt, Watt rejects critical studies that portray the broadside ballad as appealing only to lower-class sensibilities, and argues that the ballads also made their way into "respected" culture as they served important social and cultural needs.*]

My decision to begin research in early modern English history was inspired by studies published over the past fifteen years which are loosely described as works on 'popular culture'.[1] Margaret Spufford's work on the late seventeenth-century chapbook trade, in particular, raised a challenging set of questions.[2] How far back could this trade be traced? When did publishers begin to produce and distribute reading material consciously aimed at the humblest members of the literate public? The criterion of 'cheapness' seemed the best place to start, since price was the major constraining factor in book buying, after literacy. In this period up to 75% of the cost came from the paper, so the shortest works were the cheapest works: the one-page broadside and the tiny octavo chapbook.[3] This 'cheap' print, once identified, would provide an insight into popular culture and popular religion.

To some extent, these expectations were satisfied. There was, indeed, an increasing degree of specialization at the bottom end of the publishing trade in the decades before 1640, reaching, it would appear, a rapidly widening market. However, it would be misleading to describe this as a 'popular' printed culture, if 'popular' is taken to imply something exclusive to a specific social group. Ballads were hawked in the alehouses and markets, but in the same period they were sung by minstrels in the households of the nobility and gentry, who copied them carefully into manuscripts. Pictorial themes which appeared in the crudest woodcuts were also painted on the walls of manor houses. Chapbooks which sold for twopence, and appealed to 'honest folks that have no lands', were also bought by a Staffordshire lady and carefully left in her will to her clergyman son.[4] In the process of research, 'cultural homogeneities' appeared as often as cultural divisions.[5]

The model of a binary opposition of 'popular' and 'elite' has already been criticized, modified and sometimes disowned by recent social historians. Tim Harris points out that the two-tiered model fails to match the reality of a multi-tiered social hierarchy, with substantial numbers of households in the 'middling' levels. He argues that 'vertical antagonisms', especially the divisions caused by religion, were as important as horizontal divisions in seventeenth-century London.[6] Martin Ingram emphasizes the converse argument, describing areas of cultural 'consensus' which united those at all social levels.[7] While these critics doubt the explanatory value of the model, Roger Chartier attacks the theoretical premise which underlies it: the assumption 'that it is possible to establish exclusive relationships between specific cultural forms and particular social groups'. This assumption has led historians to pre-define certain cultural cleavages, which they have then proceeded to describe.[8]

Should we completely abandon the concept of 'popular culture', or can we find a more constructive way of using it? Peter Burke's 'asymmetrical' definition provides a start: for him, the 'great' tradition was the closed culture of the educated elites, while the 'little' (or popular) tradition was open to everyone, including those elites.[9] This inclusive definition is helpful, but, as Bob Scribner points out, the language tends to reduce the 'little' tradition to a 'residual or marginalized category'. Scribner suggests that we must think of popular culture as a 'total, unified culture': a system of shared attitudes and values, and the performances

or artefacts in which they are embodied.[10] We cannot ignore the existence of social stratification, nor of subcultural identities (such as apprentices or vagrants), but we must see how these overlapping segments somehow made up a functional whole.[11]

Scribner's concept of culture is harder to grasp and to use than the model of simple binary opposition, but it is more faithful to the complexities of past societies. In the present study, I will try to explore what we may describe as 'shared values', 'widespread attitudes' or 'commonplace mentalities': not a homogeneous, articulated set of doctrines, but a mosaic made up of changing and often contradictory fragments.

We may choose to call this mosaic 'popular' belief, but only if the term is understood inclusively. As historians used to the 'almost tyrannical preeminence of the social dimension'[12] we may be uncomfortable with the lack of evidence to pinpoint the audience for cheap print, and to locate it precisely on the social scale. We may be frustrated with the inability of the printed artefacts to help us differentiate between the views of the gentry, the 'middling sort' and the labouring poor. But this idea that the broadsides and chapbooks were aimed at and consumed by a definable social group may be a myth. The audience presupposed within the cheap print itself appears to be inclusive rather than exclusive, addressed both as 'readers' and as 'hearers'; as substantial householders expected to employ labourers, and as couples 'whose whole stocke could hardly purchase a wedding ring'.[13] Of course, this cheap print is not homogeneous: some items like the copper engravings and plague broadsides appear to have been produced for a market of middling Londoners, while other ballads and chapbooks inhabit the world of poor Northumberland men, west-country lasses, serving-men, chambermaids and 'poor and plaine people' living in 'remote' parts of the country.[14] As literacy increased, the market for cheap print expanded, and there may sometimes have been gaps between authorial intention and audience consumption. But the buyers remained socially variegated: in the early seventeenth century gentry collectors were still copying ballads into their commonplace books; probably the same ballads which were to be found on the walls of 'honest alehouses', in 'the shops of artificers' and in 'the cottages of poor husbandmen'.[15]

Admittedly, no matter how we define 'popular belief', it is impossible for the historian to get 'directly at' this mosaic of values and attitudes. Bob Scribner is particularly sceptical about the source materials used in studies of popular culture (including printed broadsides and chapbooks), arguing that they reveal only 'forms of downward mediation by educational or literate elites'.[16] The present study is more positive about the value of looking at printed wares, provided they are set in their cultural context. In our approach to printed sources, Roger Chartier's notion of cultural 'consumption' may be useful. For Chartier 'consumption' should be taken as 'a form of production which, to be sure, manufactures no object, but which constitutes representations that are never identical to those that the producers (the authors or artists) have introduced into their works'.[17] Although we cannot recover the reaction of the individual buyer, we will be looking at how the collective responses of cheap-print 'consumers' exercised an influence on what was printed, and especially what was reprinted. For example, in chapter 3 we will look at a body of long-enduring ballads which was to some extent 'produced' by the consumers through the process of selection. This examination will suggest ways in which the propaganda of Protestant reformers was modified by the more conservative religious outlook of the larger public.

There are undoubtedly certain sources which can bring us closer to ordinary people as cultural 'creators' rather than as creative 'consumers'.[18] Historians are paying increasing attention to records of slanderous rhymes, skimmingtons and other ritualized protests or festivities which show people using established symbols in a resourceful way.[19] However, the ballads, woodcuts and chapbooks provide a window on a particular element in the 'process of culture formation':[20] the role of print. This is an important issue in an era of increasing literacy, and in a country whose religion placed so much emphasis on words and reading. The past decades have seen a number of influential studies on the impact of print in the early modern period.[21] But we still need more careful investigation of the ways in which print interacted with other forms of communication in the specific cultural context of post-Reformation England.

Clearly not all printed sources are equally good as windows on the process by which cultural values were disseminated and absorbed (or modified) by the wider society. The notion of 'cheap print' is a valid one, if used as a neutral category, not as a genre aimed exclusively at a definable social group. Although we should try to avoid assumptions about the readership, we must also take account of the basic social and economic realities which limited contact with printed texts for much of the populace. These realities included the cost of a work, its geographical distribution, and the level of reading skills which it presupposed. During our period, publishers themselves were increasingly adopting strategies to match these realities: by organizing a syndicate for the distribution of ballads, by using woodcut pictures to appeal to those on the fringes of literacy, by condensing longer stories into an inexpensive 24-page octavo format.[22]

The growing specialization of publishers in printed works targeted for humble readers could be seen as an agent of 'polarization'; of a growing gap between patrician and plebeian culture, as described by Anthony Fletcher and John Stevenson.[23] Yet, if the culmination of this process was the creation of a separated body of 'chap' literature for an identifiably 'plebeian' audience, this did not occur within the period under study here, and possibly not until the eighteenth century. Before 1640, it is likely that a large proportion of the buyers were drawn from the middling ranks of yeomen, husbandmen and tradespeople, and that even gentry readers were not uncommon.[24] If publishers did increasingly 'target' humbler readers, this should not necessarily be seen as a divisive phenomenon. Cheap print in this period was just as likely to be an instrument of social cohesion, as more people were brought into the reading public, and as stories, images and values permeated the multiple tiers of English society.

This 'shared culture' was disseminated along lines of communication which connected the country, both socially and geographically. The distribution of cheap print relied especially on a network of wayfarers: minstrels, broadside ballad sellers, interlude players, petty chapmen. Texts and their effects radiated outward to local communities from certain focal points: the marketplace, the parish church, the godly household, the inn or alehouse.[25]

The cultural historian Roger Chartier, while attacking the elite-popular divide, has set up a new dichotomy which seems equally rigid: that of city versus country. In the cities, print was 'everywhere present, posted, exhibited, cried in the streets, and highly visible'; but in the seventeenth century this 'familiarity that was the beginning of literacy' was almost exclusively the privilege of urban dwellers.[26] This may well be true of France, but in England there can be no doubt that texts of one kind or another were familiar in all parts of the realm. From the beginning of Elizabeth's reign, injunctions required that the Lord's Prayer and other biblical sentences be painted in every parish church, and this order was reinforced by visitations.[27] In a Protestant country there was greater incentive to encourage literacy, and most parishioners had some contact with bibles, catechisms, prayer books or psalters, which were read aloud in church, and probably handled, if not actually owned.[28] Broadside ballads were commonplace from deepest Cambridgeshire to Lancashire, to the western counties; and literature of the period most typically depicts the ballad seller in a rural setting. Although early Elizabethan ballads were sometimes billed as 'A warning to London' or addressed to 'London dames', by the second quarter of the seventeenth century they were much more commonly given titles like 'The cooper of Norfolke' or 'A pleasant new northerne song, called the two York-shire lovers'.[29]

Some of these stories and their tunes may well have been picked up in the alehouses of Norfolk and Yorkshire by the same pedlars and travelling performers who later disseminated the printed ballads.[30] Even when they were concocted in London by an anonymous hack, these printed wares were not finished products like gloves or combs, to be used in much the same way by each purchaser. If we are to choose a metaphor from the chapman's pack, print was more like the 'scotch cloth' or 'coarse linen', sold by the yard, to be made into something by the buyer.[31] In the parlance of the new cultural history, we should not look at print in isolation, but at how it was 'appropriated'.[32] Much of this study will focus on the singlesheet broadside, chosen at first because, at a penny or less, it was the cheapest form of print. Yet the broadside was not only a text to be read. It was also, in fact primarily, a song to be sung, or an image to be pasted on the wall. In these oral and visual forms, it had the potential to reach a much wider audience than its original buyers and its 'literate' readers.

The question of literacy is, of course, central to any study of print in this period. We know that by the 1640s roughly 30% of adult males in rural England could sign their names, with up to 78% fully 'literate' in London.[33] David Cressy's evidence shows how the ability to sign one's name was closely tied to social status, with marked differences across geographical regions. In 1600, 52% of East Anglian tradesmen and craftsmen could sign, compared with 80% in London. East Anglian yeomen and husbandmen were 61% and 21% 'literate', while in Durham and Northumberland the figures were much lower, at 23% and 13% respectively. Statistics for labourers are thin on the ground, but in the diocese of Norwich over the entire period 1580-1700, 15% could sign their names. This was a little better than the women, whose showing was only 11%.[34]

However, as Margaret Spufford has convincingly argued, these statistics are probably gross underestimates of *reading* ability.[35] Reading was taught before writing, and it is likely that many more rural people could get through the text of a broadside ballad than could sign their names to a Protestation Oath. In Sweden, a tradition of teaching reading alone, without writing, survived well into the nineteenth century, and the gap between these skills is verified in church examination registers.[36] Cressy's figures for early modern England may only represent the proportion of each group which remained in school from age seven to eight when writing was taught. Amongst husbandmen and labourers especially, there may be a large number who attended school up to the age of six, and learnt the primary skill of reading, but who were whisked away to join the labour force 'as soon as they were strong enough to contribute meaningfully to the family economy'.[37] The 'literacy' statistics should be taken as minimum figures, not as certainties.

Nevertheless, in a partially literate society, the most influential media were those which combined print with non-literate forms. Recent studies on the impact of the printing press have viewed the sixteenth and seventeenth centuries as a period in which oral and literate modes of communication were closely intertwined.[38] Printed works were disseminated by word of mouth, transforming the culture of the 'illiterate', and oral modes of communication shaped the structure of printed works. The interesting process was not only the spread of literacy and readership, but the complex interweaving of the printed word with existing cultural practices. In Part I, we will look at how the broadside ballad interacted with oral and musical traditions. In Part II, we will see the broadside picture against the visual background of domestic wall painting and painted cloth. Only in Part III will we follow the development of 'cheap print' intended primarily for reading; first surveying a variety of short pamphlets, and then charting the beginnings of the 'penny chapbook' as a specialized product.

The dissemination of Protestant ideas will be used as a focus for this investigation. However, to describe these ballads, woodcuts and chapbooks as thoroughly 'Protestant' would be to overlook the way they blended the new ideas with older attitudes to religion and morality, just as they embraced existing oral and visual traditions. Protestant concepts and images were, like printed texts, the raw material which the purchaser could choose and shape as he wanted, according to his own needs and beliefs. We can only approach the buyer's perspective indirectly, by comparing the initial polemic of Protestant reformers with the religious ballads and chapbooks which found long-lasting commercial success.

There is little in this cheap godly print (and therefore in this study) about double predestination, ecclesiastical vestments, the position of the altar, or the prerequisites for communion. We should not assume that the audience had no interest in these matters, but that, when they did, it was satisfied elsewhere; in black-letter sermons and treatises, or discussions with neighbours, or catechizing sessions. The printed works in this study operated largely outside the sphere of the church. They were bought for entertainment, or to satisfy needs which the reader might not necessarily have defined as 'religious': the need for role models, for inspirational stories, for behavioural rules to give to their children, for guidance on the approach to death. As the cheap print trade developed and became more specialized, it seems to have become increasingly responsive to these needs, and therefore of particular interest to the 'social and cultural' historian, as well as to the historian of 'religion'.

Notes

1. For example, Robert W. Malcolmson, *Popular recreations in English society 1700-1850* (Cambridge, 1973); Keith Thomas, *Religion and the decline of magic* (1971); Natalie Zemon-Davis, *Society and culture in early modern France* (Stanford, 1982 edn); Robert Scribner, *For the sake of simple folk* (Cambridge, 1981). Not all of these historians have used the term 'popular culture' themselves.

2. Margaret Spufford, *Small books and pleasant histories. Popular fiction and its readership in seventeenth-century England* (1981).

3. Philip Gaskell, *A new introduction to bibliography* (Oxford, 1972), p. 177.

4. See chs. 1, 5, 8.

5. Martin Ingram, 'Ridings, rough music and the "reform of popular culture" in early modern England', *Past and Present,* 105 (Nov. 1984), p. 113.

6. Tim Harris, 'The problem of "popular political culture" in seventeenth-century London', *History of European Ideas,* 10 (1989), pp. 43-58.

7. Ingram, 'Ridings, rough music and the "reform of popular culture"', pp. 79, 112-13; Martin Ingram, *Church courts, sex and marriage in England, 1570-1640* (Cambridge, 1987), p. 167.

8. Roger Chartier, *The cultural uses of print in early modern France,* trans. Lydia C. Cochrane (Princeton, 1987), p. 3; Roger Chartier, *Cultural history. Between practices and representations,* trans. Lydia C. Cochrane (Cambridge, 1988), p. 30.

9. Peter Burke, *Popular culture in early modern Europe* (1978), p. 28.

10. Bob Scribner, 'Is a history of popular culture possible?', *History of European Ideas,* 10 (1989), pp. 181-2. The definition is that used by A.L. Kroeber to define 'culture' as a whole.

11. *Ibid.,* pp. 183-4.

12. Chartier, *Cultural history,* p. 30.

13. John Andrewes, *The converted mans new birth: describing the direct way to heaven* (1629), sig.A2. 'A most excellent new dittie, wherein is shewed the sage sayings, and wise sentences of Salomon' (1586). *Cupids schoole: wherein, yongmen and maids may learne divers sorts of complements* (1632), sig.C3. See pp. 311, 100, 295.

14. Engravings and broadsides discussed in ch. 6. Martin Parker, *The king and a poore northerne man* (1633). 'The crafty lass of the west', Pepys, IV, 7. *Cupids schoole.* Richard Hawes, *The poore-mans plaster-box* (1634). See pp. 299, 294-5.

15. B M Addit. MS 15,225; Shirburn. Izaak Walton, *The complete angler; or, the contemplative man's recreation* (1653), facs. edn (1976), p. 49. Nicholas Bownde, *The doctrine of the sabbath* (1595), p. 242.

16. Scribner, 'Is a history of popular culture possible?', p. 177.

17. Chartier, *Cultural history,* p. 40.

18. Bob Scribner criticizes Chartier's theory of 'consumption' for its failure to show ordinary people as creators. Scribner, 'Is a history of popular culture possible?', p. 184.

19. For example, Ingram, 'Ridings, rough music and the "reform of popular culture"', pp. 79-113; Buchanan Sharp, 'Popular political opinion in England 1660-1685', *History of European Ideas,* 10 (1989), pp. 13-29; David Underdown, *Revel, riot and rebellion. Popular politics and culture in England 1603-1660* (Oxford, 1985).

20. Scribner, 'Is a history of popular culture possible?', p. 184.

21. Elizabeth L. Eisenstein, *The printing press as an agent of change* (2 vols. in 1, Cambridge, 1980 edn). Marshall McLuhan, *The Gutenberg galaxy* (Toronto, 1962). Walter J. Ong, *Rhetoric, romance and technology* (1971); Walter J. Ong, *Orality and literacy: the technologizing of the word* (1982).

22. See chs. 3, 4, 7.

23. A.J. Fletcher and J. Stevenson, 'A polarised society?', in Fletcher and Stevenson, eds., *Order and disorder in early modern England* (Cambridge, 1985), pp. 1-15.

24. See Frances Wolfreston, pp. 315-17.

25. See chs. 1, 5.

26. Chartier, *The cultural uses of print,* pp. 347, 158-9, 166, 176.

27. See pp. 217-18.

28. On the importance of the Book of Common Prayer as a unifying force and an encouragement to literacy, see John N. Wall jnr, 'The Reformation in England and the typographical revolution: "By this printing . . . the doctrine of the Gospel soundeth to all nations"', in Gerald P. Tyson and Sylvia Wagonheim, eds., *Print and culture in the Renaissance: essays on the advent of printing in Europe* (1986).

29. 'A warning to London by the fall of Antwerp' [1577?], Collmann no. 69. 'A proper new balade expressyng the fames, concerning a warning to al London dames' [1571], Collmann no. 71. 'The cooper of Norfolke' [*c.* 1627], Pepys, I, 400. 'A pleasant new northerne song' [*c.* 1630], Pepys, I, 240.

30. John Taylor collected anecdotes from victualling houses for his *Wit and mirth. Chargeably collected out of tavernes, ordinaries, innes . . .* (1626).

31. On the contents of the pedlar's pack, see Margaret Spufford, *The great reclothing of rural England: petty chapmen and their wares in the seventeenth century* (1984).

32. Chartier, *The cultural uses of print,* p. 6.

33. David Cressy, *Literacy and the social order. Reading and writing in Tudor and Stuart England* (Cambridge, 1980), p. 72.

34. *Ibid.,* pp. 146, 150, 152, 119.

35. Margaret Spufford, 'First steps in literacy: the reading and writing experiences of the humblest seventeenth-century autobiographers', *Social History,* 4 (1979), pp. 407-35. See also Keith Thomas, 'The meaning of literacy in early modern England', in Gerd Baumann, ed., *The written word. Literacy in transition* (Oxford, 1986), p. 103.

36. Egil Johansson, 'The history of literacy in Sweden', in Harvey J. Graff, ed., *Literacy and social development in the West: a reader* (Cambridge, 1981), pp. 181-2.

37. Spufford, *Small books,* p. 26.

38. Eisenstein, *The printing press as an agent of change,* p. 129. Roger Chartier, 'Culture as appropriation: popular cultural uses in early modern France', in Stephen L. Kaplan ed., *Understanding popular culture: Europe from the middle ages to the nineteenth century* (Berlin, 1984), pp. 229-53. Ong, *Rhetoric, romance and technology,* pp. 23-47; Ong,

Orality and literacy. Tyson and Wagonheim, eds., *Print and culture in the Renaissance.*

Abbreviations

Arber: Edward Arber, ed., *A transcript of the registers of the Company of Stationers of London 1554-1640* (5 vols., 1875-94).

BL: British Library.

BM Prints: Department of Prints and Drawings, British Museum.

BM Satires: Collection of prints in the Department of Prints and Drawings, British Museum. All pre-1640 prints described in *Catalogue of prints and drawings in the British Museum. Division 1. Satires. Vol. 1. 1320-1689,* ed. Frederic G. Stephens (1870).

Child: F. J. Child, *The English and Scottish popular ballads* (5 vols., 1882-98).

Collmann: H. L. Collmann, ed., Ballads and broadsides chiefly of the Elizabethan period . . . now in the library at Britwell Court (1912). Collection now in the Huntington Library, California.

Crawford: Collection of ballads and broadsides owned by the Earl of Crawford, on deposit at the John Rylands Library, Manchester. Listed in *Bibliotheca Lindesiana: catalogue of a collection of English ballads of the XVIIth and XVIIIth centuries* (1890; facs. edn, 1962).

Dicey catalogue 1754: William and Cluer Dicey, *A catalogue of maps, histories, prints, old ballads, copy-books, broadsheets and other patters, drawing-books, garlands &c.* (1754). Reprinted in R. S. Thomson, 'The development of the broadside ballad trade and its influence upon the transmission of English folksongs' (Cambridge PhD, 1974), App. C.

DNB: The Dictionary of National Biography.

Douce: Francis Douce collection of ballads in the Bodleian Library, Oxford.

ent.: Entry in Stationers' Register.

Euing: Collection of ballads in Glasgow University Library. Reprinted in John Holloway, ed., *The Euing collection of English broadside ballads* (Glasgow, 1971).

Eyre: G. E. B. Eyre, ed., *A transcript of the registers of the worshipful Company of Stationers 1640-1708* (3 vols., 1913-14).

Hind: Arthur M. Hind, *Engraving in England in the sixteenth and seventeenth centuries* (3 vols., vol. III compiled by M. Corbett and M. Norton, Cambridge, 1952-64).

Huth. 50: Collection of ballads in the British Library. Reprinted by Joseph Lilly, 1867.

Lilly: Joseph Lilly, ed., *A collection of 79 black-letter ballads and broadsides printed in the reign of Queen Elizabeth* (1867). Now in the British Library, Huth. 50.

Manchester: Manchester Central Library, collection of ballads, 2 vols.

MS Ashmole 48: Manuscript volume of ballads in the Bodleian Library, Oxford. Reprinted in Wright. ed., *Songs and ballads, with other short poems, chiefly of the reign of Philip and Mary* (1860).

Norris and Brown 1712: List of stock ballads and chapbooks registered on 20 September 1712 to Thomas Norris and Charles Brown. Reprinted in Thomson, 'Development of the broadside ballad trade', App. B.

'partners': The 'ballad partners' syndicate (with changing membership) for the publication and distribution of ballads throughout much of the seventeenth century.

Pepys: Ballad collection of Samuel Pepys, Magdalene College, Cambridge, 5 vols.

PRO: Public Record Office.

Rawlinson 566: Rawlinson Collection of ballads in the Bodleian Library, Oxford.

RB orig.: Roxburghe collection of ballads in the British Library, 3 vols. Virtually all pre-1640 items have been reprinted in 'RB repr.'.

RB repr.: William Chappell and J. Woodfall Ebsworth, eds., *The Roxburghe Ballads* (8 vols., 1871-97).

RCHM: Royal Commission on the Historical Monuments of England.

REED: *Records of Early English Drama* (Toronto, 1979-).

Rollins Index: Hyder E. Rollins, *An analytical index to the ballad-entries in the Stationers' Registers: 1557-1709* (1924; 2nd edn with intro. by Leslie Shepard, Hatboro, 1967).

SA: Collection of Broadsides in the Society of Antiquaries, London. Catalogue by Robert Lemon, 1866.

Seng: Peter Joseph Seng, ed. *Tudor songs and ballads. From MS Cotton Vespasian A-25* (Cambridge, Mass., 1978).

Shirburn: Andrew Clark, ed., *The Shirburn ballads* (Oxford, 1907). From a MS in the library of Shirburn Castle, Oxfordshire.

Simpson: Claude M. Simpson, *The British broadside ballad and its music* (New Brunswick, New Jersey, 1966).

STC: *A short-title catalogue of books printed in England, Scotland & Ireland and of English books printed abroad 1475-1640* (first compiled by A. W. Pollard and G. R. Redgrave; 2nd edn, revised and enlarged, begun by W. A. Jackson and F. S. Ferguson, completed by Katherine F. Pantzer, 2 vols., 1976-86).

Wing: *Short-title catalogue of books printed in England, Scotland, Ireland, Wales and British North America and of English books printed in other countries 1641-1700* (compiled by Donald Wing, vol. III, New York, 1951;

2nd edn, revised and enlarged by the Index Committee of the Modern Language Association of America, vols. I-II, New York, 1972-82).

Wood: Anthony Wood's collection of ballads in the Bodleian Library, Oxford.

Wright: Thomas Wright, ed., *Songs and ballads, with other short poems, chiefly of the reign of Philip and Mary* (1860).

CHAPBOOKS, JESTBOOKS, PAMPHLETS, AND NEWSPAPERS

Matthias A. Shaaber (essay date 1929)

SOURCE: "Personal News," in *Some Forerunners of the Newspaper in England, 1476-1622,* University of Pennsylvania Press, 1929, pp. 13-34.

[*In the following excerpt, Shaaber shows that broadside ballads and other inexpensive verse often served as a means of disseminating news about the British royalty and popular heroes, and he notes that these publications eventually evolved into newspapers.*]

Personal news, as we may call it, is probably the oldest kind. It is a record or, more often, merely a celebration of the achievements of a personage of importance, from the sovereign himself to a prominent London merchant, written by one of his liegemen, retainers, or clients, or by an admirer whom his attainments have inspired at a distance. Sometimes encomia of this sort were written from motives little better than selfish, for the courtier who wrote a poem glorifying the virtues of his master might reasonably expect a reward, and indeed the court poet whom a royal or noble master kept, clothed, sheltered, and even pensioned customarily discharged his obligation by this kind of employment. Thomas Love Peacock's ironical outline of the business of the official poet is by no means altogether inaccurate and it furthermore points out the antiquity of his calling:

> The natural desire of every man to engross to himself as much power and property as he can acquire by any of the means which might makes right, is accompanied by the no less natural desire of making known to as many people as possible the extent to which he has been a winner in this universal game. The successful warrior becomes a chief; the successful chief becomes a king; his next want is an organ to disseminate the fame of his achievements and the extent of his possessions; and this organ he finds in a bard, who is always ready to celebrate the strength of his arm, being first duly inspired by that of his liquor. This is the origin of poetry, which, like all other trades, takes its rise in the

demand for the commodity, and flourishes in proportion to the extent of the market.

> Poetry is thus in its origin panegyrical. The first rude songs of all nations appear to be a sort of brief historical notices, in a strain of tumid hyperbole, of the exploits and possessions of a few pre-eminent individuals. They tell us how many battles such an one has fought, how many helmets he has cleft, how many breastplates he has pierced, how many widows he has made, how much land he has appropriated, how many houses he has demolished for other people, what a large one he has built for himself, how much gold he has stowed away in it, and how liberally and plentifully he pays, feeds, and intoxicates the divine and immortal bards, the sons of Jupiter, but for whose everlasting songs the names of heroes would perish.[1]

Verses of this kind, then, were no novelty at all at the beginning of the era of printing, and they served to spread whatever news they contained merely by being printed. Examples of personal news written in England not long before our period can be found in the works of Laurence Minot in the fourteenth century and of John Lydgate in the fifteenth.

Laurence Minot was probably a minstrel, possibly a court minstrel, and certainly an enthusiastic admirer of his king, Edward III.[2] Each one of his eleven poems is the celebration of a battle of the king's against the Scots or the French, an account which, even if it is sometimes unhistorical, gives much information about what took place. "Political journalism in rhyme" Ker calls these pieces.[3] During the reign of Henry VI, or at least until the fortunes of the king began to decline, Lydgate wrote verses in celebration of nearly every important public occasion in the life of his master, no less than four pieces, for instance, at the time of his coronation in 1429. In discharge of this duty, he became, consciously or unconsciously, a writer of news, for it would be well-nigh impossible for any one to glorify the triumphs of his master without occasionally deviating into the particulars thereof. The best example of this kind of news from Lydgate's pen is the poem which he wrote in 1432, when the king returned to London from France, recounting in 544 lines full of exact detail the municipal reception offered him.[4] This is a genuine piece of reporting: Lydgate is even so accurate as to reproduce two addresses by the lord mayor in the prose in which they were spoken.

On the other hand, these verses were sometimes written and published out of mere literary vanity, especially after the Renaissance made poetry fashionable; the coronation of a king or the birth of an heir was an acceptable subject ready made to the hand of the poetical amateur. At the same time, the professional versifier, a man who had his living to make by the pen, rather than a dependent, a poetical pensioner, or a courtier with a taste for verse-making, would also seize upon the same sort of occasion to exercise his wits, for the sake of whatever he could get for his verses from a publisher (which was usually little enough) and for the sake of whatever honorarium he could flatter out of his subject or the worthy to whom he dedicated his piece. When such a writer wrote his topical verses with the expectation of profiting by their publication, he is indistinguishable from a journalist.

These verses, rarely inspired, sometimes easy and elegant, more often conventional and insipid, were compounded of eulogy and news in varying proportions, but the traces of the latter revealed by analysis are as a rule slight and sometimes negligible. Yet even those which impart no information at all are still to be considered journalistic, for they were called forth by a passing event—an anniversary, a battle, an edict or decree, a marriage. Even if the motives which moved their authors to compose them were not always journalistic, as soon as they were printed and offered for sale they took on a journalistic color, for it could seldom have been anything but their pertinence, their dependence upon an interesting recent event, which found buyers for them.

The chief subject of personal news would naturally be the reigning sovereign himself. He was not only the most important and the most conspicuous person in the realm, but one of the most liberal patrons of poetry as well. Furthermore, most of the Tudor rulers enjoyed a good deal of personal popularity, so that it was not always mere policy which produced verses of personal praise and records of their glory. The chief occasions for composing and publishing them were, again naturally, such epoch-making events as the coronation, the marriage, or the death of the sovereign. The earliest of these which I have found were occasioned by the death of Henry VII in 1509. Only a fragment of the elegy attributed to John Skelton and printed by Wynkyn de Worde has survived, but there are copies of two editions of Bishop Fisher's funeral sermon,[5] which was probably interesting in the same way as verses lamenting the same misfortune. Much more typical of the effusions of the official poet is Stephen Hawes's *Joyfull medytacyon of the coronacyon of Henry the eyght,*[6] which describes the author as "sometyme grome of ye chambre of our late souerayne lorde kynge Henry ye seuenth." As a matter of fact, if that practitioner and patron of poetry, King Henry VIII, inspired a great deal of this sort of eulogy, an unusually large proportion has been lost, for I have found only two panegyrics printed during his reign and one lamentation for his death. There is also a prose account of the coronation procession of Queen Anne Boleyn,[7] but this is quite as much a description of a sumptuous municipal pageant as anything else, for all its doting on the graciousness of the lady. No one in England dared speak a good word for the divorced Queen Katharine when she died in 1536, but far away, in Mainz, Bishop Nausea printed a tribute to her memory.[8] Both Edward VI and Mary, however, did not lack admirers in print, the untimely death of the former in particular exciting the compassion of the poets, even though it became dangerous to express one's regard for the defender of the Protestant faith as soon as his sister had gained the throne. This sentiment, however, persisted into the reign of Elizabeth, and during her early years the printing presses bore a fresh crop of epitaphs on the decease of the king.

It is in the time of Elizabeth and James I, however, that addresses in praise of the sovereign and reports of personal history become most numerous. Several reasons suggest themselves: in the first place, there was more verse-making and more printing of all sorts; again, both monarchs had a weakness for flattery; and besides, Elizabeth's real popularity and King James's peculiar susceptibility to praise from the learned and the ingenious probably added to the tale. But the most significant reason is that by this time versifiers of a humbler sort, the ballad-writers, had joined the chorus formerly raised by the court poets alone and considerably swelled its volume. Now the meanest poetaster's artless verses might see the light just as well as the courtier's elegant encomium, and, if only they were fervent enough in praise of the queen, no doubt they were equally acceptable to her majesty's loyal subjects. In consequence, though the courtier by no means ceased expressing his duty to his queen in verse, his panegyrics were now out-numbered by those of the ballad-writer. The most curious and the best known of these is the ballad beginning, "Come ouer the born Bessy," by William Birche, "a dyologe sett furthe by twene the quenes maiestie and Englonde"[9] in terms of the most delightful intimacy.

During the reign of Elizabeth the custom also grew up of publishing laudatory ballads and verses for the anniversary of her coronation, 17 November, which was usually celebrated with tilting and pageantry. Though only a few of these pieces have been preserved, so many of them were entered in the Stationers' registers as to warrant the supposition that no anniversary after about the middle of the reign was left unmarked by simple and hearty tributes of this kind. Furthermore, the proportion of real news in them is often higher than in most of the productions of the class under consideration, for an account of the tournament held in honor of the day was sometimes made the substance of the whole piece. George Peele's *Polyhymnia*[10] (courtly in tone, of course) is a book of verses of this sort. Again, in 1588, a book of verses called *The blessednes of Brytaine,* by Maurice Kyffin, which had been printed for the coronation day of the preceding year, was reissued "with a new addition containing the late Accidents and Occurrents of this yeere 88. being the Thirtieth of hir Maiesties Raigne."[11]

When Queen Elizabeth died, all the grades of the poetical academy were heard from, beginning with the learned scholars of the University of Oxford and men like Bishop Hall and descending in the scale through ready and needy wits like Thomas Churchyard, Henry Chettle, and Samuel Rowlands to the anonymous ballad-writers. Here again we find, in the books by Chettle,[12] Richard Niccols,[13] and Henry Petowe,[14] indubitable news in the form of an appendix describing the queen's funeral. But in their pardonable preoccupation with the living rather than the dead, the poets saluted the accession of King James even more industriously. Frequently they handled both subjects at the same time and thereby produced books with titles ingeniously looking both ways, such as *Sorrowes Ioy*[15] and *Weepe with*

Ioy.[16] These welcomes to King James are but the beginning of a steady shower of panegyric which rained upon that impressionable monarch as long as he sat on the throne of England.

In fact, the London journalists' interest in King James had begun long before he succeeded to the throne of England. In 1581 William Elderton's ballad beginning, "Iesus God what a griefe is this," which tells the story of an attempt against the king's life and his rescue by an English serving-man, was entered in the Stationers' register.[17] There is no historical foundation for this legend, but it was very probably believed as news. A book concerning another attempt on the king's life was published in 1585,[18] and still another in 1593.[19] At the time of his marriage in 1590, no less than four ballads on the subject were entered in the Stationers' register,[20] and in 1594 two pieces describing the baptism of his heir, a book[21] and a ballad,[22] were published. Again in 1600, when the Earl of Gowrie attempted to assassinate the king, an account of the incident was published in London.[23]

After the death of Queen Elizabeth, the belauding of King James began the moment he left Edinburgh for London, and almost every stage in his journey was marked by the publication of a book or a ballad. It reached its climax at the time of his coronation in midsummer, when scarcely a detail of the ceremonies could have gone unrecorded. These pieces are not mere panegyric; some of them describe the king's movements in considerable detail. All told, the output of the London presses at this time includes ballads full of a holiday spirit of naïve delight, grave compliments from the universities, exultant outbursts from his patriotic countrymen pluming themselves on a Scotchman's ascending the throne of England, weighty discourses by the soberminded on the advantages of the union of the two kingdoms, addresses of congratulation by major poets such as Drayton and Daniel, and fearful and wonderful concoctions in Latin or Greek or both, probably designed to flatter his majesty's pretensions to learning. The eulogists, hackwriters, and booksellers expended their ingenuity liberally in devising novel ways of honoring the king. Several royal genealogies were printed, as indeed usually happened on an occasion of this kind; new editions of old books somehow relevant to the occasion, such as the account of the baptism of Prince Henry, that of the popish conspiracy of 1593, and that of the Earl of Gowrie's attempt mentioned above, and the description of Queen Elizabeth's progress to her coronation which Tottel had published in 1559,[24] were printed; and one "Britanno-Scotus," with exquisite tact, even composed a broadside *In effigiem Mariæ Reginæ, Iacob. Magni Britan. Reg. matris.*[25] Some of these pieces must certainly have been dictated by self-interest as much as by loyalty. One Robert Fletcher, for example, wrote *A briefe and familiar epistle shewing his maiesties . . . title to all his kingdomes; with an epitaph for the late maiestie; and lastly a prayer for his maiesties most happy succession, and for the queene and their children.*[26] This worthy subscribed himself "Yeoman purueyor of carriages for remooues of our sayde late

soueraigne Lady the Queene," and thereby exposed himself to the charge of having his eye on the main chance. The somewhat miscellaneous nature of the contents of this book is not unusual: many of these effusions were made up of several pieces; some are in both verse and prose; some were written by several authors; and some were even padded with unrelated further specimens of the author's poetical vein.

Another occasion sure to be reflected in print was a visit by the sovereign, in progress through the country, for instance, or his passage in state through the city. Some of the printed pieces thus called into being are mere bubblings-over of popular enthusiasm, but many of them are more or less exact descriptions of what actually took place. Some of the books describing the progresses of Queen Elizabeth were published by the authors of the entertainments in her honor and amount to nothing less than *scenari* or librettos. Such are *A Discourse Of the Queenes Maiesties entertainement in Suffolk and Norfolk: With a description of many things then presently seene. Deuised by Thomas Churchyarde Gent. With diuers shews of his own inuention sette out at Norwich: And some rehearsal of hir Highnesse retourne from Progresse,* printed by Henry Bynneman in [1578]; and *Certaine Deuises and shewes presented to her Maiestie by the gentlemen of Grayes-Inne at her Highnesse Court in Greenwich,*[27] which consists chiefly of the text of Thomas Hughes's *Misfortunes of Arthur,* but includes also the ceremonious speeches introducing the play and notes on the manner of performance. The formal addresses made to the queen on her visits were sometimes printed too.[28] The best-known descriptions of royal visits are the famous letter of that mad wag, Robert Laneham, an humble member of the queen's suite, describing her entertainment at Kenilworth in 1575,[29] *The Princelye pleasures, at the Courte at Kenelwoorth,* on the same event,[30] and Thomas Deloney's lively ballad of *The Queenes visiting of the Campe at Tilsburie with her entertainment there,*[31] published during the summer of the Armada's coming, when the English army was encamped on Tilbury plain. King James's movements were followed by the press with the same persistance, his visit to Scotland in 1617 in particular producing a torrent of encomia from his excited countrymen.[32]

The popular interest in the sovereign extended to the other members of the royal family as well, and we also find printed records of their activities and verses in praise of their virtues. A very early example is the prose account written by Petrus Carmelianus, Henry VII's Latin secretary, of the marriage by proxy of Prince Charles of Castile (later the Emperor Charles V) and the Princess Mary, the king's daughter, in 1508. Richard Pynson printed two versions of this narrative, one in Latin,[33] the longer and more elaborate, and the other in English[34] in the same year. They are a detailed and particular account of the reception of the embassy from the Emperor Maximilian, Charles's grandfather, the agreements entered into, and the marriage by proxy. During Henry VIII's reign it was often a little uncertain whether his children belonged to the royal family or not, and during the next three reigns there was no royal family. King Philip of Spain, however, was greeted with exquisite courtly flattery in print when he came over to marry Queen Mary, and there is a curious ballad which was printed on the queen's persuading herself, on insufficient grounds, that she had conceived an heir in 1554.[35] But the children of King James were favorite subjects for the ballad-writers and courtly poets, and Prince Henry and Princess Elizabeth must certainly have attracted a genuine popularity. Prince Henry was sometimes included in the congratulations offered the king on his accession. In 1610 two reports of the celebration of his creation as prince of Wales were printed.[36] But it was his premature death in 1612 that provoked the loudest and most prolonged outburst of sentiment. Before the end of the year, seven weeks after his death, eighteen laments had been entered in the Stationers' register,[37] and there are at least eight more bearing the date of that year which do not appear to have been entered or were printed outside London.[38] And this was not the end: the next year eight or more additional pieces were printed.[39] A list of the authors of these epicedia makes a very respectable poetical galaxy: it includes poets such as Chapman, Wither, the Earl of Stirling, Webster, Joshua Sylvester, John Davies of Hereford, Christopher Brooke, Thomas Heywood, and Cyril Tourneur, to say nothing of pedants like Alexander Julius or of John Taylor the water-poet and the ballad-writers. Conventional as these laments are in a sense, the spontaneity with which they were produced alone argues some sincerity. And now and then we find in them news as well as mourning sorrow, in the form of a history of his life or a description of his funeral. Even Chapman's *Epicede* was pieced out, more likely by the publisher than by the author, with an account of the funeral and a "Representation of the Herse of the same . . . Prince."[40] Furthermore, with the enterprise and adaptability that we must expect of a journalistic publisher, Mrs. White entered in the Stationers' register on 12 January 1613 a ballad of *Great Brytaynes greatest comfort. or Brytaynes hope for the roiall prynce Charles prynce of great Brytayne and Ireland Duke of York and Albany.*[41]

By an unfortunate coincidence, the death of Prince Henry occurred just as preparations were going forward for the marriage of the Princess Elizabeth and the Count Frederick, Palsgrave of the Rhine. But it does not seem to have set back these preparations in any way, and it certainly did not diminish one whit the popular enthusiasm for this Protestant alliance or the expression thereof in print. The journalists of the day followed the ceremonies step by step—from the arrival of the Palsgrave, through the ceremony of betrothal in the chapel at Whitehall, the shows and pageants displayed in his honor, the marriage itself, celebrated with an ingenuous appropriateness on St. Valentine's Day, the tournament on 24 March, to the departure of the married pair and their arrival in their principality on the Rhine—and apparently missed nothing. Among many nuptial poems and verses of mere praise, we find a good deal of description of events, *i.e.*, a good deal of news.

Two other occasions later in the reign of King James brought forth more celebrations in print of the same order. The first of these was the creation of Prince Charles as prince of Wales in 1616: the program of the municipal water-pageant arranged by Thomas Middleton[42] and "a true Relation of the Solemnity held at Ludlow in the Countie of Salop, vpon the fourth of Nouember . . . Being the day of the Creation of . . . Charles, Prince of Wales, . . . in his Maiesties Palace of Whitehall"[43] were both promptly printed. The second was the death of Queen Anne in 1619, which seems to have produced nothing but memorial verses in the most conventional style.

Another occasion which sometimes produced laudatory verses by the courtly poets was the visit of a foreign potentate or the reception of an embassy. These occasions also produced books of news describing the entertainments offered the visitors, and again the two were sometimes combined. Of the first kind are John Davies of Hereford's *Bien Venu. Greate Britaines Welcome to . . . the Danes*,[44] published at the time of the visit of King Christian IV, King James's brother-in-law, in 1606, Henry Roberts's *Englands Farewell to Christian the fourth*,[45] of a few months later, and John Ford's *Honour Triumphant, . . . Also the Monarches Meeting; Or the King of Denmarkes welcome into England.*[46] Of the second kind are Henry Roberts's *Most royall and Honourable entertainement of . . . Christiern the fourth*,[47] and *The king of Denmarkes vvelcome: Containing his ariuall, abode, and entertainement, both in the Citie and other places.*[48] The earliest known piece on a royal visit is a book of Latin verses composed by the celebrated grammarian William Lily and spoken by his pupils on the occasion of the reception to the Emperor Charles V at London in 1522.[49] They were printed with an English translation by an anonymous admirer and sets of introductory and valedictory verses full of unstinted praise. Among others, we find a fulsome description of the meeting of Henry VIII and Francis I of France between Calais and Boulogne in October 1532.[50]

Dropping several degrees in the social scale, we come now to the honoring in print of popular characters outside of royal circles. Verses and other pieces of this sort begin to appear early in the reign of Elizabeth. Some of them are written in precisely the same style as the verses of the courtly poets mentioned above. Composed or titled in Latin, making a great show of elegance, they are indistinguishable in manner from those addressed to a king. For example, in 1585, when a daughter was born to Sir Philip Sidney, an Italian named Scipione Gentile wrote and John Wolfe printed a commemoration of the event entitled *Nereus siue de Natali Elizabethæ illustris domini Philippi Sydnaei Filiæ.* This strain of courtly compliment was, of course, reserved chiefly for the magnates of the realm, men like the Earl of Leicester, but appears even in a eulogy of that bluff seaman, Sir Francis Drake, written by a Dane named Joannes Hercusanus.[51] The same manner appears sometimes in English verses, such as those of Bernard Garter to the Duke of Norfolk,[52] or George Peele's celebration of the conferring of the Order of the Garter on the Earl of Northumberland in 1593,[53] or his *Eglogue Gratulatorie. Entituled: To the right honorable, and renowmed Shepheard of Albions Arcadia: Robert Earle of Essex and Ewe, for his welcome into England from Portugall.*[54]

But as it was popular heroes to whom these pieces were addressed, it was in a popular style, that of the broadside ballad, and by popular rather than courtly poets that they were much more often written. These popular heroes were almost invariably soldiers, sailors, and adventurers. Among the soldiers we find men like the Earl of Sussex, Sir John Hawkins, Lord Grey de Wilton, and Lord Mountjoy. Ballads on the Elizabethan seaman are more numerous; the voyages of Frobisher and Drake were punctually marked by ballads of adieu and welcome.[55] Lesser men such as Stukeley and Cavendish received their meed of praise too. The Shirley brothers, famous travelers and adventurers at the beginning of the seventeenth century, were frequently celebrated in print, chiefly by narratives of their exploits.[56] It is interesting to notice, as a sign of journalistic alertness, that on 7 June 1616, just when he was rising rapidly to the position of royal favorite, *The picture or portrature of Sir George Villiers* was entered in the Stationers' register.[57] An unusual sort of pamphlet, *The Charterhouse with the last vvill and Testament of Thomas Sutton,*[58] which was published in 1614, about three years after Sutton's death, is probably a testimonial of the esteem in which this philanthropist came to be held on account of his benefactions. It consists of a pious exordium on the virtue of charity, a brief history of the purchase of the Charterhouse property, a list of the endowments which Sutton settled upon his hospital, and a copy of his will, "taken out of the Prerogatiue Court."

Among the personal news of our period, the numerous epitaphs and elegies published on the death of a prominent personage must be mentioned. In these laments we shall not always find news and we shall almost never find a great deal of news, but it does sometimes appear in the form of a review of the life of the late worthy or a description of his funeral. For the most part they are simply poetical exercises on a doleful theme, full of weeping and wailing and almost barren of information. Indeed, we are likely to find more solid fact in the elaborate titles prefixed to them than in the verses themselves. Consider, for example, an epitaph printed in 1578 on the death of the Countess of Lennox: *An Epitaphe on the death of the right noble and most vertuous Lady Margarit Duglasis good grace, Countisse of Liuinox (and Daughter to the renowmed and most excellent Lady Margarit Queene, Sister to the magnificent and most mighty Prince Henry the eight of England, Fraunce and Ireland, Kinge, and by Gods permission Queene of Scotland,) who disceased this life the ninth day of March. Anno. 1577. at hir mannoure in Hackny in the countye of Midelsex and lieth enterred the.3. day of April at Westminster in the Chaple of King Henry the seuenth, her worthie Grandfather of Englande, Fraunce and Ireland King. &c. The yeare of our Lorde God. 1578, and in the.20. yeare of our soueraigne Lady Queene Elizabeth by the grace of God of Englande, Fraunce and Irelande, Queene, defendour of the faith. &c.*[59] This alone is a fairly satisfactory obituary notice.

Many of these epitaphs are in the style of courtly compliment with which the great were honored while still alive. These are likewise the work of courtiers and scholars, written often in Latin, a labor of duty quite as often as of love, and sometimes mere poetical apprentice-work. Epitaphs of this kind were usually published in book form. The earliest I know of is *The Epitaffe of the moste noble & valyaunt Iasper late duke of Beddeforde,* a book of ten leaves printed by Richard Pynson in 1496. The verses are signed "Smerte, maister de ses ouzeaus," but they have sometimes been attributed to Skelton. The subject was Henry VII's uncle, who had died in the last month of the preceding year. It hardly seems possible that nothing else of this sort was published until 1542, but that is the date of the next epitaph I am able to cite. Much more likely, those which were published in the meantime have been lost, though doubtless the idea of honoring in print eminent personages outside the royal family took root only gradually. Sir Thomas Wyatt, the poet, is the subject of two memorial pieces published on his death in 1542, one in Latin by John Leland, the antiquary,[60] and another in English.[61] Many of these verses were written by genuine poets—Daniel, Chapman, John Ford, Joshua Sylvester, Cyril Tourneur, Thomas Watson, for instance; indeed, it is even possible to bring Spenser into the story of English journalism by citing his *Daphnaida,* published in 1591, a few months after the death of Lady Douglas Howard. Certain writers seem almost to have specialized in dirges of this kind: Thomas Churchyard was always ready to lament the death of a hero of the sort he admired, and George Whetstone, between 1577 and 1587, published verses on Gascoigne,[62] Sir Nicholas Bacon,[63] the Earl of Sussex,[64] Sir James Dyer,[65] the Earl of Bedford,[66] and Sir Philip Sidney.[67] The universities of Oxford and Cambridge and their colleges individually were accustomed to publish corporate tributes to the heroes of the day and to their own members. Occasionally, even as early as 1551, books of epitaphs, made up of contributions by a group of writers, were published.

Even more numerous were epitaphs of a less pretentious kind, written in loping ballad measures by the humbler sort of versifiers, especially poetically-inclined clergymen and the semi-professional ballad-writers, and published in broadside form. In style and substance they are highly conventional, so that it is indeed difficult to distinguish one from another. Sometimes they bewail the death of persons of the same quality as the courtly epitaphs just mentioned: Bishop Jewel, Sir Nicholas Bacon, the Earl of Bedford, the Earl of Leicester, Sir Philip Sidney, and the Earl of Derby, in dying, elicited lamentations of both kinds. But the subject of the popular epitaphs is much more often a lord mayor, a great city merchant, a popular preacher, or some other personage a little closer to the popular admiration. Sir Philip Sidney's death, in 1586, seems to have excited greater compassion than any other, if the number of memorial pieces printed is a true index. It is said that two hundred elegies were written on this occasion, but of course most of these were never printed: no less than eleven books and broadsides, however, did appear soon after the news reached England.[68] The Earl of Pembroke's death in 1570 called forth at least six,[69] and the Earl of Derby's in 1593 five.[70] The execution of the Earl of Essex in 1601, although the fact that he did not die a natural death made the event all the more exciting to popular interest, probably produced more regret than any of these, but at the moment it was dangerous to print a lament which showed any sympathy for the traitor. We hear from contemporary testimony that epitaphs were printed at the time, only to be suppressed at once, but none of them seems to have been preserved, at least in its original form. Within two months, however, of Queen Elizabeth's death, on 18 May 1603, Margaret Allde entered in the Stationers' register the ballad-epitaph beginning "Sweet Englands pride is gone,"[71] which she printed as *A lamentable Dittie composed vpon the death of Robert Lord Deuereux late Earle of Essex, who was beheaded in the Tower of London vpon Ashwednesday in the morning. 1601,* a ballad which was reissued several times during the seventeenth century. Many other memorials of Essex were subsequently printed as well.

Another reason for the popularity of broadside epitaphs is probably to be found in the pious custom of hanging them on tombs. Puttenham describes them as "large tables . . . hanged up in Churches and chauncells over the tombs of great men and others," and further complains that they were

> so exceeding long as one must have halfe a dayes leasure to reade one of them, & must be called away before he halfe come to the end, or else be locked into the Church by the Sexten, as I my selfe was once served reading an Epitaph in a certain cathedrall Church of England.[72]

Notes

1. *The four ages of poetry.*

2. See *C. H. E. L.,* I. 398 ff.

3. *English literature medieval,* p. 151.

4. Reprinted by Halliwell: *Selections from the minor poems of Dan John Lydgate,* Percy Society, 1840, II. 1.

5. *This sermon folowynge was compyled & sayd in the Cathedrall chyrche of saynt Poule . . ., the body beynge present of . . . Kynge Henry the .vij. the .x. daye of Maye, . . . m.ccccc.ix. . . .* Wynkyn de Worde, 1509. (All printed pieces mentioned in this treatise should be understood to have been printed at London, unless a different place is stated.)

6. Wynkyn de Worde, [1509].

7. *The noble tryumphaunt Coronation of Quene Anne, Wyfe vnto the most noble kynge Henry the viii.* For Iohan Goughe, [1533].

8. *Friderici Nauseæ . . . in diuam Catharinam . . . Funebris Oratio.* Moguntiæ: Ivo Scoeffer.

9. It is thus that the ballad was described in the Stationers' register when it was entered by William Coplande in 1558-9 (Arber, I. 96). The copy in the library of the Society of Antiquaries of London was printed by William Pickringe and is entitled *A songe betwene the Quenes maiestie and Englande.* Pickering entered the ballad again on 4 September 1564 (Arber, I. 262).

10. Richard Ihones, 1590.

11. The 1587 edition was printed by Iohn Windet; the second by Iohn VVolfe.

12. *Englandes Mourning Garment: Worne here by plaine Shepheardes; in memorie of their sacred Mistresse, Elizabeth . . . To which is added the true manner of her Emperiall Funerall . . .* For Thomas Millington, 1603 (2 issues).

13. *Expicedium. A funeral Oration, vpon the death of . . . Elizabeth . . . Whereunto is added, the true order of her . . . Funerall.* By Infelice Academico Ignoto. For E[dward] VVhite, 1603 (2 edd.).

14. *Elizabetha quasi viuens, Eliza's Funerall. . . . (The order and formall proceeding at the funerall of . . . Elizabeth . . .)* For Matthew Lawe, 1603 (2 edd.).

15. Cambridge: Iohn Legat, 1603.

16. Broadside. For Edmund Mutton, 1603.

17. Arber, II. 393. It was printed for Yarathe Iames, presumably in the same year, as *A new Ballad, declaring the great Treason conspired against the young King of Scots, and how one Andrew Browne an Englishman, which was the Kings Chamberlaine, preuented the same.* There is an oral ballad, *King James and Brown,* apparently the work of a minstrel, on the same subject (Child: *English and Scottish Popular Ballads,* III. 442).

18. *Treason Pretended against the king of Scots, by certaine Lordes and Gentlemen . . . With a declaration of the Kinges Maiesties intention to his last Acts of Parliament . . .* For Thomas Nelson.

19. *A Discouerie of the vnnaturall and traiterous Conspiracie of Scottish Papists . . .* For Iohn Norton, 1593 (reprinted from the edition printed at Edinburgh by R[obert] Walde-graue). Reprinted in 1603.

20. Arber, II. 548-9.

21. *A true reportarie of: . . . the Baptisme of . . . Frederik Henry, . . . Prince of Scotland . . .* Edinburgh: R[obert] Walde-graue, [1594?]. Entered 24 October 1594 by Johane Butter (Arber, II. 662). Reprinted in 1603.

22. Arber, II. 663.

23. *The Earle of Gowries conspiracie against the Kings Maiestie of Scotland. . . .* Valentine Simmes, 1600

(from the edition printed at Edinburgh by Robert Charteris). Reprinted in 1603.

24. *The passage of . . . Quene Elyzabeth through the citie of London to westminster the daye before her Coronacion. Anno. 1558 [/9].* (2 edd.) There are two issues of the reprint: 1) for Ione Millington, 1604; 2) for Iohn Busby, [n.d.].

25. By Io. Gordonius. Typis Iohannis Norton, [1603].

26. For Iohn Harrison, 1603.

27. Robert Robinson, 1587.

28. 1) *Carmen Gratulatorium Aedium Cecilianarum in aduentū . . . reginæ . . .* By William Cecil, Lord Burghley. Broadside. [Henry Bynneman? 1571?] 2) *Ad illus^m R. Elizabetham, L[aurence] H[umphrey] Vicecan. Oxon. oratio Woodstochiæ habita. . . .* Apud Iohannem Dayum, 1572; another edition in 1575. 3) *The Speeches and honorable Entertainment giuen to the Queenes Maiestie in Progresse, at Cowdrey . . ., by . . . the Lord Montacute. 1591.* Sold by William Wright, 1591. 4) *Speeches deliuered to her maiestie this last progresse, at . . . the Lady Russels, at Bissam, . . . the Lorde Chandos at Sudley, at . . . the Lord Norris, at Ricorte.* Oxford: Ioseph Barnes, 1592.

29. *A Letter whearin part of the entertainment vntoo the Queenz Maiesty at Killingwoorth Castle . . . in this Somerz Progress 1575 is signified . . .* [1575.]

30. [By George Gascoigne and others.] Richard Ihones, 1576.

31. Broadside. For Edward White, 1588.

32. The annual lord mayor's show in London was another occasion of pageantry somewhat resembling the entertainments given to royalty. A book containing all or part of the *scenario* was usually published. Copies of the following are extant: the pageants for 1585, 1588, and 1591 by George Peele; 1590 by Thomas Nelson; 1605, 1609, 1611, 1614-6, 1618 by Anthony Munday; 1612 by Thomas Dekker; 1613, 1617, 1619, 1621 by Thomas Middleton; 1620 by John Squire.

33. *Hoc presenti libello . . . Cōtinentur . . . Solemnes cerimonie & triūphi nuper habiti In suscipie[n]da . . . Maximiliani Romanorum Imperatoris . . . et . . . sui filii Karoli Principis castelle Archiducis austrie Legatione . . . pro sponsalibus et matrimonio inter . . . principem Karolum et . . . Dominam Mariam . . .*

34. *The solempnities and triumphes doon at the spousells of the kyngs doughter.*

35. *Nowe singe, now springe, oure care is exil'd Oure vertuous Ouene is quickned with child.*

W[illiam] Ryddaell, [1554].

36. 1) *The Order and Solemnitie of the Creation of . . . Prince Henrie . . . Prince of VVales, . . . Together with the Ceremonies of the Knights of the Bath . . .* *Whereunto is annexed the Royall Maske* [*i.e.,* Daniel's *Tethys Festival*]. For Iohn Budge. 2) *Londons loue, to the royal Prince Henrie, meeting him on the riuer of Thames . . . the last of May, 1610. With a breife reporte of the water Fight, and Fireworkes.* For Nathaniell Fosbrooke.

37. Arber, III. 501-10.

38. 1) *An Elegie on the Death of Prince Henrie.* By William Alexander, Earl of Stirling. Edinburgh: Andro Hart, 1612, 1613. 2) *Epicedium Cantabrigiense in Obitum . . . Henrici . . .* Cambridge: Ex officina Cantrelli Legge, 1612 (2 edd.). 3) *Iusta Oxoniensium.* Iohannes Bill, 1612. 4) *In Henricum Fridericum . . . lachrymæ.* By Alexander Julius. Edinburgh: Thomas Finlason, 1612. 5) *Memoriæ Sacra . . . Henrici . . . Laudatio Funebris.* By Sir Francis Nethersole. Cambridge: Cantrell Legge, 1612. 6) *Eidyllia in Obitum Fulgentissimi Henrici . . .* Oxford: Iosephus Barnesius, 1612. 7) *Luctus Posthumus: sive, . . . Magdalenensium officiosa Pietas.* Oxford: Iosephus Barnesius, 1612. 8) *Gloucesters myte for the remembrance of Prince Henrie.* By Thomas Rogers. For Ionas Man, 1612.

39. 1) *Two Elegies . . .* By C[hristopher] Brooke and W[illiam] B[rowne]. For Richard More, 1613. 2) *Mausoleum . . .* Edinburgh: Andro Hart, 1613. 3) *A funerall elegie upon the death of Henry . . .* By Thomas Heywood. For William Welbie, 1613. 4) *Illustrissimi Principis Henrici Iusta.* By David Hume. For Richard Boyle & William Iones, 1613. 5) *A monumental Columne . . .* By Iohn Webster. For William Welby, 1613. 6) *The Period of Mourning . . .* By Henry Peacham. For Iohn Helme, 1613. 7) *In Obitu summæ spei . . . Lessus.* By David Wedderburn. Edinburgh: Andreas Hart, 1613. 8) *Sundry Funeral Elegies . . .* Humphrey Lownes, 1613.

40. For Iohn Budge, 1612, 1613.

41. Arber, III. 511.

42. *Ciuitatis amor. The Cities Loue. An entertainement by water, at Chelsey, and White-hall. . . .* For Thomas Archer, 1616.

43. *The loue of VVales to their soueraigne Prince . . .* By Daniel Powell. Nicholas Okes, 1616.

44. For Nathaniel Butter.

45. For William Welby.

46. For Francis Burton.

47. Sold by William Barley.

48. Edward Allde.

49. *Of the tryūphe / and the vses that Charles themperour / & the . . . kyng of England / Henry the .viii. were saluted with / passyng through London.* Richarde Pynson, [1522].

50. *The maner of the tryumphe at Caleys and Bulleyn.* For I. Gowgh, [1532] (2 edd.).

51. *Magnifico . . . viro D. Francisco Draco Anglo Equiti Aurato.* Broadside. For Robert Wallie, 1587.

52. *A dittie, in the worthie praise of an high and mightie prince.* By Ber. Gar. Broadside. Alexander Lacy, [1566].

53. *The Honour of the Garter.* . . . For Iohn Busbie, [1593?].

54. Richard Iones, 1589.

55. Arber, II. 312, 314, 327, 386, 505.

56. 1) *A true report of Sir Anthony Shierlies iourney ouerland to Venice.* For Iohn Iaggard, 1600. 2) *A new and large discourse on the Trauels of sir Anthonie Sherley.* By William Parry. For Fletcher Norton, 1601. 3) *A true Journall of the late voyage made by . . . Sir Thomas Sherley the yonger . . . on the Coaste of Spaine &c.* Book. Entered 20 August 1602 by Thomas Pavyer (Arber, III. 214). 4) *The three English Brothers.* . . . By Anthony Nixon. Iohn Hodgets, 1607 (2 issues). 5) *Sir Robert Sherley, sent ambassadour in the name of the King of Persia, to Sigismond the third, King of Poland and Swecia . . . His Royall entertainement into Cracouia . . ., with his pretended Comming into England.* By Thomas Midleton. For Iohn Budge, 1609. 6) *Sir Antony Sherley his relation of his trauels into Persia.* For Nathaniel Butter & Iohn Bagfet, 1613.

57. By Laurence Lisle (Arber, III. 590).

58. For Thomas Thorp.

59. By I[ohn] Phillips. Broadside. For Edward White, [1578].

60. *Naeniæ in mortem Thomae Viati Equitis incomparabilis.* [Reginald Wolfe,] 1542.

61. *An excellent Epitaffe of syr Thomas Wyat, with two other compendious dytties . . .* For Roberte Toye, [1542].

62. *A remembraunce of the wel imployed life and godly end of George Gaskoigne Esquire, who deceased at Stalmford in Lincolne Shire, the 7 of October 1577. The reporte of Geor. Whetstone, Gent., an eye witnes . . .* For Edward Aggas, [1577].

63. *A Remembraunce of the woorthie and well imployed life of . . . Sir Nicholas Bacon . . .* For Myles Iennyngs, [1579].

64. *A Remembraunce of the Life, Death, and Vertues of . . . Thomas, . . . Erle of Sussex . . .* Iohn Wolfe & Richard Iones, 1583.

65. *A Remembraunce of the precious vertues of . . . Sir Iames Dier, . . . Lord Cheefe Iustice of the Common Pleas . . .* Iohn Charlewood, [1583].

66. *A Mirror of Treue Honnour and Christian Nobilitie: . . . Frauncis Earle of Bedford, . . . who deceased . . . the xxviii of Iune, 1585. . . . Whereunto is adioyned a Report of the Vertues of . . . S.*

Frauncis, Lord Russell, Sonne and Heire Apparent of the . . . Earle, . . . slaine . . . the 27 day of the said month of Iune. Richard Iones, 1585.

67. *Sir Phillip Sidney, his honorable Life, his valiant Death, and his true Vertues . . .* For Thomas Cadman, [1587].

68. 1) *The Epitaph of Sir Phillip Sidney . . .* By [Thomas] Churchyard. For Thomas Cadman, [1586]. 2) *A dolefull dytie of the death of Sir P. Sydney.* [Ballad.] Entered 22 February 1587 by Henry Carre (Arber, II. 464). 3) *Vpon the life and death of . . . Sir Phillip Sidney . . .* By A[ngel] D[ay]. Robert Walde-graue, [1586]. 4) *The Life and Death of Sir Phillip Sidney . . .: His funerals . . .; with the whole order of the mournfull shewe, as they marched thorowe the citie of London . . .* By Iohn Philip. Robert Walde-graue, 1587. 5) *The buriall of Sir Phillip Sydney.* Ballad. Entered 27 February 1587 by William Bartlet (Arber, II. 464). 6) Whetstone's book mentioned above. 7) *The mourninge muses of Lod Bryskett vpon the Deathe of . . . Sir Phillip Sydney . . .* [Book.] Entered 22 August 1587 by John Woulfe (*ib.,* II. 474). 8) *Academiæ Cantabrigiensis lacrymæ, tumulo . . . Philippi Sidneii sacratæ per Alexandrum Neuillum.* Impensis Thomæ Chardi, 1587. 9) *Exequiæ . . . Phillippi Sidnaei . . .* Oxford: Joseph Barnes, 1587. 10) *Peplus . . . Philippi Sidnaei . . . honoribus dicatus.* Oxford: Joseph Barnes, 1587. 11) *Sequitur celebritas & pompa funeris . . .* Latin & English. By Tho[mas] Lant. Grauen in copper by Derick Theodor de Brij, 1587.

69. Arber, I. 411-3.

70. *Ib.,* II. 637, 639, 642, 647. Also *Epicedium in obitum . . . Comitis Derbeiensis . . .* By M. G. Oxford: Joseph Barnes, 1593.

71. Arber, III. 234.

72. *Arte of Poesie,* Lib. I, Chap. XXVIII.

P. M. Zall (essay date 1970)

SOURCE: "The Blending of Wit and Jest: An Introduction," in *"A Nest of Ninnies" and Other English Jestbooks of the Seventeenth Century,* edited by P. M. Zall, University of Nebraska Press, 1970, pp. ix-xvii.

[In the following excerpt, Zall traces the evolution of jests and puns in English printed materials beginning in the 1400s, examining in detail works from the seventeenth century.]

THE BLENDING OF WIT AND JEST

. . . [The] making of jestbooks became an industry in the seventeenth century, expanding with the development of a larger reading public. Jestbooks flourished throughout the land, feeding one upon another in a happy self-sustaining cycle. Badly printed, crudely written, they were welcome alike in parlor and pulpit, playhouse and pub. Aside from their value in sparkling conversation and repartee, they provided preachers with pithy parables, pundits with pungent wit, and a rising middle class with instant culture. It would not be surprising, then, if more people read jestbooks than read the works of Chaucer, Spenser, and Milton combined.

A legion of nameless hackwriters during the previous century had patiently turned out collections like *A Hundred Merry Tales* and *The Jests of Skelton.* In the seventeenth century they worked on quietly industrious as ever, with such results as are represented here by the *Banquet of Jests* and the books about Scogin, Tarlton, Peters, and Hind. But now came a new kind of jestbookmaker from a growing group of entertainers proud of their authorship and eager to capitalize on the advertising of their skills that would accrue from such popular publication. There were semi-professional entertainers also, university wits and impoverished gentlemen, for whom jest-books might have made the difference between abject and genteel poverty. The identifiable authors represented here, then, make up a highly diversified cast of characters:

> Anthony Copley, impoverished gentleman, distant relative of Queen Elizabeth (but a secret agent in the service of the King of Spain), whose *Wits, Fits, and Fancies* provided a well-stocked larder for jestbookmakers throughout the century.

> Robert Armin, comedian in Shakespeare's company, an innovator in comic acting, whose *Nest of Ninnies* used jests as a means to study comic character types.

> George Wilkins and Thomas Dekker, among the foremost hackwriters of the day, for whom jestbooks were part of their stock in trade—and collaboration, as in *Jests to Make You Merry,* part of their way of life.

> John Taylor the Water Poet, a professional entertainer in verse and prose, whose *Wit and Mirth* was another fruitful repository from which other writers, and he himself, drew for later books.

> Robert Chamberlain, university wit of meager means, whose *Conceits* may well have been the first jestbook in English to specialize in puns.

> Captain William Hicks, a pseudo-university wit, a tapster in an Oxford tavern, whose *Oxford Jests* applied the brevity of puns to the telling of tales.

> Abel Boyer, lexicographer and pedant, whose *Ingenious Companion,* with its French and English texts on facing pages, made ingenious use of jests and, through its wide ranging selection, in effect recapitulated the history of jests to the end of the century.

This new breed of jestbookmaker brought a new approach to the writing of jests. Not content, as conventional jestbookmakers had been (and continued to be), with simply reprinting old jests and perhaps changing only names and places, they searched for new sources and reworked the old ones. Copley, for instance, translated a compendium of jests from the Spanish and added many more picked up during his travels on the Continent and in England. Dekker, Wilkins, and Armin exploited theatrical sources. Taylor, openly rejecting bookish sources, plucked his jests from the air of metropolitan London, while Chamberlain and Hicks plucked theirs from university common rooms and taverns. Still, the bulk of their jests were traditional, reworked in a more artful way.

The new approach was not innovative so much as representative of a different tradition of jests, one that we can call classical as distinct from the medieval tradition of conventional jestbooks. This distinction is less historical than stylistic, for the two traditions were coeval. Medieval jests, on the one hand, are discursive, diffuse, explanatory, and emphasize deeds rather than words. Classical jests are direct, concise, more subtle, and emphasize words rather than deeds. The difference is seen in this comparison between a classical jest from Copley and a Medieval jest from *Scogin:*

> In the North of Ireland, where they eat but Oaten-cake bread, there was a Kern's mother, hearing that her son was slain in fight against the Englishmen, came the morrow after into the field, and finding her dead son there, after much moan and lamentation over him, she chanced to cast her eye aside and thereby espied a dead Englishman. Then up she rose and, much accursing our nation for the death of her son, in the end she stripped him of his apparel and chanced to find a stale loaf of bread in his breeches—which was of the provision he brought with him from the English pale—which after she had a good while well viewed and wondered at, in the end burst forth into fresh tears and said, "No marvel though my dear son be slain by one that voids so hard and huge a turd!"
>
> (from Copley, *Wits, Fits, and Fancies*)

Scogin had a great Hare's skin that was new killed, and he went to a Wheatland that was an handful and a half high and did lay there a foul great Mard (they that can speak French can tell what a Mard is), and couched the Hare's skin over it, and set up the Hare's ears. And then he came to Oxford and said to them that used hunting that he had found a Hare sitting. They ran for their Greyhounds to kill the Hare, and Scogin went with them to the land where the Hare did sit. At last, one espied the ears and the head of the Hare and said, "So how!" "Stand you there," said the other, "and give her the law of the game."

Scogin got him home to Oxford, and one that came to see the game was bid to put up the Hare. And when he came almost at the Hare, "Up whore!" he said, "or I will prick you in the buttock by and by." But the Hare did not stir. At last, when he came to the place, he thrust his staff at the Hare's skin and did turn it over, and under it was a great Mard. He returned again as if he had a flea in his ear to Oxford. "Why," said they, "do you not put up the Hare?" "Go put her up yourself, with a vengeance," said he and went home in a fury.

They that held the Greyhounds did marvel what he meant, and that Scogin was gone. They went to see where the Hare should sit, and they found a Hare's skin and a great Mard. "Well," said they, "we can never beware of Scogin's mocks and jests. Would part of this Hare were in his mouth." And so they departed. Whereby you may see that fair words make fools fain.

(from *Scogin's Jests*)

The differences seen here flourished side by side throughout the century, but there was a strong tendency for the medieval and classical elements to blend, combining the exuberant story-telling quality of the one with the concise economy of the other, producing a hybrid with roots centuries deep.

Typical of the ancestry of the medieval style was the collection of erotic stories called Milesian Tales that were extremely popular in the ancient world. Barbarian chiefs were shocked when they found that Roman legionaries carried such tales into battle, but by the eleventh century they were considered decent enough to hold a steady place in Peter Alphonso's *Disciplina Clericalis,* or Priest's Handbook. In this vehicle they were carried throughout the western world, wherever missionaries wandered, from Spain to Iceland. Embellished with appropriate moral taglines, they served as the root stock of every medieval preacher's collection of "exempla," and every story-teller's collection of merry tales. Versified, they spread into more formal literature as fabliaux and, with the coming of printing, they were translated back into prose for jests in vernacular French, German, Spanish, and English.

Coeval with collections of such realistic, often scatalogical tales were collections of verbal wit accumulating especially in textbooks on the art of rhetoric, where rules for effective public speaking were illustrated by the practice of past masters. In an age when education consisted chiefly of rhetorical training, no educated man could escape being exposed to such examples as these, from Cicero's *De Oratore:* A citizen, hearing about the death of his neighbor, exclaims, "What a fool! Just as he starts making money he dies." A politician, pointing graciously at his opponent, asks, "What does this noble man lack—except cash and character?" It was only a question of time before such examples would be accumulated for their own sakes as collections of bons mots, repartee, choice insults, and witty remarks. Some collections specialized, like the tenth-century manuscript now known as *The Jests of Hierocles* (about Hierocles rather than by him), consisting of one- or two-line profiles of an absent-minded professor: told that a friend's ancestors drank from a deep well, the hero says, "My, what long necks they had!" He meets a friend reported to have died, and the friend cannot convince him that the report had been exaggerated; our hero persists, "The man who told me so was much more reliable than you."

During the Middle Ages, the more leisurely merry tales spread across the land while collections of concise, witty jests lay dormant. But the classical jests bloomed again in the Renaissance, especially after the appearance of Poggio

Bracciolini's *Facetiae* in 1477. Poggio, discoverer of some of the finest classical manuscripts in northern Italy, renewed Cicero's emphasis on epigrammatic economy, applying it to both merry tales and witty sayings. Thus in sixty words we hear the wily father assuring the prospective suitor that his daughter is neither too young nor too innocent to wed, having already had three children by the parish clerk. And we hear of the sad husband whose wife has fallen into a rushing stream, looking for her upstream rather than downstream, because he knew her to be the most perverse woman alive. Disseminated more widely than ever thanks to printing, such pointed jests served subsequent generations of Humanists as a vehicle for wit and wisdom. Many of them, like Erasmus and More, turned classical epigrams into prose jests and prose jests into classical epigrams as a means to practicing a clean Latin style; others used merry tales as a vehicle for spreading "the new learning," mixing classical wit and medieval tales for sweetness and light. Towards the end of the sixteenth century the cosmopolitan Copley had little trouble in quickly compiling 1125 classical jests for *Wits, Fits, and Fancies.*

The dramatic quality of the classical jest was of course congenial to theater people like Dekker, Wilkins, and Armin, with their knack for dialogue, irony, and colloquial language:

"Dear heart," said a Gentleman to his bride, "shall we have our pleasure or our dinner first?"

"Do just as you like, dear, and then we can dine."

(Poggio, *Facetiae,* 1477)

One called a Captain coward and said he had no heart. "It's no matter," quoth the Captain, "I have legs."

(Wilkins and Dekker, *Jests to Make You Merry,* 1607)

Their knack for scene and dialogue expanded simple jests into comic skits, modern "blackouts." A jest of Copley's reads:

One being in danger of drowning, another standing on the shore said unto him, "Get to yonder stooping tree and you are safe."

"Tut," he answered, "tell not me of getting or gaining, for I care only to save myself at this time."

Wilkins and Dekker's *Jests to Make You Merry* renders it thus:

A couple of Servingmen, having drunk hard in Southwark, came to take water about ten or eleven of the clock at night at Saint Maryovary's stairs. But the moon shining, and a puddle of water lying before them which they could not perfectly discern (without better eyes) by reason that their shadows hid it, one of them fell in, laboring with his hands and feet as if he had been a-swimming.

His fellow stood (so well as a man in his case could stand) looking upon him and said, "Art thou gone? Art thou gone? Jesus receive thy soul. Yet if thou canst but get the Temple stairs, there's some hope thou shalt do well enough."

"Tush," says the other that was down, "I look not to *get*. So I may save myself, I care for no more."

Such skilful use of scenic detail boded well for the development of artistry in jests that would have combined the story-telling appeal of the medieval tradition with the style of the classical tradition.

But the wordplay of the classical tradition attracted popularity for its own sake. By 1639 Chamberlain's *Conceits* accumulated close to 150 one- or two-line puns: "Smiths of all handicraftsmen are the most irregular, for they never think themselves better employed than when they are addicted to their vices." Little dramatic quality here, and no narrative, yet its brevity must have been considered ample compensation, and over the century we can see a developing preference generally for economy at any cost. The effect is apparent in this comparison:

> Two Countrymen keeping company till night, it happened that one of the Countryman's heels were lighter than his head; and going under a Signpost this Countryman lifted his leg very high. The other demanded why he did so. He told him it was to go over the stile, and pointed to the Sign.
>
> "Stile!" quoth his friend, "thou fool, it is a Sign!"
>
> "A Sign?" quoth he. "What Sign?"
>
> "Marry," quoth he again, "a sign that thou art terribly drunk."
>
> (from *A Banquet of Jests,* 1633)

> A drunken fellow coming by a shop asked a 'prentice boy what their sign was. He answered, it was a sign he was drunk.
>
> (from *A Choice Banquet of Witty Jests,* 1660)

Those responsible for this kind of epitome were interested more in what was said than in how it was said, but fortunately there were also writers like Taylor, Hicks, and Boyer who tried for a more artful balance. They adapted the direct style and subtlety of classical jests to medieval jests, imposing order, point, and thus effective economy with happier results. And, incidentally, they developed a plain, simple narrative style that helped to prepare the tastes of a growing body of readers for the higher art of Defoe, Swift, and Fielding in the ensuing years. It is instructive that one of Boyer's best jests would hold place in the most influential jestbook of them all, *Joe Miller's Jests* (1739) with hardly any change:

> A modest Gentlewoman being compelled to accuse her Husband of defect and being in the Court, she humbly desired the Judge that she might write what she durst not speak for Modesty. The Judge gave her that liberty and a Clerk was presently commanded to give her Pen, Ink, and Paper; whereupon she took the Pen without dipping it into the Ink, and made as if she would write. Says the Clerk to her, "Madam, there is no Ink in your Pen."

"Truly, Sir," says she, "that's just my Case, and therefore I need not explain myself any further."

A style like this blends the best of the classical and medieval traditions.

There was a comparable development in integrating classical and medieval traditions in jest-biographies, those jest-books that focused their jests on the words and deeds of one man. Diogenes Laertes' *Lives of the Philosophers* (Ca. 250 A.D.), a typical progenitor of the classical tradition, compiled all known anecdotes about historical figures like Diogenes the Cynic, providing us with such well-known jests, for example, as Diogenes warning a bastard who was throwing rocks into a crowded street, "Be careful, lad, the man you hit may be your father." Written with the economy of classical jests, such episodes acquire a certain integrity from being focused on one consistent personality. By contrast, *Howleglas* (the English version of *Til Eulenspiegel*) makes no pretense of fact or integrity. A random collection of medieval jests is hung about the hero's neck, and he plays a variety of inconsistent roles—now a fool, then a shrewd peasant, next a rogue, and then a country bumpkin or a pilloried apprentice. The only element holding one jest to another, besides the hero, is his passage from the cradle to the grave. *Scogin's Jests* is representative of such medieval jest-biographies.

Armin's *Nest of Ninnies* is an attempt early in the century to bring some balance into jest-biographies, combining the conciseness and plausibility of the *Lives of the Philosophers* with the lively story-telling of *Howleglas*. Fortunately we have the *Nest of Ninnies* in three successive stages and can see how the author transformed it from an earlier jestbook entitled *Foole upon Foole,* achieving integrity of six different biographies by imposing upon them the linking dialogue between the cynical Puritan Sotto and the lively lady named World. By some such process as this, jest-biography was easily absorbed into fictional biography, a genre that became increasingly popular as the century wore on, culminating in *Robinson Crusoe* and *Moll Flanders*.

Meanwhile, however, more conventional jest-biography continued popular also. *Tarlton's Jests* and the books about Hind (*No Jest Like a True Jest*) and Peters, even though concerned with nationally known figures only recently dead, still mix traditional jests with historical fact. But when the jests are treated in a style associated with the classical tradition, they are given the appearance of historical truth, making such jest-biography a natural tool for propaganda. A mixture of jest and factual record could easily create a noble rogue or a vicious monster. The books about Hind, the Cavalier hero, and Peters, the Puritan regicide, are clear cases in point. Modern conceptions of both men derive from their jestbiographies, even though there is ample evidence to prove them calculated myths.

In random collections as well as in jest-biographies it became increasingly harder to separate man from myth, especially when their styles no longer gave a clue to which was which or who was who. Pseudonymous jestbooks continued popular, and so did the practice of assigning jestbooks to notorious figures like Long Meg of Westminster or Mother Bunch. But now in the boldness born of competition, booksellers carelessly assigned jestbooks to people still living, like the court jester Archee Armstrong. As with Hind and Peters, the myth has outlived the man and Archee's modern reputation as a jolly good fellow derives from his association with the *Banquet of Jests*—a mythical association spawning another myth, since Archee was neither jolly nor good nor the author of the *Banquet of Jests*.

Stephen S. Hilliard (essay date 1986)

SOURCE: "The Devil's Orator: *Pierce Penniless*," in *The Singularity of Thomas Nashe,* University of Nebraska Press, 1986, pp. 62-89.

[*In the following excerpt, Hilliard examines why Thomas Nashe's 1592 pamphlet* Pierce Penniless, *with its satire of Elizabethan ideals, opened the author up to widespread criticism.*]

A suggestion of how Nashe's career appeared to his contemporaries exists in a fictionalized portrait in *The Three Parnassus Plays,* a sequence of comedies performed at Cambridge around the turn of the century. Ingenioso, who barely survives on the fees he collects from his printer John Danter (Nashe's printer), alternately fawns and rails at the misers to whom he dedicates his works and the fops for whom he ghostwrites erotic poems. He curses his bad fortune and his failure to find a liberal Maecenas, but he does not blame himself. He tells his companions:

> Nay sighe not men, laughe at the foolish worlde:
> They have the shame, though wee the miserie.

>   (211)

Like Ingenioso, Nashe projects his failures on the injustice of the world rather than doubting the wisdom of his course. Except for brief periods, he never achieved the support he thought was his due; instead he remained a marginal author, outside the order he defended. His satire was intended to serve orthodoxy, but his bitterness and sharp eye for social abuses tempted him to arrogance and excess.

Nashe's frustrations are depicted in *Pierce Penniless His Supplication to the Devil* (1592), a satiric pamphlet about the despair and anger of the title character at the unjust society that rejects him. It was a remarkably successful work, going through at least five editions by 1596. Part of its appeal was Nashe's bold reversal of the popular prodigal formula (Helgerson, 1-15). Although Pierce has wasted his youth in folly and surfeited his mind with vanity, he has repented and applied himself to mending his fortunes. "But all in vaine, I sate up late, and rose earely, contended

with the colde, and conversed with scarcitie: for all my labours turned to losse, my vulgar Muse was despised & neglected, my paines not regarded, or slightly rewarded, and I my selfe (in prime of my best wit) laid open to povertie" (1:157).[1] Unlike a prodigal, Pierce blames society rather than himself: "I grew to consider how many base men that wanted those parts which I had, enjoyed content at will, and had wealth at commaund" (158). Despair and anger at fortune give way to a review of Elizabethan England in terms of its failure to live up to its own ideals.

The short first section of *Pierce Penniless* introduces Nashe's persona and the situation that prompts him to pen a supplication to the devil. Pierce's search for a messenger to convey his supplication is the occasion for some preliminary satire on the devil-like operation of the merchant exchange and the law courts. The longer second section is the supplication itself, which is not so much an appeal to the devil as a complaint about how the seven deadly sins are manifested in contemporary England. In the third section the devil's messenger, a knight of the post (or professional perjurer) who is a devil in disguise, discourses on the nature of spirits in response to Pierce's asking whether they are imaginary. After the messenger has departed, Nashe speaks for himself and concludes with a rambling apology for the work's deficiencies which turns into a belated epistle to the reader and a dedication. The whole is held together by Pierce's personality and by its lively free-flowing style, which reflects Pierce's stance as a sometimes bitter, sometimes exuberant observer of the London life that excludes him from a significant role.

AUTHOR AND PERSONA

Nashe's invention of Pierce Penniless, the impecunious university wit who mixes personal bile into his satire, allowed him to anchor his extemporaneous style to a fictional persona and give order to his diffuse thinking about society. Pierce is also presented with an irony that enables Nashe to distance himself from his character's more controversial statements. When Gabriel Harvey criticized the arrogance of *Pierce Penniless,* Nashe could excuse "the Methode of my demeanour": his "principall scope" in the work was a "most livelie anatomie of sinne," so, to give the satire a source, "I introduce a discontented Scholler under the person of Pierce Pennilesse, tragicallie exclaiming upon his partial-eid fortune, that kept an Almes boxe of compassion in store for every one but him-selfe" (1:306). Pierce initially functions as a comic exaggeration of his author's emotions and attitudes: "(In a malecontent humor) I accused my fortune, raild on my patrones, bit my pen, rent my papers, and ragde in all points like a mad man" (157). But later the persona becomes a transparent mask through which Nashe can express his own views. Pierce Penniless rapidly became Nashe's nickname in an age given to sobriquets; in later works he used Pierce as a fictional name for himself without any suggestion that Pierce is in some sense a separate character.

Nashe's use of a persona reflects Elizabethan self-consciousness about social roles and the age's uncertainty about the nature of authorship. In ceremonial social inter-actions, imaginary roles concealed real intentions; a well-known example is the Duke d'Alençon's courtship of Queen Elizabeth, in which political issues were masked in a charade of courtly love. In the tournaments that were a regular part of court life the participants assumed chivalric names that were intended to reflect aspects of their charac-ters and their social roles. This use of sobriquets shaded into its literary counterparts: Sir Philip Sidney was Phili-sides or Astrophil in his works and in the imaginations of his admirers. Gabriel Harvey invented a number of perso-nas that expressed potential versions of himself, such as Axiophilus the poet, Angelus Furius the man of action, Eutrapelus the rhetorician, and Eudromus the pragmatist (Stern, 175-90). The fact that these personas were known only to the few who could decode them in Harvey's mar-ginalia is evidence that the social and literary custom of assuming roles had a psychological dimension. In practice the social, literary, and psychological uses of personas merged in complex ways: Sidney's Astrophil is a product of literary conventions, of the courtship games of Eliza-beth's court, and probably of Sidney's own ambivalence about erotic love.

In literature a writer assumed the role of author, a role most often validated by the professional authority of the writer or by his subordination of his views to the authori-ties he cited. But the growth of a popular readership changed the nature of authorship; there was an increased interest in the personal voice or ethos of a writer aside from any question of his credentials. The conventions of genre and decorum were powerful, but traditional rhetori-cal conceptions of authorship were yielding to a more ex-pressive conception of literature that saw works in terms of the opinions and personalities of their authors.[2] Implicit was the fragmenting of received wisdom and an increased emphasis on the individual as the source of his or her so-cial roles. Thus Harvey can conflate John Lyly with his personas: "Surely Euphues was someway a pretty fellow: would God, Lilly had alwaies bene Euphues, and never Pap-hatchet" (*Pierce's Supererogation*, sig. 14r). This de-nial of the fictional status of Lyly's personas is a reversal of Lyly's denial of Martin Marprelate's sincerity. Pierce Penniless's fictional status in relation to Thomas Nashe troubled contemporaries and is not finally resolvable. In *Four Letters* Harvey hoped that Pierce was just a disrepu-table persona adopted by the proper young man Nashe be-cause of Greene's bad example; later in *Pierce's Supererog-ation* he decides Pierce is Nashe and becomes more personal in his criticisms.

To some extent Pierce was a literary persona, a "satyricall disguise" modeled on the precedent of classical satirists. Partly because of a false etymology, the Elizabethans thought of classical satire as the donning of the mask of a satyr—that is, as adopting a rough, crude, and often ob-scene persona. This view of satire seemed to account for the difficulties of Juvenal and Persius and for the rustic el-ements in works like *Piers Plowman,* the ultimate source of Pierce's name. Nashe himself cites classical precedents

since that was the respectable thing to do, particularly since his adversary was the classicist Gabriel Harvey, but his claim that he imitates them is not borne out by evi-dence of their influence. Only by the most general analogy was Nashe a "young Juvenal." Harvey was closer to the truth when he accused Nashe of deriving his style and au-thorial stance from Martin Marprelate and Lyly, and from Tarlton and Greene. The general influence of the Elizabe-than conception of classical satire must be given its due, but Pierce's origins and popularity are better understood by examining his domestic antecedents.

As Tarlton's name suggests, Pierce is not exclusively liter-ary in origin. Richard Tarlton perpetuated on the stage a tradition of irreverent buffoonery, similar to the license of the professional jester. He was famous for his witty impro-visation—he often said more than was set down for him—and for his rapport with his audience. Like the Lords of Misrule who reigned during holiday celebrations, Tarlton voiced the complaints of the subordinate ranks of society in an acceptable comic fashion (Bradbrook, 162-77; We-imann, *Shakespeare,* 185-92). He was cocky and feisty in an exaggerated manner that mocked his own pretensions. To the traditional role of the clown he added a personal el-ement that made him the most popular actor of his day. His style was imitated by Martin Marprelate, by the anti-Martinists, and by Nashe, who also says Tarlton consulted him on matters of wit (1:319). In particular, his imitators followed his practice of breaking frame and violating the decorum of a performance. This the pamphlet writers ac-complished by the use of asides to the reader, often printed as marginal comments. As on the stage, these printed asides engage the audience, but they also suggest that the main performance of the persona or character is a mere act. The device is analogous to a wink directed at a third party in a conversation.

Like a wink, Tarlton's asides enhanced his characterization as Tarlton the clown even if they distracted from the veri-similitude of the specific dramatic role he played. His stage personality became conflated with his roles and with his private self. His public personality became like that of the professional jester in that it was a continuous perfor-mance made up of lesser bits of comic role playing. Mar-tin Marprelate also created the effect of a central personal-ity holding together the egregious routines he used to bait his opponents. Nashe joined the other anti-Martinists in denying Martin's sincerity, but he adapted Martin's tech-niques to his own purposes in *Pierce Penniless* and per-fected them in the pamphlets he wrote against Harvey. From Tarlton (and Martin) he learned to mock his own "tragical exclaimings" and break the coherence of his per-formance with asides: "Marke these two letter-leaping Metaphors, good people" (1:181). Role playing for Tarlton and his imitators was a matter, not of consistent impersona-tion, but of a set of interlocking routines that meshed into a credible overall personality.

After his death Tarlton's persona lived on in anecdotes, jest books, and even on the signs of inns. Such an afterlife as a legend had been achieved by earlier clowns and jesters such as Scogan and Will Summers. These legendary folk heroes joined a number of fictional characters in the popular imagination as symbols of a sort of enlightened roguery. Like Puck and Robin Hood, they violated social decorum in ways that were ultimately just, even if their motivation was questionable. The immorality of these legendary heroes was not an issue in itself but a way of exposing their ethical and social betters to ridicule and laughter. Scogan, Summers, and Tarlton became imaginary folk heroes who cut eccentric trajectories across the too rigid frame of order.

Robert Greene, with his university degrees, moved such irreverent roguery up the social scale, much to the disgust of his critics. His romances seem innocuous enough to modern readers, and his rogue pamphlets claim to expose criminality, but to his contemporaries Greene's career was a scandal. Apparently his notoriety derived in part from the figure he cut in the world of London taverns. In his repentance pamphlets he confesses that he has been a reprobate and an atheist, but his repentance is not very convincing and the last pamphlet attributed to him, *Greene's Groats-worth of Wit* (1592), included libelous allusions to Marlowe, Shakespeare, and others. Greene's various works were popular well into the 1590s; his was still a name to conjure with long after his death. Harvey was to argue that Greene was Nashe's master and the source of a strain of corrupt writing that polluted the press and misled the youth of London.

Greene's notoriety contrasts with that of Martin or Lyly in that its literary component is based on an ethos who is frankly Greene, rather than a persona. He spoke for himself, rather than masking his thoughts with a traditional figure like Tarlton the clown or Colin Clout the shepherd. This is particularly true of his repentance pamphlets, which contribute to the characterization of Pierce Penniless as a reformed prodigal who still cannot find employment. But Nashe was more influenced by Greene's career and his conception of himself as an author than he was by specific works. He came to see Greene's life as a valid although not admirable response to the hostile conditions young intellectuals encountered in London. Like Harvey, Nashe saw Greene's life as symbolic, but for him Greene's dissolution was a result, not a cause, of social disorder.

Greene and Nashe were not the only displaced academics about town, although evidence about the "university wit" as a social type is anecdotal. These "good fellows," as they were called, had the status of their educations but lacked suitable careers. Several tried their hands at writing, but few achieved even the limited success of Lyly, Greene, or Nashe. Often malcontented without being seditious, their lives were irregular without being criminal like those of lower-class rogues. Their lot was not as destitute as that of the uneducated, masterless men who congregated in the city looking for employment, but poverty is relative to expectations, and the bitterness of failure is likely to find expression in cynicism and hostility. Greene

saw his own lapse into profligacy and skepticism as typical of contemporary prodigality. The characterization of Pierce Penniless reflects the experience of this new class of alienated intellectuals (Curtis, "Alienated Intellectuals"; Helgerson 22-24).

Although Pierce is in this sense a spokesman for the 1590s, there is also substance in Harvey's view that Pierce is an expression of Nashe's own discontents. Discounting any irony, Harvey links the persona with Nashe himself, Greene's inwardest companion "cruelly pinched with want, vexed with discredite, tormented with other mens felicitie, and overwhelmed with his owne miserie; in a raving, and franticke moode, most desperately exhibiteth his supplication to the Divell" (*Four Letters*, sig. D3v). Harvey saw Nashe's pamphlet as the latest example of the arrogance that infected printing because of the Marprelate controversy and Greene's bad influence. Like his predecessors, Nashe advances his egocentric opinion without humility: "Every Martin Junior, and Puny Pierce, a monarch in the kingdome of his own humour: every pert, and crancke wit, in one odd veine, or other, the onely man of the University, of the Citty, of the Realme, for a flourish or two: who but he, in the flush of his overweening conceit?" (sig. H1v). Nashe objected to this literal reading of his text, but Pierce is in many ways Nashe, and his satire does verge on arrogant self-assertion.

In the first section of the pamphlet Pierce is a comic exaggeration, and in the last section Nashe speaks as author to apologize for the work's deficiencies and dedicate its good qualities to a patron. He uses Pierce to excuse the long section on spirits: "I bring Pierce Penilesse to question with the divel, as a yoong novice would talke with a great travailer." If the discussion becomes tedious, "impute it to Pierce Penilesse that was importunate in demanding" (1:240). But this ironic distance is not maintained in the long supplication, where the personal pronouns often refer to Nashe rather than to Pierce, as in the attack on Richard Harvey. In his response to Gabriel Harvey, Nashe undercuts his own argument that Pierce is a fictional persona when he lapses into the first person: "I expostulated, why Coblers, Hostlers, and Carmen should be worth so much . . ., and I, a scholler and a good-fellow, a begger" (323). In short, Pierce is an exaggerated version of Nashe, not an objectified character with opinions and attitudes of his own.

Although Pierce merges into Nashe during the course of the pamphlet, Nashe's projection of his satiric impulses onto a persona does free him to express his anger in a way acceptable to his readers. If Nashe cannot hide behind Pierce, he can at least use the persona as a way of softening his arrogance by self-mockery. Without Pierce, he would have no defense against the accusations of both Richard and Gabriel Harvey that he sets himself up as a critic of the folly of others. By expressing discontent, a satirist ran the risk of encouraging discontent in others, but this danger was mitigated when the satirist presented himself as a comic character. Thus Jaques in *As You Like It* thinks the motley of a fool will free him to expose sin and folly. *Pierce Penniless* is an improvement on *The Anatomy of Absurdity* in part because the inclusion of the satirist in the text as a comic character gives the satire a center and helps dissipate its inherent presumption.

Pierce's irony represents a new personal stance; he is not just a literary device. He overcomes his despair through the exercise of his own wit. Rather than seeking to reform himself, he exhorts his readers to amend their ways. The wit is functional to the exhortation, but it also allows him to translate his own frustration and anger into humor. There is nothing about the consolations of philosophy or religion, but there is consolation of a sort in the free play of wit. Pierce through his supplication and Nashe through Pierce use wit and irony as a way of exorcising despair as well as appealing for reform. In later works Nashe appears to have incorporated this ironic projection of himself back into his self-image; at least the ethos of "Nashe" in the later pamphlets continues to exhibit the ironic stance introduced in Pierce.

PIERCE'S SUPPLICATION AND TOPICAL SATIRE

Pierce Penniless is also an improvement on *The Anatomy of Absurdity* in its depiction of social vices and in the sharpness of its satire. Nashe's experience of London life fleshes out his polemics; he achieves *copia,* or richness in style, by piling up satiric details rather than by the schemas and allusions of euphuism. Since the details are exaggerated and frequently grotesque, the effect is analogous to Flemish art or Rabelais. Nashe's account of London life is "realistic" if one takes realism to mean verbal references to the everyday stuff of life. Because of this, Renaissance scholars have mined Nashe's works as a source of information about Elizabethan culture. This verisimilitude accounts for the continuing appeal of *Pierce Penniless,* but the journalistic details do not add up to a realistic portrayal of Elizabethan life in the sense that we associate with novels. A realistic novel claims that its plot and characters have a referential truth similar to that of its details, but the kinds of vice Nashe describes and his framework of the seven deadly sins have a "reality" that precedes and is not dependent on personal experience. Literary conventions and the categories of human experience were "real" like the hierarchy of nature, not a matter of human contrivance subject to revision (Manley, 106-33). Nashe was an empiricist in his shrewd observation of London life, but he did not develop new hypotheses on the basis of what he saw. On the contrary, his emphasis is always on the discrepancy between the selfish behavior of his contemporaries and the ordered society that *ought* to exist.

The anger and satire focus on violations of the ideal: a cobbler who was worth five hundred pounds violated the proper order of the commonwealth, as did a patron who neglected to reward merit. At times Nashe comments on the economic changes that interest modern historians, but he saw their cause to be the corrupt desires of presumptuous individuals, not new economic conditions. He was similar to his Puritan adversaries in this view that social change was caused by private vice, but for him vice was more a matter of violating norms and less a matter of personal sin (Peter, 60-103). This difference in emphasis is evident in his argument that an unthrift or prodigal is better than an idle glutton caught up in the vice of acquisitiveness because the unthrift acquires wit by seeing plays and associating with poets. "Nowe tell me whether of these two, the heavie headed gluttonous house dove, or this livelie, wanton, yoong Gallant, is like to proove the wiser man, and better member in the Common-wealth?" (1:210). In preferring the young prodigal Nashe challenges the priorities of the Puritans, and he reasserts his commitment to humanism in seeing service to the commonwealth as the goal of virtue. Conversely, evil is antisocial behavior such as the selfish withdrawal of the glutton. Nashe's account of the seven deadly sins is for the most part conventional, but the emphasis is on those vices that disrupt society rather than on private sins.

Always implicit is the unfairness of a situation that allows selfish people to prosper, while true merit, like that of Nashe, lies unregarded. Nashe's assumption of merit outraged Harvey, but it is not as arrogant as it sounds, given Nashe's orthodox emphasis on a person's social role. His claim for a higher status was based on the importance he ascribed to education and his exalted conception of the writer's vocation. The central role he attributed to the poet followed from his idealistic conception of society. If human behavior is a product of the abstract ideas people hold about themselves, then writers, who deal with images of human behavior, are unacknowledged arbiters and perhaps legislators. Persuading readers to virtue and shaming them from vice required great rhetorical skill, given the recalcitrance of human nature. Thus the account of poetry in *Pierce Penniless* is not really a digression, since literature should be the best way to inspire the populace to greater civic virtue. Unfortunately, poetry is debased by uneducated writers, "so simple they know not what they doe" (1:194), and is under attack by the Puritans. The enmity of "dull-headed divines" is caused by professional jealousy: their own secondhand sermons fail to persuade their auditors to a better life. "Silver-tongued" Smith is an example of an effective preacher who uses the resources of poetry to move the people to repentance. Nashe begins the pamphlet by evoking the memory of Sidney and ends it with praise of Spenser's *Faerie Queene:* these writers embody in their works the sort of heroic, inspirational literature that should be published and that Nashe aspires to write himself.

In a similar vein he defends drama against its critics, a bold undertaking at the time Nashe wrote. Plays are a less vicious pastime than activities such as gaming, drinking, or harlotry. This new pragmatic defense was developed by Chettle and rejected indignantly by the City fathers in their next request to the Privy Council that the theaters be shut down (Chettle, 39-48; Chambers, 4:316-17). But Nashe goes further: "Nay, what if I proove Playes to be no extreame; but a rare exercise of virtue?" (1:212). Like poetry, drama has purified the language of the common people and offered them inspirational models of heroic behavior. The Puritans who object to drama have a narrow and acquisitive conception of virtue: "What do we get by it?" Heroic deeds depicted on the stage stir the audience to emulation, but the opponents of drama respect "onely their execrable luker, and filthie unquenchable avarice" (213). This outspoken defense of drama provoked an angry response from Thomas Bowes in an epistle published as an introduction to a translation of La Primaudaye in 1594: even though "godly learned men, and some that have spoken of their owne experience, have in their bookes that are allowed by authority, termed Stage-playes and Theaters, *The schoole of abuse, the schoole of bawdery, the nest of the devil & sinke of all sinne, the chaire of pestilence, the pompe of the devil, the soveraigne place of Satan,* yet this commendation of them hath lately passed the Presse, that they are rare exercises in vertue" (La Primaudaye, sig. B4v). Bowes calls for pamphlets like Nashe's to be burned in Paul's Churchyard.

The humanistic view of the social order that lies behind these defenses of poetry and drama is also evident in Nashe's praise of the flexibility of the English system. In Denmark all ranks are fixed in a caste system: "None but the son of a Corporall must be a Corporall, nor any be Captaine, but the lawfull begotten of a Captaines body" (1:178). In England, on the other hand, "vertue ascendeth by degrees of desert unto dignitie" (176). The possibility that an ordinary divine may become a bishop, or a common lawyer rise to be a member of the Privy Council, inspires excellence. "You all knowe that man (insomuch as hee is the Image of God) delighteth in honour and worship, and all holy Writ warrantes that delight, so it bee not derogatory to any part of Gods owne worship: now take away that delight, a discontented idlenesse overtakes him" (179). For simple hire, one gets only day labor. Society should be governed by a desire for honor; contention and emulation are the springs of virtuous action, although one should beware of envy.

Ideally the distribution of wealth should reinforce the meritorious social order Nashe envisions; instead, gold is in the hands of the undeserving and the avaricious. The humble are made proud, and those who have a right to honor are humiliated. Affectations—like those of Mistress Minx, a merchant's wife, or of obscure upstart gallants—are external evidence of a distorted value system. Antiquarians squander money on gewgaws: "This is the disease of our newfangled humorists, that know not what to doe with their welth" (183). Italianate Englishmen and epicurean feasts are further evidence of distorted values. The more ostentatious vices of the sort that were covered by the futile Elizabethan sumptuary legislation are fueled by the faulty distribution of wealth and the corrupt values of the people. The solution is a reaffirmation of the proper order of the commonwealth and its decorum of social roles. In his earliest writings Nashe argued for the importance of good literature in reaffirming proper social values and exposing abnormalities; in *Pierce Penniless* he widens his scope to anatomize the social order that needs the better guidance of writers like himself.

The problem for Nashe was to expose the follies of his society without so offending those he criticized that they would harass and discredit him. This is apparent in his circumspection about the aristocracy. The sloth and luxury of some nobles brings them into contempt. "Is it the loftie treading of a Galliard, or fine grace in telling of a love tale amongst Ladies, can make a man reverenst of the multitude? no, they care not for the false glistering of gay garments, or insinuating curtesie of a carpet Peere" (210). In describing the prevalence of lechery he includes the court by a rhetorical trick: "The Court I dare not touch, but surely there (as in the Heavens) be many falling starres, and but one true Diana" (216). At the very end of the pamphlet, when he decries the lack of patrons, he becomes so outspoken that his diatribe threatens to become an attack on the aristocracy:

> We want an Aretine here among us, that might strip these golden asses out of their gaie trappings, and after he had ridden them to death with railing, leave them on the dunghill for carion. But I will write to his ghost by my carrier, and I hope hele repaire his whip, and use it against our English Peacockes, that painting themselves with church spoils, like mightie mens sepulchers, have nothing but Atheisme, schisme, hypocrisie, & vainglory, like rotten bones lie lurking within them.
>
> (242)

Aware that such railing might seem seditious, Nashe immediately qualifies his denunciation: "Far be it, bright stars of Nobilitie, and glistring attendants on the true Diana, that this my speech shoulde be anie way injurious to your glorious magnificence."

The invocation of Aretino is a reminder that Elizabethans had two conceptions of satire, both of which appealed to Nashe. There is little specific borrowing from Aretino in Nashe's works, but he was inspired by the Italian satirist's style and career (Rhodes, 26-36). Thomas Lodge labeled Nashe "our English Aretine." Aretino's frequent resort to invective, however, conflicted with the more humanistic conception of satire. A shibboleth for almost all Elizabethan satirists was that they attacked vice in general, not particular people, but Aretino had made his reputation naming names. His specialty was railing, often in a deliberately scurrilous and obscene fashion. Rather than begging, he extorted support from patrons, as Nashe does when he threatens retaliation against anyone who sends him "away with a Flea in mine eare" (1:195). Both sides in the Marprelate controversy had used invective in the manner of Aretino because they intended to discredit their opponents as well as argue the issues, but personal attacks were reluctantly adopted as a strategy. As an orthodox humanist Nashe was committed to impersonal satire; thus his later claim that he intended *Pierce Penniless* as a lively anatomy of sin and his frequent disavowels of topical allusions. But this idealistic posture does not square with the passages of invective in the pamphlet nor with the patent topical references. Moreover, the tone is often belligerent and sometimes irate; Nashe cannot maintain the ironic distance established at the start by his use of a persona.

The epistle "The Author to the Printer," added in the second edition, indicates Nashe's conflicting sentiments as a satirist. It pretends to be a private letter but was probably intended for publication; the subterfuge is required by the witty device of putting the prefatory material at the end of the pamphlet. In the letter, Nashe first attempts to allay the arrogance of his satire by the common Elizabethan device of confessing the work "to be a meer toy, not deserving any judicial mans view" (153). At the same time he is angered at the knavery of those rumored to be planning an unauthorized sequel to his work. His main purpose in the epistle is to deny any topical content in his satire. He also denies that he is the actual author of *Greene's Groatsworth of Wit*, "a scald trivial lying pamphlet," which was notorious because of its insulting allusions to Shakespeare and others. He warns off topical interpreters of his work, but promises to counterattack if criticized: "Write who will against me, but let him look his life be without scandale: for if he touch me never so litle, Ile be as good as the Blacke Booke to him & his kindred" (155). Thus he threatens to write personal invective even as he disowns any such intention in the present work.

Pierce Penniless ran into trouble in three different areas: its criticisms of certain classes of people, its putative topical allusions, and its attack on Richard Harvey. In each case Nashe anticipates the difficulty and tries to avoid hostile reactions. Antiquarians were apparently offended by his ridiculing their interest in "worm-eaten Elde," so he claims in the epistle to the printer that the criticism is directed only at a few foolish antiquarians. He also backs off from potentially offensive criticisms in the text itself, as in his qualification of the indictment of English Peacocks among the nobility. Satire on dull-headed Divines is softened by a marginal note: "Absit arrogantia, that this speeche shold concerne all divines, but such dunces as abridge men of their lawfull liberty, and care not howe unprepared they speake to their Auditorie" (192). In one case there is specific evidence that Pierce's satire on a group of people did provoke offense. Robert Beale, clerk of the Queen's Council and bitter opponent of Whitgift, thought he detected political mischief: "That one of these subjects [presumably of Whitgift's] in his book entitled, *A Supplication to the Devil,* so reviled the whole nation of Denmark, as every one, who so bore any due respect to her Majesty and her friends, might be sorry and ashamed to see it" (quoted by McKerrow, 5:142). The motivation and purpose of the lengthy attack on the pride of the Danes are obscure, but Beale thought it dangerous invective.

In spite of his denials, Nashe was also accused of including allusions to specific persons. A letter of April 1, 1593, reports gossip that he had dared criticize Lord Burghley: "In a late pamphlet entytuled *A Suplication to the Divill* he is girded at, thoughe not somuch as in *Mother Hubberd's Tale*" (Petti, "Political Satire," 141). The comparison with

Spenser's controversial poem is a reminder that Nashe's interpolated beast fable, "The Bear and the Fox," would have been read as topical allegory by Elizabethans; Harvey so read it, also comparing it to Spenser's poem. Defending himself, Nashe continued to deny that he had set down "the least allusion to any man set above mee in degree, but onely glanc'st at vice generallie" (1:320). He is explicit about the beast fable:

> The tale of the Beare and the Foxe, how ever it may set fooles heads a worke a farre off, yet I had no concealed ende in it but, in the one, to describe the right nature of a bloudthirsty tyrant, whose indefinite appetite all the pleasures in the earth have no powre to bound in goodnes, but he must seeke a new felicitie in varietie of cruelty, and destroying all other mens prosperitie; for the other, to figure an hypocrite: Let it be Martin, if you will, or some old dog that bites sorer than hee, who secretlie goes and seduceth country Swaines.
>
> (320-21).

Even in its own terms this disclaimer is not very convincing, since it hints that the fox is a specific person, presumably the arch-Puritan Thomas Cartwright; moreover, the tale itself contains pointed allusions that invite an allegorical reading. It is cautious enough, however, to defy exact interpretation, and it was probably ambiguous for Elizabethans as well. It is introduced by the Knight of the Post as part of a discussion of hypocrisy, which he defines as all "Machiavilisme, puritanisme, and outward gloasing with a mans enemie" (1:220). The tale clearly refers to the Puritan campaign, as when it recounts how the Fox persuaded the simple swains that their honey bees were in fact drones, that nothing was canonical but what he and the Chameleon spoke. We are told, "The Fox can tell a faire tale, and covers all his knaverie under conscience" (226). Such sentences ask for topical application.

If the Fox is an allegory for Thomas Cartwright, Whitgift's adversary, then the Bear may well be Cartwright's patron, the earl of Leicester, whose device was the bear and ragged staff. Since Leicester had died in 1588, Nashe could gird at him with relative impunity, although he was indeed, as Harvey warned him, risking a "parlous Tale." Such an attack on Leicester's sponsorship of the Puritans would not mean that Nashe was a crypto-Catholic, although we have no way of knowing his private beliefs (but see Nicholl, 112-21). Insofar as the tale can be interpreted, it is Nashe's usual vehement anti-Puritanism. More detailed readings of it quickly become speculative (McGinn, "Allegory"; Petti, "Beasts"; Petti, "Political Satire"). There is, however, one piece of previously neglected evidence that does indicate Nashe alluded to Leicester. In 1594, in the epistle to his translation of *The Second Part of the French Academy,* Thomas Bowes attacks the licentious pamphlets of Greene and his followers. I have already quoted his scornful rejection of Nashe's defense of stage plays. That specific reference and a complaint that lewd books have recently gathered "under the devils banner" are evidence that Nashe was very much on his mind. So he probably believed that the Bear was a reference to Leicester when he wrote, "Are they not already growen to the boldnes, that they dare to gird at the greatest personages of all estates and callings under the fables of savage beasts, not sparing the very dead that lie in their graves?" (La Primaudaye, sig. B4v). An alternate view, that this line is a reference to Lodge's *Catharos* (1591), has much less to recommend it (A. Walker, 266-67).

The quotation from Bowes also shows how scandalized the Elizabethans were by topical satire. As the charges and countercharges of the Marprelate controversy show, libel was a serious offense, involving personal honor as well as the respect due to social classes and offices. Libel was a relatively new offense, since it depended on the growth of printing, so it was often handled by the Star Chamber rather than by the lower courts. The Star Chamber was regarded as an "arm of sovereignty" whose charge it was to punish "errors creeping into the Commonwealth, which otherwise might prove dangerous and infectious diseases" (Holdsworth, 1:504). As printed defamation, libel could be a simple tort handled under common law, but libel of a public person was seen as seditious. Even libels of private persons were regarded as punishable crimes, since they tended to provoke breaches of the peace. Neither the truth of the libel nor the death of the person defamed were defenses in the Star Chamber. So if Nashe could have been proved to have libeled Burghley or Leicester, he would have faced severe penalties, as he did when the Privy Council forced him to flee London for his part in *The Isle of Dogs* a few years later. The Star Chamber was, after all, authorized to use torture in its investigations, and in the 1590s it was increasingly concerned with libel (Holdsworth, 5:205-12; Sisson, 6-11, 186-88).

The third controversy surrounding *Pierce Penniless,* which opened Nashe to the charge that he was more an Aretino than an Erasmus, was his attack on Richard Harvey. Since Nashe could not deny that it was personal invective, he introduces it as only an example of railing, a sample of his quality as a rhetorician. He asks his readers to "put case (since I am not yet out of the Theame of Wrath) that some tired Jade belonging to the Presse, whom I never wronged in my life, hath named me expressely in Print" (which Richard Harvey had done in *The Lamb of God*). "To shewe how I can raile, thus would I begin to raile on him" (1:195). Nashe concludes the detailed lambasting of Richard Harvey by returning to the ironic claim that the invective is merely a demonstration of his skills: "*Redeo ad vos, mei Auditores,* have I not an indifferent prittye vayne in Spurgalling an Asse? if you knew how extemporall it were at this instant, and with what hast it is writ, you would say so. But I would not have you thinke that all this that is set down heere is in good earnest, for then you goe by S. Gyles, the wrong way to Westminster: but onely to shewe howe for a neede I could rayle, if I were throughly fyred" (199). The impudence of this evasion and the exuberance of the style during the passage of invective cannot mask Nashe's cruelty and vindictiveness.

The title page of *Pierce Penniless* calls attention to the inclusion of "conceipted reproofes," suggesting that the attack on Richard Harvey was important to the pamphlet's popularity. However much the Elizabethans said that satire should reprehend vice but not criticize individuals, in fact they appreciated another tradition that saw the satirist's task as more personal and destructive. The ancient satirist Archilochus was said to have provoked the suicides of his victims Lycambes and his daughter. This and other stories of the power of satire sanctioned the view that satire attacked specific people in a vindictive manner (Elliott, 257-75). For example, Nashe threatens to attack anyone who writes against him or patrons who scorn his efforts. Throughout his career he was accused of concealing topical satire in his works, and of course, in his controversy with Gabriel Harvey invective became his central purpose. Thus his reputation as encapsuled in an epigram after his death:

> Nash had Lycambes on earth living beene
> The time thou wast, his death had bin al one,
> Had he but mov'd thy tartest Muse to spleene,
> Unto the forke he had as surely gone:
>   For why there lived not that man I thinke,
>   Usde better, or more bitter gall in Inke.
>
> (Nashe, 5:153)

Elizabethans appear to have delighted in vituperation even though they disapproved of it as a violation of Christian charity.

Gabriel Harvey uses Nashe's lapses into personal satire to discredit *Pierce Penniless.* In his *Four Letters* he acknowledges Nashe's talent, but lectures him that the best use of poetry is in praising virtue:

> Good sweete Oratour, be a devine Poet indeede: and use heavenly Eloquence indeede: and employ thy golden talent with amounting usance indeede: and with heroicall Cantoes honour right Vertue, & brave valour indeede: as noble Sir Philip Sidney, and gentle Maister Spencer have done, with immortall Fame: and I will bestow more complements of rare amplifications upon thee, then ever any bestowed uppon them: or this Tounge ever affoorded; or any Aretinish mountaine of huge exaggerations can bring-foorth.
>
> (sig. F4v)

Harvey's rejection of personal satire as a mode (even as practiced by his friend Spenser in *Mother Hubberd's Tale*) is based on a conception of literature similar to Nashe's own. Both saw the poet as someone who should contribute to the good order of the commonwealth, primarily through the celebration of virtue. Harvey argues that invective and libel only contribute to disrespect and disorder: "Honour is precious: worship of value: Fame invaluable: they perillously threaten the Commonwealth, that goe about to violate the inviolable partes thereof" (sig.B1r). Because a spirit of contradiction reigns in "this Martinish and Counter-martinish age," it is better to remain mute than resort to railing. "Aretine, and the Divels oratour might very well bee spared in Christian, or Piliticke [*sic*] Comonwealthes: which cannot want contagion inough, though they bee not poysened with the venemous potions of Inckhorne witches" (sigs. E3r-E3v). Harvey sees Nashe as a "backbiter" who writes "gross scurility and impudent calumny," not as a humanistic reformer of vice.

The other complaints about *Pierce Penniless* mentioned earlier support Harvey's contention that the work contains too much personal satire to pass muster as a humanist tract. It lapses into personal attacks that are tangential to any corrective purpose the work has, and much of the satire seems to reflect the resentment of Thomas Nashe, for all that it is filtered through the persona of Pierce. In claiming that the work is an "anatomy of sin," Nashe was pretending to an objectivity that is belied most obviously by the attack on Richard Harvey, but also by other passages of invective, such as the beast fable or the railing on stingy patrons. The satire often becomes vituperative and destructive rather than charitable and reformist, although the work is too good-humored to become sour. Potential patrons like "Amyntas" were probably reluctant to associate themselves with Nashe's boldness, even if they were entertained by his wit. To the extent that patrons purchased credit and a reputation for service to the commonwealth, Nashe had little to offer. Harvey was biased, but his rejection of Nashe's claim that *Pierce Penniless* is humanistic satire is compelling. Moreover, such criticisms must have stung Nashe, since his scandalous pamphlet hardly fit his own exalted conception of the function of literature.

THE DEVIL: CREDULITY AND SKEPTICISM

After the long supplication has been read, Pierce asks the Knight of the Post to draw on his experience as a devil and acquaint him "with the state of your infernall regiment: and what that hel is, where your Lord holdes his throne" (1:217). The Knight of the Post's account of spirits and demons has been seen as an irrelevant interpolation, added to pad out *Pierce Penniless.* Most of it is a translation, with some paraphrase, omissions, and a few minor additions, of an obscure Latin demonological tract by Georgius Pictorius, published in 1563. Copying from a single source without acknowledgment is hardly scholarship, even in an age where originality was not prized, but Nashe was not simply filling space while his invention flagged. A mock supplication to the devil was potentially offensive at a time when devils were still believed to be threatening presences. As a popular pamphlet writer and friend of Greene and Marlowe, Nashe took a risk in joking about traffic with the devil, even though there was a literary tradition of mocking the devil, as can be seen in a number of Tudor interludes. The passage on devils, as dull as Nashe himself admits it to be, serves as an avowal of orthodoxy. It may be secondhand, but he could hardly draw on his own experience or make it up out of whole cloth.

In calling Nashe the "Devil's Orator," Gabriel Harvey sought to portray him as a writer who served the devil's ends, however much he professed orthodoxy. Harvey evokes the ghosts of Aretino, Tarlton, and Greene in admonishing Nashe not to play wantonly "with the highest and deepest subjectes of spirituall contemplation: Heaven, and Hell, Paradise, and Purgatory." There is enough in the world to engage Nashe's invention without his offering "vayne Hyperboles of the reverende mysteries of God" (*Four Letters,* sigs. F4r-F4v). Harvey is probably pretending to a greater concern with irreverence than he feels in an effort to discredit Nashe, but the charge was serious at a time when Puritans believed Satan was using profane books to undermine religion. Harvey also represents himself as seeking Nashe's personal salvation in his effort to reform his mode of writing. His accusation that the work is diabolical may be a result of deliberate misreading or a critical judgment that the work is in fact unorthodox.

The accusation was damaging enough to provoke Nashe's *Strange News,* which was retitled *The Apology of Pierce Penniless* in a 1593 reissue. In addition to denying that Pierce is simply himself or that he included topical allusions, Nashe denies that his work is a "diabolicall Discourse," except in the sense that it treated the nature of spirits; "in that far fetcht sense may the famous *defensative against supposed Prophecies* and *the Discoverie of Witchcraft* be called notorious Diabolicall discourses, as well as the *Supplication,* for they also intreate of the illusions and sundrie operations of spirits" (1:308-9). Both of these works were in fact important documents in the growth of rationalism. Henry Howard, earl of Northampton, wrote *A Defensative Against the Poison of Supposed Prophecies* (1583) in an effort to discredit all spurious predictions of future events. The work was written because Howard's ancestors had been disastrously misled by prophecies, but it was published because of the "great disorder" caused by Richard Harvey's *Astrological Discourse,* "chiefly among the simple and unlearned people."[3] Nashe, who had ridiculed Richard Harvey's predictions himself, shared Howard's skepticism about astrology and borrowed frequently from *A Defensative* (Harlow, "A Source"). Reginald Scot's *Discovery of Witchcraft* (1584) is unique for its time in its wholesale rejection of witchcraft as a fraud and delusion. Scot's work is in fact so skeptical that it was judged a diabolical discourse by its many opponents (Anglo).

In *Pierce Penniless,* the discussion of devils and spirits is introduced as a refutation of skepticism. Pierce asks the Knight of the Post whether hell is the place of legend, where the usurer has to drink molten gold and the glutton eat nothing but toads, or "whether (as some phantasticall refyners of philosophie will needes perswade us) hell is nothing but error, and that none but fooles and Idiotes and Machanicall men, that have no learning, shall be damned" (1:218). In this way Nashe contrasts credulity with skepticism, before offering a middle way with his translation of Pictorius's pseudoscientific demonology. The Knight of the Post discounts imaginative speculation about the nature of hell, then explains how the skeptical view can reduce devils to moral allegories: "Some men there be that, building too much upon reason, perswade themselves that there are no Divels at all, but that this word *Daemon* is such another morall of mischeife, as the Poets Dame Fortune is of mishap . . . so that the Divell (as they make it) is onely a pestilent humour in a man, of pleasure, profit, or policie, that violently carries him away to vanitie, villanie, or monstrous hypocrisie" (219-20). This rationalistic explanation of moral or "earthly" devils is presented as a useful descriptive approach to human behavior, but Nashe follows Pictorius in rejecting its skeptical implications.

Demonology was a vexing problem for the Elizabethans, an area where conflicting opinions were more the rule than a firm set of beliefs. The Reformation had sought to purge religion of magic: both Puritans and Anglicans were scornful of the more superstitious aspects of medieval folk religion. Purgatory was dismissed as a myth, the saints were reduced to heroes, and ceremonial remissions of sin were abandoned. The Puritans wanted yet further reformation, but at the same time they had a vivid sense of the devil's imminence and active role in human life, so were fearful of witchcraft. Tracts on witchcraft and demons advanced a variety of opinions, ranging from Scot's skepticism to the rather credulous accounts of witchcraft trials. Most Protestant works tried to assert that devils were real and witchcraft possible but that the devil worked more through illusions than through miraclelike interventions. Occultists and Neoplatonists sought to incorporate demons into their cosmologies in pseudoscientific fashion (West, 15-53).

This intellectual debate over the nature of demons intersected with traditional folk beliefs and superstitions. Whatever his role in Christian theology, in village life the devil served to explain apparently preternatural happenings, particularly untoward misfortunes. An inexplicable illness or a crop failure might be evidence of witchcraft, particularly if there was a malevolent old woman in the neighborhood who bore a grudge against the victim. Village witchcraft was more a matter of black magic than of heresy, and as such it was part of a complex system of superstitious magic that was often quite tangential to Christian doctrine. Theologians saw all such magic as trafficking with the devil, although in practice the devils involved were the semicomic figures of folk myth rather than that embodiment of evil, Satan (K. Thomas, 435-583). Puritans and Anglicans alike were as interested in exorcising such superstitions as they were in exorcising devils. Nashe himself made a minor contribution to the effort in his *Terrors of the Night,* which questions folk superstitions.

Caution was necessary, though, because the devil was considered theologically necessary, even if belief in his existence was cluttered with superstitions. Sir Thomas Browne put it succinctly in the next century: "I have ever beleeved, and doe now know, that there are Witches; they that doubt of these, doe not onely deny them, but Spirits; and are obliquely and upon consequence a sort, not of Infidels, but Atheists" (29). King James accused Reginald Scot of Sadduceeism, a heresy that denied spirits, and was reported to have ordered all copies of *The Discovery of Witchcraft*

burned. Scot himself was careful to assert his orthodox belief in the existence of spirits, although he defined them as being incapable of any interaction with the physical world. But his position was unusual: most Elizabethans apparently experienced the devil as a personal threat. Through witchcraft and magic, possession and temptation, Satan and his cohorts played an active role in Elizabethan life. Mocking the devil was courageous, if foolhardy; mocking belief in the devil would have been doing the devil's work: "It is a policy of the Devil to persuade us that there is no Devil" (K. Thomas, 476).

Since *Pierce Penniless* was written in English in a popular format, it ill behooved Nashe to let his mockery of "the high and mightie Prince of Darknesse, Donsell dell Lucifer" seem to be scoffing at belief in the devil. The passages from Pictorius are included to offset any such implication. Nashe's labors as a translator were also necessary because his conception of evil does tend to be rationalistic rather than diabolical. The image of London life in *Pierce Penniless* is more a matter of "wit's misery and the world's madness" than of "discovering the devils incarnate of this age"—to quote the title and subtitle of a 1596 work by Thomas Lodge which also tries to amalgamate a theological and rationalist explanation of evil. Pierce's supplication is a complaint that people have usurped the devil's role as a source of evil: he tells the devil that a number of uncharitable cormorants have "incurd the daunger of a *Praemunire* with medling with matters that properly concerne your owne person" (1:165). Nashe is being witty, but his conception of vice is of a humanly motivated malignancy.

The medieval format of the seven deadly sins in *Pierce Penniless* is used in ways that anticipate social psychology. The emphasis is on how a perturbation of the mind like envy or wrath causes men and women to pervert or abuse their social roles. The effect can be subtle and perceptive, as in the description of a typical young prodigal:

> A yoong Heyre or Cockney, that is his Mothers Darling, if hee have playde the waste-good at the Innes of the Court or about London, and that neither his Students pension, nor his unthrifts credite, will serve to maintaine his Collidge of whores any longer, falles in a quarrelling humor with his fortune, because she made him not King of the Indies, and sweares and stares, after ten in the hundreth, that nere a such Pesant as his Father or brother shall keepe him under: hee will to the sea, and teare the gold out of the Spaniards throats, but he will have it, byrlady.
>
> (1:170-71).

Such passages anticipate the vogue of Theophrastian characters, which, in their emphasis on the individual playing social roles, were more psychological than medieval "estates" satire (Boyce, 69-71). The specific details quite naturally entice readers into supposing that an actual person is intended; in this case Thomas Lodge has been proposed by modern critics (McKerrow, 4:100; Nicholl, 59-60; Tenney, 130-31).

Pierce Penniless is rationalistic in its emphasis on how people through folly or hypocrisy make themselves into social stereotypes; even viciousness is likely to be an extreme affectation in Nashe's London. In such a world the devil's role is secondary; people are more free agents than agents of the devil. Pierce asks Satan: "You goodman wandrer about the world, how doe yee spende your time, that you do not rid us of these pestilent members? you are unworthy to have an office, if you can execute it no better. Behold another enemy of mankinde, besides thy selfe, exalted in the South, Philip of Spaine" (1:184). Nashe was hardly a philosopher and probably would have been unable to account for any discrepancy between his orthodox beliefs and his perception of the way people act in society. At issue are complex questions about how the devil is manifested in the world that are not to Nashe's purpose. His tendencies toward rationalism were a product of common sense and alienated cynicism rather than philosophical inquiry. For all that he paraded his learning, he was street wise, to use a modern term, rather than book wise. He presumably had no personal difficulty in squaring his orthodoxy with his secularized attitudes towards social behavior.

Nashe was not a systematic thinker, but skepticism was fashionable, and many of its attitudes met his needs. Barnaby Rich commented scornfully on the way young gentlemen affected "to be curious in cavilling, propounding captious questions, therby to shew a singularitie of their wisedomes: for the helping whereof, they diligently studie bookes for the purpose, as Cornelius Agrippa, *de vanitate scientiarum,* and other like" (sigs. H1v-H2r). Marlowe and Greene, as well as Raleigh and his circle, all dabbled in this fashionable skepticism without being full-fledged Pyrrhonists or forming a "school of night." From Agrippa's *Of the Vanity and Uncertainty of Arts and Sciences,* one of his most quoted books, Nashe acquired an easy cynicism about other people's learning. He even knew a translation of Sextus Empiricus (Sprott). Nashe would have disavowed any heterodox intentions, but the attitudes of skeptical authors found their way into his works. The account of spirits in *Pierce Penniless* claims to be a refutation of skepticism and of those who build too much on reason, but this encapsuled expression of orthodoxy cannot offset the playful skepticism of the rest of the pamphlet.

This playfulness, the impudency, and the singular style have a melancholic undertone, although Pierce's discontent is initially presented in a comic fashion. Nashe tries to distinguish Pierce's irony from the estrangement of the true malcontent, a social type who receives one of his earliest portraits in this work. The malcontent starves himself so he can dine once or twice a term at an expensive ordinary and affects "a scornfull melancholy in his gate and countenance." He talks "as though our common welth were but a mockery of government, and our Majestrates fooles, who wronged him in not looking into his deserts, not imploying him in State matters, and that, if more regard were not had of him very shortly, the whole Realme

should have a misse of him, & he would go (I mary would he) where he should be more accounted of" (1:170). At the start of the pamphlet Pierce also threatens to exile himself in his discontent. Pierce is more ironic and orthodox in his beliefs, but he is also a malcontent. Scornful melancholy and a feeling of personal grievance show through in spite of Nashe's efforts to use his persona to diffuse his anger.

Pierce Penniless is not a diabolical discourse, except in the eyes of Gabriel Harvey and of those Puritans who regarded all profane pamphlets as the devil's work. For the most part it is too conventional and playful to pose much threat to the orthodoxy of its readers. But not all of its satire was directed at approved targets, and often the destructive potential of the mode shows through as anger and envy (Lecocq, 299-315). Moreover, Nashe's mastery of Pierce is incomplete: instead of being a comic character, Pierce becomes a spokesman for discontent with Elizabethan society. Elizabethan ideology was uncomfortable with any criticism, particularly criticism disseminated among the lower ranks of society. Thus, the charge that Nashe was the devil's orator was damaging, although overstated. When the Harveys linked him with Martin Marprelate and the traitor Babington, they were being grossly unfair to his manifest orthodoxy, but *Pierce Penniless* was too outspoken and singular to be entirely safe, or to gain Nashe the respectability he needed if he was to receive sustained patronage.

Notes

1. All parenthetical citations to Nashe's work are taken from McKerrow, Ronald B., ed., *The Works of Thomas Nashe,* 5 vols., 1904-1910; rpt. Oxford University Press, 1958.

2. The view that the satirist's persona is conventional was argued by Mack, "The Muse of Satire," and developed for the Elizabethan period by Alvin Kernan in *The Cankered Muse.* This view of the persona as a literary device is questioned by Ehrenpreis, Gill, and Lecocq.

3. McKerrow doubted that the work was a reply to Richard Harvey (5:166-67), and Don Cameron Allen saw it as a reply in a general sense (*Star-Crossed Renaissance,* 112-16). Although most of *The Defensative* was written before Richard Harvey published his predictions, the title page alludes to the recent controversy. Near the end of the book Howard writes, "I could adjoyne the pregnaunt follies of some other freshe in memorie . . . saving that it is the part of no good nature, eyther to insulte on those, that are alreadye overthrowne with shame, or to agravate, affliction and miserye" (sigs. 2G4v-2H1r). Howard notes that he has been collecting material for his book since he was fifteen, but is now forced into publication by circumstances (sig. 2K1r). Thus, there may be an ironic edge to Nashe's mentioning this book in a pamphlet answering Gabriel Harvey, although Gabriel himself had reservations about his brother's astrology.

Works Cited

Bradbrook, M. C. *The Rise of the Common Player: A Study of Actor and Society in Shakespeare's England.* Cambridge: Harvard University Press, 1962.

Chambers, E. K. *The Elizabethan Stage.* 4 vols. Oxford: Clarendon Press, 1923.

Chettle, Henrie. *Kind-Hartes Dreame—1592.* And William Kemp. *Nine Daies Wonder—1600.* Bodley Head Quarto. Ed. G. B. Harrison. New York: E. P. Dutton, 1923.

Curtis, Mark H. "The Alienated Intellectuals of Early Stuart England." *Past and Present.* 23 (1962): 25-41.

Eliott, Robert C. *The Power of Satire: Magic, Ritual, Art.* Princeton: Princeton University Press, 1960.

Helgerson, Richard. *The Elizabethan Prodigals.* Berkeley and Los Angeles: University of California, 1977.

Holdsworth, W. S. *A History of English Law.* Vols. 1 and 5. Boston: Little, Brown, 1922, 1924.

Manley, Lawrence. *Convention, 1500-1750.* Cambridge: Harvard University Press, 1980.

McKerrow, Ronald B., ed. *The Works of Thomas Nashe.* 5 vols. 1904-10; rpt. with correction and a separately paged "Supplement," ed., F. P. Wilson. Oxford: Basil Blackwell, 1958.

Nicholl, Charles. *A Cup of News: The Life of Thomas Nashe.* London: Routledge and Kegan Paul, 1984.

Peter, John. *Complaint and Satire in Early English Literature.* Oxford: Clarendon Press, 1956.

Rhodes, Neil. *Elizabethan Grotesque.* London: Routledge and Kegan Paul, 1980.

Sisson, C. J. *Lost Plays of Shakespeare's Age.* Cambridge: Cambridge University Press, 1936.

Stern, Virginia. *Gabriel Harvey: His Life, Marginalia, and Library.* Oxford: Clarendon Press, 1979.

Tenney, Edward Andrews. *Thomas Lodge.* Cornell Studies in English, 26. Ithaca: Cornell University Press, 1935.

Thomas, Keith. *Religion and the Decline of Magic.* New York: Scribners, 1971.

Walker, Alice. "The Reading of an Elizabethan: Some Sources of the Prose Pamphlets of Thomas Lodge." *Review of English Studies* 8 (1932): 264-81.

Weimann, Robert. *Shakespeare and the Popular Tradition in the Theater: Studies in the Social Dimension of Dramatic Form and Function.* Ed. Robert Schwarz. Baltimore: Johns Hopkins University Press, 1978.

West, Robert Hunter. *The Invisible World: A Study of the Pneumatology in Elizabethan Drama.* Athens: University of Georgia Press, 1939.

John Simons (essay date 1998)

SOURCE: "Introduction: Why Read Chapbooks," in *Guy of Warwick and Other Chapbook Romances,* edited by John Simons, University of Exeter Press, 1998, pp. 1-18.

[*In the following excerpt, Simons discusses how broadsides were created and produced and illustrates how they slowly changed the social aspirations of English commoners.*]

[Chapbooks were] the flimsy and often poorly printed booklets which were a major source of literature for the English poor in the eighteenth century and early nineteenth century.[1] There is a full discussion of the nature and form of chapbooks below as well as some analysis of their history and readership, but here I wish to set out some of the reasons for being interested in such apparently ephemeral objects and to comment on some aspects of the relationship between work on popular literature and culture and more mainline literary-historical studies.

Chapbook readers left few records of their tastes or opinions. They were, for the most part, in dire economic necessity and therefore did not have the leisure to record their thoughts, or else they were children and did not have the power.[2] To read chapbooks is, therefore, to enter a one-sided conversation with the past. We can listen to the chapbooks as they speak to their long-dead readers, but we cannot easily hear the readers speaking back. It is true that many people who were probably chapbook readers did leave autobiographical writings, but these tend to relate narratives of personal and political development. Only very rarely are details of aesthetic response recorded. Chapbooks thus force us into the reconstitution of the mentality of groups who left few relevant traces of themselves. When we read chapbooks we must constantly ask ourselves what pleasure they offered to a reader whose access to print was limited and what sense the picture of the world they offer would have made to him or her.

Such reconstructive studies are necessary if we are going to maintain any feeling for historical continuity. Only such a feeling will enable us to remember and understand the lives of people whose access to privileged forms of communication was limited or non-existent. They provide a salutary reminder that poverty of information is not necessarily a recent phenomenon and that it visits its ill effects on future generations just as surely as do years of bad nutrition. Such studies are also necessary if many contemporary students of English Literature are to be enabled to position themselves autobiographically in the continuum of their studies. A very large number of those who now work at all levels of the higher education system—as teachers, researchers or undergraduates—have personal and family histories which offer them little or no stake in the high culture which forms the core of their academic work. It is at least desirable that they should have some access to the artefacts which produced their ancestors' world-view rather than that of their ancestors' masters.

Chapbooks offer an exemplary body of texts for this purpose and they allow us to begin to grasp the textures of the world of the pre-industrial rural and urban poor as it appears through their common reading. Most people who begin to look at chapbooks seriously appear to find that they also offer some pleasures to the modern reader. These little paper objects were valued and loved by those who bought them both in childhood and maturity. Anyone handling them today cannot fail to be moved by the disjunction between their size and fragility and the status they appear to have held in the poor reader's mind. More than anything else it is this disjunction between monetary and affective value that speaks eloquently of the struggles of ordinary people to gain some pleasure and education from reading in a world which must, for most of them, have offered few opportunities for hope or self-realisation.

The Form and Cultural Contexts of Chapbooks

Before discussing in detail the chapbooks edited below, I will describe exactly what a chapbook is. There will then be a brief exploration of some of the salient features of the history of this kind of book, which formed a body of reading matter enjoyed across the social spectrum in England, Wales, Scotland and Ireland from the late seventeenth to the mid-nineteenth century. Chapbooks also crossed the Atlantic and were read both in the American colonies and in the early years of the United States.[3] Yet chapbooks are hardly known outside of specialist bibliographical studies.

This volume is not designed as a full history of chapbooks, but it is worth mentioning that they are not exclusive to Anglophone cultures or to those countries (like Wales) where chapbooks in the native language flourished alongside chapbooks in English. Texts which share many features in common with the chapbooks edited here can be identified from the early modern period to the nineteenth century in Germany, Russia, Italy, Spain and, most famously, in France through the series commonly known as the *bibliothèque bleue*.[4] In the twentieth century, texts which may fairly be described as chapbooks were produced in Judaeo-Spanish and are still available in the *folhetos* of modern Brazil and the productions associated with the town of Onitsha in Nigeria.[5]

The heyday of the English chapbook was the eighteenth century. There are frequent allusions to chapbooks in commentaries on the literature and popular culture of this period, but few people have troubled to acquaint themselves fully with their form and content, and such longer studies as do exist have mainly concentrated on bibliographical and commercial history.[6] Anyone familiar with writing on the eighteenth century will generally find chapbooks mentioned as cheap, small books, containing highly traditional materials, and read by the poorest strata of society and by the children of the gentry. The term chapbook is also frequently and inaccurately applied to any small book, even, it seems, to those parts of longer texts which were published in serial form. The chapbook reader is often depicted as an individual of low sophistication, low intellect and meagre literacy.[7] The purpose of these initial remarks is to correct some of these misconceptions and to sketch out the conditions of production and readership which determined the chapbook's distinctive form.

It must be first said that a chapbook was not a cheap book. Chapbooks usually retailed at the price of one old penny (about 0.4p). In 1795 an agricultural labourer in the south of England had a weekly income of about 40p. The bare necessities of life (bread, salt, meat, tea, sugar, butter, soap, candles, thread) sufficient to support a family cost 9s 7½d (48p).[8] The risking of even one old penny in this state of misery might be seen as an extravagant gesture, and to the vast majority of English labourers chapbooks were certainly not cheap: indeed they may be seen as a luxury quite beyond reach. However, there is evidence that in better times labourers did buy and read chapbooks.[9] There is also plenty of evidence that chapbook readers were to be found at other levels of English society, and when, for example, gentlemen like James Boswell or Sir Walter Scott (who in 1808 was offered a thousand guineas for one poem) made their important collections of chapbooks, we may truly say that, to them, they were cheap.[10]

A chapbook is best defined strictly and briefly thus: a single sheet of paper printed on both sides and then folded so as to make a book of twelve leaves or twenty-four pages.[11] It is possible to find chapbooks which have thirty-six pages and also slimmer ones of, for example, eight pages, but the commonest form was the twenty-four pager and anyone reading chapbooks will probably encounter more of this sort than any other. Whatever the number of pages, chapbooks have the following features in common: they were sold unopened (a large number of specimens that have survived are still in this state unless they have been bound up as parts of collections), they often include one or more woodcuts or wood engravings, and they are usually fragile and printed on poor quality paper. It is tempting to lump together a whole host of other small books under the blanket term of chapbooks, but this is misleading. Chapbooks have a very specific history of production and distribution, and it is this which enables us to understand them as a genuine form of literary and intellectual culture.

When the virtual monopoly on printing which had been enjoyed by London since the incorporation of the Stationers' Company in 1557 came to an end in 1695, presses began to spring up across the country. Many provincial printers tried their hand at the chapbook form—one can find chapbooks from Kendal, Whitehaven, Wigan, and Falkirk for example—but there were certain centres which gained and retained their prominence throughout the period. London, Newcastle, York, Glasgow (especially in the nineteenth century) and Banbury (represented by the work of John Cheney and the somewhat artistic productions of the Rusher family) were the most important of these.[12] A web of travelling pedlars known as chapmen spread from these regional centres where, particularly in London, print-shops were supported by fully stocked warehouses. It was largely through this web that the chapbooks were carried all over the British Isles and reached the rural communities with which they are most commonly associated.[13] Thus the regions could be served with a range of chapbooks which not only linked them to national culture (for example, through chapbook texts of novels like *Robinson Crusoe* and *Moll Flanders*) but also satisfied local tastes (for example, the range of religious chapbooks produced at York or the highly colourful Scottish chapbooks of Dougal Graham, 'the bellman of Glasgow').[14] In this way, chapbooks provided one of the links which enabled national consciousness to grow within a culture which was still tolerant of regional difference. It has been very properly said that 'the importance of the printing press in unifying Great Britain and in shaping its inhabitants' view of themselves' has not been fully understood.[15]

Economic hardships made it unlikely that chapbooks would have formed a regular purchase in labouring households even in better times. However, we know from the autobiographical writings of such as John Clare, Samuel Bamford and Thomas Holcroft that chapbooks were a fairly familiar commodity among the rural poor.[16] It should be remembered that in pre-industrial societies (or in societies where industrialisation has not severely impacted on the details of daily life and culture) the lack of means to possess or read a text does not by any means preclude access to writing. Events where readings to village communities formed a common entertainment are well recorded for early modern France and Italy, and the bookseller James Lackington hinted at similar pastimes in eighteenth-century England when he wrote of:

> The poorer sort of farmers and even the poor country people in general, who before that spent their evenings in relating stories of witches, ghosts, hobgoblins etc., now shorten the winter nights by hearing their sons and daughters read tales, romances etc.[17]

Even so, it is probably safest to assume that the regular purchase and collection of chapbooks was available only to those members of rural communities who lived in relative comfort (say on 10s a week) and that these families played the part of culture brokers. They mediated between the national life based in literacy and the oral tradition which formed the fine texture of understanding and belief in the mass of the population.[18] There are plainly many things to be said against this simple model, but it is difficult to see how the hard facts of economic life in pre-industrial England square easily with any other interpretation. We should certainly not assume that chapbooks were ephemera which could be read and discarded. If only a smallish number has survived, this may well be due to the process of 'reading to bits' and also the lack of affection for these traditional texts which set in when the mass production of genuinely cheap books and periodicals, often in penny and twopenny issues, drove them from the urban market at least in the 1830s and 1840s.

We also know that, while the labourers read chapbooks in their cottages, the children of the gentry also avidly consumed them in the great houses. Through these children, the many servants who laboured to support landowners, rural merchants and industrialists may also have had access to them. Sir Richard Steele, James Boswell, Sir Walter Scott and George Borrow all read chapbooks as children,

and in Boswell's case collected them in maturity. Thackeray bought and enjoyed chapbooks on his tour of Ireland.[19] One of the most intractable problems of chapbook scholarship is that the best and most extensive bases of evidence for chapbook readership comes not from the rural poor, who plainly did provide a huge and diverse market for them, but from the gentry. This need not disturb us too much if we remember that it was possible to be able to read and to have access to chapbooks even if you were only supported by a relatively low economic base and a restricted set of cultural opportunities. To have been able to write, however, especially to have been able to write with the kind of leisure that is implied by the ability to make records of personal literary taste, was an entirely different order of accomplishment. Put bluntly, it was a luxury which was even further beyond the reach of the English poor than the penny chapbook.

I remarked above that it is too often said that popular literature, and especially popular literature which has the low status ascribed to chapbooks, is designed to appeal to a reader of low sophistication and low intellect. Part of my purpose in producing this edition is to counter this highly prejudiced view. It is true that chapbooks do not speak to a world thronged by readers who were conversant with high literary culture or the finer points of literary discrimination. At the same time, the chapbooks themselves do not suggest a reader of low literacy. The texts presented here do not, to my mind, make concessions where literacy is concerned. They make the occasional blunder which may amuse a contemporary reader but which is understandable to anyone who can comprehend that a reasonable level of intelligence may readily combine with poor education.

Anyone who could read a *Moll Flanders* chapbook was certainly sufficiently literate to read *Moll Flanders*. What he or she may well not have been able to do was BUY *Moll Flanders* in any but its penny form. Chapbooks do not speak of a world of intellectual limitation but of a world of economic hardship and lack of opportunity. Working-class autobiography of the nineteenth century is a record of the consistently heroic effort to gain access to the products of the official literate culture. We should not be too quick to assume, especially when considering a world where hard work from childhood onwards left little room for education (even if this were an available option), that lack of money implies anything more than poverty and all the waste of human intellectual and sensual resources that poverty brings with it.

THE CONCERNS OF CHAPBOOKS

Although chapbooks are most readily associated with highly traditional materials, this view does not do anything like justice to their range of interests. Indeed a chapbook collector could have assembled a library in miniature which comprehended almost the entire range of polite knowledge. In order to give some meaningful contexts to the chapbook romances edited below it will be helpful to review briefly the sorts of chapbook which their readers might also have owned and enjoyed.

Chapbooks were often of practical as well as recreational interest, so we may begin with mentioning the various almanacs and prognostications which were found in this form from the late seventeenth century onwards. Almanacs offered obvious guides to life in rural surroundings, but their purely practical uses were supplemented by more exotic books of prophecies. The most celebrated were probably those of *Mother Shipton* and *Mother Bunch,* with *Nixon's Cheshire Prophecies* coming a close third. These chapbooks blended folkloric material with obscure prophecy and biographies of the prophets.[20] It is hard to say how far such texts were used in a genuinely practical manner. They were certainly just the sort of work which gave chapbooks their bad reputation in the official culture where more reputable astrologers such as Partridge had long been the butt of fashionable jokes and had themselves passed into chapbook form. I suspect that many chapbook readers would have seen this kind of text as entertaining and absurd but containing much useful material and being of some historical interest.

More obviously practical were various guides to divination: the interpretation of dreams, the significance of the placement of moles on the face and body, physiognomy and palmistry. These sorts of popular sciences were the common currency of travelling fairs and would have been very familiar to rural readers who may have tried various sorts of divination for themselves—especially where the choice of a marriage partner was concerned. Indeed the key and Bible ceremony was a common popular practice (corresponding with the more polite *sortes Virgilianae*) and David Vincent has written an account of a *Guy of Warwick* chapbook being used in a divination ceremony where a Bible was lacking.[21] In addition to exploring the various supernatural forms of choosing a partner, chapbook readers could learn how to cement a relationship by reference to chapbooks which taught them how to write letters. This kind of chapbook, where a series of letters shows both the progress of a relationship and various other types of family situation, is particularly interesting for two reasons. The first is that such chapbooks do tend to have the force of miniature epistolary novels: the examples I have seen seem to lose sight of their practical purpose and become engrossed in the progress of the courtship which they are mapping. The second is that Samuel Richardson, the great exponent of the epistolary form in the mideighteenth century, served his apprenticeship with a chapbook printer and may have found his initial stimulation in his experience of producing chapbooks. It is probably no coincidence that Mr Colbrond, the tormentor of Richardson's heroine Pamela, shares his name with one of the major enemies of Guy of Warwick, a most durable chapbook hero whose adventures are edited in two versions below.[22] We see here just how dangerous it is to build watertight compartments between the different levels of cultural production, for just as it is certain that all late eighteenth-century adults are likely to have used opium for medicinal or recreational purposes at some point in their life, it is also certain that all polite adults are likely to have read chapbooks

during their childhood and would have known very well the source of Richardson's villain.

Religious chapbooks were also common, though here we must exercise some care in distinguishing chapbooks from tracts. In the 1790s the Society for Promoting Christian Knowledge produced, through the work of Hannah More and others, tracts in forms which very precisely mimicked those of the chapbook.[23] Indeed, antiquarian booksellers who offer chapbooks for sale are frequently in possession of collections of these tracts rather than of chapbooks proper. This tractarian marketing ploy was so successful that there is the real probability that it forced chapbooks into a decline from which they never fully recovered (in the south of England at least). There were, however, also genuine chapbooks with a religious content. I have already mentioned the religious chapbooks which circulated in Yorkshire, but chapbooks which told biblical or quasibiblical stories were well known and must have supplemented Bible reading and provided useful examples which could be easily recalled and discussed.

Related to religious chapbooks, especially to those of Hannah More, are the radical political tracts which were produced by Thomas Spence, also in the 1790s.[24] Spence was plainly concerned with the issue of literacy and actually attempted the publication of a phonetic Bible to be sold in penny instalments. Thomas Paine's *The Rights of Man,* by far the most influential radical work of its time, also appeared in chapbook form.[25] By 1805 the publisher Thomas Harris had also begun to appropriate the forms of the children's chapbook in order to produce political satire.[26] The relationship between Blake's illuminated books, chapbooks and late eighteenth-century London radicalism should also be recognised and gives another important insight into the role which chapbooks had in mediating between different levels of cultural activity.[27]

One of the most difficult kinds of chapbook to place is that which contains a collection of songs. These collections are usually known as 'Garlands' and formed a very large part of the output of chapbook printers, particularly in London and Newcastle.[28] Frequently such texts do not run to the full twenty-four pages, but in all other respects they are true chapbooks in that they satisfy the formal criteria I outlined above. They are probably best seen as offering a parallel (and better value) form to the broadside ballads which are especially associated with the printers in the Seven Dials area of London and which would also have been available from chapmen.[29] Many Irish chapbooks, for example those printed by Walter Kelly of Waterford or William Gogarty of Limerick, are collections of songs in the Garland format.[30] Chapbook readers would certainly have been familiar with Garlands and probably bought them to supplement their collections, but the material contained in them is certainly different from that in other kinds of chapbook as it obeys formal conventions which are sometimes far removed from the traditional world of village culture.

Current affairs were frequently explored through broadside ballads, especially those which dealt with violent crime, accidents or the execution of notorious murderers. Chapbooks too reflected eighteenth-century society's obsession with crime. This obsession comprehended crime's potential as a subject both for exciting and romantic stories and for edifying narratives of penitence and punishment. The lives of pirates and famous highwaymen are represented in the chapbook stock and there are also chapbooks which provide awful warnings of the dangers of filial disobedience, avarice and inebriation—especially in combination. This kind of chapbook offered not only pious examples but also genuinely entertaining narratives, and must surely have been read as much for the enjoyment of prose fiction as for the guidance which they presented. Indeed this dual function can be readily recognised in the early eighteenth-century novel. Defoe plainly drew on the genre of Newgate biography for *Moll Flanders* and on sailors' memoirs for *Robinson Crusoe,* and it is no surprise to find that both of these texts were commonly produced in chapbook form. It is interesting to speculate, there being little formal difference between the biographies of genuine rogues and that of the fictional Moll Flanders, whether or not chapbook readers—who almost certainly would not have heard of Defoe—would have read these texts as pure fiction or whether they happily, or anxiously, assumed that they had a solid, if colourful, factual basis.

With rogue biographies we are approaching fiction proper and we may pass over chapbooks with a historical content and jest books (a hardy Tudor form which survived well into the eighteenth century through the chapbooks) and encounter fiction proper. I have already mentioned chapbooks of Defoe's novels, and there were also chapbook versions of work by Fielding. However, the core of chapbook fiction divides into three sections. The first contains romances, which form the subject of this edition and will be dealt with in detail below. The second consists of short self-contained anecdotes based on the life of a particular hero. The third is based on a range of traditional narrative. The second category usually has its sources in late medieval and Renaissance writing and concentrates on the lives of well-known figures such as Faustus, Fortunatus, Dick Whittington (though Whittington chapbooks arguably belong to the genre of historical biography), Reynard the Fox, or Robin Hood. The third category contains some of the most interesting and charming narratives and is most frequently cited by readers who were remembering their childhood experience of chapbooks. In this category we find Jack the Giant Killer, Thomas Hickathrift and Tom Thumb. In these fascinating stories can be seen many strata of the history of English narrative. Elements drawn from Middle English romance jostle with apparently polite commentary and material which appears to derive from an oral tradition of story telling. We can usually assign definite early printed sources to parts of most of these texts, but there remains a residue that tantalisingly reminds us of the voices which once breathed through a now entirely dead culture.

It will be seen from the latter part of this very brief, highly descriptive and by no means exhaustive account of the range of chapbooks that, where fiction is concerned, it is extremely hard to draw a line which defines authoritatively where a text as record of historic fact ends and a text as record of imaginative creation begins. The lack of named authorship which is a feature of most chapbooks (the Scottish writers Dougal Graham and James Hogg are extremely rare examples of known chapbook authors) leaves the reader bereft of the usual markers which enable him or her confidently to place books into the various categories which make the modern mind feel comfortable. Such taxonomic anarchy is, to some extent, a general characteristic of pre-industrial literature, but it is magnified by chapbooks which teach us just how much highly literate readers depend on extra-textual prompting in the act of interpretation. The notion that we might fully be able to understand a text solely through the encounter with its words and its rhetorical and syntactic devices becomes even more of a critical chimera.

It is often said that the traditional nature of chapbooks supported a cultural conservatism which hindered the potential of the rural poor to offer a radical critique of the world in which they found themselves. This opinion is one that derives largely from comment on the French *bibliothèque bleue,* but it is possible to extrapolate from this range of scholarship in order to speak of chapbooks. The first thing to be said about this view is that there is no evidence whatsoever that the chapbooks enshrined any conscious ideological project to keep the poor in happy ignorance. If anything, polite thinkers worried that traditions of rural life prevented the country people from cultivating the attitudes which would enable efficient work and the disciplines necessary for industrial progress. Secondly, poverty and suffering are not things of which you remain ignorant as you are experiencing them, especially when examples of luxury and ease are daily visible. The history of rural England in the eighteenth and nineteenth centuries may be read as marked as much by popular protest of an often violent kind as by the peaceful continuation of the seasonal rituals of Merry England which were increasingly under attack by the twin forces of the Protestant settlement and the rationalism of the Enlightenment.[31] Thirdly, just because the forms and expression of a culture appear to have deeply traditional affiliations, that does not mean that the function of those expressions cannot be absolutely modern in its particular applications.

What this signifies is that pre-industrial people were not the slaves of their traditions any more than modern people are the slaves of their clothes. Tradition provides a vocabulary and a structure, but it provides rather than precludes ways of understanding the challenges of changing social conditions. Chapbooks do not offer a uniform worldview. Rather they show how readers who were cut off from access to the mainstream of learning were able to make some strides towards it. Chapbooks offered poor readers a range of literate experiences. However, we should not patronise them by assuming that they could not make sense of them in any but an uncritical way. We might also remember that the conservative world-view which is frequently associated with rural tradition may be, for the most part, a construct of modern scholarship.

CHAPBOOKS AND THE ROMANCE TRADITION

Perhaps the most extraordinary feature of chapbooks is their preservation of texts whose history can be traced back to the thirteenth century if not further in extremely faithful, truncated versions. The readers of the eighteenth and nineteenth centuries were, apparently, finding plenty to entertain them in narratives which were first read in the regional courts of England in the high Middle Ages. In order to understand how this came about it is worth standing back for a moment and considering the history of the transmission of Middle English romances. This history includes the growth, during the sixteenth century, of a new corpus of romance which drew both on the domestic tradition and on the fashionable narratives of the massive cycles of Spanish and Portuguese chivalric adventure stories.

Between 1200 and 1500 the romance of chivalry was probably the genre of secular narrative that was most extensively produced and read.[32] Romances could take many forms and were derived from many sources. In the earlier part of this long period they were almost always in some form of verse—couplets, stanzaic, tail-rhyme, or alliterative long line—and can usually, but by no means always, be traced to originals in Anglo-Norman or Old French. In the later period prose became more common and the influence of the Vulgate cycle of Arthurian narratives and the fashionable French prose romances which were imported from the court of Burgundy can readily be seen.[33] There have been attempts to claim some of the romances, especially some of the cruder or knockabout couplet and tail-rhyme specimens, as popular. However, there can be little doubt that in the social conditions which prevailed, such lengthy texts, preoccupied as they were with the details and ethic of chivalric adventure, could only have been accessible to readers who were themselves courtly or who were in close contact with courtly society. There is clear evidence for a courtly readership, and if the major codices of romance are not among the most *de luxe* productions, they are still of sufficient size and extent to suggest patrons who were very far removed economically from the mass of the English people.

Romances were among the first books to be printed in English, but as printing became more common and books cheaper it is noticeable that the printers who catered for the more courtly end of the publishing market gradually ceased to produce versions of these old texts. However, the growth of printing enabled a growth in literacy and, by the later sixteenth century, there is no doubt that, in London at least, a readership with a broader base had developed. This consisted mainly of citizens who were engaged in trade and manufacture and their families. It is at about this time that we also begin to see books which are dedicated not to wealthy individuals but to craft guilds. There is little doubt that authors were beginning in a truly modern fashion to depend for their success not on the good word and munificence of a few powerful individuals but on market forces.

The printers who catered for this new audience included among their productions modernised versions of the old romances which had dropped from favour with the courtly audience. This audience had now turned to Europe, especially to Italy and France, for its cultural models. At the same time, a group of citizen writers, such as Richard Johnson, Thomas Deloney and Henry Robarts, was also producing entirely new romances which drew extensively on the narrative structures of the Middle English texts and incorporated many of their incidents.[34] These texts, among which we can clearly discern the origins of the novel, included adventures in which merchants and craftsmen played the leading roles. These citizen heroes went through the same trials as the medieval knights, but now in order to explore the ethics of Protestantism and commerce, rather than those of Roman Catholicism and chivalry.

By the middle of the seventeenth century these texts too were being replaced, as far as polite and middle class readers were concerned, by the books which form the earliest examples of English Literature as this term is generally understood by modern readers. They did, however, continue to be printed in cheap forms and it was these that eventually metamorphosed into the chapbook, which appears by the 1670s. Thus, chapbooks continued to transmit a tradition of narrative which, by the turn of the eighteenth century, was already at least five hundred years old. This extraordinary fact should, if it does nothing else, alert us to the dangers of unduly rigorous periodisation. What it particularly teaches us is that the division of the continuum of English Literature into discrete historical moments is possible only when we view it from a single perspective: that of the educated or privileged reader who engaged with the texts which we now value as the most typical and best of their time. But even this simple model does not hold true. If it did, Bowles, Campbell and Tom Moore would be very familiar to us while Coleridge, Wordsworth and Keats would be represented only by a poem or two in the larger anthologies. It would appear that to maintain the coherence of literary criticism as a practice which confronts literary history we need also to maintain the convenient fiction that the readers of the past admired the same texts which we now canonise. By this means we can make the past legible as an unbroken preamble to our present.

The fact is, however, that literary history, like all other types of history, has the property of being seen to move at different speeds depending on what aspects of it are being studied and from what notional vantage point.[35] What is really fascinating is how it comes about that whole bodies of texts make the transition from one readership to another and how the very same internal structures can offer to different readerships in different social conditions convincing and entertaining pictures of both the material and the mental world. Early nineteenth-century weavers could, plainly, not have understood a chivalric romance in the same way that fourteenth-century courtiers did even though the core narrative was identical. It is amazing that they understood it at all, but we must assume that they did for otherwise we could not explain the apparent popularity of traditional romances drawing on medieval or Elizabethan originals within the chapbook corpus.

One explanation of the transmission of romance is purely economic. As polite audiences developed new tastes the texts they once valued became available to printers in a more humble sector of the market. This process even affects the mechanism of the printing industry itself and it can be seen that by the seventeenth century when prestigious printers had shifted almost exclusively to roman and italic founts ('white letter') those who produced cheaper books remained faithful to the Gothic 'black letter' and often used second-hand type which shows increasing signs of wear.[36] Thus, we can trace the transmission of romance from the expensive hand-produced manuscript through the equally expensive incunabulum, thence to mass-produced books of various qualities and prices, and so to the chapbook. At each phase in this shift we can identify an audience which is gradually shifting downwards in educational opportunity and purchasing power.

This account of the process seems to work (though in the later period we have to discount children who, for the purposes of this argument, have to be classed with the poor even if they came from rich households) but it cannot explain how the texts themselves continued to be viable as they shifted through time and audience. Of course, texts underwent substantial revision—notably modernisation of language and abridgement of content—during these transitions, but the core of their narratives remained the same. This shows us very clearly that readers do not use texts as they would maps. In other words, the 'meanings' and pleasures of texts are not to be found in the reader's attempt to treat them as if they were interpretations of an imagined world. Rather, chapbook romances show us how readers constantly adjusted the relationship between themselves and the imagined world manifested to them in narrative so as to discover credible pictures of human life in the printed page. These pictures provided, on the one hand, a contrast to their own experience and, on the other, could have been used to stimulate an internal commentary and debate on the values which that experience enshrined.

I strongly disagree with arguments that try to claim that the romances were a form of literature that enabled poor readers to escape from the humdrum or miserable circumstances in which they found themselves. Escapism seems to me a peculiarly modern conception and one which speaks of luxury and leisure. It is quite different from that imaginative stimulation in which contrasting manners and values are explored in order to enrich or extend the reader's inner life. I believe that chapbooks offered just this kind of stimulation. The fourteenth-century courtier may have read romance because of his or her interest in the nice questions of chivalric and religious duty and amorous procedure which it set for the heroes and heroines. The

sixteenth-century citizen enjoyed the same romance text for its power to demonstrate the virtues of patriotism and industry by its location of commercial values in the very narrative space from which pure chivalric adventure had been displaced.[37] But eighteenth-century villagers or early nineteenth-century craft workers found imaginative stimulation, contrast, and, perhaps above all, the precious sense that by reading such texts they were participating in the world of literary and education to which they were only marginally connected. The history of working-class self-improvement in the later nineteenth century shows that this connection was an object of undoubted and hard-fought aspiration.

Notes

1. The only example of chapbook texts currently available is John Ashton's *Chapbooks of the Eighteenth Century* (London, 1882; repr. London, n.d. 1991?). This gives texts of some chapbooks but is largely of antiquarian rather than scholarly interest and consists mainly of plot summaries and reproductions of woodcuts. R. H. Cunningham, *Amusing Prose Chap-books* (London, 1889) gives fuller texts and V. E. Neuburg, *The Penny Histories* (London, 1968) contains seven facsimiles.

2. The issue of children as chapbook readers is by no means fully addressed in this volume but it is a vital area of chapbook research.

3. The best general treatments of the topic remain those of H. B. Weiss, *A Book about Chapbooks* (Trenton, 1942) and V. E. Neuburg, *A Chapbook Bibliography* (London, 1964). On America see H. B. Weiss, 'American Chapbooks 1722-1842', *Bulletin of the New York Public Library*, 49 (1945), pp. 491-8 and 587-98, W. L. Joyce et al. (eds), *Printing and Society in Early America* (Worcester, Mass., 1983), and V. E. Neuburg, 'Chapbooks in America', in C. N. Davidson (ed.), *Reading in America* (Baltimore, 1989).

4. See, for example, P. Burke, *Popular Culture in Early Modern Europe* (London, 1978), D. E. Farrell, 'The Origins of Russian Popular Prints and their Social Milieu in the Early Eighteenth Century', *Journal of Popular Culture*, 17 (1983), pp. 9-47, W. E. A. Axon, 'Some Twentieth-Century Italian Chapbooks', *The Library*, new series, 5 (1904), pp. 239-55, F. J. Norton and E. M. Wilson (eds), *Two Spanish Verse Chapbooks* (Cambridge, 1969), R. Darnton and D. Roche (eds), *Revolution in Print* (Berkeley, 1989), D. T. Pottinger, *The French Book Trade in the Ancien Regime* (Cambridge, Mass., 1958), R. Chartier, *The Cultural Uses of Print in Early Modern France* (Princeton, 1987), and R. Mandrou, *De La Culture Populaire au dixhuitième Siécle* (Paris, repr. 1985). R. W. Scribner, *For the Sake of Simple Folk* (Oxford, 1994) is a valuable study of popular literacy during the German Reformation.

5. See G. Armistead and J. Silvermann (eds), *The Judaeo-Spanish Chapbooks of Yacob Abraham Yona* (Berkeley, 1971). On *folhetos* see P. Burke, 'Chivalry in the New World', in S. Anglo (ed.), *Chivalry in the Renaissance* (Woodbridge, 1990), pp. 252-62, and W. Rowe and V. Schelling, *Memory and Modernity* (London, 1991), pp. 85-94. On Nigerian chapbooks see B. Lindfors, 'Heroes and Hero-Worship in Nigerian Chapbooks', *Journal of Popular Culture,* 1 (1967), pp. 1-22, and E. N. Obiechina, *Onitsha Market Literature* (London, 1972).

6. A few scholars have recently looked at the wider implications of popular reading. See M. Spufford, *Small Books and Pleasant Histories* (Cambridge, 1981), a fascinating and invaluable study based on Samuel Pepys's collection of chapbooks and other popular texts. See also D. Vincent, *Literacy and Popular Culture 1750-1914,* (Cambridge, 1989), T. Watt, *Cheap Print and Popular Piety 1550-1640* (Cambridge, 1991), J. Friedman, *Miracles and the Pulp Press during the English Revolution* (London, 1993), P. Anderson, *The Printed Image and the Transformation of Popular Culture 1790-1860* (Oxford, 1991) and B. E. Maidment, *Reading Popular Prints, 1790-1870* (Manchester, 1996).

7. For a discussion of the transmission of polite literature into chapbook form see P. Rogers, *Literature and Popular Culture in Eighteenth-Century England* (Brighton, 1985) and 'Classics and Chapbooks', in I. Rivers (ed.), *Books and their Readers in Eighteenth-Century England* (Leicester, 1982), pp. 27-46. On serial publication see E. W. Pitcher, 'The Serial Publication and Collecting of Pamphlets, 1790-1815', *The Library,* 5th series, 30 (1975), pp. 322-9. J. P. Hunter, *Before Novels* (London, 1990) gives a good account of studies in the growth of literacy 1600-1800 on pp. 61-85. Hunter suggests that by 1800 60-70 per cent of adult men in England and Wales were literate with a rate of 88 per cent for Scotland. Female literacy was probably between 40-50 per cent. Literacy was higher in towns than in the country and highest in London, the south-east and the north. In 1832 *The Penny Magazine* first appeared and the preface to the first volume estimated a sale of two hundred thousand copies and a million readers.

8. Rule, *The Labouring Classes in Early Industrial England, 1750-1850* (London, 1986), pp. ix-x.

9. See Vincent, *Literacy and Popular Culture* and *Bread, Knowledge and Freedom.*

10. See D. Vincent, 'The Decline of the Oral Tradition in Popular Culture' in R. D. Storch (ed.), *Popular Culture and Custom in Nineteenth-Century England* (London, 1982), pp. 20-47, and D. Harker, *Fakesong* (Milton Keynes, 1985), pp. 40-41.

11. See P. Stockham, *Chapbooks* (London, 1976) and A. R. Thompson, 'Chapbook Printers', *Bibliotheck,* 6 (1972), pp. 76-83.

12. See, for example, V. E. Neuburg, 'The Diceys and the Chapbook Trade', *The Library,* 5th series, 24 (1969), pp. 219-31, F. M. Thompson, *Newcastle Chapbooks* (Newcastle, 1969), P. G. Isaac, *Halfpenny Chapbooks by William Davison* (Newcastle, 1971), S. Roscoe and A. Brimmel, *James Lumsden and Son of Glasgow* (London, 1981), F. W. Ratcliffe, 'Chapbooks with Scottish Imprints in the Robert White Collection', *Bibliotheck,* 4 (1964), pp. 88-174, E. Pearson, *Banbury Chapbooks* (Welwyn Garden City, 1970), P. Renold, 'William Rusher: A Sketch of his Life', *Cake and Cockhorse,* 11 (1991), pp. 218-28, P. Ward, *Cambridge Street Literature* (Cambridge, 1978), pp. 33-9.

13. The most detailed study of chapmen is M. Spufford, *The Great Reclothing of Rural England* (London, 1984). See also R. Leitch, 'Here chapman billies tak their stand', *Proceedings of the Society of Antiquarians of Scotland,* 128 (1990), pp. 173-88 and P. Rogers, 'Defoe's *Tour* (1742) and the Chapbook Trade', *The Library,* 6th series, 6 (1984), pp. 275-9.

14. See Rogers, 'Classics and Chapbooks', C. A. Federer, *Yorkshire Chapbooks* (London, 1899), G. MacGregor (ed.), *The Collected Writings of Dougal Graham,* 2 vols (Glasgow, 1883), W. Harvey, *Scottish Chapbook Literature* (Dundee, 1903).

15. Colley, *Britons* (London, 1992), p. 40. See also R. A. Houston, *Scottish Literacy and the National Identity* (Cambridge, 1985).

16. John Clare, *Autobiographical Fragments,* ed. E. Robinson (Oxford, 1986), pp. 56-7, Samuel Bamford, *Early Days* (London, 1849), Thomas Holcroft, *Hugh Trevor,* ed. S. Deanes (Oxford, 1973), p. 41. See also G. Deacon, *John Clare and the Folk Tradition* (London, 1983).

17. Cited by R. Porter, *English Society in the Eighteenth Century* (Harmondsworth, 1982), p. 253. E. P. Thompson, *The Making of the English Working Class* (Harmondsworth, 1963) records cases of labourers reading to their colleagues. See also D. Worrall, *Radical Culture* (London, 1992).

18. Burke, 'The "Discovery" of Popular Culture', in R. Samuel (ed.), *People's History and Socialist Theory* (London, 1981), pp. 216-21. Louis James, *Fiction for the Working Man* (London, 1963) argues convincingly for the formation of a new urban literate culture which 'was not a continuation of the old popular cultures which expressed themselves in broadsheets, chapbooks and popular drama' (p. 1). From the 1820s onwards this new culture, specifically urban in character, was provided with a host of cheap books and periodicals such as *The Penny Magazine* (see note 7 above). These new publications covered much of the same ground as chapbooks but often with a more explicitly educational purpose. However, even *The Penny*

Magazine drew attention to the fact that 'some of the unexampled success of this little work is to be ascribed to the liberal employment of illustrations, by means of Wood-cuts' (Preface to issue 1).

19. See, for example, R. Steele, *The Tatler,* no. 95, J. Boswell, *Boswell's London Journal,* ed. W. A. Pottle (London, 1950), p. 299, George Borrow, *Lavengro* (Oxford, 1982), p. 67, J. C. Corson, 'Scott's Boyhood Collection of Chapbooks', *Bibliotheck,* 3 (1962), pp. 202-18, W. M. Thackeray, *The Irish Sketch Book,* 2 vols (London, 1843), I, p. 7 and II, pp. 273-4.

20. Ashton, *Chapbooks of the Eighteenth Century,* gives examples of these. See also D. Valenze, 'Prophecy and Popular Literature in the Eighteenth Century', *Journal of Ecclesiastical History,* 29 (1978), pp. 75-92 and B. Capp, *Astrology and the Popular Press* (London, 1979).

21. Vincent, *Literacy and Popular Culture,* p. 177.

22. Simons, 'Romance in the Eighteenth-Century Chapbook' in J. Simons (ed.), *From Medieval to Medievalism* (London, 1992), pp. 122-43, p. 130.

23. See V. E. Neuburg, *Popular Literature* (Harmondsworth, 1977), pp. 249-64.

24. On Spence see M. Wood, *Radical Satire and Print Culture* (Oxford, 1994), pp. 86-95.

25. Ibid., p. 94

26. Ibid., pp. 222-5

27. On Blake and chapbooks see G. Summerfield, *Fantasy and Reason: Children's Literature in the Eighteenth Century* (London, 1983) and P. Ackroyd, *Blake* (London, 1995), pp. 24-5.

28. See Thompson, *Newcastle Chapbooks.*

29. For surveys of these genres and many examples see C. Hindley, *Curiosities of Street Literature* (Welwyn Garden City, 1969), L. Shepard, *The History of Street Literature* (Newton Abott, 1973), L. James, *Print and the People* (Harmondsworth, 1978), L. Shepard, *The Broadside Ballad* (Wakefield, 1978), C. M. Simpson, *The British Broadside Ballad and its Music* (New Brunswick, 1986).

30. On these printers see J. Simons, 'Irish Chapbooks in the Huntington Library', *Huntington Library Quarterly,* 57 (1995), pp. 359-65

31. See D. Cressy, *Bonfires and Bells* (London, 1989), E. P. Thompson, *Customs in Common* (Harmondsworth, 1991), R. Hutton, *The Rise and Fall of Merry England: The Ritual Year 1400-1700* (Oxford, 1994), Hunter, *Before Novels,* pp. 138-64. Hunter points out (p. 147) that John Locke was so traumatised by the folk stories told him by his childhood nurse that he was scared of the dark and the hobgoblins that lurked there throughout his life.

32. The most recent general survey is that of W. R. J. Barron, *English Medieval Romance* (London, 1987).

33. See G. Doutrepont, *Les Mises en Prose des Epopées et Romans Chevaleresques* (Brussels, 1939), N. F. Blake, 'William Caxton's Chivalric Romances and the Burgundian Renaissance in England', *Essays and Studies,* 57 (1976), pp 1-10, and N. F. Blake, 'Lord Berners: A Survey', *Medievalia et Humanistica,* 2 (1971), pp. 119-32.

34. Simons, 'Medieval Chivalric Romance and Elizabethan Popular Literature' (Exeter University unpubl. Ph.D., 1982).

35. See F. Braudel, *The Mediterranean in the Age of Philip II,* 2 vols (London, 1975).

36. Mish, 'Black Letter as a Social Discriminant', *Publications of the Modern Language Association of America,* 68 (1953), pp. 627-30.

37. See J. Simons, 'Open and Closed Books: a Semiotic Approach to the History of Elizabethan and Jacobean Popular Romance', in C. Bloom (ed.), *Jacobean Poetry and Prose* (London, 1988), pp. 8-24 and J. Simons, 'Transforming the Romance: Some Observations on Early Modern Popular Narrative', in W. Gortschacher and H. Klein (eds), *Narrative Strategies in Early English Fiction* (Lewiston, 1995), pp. 273-88.

FURTHER READING

Criticism

"Introduction." In *Black-Letter Ballads and Broadsides, Printed in the Reign of Queen Elizabeth, Between the Years 1559 and 1597.* Detroit: Singing Tree Press, 1968, pp. v-xxxi.

Analysis of British chapbooks and broadside ballads published in the last half of the sixteenth century. The critic distinguishes between those works with literary merit and others concerned with more topical issues like politics and everyday life.

Bryant, Frank Egbert. *A History of English Balladry and Other Studies.* Boston: The Gorman Press, 1913, 222 p.

Comprehensive discussion of English ballads from 1400 to the end of the sixteenth century, concentrating on broadside ballads collected in Francis James Child's ten-volume *The English and Scottish Popular Ballad.*

Burke, Peter. *Popular Culture in Early Modern Europe.* Hants, England: Scholar Press, 1994, 377 p.

Extensive study of European popular culture from 1500 to 1800 with frequent references to chapbooks and broadsides as both primary influences on and reflections of attitudes and values.

Capp, Bernard. "Popular Literature." In *Popular Culture in Seventeenth-Century England,* edited by Barry Reay, pp. 198-243. London: Croom Helm, 1985.

Traces the most popular topics of seventeenth-century broadsides and ballads, including romance, religion, legends, drinking, and other earthly pleasures. Capp concludes that the ballad remained the dominant peasant art of England until print journalism began to replace it by the last third of the seventeenth century.

Darton, F. J. Harvey. "The Pedlar's Pack: 'The Running Stationers.'" In *Children's Books in England: Five Centuries of Social Life.* Cambridge: Cambridge University Press, 1982, pp. 68-84.

Credits the chapbook, a genre commonly treated as substandard, as being the only reason beloved fairy tales and nursery rhymes are remembered at all today.

Friedman, Albert B. *The Ballad Revival: Studies in the Influence of Popular on Sophisticated Poetry.* Chicago: The University of Chicago Press, 1961, 376 p.

Examines the British ballad from its roots as common entertainment in the sixteenth century to its increasing acceptance and influence on more critically acclaimed poetry and literature through the end of the 1800s.

Harvey, William. *Scottish Chapbook Literature.* Paisley: Alexander Gardner, 1903, 153 p.

Divides seventeenth- and eighteenth-century Scottish chapbooks into ten categories, including romance, songs, humor, and instruction, to show that chapbooks did not comprise a monolithic genre and responded to a wide range of human interests.

Holloway, John and Joan Black. Introduction to *Later English Broadside Ballads.* London: Routledge & Kegan Paul, 1975, pp. 1-11.

Examines the evolution of eighteenth-century printed ballads in England, arguing that there is an important link between the early ballad singer and the British theater.

Kunzle, David. "England (c. 1605-1710)." In *The Early Comic Strip: Narrative Strips and Picture Stories in the European Broadsheet from c. 1450 to 1825.* Berkeley: University of California Press, 1973, pp. 122-53.

Discusses such historical events as the English Civil War, the Horrid Popish Plot, and the Glorious Revolution as represented in comics and playing cards produced between 1605-1710.

Neuburg, Victor E. "'The Old Classics of the Nursery,'" In *The Penny Histories: A Study of Chapbooks for Young Readers over Two Centuries.* New York: Harcourt, Brace & World, Inc., 1968, pp. 1-20.

Describes how chapbooks, originally published as an inexpensive and entertaining alternatives to religious texts, kept alive much older literary traditions such as medieval folk tales, legends, and fairy tales, as well as introduced even the poorest British citizens to abridged versions of literary classics.

Pearson, Edwin. *Banbury Chap Books and Nursery Toy Literature of the XVIII and early XIX Centuries.* New York: Burt Franklin, 1890, 117 p.

Concentrates on chapbook woodcut illustrations commonly called "Banbury Blocks," with analysis of many accompanying stories.

Pories, Kathleen. "An Intersection of Poor Laws and Literature in the Sixteenth Century: Fictional and Factual Categories." In *Framing Elizabethan Fictions: Contemporary Approaches to Early Modern Narrative Prose,* edited by Constance C. Reliham,, pp. 17-40. Kent, Ohio: The Kent State University Press, 1996.

Argues that sixteenth-century English pamphlets about criminality and poverty often blurred the lines between fact and fiction, and had profound effects on both British literature and government legislation.

Pound, Louise. *Poetic Origins and the Ballad.* New York: The MacMillan Company, 1921, 247 p.

Study of the poetic evolution of British ballads from the Middle Ages to their migration to nineteenth-century cowboy America, with a concentration on British ballads of the seventeenth and eighteenth centuries.

Rogers, Pat. "Classics and Chapbooks." In *Literature and Popular Culture in Eighteenth-Century England.* Sussex: The Harvester Press, 1985, pp. 162-82.

Discusses many of the abridged versions of literary classics published in eighteenth-century chapbooks, including favorites like *Tom Thumb, The Pilgrim's Progress, Robinson Crusoe, Moll Flanders,* and *Gulliver's Travels.*

Rollins, Hyder E. Introduction to *Cavalier and Puritan: Ballads and Broadsides Illustrating the Period of the Great Rebellion, 1640-1660.* New York: The New York University Press, 1923, 532 p.

Argues that civil war and rebellion in England between 1640 and 1660 changed the general tone of broadside ballads from entertaining songs to increasingly pointed and often satircial political journalism and commentary.

Valenze, Deborah. "Prophesy and Popular Literature in Eighteenth-Century England." *Journal of Ecclesiastical History* 29, No. 1 (January 1978): pp. 75-92.

Examines the place of eighteenth-century English prophetic chapbooks, arguing that these popular guidebooks preserved age-old beliefs that otherwise would have disappeared from memory or record.

Weiss, Harry B. *A Book About Chapbooks: The People's Literature of Bygone Times.* Hatboro, Penn.: Folklore Associates, Inc., 1969, 149 p.

Demonstrates that British and American chapbooks from the eighteenth and nineteenth centuries covered almost every conceivable topic from popular biography and history to prose and dramatic story telling.

The Epistolary Novel

INTRODUCTION

A genre of fiction which first gained popularity in the seventeenth and eighteenth centuries, the epistolary novel is a form in which most or all of the plot is advanced by the letters or journal entries of one or more of its characters, and which marked the beginning of the novel as a literary form.

Epistolary fiction dates back at least to ancient Roman times, but the epistolary novel as a distinct genre first gained prominence in Britain in the mid-eighteenth century. In the late seventeenth and early eighteenth centuries, Aphra Behn in Britain and Charles Louis de Montesquieu in France produced works of fiction told through the medium of letters, but many scholars still regard Samuel Richardson's *Pamela* (1740) to be the first example of the epistolary novel—and indeed the first mature novel to be written in English. Richardson's ground-breaking work is marked by a coherence of characterization, plot, and theme that had been missing in earlier fictional efforts, and his use of the epistolary form lends realism, complexity, and psychological subtlety to his story. The epistolary novel enjoyed its greatest popularity in England and France from the mid-1700s to the end of the century, a time when literacy was on the increase and the public sought literary works with more depictions of ordinary experience and greater psychological realism than were found in the old heroic romances. With its reliance on subjective points of view, the epistolary novel by its very nature offers intimate insight into characters' thoughts and feelings without interference from the author, and advances the plot with dramatic immediacy. Epistolary authors commonly wrote about questions of morality, and many epistolary novels are sentimental in nature. Because of the "private" nature of the form, with the depiction of domestic and personal concerns, much epistolary fiction was written by or about women, and the letter-novel was one of the earliest avenues for women writers to achieve public recognition for their art.

Female characters in the novels often wrestle with sexual temptation and moral propriety and find that the only way to express themselves honestly and thoroughly is by confiding in a trusted friend through letters. Many critics in Richardson's day regarded the letters he wrote in the voices of his female protagonists to be the finest expression of feminine concerns and sensibilities of the period. Genuine female voices are also to be found in the some of the most popular and best-known epistolary novels of the eighteenth century. Mary Davys, one of the first women to support herself through her writing, produced several epistolary works, including *The Reform'd Coquet: or Memoirs of Amoranda* (1724), which tells of the "taming" of Amoranda, a good but flighty young woman, and *Familiar Letters Betwixt a Gentleman and a Lady* (1725), a satire about politics and women's place in society. Fanny Burney's *Evelina: or the History of a Young Lady's Entrance into the World* (1778) is a novel of manners that explores a young, innocent woman's entrance into society. Marie-Jeanne Riccobini's highly successful *Les Lettres de Mistriss Fanni Butlerd* (1757), an exchange of letters between a simple young Englishwoman and her aristocratic lover, makes clear the division between private and public spheres that were a feature of women's social reality in the eighteenth century. Many women writers of the period in their novels point out women's exclusion from public matters, and often their female characters seek to transcend social barriers by making their own autonomous decisions.

While women novelists were certainly read during the eighteenth century, the bias prevailed that serious literary work was conducted by men. The acknowledged great British epistolary novelists of the period included Richardson, Henry Fielding, and Tobias Smollet. Richardson had enjoyed a career as a successful printer, and was asked to compose a guide to letter writing. He worked around a central theme and the result was his moral novel *Pamela: or, Virtue Unrewarded,* the story of a servant girl's victorious struggle against her master's attempts to seduce her. The work was an unprecedented popular and critical success and spawned dozens of imitations and burlesques, the best-known of which was Fielding's *An Apology for the Life of Mrs. Shamela Andrews.* Fielding with his parody points out some of the inherent problems with the epistolary form, including the fact that simple, uneducated characters convey their sentiments through sophisticated literary means. Still, Richardson continued to favor the form, declaring that it was much better suited to realistically portraying the lives and dilemmas of characters than straightforward narrative fiction. The fact that the important and well-respected novelist Tobias Smollet, who had already achieved fame with his narrative fiction, turned to the epistolary form with *The Expedition of Humphry Clinker* (1771) indicates the popularity of the genre in England in the last decades of the eighteenth century.

Fiction told through the medium of letters was also popular on the European continent, and by the mid-sixteenth century in Spain and Italy letters were often used to tell stories of the trials of illicit and prohibited love. Over the next 150 years, letter-writing became increasingly popular in travel books, news stories, and published personal correspondences. The rise of the epistolary novel as a form on the continent roughly parallels its development in England. Charles Louis de Montesquieu's 1721 *Lettres persanes* and Claude Prosper Jolyot de Crébillon, *fils*'s 1735 *Lettres de la Marquise de M*** au Comte de R**** lacked the realistic novelistic structure and complexity of Richardson's fiction, but those works certainly influenced Richardson as well as later French epistolary writers. Some of the great French epistolary novels in the eighteenth century include Jean-Jacques Rousseau's *La Nouvelle Héloïse* (1761) and Choderlos de Laclos' 1782 *Les Liaisons dangereuses*. These novels, like their English counterparts, are redolent with sentimental romance and melodrama, and a great deal of attention is paid to questions of morality. Several popular but little-remembered epistolary novels appeared in the United States at the end of the century, just as the greatest vogue of the genre was past in Europe and Britain. As the century drew to a close the novel letter as a form had fallen into disfavor, as readers and writers of popular fiction increasingly turned to Gothic romances, and serious novelists, too, adopted the more straightforward narrative form.

REPRESENTATIVE WORKS

Anonymous
Olinda's Adventures: Or the Amours of a Young Lady 1693

Frances Burney
Evelina: or the History of a Young Lady's Entrance into the World 1778

Claude Prosper Jolyot de Crébillon, fils
Letters from the Marchioness de M*** to the Count de R*** 1735

J. Hector St. John de Crèvecoeur
Letters from an American Farmer 1782

Mary Davys
The Reform'd Coquet: or Memoirs of Amoranda 1724
Familiar Letters Betwixt a Gentleman and a Lady 1725
The Accomplish'd Rake: or a Modern Fine Gentleman 1727

Henry Fielding
An Apology for the Life of Mrs. Shamela Andrews [*Shamela*] 1741

Choderlos de Laclos
Les liaisons dangereuses [*Dangerous Liaisons*] 1782

Charles Louis de Montesquieu
Lettres persanes [*Persian Letters*] 1721

Marie-Jeanne Riccoboni
Les Lettres de Mistriss Fanni Butlerd 1757

Samuel Richardson
Pamela: or, Virtue Unrewarded 1740
Clarissa: or the History of the Young Lady 1747
History of Sir Charles Grandison 1750

Jean-Jacques Rousseau
La Nouvelle Héloïse 1761
Letters of an English Nun and an English Gentleman 1781

Tobias Smollett
The Expedition of Humphry Clinker 1771

OVERVIEWS AND GENERAL STUDIES

Godfrey Frank Singer (essay date 1933)

SOURCE: "Epistolary Fiction (Particularly the Novel) in France and in Italy," in *The Epistolary Novel: Its Origin, Development, Decline, and Residuary Influence*, Russell & Russell, 1963, pp. 181-94.

[*In the following excerpt from a work originally published in 1933, Singer examines the popularity of the epistolary genre in France, Italy, and Germany, countries whose works he says most critics neglect because of the prominence of Samuel Richardson and other English authors.*]

The casting of narrative works of fiction, which we have designated novels, into epistolary form, was a practice by no means limited to the land which gave the greatest examples of the art any more than it was to the century which produced its most distinguished proponents and in which the mode reached its highest peak of development and achievement. Novels were written in this form by French, Italian, American, German, Russian, and other authors. In Brian W. Downs' book on Samuel Richardson, there is included a chapter on "The Consequences of Richardson,"[1] wherein Mr. Downs has included a list of novels in letter form in various other literatures in Europe. He has, however, omitted America from his census, and has treated epistolary fiction in Italy rather slightingly. It may be argued, of course, that the use of this form was not a "consequence" of Richardson, or that Richardson did not introduce into Italy the novel in letters, although admittedly he made it fashionable there. But when one considers the epistolary epidemic, as it may be termed, and sees the germinal *poste restante* marked "England" and knows further than that that Richardson connotes the word "epistolary" in England, one can well feel that he is not jumping to conclusions rashly in ascribing to Richardson the impulse giving strength to the novel in letters and its imitators in England and outside England.

If one were anxious to investigate the subject of the epistolary novel in France completely, the compass of a volume would be necessary. Aside from those works listed by Mr. Downs in his aforementioned chapter, M. Philippe Van Tieghem's edition of *La Nouvelle Héloise; ou Lettres de deux Amants habitans d'une petite Ville au pieds des Alps,* of Rousseau (first exposed for sale in 1761 in Paris), contains the best list collected in one spot convenient to the finger tips.

In 1751, three years after its appearance in England, *Clarissa* appeared in French as *Lettres Angloises ou Histoire de Clarissa Harlove.* In 1755-56 we may note the appearance in French of *Nouvelle Lettres Angloises ou Histoire de Chevalier Grandisson.* These translations are both attributed to Abbé Prévost, the author of *Manon Lescaut.* As early, however, as 1742, there is noted a work which shows that *Pamela* had already made its mark upon the French literary consciousness, for *Antipamela; or Mémoires de M.D.*—appeared at this time, published in London. In 1743, *Anti-Pamela; or, Feign'd Innocence Detected: In a Series of Syrena's Adventures,* possibly by Mrs. Haywood (opines Mr. Downs) was translated into French. The translation of *Pamela* itself appeared in 1742, but this is a book less to the fancy of the French than are Richardson's two later novels. From this date on, through the eighteenth century, as in England, France having looked upon the epistolary mode and having liked it, its popularity was assured. Many imitations of *Pamela,* aside from those already noted, appeared in French. Mme. de Beaumont, who has been previously mentioned for her epistolary fiction, was a Frenchwoman prolific in her imitations of Richardson. Francois-Thomas de Baculard d'Arnaud was another such author. Diderot's *La Réligieuse* is one of the most outstanding instances of Richardson imitation and was published in 1760, almost twenty years after the appearance of *Pamela.* Laclos' *Liaisons Dangereuses* (translated into English as *Dangerous Connections*) was another.

The true Richardson of France was, however, Jean-Jacques Rousseau. *La Nouvelle Héloise* (1761), is, like others of his works, in letters. This work in particular may be compared with those of Richardson because it, too, had a long train of imitators. Of great interest, however, is Rousseau's version of the *Portuguese Letters* in a volume called, *Letters of An Italian Nun and an English Gentleman* (1781), a series of sentimental and pathetic letters which are extremely well written, graceful in phrasing, and of an insistent sadness. The influence of these on English sentiment was great.

Among the many works which were composed in imitation of the *Nouvelle Héloise,* M. van Tieghem has listed: *La Philosophe par Amour; ou, Lettres de deux Amants Passionnés et vertueux* (1765); *Henriette de Wolmar; ou, la Mere jalouse de sa Fille, pour servir de suite à la Nouvelle Héloise* (1768); *Le Nouvel Abailard; ou, Lettres de deux Amants qui ne se sont jamais vus* (1778), by Réstif de la Bretonne; *Sophie; ou, Lettres de deux Amies recueillies et publiées par un citoyen de Genève* (1779); *Lettres de deux Amants habitants de Lyons, publiées par M. Léonard* (1783); *La Dernière Héloise; ou, Lettres de Junie Salisbury recueillies et publiées par M. Dauphin, citoyen de Verdun* (1784); and *Amours ou Lettres d'Alexis et Justine* (1786).

It is not to be thought, however, that the epistolary impulse in France was entirely dependent upon Richardson. As early as 1607-1619 Honoré d'Urfé's *L'Histoire d'Astrée,* was a model for epistolary correspondence in France in the seventeenth century. It was of such tremendous influence that its use in the eighteenth century as a representative gem of the epistolary art is not to be wondered at. Then, too, there were *Lettres Persanes* (1721), by Charles Louis de Sécondat, Baron de la Brède et de Montesquieu, full of a graceful humor, a piquancy of phrasing and a perspicacity of observation that render them particularly lively. If Oliver Goldsmith could copy this work forty years later in his *Citizen of the World,* surely its widespread use at home need not be thought surprising. The intermixture of the serious with the light vein in these letters keeps them delightful. They are, moreover, valuable as an informative treatment of the manners and customs of Europe as these might be seen through the eyes of two Asiatics. John Davidson, the English poet, made a sympathetic translation of them late in the nineteenth century. Directly in imitation of these are the letters of the French patriot, Jean Paul Marat, *Lettres Polonaises,* written about 1770. In these letters, a young Polish prince traveling through the countries of Europe incognito, writes his extended criticisms of the manners and customs, especially of the social conditions, of the countries through which he has traveled, and sends them chiefly to a friend and to a brother. The letters are, of course, an excuse for Marat to air his opinions of the existing social order.

Not entirely in the same vein, but created by the same impulse as were the *Lettres Persanes* were those two epistolary works which formed a background in France to the development of sentimental fiction in the epistolary form, Alcoforado's *Lettres Portugaises* (1669), and Mme. de Graffigny's *Lettres Peruviennes* (1747), both of great popularity.

When the influence of Richardson on the French epistolary novel is being argued, it must be remembered that there is a high possibility of the existence of an original French epistolary influence on Richardson. Marivaux's two major works of fiction, *La Vie de Marianne* (1731-41), completed after Marivaux's death by Mme. Riccoboni, and *Le Paysan Parvenu* (1735-36), are both in letter form. It was this author, Pierre Carlet de Chamblain de Marivaux, who endeavored to bring back his countrymen to nature, as has already been mentioned (p. 75). In like manner, Samuel Richardson made strong endeavor to turn the tide of fiction into the channels of realism, of everyday occurrences and everyday lives. He succeeded undoubtedly beyond the dreams of Marivaux, and the works of the latter author are, by comparison with those of the English writer, fanciful and light. Yet there are resemblances to be noticed between the attempted realism of Marivaux and the successful realism of Richardson, resemblances that suggest the possibility of Richardson's having somewhat followed the lead of the Frenchman. *Marianne* is, however, episodic. The Richardson book it most suggests, *Clarissa*, is, on the other hand, a history in which the events of the heroine's life follow each other in an uninterrupted succession. Here is one of the chief differences between Richardson and Marivaux. There is no doubt that Richardson had before him the example of Marivaux's novels in the epistolary form. That he was led to couch his own works in that form because of the example of Marivaux is, on the other hand, doubtful, if not entirely incredible.

Even before Marivaux, however, and following in the trail of the *Lettres Portugaises* rather than in that of Marivaux's early work, are such series of love letters as *Lettres de la Marquise de M——— au Comte de P———* (1732) and *Lettres Athéniennes* (1732), both the work of Claude Prosper Jolyot de Crébillon (Crébillon *fils*). The latter work may be placed beside Landor's tale of classic love in letters, *Pericles and Aspasia*. In the French work the letters are exchanged between Alcibiades and Aspasia.

To almost the same period of years as the two important epistolary works of Marivaux belong the epistolary works of Madame de Tencin, *Le Comte de Comminge* (1735) and *Malheurs de L'Amour* (1747), two sprightly novels written with a moral purpose but not a great deal of dignity. Already considered as French epistolary authors whose work was translated into English are Mme. Riccoboni and Mme. Elie de Beaumont. The former is the author of *Lettres de Julie Catesby* (1759), and the latter the author of *Lettres du Marquis de Roselle* (1764), both written in the epistolary form. It might be noted that Mesdames Tencin, Riccoboni, and de Beaumont, along with Mme. de Charrière, author of *Lettres neuchateloises* (1784), and *Caliste; ou Lettres écrites de Lausanne* (1786), and Mme. de Souza, who wrote *Adèle de Senanges* (1794), form a sort of epistolary school of sensibility which extends over a period of some sixty years and is comparable to the similar school of sensibility already considered in the English epistolary novel of the eighteenth century. These French books are, upon the whole, although the works of Mme. Riccoboni and Mme. de Beaumont are thoroughly pleasant, rather pedestrian and uninspired creations, sometimes relieved by a flow of graceful and exquisite writing, but usually overladen with sentiment and sensibility.

Voltaire is the author of an epistolary work in *Les Lettres d'Amabed, traduites par l'Abbé Tamponet,* a piece that may be considered minor in every respect. This was published in 1769. Dependent upon the work of Marivaux for its title and its moral indignation is *Le Paysan Perverti; ou, les Dangers de la ville—histoire récente mise au jour d'après les véritables lettres des personages,* by Réstif de la Bretonne (already mentioned for his imitation of Rousseau), published in 1775. . . .

Turning to epistolary expression in Italy, we find that *Pamela* appeared in translation in 1744-46, and the heroine of

the novel had her story made famous in that country by Goldoni's *Pamela Fanciulla* (or *Pamela Nubile*) (1750). Goldoni followed this play with *Pamela Maritata* (1750). *Clarissa* was translated, in novel form, in 1783-86; *Grandison* in 1784-89. Thus we find that the epistolary novel reached Italy, from England, save in the case of *Pamela*, rather later than it had France, where Richardson's novels were completely translated by the close of the fifties. In Germany, too, the fifties saw Richardson completely translated. But in Italy the drama was at this time more popular than the novel, and so it was that Pamela became a stage rather than a page heroine. Incidentally, these plays of Goldoni were translated into English and published in London in 1756. Chiari, in 1759, also published a *Pamela Maritata,* and his novel *Francese in Italia* he based on *Clarissa*.[2] One finds here not so much the definitely moralistic tone that was so peculiarly Richardson's; but the impulse of the epistle came from him. Of course Rousseau was, in France, a nearer neighbor to Italy, and Goethe's *Werther* was also very popular with the Italians, but since all go back to Richardson as the fountainhead we may say of Chiari that he, too, does. Mr. Downs has taken from Arturo Graf the statement that Richardson, though he did not introduce the epistolary form into Italy, made it popular there.[3] This is unquestionably a good phrase, but one that seems upon the whole a trifle vague, for the translation of *Pamela* dates 1744-46; Chiari's *Francese in Italia* dates 1762. Richardson was there eighteen years before Pietro Chiari! And in Chiari's *La Viaggiatrice* there is a very clear influence of *Pamela*. It is in epistolary form as are three of his other novels: *La filosofessa italiana; La Cantatrice per disgrazia;* and *La Donna che non si trova* (1762), which is in imitation of *La Nouvelle Héloïse*. As a matter of fact, Albergati had had it in mind to imitate this Rousseau work in an epistolary novel but did not do it, and published instead the *Lettere Capricciose piacevoli e varie* in collaboration with Zacchiroli, Compopioni, and Bertalozzi. Thus, if Richardson did not "introduce" the epistolary form into Italy, but merely made it "fashionable," then to Chiari must be given the honor of introducing it. But since Richardson was most often his model, we may conclude that the introduction was at least under the influence of Richardson if that author was not himself the immediate impulse. Of course, Richardson did not introduce epistolary fiction into England, but he made it popular there.

Earlier too, of course, than Chiari are certain other works. It has been claimed for Italy that the origins of the epistolary novel are Italian. Europe knew the epistolary novels of Montesquieu, Richardson, Rousseau, and Goethe. But in 1569 there was already an epistolary novel in Italy, the *Lettere Amorose* of Aloise Pasqualigo, which is the basis for this distinguished claim. In 1684 we have Marana's *L'Esploratore turco e le diliu relazioni segrete alla Porte Ottomana* (Paris). This has been thought to be of French origin, but Natali refutes this conclusively.[4] It is, like Montesquieu's *Lettres Persanes*, a survey of politics and society. It was very popular and appeared in English in the first decade of the eighteenth century. In almost direct imitation of the early work by Marana is *Lo Spione Italiano; ossia corrispondenza segreta e familiare fra il Marchese di Licciocara e il Conte Pifiela, tutti e due viaggiatori incogniti per i diverse corti d'Europa* (1782).

It is, in the final analysis, however, Pietro Chiari who is the leading proponent of the epistolary form in Italy, as has already been intimated. Certainly this is indisputably true of his place in the eighteenth century, if it is not equally true of his place in all Italian literature. It is interesting to note that the general machinery of his epistolary novels is, indeed, very much like that of the sentimental moralistic novel in letters in England. The same extravagances, the same plethora of gallant intrigues, surprises, duels, flights, and of the course, tears, are employed in these novels almost as plentifully as they were in England's epistolary works of fiction. I have already indicated that the novel was not the most important form in Italy in the literature of the eighteenth century. It was not, indeed, until the appearance of *Le Ultime Lettere di Jacopo Ortis* in 1799-1802 that the novel became a truly popular form in that country. In other words, Chiari was persistently writing in a form that was not entirely popular during the period in which he wrote. By 1757 he had begun his career as a writer of the picaresque tale with the *Storia di Luigi Manderine,* based on a French original. Thus Concari sums up this really important writer:

> *Non credo che giovi di saperne oltre di codesti romanzi di venture fondati in capricciose combinazioni accozzate senza logica ne arte; il fin qui detto da un idea dei propisiti dell' autore, che pure scrive per dilettare e istriure, e non ha ne rettitudine ne moralita, se non pervana ostentazione nelle massime e nei discorsi.*[5]

Yet this is the man who did so much in Italy to keep the novel alive! . . .

Of the work which saw the light in Italy in this form, it may be said that there is only one of lasting importance, and that is Ugo Foscolo's *Lettere Ultime di Jacopo Ortis.* The other novels in epistolary form are more or less transitory in tissue and general worth. But when one remembers that a country which had very little fiction in novel form which was its own before 1830 gave birth to a goodly dozen of epistolary novels, the virulence of this trans-European epidemic can be estimated.

The same general statement may be made of German literature, in which there is to be found, among the several existing epistolary novels, but one that is of true worth and importance. This is, of course, *Die Leiden des Jungen Werthers,* by Johann Wolfgang von Goethe, a novel in letters which first appeared in 1774. Since it was preceded by the epistolary works of Samuel Richardson and Jean-Jacques Rousseau, it is a safe and natural assumption to suppose that Goethe derived at least the suggestion for the form of his work from the novels in letters of Richardson and Rousseau. Goethe followed the path of Rousseau in the spirit that he established in his work and succeeded in setting up a new mode of thought in German social rela-

tions and in literature. In that the book encouraged sentimental youths to commit suicide, it achieved a sort of notoriety as well as fame; yet its intrinsic value is a high one. The philosophy, the sentimentality, and the social ethics of the book are derived from Rousseau. On the other hand, the style in which the letters are written; their naturalness; their faithfulness to character (especially in the case of the letters which Werther writes, full as they are of philosophic ramblings and sentimental self-pityings); their attempted simple presentation of bourgeois life, are all more closely allied to the work of Richardson than to that of Rousseau.

The book itself is important as a literary work as well as an epistolary one. In this novel, says Wilhelm Scherer, Goethe "protested against a society, which did not understand how to use the brilliant talents of an impetuous young man; he protested against established inequality, against the pride of the nobility . . . ; he protested against prevailing morality, that did not even look upon suicide with compassion; he protested against conventional pedantry of style and against aesthetic rules . . . ; and he protested against the established speech, which the author employed, as a matter of fact, not only with freedom, but even arbitrarily."[6] Whatever else may be said of the book, it must stand undoubtedly as one of the most remarkable and influential of epistolary novels in literature and one as important in its effects as the epistolary novels of Richardson and the *Nouvelle Héloise* of Rousseau.

Notes

1. *Richardson,* London, New York, 1928, p. 218.

2. Arturo Graf, *L'Anglo-Mania e L'Influsso Inglese in Italia nel secolo XVIII,* Torino, 1911.

3. Graf, *op. cit.,* p. 282; Downs, *op. cit.,* p. 233.

4. *Il Settecento.* In *Storia Letteraria D'Italia.* Scritta da una Società di Professori, Milan, 1929.

5. "I do not think it is necessary to enquire any further into such romances of adventure revolving about whimsical combination, thrown together without either logic or art. What has been said thus far gives an idea of the purposes of the author who writes to delight and to instruct, and yet does not possess either righteousness or morality, except to display them in his maxims and discourses." T. Concari, *Il Settecento.* In *Storia Letteraria D'Italia.* Scritta da una Società di Professori, Milan, N. D., p. 398.

6. Wilhelm Scherer, *Geschichte der Deutschen Literatur,* Berlin, 1883, p. 500.

Charles E. Kany (essay date 1937)

SOURCE: "The Sixteenth Century: The First Epistolary Romances in Prose," in *The Beginnings of the Epistolary Novel in France, Italy, and Spain,* University of California Press, 1937, pp. 69-79.

[*In the following excerpt, Kany discusses two sixteenth-century Spanish works that he considers to be the first true epistolary novels, and he examines their influence on European romantic and pastoral literature.*]

In 1548 . . . there appeared in Spain the *Processo de cartas,* a full-fledged epistolary novel made up entirely of prose letters. Fifteen years later (1563) a still longer romance wholly in letter form, Pasqualigo's *Lettere amorose,* appeared in Italy. These are the only two examples which we have inherited from that period.

Premature efforts at best, their technique fell far short of perfection, and their significance is wholly premonitory. Nor is it surprising that they gave rise to no immediate and direct imitation. The inserted letter of the romance continued its fixed course and shows no startling change such as might have been brought about by the impinging influences of the *Processo de cartas* and the *Lettere amorose.* These two romances are, then, to be regarded as pioneer works which cleared a path for the advance of the epistolary novel.

PROCESSO DE CARTAS (1548)

The fuller title of this Spanish romance is: *Processo de cartas de amores que entre dos amantes passaron.* Of the author, Juan de Segura, nothing is known. Alfonso de Ulloa printed the *Cartas* anonymously in Venice in the year 1553.[1] Juan de Segura's name, however, appears in the editions of 1548, 1553 (Alcalá), and 1564.[2] Ticknor (I:426, note 13), who knew only the 1553 anonymous edition, suspected that the *Cartas* were written by Diego de San Pedro, according to a phrase in the latter's *Desprecio de la fortuna* where he speaks of "aquellas cartas de Amores, escriptas de dos en dos." But this statement must refer to some other work. . . .

Perhaps the best way to demonstrate how the simple plot is developed in this first of epistolary novels, will be to give a brief summary:

Not until the lover has written his lady three letters (signed *Captivo*) protesting his deep affection does she deign to reply (number 4), telling him that since pity is natural to women, she responds to this inner voice, but she warns him not to write again. Overjoyed, he begs her (5 and 6) to pronounce his doom. She will not give him the satisfaction of ordering his death and rejoices in his torment (7). If he prove sufficiently long-suffering and worthy she may reply to his question. Until then she wishes to hear no more from him, though she admits that his epistolary style is agreeable.

In letters 8 and 9 he is despondent as any condemned man, reading and rereading her cruel sentence. Finally she relents (10), "opening the door" to his desire but enjoining upon him the utmost discretion. This reply inflames his passion (11). Since she has opened to him the gate of commiseration, he will neglect nothing to obtain still greater favors. He begs her (12) to write when she can, for

he sees her so seldom. She confesses (13) that she is won and promises to meet him at a place he frequents.

Subsequently he tells her (15) how much their interview delighted him and asks whether he may not enjoy her conversation undisturbed some evening, for he has now served her for two years. At this she reproaches him for his haste and inexperience in love (16). He, in turn, curses his hand and his tongue for the offense they have given (17).

After six days he writes again (18), begging her to visit the place where his body will soon be buried. She replies (19) that since she has been the cause of his misfortune, she will remedy it as soon as an opportunity presents itself. After two rapturous letters from him (20 and 21) she informs the ecstatic lover (22) that she has not forgotten her promise and that she and her mother will watch at Nuestra Señora de Gracia early that very evening.

He is grateful for the all too short interview (23). Now that he has spoken with her and enjoyed her sweet and instructive conversation as well as her beauty, he is lost indeed (24). She is pleased with his letters (25) and would consider herself most ungrateful if she did not accord him her favors. At their last meeting she noticed his downcast eyes and his silence. This shyness she attributes to excessive love. She will meet him in the afternoon at the usual place. All his joy consists in seeing her at the appointed hour (26).

Would that she had not seen him (27), for the fire in his eyes has kindled her heart and won her completely; but he must speak to her brothers about their union, since she is obedient to their will.

He reports (28) that he has asked for her hand but has been refused. She writes (29) that his last letter proposing an elopement has been intercepted by her brothers and that they are planning to take her away. She begs him to find some means to write. She is sending this letter by a maid who will serve them in their future correspondence. If he is deprived of the sight of his lady, he cannot live an hour (30). Her afflicted heart undergoes tortures during the hours when she used to see him (31).

He sends her silks of various colors (32). She thanks him for his letter and present (33). She is confined to a convent and wishes him to send a gift to one of the "devotas señoras," whom she has chosen for her confidante, and whom she hopes to win over to their side.

Not hearing from him for two weeks, she reproaches him severely (34). Sickness has prevented him from writing (35). He sends cloth for a robe and twenty *escudos* for hoods as a gift to her confidante. She writes that Doña Juliana is grateful (36) and sends him some pastries in return. She wishes he would serenade her but warns him to sing softly.

She writes (38) that Orpheus could never equal the sweetness of his music, which the nuns thought to be the voice of an angel from Heaven. He replies that the source of his music is her beauty (39). She writes (40) that her parents and brothers, having learned of the serenading, are determined to take her far away, she knows not whither.

After his lady is taken from him, he writes to Doña Juliana (41) requesting her to send him certain promised relics. Doña Juliana replies (42), enclosing a cloth which bears a few drops of blood left for him by his lady, and tells him there is no hope for his love.

In his misery, he writes to a loyal friend (43), seeking advice. He wishes to put an end to his wretched life. His friend attempts to console him (44) by sending a copy of the story of Luzindaro and Medusina, similar to his own. The romance has this title: *Quexa y aviso de un cavallero llamado Luzindaro, contra amor y una Dama, y sus casos, con deleytoso estilo de proceder, hasta al fin de ambos: sacado del estilo Griego en nuestro Castellano.* It is a mixture of sentimental discourses, allegory, and fantastic adventures:

A king of Greece, versed in astrology, imprisons his daughter in a tower in order to prevent the fulfillment of her destiny as predicted by the stars. But the wise Acthelasia frustrates his plans by making Luzindaro, son of the king of Ethiopia, fall in love with the unhappy princess after beholding her in a vision. With the aid of a magic ring, Luzindaro makes his way into the tower. At first unsuccessful in his suit, he is later much favored. But he must undergo shipwreck and many other adventures before he is united in marriage to Medusina. After a brief period of happiness, the princess dies. Luzindaro, in despair, starves himself to death, after having devoured the ashes of his beloved.

Thus end the story and the *Processo.*

It is interesting to consider in the *Processo* how the action taking place outside the letters proper is incorporated into the general scheme. The method lacks smoothness and finish, to be sure, in this first effort; but the attempt is worthy of note. Not until letter 12, for instance, do we learn that the lover sees his lady from time to time. Up to this point the reader assumes the relationship between the two lovers to be wholly epistolary. Again, in letter 13, she arranges to meet him; in letter 15 he tells how much he enjoyed meeting her. The interview itself, which we are to infer took place, is nowhere described. In letter 22 she informs him of her intention of going to church with her mother; in letter 24 he speaks of having enjoyed her sweet conversation, etc.; in letter 25 she makes a casual remark about his conduct at that meeting. In the same letter, she arranges for another tryst, the emotional result of which we learn in letter 27. The brothers' refusal to grant the request of the lover and their later action in bringing about the dénouement are treated in greater narrative detail, yet not so completely as might be desired.

Although the work contains many letters that teem with extravagant conceits of the time, it is nevertheless of great importance in the development of the genre, for it is the first modern novel made up entirely of letters. Juan de Segura, having generalized the procedure of Aeneas Silvius, Diego de San Pedro, and even older authors, has thus honored the literature of Spain. Save for its mention in histories of Spanish literature, Spain's claim to priority in the epistolary novel has never been sufficiently recognized.[3]

Though the work enjoyed four editions in Spain, only its appendage, the story of Luzindaro and Medusina, seems to have been translated into French.

LETTERE AMOROSE (1563)

The second epistolary novel is Alvise Pasqualigo's *Delle Lettere amorose libri due ne quali leg gendosi una historia continuata d'uno amor fervente di molti anni tra due nobilissimi amanti, si contien ciò che puo in questa materia a qualunque persona avvenire.*[4]

The *Processo de cartas* is a mere tale compared with this, for here we have 557 letters, divided into two books. Since a detailed account of them would be impossible, not to say inexpressibly dull, I shall trace only the main facts of the story.[5]

The nobleman Alvise Pasqualigo, returning to Venice after a seven years' absence during which he has tried to forget Madonna Vittoria, attempts through frequent writing to revive what had been an unsuccessful affair. Vittoria, wife of a young count, is overwhelmed by Alvise's importunities and finally promises to love him as a brother. But he insists in many letters upon seeing her secretly; and she, chary of her reputation, entreats him not to show her portrait to anyone nor to breathe a word about her.

She remains implacable, doubting the sincerity of his love; whereupon Alvise threatens to kill himself. Convinced of her lover's constancy by this threat and regretting her doubts, Vittoria meets him clandestinely one day in order to reassure him of her affection. From that day on, the letters of Madonna are poignantly sad and bitter. Anonymous letters (97, 105) are written by an admirer for the purpose of inciting the jealousy not only of her husband, but of Madonna herself.

Vittoria soon becomes pregnant (163) and her jealousy and discontent increase (218, 249). In vain does Alvise attempt to convince her that he uses the other ladies of his acquaintance as a screen for their own love; she continues to live in anxiety and desires death:

> . . . per esser io donna priva d'ogni conversazione & si puo dire confinata in casa, & per convenirmi pensar sempre di quella cosa che più m'è cara, non havendo con alcuna sorte di trattenimenti da rompere il mio fisso pensiero, o pur da sviarlo per qualche momento.
>
> (240)

Her greatest woe is that she must live with her husband, "chi mortalmente m'odia" (322). He has charged a certain

Fortunio to keep strict watch over all the household. During this time the lovers, unable to see each other, find consolation in epistolizing. Finally, assuming girl's attire and accompanied by a lady, Alvise spends happy moments sitting beside Vittoria in church (346-347).

The situation becomes so perilous that Alvise never leaves the house without the accompaniment of three noblemen. Yet his lady's love does not diminish. She falls dangerously ill on learning that, to avoid marrying a girl of his parents' choice, he plans to leave the city for a month (450-451); she would rather that he marry the girl than that he go so far away. Alvise, however, thinks best to depart.

Here ends the story as told in the 1563 edition, which is probably the first. Without mentioning this edition, Albertazzi (pp. 55-56) and Wiese simply say that the letters appeared before 1569 under the title of *Lettere di due amanti*.[6] Natali in his monumental *Settecento* (1929, II:1095) mentions only the 1569 edition in attempting to corroborate his erroneous statement that the first epistolary novel was Italian.[7] In the 1569 and 1607 editions, the work was called *Lettere amorose di Messer Alvise Pasqualigo*. Albertazzi for his analysis probably used the 1607 edition, which is divided into four books and contains the dénouement of the romance. Since I had access to the 1563 edition only, I shall give a brief account of the dénouement as related by Albertazzi:

Returning to Venice after a four months' absence, Alvise finds Madonna Vittoria a changed person, quite secure against all temptation. She reassures him of her Platonic affection but adds that the long separation has cured her of culpable love. The truth, however, is gradually revealed. Vittoria in the interim has had another lover, and indeed no other than Fortunio, the spy. Since her attempts at denying it are futile, she reluctantly confesses her misdeed. Derided by his friends, Alvise finally challenges Fortunio and wounds him in a duel. Vittoria intercedes for him, showing Alvise a letter in which Fortunio consents to leave her, since she so desires. But this is in vain. Alvise leaves her to despair.

It is thought that these were real letters, written, copied, and preserved with the intention of being published, "quasi a modello di epistolario amoroso."[8] The writers therefore took precautions: proper names are never given in full, the husband is usually referred to as "amico" (24, 47, 54, 81), "matto" (530), "nemico" (163), etc. The letters embody many disquisitions on love, which was characteristic of the period. The current question whether a lover ought to be favored by many or by only one lady forms the subject-matter of four letters (210-213); nor are arguments for and against jealousy lacking (218, 249, 263, 342, 362). The letters are too repetitious in thought and in sentiment to make very pleasant reading—probably owing to the fact that they are genuine and not fictitious. The constant reiteration of mutual faith, the exaggeration of mood and emotion, the endless adjurations, and the eternal protests

are unfavorable to that sense of selection and progress demanded in a conscious work of art. In spite of the extremists in contemporary literature, it seems reasonable to expect the novel to have a less private and limited appeal than any collection of actual correspondence. But whatever its limitations as a work of art, the *Lettere amorose* takes its place with the *Processo de cartas*, Spain's strangely neglected contribution to the history of literature.

PASTORAL ROMANCES

In dealing with the pastoral romances I shall choose as examples only such episodes as show a continuation of, or an advance over, the use of the letter as last seen in the Italian erotic romances.

The device by which the individual episodes are made to fit into the whole work is nearly always the same: a company of shepherds come upon another shepherd, who is lamenting his amorous misfortunes and who, upon their request, recites his tale of woe.

The Italian pastorals, the *Ameto* and Sannazaro's *Arcadia* (1504), offer no letters. Even the first Spanish pastoral, Montemayor's *Diana* (1558), has nothing of the particular interest. Though it contains nine letters, they are not of sufficient importance to warrant their consideration here. Gil Polo's *Diana enamorada* (1564) falls into the same category.

The *Segunda parte de la Diana de Jorge de Montemayor*, on the other hand, written by Alonso Pérez (1564), has twelve letters which serve to advance the plot. I shall give in brief form the contents of one of the episodes in this pastoral:

Disteo receives a letter (p. 398 in the 1622 edition) from Palna, his "madre de leche," in which she explains why she has suddenly left him, whom she calls her "only consolation." She begs him to have patience until she can make full explanation. Sagastes has persuaded her with promises and gifts to become the confidante of his sister Dardenea, whom Disteo loves. After some time Disteo replies to Palna (p. 400), pardoning her desertion.

Because of his love for Dardenea, Disteo avoids all companionship and is sunk in melancholy. Attributing his plight to her absence, Palna is deeply grieved and writes him a letter (p. 401, not given in full), reminding him of his promise to be patient. She exhorts him to banish his sorrow and to exercise himself in arms. Disteo replies to this (p. 401, not in full) that since she is near his Dardenea, he is content. Finally, at his request, she arranges a tryst with Dardenea. He disguises himself as Palna's nephew Placindo, whose place he takes as the bodyguard of Sagastes, about to engage in a fierce nocturnal adventure. Thanks to Disteo, Sagastes is successful and is proclaimed a hero.

The following day Disteo sends a letter to Palna (p. 414), describing the adventure. Palna, in turn, relates the whole story to Dardenea, who, thinking her honor involved, forbids Disteo her house. She relents only after Disteo has acquired a reputation throughout the kingdom for his heroic deeds.

Disteo writes Palna again, enclosing a letter for Dardenea. But Palna, not daring to deliver the missive directly, resorts to a cunning trick. She arouses Dardenea's curiosity by shutting herself continually in her room. Dardenea, having discovered that Palna is engaged in reading and writing letters, one day undertakes a search for the epistles, and this is what she finds (pp. 420ff.):

(1) Letter from Disteo to Palna, in which he laments her loss and begs her to give Dardenea the enclosed note.

(2) Letter from Palna to Disteo, in reply to (1), in which Palna thanks him for his kind thoughts, but will return his note lest it displease her mistress.

(3) Letter from Disteo to Dardenea (in *terza rima*), in which he writes that he is bidden by Amor to admonish her lest she anger Cupid or Nature. If she will not requite his love, he will seek death.

Aroused, Dardenea addresses him (pp. 425-428, *terza rima*) as "el más de los hombres atrevido." If she thought a reply were dishonorable, she would sooner take up the sword to find death than the pen to answer him. Relenting somewhat, she says she cannot prevent his loving her; if he uses force she must needs consent in spite of herself. But since hope is uncertain, and evil and harm are sure to result, it would be better to "open the door to forgetfulness and disdain."

Now Palna, who has been allowed to read this reply, sends another letter to Disteo (p. 428), lest Dardenea's harshness discourage him. She urges him to persevere, since his beginning is so favorable. Dardenea, however, will not consent to speak with Disteo until he promises to marry her. After the exchange of many more letters (p. 428, not noted individually), Disteo expresses his desire to wed her, and he is allowed to see her one evening. Discovering that Palna has unwittingly left the door unlocked, Disteo returns furtively to his beloved. Later Dardenea's brother enters the room unexpectedly, but Disteo, with more ingenuity than clothing, manages to escape unrecognized. A happy ending is indicated when the two lovers and Palna flee from the closely guarded city to live the peaceful life of shepherds.

Although this romance was cast into the bonfire in the examination of Don Quixote's library because the author had not followed the plan of Montemayor, it is of greater interest for our purposes than the *Diana* itself.

We may pass by Montalvo's *Pastor de Fílida* (5 letters), Cervantes' *Galatea* (10 letters), and many others, but we owe some attention to Lope de Vega's *Arcadia* (1598). This pastoral begins with a rhapsodic love letter from the shepherd Anfriso to his love Belisarda (pp. 92-95 in the 1653 edition). Belisarda answers fondly (p. 104), telling him that she is to be alone that evening, and sending him a lock of hair.

But Anfriso has rivals who make his life miserable. He goes off into the mountains to forget his shepherdess, sending two shepherd boys to keep him posted on events in town. They write him a full account, with special emphasis on the constancy of Belisarda. In the solitude of his retreat, Anfriso is consoled by reading the innumerable letters from his love. But the shepherd boys bring him news of Belisarda's departure for Cilene. Anfriso finds means to write to her, and she replies (p. 109). Then Anfriso, reassured by her letters, abandons the mountains and journeys to Cilene. Shortly after his arrival he receives a letter from Belisarda (p. 109) saying that she is arranging to meet him. They spend several days in festivities and entertainment, nevertheless still exchanging love letters (p. 116).

Then Belisarda asks Anfriso, for the sake of their mutual tranquillity, to leave her. Dressed as a pilgrim, the sorrowful shepherd wends his way to Italy, and the rest of the story deals with his wanderings. The unfaithful Belisarda marries another.

Though many of the letters in the *Arcadia* are not given in full, their contents are indicated. This was the common practice in writing pastorals, which were not generally of great length. Occasionally, however, we find the letters given in their entirety, as they are in the heroic-gallant novels of the XVIIth century. One of these rare exceptions is Antonio de lo Frasso's *Diez libros de fortuna de amor* (1573). This work is less episodic than the ordinary and has a connected plot, which is, however, too long to be included here.

Although the *Diez libros de fortuna de amor* is ridiculed by Cervantes (*El Quijote*, I, 6) and characterized by Ticknor (III, 45, n.) as "absurd" and full of "so much bad verse," nevertheless, so far as it relates to the epistolary genre, it has more merits than any of the other pastorals. It is free from the host of disconcerting and disrupting episodes that characterize the type. It can therefore develop its own action, scanty as that may be, to its full extent, and give free play to a long series of letters and verses which would probably have found only passing mention in the condensed episodes of other pastorals.

It is interesting to note the methods employed by the very late pastoral writers, such as Florian (1755-94). By the middle of the XVIIIth century, the pastoral had long since fallen into disrepute. The very name of the pastoral was somniferous: "dès que l'on annonce un ouvrage dont les héros sont des bergers, il semble que ce nom seul donne envie de dormir."[9] The cause of this "dégout" for the shepherd romances was probably their remoteness from real life, their prolixity, and their countless episodic digressions. Florian therefore reduced his charming *Galatée* written in imitation of Cervantes' *Galatea* to one hundred pages, about one-third the length of the original, and inserted but one letter; his *Estelle* (132 pages) likewise contains but one.[10] This paucity of inserted missives is partly due to the fact that the letter device had long since become strong enough to exist independently, and had therefore been dismissed from the romance to form an entity of its own. The pastorals had contributed their part toward the development of the epistolary genre. They adopted the letter from the sentimental and erotic romances,[11] kept or increased its vigor, then passed it on to the heroic-gallant novels. The important channel through which the letter was conveyed to these XVIIth-century romances is the pastoral par excellence, the *Astrée*.

Notes

1. Such is the copy in the Ticknor collection (Boston Public Library).

2. Cf. *Orígenes,* I:cccxxxviii.

3. Singer, for example, in his recent work *The Epistolary Novel* (1933), not only ignores the existence of the *Processo* but makes this rash statement (p. 214): ". . . no great literature, with the possible exception of the Spanish, seems to have escaped completely from the [epistolary] impulse." It might be noted here that the picaresque novel, engendered in Spain, may well have contributed its share of intimate narrative in the first person to the popularity of the equally self-revealing memoirs, journal-books and letters which eventually led to the epistolary novel.

4. Venetia, Fr. Rampazetto (1563), ed. by Francesco Sansovino. Reynier (p. 256, note 3) mentions a collection of letters that appeared in Venice in 1562: *Lettere amorose di Mad. Celia scritte al suo amante.* This exceedingly rare work I have not seen.

5. In the preface to the 1563 edition, Francesco Sansovino states his purpose in publishing the letters: to expose woman's fickleness in affairs of the heart and to warn noblemen against the snares of love. He thinks the following moral may be drawn from the work:

   che lo huomo nobilissimo tra tutte l'altre cose del mondo, mal fa quando si dà in preda all'affetto amoroso, & che egli dee cercare di spendere il tempo in cose di valore & non d'Amore, & ch'il Petrarca ben disse il vero quando lasciò scritto,

   Femina è cosa mobil per natura
   Ond' io so ben ch'un amoroso stato
   In cor di donna picciol tempo dura.

6. Cf. Wiese and Pèrcopo, *Geschichte der ital. Litt.* (1899), p. 379.

7. ". . . le origini del romanzo epistolare sono italiane; noi avemmo le *Lettere amorose* di Alvise Pasqualigo sin dal 1569."

8. Albertazzi, p. 57, and Letter 416.

9. Cf. Florian, *uvres* (Paris, 1838), I:162.

10. *Ibid.,* I, *Galatée* (1783), *Estelle* (1788).

11. The French sentimental novel at the turn of the century looks back to works already discussed; space prohibits mention of their relatively unimportant imitations.

Bibliography

Albertazzi, A. *Romanzieri e romanzi del cinquento e del seicento* (Bologna, 1891).

Florian. *uvres* (Paris, 1838).

Natali, G. *Il Settecento* (*Storia letteraria d'Italia,* Milan, 1929, 2 vols.).

Pasqualigo, Alvise. *Delle Lettere amorose libri due* (ed. F. Sansovino, Venetia, 1563).

Reynier, G. *Le Roman sentimental avant l'Astrée* (Paris, 1908).

Segura, Juan de. *Processo de cartas de amores que entre dos amantes passaron* (Venice, 1553).

Singer, G. F. *The Epistolary Novel, Its Origin, Development, Decline, and Residuary Influence* (Univ. of Pennsylvania Press, 1933).

Ticknor, George. *History of Spanish Literature* (New York, 1849, 3 vols.).

Wiese and Pèrcopo. *Geschichte der italienischen Litteratur* (1899).

Dorothy R. Thelander (essay date 1963)

SOURCE: Introduction to *Laclos and the Epistolary Novel,* Librairie Droz, 1963, pp. 11-17.

[*In the following introduction to her study of Choderlos de Laclos'* Les Liaisons dangereuses, *Thelander discusses in general terms why the epistolary form was thought to be more realistic than narrative fiction and how it allowed the author to depict characters from multiple perspectives.*]

Today, so few epistolary novels are published that we tend to forget that the genre is more than another eighteenth-century phenomenon like the mania for *parfilage* which, one year, threatened all the epaulettes of Paris. Long before Richardson, the basic premises of the novel by letters had been established; the techniques employed by eighteenth-century writers cannot be considered as original. Ancient models were known and copied during the Middle Ages and the Renaissance when other forerunners of the epistolary novel were composed. Ovid's *Heroides,* a series of letters in verse from heroines of literature, history, and mythology to their absent lovers which contain the entire story of the romance in a few lines, went through twenty-five editions or reprints before 1789, according to the Bibliothèque Nationale catalog; the translations of Octavien de Saint Gelais were reprinted seven times by 1546. There were even new "heroides" written by Radulf de la Tourte,[1] Guilbert de Nogent,[2] and Baudri de Bourgueil. The replies from the lovers to three of the letters composed by the fifteenth-century poet Angelus Sabinus[3] were popularly attributed to Ovid himself. It is against this tradition that is much older than the eighteenth century that Laclos wrote *Les Liaisons dangereuses* and it is against this background of continued use that his novel (or any other epistolary novel) must be assessed.

In order to write an epistolary novel, an author must be able to see that real or fictional letters can be arranged in a series in order to carry the narrative element of a story. By this definition, there were no classical epistolary novels which survived to influence later fiction, although Reinhold Merkelbach believes that one of the sources of the *Life of Alexander of Macedon* in the Pseudo-Callisthenes version (c. 300 A.D.) was an epistolary novel composed about 100 B.C.[4] Letters were used for brief narration in the Bible and in early Christian literature, as well as in the Greek letter collections of ælian and Alciphron. The letters of Héloïse and Abelard, which contain narrative portions, were so immensely popular that they were retranslated and rewritten straight through the eighteenth century. One of the weapons in the Reuchlin case was a collection of satiric letters called the *Epistolae Obscurorum Virorum,* where there is occasional narration. Writers of seventeenth-century romances even followed the Greek tradition when they used letters within their narrative to emphasize important facts or events or to add to the credibility of their stories.

In the previous paragraph, no distinction was made between fictional letters and real letters because the emphasis has been on the letter as a popular form which could be used for narration. Before discussing the peculiar properties of the epistolary novel, it might be well to define the fictional letter and to consider its stylistic requirements. A real love letter may contain an extravagant account of the beloved's charms, employing all of the stock metaphors; it may even be written in verse. At least in the eyes of the writer and recipient, it is not a fictional letter. The short essay with a salutation and a complimentary close is also not automatically a fictional letter: if the writer and recipient are both real people who use the mail services of their time to communicate, it is a special category of the real letter. Thus Voltaire's letter to Rousseau on "natural man" is a real letter. A fictional letter may be either well or poorly written, just as a real letter may be. The basic characteristic of a fictional letter is that either the writer or the recipient are not historical people, or that the historical personage to whom the letter is attributed did not write it. In short, the only way in which a fictional letter is distinguished from the real one is that it is fiction.

However, the fictional letter loses its effectiveness unless the reader is willing to forget for the moment that what he is reading is not a real letter. The fictional letter must thus meet various criteria of credibility. The most obvious method of judging the letter is its length, as Frank Gees Black has said.[5] While our practical experience tells us that the amount of time any individual can and will devote to correspondence varies, still, when we are asked to believe that the heroine of Mme Riccoboni's *Lettres d'Adélaïde de Dammartin* writes a letter equivalent to over twenty printed pages, we may well be incredulous. In contrast to the relatively short letters in early epistolary fiction, those in the eighteenth-century novels tend to excessive length either in their own right or by the inclusion of diaries and journals faithfully copied by the characters to provide their correspondents with background. Though the real letters of the period were often long, the writers at least seemed aware that they might tire or bore the recipients, as shown by Diderot's repeated apologies to Sophie Volland. The eighteenth-century fictional-letter-writer tended to be immune to writer's cramp and insensitive to his reader.

Besides length, there are other criteria which we apply to epistolary fiction, consciously or unconsciously. The author of the letters in III Maccabees, for example, was careful to observe the correct chancellory form in order to give to his epistles the outward trappings of reality. On a more subtle level, while Ovid's claim to have been the originator of a new literary form in the *Heroides* "Vel tibi composita cantetor epistola uoce / Ignotum hoc aliis ille nouauit opus," *Ars Amandi,* iii, 345) may be disputed, these imaginary letters establish the basic criteria of style in epistolary fiction. Ovid took the idea for the *Heroides* from the grammarians and rhetors under whom he had studied.[6] With the rhetors, he had composed monologues or speeches for a designated person employing language suitable to their social position, age, and emotion. Substituting letter for speech, the bases for inner reality and for characterization in the epistolary novel are established. These criteria, unconsciously used by the reader, even became critical weapons in the late seventeenth century during the British phase of the *Querelle des anciens et des modernes,* as when Bentley argued against the authenticity of the epistles of Phalaris because of inconsistencies in the letters themselves.

Thus, the letters in an epistolary novel define the character of the fictional author by their style. If an author is to take full advantage of the documentary aspect of the letter, he must place his characters in such a situation that the letters they write are credible. Although we may wonder at the high degree of literacy among Alciphron's farmers and fishermen, once we grant this premise, there is nothing illogical about their letters. By contrast, as has been pointed out so often, the letter which Saint-Preux writes in Julie's boudoir is not credible.

The correspondence in an epistolary novel must somehow be motivated. This is only one of the technical problems facing the author. Another is the relationship between the letterwriters and the plot—are the characters writing about events which they have witnessed or in which they have taken part? Obviously, the letterwriter can be completely removed from the events which he supposedly narrates, but then the epistolary form loses part of its strength. There is also the "time lapse" problem. Events must be arranged in such a way that the narrator or narrators seem to be kept busy narrating. One solution is simply to indicate the passage of time by a change in the date assigned to the letter. A second is to insert material, not necessarily connected with the main plot, so that time may seem to pass for the reader. The addition of diaries of comparative strangers in some eighteenth-century novels can be directly traced to the need of the author to give his main characters time to travel or for the plot to develop behind the scenes without abruptly shifting dates and thus confusing the reader. And, if more than one person is narrating, the author must somehow arrange his correspondents so that the same event is never seen twice in the same way. One solution here is to have a supposed editor who tells the reader in a footnote that he had deleted useless letters. Another, which presents far more interesting possibilities, is to utilize the double narration, as Alciphron did, either by permitting one character to write two contradictory letters or two characters to write from different points of view, allowing the reader to make up his own mind about the event.

Although the epistolary technique, with its stylistic requirements, is surely not the easiest way to tell a story, it does present subtle possibilities to the skilful writer. A letter is a personal document—it is written by one individual with a definite personality which he reveals consciously or unconsciously. We need not go as far as Giraudoux in saying that a letter is in essence a confession or an improvisation;[7] yet, at the same time, a letter is written to someone with another personality, with whom the author is attempting to communicate for some purpose. He tries to place his case before the recipient in such a way that the latter will be moved to accept the writer's position or to take the action which the writer desires. In the case of a letter to a distant friend, the writer is usually looking only for a sympathetic audience or for advice which he will find acceptable. When the recipient is in a position to help the writer actively, it is most important for him to realize what the writer is attempting to do.

In this way, the letter presents a dual abstraction from reality. Events are first passed through the prism of the writer's own personality then through a second prism: his knowledge of the recipient's character and his desire to influence him. It is more than a question of varying social distance, as M. Seylaz[8] claims; the social distance maintained is a result of the wish to exert pressure on the recipient. In this sense, there would be, at least in theory, a difference between an epistolary novel which presents only one side of a single correspondence and a novel in the form of a diary. We do agree with M. Seylaz that the major strength of the epistolary technique lies in its ability to present several views of an evolving situation. They may come from the same person, a device used as early as Alciphron in his three Baccis letters; many individuals may give us a picture of a single person, as in the guilt-by-association technique of the *Epistolae Obscurorum Virorum;* or they may be combined so that we get multiple views of several individuals.

If the author of an epistolary novel has been successful in his creation of illusion, the reader, at least for the moment, accepts the letters as documents. From the multiple views, he must create his own version of the truth and must correct it as he goes along with the new information he receives. While in a sense the reader may be said to recreate any novel for himself, he does so with minimal guidance from the author in this *genre,* much as he is forced in daily life to probe not only what is said or written or done by several people, but what is omitted. M. Seylaz, has corrected the opinion of Yvon Belaval that the flowering of the epistolary technique in the eighteenth century reflects the social preoccupation with memoirs and letters. M. Seylaz suggests that the authors wanted to make us forget that they were makers of stories in order to give us the illusion of communicating directly with real people and to take no responsibility for the work *vis-à-vis* the reader (pp. 15-16). Both of these suggestions are attractive, but there is a third reason for the appeal of the epistolary technique which lies in the special relationship between the reader and the novel. Throughout the "Eloge de Richardson," Diderot elaborates in a more sophisticated fashion his early statement: "Combien de fois ne me suis-je pas surpris, comme il est arrivé à des enfants qu'on avait mené au spectacle pour la première fois, criant: Ne le croyez pas, il vous trompe . . ."[9] The illusion of reality is complete for Diderot. The growth of the scientific spirit, the developing interest in man related to his environment throughout the eighteenth century meant an increasing importance for factual evidence. From the Biblical examples onwards, letters are documents, the exhibits which the lawyer produces to prove his case.

Yet neither the strengths of the epistolary technique nor its continuing popularity from Ovid to the writers of historical romances quite prepare us for the "after *Pamela,* the deluge" effect which sets literary historians to tracing the family trees of the four major works in the *genre* which appear in the eighteenth century at about twenty-year intervals: *Les Lettres persanes* (1721), *Pamela* (1740), *La Nouvelle Héloïse* (1761), and *Les Liaisons dangereuses* (1782). The familiar story that Richardson sat down to compose a manual on the art of writing letters and ended up with *Pamela* hides a premise which is perhaps more instructive than the novel: people, not necessarily of the highest classes, were sufficiently interested in writing letters themselves to buy a book that would tell them how.[10] Writers could cater to this interest and turn an ancient form into a stylish *genre.*

Something is needed to produce an epistolary novel besides the idea that a letter can narrate and that it can be faked. Unless that novel is to be nothing more than a first-person narrative in long installments, the writer must be able to mirror a society in which people can and do communicate with each other by means of letters with some degree of ease. One extreme form of this problem appears in Mme de Graffigny's *Lettres d'une Péruvienne,* a very popular eighteenth-century epistolary novel. The thoughts expressed in the letters by the young Peruvian exposed to western civilization for the first time seem perfectly natural. We do not even doubt that messages were common among the Peruvians. However, even in a world where machines can be fed complicated instructions with only two signals, the idea that *quipus* (cords with knotted strings) could be used to record such nuanced thoughts is slightly ridiculous.

During the seventeenth and eighteenth centuries, a climate was developing in England and in France in which an epistolary novel would not seem like a science fiction story. The crude postal systems of the Middle Ages and Renaissance were turning into efficient organizations delivering mail on a regular basis. By 1677, the British postal system was well organized, and the London Penny Post was founded in 1680. In France, the postal system was first formed in 1672. However, it was not until 1758 that the Parisian Petite-Poste was established.[11]

Once a postal system is in common use, it is possible to write an epistolary novel with someone other than Alexander the Great as the hero. The success of such a novel will depend in part on the degree to which letters do imitate real life. It caters to that very human desire to read other people's mail. M. Seylaz has constructed a theory about the appeal of the epistolary novel, especially *Les Liaisons dangereuses,* based on eroticism in which the reader becomes a sophisticated *voyeur.*[12] While the Peeping Tom element may be concealed in the pleasure derived from reading another's letters, the late seventeenth-century British "rifled mailbox" collections, the popularity of the travel letter where the sexual element is often minimal, and the severe penalties imposed by law for tampering with the mail all suggest that people will read almost anything provided that they are not the addressees.

Notes

1. On Radulf or Raoul de La Tourte, see F. J.. E. Raby, *A History of Secular Latin Poetry from the Beginnings to the Close of the Middle Ages* (Oxford, 1934) II, 23.

2. On Guilbert de Nogent, see Phyllis Abrahams, *Les uvres poétiques de Baudri de Bourgueil* (Paris, 1926), p. 37.

3. J. Wright Duff, *A Literary History of Rome . . .* (London, 1909), p. 592.

4. *Die Quellen des Griechischen Alexanderromans* (Munich, 1954), p. 188.

5. *The Epistolary Novel in the Late Eighteenth Century, a Descriptive and Bibliographical Study* (Eugene, 1940), p. 8.

6. Ovid, *Heroides* (Paris, 1928), tr. Marcel Prévost, ed. Henri Bonecque, p. xi.

7. Jean Giraudoux, "Choderlos de Laclos," *Littérature* (Paris, 1941), p. 67. Mme de Merteuil really

answers this definition when she writes to Cécile (Letter CV, Vol. III, p. 119): "Vous écrivez toujours comme un enfant. Je vois bien d'où cela vient; c'est que vous dites tout ce que vous pensez, et rien de ce que vous ne pensez pas." Miriam Allott, *Novelists on the Novel* (New York, 1959), p. 189 concludes that the *genre* is excellent for the "interpretation of private feeling and the power of individual self-expression," and that "it was handled best by the French novelists—most devastatingly, perhaps, by Choderlos de Laclos . . . in *Les Liaisons Dangereuses . . . ,* where it served with splendid success his Gallic gift for the unflinching analysis of devious motive and perverse emotion."

8. Jean-Luc Seylaz, *"Les Liaisons dangereuses" et la création romanesque chez Laclos* (Geneva, 1958), p. 61.

9. Denis Diderot, *uvres,* ed. André Billy (Paris, 1946), p. 1090.

10. Rudolph Hercher, ed., *Epistolographi Graeci* (Paris, 1873), pp. 6-12 gives the classifications (41) and examples of letters of Proclius Platonicus (7th century A.D.?). These examples are, however, quite different from later ones as this sample love letter will show: "Amo, amo per Themidem, pulchram tuam ct amabilem formam, nec pudet me amoris: nam pulchras amare non est turpe. Sin autem qui omnio me reprehendat ut amantem, rursus ut pulchram petentem praedicet." (p. 12).

11. One of the reasons Mme de Merteuil gives for forcing Cécile's mother to take her to the country is that she might think of using the *Petite Poste* for her letters to Danceny.

12. Seylaz, pp. 22-23, observes that Valmont often refers to the drafts of his letters. How much this reflects Laclos' need to give some logical explanation for their existence in the collection and how much the desire to inform us that these letters are not to be read as spontaneously written documents, as M. Seylaz feels, might be disputed.

Elizabeth Heckendorn Cook (essay date 1996)

SOURCE: "The Eighteenth Century Epistolary Body and the Public Sphere," in *Epistolary Bodies: Gender and Genre in the Eighteenth-Century Republic of Letters,* Stanford University Press, 1996, pp. 5-29.

[*In the following excerpt, Cook discusses Charles Louis de Montesquieu's 1721* Lettres persanes, *Samuel Richardson's 1747* Clarissa, *Marie-Jeanne Riccoboni's 1757* Fanni Butlerd, *and J. Hector St. John de Crèvecoeur's 1782* Letters from an American Farmer, *works which, she argues, illustrate the epistolary genre's evolving concern for the boundaries between public and private domains.*]

LETTER AND CONTRACT: THE BODY OF WRITING

If the rhetorical structure of the letter always makes us ask, "Who writes, and to whom?", the eighteenth-century letter-narrative provokes a more specific question: "What does it mean to write from the crossroads of public and private, manuscript and print, at this particular historical moment?"

In his essay "What Is an Author?" Michel Foucault makes an assertion about the forms I explore in this study that suggests some provisional responses.

> The author's name manifests the appearance of a certain discursive set and indicates the status of this discourse within a society and a culture. It has no legal status, nor is it located in the fiction of the work; rather, it is located in the break that founds a certain discursive construct and its very particular mode of being. As a result, we could say that in a civilization like our own there are a certain number of discourses that are endowed with the "author function," while others are deprived of it. A private letter may well have a signer—it does not have an author; a contract may well have a guarantor—it does not have an author. . . . The author function is therefore characteristic of the mode of existence, circulation, and functioning of certain discourses within a society.[1]

Foucault's essay is intended to serve as "an introduction to the historical analysis of discourse," an analysis sensitive to transformations in both the "author function" and in the narratives legitimated by that function.[2] The eighteenth-century epistolary fictions examined here, however, make it necessary to reconsider Foucault's claim that letters and contracts are among discourses lacking the "author function." The *Letters persanes, Clarissa, Fanni Butlerd,* and *Letters from an American Farmer* challenge both Foucault's historical chronology and his taxonomy of the author function. In the first two-thirds of the eighteenth century, I argue here, a "discursive set" existed that coordinated the concept of authorship with both of the written forms that Foucault claims exclude it "in a civilization like our own."

Not coincidentally, Foucault's categorization of modern discourses matches the conventional division of human experience into separate orders of public and private, a division that was consolidated and naturalized in the course of the eighteenth century. Against the swarm of public print forms that proliferated in the early decades of the century, the letter became an emblem of the private; while keeping its actual function as an agent of the public exchange of knowledge, it took on the general connotations it still holds for us today, intimately identified with the body, especially a female body, and the somatic terrain of the emotions, as well as with the thematic material of love, marriage, and the family. In the same period, the contract became the representative instrument of that other great aspect of the private, the range of economic activities we still call "private enterprise."[3] In general, literary critics are only now beginning to analyze more attentively the connections between on the one hand the capitalist economic system, formalized by the late-seventeenth-century financial revolution, and on the other the nuclear family, affirmed by eighteenth-century culture: the two major divi-

sions of the domain of the private acknowledged by the Enlightenment.

As a result of being at last so thoroughly identified with the private order, the cultural history of both letter and contract has rarely been acknowledged or explored. It is often assumed that they have always been the private, "authorless" discourses Foucault describes, transparent forms that signify only constatively. In the eighteenth century, however, on the cusp between manuscript and print cultures, both these forms came into prominence in the cultural imagination. Functioning symbolically as well as semantically, they operated not to reflect a preexisting subjectivity but rather to produce and organize it in various ways. In so doing, they also delineate the modern historical trajectory of the metaphor of the Republic of Letters and of the citizen-critic who inhabits that republic. The *Letters persanes* (1721) uses the polyphonic epistolary form to train its readers in the new critical activities proper to subjects of the Republic of Letters. In *Clarissa* (1747-48), Richardson co-opts and reconstructs Montesquieu's public sphere of letters as a "quasi public" modeled on the affective relations of the private family. Where Richardson's novel exploits the ideology of the private, *Fanni Butlerd* (1757) exposes its crippling effects and transforms voyeuristic readers of private letters into parties to a (feminist) literary contract. Near the end of the century, the *Letters from an American Farmer* (1782) mourns the collapse of the public sphere that made such a contract theoretically possible. In each case, the forms of letter and contract not only define the boundaries of authorship but also construe their readers in very specific ways in relation to the categories of public and private.

In response to Foucault's definition of authorship, then, we can draw two counterconclusions for the study of eighteenth-century epistolarity. First, the eighteenth century was in important ways *not* "a civilization like our own," and the real historical and cultural differences should not be flattened out when we read texts from the period. Second, those discursive modes haunting the borders or margins of established literary taxonomies, such as the epistolary narrative, constitute the richest terrain for the exploration of such differences.

The epistolary genre was central to the construction and definition of the categories of public and private that we have inherited from Enlightenment social and political traditions, and to the construction and definition of the bodies held properly to inhabit those categories. However, in part because an ideological investment in the existence of a gendered private order continued to deepen in the post-Enlightenment period, the critical histories of the narratives I examine here have consistently returned them to the realm of the private from which their characters strive, in different ways, to free themselves. This critical relocation persisted even though, in each case, the narrative of *epistolarity* that accompanies the epistolary narrative clearly claims its place in the Enlightenment public sphere.[4] In order to elude the hermeneutic cul-de-sac produced by this ideological effect, eighteenth-century epistolary fictions must be read both through and against that Enlightenment cultural framework. By expanding formalist models of epistolarity in the directions to which Foucault points, examining such specific institutions of eighteenth-century print culture as the author function, the literary public sphere, and the ideal of the citizen-critic, we can begin to recover the full epistolary body of the Enlightenment Republic of Letters.

PUBLISHED LETTERS AND PUBLIC SPHERE THEORY

Eighteenth-century epistolary fictions allow us to examine the Enlightenment ideal of a Republic of Letters precisely because the letter-narrative exposes the private body to publication.[5] The letter-narrative is formally and thematically concerned with competing definitions of subjectivity: it puts into play the tension between the private individual, identified with a specifically gendered, classed body that necessarily commits it to specific forms of self-interest, and the public person, divested of self-interest, discursively constituted, and functionally disembodied. This is the citizen-critic who is the proper subject of the Republic of Letters.

Jürgen Habermas's groundbreaking sociological work *The Structural Transformation of the Public Sphere* (1962) defined the invention of a certain kind of publicness as the central event of Enlightenment.[6] If the private spaces of the conjugal family and of commodity exchange (the market) are opposed to the public terrain of the court and the modern state, then the "public sphere" (as Habermas's *Öffentlichkeit* has been translated) refers to a social space that is independent of *both* the private and the public categories of human experience. . . .[7]

As Habermas describes it, the public sphere itself develops out of and remains structurally related to the realm of the private, but the crucial distinction between the two lies in his definition of the public sphere as a zone in which participants leave behind that self-interestedness that necessarily enters into their consideration of matters of production and reproduction. Private individuals come together in the public sphere as citizens employing disinterested reason to consider matters of public concern. The innovativeness, and indeed the optimism, of Habermas's model stands out against other theories of modern publicness. For example, Hannah Arendt claims that the classical distinction between public and private is corrupted by the rise of what she calls the "social," the realm of "housekeeping," as she also tendentiously terms it.[8] The current revaluation of so-called women's work would require us to rethink Arendt's dismissive assessment of this category of experience even had Habermas not mapped out the radical inversion of values that distinguishes classical notions of public and private from those of the Enlightenment. In the Greek model, the private stands as the space of deprivation, against which the public represents the space of freedom for the self. In contrast, in early modern Europe the idea began to take hold that only in the private realm of the af-

fectively organized family did one evolve an "authentic" subjectivity. Now the privileges of privacy were to be defended against the encroachment of the state.

For Habermas, then, the public sphere existed in eighteenth-century Europe as a conceptual space in which reasoning individuals, abstracted from their private interests, arrived at a consensus on public affairs through their discussions, letters, speeches, books, and essays. This free, rational, and disinterested consensus effectively counterbalanced the growing influence of state- and class-based institutions and of conflicting private interest groups until its dissolution under the pressures of market capitalism in the latter part of the nineteenth century.[9]

Habermas does not acknowledge, however, that while the Enlightenment public sphere was ostensibly accessible to every literate human being, it functionally excluded subjects who were not white upper-class males. Here the limitations of *Structural Transformation* can be addressed by incorporating into public sphere theory the central insight of feminist criticism that these categories of human experience were constituted as gendered even as they evolved. Eighteenth-century epistolary fictions, formally and thematically preoccupied with the gendered private body as they are, necessitate the revision of Habermas's model on these grounds.[10]

Of particular importance to literary studies is Habermas's argument that the spread of literacy and the informal practice of amateur literary and art criticism in the salons, coffeehouses, and reading societies of Enlightenment Europe prepared the grounds for the forms of political critique that led to full civic engagement: the Republic of Letters made possible the political republics of the late eighteenth century.[11] Especially in the last decade, critics have begun to explore the extent to which eighteenth-century literature was conscious of its intimate relation to the structures, conventions, and material bases of the public sphere, to the political contexts of liberalism and nationalism as these evolved in the course of the century, and to the new forms of subjectivity, including both the citizen-critic and the private individual, that inhabited these spaces.

From this perspective, however, a problem arises with Habermas's description of the historical trajectory of the public sphere. Although Habermas does not consistently do so, it is both legitimate and essential to distinguish between the public sphere in the world of letters and the public sphere in the political realm. Habermas's failure to distinguish between these two is the more striking in that his own analysis brilliantly shows that precisely this conflation is the foundation of liberal ideology. The emphasis of *Structural Transformation* is in general on the political, whereas my study is focused on the literary; as a result, the two projects propose different chronologies of the public sphere. For Habermas, between the 1770s and the 1870s, "civil society as the private sphere [was] emancipated from the directives of public authority to such an extent that at that time the *political* public sphere could attain its full development in the bourgeois constitutional state," particularly in British parliamentarianism,[12] In contrast, I focus here on the transnational ideal of a *literary* public sphere, formulated in part in epistolary fictions between the 1720s and the 1770s. I am of course concerned with the political resonances implicit in the metaphor of the Republic of Letters, and the last chapter of this work examines the rupture between literary and political public spheres in revolutionary America, but my study remains bounded by the Enlightenment ideal of the public sphere, which could not be accommodated by the nationalist cultures that increasingly shaped political states from around 1775.

Other important differences not discussed by Habermas between the public sphere of letters and the political public sphere appear when public sphere theory is reread from a feminist perspective, as I have already suggested. At the simplest level, one difference is evident in the fact that many individuals who did claim access to a literary public sphere were excluded from the political public sphere under British parliamentarianism and American and French constitutionalism. The full rights of citizenship institutionalized by the Bill of Rights or the Declaration of the Rights of Man were generally limited to white property-owning males and invoked a far less inclusive notion of citizenship than did the model of open access to the domain of reason implicit in the Enlightenment metaphor of the public sphere.

The elision of sex and class in Habermas's early formulation of the public sphere explains the insistence here on the body in print culture. Consider again the example of Lady Bradshaigh's *Clarissa,* described in the Introduction, which simultaneously invokes and resists the model of the citizen-critic's disembodied disinterestedness. Here the gendered private body and its desires, literalized by Bradshaigh's scrawl, are insistently held before our eyes against the publicity and the decorporealization implicit in the printed text. The extended, marginalized letter that is Bradshaigh's impassioned critique makes present by analogy the private letters of Clarissa, Lovelace, the Harlowes, Belford, and Anna that are understood to lie behind the published book and to sustain its public form. Other eighteenth-century letter-narratives manifest the same oscillation between private and public, script and print, which is also implicitly an oscillation between a corporealized, gendered writing subject and the disembodied voice of the citizen-critic.

The eighteenth-century epistolary novel played an important part in the reconfiguration and redefinition of concepts of private and public, for it represents the paradoxical intersection of these apparently opposed orders. Consisting of personal letters, very often those of women, that are brought into the public sphere of print culture, epistolary narratives are necessarily concerned with determining the boundaries of public and private—and with questions of gender and corporealization that are inextricably involved in this definition. Indeed, as I'll argue, the oscillation ex-

emplified in Bradshaigh's *Clarissa* is formally as well as thematically inherent in the genre at this historical moment, in which broad social redefinitions of bodies and subjectivities, and of the spaces that these properly inhabit, are evolving with and against each other in the context of the institutions and material bases of print culture.[13] The modern body-subject, as we might call it—that notion of the self as represented and bounded by the body and what it does and makes—is brought into play in epistolary narratives in particularly rich and complicated ways. Inflecting these are the concepts of public and private, bound up with liberal political theory as it evolved in this period, and such associated notions as publicity, publication, privacy, privilege, and privation. The ways in which eighteenth-century letter narratives deploy this constellation of concepts maps out the definition, contestation, and eventual collapse of the Enlightenment ideal of the public sphere; in this sense, the epistolary narrative is the central cultural form of Enlightenment.[14]

CULTURAL CONTEXTS: THE FATHER AND THE CONTRACT

The death of the Father would deprive literature of many of its pleasures. If there is no longer a Father, why tell stories?

—Roland Barthes, *The Pleasure of the Text*

I have seen the morals of my time, and I have published these letters.

—Jean-Jacques Rousseau, *Julie, ou la nouvelle Héloïse*

The modern outlines of the cultural categories of public and private took shape in the eighteenth century. The concept of publicness is necessarily defined against the complementary notion of the private; like all oppositional pairs, public and private make up a cultural system, a connotational network that with the rise of print culture began to implicate such related ideas as publication and publicity. Among the philosophical and political theories and the sociological and technological developments that affected how these categories were understood, the accelerating growth of print culture around the beginning of the century is especially significant. This is because the Enlightenment ideal of a public sphere was supported by a discursive network of publications: letters, speeches, sermons, treatises, engravings, political cartoons, books, broadsheets, and essays, all widely circulated in print. Together these made up the visible manifestation of the eighteenth-century Republic of Letters.

In what follows, I connect the ideas of public and private implicit in the metaphor of the Republic of Letters with one of the important myths of liberal political theory, a narrative about the origins of the civil state that was most clearly articulated in Great Britain near the end of the seventeenth century, although it had widespread European currency. This myth exposes a key difference between earlier notions of the public/private dichotomy and the predominant eighteenth-century model—a difference having to do with a changing sense of the cultural authority of the father.

The narrative goes something like this. For centuries, Western political theory assumed an analogy between paternal authority and that of the ruler and assimilated all power relations to this model. This conventional analogy was strengthened in seventeenth-century absolutist political theory, which assigned to the ruler a power over his subjects as innate and as complete as that of the patriarchal father over his child. Since paternal and political power were analogous, the Father-King was understood to be divinely ordained to rule both as political authority and as head of the family constituted by his people.

In direct opposition to this idea, Enlightenment contractarian theory denied the patriarchal justification of political power.[15] As opposed to the assumption of continuity implicit in patriarchal political theory, which imagined no transformation of the basic structure of authority from the origins of mankind to the present, the story of civil origins told by contractarian theory assumed a foundational discontinuity. According to this narrative, the civil state brought into being by the social contract originated in a rupture of the father's patriarchal authority (through his death or replacement). In the ensuing structural reconfiguration, his sons entered into relatively egalitarian contractual relations with one another as brothers. Locke, for example, acknowledges that while patriarchal rule was undoubtedly the general form of government in earliest times, when the "natural" and customary rule of the father was tacitly accepted by members of an extended family, nonetheless a social contract and the civil society that is its product emerged when patriarchal authority was disrupted, by death or otherwise: "But when either the Father died, and left his next Heir for want of Age, Wisdom, Courage, or any other Qualities, less fit for Rule: or where several Families met, and consented to continue together: There, 'tis not to be doubted, but they used their natural freedom, to set up him, whom they judged the ablest, and most likely to Rule well over them."[16]

Contractarian theory's disruptive narrative of the origins of civil society has crucial implications for the Enlightenment model of public and private that concerns us here, for it implies the decentering of the paternal role—or, to use Barthes's phrase, the death of the Father. Because the patriarchal Father-King structurally united the domains of government and the family, the dislocation of this figure meant that the political (public) and domestic (private) spheres once conjoined by the body of the patriarch split apart into differentiated domains of human experience, each of which had now to be separately regulated. The fiction of the social contract addresses only the *public* domain: the contract organizes the political relations of the brothers and produces the civil state, but it does not govern the private domain of the family. Enlightenment political theory provided no comparable fiction to order the family's relations, which were understood to be affectively rather than politically grounded.[17] As a result, the emergent domain of private experience, no longer controlled by a larger, unifying social structure, could now be perceived as dangerously unregulated.

In direct contradiction to Barthes's (perhaps ironic) suggestion that narrative is pointless in the absence of the Father, I propose that in fact the telling of stories became much more important after the demise of the authority structures implicit in a patriarchal epistemology. In the extended cultural transition of the late seventeenth and early eighteenth centuries, the institutions of print culture generally and individual works of literature in particular can be understood as efforts to explain and compensate for the effects of the death of the Father. In particular, the question of how to harness what were now seen as the private energies and appetites of individual men and women was answered not by political theorists but by writers of fiction: the novel, and particularly the epistolary novel, developed as a direct response to a new anxiety about the private at the very heart of the Enlightenment. The private sphere of affective relations required an ordering principle analogous to the social contract that ordered the public, civic domain. Just as the social contract produced citizens of political republics, then, the literary contract of the epistolary novel invented and regulated the post-patriarchal private subject as a citizen of the Republic of Letters.

THE EPISTOLARY CONTRACT: EIGHTEENTH-CENTURY LETTERS

Genres are essentially literary *institutions* or social contracts between a writer and a specific public, whose function is to specify the proper use of a particular cultural artifact.

—Fredric Jameson, *The Political Unconscious*

What was the "proper use" of an epistolary narrative in the eighteenth century? The claim I make about the cultural role of letter-fictions will be more readily accepted if both the epistomological status and something of the discursive range of the letter in eighteenth-century writing are established—if, that is, we specify some aspects of the contract in which Enlightenment readers understood themselves to be participating as they read an epistolary narrative.

The letter as such carried two contradictory sets of connotations in this period. On the one hand, it was considered the most direct, sincere, and transparent form of written communication, a notion expressed in the title of Thomas Forde's early letter-collection *Foenestra in pectore, or, Familiar Letters* (Window in the breast, or . . . ; 1660). The same idea is exploited in Lovelace's phony etymology of *correspondence:* "writing from the heart (without the fetters prescribed by method or study)." It also appears in Dr. Johnson's often-cited remark that "a man's letters . . . are only the mirror of his breast." But the letter was simultaneously recognized as the most playful and potentially deceptive of forms, as a stage for rhetorical trickery, the "calm and deliberate performance" that Johnson, reviewing the scandal over the publication of Pope's correspondence, describes in his *Life of Pope* (1779).[18]

True to this epistemological ambiguity, in the eighteenth century the letter-form was used in every kind of writing, from scientific treatises to novels, from conduct books to political essays, as well as in exchanges between ordinary people facilitated by the development of postal institutions across Europe.[19] The ways in which the letter saturated Enlightenment culture make it clear that studies of eighteenth-century epistolarity must begin by rejecting an anachronistic distinction between literatures of fact and fiction.[20] While this dichotomy has become a basic principle of our textual taxonomies, a brief examination of various published uses of the letter in the eighteenth century shows no consistent distinction between "real" and "fictional" letters. Aside from the epistolary novel per se, there were poetical epistles, letters on botany, and monthly newsletters on literature, fashion, and business conditions. Such periodicals as the *Gentleman's Magazine* and Henry Fielding's *Covent-Garden Journal* might be largely made up of letters, often generated by the editor to evoke the impression of a community of readers.[21] There were travel letters, letter-writing manuals, and letters "from the dead to the living." There were editions of the letters of classical authors and of a few modern political and literary figures, though it was not yet considered acceptable to publish one's own correspondence during one's life.[22] Particularly toward the end of the century, letters became identified with a radical political agenda; published letters appeared under such titles as "An Open Letter to the People of England," and anonymous unpublished letters threatened landlords with fire and destruction.[23]

The implications of what I've characterized as the letter-form's ontological ambiguity become clearer when we consider this form's importance in Enlightenment scientific discourse. The letter's contemporary connotations of directness, transparency, and sociability made it arguably the crucial genre of the New Science, for where the tendency of classical and Renaissance natural philosophy had been to devise elaborate universal systems that had to be explained in book-length treatises, the empirical New Science emphasized the proposition and affirmation of limited hypotheses and specific facts. The letter encouraged the swift dissemination of discrete chunks of information such as accounts of individual experiments. Letters could be easily transmitted across national borders, escaping the kinds of censorship imposed on full-length books; they could be rapidly translated into the variety of national languages in which the New Science was now being discussed; and they could be swiftly and inexpensively printed and widely distributed.[24]

Furthermore, the letter-form encouraged the participation of nonspecialists in scientific endeavors. The correspondence columns of general-interest journals often contained letters on natural history observations or mathematical questions, and submissions to *Philosophical Transactions,* the journal of the Royal Society, appeared as letters. Under the rubric of epistolary sociability, the correspondence published by these journals composed a scientific community that linked rural subscribers with city dwellers and amateurs with experts.

Book-length scientific works used the letter for similar reasons, and here we begin to see how the implied authenticity of the letter-form, reinforced by its documentary function in the New Science, tended to blur the boundaries, not yet firmly established in the early eighteenth century, between fact and fiction. Arthur Young's *The Farmer's Letters to the People of England* (1768) recommended the practical agricultural innovations generated by Enlightenment science through the proto-persona of an educated farmer. Gilbert White's *Natural History and Antiquities of Selborne* (1789), presented as an orderly series of letters, was actually patched together from a variety of sources: formal essays composed for the Royal Society, entries made over a period of thirty years in White's garden note-books and natural-history journals, and scraps of actual correspondence dating back to midcentury. Daniel Defoe's *The Storm* (1704), a survey of the effects of the previous year's disastrous tempest, combined real letters from correspondents all over Great Britain with supplementary "letters" written by himself under a variety of pseudonyms to round out the report. Its subtitle makes explicit its documentary claim: *A Collection of the most remarkable casualties and disasters, which happen'd in the late dreadful tempest, both by sea and land, on Friday the twenty-sixth of November, seventeen hundred and three.* However, the lengthy, vehement insistence of its preface on the literal authenticity of the letters suggests that readers were deeply suspicious of that authenticity.

These examples of ontological ambiguity are related to the notorious blurring of fact and fiction in what we would now classify as properly literary epistolary works, such as the early editions of Samuel Richardson's letter-novels. Although the prefatory material of *Pamela* (1740) claims that the text is based on real letters, both the plot and the epistolary form of this novel grew out of an explicitly didactic model-letter manual Richardson was writing. The ontological confusion expands with his later epistolary novels, *Clarissa* (1747-48) and *Sir Charles Grandison* (1754): each of these generated extended written exchanges among Richardson's circle of correspondents, who offered advice on the work in progress, detailed their responses to events and characters in the novel, transcribed into their own correspondence useful moral apothegms distilled from the fictional letters, and occasionally wrote as though they were themselves those characters.[25]

The letter continued to inhabit an indeterminate space between fact and fiction to the end of the century, and this indeterminacy came to be recognized as a characteristic of the genre. Notoriously, both Rousseau in the second preface to *Julie, ou la nouvelle Héloïse* (1761) and Choderlos de Laclos in the Publisher's Note and Editor's Preface to *Les Liaisons dangereuses* (1782) ironize the trope of the "real" letter-collection, completing the genre's ontological destabilization. Crèvecoeur's *Letters from an American Farmer* (1782) . . . amalgamates a rich mixture of narrative genres, from the documentary travel account to political allegory disguised as authentic natural history observations to historical and ethnographic anecdotes, framed as an exchange of letters between a simple, ill-educated frontier farmer and a rich and cultured European gentleman.

In the face of such generic variety, the question of whether Crèvecoeur's *Letters* is "fact" or "fiction" has little pertinence. Although I do not make precisely the same assertion about *Pamela* or the *Liaisons dangereuses,* I do suggest that viewing the genre as a continuous spectrum that runs from, say, *Selborne* at one end to *Clarissa* and *Julie* at the other will result in a much richer and more historically accurate understanding of it. In short, I am arguing that, contrary to what is implied by the title of one important modern study of the genre, epistolary narratives are not simply stories "told in letters."[26] Because of their intimate relation to the contexts of print culture, and because of their ontological ambiguity, letter-fictions require a critical apparatus specifically adapted to their formal and thematic idiosyncrasies. In the remainder of this chapter, I define a critical *epistolarity* to take the place of traditional approaches to epistolary literature.

THE HISTORY OF EPISTOLARY CRITICISM: PROBLEMS OF GENEALOGY

The need for such a critical apparatus has not always been recognized. Too often, epistolary criticism has been based on assumptions about the genealogies of letter-narratives that distort their contexts, or on anachronistic premises that ignore the contemporary significance of the form or assimilate it to third-person narrative. Surveys of the eighteenth-century novel, for example, often discuss epistolary narrative only as a kind of subplot or parenthesis in the "development" of prose fiction. For the last three decades, accounts of that development have been heavily influenced by Ian Watt's *Rise of the Novel* (1957). Declaring the novel of "realism" to be the dominant prose-fiction tradition, Watt traces an evolution from Defoe through Richardson, who holds "the central place in the development of the technique of narrative realism," on to Austen and so through to the great nineteenth-century novelists. Left to languish as cul-de-sacs of this evolutionary model are not only the "stylistic virtues" of Fielding and those British novelists who follow his "external" approach to character but also, even more sweepingly, all of "French fiction from *La Princesse de Clèves* to *Les Liaisons dangereuses,*" which, according to Watt, "we feel" to be "too stylish to be authentic."[27]

Watt's teleological model of literary development continues to shape recent studies of the novel, even those that recognize the pit-falls of reading eighteenth-century novels as the imperfect precursors of nineteenth-century works. Michael McKeon's magisterial *The Origins of the English Novel, 1660-1740* (1987) explicitly positions itself as a revision of Watt's study, redefining the nature and function of literary genres dialectically rather than teleologically. Certainly, McKeon's approach offers a more intricate understanding of the relation between literary works and social contexts than does Watt's model of simple analogy between philosophical and literary "realisms," and further-

more it provides an explanation of the naturalization of the novel form that does not rely on a retrospective view from Austen's parlor window. Although McKeon begins by surveying a wide range of pre-eighteenth-century prose narratives crucial to the formation of the genre, however, the extended close readings making up the latter part of his book are devoted to British authors already certified as canonical by the academic culture industry: after Cervantes, Bunyan, and Swift comes the triad of Defoe, Richardson, and Fielding discussed by Watt. One is left to infer that "the novel" before 1740 was exclusively the product of these writers, for the implications of this selection of authors is not discussed.[28]

Even as professedly radical a rereading of the diachronic development of the genre as Nancy Armstrong's *Desire and Domestic Fiction: A Political History of the Novel* follows Watt's canonical lead. The elision that occurs between Armstrong's title and her subtitle, by means of which "domestic fiction" implicitly comes to stand for "novel," exemplifies one of the governing critical assumptions about eighteenth-century prose fiction that is problematic in epistolary criticism. Like Watt and McKeon, Armstrong opens her study with a survey of certain extra-canonical nonfiction prose forms that help shape the novel—in this case eighteenth- and nineteenth-century conduct books. Again, like Watt's and McKeon's, her close readings are devoted to a very traditional group of British authors: Richardson, Austen, and the Brontës. Her chapter on *Pamela* borrows Watt's title, "The Rise of the Novel," without distinguishing her own project from the teleological account of the earlier study.

The juxtaposition of extraliterary discourses with canonical fictions—a strategy that New Historicist critics have employed very effectively—can be a way of challenging the authority of a literary canon. It is particularly useful insofar as that authority has been assumed to derive from an autonomous, ahistorical, and pancultural sphere of literary values that has little or nothing to do with social and political contexts. While challenging the principles by which canonical *inclusion* is legitimated, however, such a critical practice often ignores the category of literary works that have been *excluded.* In the case of prose-fiction criticism, the story of the "rise of the novel" still centers almost exclusively on the novels of private life, those drawing on the thematic material of the family, sex, and marriage that is central to what could be called (conflating Watt's and Armstrong's terms) the "realist-domestic novel." Such a reading presents Samuel Richardson as the ancestor of the novel of private life that is at last perfected in the nineteenth century, rather than as one among a group of eighteenth-century authors who explore the thematic and generic possibilities of the epistolary form in the specific cultural contexts of the Enlightenment Republic of Letters. In contrast, the critical perspective proposed by this study takes Richardson as, among other things, Montesquieu's successor, rather than as merely Austen's precursor.

Along with retrospective constructions of the genre's genealogy, traditional epistolary criticism has essentialized its gender. Since the late seventeenth century, when the astounding popularity of the anonymous *Lettres portugaises* (1669) was followed by equally popular vernacular translations of the correspondence of Heloise and Abelard, the epistolary genre has been particularly identified with women and with what are often seen as women's concerns. The critical valence of the genre so defined is grounded in a complex ideological arrangement that valorizes "authenticity" and "sincerity" in women's writing, most frequently coded as the ostensibly natural expression of passionate emotion, the model for which can be found in Ovid's *Heroïdes* and Heloise's letters.[29] Despite this more or less respectable ancestry, such values are in many ways at odds with the ideology of professional authorship that came into being with the rise of print culture. Thus epistolary works matching this profile were relegated by generations of professional critics to the second ranks of "literature"—or were simply forgotten.

Beginning in the 1970s, however, literary scholars "rediscovered" epistolary fiction and began to work out critical approaches under two different rubrics that took into account its formal and thematic specificities. On the one hand, feminist criticism exposed the cultural construction of the hierarchies of gender and genre that structure letter-narratives and their reception, and reopened the question of sociohistorical contexts; on the other, the attention of deconstructionist criticism to thematizations of textuality in literary works made accessible a crucial preoccupation of eighteenth-century letter-narratives. The salient example is Jacques Derrida's *La carte postale: de Socrate à Freud et au delà* (1980), an exploration of what might be called the sublime of epistolary poetics. *The Post Card* provides what was for a while the epigraph *de rigueur* for studies of the epistolary genre: "the letter, the epistle, which is not a genre but all genres, literature itself."[30] Appearing on what seems to be the terminal cusp of print culture, Derrida's monologic epistolary text redeploys every trick in the Scriblerian/Sterneian repertoire of typographical puns, from intrusive footnotes to textual gaps of the "hic multa desiderantur" variety. The letter-writer muses on travel, telephoning, and translation; on the history of postal institutions; and on Poe's, Freud's, and Heidegger's relations to epistolary intercourse. A thinnish subplot even works in the generic motif of the missing love letter. But these allusions remain superficial; Derrida's real interest is the perverse textual relation between Plato and Socrates at the heart of Western culture that is exposed on the eponymous postcard. As the phrase cited above indicates, Derrida here uses the letter as a trope for all writing. In contrast, my interest is precisely to distinguish the letter from other literary genres—to define its epistolarity—within Enlightenment print culture.

While feminist criticism and deconstruction made epistolary narratives legible again, they sometimes did so by simply inverting the hierarchy of values that formerly marginalized the epistolary novel, producing similarly limited definitions of the genre. Consider the critical history of Montesquieu's *Lettres persanes* (1721) as a case study. Scholarship on the *Lettres persanes* has perennially focused on the question of genre. For many years, the work was studied primarily by intellectual historians and students of political philosophy as a kind of warm-up act for the *Esprit des lois* (1748). From this perspective, those letters that set up the project of cultural critique by comparing forms of governments or demystifying the origins of customs and religions had the greatest value. Letters relating to the harem, to the sexual pleasures and frustrations of Usbek, his wives, and his eunuchs, were dismissed as superficial vestiges of contemporary rococo eroticism. This material merely veiled what was assumed to be Montesquieu's serious purpose, a liberal indictment of French absolutism. Even when the harem material was read as political allegory, the subordination of literary form to intellectual content remained the same.

Eventually the *Lettres persanes* was claimed by literary critics, who tended to reverse the emphasis of social scientists by focusing almost exclusively on the harem material. These critics sought a unity in the text that would allow its categorization as a novel, and they found it in the story of the harem's collapse. The other hundred and thirty-odd letters, those on comparative religion, depopulation, Parisian customs, notions of justice, and so forth, become obfuscatory secondary material that simply defers the story of sexual passion at the text's heart.[31]

This way of reading the *Lettres persanes* is intended, of course, to rescue it from a scholarship that subordinates literary form to philosophical content, but it generates its own problems. Specifically, when the epistolary genre is seen as limited to the sentimental epistolary plot of feminine passion, the exclusive identification of women and letters reaffirms essentialist concepts of gender and sexuality, as well as replicating an artificial division of human experience into separate and gendered public and private spheres. Such a confusion of classificatory principles can only further obscure our understanding of the interrelation of gender and genre, and our awareness of the cultural construction of both.[32]

As these summaries suggest, the contrasting approaches to the *Lettres persanes* of historians and literary critics share a structural feature: both treat those letters that emanate from and return to the harem as fundamentally different from the letters associated with the project of cultural critique. The distinction seems to result from assumptions about the gendering of discourses: when the *Lettres persanes* is classified as political philosophy, its novelistic or literary aspects may be ignored on the assumption that a literary genre linked to "feminine" values will not be relevant to a "masculine" political discourse. On the other hand, when the *Lettres persanes* is treated as a forerunner of the "domestic-realist" novel, its satirical and political elements are erased, for the plot of feminine passion is held to belong to a private sphere of human experience that excludes political and philosophical issues.

Thus, as long as gender is assumed to be the primary analytical category for reading the *Lettres persanes,* we will necessarily reproduce variations of the gendered dichotomies that split the text apart unsatisfyingly. In contrast, as the next chapter argues, when the network of issues implicit in eighteenth-century notions of public and private is taken as an organizing principle of the *Lettres persanes,* the legibility and coherence of Montesquieu's text is uncovered on its own terms, and its central importance in a reconstructed epistolary tradition becomes clear. Such a reading, which recognizes that gender is necessarily implicated in other cultural categories, also opens up more generically stable epistolary works, as we will see with *Clarissa.*

MARGINS AND FRAMES: PRINT CULTURE AND THE STORY OF THE LETTERS

> All margins are dangerous. If they are pulled this way or that, the shape of fundamental experience is altered. Any structure of ideas is vulnerable at its margins.
>
> —Mary Douglas, *Purity and Danger*

Each of the following chapters is devoted to an eighteenth-century letter-narrative that challenges the boundaries of the epistolary genre and reconstructs it in important ways. My investigation of these fictions is shaped by their engagement with the technological and sociological contexts of the Republic of Letters. My central concern with print culture has to do with certain features of contemporary texts that are often overlooked: the material that frames the body of the letter-narrative, where the editorial apparatus offers the (fictional or actual) history of the letters' transformation from private documents into published texts.[33] This strategic relocation of editorial frame to textual center works to defamiliarize these products of an earlier, transitional moment of print culture. Thus we read them not only as the private histories of individuals like ourselves, recorded by hand on scraps of paper and then ushered into the public world of print by an authoritative editor, but also, to some extent, as allegories of the Republic of Letters: stories about putting private life into publication that were written before this came to seem the "natural" way of telling stories.

I examine here what these works have in common as eighteenth-century epistolary narratives, linked by the thematics of publication and privacy. To that extent this study is an attempt to rewrite our definition of the genre as a whole through Enlightenment print culture. It is also, however, an examination of the contestations and reformulations of generic boundaries by four particular texts that claim very different relations to the Anglo-European public sphere, each of which represents an important contestation of the Republic of Letters. Thus this study also surveys the transformation of the epistolary genre over the course of the century as the generic contract is rewritten by historical contexts.

On the model of the abandoned lover's epistolary complaint established by the *Heroïdes,* writing a letter can be understood as the attempt to construct a phantasmatic body that in some measure compensates for the writer's absence. In this sense, the body is always central to the letter-narrative. As the following chapters will make clear, that body will be imagined differently, not only for different rhetorical purposes, but also at different historical moments. In this sense, Montesquieu's *Lettres persanes* represents a radical construction project: the creation of a masculine citizen-critic from within the symbolic field of early eighteenth-century French absolutism. Bringing together the registers of political power, gender, and publication, Montesquieu seeks to produce simultaneously the discourse of citizenship (the public sphere) and a properly male subject. The desired result appears in the distinction between a collection of letters and a published book. On the one hand, the Persians' letters describe the collapse of erotic relations; their epistolary strategies fail adequately to represent the absent phallus and instead disseminate only the various figures of lack that haunt the text. On the other hand, . . . the *Lettres persanes* itself successfully stages an antiabsolutist reconstruction of gender and power relations by helping to define the Enlightenment ideals of the public sphere and of the citizen-critics who inhabit it.

Montesquieu's second preface to the *Lettres persanes,* written 33 years later, makes it clear that the generic identity of the epistolary narrative was redefined by midcentury, following the success of the Richardsonian sentimental epistolary novel. Despite this rewriting of the generic contract, the material institutions of the Republic of Letters—the printing press, the post office, the periodical—remain the necessary contexts of epistolary narrative throughout the century, and so too the tradition of cultural and political critique associated with earlier epistolary narratives like Montesquieu's remains present in sentimental epistolary fictions of feminine passion. My juxtaposition of the picaresque-epistolary *Lettres persanes* with Samuel Richardson's sentimental-epistolary *Clarissa* (1747-48) . . . is intended to restore to view the full generic identity of the epistolary novel. Resituating *Clarissa* within the extended generic tradition, we are able to perceive that Richardson transformed and redeployed certain features of an already well-established genre and that he redefined the implications for society and literature of the idea of the Republic of Letters. If Montesquieu's answer to the Enlightenment conflict between private passion and public order is the creation of (male) citizens of the Republic of Letters, Richardson's relation to the democratizing effects of print culture is less straightforward and implies an alternative gendering of the epistolary body.

The uneasy accord between public and private worked out in *Clarissa* is complicated by Richardson's ambivalences, first, about his own relation as a printer and novelist to literary tradition and, second, about what he found to be the exceedingly difficult question of women's place in the public sphere. These vexed issues come to the fore in the debate over Clarissa's allegorical "father's house" letter. The Christian heroine's final explanation of her sufferings, "GOD ALMIGHTY WOULD NOT LET ME DEPEND FOR COMFORT UPON

ANY BUT HIMSELF," can also be read as Richardson's solution to the dangerous separation of public and private spheres. By means of his manipulation of the relation between epistolary text and editorial frame, a version of patriarchal authority undermined by Montesquieu is reaffirmed in secular novelistic form through the figure of the author-editor who appropriates, fragments, and disseminates private letters as a branch of public morality. Like Clarissa's God, Richardson is reluctant to permit his readers to depend for epistemological and moral certainty upon any but himself.

Marie-Jeanne Riccoboni's *Les Lettres de Mistriss Fanni Butlerd* (1757) . . . frames similar issues very differently. Drawing explicitly on Enlightenment political theory, as well as implicitly on her own experience as a professional actress, Riccoboni's novel provides an analysis of how the concept of the private enables men's exploitation of women. *Fanni Butlerd* shatters the sentimental epistolary convention according to which the private letters of women are (re)authorized by male editors. In her letters to her aristocratic lover, the young Englishwoman Fanni refuses the agonistic model of sexual relations in which men conquer women and insists on her free decision to give herself to her beloved. In precisely the same way, she refuses the exploitational implications of the sentimental epistolary tradition, from the *Lettres portugaises* to Richardson's novels. After being abandoned by her lover, Fanni transforms herself from private victim to public author by publishing her own letters, first in a newspaper, then as a book.

In so doing, Fanni removes the epistolary tradition from the hermetic privacy of the convent and the boudoir to what the French (and many English) idealized as the wide-open spaces of the English press. Converting a dangerous private passion into the public denunciation of social corruption through the Enlightenment technology of print, Fanni establishes a literary contract between herself and her readers by means of which sympathy of taste will reform society, producing not only more just and equal relations between the sexes but also model citizen-readers, both male and female, of the novel. In contrast to the *Lettres persanes* and *Clarissa,* both the publication history of this novel and its fictionalized frame imply the possibility of full female citizenship in the Republic of Letters. In this sense, *Fanni Butlerd* is an optimistic—and feminist—parable of the rise of the public sphere in a mass print culture.

Riccoboni's optimism did not, of course, bring about the egalitarian transformation of Anglo-European societies. The ideal of the Republic of Letters came into general question under the political pressures of the 1770s and 1780s, to be generally discredited in the 1790s through its identification with political radicalism.[34] Because a founding principle of the public sphere is that of the participants' disinterestedness and non-factionalism, such an identification necessarily meant the end of its emancipatory potential as a cultural concept.

The trajectory of the loss of an Enlightenment faith in correspondence can be traced in Crèvecoeur's *Letters from an American Farmer* (1782), which I read . . . as a narrative of the decline of the Republic of Letters under the pressures of a developing nationalism that replaces the cosmopolitanism of the older ideal. The politically masculine (but ostensibly disembodied) citizen-critic constructed by Montesquieu, uneasily set aside by Richardson, and triumphantly redefined as female by Riccoboni returns in Crèvecoeur's *Letters* to a problematic corporeality that clashes with the requirements of disembodiment and anonymity necessary to citizenship in the Republic of Letters. The rupture of correspondence at the close of *Letters from an American Farmer* marks not only the end of the Enlightenment ideal of a cosmopolitan civic exchange but also the end of Enlightenment epistolarity.

Notes

1. Foucault, "What Is an Author?" p. 108.

2. Ibid., p. 117.

3. This use of the adjective "private" often masks the long ideological collaboration between an ostensibly individualistic "exploring spirit" and more or less officially sponsored economic imperialism, the profound entanglement of so-called private and public motives that underwrote, for example, the history of the East India Company. For a synopsis of the various ways in which economic activity has been classified in relation to the public-private dichotomy, see Jeff Weintraub's "The Theory and Politics of the Public/Private Distinction," excerpted in Bruce Robbins's "Introduction" to *The Phantom Public Sphere,* p. xiii.

4. The term is Janet Gurkin Altman's; she defines it as "the pressure exerted by form upon meaning" (*Epistolarity,* p. 189).

5. The metaphor of the Republic of Letters is of course much older than the eighteenth century, but I am concerned here with its Enlightenment connotations, inflected by the proliferation of print (although such non-written discursive exchanges as speeches, sermons, and public rituals are also relevant to it). A study of eighteenth-century European uses of the ideal might begin with Pierre Bayle's *Dictionnaire Historique et Critique* (1695) and extend through Kant's *Was ist Aufklärung?* (1794); my investigation concerns the appropriation of the term by "polite literature."

6. The full text of Habermas's work, originally published in 1962 as *Strukturwandel der Öffentlichkeit,* was not translated into English until 1989. His models reached non-German-reading scholars earlier through several channels: a French translation appeared in 1978, and selections in English were published in *New German Critique* in the 1970s and 1980s.

7. This graphic representation may have encouraged reductionist readings of Habermas's theory, which

does not propose a static, constant relation between these spaces but traces their dialectical development. Dena Goodman discusses slight differences between the diagrams in the German and English editions that may affect their interpretation in her article "Public Sphere and Private Life."

8. I find the metaphor of housekeeping very suggestive in relation to the question of the citizen-critic's gender. See Arendt, *The Human Condition,* p. 38. Although Habermas revalorizes the private, he, like Arendt, echoes the Frankfurt School view that the rise of mass culture destroys the emancipatory political potential of Enlightenment publicness. Peter Uwe Hohendahl's *Institution of Criticism* surveys important critiques of Habermas's work from the 1960s and 1970s, including those of Peter Glotz, Oskar Negt and Alexander Kluge, Wolfgang Jäger, and Niklas Luhmann. Richard Sennett's use of Habermasian public-sphere theory in *The Fall of Public Man* tends to generalize, even romanticize, and thus distort issues that Habermas treats more carefully. The essays in Craig Calhoun's *Habermas and the Public Sphere* and in Bruce Robbins's *The Phantom Public Sphere* have suggested other ways of rethinking, refining, and developing Habermas's models. I find particularly valuable Nancy Fraser's analyses of Habermas's disregard of questions of gender and Michael Warner's emphasis on the significance of anonymity and disembodiment in the public sphere. See Habermas's comments on these and other critiques in "Further Reflections on the Public Sphere," in Calhoun, ed., *Habermas.* Despite its flaws, Habermas's book has proved to be, as Calhoun asserts in *Habermas,* "an immensely fruitful generator of new research, analysis, and theory" (p. 41).

9. A related focus on the role of Enlightenment criticism is found in Reinhart Koselleck's *Critique and Crisis.* The distinctions between Koselleck's negative reading of the Enlightenment politicization of criticism and Habermas's celebration of that development are analyzed by Goodman in "Public Sphere and Private Life."

10. Here my study joins an existing body of feminist theory and criticism on the public sphere. Important examples include Joan Landes's *Women and the Public Sphere in the Age of the French Revolution* and Nancy Fraser's essays "What's Critical About Critical Theory?" and "Rethinking the Public Sphere."

11. Henry Fielding's *Covent-Garden Journal* illustrates the contemporary currency of the metaphor of the Republic of Letters in the field of polite literature. In a recurring column headed "A Journal of the Present War Between the Forces Under Sir Alexander Drawcansir, and the Army of Grub-Street," Fielding attributes "the present dreadful condition of the great Empire of Letters" to the corruption of critical standards. In the first two

numbers, the "Journal of the Present War" describes skirmishes in and around the various coffee-houses and theaters of London; in the third number, it reproduces a treaty between Sir Alexander and "their Lownesses the Republic of Grub-Street." The treaty establishes Sir Alexander's Court of Censorial Inquiry and assigns it the right "to hear, and determine, all manner of Causes, which in anywise relate to the Republic of Letters." Subsequent issues offer critical reviews in the guise of court hearings and letters to the Censor ostensibly from readers. See *The Covent-Garden Journal,* pp. 39, 45.

12. Habermas, *Structural Transformation,* p. 79, my emphasis.

13. In *Desire and Domestic Fiction,* Nancy Armstrong describes how sexual desire, and more generally subjectivity itself, is constructed in the "domestic novel" as a domain of experience wholly separate from the political. While our projects intersect at several points, I argue that an exclusive focus on the "domestic novel" produces an inadequate understanding of the epistolary genre.

14. I am proposing that the letter is the "symbolic form" of the Enlightenment, as Panofsky takes perspective to be for the Renaissance. See Erwin Panofsky, *Perspective as Symbolic Form.*

15. These positions are respectively expressed in Sir Robert Filmer's *Patriarcha* (1680) and John Locke's *Second Treatise of Government* (1689). Because my interest here is in linking political and literary ways of making social order rather than in rehearsing an argument in political philosophy, and because my claim is about competing cultural mythologies rather than about the specific influence of any one text or individual, I will not review here the debate over the relation between the Glorious Revolution and contractarian theory claimed by Whig readings of history. See Peter Laslett's extensive introduction to his edition of *Two Treatises of Government,* and J. C. D. Clark's revisionist discussion in *English Society 1688-1832,* pp. 44-59.

16. Locke, *Two Treatises of Government,* p. 381.

17. My discussion of the social contract is indebted to Carole Pateman's extremely suggestive analysis of the ideology of liberal contractarian theory. Pateman describes, behind and prior to the fiction of the social contract, a hidden sexual contract. Women, exchanged between males to symbolize and seal homosocial relations, are not parties *to* this sexual contract, but instead are the objects *of* it. Though political theorists have traditionally assumed that patriarchal power is eliminated by modern contractual society, Pateman argues that it is simply reorganized: a modern, fraternal, and contractual version of (sexual) patriarchal power continues to operate in the private sphere of the family, a realm excluded from the civil contract. See *The Sexual Contract,* especially chapter 4.

18. In Chapter 3, I show that the context of Johnson's remark makes clear that it was intended ironically. See the full text of his letter to Mrs. Thrale, dated Oct. 27, 1777, in *Letters,* pp. 89-90. For Lovelace's remark, see *Clarissa,* vol. 2, p. 431. The passage from the *Life of Pope* appears on p. 207 of the *Lives of the Poets.*

19. For accounts of these institutions in Great Britain and Europe, see Howard Robinson's *The British Post Office* and Kenneth Ellis's *The Post Office in the Eighteenth Century.*

20. On the development and institutionalization of this distinction, see Lennard Davis's *Factual Fictions.*

21. On how the periodicals constructed a certain type of eighteenth-century reader in part through such letters, see Jon P. Klancher's *The Making of English Reading Audiences, 1790-1832,* pp. 18-26.

22. In the *Life of Pope,* Johnson emphasizes the novelty of Pope's correspondence having been published. The only English precedents, he claims, are the (posthumous) letter collections of Howell, Loveday, Herbert, Suckling, and "Orinda" (Katherine Philips).

23. E. P. Thompson discusses the latter in "The Crime of Anonymity," as does Mary A. Favret in *Romantic Correspondence.*

24. For example, Sir Isaac Newton's physico-theological letters to Dr. Richard Bentley, arguing the existence of God from the structure and function of the creation, were cheaply and widely available in pamphlet form and were reprinted through much of the century. The role of letters in the New Science is sketched in Daniel J. Boorstin's *The Discoverers,* pp. 387-93.

25. This intertwining of fictional and nonfictional correspondence has a posthumous phase: some of these letters were eventually published along with Richardson's own in a hagiographic six-volume edition of his correspondence edited by Anna Laetitia Barbauld in 1804; an example is discussed in more detail in Chapter 3. Discussing a related kind of ontological confusion, Madeleine Kahn analyzes Richardson's own habit of "quoting [his characters'] views to reinforce his stated opinions, as if he had not also penned the text from which he now cites as from some unimpeachable source" (*Narrative Transvestism,* p. 118).

26. I refer to Robert Adams Day's *Told in Letters: Epistolary Fiction Before Richardson.*

27. Watt, *The Rise of the Novel,* pp. 26, 291, 30.

28. Despite his explicit disagreement with Watt's linearity, McKeon nonetheless refers in his conclusion to a "climax" of "the origins of the English novel" (*Origins,* p. 410). The unusual syntactic awkwardness perhaps marks his discomfort at reverting momentarily to a model he has explicitly disowned, and suggests the power of the teleological paradigm in our thinking about literary history. Surprisingly in such a consciously self-reflexive work of criticism, the word "canon" does not appear in McKeon's index.

29. On the publication and reception history of the *Lettres portugaises,* see excellent complementary essays by Peggy Kamuf and Nancy K. Miller, respectively: "Writing Like a Woman" and "'I's' in Drag: The Sex of Recollection." Both are exquisitely aware of the ironies implicit in the present-day attribution of the *Lettres portugaises* to Gabriel de Lavergne de Guilleragues, a minor literary figure and diplomat. The Heloise-Abelard letters were published in French in 1695 and in English in 1714; Latin versions and partial translations circulated from the thirteenth century on. Their publication and critical history from the twelfth century to the present are discussed in Linda S. Kauffman's *Discourses of Desire,* pp. 84-89. Kauffman's study surveys the "Heroïdean" epistolary type, linking women, love, and letters, from Ovid to the "three Marias" (Barreño, Horta, and Velho da Costa) who co-authored the *New Portuguese Letters* (1971). While she is sensitive to the larger political implications of Heroïdean epistolary poetics, Kauffman does not relate these to the historically specific contexts of Enlightenment print culture. Ruth Perry's *Women, Letters, and the Novel* examines social, economic, and psychological reasons for the identification of the letter-novel with aspects of female experience in the seventeenth and eighteenth centuries.

30. Derrida, *The Post Card,* p. 48. Some of the implications of the transformation from a culture of print to one of telecommunications are traced in Friedrich Kittler's *Discourse Networks 1800/1900* and Avital Ronell's *The Telephone Book.* Consider also Nicholson Baker's telephone-sex novel *Vox.* Beyond *Vox,* which is after all still a book, lies the brave new world of such digitalized sexual/conceptual prostheses as "Virtual Valerie."

31. The major trends in this history are summarized in the opening paragraphs of Alan J. Singerman's "Réflexions sur une métaphore." As examples of unifying readings, see the essays of Roger Laufer, "La Réussite romanesque," and Pierre Testud, "*Les Lettres persanes,* roman épistolaire." Paul Valéry's essay on the *Lettres persanes* appears in *Variétés II* (Paris, 1930), p. 71. On the eunuch, see, e.g., Aram Vartanian's "Eroticism and Politics in the *Lettres persanes*" and Michel Delon's "Un Monde d'eunuques." Among feminist readings, Suzanne Rodin Pucci's "Letters from the Harem: Veiled Figures of Writing in Montesquieu's *Lettres Persanes*" examines the wives' letters.

32. Connections between gender and genre are examined in Derrida's "La Loi du genre," translated as "The Law of Genre." Shari Benstock also makes this point in her essay "From Letters to Literature."

33. This concern is implicit in Tzvetan Todorov's suggestion that the most interesting subject of eighteenth-century epistolary fictions is how the story *in* the letters becomes the story *of* the letters. Todorov describes the relation between "l'histoire du roman et l'histoire dans le roman" in terms that imply the generalizability of this insight to all novels, a claim perhaps inspired by a New Critical assumption of an organic unity inherent in all texts: "The underlying story of the novel is precisely that of its creation; that story is told through the other story . . . the meaning of a work consists in speaking itself, speaking to us of its own existence" ("Le Sens des lettres," p. 49). In contrast, I limit the claim to the eighteenth-century epistolary novel as the product of a historically specific, self-reflexive moment of print culture.

34. On the transformation of models of readership in the 1790s, see Klancher's *The Making of English Reading Audiences* and Favret, *Romantic Correspondence,* especially chapter 2.

Works Cited

Altman, Janet Gurkin. *Epistolarity: Approaches to a Form.* Columbus: Ohio State University Press, 1982.

Arendt, Hannah. *The Human Condition.* Chicago: University of Chicago Press, 1958.

Armstrong, Nancy. *Desire and Domestic Fiction: A Political History of the Novel.* New York: Oxford University Press, 1987.

Baker, Nicholson. *Vox.* New York: Random House, 1992.

Benstock, Shari. "From Letters to Literature: *La Carte Postale* om the Epistolary Genre." *Genre* 18, 3 (1985): 257–95.

Boorstin, Daniel J. *The Discoverers: A History of Man's Search to Know His World and Himself.* New York: Vintage-Random House, 1985.

Clark, J. C. D. *English Society 1688–1832.* Cambridge, Eng.: Cambridge University Press, 1985.

Davis, Lennard. *Factual Fictions: The Origins of the English Novel.* New York: Columbia University Press, 1983.

Day, Robert Adams. *Told in Letters: Epistolary Fiction Before Richardson.* Ann Arbor: University of Michigan Press, 1966.

Delon, Michel. "Un Monde d'eunuques." *Europe* 55, 574 (1977): 79–88.

Derrida, Jacques. "The Law of Genre." Trans. Avital Ronell. In W. J. T. Mitchell, ed. *On Narrative.* Chicago: University of Chicago Press, 1981.

———. *The Post Card: From Socrates to Freud and Beyond.* Trans. Alan Bass. Chicago: University of Chicago Press, 1987.

Favret, Mary A. *Romantic Correspondence: Women, Politics, and the Fiction of Letters.* Cambridge, Eng.: Cambridge University Press, 1993.

Fielding, Henry. *The Covent-Garden Journal and A Plan of the Universal Register-Office.* Ed. Bertrand A. Goldgar. Middletown, Conn.: Wesleyan University Press, 1988.

Foucault, Michel. "What is an Author?" In Paul Rabinow, ed., *The Foucault Reader.* New York: Pantheon Books, 1984, pp. 101–20.

Fraser, Nancy. "Rethinking the Public Sphere: A Contribution to the Critique of Actually Existing Democracy." In Bruce Robbins, ed. *The Phantom Public Sphere.* Minneapolis: University of Minnesota Press, 1993.

———. "What's Critical About Critical Theory?" In Seyla Benhabib and Drucilla Cornell, eds. *Feminism as Critique.* Minneapolis: University of Minnesota Press, 1988, pp. 31–56.

Goodman, Dena. "Public Sphere and Private Life: Toward a Synthesis of Current Historiographical Approaches to the Old Regime." *History and Theory* 31, 1 (1992): 1–20.

Habermas, Jürgen. *The Structural Transformation of the Public Sphere: An Inquiry into a Category of Bourgeois Society.* Trans. Thomas Burger and Frederick Lawrence. Cambridge, Mass.: MIT Press, 1989.

Hohendahl, Peter Uwe. *The Institution of Criticism.* Ithaca, N.Y.: Cornell University Press, 1982.

Johnson, Samuel. *Letters.* 3 vols. Ed. Bruce Redford. Princeton, N.J.: Princeton University Press, 1992.

———. *Lives of the English Poets.* 3 vols. Ed. G. B. Hill. Oxford: Clarendon Press, 1905.

Kahn, Madeleine. *Narrative Transvestism: Rhetoric and Gender in the Eighteenth-Century English Novel.* Ithaca, N.Y.: Cornell University Press, 1991.

Kamuf, Peggy. *Fictions of Feminine Desire: Disclosures of Heloise.* Lincoln: University of Nebraska Press, 1982.

———. "Writing Like a Woman." In Sally McConnell-Ginet, et al., eds., *Women and Language in Literature and Society.* New York: Praeger, 1980.

Kauffman, Linda S. *Discourses of Desire: Gender, Genre, and Epistolary Fictions.* Ithaca, N.Y.: Cornell University Press, 1986.

Kittler, Friedrich. *Discourse Networks 1800/1900.* Trans. Michael Metteer with Chris Cullens. Stanford, Calif.: Stanford University Press, 1990.

Klancher, Jon P. *The Making of English Reading Audiences, 1790–1832.* Madison: University of Wisconsin Press, 1987.

Koselleck, Reinhart. *Critique and Crisis: Enlightenment and the Pathogenesis of Modern Society* (1969). Cambridge, Mass.: The MIT Press, 1988.

Landes, Joan B. *Women and thePublic Sphere in the Age of the French Revolution.* Ithaca, N.Y.: Cornell University Press, 1988.

Laufer, Roger. "La Réussite romanesque et la signification des *Lettres persanes* de Montesquieu." *Revue d'Histoire littérature de la France* 61, 2 (1961): 188–203.

Locke, John. *Two Treatises of Government.* Ed. Peter Laslett. Cambridge, 1960; rprt. New York: Mentor-Penguin Books, 1965.

———. *Two Treatises of Government.* Ed. C. B. MacPherson. Indianapolis, Ind.: Hackett, 1980.

McKeon, Michael. *The Origins of the English Novel, 1600–1740.* Baltimore: Johns Hopkins University Press, 1987.

Miller, Nancy K. *The Heroine's Text: Readings in the French and English Novel, 1722–1782.* New York: Columbia University Press, 1982.

———. "'I's' in Drag: The Sex of Recollection." *The Eighteenth Century: Theory and Interpretation* 22, 1 (1981): 47–57.

Panofsky, Erwin. *Perspective as Symbolic Form.* Trans. Christopher S. Wood. New York: Zone Books, 1991.

Pateman, Carole. *The Sexual Contract.* Stanford, Calif.: Stanford University Press, 1988.

Perry, Ruth. *Women, Letters, and the Novel.* New York: AMS, 1980.

Pucci, Suzanne Rodin. "Letters from the Harem: Veiled Figures of Writing in Montesquieu's *Lettres persanes.*" In Elizabeth C. Goldsmith, ed., *Writing the Female Voice.* Boston: Northeastern University Press, 1989, pp. 114–34.

Richardson, Samuel. *Clarissa, or the History of a Young Lady.* Ed. Angus Ross. New York: Viking Penguin, 1985.

———. *Clarissa, or the History of a Young Lady.* 4 vols. London: Dent, 1962.

———. *Correspondence of Samuel Richardson.* 6 vols. Ed. Anna Letitia Barbauld. London, 1804.

Robbins, Bruce, ed. *The Phantom Public Sphere.* Minneapolis: University of Minnesota Press, 1993.

Robinson, Howard. *The British Post Office: A History.* Princeton, N.J.: Princeton University Press, 1948.

Ronell, Avital. *The Telephone Book: Technology, Schizophrenia, Electric Speech.* Lincoln: University of Nebraska Press, 1989.

Sennett, Richard. *The Fall of Public Man: On the Social Psychology of Capitalism.* New York: Vintage Books, 1978.

Singerman, Alan J. "Réflexions sur une métaphore: le sérail dans les *Lettres persanes.*"*Studies on Voltaire and the Eighteenth Century* 185 (1980): 181–98.

Testud, Pierre. "*Les Lettres persanes,* roman épistolare."*Revue d'Histoire littérature de la France* 66, 4 (1966): 642–56.

Thompson, E. P. "The Crime of Anonymity." In Douglas Hay et al., eds., *Albion's Fatal Tree: Crime and Society in Eighteenth-Century England.* New York: Pantheon-Random House, 1975, pp. 255–344.

Todorov, Tzvetan. "Le Sens des lettres." In his *Littérature et signification.* Paris: Larousse, 1967.

Vartanian, Aram. "Eroticism and Politics in the *Lettres persanes,*"*Romanic Review* 60 (1969): 23–33.

Warner, Michael. *The Letters of the Republic: Publication and the Public Sphere in Eighteenth-Century America.* Cambridge, Mass.: Harvard University Press, 1990.

Watt, Ian. *The Rise of the Novel.* Berkeley: University of California Press, 1957.

WOMEN AND THE EPISTOLARY NOVEL

Robert Adams Day (essay date 1969)

SOURCE: Introduction to *Olinda's Adventures: Or the Amours of a Young Lady,* William Andrews Clark Memorial Library, University of California—Los Angeles, 1969, pp. i-vii.

[*In the following introduction to his edition of the anonymous 1693 epistolary narrative* Olinda's Adventures, *Day claims that the story is interesting because it contains many elements that precede the works of Daniel Defoe and Samuel Richardson and that anticipate aspects of later realistic novels.*]

A standard modern history of the English novel speaks of "the appearance of the novel round about 1700. Nothing that preceded it in the way of prose fiction can explain it."[1] Though today many scholars would assert that "nothing" is too strong a term, just how much of the original fiction written under the later Stuarts could "explain" Defoe and Richardson? Most late seventeenth-century novels, it is true, are rogue biographies, scandalchronicles, translations and imitations of French *nouvelles,* or short sensational romances of love, intrigue, and adventure with fantastic plots and wooden characters. Only occasionally was a tale published which showed that it was not examples of the novelist's craft that were wanting to inspire the achievement of a Defoe, but rather the sustained application of that craft over hundreds of pages by the unique combination of talents of a Defoe himself.

Such a novel is *Olinda's Adventures,* a brief epistolary narrative of 1693, a minor but convincing demonstration of the theory that a literary form such as the novel develops irregularly, by fits and starts, and of the truism that a superior mind can produce superior results with the most seemingly ungrateful materials. Of Defoe, *Olinda's Adventures* must appear a modest precursor indeed; but measured, as a realistic-domestic novel, against the English fiction of its day, it is surprisingly mature; and if we believe the bookseller and assign its authorship to a girl of fourteen, we must look to the juvenilia of Jane Austen for the first comparable phenomenon.

Olinda's Adventures seems to owe what success it had entirely to the bookseller Samuel Briscoe. It appeared in 1693 in the first volume of his epistolary miscellany *Letters of Love and Gallantry and Several Other Subjects. All Written by Ladies,* the second volume following in 1694.[2] It may have been the nucleus of the collection, however, since it begins the volume, and since Briscoe states in "The Bookseller to the Reader" (sig. A2) that various ladies, hearing that he was going to print Olinda's letters, have sent in amorous correspondence of their own—a remark that could indicate some previous circulation in manuscript. Another edition (or issue) of the miscellany, with a slightly altered title, was advertised in 1697, but no copy of this is recorded.[3] Nothing further is heard of *Olinda* for some years, but meanwhile Briscoe became something of a specialist in popular epistolary miscellanies, perhaps because he was a principal employer of Tom Brown, much of whose output consisted of original and translated "familiar letters." In 1718 Briscoe assembled a two-volume epistolary collection with the title *Familiar Letters of Love, Gallantry and Several Occasions;* this collection was apparently made up of the best and most popular items in his miscellanies of the past twenty-five years.[4] Here *Olinda* appears in much more impressive company than the anonymous "ladies," for the collection includes the first letter of Heloise to Abelard (said to be translated by L'Estrange) with actual correspondence and epistolary fiction by Butler, Mrs. Behn, Dennis, Otway, Etherege, Dryden, Tom Brown, Mrs. Mary Manley, Farquhar, Mrs. Centlivre, and other wits. Another edition (or issue) was advertised for W. Chetwood in 1720; and if the edition of 1724 ("Corrected. With Additions") is really the sixth, as Briscoe's title-page states, *Olinda* must have reached a respectable number of readers.

Olinda enjoyed another distinction, nearly unique for English popular fiction before 1700. While by the middle of the eighteenth century novel-readers in France were reveling in the adventures of the English epigones of Pamela and Clarissa, defending their virtue or exhibiting their sensibility in translation, the current of literary influence before Defoe ran overwhelmingly in the opposite direction. *Olinda* anticipated the Miss Sally Sampsons of sixty years later by appearing in 1695 in a French translation as *Les Amours d'une belle Angloise: ou la vie et les avantures de la jeune Olinde: Ecrites par Elle mesme en forme de lettres à un Chevalier de ses amis.*[5] Whether merit or mere chance accounted for this unusual occurrence it is impossible to say; the translation of *Olinda* is a faithful one, though the

text is at times expanded by the insertion of poems into Olinda's letters, with brief interpolated passages which rather awkwardly account for their presence. Curiously, the volume closes with a list of books printed for Briscoe, indicating either that the French translator would do anything to fill up space, or that Briscoe may have been exploring the possibilities of a French market for his wares.

While *Olinda* was ascribed merely to an anonymous "young lady" in the first edition, the editions of 1718 and 1724 gave it to "Mrs. Trotter." This lady, who since 1707 had been the wife of the Reverend Patrick Cockburn, a Suffolk curate, was then living in relative obscurity (her husband, having lost his living at the accession of George I, was precariously supporting his family by teaching), though she had enjoyed a certain literary success in King William's time and would later be heard from as a "learned lady" and writer on ethics. The fact that her maiden name was used, though not likely in 1718 to add very much luster to Briscoe's collection, and the similarities between the heroine's situation and Mrs. Trotter's own early life . . . make Briscoe's attribution seem worthy of acceptance. It is true that if Mrs. Trotter wrote *Olinda* she did it at fourteen. But she had been a child of astonishing precocity; she had produced a successful blank-verse tragedy at sixteen, and both Lady Mary Wortley Montagu and Jane Austen were to perform similar novelistic feats (to say nothing of Daisy Ashford).

Catherine Trotter (1679-1749)[6] was the daughter of David Trotter, a naval commander who died on a voyage in 1683, and Sarah Bellenden (or Ballenden), whose connections with the Maitland and Drummond families seem to have helped support her and her daughter in genteel poverty until she gained a pension of £20 per year under Queen Anne; Bishop Burnet was also her friend and patron. Catherine, a child prodigy, learned Latin and logic, and is said to have taught herself French; she extemporized verses in childhood, and at fourteen composed a poem on Mr. Bevil Higgons's recovery from the smallpox which is no worse than many "Pindarics" of the period. In 1695, however, Catherine Trotter established herself as a female wit with the impressive success of her tragedy *Agnes de Castro,* adapted from Mrs. Behn's retelling of an episode from Portuguese history. It was produced at the Theatre Royal in Drury Lane in December, with a prologue by Wycherley and with Mr. and Mrs. Verbruggen and Colley Cibber in the cast. *The Fatal Friendship,* a tragedy produced at Lincoln's Inn Fields in 1698, had a moderate success; two later plays did not. But Mrs. Trotter gained the acquaintance of Congreve, Dryden, and Farquhar, and was well enough known to be lampooned in *The Female Wits* (1704; acted 1696) along with Mrs. Pix and Mrs. Manley. In 1702 she turned to more serious writing, and her *Defence of the Essay of Humane Understanding* and other treatises defending Locke's theories against the charge of materialism were impressive enough to earn her a flattering letter from Locke himself; she also corresponded with Leibniz, who analyzed her theories at some length. *The History of the Works of the Learned* printed an essay of hers on moral obligation in 1743, and in 1747 Warburton contributed a preface to one of her treatises.

If we are willing to admit that *Olinda* is Mrs. Trotter's work, its virtues may be explained in part by seeing it as romanticized autobiography. Olinda, like Mrs. Trotter, is a wit and something of a beauty in adolescence, a fatherless child living with a prudent mother who is anxious to marry her off advantageously, and a solicitor of favors from noble or wealthy connections. Of the details of her character and circumstances at this time, however, no information is certain, and we must rely upon two presumably biased contemporary portraits. Mrs. Trotter gets off lightly in *The Female Wits;* she is represented (in "Calista," a small role) as being somewhat catty and pretentious, vain of her attainments in Latin and Greek (she has read Aristotle in the original, she says), but her moral character is not touched upon.[7] Another account of her early life, in Mrs. Manley's fictionalized autobiography and scandal-chronicle, *The Adventures of Rivella* (1714), may be entirely unreliable; but its author was certainly well acquainted with Mrs. Trotter, and what she says of her life in the 1690's, what is narrated in *Olinda,* and what Mrs. Trotter's scholarly memoirist Thomas Birch relates are similar in outline, similar enough so that we may speculate that the same set of facts has been "improved" in *Olinda,* perhaps maliciously distorted in *Rivella.* Cleander, the Platonic friend of the novel, Orontes, the kidnapped bridegroom, and Cloridon, the inconveniently married noble lover, appear to be three aspects of the same person; for Mrs. Manley tells at length (pp. 64-71) of "Calista's" relationship with "Cleander" (identified in the "key" to *Rivella* as Mrs. Trotter and Mr. Tilly).[8] John Tilly, the deputy warden of the Fleet prison, whose mistress Mrs. Manley became and remained until 1702, first met her, she says, through Mrs. Trotter, who sought her aid in interceding with her cousin John Manley, appointed chairman of a committee to look into alleged misdemeanors of Tilly as prison administrator. Mrs. Trotter, says Mrs. Manley, was a prude in public, not so in private; she was the first, "Cleander" said, who ever made him unfaithful to his wife. Mrs. Manley goes on, with a tantalizing lack of clarity (pp. 101-102):

> [Calista's] Mother being in Misfortunes and indebted to him, she had offered her Daughter's Security, he took it, and moreover the Blessing of one Night's Lodging, which he never paid her back again. . . . [Calista] had given herself Airs about not visiting *Rivella,* now she was made the Town-Talk by her Scandalous Intreague with *Cleander.*

Whatever the truth about Mrs. Trotter's adolescent amours may have been, or whether they have any connection with Olinda's fictional ones, must remain a matter for speculation; but the artistic merits of *Olinda* are in no such doubt. Although technically it may be called an epistolary novel, its author is no Richardson in marshalling the strategies of the epistolary technique. Nevertheless, although it is actually a fictional autobiography divided somewhat arbitrarily into "letters," the postponement of the letter to Cloridon until the end, the introduction of what might be called a subplot as Olinda tries to promote Cleander's courtship of Ambrisia and notes its progress, the breaking off of the letters at moments of (mild) suspense, the bringing up of the action to an uncompleted present, all these show an awareness of fictional mechanics that is far from elementary. Indeed, a contemporary critic might go so far as to see in the novel's conclusion an anticipation of the "open-ended" realism of plotting so much applauded at present; for though Orontes has been got out of the way, Olinda has not yet been rewarded with Cloridon's hand by a similarly happy turn of fate, and must patiently await the demise of his inconvenient wife as anyone outside of melodrama might have to do. The contretemps and misunderstandings, the trick played on Olinda with regard to Cloridon's fidelity and her subsequent undeceiving, the closet-scene and its embarrassments, may smack of the hackneyed devices of stage comedy, but they are not clumsily handled, and they never make emotional mountains out of molehills.

Perhaps the most salient qualities of *Olinda,* in contrast to the fiction of its day, are restraint and control. With the exception of the rather ridiculous way in which the complications are resolved at the end (Orontes's sequestration and death from smallpox), everything in the novel is planned and motivated with some care. Inclinations develop slowly and believably; the spring of action, barring a few not very fantastic coincidences and accidents, are anti-romantic—almost too much so. Indeed, such criteria of the "modern novel" as those proposed by Ian Watt[9] are all modestly but adequately met. Most important, the situation and behavior of the heroine, her values, and the world in which she lives are (but for their sketchy development) what a reader of Jane Austen might take for granted, yet are all but unique before 1740.

Here is a middle-class heroine who is fully as moral as Pamela, but with a wry sense of humor; she defers to her mother as a matter of course when marriage is in question, yet would willingly evade parental decrees; she is capable of Moll Flanders's examinations of motive, yet sees through her own hypocrisies; she lives in London in reduced circumstances and agrees to a marriage of convenience although tempted to engage in a dashing adultery; and she endures the onset of both love and jealousy without melodramatic or sentimental posturings.

Other technical achievements of *Olinda* aside, the portrait of the heroine as she reveals herself to her confidant is the novel's most significant feature. A fictional heroine of this early date who can be sententious without being tedious, who is moderately and believably witty, who is courted by a gold-smith (even though, conformably to the times, he is named Berontus) rather than a prince borrowed from *Astree,* and who satirizes herself soberly for scorning him, who meets her ideal lover with a business letter rather than in a shipwreck, and who level-headedly fends him off because he is both married and a would-be philanderer, is a rarity indeed.

Olinda commends itself to the student of English literary history principally for two reasons: because it so ably anticipates in embryo so many features which the English domestic and realistic novel would develop in its age of maturity and popularity, and because we do not yet understand, and need to investigate, the cultural factors-literary, social, and economic—which prevented the kind of achievement it represents from being duplicated with any frequency for several decades.

Notes

1. Walter Allen, *The English Novel* (New York, 1968), p. 4.

2. Advertised in the *Term Catalogues,* Trinity Term, 1693 (II, 466); Wing L1784, L1785.

3. It is listed in Harold C. Binkley, "Letter Writing in English Literature" (unpublished Harvard dissertation, 1923).

4. They included *Familiar Letters [of] Rochester* (2 vols., 1697), *Familiar and Courtly Letters [of] Voiture* (2 vols., 1700), *A Pacquet from Will's* (2nd ed., 1705), *The Works of Mr. Thomas Brown* (2-4 vols., 1707—), and *The Lady's Pacquet of Letters* (1710). Briscoe was not in every case the printer of the first edition.

5. "A Cologne. Chez ***. MDCXCV." A copy of the volume is in the Bibliotheque de l'Arsenal in Paris.

6. See *DNB, s. v.* "Cockburn, Catherine"; Edmund Gosse, "Catharine Trotter, the First of the Bluestockings," *Fortnightly Review, N. S.,* No. 594 (June 1916), pp. 1034-1048; Alison Fleming, "Catherine Trotter—'the Scots Sappho,'" *Scots Magazine,* XXXIII (1940), 305-314. The source from which all three are derived is Thomas Birch's *The Works of Mrs. Catherine Cockburn* (2 vols., 1751), including letters and a prefatory biography.

7. The play is reproduced in the Augustan Reprint Society's Publication No. 124 (Los Angeles, 1967), with an introduction by Lucyle Hook.

8. Page references are to the "second edition" of 1715. See Paul B. Anderson, "Mistress Delariviere Manley's Biography," *MP,* XXXIII (1935-36), 270-271, for further details.

9. *The Rise of the Novel* (London, 1957), Chapter I.

Ruth Perry (essay date 1980)

SOURCE: "Letter Fiction and the Search for Human Nature" and "Romantic Love and Sexual Fantasy in Epistolary Fiction," in *Women, Letters, and the Novel,* AMS Press, 1980, pp. 1-26; 137-67.

[*In the first excerpt below, Perry describes the social and economic conditions of early eighteenth-century England and their influence of the surging popularity of epistolary fiction, a literary genre that offered unprecedented opportunity for women writers and their concerns. In the second* excerpt, *she discusses the changing sexual mores of the late seventeenth and early eighteenth centuries and how this was depicted in the romantic fantasies of epistolary fiction.*]

London was a brutal and disorderly place in the late seventeenth and early eighteenth centuries. Ruffians lurked in the dirty, badly lit streets to rob and harass the wealthier citizens. John Evelyn was robbed several times at home and on the road. Samuel Pepys reports lying afraid in his bed at night, sure that the sounds he was hearing were thieves breaking into his house to steal his beloved possessions. Although the laws against theft were extreme—stealing a kerchief could be punished by death[1]—there continued to be a sizable criminal sub-culture of the sort described by Defoe in *Moll Flanders.*

In 1705 London's Common Council appointed more watchmen to keep peace in public streets; this action did not have its desired effect, though, for five years later it was reported that

> of late many loose, idle, and disorderly Persons have used in the Evenings, in a riotous and tumultuous Manner, to gather together in the Streets and other Passages of this city, and the Suburbs thereof; where they make Bonfires and Illuminations, stop the Coaches and assault the Persons of the Inhabitants, and other her Majesty's subjects who happen to pass by on their lawful Occasions, insult their Houses, break their Windows, forcibly and illegally demand Money of them. . . .[2]

In 1718 the City Marshall reported

> the general complaint of the taverns, the coffee-houses, the shop-keepers and others that their customers are afraid when it is dark to come to their houses and shops for fear that their hats and wigs should be snitched from their heads or their swords taken from their sides, or that they may be blinded, knocked down, cut or stabbed; Nay, the coaches cannot secure them, but they are likewise cut and robbed in the public streets, etc.[3]

Some of this crime was malicious, willful, unmotivated by material need. There were, for instance, a band of local hoodlums,

> who call themselves Hawkubites, and their mischievous invention of the work is, that they take people between hawk and buzzard, that is, between two of them, and making them turn from one to the other, abuse them with blows and scoffings; and if they pretend to speak for themselves, they then slit their noses, or cut them down the back.[4]

There were also a growing number of prostitutes, supplied by the influx of country girls who came to London, helpless and unsuspecting as one depicted in Hogarth's *The Harlot's Progress,* unable to survive the disruptions of enclosure and industrialization in their native towns, and seeking employment as servants in the growing city.[5] The many remedies for venereal disease advertised in the London newspapers in the 1720s is probably a good index of their increased activity.[6] And along the road leading out of London lay an appalling number of abandoned children, both dead and alive.[7]

In fact, living conditions in London in 1700 were so bad that the death rate (one in twenty-five) far exceeded the birth rate, a fact which alarmed a number of natural philosophers who wrote about the necessity for marriage and having more children.[8] This extraordinarily high waste of life in the city occurred because of too much poisonous gin (more stringent liquor licensing laws were not passed until 1751), unsanitary quarters, bad food, disease, etc. Throughout the eighteenth century the population of London had to be continually replenished by people pouring in from other towns and from the countryside.[9]

The rising numbers of marginal individuals without community or respectable work, and the squalor into which the city absorbed them, were signs of a society moving from an agricultural economy toward an industrial one. In many ways, the intellectual and philosophical changes in the culture were reflections of this critical economic shift. The old authorities were gone: the seventeenth century witnessed both the execution of the legitimate king and widespread religious dissent from traditional theology; nor had these orthodox sources of truth yet been repaired or replaced. It was an era in which abundant satire testified to the moral confusion, to the hypocritical gaps between pretended and actual standards. The culture paid lip service to the comfortable philosophy of the "great chain of being," in which individuals were required to blindly live out their parts in a Divine Plan so complicated that no one but God could understand its entire and perfect justice. Yet this philosophy was at odds with the newer spirit of entrepreneurial individualism which accompanied expanding trade and capitalism.

The literature is full of these contradictory signals. Robinson Crusoe, Pamela Andrews, Clarissa Harlowe, Tom Jones, all begin their adventures by leaving home, going off on their own, but each suffers for that willfulness and each is made to see the impossibility, in a social world, of doing exactly as one pleases. In each case, however, their enterprising spirit is rewarded as each achieves a higher station in life than that in which he or she began. This pattern is perhaps clearest in *Robinson Crusoe* where the sin committed by the hero—self-determination—is punishable by twenty-odd years of solitude and then rewarded with wealth.

Many of the criminal biographies, so popular in the early part of the eighteenth century, were shaped the same way, making it clear that each scoundrel's first important misstep had been "individualism," ignoring Providence, and believing too exclusively in himself. Certainly this was the cause of Moll Flanders' unhappiness as well as of her success, and Defoe shows his readers at the end of that book that the only way to win personal salvation and public acclaim was to submit to the laws of God and of society. Similarly, the later parts of *Pamela* and of *Robinson Cru-*

soe are about the reclaiming of the individual by society: Pamela must learn to be the mistress of a bourgeois establishment, to fit into society at her new station, and Robinson Crusoe must cope with his sailors and the colony established on his once isolated and peaceful island. The attempt was to strike a new balance, to redefine the relation between needs of individuals and the rules of the larger society.

In the midst of these confusions, without clear ethical standards for living or unalterable social and economic places in which to fit, there was a growing belief that reason, aided by facts collected empirically, could supply the answers no longer provided by traditional religion or a divine-right monarchy. It was believed possible to understand human nature and prescribe rules for a healthy life through study and analysis rather than through revelation. After all, the seventeenth century had seen the discovery of the laws governing the universe; now it was time to do the same for humankind. As Ernst Cassirer observes:

> The whole eighteenth century is permeated by this conviction, namely, that in the history of humanity the time had now arrived to deprive nature of its carefully guarded secret, to leave it no longer in the dark to be marveled at as an incomprehensible mystery but to bring it under the bright light of reason and analyze it with all its fundamental force.[10]

The Royal Society, operating since 1660 with its studies of mathematics, astronomy, chemistry, and the natural sciences, was the institutional manifestation of the faith in the new methods of pursuing knowledge. Swift's materials for the satire of the experimenting mania in book III of *Gulliver's Travels* were not invented by him but came from the pages of *Philosophical Transactions*. Robert Boyle, for example, (who first enunciated the law that the volume of a gas varies inversely with pressure) was one of those who supplied him with instances in which the drive to corroborate scientific constructs with systematically gathered information exceeded the bounds of common sense. When Boyle described a blind Dutchman who could distinguish color by touch, "his most exquisite perception is in his thumb," and described his data with as much precision as in his more plausible experiments, Swift transformed the report into the blind man in Lagado who mixed colors for painters.[11]

Nor was curiosity the exclusive quality of a specialized group of academics. There was, at that time, a thirst for information among all those with the leisure and means to pursue it. The educated Englishman characteristically wanted to know more about the world in which he lived and about the people who inhabited it. A Frenchman visiting London in the early part of the century was struck by how universal was the English appetite for information and wrote home about it in this way:

> There are many shabby cafes in London with furniture which is worn because of the numbers of people frequenting them . . . What attracts the people to the ca-

fes are the gazettes and other public papers. The English are great newsmongers. Most workers begin their day by going to a cafe to read the news. I have often seen bootblacks and others of that sort getting together to buy each day's gazette for a half-farthing and to read it together . . . There are a dozen different gazettes in London, some which come out every day, some twice a week and some weekly. One can read the news from other countries usually taken from the *Holland Gazette*. The articles on London are always the longest, one can learn of the marriage and death of people of quality, of civil, military and clerical appointments, and anything else of interest, comic and tragic, in this great city.[12]

The tastes of an increasingly literate public were beginning to determine what was printed in England, unlike in earlier times when writing was an aristocratic pursuit for a very select audience. Writers had to convince booksellers that their works could sell widely; it was no longer a matter of simply pleasing an aristocracy. Visual art, too, was moving toward public subscription rather than the patronage system with the establishment of the first academy of painting in 1711.[13] Newspapers were one of the visible signs of the demands of this new, broader audience. Indeed, modern notions of journalism—of simple, factual, objective, informative reporting—can be traced to this period. The lapsing of the Licensing Act in 1695 which had been a curb to publishing also encouraged the proliferation of this cheap reading matter. Coffee houses attracted customers by supplying newspapers to their clientele along with the latest beverages from the New World.

The popular demand for informative reading is also recognizable in the longer literary forms which sold well during the early part of the century. There were tales of travel, secret and not so secret histories of lives, and collections of letters. Certain terms recurred again and again in the titles of fiction: "history," "memoirs," "life," "voyage," "adventure," "account," "letters."[14] All of these forms were supposedly derived from materials which were authentic rather than fictional, for the public seemed to want to be informed about all the strange and marvelous permutations possible in real life.

The travel books were partly the result of the growth of capitalism: the impulse to accrue and the necessity for finding new business sent Englishmen all the way around the world, to return to talk of new lands and foreign people. As early as 1680 The Royal Society had shown an official interest in the accounts of travelers[15] and Evelyn's diary of August 6, 1698 reports the excitement of dining "at Mr. Pepys, where was Cap: Dampier, who had been a famous Buccaneere, brought hither the painted Prince Jolo, printed a Relation of his very strange adventures," discussing the errors in existing maps of the South Pacific.[16] Of course by 1720, this interest in the exotic South Pacific had grown sufficiently to blow up the famous South Sea bubble.

The letter, as form, was a perfect frame for travel reports or essays of any length and on any subject in this new age which so valued collecting information. (Indeed, the earliest newspapers were no more than batches of informative letters published together.)[17] Tone could range from impersonal journalistic human interest stories, to pedantic ethnographies, to ponderous theological debates, to sensational disclosures. Edward Ward, for example, was a hack writer who liked to masquerade his sensational exposés as on-the-scene reports back home in the form of letters.[18] While some had recourse to letters to debate the tenets of Quakerism or to detail foreign cultures, popular writers like Ward framed anything that might sell in a letter format.

Travel books were so popular by that time that after theology books they were the second most numerous kind of book published. But stories of voyages are also metaphoric expressions of testing limits. They are quite literally about how far one can go, pushing at boundaries, reducing unknowns to knowns. The travel literature which provided the public with anthropological lore about other civilizations often compared them to English society with an eye to finding out what was considered natural in other cultures, what customs corroborated one's own certainties about human limitations. Other environments were especially interesting for what they could show individuals about their own world. English courtship and marriage customs, in particular, were often compared to other cultures as if these differences could teach one how all of it ought to be done. Travel stories were also suitable as allegories of the favorite Puritan sort about losing and then finding one's way—wrestling with one's rebellious mind, straying into psychically alien territory, but finally turning homeward to the proper English way of life.

Pirate tales and criminal biographies, also very popular in the early part of the century, helped define good and evil in ways it would be hard to duplicate, with their examples of gratuitous and unreasoning violence at the extremes of human cruelty.[19] Indeed, the very interest in criminality presupposes an allegiance to law and order; it assumes that there is some basic standard from which deviations are made. There was an interest in unlawfulness for the same reasons that there was an interest in making up rules for living. Because man was still the most uncontrollable and unpredictable element in his own world, there was a need to examine the outer edges of human experience, in order to define the natural limits of the passions. So although the success of the criminal biographies can be explained by popular craving for the lurid and sensational, it could also be argued that these biographies satisfied a taste for the details about those who ended on the gallows, a curiosity as to how their lives led in that direction, what their experience consisted of, and how they came to be what they were. In fact, these accounts often did come from the records kept and published by the institutions processing these criminals, from reports of the trials at Old Bailey, and from published accounts which Newgate prison chaplains wrote about the last hours and confessions of criminals they had worked with. These chaplains sold their accounts for money and for the glory they earned with stories of their spiritual prowess in last minute conversions.[20]

It was an age of sermons, laws, rules, and fictionalized explorations of conduct and consequences, an age that believed reason could educate feeling. Therefore a market existed for books of advice on how to behave in even the most intimate moments of one's life. Popular writers of the day were certainly aware of that audience: John Dunton's *The Athenian Spy* (1704) was ready "to direct the Bachelor and the Virgin in their whole amour"[21] and Edward Ward's *Marriage Dialogues* (1708) meant to show those "unhappy in the Marry'd State" "where the fault lies." Defoe, always willing to supply the needs of the reading public, contributed *The Family Instructor* (1715), a collection of sample dialogues for sticky situations which might occur between a father and son, or a mother and daughter—a "how-to-do-it" manual for family life—and *Conjugal Lewdness* (1727) which warns married couples at great length against too heavy an emphasis on the sexual side of their union. It should be remembered, too, that Richardson's letter-writing manual offered directives to its readers for a good deal more than style. It would seem that many readers were looking for instruction in how to think and feel.

The many tales of love affairs bought eagerly by the public at this time often featured a moralizing editorial statement between the episodes of passion, dwelling on the degree to which emotion could obliterate conscience and pervert social relationships. Love always broke all the rules, and created lawless behavior. As one novelist put it,

> Reason, Religion, and even the Will is subservient to that all-powerful Passion which forces us sometimes to Actions our Natures most detest; Mother against Daughter, Father against Son, contrives; all Obligations of Blood and Interest are no more remember'd; over every Bound we leap, to gratify the wild Desire, and Conscience but vainly interposes its Remonstrances.[22]

Perhaps there was a delicious horror in reading about such "wild Desire" for the issue of what "our Natures most detest" or the "Obligations of Blood and Interest" were not easily defined. Stories of anarchic emotion teased the imagination with the real range of human choices. Excessive desire, difficult to control and predict at best, could push a person beyond self-control. Thus an early marriage manual advises against incest "lest the Friendship a Man bears to such a woman be immoderate; for . . . if the conjugal Affection be full and betwixt them as it ought to be, and that it be over and above surcharged with that kindred too, there is no doubt but such an Addition will carry the Husband beyond the Bounds of Reason."[23] Love could lead to madness; indeed it was seen as a kind of temporary insanity in which "Rape, Murder, everything that is shocking to Nature, and Humanity had in them Ideas less terrible than what despairing love presented . . ."[24] Thus such tales demonstrated what social philosophers believed at that time—that people were held in check only by the laws and customs which regulated individual passions, that they were creatures of appetite whose instincts headed them toward chaos but for the restraints of reason.

Sometimes these love stories were offered up in a spirit of scientific humanism, as case studies in emotion. Like the criminal biographies they offered a close up view of the uncivilized side of human nature. This rationale was all the more convincing as the conventions which defined fiction became increasingly realistic; for as one popular writer pointed out, moral prescriptions based on fictional lives are more likely heeded when "fear of falling into the like Misfortunes, causes us to interest ourselves more in their Adventures, because that those sorts of Accidents may happen to all the World; and it touches so much the more because they are the common Effects of Nature."[25] The public wanted more of the sense that such stories were based on "real life" and that one could learn from individual cases. In 1705 Mrs. Manley announced this literary trend: the fad for French romances was "very much abated" and "Little Histories" had taken their place.[26] In 1719 Defoe assured his readers that "a private Man's Adventures in the World were worth making Publick."

Some of the "Little Histories" of that time strain the modern sense of realism considerably. Take, for example, this letter from a servant girl asking advice of an all-knowing seer about her affair with her master:

> I believe, indeed, he has a great Respect for me, for he always takes care to cut the best bit of the Meat, or Fowl, or whatever we have for our Dinner, and lay it on his Plate as if he design'd to eat it himself, and leaves it for me.[27]

This detail, touching in its homeliness, is meant to testify to the everyday reality of the tale and to give the reader some insight into the experience of the character. Yet in its own way, it is as naively romantic as a story of a damsel saved from distress.

Nevertheless, the effect of writing vignettes about probable characters rather than allegorical sequences or fantastic adventures, of focusing on concrete physical details rather than falling back on indistinct, stylized descriptions, of shortening length and deflating style, was to blur distinctions between fantasy and mundane reality and make it seem possible to move romance into the realm of daily life. The outlandish and fanciful names of characters in the romances began to be used as the pseudonyms in epistolary fiction, assumed by clandestine correspondents to avoid detection in case their letters were intercepted. It also was becoming literary fashion to write about middle-class heroes and heroines, a practice which the very prolific Eliza Haywood defended in this way:

> Those who undertake to write Romances, are always careful to give a high Extraction to their *Heroes* and *Heroines;* because it is certain we are apt to take a greater Interest in the Destiny of a *Prince* than of a *private Person.* We frequently find, however, among those of a middle State, some, who have Souls as elevated, and Sentiments equally noble with those of the most illustrious Birth: Nor do I see any Reason to the contrary; *Nature* confines not her Blessings to the *Great* alone . . . As the following Sheets, therefore, contain only real Matters of Fact, and have, indeed, something so very surprising in themselves, that they stand not in

need of any Embellishments from Fiction: I shall take my *Heroine* such as I find her, and believe the Reader will easily pass by the Meanness of her Birth, in favour of a thousand other good Qualities she was possess'd of.[28]

In arguing that human qualities which are worth emulating can be found throughout the population, she at once announces that her book has a moral function and heightens the impression that her characters come from life, that her stories "contain only real Matters of Fact" and "stand not in need of any Embellishments from Fiction." Nor is this example unique. A passage from the translation of Marivaux' *The Life of Marianne* (1736) strikes the same notes: there is an inverse snobbishness aimed at those who do not like to read about ordinary people and an implication that the story of a tradesman or commoner is as valuable a "History of the human Heart" as anyone could wish, and probably truer:

> There are People whose Vanity creeps into every Thing they do, even into their very Reading. Lay before them the History of the human Heart, among People of great Quality; no Doubt they will think it an important Matter, and well worth their Attention . . . No Matter for all the rest of Mankind. They barely allow them to live, but judge them with no further Notice. They would even insinuate, that Nature might very well have spared the Production of such Creatures, and that Tradesmen and Commoners are but a Dishonour to her. You may judge then with what Scorn such Readers as these would have looked upon me.[29]

The day of the poor but honest heroine had arrived, thanks to the demands of a less aristocratic reading public who wanted to read more stories about people from their own class staunchly upholding strict moral codes.

The audience for whom these early novels were written were generally Londoners with enough education and leisure to read, and enough money to buy the books. Since they cost six pence to six shillings at that time (one or two shillings being the common price), they were out of range of all but the well-to-do. Epistolary fiction, sometimes printed piecemeal in magazines, was a little cheaper, installments running only six to twelve pence a week that way.[30] The effect of watching the story unfold, of waiting for the next installment, was particularly well suited to the form of a novel told in letters. But whether serially or by volume, reading novels was a taste that only the comfortable classes could indulge. Private entertainment is expensive, and reading one's own book cost a good deal more than communal theater-going which had been the literary amusement of an earlier generation. Still, books were selling better than ever before, and the increased volume of sales kept their price stable in spite of a steady rise in the cost of printing.[31]

Although these books were fairly expensive, the main audience for them was not aristocratic. For one thing, the villainous rakes most often cast as the enemy in these stories came from that class, and the satire tends towards mockery of class distinctions from a middle-class point of view. For example, in Mrs. Davys' *Familiar Letters Betwixt a Gentleman and a Lady,* there is a butler whose proof of being "a very well-bred Man" is that he "drinks, whores, and games and has just as much Estate as will qualify him for a vote," as well as an impoverished peer who has gambled away his estate and whose hovel is satirically called "my Lord's chamber."[32] The focus on the heroines in these novels also betrays a particularly middle-class concern, for it was the only class in which men worked and women did not. (Among the laboring classes men and women both worked; aristocratic men and women had similar requirements in the way of duties.) This divergence of role led to great controversy about the nature of their relationship to one another. Then, too, the growing need in landed aristocratic families for middle-class cash made middle-class women upwardly mobile as they had never been before. This intensified the middle-class interest in themes of love, marriage, and the etiquette of sexual fencing.

The letter novel thrived in this context. Middle-class readers could identify with characters who sat down to write letters which told of the agonies of love, or reported experiences of traveling, or revealed secrets, or gave advice, or arranged intrigues. They could read about the thoughts and experiences of these literate heroes and heroines with the appealing illusion that they came directly from the minds of the participants rather than being filtered through the sensibility of an omniscient narrator. The language generally used in epistolary fiction was common rather than literary, and the characters who wrote news to their families or advice to their friends were all plausible types. The letters themselves seemed to be proof that such people really existed and that following their lives was not merely self-indulgent escape, but informative reading about first-hand experience.

Certainly the most interesting experiments in realistic fiction of the day were books written like autobiography— *Moll Flanders* or *Robinson Crusoe* or letter novels. The public must have enjoyed such first-hand writing, for columns of letters of complaints, advice, or confession written to editors of newspapers and gazettes by private individuals were so successful that editors imitated them, and featured professionally written ones concocted to read like unsolicited letters. It was simply easier to commission them than to collect them, and the public was always curious about others like themselves, isolated in their separate lives within the big city.

Because letters were the obvious medium for exchanging informal and personal news between intimates, they also perfectly illustrated stories of relationships. The epistolary mode gave an objective cast to such stories, as if they were data collected from actual experience demonstrating the natural extremes of feeling and depicting human problems. Even the titles of epistolary novels sometimes seem to lay claim to special truth about human states like curiosity or love or constancy or jealousy or innocence, as if the letters made it possible to abstract and isolate them for special study in each story: "The Masqueraders, or *Fatal Curiosity*," "Fantomina, or *Love in a Maze*," "The Fatal Secret or *Constancy in Distress*," "The Penitant Hermit or *The Fruits of Jealousy*," "The Player's Tragedy or *Fatal Love*," "The Brothers or *Treachery Punish'd*" (italics mine).

This kind of epistolary writing tended to be very much in demand in the forty years or so which preceded Richardson's *Pamela*, perhaps because it satisfied the public taste for "realism" or seemed to provide documentation for moral dilemmas, and because it was written not as literary art but to sell to the middle class readers whose values and interests it reflected. In any case there were between 100 and 200 epistolary works published and sold in London during the early eighteenth century, many of them very popular, running through many editions. Some of them were collections of separate, unconnected letters, each of which was exemplary, amusing, or informative; some were novels constructed entirely with letters; some were intermediate cases—collections of "real life" letters which were sequential but did not quite tell a story, or novels with interpolated letters but with plots much too complicated to be narrated through the indirection of letters. This cluster of letter fiction provides the seeding for the subsequent development of English novels; close inspection of the form in later chapters will show how the letter format encouraged certain tendencies in fiction, made it possible for women to do such writing professionally, and because of the inevitable assumptions and themes of stories told in letters, made fashionable the tales of endless maneuvering between men and women.

All of the best selling Grub Street hack writers dealt in letters: Defoe, Dunton, Ward, Brown, D'Urfey, and by the 1720s, Eliza Haywood and Mary Manley as well. They translated them, edited them, "presented" them or wrote them outright; many letters were passed off as authentic, some were facetious, some were fictional. Eliza Haywood alone issued eighteen volumes of epistolary work between 1724 and 1727 which means that there was a great demand for them, for her livelihood depended on writing what would sell. Edmund Curll, the most famous, successful, and unscrupulous bookseller of this period was making most of his money by 1719 on letter collections and fictive autobiographies.[33] This was the same bookseller called "unspeakable" by Pope in his denunciation of the whole new upstart literary industry which was upsetting the tradition of literature as an aristocratic occupation. A later critic of the period wrote more kindly of Curll's propensity to print private papers as his "indefatigable industry in preserving our national remains."[34]

But not only did the middle class profit from the opening up of the literary profession. Educated women, too, now found it possible to make a living writing stories according to the popular formula, or publishing diaries or letters in a culture which thought it anomalous for a gentlewoman to produce anything more public. Women's writing, of course, was not taken seriously but thought of as a new, pleasant way for women to busy themselves. A reader wrote to *The Spectator,*

> You lately recommended to your Female Readers, the good old custom of their Grandmothers, who used to lay out a great Part of their Time in Needle-work: I entirely agree with you in your Sentiments, . . . I would, however, humbly offer to your Consideration the Case of the Poetical Ladies; who, though they may be willing to take any Advice given them by the *Spectator,* yet can't so easily quit their Pen and Ink, as you may imagine.[35]

The Preface to Lady Mary Wortley Montagu's *Turkish Letters,* written in 1724 by the first English feminist, Mary Astell, was unusual in its warm praise of the female sensibility. Mary Astell, who had long decried women's servitude, pressing for women's right to a real education, asked her audience to set aside their prejudices against women's writing and be "pleased that a *woman* triumphs, and proud to follow in her train."[36] The woman she championed, Lady Mary Wortley Montagu, was one of the few women in the intellectual circles of the day. She was a gifted writer and an astute conversationalist, at one time very much admired by Pope, although later estranged from him. Mary Astell claimed that her letters from Turkey were proof that ladies traveled "to better purpose" than their lords, and that while the public was "surfeited with *Male Travels,* all in the same tone, and stuft with the same trifles; a lady has the skill to strike out a new path, and to embellish a worn-out subject, with a variety of fresh and elegant entertainment."[37] Certainly Lady Mary traveled "to better purpose" than even elegant entertainment, for it was she who brought back to England the practice of innoculation against small-pox.

Indeed, there were a number of successful woman novelists in the decades preceding the publication of Richardson's *Pamela,* in spite of the fashionable derision of "Literary Ladies." Interestingly, all of them—Behn, Manley, Davys, Haywood, Rowe—wrote at least some of their fiction in the form of letters. One of the reasons women were encouraged to try their hands at epistolary fiction was because it was a format that required no formal education. It did not treat traditional literary problems, it necessitated no scholarly training. Its success largely depended on a simple, personal, letter-writing style. This was, in fact, one of the few kinds of writing which had long been encouraged in women since—to make the appropriate distinction—letter-writing had always been thought of as an accomplishment rather than as an art.

But it is important to remember that women did not dominate this new sort of fiction although they wrote a good deal of it. The most authoritative checklist of pre-Richardson epistolary fiction includes seventy-two volumes written by men and fifty-four volumes written by women, of which Eliza Haywood alone wrote twenty-nine.[38] It is possible, of course, that women contributed more to epistolary fiction than we can ever know, for sixty-eight of those 200 or so early epistolary works[39] have no known authors and it is often thought that respectable women took refuge behind the label "anonymous."

At the same time that women began to write professionally, they also became a significant new audience for the fiction and light reading coming from the new Grub Street industry. Certainly the proportion of women readers in the audience had been much less half a century earlier. A study of 262 works printed in a ten-year span in the middle of the seventeenth century shows that although twenty-nine were dedicated to specific women, only nine of the books were explicitly intended for a female readership.[40] Nor had women been the main audience for the romances of the seventeenth century. William Temple recommended several long romances to Dorothy Osborne in the course of their courtship; Samuel Pepys read romances and even tried his amateur's hand at writing one. On January 30, 1664 his diary entry reads:

> This evening, being in the humour of making all things even and clear in the world, I tore some old papers; among others, a romance which (under the title of 'Love a Cheate') I begun ten years ago at Cambridge; and at this time reading it over tonight I liked it very well. . . .

But by the beginning of the eighteenth century, a sizable female audience was beginning to be assumed for fiction of all sorts. The preface to Mme. D'Aulnoy's *The Present Court of Spain* calls attention to its female writer because it "will go a great way you know with the Ladies and admirers of Ladies. . . ."[41] Edward Ward's *Female Policy Detected: or The Arts of a Designing Woman Laid Open* (1695) was certainly written because of the growing market for books about women. Dunton, never one to miss a good commercial opportunity, advertised a book of "600 letters pro and con, on all the Disputable Points relating to Women" called *The Female Warr.* It is interesting that he thought the letter the most believable way of presenting women's voices. Steele, too, considered his treatment of women's topics in *The Spectator* as new and daring since no other magazine had ever set out to "treat on Matters which relate to Females, as they are concern'd to approach, or fly from the other Sex, or as they are tyed to them by Blood, Interest, or Affection."[42] The novelty of his venture is partly visible in the uncertain tone with which he treats women's issues. On the one hand he professed an interest in elevating them to a shared intellectualism with men, deploring the lack of opportunities for women's education and recognizing the harmful effects of the differential attitudes of parents towards their girl and boy children. On the other hand, he patronized, with amusement, the diminished world which women inhabited:

> I have often thought there has not been sufficient Pains taken in finding out proper Employments and Diversions for the Fair ones. Their Amusements seem contrived for them rather as they are Women than as they are reasonable Creatures; and are more adapted to the Sex than to the Species. The Toilet is their great Scene of Business, and the right adjusting of their Hair the principal Employment of their Lives . . . Their most Serious Occupations are Sowing and Embroidery, and their greatest Drudgery the Preparation of Jellies and Sweet-meats.[43]

The new audience for the incidental prose of letter collections, magazines, and epistolary fiction in the early eighteenth century also continued to include many men. Dudley Ryder for instance, a pleasant middle-class young man whose diary survives, was an avid reader both of letter collections and of essays from *The Spectator* and *The Tatler* for their sensible "reflections and observations upon the passions, tempers, follies and vices of mankind."[44] One hundred and eighty-six of the 309 names of people engaged to buy a copy of *Letters From a Lady of Quality to a Chevalier* (costing three to five shillings depending on the binding) are men's names;[45] seventy-four percent of the names on the subscription list bound with the 1730 edition of *Some Memoirs of the Amours and Intrigues of a Certain Irish Dean* are men's names; 198 out of 332 subscribers for Elizabeth Boyd's *The Happy Unfortunate or The Female Page* (costing two shillings six pence in advance and an equal sum upon delivery) are men; in five out of six of the subscription lists for epistolary novels reported on by Robert Day, men subscribers outnumber women subscribers two to one.[46] It would seem that in spite of the increasing number of women's voices and women's issues reaching the public, men were still the main purchasers of literature in that period. Part of the explanation for this, no doubt, is that men tended to control the money in a family. Furthermore, booksellers' shops, like coffee houses, were still men's territory, unusual places for a gentlewoman to be found.

Considering that men still dominated the world of popular literature it is remarkable how many of the central characters in these novels are women. The stories are created so that the reader watches their dilemmas, which are usually sexual, unfold. In the older chivalric romances it had always been a man's honor which was tested, not a woman's—and that honor had altogether different properties from those at issue in the eighteenth-century novel. In the tradition of Adam and Eve, Samson and Delilah, Aeneas and Dido, it had always been the woman who seductively lured the man from his higher purpose, his noble mission. When Sir Gawain in the Arthurian romance *Sir Gawain and the Green Knight* allowed himself to be seduced by a woman it was a punishable weakness in his knightly character, a flaw in his single-minded perseverance. In the literature of chivalry, a man's honor resided in his physical prowess and his spiritual enlightenment which were his weapons against the forces of evil often tempting him in the form of a sexually inviting woman. By the time of Richardson, these roles had been very much reversed, and without any sense of strain the public read its way tearfully through 2,000 pages of an unscrupulous rake trying to seduce a poor, defenseless woman. As a social philosopher at the turn of the century noted, "Men are now the Tempters, and *Women* . . . are first *ashamed* of their *offense.*"[47] No longer were men expected to test their mettle by stoic endurance against tremendous odds—dragons, sorcery, hostile bands of knights. No longer did a man display his "greedy hardiment" by eager combat with challengers. The contest had narrowed considerably by the end of the seventeenth century; a man's trophies were his sexual conquests, and it was the woman who fought the holy struggle to preserve her chastity.

In these fictions, a woman's chastity stood for a more profound inviolability, for being able to hold onto one's convictions and not buckle under pressure. It was her passive endurance, her ability to keep saying "no" in the face of increasingly extreme pressure that was being tested. An early epistolary story by Thomas Brown, for example, shows the connection between chastity and independence; for as long as the husband could not possess his wife sexually he could not "invade" her in any other way either. Only when "the Castle surrender'd" after two months, could the husband control her entirely.[48]

One feels certain that these sexual conflicts were about power rather than desire because the male sexuality is so aggressive. In Crébillon *fils'* novel *Letters from the Marchioness de M**** as in *Clarissa,* the woman actually dies of the sexual invasion. The military metaphors in *Captain Ayloffe's Letters* which are standard in the eighteenth-century language of love, are very much to the point; that is, the object of the game was winning as much as pleasure. "Women are like Commanders in small Garrisons," reads Captain Ayloffe's advice to his friend, "reject the *Carte Blanche,* and pretend to maintain the last Man; but when your Approaches are made, and the Batteries play smartly upon 'em, they'l hang out the Flag, and that Town is not far from Surrendring, which begins to Parley."[49] Or take this letter which a man writes to the woman he loves in *Love-Letters Between A Nobleman and His Sister.* He is telling her of a dream he has just had:

> . . . it was then, and there me thought my *Sylvia* yielded, with a faint Struggle and a soft Resistance; I heard her broken Sighs, her tender whispering Voice, that trembling cry'd—Oh! Can you be so cruel.—Have you the Heart—Will you undo a Maid because she loves you? Oh! Will you ruin me because you may? My faithless—My unkind—then sigh'd, and yielded, and made me happier than a triumphing God! But this was still a Dream, I wak'd and sigh'd, and found it vanish'd all![50]

He dreams about "triumphing," fighting and taking and being deified, potent as a God! Like most of the seduction struggles, this one too is really a power struggle.

One of the reasons for this sexual aggressiveness against women in epistolary novels is because it is precisely the impotent suffering of the embattled heroine which produces the anguished consciousness that needs the release of writing letters. In these stories, women are imprisoned, seduced, abducted, raped, abandoned, and their passively outraged responses to these developments are carefully detailed. Because the woman's role is stereotypically reactive rather than active, the woman's side of things maximizes emotional self-examination. After each encounter, each new plot development, the heroine is given no recourse but to retire to the privacy of her writing closet and react on paper.

Indeed, these epistolary novels are often plotted like experiments performed on isolated individuals. The characters are almost systematically manipulated and their reactions under pressure carefully preserved in their letters or journals. Both Pamela and Clarissa are put through paces to see if they pass the test of virtue. Certainly in a civilization steeped in the Christian tradition of wanderings in the wilderness and of finally finding salvation, stories of trials are no novelty. Yet these references to tests and trials are not so allegorical in tone as they are experimental. One of Aphra Behn's women writes "I'll die before I'll yield my Honour . . . if I can stand this Temptation, I am Proof against all the World."[51] "If it had not been for this Trial to get the Mastery of my Passion," states another embattled heroine in another epistolary novel, "I should never have understood the force of it."[52] The books direct the reader's attention to the heroine's responses as she confronts difficulty after difficulty, to be recorded in her letters, as if the emotional particulars of each case are what is important rather than any temporary outcome in the plot.

Perhaps it was because women were so separated from the rest of society, so very much on their own psychologically, that they came to be the symbolic figures who battled for integrity in the new forms of fiction. Even if a woman conformed totally to the expectations her family held for her, she never was really established securely. Her position was so perennially marginal that one misstep could always lose her everything, and she usually had nothing but her own strength of will and character to pull her through. No one in the society was as alone as a woman; she had no personal power, no resources, and if cut off from her parents, no allies. This defenselessness is apparent enough in a Pamela or a Moll Flanders, but a married woman, too, out of favor with her husband, could be as isolated as described in *The Fatal Amour Between a Beautiful Lady and a Young Nobleman*: "She saw herself in the Hands of an angry Husband, who had an absolute Power over her: And had no body to advise or comfort her."[53] Often these fictional heroines are orphans, lonely individuals standing outside the culture who therefore can be the test cases for working out a new balance between society's regulation and individual desire.

When fictional heroines vacillated about leaving their parental homes and making their own choices, or when fictional rakes debated internally about indulging their desires or following the community's moral codes, they were reflecting dilemmas new to the culture. In part, these were caused by economic changes.[54] For example, the issue of whether to marry for reasons of estate or for individual preference was a very real question in England at that time. But other problems were metaphorically tested in tales of women's virtue and desire as well: whether or not there were natural moral limits, whether the claims of society and traditional authority ought to come before the needs and passions of an individual.

In the epistolary story by Aphra Behn called *Love-Letters Between A Nobleman and His Sister* (1694), these things come together clearly. It is about an incestuous and adulterous passion which is discussed for a long time in letters before finally being consummated near the end of the story. In his verbal agonies, the hero Philander often writes about what is natural and what is artificially imposed upon man by misguided social codes. He is made to be a spokesman for the more "natural," animal side of human nature, envying the freedom of wild birds who are not restrained by "troublesome Honour:"

> Man, the Lord of all! He to be stinted in the most valuable Joy of Life; Is it not pity? Here is no troublesome Honour, amongst the pretty Inhabitants of the Woods and Streams, fondly to give Laws to Nature, but uncontroul'd they play, and sing, and love; no Parents checking their dear Delights, no Slavish Matrimonial Ties to restrain their nobler Flame. No Spies to interrupt their blest Appointments. . . .[55]

He questions the social definitions of what is acceptable, and proclaims his right to "incestuous" love. Indeed, when one looks closely at the nobleman and his mistress-sister, Sylvia, it is clear that there are some extenuating circumstances. For one thing, Sylvia is not Philander's actual blood sister but his wife's younger sister, although that relationship still has an incestuous feel to it. For another, his wife is cuckolding *him* with someone else. But Sylvia argues "False as she is, you are still married to her."[56] Because the social codes are taken seriously, the novel is shaped by that struggle over morality.

The characters all realize that there are laws which feeling does not sweep away; throughout there are references to the affair as being "criminal," "monstrous." When they are discovered, Sylvia writes to her lover:

> *Philander,* all that I dreaded, all that I fear'd is fallen upon me: I have been arraign'd and convicted; three Judges, severe as the three infernal ones, sate in Condemnation on me, a Father, a Mother and a Sister. . . .[57]

Her love affair is an illegal one, and she sees in her family's condemnation the disapproval of the larger society. Sylvia's legalistic metaphor foreshadows the real legal action which follows, too, for the larger society does seek to punish the illicit lovers. Philander is pursued by lawsuits for rape and incest. Finally they solve their problem by marrying Sylvia off to one of Philander's lackeys, who agrees to be married in name only, acting as a front for Philander himself. The only way to appease the outraged society is to mimic its conventions, even in travesty.

Although the lovers hide from their parents, and try to outwit the conventions of society, there is no gaiety about this truancy. Throughout this book there is a deep fear of the breakdown of authority. Although Philander decries the social codes, at the same time the reader feels how much they are needed to hold together the society. Vague and shadowy, the execution of Charles I hovers in the background as a warning of where disrespect for law and order can lead. Philander is a political rebel as well as a sexual one; Sylvia denounces his secret revolutionary activities because they could lead to king-killing and sacrilege. She writes to Philander as if there were a mystical and religious sanction against questioning authority: "I am certain that should the most harden'd of your bloody Rebels look him in the Face," she says, referring to the king, "the devilish Instrument of Death would drop from his sacrilegious Hand, and leave him confounded at the Feet of the Royal forgiving Sufferer . . ."[58] Certainly this passage is naive; but more than that, it is invested with great religious fervor suddenly and sharply felt. In fact, the energy seems to come from Sylvia's anxiety and displaced sexual intensity, expressed in these political issues. Her exaggerated reaction connects the breaking of the two kinds of rules.

This story of crime, both incest and treason, told in the love letters between Philander and Sylvia, looks much like the same old seduction story. Philander convinces Sylvia, against law and common sense, that their desire for one another is more important than anything else. But closer to the surface than usual, the concerns of a culture in flux can be seen, trying to mediate in its fiction between the claims of the traditional and the individual's questioning of these conventions.

Because the epistolary novel grew in response to certain specific social conditions—a new literary industry, broader literacy in the population, the evolution of the female audience, the development of a few writers among middle and upper class women—it was a form well suited to a detailed working through of moral issues. Characters who spent their fictional lives writing letters to each other about their confusion and ambivalence contributed to an illusion of realism; these emotional outpourings were the literary residue of deeply felt experience and thought from which a reader might learn something of use in order to deal with his own moral dilemmas.

. . . . .

It is not simple coincidence that the novel, and especially the epistolary novel, came into vogue at roughly the same time as women's preoccupations began to have less to do with how they actually lived their lives and more to do with the fantasies of love and romance which were the most they could expect as women, if they kept themselves graceful and attractive. The novel must be understood as a form of literature which developed at a time of dislocating social changes. The growth of cities and the beginnings of industrialism caused new divisions of function in the society on the basis of sex as well as class, and this seriously affected the condition of women in the literate classes. These city women no longer were the economic partners of men, for the new capitalistic modes no longer made public use of their labor, but separated them from the active concerns of life into a pretend world of romantic love and fantasy relationships. It is at this point that the novel came into its own—at a time in history when urban women of the middle and upper classes no longer had any economic power, when they no longer participated in the means of production of the society.

Novels fit into this changing social scene as the means for circulating the comforting affirmation that women were not meant to be grocers or haberdashers or wooldrapers (let alone doctors or scholars), but were intended solely for the business of romantic love. Indeed, if a novel had a male protagonist it could be about almost any sort of subject and circumstance, but if it was about a woman, it was almost certainly about her relation to a man; nothing else was germane. Most of these novels about women start as Thomas Brown's *The Adventures of Lindamira* (1702) does: "I shall pass over those little Occurances of my life till I arrived to my 16th Year, during which time nothing remarkable hapned [sic] to me," beginning at the point when the heroine becomes a sexually vulnerable figure, open to the temptations, delusions, and ecstasies of romantic love.[59]

The epistolary novel was the perfect vehicle for stories of romantic love because its very format demanded a subject matter in which emotional states were most prominent. Long distance epistolary involvements, like romantic love, required a taste for sentimentalized fantasy relations, and an ability to shut out humdrum reality. Created to seem possible and true to life, stories in letters portrayed characters who resembled their respectable readers, but who escaped their urban isolation by reading and writing their way into exciting amorous adventures.

Fantasies about love and marriage flourished in this environment not only because they justified the empty lives of middle and upper class women, but because the culture inhibited any realistic and easy relations between the sexes. Marriageable women were rarely alone with the men they imagined themselves to love; such a lack of access could only have encouraged idealized dreams of romance. Many courtships were carried on in letters fuelled by the imaginative process of writing, because written correspondence was the most direct and private way that unmarried men and women had of communicating with one another. We know, for instance, that John Evelyn's eldest daughter Elizabeth appalled her parents by eloping after a long-standing, clandestine correspondence. Dorothy Osborne and William Temple wrote to each other for seven years, despite his father's efforts to find a richer match as well as her relatives' disapproving judgment of William as an adventurer. Finally, after her father died and she survived the smallpox, which disfigured her, they married.

The danger of such relationships was that the distance made it easier to imitate the conventions of the fictions which furnished the ideal versions of such love affairs, and to ignore the obvious disparities between novelistic romances and the experiences of life. *The Spectator* warned, "We generally make Love in a Stile, and with Sentiments

very unfit for ordinary Life: They are half Theatrical, half Romantick. By this Means we raise our Imaginations to what is not to be expected in humane life . . . because we did not beforehand think of the Creature we were enamoured of as subject to Dishumor, Age, Sickness, Impatience, or Sullennes. . . ."[60] As long as such romantic expectations had been attached only to those special relationships outside of the daily round of married life, the stories which promulgated them could have no pernicious effects. But in the fictions of love being written by the end of the seventeenth century, realistic characters were always working through crises, falling in and out of love, managing to live their lives at the emotional pitch which the new clichés about love and marriage celebrated, but which never quite came true for their readers.

The epistolary courtship of Dorothy Osborne and William Temple does not seem to have misled them, for their marriage appears to have been a contented one, despite their early prolonged separation. But other stories from real life did not end so happily. Lady Mary Wortley Montagu, for example, enjoyed her courtship with Wortley and arranged to elope with him by letter, because she was forbidden to see him. Her clandestine correspondence, which ended in an unhappy marriage, is very dramatic, even reading like a novel. In fact, when she was an older woman she told her daughter that Richardson's *Clarissa* reminded her of her own youth. She wrote: "I was such an old Fool as to weep over Clarissa Harlowe like any milkmaid of sixteen over the Ballad of the Ladie's Fall [a broadside written circa 1680]. To say truth, the first volume soften'd me by a near ressemblance of my Maiden Days. . . ."[61]

And it is true—the letters from these "Maiden Days" do read like *Clarissa*. Lady Mary's parents tried to push her into a loveless marriage to add to the family's wealth, and although she argued and appealed to relatives to intercede for her, she finally had no other recourse but to make a stealthy escape. It was almost forty years before *Clarissa* when Lady Mary ran off with her lover; at that time most people did not yet consider love either a necessary or a sufficient condition for marrying. Lady Mary, who did not want to marry against her own inclinations, was advised to do so by her relatives, ordered to do so by her father, and considered "a little Romantic" by her friends. She was sure that even her friend Phillipa would think her mad to run away from an arranged marriage.

I give here most of the sequence which Lady Mary remembered so vividly in her later years, both for the sake of showing the degree to which fiction made use of the conditions of women's lives and because such an actual document throws some light on the fiction it resembles.

To Wortley, June 11, 1712:

> . . . My Family is resolv'd to dispose of me where I hate. I have made all the Opposition in my power; perhaps I have carry'd that opposition too far. However it is, things were carry'd to that height, I have been assur'd of never haveing a shilling, except I comply.

Since the Time of Mandana's we have heard of no Lady's ran away with, without fortunes.[62]

To Wortley, July 26, 1712: she tells him that she has written an importunate letter to her father and

> . . . said every thing in this Letter I thought proper to move him, and proffer'd in attonement for not marrying whom he would, never to marry at all. He did not think fit to answer this letter, but sent for me to him. He told me he was very much surpriz'd that I did not depend on his Judgement for my future happynesse, that he knew nothing I had to complain of etc., that he did not doubt I had some other fancy in my head which encourag'd me to this disobedience, but he assur'd me if I refus'd a settlement he has provided for me, he gave me his word, whatever proposalls were made him, he would never so much as enter into a Treaty with any other; that if I founded any hopes upon his death, I should find my selfe mistaken. . . . I told my Intention to all my nearest Relations; I was surpriz'd at their blameing it to the greatest degree. I was told they were sorry I would ruin my selfe, but if I was so unreasonable they could not blame my F[ather] whatever he inflicted on me. I objected I did not love him. They made answer they found no Necessity of Loveing; if I liv'd well with him, that was all was requir'd of me, and that if I consider'd this Town I should find very few women in love with their Husbands and yet a manny happy. It was in vain to dispute with such prudent people; they look'd upon me as a little Romantic, and I found it impossible to persuade them that liveing in London at Liberty was not the height of happynesse. . . .[63]

To Phillipa Mundy, August 1712:

> For my part, I know not what I shall do; perhaps at last I shall do something to surprize everybody. Where ever I am, and what ever becomes of me, I am ever yours. Limbo is better than Hell. My Adventures are very odd; I may go into Limbo if I please, but tis accompanny'd with such circumstances, my courage will hardly come up to it, yet perhaps it may. In short I know not what will become of me. You'l think me mad, but I know nothing certain but that I shall not dye an Old Maid, that's positive. . . .[64]

To Wortley, August 17, 1712:

> Every thing I apprehended is come t[o p]asse. 'Tis with the utmost difficulty [and d]anger I write this. My father is in the house. . . . I am frighted to death and know not what I say. I had the precaution of desiring Mrs.— to send her servant to wait here for a Letter, yet I am in apprehension of this being stopp'd. If tis, I have yet more to suffer, for I have been forc'd to promise to write no more to you.[65]

To Wortley, August 18, 1712:

> . . . If you can come to the same place any time before that, I may slip out, because they have no suspicion of the morning before a Journey. Tis possible some of the servants will be about the house and see me go

off, but when I am once with you, tis no matter.—If this is impracticable, Adieu, I fear for ever.[66]

To Wortley, August 18, 1712:

> I would not give my selfe the pain of thinking you have suffer'd as much by this misfortune as I have done. The pain of my mind has very much affected my body. I have been sick ever since, yet tho' overcome by fateigue and misfortune I write to you from the first Inn. . . .[67]

The similarity of Lady Mary Wortley Montagu's experience to those of Richardson's celebrated heroine is startling. It makes the interchange between art and life more tangible: Richardson's art seems more genuinely borrowed from the life of his day, while Lady Mary's letters seem more dramatic than life usually is. The energy in these letters comes not only from her fine independent spirit dealing with difficulties, but also from the theatrical touches in her writing which betray interest in the melodrama of her situation. The way she compares her plight to that of Mandane in the romance by Scudéry, the ironic self-consciousness of writing "Hell" to mean spinsterhood and "Limbo" for an uncertain elopement, and the flamboyance of her declarations give one the impression that she thinks her life comparable to that of a fictional heroine.

The excitement of Lady Mary's courtship with Edward Wortley Montagu must have been heightened by their separation, by their constant brooding about one another, and, of course, by the correspondence that they had to resort to. Their meetings had all the trappings of forbidden adulterous affairs: fear of suspicion, arrangements for passing letters, and for properly spaced meetings in larger gatherings. Their letters are all about missing each other, sudden jealousies, and the designing of future *tête-à-têtes*. Behind their relationship was the titillation of checking over one's shoulder, of defying parents, of living out a romance—all the elements of an epistolary relationship. The passion with which they invested their relationship was manufactured out of their fantasies about love and about each other rather than growing gradually out of direct experience of the other.

Lady Mary's marriage was evidently not a happy one, and she must have speculated on the degree to which the imaginings of love reckoned in her own youthful folly. Throughout her later letters she reiterates the maxim that passion keeps better in the imagination than in reality, that long possession of any woman inevitably cools a man's desire for her. In the wisdom of age, having lived through her own difficulties, her final response to Richardson's novel was unsympathetic. She wrote to her daughter:

> Even that model of Perfection, Clarissa, is so faulty in her behavior as to deserve little Compassion. Any Girl that runs away with a young Fellow without intending to marry him should be carry'd to the Bridewell or Bedlam the next day. Yet the circumstances are so laid as to inspire tenderness, not withstanding the low style and absurd incidents, and I look upon this and Pamela

to be two Books that will do more general mischief than the Works of Lord Rochester.[68]

The mischief of which she spoke, no doubt, was the sort that followed from too close identification with such fictional heroines. Novels like *Clarissa* sowed false expectations of romance in young women, as well as such sympathy for her yearnings as might lead them to share her downfall. While Lord Rochester only wrote lascivious verses whose original impulse was clear and whose effects predictable, Richardson wrote books which lured the reader into a world in which right was not so very distinguishable from wrong, because the verisimilitude of the characterizations roused an empathy in the reader which confused the issues. The epistolary format, especially, created a genre in which each character spoke for him or herself, from his or her own point of view; as Clarissa put it to her friend Anna Howe: "there would hardly be a guilty person in the world, were each *suspected* or *accused* person to tell his or her own story and be allowed any degree of credit."[69]

The trouble was that there was not sufficient ballast in women's lives to keep their feet on the ground. The work they did became progressively more ornamental and less functional in the course of the seventeenth century. Like the heroines of epistolary novels, they merely filled their time while waiting for something exciting to happen. Elizabeth Pepys, for example, the wife of the famous diarist, suffered from having nothing to do while her husband was off with friends or at his office. Samuel Pepys seems to have understood what a strain such interminable inactivity was on his wife, although he could not do much about it:

> Up and began our discontent again, and sorely angered my wife, who indeed do live very lonely, but I do perceive that it is want of work. . . . Then to my office late, and this afternoon my wife in her discontent sent me a letter, which I am in a quandry what to do, whether to read it or not, but I propose not, but to burn it before her face, that I may put a stop to more of this nature. But I must think of some way, either to find her some body to keep her company, or to set her to work and by employment to take up her thoughts and time.[70]

With four or five servants and no children, Elizabeth Pepys had little to do but write complaining letters to her husband, who for his part was always hiring some new maid to keep his wife company, or taking her to visit her mother, or engaging a music teacher or a dancing master to keep her occupied.

The situation was no better for brave Lady Mary Wortley Montagu who wrote this letter to her new husband, describing her occupations in his absence:

> I write and read till I can't see, and then I walk; sleep succeeds; thus my whole time is divided. If I was as well qualified in all other ways as I am by idleness, I would publish a daily paper called the *Meditator*. . . . Till today I have had no occasion of opening my mouth to speak, since I wished you a good journey. I see noth-

ing, but I think of every thing, and indulge my imagination, which is chiefly employed on you.[71]

Nor was her case unusual. The editor of *The Tatler* claimed he knew twenty families by name "where all the Girls hear of in this Life is, That it is Time to rise and to come to Dinner; as if they were so insignificant as to be wholly provided for when they are fed and cloathed." With an understanding rare to his time, he continued: "It is with great Indignation that I see such Crowds of the Female World lost to humane Society and condemned to a Laziness, which makes Life pass away with less Relish than in the hardest Labour."[72]

Woman's domain had been reduced to her own small nuclear family, for which she was provided with necessities (cloth, food) by professionals in a wage economy which increasingly excluded her. The new cultural emphasis on childhood and childrearing which Philippe Ariès dates from the end of the seventeenth century probably grew out of this social dysfunction. It was then that childhood began to be understood as qualitatively different from adulthood: children stopped being dressed exactly like adults, and painters stopped painting them as scaled-down adults.[73] The new consideration given to the education and training of children made motherhood into a kind of profession, creating new responsibilities for women, and providing them with new leverage within the evolving family.

But these were not roles which required formal education and rarely were women trained to read further than the semi-literate assortment of novels, romances, and plays available to them. Even wealthy women were expected to improve their time with needlework rather than in the pursuit of learning. Mary Astell, who petitioned Queen Anne to set up schools for women, felt that this cultural neglect of women's minds was the root symptom of the prejudice against them, and that to it could be traced their characteristic boredom, frivolity, and expense. An intellectual life was the highest good, she believed, and leisure was best filled with serious study and charitable works. She felt that women needed education to help right the balance in their lives, to promote reason over passion, and reality over fantasy. But in advocating women's schools, she could not always keep an ironic note from her writing, for she knew she was demanding it in a social vacuum:

> But to what Study shall we apply ourselves? some Men say that Heraldry is a pretty Study for a Woman, for this reason, I suppose, That she may know how to Blazon her Lord and Master's great Atchievements! They allow us Poetry, Plays, and Romances, to Divert us and themselves; and when they would express a particular Esteem for a Woman's Sense, they recommend History; tho' with Submission, History can only serve us for Amusement and a Subject of Discourse. [For] . . . how will this help our Conduct or excite us in a generous Emulation? since the Men being the Historians, they seldom condescend to record the great and good Actions of Women; and when they take notice of them, 'tis with this wise Remark, That such Women *acted*

above their Sex. By which one must suppose they would have their Readers understand, That they were not Women who did those Great Actions, but that they were Men in Petticoats![74]

With so little to give their lives meaning and stability, it is no wonder that women were given to illusory brooding about romance. A sophisticated character in a French epistolary novel later in the century shuddered for the susceptibility of idle women whose energies centered on love:

> Tremble above all for those women, active in their idleness, whom you call "tender," of whom love takes possession so easily and with such power; women who feel the need to occupy themselves with it even when they do not enjoy it and who, abandoning themselves unreservedly to the ebullition of their ideas, give birth through them to those sweet letters which are so dangerous to write; women who are not afraid to confide these proofs of their weakness to the person who causes them; imprudent women, who cannot see their future enemy in their present lover.[75]

"Those sweet letters" to which epistolary heroines abandoned themselves, were "dangerous to write" because they fanned the flames of love and encouraged solitary dreaming. Writing kept a woman on the string, imaginatively involved in the love affair, no matter what the distance, no matter what the obstacles. As the famous letter-writing Portuguese Nun observed: "a man should rather fix upon a Mistress in a Convent than anywhere else. For they have nothing there to hinder them from being perpetually Intent upon their Passion. . . ."[76]

The unreality of women's lives was also perpetuated by such training and direction as they did get. Lord Halifax's famous letter to his daughter, a distillation of the soundest precepts of his time, advised her "to have a perpetual watch upon your Eyes, and to remember, that one careless Glance giveth more advantage than a hundred words not enough considered."[77] He warned her to avoid gambling because she might get caught up in the game and forget to compose her face. Everywhere he reminds her that her reputation is her most important possession, in a hostile world where everyone is after her virtue. "The Enemy is abroad and you are sure to be taken if you are found stragling."[78] He preached constant vigilance and mastery of inference, of indirect expression, of innuendo. Indeed, his advice could also have been aimed at training for seduction, so much did he emphasize the possible effects of the smallest sign or gesture of real feeling.

Steele satirizes this trained coquetry in the complaints of a fashionable London lady about her visiting country cousin, in *The Spectator.*

> She is very pretty, but you can't imagine how Unformed a Creature it is. She comes to my Hands just as Nature left her, half finished, and without any acquired Improvements. . . . She knows no Way to express her self but by Tongue, and that always to signifie her Meaning. Her Eyes serve her yet only to see with, and

she is utterly a Foreigner to the Language of Looks and Glances. In this I fancy you could help her better than any Body. I have bestowed two Months in teaching her to Sigh when she is not concerned, and to Smile when she is not pleased: and am ashamed to own she makes little or no Improvement. . . . I could pardon too her Blushing, if she knew how to carry her self in it and if it did not manifestly injure her Complexion.[79]

Although Steele humorously overdoes his thesis that city women are caricatures of all that is unnatural, always playing a part, still he suggests how genteel women of his time did violence to their own feelings of reality. He also describes the upbringing which trained them to control their feelings, expressions, and actions, to ignore discomfort for beauty, and to choose an immediate pain in the expectation of a future pleasure:

> When a Girl is safely brought from her Nurse, before she is capable of forming one simple Notion of anything in Life . . . [she] is taught a fantastical Gravity of Behaviour and is forced to a particular Way of holding her Head, heaving her Breast, and moving with her whole Body; and all this under the Pain of never having a Husband; if she steps, looks, or moves awry. This gives the Young Lady wonderful Workings of Imagination, what is to pass between her and this Husband, that she is every Moment told of, and for whom she seems to be educated.[80]

This is an important point: women were being brought up to live imaginatively in the future; nothing else in their lives justified such training as they got.

By assuming that women were meant primarily for romantic attachment, society condemned them to it. Gone were the earlier straightforward contractual relations between the sexes, supplanted by the mystification of idealized relationships. The only appropriate ambition of a lady of quality was to bend all efforts to the art of pleasing. This constant recourse to the judgments of others was to take the place of living for them and fill the gaps of education and career. "'Tis much more natural for women to please men than do any other thing," states a pamphlet published in 1696. "And this desire which is so innate to the Sex, makes them live without action."[81] Women were instructed to treat themselves as mirrors, to reflect others rather than to have any self. They were to live in their imaginings of others' thoughts rather than in their own reality. "True Love," began "Mrs. Steele" ominously in the third volume of *The Ladies Library,* "in all Accidents, looks upon the Person beloved, and observes his countenance, and how he approves or disapproves it, and accordingly looks sad or cheerful."[82] Since love was to be the basic inspiration of a married woman's life, she was to experience everything in terms of another's wishes, and filter her life through the construct of her husband's mind.

Not only did this society demand that women move carefully and watchfully through life, guided by their conscious minds and not their instincts, but it denied their physical reality, the enjoyment of their bodies. Their visible constraint was even remarked by a foreign visitor:

Walking is likewise a great Diversion among the Ladies, and their Manner of doing it is one way of knowing their Character; desiring only to be seen, they walk
together, for the most part, without speaking: They are
always dress'd, and always stiff; they go forward constantly, and nothing can amuse or put them out of their
way; I doubt they would not stoop to take up a Flower
from under their Feet: I never saw any of them lie on
the Grass, not shew the least Inclination to sing. . . .[83]

The ultimate physical repression, of course, was the culture's denial of female sexuality. Although trained to attract men, even in a sexual way, the love women were to
bear their husbands was to exclude the natural reason that
men and women mate. The author of *The Present State of
Matrimony* suggested that women have "*an inexpressible
Desire of Children,* which we rudely, and wrongfully term
Lust . . . This Passion for young Children, is beyond
Imagination. The most chaste Virgin in the World can
scarce contain herself at the Sight of a beautiful Child; but
is ready to devour it with her Kisses."[84] Any feeling more
distinctly physical than that in a woman was thought degenerate. Many critics have taken Clarissa's vacillations as
a sign of her neurosis, but it was characteristic of the period to assume that women only endured sex for money or
security. Even Moll Flanders only used sex for these ends.
The early novels are filled with heroines who are wood-
enly unconscious of their own desire—a convention which
demonstrated their decency and modesty as well as the expectations of polite society. Defoe, who chides his male
readers in *Conjugal Lewdness* for marrying solely for
"Money and Maidenhood," never admits the possibility of
women's marrying for sexual reasons. But he does warn
prospective husbands that they would be fools to marry
any woman who granted the ultimate favor before the
wedding night, because such appetite proved them unfit
for marriage.

These attitudes had not always prevailed—even in England. In Chaucer's time, for example, the sexuality of
that gat-toothed woman, the libidinous Wife of Bath, was
portrayed without embarrassment, ugliness, or shame. Her
lustiness was a sign of vitality and readers were to delight
in it, to admire her for having had the world in her time.
In the Renaissance, too, a woman's sexual appetite was
recognized and even feared. For once she was introduced
to sexual pleasure by her conjugal duties and her natural
passion aroused, one could not depend on her chastity.
Husbands were therefore advised to limit sexual activity
with their wives, "even to the point of deprecating pleasure,"[85] and not awaken this dangerous appetite. Certainly
the Renaissance conventions of adulterous passion, a system which separated love from marriage, implicitly recognized women's desires. But by the eighteenth century, decent women were no longer expected to enjoy their
sexuality. In 1714 a woman, shielded by anonymity, lamented in *The Spectator* "that Men may boast and glory in
those things that we must think of with Shame and Horror!"[86]

The public promotion of contraceptives made this denial
all the more double-edged inasmuch as it clarified the dis-

tinction between sex for pleasure and sex for reproduction.
Although contraceptives had been used in many cultures
for centuries, public notice of them was new.[87] The first
mention of them in print came in 1708, in *The Charitable
Surgeon,* by "T. C. Surgeon" (pirated from John Marten)
which offered "The certain easy way to escape Infection,
tho' never so often accompanying with the most polluted
Companion," and went on to hint that it might keep young
ladies from "a great belly."[88] A year later *The Tatler* jogged
the public memory by touting him who "invented an Engine for the Prevention of Harms by Love Adventures" as
a great "Promoter of Gallantry and Pleasure."[89] These notices amounted to a public recognition that sex could be
indulged in exclusively for pleasure. Indeed, Defoe
frowned upon their use in marriage as encouraging improper attitudes towards sexual relations.[90]

It is important to know these facts about women's lives if
one is to make sense of Clarissa's endless ambivalence,
Pamela's investment in her simple style of dress, the interminable letters which they wrote, or the reading public's
fascination with long stories of women's seduction. The
speakers in many early novels were women: Moll Flanders,
Roxana, Pamela, Clarissa, Evelina; and their moral, economic, and social choices were symbolized almost exclusively in sexual terms because increasingly, that *was* the
only option in women's lives. Unlike the dazzling but
faceless damsels of earlier romances, these self-involved
heroines focused minutely and lengthily on their own feelings, for they evolved when their genteel counterparts in
life were bored, inactive, badly educated, and without real
work. It is no wonder that women's lives furnished the
materials for a genre whose subject matter was deferred
experience and emotional description.

But the inventors of such heroines had to be careful not to
outrage polite readers of their fictions. Their characters
had to have the fire and imagination for the ardent love affairs readers wanted to experience by proxy, but enough
discretion to inhibit these impulses like properly bred
women. The solution was to let art imitate life, and to portray women who enacted in fantasy what they were denied
in actuality. One of Mrs. Manley's heroines, for instance,
confides to her lover that

> Fancy has brought you near, nay so very near, as to my
> Bosom; there this Morning I dream'd you were, and
> the Imagination was so strong, that starting out of my
> Sleep I left my Dream imperfect; my Senses, had their
> Concern been less, had not so soon rous'd themselves
> to find whether the Object were a real or imaginary
> Happiness. And I perhaps had longer seen you, nay, I
> more than saw you, forgive the Pleasure I take in writ-
> ing freely. . . .[91]

The unconsciousness of the dream state not only relieved
her of responsibility for her sexual desire, but also proved
her moral strength. For virtue is cheap if there is no passion to overcome, no struggle to win. Héloise's letters,
too, report living through moments from the past she
shared with Abelard in a precious, recurring dream:

During the still Night, when my Heart ought to be quiet in the midst of sleep, which suspends the greatest Disturbances, I cannot avoid those Illusions my Heart entertains. I think I am still with my dear Abelard. I see him, I speak to him, and hear him answer. Charmed with each other, we quit our Philosophick studies to entertain ourselves with our Passion. . . .[92]

The dream itself is about surrender to passion, the relaxation of vigilant reason, that moment when a woman puts down her book and stops studying. And that is when the remembrance comes to Héloise—when her guard is down, when her fantasies are available to her, unlocked by sleep.

As Eliza Haywood told her readers "whatever Dominion, Honour, and Virtue may have over our waking Thoughts, 'tis certain that they fly from the clos'd Eyes, our Passions then exert their forceful Power, and that which is most Predominant in the Soul, Agitates the fancy, and brings even Things Impossible to pass: Desire, with watchful Diligence repell'd, returns with greater violence in unguarded sleep, and overthrows the vain Efforts of Day."[93] Haywood herself has a delightful example of it in *Love in Excess,* when during her sleep "Melliora in spite of herself, was often happy in Idea, and possest a Blessing, which shame and Guilt deter'd her from in reality."[94] We see Melliora enact in dumbshow, still asleep, the motions of her desire while calling out: "too too lovely Count—Ecstatic Ruiner!" What is all the more delicious, the Count himself is present in the room with her, holding her and kissing her as she sleeps. Melliora can enact her impulsive desires but without any moral responsibility for them because she is asleep. Meanwhile, the chaste reader, too, could have the satisfaction of both admiring an honorable heroine and of vicariously enjoying her less-than-honorable embraces.

Such a scene testifies to the increasing gap in early eighteenth-century culture between private sexual indulgence and public emphasis on chastity; it shows the hypocrisy of an age in which men had the reputations of libertines, while women denied and were denied their sexuality. Nor was the effect of this public prudery to dismiss questions of sex from the public consciousness but rather to focus it more sharply on the mildest of actions. By the time Fanny Burney wrote *Evelina,* her readership was titillated by the effrontery of a man who took the arm of a decent woman unbidden. Innuendo and metaphor began to make up the deficits in explicit storytelling in these stories of thwarted love: when Melliora stuffs the keyhole to her room to prevent the Count from using his key, there is no doubt about what these images stand for; the nun in Jane Barker's *A Patch-work Screen For The Ladies* touches off a fire in her convent as she runs away with her lover—the convent and her passion simultaneously burst into flames.

Inevitably, it was feared that such reading would have bad effects on the suggestible minds of young women who were learning to read in greater numbers all the time. Take this warning, for example, the donné of a story by Jane

Barker: wealthy Dorinda is so blinded and misled by the romantic fiction with which she has been filling her head that she makes the terrible mistake of marrying her footman, sure that he is a prince in disguise. However once he has the legal prerogatives of a husband he proves to be a brute, taking over her property and even pushing her out of the house. She finally blames fiction for the illusions which led her into folly.

It was such Romantick Whimsies that brought upon me the Ruin and Distress in which you behold me; I had read Plays, Novels and Romances; till I began to think myself a Heroine of the first rate; and all Men that flatter'd, or ogled me were Heroes; and that a pretty well-behaved foot-man or Page must needs be the Son of some Lord or great Gentleman.[95]

In Defoe's *The Family Instructor* (1715), the exemplary dialogue between mother and daughter focuses on this problem as if it were a standard reason for the maternal admonitions of young ladies. At the end of the ideal scenario between mother and daughter, the repentant daughter makes an enormous bonfire of all her plays, romances, and novels, in a blaze of religious fervor. The transgressions of the son in this fictively typical family were profligacy, drinking, play-going, and swearing; no one was concerned about the delicate balance of *his* mind. Not until fifty years later was there a male character, Rousseau's St. Preux, who was encouraged in his deceptions about romantic love by reading too many novels.

Parents recognized that novels set improper examples and encouraged improper feelings, that the passions in these fictions "are apt to insinuate themselves into unwary Readers, and by an unhappy Inversion a copy shall produce an Original. . . . Indeed 'tis very difficult to imagine what vast Mischief is done to the World by the False Notions and Images of Things, particularly of Love and Honour, those noblest concerns of Human Life, represented in these Mirrors."[96] In fact, epistolary fictions were always calling the attention of readers to these dangers. It was as if they advertised their product and testified for it themselves. In a conversation in *Love in Excess,* it was averred that "these sort of Books were, as it were, preparations to Love, and by their softening Influence melted the Soul, and made it fit for Amorous Impressions."[97] In other words, one was more open to real sexual experience if one had lived through it once already in the imagination.

There is a letter in the fictional collection, *The Post-Boy Rob'd of His Mail,* in which a libertine instructs a complicitous maid by letter to help him time his amorous attacks:

Watch her softest hours, when her Soul's in tune to join with the Harmony of Love: After her Mind has been employed in Romances, Plays, and Novels, then nought but sweet Ideas fill her Soul, and Love can't be denied admittance, those having so well prepared the way.[98]

He subscribes to the theory that these stories of love will stimulate the woman's sexual impulses and he wants to strike, so to speak, when the iron is hot. In another fiction, an experienced woman writes a letter to a friend, in which she describes seducing a young man by lending him some books. The volume that seemed most effective, significantly enough, is a collection of letters:

> We chanced one day to light upon Brown's Translation of *Fontenel's* and *Aristaenetus's* Letters; he seem'd mightily pleas'd with 'em; there was one from a Lady who permits a Lover all but the Last Favor, and gives him leave to touch her Breast, to Kiss her Eyes, her Mouth, and squeeze her with her stays off; he could not imagine what Pleasure could be taken in that. . . .[99]

Certainly the epistolary author is asking the reader-at-home to "imagine what Pleasure could be taken in that," as well as telling the story. Books do lead one into sexual thoughts. The sequence is reminiscent of Dante's lovers Paolo and Francesca seduced by the kiss in their book. Needless to say, the heroine soon shows the naif what he has been missing. But it is clear that the seeds of his seduction were planted not by any real touching, but by the imagined touching which he experienced through the printed page. This is the point at which the experience of the reader in the fiction is shared exactly by the reader-at-home.

The same seductive technique is employed by the Duke in the *Secret Memoirs . . . from New Atalantis* when, attracted to his beautiful young ward Charlot, he decides to stop playing guardian to her virtue and to corrupt her. Like Milton's Satan, he knows that the surest way is to appeal to her imagination, to offer the intangible. He leads her to the library and directs her to read romances and novels and various works which focus on love. Then he leaves for several days, to give the poison a chance to work:

> The Duke was an Age absent from her, she could only in Imagination possess what she believed so pleasing. Her Memory was prodigious, she was indefatigable in Reading. The Duke had left Orders she shou'd not be controul'd in any thing: Whole Nights were wasted by her in the Gallery; she had too well inform'd her self of the speculative Joys of Loves. There are Books dangerous to the Community of Mankind; abominable for Virgins, and destructive to Youth; such as explains the Mysteries of Nature, the congregated Pleasures of Venus, the full Delights of mutual Lovers, which rather ought to pass the Fire than the Press.[100]

The episodes which follow are predictable. Charlot succumbs to temptation and becomes the Duke's mistress upon his return. Advertising her book as the apotheosis of passion, Mrs. Manley unconsciously burlesques the scene, promising her readers a "young and innocent Charlot, transported with the powerful Emotion of a just kindling Flame, sinking with Delight and Shame upon the Bosom of her Lover in the Gallery of Books."[101] It is a wonderful image, a perfect emblem of the warning and fascination for books which describe love, illustrating how stories about passion induce passion, that vicarious experience enjoyed in the reading could have consequences in real life.

Again and again in epistolary novels, there are scenes which do not advance the plot but seem especially prepared, garnished, and served as inducements to fantasy. Reported in letters, they are twice as suggestive, for they carry with them the motives of the fictive correspondents who want to re-experience their moments of passion by writing about them. Sylvia, for instance, in *Love-Letters Between A Nobleman and His Sister,* writes to her lover:

> What tho' I lay extended on my Bed undrest, unapprehensive of my Fate, my Bosom loose and easy of Access, my Garments ready, thin and wantonly put on, as if they would with little Force submit to the fond straying Hand. . . .[102]

There is no narrative reason for Sylvia to tell Philander all this since both he and his "fond straying Hand" were present at the time. The reader can only understand it as a daydream, a delicious moment Sylvia wants Philander to live through again with her in the imagination. But the passage is also designed to allow the audience a chance to imagine themselves into such a moment. Another letter-writing character, almost as blatant, urges his sister to think of him at the moment he takes his new bride to bed: "I conjure you, Sister, by our Friendship, in your Imagination to time my Joys, when all transported I shall naked clasp her fair, soft, sweet, enchanting Body to my Bosom. . . ."[103] Such letters are explicit invitations to the reader-at-home, too, to indulge in voyeuristic fantasy. Imagine, for instance, a solitary reader at home in 1730 reading these words written by a solitary character having an epistolary love affair:

> The thoughts of your Return, and our happy Meeting again, fills me with Ideas too ravishing to admit Allay. . . . Instead of amusing myself with any thing that might make me forget you, I take no Delight but in remembering you: Recollections presenting me with ten thousand nameless Softnesses your dear Society blest me with, and I injoy them over again in Theory. . . .[104]

The unspecific language could fit almost anyone's fantasy of love. And the reader could certainly "injoy them over again in theory" as often and as imaginatively as the epistolary heroine herself.

Even the plot structures of epistolary novels have a sexual rhythm, building towards the moment of sexual release. "I could grow old with waiting here the blessed Moment," writes Philander in *Love-letters Between a Nobleman and His Sister,* focusing his entire attention, and the reader's as well, on that moment.[105] The characters in epistolary novels stimulate and tease themselves, as well as the reader, with their longings for one another, their jealousies, and the possibilities of their next meeting. The culmination of this epistolary activity is usually their sexual union, the non-verbal end to which the writing is directed. The hindrances to this consummation, the obstacles in the way, then become a kind of titillating foreplay the author and reader engage in. As one of Mrs. Manley's epistolary characters asks, "what can be more exquisite than delay'd Enjoyment?"[106]

In Aphra Behn's *Love-Letters Between A Nobleman and His Sister,* for instance, although we know from the start that Philander and Sylvia are destined for each other, three quarters of Part I goes by before they manage to go to bed together. Until then, most of their writing has to do with the planning and anticipation of that moment. Many pages, written to tantalize and heighten the suspense, elapse after Sylvia agrees to it. And then, after all that, Sylvia faints and Philander becomes impotent; the tryst is a failure and the lovers begin to plan for another one. And so the novel itself becomes a paradigm of sexual play: building up the audience for the big moment, delaying it, and building up again.

The same rhythm is worked out in Eliza Haywood's *Love in Excess.* Many times before the dénouement, the sexual act is averted at the last minute. The would-be lovers are interrupted at the crucial moment many times and finally even separated by nunnery walls before the actual reunion and marriage take place. There is even one scene in which the Count, about to be seduced by a wealthy, corrupt, alluring woman, is saved at the eleventh hour when a messenger bursts into the room. The scene is unintentionally laughable, for the Count has already come to the brink of intercourse so many times with the lovely Melliora that his near seduction seems like an unintended parody of those scenes: virtue is always being saved just in the nick of time. Not that there is ever any question about the eventual outcome. One of the characters even carries around a wedding gown in a trunk, as Haywood carried the ending in her mind from the start, and makes a dramatic entrance in it at the triple marriage which ends the book.

Interestingly, overt pornography was developing at the same time as these epistolary tales of love and sex. Certainly they came out of the same socio-economic facts: growing literacy and book production, an increased emphasis on women as sexual objects along with greater restraints than ever on their availability, and arrangements for privacy in urban dwellings. This was a context which bred a taste for sexual fantasy, and in it the pornographic novel grew up side by side with the polite novel.

There had always been a place for the bawdy in literature, for the telling of dirty stories for raucous enjoyment. But this new kind of book had a very different effect on its readers. Here is an account which Pepys gives of finding a copy of *L'Ecole des Filles* unexpectedly:

> Jan. 13, 1668
>
> . . . stopped at Martin's, my bookseller, where I saw the French book which I did think to have had for my wife to translate, called 'L'eschollle des filles,' but when I come to look at it, it is the most bawdy, lewd book that I ever saw, rather worse than 'Putana errante,' so that I was ashamed of reading it.[107]

But the fascination outlasted the shame, and a month later Pepys returned to his bookseller's shop and

> . . . bought the idle rogueish book 'L'eschollle des filles,' which I have bought in plain binding, avoiding the buying of it better bound, because I resolve, as soon as I have read it, to burn it, that it may not stand in the list of books nor among them, to disgrace them if it should be found.[108]

The next day, having read his new book, Pepys says that

> it is a mightly lewd book, but yet not amiss for a sober man once to read over to inform himself of the vilany of the world. . . . I to my chamber where read through 'L'escholle des filles,' a lewd book, but what do no wrong once to read for information sake. . . . And after I had done it I burned it, that it might not be among my books to my shame, and so at night to supper and to bed.[109]

Pepys's response to the book distinguished it from the bawdy of earlier periods: by 1668 sexuality had the power to entice and to shame. It counted among the villainies of the world, and a reader had to somehow justify his reading such books by claiming for them some redeeming social value.

Both pornography and novels shared an emphasis on the flammable imagination, on the dimension of mental activity in sexual matters. But whereas polite prose fiction emphasized women's sexuality by means of prudish abhorrence of it, by imagining women as protectors of the honor of their families, pornographic books were exclusively about the other side of women's nature. *La Puttana Errante* (1650) was a discussion between whores on the means to sexual pleasure; *L'Ecole des Filles,* published five years later, linked sex to romantic love in a radical departure from conventional mores. By 1660 there was a book out which specialized in perversions, including sections on the young, group intercourse, whipping and lesbianism.[110] Women were viewed as angels in one form of prose fiction and as whores in another—in both cases in exclusively sexual terms.

Epistolary fiction, in which characters tried expressly to share their experiences with one another, capitalized on these trends. After all, the purpose of a letter is to make one person's consciousness available to another. Epistolary characters are always trying to make people far away catch fire, to make their friends and lovers feel what they feel. Sometimes this intention is explicit, as with Edward Ward's young man who employs "*Loves* common confident, The *Pen*" as a "means of kindling the like Desires in my new found Angel . . ."[111] Or there is Mary Davys' gentleman who also thinks a pen the most effective way to woo a lady. "Methinks," replies this man's intended victim, warning him that she is not susceptible to his sweet words, "you write as if you had a mind to draw me in, as you pretend Love has done you, by Wheedle."[112]

Since all the relationships in an epistolary novel are verbal, people fall in love with one another's words, tempt each other at long distance by writing seductive things, and spy on each other's words. The novels set out to dramatize the relation of imagination to life, the way the words on a page can play havoc with the emotional state of a reader. And because the novel reader is also privy to these very powerful words, he or she is also open to their effects.

Indeed, epistolary fiction often encouraged readers' identification by providing a third figure in the novel who also read the letters, who was privy to the action, and who comprehended the intimacy between the major correspondents. This third person, sometimes a confidante of the hero or heroine, sometimes part of a love triangle, opened up the tale to the reader-at-home by doubling his or her role as spectator to the emotional action.

There is an example of this provocation to voyeurism in *The Unnatural Mother and Ungrateful Wife,* a story in which daughters triumph over their mothers. It comes in a central scene in which the kindly woman who is being betrayed by her adopted daughter is alerted to this state of affairs by her waiting maid. She watches through a keyhole and sees her husband come into evil Nelly's room at midnight "with nothing on him but his Shirt and a Night-Gown flowing loose about him." Then the faithless man "threw himself on her Bosom with eager Haste, seem'd ready to stifle her with burning Kisses, while his wanton Hands were preparing to consummate the last guilty Rites of lawless Passion."[113] As the betrayed wife watches the two lovers enact their passion, the reader notices, with a kind of jealous and guilty shock, that he or she is also watching. The scene, then, is structured to duplicate, for the reader, the voyeurism and to intensify the feelings it engenders.

René Girard, writing theoretically about the novel, describes and explains this "triangulation of desire" as he calls it.[114] Triangulating desire, arranging a three-way love interest rather than a simple two-way mutual attraction, keeps the desire from being a simple, direct relation between the one who loves and the object of desire. A triple relationship is mediated by someone else's responses, and this mediation, this awareness of a third person's implication in the love affair intensifies the desire, for the rivals imitate each other, reinforce their own fixations by imagining the other's feeling. In other words, the force of triangular desire comes from the mind, as it were, rather than from the viscera; its power can be attributed to the intensified consciousness which jealousy provokes. Such triangulation is almost standard in epistolary novels, in which letters between lovers or confidantes are always being forged, intercepted, or even just read, legitimately, by a third person.

The experience of vicariously sharing the lives of fictional characters is undoubtedly familiar to long-time novel readers. By now we have all grown up knowing that feeling of becoming absorbed in another world, of escaping through the printed page, of going into that reading trance which substitutes the reality of the world on the page for the world around us; but this is a relatively recent notion of the way literature can function. It was not until the early

epistolary novels, with their long-distance relationships, their emotional realism, their stories of amateur writers trying to let one another in on essential experiences, that books were turned to such a use. Until then literature was used to delight and to instruct, but not to confound a storybook realm with real life.

Nor were books the proper medium for light entertainment until literacy and book production put them in the hands of a much larger proportion of the population. Printed literature had always been the province of a small number of educated aristocrats until the late seventeenth century, with traditions going back to the Bible or the classical writers. The issues of these novels—the search for personal happiness in romantic love and marriage, and the sanctification of the individual consciousness (the resistance to seduction or persuasion, the need for privacy)—these had not mattered to earlier cultures. Not until the economic and cultural changes of the seventeenth century, with the consequent reshaping of community and family life, altered social patterns was there need for a literature with another audience, another purpose, another set of strategies.

One of the earliest critics to consider the "origin and progress of novel-writing," the first editor of Richardson's letters, describes what is special about the way Clarissa works:

> We do not come upon unexpected adventures and wonderful recognitions, by quick turns and surprise: we see her fate from afar, as it were through a long avenue, the gradual approach to which, without ever losing sight of the object, has more of simplicity and grandeur than the most cunning labyrinth . . . As the work advances, the character rises; the distress is deepened; our hearts are torn with pity and indignation; bursts of grief succeed one another, till at length the mind is composed and harmonized with emotions of milder sorrow; we are calmed into resignation, elevated with pious hope, and dismissed glowing with the conscious triumph of virtue.[115]

Moment by moment the experienced novelist guides us into a world which is familiar and simplified. Gradually he draws us into believing in it, meshes its assumptions with our own, arranges for us to live in his world long enough until it takes over our entire consciousness and "our hearts are torn with pity and indignation" and all the rest of it.

In letter fiction, because writer and reader are already part of the fictional reality, a reader-at-home is that much closer to full suspension of disbelief. Whereas in the epics or tragedies of the Greeks, *catharsis* was achieved by ritual progress through symbolic action, here it is achieved by identification with the particular plight of a particular individual. We feel the dilemma because we care for Clarissa. The participatory *action* of reading letters, the attempt to re-create the world of the letter-writer so as to make sense of the letter, encourages this empathy. And for the reading audience of these early novels, used to maintaining emotional connections with family and friends by mail for long periods of time, the effort must have been a familiar one.

Letters have the natural property of suspending attention from the world of objects and turning it inward to imagined people and relationships. These attention-riveting qualities of letters are apparent simply by picking up a modern day letter manual and skimming some samples. The words on the page, with their implication of direct, personal communication, have the power to take precedence over the immediate world. It is not necessary to have a personal connection to the circumstances of these writings to participate in the fictional world from which they arise; one naturally tries to fill in the qualities of the letter-writer and the relationship with the interlocutor from the tone and style of the letter.

These effects influenced the developing novel. A fiction presented "unedited" in a series of letters could lure a reader into putting the story together, into caring about the characters behind the letters. The adventures and relationships of solitary letter-writing characters in fiction were more available to solitary readers at home for delectation and escape than those offered in a more conventional narrative form. Letter novels, like letters themselves, could take you vicariously where you could not go in life.

But this could also be a moral advantage, as Richardson convinced the reading public. One could live through others' mistakes and emerge unscathed but chastened. The experience of an exemplary consciousness—that of a Pamela or a Clarissa—could inspire, uplift, change a reader. "Many a young woman has caught from such works as *Clarissa* or *Cecilia,* ideas of delicacy and refinement which were not, perhaps, to be gained in any society she could have access to," wrote Anna Letitia Barhauld in her early nineteenth-century eulogy of Richardson. In an anecdote included in the introduction to the second edition of *Pamela,* this sorcery of the novel, this power to take over the reader, is held up as its special advantage:

> The first Discovery we made of this Power over so unripe and unfix'd an Attention, was, one Evening, when I was reading her [Pamela's] Reflections at the *Pond* to some Company. The little rampant Intruder, being kept out by the Extent of the Circle, had crept under my Chair, and was sitting before me, on the Carpet, with his Head almost touching the Book, and his Face bowing down toward the Fire.—He had sat for some time in this Posture, with a Stillnes, that made us conclude him asleep: when, on a sudden, we heard a Succession of heart-heaving Sobs; which while he strove to conceal from our Notice, his little Sides swell'd, as if they wou'd burst, with the throbbing Restraint of his Sorrow. I turn'd his innocent Face, to look toward me; but his Eyes were quite lost, in his *Tears.* . . . [He] is perhaps the youngest of *Pamela's Converts.*[116]

This passage is a testimonial to the novel's success, proof that it has the desired effect, that it can do its appointed job properly. That stillness which seemed like sleep is a sign of the spellbinding, the transfixion of the boy in another consciousness. The fact that we are told he also "has got half her sayings by heart, talks no other language but hers . . ." demonstrates, too, the extent to which he has

entered Pamela's mind, or perhaps let her enter his. A new era of fiction had begun; now a book was expected to do more than just tell a story.

Letters, by virtue of their place in the culture, their literary effects, and their implicit fiction of a single, personal voice, had been an important link in the process which evolved the modern novel. The experience of long-distance correspondence made it possible for the reading audience to imagine carrying on an emotional life at some remove, or to maintain a one-sided relationship in the imagination rather than to live it out in the social world. This new kind of literature encouraged readers to dream themselves into the lives they found in books, lives of characters for whom reading and writing were their most significant acts.

The epistolary mode also made plausible a new kind of heroine—literate, isolated, unhappy—who symbolized in a purer form the dilemmas of the current culture than the heroes of earlier romances and epics. Such heroines, who poured out their hearts on paper, valued their individual happiness above social approval and assumed that this happiness was to be found not in work or religion but in a perfect sexual union whose institutional form was marriage. These were assumptions which, however widely adopted by middle-class English society, belonged particularly to the women of that class, for the economic and social reorganization which took place in England in the course of the seventeenth century had abridged many of their functions. Novels not only filled the leisure of those without serious work but provided romantic fantasies to give meaning to their lives. Even the intoxication of reading novels resembled the intoxication of romantic love; the epistolary formula, in particular, was a perfect one for stories of romantic love ending in "happily ever after" marriages. In this way, epistolary novels perpetuated the myth of romance in everyday life by telling such stories as if they were true, by giving them wider circulation and making them part of the popular culture, and by inviting readers in their very form, to partake of the pleasures of fantasy.

Notes

1. J. H. Plumb, *England in the Eighteenth Century* (Harmondsworth, 1950), p. 17.

2. W. Maitland, *A History of London* (London, 1739), pp. 322-324.

3. M. Dorothy George, *London Life in the Eighteenth Century* (New York, 1965), pp. 10-11.

4. Philip Pinkus, *Grub Street Stripped Bare* (New York, 1968), p. 285. This is quoted from a contemporary broadsheet.

5. Margaret Cole, *Marriage: Past and Present* (London, 1938), p. 86.

6. Ronald Paulson, *Hogarth: His Life, Art and Times,* 2 vols. (New Haven, 1971), I, 254.

7. David Owen, *English Philanthropy* (Cambridge, Mass., 1964), p. 53.

8. M. Dorothy George, *London Life in the Eighteenth Century,* p. 25. See the work of early demographers such as John Graunt and William Petty or the pamphlet *Marriage Promoted: In a Discourse of Its Ancient and Modern Practice both under Heathen and Christian Commonwealth* (London, 1690), described below.

9. William Black, *Observations Medical and Political on the Small Pox and the Mortality of Mankind at Every Age in City and Country* (London, 1781), p. 154.

10. Ernst Cassirer, *The Philosophy of the Enlightenment,* trans. Fritz C. Koelln and James Pettegrove (Princeton, 1951), p. 47.

11. Marjorie Nicolson and Nora Mohler, "The Scientific Background of Swift's Voyage to Laputa," *Annals of Science,* 1937, II, 299-334. See especially pp. 322-323.

12. César de Saussure, *Lettres et Voyages* (Laussane, 1903), Lettre VI, pp. 166-167.

13. Ronald Paulson, *Hogarth: His Life, Art, and Times, I,* p. 92.

14. William M. McBurney, *A Checklist of Prose Fiction, 1700-1739* (Cambridge, 1960), p. viii.

15. E. S. de Beer, ed., *The Diary of John Evelyn* (London, 1959), p. 689. Entry dated August 27, 1680.

16. *Ibid.,* p. 1027.

17. These newsletters were like the European *relations* or reports of topical events. See Joseph Frank, *The Beginnings of the English Newspaper, 1620-1660* (Cambridge, 1961).

18. For Ward's sensational "letters" describing the pleasure-seekers of Tunbridge or the wicked colonists of New England, see Edward Ward, "A Packet from Will's" in *Letters of Love, Gallantry, and Several Other Occasions,* 2 vols., by Voiture, Brown, Dryden, Congreve, etc. (London, 1724) II; also *A Trip to New England* (London, 1699). This and "A Letter From New England" are reprinted by the Club for Colonial Reprints, ed. George Parker Winship (Providence, 1905).

19. John J. Richetti, *Popular Fiction Before Richardson: Narrative Patterns 1700-1739* (Oxford, 1969), p. 77.

20. *Ibid.,* p. 77.

21. Philip Pinkus, *Grub Street Stripped Bare,* p. 92.

22. Eliza Haywood, *The Agreeable Caledonian* (London, 1728), p. 84.

23. Thomas Salmon, *A Critical Essay Concerning Marriage* (London, 1724), p. 165.

24. Eliza Haywood, "Good Out of Evil; or, The Double Deceit" appearing in Eliza Haywood, *Love in Its Variety; Being a Collection of Select Novels written in Spanish by Signior Michael Bandello* (London, 1727), p. 67.

25. Mary Delariviere Manley, *The Secret History of Queen Zarah* (London, 1705), Preface.

26. *Ibid.,* Preface.

27. *A Spy Upon the Conjurer,* author uncertain, possibly Daniel Defoe or Eliza Haywood (London, 1724), Part III.

28. Eliza Haywood, *The Disguis'd Prince or, The Beautiful Parisian* (London, 1728), pp. 1-2. This is a translation of a French book written in 1679 by Jean de Préchac.

29. Pierre Corlet de Chamblain de Marivaux, *The Life of Marianne* (London, 1736), Part II, 83-84.

30. Robert Adams Day, *Told in Letters* (Ann Arbor, 1966), p. 71.

31. A. S. Collins, 'The Growth of the Reading Public During the Eighteenth Century," *Review of English Studies,* II(1926), 284-294.

32. Mary Davys, "Familiar Letters Betwixt a Gentleman and a Lady," in *The Works of Mrs. Davys,* 2 vols. (London, 1725), II. Also available in publications of *Augustan Reprint Society,* #54, 1955.

33. William Henry Irving, *The Providence of Wit in The English Letter-Writers* (Durham, 1955), p. 145.

34. David Nichols, *The Correspondence of Dean Atterbury,* 5 vols. (London, 1783-1790), I, iv.

35. *The Spectator,* No. 632, Dublin, Nov. 30, 1714.

36. *The Complete Letters of Lady Mary Wortley Montagu,* ed. Robert Halsband, 3 vols. (Oxford, 1965), I, Appendix I, 467.

37. *Ibid.,* p. 467.

38. Robert Day, *Told in Letters,* pp. 239-258.

39. This is Day's figure. Actually there were somewhat fewer for some of the works on his bibliography are duplicates: the same book reprinted later with a new title page, or individual pieces of a collection listed individually and also together.

40. An unpublished Radcliffe thesis by Ruth Stauffer in 1942.

41. Mme. D'Aulnoy, *The Present Court of Spain,* trans. Thomas Brown (London, 1693), Preface.

42. *The Spectator,* No. 4, March 5, 1711.

43. *The Spectator,* No. 10, March 12, 1711.

44. *The Diary of Dudley Ryder (1715-1716)* ed. William Matthews (London, 1939), p. 119. Entry dated October 14, 1715.

45. George Frisbie Whicher, *The Life and Romances of Eliza Haywood* (New York, 1915), p. 11.

46. Robert Day, *Told in Letters,* p. 74.

47. *Marriage Promoted: In a Discourse of Its Ancient and Modern Practice both under Heathen and Christian Commonwealth,* anonymous pamphlet (London, 1690), p. 27.

48. *The Works of Mr. Thomas Brown,* 2 vols. (London, 1707), I, 337-340.

49. "Captain Ayloffe's Letters," in Abel Boyer's *Letters of Wit, Politics, and Morality* (London, 1701), reprinted in Natascha Würzbach, *The Novel in Letters* (Coral Gables, 1969), p. 27.

50. Aphra Behn, *Love-Letters Between A Nobleman and His Sister* (London, 1694), Part I reprinted in Natascha Würzbach, *The Novel in Letters,* p. 206.

51. *Ibid.,* p. 217.

52. *Five Love-letters From a Nun to a Cavalier,* trans. Sir Roger L'Estrange (London, 1678), reprinted in Natascha Würzbach, *The Novel in Letters,* p. 17.

53. Anonymous, *The Fatal Amour Between a Beautiful Lady and a Young Nobleman* (London, 1719), p. 64.

54. Chapter 2, *passim.*

55. Reprinted in Natascha Würzbach, *The Novel in Letters,* p. 221.

56. *Ibid.,* p. 215.

57. *Ibid.,* p. 265.

58. *Ibid.,* p. 225.

59. *The Adventures of Lindamira,* Revised and Corrected by Mr. Thomas Brown (London, 1702), p. 2.

60. *The Spectator,* No. 479, September 9, 1712.

61. *The Complete Letters of Lady Mary Wortley Montagu,* ed. Robert Halsband, 3 vols. (Oxford, 1965), III, 8-9. Letter to Lady Bute, March 1, 1752.

62. *Ibid.,* I, 123n. Mandane is the runaway heroine of Madelaine de Scudéry's *Artamène ou le Grand Cyrus* (1649-1653), which Lady Mary read as early as 1705.

63. *Ibid.,* I, 133-134.

64. *Ibid.,* I, 149-150. The exact date of this letter is unknown. Phillipa Mundy was a close friend of Lady Mary's age: she was Lady Mary's "Anna Howe."

65. *Ibid.,* I, 163-164. In the heat of this excitement, Lady Mary was writing Wortley twice a day: two letters on August 15, two letters on August 16, and an earlier one on August 17 precede this letter. Weary students of epistolary fiction should take note that people *did* write an extraordinary number of letters.

66. *Ibid.,* I, 164.

67. *Ibid.,* I, 164.

68. *Ibid.,* III, 9. Letter to Lady Bute, March 1, 1752.

69. Samuel Richardson, *Clarissa,* 4 vols. (London, 1748), I, 186.

70. *The Diary of Samuel Pepys,* ed. Henry B. Wheatley, 2 vols. (New York, 1893), I, 513-514. Entry dated November 13, 1662.

71. *The complete Letters of Lady Mary Wortley Montagu,* ed. Robert Halsband, I, 175. Letter to Wortley, December 8, 1712.

72. *The Tatler,* No. 248, November 8, 1710.

73. Philippe Ariès, *Centuries of Childhood,* trans. Robert Baldick (New York, 1962) pp. 349-350 and *passim.* Lawrence Stone disagrees about the evidence of children's dress styles, but generally supports Ariès' conclusions that England was moving towards a more child-oriented society. Lawrence Stone, *The Family, Sex, and Marriage* (New York, 1977), pp. 405-449.

74. Mary Astell, *The Christian Religion as Profess'd by a Daughter of the Church of England* (London, 1705), pp. 292-293.

75. Choderlos de Laclos, *Les Liaisons dangereuses.* trans. Richard Addington (New York, 1962), p. 178.

76. *Five Love-Letters From a Nun to a Cavalier,* trans. Roger L'Estrange (London, 1678), reprinted in Natascha Würzbach, *The Novel in Letters,* p. 19.

77. "The Lady's New Year Gift, or Advice to a Daughter," *The Life and Letters of Sir George Saville, Bart. First Marquis of Halifax,* 2 vols. ed. H. C. Foxcroft (London, 1898), II, 410.

78. *Ibid.,* II, 408.

79. *The Spectator,* No. 66, May 16, 1711.

80. *Ibid.*

81. Anonymous [possibly Judith Drake], *A Farther Essay Relating to the Female Sex* (London, 1696), p. 59.

82. Anonymous [possibly Mrs. Steele], *The Ladies Library,* 3 vols. (London, 1714), III, 90.

83. Béat de Muralt, *Letters Describing the Character and Customs of the English and French Nations* (London, 1726), p. 35.

84. Philogamous, *The Present State of Matrimony* (London, 1739), p. 67.

85. Ruth Kelso, *Doctrine for the Lady of the Renaissance* (Urbana, 1965), p. 105.

86. *The Spectator,* No. 611, October 24, 1714.

87. Peter Laslett dates the use of contraceptive devices to Geneva at the end of the seventeenth century. *The World We Have Lost* (New York, 1965), p. 132.

88. T. C. Surgeon, *The Charitable Surgeon* (London, 1708), p. 58.

89. *The Tatler,* No. 15, May 13, 1709.

90. Daniel Defoe, *Conjugal Lewdness* (London, 1727), p. 132.

91. Mary Delariviere Manley, *Court Intrigues* (London, 1711), p. 138.

92. *The Letters of Abelard and Héloise,* trans. John Hughes (London, 1743), p. 185.

93. Eliza Haywood, *Love in Excess* (London, 1719), Part II, 47.

94. *Ibid.*

95. Jane Barker, *The Lining to the Patch-work Screen* (London, 1726), p. 106.

96. Anonymous [possibly Mrs. Steele], *The Ladies Library,* II, 46.

97. Eliza Haywood, *Love in Excess,* p. 36.

98. Charles Gildon, *The Post-Boy Rob'd of His Mail* (London, 1692), p. 237.

99. Mary Delariviere Manley, "From a Lady To a Lady," Letter XXXIII in *Court Intrigues* (London, 1711), reprinted in Natascha Würzbach, *The Novel in Letters,* p. 44.

100. Mary Delariviere Manley, *Secret Memoirs and Manners of Several Persons of Quality of Both Sexes From New Atalantis* (London, 1709), p. 67.

101. Mary Delariviere Manley, *Rivella,* p. 4, bound with *Court Intrigues* (London, 1711).

102. Aphra Behn, *Love-Letters Between A Nobleman and His Sister* (London, 1694), reprinted in Natascha Würzbach, *The Novel in Letters,* p. 246.

103. Mary Delariviere Manley, *Court Intrigues,* p. 36.

104. Eliza Haywood, *Love-Letters on All Occasions* (London, 1730), p. 103.

105. Aphra Behn, *Love-Letters Between A Nobleman and His Sister,* reprinted in Natascha Würzbach, *The Novel in Letters,* p. 230.

106. Mary Delariviere Manley, *Court Intrigues,* p. 36.

107. *The Dairy of Samuel Pepys,* II, 768-769. Entry dated January 13, 1668.

108. *Ibid.,* II, 790. Entry dated February 8, 1668.

109. *Ibid.,* II, 790.

110. David Foxon, *Libertine Literature in England, 1660-1745* (New York, 1965) p. 48.

111. "The Dancing School," *A Collection of the Writings of Mr. Edward Ward,* 6 vols. (London, 1717-1718), II, 237.

112. Mary Davys, "Familiar Letters Betwixt a Gentleman and a Lady", *The Works of Mrs. Davys,* 2 vols. (London, 1725), II, 299.

113. Anonymous, *The Unnatural Mother and Ungrateful Wife* (London, 1730), p. 11.

114. René Girard, *Deceit, Desire, and the Novel* (Baltimore, 1965), Chapter 1.

115. Anna Letitia Barbauld, "Richardson," *The British Novelists,* 50 vols. (London, 1810), I, xiv. Barbauld, besides being a great admirer of Richardson's technique, was the first editor of *his* letters.

116. Samuel Richardson, *Pamela, or Virtue Rewarded,* 2nd edition (London, 1741), Introduction, pp. xxiv-xxv.

Irene Tucker (essay date 1993)

SOURCE: "Writing Home: *Evelina,* the Epistolary Novel and the Paradox of Property," in *ELH,* Vol. 60, No. 2, Summer 1993, pp. 419-39.

[*In the following essay on Frances Burney's* Evelina, *Tucker discusses issues the story raises concerning intellectual property rights and personal identity.*]

On June 4, 1741, Alexander Pope filed suit against Edmund Curll, the prominent London bookseller who had just published *Dean Swift's Literary Correspondence, for Twenty-Four Years,* a volume comprised of letters written by Pope as well as those he received from such literary luminaries as Swift, Gay and Bolingbroke.[1] Pope claimed rights over not only his own letters, but also over the letters he had received from Swift, and, on the basis of this claim, sought to prevent Curll from continuing to sell the book. Because he had never relinquished his rights to his writing, authorial rights established thirty years earlier by the 1710 Statute of Anne, Pope argued that his rights as author had been violated by Curll's failure to get permission to publish the letters.[2] For his part, Curll maintained he had received the letters included in the volume from "the several Persons by whom & to whom they severally Purport to have been written & addressed," and argued that, as a result, "the Complainant is not to be Considered as [both] the Author & proprietor of all or any of the said letters."[3]

In his decision, handed down two weeks later on June 17, Lord Chancellor Hardwicke ordered Curll to halt sale of the book, partially upholding Pope's claim to the letters. In awarding Pope control over only the letters the poet himself had written, Hardwicke rejected Curll's contention that a letter constitutes a gift from sender to receiver. Still, the strange quality of Hardwicke's ruling, which awarded the recipient control over the material contents of the letter—the ink and the paper written on—while giving the author control over the intangible ideas and expression contained within, strikingly highlights certain contradictions implicit within the liberal notion of property that otherwise escape notice. Hardwicke writes, "It is only a special property in the receiver, possibly the property of the paper may belong to him; but this does not give a licence to any person whatsoever to publish them to the world, for at most the receiver has only a joint property with the writer."[4] What Mark Rose argues, persuasively to my mind, is that the Hardwicke decision, through its deliberate splitting of the material and ideal qualities of the letter, marks the creation of a new form of property—immaterial, intellectual property. The force of the ruling not only invests Pope with the right to control the fate of his writing, but, in separating the author's ideal "text" from its material manifestation as a particular "manuscript," the Hardwicke decision delineates the otherwise obscure relations of the concept of copyright by creating the legal and ontological justification for the mass production and circulation of a potentially infinite number of these manuscripts.[5] But, paradoxically, this material/ideal bifurcation threatens to subvert the very notion of property it is designed to shore up. If the material and the ideal can be separated from one another, then the possibility of acting willfully to change the material world—a possibility central to the liberal conception of property, as I will explain—is revealed to be contingent; a text happens to appear in the form of a manuscript, but need not necessarily do so.[6] In attempting to secure property by freeing it from the limitations of its materiality, the concept of intellectual property created by the Hardwicke ruling opens up the terrifying possibility latent in all forms of liberal property—that actions performed, when not limited by the material world, are finally and fundamentally irrelevant to that world.

The natural rights personality theory of property set out by Locke in *The Second Treatise of Civil Government* has long served as the theoretical basis of liberal thought. According to Locke's formulation, individuals' rights to property are based upon their natural and inalienable right to their own person. Humans gain rights over materials outside the boundaries of their individual bodies by virtue of this self-ownership, since by acting on nature with the labor of one's body, one changes nature, and, in so changing it, one effectively produces this newly-reborn nature into an extension of oneself:

> The labour of his body and the work of his hands, we may say, are properly his. Whatsoever then he removes out of the state that nature hath provided and left it in, he hath mixed his labour with, and joined to it something that is his own, and thereby makes it his property. It being by him removed from the common state nature hath placed it in, it hath by this labour something annexed to it that excludes the common right of other men. For this labour being the unquestionable property of the labourer, no man but he can have a right to what that is once joined to, at least where there is enough and as good left in common for others.[7]

Locke here posits a model of property in which the self represents itself in the form of its productions and then owns these productions. Property is thus an extension of the self and the right to property is figured as being just as "natural" and "inalienable" as the right to own one's self.

Locke seizes upon the peculiar, part-literal, part-figurative quality of metonymy in order to develop his argument here. The central metonym of the passage, that relating labor to the body, enables Locke to move from the material to the ideal and back to the material—from the body that is owned by the self to the labor that is "mixed" (but only figuratively) with the material world back to the material world having been transformed by labor (and hence "owned")—while eliding the oscillation between literal and figurative, between material and ideal. But since the possibility of acting upon nature with one's labor presupposes the separation of that nature from oneself, property marks not only the extension of the self but its limits as well. One asserts control over property by sending it away; the potential alienability of property paradoxically becomes the only possible proof of the inalienability of the right to it.[8]

Viewed within the Lockean context, the 1741 debate over the ownership of letters seems particularly scandalous precisely because it threatens to expose the paradox implicit in the natural rights conception of all property. If property not only serves as self-representation/self-production but also marks what is not the self, then the paradox of the ownership of letters serves as a dramatic literalization of the paradox of property. Pope's fascination with the possibility that he might lose property rights over his letters by sending them away from himself dramatizes the compelling irresolvability of the natural rights model of property, a model in which the moment of self-representation is simultaneously the moment of self-loss.

Frances Burney published her epistolary novel *Evelina, or the History of a Young Lady's Entrance into the World* in January 1778, thirty-seven years after Hardwicke rendered his decision in *Pope v. Curll*. Insofar as Hardwicke's verdict had been simply a restatement of, rather than a solution to, the paradox of property, the question of the ownership of letters seems to have remained a source of considerable interest. In choosing the form of the epistolary novel to tell the story of Evelina, Burney generalizes the paradox of owning letters into a paradox about property, representation and, ultimately, the nature of the self. Burney, in offering the story of a young, half-orphaned, incompletely owned woman who leaves her guardian in the provinces to go out into the world, seizes upon these very paradoxes as instruments for delaying the inevitable closure of the marriage plot she nonetheless feels compelled to weave.[9] Moreover, Burney, who published the novel anonymously, refigures her relationship as author to her own artistic production and to the audience that would receive it in ways that generalize the particular vulnerabilities of her position as a woman writer into a critique of the liberal notion of property.

If the relationships among the writing self, the letter and the recipient of the letter are complex, the complexities of those relationships multiply exponentially when the selves and the letters in question are part of an epistolary novel. In his introduction to a special edition of *Yale French Studies* on literary letters entitled, "Men/Women of Letters," Charles Porter analyzes the components of a letter that characterize it as letter.[10] While Porter's analysis is an attempt to describe actual letters as opposed to letters within an epistolary novel, it nonetheless offers a detailed structure from which to begin to analyze both the particular representational paradoxes of the letter form and the ways in which these paradoxes are complicated by being placed within the frame of a novel:

1) The letter has an author known to and readily identifiable (even if vaguely) by the intended reader. Likewise the letter is addressed by that author (even if at times only implicitly) to an identifiable person or collectivity, sometimes well-known to the author, and is usually addressed *only* to that person or collectivity. Porter contrasts the letter with its related forms, the diary, which is normally addressed only to its author, and the autobiography, which does not have a single, identifiable addressee.

The epistolary novel departs most strikingly from its "real-life" counterpart with regard to the identities of author and reader. The form of the epistolary novel is characterized by an implicit doubleness of both, since along with the writer and addressee of any given letter within the novel there exists a second writer and addressee—the author of the novel and the novel's readers.[11] If we recall the ways in which the presence of a letter's recipient within the representational economy of the letter draws attention to the paradoxes and limitations of property as a form of representation, then the presence of a second writer and a second, largely undefined audience within the epistolary novel makes the representative relationship between writing self and letter even less tenable. Within the epistolary frame, the letter is limited as an act of self-representation of its author within the text not only because it must be received and read before it can effectively represent, but also because it is literally the representation of another author—the author of the novel.

2) The letter is written out of its author's experiences or wishes or aspirations. "I" refers to the author, even if it is not fully identifiable with that author. Within the epistolary novel, the fictionality of subject position is both emphasized and complicated by the fact that the person behind the "I" is a fictional construction of the novel's author. Furthermore, the novel most often boasts a variety of "I"'s within its implicit wholeness, simultaneously depending upon and subverting the identification between letter and writing self.

3) Letters are dated or presumably datable. While the dates of actual letters are intended to identify the time of composition and, in so doing, emphasize and implicitly privilege the act of writing, dates in epistolary novels, when they are present, serve primarily as an ordering device. Dates also serve to ally the narrative movement of the story with a certain inexorability associated with the passage of time. At the same time the dates within an epistolary novel draw attention to the coincidence of a "natural" passage of time and the novel's narrative motion, however, the juxtaposition of the two time frames also accentuates the differences between the two. The temporal disjunctions created by the epistolary form suggest the extent to which human action (and the [autobiographical] representation of that action) depends upon the disruption of the "natural" passage of time, or, further, the way in which that passage of time only gains meaning through its disruption.

In apparently privileging the moment of writing, the presence of the date hides the temporal doubleness of any letter—the gap between the time a letter is written and the time it is read. If a letter is an act of self-representation, at what time precisely can that act of self-representation be said to occur? The temporal gap opened up by the act of transmitting the letter is the paradox of property converted into narrative terms, the function of property as both extension and limitation of the self mapped across time. The temporal doubleness implicit in the form of the letter is further complicated by the doubleness of the epistolary novel's author/reader structure. As readers of the novel, we can never be certain whether we are reading the letters as they are written, as they are being read by their recipient within the novel, or at some moment entirely independent of either of the two events.[12]

4) A series of actual letters is written "forward," but the author of the letters lacks certainty about the future. These letters are thus unable to forecast or trace out a destiny, making them by nature discontinuous, multi-directional, fragmented. Porter contrasts the discontinuity of a series of letters with the implicit continuity of diary entries, arguing that while each letter is designed as an independent entity, created around a precise intention, a diary entry is supposed to be a state in an overall narrative of self-understanding.

In an epistolary novel, the fragmented quality of the letter form is consciously placed in tension with our knowledge as readers that the letters are part of a progression that, by virtue of its status as the production of a single author and as a formal whole, is meant to be understood as more or less unified. This tension subverts any clean opposition between the unified and the fragmentary. Within *Evelina,* this collapse of the unified/fragmentary opposition is manifested by a simultaneous recognition of the inevitability of the marriage plot that characterizes the eighteenth-century novel and the temporary subversion of that plot figured by the discontinuity of the individual letters.

5) Letters are identifiable by certain material forms (salutation, address, stationary, seal, etc.). These material forms are simultaneously present and conspicuously absent in the epistolary novel, since the novel invokes some of these forms—the salutation and structure of letter—in order to identify the letters in the novel as letters, yet in so doing, makes obvious the absence of other forms (the fact that the letters are printed rather than handwritten, that there are no envelopes or seals). This splitting of material and ideal forms of the letter—the idea of the letter is invoked, while many of the material aspects are held in abeyance—recalls Hardwicke's strange decision in *Pope v. Curll* to preserve the letter writer's rights of ownership by separating the material and ideal aspects of the letter.[13] The status of *Evelina* as a published, copyrighted work ought not to be ignored in this context. The materiality of the book comes into being only by the act of separating the text from the matter of the letter. Textual property exists at the vanishing point of matter, but it is precisely at this point that material transformation can occur.

If the epistolary novel as a form serves to highlight the contradictions intrinsic to a natural rights theory of property and, more fundamentally, the pitfalls associated with traditional forms of self-representation, then *Evelina,* as a particular example of the epistolary form, seizes upon these contradictions with a vengeance. Writing as a woman within a society whose system of patrilineal inheritance made the relation between identity and property oblique at best, Frances Burney creates in Evelina a protagonist whose position as disowned heiress places her at the center of the contradictions regarding property and identity.[14] Evelina first appears surprisingly late in the novel that bears her name; her appearance (in the form of her first letter) is delayed by a protracted exchange of letters in which Evelina's guardian, the Reverend Arthur Villars, resists then finally yields to the urgings of a female representative of Evelina's maternal grandmother to allow his ward to leave his home in the provinces in order to visit the grandmother in London. Evelina's initial identity within the novel is thus produced in her absence; in order for her to acquire the voice necessary for self-representation, she must absent herself from the site of this initial making.

As the letters are presented in the novel, each one labeled with its author and recipient, they are clearly established as the self-representations of their authors, yet the unavoidable presence of the recipient in the identification of the letter introduces the limitations of the letter as a form of self-representation at the same moment its possibilities appear. Moreover, as the opening epistolary dialogue of the novel makes clear, Villars views not only the letters he writes but the ward whose fate those letters negotiate as instances of his own moral production. Because Evelina is unclaimed by her own father, she is free to be appropriated by her guardian as his representation.[15] Thus the prospect of sending Evelina away from the self-enclosed paradise in which the two of them have lived strikes him much as the prospect of sending off a carefully crafted letter might; the act of self-representation is only able to function by being made public, yet the step of making that representation public means that it is no longer fully Villars's own:

> The mind is but too naturally prone to pleasure, but too easily yielded to dissipation: it has been my study to guard [Evelina] against their delusions, by preparing her to expect,—and to despise them. But the time draws on for experience and observation to take place of instruction: if I have, in some measure, rendered her capable of using the one with discretion, and making the other with improvement, I shall rejoice myself with the assurance of having largely contributed to her welfare.[16]

Evelina's behavior becomes, within the terms her guardian sets out, the possibility of Villars's celebration of himself. Furthermore, the movement into time—into narrative and into experience—manifested by both the letter and Evelina herself is figured simultaneously as a necessary precondition for Villars's self-representation and as a condition that guarantees the impossibility of complete, owned self-representation.

In the letter immediately following, the contradictory elements of the letter as a structure of self-representation are made even more evident as they begin to be wrenched apart from one another. As she leaves Villars's home in the provinces bearing the letter that gives her permission to leave, Evelina effectively stands as the bearer of the letter of permission and that letter itself. That she has completed her act of delivery necessarily indicates that she has been allowed to leave, yet the fact that she functions both as the representation of Villars's authority as a moral educator and as the bearer of that representation testifies that she is fully neither. The language of Villars's letter marks his growing alienation from his ward that necessarily accompanies the sending of the letter, as the progression of appositives reveals the increasing tenuousness of his claim to Evelina. "This letter will be delivered to you by *my child,—the child of my adoption,—my affection* (20, emphasis added). Within this structure, it is the sociality of the letter form and, by extension, of the act of self-representation that brings about Evelina's fall into narrative, into experience and history, into the material. Without the demands of the social, both Evelina and the letter she carries might remain within their provincial glade, forever unaffected by "the experience and observation [that] takes place of instruction." Granted, the moral instruction Villars imparts unto Evelina within the privacy of his own estate is itself a social relation, but it can only be of limited consequence as long as that instruction remains outside of the public eye; Evelina can only function as Villars's representation once he consents to allow her to be seen within a wider public sphere. Only retrospectively, from a position outside Villars's enclosure, can the sociality of his relationship with Evelina be recognized and made to mean. (Significantly, it is not until Evelina leaves home that we hear anything of her own voice, since she has no need to write letters until she is separated from acquaintances.)

The doubleness of the novel's title pithily encapsulates the tension between Villars's prelapsarian fantasy—the promise of a perfect, transcendent identity implied by the concept of the name—and identity as a narrative, socially produced and historically contingent. But even the terms of the opposition between name and narrative laid out within the title *Evelina, or the History of a Young Lady's Entrance into the World* are immediately set into motion. The reference to "entrance" suggests the way in which both Evelina's and Villars's identities are formed by the process of moving away that mutually marks the outer limits of the selves, yet the transformation of that process into an entity called history that is itself the history of a type—"a Young Lady"—further suggests the fundamental inextricability of the two aspects of identity.

I am proposing that Burney establishes the letter from the outset of the novel as the emblem of the paradoxes implicit in both identity and in property as a form of self-representation. It is important, then, to examine the ways in which the form of the letter changes over the course of *Evelina,* for these shifts can be read as an attempt to trace the outer edges of the apparently opposing models of identity. While the letters at the opening of the novel are relatively short and "letter-like," as the novel progresses and Evelina begins to establish a social world for herself apart from the one that had been defined for her by her guardian, the letters lose much of their letter-like quality, becoming considerably longer than the early examples and taking on many of the characteristics of non-epistolary narrative forms.[17] (Many of these later letters are labeled, confusing if tellingly, "Evelina in continuation.") A short, letter-like letter is necessarily more fully characterized by its "Sender to Recipient" label, suggesting a model of the self that becomes representative in being presented to, and hence limited by, an other. But, importantly, the shorter the letters are—the more completely they are identified by their label as the self-representation of their author—the greater the significance of the time gap created by the letter's transmission. The shorter and less narrative the letters are—the more like letters they are—the more they become subject to the temporal gaps brought about precisely by their status as letters—the time necessary for them to travel from London to the provinces and back again. Conversely, while the long, more narrative letters are proportionately less affected by the fact of their transmission, their narrative qualities at the time undermine the claims they might make to identify their authors, insofar as identity is most purely expressed in the form of an isolated name. Authorship, then, is figured as an assertion of control over interpretation—here, the interpretation of how the space of time is to be understood. This opening out of time introduces the possibility—clearly a frightening one—that the letter won't be read, that a reply will not be forthcoming.

But we ought to keep in mind that, in an epistolary novel as opposed to an actual letter, the author and reader of any given letter are not only the people whose names are affixed to the letter's text, but the novel's author and readers as well. Not only does this doubleness serve to undermine the simple notion of letter as self-representation to which Villars would willfully cling, but it draws our attention to the temporal doubleness implicit in the epistolary novel. Since we as readers are never certain at exactly what point in its circuit of production we gain access to a given letter, the authority—both in the sense of authorial identity and in the sense of force of law—that any letter commands is called into question. This subversive potential made possible by the form's temporal doubleness is most clearly manifested near the middle of the novel, when Villars condemns his ward's growing intimacy with Lord Orville, a man she has become acquainted with in London. When, having already read Villars's condemnation of the connection, we read Evelina's description of her continuing pursuit of the relationship, we are led to believe that she is willfully disregarding her guardian's wishes. Soon enough we learn that Evelina's apparent disregard of Villars's desires is merely an illusion created by the temporal doubleness of the epistolary novel: we have read Villars's letter before she has. Nonetheless, the lesson of the incident is marked indelibly. Once again, the very sociality of the construction of identity—whether the identity takes the form of authority, property or written self-representation, that makes it necessary for the letters to be transmitted to gain their meaning—also figures the limitation of that authority.

Thus far we have traced the trajectory of the novel according to the way it calls into question with increasing force

Villars's authority and structures of identity. But the novel's development can be figured equally well in terms of Evelina's developing voice as a letter-writer, even as the valuation we normally lend such a development is called into question. Most obviously, Evelina's letters to Villars stand as a sign of her growing distance from him, both geographically and ontologically. Initially, Evelina is reluctant to write, recognizing that writing signals her ontological break from him:

> My dear Sir, I am desired to make a request to you. I hope you will not think me an encroacher; Lady Howard insists upon my writing!—and yet I hardly know how to go on; a petition implies a want,—and have you left me one? No indeed. (23)

Here, as in the novel's opening pages, Evelina serves both as message and as the means of transmission for that message. The parallels between these two moments ought to alert us to their crucial difference, however: while in the first instance Evelina is sent away from Villars as if she were a letter, here, the letter returns to Villars as if it were Evelina. The substitution of the ideality of the letter for the materiality of Evelina's actual body hence becomes a necessary condition of her developing autonomy. The act of self-definition is explicitly figured as a definition of the limits of property; it is her conception of a want, of the possibility of lack, that marks her break from Villars. Still, just a few paragraphs later in the same letter, Evelina has already begun to conceive of her relationship to her erstwhile guardian differently, with his authority over her desires transformed into a legal control rather than a control emerging from their mutuality of identification or desire. She asks him, "Ought I to form a wish that has not your sanction?" (23). She marks the transitory state of her identity at this moment by refusing to mark, signing her letter with a blank space whose significance will become clearer later.

Villars responds, not unexpectedly, with an attempt to assert his imaginative authority to recreate the time in which the unity of their identities—his moral, emotional and financial possession of Evelina—produced the illusion of satiation, of limitlessness. "To see my Evelina happy is to see myself without a wish" (25). But Villars clearly, if reluctantly, recognizes the increasing untenability of his position, an untenability brought on by the fact that his self-representation in the form of Evelina has already been made public. To the extent that Evelina has become a writing subject, someone engaged in her own self-representation, she has become irreducibly different from Villars. His solution, acknowledgedly ideal, is to cancel her identity as letter-writer by eliminating the geographical (and, implicitly, the temporal) space that separates them. "To follow the dictates of my own heart, I should instantly recall you to myself, and never more consent to your being separated from me; but the manners and opinions of the world demand a different conduct" (129). Even this ideal, admittedly unachievable, solution is a fallen one, however, as Villars figures the unity between them as consent given or withheld rather than as a form of organic identity.

What is crucial to keep in mind is the way in which, throughout most of the novel, the paradox of identity and property is inflected differently across gender lines. If Evelina is schooled in the possibilities for subversion by witnessing the forms her own movement away from Villars takes, she is nonetheless, as a woman, placed differently from her guardian within the conflicting and intersecting lines of power that define identity and property. As the novel makes clear, Evelina's vulnerability to being appropriated as the site of Villars's moral self-production—her appropriateness to being made both the material and limit of others' self-representation—depends in large part upon her status as orphan, or, more accurately, as unowned heiress. Paradoxically enough, however, while her unconnectedness is what allows her to be seized as the stuff out of which others' self-production is made, Evelina nonetheless needs to imagine an absence of connection (at least of connection to men) as the foundation of her own identity. Faced with an array of competing suitors at her first public ball, Evelina tells each of them she is engaged to another to avoid having to commit herself to any of them. Where Villars uses his (and Evelina's) isolation from the world to justify his appropriation of her as a representation before the world, Evelina's fiction is a negative one, one that describes something that is not there. If the paradoxes of property and identity make clear the way in which the oppositions of autonomy and sociality tend to collapse into one another, men and women within the novel still begin at different places within the ever-intertwining set of terms. Rather than using control over others to represent identity before the world as Villars does, Evelina creates a fiction of connectedness in the form of her story to the suitors, intended to create for her the possibility of an autonomy that otherwise would not exist. To the extent to which personal autonomy is either possible or desirable (Burney is clearly wary on both counts), women seem only able to approach such autonomy under the cover of sociality.

The threat posed by Evelina's lie at the ball resounds throughout the novel. Just as Evelina's lack of familial connection both allows her appropriation by Villars and figures her identity as possible (and, from Villars's point of view, threatening) in its very fluidity, her social fiction-making, her telling of stories deliberately *unrepresentative* of and unconnected to her social reality, creates in part the possibility of her selfhood. Evelina clearly recognizes the power of the threat presented by her capacity to lie, particularly as that capacity remakes her relationship with Villars. She deliberately sets that threat into motion as she withholds information from Villars and then flaunts that act of withholding:

> Will you forgive me if I own that I have *first* written an account of this transaction to Miss Mirvan?—and that I even thought of *concealing* it from you?—Short-lived, however, was the ungrateful idea, and sooner will I risk the justice of your displeasure, then unworthily betray your generous confidence. (249)

Here, the capacity to lie that Evelina first demonstrates at the ball is clearly associated with the structure of temporal

doubleness associated with the letter in the epistolary novel. Evelina demonstrates her acumen as a reader of *Evelina.* To write letters is to prove that one is capable of lying. Evelina, who is characterized in the early sections of the novel explicitly by her lack of guile, learns to lie by coming to understand the operation of the letter. Inasmuch as her mendacity marks a deviation from her early character, writing letters would seem to serve to make Evelina less, rather than more, herself. Clearly, however, Burney holds no stock in the possibility of personal "essence"; not only do the novel's letters signal Evelina's growing independence from Villars, but autonomy in general, to the extent to which it is possible, is shown to be borne of the capacity to misrepresent. In *Evelina,* the act of lying becomes an assertion of the possibility of choice.[18]

Even more fundamentally, the association between lying and letter writing points up the extent to which the fact of human distance and separateness—the distance between London and the provinces that compels Evelina and Villars to communicate by letter and opens the temporal gap that makes it impossible for either to own their communication—coupled with the sociality of meaning, creates the possibility, indeed, the inevitability, of misrepresenting. There seems no position from which letters may be owned, from which they can even confidently be read. To assert that one is capable of either owning or reading is therefore to assert a fiction, to write a letter, to lie. Within the novel, sending, withholding and receiving information are not fundamentally different acts, but simply different moments in a single circuit. But as our experience as readers of the epistolary novel teaches us, we can never know exactly where in the circuit we are.

For Evelina, such undecidability is opportunity. Toward the end of the novel, as the inexorable marriage plot narrows around her, systematically closing off all avenues of escape, Evelina seizes upon the temporal undecidability made so evident by the epistolary form in one final, desperate effort to postpone the closure of marriage. When Lord Orville proposes marriage, "to make [his] devotion to [her] public," Evelina begs for more time, asking his deference to a secret she is not currently in a position to reveal. "There is *nothing,* my Lord, I wish to conceal;—to *postpone* an explanation is all I desire" (354). Her secret is, of course, the mystery of her personal history, the explanation of her status as "orphan," and the ostensible purpose of her delay is to await an opportunity for presenting herself to her father, Sir John Belmont, to be owned. Evelina invokes the conditions of her dependence as a further means of delaying her marriage. She informs Lord Orville she must write away to Villars for permission to marry:

> I told [Lord Orville] I was wholly dependent upon you, and that I was certain your opinion would be the same as mine, which was that it would be highly improper should I dispose of myself forever so very near the time which must finally decide by whose authority I ought to be granted.
>
> (370)

Reading her situation as a woman in a world in which autonomy and dependence are not distinguishable ontological conditions but, rather, names for discursive strategies, Evelina invokes the impropriety of "dispos[ing] of [her] self," as a means of buying more time as she waits for Villars's response to arrive by the mails.

That the novel raises no question regarding Belmont's status as Evelina's real father is crucial, since the presumption of their relatedness shifts the issue to be resolved from one of determining natural connection to one of determining ownership. As Evelina sets off to meet her father, the question at hand is not whether Evelina is her father's daughter, but, rather, whether her father will own her as such. As the novel describes the encounter, Belmont could just as easily own her as not, a fact that explicitly empties the act of any ontological significance. As a result, Evelina's receipt of the patronym is not, as we might have expected, a moment at which her freedom to act is shut down, but, rather, one in which the strictures that might limit her action are revealed to be at their most arbitrary. Clearly, for this novel, there is nothing "natural" about owning or being owned.

If Burney labors both within and by means of the novel to represent the denaturalization of paternal ownership, she does not do so in opposition to Locke, but squarely within his terms. Until now, I have been discussing the concept of paternal property—the relationship of paternal ownership, authority and identity—as though it can be accommodated unproblematically within the general liberal model of property. While it is the Second Treatise's natural rights theory for which Locke is best known, the political and philosophical context for this model is laid out in the largely ignored First Treatise, in which Locke explicitly refutes Sir Robert Filmer's identification of the authority of absolute monarchs with the "natural" authority of fathers over their children. What becomes clear in examining Locke within the context of Filmer is the extent to which Evelina's strategy of postponement is an accord with Locke's own project to pry apart property, paternity and political authority. Insofar as this separation depends upon both the ambiguous materiality of the "labor" metaphor and the oscillation of alienability that the metaphor implies, such a move threatens the liberal form of property at the very moment it constitutes such a model; within this view, Evelina's status as disowned daughter becomes not perverse but paradigmatic.[19]

Indeed, "being Belmont" marks, if anything, the freedom that for Evelina accompanies undecidability, since her life as Evelina Belmont is almost perfectly coextensive with the period of time during which the letters requesting and granting permission for her to marry are *en route*. Within the structure of relations suggested by the names in the book, in fact, Evelina is figured as least "owned" when she has received the patronym Belmont, insofar as the surname Villars had chosen for her—Anville—linguistically emphasizes her links with both himself and with Orville. The association between her life as Evelina Belmont and her freedom from ownership is further extended through her letter to Villars in which she describes the arrival of his letter granting her permission to marry:

> Open it, indeed, I did;—but read it I could not,—the willing, yet aweful consent you have granted,—the tenderness of your expressions,—the certainty that no obstacle remained to my external union with the loved owner of my heart, gave me sensations too various, and though joyful, too little placid for observation. Finding myself unable to proceed, and blinded by the tears of gratitude and delight which started into my eyes, I gave over the attempt of reading, till I retired to my own room: and, having no voice to answer the enquiries of Lord Orville, I put the letter into his hands, and left it to speak both for me and itself.
>
> (404)

This letter, which she signs Evelina Belmont, "for the first—and probably the last time I shall ever own the name" (404), appears at first glance to mark, in the form of the arrival of Villars's letter, the final closing down of the structure of postponement that has heretofore enabled her limited freedom. Evelina is unable to read or speak, and if it was her movement beyond the status of Villars's "letter" that marked her initial break from her guardian, here she is explicitly returned to the status of his letter, "which speaks for both [her] and itself."

But in this closing section, as in the rest of *Evelina,* nothing is quite as simple as it seems, no divisions quite so easily upheld. While the force and immediacy of the description may lead us to forget the context in which it is written, we ought to keep in mind that this passage is composed by Evelina retrospectively as part of a letter to Villars recalling precisely the moment of his letter's arrival. Once again, the acts of receiving, reading and writing letters collapse into one another, so that the primacy that might otherwise have been accorded the moment of writing is transferred to this complex knot of activity in which all acts become the same act: Villars reads Evelina's writing about her reading of his writing, all of which is further complicated by the fact that we as external audience enter the circuit at some undefinable point to read Fanny Burney's writing about this knotted complex of reading and writing, sending and receiving. Not only is the moment of Evelina's apparent voicelessness and self-dissolution at least partially recuperated by our knowledge that Evelina herself has represented this disempowerment, but the act of representation itself is shown to be one that gains its meaning only in being received and read.

Viewed within the structure of the letter laid out by *Evelina,* Lord Chancellor Hardwicke's creation of the concept of intellectual property by granting copyright to the writer rather than the recipient of a letter threatens to unravel the intertwined concepts of material property and personal identity on which intellectual property right is founded. It makes no sense, in understanding the functioning of the letter, to separate the act of writing from the acts of receiving and reading; thus the legal privileging of writing has the effect of pointing up the incoherences implicit within the notion of private property. The Lockean notion of property that grounds ownership in the "natural" ownership of the body, figuring the objects of possession as extensions and representations of the self, must ignore the fact that those objects must necessarily be defined as already alienated, already different from the self, in order for them to be owned. Evelina is able to transform the letters intended to secure her ties first to guardian, then to husband into an instrument for postponing her links to either; similarly, Fanny Burney, as a woman novelist, seizes Pope's attempts to extend his control from material to immaterial property as a means of challenging his right to property in any form. In refusing as illusory the legal separation between property as self-extension and property as self-difference, the structure of the letter in *Evelina* challenges the natural rights notion of property by exposing the contradiction at its core.

But ought we to read *Evelina* simply as critique? Far from simply pointing up the paradox of property as self-representation, Burney attempts in her novel to figure a new model of authorship that implicitly suggests new relations between self, production and property. In the dedicatory poem that opens the volume, "To ——— ———," Burney once again uses the doubleness implicit in the epistolary novel to extend a discussion focused historically around the ownership of letters to apply to published writing in general as part of her larger attempt to imagine a kind of authorship that is not based on the model of possession. The blank place of the recipient, which recalls the blank signature of Evelina's first letter to Villars, most explicitly refers to Burney's status as anonymous author of the novel. Directed to the "author of my being" (1), the poem is offered as an explanation from the author to her father for her decision to publish her work anonymously.[20] "But since my niggard stars that gift refuse / Concealment is the only boon I claim; / Obscure be still the unsuccessful Muse, / Who cannot raise, but would not sink, your fame" (1). Clearly, if Burney has chosen to publish anonymously, as she claims in the poem, in order to avoid sinking her father's fame, then she cannot name him as the recipient of the poem and the novel without revealing his identity. But like Evelina within the body of the novel, Burney also seems to refuse the social structures that define the daughter as "recorder of [her father's] worth" (1), as his self-production and representation. Likewise, it is possible to read the character of Evelina as the speaker throughout the poem (the blank in Evelina's first letter to Villars helps validate such a reading), addressing to Burney her own reluctance to stand as "recorder of thy worth." With the blank place of the recipient holding both readings in suspension, Burney and Evelina, author and production, become indistinguishable from one another, an apparent fulfillment of the Lockean fantasy.

But clearly Burney has more than utopian wish-fulfillment in mind. While the blankness of the dedication conflates Burney and Evelina, if the two readings are considered at once, Burney becomes simultaneously both speaker and listener—the speaker of her address to her father, the listener of Evelina's address to her author. As soon as the validity of a natural rights notion of property is suggested by the conflation of author and artistic production, that validity is undermined by the collapse of speaker and listener that effectively challenges any move to privilege the speaker/author. The risks of such a strategy for Burney are at least equally as pronounced as the potentially liberatory effects of her subversion.[21] The possibility of self-representation is made available only with the acknowledgement that any self that might be represented has already disappeared, replaced by a system of relations uniting reader and writer, sender and recipient, speaker and listener. Finally, however, the blankness allows each of the novel's readers to become the recipient of the dedication, to take his or her place as "author of [the speaker's] being." In assuming her position as anonymous author and uncovering the infinite openness of the position of recipient/author that is implicitly characteristic of the relationship of all authors to their reading public, Burney figures a notion of authorship that is the production of all involved in the reading/writing process.[22] In sending *Evelina,* like a letter, to everyone, she belongs to no one.

Notes

This essay was first prepared in conjunction with Catherine Gallagher's graduate seminar on seventeenth- and eighteenth-century Women Writers, held at the University of California, Berkeley in the spring of 1990. I am grateful to the other participants in the seminar for their helpful comments on the earliest formulation of this piece and to Cynthia Franklin, Catherine Gallagher, Victoria Pond, Simon Stern and Elizabeth Todesco for their sensitive, astute and supportive readings of later versions. I also benefited greatly from the lively discussion that followed my presentation of this paper under the aegis of the Berkeley Graduate English Women's Caucus. My thinking about Locke has been influenced significantly by Howard Horwitz's work on the subject; I thank him as well.

1. Mark Rose, "The Author in Court: *Pope v. Curll* (1741)," *Cardozo Arts & Entertainment Law Journal* 10 (1992): 475-493. Rose cites *Pope v. Curll* as the first case in which a major English author went to court in his own name to defend his literary rights. As such, the case marks a transitional moment both in the concept of authorship and in the notion of literary property more generally.

2. Some standard works on the Statute of Anne and on the development of copyright generally are Harry Ranson, *The First Copyright Statute* (Austin: Univ. of Texas Press, 1956); John Feather, "The Book Trade in Politics: the Making of the Copyright Act of 1710," *Publishing History* 8 (1980): 19-34; Lyman Ray Patterson, *Copyright in Historical Perspective* (Nashville: Vanderbilt Univ. Press, 1968); Benjamin Kaplan, *An Unhurried View of Copyright* (New York: Columbia Univ. Press, 1967); and Marjorie Plant, *The English Book Trade* (London: George Allen & Unwin Ltd., 1939).

3. Quoted in Rose (note 1), 484.

4. Public Record Office C11/1569/29, quoted in Rose (note 1), 485-86.

5. While the Statute of Anne certainly initiated a concept of literary property, Rose, following Kaplan, contends that the statute operated within terms presumed by the economic structure of printing rather than that of authorship. That the statute mandated that violators of the law forfeit all offending books to their rightful proprietors, who were in turn, required to "Damask and make Waste Paper of them" points up the statute's emphasis on the book as a physical entity (Rose [note 1], 487).

6. In his provocative discussion of the intersections of narrative and critical literalism in *Clarissa* ("Taking Clarissa Literally: The Implication of Reading," *Genre* 21 [Summer 1988]), Stephen Melville comments that "nothing can stop this suspicion of art, fiction, reflection, once it has started. (And isn't that just the fear close reading always provokes, the fear internal to criticism that always turns its theoretical debates back into matters of detail, the accidental and essential of reading?)" (143). Indeed, *Evelina* seems to undermine any claims it (or its critics) might possibly make for the novel's representative status in its strategic exposure of the contingency signaled by the material. *Evelina* as example—whether it be as representative or unrepresentative text, whether its meaningful context be the epistolary novel, eighteenth-century fiction, or the history of women's writing—always threaten to veer into *Evelina* as random sample, with such randomness marking the point of intersection between significance and insignificance. The relationship between the historical claims I make in this paper and the evidence I adduce to support those claims, that is, a fairly detailed reading of a single novel, bears a striking resemblance to the text/manuscript knot Hardwicke tried unsuccessfully to unravel: a theoretical point happens to appear in the form of a novel, but need not necessarily do so (although, within certain professional contexts, it is only of interest insofar as it does). Finally, I think a clue to this puzzle lies in what Melville calls the epistolary novel's "seamlessness of mimesis," the fact that "we can know [the epistolary novel] to be a fiction only if we are assured in advance or by some third person that it is such" (138). The difficulty we might have in distinguishing foreground from background with regard to the relationship between the history of the Hardwicke decision and the text of *Evelina* seems to me an analytically helpful one, the difficulty of the epistolary novel's "seamless mimesis," since it suggests that such distinctions are achieved only by the intervention of either authority or personal interest.

7. John Locke, *Two Treatises of Government,* ed. Peter Laslett (Cambridge: Cambridge Univ. Press, 1988), 287-88.

8. For some discussions of the paradox of the natural rights theory of property in other contexts, see Catherine Gallagher's "George Eliot and *Daniel Deronda:* The Prostitute and the Jewish Question," in *Sex, Politics and Science in the Nineteenth-Century Novel: Selected Papers from the English Institute, 1983-84,* ed. Ruth Bernard Yeazell (Baltimore: Johns Hopkins Univ. Press, 1986), 39-62; Walter Benn Michaels's "Romance and Real Estate," in *The Gold Standard and the Logic of Naturalism* (Berkeley: Univ. of California Press, 1987), 85-112; and Howard Horwitz's *"O Pioneers!* and the Paradox of Property: Cather's Aesthetics of Divestment," *Prospects* 13 (1988): 61-93. I am interested in exploring here the ways in which the structure of the letter, within both Burney's adaptation of the tradition of the epistolary novel and the contemporary debate over the ownership of letters, makes the relations of the Lockean paradox particularly evident.

9. Mary Poovey argues that Burney identifies the courtship period as a moment at which the interests of fathers and husbands potentially come into conflict, but that she then retreats from the implications of such an analysis. See Poovey, "Fathers and Daughters: The Trauma of Growing Up Female," in *Fanny Burney's "Evelina,"* ed. Harold Bloom (New York: Chelsea House, 1988), 85-98. While Burney does seem particularly interested in this period for precisely the reasons Poovey suggests, I intend to argue that, far from backing away from such a conflict, Burney dramatizes the ways in which young women may employ it strategically to their own ends.

10. Charles A. Porter, "Forward: Men/Women of Letters," *Yale French Studies* 74 (1986): 1-14.

11. In "Of Readers and Narratees: The Experience of *Pamela,*" *L'Esprit Createur* 21 (Summer 1981): 93, Susan Rubin Suleiman identifies convincingly an additional level of narration implicit in the epistolary form—that of the editor (and editor's reader). This narrative level may be emphasized to a greater degree (as in *Les Liasons dangereuses* and *Pamela*) or to a lesser extent (as in *Clarissa* or *Evelina*). While Suleiman argues that narrators and narratees within the same narrative levels remain stable in relation to one another, the relations seem to me to get more tricky at the extranarrative levels. While the distinction between author and editor remains clear, for example, the condition of author's narratee is to aspire to become editor's narratee through the willing suspension of disbelief demanded of most realism's readers. That this relationship between narratees is so unstable, in addition to the fact Burney identifies an editor in the Preface only immediately to subsume the role of that editor

within the functions of an explicitly imaginative author, suggests that she is eager to minimize the distinction between author and editor. As I will argue, possession and authorship are figured in terms of one another and are plagued by the same incoherences.

12. Janet Gurkin Altman points out that epistolary novels conventionally emphasize the immediacy of their narration, what she terms the "pivotal, yet impossible present." The only event that can be represented with the presence the form of the epistolary novel claims for itself is the act of writing. See Altman, *Epistolarity: Approaches to a Form* (Columbus: Ohio State Univ. Press, 1982), 129. Paradoxically, the materiality of writing, the same materiality that is threatening insofar as it limits the transparency (hence, the completeness) with which writing can function as a means of self-representation, is the only thing that can be represented completely (the completeness of the representation contingent upon the transformation of writing from an act into a thing.)

13. Altman (note 12) terms the two uses of the letter "metaphoric" (by which the "message" of the letter stands in for the sender by virtue of its immateriality) and "metonymic" (by which the materiality of the letter becomes the conduit of physical contact between sender and recipient) (19).

14. Susan Staves, Patricia Meyer Spacks and Judith Lowder Newton all trace a preponderance of physical violence within the novel. See Staves, "*Evelina*; or, Female Difficulties," in Bloom (note 9), 13-30; Spacks, "Dynamics of Fear: Fanny Burney," in Bloom, 31-57; and Newton, "*Evelina*: A Chronicle of Assault," in Bloom, 59-83. This excess of violence seems to testify to the anxiety produced by these contradictions within and between property and identity.

15. Since Evelina is without a patronym, Villars has created a surname for her—Anville, an obvious variation on his own name, as well as an anagram both for Evelyn (Evelina's grandfather and Villars's pupil) and for Evelina's own name. Not only does Evelina's lack of a patronym allow Villars to construct a lineage based strictly on their legal ties to one another, but the explicit linking of Evelina's first name to this fictional ancestral line would seems to suggest the impossibility of preserving any aspect of her identity from association with this line. Still, this collapse of given name and surname into an undeniably artificial genealogy suggests that Evelina might possess, in the absence of actual family ties, an extraordinary opportunity to fashion her own identity. This oscillation between discourses of complete determinacy and a complete absence of referentiality returns repeatedly throughout the novel and seems to function, both for Evelina and for Burney, as a means of creating actual, if temporary,

freedom in the world. I will discuss this pattern in greater detail below.

16. Fanny Burney, *Evelina, or the History of a Young Lady's Entrance into the World* (Oxford: Oxford Univ. Press, 1989), 18. All further page references to the novel will be cited parenthetically within the text.

17. This retrospective, narrative (as opposed to dramatic) quality stands in sharp contrast to the forms of narration characteristic of Richardson's epistolary fiction, the narration of "writing to the moment," a phrase Richardson coined in his Preface to *Sir Charles Grandison*. "The nature of familiar letters, written, as it were, to the *moment,* while the heart is agitated by hopes and fears, or events undecided, must plead as an excuse for the bulk of a collection of this kind" (Richardson, quoted in Altman [note 12], 141).

18. Altman argues that the epistolary novel became a favorite eighteenth-century form within a cultural milieu that saw authentication as a form of "presentification . . . whereby the writer tries to create the illusion that both he and his addressee are immediately present to each other and to the action. . . . Such tendencies suggest an eighteenth-century reading public whose dominant esthetic is contemporaneity; one might speculate on the dialectical relationship between the epistolary novel so popular in the latter half of the eighteenth century and the historical novel focusing on more distant events that ushered in a new kind of narrative in the nineteenth century" (202). If we understand *Evelina,* in its tendency toward retrospectivity and postponement, to be a movement away from the classic epistolary form identified by Altman, then we might see the beginnings of a new form of authority here—the authority of fiction, of the lie. We would thus understand the emergence of this new aesthetic of fictionality as a response to the particular conditions of disempowerment that made immediacy insupportable for Burney and for Evelina—propertylessness and daughterhood.

19. Along these lines, Richard Swartz argues that the concept of patrimony—the right of fathers to will their property to their children—was frequently employed in eighteenth-century debates over perpetuity of copyright in an attempt to resolve the tension between the literary artifact's status as unique creation and its status as commodity. While Swartz's reading of the *Miller v. Taylor* (1769) copyright case tends to emphasize the diachronic aspects of the contradictions within the Lockean conception of property in distinction to my focus on the synchronic aspects, these differences, rather than being understood as opposing positions, might productively be read as offering insights into Locke's complex use of time in his natural rights model. See Swartz, "Patrimony and the Figuration

of Authorship in the Eighteenth-Century Property Debates," *Works and Days* 7 (1989): 29-54.

20. For detailed biographical accounts of the nature of Burney's relationship to her father, see Margaret Anne Doody, *Frances Burney: The Life in the Works* (New Brunswick: Rutgers Univ. Press, 1988) and Poovey (note 9).

21. Burney writes in her journal on the occasion of the publication of Evelina, "I have an exceeding odd sensation, when I consider that it is now in the power of *any* and *every* body to read what I so carefully hoarded even from my best friends, till this last month or two,—and that a work which was so lately lodged, in all privacy of my bureau, may now be seen by every butcher and baker, cobbler and tinker, throughout the three kingdoms" (Burney, quoted in Jennifer A. Wagner, "Privacy and Anonymity in *Evelina,* in Bloom [note 9], 99-109).

22. Inasmuch as books must be bought and postage must be paid, such infinite openness is only theoretical. Nevertheless, because, before the establishment of the penny post in 1840, most postage was paid by recipients of letters rather than senders, the analogy between recipients and readers still holds. See Asa Briggs, *Victorian Things* (Chicago: Univ. of Chicago Press, 1988), 332. I am thankful to Elizabeth Young for asking this question and Cheri Larsen for her help in tracking down the answer.

Martha F. Bowden (essay date 1999)

SOURCE: Introduction to *The Reform'd Coquet: or Memoirs of Amoranda; Familiar Letters Betwixt a Gentleman and a Lady; and The Accomplish'd Rake, or a Modern Fine Gentleman,* by Mary Davys, edited by Martha F. Bowden, University of Kentucky Press, 1999, pp. xxvi-xlvi.

[*In the following introduction to three eighteenth-century epistolary novels by the British author Mary Davys, Bowden discusses how* The Reform'd Coquet, Familiar Letters, *and* The Accomplish'd Rake *prefigure stories and styles later made famous by Samuel Richardson.*]

THE REFORM'D COQUET (1724)

The Reform'd Coquet tells the story of Amoranda, an essentially good but flighty young woman whose unfortunate tendency towards coquetry and carelessness of her reputation is tamed by Alanthus, the man who wishes to marry her. In order to effect the reformation, the handsome lover disguises himself as an old man, called Formator, and moves into her house as her guardian and guide. It is the first work we know Davys to have written after her move to Cambridge, and her longest to this date; only *The Accomplish'd Rake* is more extensive, and it is no more

elaborate. The preface suggests that she may have returned to writing out of financial necessity: "Few People are so inconsiderable in Life, but they may at some time do good; and tho I must own my Purse is (by a thousand Misfortunes) grown wholly useless to every body, my Pen is at the service of the Publick, and if it can but make some impression upon the young unthinking Minds of some of my own Sex, I shall bless my Labour" (5). Whatever the reasons for its creation, it is an accomplished work and shows no sign of being turned out mechanically merely for monetary reward. The dedication is addressed generally "To the Ladies of Great Britain" rather than to a particular lady from whom Davys might expect patronage; and in contrast to the flattery usual in such a document when the writer is seeking support, it contains words of admonishment and advice. She holds up her heroine as a model who, "when the Lightnesses of her mind were removed . . . became worthy of imitation" (3) and suggests that the ladies who read the book for "an hour or two of agreeable Amusement" (6) follow her example: "When you grow weary of Flattery, and begin to listen to matrimonial Addresses, chuse a Man with fine Sense, as well as a fine Wigg, and let him have some Merit, as well as much Embroidery" (3). She thus indicates her intended audience, who are young, unmarried, potentially giddy and impressionable young ladies.

The book was her first published by subscription, that is the collection of money from supporters in advance of publication to pay for the printing. The subscribers received a copy of the book and their names were printed in a list that they could have bound in the front of the volume. It was a method of ensuring publication that was widely used—Pope's edition of Homer is perhaps the most famous contemporary example—but an unusual approach to publication for novels at the time.[1] As the second novelist to make use of this mode of publication, Davys was in the vanguard of innovation. An examination of the subscription list explains the absence of a potential patron on the dedication page, for the list represented each of the social strata: the nobility and gentry, the clergy (in addition to those obviously designated "The Reverend" there are also two listed as "Dr. Anonymous" who are probably clergymen as well), the literary world, and a long list of more ordinary folk, many of whom were probably her undergraduate patrons.

The novel, while innovative and well-crafted, also reflects her previous work. Although it is not, like *Familiar Letters,* an exclusively epistolary work, Robert Adams Day includes it in his discussion of epistolary fiction, which he defines as "any prose narrative, long or short, largely or wholly imaginative, in which letters, partly or entirely fictitious, serve as the medium or figure significantly in the conduct of the story" (5). Indeed, Davys's writing is always efficient, so that all thirteen letters in the volume, like the dialogue, are not ornaments to the plot but essential devices for furthering the story. Unlike many of her contemporaries, she has little indirect discourse. The characters speak directly for themselves, demonstrating the extent to which the drama has influenced her novels.

The preface to the *Works* (1725), which precedes the text of *Familiar Letters* in this edition, is Davys's clearest articulation of the use of dramatic technique in narrative fiction: "I have in every Novel propos'd one entire Scheme or Plot, and the other Adventures are only incident or collateral to it; which is the great Rule prescribed by the Criticks, not only in Tragedy, and other Heroick-Poems, but in Comedy too. The Adventures, as far as I could order them, are wonderful and probable; and I have with the utmost Justice rewarded Virtues, and punish'd Vice" (87). In the prologue to *The Northern Heiress*, several years before both *The Reform'd Coquet* and the *Works*, Davys also alluded to the rules of the critics, specifically Aristotle, in the works of learned writers:

> . . . you Poets know, whose Brains
> Having at last produc'd with mighty Pains,
> Pieces in which not one Rule was forgot
> Of all that mighty Aristotle wrote;
> Nature in all the Characters observ'd,
> And Time and Place to Nicety preserv'd.

She had then excluded herself from this august company, claiming to have little learning and only one language.[2] But of course she has already demonstrated her familiarity with the rules, and she does so again in this novel. Like the letters and dialogue, the various subplots and interpolated stories—Callid and Froth, Lord Lofty and Altemira, Biranthus and Arentia—all work towards the purpose of the story, the "reform" of the title. They allow Amoranda to be placed in multiple dangers, which are held to be the consequence of her own over-trustfulness and carelessness, without resulting in actual rape, which would have prevented virtue's natural reward, the happy ending.[3] While Altemira's story has a technically "happy" ending—marriage to her seducer—Lord Lofty is such a loathsome character that the only happiness we can imagine for her is the restoration of her good name. The marriage, from Lord Lofty's point of view, is punishment for his mistreatment of Altemira. The wicked are chastised with a severity that verges on parody; to take all these deaths seriously would be to undermine the comic intention of the book.

Davys's use of the summerhouse is a good example of dramatic technique incorporated into the structure of the novel. Indeed, apart from its dramatic uses, its placement is rather odd: surely an estate would have a quieter, more private setting for a retreat than the side of a highway. But it can easily be imagined as a functional stage set: it is on two levels, which allows Callid and Froth to be overheard by the housekeeper when hatching their plot. Both the listening servant and the plotting beaus are visible to the audience, or the reader, but the beaus are of course oblivious of any auditors. Its front windows allow it to be used as a little theater itself—we can look in at the various scenes going on there, such as Formator and the footman beating the beaus or Lord Lofty attempting to seduce Amoranda. Froth and Callid can thus also suggest to Amoranda that she sit in it to watch "a Dance of Shepherds and Shepherdesses in the High-way by Moon-light, just at the Summer-house window" (24). The proximity to the high-

way allows the most dramatic delivery of all the letters: "a Gentleman rid by, and threw in a Glove at the Window; *Amoranda,* at whose foot it fell, took it up, and found there was something in it, which she conceal'd, but was much surpriz'd at the Action" (19). The glove contains a letter whose contents are a declaration of love, but there will be many adventures and many more letters before the mystery of this one and the man who delivers it will be revealed.

Davys's use of cross-dressing can also be linked to the theater and the breeches roles in plays like Wycherley's *The Plain-Dealer* and *The Country Wife* or Farquhar's *The Recruiting Officer.* In fact, however, her use of the device is quite different from that of the playwrights whom she obviously read with affection. There are also significant differences between media that make cross-dressing on stage and on the page two very different devices. One aim of the breeches roles in plays—the display of women's legs, a novelty in a theater where actresses themselves were a novelty—was impossible in the nonvisual medium of print. The audience perception also changes. There is no doubt that everyone in the audience knows that Fidelia in *The Plain-Dealer* is a woman dressing as a man in order to attend her lover. Similarly, few of the characters and none of the audience are fooled by Margery Pinchwife's appearance in her brother's clothes in *The Country Wife;* yet the novel reader sees only as much as the author will let her, and is no more knowledgeable than the characters. Thus, while we may have suspicions about some of the little gentlemen in both *The Reform'd Coquet* and *The Accomplish'd Rake,* we do not truly learn their identities until they are revealed to the fictional characters.

More importantly, cross-dressing is connected with transgression in Davys, in ways it is not in Wycherley, Dryden, or Farquhar. In *The Reform'd Coquet,* Altemira becomes emaciated from grief and dons men's clothes after her femininity has essentially been burned away by her experience of multiple betrayal. Despite the fact that she is essentially blameless, she has been "ruined" by her trust in Lord Lofty, and wears the clothing of a man as a kind of penance until her reputation can be restored. In the same way, Davys's use of male cross-dressing in some ways invokes the role of the stage dame but is fundamentally different in purpose.[4] The episode in which Formator and a footman, both in women's clothes, attack the unsuspecting Callid and Froth is farcical—particularly since Formator is already one level deep in disguise. Amoranda unknowingly enters into the masquerade by promising another kind of exchange of roles: "if you happen to be worsted, we'll invert the Custom, and instead of your delivering the distress'd Damsel, she shall come and rescue you" (27).

The story of Birantha, however, bears little resemblance to stage farce, and is rather linked entirely with transgression. The rape attempt is disturbing, not humorous, because Birantha/Biranthus is far more competent than the fops and appears much more likely to be successful. On the stage two women in full dress fighting with each other might have a slapstick appeal; but without physical presentation to lighten the mood, the threats are quite horrifying: "This minute, by the help of thy own Servant, I will enjoy thee; and then, by the Assistance of my arm, he shall do so too" (59). Biranthus's ending reflects his transgressive behavior. He is put out of his misery by one of the Stranger's servants, a fate no gentleman would expect or desire, and is left lying dead still in the dishonorable woman's clothes. The betrayal by Biranthus and Arentia is surrounded by imagery of the fall of man, which emphasizes the sense of transgression and further distances the incident from the world of the stage dame. Biranthus's several disguises link him with Satan's shape changes in *Paradise Lost,* as does his decision that both his interior and exterior must be hidden. He is "resolved to disguise his Mind as well as his Body" (57), the former with rhetoric, the latter with petticoats. Biranthus and Arentia are called devils by the narrator (58) and Biranthus a viper by Amoranda (59). Arentia becomes the voice of the tempter, as she urges Amoranda to comply since she is being offered the choice of forced marriage or outright rape. But Amoranda, while she shares with Eve the vulnerability that comes from separation from her mentor, recognizes and rejects the rhetoric: "Peace, Screech-Owl, *said* Amoranda, thy Advice carries Poison and Infection in it; the very Sound of thy Words raises Blisters on me, so venomous is the Air of thy Breath" (59). Finally the serpent claims his own, for Arentia, who brought the tempter into the garden, dies from the bite of an adder.

In addition to the dramatic influence in this novel, there is a connection with the world of fairy tale and enchantment, which is not developed until the end of the novel, with the arrival of Lady Betty, Alanthus's sister. Lady Betty has come looking for her brother, who seems to have disappeared: "I fancy he's got into *Fairy-Land,* he lets me hear from him, but will not tell me how he may hear from me" (82). When Formator is revealed to her as the long-lost brother, she faints: "she not expecting to find her brother there, and seeing him all of a sudden turn'd from an old Man, whom she had never seen before, to a brother whom she knew not where to find, she thought herself in some inchanted Castle, and all about her Fiends and Goblins" (83). Amoranda has a dual role in the fairy tale world. She is the enchantress, keeping Formator/Alanthus captive and transformed ("There, there's the Inchantress, who by a natural Magick, has kept me all this while in chains of love," says Alanthus), and a type of imprisoned heroine herself. As in the fairy tale "Beauty and the Beast," it is necessary for her to love Alanthus as Formator before she can see him in his true shape and thus move towards the "happily ever after" ending. The spell is broken when, being attacked by Biranthus, she calls for Formator, and Alanthus appears.

But that happy ending is itself problematic. Amoranda's character is developed in a careful and some ways conventional manner. Like many heroines, she is an orphan, whose mother dies of grief shortly after her father, leaving her alone and without direction at a critical point in her life. She has been raised in a sheltered place that has prevented her from learning the ways of the world, thus making her even more vulnerable. Davys also establishes the roots of her behavior in her flawed upbringing: her parents encourage her tendency to vanity, "under that mistaken Notion, of everything looking well in a Child" (13). But unlike many heroines in works of this nature, she has, in addition to beauty and charm, a quick wit and some of the best dialogue in any novel of the period: "Pray, my Lord, have done, *said* Amoranda, for I freely own I am not proof against Flattery, there is something so inexpressibly pleasing in it—Lard! you Men———— Come, let us catch some Fish, and divert the Subject. Hang the Fish, *said my Lord.* Aye, said Amoranda, for we shall never drown them" (17). It is unfortunate from a twentieth-century viewpoint that her "reform" directed by Formator/Alanthus through the incidents in the book should involve silencing and fear and be observable in her growing suspicion of other people. The girl who ignores a warning about the lecherous Lord Lofty becomes afraid to allow first a puny man, who turns out to be a woman, and then an obviously respectable lady into her house: "*Amoranda* had a just compassion for the unfortunate Man, and saw his Lady's Journey retarded; but the late Attempts which had been made upon her, made her afraid to desire her to come in" (69). By the end of the novel, the masks and disguises are gone—in Alanthus's words, "we are now barefac'd, and know one another" (83)—but all Amoranda's sparkle has disappeared with them. In the final happy scene she is utterly silent. Her last words, to Alanthus's sister Lady Betty who wants an explanation of her brother's white beard, are "Lord *Alanthus,* and Mr. *Traffick,* are the fittest to give your Ladyship an account, which I leave them to do, while I beg leave to go and dress me" (83). Having left her story in the male hands of her lover and guardian, she leaves the stage. When she returns and Alanthus makes his formal proposal, her answer is not recorded.

Part of the problem lies with the character of Formator, whose tendency to priggishness is obvious in his acceptance of Mr. Traffick's request, to mold the niece into the perfect woman as a preliminary to marrying her. To Amoranda he seems initially a killjoy; and his behavior in leaving her apparently to be raped by Biranthus, with the words, "Well, Madam, I am sorry for you, but I am no Knight Errant, nor do I ride in quest of Adventures; I wish you a good Deliverance, and am your humble servant" (60) in order to teach her a lesson, is not only priggish but outrageous. When Amoranda later challenges him about his desertion, he admits to conflicted feelings: "I was resolved, if possible, to cure you at once of rambling with Strangers: in order to which, I put on an Air of Cruelty, which Heaven knows! my Heart had no hand in" (80). But the reader may feel that his words are too little, too late, especially since he shows a sadistic pleasure in her pain (80-81), and Amoranda in turn seems only too quick to enjoy it (80).

The fairy tale framing allows us to suspend judgement in part on the shortcomings of his character. He is also partially redeemed through the observations of Maria, Amoranda's clever, older relation, for although her sharp eyes penetrate his disguise very quickly, she nonetheless finds him attractive, and takes the beard away with her so that she can ask potential suitors to wear it. Pictures of perfection are not easily drawn and many of us share Jane Austen's reaction to them; accusations of priggishness against Richardson's Sir Charles Grandison demonstrate the difficulty that even the greatest writers have in portraying virtue. But like the problematic nature of Amoranda's reform, the concept of Formator as perfection is bound to be questioned by twentieth-century readers. Did Davys really believe him to be so (would she choose him as a husband?) or was she reflecting the demands of the literary marketplace and her own desire to establish herself as a writer of texts that restore the "purity and empire of love"? And finally, are we supposed to see in the young man who puts on a fake beard and a lisp a spoof on the whole idea of Mentor? He certainly presents a much less dignified appearance than Athena does when, disguised as a wise man, she arrives in Ithaca to aid and strengthen Telemachus, who has to cope with his mother's unruly suitors. Davys's other writing suggests that she has enough familiarity with the classics and gift for satire to make that reading a possibility, or at least a subtext. At this distance an "authoritive" reading is both impossible and undesirable, but the wise reader will keep all these possibilities in mind.

FAMILIAR LETTERS BETWIXT A GENTLEMAN AND A LADY (1725)

While *Familiar Letters'* sole publication in Davys's lifetime was in her *Works* in 1725, there is sufficient internal evidence to date it from her days in London between 1716 and 1718. Donald Hal Stefanson (1:xi, xii) believes it was begun in the fall of 1717 and finished in 1718. He bases his date on the announcement of the birth of an heir to the Hanovers in the text (95), which he links with the birth of a son, George William, to Prince George on 2 November 1717, and "the 'Glorious Revolution' of 1689" (xii n. 5). On the other hand, because William III landed on British soil on 5 November 1688, the twenty-eight years of Whiggish rule referred to in the text might direct us to 1716. Furthermore, the child was born on 20 October, not 2 November 1717.[5] Whatever scheme one uses to date the work, it clearly comes from the London years, as the references to Flamsteed and the Reduction of the Light Horse indicate; it may have had several revisions whose chronologies have not been made consistent in the final version. There would also have been good reason not to publish it, for George William was born with a congenital weakness—a polyp in the heart—and the plaudits and good wishes for the birth of the first Hanoverian son born on English soil would have fallen rather flat in the face of the child's death in February, 1718. By the time Davys published the Works, however, William Augustus had been born (1721) in good health, and thus the compliments could flow without apology. In any event, the tributes to the so-called British heir are pure Whig apologetics, since the succession to the throne continued through the eldest

son, German-born Frederick, who did not himself rule, but whose son became George III.[6]

Robert Adams Day includes *Familiar Letters* in a list of the four novels that "represent the highest development of letter fiction before Richardson."[7] He draws attention to the realism of the text, Davys's "sense of humor and an eye for physical detail" (187), and the fact that the letters are dated at adequately-spaced intervals to allow them to arrive at their destinations through the post as it then operated (203). While not noting the serious divisions between the two characters, he commends the tone of the letters for emphasizing wit over passion: "A pair of correspondents like Artander and Berina, who manage to be witty instead of passionate while conveying the impression that they entertain tender feelings for one another, is a refreshing innovation . . . The very lack of stress on conventional passion in the letters, combined with their playful tone, makes them perhaps the most realistic letters in early English fiction" (187, 190). Their wit makes Artander and Berina particularly good company; it also suggests that their text is somehow different from the other fictions into whose company they are generally gathered. Ruth Perry describes the typical epistolary process: "Certainly within these novels, characters use their letters to re-live moments they have spent together. Not concerned with narrative progress, they describe to each other the episodes they have lived through together, dwelling on them in loving, repetitious, detail."[8] While this description is an accurate characterization of many epistolary novels, it does not describe *Familiar Letters,* where we know almost nothing about the correspondents' lives before the book and the correspondence begin.

We know that they have been in the city together, that Artander has left for his family seat in the country, and that they have agreed to be platonic friends rather than courting lovers—a situation that suits Berina much better than it does Artander. There is no dwelling on their moments together, although there are some complaints about the separation from Artander, and a reference to previous political disputes. Instead, they discuss politics, argue, describe their friends and visitors, all in the witty manner that has delighted its readers ever since. The anomalies in the book, which set it apart from the epistolary fiction of the day, also lead us to other readings. Lindy Riley's article, "Mary Davys's Satiric Novel *Familiar Letters:* Refusing Patriarchal Inscription of Women" is quite right in describing the novel as satire, although I believe she is wrong in describing it as a reverse conduct book.[9] Its satire is aimed at society rather than at exclusively gender issues. The vignettes interspersed throughout the letters paint a picture of social situations—fashion, miserliness, love, faithlessness, the pains of marriage, and death. They underline how broad a net Davys is casting. That she asserts a female Whig as the voice of reason and stability suggests where she thinks the answers to society's ills may lie.

Davys sets up a relationship between a man, Artander, who is both Tory and mildly misogynistic, and a woman,

Berina, who is a Whig and reluctant to accept the restrictions of the past, both for women and for subjects of the crown. It is significant, however, that the conduct advice she rejects is from what she calls "one of those modern Creatures call'd a *Prude* . . . being the oldest Lady in the room" (94).[10] Her reason for rejecting the injunction to cease writing to Artander is not that she feels that women should no longer be restricted in their correspondence. Rather, she rejects the "modern" and prudish idea that all relationships between men and women are sexual and makes a more ancient claim for her ties with Artander, that of friendship. She bases her decision to go on writing within the ancient and classical locus of the demands of friendship: "A Friend is not worth calling so, who dares not run the risque of so trifling a Censure, to maintain so noble a Character."[11] After a brief reference to Artander's letter, in which he describes a woman taken to task by her husband-to-be, she goes on to what will be one of the central concerns of the letters, the Tory/Whig argument, in which each tries to convert the other.

Politics and religion share the same close relationship in this text as they did in eighteenth-century England. Davy's connection with the clergy is a part of her writing persona and demands that she support the established church. Stefanson mentions that she does not seem to be particularly religious and that she makes fun of the pious. But the pious she makes fun of, particularly the woman in *The Merry Wanderer,* are dissenters, and she upholds the centrality of the *Book of Common Prayer,* as her use of November 5 makes very clear. By announcing the birth of the prince on November 5, instead of closer to the actual birth, Davys chose to link the continuity of the Hanoverian succession with two other significant events in English history, both of which confirmed in the minds of the British people that the maintenance of a Protestant monarchy was under providential control. On 5 November 1605, the Gunpowder Plot, more commonly known to us as Guy Fawkes Day, was uncovered; in 1688, William of Orange cannily arranged to land on English soil on the same day. The Gunpowder Plot had been a day of required observance in the church since 1605; after 1688, the commemoration of the Glorious Revolution was added to the service. Thus the choice of the day is deliberate, as is no doubt the day on which the correspondence begins, November 1, All Saints' Day, on which the church recognizes its unity through the ages in the community of those who have gone before.

Berina's support of the Whigs throughout the encounter, which she also describes as providential ("heaven had designed me for what I am" [97]) is a repetition of anti-Catholic and anti-Jacobite rhetoric as it was expressed in the public press and in the sermons of the day. All the parish congregations as well as the Houses of Parliament convened to commemorate the Gunpowder Plot, according to the rubrics of the *Book of Common Prayer,* and to hear a sermon that rehearsed much of what Berina asserts in her letter of November 10. The catalogue of Catholic atrocities, including Mary Tudor's persecution of the Protestants and the Irish Rebellion, was standard fare, aired in pulpits all over the country. Artander's responses—his defense and hagiography of King Charles and his repudiation of Cromwell's people, whom he calls "King Killers"—are equally those of the Tory supporters of the Stuart monarchy and divine right.

Davys, stalwart Whig and Hanoverian as she has demonstrated herself to be in her dedication to *The Northern Heiress,* deliberately presents the Tory as inconsistent, changeable and untrustworthy. For example, Artander offers to subvert the Church's construction of marriage, in which the woman promises to obey her husband: "you shall find I will out-do your own Wishes, by giving myself up so entirely to your will, that your least Inclination shall be a Command" (117). Just as he goes against their pact and speaks to Berina of love, linking it with friendship in a way that she has previously rejected as prudish and modern, so he cannot be depended upon to follow through on his principles and match the absolute monarch on the throne with one in the family. Having used the Bible to support his Tory argument (99), he proposes to subvert scripture in order to win Berina's hand. Finally, he displays his cowardice: rather than reject a marriage proposal outright, he invents a mortal illness to explain his inability to accept it.

Davys is satirizing the political argument by diminishing it to the level of a quarrel between lovers; but she is quite serious in the description of marriage that she gives Berina to articulate:

> . . . the Promise you make of inverting the God of Nature's Rules, and being all Obedience, is no Inducement to me to become a Wife: I shou'd despise a Husband as much as a King who wou'd give up his own Prerogative, or unman himself to make his Wife his Head: We Women are too weak to be trusted with Power, and don't know how to manage it without the Assistance of your Sex, tho' we oftenest shew that Weakness in the Choice of our Advisers. The notion I have always had of Happiness in Marriage, is, where Love causes Obedience on one side, and Compliance on the other, with a View to the Duty incumbent on both: If anything can sweeten the bitter Cup, 'tis that.
>
> (117-18)

There is nothing ironic in Berina's tone; what she says is consistent with her support of the King, who was also head of the church. Like her anti-Jacobite rhetoric, it reflects the Church of England view. She sees marriage as a mutual contract between husband and wife, much like the contract worked out between king and people: "When we swear Allegiance to a King, 'tis conditional; as long as he keeps his Oath, we'll keep ours. When God Almighty commanded our Obedience, he commanded his Care and Love" (100). The same *Book of Common Prayer* that mandated the commemoration of November Fifth and obedience in marriage also required that the King be prayed for at every service. Thus Berina's rejection of marriage because it too much resembles slavery is not representative of her rejection of women's obedience in marriage. On the contrary, she accepts the terms of the contract, but chooses not to enter into it herself, and therefore cannot accept marriage with Artander or anyone else. In doing so, she, unlike Artander, remains firm in the principles she espouses at the beginning: "I hate a Yoke that galls for life" (96). She is linked in her views of marriage with early feminists like Mary Astell, although given Astell's high Tory sentiments, it is unlikely that they would have much else in common. It should be remembered that Davys did not remarry, and instead chose to live thirty-four years a widow. Therefore it is probably significant that she places the words of the rational, clear-eyed Whig in the mouth of a woman, and one who fears love because she equates it with blindness and loss of control. The extent to which the satires of politics, gender, and belief, are intertwined in this novel is clear from the dynamics of the correspondence, for Berina is no more able to refrain from talking about politics and current events than Artander is from speaking of love. It is a reversal of gender roles; it also implies that the Whig/woman is more serious-minded than the Tory/man.

Day believes that Berina's laughter at Artander "grows fainter as the correspondence ends" and that "the reader is left to assume that a marriage will take place" (188). But does the reader assume any such thing? Certainly one eighteenth-century reader did so and wrote a couplet on the subject,[12] but that very couplet invokes the god of love who, represented as a blind and blinding boy, is very much a presence in the novel. Artander and the reader beware: we may be misreading the heroine. Many of my students assume that when Artander arrives in town, Berina will welcome him as more than friend, but there are dissenting voices. One student thought that Berina would set him straight and send him away; another thought that she would probably marry him, but it would be, in the student's own words, "a complete waste." Given the necessity for obedience and the expected role of the wife in the eighteenth century, the student saw Berina's brilliance snuffed out by marriage. She had not read *The Reform'd Coquet,* but she seemed to intuit Amoranda's silencing.

Davys's pattern of allusion is particularly strong in this short work; she draws in all the sites of reference that she invokes in the longer works. The density of allusion also marks it as somehow different from the other novels, and helps us to see her strategy. It is probably no coincidence that among the writers to whom she refers most often are Swift, Congreve, and Farquhar, all of whom went to Trinity College, Dublin, the first two at exactly the same time as her husband. In addition she refers to Cowley, whom Ruth Perry describes as a favorite among the women of the late seventeenth and early eighteenth century, although Davys is more drawn to his love poems than to the celebrations of retired life; retirement was not something she was ever able to enjoy.[13] The many classical references announce Davys's claim to be an Augustan wit, although her status and gender denied her a classical education. Two Scriblerians, Pope and Gay, subscribed to her work, and in *The Accomplish'd Rake,* the Belinda story is a deliberate revisioning of Pope's *Rape of the Lock.* Cervantes' hero Don Quixote and his companion Sancho Panza also appear; they were favorites among the wits of the day, particularly the Scriblerians to whom Swift belonged. It is as if, isolated both socially and geographically (after 1718) from the intellectual center, she is nonetheless attempting to write herself into it, creating in her work an association that mimics the connections of friendship and writing between the members of the Scriblerus group, to which she could never in actuality belong.[14]

THE ACCOMPLISH'D RAKE

Like *The Reform'd Coquet,* the story of Sir John Galliard is one of transformation and education. Here again Davys carefully sets up the protagonist to be a prime candidate for reform. His father dies when he is young, leaving him, like Amoranda, without a strong moral force in the family. While Amoranda's mother is physically weak and dies, leaving her orphaned, Sir John's mother, Lady Galliard, fails him morally. The psychological preparation is very astute in a pre-Freudian age, for Sir John's antipathy towards women, the vice that especially requires reform, begins with sexual betrayal by his mother when he finds her in bed with her footman. At that point he leaves the house in disgust, rejects Cambridge and the groves of academe, and instead takes the high road to London. Given the eighteenth-century pastoral/urban dichotomy, one might say he chooses to go to hell on his own terms. When at the end of the book he returns home, his mother reveals her complicity in his actions by quoting Cowley's "The Welcome." Superficially the poem seems entirely appropriate for welcoming home one's long-lost son, with its prodigal son imagery, but it is in fact the speaker's welcome to her own heart. She admits, through the poet's voice, that her own actions have initiated and participated in the progress of this particular rake.

Once in London, he falls into all the well-known vices: gambling, whoring, dandyism, falling into bad company, and spending his inheritance on luxuries before he gets it, so that he is obliged to go into debt. Particularly he attacks women, even the daughter of Mr. Friendly, his surrogate father and the man who cares most for him in the world. Attractive women are there for him to take, to seduce, to enjoy and to discard, regardless of their social status. He suffers all the usual ills of a man in his situation: he is sick, hungover, infected with venereal disease, cheated and in debt. Eventually he goes too far and rapes Mr. Friendly's daughter. From then on, even he is able to see how everything he does blows up in his face (sometimes literally) and he is forced to go home and face the consequences.

The novel repeats many of the techniques of *The Reform'd Coquet.* Here as well, letters play a significant role in furthering the plot. Of particular note are the double-talking letter from a jealous husband that lures Sir John into a trap (214) and his mother's deceptively breezy note from home which reveals to him that Nancy Friendly has given birth to a child who looks suspiciously like himself (212-13). Davys also uses the breeches role in a similar manner as before, to mark transgressive behavior; the "little gentleman" called Venture-all dresses as a man to solicit Galliard's attention, something she could not do as a woman. Yet while Venture-all appears to accomplish her goal of producing a child for her husband, her approach is transgressive in Davys's world and is not rewarded. She is not able to convince Galliard to impregnate her until she takes off her mask, and he complies only because she is beautiful; the resulting child is a girl, not the son and heir she had hoped for. When she proposes marriage, again assuming the male prerogative with male dress, he refuses her. Catherine Craft-Fairchild, in *Masquerade and Gender,* includes Davys in her consideration of the "Darker Side of Masquerade": while female cross-dressing results in empowerment, it also "seems to be a cautionary tale warning women against the dangers of female desire."[15] For her actions nonetheless confirm the roles that society dictates: "If transvestism is a woman's effort to 'move up the patriarchal hierarchy,' such a move only confirms the terms of that hierarchy and privileges 'man' at the expense of 'woman'" (45).

Among the several seduction plots, the rape of Nancy is a critical point in the reformation of Sir John, since from then on he is beset by misadventure, experiences qualms of conscience, and is eventually led to offer marriage to her. Nancy's experience is thus more important than the seduction stories in *The Reform'd Coquet,* which are designed as a cautionary tales for the heroine. The tone is significantly different from the story of Altermira and Lord Lofty—the rape is more violent, the girl more vocal, and there is no question of her ultimate happiness being fulfilled; as she says, not even marriage will restore her good name entirely, for "the good natured World knows my Fault, and it will be sure to keep it in continual Remembrance" (225). But as in the case of Altermira and Lofty, we may be compelled to question Sir John's fitness as a husband, since nothing in his previous behavior has led us to expect him to be faithful. Indeed, he hastens the marriage lest he lose his nerve, and the author admits that she has set spies upon him to make sure that he behaves. Nonetheless, the story has been resolved in the time-honored way; Sir John has returned home, faced his duties, and been granted an heir to boot.

The parallels with *Clarissa* are obvious and illustrate the way in which Richardson's novel builds upon and transforms the amatory fiction which preceded it; Davys is just as surely a forerunner of Richardson as she is of Fielding. We have a virtuous woman betrayed, raped while drugged, her life apparently ruined, and her family distraught.[16] As in *Clarissa,* this action becomes the turning point in the central male character's life, after which nothing is the same. The differences between the two lie in Clarissa's recognition of the essentially tragic nature of her situation. She refuses to marry Lovelace, although her family and Anna Howe want her to; and instead of pregnancy, a child, and redemption for both by marriage, she and Lovelace

die, in very different ways that reflect their roles in the story. Like Clarissa's, Nancy's mind becomes disordered by the event—she says that "Peace is become such a Stranger that if it were to make me a Visit I should look surprised and cry I know you not" (224). Even when she is recovered she does not want to see or meet with other people. Her concern with whether or not her door had been locked on the night of the rape anticipates Clarissa's language, and her revelation of what has happened to her is linked to the unlocked door: "Perhaps (replied the poor Lady in Tears) they broke it open when they could not awake us; but be it how it will, I fear I am ruined past Redemption" (169). Twenty years later when Clarissa describes her own catastrophe, the room is transformed into her own body: "when all my doors are fast, and nothing but the keyhole open, and the key of late put into that, to be where you are, in a manner without opening any of them."[17] Davys's world is still a comic one, however, although in Nancy's pathetic cry that "No one has done this," there is a growing recognition of the potential for tragedy.

The character of Belinda is also crucial to Sir John's reform, because she presents him with the salutary experience of a smart, attractive and articulate woman who does *not* find him irresistible. Of all the women he meets, she is most his equal. Her name is significant, for she clearly represents a reference to, and a reversal of, Pope's character in *The Rape of the Lock.* It is only after the reference to ombre, the game that proves fatal to Belinda's hair in Pope's mock epic, that the narrator rather disingenuously gives her character a name, "the common name of Belinda." However common a name it may be (and it stands out among the other characters" names—Jenny, Nancy, Dolly, Sarah, Betty, Margaret) there is only one other Belinda connected in contemporary minds with a game of ombre. Miss Wary, like Ariel and Pope's Clarissa, attempts to warn Belinda against this particular man, if not against men in general. Having established the connection, however, Davys reworks the entire encounter.

Like her predecessor, Belinda is beautiful, vivacious and involved in London society; unlike her, she is not superficial. Even when Sir John manages to get her alone in a coach on a deserted road, he is not able to carry out in actuality what the Baron does metaphorically—Belinda does not lose a lock of her hair or anything else. What is more, she has paid some attention to Miss Wary: "But how resolved so ever *Belinda* was to reject Miss Wary's Counsel, it put her upon her Guard, and she kept a constant Centry at the Door of her Virtue" (188). The celestial powers of Davys's world do not desert a lady when they see the image of a man in her heart. The greatest change, however, is in her articulate use of rhetoric: where Sir John expects a wrestling match, he gets a debate, and one the lady wins, as she could not have won the physical encounter. She does so by suggesting, in her anger and not realizing how close to the bone she is cutting, that his mother is less than virtuous and that he is a footman's bastard, since he is not behaving in a way that indicates nobility. Sir John is vanquished; he was "never so stung in his life before" (193). The encounter has the extraordinary and unique effect of changing his feeling for her; it "is now turn'd to Esteem and Respect, which shall for the future regulate all my actions towards you . . . I am ashamed of what I have done, and, which is more, you are the first woman who has ever made me so" (194). She is also the first woman with whom he has a relationship that is neither sexual nor predatory; her influence prepares him for the remorse and sense of responsibility which will result in his returning home to acknowledge his son and marry Nancy. Nancy, too, wins him by the force of her rhetoric.

While it is always dangerous to speculate on personal parallels, this novel contains several distinct instances that suggest that although Davys did not put her name on the title page or at the end of the dedication, she nonetheless left her mark in the text. I have already mentioned her reference to Cambridge and the use of the name John, which is given to the hero, as well as to his Cambridge-educated father, Mr. Friendly, the surrogate father, and the "Little Mackroon," the child whose presence in part effects the reform of Sir John's character. Teachwell, the man of "worth and learning," clergyman, scholar, and teacher, who dies tragically young, is surely a tribute to Peter Davys, who was all those things. He is of "sober mild Behaviour, affable to all, but very industrious to bring his new Charge to a Sence of those Rudiments which Neglect had made him a Stranger to" (133-34). This novel also contains most of the few instances in which Davys discusses children in an emotional way. Venture-all's brief note to Belinda announcing the illness of her daughter, "whose Life is hers" (187) is full of pathos: *MY trembling Hand is now imployed to tell you, my dear Child is extremely ill, and you well know I share the Malady, fly to see it while alive and help to comfort a distracted Sister. P.S. Dear Bell make hast*" (186). Sir John's reaction to the first sight of his own son is also notable, for it cracks his supposedly disinterested façade before he overtly accepts the boy as his own: "Sir *John* at Nature's Call, ran to meet it, took it to his Bosom and embraced it with a Father's Love" (224). Perhaps at the end of her life, Davys was finally able to think of her daughters without pain; in this work, we see her tribute to all she has lost.

Notes

1. It is the first book Turner identifies as being published in such a way in her "Catalogue of women's fiction published in book form 1696-1796," although Robert Adams Day notes one earlier example, that of *Letters from a Lady of Quality to a Chevalier,* by Eliza Haywood, published in 1721 with 309 subscribers. Turner, 152-211; Robert Adams Day, *Told in Letters: Epistolary Fiction Before Richardson* (Ann Arbor: Univ. of Michigan Press, 1966), 73-74.

2. *The Northern Heiress: or, the Humours of York* (London, 1716), 6.

3. See Susan Staves, "Fielding and the Comedy of Attempted Rape," *History, Gender and Eighteenth-Century Literature,* ed. Beth Fowkes Tobin (Athens: Univ. of Georgia Press, 1994), 86-112.

4. See John Harold Wilson, *All the King's Ladies: Actresses of the Restoration* (Chicago: Univ. of Chicago Press), 73, for the comic uses of the stage dame.

5. Ragnhild Hatton, *George I: Elector and King* (Cambridge: Harvard Univ. Press, 1978), 132, 168.

6. Stefanson thinks that Davys is attempting to win the support of George II, but the compliments are obviously aimed at George I who was still very much alive, both in the teens when the book was written and in 1725 when it was published.

7. *Told in Letters,* 177. The other four are *The Perfidious P* (1702), *Lindamira* (1702), and *Olinda's Adventures* (1693 and later).

8. Ruth Perry, *Women, Letters, and the Novel.* AMS Studies in the Eighteenth Century, no. 4. (New York: AMS Press, 1980), 123.

9. In *Cutting Edges: Postmodern Critical Essays on Eighteenth-Century Satire,* ed. James E. Gill. Tennessee Studies in Literature, vol. 37 (Knoxville: Univ. of Tennessee Press. 1995), 206-21.

10. Pope's poem "Answer to the following question of Mrs Howe: WHAT is PRUDERY?" suggests that rejecting a prude's advice is not necessarily a radical subversion of societal norms. The prude is described as "Old and void of all good-nature; / Lean and fretful; would seem wise," and thus located in a group generally marginalized by society—the old and unattractive single women. Alexander Pope, *Poetical Works,* ed. Herbert Davis (London: Oxford Univ. Press, 1966, 1967), 638, lines 6-7.

11. Davys enters an ongoing controversy as to whether or not women were capable of friendship. That Richardson should put disparaging comments about female friendship into the mouth of Lovelace is not surprising; but Clarissa's cousin Morden, a much more positive character, expresses similar convictions (see my article, "Composing Herself: Music, Solitude, and St. Cecilia in *Clarissa,*" in *1650-1850: Ideas, Aesthetics, and Inquiries in the Early Modern Era,* vol. 2, ed. Kevin L. Cope [New York: AMS Press, 1995], 185-201).

12. See below, p 242 n. 66.

13. Ruth Perry, *The Celebrated Mary Astell: An Early English Feminist* (Chicago: Univ. of Chicago Press, 1986), 126-27.

14. See Patricia Carr Brückmann, *A Manner of Correspondence: A Study of the Scriblerus Club* (Montreal and Kingston: McGill-Queen's Univ. Press, 1997) for a description of the way the relationship among the Scriblerians manifests itself in a pattern of shared allusion.

15. Catherine Craft-Fairchild, *Masquerade and Gender: Disguise and Female Identity in Eighteenth-Century*

Fictions by Women (University Park: Pennsylvania State Univ. Press, 1993), 35.

16. See Susan Staves, "British Seduced Maidens," *Eighteenth Century Studies* 14 (1980-81): 109-34, for a discussion of the way in which the seduction of a daughter affects the whole family; Mr. Friendly's decline exactly fits the pattern.

17. Samuel Richardson, *Clarissa, or, the History of a Young Lady,* 4 vols. (London and New York: Dent, Dutton, 1932, 1962), 3:210-11.

PRINCIPAL FIGURES: BRITAIN

Ian Watt (essay date 1956)

SOURCE: "Shamela," in *Fielding: A Collection of Critical Essays,* edited by Ronald Paulson, Prentice-Hall, Inc., 1962, pp. 45-51.

[*In the following essay, which first appeared in slightly different form in 1956, Watts claims that Henry Fielding's intention in* Shamela, *a satire on Samuel Richardson's* Pamela, *is to attack religious ideas of virtue and to undermine Richardson's interpretation of his heroine's character. Watts argues further that this latter purpose gives the novel its basic narrative form, as it begins and ends with letters exchanged between two parsons about Richardson's novel.*]

Pamela: or, Virtue Rewarded was published on November 6th, 1740. It immediately became the sensation of the literary season, and a swarm of attacks, parodies, and spurious continuations soon appeared to sour Richardson's remarkable and unexpected triumph; of these the first and easily the best was the eighteen-penny pamphlet *An Apology for the Life of Mrs. Shamela Andrews,* published on April 4th, 1741, under the name of Mr. Conny Keyber.

That Fielding was the author is indisputable. Horace Walpole and several other contemporaries privately recorded it as his in terms that do not suggest that there was any doubt about the matter; and in the last fifty years or so the labors of Austin Dobson, Wilbur Cross, Alan D. McKillop, Charles B. Woods,[1] and many others, have strengthened the attribution with a great deal of internal and external evidence. There is always an element of uncertainty about the authorship of any work that was published pseudonymously, remained unacknowledged by its author, and was not publicly attributed to him in his lifetime.[2] In the case of *Shamela,* however, these things are natural enough: Fielding was soon to become prominent as a novelist, journalist, and reforming magistrate, and was naturally unwilling to avow so indecent a work, especially once he knew, which he apparently did not when he wrote *Shamela,*

that *Pamela* had actually been written by Richardson, whose *Clarissa* he was later to admire, and who was, moreover, a friend of his sister Sarah's; as for the public, it was not likely to be very interested in the authorship of a minor squib which, after the three editions of 1741, was not reprinted until 1926.

One might have expected that the question would have been settled in 1804, when Mrs. Barbauld published her edition of Richardson's correspondence; for it made public a letter to Lady Bradshaigh naming Fielding as the author.[3] Nevertheless, the issue was avoided for nearly a century more, a fact which can perhaps best be explained as the result of the misplaced zeal of nineteenth century editors and scholars for Fielding's reputation or our morals, both matters, of course, which might more properly have been assumed to be no less invulnerable than Pamela's virtue.

I

Shamela, then, is Fielding's, and it is therefore his first prose fiction. The tale itself is accessible enough: the only facts it requires of its reader are those of life. Nor is the main range of satiric allusion much more recondite: it demands only a nodding acquaintance with *Pamela,* such as college easily supplies. The book opens and closes, however, with a series of secondary allusions which may call for some explanation. Any readers of the title page, for example, who do not have the works of Cibber and Middleton at their fingertips, may well wonder who is Mr. Conny Keyber?

Colley Cibber, actor, dramatist and Poet Laureate since 1730, was a very old enemy and butt of Fielding. His *Apology for the Life of Mr. Colley Cibber, Comedian, Written by Himself,* had been one of the best sellers of 1740; the title of *Shamela* is closely modeled on it, and there is, further, some similarity between Cibber's air of ingenuous self-satisfaction and the innocent self-revelation of Fielding's heroine. Here, however, the connection stops; and it is probable that Fielding used Cibber's name for his parody mainly because it would add to its topicality, and to the further discredit of a celebrity whom everyone would recognize under the patent and already established sobriquet of "keyber."

The "Conny" of "Conny Keyber" is a conflation of "Colley" and "Conyers," with the added appropriate suggestions of "coney," a dupe, and possibly of "cunny," latin "cunnus." Conyers was the given name of Dr. Middleton, Fellow of Trinity College, Cambridge, whom grateful colleagues had made "Principal Library-Keeper" of the University as some compensation for his vigorous, unsuccessful, and ruinously expensive attacks on the Master of his college, the redoubtable Dr. Bentley. Middleton had published a *Life of Cicero* early in 1741, and we know from *Joseph Andrews*[4] that Fielding had little regard for the work itself; but what drew his fire in *Shamela* was the adulatory inanity of Middleton's "Epistle Dedicatory" to his patron, John, Lord Hervey. This courtier and poetaster,

Pope's Sporus, was the Lord Privy Seal of Walpole's crumbling administration; and his effeminacy, which had already excited a good deal of satiric comment, explains the terms of Fielding's dedicatory letter "To Miss Fanny, &c."—an appellation Pope had already established. The letter is actually a very close parody of Middleton's effusion; compare, for instance, its third, sixth, and final paragraphs with these passages from Middleton:

> I cannot forbear boasting, that some Parts of my present Work have been brightened by the Strokes of your Lordship's Pencil.

> That singular Temperance in Diet, in which your Lordship perseveres . . .

> It was Cicero who instructed me to write; your Lordship who rewards me for writing.

> [*First,* then, Madam, I must tell the World, that you have tickled up and brightened many Strokes in this Work by your Pencil.

> [*Fourthly,* You have a Virtue which enables you to rise early and study hard, and that is, forbearing to over-eat yourself, and this in spite of all the luscious Temptations of Puddings and Custards, exciting the Brute (as Dr. *Woodward* calls it) to rebel. This is a Virtue which I can greatly admire, though I much question whether I could imitate it.

> [. . . it was *Euclid* who taught me to write. It is you, Madam, who pay me for Writing.]

Middleton had also commended Hervey's habit of early rising, of "spending a useful day, before others begin to enjoy it," and had recorded his own matutinal visits "when I have found you commonly engaged with the classical writers of Greece and Rome." The vignette was irresistible, and in the fifth paragraph of his dedicatory letter Fielding delightedly developed the opening afforded by the ambiguity of "engaged" into the kind of sexual innuendo appropriate to Hervey's reputation. We must agree with the verdict of Thomas Dampier, later Dean of Durham, who writes in a private letter of 1741 that "the Dedication to Lord Hervey has been very justly and prettily ridiculed by Fielding in a Dedication to a Pamphlet called 'Shamela' which he wrote to burlesque . . . 'Pamela,' a Romance in low Life."[5]

So much for the title page and dedicatory letter: the second of the "Letters to the Editor" introduces yet another polemic note. Unlike Fielding, Cibber and Middleton were both Administration supporters, and this was no doubt an added reason for Fielding's mockery: but the political issue is not specifically raised until John Puff's letter. There Fielding ironically suggests that the talents of the creator of *Shamela* might even be equal to no less a task than writing a biography of "his Honour"—Walpole, and follows this insult with an injurious explanation of that politician's notorious complaisance about his wife's infidelities. The political aspect of *Shamela,* however, is very minor, and we must pass on to the letters of the two parsons which serve as introduction and conclusion to the

narrative itself if we are to get to grips with Fielding's main intentions and appreciate *Shamela* as—among other things—a topical literary, religious, and moral satire.

When Parson Oliver, who bears the name of Fielding's early tutor, speaks of "an epidemical Phrenzy now raging in Town" over *Pamela,* we are confronted with yet another example of the Augustan rearguard action against the swelling ranks of the Grub-Street Dunces. It was bad enough that Cibber should make 1500 pounds from his *Apology* and Middleton much more from his *Cicero,*[6] especially when Fielding himself was in the literary and economic doldrums, the dramatic career ended, that of the novelist and magistrate not yet begun; but the simultaneous furor over *Pamela* must have looked like the most dangerous conspiracy of all against the Republic of Letters, since the clergy seemed to be the ringleaders.

Fielding probably had two things mainly in mind when he made Parson Oliver attack "the confederating to cry up a nonsensical ridiculous Book, (I believe the most extensively so of any ever yet published)." There was, first, Richardson's insertion of some thirty pages of laudatory letters in the second and subsequent editions of *Pamela:* puffing was ancient enough, but never had it been so copious and shameless, and Fielding could make his satirical point merely by culling the riper fatuities from the original—the passages in quotation marks in Tickletext's first letter are all, with one brief exception,[7] cited verbatim from the prefatory matter to *Pamela.*[8]

The second, and much more important thing that Fielding had in mind in attacking "the confederating to cry up" *Pamela* was the unprecedented and enthusiastic collaboration of the clergy. Dr. Benjamin Slocock had even recommended it from the pulpit of St. Saviour's Church, Southwark, and, it was rumored, had received ten guineas for the favor. When Fielding, therefore, put the rubric "Necessary to be had in all Families" on the title page of *Shamela,* and made Tickletext compare the *Whole Duty of Man* unfavorably with *Pamela,* he was only going a little further than Richardson's clerical *claque.* Pope himself, incidentally, had been numbered in the chorus, and in the charming eulogy "The Editor to *Himself*" Fielding seems to be embroidering his no doubt intentionally ambiguous encomium that *Pamela* "would do more good than many volumes of sermons."

One other religious aspect of *Shamela* perhaps calls for brief explanation. Shamela, we notice, is like her avatar in owning a little library of devotional as well as other reading; and she twice mentions *A Short Account of God's Dealings with the Reverend Mr. George Whitefield.* Whitefield had published this work in 1740 as a reply to an attack on Methodism and on him personally by Dr. Joseph Trapp in the previous year; and when Parson Williams takes as his text "Be Not Righteous Overmuch" he is following Trapp in his first sermon, which had provided the keynote for the subsequent polemics.[9] Public interest in the rise of Methodism, then, supplied Fielding with yet another set of topical allusions: and it is also, no doubt, partly responsible for the expansion of the role of Parson Williams, who is a very minor figure in Richardson, but who in *Shamela* becomes a caricature of a canting and hypocritical enthusiast.

Fielding's religious target in *Shamela,* however, is certainly not the Methodists as such, but rather those of any persuasion who are governed by what in *Joseph Andrews* he called "the detestable doctrine of faith against good works."[10] This emphasis on the social and moral virtues is typical of Fielding; and it is the central idea in *Shamela,* since it brings together Fielding's two main polemic purposes—the attack on those who had puffed *Pamela* as a book likely to promote the cause of virtue and religion, and the attack on Richardson's interpretation of his heroine's character. The domain of faith is inward and subjective: those who profess it may be deceiving themselves, or they may intentionally be deceiving others; we cannot test their professions any more than we can test the oft-protested purity of Pamela's motives; but we have a right to be suspicious, and a duty both to warn those who are duped and to expose those who sham.

II

These dual intentions give *Shamela* its basic narrative strategy. Fielding very ingeniously outdid Richardson in his pretense that he was only the editor of authentic letters: for he provided two independent sets of correspondence. We begin with a discussion between two clergymen about *Pamela;* then, once the framework of moral and literary criticism has been built up, Oliver discovers the real letters which prove his view of the case; and when these have been given, the two parallel actions—the disabusing of Tickletext and the unmasking of Shamela—are brought together in the final letter where Tickletext acknowledges that he had grievously misunderstood the whole matter, before telling us in his last postscript that justice has at last overtaken Shamela and her paramour.

Fielding's retelling of the *Pamela* story for his own purposes keeps very close to the original incidents; but gives them a contrary psychological explanation. Shamela feigns virtue only because Booby's inexperience makes her see that instead of "making a little Fortune by my Person" she can easily make "a great one by my Vartue." What changes Fielding makes are not without warrant in the original: Mr. B., for example, had noted Pamela's "lucky Knack of falling into Fits when she pleases"—it was easy enough to show that it was not luck but cunning; and even Shamela's intrigue with Parson Williams is licensed by Mr. B.'s suggestion that his interest had been amorous rather than pastoral.

This aspect of Shamela is obvious enough to any reader of *Pamela,* and has often been analyzed. But some other elements of the satire have perhaps met with less notice. Fielding parodies Richardson's manner as cruelly as his moral. He is particularly successful in hitting off the in-

congruity between Pamela's pretensions to literate gentility and the rusticity, not to say boorishness, of much of the dialogue: some of the badinage between Pamela and her "Angel" is not far removed from such a report on her master's courtship as the following from Shamela: "Says he . . . Hussy, Gipsie, Hypocrite, Saucebox, Boldface, get out of my Sight, get out of my Sight, or I will lend you such a Kick in the ——— I don't care to repeat the Word, but he meant my hinder part." The juxtaposition of exalted sentiments and inconsequential domestic details, which was a characteristic Richardsonian innovation in making the narrative seem real, is also very nicely taken off by Fielding: "And so we talked of honourable Designs till Supper-time. And Mrs. Jewkes and I supped upon a hot buttered Apple-pie." Excellent, too, is the hit at Richardson's use of present-tense narration in highly improbable circumstances: "Mrs. Jervis and I are just in Bed, and the Door unlocked; if my Master should come—Odsbobs! I hear him just coming in at the Door. You see I write in the present Tense, as Parson Williams says."

In general, then, Fielding unerringly selects the most dubious aspects of *Pamela,* and drives home its crucial moral and psychological ambiguities. The eighteenth century was a great age of burlesque; there is much to be said for the view that the best of Fielding's previous works had been burlesques such as *The Tragedy of Tragedies* and *The Grub-Street Opera;* and *Shamela* may be seen as the happy fruit of Fielding's own long experience in the genre.

But of course *Shamela* also looks forward. Like Hemingway's *Torrents of Spring,* it goes far beyond its original intention as parody, and takes on a life of its own. Not only so: Fielding, again like Hemingway, is ridiculing someone from whom he has learned much, more, perhaps, than he knows: for there is substantial truth in Richardson's assertion that "Pamela, which [Fielding] abused in his Shamela, taught him how to write to please. . . . Before his Joseph Andrews (hints and names taken from that story, with a lewd and ungenerous engraftment) the poor man wrote without being read. . . ."[11]

Shamela, of course, is not a faultless performance. Some of the details show signs of its hasty composition—there is some confusion, for example, about the extent of Mrs. Jewkes's complicity in Shamela's designs. It may also be questioned whether Shamela's very conscious hypocrisy about sexual matters is in harmony with the apparently unconscious nature of her religious hypocrisy; and there is perhaps an analogous contradiction between Tickletext's main role as a foolish dupe, and his conscious and unashamed revelation to Oliver of the aphrodisiacal effects of reading *Pamela.* At other times Fielding's love of the facetious tends to interfere with his main intention; and it is difficult to reconcile his many scabrous innuendoes with the serious didactic purpose he puts into the mouth of Parson Oliver.

Shamela, then, has many diverse elements: in matter, both coffee-house polemic and timeless satire on human folly;

in manner, both precise stylistic parody and uproarious burlesque. This diversity naturally puzzles the literary historian, who is called on to place a work that is both a footnote to the *Dunciad* and a prologue to *Tom Jones;* while the critic, recognizing much of the brilliant invention, the lively narrative pace, the human insight, and the fortifying gusto found in Fielding's novels, may well have difficulty in determining how successfully the varied aims and methods of *Shamela* have been combined. There is a further difficulty: the ultimate criteria by which so bawdy a work can properly be judged have not, to my knowledge, been satisfactorily established. Grave moral reservations are doubtless mandatory. But perhaps I should leave them to my betters, and end instead by revealing that, if perfect honesty in these matters were to be made possible by some guarantee of academic immunity, I could find one reader of *Shamela* at least willing to testify that—to use a metaphor dear to Fielding—this salty *hors d'oeuvre* is more to his taste than some of the more imposing dishes on the Pierian buffet.

Notes

1. Whose excellent article, "The Authorship of *Shamela*," *PQ,* XXV (1946), 248-272, gives full references to previous work on the subject.

2. With one exception: the catalogue of books and copyrights offered at the bankruptcy sale of the bookseller Francis Cogan, July 10th, 1746, shows that his half interest in "Shamela, by Fielding" was sold to Andrew Millar (Alan D. McKillop, *Samuel Richardson: Printer and Novelist* [Chapel Hill: University of North Carolina Press. 1936], p. 74).

3. *Correspondence of Samuel Richardson,* IV, 286; probably written late in 1749.

4. Bk. III, chap. vi.

5. McKillop, *op. cit.,* p. 73.

6. Richard H. Barker, *Mr. Cibber of Drury Lane* ("Columbia University Studies in English and Comparative Literature," No. 143 [New York: Columbia University Press, 1939]), p. 194; Conyers Middleton, *Miscellaneous Works,* 1755, I, 397.

7. On p. 3, l. 21, "innocent story" is changed into "&c"; cf. *Romeo and Juliet,* Act II, scene I, line 38. The "dear Monysyllable" toasted on p. 30, l. 29, is glossed in Eric Partridge, *Dictionary of Slang and Unconventional English.* [References are to the text of Mr. Watt's edition, which is a facsimile of the second edition of November 3, 1741. Ed.]

8. The passages, which were actually written by Aaron Hill, can conveniently be compared in the Augustan Society's valuable reprint of the Introduction to *Pamela* (ed. Sheridan W. Baker, Jr., No. 48, 1954).

9. See Sheridan W. Baker, Jr.'s Introduction to his edition of *Shamela* (Berkeley and Los Angeles: University of California Press, 1953), pp. xv-xx.

10. *Joseph Andrews,* Bk. I, chap. xvii.

11. See note 3.

David K. Jeffrey (essay date 1977)

SOURCE: "The Epistolary Format of *Pamela* and *Humphry Clinker,*" in *A Provision of Human Nature: Essays on Fielding and Others in Honor of Miriam Austin Locke,* edited by Donald Kay, The University of Alabama Press, 1977, pp. 145-54.

[*In the following essay, Jeffrey compares Samuel Richardson's* Pamela *and Tobias Smollett's* Humphry Clinker, *and argues that by using letters, the heroines of the two novels are able to create their own portraits of themselves and construct stable, artistic versions of reality that are less painful than their real lives.*]

Samuel Richardson would doubtless disapprove the mating of his first heroine with Smollett's last protagonist, but they are not, in some ways, such a strange pair. Pamela in 1740 is the heroine of the first great epistolary novel, while Humphry in 1771 is the titular hero of the last. Both begin as servants, both moralize throughout their novels, and both find themselves elevated socially at each novel's conclusion—Pamela by marriage to her former master and would-be seducer, Squire B.; Humphry by being legitimated. On the other hand, Pamela's initially violent reactions each time B. lays heavy, ineffectual hands upon her contrasts with Humphry's crude, initial (dare I say) appearance, his bare posterior inadvertently exposed. Literacy separates the two even further; Pamela writes two hefty volumes about her trials and triumphs, while Humphry pens not a word, leaving that three-volume task to members of the group he serves.

Although contemplation of this pairing amuses, the parallels are clearer between Pamela and Lydia Melford (a member of the group Humphry serves), especially in regard to their writing and the meaning of the epistolary format. Lydia is in fact one of Pamela's many daughters.[1] In character, both are young and fair, delicate and virginal creatures, much given to faints. Smollett does invert Richardson's plot, however, for the upper-class Lydia loves a man believed beneath her socially—an actor—although he too is legitimated at the novel's denouement. Lydia is not as prolific a writer as Pamela; few characters are. Lydia writes only eleven of the eighty-two letters in *Humphry Clinker;* her uncle, Matt Bramble, and her brother, Jery, write over two-thirds of the novel, while her aunt, Tabitha, writes six letters and Tabitha's maid-servant, Win Jenkins, "pursues her anal fixation"[2] through ten hilarious missives. Pamela writes all but four of the thirty-two letters and the entire one and one-half volume journal that constitute her novel.

Why anyone would want to fill two or three volumes with fictional letters puzzles the modern reader. Certainly, the other forms available to Richardson—the romance, the picaresque, the pseudomemoir—seem either far less technically crude or far faster paced. Why then settle on an epistolary format? The answer is not only that letter writing was the habit of Richardson's lifetime but that, as he explains in the Preface to *Clarissa*, the epistolary format has advantages the other forms lack: "Letters . . . written while the hearts of the writers must be supposed to be wholly engaged in their subjects . . . abound not only with critical situations, but with what may be called *instantaneous* Descriptions and Reflections. . . ." "*Much more* lively and affecting," he continues, quoting one of his characters, "must be the Style of those who write in the height of a *present* distress; the mind tortured by the pangs of uncertainty . . . than the dry, narrative, unanimated Style of a person relating difficulties and dangers surmounted, can be; the relater perfectly at ease; and if himself unmoved by his own Story, not likely greatly to affect the Reader."[3] In the Preface to *Pamela* Richardson hints at this same view, calling the format "probable," "natural," "lively," and "mov[ing]."[4] There is in Smollett no similar biographical predilection for the format, but, perhaps, he settles on it at last for the reasons Richardson states. Certainly, Smollett's four earlier novels are less successful than *Humphry Clinker* precisely because of the disparity between lively and affecting events and the dispassionate or ironic narrator who comments on them.[5] But the epistolary format, as Richardson suggests in the prefaces, resolves such disparities by locating its writer somewhere between stream of consciousness and emotion recollected in tranquillity, thus providing at once a temporal closeness to the raw experience of reality and a consciousness which reacts to that reality.

As a consequence of this positioning, the writer of letters is both isolated and unreliable. In the act of writing, he separates himself from the present and cannot fully experience it; he can recreate only the past. Because the past he recounts precedes so immediately his recording of it and because that past so movingly affects him, his record of it cannot be wholly accurate.

I

Richardson pictures his heroine at odds with both familial and social units, and her isolation from such units the epistolary format effectively mirrors. Pamela's emotional isolation from her family is suggested by her parents' response to her first letter. Although Pamela's letter contains not the slightest indication that B. has other than an honorable interest in her or that Pamela feels anything other than gratitude to him for such interest, her parents respond to it by expressing fear that their fifteen-year-old daughter will act in a "dishonest or wicked" way; "we fear," they write, "—you should be *too* grateful—and reward him with that Jewel, your Virtue, which no Riches, nor Favour, nor any thing in this Life, can make up to you" (p. 27). As a result of this extraordinary injunction, Pamela tries for most of the first volume to repress her attraction to B. Only after B.'s open admission of love for her does Pamela give way to the emotions of her own heart; only after

her marriage and midway into the second volume can she write guiltlessly of her love, no longer fearful of her parents' reactions.[6] Pamela's first letter also calls attention to her uneasy social position; through the good offices of Lady B., the squire's mother, Pamela has achieved "Qualifications above [her] Degree" (p.25), so that finding another suitable job would be difficult. But, if she is a little more than servant, she is less than B.'s kind, and she strives throughout most of the novel's first volume to escape both him and the concurrent moral and social dilemma his pursuit of her raises. Even after their marriage, she must attempt to make herself acceptable to those of B.'s class who either view her as a curiosity or openly scorn her. Not until she establishes a secure place in his social class does she lay down her pen.[7] Pamela's isolation is also suggested geographically. In the first volume she is abducted from Bedfordshire (where friendly fellow servants aid and comfort her) to Lincolnshire (a wilderness in which, friendless, she endures temptations for some forty days and nights), and her switch from the letter format in Bedfordshire to the journal format in Lincolnshire mirrors her developing isolation, an isolation that works in Pamela's favor, for it forces her to make her own decisions rather than to act as her parents enjoin her. Near the end of the novel, she returns triumphantly to Bedfordshire and stops writing in order to "apply [her]self to the Duties of the Family" (p. 387). She has established her place, both as daughter and wife, within familial and social units.

Smollett's writers face similar difficulties—as they begin their journey from Wales through England and Scotland, they are isolated not only, as a group, from societies new to them but also, as individuals, from each other.[8] Jery struggles to dominate his sister, Lydia, and views his uncle and aunt as "a family of originals" (p. 8). Matt's constipation comically reflects his emotional isolation; his bowels are as constricted as his heart. He even requests his correspondent to "lock up all my drawers, and keep the keys" (p. 6). Jery's isolation from Lydia is more literal. After some years of separation, he has "found her a fine, tall girl of seventeen . . . but remarkably simple, and quite ignorant of the world" (p. 8). In his first letter he parades his duty to the family and to her, such duty consisting, he believes, in stifl[ing her] correspondence" with the man she loves, Wilson the actor. Lydia delineates this injunction in two paired letters—the first to her school mistress, whom she thinks of as a surrogate mother (p. 9), the second to a schoolmate, Letty. As a result of that injunction, she has "promised to break off all correspondence" with Wilson "and, if possible," she adds to Letty, "to forget him: but, alas! I begin to perceive that will not be in my power" (p. 10). This injunction figures importantly in the overall structure of the novel, for the novel will not end until all its letter writers achieve harmony within a familial unit. Matt tames Tabitha during a quarrel near the end of the first volume; Matt and Jery become friendly in the second, finding common ground in their sympathy for Martin, the rakish highwayman they encounter near the beginning of the volume,[9] and in their mutual wonderment at Lismahago, the quixotic figure they encounter on the highway near that volume's end. They are not reconciled with Lydia until the last several pages of the volume, Matt when she calls him "father" in her hysterical relief that he has not drowned (p. 315), Jery soon after that, when, as Lydia phrases it, "the slighted Wilson is metamorphosed into George Dennison, only son and heir of a gentleman"—a gentleman who is also, too coincidentally, Matt's childhood friend (p. 336). The opening letters of the novel, then, introduce separate, because egocentric, consciousnesses, and the novel traces their developing union. As in *Pamela,* the geography of the novel suggests their progress. The characters journey through the urban centers of southern England (where their relationship is as constrained as Matt's bowels) to the north through Scotland (where Matt's pains ascend to his ear and where he and Jery both wax enthusiastic, but where Lydia sickens and writes nothing) to a midpoint between these geographical extremes, Dennison's rural estate, where Matt and Jery find new and even more compatible friends and where all three women—Lydia, Tabitha, and Win—fulfill themselves in marriage.

Thus to isolate a character calls attention to the existential dilemma in which he finds himself—or rather, in which she finds herself. For neither Richardson nor Smollett focuses much attention in these two novels on the existential choices of their heroes. Neither of Smollett's heroes are required to make such choices. Matt Bramble and his nephew, Jery Melford, record the mores of the places they visit but seldom mention their growing affection for each other. They do not, in any case, consciously choose to be affectionate. Squire B., on the other hand, is required to make some such choice, and critics have objected that Richardson has provided no other window into B.'s consciousness than Pamela's letters, which only record the reasons B. gives to her for his choice of her. Perhaps B.'s remarks about unequal marriages suggest reasons for the inequitable pressures only the heroines are forced to withstand. B. says, "A Man ennobles the Woman he takes, be she *who* she will; and adopts her into his own rank, be it *what* it will: But a Woman, tho' ever so noble born, debases herself by a mean Marriage, and descends from her own Rank, to his she stoops to" (p. 349). And he continues in this vein for six paragraphs. Here B. does not so much flaunt his own male chauvinism as he recognizes such chauvinism as the received social condition of his time. In such a society his roles are a given, defined by his birth into a particular class. Virtually nothing he could do would change this given, and thus his choices are essentially uninteresting and unimportant. A woman, however, is not socially defined. No matter her class, she can "debase herself" by "mean" behavior. Her place in society is thus more fluid and uneasy. Her choices are therefore vital, because she is self-defined.

II

A closer examination of the two heroines reveals important differences as well as similarities in the choices that affect their self-definition. Parental figures enjoin both

girls at the very outset of the novels, and these injunctions force the heroines to affect roles, roles that are negative and potentially destructive; until they are free from these injunctions, the girls cannot act positively, as autonomous selves, for the injunctions involve them in what transactional analysts call "losing scripts."[10] Pamela's parents conclude the injunction of their first letter thus: ". . . we had rather see you all cover'd with Rags, and even follow you to the Church-yard, than have it said, a Child of Ours preferr'd worldly Conveniences to her Virtue" (p. 28). Here, as elsewhere, Pamela's parents equate dishonor and death; thus, when B. later tells her father that Pamela "is in a way to be happy," her father replies, believing her defiled, "What! then is she dying?" (p. 248). Pamela accepts this equation for the first half of the novel, first threatening suicide (p. 126) and then nearly committing it (pp. 151-54) when she believes she cannot avoid dishonor. Her parents' script provides Pamela with only two roles, "Poor But Honest" and "The Ruined Maid." The former she must embrace, the latter avoid at any cost, even death. Throughout most of the first volume, Pamela's behavior alternates between these two roles: she describes at length either her longing to escape from B. and her preparations for servitude at home (pp. 52, 60) or alternately, and rather warmly, her resistance to B.'s advances (pp. 64-68) and her near suicide. But the trials she undergoes while alone at Lincolnshire free her from her parents' script, and when B. releases her, admitting his love, she acts contrary to her parents' injunction. Her return to B. is an assertion of her own selfhood; she has realized her desires in a winner's role, that of Cinderella.

The consequences of Lydia's choices are less fully explored, although they are similar to Pamela's. Like Pamela, Lydia begins the novel with a loser's role, one assigned her by Jery, Matt, and Tabitha. Her correspondence with Wilson precipitates her brother's attempts to duel with him, and after the lovers are separated, as Matt writes, "the poor creature was so frightened and fluttered, by our threats and expostulations, that she fell sick the fourth day after our arrival at Clifton, and continued so ill for a whole week, that her life wa despaired of" (p. 14). Enjoining her against the role of "Ruined Maid," they have instead scripted her as "Sleeping Beauty." They believe time will erase Wilson from her memory and provide her with a mate of more suitable class. Lydia accepts this role, but she hopes that "time and the chapter of accidents, or rather . . . that Providence . . . will not fail, sooner or later, to reward those that walk in the paths of honour and virtue" (p. 11). Lydia has less appeal as a character than Pamela does because Lydia never rebels against her passive role. Instead, she accepts the pain that role causes her and faints and falls ill repeatedly. Happily for her, but unhappily for the novel, "accident" does convert her loser's role into a winner's. Her lover stumbles through the Brambles that surround her and is "metamorphosed"—from Wilson the Frog into The Prince of Dennison.

So, acceptance of their losing roles leads both girls to sickness and nearly to death. Thus Lydia languishes. And thus Pamela pitifully: "And now my dearest Father and Mother, expect to see soon your poor Daughter, with a humble and dutiful Mind, return'd to you: And don't fear but I know how to be happy with you as ever: For I will lie in the Loft, as I used to do; and pray let the little Bed be got ready . . . and fear not that I shall be a Burden to you, if My Health continues . . ." (p. 45). Still, one of the roles presented to the heroines has less appeal, because less potential, than the other, as Richardson has Pamela intuit. Pamela, of course, never does return to her parents. Life in a hovel is no life for her; "if my Health continues," indeed. And Lydia's contrasting acceptance of the role chosen for her causes her many illnesses and also, intriguingly, the three-month cessation of correspondence with Letty, while Lydia journeys to and travels in Scotland, her farthest remove from Wilson. In short, acceptance of the role parental figures assign them can lead only to the stultification and stagnation of their personalities. On the other hand, flirtation with ruin—that is, with the role against which the parental figures enjoin them—provides both excitement and the greater potentiality. Pamela's flirtation with this latter role enables her to mature and, in fact, to define her own life, while Lydia's choice of the former role thwarts her maturation and, in some measure, her self-definition.

What does this mean? How do the heroines define themselves? They do so not by projecting their personalities onto an existential reality, but by projecting themselves onto paper.[11] They are, after all, doubly isolated from reality. As they write, they isolate themselves temporally, and the two authors also isolate their heroines spatially. Only Lydia of Smollett's five writers seems to correspond covertly (pp. 27, 58, 134), and Pamela, of course, retires to her writing closet at every opportunity; she even busies herself with scribbling fifteen minutes before the hymeneal night's consummation devoutly to be wished (p. 295). Peculiarly separated from the realities of time and space, the heroines' letters contrast with reality and with the scripted roles, both of which threaten the heroines' destructions.

Just as the roles her parents script would destroy Pamela, so too, of course, would B. He does not at first think of Pamela as fully human; she exists for him simply as an object for his sexual pleasure. Nor does he respond to Pamela's threats, expostulations, faints, or prayers; nothing the girl does moves him. It is her journal, her "ready . . . Talent at [her] Pen" (p. 231), that destroys his "Resolution" (p. 213) to forget her and so "mov[es]" him (p. 208) that he proposes marriage. In her journal he discovers that what he had earlier thought "artful Wiles" (p. 160) and "little villainous Plots" (p. 161) either to escape or to ensnare him were in fact "pretty Tricks and Artifices, to escape the Snares [he] had laid for her, yet all . . . innocent, lovely, and uniformly beautiful" (p. 255). Similarly, B.'s sister, Lady Davers, is somewhat reconciled to Pamela by B., but the "Sight of your Papers," she tells Pamela, "I dare say, will crown the Work, will disarm my Pride, banish my Resentment . . . , and justify my Brother's Conduct" (p. 375), will in fact "make me love you" (p. 374).

Lydia's epistles do not serve quite so dramatic a purpose, but they do render her happier than either the role she accepts or her travels with her family. For in her letters she can openly admit the real "condition of [her] poor heart" (p. 93); indeed, only in her letters does she dare to mention Wilson, who figures prominently in them all. Thus, Lydia does not write only of the reality she has experienced during her travels or the torment and sickness caused by her role; she projects in her letters the reality for which she hopes. When these hopes seem to her most unlikely to be realized, the three-month hiatus in her correspondence occurs. Seemingly deprived of the reality she desires, she ceases to exist as a personality. Her epistolary death is the inverse of Pamela's proliferative epistolary life. Richardson has a good deal of fun with this idea of Pamela's papers having life. After catching a carp, for example, Pamela retires to her garden, there to "plant Life," as she says (p. 120). What she plants, of course, is a letter to Parson Williams. Just prior to this episode, she conceals her entire packet of papers "in [her] Under-coat, next [her] Linen" "for they grow large!" (p. 120). Using the same phrase, Pamela calls attention to her epistolary pregnancy once more (p. 198.), just before B. jocularly threatens to strip her of the clothes that conceal her papers; she retires to her bedroom and complains that she "must all undress" before she can deliver the bundle (p. 204). This delivery, by the way, she "stomach[es] . . . very heavily" (p. 206).

In their letters, then, the heroines conceive of a life reality would abort, and each conceives of that life as an artist of his material. Each heroine distances herself from her own raw experience by writing letters, and each projects a more orderly version of that experience in her letters. For each girl, reality is painfully chaotic, and each can give it shape only in her letters. Each girl is rootless, tossed from Bedfordshire to Lincolnshire, around and back, carried throughout England and Scotland. Pamela's loss of and Lydia's need for a mother figure, which each mentions at the beginning of her first letter, stresses this rootlessness. Each heroine, therefore, projects a structure onto her disjointed experiences, and each is aware of doing so.

Pamela's inclusion in her letters of her poems and of her alteration of the 137th Psalm to fit her own circumstances calls attention to her conscious artistry, as does her constant worry about her little store of pen, paper, and ink—the utensils of her art. But she also calls attention to the artistry of her letters, which she writes as a "Diversion" from her troubles (p. 106). From the outset she compares herself and B. to various characters in books she has read—romances (p. 49), the Bible (p. 180), and *Aesop's Fables* (pp. 77, 162). Pamela writes also of the "Inditing" of letters (p. 37), of the "Scene[s]" in them (p. 155), of the "Part[s]" (p. 173) played by the other "Character[s]" (p. 181), of her own "Part" (p. 225), and of her style or "Language" (p. 257). She even suggests that her "Story surely would furnish out a surprizing kind of Novel, if it was to be well told" (pp. 212-13). B., at least, believes it; after reading part of her journal, he pleads with her thus to be shown the rest: "I long to see the Particulars of your Plot, and your Disappointment, where your Papers leave off. For you have so beautiful a manner, that it is partly that, and partly my Love for you, that has made me desirous of reading all you write. . . . And as I have furnished you with the Subject, I have a Title to see the fruits of your Pen.—Besides, . . . there is such a pretty Air of Romance, as you relate them, in your Plots, and my Plots, that I shall be better directed in what manner to wind up the Catastrophe of the pretty Novel" (p. 201). For Lydia, too, the artistry of her own letters provides the primary solace and order of her life. Thus she entrusts the "chapter of accidents"—in the Book of Life?—to reunite her with Wilson, and thus her "method of writing" to Letty affords her "some ease and satisfaction in the midst of [her] disquiet" (p. 307). But when Matt nearly drowns and Humphry is legitimated and Wilson stands revealed as Dennison, poor Lydia's "ideas are thrown into confusion and perplexity" so that she fears she will not be able to impart "either method or coherence" to her letter. She soon does so by settling into "a regular detail" of those events, that is, into a minute narrative of them (p. 334). Like Pamela, she creates order where she does not find it.

The epistolary format, then, enables Pamela and Lydia to structure an artistic version of reality that is less painful to them because given order by them, and both heroines are aware they are using their letters for that purpose. In the face of chaotic realities, they trust their art to provide permanence and stability in their lives. Richardson's remarks about the epistolary format suggest the validity of this interpretation: "Much more lively and affecting . . . must be the *Style* of those who write in the height of a present distress; the mind tortured by the pangs of uncertainty . . . than the dry, narrative, unanimated *Style* of a person relating difficulties and dangers surmounted, can be; the relater perfectly at ease; and if himself unmoved by his own *Story*, not likely greatly to affect the Reader" (my italics). Richardson's remarks do not stress only the psychic torment of his creations; his remarks also indicate his use of those creations as creators, artists aware of their own "Story," aware of their own "Style."

In sum, the epistolary format of *Pamela* and *Humphry Clinker* isolates the heroines from reality and thus enables them to construct their own portraits of themselves. The heroines are aware of the artistry such portraiture involves, and they use their art to structure not only their characters but also the plots of their lives. Essentially, Pamela and Lydia use the format as another of the century's great writers used his journal, and one of James Boswell's plaintive entries may serve as an appropriate epigraph for both Richardson's and Smollett's novels. Boswell wrote: "I am fallen sadly behind in my journal. I should live no more than I can record, as one should not have more corn growing than one can get in. There is a waste of good if it be not preserved. And yet perhaps if it serve the purpose of immediate felicity, that is enough."[12]

Notes

1. Robert F. Utter and Gwendolyn B. Needham, *Pamela's Daughters* (New York: Macmillan Co., 1936), esp. p. 13.

2. Sheridan Baker, "*Humphry Clinker* as Comic Romance," in *Essays on the Eighteenth-Century Novel*, ed. Robert Donald Spector (Bloomington: Indian Univ. Press, 1965), p. 163.

3. Samuel Richardson, "Author's Preface (1759)," *Clarissa*, ed. George Sherburn (Cambridge: Riverside Press, 1962), p. xx.

4. Samuel Richardson, "Preface by the Editor," *Pamela*, ed. T.C. Duncan Eaves and Ben D. Kimpel (Boston: Houghton Mifflin Co., 1971), p. 3. Subsequent references are to this edition and will be cited in the text.

5. See Tuvia Bloch, "Smollett's Quest for Form," *MP*, 65 (1967), 103-13.

6. Cf. Robert Alan Donovan, "The Problem of Pamela," in *The Shaping Vision* (Ithaca: Cornell Univ. Press, 1966), pp. 47-67.

7. Cf. John A. Dussinger, "What Pamela Knew: An Interpretation," *JEGP*, 69 (1970), 377-93; Stuart Wilson, "Pamela: An Interpretation," *PMLA*, 88 (1973), 79-91.

8. Tobias Smollett, *Humphry Clinker*, ed. Lewis M. Knapp (London: Oxford Univ. Press, 1972), p. 5. Subsequent references are to this edition and will be cited in the text.

9. Interestingly, a rake named Martin also appears in the latter half of Richardson's novel.

10. See, for example, Eric Berne, *Transactional Analysis in Psychotherapy* (New York: Grove Press, 1961) and *What Do You Say After You Say Hello?* (New York: Grove Press, 1972). The latter work Berne devotes to extensive analysis of various life plans, or scripts, finding in such classic fairy tales as Little Red Riding Hood, Cinderella, and Sleeping Beauty patterns of human behavior.

11. David Goldknopf, "The Epistolary Format in *Clarissa*," in *The Life of the Novel* (Chicago: Univ. of Chicago Press, 1973), pp. 59-78.

12. James Boswell, *The Ominous Years, 1774-1776*, ed. Charles Ryskamp and Frederick A. Pottle (New York: McGraw-Hill Book Co., 1963), p. 265.

Donald R. Wehrs (essay date 1986)

SOURCE: "Irony, Storytelling, and the Conflict of Interpretation in *Clarissa*," in *ELH*, Vol. 53, No. 4, Winter 1986, pp. 759-77

[*In the following essay, Wehr argues that deconstructionist interpretations of Samuel Richardson's* Clarissa *miss the ways the author uses irony to impose a single, moralizing narrative judgment on the story's characters and actions.*]

In recent years dour, didactic Samuel Richardson has become a proving ground for deconstructionist criticism. The epistolary mode, in which different characters read experience according to their irreconcilable value systems, interests and desires, and the author withdraws behind an editor's mask, appears to thematize "the struggles of interpretation," making *Clarissa* a tragedy of "hermeneutic anarchy . . . a cacophony of voices, a multiplicity of exegetes struggling to articulate different 'constructions' of the world."[1] This hermeneutical struggle constitutes a power struggle: Lovelace reads Clarissa so as to inscribe her into his system while she resists the "rape" of such "colonization."[2]

Though suggestive, these readings fail to register the role that irony and story play in orchestrating and evaluating the constructions of *Clarissa*'s different correspondents. What gives *Clarissa* its central importance in the development of the novel is not its dramatization of a conflict of interpretations, but the system of resolution it proposes: the story establishes, through seemingly natural or self-evident inferences, a context for irony that in turn adjudicates between the claims of competing voices. It has long been noted that the novel as a genre seeks to naturalize interpretation, to make interpretation appear to arise of itself from the narrative, as opposed to acknowledging that interpretation rests upon arbitrary, allegorical signification. (The modern prose fictions, from Sterne on, that do call attention to the ambiguities of interpretation are frequently called "anti-novels," "self-ironic," or "self-parodic.") The novel attempts to naturalize interpretation by using the story to justify a context for irony that in turn legitimates a certain reading of the story. *Clarissa* inaugurates a new genre of fiction by presenting a paradigmatic model for justifying irony through a realistic story and thus provides (or seemed to provide) a means of showing interpretation as it arises autonomously from the raw data of experience.

Instead of noting the connection between irony and story, the recent deconstructionist readings of *Clarissa* rely upon a generalized view of how the epistolary mode calls attention to the act of interpretation and thus reveals that "meanings are generated, arbitrarily, by different readers."[3] It is a small step from seeing every reading of a letter as a subjective construct to seeing the novel not as a story but as "a continuous gabble of imaginary voices," lacking "any sense of a controlling, magus-like authorial presence."[4] The problem with such generalized analyses is that it suppresses differences: the effect of an interplay of many voices in *Clarissa* is not the same as the interplay in *Wilhelm Meisters Wanderjahre* or a William Gaddis novel. Richardson makes his presence felt through the irony his story imposes upon the various correspondents. The worth or referentiality of the characters' readings of experience is judged by what happens to them, a matter over which Richardson has some say. Clarissa's fearsome determination to accept death rather than endure moral compromise

justifies her interpretation not of the world (which was grievously misguided) but of herself; it gives the lie to the readings imposed by the Harlowes and Lovelace. After all the welter of words about Clarissa, she defines herself by her conduct, a conduct that ultimately discloses her true character, the signified that all the signifiers have been clamoring to describe and penetrate. The gradual unfolding of Clarissa's story provides a context for irony toward the various correspondents' assertions, a frame of reference that is complete only when the "History of a Young Lady" has made Clarissa's true self fully present by demonstrating that she means what she has always said, that moral integrity is more important to her than anything in this world, including life itself.

Before turning to *Clarissa,* we must consider briefly the relation of story to the epistolary novel and the relation of irony to multivocal narrative. It might well seem superfluous to observe that *Clarissa* tells a story, but Terry Castle maintains that it does not.[5] Her argument rests upon the assumption, recently put forward by a number of critics, that the epistolary mode intensifies interpretive uncertainty.[6] Since there is "no identifiable single voice of narration," the reader "must piece together a sequence of actions" (a story) by himself. Letters produced by characters are the material for this construction, but "letters open themselves, promiscuously, to distortion by readers. . . ."[7] Terry Eagleton makes much the same point: "the utterance of the moment, once paralysed to print, is then secured for the most devious interpretative uses."[8] The problem with this account is that it places letters in a narrative vacuum. But each letter stands in a collection, created by an author, that shapes the way individual letters are read (on first and subsequent readings) because they are made moments in a story that unfolds progressively. Castle makes this point herself. Our interpretation of Clarissa's reading of "Mr. Doleman's" letter describing a number of London lodgings is conditioned by "Lovelace's own account" of the letter: it was dictated by Lovelace himself to delude Clarissa into choosing to go to Mrs. Sinclair's: Clarissa's "reading of the letter has been anticipated; indeed, its very rhetoric, it turns out, has been designed to incline her toward Dover Street and Mrs. Sinclair."[9] There is a simple dramatic irony at work here. Because the reader and Lovelace know more than Clarissa, they can read Doleman's letter in a way she cannot and can see that her free choice is really, ironically, predetermined. Similarly, as Castle skillfully remarks, the conception of Mrs. Sinclair's that Clarissa gathers from the letter "blinds her to the true nature of her surroundings."[10] The act of blinding and its consequences are part of a story told through a series of letters. Clarissa's view of Mrs. Sinclair is subject to irony from the context of "the *true* nature of her surroundings"; that is, her surroundings as they are revealed to be in the course of the story. There is a conflict of interpretation between Clarissa's and Lovelace's view of Mrs. Sinclair's, but Castle can say with assurance that Lovelace's interpretation is right and Clarissa's is wrong because, in terms of the story, what Lovelace sees is what is really there. Because the story creates a context which backs up or refutes the claims or values of any correspondent, it is simply wrong to say, as Castle does, that "the only events in epistolary fiction, strictly speaking, are events of language."[11] What is represented indirectly in a story is no less an event than what is represented directly. In a play characters who are killed off-stage are no less dead than those killed on-stage.

The story cannot be neglected with impunity. Although Eagleton and Castle use deconstruction to further their arguments, they both reject William B. Warner's *Reading Clarissa* on the grounds that Warner obscures the significance of what actually happens between Lovelace and Clarissa. In Warner's peculiar allegory of reading, Lovelace is a playful fellow who knows that words never signify anything and that values are a bore while Clarissa is hopelessly deluded by the mythology of a unified self and logocentrism. Lovelace's rape is an act of decentering, creatively applied, "subvert[ing] this fiction [of the unified self] by introducing a small part of himself *into* Clarissa. Thus the rape, like all Lovelace's displacements, will seek to induce the slight difference that will make all the difference."[12] Eagleton's devastating critique of Warner exposes the moral irresponsibility that arises from failing to take the story seriously: "Lovelace, whom Warner finds 'charming', moves towards the rape 'with an inexorable necessity': what else can the poor fellow do if he is out to deconstruct her? . . . Clarissa, presumably, couldn't take a joke. . . . Warner . . . regards most critics as conspiring with the prim Clarissa to judge Lovelace in such shabbily undeconstructed terms as 'seriousness, consistency, sympathy, maturity, a full deep heart, and belief in the "real"'."[13] Castle, who finds *Clarissa* "ethical" because it teaches us that readings are arbitrary and that we should "read ourselves" (presumably, arbitrarily) detects in Warner's glossing over what actually happens a failure to consider the politics of interpretation, a failure that takes the form of "ill-considered attacks" on Clarissa, "boyish expressions of admiration" for Lovelace, and a pervasive tone of "startlingly primitive misogyny. . . ."[14] What is the standard against which Warner's words are measured to judge them ill-considered and boyish? Eagleton and Castle claim that those words fail to address the represented reality: Lovelace's abduction, drugging, and rape of Clarissa—the story that is there even though Richardson tells it through a series of letters.

Because the story provides nonarbitrary benchmarks against which the readings of the multiple correspondents may be judged, it establishes a means of determining whether a certain letter, a certain interpretation, even a certain voice is accurate or is refuted by the action the novel sets forth. Lovelace constantly proclaims that his success will be measured by his ability to subdue Clarissa's will. When abduction, deceit, and intimidation fail to achieve that result, he drugs and rapes her on the assumption that once subdued, always subdued. Clarissa, in turn, maintains that her will shall never be subdued. The events—Lovelace's need to resort to drugs, Clarissa's subsequent escape and steadfast refusal to marry him despite

poverty, isolation, and ill-health—make Lovelace's boasts seem as ironically blind as Clarissa's naive conception of Mrs. Sinclair's. They back up Clarissa's claim to know her will and have the courage to hold to it. Instead of presenting mere "hermeneutical anarchy" and a "gabble of imaginary voices," the novel shows experience subjecting some words, some interpretations, to ironic refutation while confirming others. We must emphasize that the represented experience, what actually happens, is a fiction, created by Richardson. One may reject the fiction as unrealistic or ideologically mystified: Richardson was himself aware of that possibility. We will address this difficulty later; here it is important to distinguish between standing outside the story in order to reject it and viewing the function of the story within Richardson's epistolary novel. Within *Clarissa,* the story constitutes a world of experience that justifies a context for irony: irony challenges the anarchy of a gabble of voices by setting them into an order of rank, by assaying their degree of truth.

Since the work of Mikhail Bakhtin has become available in the West in the last decade, critics have sought to apply his notions of dialogic narrative and multivoiced fiction to nearly every novel, including *Clarissa.* Eagleton believes that the letter in *Clarissa* is dialogic because it is both private expression and public discourse, "overhearing itself in the ears of its addressee. . . ."[15] Bakhtin's description of Dostoevsky's novels as a "*plurality of independent and unmerged voices and consciousnesses, a genuine polyphony of fully valid voices*" stands behind the "gabble of imaginary voices" that Castle hears in *Clarissa.*[16] As frequently occurs, the ideas a major critic develops to apply in a judicious, learned manner to particular types of work are appropriated for use everywhere. For Bakhtin, Dostoevsky originates the polyphonic novel as an exception to the standard, monologic European novel. Eagleton's claim that the letter is dialogic because it is both private and public and is "speech-for-another" makes "dialogic" so general a term that it is useless. In Bakhtin, it is discourse "directed both toward the referential object of speech, . . . and toward *another's discourse,* toward *someone else's speech*" (185). Eagleton's correspondent's words are not directed toward another's speech, but toward another's subjectivity: "you must write with a wary eye on the other. . . ."[17] Emile Benveniste has argued persuasively that all language establishes an "I-thou" axis, that all language is both subjective and "speech-for-another."[18] As for letters being both private and public, Hegel has noted that all language objectifies subjectivity, externalizing the internal.

In addition to applying a trendy term so broadly that it loses its original discriminating value, critics frequently set up simple paired opposites, valorizing one side of the opposition: showing against telling; organic unity against editorial intrusions; disruptions against centeredness. Recently, multivocality has become valorized at the expense of irony. Roland Barthes argues that irony contradicts multivalence by giving speech a speaker, "the voice which would give the text its ('organic') unity. . . ." The multivalent (good) text would have a "wall of voices" not owned or subordinated and thus equally valid, whereas the classic (bad) text would order the voices into a hierarchy of value through irony.[19]

Although the conflict between multivocality and irony is real, the simple either/or paired opposition is not. To delineate how story allows irony to regulate a multiplicity of voices, we must recall Bakhtin's discussion of Dostoevsky. Whereas most European novels evoke a plurality of voices only to subordinate them to a "finalizing artistic vision" (5), Dostoevsky leaves the conflicting voices and consciousnesses unmerged, setting competing world-views alongside each other in "dramatic juxtaposition" (28). In contrast to a Hegelian artist like Goethe, who sees diverse consciousnesses as stages in a unified process, Dostoevsky conceives the diversity in "simultaneous coexistence" (29). Thus, the voices are not subordinated into a hierarchy, but are kept "fully valid" with each other in polyphonic juxtaposition. To maintain this full validity, Dostoevsky shuns "finalizing authorial words" and seeks "plot situations that provoke, tease, extort, dialogize," that remain open-ended. There is, in fact, a conflict between the "fundamental open-endedness of the polyphonic novel" and the *"conventionally monologic* ending" that Dostoevsky provides for most of his novels (39). For our purposes, the critical point is that a completed story has the same effect as "finalizing authorial words": it constrains multivocal plurality by establishing a basis for irony against which the various voices are measured and thus articulates a vision into which they are set. In the following discussion of *Clarissa,* we shall explore how story stands in for "authorial words" in Richardson's epistolary novel, how it imposes irony and thus places the heterogeneous material into a finalizing, monologic artistic vision.

The story does not merely impose a context for irony; it also justifies it. Bakhtin is led to downplay the role of plot in Dostoevsky lest the thesis of equal validity for every voice be compromised. It is unclear, at least in translation, whether the term "fully valid" (as in "a plurality of fully valid voices") refers to realism of presentation or truth of content. Still, we may ask whether it is true that Dostoevsky simply juxtaposes competing voices in a spatial manner (28). *The Brothers Karamazov* tells a story of murder. Does Ivan's role in that murder have no effect upon the validity of his voice against the voices of Dmitri and Alyosha? The novel may present the three voices as equally real while the story indicates that they are not equally true or good. To put the question in a different way, is "The Grand Inquisitor" the same story and the same work of art when it is anthologized independently as when it is a moment in the action of *The Brothers Karamazov?* Ivan's ideas (and the character, voice, and consciousness fused to those ideas) are tested by the story in which he is placed. His ideas, as well as Dmitri's and Alyosha's, are judged against the context of a represented experience just as the ideas of Lovelace and Clarissa are judged against what actually happens, the reality their story bodies forth.

The story does not merely set different voices side by side; it tests the validity of each voice against the others. Indeed, Bakhtin argues that Dostoevsky's type of narrative derives from the method of *"testing* truth" (111) in Socratic dialogue and Menippean satire. The narrative propulsion of the Socratic dialogue lies in "collectively searching for truth, in the process of . . . dialogic interaction [between people]" (110). By anacrisis, provoking the words of one's interlocutor, Socrates elucidates the implications and consequences of ideas, thus testing their validity. "The dialogic testing of the idea is simultaneously also the testing of the person who represents it" (111-12). Menippean satire, according to Bakhtin, transposes Socratic testing into a story: the plot, by means of some anacrisis (some illuminating provocation), becomes "a mode for searching after truth, provoking it, and, most important, *testing* it" (114). The application of all this to *Clarissa* is apparent: the story tests the ideas Clarissa and Lovelace represent by presenting Clarissa and Lovelace in a conflict that makes their struggle a testing of truth. In fiction, if not in life, the testing yields some result and that result takes the form of irony. Irony may be provisional or final. As we shall see, the irony the story imposes upon Clarissa is eventually superseded by a higher irony imposed upon Lovelace. Irony may be, as Wayne Booth has noted, stable or unstable.[20] It may invalidate a certain perspective by asserting the superiority of an opposite perspective, or it may juxtapose contrasting perspectives or meanings while coolly refusing to endorse any. Irony may finalize a unified, coherent worldview; it may, as in Friedrich Schlegel, endorse an ongoing interplay of separate local truths; or it may, as in Novalis and Samuel Beckett, subject every finalization to ironic subversion *ad infinitum.*[21] The type of irony a particular story's testing of truth may justify varies, but the effect of this justification is to naturalize a particular interpretation of experience and thus to legitimate some ordering of multivocality, whether that ordering involves reducing all voices to one, distributing degrees of validity, or approving anarchy. The centrality of the novel to modern society derives in no small measure from its ability to legitimate an interpretation by using story to create a natural justification of a context for irony, a process first mastered by Richardson in *Clarissa.*

Clarissa draws on a type of story that predates epistolary fiction and does not derive from Socratic dialogue or Menippean satire. In the Middle Ages, exemplary tales, based loosely on Job, subjected extraordinary virtue to extraordinary trials. In Chaucer's Man of Law's Tale, the heroine becomes an earthly image of heavenly patience as she endures a succession of calamities.[22] The metaphysical assumptions behind such storytelling are directly opposed to those underlying the "dialogic means of seeking truth," which is "counterposed to *official* monologism, which pretends to *possess a ready-made truth.* . . ." (110). Instead of testing a proposed truth against its implications and against experience, the exemplary tale seeks to illustrate a pregiven, supersensual reality. The story is exemplary because it directs attention away from the distortions of this life, picturing the essence of patience shorn of accidental dross. The notion that trials exhibit virtue led to a sub-genre of tales such as Boccaccio's "Griselda" (*Decameron*, 10.10), in which a husband contrives a series of events to test the fidelity or obedience of a wife. The story becomes problematic when its portrait of experience ceases to be clearly subordinate to the illustration of an idea (fidelity or obedience as such), when the represented reality begins to provide a context for judgment. Whereas Boccaccio describes the husband's decision to test his wife in brief, formal, impersonal terms, Chaucer's version asks the reader to consider the decision's moral propriety:

> He hadde assayed hire ynogh bifore,
> And foond hire evere good; what neded it
> Hire for to tempte, and alwey moore and moore,
> Though som men preise it for a subtil wit?
> But as for me, I seye that yvele it sit
> To assaye a wyf whan that it is no nede,
> And putten hire in angwyssh and in drede.[23]

Chaucer judges the merits of the husband's actions by their consequences in this life, while Boccaccio keeps the story focused on illustrating exemplary virtue. Richardson attempts to have it both ways. Lovelace's testing of Clarissa is a cruel attempt to be a "subtil wit" at the expense of another. By arranging to put Clarissa's virtue on trial, Lovelace seeks to attain a God-like control over experience. But Richardson's own storymaking endeavors, through showing in detail *how* virtue is rewarded, to place the reader in the God-like position of seeing through everyday events to the providential design underlying them. Richardson wishes to illustrate a received, orthodox, monologic truth, but in order to convince a skeptical public of the validity of his moral lessons, he must show that a certain (moral) interpretation arises naturally from a faithful representation of experience. The need to naturalize interpretation leads him to the testing of truth, to the development of a context for irony arising from a dramatized conflict of interpretations. Beginning with Pamela's rejection of Mr. B.'s assertion that he has a right to her, Richardson's stories test the strength of competing worldviews against the evidence of experience. By portraying how Pamela is able to move from being a servant to being an exemplary wife, by demonstrating that marriage can be an ennobling union of minds, Richardson indicates that experience legitimates the values by which Pamela defines herself. Conversely, the story endorses an interpretative framework that subjects Mr. B.'s attitudes and actions to increasing irony: the more cruelly he tests Pamela, the more thoroughly he disproves the assumptions behind the test.

Of course, the experience against which worldviews are judged is created by a story that is made up. If the story is rejected as fantastic or improbable, the context for irony it proposes is left without foundation. Fielding's parody of *Pamela* imposes a counterstory and thus endorses a quite different irony directed at Mr. Booby's victimization by the socially climbing Shamela. Richardson is keenly aware of the danger that his novels might be rejected as mere fictions. He casts his exemplary tales in the epistolary mode in order to create a sense of mimetic authenticity and immediacy, to give the reader the impression of "looking into the hearts of some [of the characters], through windows that at other times have been close shut up."[24] The mimetic illusion, reinforced in each scene, should be buttressed by a credible sequence of events.[25] The point of constructing stories faithful to ordinary experience, of eschewing the marvelous in favor of the probable, is to allow moral judgment to arise naturally from the represented situation, so that the interpretation seems to belong to the events rather than to the beliefs of the author. Of course, arguments have raged from Richardson's time on about the probability of certain characters, episodes, and plot turns. Yet the very terms of the debate ("Would Lovelace really do that?") assume that fiction may possess a type of truth that is distinct from both history and lying.[26] A story acquires the authority of representing experience by showing what *would* happen *if* there were a Clarissa and Lovelace set in battle against each other. The reader's conviction that the story does portray what would happen makes the represented experience seem true and thus allows that experience to legitimate a context for irony toward each character's reading of experience.

Clarissa's trial, like Pamela's, places worldviews in conflict. But the story does not simply disclose the victory of one perspective, nor is victory without cost. Clarissa's nobility of soul makes her vulnerable to Lovelace's manipulations even as it saves her from his power. The story imposes and displaces a succession of ironic contexts: Clarissa's filial loyalty ensures that her family will misunderstand and mistreat her; her sense of right reinforces Lovelace's determination to conquer her; despite abduction and rape, Clarissa transforms Lovelace's victories into defeats by maintaining an integrity of will he is powerless to shake. The story's termination in Clarissa's death establishes a finalized perspective in which superseded readings of experience are accorded a place.

Clarissa defines herself by attempting to realize ideal standards in daily life. Her family basks in the glow of her exemplary behavior until it challenges their worldly ambitions. By inheriting her grandfather's estate and rejecting Solmes's suit, she inadvertently puts her individual merit in the way of the Harlowes' "darling view . . . of *raising a family,*" of using great wealth to acquire a title.[27] Solmes's offer to settle his immense fortune on Clarissa would allow the Harlowes to buy their way into the nobility. Though lust for wealth and status is alien to her, obedience to parents is part of the ideal code Clarissa strives to realize. She is dutifully compliant in whatever does not compromise her moral integrity, offering to surrender her claim to the estate and never to marry against her family's will. Unappeased, the Harlowes insist that she prove her obedience by marrying Solmes. Much has recently been written about Clarissa's oppression by patriarchy, about her family's assumption that she is their property.[28] While this is undeniably true, Clarissa's own objection to being treated like disposable property centers not on the violation this entails *per se,* but on its consequences upon her own ethical conduct: "To marry a man one *cannot endure,* is not only a dishonest thing, as to the man; but it is enough to make a creature who wishes to be a *good wife,* a bad or indifferent one . . . and then she can hardly be either a *good mistress,* or a *good friend;* or anything but a discredit to her family, and a bad example to all around her" (1: 307). As Jean Hagstrum points out, Clarissa's ideal of marriage rests upon the Miltonic conception of wifely obedience *and* a free communion of spiritually attuned minds.[29] Since Clarissa's character is grounded in striving for unity of conduct and principle, the Harlowes are asking her to repudiate herself, to yield up her soul for worldly gain by introducing an ironic gap between what she is and what she ought to be.

Being thoroughly worldly themselves, the Harlowes naturally interpret Clarissa's refusal in terms of lust and self-interest. Clarissa's story hinges upon the cruel irony that all her efforts to maintain exemplary conduct turn into means by which she is brought to compromise it. She would live without introducing an ironic disjunction between principles and conduct into her being. However, the world—in the form of her family—insists upon this disjunction as the price of retaining the protection of a secure social position. Clarissa's motives are constantly misread as selfish and worldly because the idea that one might really mean to live by an ideal code is foreign to the Harlowes' conception of experience. Furthermore, since Clarissa really does mean what she says, she constantly disarms herself. To combine ideality and actuality, she must behave as an ideal daughter to her real family, which means that she must pretend not to see the ironic distance between the way an ideal family would behave and the way her real one actually behaves. Out of a sense of filial obedience, she rejects Miss Howe's advice that she assume her estate; instead, she surrenders control of it to her father. Each refusal to act according to self-interest narrows her options, rendering her more, not less, vulnerable to the demands for moral compromise voiced by the Harlowes and Lovelace. Richardson makes grimly clear that attaining a position in this life that will permit moral independence requires a degree of self-interest that compromises ideality and therefore must be rejected by Clarissa.

Unwilling to stoop in her battle against the Harlowes, Clarissa is increasingly compromised by Lovelace. After beginning a correspondence in order to prevent him from taking revenge against her family for their insults, she continues to write, despite her parents' prohibition, in hopes of averting mischief. Clarissa cannot bring herself to wash her hands of responsibility for her family, but by continuing the correspondence she slides into the very separation of principles and conduct she strives to avoid: drawn into clandestine communication with a libertine, she is forced to deceive her parents. This deception gives Lovelace a weapon he can use against her. Similarly, in renouncing her estate, Clarissa gives up the means of shielding herself from the Harlowes' plans to drag her to the altar. Finally, though Clarissa repents of agreeing to go off with Lovelace, she nevertheless decides to meet him rather than break a promise. Because she is determined to be faithful to her word, she gives him the opportunity to abduct her.

As R. F. Brissenden observes, Lovelace's treatment of Clarissa repeats the Harlowes' treatment of her in a more stark and intense way.[30] Their conflict assumes the ferocity of a death struggle because Lovelace realizes that unless he can make Clarissa accept life without moral ideality the worldview by which he defines himself will stand refuted; she realizes that Lovelace is attempting, no less than her family, to separate her conduct from her values. Like the Harlowes, Lovelace struggles to assimilate Clarissa into an interpretative context of lust and self-interest. Unlike them, he is no hypocrite, asserting outright that virtue is a mask, that pride and the will to mastery provide the keys to any penetrating analysis of behavior. Behind Lovelace lie Mandeville, Hobbes, and the cultivated cynicism of the seventeenth-century *libertinage* tradition, summarized by the Earl of Rochester's lines: "Look to the bottom of his vast design, / Wherein man's wisdom, power, and glory join: / The good he acts, the ill he does endure, / 'Tis all from fear, to make himself secure."[31] Lovelace defines himself by his skill in manipulating people's hidden, base impulses. When his power is challenged, he constructs plots to compel experience to affirm his estimation of others and of himself; in effect, he invents stories to legitimate his context for irony. Lovelace spares the innkeeper's daughter, Rosebud, because her grandmother implores him to "be merciful to her." There is no need to make a story out of her (1: 170).

Clarissa offers Lovelace different treatment: "her whole air . . . expressed a majestic kind of indignation, which implied a believed superiority over the person to whom she spoke" (2: 14). He expects her to realize that she is in his power and that thus it is in her interest to appeal to his generosity. Instead, she refuses expediencies such as a rapid agreement to marry him or even a pretense of flattery. Lovelace quickly senses that if Clarissa can be what she wishes to be, she will stand outside his context for irony and hence be living proof of the insufficiency of his vision and power. Thus, he turns his plotting against her, listing to his friend Belford a series of premises to be put on trial: "*Importunity* and *opportunity* no woman is proof against . . ."; "Is not, may not, her virtue be found rather in *pride* than in *principle?* (2: 35); "Is then the divine Clarissa capable of *loving* a man whom she ought *not* to love?" (2: 38). Lovelace hopes, by subjecting Clarissa's beliefs about herself to devastating irony, to legitimate his Hobbesian-Mandevillian premises, to confirm his own worldview. The rest of the novel, three-fourths of its bulk, describes in minute detail how Lovelace's effort to impose irony on Clarissa succeeds, ironically, in imposing irony upon him, granting Clarissa the opportunity to justify her view of herself at his expense.

At first, Lovelace's campaign follows the pattern established by the Harlowes' bullying of Clarissa. Virtue is apparently defenseless. Miss Howe urges Clarissa to realize that she has "a nice part to act," that she should try to "engage [Lovelace's] *pride,* which he calls his *honour* . . ." (2: 44), but Clarissa cannot "palliate," cannot deliberately mislead without renouncing unity of conduct and principles. In a grimly ironic manner, virtue seems to open itself for attack. Seeing her "believed superiority," Lovelace's determination to defeat her is constantly renewed. Even her vigilance seems to turn against her. Each time she resists and sees through his schemes, he is driven to more elaborate and less merciful subterfuge. In the middle sections of the novel, Richardson appears to establish a context for irony that endorses neither Lovelace's cynical worldliness nor Clarissa's faith in providence. Instead, irony seems to rest upon a tragic view of experience in which genuine, innate nobility of soul provides persecutors the weapons that allow such nobility to be manipulated, deceived, and brought low.

Lovelace constructs a world where the ironic disjunctions that Clarissa discovered at Harlowe Place between appearances and reality, ideal standards and actual behavior, are radically intensified: the pious widow Sinclair turns out to be a madam of a brothel; her uncle's friend, Captain Tomlinson, who seeks her out to arrange a reconciliation with her family, is really one of Lovelace's tools; Lovelace's lady relatives who offer to welcome her into his family are actually prostitutes hired to take her back to the brothel. As Brissenden remarks, "Lovelace brings into existence a horrible parody of the world in which Clarissa places her faith, gets her to accept it, and then destroys it."[32] Being a type of artist, Lovelace constructs a lie that discloses the truth with a sharpness and clarity it would otherwise lack: the polite world of the Harlowes is a sham, a veil for the most mercenary of designs.

Although Lovelace's artifice works sufficiently to return Clarissa to the brothel, where he drugs and rapes her, his storymaking does not work out the way he intends. Instead of leading Clarissa to confirm the rake's creed, Lovelace's deceptions subject that creed to irony by eliciting behavior for which it cannot account. Like Anselmo in Cervantes's "El Curioso impertinente," Lovelace is punished for his impious aspirations by a higher plotter. Anselmo places his wife's virtue on trial much the way Lovelace places Clarissa's virtue on trial.[33] He induces his best friend, Lotario, to prove his wife's merit by attempting to seduce her. To the surprise of all three, Lotario and Anselmo's wife fall in love. Both Anselmo and Lovelace set stories in motion whose implications they cannot control. Whereas Anselmo learns, to his grief, that no woman can incarnate the ideal of chastity, Lovelace is taught much the opposite lesson: a real woman can be virtuous out of principle alone. By testing Clarissa and the values she seeks to realize, Lovelace unwittingly subjects himself to the type of devastating irony he would impose upon her. The tragic irony that makes Clarissa's vigilance a form of vulnerability is displaced by a higher irony in which Lovelace's exploitation of Clarissa's vulnerability makes manifest the falsity of his own worldview: after the rape, Clarissa steadfastly refuses to marry him.

Instead of simply setting a number of competing consciousnesses alongside each other in a spatial manner, the story exploits the temporal apprehension of narrative in order to create in the reader a sense that the progressive penetration of experience leads to a progressive refinement and alteration of contexts for irony. The generation of irony by story in *Clarissa* cannot be explained adequately by Bahktin's spatial deployment and juxtaposition of competing voices alone. Instead, narrative extension (the *sequence* of discrete scenes) is constantly composed into provisional unities in the (temporal) course of reading. Each provisional unity is then displaced by further extension, giving rise to new, reconfigured provisional unities, followed by new displacements by extension (something more happens). In a general way, this process accords with the phenomenologies of narrative cognition explored by Ingarden and Ricoeur.[34] Each provisional unity connects the foregoing extension through some causal hypothesis, which in turn naturalizes a context for irony. The basis for irony seems to arise of itself from a realistic portrait of experience. Lovelace's ability to seduce Clarissa back to Mrs. Sinclair's suggests that virtue, no matter how scrupulous, is too good not to be vulnerable to artful, evil imposition: Clarissa simply fails to anticipate, until it is too late, that Lovelace might dress up prostitutes as his own aristocratic relatives. But once Lovelace rapes Clarissa the story's continuation, the narrative's further extension, reveals that irony against Clarissa's unworldliness is not the final irony. By tracing Clarissa's escape from the brothel and her resolute rejection of all his pleas for marriage, the story reveals that Lovelace's trickery has the ironic effect of unmasking his true character to Clarissa, which in turn ensures, ironically, that she will *not* be tricked by him, that she will never marry him.

But while Clarissa maintains her integrity against all efforts to subvert it, she becomes increasingly aware that earthly existence entails moral compromise. She was abducted by Lovelace because she refused to break a promise to meet him in her father's garden. She escapes Lovelace's power by resorting to breaking a promise in order to flee Mrs. Sinclair's brothel. When she recounts the deception to Miss Howe, Clarissa exclaims, "How hard, how next to impossible, my dear, to avoid many *lesser* deviations, when we are betrayed into a *capital* one!" (3: 20). However unwittingly, Lovelace's storymaking does subject Clarissa's desire to combine ideality and actuality to brutal irony. She strives after a greater-than-human moral conduct just as Anselmo yearns for a greater-than-human knowledge (he would *know* rather than *trust* that his wife is faithful). The effect of Lovelace's manipulations is to place Clarissa in situations where she cannot be in the right. Either the desire for ideality makes her demand, impiously, immunity from human imperfections, or her acquiescence in ambiguous actions (lying to escape Mrs. Sinclair's) makes her guilty of equivocations. In either case, her principles and conduct stand in ironic opposition. Rather than accept such a violation of her sense of herself as the price of existence, Clarissa longs for death: "and since all my own hopes of worldly happiness are entirely over; let me slide quietly into my grave . . ." (3: 374).

From Richardson's point of view, Providence kindly answers her wishes. Her death, alone, impoverished, disdaining Lovelace's offers to make amends through marriage, justifies and completes the self revealed through her writings. Richardson wisely resisted the pleas of his friends to save Clarissa. Anything less than a resolute and pious death would vindicate Lovelace's ironic worldview by showing that no matter how he has treated her, the consequences need not be serious because everything may be patched up after all. Instead, Clarissa's refusal of any compromise subjects the worldly irony of Lovelace and the Harlowes to a withering higher irony. Rather than being, as Eagleton would have it, an "aggressive onslaught on the whole social system," Clarissa's death is an assertion of the superiority of spiritual values, of her "true home," to the values of any social system.[35] In the last fourth of the novel, the testing of truth, of competing worldviews and voices, shifts from getting along in this life to the manner in which one faces the next. When the arena of conflict moves from Harlowe Place and Mrs. Sinclair's to deathbed scenes, Clarissa's apparent defenselessness and vulnerability become, ironically, the only defense and strength that matter. Just as the change of scene from Harlowe Place to Mrs. Sinclair's involves, as Brissenden observes, a deeper penetration into reality and a raising of the stakes in the battle, so does the change of scene from Mrs. Sinclair's to the deathbed. Clarissa's dying is contrasted to the dying of Lovelace's minion, Belton, Mrs. Sinclair, and eventually Lovelace himself. Whereas they babble in mindless fear, Clarissa alone speaks composedly and meaningfully.

Castle argues that Clarissa chooses the silence of death once she has lost her (naive) faith in referential language.[36] It is more accurate to say that she has discovered the sphere and the means by which she can secure referentiality for her language. Once her family has learned that she is truly ill, Uncle John Harlowe writes that her assertions had been discounted because "we know your talents, my dear, and how movingly you could write, whenever you pleased. . . ." (4: 352). Dying in an exemplary manner, Clarissa can back up her words, show that they really do refer to something, and close off at least the most slanderous misinterpretations that have plagued her. Quite simply, knowledge of Clarissa's manner of death colors a second reading of her early letters in a different way than would her marrying Lovelace, marrying Belford, escaping to her grandfather's estate, or running off to America. Far from sinking brokenly into silence, Clarissa goes on talking and writing until the hour of her death. What has changed is that all her words, past and present, come to revolve around that nodal point: her way of dying becomes the ever present signified towards which every remark, no matter how oblique, points.

The final testing of an idea and a character by experience lies in the confrontation with death. Hence Richardson

gives over so much of his novel to a picture of how Clarissa's values permit her to put this transitory life behind her. Myopic modern readings fail to take seriously the structure of *Clarissa,* which is designed to drive home that the most important thing about this life is that it is a preparation for death. Castle argues, for example, that Clarissa's refusal to bring suit against Lovelace shows that she "now mistrusts any form of linguistic self-presentation," citing as evidence not Clarissa's many explanations of her refusal, but Lovelace's jibes at lawyers and courts.[37] Clarissa is interested in a different court. Indeed, her indifference to all lower courts has the effect, ironically, of advancing her earthly vindication by giving her history yet another instance of her refusal to confuse intrinsic rightness with the opinion of the world. For this reason she is able to face an apparently sordid death (abandoned by family, deprived of friends, without money, comforted by strangers alone) with composure and pious anticipation. Richardson's story, by testing competing claims of truth until the conflict yields a portrait of ideality in experience, justifies a context for irony that sets all the previous, superseded contexts into a "finalized artistic vision."

Richardson's justification of irony by story establishes a model for naturalizing interpretation and adjudicating between the conflicting claims of juxtaposed voices and values. Such justification underpins the novelistic mode of organizing narrative, for the novel seeks to legitimate a certain reading of experience by showing, in a mimetically plausible manner, what *would* happen if fictional characters and situations were real. Confidence in this mode of demonstration underlies the historical development of the novel, and it is a faith to which novelists, however tenuously, still cling.

Notes

1. The phrase, "the struggles of interpretation," is borrowed from William B. Warner's *Reading Clarissa: The Struggles of Interpretation* (New Haven: Yale Univ. Press, 1979). The characterization of *Clarissa* as a "hermeneutic anarchy" is from Terry Castle, *Clarissa's Ciphers: Meaning and Disruption in Richardson's "Clarissa"* (Ithaca and London: Cornell Univ. Press, 1982), 21.

2. See Terry Eagleton, *The Rape of Clarissa: Writing, Sexuality and Class Struggle in Samuel Richardson* (Minneapolis: Univ. of Minnesota Press, 1982), 44-45; Castle, 26; 89; 90.

3. Castle, 45; see Eagleton, 40-51.

4. Castle, 148, 165.

5. See Castle, esp. 38-46; 148-80.

6. See Eagleton; Ronald C. Rosbottom, *Choderlos de Laclos* (Boston: Twayne, 1978); Tzvetan Todorov, *Littérature et signification* (Paris: Larousse, 1967), 39-49.

7. Castle, 41, 42, 43-44.

8. Eagleton, 49.

9. Castle, 94.

10. Castle, 94.

11. Castle, 46.

12. Warner, 49.

13. Eagleton, 67.

14. Castle, 186, 194.

15. Eagleton, 52.

16. Mikhail Bakhtin, *Problems of Dostoevsky's Poetics,* trans. Caryl Emerson (Minneapolis: Univ. of Minnesota Press, 1984), 6. Further references are to this edition and will be cited parenthetically in the text.

17. Eagleton, 52.

18. See Emile Benveniste, *Problèmes de linguistique générale* (Paris: Gallimard, 1966).

19. Roland Barthes, *S/Z: An Essay,* trans. Richard Miller (New York: Hill and Wang, 1974), 44, 45.

20. See Wayne C. Booth, *A Rhetoric of Irony* (Chicago and London: Univ. of Chicago Press, 1974).

21. See Ingrid Strohschneider-Kohrs' definitive study of irony in Friedrich Schlegel and Novalis, *Die romantische Ironie in Theorie und Gestaltung,* 2nd. ed., (Tübingen: Max Niemeyer Verlag, 1977) esp. 7-91, 100-112.

22. Chaucer's use of the genre in the Man of Law's Tale may be ironic. That question, however, supersedes the scope of this discussion.

23. Geoffrey Chaucer, "The Clerk's Tale" (ll. 456-62), in *The Works of Geoffrey Chaucer,* ed. F. N. Robinson, 2nd. ed. (Boston: Houghton Mifflin Company, 1957), 106.

24. To Lady Echlin, October 10, 1754; quoted in Donald L. Ball, *Samuel Richardson's Theory of Fiction* (The Hague and Paris: Mouton, 1971), 26.

25. See Ball's discussion of probability in Richardson's theory of fiction.

26. See Leopold Damrosch, Jr., *God's Plot and Man's Stories: Studies in the Fictional Imagination from Milton to Fielding* (Chicago and London: Univ. of Chicago Press, 1985), 10.

27. Samuel Richardson, *Clarissa,* in 4 vols. (London: Everyman, 1932), (1:53). Further citations are to this edition and will be included parenthetically in the text.

28. See Eagleton, 56.

29. See Jean H. Hagstrum, *Sex and Sensibility: Ideal and Erotic Love from Milton to Mozart* (Chicago and London: Univ. of Chicago Press, 1980), esp. 186-218.

30. R. F. Brissenden, *Virtue in Distress: Studies in the Novel of Sentiment from Richardson to Sade* (New York: Barnes & Noble, 1974), 181.

31. John Wilmot, Earl of Rochester, "A Satyr against Reason and Mankind" (ll. 153-56) in *The Complete Poems of John Wilmot, Earl of Rochester,* ed. David M. Vieth (New Haven and London: Yale Univ. Press, 1968), 99.

32. Brissenden, 181.

33. The tale, of course, appears as an inset narrative in *Don Quixote,* Part One.

34. Despite differences, both Ingarden and Ricoeur discuss the relation between narrative extension and the reader's act of (provisional) unification. See Roman Ingarden, *The Cognition of the Literary Work of Art,* trans. Ruth Ann Crowley and Kenneth R. Olson (Evanston: Northwestern Univ. Press, 1973), particularly "Temporal Perspective in the Concretization of the Literary Work of Art," 94-145; Paul Ricoeur, *Time And Narrative,* vol. I, trans. Kathleen McLauglin and David Pellauer (Chicago and London: Univ. of Chicago Press, 1984), particularly "Time and Narrative: Threefold Mimesis," 52-87.

35. Eagleton, 90.

36. See Castle, 108-35.

37. Castle, 128.

PRINCIPAL FIGURES: FRANCE

William Mead (essay date 1961)

SOURCE: "*La Nouvelle Héloïse* and the Public of 1761," in *Yale French Studies,* No. 28, 1961, pp. 13-19.

[*In the following excerpt, Mead examines the impact of Jean-Jacques Rousseau's* La Nouvelle Héloïse *when it was first published, and assesses its impact on the subsequent history of the novel.*]

Towards the middle of the 18th century, the novel—or rather, the Novel—disentangling itself from wicked nurses, stolen wills, and the adventures of terribly handsome princes, and already beginning to demonstrate by actual examples that its natural domain was what Thomas Hardy called "the presentation of the uncommon in ordinary life," faced a serious threat to its continuing development as a serious genre in the widespread human tendency to complicate simple things whenever possible. If any one thing is characteristic of advanced states of civilization, it seems to be a fatal weakness for talking about what one is doing, and enjoying the talk a good deal more than anything else. In 18th-century France, where conversation was, in the somewhat chilling words of Mme de Montpensier, "one of the greatest of the few pleasures of life," a love of talk for its own sake was a national glory; I cannot think of any more striking reflection of the century than what one finds in the absurd so-called "philosophical" novels of the Marquis de Sade, where the characters, with an almost touchingly dogged persistence, work their way in a page or so through one or another of a methodical series of couplings and then calmly sit down for fifty or a hundred pages of the discussion it is obvious they find much more satisfactory. Such a fondness for talk, however, goes far toward explaining how it happens that, while there already existed in France admirable models of the sort of work the genre as a whole was then struggling to achieve, and would eventually achieve on all sides in the following century, these models—Mme de Lafayette's *La Princesse de Clèves,* for example, Crébillon Fils' *Lettres de la Marquise de M—— au Comte de R——* remained without influence, and the majority of people who bothered themselves about novels from 1700 or so on, including, one is sorry to say, a great many of the people writing them, spent a large part of their time worrying about such red herrings as the differences between the Novel and the Epic and the Romance and, whether they managed to sort these out or not, an even greater amount of time worrying about the 18th-century equivalent of Mr. Podsnap's daughter, that formidable "young person" whom a novelist was under no circumstances to cause to blush, and who blushed with such alarming readiness. But progress in art, after all, rarely has much to do with art. It is something great artists and minor artist alike usually achieve because they are interested in something else, and easily manage to swallow the largest camel around at the moment while manfully setting their lips against some, to us, quite insignificant gnat. In 1761, the largest camel of this sort anywhere, if I may keep up this metaphor briefly, was Jean-Jacques Rousseau's *La Nouvelle Héloïse,* and if ever a novel came at a moment when it was most needed and served both the novel and the novelist a good turn, this is that novel. As a camel, the *Nouvelle Héloïse* was the embodiment of everything in the form that at the time was new and revolutionary—it pretended to depict ordinary life, it claimed to be moral, it appealed to the heart. As a gnat, it violated every accepted canon of taste from common sense to common decency. And this was immensely to the good; for in view of its unheard-of popularity, the duty of every self-respecting novelist in Europe was plain. With people lining up in the streets outside the bookshops for a chance to spend half an hour reading it, *La Nouvelle Héloïse* clearly was not a book one simply talked about. It was a book one rewrote. And once these hundreds of ambitious, insignificant, exasperated pens were at work, the future of the novel was safe.

The crisis which marks and determines the history of the novel in the 18th century comes above all from a general and growing conviction that, in spite of its past, the novel *ought* to be a major genre. Heaven and Matthew Arnold alone can say what the term "major" when applied to literary works really means, but it is a fact that everyone who wrote novels from at least 1730 on, and possibly a great many of those who read them, felt some sort of resentment that people as a rule didn't thinks novels major at all, although tragedy was, and the epic was, and many kinds of perfectly silly poetry were. Weren't novelists, after all—wasn't even a lowly hack like Mme de Gomez, scribbling fiction in a rented room to keep meat in the pot and at least one decent velvet dress—writing about human beings in critical situations exemplifying moral truths? "If these are not pigeons, what are they?" as Gertrude Stein said. The century, however, remained largely unconvinced. Between novels for ladies which were elevated but incredible, and novels for men which were credible, all right, but not elevated, one had clearly no choice if one was a person of taste—as who indeed wasn't?

Samuel Richardson's *Pamela* (1740) and above all his *Clarissa* (1747) at last provided the novelists themselves with the models they were seeking, models hallowed as it were and made authoritative by popular acclaim. Here were works which at the same time presented believable pictures of everyday, ordinary life, full of the housekeepers and hackney coaches for which novelists felt so natural an attraction, and yet which were also overwhelmingly moral, specifically intended in fact for the edification of Miss Podsnap, since, in Richardson's own words, they were "published in order to cultivate Principles of Virtue and Religion in the Youth of Both Sexes," being "Entirely Divested of All those Images which, in too Many Pieces calculated for Amusement only, tend to inflame the Minds they should Instruct." If, however, these sanctimonious narratives at last gave the general run of novelists a leg to stand on, the leg was nevertheless a wooden one. Richardson made the novel into something young ladies and their papas could unashamedly read in the parlor; but he did so by pretending that the novel was something it was not, thereby setting a precedent which has been faithfully adhered to ever since by any sort of fiction that is designed to sell. Today our commercial novelists pretend to be investigating social problems and making comments on life. Richardson simply pretended he was not writing novels. What he published, he said, were collections of real letters from real people to real people, and as you read them and wept, you said, with far greater feeling than mere art could ever evoke in you, there, but for the grace of God and the timely lesson this book has taught me, go I. Reading fiction, indeed, might be an idle pastime, but was this fiction? Surely if Clarissa's cousin Colonel Morden had not hunted down her vile seducer and run him through, many a young man would have recognized Lovelace in a back lane and drawn his sword on some unfortunate stranger in the name of Clarissa, of purity and of England.

In France, too, this "willing suspension of disbelief" eventually took hold: Diderot, in his *Eloge de Richardson,* speaks of a lady who asks an acquaintance leaving for England to convey her respects to Clarissa's friend Miss Howe, if he can find her, and if she still lives. But to the French of 1750, Richardson was still largely a *foreign* curiosity. The French, it would seem, could not come by the ability to swallow this particular camel—I mean this pretense on the part of the writer that he wasn't writing, and thus that his work should be judged morally as life is, rather than aesthetically—quite so easily as the already more sentimental English. That climate of immediate, enthusiastic, undifferentiating response which is the hothouse, so to speak, of all really significant spiritual transformations was slow to develop in the temperate atmosphere of the salons. The talkative French intelligence found in Richardson above all a further incentive to talk: about the odd ways of foreigners, their curious genius and their hopeless want of taste, all of which really left the novel just about where it was before, since one could scarcely look upon anything the English had done as literature.

With the 18th century, the old distinction between female and masculine readers had tended gradually to break down. French women had become intellectually emancipated, French men had become polished, and there had come into existence a neutral but hungry public which accepted as a novel anything and everything that called itself one, from *La Vie de Marianne,* which was a novel, to Mme de Graffigny's *Lettres Péruviennes,* which wasn't, and although it considered them all more less trifling if you put a fine edge on it, it really didn't much care, and couldn't be roused to make much of a fuss about the matter, except in the salons, where one could argue about anything and had, after all, to argue about something. Distinctions between the Epic and the Romance and speculations about moral usefulness are admirably suited to salon conversations because they are almost ideally gratuitous, and in any case it is more than doubtful that, in that blessed pre-Bovary era, anyone actually had anything whatsoever *happen* to his morals as the result of reading a work of fiction, or ever seriously entertained the idea that such a thing was possible. It was on the contrary merely something one said one thought was possible.

But as I said, if the novel was to grow and thrive and blossom and bear fruit, there had to be some sort of a fuss—not a lot of animated but empty controversy, but a real disturbance generating a good deal of heat and moisture, and producing in time an atmosphere so humid that, while anything would grow in it, it would be excessively difficult to see through it distinctly. Taking it all in all, this precisely what first Richardson and then Rousseau managed to accomplish.

Subversive is surely the best word for both as novelists. Richardson was perhaps the first great novelist who could not be dismissed either because he was merely an artist doing something ideally admired from a distance, or because he wasn't an artist, and thus failed to come up to scratch. He was the first great novelist whose principal function was that of making his audience uncomfortable by doing with it what it was ready to have done with it, but didn't readily know how to assimilate or discount. By most standards—and I mean *French* standards—Richardson was no artist at all. He wrote too much, he said too little, he played havoc with order, clarity, coherence, truth and common sense. Prévost's admiring translation of *Clarissa* is only occasionally a translation in the ordinary sense of the word; one thinks of Mme de Boufflers reading the Bible and remarking on its style: "What a pity the Holy Ghost was so lacking in taste."

But how troubling *Clarissa* was. How moving in spite of everything. How true to what truth should be. You could laugh at Richardson if you liked, but you somehow couldn't laugh him away. Perhaps you did not feel more virtuous when you had finished reading him, but you felt you ought to be. Reading a romance, you might reflect that no one could ever embody the Illustrious Mandane or the Matchless Charicléa or the Divine Clélie, and sigh with pleasurable melancholy and that would be the end of it; but when you put down the tale of the Incomparable Clarissa you did so with an uneasy consciousness that your being incomparable to her was something for which you had no one but yourself to blame.

And thus, even in a public intellectually trained to look upon the novel as an "entertainment," and naturally inclined to be severe in matters of taste as well as sceptical in matters of feeling, there is gradually built up a residuum of semi-vicarious sentimental experience, a vague backlog of doubts, uncertainties, unexpressed aspirations, half-formed and unknown yearnings, an indefinite awareness of something in the self that is as yet imperfect, unrealized, unfulfilled. There is a pronounced strain of masochism in the 18th-century novel-reading public; an agreeable sensation of guilt is quite as natural to the 18th-century novel-reader as his bag-wig and slippers.

Richardson, however, was, as I said, a foreigner, and since this was a misfortune which could not possibly be remedied, had there been no one of his kind *but* Richardson, it is doubtful whether the as yet unformulated appetite he aroused for the spectacle of high seriousness in lowly circumstances would have soon come to much in the France of Mme de Pompadour. If Jean-Jacques Rousseau was also foreign, he was, by the time he wrote the *Nouvelle Héloïse,* only foreign to the world of the Paris salons, and at that more in his own imagination than in reality. No one, I think, has ever had a more perfect, instinctive grasp of the mind of the public for whom he was writing. No one has ever chosen a more strikingly opportune moment to give the public what, unbeknownst to itself, it had so deep a longing to read. The explanation is not hard to come by, since Rousseau, as a reader of Richardson, wrote for the most representative of all readers of Richardson, himself, and was prompted by a desire to succeed where Richardson had failed—that is to say, to Rousseau's way of thinking, as a moralist. Richardson as an artist was of no interest to Rousseau, who sincerely believed he believed that art was generally beneath contempt; but Richardson, in attempting to be moral, had given his readers, in the person of his heroine, a paragon of virtue so awe-inspiring as to discourage any of the commonplace weaker vessels who stood in such need of good examples to keep them in the paths of righteousness. To call this moral was positively absurd, positively criminal. A genuine moralist has a better grasp of human nature. He, Jean-Jacques Rousseau, Citizen of Geneva, would write the perfect moral novel, defeating Richardson on his own terrain, presenting his readers with the far more useful history of Julie, an ordinary (if not common-place) woman who was tempted, as women are, and fell as women do and will, but *who was redeemed,* as any woman can be and so few, alas, are: redeemed by understanding, by Nature and by voluntary submission to Divine Providence, as it lies within the grasp of any creature, however abandoned, to be. This, at last, would be truly moral fiction. And to do Rousseau the credit he deserves, the public, the suddenly vast public of young ladies with tear-stained cheeks and fathers of families past forty blowing their noses into immense handkerchiefs and of great ladies and of young men with pale faces and glittering eyes—the lacrymose public of 1761 which seemed, to the incredulous and die-hard rationalists of the salons, to have sprung up out of nowhere, welcomed *La Nouvelle Héloïse* with an enthusiasm that had never been seen before, and has not, I believe, been given to any work since that time, including *My Fair Lady.*

A résumé of the *Nouvelle Héloïse,* while it is likely to be quite amusing, a claim I am afraid I could not honestly make for the novel itself, would *not* convey what I am essentially dealing with here, the insidious and subversive play of the novel upon the reader's nerves and areas within himself of which he is scarcely conscious. Using again the pretense that the book has no author but was written as it was lived by the characters themselves, Rousseau gradually subverts the reader's objective determination to read the novel as a novel, gradually involves him, entangles him, commits him to love and hate, to long and enjoy, to such an extent that, although at any moment he can shake off the illusion and remind himself sternly that this is absurd, tedious, bad, he cannot really resist abandoning himself to the power and passion which so mysteriously and yet so splendidly animate the whole. It would be difficult for me to point to any one passage in the book which justified this abandonment or explained this seduction; but the ultimate experience, the effect of the whole, is undeniably that of beauty.

And it is precisely this aspect of the book I have wished to emphasize, this inequation between the whole and its parts. If one imagines for a moment ourselves as a group, cultivated, sensitive, clever, responsible people that we are, carried back into the intellectual atmosphere of April, 1761, what do we find ourselves doing? Why, I suppose we more or less resemble those advertisements in which one man is shouting at an octopus descending from a flying saucer and everyone else is buried in the *Philadelphia Bulletin.* Someone among us may be worrying about the seven years war or the common cold, but everyone else is reading *La Nouvelle Héloïse,* and most of us, I imagine, are on the point of doing something about it, because there never was yet a book that raised one in his own estimation to such an exalted height of feeling and gave one such a sight of what had to be done again, and done better, and of what, above all, remained to be done for the first time. I

pay us the natural compliments of supposing that we would not have liked the book very much. Educated people in 1761 did not generally care for *La Nouvelle Héloïse.* Even if they read it four times, like Mme du Deffand, they didn't like it, and they had all sorts of excellent reasons. Of course they were wrong, some as I said because it was in their best interests and ultimately those of the genre not to see in it another masterpiece in whose shadow the novel would wither and die as tragedy had in the shadow of Racine, and some because, like most critics since that time, they misread it entirely and supposed it to be a defense of the rights of passion, a thing they most properly deplored. The great public, however, was not so misguided, and took from it no passion but a passion for goodness, an insatiable craving for more and more and more tableaux of the struggles of generous but fallible beings to rise above the snares of worldliness and the torments of the flesh into the pure, fresh, fantastic realm of Rousseau's imagination.

Rousseau, in telling this story, had managed to suggest not only that it had happened, but that it had happened to him, and that he who called himself Saint-Preux was that most outstandingly virtuous of men, the Citizen of Geneva. To satisfy their readers' new passion for virtue, novelists on every hand went industriously to work on tales crowded with sublimity, sacrifice and sermonizing; but they did not fail to include housemaids and hackney-coaches, and they did not miss the hint Rousseau had given them that the key to success was to make a prominent if disguised appearance themselves among the cast of characters. Thus, innocently—or is it slyly?—for reasons that have little or nothing to do with art, as such, and which spring even less from a concern for the perfection of the novel, the concept of subjective first-person narrative, which will soon prove so invaluable as a means of expression for the self-centered romantic temperament, is somehow established in works which purport to be serious studies of society as a whole and contributions to the betterment of public morality. Soon *The Sorrows of Werther,* the *Last Letters of Jacopo Ortis,* the fiery fantasies of Mme de Staël, the melancholy memoires of René will seize upon this discovery and exploit it to the full, creating in their turn new appetites in the public and new imitators hopeful of satisfying them; and so, eventually, the inheritance of the *Nouvelle Héloïse* will pass over into the next century to become a by then obscured but none the less vital part of the substance of Balzac, Stendhal, and the modern novel as a whole.

I love men too much to need to choose among them; I love them all, and it is because I love them that I hate injustice; it is because I love them that I flee them. I suffer less from their miseries when I do not see them.

                                            LETTER OF 28 JANUARY, 1762

Josephine Grieder (essay date 1972)

SOURCE: Introduction to *Letters From the Marchioness de M*** to the Count de R***,* by Claude Prosper Jolyot de Crébillon *fils,* Garland Publishing, 1972, pp. 5-10.

[*In the following introduction to a modern edition of Crébillon's novel, Grieder points out that the epistolary novel
did not originate with Samuel Richardson in England, and
explains how Crébillon's work uses the genre's strengths
to build up sympathy for an amoral woman.*]

The reader acquainted with the epistolary novel only
through *Pamela, Clarissa,* or *Sir Charles Grandison* may
be tempted to assume that the form sprang full blown like
Athena from the brow of Samuel Richardson. Such is not
the case, as Robert Adams Day thoroughly demonstrates
in *Told in Letters;* and the *Letters from the Marchioness de
M*** to the Count de R**** (1735) by Crébillon *fils* is a
good example of an earlier effort in the genre.[1] The title
page, in its quotation from the *Journal Littéraire,* indicates
the work's immediate antecedents, the *Lettres portugaises*
(1669) and the *Lettres galantes du Chevalier d'Her*** by
Fontenelle (1683 and 1687); but Crébillon creates a heroine more sentimental and worldly than the passionate Portuguese nun and focuses less on satirical portraits of the
beau monde, Fontenelle's chief interest, than on the Marchioness' inner joys and torments.

The technical problems involved in the composition of an
epistolary novel—how to present differing points of view;
how to provide the characters with enough motivation, leisure, paper, and ink to write—are here reduced to the
minimum. The sole correspondent is the Marchioness. The
sole recipient is the Count, whose alternating assiduity and
indifference to his mistress occasion her correspondence.
Short billets, generally setting assignations, contrast with
longer letters concerning her emotions; she enlivens her
pages with gossip about friends, her husband, and other
suitors. Sometimes she writes to request his help in an
amorous affair; sometimes to assure him of her feelings;
and very frequently to reproach him for his coldness or inconstancy.

But Crébillon, in employing the epistolary form, seized on
its essential virtue: because the reader sees without an intermediary the feelings of the Marchioness, he is directly
engaged emotionally with her. The translator, Samuel
Humphreys, makes this clear in his preface.[2] He anticipates that those ladies "who pretend to be devoted to the
severest Sanctity" will no doubt disapprove of the work,
but "The amiable and generous Part of the Sex, will be
soften'd into Compassion, for the Frailties of a Lady who
was too lovely to be exempted from the Ensnarements that
result from blooming Beauty, and shining Wit." The Marchioness indeed deviates from virtue, but a consideration
of circumstances "shall easily permit our Constructions of
her Conduct to be moderated by the Sentiments of Humanity." And particularly on reading of her death, "we in-
termix our Tears with hers; we intreat Heaven to be propi-
tious to her . . . and wish to see her wafted, by Angels, to
those blissful Regions where all Sorrows shall for ever
cease, and where the Infirmities inseparable from the
present State of human Nature, will no more be repeated"
(no pp.). Such participation on the part of the reader is
particularly necessary in a story where sentiment is the

chief interest and morality depends rather on nuances of
feeling than on rigid interpretation of actions.

The Marchioness is, as we first see her, a delightful, witty
coquette, intrigued by the Count's passion. Men's "Follies
contribute to my Amusement," (p. 10), she declares;
though she is not "insensible" to his charms, she suggests
that he "endeavour to refine your Heart from this unavail-
ing Passion" (p. 15) and try elsewhere. Besides, her idea
of love as "a mutual Confidence, an untainted Friendship
and a perpetual Sollicitude to please" does not correspond
to the modern idea; "That Passion, as it is now conducted,
is no more than a frail Intercourse formed by Caprice;
cherished awhile, by a Cast of Mind, still more contemptible; and, at last, extinguished by both" (p. 22).

Nevertheless, little by little, passion makes inroads on this
confidence. She finds in herself "something more lively
than Friendship" (p. 27). In response to his reproaches on
her sarcasm, she tergiversates: "How do you know but that
the Vivacity you complain of, may be my only Expedient
to conceal half your Happiness from you, and to preserve
me from the Confusion of declaring that I love you?" (p.
37). She becomes seriously annoyed at his apparent infidelity and exclaims, "Good God! can I be weak enough to
wish you may be able to justify yourself!" (p. 49). Finally,
conscious of being led into "a dreadful Abyss . . . the fatal Gulph" (p. 51), she admits the force of her feelings: "O
Heavens! whither shall I fly from such a Combination of
fatal Foes! My Sighs and Tears, and even my strongest
Oppositions, give new Vigour to my unhappy Passion" (p.
52).

Assured of her love, the Count urges her, as we learn indirectly, to grant the "last favours." She is caught in the in-
extricable female dilemma: "How happy is your Sex, in
their Prerogative to pursue their Inclinations without the
Checks of Shame and Confusion! whilst we, who are under the Tyranny of injust Laws, are compell'd to conquer
the Impulse of Nature, who has implanted, in our Hearts,
the same Desires that predominate in yours, and are so
much the more unfortunate as we are obliged to oppose
your Sollicitations and our own Frailty" (p. 58). Nevertheless, she marshalls the usual prudent arguments against
such a step. First, man's nature is inevitably inconstant;
and she is "persuaded it would be better to lose a Lover
who is dissatisfied with our Cruelty, than one who is satiated with our Favours" (p. 63). Second, she fears her conscience. The Count's discretion might be able to conceal
their arrangement, "but alas! who would have the Power
to screen me from the Remorse of my own Heart?" (p.
67). She temporarily concludes that "the Emotions of the
Heart are not subordinate to the Judgment: But, surely, I
have the Ability to be virtuous; and we never cease to be
so, against our Inclinations" (p. 67).

Does the Marchioness actually capitulate? Her Letter XX-
VII informs the Count that "your impatient Ardours had
almost surprized me into an absolute Insensibility of my
Duty" (p. 106) when the arrival of her husband fortunately

saved her virtue, and she swears never to have another such interview with him. But relenting, "You see the Perplexity in which I am involved," she declares; "your Lordship in one Scale, and Virtue in the other: How difficult is it to adjust the Ballance! (109). Two quick billets follow, the second arranging an assignation; "Some Letters are here suppress'd" (p. 111), the editor informs us. And in the next letter, the Marchioness reproaches R*** for too warm a declaration of his affection in public. Crébillon originally wrote at this point, "Voulez-vous faire deviner à tout le monde que vous m'aimez, et qu'il ne manque rien à votre bonheur?" Mr. Humphreys chooses to translate this ambiguously: "Would you have all the World suspect your Passion for me; and are you desirous they should believe you want nothing to render your Happiness compleat . . .?" (p. 113).

Whatever the English reader may choose to decide, the Marchioness knows from this point on all the worries that a mistress is subject to. In order to keep him interested, she gives him frequent cause for jealousy because "I have observed that it is good to awaken your Passion" (p. 129); satirical portraits of amorous tax collectors, an old marquis, her philosophy professor, a fop, and a prince enliven her letters. She is concerned about her reputation—"From the first moment I lov'd you, every Instance of my Conduct has been a Deviation from my Duty" (p. 169)—but her husband troubles her less as a watchdog than as a person whose justifiable amorous solicitations prove troublesome to her passion. She is continually in dread of the Count's inconstancy and reproaches him for it, though she asks him to "Pity me, in some tender Moments; for I cannot presume to require, from you, any Sentiments that are more ardent" (p. 230). Hoping by her coldness to revive his interest, she declares to him that "I once lov'd you to Adoration, and my Passion was incapable of a Moment's Insincerity; but you have, at last, caus'd it to expire" (p. 258).

An unexpected event—her husband's promotion to a post abroad—triggers the denouement: the Marchioness' death from anguish at being obliged to part from the Count. All her guilty feelings now come forward to torment her: "I am constantly haunted by the most criminal Ideas, and find it impossible to chase them from my Remembrance" (p. 297). She is repentant—and yet she loves. "It is no longer the frail Person enslav'd by a fatal Passion, who writes to you now. It is an unfortunate Creature, who repents of all her Crimes; who reviews them with Horror; who is sensible of all their Weight, and who yet is unable to refuse you new Proofs of her Tenderness" (p. 302). She is, in fact, more concerned about the Count's despair at her death than about her own situation and urges him to be steadfast. At the end, she neither loses dignity nor recants her love. "I am now come to the last Period of my Days, and am preparing to end them with Fortitude. Adieu! Adieu! Adieu! for ever!" (p. 304).

The ordinary reader will see in these letters the progress of feminine sensibility from coquetry to a tender and sincere passion. The perspicacious reader will see as well a comment on woman's ambiguous position in contemporary society. The novel presents, in effect, a *ménage à trois*. But the husband is impossible: free to engage in the amours which please him; delighted to retail to her the history of his conquests; yet out of boredom capricious and demanding of his marital rights. The much-loved Count is scarcely less agreeable on close inspection. He parades his mistresses before the Marchioness; he brags to others of his inconstancy; he neglects her "with no other View than to satisfy your Curiosity whether the Loss of you will affect me" (p. 253); he neglects her for no reason whatever. But the Marchioness tacitly accepts the current code and lives as honorably as possible with it. Unlike later heroines who lament and repent at length their fall from virtue, she has no recriminations until the moment of her death. This perhaps makes her technically "immoral"; that she continues faithful and tender in such a situation makes her, however, extremely admirable and even lovable.

Notes

1. The complete title of Mr. Day's work is *Told in Letters: Epistolary Fiction before Richardson* (Ann Arbor: University of Michigan Press, 1966); a brief discussion of the *Letters* will be found in pages 107-109.

2. Humphreys (1698?-1738) was a poet and a respected, if minor, figure in the world of letters: he provided the texts to several of Handel's most celebrated oratorios; and he did translations from Italian and French, including Gueulette's *Peruvian Letters* (1734) and pieces from La Fontaine.

Elizabeth Heckendorn Cook (essay date 1996)

SOURCE: "The End of Epistolarity: 'Letters from an American Farmer,'" in *Epistolary Bodies: Gender and Genre in the Eighteenth-Century Republic of Letters,* Stanford University Press, 1996, pp. 140-72.

[*In the following excerpt, Cook contends that J. Hector St. John de Crèvecoeur's* Letters from an American Farmer *laments the ending of the epistolary genre as it records life and customs in the newly independent United States.*]

What the *Lettres persanes* has been for scholars of European Enlightenment, [J. Hector St. John de] Crèvecoeur's *Letters from an American Farmer* (1782) has been for American studies: a generic anomaly that generates ongoing intradisciplinary contestation. The terrain of the debate is familiar: while the book deploys some of the narrative techniques of conventional prose fiction, it is composed of a series of letters that provide cultural and natural-historical information about the American setting and events, to which plot and character development are subordinated. As a result, the *Letters* have often been treated as a collection of loosely related essays. Selections from the work are anthologized according to the ideological currents of the moment, while the rest is dismissed unread. For example, Gary B. Nash has examined how Letter III, "What Is an American?" has been used by American literature and history courses to support a "myth of a classless prerevolutionary American society . . . a sentimentalized, idealistic vision of a vanished, egalitarian America" (216). As Cathy Davidson points out, "predictably . . . the later sections of Crèvecoeur's classic are anthologized far less often than the exultant (if unrealistic) Letter III. For most readers of Crèvecoeur (who typically encounter his work in anthologies, if at all), the important analysis of American racism set forth in the latter portions of the book simply does not exist. It is not part of our literary inheritance."[1] The *Letters from an American Farmer* is seldom examined as a novel; it is even less often treated as an epistolary narrative. In fact, its epistolarity—its generic context and codes—is almost always ignored.[2] As a result, no one has put to the *Letters* the questions that eighteenth-century epistolary narratives consistently raise about the meaning of publication itself. As this study has been concerned to demonstrate, contemporary print artifacts of all sorts existed in dialogue with a liberal ideology that bound together publication, civic identity, and subjectivity, so that this dialogue is formally and thematically implicated in the question of what any eighteenth-century letter-narrative "means."

In a recent study of eighteenth-century American writing, Michael Warner claims that the concept of a print culture is crucial to all contemporary American literature. Warner shows that the colonies' identity was intimately tied to print, and that print was insistently thematized in all sorts of American publications, from ephemeral pamphlets to conduct books to the U.S. Constitution. American novels in particular differ from the Anglo-European models that literary critics have traditionally used as touchstones: "American novels before Cooper are all anomalous from the perspective of literary criticism." These novels must be read in the context of American print culture: they are "better accounted for by treating them as features of a republican public sphere rather than a liberal aesthetic."[3] In other words, instead of invoking such literary critical concepts as organic unity, characterization, or narrative voice, we should rather attend to how these works thematize publication, privacy, civic virtue, and the gendered body of the citizen, issues that preoccupy contemporary letter-narratives. Here such attention makes visible a transformation over the course of the century in attitudes toward the Enlightenment ideal of a public sphere. This final chapter examines how an American letter-narrative written in the last decades of the century comments on the political and cultural values implicit in Enlightenment print culture.

In many ways, Crèvecoeur's letter-narrative is even more anomalous than the novels Warner examines, for one could argue that it is neither a novel nor American in any meaningful sense. The *Letters* was composed (apparently largely in America) by a naturalized British citizen and landowner who used the name J. Hector St. John; it was published first in England (1782) and then in Ireland. Translated, revised, much extended, and rededicated, it came out in France two years later, by which time its author had resumed his original French citizenship and name, Michel Guillaume St. Jean de Crèvecoeur, and was back in the state of New York serving as French consul.[4] It was not published in the United States until 1793, three years after Crèvecoeur returned to the Continent, but by this time its vogue had passed, and for many years the *Letters* remained unread by any but a few scholars.

The formal peculiarities and the odd publication history of the *Letters from an American Farmer* make perfect generic sense when it is read within the Anglo-European tradition of epistolary narrative defined by the thematization of the public sphere. The *Letters from an American Farmer* appeared as the popularity of the epistolary genre began to decline, and thus it can be read as an elegy for the political and cultural ideologies that had been implicit in the genre through the century. Americanists have long read Crèvecoeur's text primarily as commenting on the future of the American republic; however, returned to its generic context, the *Letters* is clearly about that republic's past: it mourns the end of the transatlantic Republic of Letters and of the cosmopolitan citizen-critic imagined and constructed in its narratives.

Michael Warner describes postrevolutionary America as a period of transition from an old paradigm of readership to a new one. The earlier paradigm, which he calls "republican," imagines a reading subject resembling the one that I have argued is produced by the *Lettres persanes:* the republican text invents a disembodied citizen-critic whose reading is an act of public civic virtue. In contrast, the second paradigm of readership, which he calls "nationalist," invokes a private subject, embodied in history and therefore necessarily gendered and classed, whose reading is above all sympathetic.[5] In what follows, we will see that the *Letters from an American Farmer* stages the cultural transformation from republican to nationalist readership, and in so doing, it stages the eclipse of the Enlightenment ideal of the Republic of Letters and of its cosmopolite, supranational citizen-critic.

Letter III, famously, opens with the question, "What is this new man, this American?" Crèvecoeur shows that as "America" rewrites itself into the United States through a bloody internecine struggle, it distinguishes this "new man" from a figure like the cosmopolitan citizen-critic produced by Montesquieu. The distinction reveals the alienation from Enlightenment values inherent in the new notion of national citizenship. For Montesquieu, the roles of father, husband, political subject, and critic mutually complement one another, and their complementarity regulates both the political and the domestic orders. In contrast, in a country "convulsed" (to use Crèvecoeur's repeated expression) by civil war, private and public aspects of the self are in direct and radical conflict: public and private categories of identity represent mutually exclusive subject-positions. Corporeality can no longer be abstracted or transcended, its politically masculine status guaranteed by participation in the public sphere. Instead, the body in all its vulnerable materiality—resembling in this way the body of the Richardsonian epistolary heroine, ever subject to invasion and violation—returns to center stage as the site of a cultural anxiety about power and authority. The post-Enlightenment subject is definitively embodied, and is thereby consigned to the private sphere of particularity and self-interest. In a period of national revolution, which in Crèvecoeur's depiction closely resembles a Hobbesian state of nature, the ideal of open public exchange between disinterested citizens whose reason qualifies them to debate the actions of the state is necessarily discredited.

Against this transformation of the significance of public and private, the *Letters* defines the American subject at the end of a certain mode of transatlantic correspondence. Crèvecoeur's elegiac project is anchored by three figurations of the body/subject: the colonist's wife in Letter I; the slave in the cage in Letter IX; and George III in Letter XII. The bodies of women, slaves, and the monarch pose specific and intractable challenges to the ideology of anonymity and disinterestedness that sustains the Enlightenment public sphere; these challenges help explain the demise of both the public sphere and the epistolary genre in the new nation.[6] . . .

THE WRITING SUBJECT: PUBLICNESS AND REPRESENTATION IN THE NEW NATION

The title of the much-anthologized Letter III of the *Letters* poses the compelling question "What Is an American?" In 1782, one answer might have been that an American is someone who has successfully negotiated a complicated transition from being a subject in the political sense to being a subject in the modern psychological sense: the movement is simultaneously from subject to citizen and from political subjecthood to psychic subjectivity. The American is someone who has come to live under the linked signs of personal identity and personal property that we now think of as making up possessive individualism.[7] In Europe, the *Letters* tells us, immigrants "were not numbered in any civil lists of their country, except in those of the poor; here they rank as citizens. . . . The laws . . . protect them as they arrive, stamping on them the symbol of adoption; they receive ample rewards for their labours; these accumulated rewards procure them lands; those lands confer on them the title of freemen, and to that title every benefit is affixed which men can possibly require" (68-69). In colonial and revolutionary America, this transition from statistical cipher to individual freeman takes place through the power of the printed word to create the citizen-critic: "As citizens it is easy to imagine that they will carefully read the newspapers, enter into every political disquisition, freely blame or censure governors and others" (71).[8] Against a critical tradition that dismisses the *Letters* as generically anomalous and aesthetically uneven, I argue that a reading focusing on the complicated intersection between (political) citizen and (psychological) subject mediated by writing will reveal the order and clarity—the secret chain, we might say—of Crèvecoeur's rich and peculiar letter-narrative.

The first letter introduces this constellation of issues. Here, James the self-taught colonial must negotiate an epistolary identity for himself between the history, politics, and linguistic conventions he inherits from the Old World and the as-yet untested frontiers of the New. This negotiation is both the subject and the effect of the act of writing that constitutes the *Letters from an American Farmer* as a whole, for the print artifact we are reading is made up of James's letters describing the natural and civic terrain of America to Mr. F. B., the "enlightened European" gentleman who has solicited this letter-exchange after staying with the family during an American tour (51). The first letter establishes how much is at stake in this proposed epistolary engagement by putting into print the debate about it between James, his wife, and the local minister. Their language frames the correspondence as a kind of dangerous expedition between opposed social and political allegiances. In the eighteenth-century generic context, we could see the eastern trajectory of James's letters as reversing the journey to the West undertaken by Usbek and Rica. The farmer's letters sketch a return to the East, albeit one that will be canceled out by his family's western flight at the close of the narrative. James defines his epistolary offerings as recompense for the discursive tour of the Old World that Mr. F. B. gave him during that gentleman's visit to America: "You conducted me, on the map, from one European country to another; told me many extraordinary things of our famed mother country, of which I knew very little, of its internal navigation, agriculture, arts, manufactures, and trade; you guided me through an extensive maze, and I abundantly profited by the journey" (39).

This model of complementary exchange is challenged by one party to the three-cornered debate staged in Letter I. James's wife insists on Mr. F. B.'s radical difference from James; his extensive travels, she thinks, make it unlikely that he really wants to read James's homely letters.

> Only think of a London man going to Rome! Where is it that these English folks won't go? One who hath seen the factory of brimstone at 'Suvius and town of Pompeii underground! Would'st thou pretend to *letter it* with a person who hath been to Paris, to the Alps, to Petersburg, and who hath seen so many fine things up and down the old countries; who hath come over the great sea unto us and hath journeyed from our New Hampshire in the East to our Charles Town in the South; who hath visited all our great cities?
>
> (40; my emphasis)

The wife's description of Mr. F. B.'s and James's relationship as "letter[ing] it" links cultural capital to correspondence as an index of difference that precludes correspondence between subjects of different nations and classes. In contrast, the minister suggests that for such readers as Mr. F. B., letters work in lieu of actual travel to unite individuals discursively across difference. He assures James that even if his American anecdotes "be not elegant, they will smell of the woods and be a little wild; I know your turn, they will contain some matters which he never knew before. . . . We are all apt to love and admire exotics, though they may be often inferior to what we possess" (41-42). Mr. F. B. reading James's letters—and by analogy the British readers of Crèvecoeur's *Letters*—will undertake a discursive voyage to the New World more instructive than any continental tour:

> Methinks there would be much more real satisfaction in observing among us the humble rudiments and embryos of societies spreading everywhere. . . . I am sure that the rapidity of their growth would be more pleasing to behold than the ruins of old towers, useless aqueducts, or impending battlements. . . . I am sure I cannot be called a partial American when I say that the spectacle afforded by these pleasing scenes must be more entertaining and more philosophical than that which arises from beholding the musty ruins of Rome. . . . For my part, I had rather admire the ample barn of one of our opulent farmers, who himself felled the first tree in his plantation and was the first founder of his settlement, than study the dimensions of the temple of Ceres.
>
> (42-43)

In short, the ideal enlightened reader is understood to possess a cosmopolitan benevolence that makes the print representation of America a source of pleasure regardless of nationality. Indeed, James later asserts that American identity is effectively transnational: "We know, properly speaking, no strangers; this is every person's country" (80). In this sense, the discursive representation of America would be the natural topos of the Enlightenment Republic of Letters.

This representation of the Republic of Letters as transnational is itself bound to a particular historical moment. Taken as a whole, the *Letters* invites us to consider what happens to the Enlightenment ideal of the public sphere when political conditions preclude the fulfillment of the citizen-critic's rights and responsibilities. Specifically, the *Letters* exposes the challenges to the ideology of cosmopolitan citizenship that arise when the meanings of "private" and "public" are rewritten in the political context of the 1770s and 1780s. For instance, James's sharp-witted, cautious wife fears that if the epistolary exchange is publicized, her husband will be persecuted by suspicious neighbors and royal agents as "the scribbling farmer" (49). She urges that the correspondence be kept secret, because, as we gradually learn, the American "public" described in the *Letters* is not a rational forum of disinterested citizens, but rather a battleground of private interests.[9] The wife is particularly alert to how self-interestedness may color interpretations of the act of writing.[10] She urges, "For God's sake let [the correspondence] be kept a profound secret among us; if it were once known/abroad that thee writest to a great and rich man over at London, there would be no end of the talk of the people: some would vow that thee art going to turn an author; others would pretend to foresee some great alterations in the welfare of thy family; some would say this; some would say that. Who would wish to become the subject of public talk?" (47-48). Her anxiety about the figure of the writing farmer makes it clear that criticism according to properly literary criteria is impossible in this political context:

> Wert thee to write as well as friend Edmund, whose speeches I often see in our papers, it would be the very selfsame thing; thee would'st be equally accused of idleness and vain notions not befitting thy condition. Our colonel would be often coming here to know what it is that thee canst write so much about. Some would imagine that thee wantest to become either an assembly man or a magistrate, which God forbid, and that thee art telling the king's men abundance of things. . . . Therefore, . . . let it be as great a secret as if it was some heinous crime.
>
> (48)

In the crippled society of colonial America, with its divided proto-public of individuals who are not yet fully citizens, publicity is symptomatic of political transgression rather than of republican transparency, as it was for Montesquieu's limping woman. In such a culture it is assumed that one writes to promote one's private interests, rather than the public good; on these grounds James's wife recommends that he retain the private status (and, implicitly, the political gender) of that female figure crippled by publicity.

Unlike the *Lettres persanes,* however, Crèvecoeur's *Letters* does not propose a utopian restoration of the proper body through the public exercise of critical reason. Indeed, for James's wife, writing belongs to a world to which Americans have no access.[11] "Great people over sea may write to our townsfolk because they have nothing else to do. These Englishmen are strange people; because they can live upon what they call bank notes, without working, they think that all the world can do the same. This goodly country never would have been tilled and cleared with these notes" (48). In contrast to America, England operates on a strange hybrid economy of paper money standing in for gold: "if they have no trees to cut down, they have gold in abundance, they say; for I have often heard my grandfather tell how they live there by writing. By writing they send this cargo unto us, that to the West, and the other to the East Indies." This magic circulation of paper is utterly foreign to the American economy: "But, James, thee knowest that it is not by writing that we shall pay the blacksmith, the minister, the weaver, the tailor, and the English shop" (49). According to the wife, America is still a precapitalist agrarian economy in which value is generated by labor, not paper. Her description sounds very much like Locke's explanation of how property rights precede money: when the laborer mixes his body's labor capacity with the earth, the resulting product (say, the tilled field) belongs to him.[12] The wife insists, "I am sure when Mr. F. B. was here, he saw thee sweat and take abundance of pains; he often told me how the Americans worked a great deal harder than the home Englishmen; for there, he told us, that they have no trees to cut down, no fences to make, no Negroes to buy and to clothe" (48-49).[13] In the context of the politically and economically self-regulating and self-sufficient society she describes, writing, linked to an illusory paper economy, is inherently anomalous and even scandalous: "How would'st thee bear to be called at our country meetings the man of the pen? If this scheme of thine was once known, travellers as they go along would point out to our house, saying, 'Here liveth the scribbling farmer'" (49).

Larzer Ziff emphasizes that the wife's position is complicit with the dominant political powers: "From the authorities' viewpoint, a writing farmer indicates a disordering of the hierarchy on which political stability rests."[14] But the wife seems even more concerned about the opinions of her neighbors than she is about those of the authorities. Ziff may be correct in reading these passages as evidence of the wife's understanding of writing as linked to society's secular fall, but we need not also infer a rejection of writing on Crèvecoeur's part. Read in relation to the Enlightenment ideal of the public sphere, it becomes clear that the *Letters* here draws attention to the dangerous absence of the civic conditions enabling publication to be part of a transparent order where citizens, divested of personalities and private interests, discuss public affairs.[15]

According to the ideal of the public sphere, to write is to participate in a public debate. Mr. F. B. invokes the epistolary trope that "writing letters is nothing more than talking on paper," and the minister significantly develops the comparison into a kind of public performance. "Imagine, then, that Mr. F. B. is still here and simply write down what you would say to him. Suppose the questions he will put to you in his future letters to be asked by his viva-voce, as we used to call it at the college; then let your answers be conceived and expressed exactly in the same language as if he was present" (41). Here the domain of writing is constituted neither as a corrupter of idealized pure presence nor as its successful reconstitution, but rather as a formal technology of exchange.[16] This epistolary exchange does not testify to a nostalgia for "immanence," to use Ziff's word, but rather to a republican paradigm of writing as the forum of objective, disinterested debate and discussion under the supervision of the public. If the wife describes a society in which writing is a sign of divisive self-interest, then in contrast, the epistolary project envisioned by James, the minister, and Mr. F. B. would allow citizen-critics to shape and affirm a Republic of Letters through writing. This vision stands at the head of the text, but as we will see, it cannot be sustained in the warring state of nature to which we see America reduced in Letter XII, in which self-interest has become fatally paramount.

The wife's doubts articulate, in displaced and domesticated disguise, Crèvecoeur's own fears about how public authorial status can be established in the context of a literary and political culture in the throes of "convulsion"—a word he returns to again and again. Can one be a citizen of a transatlantic Republic of Letters when one's own society is in political turmoil? And if this ideal is no longer possible, how can authorship be imagined differently? We will return to these questions, but first let us consider the final disposition of Mr. F. B.'s proposal.

The three readers in this opening scene are preoccupied by the question of whether language is transparent: that is, does Mr. F. B. mean what he writes? The text for this exercise in group reading is a handwritten, private letter from an acquaintance and potential patron, but it nonetheless calls on its readers' highest exegetical skills, as though it were Holy Scripture. The wife exclaims, "James, thee must read this letter over again, paragraph by paragraph, and warily observe whether thee canst perceive some words of jesting, something that hath more than one meaning" (41). She then, as James tells Mr. F. B., "read it herself very attentively; our minister was present, we listened to and weighed every syllable; we all unanimously concluded that you must have been in a sober earnest intention, as my wife calls it, and your request appeared to be candid and sincere. . . . Our minister took the letter from my wife and read it to himself; he made us observe the two last phrases, and we weighed the contents to the best of our abilities. The conclusion we all drew made me resolve to write" (41). This community debate mirrors a miniaturized public sphere reinforced by public reading, a publicness that, James vows to the minister, will continue: "my letters shall not be sent, nor will I receive any, without reading them to you and my wife; . . . it will not be the first thing which I have submitted to your joint opinions. Whenever you come to dine with us, these shall be the last dish on the table" (45-46). With this guarantee, the epistolary engagement is accepted: James will represent America for Mr. F. B. In the process, Crèvecoeur seems to suggest, he will also write himself into being, as a subject of Enlightenment print culture and as a citizen of the Republic of Letters.

By thus defining and staging the literary construction of the private subject at this early moment of national history, Crèvecoeur distances the anxiety he himself shares with his readers about the definition and status of American authority in the 1780s. By the end of the letter-narrative we will see James not as the contemptible "scribbling farmer" his wife imagines, but instead as the full-blown "farmer of feelings," Mr. F. B.'s "refined" denomination for his correspondent (53). Despite this apparently successful negotiation of the boundary between public and private at the level of individual subjectivity, the strategies that allowed earlier epistolary authors to employ the paradigms of the Republic of Letters in the construction of their authorial identities no longer serve James or Crèvecoeur himself in the same way. The "farmer of feelings" is not the citizen-critic: the image appeals to a very different paradigm of reading and interpretation, one that problematizes correspondence instead of idealizing it.

This problematization becomes evident in the imbalances of the epistolary exchange charted here. Although James and the minister suggest in Letter I that correspondence can circumvent class and national differences, it does not necessarily produce egalitarian relations or a true public sphere. Particularly where the American is anxious to prove himself on the European's intellectual terrain, his correspondence becomes vulnerable to charges of self-interest. This may be the case even when the American's own landscape is the basis of the epistolary exchange, as it so often is in the *Letters*. Laura Rigal has described how eighteenth-century American natural historians depended on a European "network of men of letters" who provided letters of introduction and recommendation, as La Rochefoucauld did for Crèvecoeur. On her account, Crèvecoeur's *Letters* illustrates how the claim to properly "American" independence and thus to an idealized republican moral purity is actually undermined by the workings of correspondence:

> In Crèvecoeur's fiction, the letters themselves come to be objectified properties, serving, in effect, as heraldic devices which legitimate, and even prove the virtuous existence of the Pennsylvania yeoman. However, legitimation by letters to and from Europe is accomplished only at the expense of continuity with the Old World civilization in respect to which the Pennsylvanian hopes to distinguish himself. While serving as evidence of his virtuous character, therefore, the farmer's letters also serve to document the corruption and "interestedness" which are implicit in his trans-Atlantic social connections, and which reflect his own social origin.[17]

Rigal examines this collapse of a crucial distance between Old and New World in Letter XI, which recounts the visit to John Bartram of a Russian traveler named Iwan. Bartram is not ashamed to be found working beside his laborers, thus demonstrating his unpretentious, democratic "American" values, but he proudly cites his epistolary links with European aristocrats and royalty. He has corresponded with the British king about Florida; with Queen Ulrica of Sweden, whose "kind epistle" in Latin he displays to Iwan; and with various distinguished Europeans, exchanging seeds and specimens. The coat of arms of his French father's family, a token of his continued engagement with the values of the Old World, hangs in his study.

The idea of correspondence resonates throughout Letter XI in various ways. Iwan's desire to meet Bartram was stimulated by "the extensive correspondence which I knew he held with the most eminent Scotch and French botanists" as well as with Queen Ulrica (188), and Bartram was not surprised by Iwan's visit because he had received advance notice of his arrival from another correspondent. Bartram's transformation from a colonial farmer to a world-famous botanist who "walk[s] in the garden of Linnaeus" (194) with princesses and nobles is due to his knowledge of Latin, which permits him not only to grasp the "universal grammar of plants through the Linnaean system" but to correspond with a queen. Latin makes him a cosmopolitan citizen of the Republic of Letters; it also makes him botanically at home not only "all over [his] farm" but throughout North America, until by now, he says modestly, "I have acquired a pretty general knowledge of every plant and tree to be found in our continent" (195). This knowledge anchors a self-perpetuating chain of correspondence: Bartram's autobiographical account ends triumphantly, "In process of time I was applied to from the old countries, whither I every year send many collections,"

and he offers to add Iwan to his list of natural-historical correspondents.

While Iwan's account emphasizes the reciprocality of Bartram's epistolary exchanges, the underlying hierarchialism implicit in them becomes clear when the epistolary metaphor is extended to Bartram's household economy, which Iwan describes as "the mutual correspondence between the master and the inferior members of his family" (195). Bartram's household is represented as an ideal patriarchy. Assembled around the dining table, its members exemplify the orderly Great Chain of Being, rising from "Negroes" and "hired men" to family and guests up to "the head, [where] the venerable father and his wife presided" (189). Here, the idea of correspondence accommodates a highly stratified social model, rather than that of an egalitarian exchange between citizens of the Republic of Letters.

Iwan ends the letter about his visit to Bartram by thanking his own correspondent for a letter of introduction: "It was to the letter you gave me that I am indebted for the extensive acquaintance I now have throughout Pennsylvania" (199). Rigal's reading asks us to de-figure this economic metaphor, in the sense of returning it to its literal meaning: such letters are indeed debts, for they entangle the American naturalist in the social hierarchies of the Old World and carry its corrupt values into the ostensibly objective, scientific study of the New World. As a result, the ideal of the disinterested citizen-critic is undermined. In this sense, Letter IX raises questions about correspondence between the New World and the Old that prepare us for the disastrous epistolary rupture that concludes Letter XII.

THE AMERICAN EMBODIED

The fantasy of benevolent paternalism suggested in Iwan's image of the Bartram dinner table is crystallized in the figure of Mr. F. B., who authorizes, though he does not author, the correspondence that becomes the *Letters from an American Farmer*. As the narrative develops, however, this fantasy is disrupted by a series of challenges to the crucial guarantee represented by the father's body. In Montesquieu's work, the Persians' letters repeatedly invoke a real paternal body as the anchor of language and of narrative, but the *Lettres persanes* itself seeks to eliminate the connection between discourse and (gendered) body so as to open up a space for the disembodied citizen-critic. In the *Letters from an American Farmer*, the narrator's attempts to locate and affirm the inherency of meaning in the father's body are also exposed as fruitless. James's anxious discourse seeks the origin of language and property, and ultimately of the new nation itself, in corporeality. The anomalous body of the slave, however, calls into question the Lockean connections between body, property, and society.

In Locke's *Second Treatise of Government*, America as a concept is a sort of thought-laboratory in which the origin of society can be worked out: "in the beginning all the world was America."[18] In this Edenic New World, the individual exists very precisely as a body/subject: subjectivity and corporeality are coextensive and indivisible. This is clear in the famous passage on the origin of property:

> every man has a *property* in his own *person;* this no body has any right to but himself. The *labour* of his body, and the *work* of his hands, we may say, are properly his. Whatsoever then he removes out of the state that nature hath provided, and left it in, he hath mixed his *labour* with, and joined to it something that is his own, and thereby makes it his *property.*[19]

Locke asserts that the body's physical limitations ensure the essential fairness of the property system established by God. So long as there is no waste, defined by the limits of the capacity of the body to consume, the concept of property is unproblematic:

> The same law of nature, that does by this means give us property, does also *bound* that *property* too. *God has given us all things richly,* 1 Tim. VI. 12 is the voice of reason confirmed by inspiration. But how far has he given it us? *To enjoy.* As much as any one can make use of to any advantage of life before it spoils, so much he may by his labour fix a property in: whatever is beyond this, is more than his share, and belongs to others. Nothing was made by God for man to spoil or destroy.[20]

When this law is observed, property is justified by nature itself:

> The measure of property nature has well set by the extent of men's labour and the conveniencies of life: no man's labour could subdue, or appropriate all; nor could his enjoyment consume more than a small part; so that it was impossible for any man, this way, to intrench upon the right of another, or acquire to himself a property to the prejudice of his neighbour, who would still have room for as good, and as large a possession (after the other had taken out his) as before it was appropriated. This measure did confine every man's possession to a very moderate proportion.[21]

These passages justify property as a by-product of the body/subject. However, a categorical difficulty arises when another kind of body is considered: that of the servant. Initially, Locke presents the servant's body as simply a kind of prosthesis. In a passage summarizing how labor makes property out of nonproperty, he writes, "Thus the grass my horse has bit; *the turfs my servant has cut;* and the ore I have digged in any place, where I have a right to them in common with others, become my *property* without the assignation or consent of anybody."[22] The parallelism finesses a troubling question about the extension of agency through servitude, for the service of another, whether wage laborer, indenturee, or slave, is not the same as the pure effects of one's own bodily labor that provide an inalienable right to property. Such service must instead be a result of the invention of money, which replaces the natural corporeal index of legitimate consumption and waste by an artificial measure that allows the unjust distribution of goods: "this I dare boldly affirm, that the same *rule of pro-*

priety, (viz.) that every man should have as much as he could make use of, would hold still in the world, without straitening any body; . . . had not the *invention of money,* and the tacit agreement of men to put a value on it, introduced (by consent) larger possessions, and a right to them."[23] The category of the servant's labor represents a point of entanglement in Locke's argument about the origins of property; it also underlines a confusion about the concept of the body in eighteenth-century Enlightenment culture.

The problem of the servant's labor, unresolved in Locke, becomes urgent in Letter IX, for what ultimately undermines the optimistic representation of America in James's early letters is the paradoxical body of the slave. In the New World, which Locke represents as the scene of property's legitimate birth, the slave's body stands as an emblem of the ethical, even the ontological, dubiety of property. It is also an emblem of the loss of civic values that leads to the despairing conclusion of the *Letters.* The themes of Letter IX echo the reflections of Montesquieu's Usbek on the rise of despotism, for both emphasize the cyclic decay of civic values and link bodily and economic health. James begins his description of Charles Town by referring to the "valetudinarians from the West Indies" he sees there, "at thirty, loaded with the infirmities of old age" (167), their health destroyed by the luxuriousness of their climate and the ease of their life. The idyllic climate of Charles Town encourages the excesses of its citizens, who resemble West Indian planters, notorious for dissipation and cruelty, in their moral and physical debility: "The rays of their sun seem to urge them irresistibly to dissipation and pleasure" (167). Land values there are very high, because of the "narrowness of the neck on which it stands"; nonetheless, this value does not remain in the land, but is progressively drained off into the hands of lawyers, a class that figures parasitical nonproductivity to James. "In another century, the law will possess in the north what now the church possesses in Peru and Mexico" (168).

These comparisons between the West Indies, Mexico, and Peru, all Enlightenment tropes for colonial despotism, set in play the question of slavery that dominates the rest of this letter. In Charles Town, James observes, slaves' bodies are invisible to their owners: "Their ears by habit are become deaf, their hearts are hardened; they neither see, hear, nor feel, for the woes of their poor slaves, from whose painful labours all their wealth proceeds. Here the horrors of slavery, the hardship of incessant toils, are unseen, and no one thinks with compassion of those showers of sweat and of tears which from the bodies of Africans daily drop and moisten the ground they till" (168). The passage invokes obliquely, in relation to the slaves, the Lockean image of the mixture of the body's labor with the earth that constitutes and legitimates property; at the same time, it emphasizes how the invention of money makes that justification of property irrelevant. Because of the rise of a market in human bodies as slave labor made possible by money, the mixing of the human body with the earth, by its emissions of sweat and tears as well as by its labor capacity, no longer performs its proprietary magic. The wealth of Charles Town's planters derives less from agricultural productivity than from the gold-driven triangle trade that circulates from Peru to Guinea to North America, bringing captured Africans "to toil, to starve, and to languish for a few years on the different plantations of these citizens" (169). The slaves are not subjects in a money economy but objects of it, laboring for people "who have no other power over them than that of violence, no other right than what this accursed metal has given them!" (169).

In such a context, even paternity, that basic bodily function that anchors and stabilizes society for James and for Usbek, becomes an index of dehumanization. That the slave's body is not that of a body/subject is clearest when it is considered against contemporary models of fatherhood. By definition, the slave can never fully participate in the Enlightenment triad of masculine identity-categories celebrated by Usbek, that of husband, father, and citizen. James notes:

> If Negroes are permitted to become fathers, this fatal indulgence only tends to increase their misery; the poor companions of their scanty pleasures are likewise the companions of their labours; and when at some critical seasons they could wish to see them relieved, with tears in their eyes they behold them perhaps doubly oppressed, obliged to bear the burden of Nature—a fatal present—as well as that of unabated tasks. How many have I seen cursing the irresistible propensity and regretting that by having tasted of those harmless joys they had become the authors of double misery to their wives . . . they are not permitted to partake of those ineffable sensations with which Nature inspires the hearts of fathers and mothers; they must repel them all and become callous and passive. . . . Their paternal fondness is embittered by considering that if their children live, they must live to be slaves like themselves. . . . The very instinct of the brute, so laudable, so irresistible, runs counter here to their master's interest; and to that god, all the laws of Nature must give way. Thus planters get rich.
>
> (169-71)

The bodily paradoxes of slavery counter the Lockean representation of the New World as the space in which liberal humanism, founded on democratic capitalism, can freely unfold.

Slavery's corrosive effects on liberal idealism are most memorably presented in Letter IX's appalling spectacle of the slaves in the cage. This scene is traditionally read as an allegory of the excesses of revolution, but the suicide of Montesquieu's Roxane has taught us not to move too quickly from the body to its exegesis. The passage opens with a familiar Enlightenment evocation of the benign relations between humans and the natural world. On his way to a friendly dinner with a plantation owner, our narrator rambles through a pleasant pastoral landscape. However, this landscape is abruptly invaded by the tropes of despotism. The image of the caged and dying slave enacts the

reversals of value that despotism sets into motion: in this terrible image of a World Upside Down, a man is trapped in a cage, while birds outside struggle to get in to feed on him. The caged slave's body is written over by wounds; since despotic power always leaves its signature on the eyes, the narrator observes that "the birds had already picked out his eyes; his cheek-bones were bare" (178). The birds have torn the slave's face so that he is literally "disfigured."[24]

The effect of this spectacle on the beholder is just what the despot would desire: in the presence of these signs of absolute power, the narrator experiences a sublime disruption of apprehension and expression. The body/subject is disarticulated: "I found myself suddenly arrested by the power of affright and terror; my nerves were convulsed; I trembled; I stood motionless, involuntarily contemplating the fate of this Negro in all its dismal latitude." In a pidgin English that signals his marginality to humanity itself, the caged slave utters "a few inarticulate monosyllables" (177). When he begs for a sip of water and then for the greater kindness of death, the goal of despotism—to display its absolute authority over the bodies of its miserable subjects—has been accomplished. That Crèvecoeur's slave must beg for his death marks how much greater is his abjection than that of Montesquieu's Roxane, who is able, at least, to end her own life. Even his death is not at the slave's disposal.[25]

Facing this spectacle, the narrator realizes that the ideals of Enlightenment are not sustainable in the face of human greed and cruelty. So-called Oriental tyranny exists even in the New World, and there is no escape from it: "History perpetually tells us of millions of people abandoned to the caprice of the maddest princes, and of whole nations devoted to the blind fury of tyrants. Countries destroyed, nations alternately buried in ruins by other nations, some parts of the world beautifully cultivated, returned again into their pristine state, the fruits of ages of industry, the toil of thousands in a short time destroyed by few" (173). Human societies are always in a state of nature: "Everything is submitted to the power of the strongest; men, like the elements, are always at war; the weakest yield to the most potent; force, subtlety, and malice always triumph over unguarded honesty and simplicity" (174). As Usbek's Troglodyte fable suggested, every political order eventually degenerates back into despotism: "Republics, kingdoms, monarchies, founded either on fraud or successful violence, increase by pursuing the steps of the same policy until they are destroyed in their turn, either by the influence of their own crimes or by more successful but equally criminal enemies" (177). While civilized society at its best may allow a degree of political stability, perhaps even temporary felicity, nonetheless human society "is a strange heterogeneous assemblage of vices and virtues and of a variety of other principles forever at war, forever jarring, forever producing some dangerous, some distressing extreme" (177). With this realization, the Enlightenment vision of an emancipatory public sphere of reasoning, disinterested citizens is exposed as an empty ideal. What follows is a depiction of the end of the Republic of Letters and of the correspondence that symbolized it.

The visit to Charles Town described in Letter IX offers a counter-Enlightenment narrative about the corrupting effects of the despotic tendency in human society. This narrative prepares us for the final phase of James's story: a vivid depiction of the actual "convulsion" of American society. If the ideal society is that in which the roles of husband, father, and citizen are mutually self-reinforcing, so that self-interest and public interest are the same, in a society in "convulsion" these roles become radically incompatible. In his last letter, James describes the anguish of this experience, which threatens the dissolution of the body/subject:

> Never was a situation so singularly terrible as mine, in every possible respect, as a member of an extensive society, as a citizen of an inferior division of the same society, as a husband, as a father, as a man who exquisitely feels for the miseries of others as well as for his own! . . . When I consider myself as connected in all these characters, as bound by so many cords, all uniting in my heart, I am seized with a fear of the mind, I am transported beyond that degree of calmness which is necessary to delineate our thoughts. I feel as if my reason wanted to leave me, as if it would burst its poor weak tenement.
>
> (201)

What is lost in the storm of revolution is the quintessentially human desire for sociability, for "of all animals that live on the surface of this planet, what is man when no longer connected with society, or when he finds himself surrounded by a convulsed and a half-dissolved one? He cannot live in solitude; he must belong to some community bound by some ties, however imperfect" (201). Now, however, "every one feels . . . for himself alone"; no man is truly a citizen in the Enlightenment's fullest sense of the word. Symptomatically, the gendered identity that underpins citizenship now becomes unstable: James's response to the dangers of attack is a kind of lability of gender. "Sometimes feeling the spontaneous courage of a man, I seem to wish for the decisive minute; the next instant a message from my wife, sent by one of the children, . . . unmans me; away goes my courage, and I descend again into the deepest despondency" (202). In the context of revolution, the roles of husband, father, and citizen clash and undermine one another. The Republic of Letters, grounded on that complementary trilogy, collapses in its absence.

At the end of the *Letters,* then, we return to the question raised in the first letter by the wife's anxiety about writing. How can a public authorial status be established in a society in the throes of "convulsion"? In this study's terms, the question can be framed even more specifically: how can one be a citizen of a transatlantic Republic of Letters when one's own nation is in political turmoil, so that local and larger identities clash? And if this ideal is no longer possible, how can authorship be imagined otherwise? James's reference to the conflict he experiences between being "a member of a large society which extends to many parts of the world" and "a citizen of a smaller society" (203) describes the author's dilemma as well as that of the colonial.

Letter XII describes life in America during this civil conflict as essentially unrepresentable. The loss of representability threatens the existing relation between author and reader, grounded in a model of readership that appeals above all to the exercise of reason. Up till now, a reading model based on sympathy and identification has been only implicit in the text, but here the interpellation of the disinterested, disembodied citizen is replaced by an interpellation that demands embodied identification.[26] Since the representation of the distresses of civil war strains rational language past its limits, the *Letters* at last turns to the language and paradigms of sympathy and identification that Warner sees as characteristic of a nationalist model of readership: "men secure and out of danger are soon fatigued with mournful details: can you enter with me into fellowship with all these afflictive sensations; have you a tear ready to shed over the approaching ruin of a once opulent and substantial family? Read this, I pray with the eyes of sympathy" (203).

In this new kind of reading, the reader is deliberately invited to import self-interest into the text. Sympathetic reading calls on the reader not in the abstract, as one of the many anonymous and disinterested readers of print artifacts who constitute a public, but as a private person whose body necessarily engages his or her special interests. In short, what we might call the writing of sympathy creates its addressees as those body/subjects that Montesquieu, as I argued in Chapter 2, sought to deconstruct. As a result, the experiences of private subjectivity, not those of public criticism, become predominant. The concept of a disinterested civic debate in a public sphere defined by abstraction and impersonality becomes irrelevant, and the abstract tenets of jurisprudence and political philosophy are brushed aside as citizens are reduced to their bodies. The following passage maps out the transformation from impartial, disinterested, disembodied "spectator" and "citizen" to corporealized colonist:

> The cool, the distant spectator, placed in safety, may arraign me for ingratitude, may bring forth the principles of Solon or Montesquieu; he may look on me as wilfully guilty; he may call me by the most opprobrious names. Secure from personal danger, his warm imagination, undisturbed by the least agitation of the heart, will expatiate freely on this grand question. . . . To him the object becomes abstracted. . . . But let him come and reside with us one single month; let him pass with us through all the successive hours of necessary toil, terror, and affright; let him watch with us, his musket in his hand, through tedious sleepless nights, his imagination furrowed by the keen chisel of every passion; let his wife and his children become exposed

to the most dreadful hazards of death; let the existence of his property depend on a single spark, blown by the breath of the enemy; . . . let his heart, the seat of the most affecting passions, be powerfully wrung by hearing the melancholy end of his relations and friends; let him trace on the map the progress of these desolations; let his alarmed imagination predict to him the night, the dreadful night when it may be his turn to perish, as so many have perished before. Observe, then, whether the man will not get the better of the citizen, whether his political maxims will not vanish! Yes, he will cease to glow so warmly with the glory of the metropolis: all his wishes will be turned toward the preservation of his family!

(206)

The convulsion that reduces citizens to bodies acts even on monarchy. James assures himself that if George III found himself transported to America at this moment, he too would act as a father rather than as a ruler:

If a poor frontier inhabitant may be allowed to suppose this great personage[,] the first in our system[,] to be exposed but for one hour to the exquisite pangs we so often feel, would not the preservation of so numerous a family engross all his thoughts; would not the ideas of dominion and other felicities attendant on royalty all vanish in the hour of danger? The regal character, however sacred, would be superseded by the stronger, because more natural one of man and father. Oh! Did he but know the circumstances of this horrid war, I am sure he would put a stop to that long destruction of parents and children. I am sure that while he turned his ears to state policy, he would attentively listen also to the dictates of Nature, that great parent; for, as a good king, he no doubt wishes to create, to spare, and to protect, as she does.

(207)

Here the image of the paternal Farmer George meets that of an implicitly maternal Nature to create a natural family out of all the king's subjects, metropolitan as well as colonial.

This powerful invocation of the secular, corporeal, domestic aspect of the king's double body sets up the rhetorical climax of this letter, in which the vulnerable bodies of James's own family clinch the appeal to sympathy. Here again, the destructiveness of civil war is measured by how it opposes the body of the father and husband to the ideal of the disembodied citizen, defining these roles as radically at odds instead of mutually complementary:

Must I then, in order to be called a faithful subject, coolly and philosophically say it is necessary for the good of Britain that my children's brains should be dashed against the walls of the house in which they were reared; that my wife should be stabbed and scalped before my face; that I should be either murthered or captivated; or that for greater expedition we should all be locked up and burnt to ashes as the family of the B———n was?

(207)

These violent images of destruction and dismemberment testify to the end of the idealized disembodiment of the Enlightenment. If in 1721 Montesquieu uncoupled body from subjectivity to create the citizen-critic, 60 years later, in the collapse of the public sphere that is the subtext of the *Letters from an American Farmer,* Crèvecoeur obsessively returns to the body and mourns the death of the citizen. In a world barely distinguishable from the state of nature, the body becomes the vehicle of sympathy, which is all that is left in a society where citizenship is impossible.

Letter XII charts the destruction of the conditions that sustain the proper citizen-critic, and rematerializes the body as the site of civic anxiety. Symptomatically, unlike the *Lettres persanes, Clarissa,* or *Fanni Butlerd,* this letter-narrative does not close with an explanation of its own publication, a self-inscribed textual history. It records instead the rupture of the correspondence between Europe and America, the end of the narrative of epistolarity as well as of this particular epistolary narrative. James at last resolves to flee the war zone, taking his family west to the Indian villages far from the European settlements and their institutionalized connections with the Old World.

His final letter is oddly broken up by dashes standing for the names of the Indian tribes and their villages where his family will soon live. These blanks serve as typographical icons of the end of correspondence: the unmapped new spaces beyond the frontier are not on the embryonic postal routes of the new nation. In despair, James asks Mr. F. B., "Shall we ever meet again? If we should, where will it be? On the wide shores of ———." The unnamable destination that concludes James's query stands, as it were, for "address unknown." The elision marks both the expulsion of epistolarity from this troubled Eden and the passing from cultural authority of an entire constellation of images and values bound up with the idea of correspondence.[27] With the fall of the Republic of Letters, transatlantic postrevolutionary and post-Enlightenment print culture will have to devise new metaphors of exchange, communication, and authorship, as well as new definitions of citizenship and indeed of subjectivity itself.

Notes

1. Nash, ed., *Class and Society in Early America,* p. 21, cited in Cathy Davidson, *Revolution and the Word,* pp. 216-17. For a discussion of the publication history and critical reception of the *Letters,* see Thomas Philbrick, *St. John de Crèvecoeur,* pp. 161-64, and Davidson, p. 257.

2. Among the few exceptions to the suppression of the *Letters'* epistolarity are Philip D. Beidler's "Franklin's and Crèvecoeur's 'Literary' Americans"; Jean F. Beranger's "The Desire of Communication"; and Manfred Putz's "Dramatic Elements and the Problem of Literary Mediation." These essays do not consider the relation between the epistolary genre and print culture that focuses my study.

3. Michael Warner, *The Letters of the Republic,* pp. 151-52. Warner examines a wide range of print

artifacts, including pamphlets on such political matters as the 1765 Stamp Act; an account of a libel trial against a printer; Franklin's epitaph and *Poor Richard's Almanac;* and Charles Brockden Brown's novel *Arthur Mervyn* (1799-1800). While his treatment of each of these is valuable, I found particularly useful for my interests here his treatment of Franklin's periodical Silence Dogood letters of 1722.

4. In the French edition, a dedication to Lafayette replaced the original dedication to the Abbé Raynal.

5. See Warner, chap. 5.

6. While the body of the citizen-critic is functionally gendered male, this serves not to particularize the citizen but to link him to the abstract "norm" from which all those who are not literate white male property-holders deviate into particularity. Warner explores the collapse of this model, the undoing of "the citizen's literate transcendence of his unacknowledged male body," in Charles Brockden Brown's *Arthur Mervyn,* another narrative about the crisis of the public sphere (170).

7. C. B. MacPherson's *The Political Theory of Possessive Individualism* provides an indispensable discussion of the connection between capitalism and liberalism.

8. This sense of Americans' self-definition through print culture has been explored, sometimes brilliantly, in American studies over the last decade. Examples include Davidson's *Revolution and the Word,* Larzer Ziff's *Writing in the New Nation,* and Warner's *Letters of the Republic.*

9. Obviously, this public resembles the oppressive, tyrannical majorities of ignorant individuals envisioned, in somewhat different ways, by Rousseau, J. S. Mill, and Tocqueville. See Habermas's discussion in *Structural Transformation,* pp. 98-99, 132-38.

10. In the *Sketches,* Crèvecoeur portrays such self-interestedness in his Patriot characters, whose desire to appropriate the goods of others is only thinly veiled by their hypocritical republican rhetoric. In the Fifth Landscape, a Patriot official's wife helps herself to the belongings of a Loyalist's widow and children, ostensibly to shield them from accusations of ill-gotten wealth when their household goods are publicly displayed for auction. This satirical depiction of self-interest in a feminized and domesticated mode suggests a powerful if displaced indictment of Patriot motives and actions.

11. Larzer Ziff argues that the wife connects writing with the realm of market values, paper money, credit, and "representation," as opposed to "immanence"; see *Writing in the New Nation,* p. xi.

12. Locke's well-known discussion of labor and property is cited and discussed later in this chapter; see note 29.

13. Her rhetoric makes slave-owning a self-justifying institution, analogous to the examples of labor Locke gives as the basis of the division of objects held in common into individual property before the invention of money. Just as the labor of one's body is combined with the tree by the act of cutting it down and with the fence by the act of building it, making the tree and the fence one's property, so slaves, she implies, become one's property through the labor of clothing them. However, the mention of *buying* Negroes smuggles the concept of money into the wife's precapitalist world somewhat as it is smuggled into Locke's justification of property in the *Second Treatise of Government.* In both contexts, a money economy complicates the justification of property, as I show below.

14. Ziff, *Writing in the New Nation,* p. 28.

15. Ziff's conclusion suggests something like a Whig reading of eighteenth-century history: the *Letters* is positioned at a "turning point" in a cultural teleology, necessarily bearing the traces of a representational economy's corruption but looking ahead to a post-Revolutionary Restoration through nature (33). It is not always clear whether Ziff intends to attribute the vocabulary of progress and nostalgia employed in this discussion to James or Crèvecoeur, or whether it is his own. To anticipate my conclusion, I emphatically disagree with Ziff's idea that James's flight to the Indian villages is simply a relocation of the happy society, which he justifies by asserting that there was no "idea of ruin in the [American] culture" (33). The *Letters* is itself vivid evidence to the contrary: the public sphere destroyed by "convulsion" won't be reconstructed in the anticivic space beyond the frontier to which James's family eventually flees.

16. In this context the scholarly catechism could be linked to the contemporary use of the natural history questionnaire, which, with its set questions about soils, topography, ad flora ad fauna, was circulated to a range of informants and then collated to avoid the distorting effects of subjective, idiosyncratic observation. Perhaps the first such questionnaire in English was Robert Boyle's "General Heads for a Natural History of a Countrey, Great or Small," printed in the first volume of the Royal Society's *Philosophical Transactions* (1666). The questionnaire continued to be used in assembling natural histories through the early nineteenth century. Also relevant to the idea of the oral examination is Warner's discussion of the principle of supervision in the republican public sphere (*Letters of the Republic,* chap. 2) and James's interrogation of Andrew the Hebridean in Letter III.

17. Rigal, "An American Manufactory: Political Economy, Collectivity, and the Arts in Philadelphia, 1790-1810," pp. 188-89. Rigal discusses this aspect of the letter in a chapter on William Bartram's *Travels through North and South Carolina, East and*

West Florida. I thank her for making available to me an early version of this material, which I cite here. A more prosaic example of potential self-interest in James's correspondence with Mr. F. B. appears in the minister's comment, "You intend one of your children for the gown; who knows but Mr. F. B. may give you some assistance when the lad comes to have concerns with the bishop. It is good for American farmers to have friends even in England" (44).

18. Locke, *Second Treatise of Government,* ed. MacPherson, p. 29.

19. Ibid., p. 19. Locke's pronominal use is appropriate: his analysis applies to males only. Here and elsewhere, the italics that signal the key terms suggest the paradoxes of print culture: while the labor of the hand that made the manuscript is effaced by the conventions of typography, the italicization of the word "labor" calls attention to the artificiality of those conventions.

20. Ibid., pp. 20-21.

21. Ibid., p. 22.

22. Ibid., pp. 19-20, emphasis mine.

23. Ibid., p. 23.

24. These references to despotism look back to the work of Alain Grosrichard discussed in connection with the *Lettres persanes.* The word "disfigured" resonates particularly richly for a native speaker of French like Crèvecoeur, given the range of meaning of the word "figure" in that language. I also recall here de Bolla's attention to "disfiguration" as a strategy that empties the represented body of figural meanings in order to return it to what is held to be its "original" significance. This strategy also militates against an allegorical reading of the disfigured slave.

25. In *The Body in Pain,* Elaine Scarry defines slaves in Lockean terms as those who have "ceased to exercise political autonomy over their own most intimate property, the human body" (156).

26. The term "interpellation" is Althusser's, explained in his "Ideology and Ideological State Apparatuses," p. 173-76.

27. What Jay Fliegelman describes as "the sealing of the garden" in late-eighteenth-century America comes about in part as a result of this expulsion of epistolarity. See his *Prodigals and Pilgrims,* pp. 227-67.

Works Cited

Althusser, Louis. "Ideology and Ideological State Apparatuses." In *Lenin and Philosophy and Other Essays.* Trans. Ben Brewster. New York: Monthly Review Press, 1971.

Beidler, Philip D. "Franklin's and Crèvecoeur's 'Literary' Americans."*Early American Literature* 13 (1978): 50–63.

Beranger, Jean F. "The Desire of Communication: Narrator and Narratee in *Letters from an American Farmer.*" *Early American Studies* 12 (1977): 73–85.

Davidson, Cathy. *Revolution and the Word: The Rise of the Novel in America.* London: Oxford University Press, 1986.

Fliegelman, Jay. *Prodigals and Pilgrims: The American Revolution Against Patriarchal Authority 1750–1800.* Cambridge, Eng.: Cambridge University Press, 1982.

Grosrichard, Alain. *Structure du sérail: La fiction du sepostisme asiatique dans l'Occident classique.* Paris:Éditions du Seuil, 1979.

Habermas, Jürgen. *The Structural Transformation of the Public Sphere: An Inquiry into a Category of Bourgeois Society.* Trans. Thomas Burger and Frederick Lawrence. Cambridge, Mass.: MIT Press, 1989.

Locke, John. *Two Treatises of Government.* Ed. Peter Laslett. Cambridge, 1960; rprt. New York: Mentor-Penguin Books, 1965.

———. *Two Treatises of Government.* Ed. C. B. MacPherson. Indianapolis, Ind.: Hackett, 1980.

MacPherson, C. B. *The Political Theory of Possessive Individualism, Hobbes to Locke.* Oxford: Clarendon Press, 1962.

Nash, Gary, ed. *Class and Society in Early America.* Englewood Cliffs, N.J.: Prentice-Hall, 1970.

Philbrick, Thomas. *St. John de Crèvecoeur.* Boston: Twayne, 1970.

Putz, Manfred. "Dramatic Elements and the Problem of Literary Mediation in the Works of Hector St. John de Crèvecoeur."*Yearbook of Research in English and American Literature* 3 (1985): 111–30.

Rigal, Laura. "An American Manufactory: Political Economy, Collectivity, and the Arts in Philadelphia, 1790–1810." PhD. Diss., Stanford University, 1989.

Scarry, Elaine, *The Body in Pain.* Oxford: Oxford University Press, 1985.

Warner, Michael. *The Letters of the Republic: Publication and the Public Sphere in Eighteenth-Century America.* Cambridge, Mass.: Harvard University Press, 1990.

Ziff, Larzer. *Writing in the New Nation: Prose, Print, and Politics in the Early United States.* New Haven, Conn.: Yale University Press, 1991.

FURTHER READING

Criticism

Ball, Donald L. "Richardson's Statement of His Theory of Fiction." In *Samuel Richardson's Theory of Fiction.* The Hague: Mouton & Co., 1971, pp. 23-30.

Clarifies the principal reasons Richardson prized the epistolary form over narrative fiction: because letters are by nature rooted in the present and because they most actively engage the attention of the reader.

Brophy, Elizabeth Bergen. "Epistolary Form: An Easy and Natural Style." In *Samuel Richardson: The Triumph of Craft.* Knoxville: The University of Tennessee Press, 1974, pp. 38-49.

Examines Richardson's reliance on the epistolary genre and claims that that Richardson found the form more realistic, flexible, and morally instructive than the narrative novel.

Cohan, Steven M. "Clarissa and the Individuation of Character." *ELH* 43 (1976): 163-83.

Examines how Richardson uses the epistolary convention to explore the difficulties in understanding a complex human personality.

Day, Robert Adams. *Told in Letters: Epistolary Fiction before Richardson.* Ann Arbor: University of Michigan Press, 1966, 241 p.

Comprehensive study of the epistolary genre; includes a chronological list of English letter fiction from 1660 to 1740 and provides notes on epistolary miscellanies as well as discussions of novels and major figures.

Doody, Margaret Anne. *A Natural Passion: A Study of the Novels of Samuel Richardson.* Oxford: The Clarendon Press, 1974, 410 p.

Discussion of all of Richardson's novels, emphasizing the author's creative genius as revealed through the differences among the works.

Epstein, Julia L. "Fanny Burney's Epistolary Voices." *The Eighteenth-Century: Theory and Interpretation* 27, No. 2 (Spring, 1986): 162-79.

Examines Burney's narrative strategy, paying special attention to the voices of female characters in her fiction.

Flynn, Carol Houlihan. *Samuel Richardson: A Man of Letters.* Princeton, N.J.: Princeton University Press, 1982, 342 p.

Examines the tension between Richardson's moral and aesthetic principles in his novels and personal letters.

Gelley, Alexander. "The Two Julies: Conversion and Imagination in *La Nouvelle Héloïse.*" *Modern Language Notes* 92, No. 4 (May 1977): 749-60.

Discusses the apparent discrepancies between the passionate and witty Julie D'Etagne of the early part of *La Nouvelle Héloïse.* to the preachy, mystically inclined Mme. de Wolmar of the last half of the work.

Gillis, Christina Marsden. *The Paradox of Privacy: Epistolary Form in* Clarissa. Gainesville: University Presses of Florida, 1984, 173 p.

Examination of the historical and dramatic space of the novel followed by a literary-historical approach to Richardson's epistolary form.

Jensen, Katharine Ann. *Writing Love: Letters, Women, and the Novel in France, 1605-1776.* Carbondale: Southern Illinois University Press, 1995, 217 p.

Investigates literary and sexual inequality as depicted in feminine epistolary in *ancien régime* France.

Kinkaid-Weekes. *Samuel Richardson: Dramatic Novelist.* Ithaca, N.Y.: Cornell University Press, 1973, 506 p.

Interpretive readings of Richardson's novels followed by a general discussion of their social realism, psychology, and form.

Lindquist, Carol A. "Aphra Behn and the First Epistolary Novel in English." *Publications of the Arkansas Philological Association* 3, No. 2 (1977): 29-33.

Views Behn's *Love Letters Between a Nobleman and His Sister* as the first English epistolary novel.

Preston, John. "*Les liaisons dangereuses*: An Epistolary Narrative and Moral Discovery." *French Studies: A Quarterly Review* 24 (1970): 23-36.

Explores the narrative method used to convey moral lessons in Laclos's novel.

Singer, Godfrey Frank. *The Epistolary Novel: Its Origin, Development, Decline, and Residuary Influence.* New York: Russell & Russell, Inc., 1963, 266 p.

Broad survey of the form that examines hundreds of epistolary works and discusses their place in the history of the genre.

Thelander, Dorothy R. *Laclos and the Epistolary Novel.* Geneva: Droz, 1963, 167 p.

Examines Laclos's novel *Les liaisons dangereuses* against the background of the European tradition of letter fiction.

Visconti, Laura. "The Beginnings of the Epistolary Novel in England." In *Contexts of Pre-Novel Narrative: The European Tradition.* Berlin: Mouton de Gruyter, 1994, 397 p.

Traces the development of the epistolary form in its social and cultural contexts.

Warner, William Beatty. *Reading* Clarissa. New Haven, Conn.: Yale University Press, 1979, 274 p.

Interpretation of Richardson's *Clarissa,* followed by a survey and analysis of previous critical approaches.

Würzbach, Natascha, ed. *The Novel in Letters: Epistolary Fiction in the Early English Novel, 1678-1740.* Coral Gables, Fla.: University of Miami Press, 1969, 288 p.

Examines the use of letters in fiction before Richardson.

Zaczek, Barbara Maria. *Censored Sentiments: Letters and Censorship in Epistolary Novels and Conduct Material.* Newark: University of Delaware Press, 1997, 209 p.

Examines the censoring practices that influenced female epistolary writing in the eighteenth century.

Pastoral Literature of the English Renaissance

INTRODUCTION

The pastoral is a literary style or type that presents a conventionalized picture of rural life, the naturalness and innocence of which is seen in contrast to the corruption and artificiality of city and court. Although pastoral works are written from the point of view of shepherds or rustics, they are always penned by highly sophisticated, urban poets. Some major, related concerns in pastoral works are the tensions between nature and art, the real and the ideal, and the actual and the mythical. English Renaissance pastoral has classical roots, but contains distinctly contemporary English elements, including humanism, sentimentality, depictions of courtly reality, a concern with real life, and the use of satire and comedy.

Pastoralism figured prominently in English poetry, prose, and drama from the mid-sixteenth to the mid-seventeenth century. English pastorals of this period were modeled after classical Italian and Spanish works, which in turn looked back to the ancients, whose pastoral poetry stemmed from the folk songs and ceremonies that honored the pastoral gods. The earliest extant pastoral poetry, the *Idylls,* was written by Theocritus in the third century B.C. Theocritus's works contain all the elements that were later conventionalized into the pastoral form or style: his rustic characters discuss the pleasures of country life, engage in impromptu singing contests, recount folktales, lament the loss of loved ones, and offer elegies on the deceased. His characters Daphnis and Amaryllis became fixtures of pastoral works. The Roman poet Virgil adopted the pastoral mode in his first-century B.C. *Eclogues,* adding mythical and political dimensions to his poetry and introducing the self-conscious questioning of the pastoral convention itself, with its tension between the real and the mythical. Few pastorals were written during the Middle Ages, but the form became popular with Italian Renaissance humanists such as Petrarch, Mantuan, and Boccaccio, who experimented with Latin forms. One of the earliest dramatic pastorals is *Orfeo,* by Politian, performed at the court of Mantua about 1471. Others include *Aminta* (1573) by Torquato Tasso and *Pastor Fido* (1590) by Giovanni Guarini. Nondramatic pastorals of sixteenth-century Italy include the romance *Arcadia* (1504) by Jacopo Sannazzaro. The pastoral also flourished at this time in the poems of the Portuguese writer Gil Vicente and the Spanish writers Juan del Encina, Miguel de Cervantes Saavedra, and others.

English poets such as Alexander Barclay and Barnabe Googe, who wrote in the first decades of the sixteenth century, were, like the Continental poets, influenced by the Latin eclogues. The first true pastoral work from the pen of an English writer, however, was *The Shepheardes Calender* (1579) by Edmund Spenser. Spenser used many of the conventions established by Theocritus, Virgil, Mantuan, and Sannazzaro in his twelve eclogues (one for each month of the year) that subtly satirize the political and religious figures of his day and draw attention to the artificiality of the courtly world. The poem has very little real action or narrative progression, but sustains interest as Spenser's shepherds contemplate a number of subjects and use a variety of poetic forms, such as amorous complaints, fables, singing matches and debates, an encomium, a funeral elegy, and a hymn to the god Pan. Spenser also added important innovations to the traditional pastoral form in *The Shepheardes Calender,* as his eclogues use a wide range of different meters and experiments in prosody and use allegory to discuss political themes. Spenser's other pastoral works include *Colin Clouts Come Home Againe* (1595), an allegory dealing with a journey to London and the vices of court life, and his unfinished masterpiece *The Faerie Queene* (1596).

The other great pastoral poet of the Elizabethan period was Philip Sidney, the man to whom Spenser dedicated *The Shepheardes Calender.* Sidney's *Arcadia* is a mixed-mode romance that intersperses pastoral lyrics in a tale of courtly love, as two princes set off to find love in Arcadia, fall in love with two princesses, and eventually marry them. Along the way, the major characters must spend much of their time disguised as shepherds. The major theme of the work is the life of action and responsibility versus the life of contemplation and love, a common pastoral motif. Another familiar trope is that of the mythic "Golden Age." As with other Renaissance pastorals, *Arcadia* also presents sophisticated ideas in the words of common, rustic characters, thus simplifying difficult concepts and emphasizing the universality of human nature. The eclogue "Ye Goatherd Gods" contained in *Arcadia* is especially admired for its originality of meter and ornate amplification.

Most of the other figures writing on pastoral themes in the early Renaissance were lyric poets and dramatists. The most famous of the lyricists were Walter Raleigh, Christopher Marlowe, William Browne, Richard Barnfield, George Wither, and Michael Drayton, many of whom modeled their verses after Spenser's eclogues but treated less weighty themes.

Pastoral themes were also popular in Elizabethan drama, particularly in court masques. These comprised a distinctively courtly form of dramatic spectacle that was characterized by the use of masks and the mingling of actors and spectators, as well as an emphasis on music and dance.

Sidney's *Lady of May* (1578), about a young woman who cannot choose between two men who want to marry her—a rich shepherd of "smale Desertes and no faultes" and a woodsman of "manie Desertes and manie faultes"—has the elements of gaiety and lightness that mark these types of dramas. Dramatists of the later Renaissance, including William Shakespeare, began to react against hackneyed pastoral conventions in their "antipastoral" pastorals. Shakespeare employed and yet overturned pastoral ideas and themes in in *As You Like It* (1598), *The Winter's Tale* (1609), and *The Tempest* (1611). The idea that the bucolic existence of the countryside offers an alternative to the corruption of the courtly life was simply not an economic reality by the end of the Renaissance, and in Ben Jonson's *Sad Shepherd* (1640) it becomes clear that the material realities of an age of commerce and exploration make it impossible to depict the court in simple terms or to hold up the countryside as a paradisaical world of innocence and harmony.

Many lyric poets of the later Renaissance moved away from the use of pastoral conventions in their verse, or they more self-consciously explored in their work the meaning of pastoral themes for a changing world. Some writers, such as Robert Herrick, with his realistically detailed descriptions of rural festivals and life, did present pastoral idealizations of the country. For other poets, the greater concern was to reflect in their poetry the transformation of the land and changing conditions of the countryside—in which increasingly landowners hired workers to tend their property and contented shepherds did not populate the hillsides. The two great pastoral poets of the later Renaissance, John Milton and Andrew Marvell, used many pastoral elements in their work, often to point to the passing of an age. While the English Renaissance pastoral had always contained an element of self-conscious exploration of its own conventions, Marvell's poetry is deeply self-reflexive and internalized, and in many of his posthumously published poems, such as "The Garden" and "The Mower Against Gardens" (1681), the idealized world he longs for seems to be a state of inner, individual harmony and not the outer, physical retreat of nature. Milton used pastoral elements in several of his works, including the poem "Lycidas" (1638) and Books IV and IX of *Paradise Lost* (1668). "Lycidas," a moving pastoral elegy for Milton's acquaintance Edward King, is very close in structure to Virgilian eclogues, but in the poem Milton mingles classical and Christian myths and creates a sense of unrest atypical of pastoral poetry that is quelled only when Lycidas is raised to heaven. Many critics have viewed "Lycidas" as Milton's farewell not only to his friend but to his youth, to the ideas and ideals of a past age, and to pastoralism in general. In *Paradise Lost,* too, Milton is less concerned with pastoral landscapes and lost paradises than with a "paradise within." Restoration writers clearly rejected and even ridiculed the pastoral impulse, and it would more than a century before the ideals of the pastoral, again transformed, would again respectibility in the works of Romantic writers.

REPRESENTATIVE WORKS

Richard Barnfield
The Affectionate Shepherd (poem) 1594

William Browne
Britannia's Pastorals (poem) 1613-16
The Shepheards Pipe (poem) 1614

Michael Drayton
Idea, the Shepherd's Garland (poem) 1593

Ben Jonson
The Sad Shepherd (play) 1640

Christopher Marlowe
"The Passionate Shepherd to His Love" (poem) 1599

Andrew Marvell
"Ametas and Thestylis Making Hay-Ropes" (poem) 1681
"Bermudas" (poem) 1681
"Damon the Mower" (poem) 1681
"The Garden" (poem) 1681
"The Mower against Gardens" (poem) 1681

John Milton
"Comus" (poem) 1634
"L'Allegro" (poem) 1634
"Lycidas" (poem) 1637
Paradise Lost (epic poem) 1667

Walter Raleigh
"The Nymph's Reply to the Shepherd" (poem) 1600

William Shakespeare
As You Like It (play) 1598
The Winter's Tale (play) 1609
The Tempest (play) 1611

Philip Sidney
Lady of May (masque) 1578
Arcadia (epic poem) 1590
Astrophel and Stella (sonnet sequence) 1591

Edmund Spenser
The Shepheardes Calender (eclogues) 1579
The Faerie Queene (epic poem) 1595

OVERVIEWS AND GENERAL STUDIES

William Empson (essay date 1935)

SOURCE: "Proletarian Literature," in *Some Versions of Pastoral,* New Directions, 1968, pp. 11-15.

[*In the following excerpt from a work first published in 1935, Empson contends that pastoral literature reflects an impulse to clarify difficult issues by restating them in terms spoken by common folk, thus emphasizing their universal nature.*]

The essential trick of the old pastoral, which was felt to imply a beautiful relation between rich and poor. was to make simple people express strong feelings (felt as the most universal subject, something fundamentally true about everybody) in learned and fashionable language (so that you wrote about the best subject in the best way). From seeing the two sorts of people combined like this you thought better of both; the best parts of both were used. The effect was in some degree to combine in the reader or author the merits of the two sorts; he was made to mirror in himself more completely the effective elements of the society he lived in. This was not a process that you could explain in the course of writing pastoral; it was already shown by the clash between style and theme, and to make the clash work in the right way (not become funny) the writer must keep up a firm pretence that he was unconscious of it. Indeed the usual process for putting further meanings into the pastoral situation was to insist that the shepherds were rulers of sheep, and so compare them to politicians or bishops or what not; this piled the heroic convention onto the pastoral one, since the hero was another symbol of his whole society. Such a pretence no doubt makes the characters unreal, but not the feelings expressed or even the situation described; the same pretence is often valuable in real life. I should say that it was over this fence that pastoral came down in England after the Restoration. The arts, even music, came to depend more than before on knowing about foreign culture, and Puritanism, suspicious of the arts, was only not strong among the aristocracy. A feeling gradually got about that any one below the upper middles was making himself ridiculous, being above himself, if he showed any signs of keeping a sense of beauty at all, and this feeling was common to all classes. It takes a general belief as harsh and as unreal as this to make the polite pretence of pastoral seem necessarily absurd. Even so there was a successful school of mock-pastoral for so long as the upper and lower classes were consciously less Puritan than the middle. When that goes the pastoral tricks of thought take refuge in child-cult.

One strong help for the pastoral convention was the tradition, coming down from the origin of our romantic love-poetry in the troubadours, that its proper tone is one of humility, that the proper moments to dramatise in a love-affair are those when the lover is in despair. (Much theorising might be done in praise of this convention; some of it comes into Poe's absurd proof that melancholy is the most poetical of the tones. For one thing the mere fact that you don't altogether believe in the poet's expressions of despair makes you feel that he has reserves of strength.) Granted this, the low man has only to shift his humility onto his love affairs to adopt the dignity of a courtly convention. There is a good example in *As You Like It*; we see Corin for a moment bewailing his hopeless love with an older shepherd, and then the gentry try to get food out of him.

> CLOWN. Holla! you, clown!
> ROSALIND. Peace, fool, he's not thy kinsman.
> CORIN. Who calls?
> CLOWN. Your betters, sir.
> CORIN. Else they are very wretched.

Rosalind has heard the previous conversation, but no doubt she would understand this anyway; the shepherd is giving himself airs rather than being humble, but he has every right to it, and the court clown is silenced for the rest of the scene.

The convention was, of course, often absurdly artificial; the praise of simplicity usually went with extreme flattery of a patron (dignified as a symbol of the whole society, through the connection of pastoral with heroic), done so that the author could get some of the patron's luxuries; it allowed the flattery to be more extreme because it helped both author and patron to keep their self-respect. So it was much parodied, especially to make the poor man worthy but ridiculous, as often in Shakespeare; nor is this merely snobbish when in its full form. The simple man becomes a clumsy fool who yet has better 'sense' than his betters and can say things more fundamentally true; he is 'in contact with nature,' which the complex man needs to be, so that Bottom is not afraid of the fairies; he is in contact with the mysterious forces of our own nature, so that the clown has the wit of the Unconscious; he can speak the truth because he has nothing to lose. Also the idea that he is in contact with nature, therefore 'one with the universe' like the Senecan man, brought in a suggestion of stoicism; this made the thing less unreal since the humorous poor man is more obviously stoical than profound. And there may be obscure feelings at work, which I am unable to list, like those about the earth-touching Buddha. Another use of the clown (itself a word for the simple countryman) should be mentioned here; the business of the macabre, where you make a clown out of death. Death in the Holbein Dance of Death, a skeleton still skinny, is often an elegant and charming small figure whose wasp waist gives him a certain mixed-sex quality, and though we are to think otherwise he conceives himself as poking fun; he is seen at his best when piping to an idiot clown and leading him on, presumably to some precipice, treating this great coy figure with so gay and sympathetic an admiration that the picture stays in one's mind chiefly as a love scene. It is a far cry from pastoral, but the clown has such feelings behind him among his sources of strength.

Thus both versions, straight and comic, are based on a double attitude of the artist to the worker, of the complex man to the simple one ('I am in one way better, in another not so good'), and this may well recognise a permanent truth about the aesthetic situation.

Frank Kermode (essay date 1952)

SOURCE: Introduction to *English Pastoral Poetry: From*

the Beginnings to Marvell, edited by Frank Kermode, George Harrap and Company, 1952, pp. 11-44.

[*In the following excerpt, Kermode looks at the scope of the pastoral form, especially as it was used by English Renaissance poets; outlines its history and its critical and philosophical background; and discusses the general theory of Imitation as it relates to the pastoral.*]

> Jove, Jove! this shepherd's passion
> Is much upon my fashion.
>
> > *As You Like It,* II, iv, 56-57.
>
> Hast any philosophy in thee, shepherd?
>
> > *Ibid.,* III, i, 21.

Pastoral is one of the 'kinds' of poetry, like Epic, Tragedy, and Satire. We still know what these 'kinds' are, though we probably attach less importance to them than earlier readers did. To an Elizabethan critic they were natural; men had discovered, not devised, them. A poet who wrote in some novel form not recognized as a 'kind' was liable to be called to account, and accused of a breach of decorum, which is an offence against nature. Pastoral, though it ranked below some of the other 'kinds' of poetry, had, during the period which most concerns us, this official protection, and the Elizabethan schoolboy learned its laws as part of his rhetorical training. Yet to Dr Johnson it was a form "easy, vulgar, and therefore disgusting"—he was writing about *Lycidas*—and to us it probably suggests the word 'artificial' rather than the word 'natural.'

We can perhaps learn something from the use of the word 'artificial' in this connexion. For us it suggests mannerism, triviality, lack of seriousness, possibly even the *ersatz.* But for the Elizabethan it was usually high praise. "Our vulgar Poesie," says Puttenham, a good critic,

> cannot shew it selfe either gallant or gorgious, if any lymme be left naked and bare and not clad in his kindly[1] clothes and coulours,[2] such as may convey them somewhat out of sight, that is from the common course of ordinary speach and capacitie of the vulgar iudgement, and yet being artificially handled must need yeld it much more bewtie and commendation.

And Puttenham is speaking, not merely of Pastoral, but of all poetry. He is recommending the poet to be as 'unnatural' as possible, though he would not have used that word. He meant that to do the work of Art the poet must be artificial; and the work of Art was no less than the improvement or development of Nature. There are great difficulties in this word 'Nature,' as the Elizabethans themselves realized. They would argue, for example, that Art itself is an instrument of Nature. But the chief meaning, as it concerns us here at the moment, may best be expressed as 'the antithesis of Art,' the wild or savage as opposed to the cultivated, the material upon which Art works. And this opposition is nowhere so evident and acute as in Pastoral, for in this 'kind' the cultivated, in their artificial way, reflect upon and describe, for their own ends, the

natural life. For reasons we shall have to consider, this natural life was normally associated with shepherds.

At first sight it must seem odd that so considerable a proportion of European literature should concern itself with rustics, and even odder that it should concentrate on a small class of rustics. It will probably be easier to understand if we devote a little time to the history of the kind, and its critical justification. It must not be forgotten that when a new kind is founded its literary momentum may carry it far beyond the particular situation from which it took its origin; that is to say, the literary tradition is carried on by one writer imitating another despite the fact that the world of the second is different from that of the first. He is asking his readers to judge him by a purely literary criterion, and his mind is working in accordance with one of the laws of literary history which lays it down that to imitate a classic writer is the same as imitating Nature. Nature and Homer, so Pope tells us, are the same. The theory of Imitation has for good or ill a great deal to do with pastoral poetry, and it needs to be expounded in connexion with our present purposes. It seems, therefore, that this approach to the Pastoral of the English Renaissance involves three main considerations, which are in fact closely related to each other: we must look at the history of the kind, at its critical and philosophical background, and at the general theory of Imitation as it affects Pastoral. But first, we must try to understand its scope and fertility.

THE NATURE OF PASTORAL POETRY

Some modern writers use the term 'Pastoral' to describe any work which concerns itself with the contrast between simple and complicated ways of living; its method is to exalt the naturalness and virtue of the simple man at the expense of the complicated one, whether the former be a shepherd, or a child, or a working-man. This is perfectly justifiable, although the title given to the kind emphasizes that the natural man is conventionally a shepherd. There were reasons for this, but when the old feeling about shepherds, about which I shall be speaking shortly, faded, the preoccupation of the Pastoral with them tended to increase its 'artificiality.' [A necessary result of this is that there is much pastoral poetry which must be sympathetically read with reference to the convention in which it is written; otherwise it will certainly seem a barren or frigidly ornamental literary exercise, as *Lycidas* did to Johnson. Milton could not impress *him* by claiming that he and King "drove a field" and 'battened their flocks with the fresh dews of night'; "we know," says Johnson, "that they never drove a field, and that they had no flocks to batten."[3] And to Johnson it seemed that Pastoral was useful only to give young poets something to cut their teeth on. "It seems natural for a young poet to initiate himself by Pastorals, which, not professing to imitate real life, require no experience . . ."[4] If we are to avoid Johnson's mistake we must be aware of what the poets who wrote artificially about shepherds were trying to do; clearly they had in mind a great deal of earlier pastoral writing which had established the conventions within which they worked, and assumed in their readers a knowledge of the history of the kind. That is why our historical inquiry must be directed, not only upon the general situation which produces significant contrasts between the natural and the cultivated, but upon the tradition of literary Pastoral which is carried on by one poet's imitating another. But first, the more general topic of the scope of Pastoral.

The first condition of pastoral poetry is that there should be a sharp difference between two ways of life, the rustic and the urban. The city is an artificial product, and the pastoral poet invariably lives in it, or is the product of its schools and universities. Considerable animosity may exist between the townsman and the countryman. Thus the 'primitive' may be sceptical about the justice of a state of affairs which makes him live under rude conditions while the town-poet lives in polite society. On the other hand, the town- or court-poet has a certain contempt for the peasant (sometimes very strong); and both primitive and court-poet write verse which reflects these attitudes. Occasionally there is a certain similarity of subject. Townsman and rustic alike may consider the idea that at a remote period in history nature gave forth her fruits without the aid of man's labour and worship. Perhaps, somewhere, she still does so. This idea that the world has been a better place and that men have degenerated is remarkably widespread, and a regular feature of pastoral poetry. We have abused Nature, by breaking its laws or falling into sin, and we are therefore steadily deteriorating so that our only hope is for a fresh start, after some kind of redemption. The restoration of the Golden Age is a theme of Virgilian Pastoral, and was naturally taken over in the Pastoral of the Christian era. All such ideas are more ancient than the pastoral convention, but they naturally became attached to it in the course of time. They occur in primitive poetry as well as in the poetry of the cultivated, but this should not deceive us into thinking that there can be primitive Pastoral. The first condition of Pastoral is that it is an urban product.

Nevertheless, it is as closely connected with earlier poetry as the Epic is with the lays of the 'heroic age.' For example, although the literary tradition of the Golden Age is securely rooted in Virgil, Ovid, Seneca, Juvenal, and Boëthius, we may be sure that the primary impulse, human resentment at the conditions and struggles of life, vitalizes the myth in its literary form and establishes its kinship with similar primitive myths which occur in almost every recorded culture from Mycenæan to American Negro. Something better must have existed, and for some folly or sin we can easily recognize in ourselves we have been turned out of the garden and can only hope to return.

Satire, also an urban 'kind,' assumes that in its own milieu, the metropolis, it discovers the extremest forms of degeneracy, which it exposes by contrasting it with some better way of life—that is, some earlier way of life; the farther back you go the better. One would expect Satire to get better and better, as the conditions grow more odiously stimulating; and in Rome this happened, for from being a

comparatively good-humoured affair it took over various rights from other forms, including that of direct and vigorous attack on the vices of society and individuals, and culminated in the fierce and gloomy Juvenal, who is the genuine prototype of European Satire, though the last of the considerable Roman practitioners. In the heyday of English Pastoral the satirist, with Juvenal never far from his thoughts, is always at hand, flogging away with his scourge of untrimmed decasyllables; sometimes, by a pardonable etymological confusion, imagining himself a satyr, but never to be reconciled to the loss of virtue always entailed in wresting a metropolis out of the gentler countryside. *Pietas, gravitas, virtus*—these are qualities which wither in acquisitive communities; leisure increases, and with it the arts and the vices. By contrast the rural nation of a few generations back appears as free of vice as it is of culture in the narrow sense of a refined minority pursuit. Society outside the town walls is still comparatively simple, and still natural—especially in properly pastoral areas, where the country has to be rich and fresh—whereas the town has viciously supplied imagined wants in nature with the art of brick and stone. Obviously there is common ground between Pastoral and Satire; but Pastoral—here I limit the meaning of the word to literature which deals with rural life, and exclude other 'versions' of Pastoral—Pastoral flourishes at a particular moment in the urban development, the phase in which the relationship of metropolis and country is still evident, and there are no children (as there are now) who have never seen a cow.

Heroic poetry celebrates the achievements of an age of heroes in the verse of sophisticated poets like Homer. "The result," writes Professor G. Thomson,[5] "was a dynamic tension between them [the poets] and their material, and so deeply had they absorbed their material that this tension appears as something internal in the heroes of the story." He then quotes a speech of Sarpedon's which certainly justifies the comment that it is "not the voice of a robber chief."[6] The heroic poet, believing in his right, and that of his patrons, to the heroic life, and yet experiencing a complex response to the recounting of that life which the heroes themselves could not have imagined, is under extraordinary pressure. The position of the pastoral poet is even less simple than that of the heroic poet; although his rustics are in a way contemptible in their simplicity and coarseness, they have a way of life which is admirable because it is natural, and are, in fact, a local and contemporary version of Golden Age humanity, without the intrigues of the Court and the money-grubbing of the city. The shepherd in particular leads a deliciously idle life and whiles away the time playing a pipe. He became the type of the natural life, uncomplicated, contemplative, and in sympathy with Nature as the townsman could never be. He is the measure of the cultivated man's unnaturalness: he has plenty of time for thought; when he weeps the Nature with which he lives in such sympathy weeps also. Unlike the townsman, he does not meddle with Nature. (Of course, one believes this only in a certain frame of mind, or when striking a certain attitude, like that adopted by Marvell in

The Mower against Gardens, or by the seventeenth-century French poet Theophile when he said:

> La nature est inimitable
> Et dans sa beauté véritable
> Elle éclate si vivement
> Que l'art gaste tous ses ouvrages,
> Et luy fait plustost mille outrages
> Qu'il ne luy donne un ornement.[7]

Unlike the townsman, he lives a contemplative and not an active life. This, as everybody knew from the story of Cincinnatus, and as Cicero had said of Scipio Africanus, was the best preparation for virtue. God preferred Abel before Cain, the contemplative life of the shepherd before the active life of the farmer. In Hesiod as well as in the Gospels a divine nativity is announced to shepherds. Their craft endows them with a kind of purity, almost a kind of holiness.

The simplest kind of pastoral poetry assumes that the quiet wildness of the country is better than the cultivated and complex life of the hurrying city and court. These places are unfortunate islands of luxury in a green sea of simplicity; Nature's handmaid, Art, has driven Nature out, and at best the city is a garden, tortured by artist-gardeners who

> . . . the cherry vex
> To procreate without a sex;

while, in the fields beyond,

> Every mower's wholesome heat
> Smells like an Alexander's sweat.

It does not concern itself with the subtleties which Polixenes offers to the reluctant Perdita. Living in his city garden with its sophisticated philosophies, its exotic plants, its cultivated music, the poet contemplates the life he has rejected, the life of the healthy countryside, with its simple manners, natural flowers, and rude pipings. The die is cast; in the great no man's land of the fields even the grasshoppers will mock him—as Marvell said in his lines on Nun Appleton House. There is no going back; the Golden Age is a moving fiction, the *vendange* and the hock-cart are charming and interesting, and upon them one may construct the amusements of a polite society; but the gentleman is now committed to another way of life. And always at the back of this literary attitude to Nature is the shadow of its opposite; the knowledge that Nature is rough, and the natural life in fact rather an animal affair; by long cultivation men have improved the natural breed, and the difference between the cultivated and the natural is the difference between a Ferdinand and a Caliban.[8] It is surely inevitable that in such a situation the poet should allow his complexities to colour his talk of the rustic subject, as the Epic poet projected his intellectual tensions on to the hero. Sarpedon appeared as a man of extraordinary sensibility; the shepherd appears as philosopher and poet.

Provided, then, that one does not allow the hard view of Nature as crude and rough to overset the dreamier view of its as uncorrupt,[9] one may well find that the rustic, and in particular the shepherd, has fascinating possibilities for the cultivated poet. A natural piper and singer, he is easily made to stand for the poet. It may be that the cultivated poet at a very early date learned his themes from the rustic primitive. In Ancient Greece and in the Europe of the Middle Ages the women at the corn-mills sang their *cantilen molares,* songs which told of a former Age of Gold, under the reign of a peaceful king whose sudden death brought it to an end; they dreamed of rest as a hungry man does of food. Another theme of the peasant singer was the encounter of rustic and courtier, in which the rustic triumphed. This was a kind of song which certainly had its origin in sheep-country, as modern French scholars have shown. Both of these themes, sophisticated and given a new orientation, belong to the stock of the pastoral poet. He will also observe that the figures of the shepherd and the shepherd-king have accumulated through the ages new and deeper meanings; if the pastoral poet is late enough in time he will never be unconscious of the persistent pastoral imagery of Christ,[10] in sermon and parable, or of the manner in which the Church has adapted that imagery. (The connexion between this imagery and that of the formal Pastoral was made explicit by Petrarch.) The Christian Pastoralist will also remember that the Song of Solomon, with all its unfathomable significance to the allegorical divine, is an epithalamium cast in the form of a dream-Pastoral. The poet's language is therefore capable of venturing close to, and across, that vague frontier which in the great periods of poetry separates secular and religious imagery.

These are merely a few random hints as to the complexity of Pastoral, treated abstractly. In the England of 1600, which produced most of the poetry in this collection, the relationship between the poet and his theme was governed in these and in many other ways, and affected by more specific religious, political, and economic tensions. Evidently it cannot be properly understood in isolation from the 'kind' within whose conventions it is written.

These general remarks might be summed up as follows. Pastoral depends upon an opposition between the simple, or natural, and the cultivated. Although this opposition can be complex, the bulk of pastoral poetry treats it quite simply, and assumes that natural men are purer and less vicious than cultivated men, and that there exists between them and Nature a special sympathy. The natural man is also wise and gifted in a different way from the cultivated man. By reason of his simplicity he is a useful subject for cultivated study, since his emotions and virtues are not complicated by deterioration and artificiality. The themes of the cultivated poet may be connected with those of the primitive poet, much as the garden is related to the open countryside, but the cultivated poet sophisticates them and endows them with learned allusions. Thus the Pastoral can become a vehicle for poetic speculation on religious mysteries, on the hierarchy of the Church, and also on poetry itself.

Origins and Development of the 'Kind'

There are extant very old songs concerning shepherds, which may be connected with pastoral poetry. One dates from the early (*i.e.,* Sumerian) civilization of Mesopotamia; in it a girl prefers a farmer (socially superior because economically more highly organized) to a shepherd:

> Never shall the shepherd marry me;
> Never shall he drape me in his tufted cloth;
> Never shall his finest wool touch me.
> Me, the maiden, shall the farmer,
> And he only, take in marriage—
> The farmer who can grow beans,
> The farmer who can grow grain.[11]

The shepherd spurned here is quite like the rejected swain in the Twentieth Idyll of Theocritus. The simplicity which accompanies the poverty of the shepherd is celebrated in many pre-Pastoral myths; in particular, there is the myth of the royal child (to the Christian, the type of Christ), cast away or exiled in infancy, who "receives the ministrations of shepherds, and is reared by a foster-father of humble birth";[12] a myth later treated in pastoral poetry by many poets, and especially by Spenser and Shakespeare.

The connexion between myth of this kind and the beginnings of Pastoral is obscure. Little is known about the sources of Theocritus, the first pastoral poet, who was born in Syracuse about 310 B.C., and lived in Alexandria under the patronage of Ptolemy Philadelphus. These sources may have had local characteristics which Theocritus generalized when he established the form. It is impossible to guess what these might have been. It may, however, be supposed that some pastoral themes, like those of gift-bringing and song-contest, originated in the sheep-pastures of Sicily. It is known that Theocritus, in those Idylls which deal with country life, made a fairly thorough attempt to write in rustic language, 'placing' his rustics socially by using the Doric dialect, and allowing their hexameters to be occasionally the vehicles of coarse or bawdy expressions. Theocritus found that the country folk were interesting in themselves, and worth recording in these relaxed hexameters. He did not himself do much by way of refining the poetic-philosophic potentialities of the Pastoral, but simply offered a courtly version, presumably substantially accurate, of certain rustic activities as he had observed them in Sicily and on the island of Cos. This in itself was an achievement related to, and in a sense bred out of, the needs of his time. "Theocritus," says Professor Jackson Knight, "brought the country itself out from the mere relief of the choric ode, and normal, active love out from the background of a story, on to the central stage, where highly complex urban communities needed it most."[13]

We find in Theocritus the court-poet, dependant of tyrants, habitué of the advanced literary communities of Alexandria, many signs of the typical pastoral attitude. In his First Idyll he celebrates the death of the shepherd-hero Daphnis, which in folklore had represented the annual death of Nature itself. Thus the "pathetic fallacy," as Ruskin called the convention by which Nature is made to share human sorrow, enters the pastoral tradition at the very beginning. From this Idyll developed the whole elaborate convention of the Pastoral Elegy, which perhaps reached its climax in Milton's *Lycidas* and in his *Epitaphium Damonis*. Yet Daphnis could have meant little to Theocritus except in the vicarious way in which the townsman enjoys the serious rites of the countryside. The pastoral flute was an instrument not of utility but of nostalgia, the nostalgia of a sophisticated poet for an art which was not yet a matter for hair-splitting and casuistry. And although Theocritus was more content than any pastoral poet up to the time of the Elizabethans to give his readers a straightforward account of the simple completeness of bucolic culture, and let them draw from it the conclusions to which he himself had come, he did not always avoid that projection of his own values and interests on his characters which we have noted as being characteristic of Pastoral. In the Seventh Idyll, for instance, the emphasis in the description of the harvest festival in Cos is on the fact that the city poets are playing at shepherds in this rich and authentic autumn setting. Actual poets are discussed under fancy names.

> So 'shepherd' can on occasion mean 'poet'; to sing or play in shepherd fashion is to write or publish poetry. . . . The first step had been taken towards the days when, if anyone was called a shepherd in poetry, it would have been a startling discovery to find that he really was a country fellow who got his living by looking after actual sheep and had never published or tried to publish anything in his life.[14]

Kinds of poetry are not unchangeable entities, though the Renaissance found that easy to believe. Theocritus is obviously a pastoral poet, and in some ways the most accomplished of all who explore the form; but conditions which later became inseparable from the kind are only sketched and hinted at in its earliest exponent.[15] The work of developing these hints fell to a line of comparatively undistinguished poets who were writing between the time of Theocritus and the time of Virgil. For these poets Theocritus was the model, and from him they derived authority for the manner of their writing, giving him the status of a classic. Their themes, their metre (the hexameter), and their dialect (the Doric) they derived from him.

The position of Theocritus thus resembles in some respects that of Homer. He is the acknowledged classic of pastoral poetry, though his influence upon the tradition is less direct and in the long run less formative than that of Virgil. But he quickly became a true classic, the subject of imitation by later poets working in the same line.

Imitation is one of the fundamental laws of literary history, for it arises whenever a poet contemplates poetry. It is the function which gives literary history a meaning in terms of itself, and provides the channels of literary tradition. It is a wide concept, covering many related aspects of literary activity, and when used dogmatically it has often had very damaging and confusing consequences. But when that is said it must still be remembered that Imitation, in so far as it implies the need for an awareness of the best that has been thought and said, and the best ways of thinking and saying it, an awareness of what a classic is and how it should modify later work, is a doctrine of prime import for the study of literature, and particularly of modern literature; for it was during the Renaissance that the characteristic modern attitude to the ancients (the classics) was adopted and defined.

The critics of the Renaissance sometimes named the poet's chief requirements as being Art, Imitation, and Exercise; these requirements relate to the knowledge, study, and practice of the best models and methods of their medium. Another requirement, that of native genius, is also mentioned; unfortunately, not all practitioners of poetry have this, and the result was a good deal of poetry which depended upon critical laws and the pedantic imitation of detail. The consequence is a degree of tedium which has tended to bring the whole doctrine into disrepute as a dreary rhetorical substitute for poetry. This bad kind of Imitation is not confined to poetry; two great, but very different, humanists, Politian and Erasmus, were driven to complain of the absurdities into which those neo-Latinists fell who insisted upon the closest imitation of Cicero's style down to the last *esse videatur.* If we consider the degree to which Imitation penetrated the educational systems of the Renaissance and shaped the minds of all its writers we shall not be surprised that it occasionally had such dull and mechanical consequences. But not with the true scholar and poet who had laboured to understand it in ancient criticism and ancient literature—who understood that, although the letter may kill, the spirit will always give life, and that the doctrine was, among other things, a rational interpretation of the true relationship between the ancient and the modern world. Not, in fact, with Jonson, whose many and close imitations of Horace, Juvenal, and other poets require far more explanation than that they happened to have said already whatever it was he proposed to say. They were his guides, he said, not his commanders. Like Pope and Milton, he distinguished between the essence and the accident in his model; like Pope, he inhabited the critical and moral environment of the classic civilization without forfeiting citizenship of his own. He understood Imitation, and I have sometimes felt that it is through Jonson that we, in a rather different world, might hope best to understand it, and to understand how it can be held responsible on the one hand for mountains of dullness and on the other for *Volpone* and *Lycidas.* To conclude this digression, it may be said that a measure of the importance of the doctrine historically is the possibility of maintaining that the great seventeenth-century war of Ancients and Moderns was really fought on divergent interpretations of Imitation, in the widest sense of the term.

But Imitation, even in its narrowest rhetorical sense, is not a modern doctrine; it was current in the schools of Alexandria and Rome. The imitators of Theocritus did not, so far as is known, explore, using him as a guide; they repro-

duced. The best-known Greek pastoral poem outside Theocritus is the elegy written for Bion, a second-century Alexandrian poet, which was formerly, but it seems incorrectly, attributed to Moschus, under whose name it still goes. This poem is the next link in the chain connecting the First Idyll of Theocritus with Milton.[16] It is written in literary Doric, with many allusions to Theocritus. Its connexion with rustic life is purely formal. Bion is a shepherd-poet who had gladdened Pan with his pipe and his songs; pastoral details are given allegorical significances by now very obscure. These details, however, themselves descended from Theocritus, who was already an edited classic, and perhaps the subject of commentary not merely philological but of the laboured and far-fetched sort that Virgil was later to receive. In Moschus there are in full measure those artifices of allegory and myth and language which, when they are separate from the genuine emotional and intellectual interests of Pastoral, give the kind its reputation as a matter of frigid ornament. His *Lament* is, in fact, the kind of poem Johnson thought *Lycidas* was.

There is no need, for our purposes, to say any more of post-Theocritean Greek pastoral poetry, or, indeed, of the dependent Latin tradition. "It would seem," says H. J. Rose, "that by the time of Nero one of the stock rhetorical exercises, a thing of which every passman was supposed to be capable, was to describe a country feast or praise the life of the countryman."[17] But meantime Virgil had intervened to change the merely rhetorical tradition.

Virgil seems to have gone straight to Theocritus for the model of his Imitation. He used him as a guide, not as a commander, and the result is poetry which it would be impossible to study as merely part of a rhetorical tradition. It is pastoral poetry which, for the first time, complicates the simple town-country contrast with serious reflections upon that contrast; which cultivates simplicity in decorated language; and which uses the country scene and rustic episode for allegorical purposes.

Robert Graves speaks of "the Virgilian pseudo-shepherd,"[18] and there would be no objection to the phrase if its tone were not slightly disparaging. The pastoral figures of the youthful Virgil are as sophisticated as his later Trojan emigrants. He places them in a remote paradise which he calls Arcadia, though in fact Arcadia was and is a rugged and unparadisial place; he could not use Sicily, as Theocritus had done, because it was over-familiar, though his Muses are the Pastoral Muses of Theocritus—*Sicelides Musæ.* Some of his most exquisite passages refer, as Mr Graves suggests, to vulgar and unpoetic contemporaries; he discusses contemporary agrarian questions; he flatters powerful men; he celebrates in exalted language homosexual love (though it should be remembered that this passion was not at the time regarded as peculiarly vicious). In fact, Virgil develops the hints of Theocritus in a very thorough way; he is derivative, and often translates (sometimes, it has been argued, even mistranslates) his master. Indeed, there seems to be a case for dismissing Virgil as a particularly 'artificial' writer of Pastoral, who simply "used the pastoral situation as a convenient rostrum for moral philosophy"[19] and for other even less reputable purposes. If the charge is fair it is a poor look-out for the remainder of the European bucolic corpus, in which Virgil is by far the most potent influence; one of the eclogues, the fourth, has perhaps the best claim of all pagan poetry to be considered, with respect to the whole culture of Christian Europe, seminal. Clearly this account of Virgil is incomplete.

Daphnis, the figure whom Virgil borrowed from Theocritus to do duty for Gallus, a friend lamenting his desertion by professional mistress, had a place in the Sicilian mythology that corresponds to that of various more familiar figures like Thomas the Rhymer, who took fairy brides under odd and stringent conditions. The similarity between the Greek Daphnis and the sensitive but worldly Gallus is of course somewhat remote, and Virgil does not force it, preferring to convey it by delicate allusion to the Theocritean character. But it is surely wrong to suggest that he was indifferent to the ultimate propriety of the analogy. A soldier-poet distressed by the defection of "an actress in low comedy who has left him to go off with a soldier"[20] may very well be celebrated in these terms, as the scheming monopolists of Elizabeth's court were glorified in great poetry as knights of chivalry. There is a basic similarity in the situation of Gallus and Daphnis. Again, the lament for the dead Daphnis in Eclogue V may be about Julius Cæsar; both were gods, and both were shepherds—Cæsar of his people. To adherents of Octavian Cæsar was also a saviour. The Pastoral is a leveller—it has to assume that "you can say everything about complex people by a complete consideration of simple people."[21] But in order to do so you must project polite complexities on the rude pastoral situation. When the peasant is nothing but a courtier in disguise, when the sillabubs are, as it were, pasteurized, there is nothing left but an emptily artificial Trianon masquerade. Despite Virgil's polite projections and his well-groomed hinds, he has not done this; he has left the situation intact, and the characteristically urban plight of Gallus, as well as the political murder of Julius Cæsar, yield a fuller significance when they are appraised in terms of a world schematically simple and sensitive to magic and poetry.

Virgil's is the supreme achievement of classical Pastoral; the virtues of his English rivals derive from a revaluation of the relationship between the actual town-country situation and the poetic tradition. He is perhaps as far removed from the facts of rural society as it is safe to go; his imitators support this suggestion by adopting a sterile pose even farther removed Virgil's influence is therefore not without its dangers; it is easier to reproduce the letter than the spirit. The best of later pastoral poetry arduously achieved the Virgilian feat of rediscovering the true impulse of the classical form.

The most influential of Virgil's eclogues is the fourth. This poem, with its hundred problems for the scholar, has a hundred virtues for the poet. It conquers new and legiti-

mate territory for the Pastoral, and gives licence for a new and more authoritative tone—*paulo maiora canamus.* Above all, it suggests to other poets an unsuspected complexity in the 'pseudo-shepherd' and his associated imagery, a suggestion partly responsible for the profundity characteristic of so many later poems. The view of this eclogue generally held during the formative period of modern Pastoral was that, by employing the dicta of the Cumæan sibyl, Virgil had been enabled to prophesy the birth of Christ a few decades later, and some modern scholars have found traces of evidence that he was in fact indebted to the sibylline remains. But that does not matter. The enormous influence of Virgil in the Renaissance derives in some degree from his strange medieval reputation as a mage and pre-Christian prophet, and this reputation is undoubtedly dependent to some extent on the acceptance of the 'Messianic' Eclogue as a pagan prophecy of Christ—an acceptance made with the authority of St Augustine. In the official hierarchy of kinds Pastoral was always classed as one of the lower manifestations of poetry on account of the ostensible meanness of its milieu and characters; the Fourth Eclogue authorized an occasional 'unkindly' majesty of diction, of which later poets were to take advantage. The influence of this poem extends far beyond the pastoral kind, but within that kind it is often at work when there is no explicit reference to Virgil. It is the point at which the Golden Age of Saturn, the return of which the poet foresees, mingles with the Christian vision of man in paradisial state before Adam's sin, and after redemption is complete.

Virgil may therefore be regarded as a liberator of the Pastoral. The immensity of his achievement did nevertheless induce in his imitators a servility which, if unaccompanied by a proper sense of the fullness of that achievement and an awareness of what each poet needs to do again for himself, gave rise to the bad kind of imitation, which imitated the letter and not the spirit. This was not Virgil's fault. He did for Theocritus what he was to do for Homer; he established the classical poem and suggested many of its recognized variant forms. These remarks, which must conclude the scanty appraisal of the Eclogues which is all we have space for here, really say no more than that Pastoral would have been another, and a lesser, thing had Virgil never applied himself to the exploration of its problems and possibilities. . . .

RENAISSANCE THEORIES OF PASTORAL

A reasonable idea of the normal Renaissance definition of Pastoral may be derived from Puttenham's remarks on the Eclogue in his *Arte of English Poesie:*[22]

> the Poet devised the *Eglogue* . . . not of purpose to counterfait or represent the rusticall manner of loves and communication: but under the vaile of homely persons, and in rude speeches to insinuate and glaunce at greater matters, and such as perchance had not bene safe to have disclosed in any other sort, which may be perceived by the Eglogues of *Virgill,* in which are treated by figure matters of greater importance then the

loves of *Titirus* and *Corydon.* These Eglogues came after to containe and enforme morall discipline, for the
amendment of mans behaviour, as be those of *Mantuan*[23] and other modern poets.

Puttenham, as usual, displays considerable common sense.
He avoids the doctrine that the Pastoral is the oldest of
genres because of its association with primitive rustic
communities, and confines himself to a description of what
it was really like in the hands of authors like Mantuan,
who imitated Virgil and included topical references and
ecclesiastical allegories. He insists on the paradox inherent
in the kind; though rudely written, it deals with great matters. Decorum insists that the proper style for Pastoral is
low, or rude, though there is precedent (invoked by Spenser
and Milton) for higher flights. Sidney, who in his own *Arcadia* wrote a heroic Pastoral, a blend of two kinds, pretends in his *Apologie for Poetrie* that Pastoral is a possible
weak point in the defences of poetry, where its opponents
may choose to assault it, "for perchance where the hedge
is lowest they will soonest leap over." Webbe says that,
despite its lowness, the Pastoral can offer much profitable
delight, and in this he includes both flattery and inveighing
against abuses. Although poets preferred to use a decora-
tive licence, decorum nevertheless insisted that Pastoral,
like Satire, belonged to the base style, "to be holden within
their tether by a low, myld and simple maner of utterance,
creeping rather then clyming, & marching rather then
mounting upwardes." This tenet explains in a general way
the provincialisms and archaisms conscientiously used by
Spenser in his Eclogues. Although they descend ultimately
from the Doric of Theocritus, it is not even certain that
Spenser knew the Greek poet at first hand; he is showing
his familiarity with the laws of poetry and the practice of
the best modern French poets.

The most thorough examination of the status of the kind
was that undertaken by the Italian dramatist Guarini, his
supporters, and his opponents, in a long controversy about
Guarini's pastoral drama, *Il Pastor Fido,* towards the end
of the sixteenth century. Guarini had been challenged by a
certain Jasone de Nores, who held that pastoral drama was
socially and morally useless, and also that it contravened
the ancient laws of poetry. Pastoral, said de Nores, was
not only useless to town-dwellers, but might even do harm
by inducing them to live in the country; if the pastoral life
was unfavourably treated, then harm was done to the rustics as well. He thought shepherds particularly poor subjects for drama, since they were lazy and lacking elaborate
manners and customs. The Ancients avoided these difficulties; for one thing, their pastoral poems were all short
eclogues which did not infringe the laws of probability, or
make shepherds talk like princes or philosophers. Guarini's reply is interesting because he was forced to make explicit the rationale of Pastoral. He relies upon the historical argument that the pastoral society is the earliest of all,
and that when every one was a shepherd there must have
been shepherd kings, shepherd poets, shepherd warriors,
and so on, so that in writing about shepherds one can
write freely about the concerns of the modern world. They
are all reflected in a very simple form in the hypothetical

pastoral community. He is at some pains to explain that
love, a special concern of Renaissance Pastoral, can be
easily and pleasantly studied in this context.[24]

Such arguments are of little interest save in that they show
a certain concern about the historical justification of this
apparently somewhat arbitrary form. Although Guarini
shows some independence of the strict classicist interpretation of the kind, he is a poet of the second or third rank,
and shows no real understanding of the true philosophic
importance of the kind, or of the peculiar contribution
which his age was able to make to it. His countryman
Tasso, in his *Aminta,* is much closer to such an understanding, and in France the kind was patiently and successfully investigated; but it is not until we consider English Pastoral that we can recognize an appreciation,
almost intuitive and certainly remarkably complete, of
pastoral poetry as it was shaped by the pressure of the
age's thought and sensibility. For this understanding we
look not to critics, but to poets. . . .

NATURE IN THE RENAISSANCE PASTORAL

When Marvell, at the end of our period, wrote about a
mower's hatred of gardens, he was representing the world
of Nature, the uncultivated, the pure, by the untamed, un-
corrupted fields; and the world of Art, the civilized, the
cultivated, the sphere in which men had meddled with Nature, by the garden. He was, of course, simplifying for his
own purposes a difficult philosophical opposition between
Art and Nature, but he is none the less putting, with considerable subtlety, a point of view which was frequently
expressed in the Renaissance, and which recurs with some
persistence in the history of our literature. Probably the
contrast between town and country—the social aspect of
the great Art-Nature antithesis which is philosophically the
basis of pastoral literature—was more poignant at that
time than it has been since. London was becoming a modern metropolis, with a distinctively metropolitan ethos, before the eyes of its citizens, who were by tradition and
even by upbringing much more rural than any town-
dweller can now be. The plays of Jonson, and some of
Shakespeare's too, contain many references to the new
morality, the new men, the new social standing of the
commercial classes, the growth of wealth not based upon
the soil; and the death of an old order which hated usury
and did not imagine that cakes and ale were hostile to virtue. The great Astrophel himself, like many other courtiers, was deeply in debt, and consciously living the life of
a dead and lamented epoch—a kind of golden age of chivalry—in the age which saw the inauguration of modern
capitalist finance. Puritanism, at its best a way of life and
worship worthy of fine minds, was legitimately associated,
by Jonson and others, with a tendency to hypocritical self-
aggrandizement and to a mean interference with the traditional pleasures and customs of others. Essentially an urban growth, it was suspicious of country matters, and its
hatred for the maypole and its associated sports, which Puritans rightly conjectured to be descended from pagan religious rites, was logical in a religious attitude which also

condemned the drama. The satirist looked about him in a town which was turning into a metropolis, and observed that its citizen body was stratifying into new classes, actively discontented with the old dispensation, and living under a municipal authority predominantly Puritan. The court was held to be corrupt and affected; the increase in luxury and artificiality visible in the lives of courtier and burgher alike deeply troubled Jonson, who found that the language was imitating "the public riot." When Jonson turned from Satire to Pastoral, at the end of his career, he lamented the death of an order as old, he thought, as the countryside; a way of life in which generosity, in the fullest sense of that word, accompanied a purity of life and pleasure which the Juvenalian town had exchanged for disease, obscurantism, affectation, and bigotry.[25] The moving passage from his *Sad Shepherd . . .* is one of the themes which occur frequently in Elizabethan Pastoral.

The contrast between town and country is frequently expressed in the literature of the period. There was a tendency to laugh at country folk, and this was a traditional activity; but there was also a tendency to idealize them. Overbury writes of a milkmaid:

> The golden ears of corn fall and kiss her feet when she reaps them, as if they wished to be bound and led prisoners by the same hand that felled them. Her breath is her own, which scents all the year long of June, like a new made haycock. She makes her hands hard with labour, and her heart soft with pity: and when winter evenings fall early (sitting at her merry wheel) she sings a defiance to the giddy wheel of fortune. . . . The garden and bee-hive are all her physic and chirurgery, and she lives the longer for it. . . . Thus lives she, and all her care is she may die in the spring-time, to have store of flowers stuck upon her winding-sheet.[26]

Something of the Elizabethan sense of the urgent beauty of the country life emerges in Nicholas Breton's dialogue, "The Courtier and the Countryman." The Countryman speaks:

> Now for the delight of our eyes, we have the May—painting of the earth, with flowers of dainty colours, and delicate sweets: we have the berries, the cherries, the peas and the beans, the plums and the codlings, in the month of June: in July the pears and the apples, the wheat, the rye, the barley and the oats, the beauty of the wide fields, and the labours with delight and mirth, and merry cheer at the coming home of the harvest cart. We have, again, in our woods the birds singing: in the pastures the cow lowing, the ewe bleating, the foal neighing, which profit and pleasure makes us better music than an idle note and a worse ditty, though I highly do commend music, when it is in the right key. Again, we have young rabbits that in a sunny morning sit washing their faces, while as I have heard there are certain old conies that in their beds sit painting of their faces. . . .

To all this, the worsted Courtier replies, "I can the better bear with your humour because it is more natural than artificial, yet could I wish you would not so clownify your

wit, as to bury your understanding under a clod of earth." Which earns him the reproof, "Now for your Nature and Art, I think better of a natural Art than an artifical Nature"; for this is a pastoral countryman, who understands the terms of the town. We might note what he has to say about love, the passion which occupies so much space in Elizabethan pastoral poetry:

> And for love, if it be in the world, I think it is in the country, for where envy, pride, and malice and jealousy makes buzzes in men's brains, what love can be in their hearts, howsoever it slip from their tongues? No, no, our turtles ever fly together, our swans ever swim together, and our loves live and die together. Now if such love be among you, it is worthy to be made much of, but if you like today and loathe tomorrow, if all your love be to laugh and lie down, or to hope of gain or reward, that is none of our love. . . .

Here is the Golden Age envisaged in the countryside, all the more poignantly because the countryside is still very near one's own doorstep. This tension between town and country seems to be productive of the special kind of literature we call Pastoral. Poets were interested in the contrast between the wild and the cultivated. But their interest was not dependent entirely upon social changes and the discovery of ancient Pastoral; the interest of Renaissance poets in Nature was stimulated by the discovery of countries in which men were living in a state of nature, unaffected by Art, and outside the scope of Grace. Anyone who turns to Montaigne's essay *Of Cannibals* may read an account of one sensitive and subtle reaction to the news from the New World. The travellers came back with their accounts of the natives, or even brought the savages back with them—Montaigne conversed with some. But, because there were two opinions about natural men, one holding that they were virtuous because unspoilt, and the other that they were vicious because they belonged to what the theologians called the state of nature as opposed to the state of grace, the travellers emphasized the evidence which suited the theory they favoured; some reported the New World savages to live in perfect concord and happiness (as Montaigne says they did), but others found them treacherous and devil-worshipping. Both these views fell in neatly with preconceptions already held and already expressed in literature and philosophy. On the one hand there is the classic expression of Golden Age happiness in the much-imitated chorus of Tasso's *Aminta;* this could easily be extended to the 'naturalist' libertine poetry of Donne and Carew and Randolph, which Marvell subtly countered in his poetry. On the other hand there is the deeper examination of Nature and its true relationship to Art and Grace which Spenser in *The Faerie Queene,* Shakespeare in his last comedies, and Milton in *Comus* undertook. Each of these poets sometimes presents Nature for what it is—that state from which men, by nurture and grace, have been led away. The generous 'salvage man' in Spenser is so by reason of the cultivated stock from which he sprang; his nature is improved by the action of grace. The King's sons in *Cymbeline* cannot suppress their nobility, and Caliban is natural and vile in contrast with Miranda, who has the virtues of nobility; *nobile,* it was believed, was a contraction of *non vile.* Comus rules over the realm of Nature, and attempts to deprave the lady, who is clad in the magical armour of nobility and chastity, by using the very arguments of the 'naturalist.'

This is only a very hurried glimpse of the serious philosophic element which penetrates the English Pastoral of the Renaissance. In the longer poems, and in the plays, it is rarely far from the surface—as, for example, in Fletcher's *The Faithful Shepherdess.* It mingles with serious attempts to reproduce the ancient tradition in the modern Eclogue by inventing a native Doric and adapting the equipment of the Sicilian shepherd to his English equivalent; with studious adaptations and translations of modern authors like Mantuan, Sannazaro, Marot, Ronsard, Montemayor, Tasso, and Guarini. Every device of literary Pastoral is found in some form or other in the poetry of this period; every use to which the kind can be put is exploited, from the ecclesiastical allegory which Googe derived from Mantuan to the elegies which Bryskett and Milton derived from Moschus. All the moral and scientific interests of the time found expression in the form, and the age's passion for allegory found the Pastoral a particularly congenial form of expression. In Spenser alone one may study almost every aspect of Renaissance Pastoral.[27] It is generally acknowledged that the publication of *The Shepheardes Calender,* in 1579, was one of the most important events in the history of English poetry, and not only in the history of Pastoral. In this work Spenser, while not ignoring the charms of the English pastoral scene, which often gave the work of his contemporaries a fresh, unstudied charm, brought into the tradition of English poetry the influence of every great pastoral poet of the past, from Theocritus to the modern French poets. As E. K. says, after a roll-call of the bucolic poets of the past, Spenser follows their "footing" everywhere, "yet so as few, but they be wel sented, can trace him out." Spenser's imagination worked freely within the classical tradition, which he explored in depth, but he was also capable of sustained efforts in heroic Pastoral of a sort not contemplated by the ancient poets. In the Sixth Book of the *Faerie Queene,* which is the Legend of Courtesy, we have the richest and most impressive example of a distinctively English development of the pastoral tradition, which was later imitated by Shakespeare and Milton.

But it is not only the great who engage us. Hundreds of poets wrote Pastoral in one form or another, and the general level of achievement was almost incredibly high; never had Pastoral seemed a more natural mode of song. And when its summer had passed, and poets had for a while contented themselves with re-examining the formal Eclogue, there came Herrick, who seemed to look back on all the richness of the Elizabethan Pastoral and distil from it a nostalgic essence, and Marvell, whose handful of poems seem to sum up the whole story of the English Pastoral, inexhaustibly rich in their solemn undertones.

With Marvell the story really ends, for the later Pastoral lived in a quite different atmosphere, and in a quite different relationship to its readers. Marvell's lyrics, whenever they were written, were not published until the tradition in which they existed was already being forgotten. Dryden's translations of Theocritus are pert, as Theocritus never was; the true impulse of rustic Pastoral petered out; it was something the Giant Race had understood. The Pastorals of Pope show how much and how little the new poetry could do in this kind; in Pope there is a union, impossible a century earlier, between the practice and the academic theory of Pastoral. The eighteenth century excelled in the mock-Pastoral, which is a kind of pantomime following the great play. The Augustans were often conscious of their defects, and Pope understood the significance of his addiction to mock-Epic; the *Dunciad,* he said, was a kind of satyr-play appended to the great trilogy of Homer, Virgil, and Milton. It is not too difficult to see an analogy with mock-Pastoral. Human needs had, perhaps, not changed; but certain things of importance had reduced the relevance of the old Pastoral. London had lost the country; its maypole, as Pope observed, had been taken down. The literary and philosophical preoccupations of the Renaissance poets had largely given way to a new, or newly expressed, set of problems. The old poetry, and everything that gave it its peculiar richness, had been largely forgotten by the time Johnson expressed his rational objections to *Lycidas.*

Conclusion

To some extent, the conditions under which the pastoral poetry of the English Renaissance was written were similar to those which give rise to the first pastoral poetry in Theocritus; but many other factors worked upon it to make it different, though of the same 'kind.' For one thing, the Renaissance poets were aware of their great ancient progenitors, as Virgil had been aware of Theocritus. Not only was Imitation a part of their accepted rhetorical and educational system; it was also a leading principle in their poetic, it controlled their attitude to their Art. The best poets would imitate the spirit which gave life, and adapt the work of their masters to a new world. This new world was not unconscious of the ages of poetry which filled the time between Theocritus and itself; during that time there had been other kinds of poetry relevant to the pastoral kind, and the language of shepherds had been applied variously to greater concerns, notably to the government of the Church, and the worship of God and the Blessed Virgin. Pastoral poetry concerns itself with the relationship between Nature and Art, and Renaissance views of Nature had been enlarged by new knowledge. The object of the pastoral poet's contemplation was no longer merely the happy peasant or shepherd, but the true natural man of the New World. Old modes of thinking about Nature and Art did, however, survive, and led a lively existence in the thought of the Renaissance. Montaigne's reaction to the accounts he had heard of the New World and its inhabitants were conditioned by all he knew of the old pastoral myths of the Golden Age. A 'naturalist' philosophy induced poets to portray that age as hedonistic and sinless, though wanton; in reply, the more moral poets asserted supernatural values, and described Nature as corrupted by the sin of Adam. Furthermore, even more keenly than Theocritus, perhaps, the English poets of the Renaissance found a pure though nostalgic pleasure in contemplating the life of the countryside. This is, in essence, the same delight that all ages know, and which is so keenly expressed in Chaucer. Country sports and country loves were interesting for their own sake, as well as being a kind of comment on the sophistication of the city. Flowers were valued not only as decorations for the laureate hearse of a dead shepherd-poet, but for their own beauty. Although, in thoughtful mood, the poet might think of Nature as God's Book of the Creatures, the more usual reaction of the Elizabethan poet is one of spontaneous pleasure. This pleasure, and the nostalgia of which I have spoken, combine with the critical and philosophical elements in the pastoral tradition to produce the rich profundity of English pastoral poetry.

Notes

1. *I.e.,* Appropriate to its kind, or *genre.*

2. *I.e.,* Figures of rhetoric.

3. *Lives of the Poets:* "Life of Milton" (World's Classics edition, I, 116; Oxford University Press, 1906).

4. *Lives of the Poets:* "Life of Pope" (*ibid.,* II, 324). The tradition that poets profitably commence their careers with Pastoral developed from Virgil's *Eclogues.*

5. *schylus and Athens* (Lawrence and Wishart, 1941), p. 66.

6. *Iliad,* XII, 310-328.

7. "Nature is inimitable; and in her real beauty she bursts forth with such vigour that Art can merely spoil all her works, committing upon her a thousand outrages for every ornament it manages to bestow." This is the opinion that is orthodoxly confuted by Polixenes in *The Winter's Tale.*

8. This is a topic of endless discussion. The reader might consult Castiglione, *The Courtier,* for a characteristic debate upon it. Shakespeare's *Tempest* treats the theme allusively but very fully.

9. This hard view is as old as the soft one; both are pre-Christian, though Christian views on Nature tend to prefer the hard view, when by Nature is meant that which Adam's fall corrupted, and which is opposed to Grace. But this is a complicated subject.

10. See, for example, John X, 11-16.

11. Frankfort, Frankfort, Wilson, and Jacobsen, *Before Philosophy* (Penguin, 1949), p. 180.

12. See A. J. Toynbee, *A Study of History,* abridged D. C. Somervell (Oxford University Press, 1946), pp. 219 ff.

13. *Roman Vergil* (Faber and Faber, 1944), p. 31.

14. H. J. Rose, *The Eclogues of Vergil* (Cambridge University Press, 1942), p. 11.

15. Some scholars believe that Theocritus found in Cos a school of pastoral poets, whom he imitated; but none of these poets has survived.

16. It is not included here, for lack of a suitable English translation.

17. *The Eclogues of Vergil* (Cambridge University Press, 1942), p. 16.

18. *The Common Asphodel* (Hamish Hamilton, 1949), p. 253.

19. Graves, *op. cit.,* p. 252.

20. Graves, *op. cit.,* 253.

21. W. Empson, *Some Versions of Pastoral* (Chatto and Windus, 1935), p. 137.

22. Edited by G. D. Willcock and A. Walker (Cambridge University Press, 1936), pp. 38-39.

23. The *Eclogues* of Baptista Spagnuoli, known as Mantuanus, were published in 1498, and won him a great reputation as a Latin poet. His bucolics were standard in the Renaissance; when Holofernes misquotes him in *Love's Labour's Lost,* IV, ii, 95-96, the implication is that Holofernes is a dunce. Mantuan was one of Spenser's many models in *The Shepheardes Calender,* and hundreds of other eclogues are indebted to him. He is one of the authorities for the attack on unworthy pastors in *Lycidas.* The earliest English writers to be affected by him were Barclay and Googe. He is represented in this book by one of his Eclogues in the translation of Turberville.

24. Pastoral drama as such has been excluded from this collection; it is too bulky to be properly represented. But it is none the less an important Renaissance development of Pastoral. When an extract from it seems to make an important point about Pastoral I have not hesitated to use it.

The other great formal development of Renaissance Pastoral was the prose or verse-and-prose romance. The chief writers in this kind were Sannazaro (1456-1530), in Italian; Montemayor (1520-61), in Spanish; and Sidney in English. Their starting-point was the Hellenistic romance, and generally speaking they are more concerned with narrative values than with specifically pastoral values. They have their place in the history of the novel, and in the history of Epic, as Sidney's comments in the *Apologie* suggest. Sannazaro, with his polished melancholy and his insistence on the "pathetic fallacy" whereby he makes the whole of Nature lament with the unhappy lover, was enormously fashionable, and Sidney even borrowed his title, *Arcadia.* He was probably very well known in England. So was Montemayor, who provided Shakespeare with at least one, and probably two, plot-ideas. Sidney was likewise used, but was equally thought of as a pastoral poet, and his death stimulated a large number of pastoral elegies in the tradition of Theocritus, Moschus, and Virgil.

25. Characteristically, Jonson chose the Robin Hood legend as the theme of his *Sad Shepherd*. This hero of the dead golden world of England echoes throughout Elizabethan Pastoral.

26. This Character, with others of the same kind, may be found in J. Dover Wilson's *Life in Shakespeare's England* (Cambridge University Press, 1925; Penguin, 1949).

27. See the very valuable appendices in Volume I of the Minor Poems in the *Variorum Spenser* (ed. Greenlaw and others) (Oxford University Press, 1933-47).

S. K. Heninger, Jr. (essay date 1961)

SOURCE: "The Renaissance Perversion of Pastoral," in *Journal of the History of Ideas*, Vol. 1, No. 2, April-June 1961, pp. 254-61.

[*In the following essay, Heninger claims that in the sixteenth century the classical pastoral was "perverted" to express moral, satirical, and sentimental themes, and that this adaptation was the result of a humanist desire to explore real life in a form that was originally developed to reflect the ideal.*]

When the youthful Alexander Pope had finished his pastorals, he wrote a "Discourse" which offers both an encomium of the pastoral tradition and an apologia for his interpretation of it. He began with a characteristically waspish declaration, made with the confidence and careful balance of impeccable authority:

> There are not, I believe, a greater number of any sort of verses than of those which are called Pastorals, nor a smaller, than of those which are truly so.[1]

With a neo-classical eye, Pope had surveyed his predecessors in pastoral, using Theocritus and Vergil as norms. Quite rightly he found little genuine pastoral since classical times, because the Renaissance had violently perverted both its purpose and its method, both its content and its form.

Pastoral was rife during the Renaissance, but not as the ancients had practised it. The idyll and eclogue persisted, but not with the former sweetness and beauty. Instead, the shepherd spoke with a dread voice that shrank the streams of Sicily and blasted the spreading beeches of Arcadia. The setting still purveyed the well-known delights of pasture and forest, but beneath this superficial loveliness rankled the wretchedness of man. The eclogue became a favored form for satire and sarcasm, while idyllicism itself moved over to other literary forms.

To understand the renaissance perversion of pastoral, we must of course first understand the mode in its pure form. This is difficult—rather like trying to isolate a melodic

theme from symphonic variations on it. But there is a sizable corpus of critical opinion upon which we may draw. Recent critics, speaking to the theory of pastoral, have emphasized its optimistic simplicity, its denial of reality by simplifying confusion and complexity to an irreducible orderliness. W. W. Greg makes the statement categorical:

> What does appear to be a constant element in the pastoral as known to literature is the recognition of a contrast, implicit or expressed, between pastoral life and some more complex type of civilization.[2]

William Empson likewise insists upon this single criterion for pastoral; in *Some Versions of Pastoral,* he includes any work which involves the "process of putting the complex into the simple."[3] So pastoral depicts some imagined life in contrast to the complexity of real life. As Greg reiterates a few pages later, it is "the reaction against the world that is too much with us."[4]

This is certainly the understanding of pastoral that Spenser promulgates in the Pastorella episode in Book VI of *The Faerie Queene*. There Sir Calidore interrupts his pursuit of the Blatant Beast for an amatory interlude with Pastorella, an obvious allegorical figure representing the perfection of pastoral existence. After sampling the simple pleasures of country life, Calidore

> Gan highly to commend the happie life,
> Which Shepheards lead, without debate or bitter strife.
> How much (sayd he) more happie is the state,
> In which ye father here doe dwell at ease,
> Leading a life so free and fortunate,
> From all the tempests of these worldly seas,
> Which tosse the rest in daungerous disease;
> Where warres, and wreckes, and wicked enmitie
> Doe them afflict, which no man can appease.
>
> (VI.ix.18.8-9, 19.1-7)

This same interpretation of pastoral is advanced by Voltaire, though diametrically opposed to Spenser in artistic temperament and purpose. Candide, disillusioned after testing innumerable ways of life in both the Old World and the New, finds permanent value only in the conduct of the good old man taking the air at his door within a bower of orange-trees, eloigned from worldly affairs. By self-sufficient management of his twenty acres, he has staved off the three great evils of *l'ennui, le vice, et le besoin.*

This smug atmosphere has pervaded literary pastoral from the time of its inception. Theocritus revolutionized hexameter verse by the use of mime, and prepared the way for the Arcadian pastoral that was to follow. Writing under the influence of a sophisticated coterie in Cos and later under the stultifying patronage of Ptolemy Philadelphus in overcivilized Alexandria, he composed fragile little poems about simple folk in a dulcet setting of his native Sicily. He depicted a real rural scene in the sense that actual flora and fauna and place-names are recognizable, and he simulated a Doric dialect to suggest genuine rusticity. But it is reality refined, purified of sordidness. The only ugliness appears as naïveté, and pain—such as unrequited love or grief for a dead friend—even pain is etherealized into an exquisite masochism.

So from its inception, pure pastoral has described some half-remembered place in archaic terms, a nostalgic reminiscence of an idealized child-scape, an Eden-like state of innocence and harmonious perfection. Any realistic elements in pastoral appear within this carefully constructed frame of psychological reference, from a carefully prescribed psychological distance. The milieu is Arcadia in terms of space, or the Golden Age in terms of time. But all takes place at least one remove from the here-and-now. The purpose of pastoral, as it developed from Theocritus, is to create an ideal existence in contradistinction to the real world. This is precisely the dichotomy which Vergil stresses so pointedly in his very first eclogue: Tityrus, piping beneath the beech tree, is secure in his bucolic bliss, while the displaced Meliboeus goes sadly forth to travail in a non-pastoral life.

Pastoral depends upon this distinction between ideal and reality; but equally important, it insists upon juxtaposition of the two worlds. The boundaries are contiguous, and the frontiers must be crossable. Meliboeus is evicted from his farm to become an urbanite; or moving in the other direction, the courtier Sir Calidore can sport with Pastorella in the shade. This intercourse between actual and ideal, for another example, is the point of Shakespeare's *As You Like It*. The banished Duke and his retainers live blissfully in the Forest of Arden, where there are also Silvius and Phebe, Arcadian rustics, contrasted with Audrey and William, realistic rustics. At the end, all return to the court and to happiness, having benefited from a pastoral interlude.

This is the optimistic spirit of pastoral. It is available to all. Arcadia is always just over the next hill, or a new Golden Age is just around the next corner. This easy access between reality and illusion, though only by means of some mental freeway, is essential to pure pastoral. The psychology of the Arcadian experience is described by Andrew Marvell in "The Garden":

> Here at the Fountains sliding foot,
> Or at some Fruit-trees mossy root,
> Casting the Bodies Vest aside,
> My Soul into the boughs does glide.
>
> (lines 49-52)

Marvell explains man's predilection for pastoral: "The Mind . . . / Withdraws into its happiness," "annihilating all that's made / To a green Thought in a green Shade." Or as Keats said, it is "a thing of beauty" that "keep[s] a bower quiet for us." This haven of perfection provides refuge from the disappointments and depravity of our real lives. John Hughes, the XVIIIth-century editor of Spenser, emphasized this temporary return to radical innocence in his "Remarks on the *Shepherd's Calendar*":

> [Pastoral] is a wonderful Amusement to the Imagination, to be sometimes transported, as it were, out of

modern Life, and to wander in these pleasant Scenes which the Pastoral Poets provide for us, and in which we are apt to fancy our selves reinstated for a time in our first Innocence and Happiness.[5]

One function of pure pastoral is to provide such solace through escape into a system of pristine goodness. It is escapist literature in a therapeutic sense.

Transcending this individual response, yet as a corollary to it, there is a sociological explanation for pastoral's genesis: it is art as compensation for what a culture lacks, rather than art as expression of what a culture has achieved. Art is often cultural compensation. For instance, the serenity of Greek architecture belies the political turmoil of the city-states, and the saccharine sentimentality of German *lieder* is clearly antithetical to Prussian militarism. Just so, it is the city-dweller who writes pastorals. When love and leisure are in short supply, pastoral provides these staples—in fiction if not in fact. The pastoralist voices man's inherent longing for the tranquillity of Arcadia, for the innocence of a lost Golden Age. This accounts for the usual charge of artificiality: pure pastoral must be artificial because it describes what is not.

Pastoral, then, is not so much a literary genre—like epic or tragedy or the novel—as a state of mind, a euphoria. Nonetheless, the pastoral exhibits several traditional features of method, conventions introduced by Theocritus and confirmed by Vergil. The idyll or eclogue, the form of pastoral in classical times, has a poetic structure more elaborately articulated than the lyric but less formal than the ode, and in many cases comparable to the drama. It is always a dramatic monologue or a dialogue between shepherds, usually two. The metre is normally the stately hexameter. The theme is consistently love—of woman, of man, of nature—expressed often in set-pieces, such as the singing-match, the amorous complaint, and the dirge. The context is harmonious nature, animate and inanimate, described in realistic detail but without unpleasantness. The prevailing tone approaches the serious mock-heroic, if I may be permitted an oxymoron: our gravest griefs and most earnest joys are presented with straight-faced intensity in the silly activities of shepherds.

So much for the purpose and method of pastoral as the Renaissance found it. It had not been a dominant theme among the ancients: there were Theocritus and his disciples, Moschus and Bion, then Vergil and a few insignificant imitators. Pastoral was unknown among the classical Greeks, and neither Aristotle nor Horace had mentioned it. But in the Renaissance every major author tried his hand at it—from Dante, who wrote two eclogues, to Milton, who offered pastoral in several forms. And the changes rung on the traditional theme were sometimes sonorous, sometimes giddy.

In the Renaissance the pastoral suffered a dissociation between its classic purpose and its standardized method. Poets often ignored the original intention of pastoral, though they continued to use its means—its accoutrements and conventions—for other ends. There are, in consequence, perversions of purpose and perversions of method. In the first category the literary pastoral assumed new rôles as satire, as moral allegory, and as sentiment; in the second category the pastoral spirit assumed new forms of prose, drama, and verse.

The signal perversion of pastoral was its adaptation for the purpose of satire. Those for whom the world really was too much took the pessimistic view that Arcadia does not exist and therefore is available to no one. Renaissance reformers with malice aforethought conceded that pastoral expressed an unattainable ideal, meaningful only as a foil to set off sharply the defects of reality. The speculum of the Golden Age provided a norm against which to measure the degree of man's degradation in this last and worst Age of Iron.

The purpose of pastoral was easily corrupted to satire because it contained a ready-made mechanism for personal allusion. The guise of shepherds was a handy camouflage for actual men. In the ten pastoral poems of Theocritus there is no covert identification except in Idyll VII, "The Harvest-Home," where several fellow poets appear as shepherds.[6] But other poems by Theocritus, published regularly with the pastorals to make up the thirty idyllia, contain undisguised names of patrons: for example, Idyll XVI is a plea for patronage addressed to Hiero II of Syracuse, and Idyll XVII is a panegyric of Ptolemy Philadelphus. Vergil took this as license to expand the use of personal allusion,[7] both covert and open, so that even the earliest scholiasts explicated many of the eclogues as historical allegory.[8] Not until the Renaissance, however, not until Petrarch and Boccaccio revived the eclogue, was personal allusion an indispensable feature of pastoral.[9] Then every shepherd embodied an historical personage; every episode recorded an historical event. Rather than being a graceful ornament, personal allusion became the raison d'être for pastoral. E. K. Chambers confides the rationale behind Spenser's *Shepheardes Calender:* "He chose rather to unfold great matter of argument covertly . . . which moved him rather in glogues, then other wise to write."[10]

Moreover, in antiquity hidden reference had been no more than a pretty compliment to a friend or patron. It was an aristocratic masquerade. But in the Renaissance, covert identification offered a disguise for dissent in an age of political and ecclesiastical turbulence; not only did it permit a panegyric for a patron, but also a philippic against an opponent. Pastoral turned from compliment to abuse. And following the example of Petrarch, malcontents for three centuries proclaimed their bitterest denunciations in the uncongenial and ridiculous garb of shepherds.

A fortuitous circumstance conspired to make pastoral a vehicle of satire. The Renaissance was quick to adapt pastoral terminology to religious meanings, so that shepherd = pastor, the flock = the congregation, and Pan = Christ, the All-inclusive and All-powerful.[11] This fusion of classical and Christian iconography, abetted by a syncretic etymology, gave pastoral an inherent advantage for religious satire. Petrarch was the first to utilize this advantage, but it was exploited most notably by Mantuan in Italy, Marot in France, and Spenser in England.

An outgrowth of the pastoral perverted to religious satire was pastoral as moral allegory. Both share the purpose of encouraging goodness in its struggle with evil. Chambers, classifying Spenser's twelve eclogues, claimed that the largest number (5) are "Moral: which for the most part be mixed with some Satyrical bitterness."[12] Puttenham imputed a didactic intention to Vergil, whose eclogues "containe and enforme morall discipline, for the amendment of mans behaviour."[13] But the later Mantuan is the first to make a decided point of moralizing in pastoral, which may account for the widespread use of his eclogues as a textbook. Moral allegory in the guise of pastoral was especially dear to the Puritans; it figured prominently in Spenser's *Shepheardes Calender,* and after a brief career culminated in Milton's *Comus.*

But clearly satire and allegory are side-tracks for pastoral, which properly depicts an ideal, not a particular nor even a universal. Therefore satire, which depends upon particular reference, and allegory, which implies a universal reference, are foreign to the true pastoral spirit. Pastoral as satire never rose above ingenious raillery, and therefore sticks in the mire of polemics; while pastoral as moral allegory, even that conceived by Milton, remains platitudinous.

In the XVIth century the perversion of pastoral for purposes of satire was paralleled by an equally strong tendency in an opposite direction: the utilization of pastoral for generating sentiment. A precedent for a sentimental love-story in the pastoral milieu had been set by Longus' *Daphnis and Chloe,* a Hellenistic tale of refined passions, dangers to both life and virtue, and revelations of unsuspected aristocratic lineage. But in the Renaissance the innovator of pastoral as sentiment was Sannazaro, whose authorized *Arcadia* appeared in 1504. The prose narrative interspersed with twelve eclogues seems to have no purpose but decorous emotionalism. Tasso's *Aminta,* acted in 1573, inaugurated the sentimental pastoral in dramatic form, soon to be seconded by Guarini's *Pastor Fido,* acted in 1585. These genuine artists engendered a languid sentiment that brooded on the mutability of lovely things. They knew that in Arcadia, the very kingdom of delight, veiled melancholy has her sovereign shrine. But in the hands of imitators, this wakeful wistfulness rapidly degenerated to maudlin affectation.

Those are the distinguishable perversions of the purpose of pastoral, intentions beyond the ken of ancient practitioners in the mode. The Renaissance likewise revamped the method of pastoral. The set-pieces were generally ignored, and the eclogue, traditional form of the pastoral, became less and less common. Although Petrarch, Boccaccio, and Mantuan faithfully perpetuated the classical eclogue, the pastoral mode was most often expressed in other forms.

Pastoral drama, for example, became a distinct genre.[14] As early as 1472, Poliziano presented the tragedy of *Orfeo* within a pastoral setting; and after a somewhat discontinuous evolution, pastoral drama reached its greatest triumphs in Tasso's *Aminta* and Guarini's *Pastor Fido*. Pastoral also appeared prominently in the masque, a late sub-dramatic form, such as Ronsard's *Bergerie* and Jonson's *Sad Shepherd*.

Another distinct genre in the pastoral milieu was the multiplot prose romance, inaugurated by Boccaccio's *Ameto* and solidified into convention by Sannazaro's *Arcadia*. A half century later Montemayor amalgamated pastoral and the medieval chivalric romance to produce *Diana,* and Sidney followed the same formula for his *Arcadia*. In these works, shepherds began to posture strangely in courtly and heroic attitudes. From there, the pastoral romance sank ever deeper into banality, from which not even *Don Quixote* could shame it.

There were pastoral elegies, such as Marot's dirge for Louise de Savoye and Milton's "Lycidas," both contaminated with satire; pastoral odes, such as Ronsard's "Aux Cendres de Marguerite de Valois" and Spenser's "April"; and pastoral verse-narrative, such as Boccaccio's *Ninfale fiesolano* and Drayton's *Endimion and Phoebe*. The lyric, though, became the most prevalent verse form assumed by pastoral, and certainly it is the form which has had enduring popularity. In the lyric the true spirit of pastoral found a resting-place. Freed from the metrical demands of the Latin eclogue, the shepherd sang seductively in his vernacular: Come live with me in a constant round of pleasures. The pastoral lyric had been a standard feature in the shepherd-mimes of *Theocritus,* and it developed in the Renaissance as a graceful adjunct to the prose narrative of the romances. Under the stimulus of Lorenzo de Medici, it also achieved an autonomous existence.[15] The Pléiade brought the pastoral lyric to high art, and Elizabethans in the poetical miscellanies refined it to a curiously elegant simplicity.

But Marlowe's "Passionate Shepherd" was too self-consciously a city-dweller; he promised gold buckles and madrigals rather than cheese and music on the pipes. And Raleigh's "Nymph's Reply" was a well-known rider on any proposition to lead the pastoral life, a rider inevitable in the world-weary later Renaissance. Moreover, the metrics of the "Passionate Shepherd" are an adaptation of the standard ballad stanza, so the song has more affinities with the vulgar ballad than with the dignified hexameter. When Pope sat down to write pastorals, he found a multitude of works feigning loyalty to this time-honored tradition, but he rightly noted that almost none were pastoral in both purpose and method.

Pastoral had irresistibly attracted the greatest renaissance poets because, like tragedy, it offers the opportunity of juxtaposing the ideal and the actual in a single neat system. The ancients had developed the ideal aspects of pastoral; for them it served as an escape mechanism. Such an interpretation presupposes that literature and life are separate experiences, however, that literature provides a haven from life. So the renaissance humanist could not accept this facile dichotomy which fragmented man rather than making him whole. He wanted real literature as well as an ideal life. Literature, like life, must take form within the human sphere; yet it should reflect the perfection glimpsed by the poet in his moment of ecstasy. The humanist was forced to concede that man is limited—Genesis established this fact as well as its wherefore; yet under optimum conditions man is still capable of conceiving the ideal and affirming it. Then the ideal momentarily becomes actual. Although the ideal, like Adam, is mortal, mortality is its only imperfection. And for the circumscribed period of its existence, the ideal is a unique, unqualified value. In fact, awareness that the ideal is limited to an ephemeral existence makes it all the more to be cherished—an attitude developed later by the romantics.

The Renaissance, though, most frequently expressed the enigma of perfection's finitude in terms of mutability: time brings inevitable change, but this change is itself part of the pattern, indeed is essential to realizing the pattern. This cognizance of finitude haunted the poet, and frightened him into explaining it—hence, Spenser's "Cantos of Mutabilitie." The theme intruded even into the realm of pastoral, and shepherds for the first time in the Renaissance recovered moldering tombstones from the Golden Age with the pointed inscription, *"Et in Arcadia ego,"* where the speaker is clearly Death.[16] Arcadia invaded by Death is Eden delimited by sin—but each is itself an untarnished ideal. And if man, though debased, can somehow re-enter Paradise—if only through the artifice of pastoral—he will regain a measure of his pristine goodness and will comprehend the reasons for his fall from such a blissful seat. The pastoral world provides a literary Eden where man fallen cohabits with man innocent. Pastoral can present the mystery of man's relation to this harmonious universe, the paradox of his simultaneous mortality and godlikeness. When handled properly, pastoral can place the immediate in a cosmic context—witness Milton's "Lycidas."

But only rarely did pastoral build the lofty rhyme. There were some dizzy raptures in the lyrics and a few aching joys in the drama; but then the still, sad music of humanity smothered all, even the carping of the malcontents, so that pastoral petered out in self-conscious dirges . . . *Astrophel . . . Adonais . . . Thyrsis*. Pastoral failed to achieve greatness in the Renaissance, when the humanistic poet could have given substance to its wavering vision of man's nature. Instead, pastoral was perverted to satire, moral allegory, and sentimental narrative; it assumed modish, superficial forms. Unlike tragedy, pastoral never realized its potentiality.

Notes

1. Pope, *Prose Works,* ed. Norman Ault (Oxford, 1936), 297.

2. W. W. Greg, *Pastoral Poetry & Pastoral Drama* (London, 1906), 4.

3. (London, 1935), 23, 53. Empson's purpose—a sociological one—is perspicaciously summarized by J. E. Congleton, *Theories of Pastoral Poetry in England, 1684-1798* (Univ. of Florida Press, 1952), 4-5; and later, Congleton cites several XVIIth- and XVIIIth-century critics who similarly discussed pastoral as the ultimate simplification of complex reality (169-177).

4. *Pastoral Poetry,* 6.

5. *The Works of Mr. Edmund Spenser* (6 vols.; London, 1715), I, ci-cii.

6. H. J. Rose pinpoints the importance of this idyll in the development of pastoral as personal allegory (*The Eclogues of Vergil* [Univ. of California Press, 1942], 10-11).

7. See John S. Phillimore, *Pastoral and Allegory, a Re-reading of the Bucolics of Virgil* (Oxford, 1925), 13ff.

8. The inability of scholars to agree upon the identity of prominent figures—such as the expected child in Eclogue IV and Daphnis in Eclogue V—proves that personal allegory in Vergil is not cut-and-dried, however, and suggests strongly that personal allegory is not intended in every eclogue. Allegory was merely one step which Vergil took in the direction of generalizing his thought or emotion. In his chapter on "Vergil and Allegory," Rose concludes: "There is in the Eclogues rather less than one might expect of hidden meaning, and especially of figurative allusion to the author's own circumstances" (*Eclogues of Vergil,* 138). When Vergil intended unmitigated personal allusion, he used real names—e.g., Pollio and Varus and Gallus.

9. Both Petrarch and Boccaccio are explicit on this point; see Greg, *Pastoral Poetry,* 18 (n. 1), and Congleton, *Theories of Pastoral,* 15, 172-173.

10. *Variorum Spenser, Minor Poems* (Johns Hopkins Press, 1943), I, 10

11. For other affinities between pastoral and the Christian tradition, see E. K. Chambers, *English Pastorals* (London, 1895), xxv-xxvi.

12. *Minor Poems,* I, 12. Cf. Philip Sidney's comments on pastoral in the *Defence of Poesie* (in *Complete Works,* ed. Albert Feuillerat [4 vols.: Cambridge Univ. Press, 1922-1926], III, 22).

13. *The Arte of English Poesie,* ed. Gladys D. Willcock and Alice Walker (Cambridge Univ. Press, 1936), 39.

14. For the details of this evolution, see Greg, *Pastoral Poetry,* 155ff.; Enrico Carrara, *La Poesia pastorale* (Milan, 1909), 205ff. and 297ff.; and Louis E. Lord, tr., *The "Orpheus" of Angelo Politian and the "Aminta" of Torquato Tasso* (Oxford Univ. Press, 1931), 54-60.

15. See Greg, *Pastoral Poetry,* 33-36; Carrara, *Poesia pastorale,* 164ff., 225ff., and 415ff.; and Lord, tr., *"Orpheus" of Politian,* 52.

16. See Erwin Panofsky, "*Et in Arcadia Ego:* Poussin and the Elegiac Tradition," in *Meaning in the Visual Arts* (New York, 1955), 295-320.

Laurence Lerner (essay date 1972)

SOURCE: "The Pastoral World: Arcadia and the Golden Age," in *The Pastoral Mode: A Casebook,* edited by Bryan Loughrey, Macmillan Publishers Ltd., 1984, pp. 133-54.

[*In the following excerpt from an essay first published in 1972, Lerner argues that the pastoral, as a representation of the provincial mediated by courtly writers seeking relief from the problems of a sophisticated society, is poetry of illusion and thus of wish-fulfillment.*]

Every culture has one or more centres of social, artistic and moral standards, a place where the educated people live, where the King's English, or its equivalent, is spoken, where the theatres perform and the political decisions are taken. In the sixteenth and seventeenth centuries this centre was the court; by the nineteenth it was the city; in modern America it is becoming the university. Most literature is written from and for this centre; but there are always corners of society, rural or provincial pockets, lower social levels, with their own less articulate, less sophisticated traditions, sometimes imprinted by old-fashioned court mores, sometimes seeming to live an older, more unchanging life of their own. It used to be true that the literature of the centre was written, that of the corners oral, but literacy and radio have changed that.

To describe this contrast, we can speak of court, or metropolitan or (more generally) centric literature, and set it against unsophisticated, rural, popular or (more generally) provincial literature. To this can be added another contrast, concerning the way in which a poem sees the world it describes. It may present that world as it is, through the eyes of a familiar and an expert, subjecting it to none of the distracting expectations of the outsider. This I will call the direct vision. Or it may deliberately see its world as answering to the illusions or discontents of an outsider, as a projection rather than as the object of the matter-of-fact gaze of the inmate; this I will call the mediated vision. Now, by using these two pair of contrasts, we arrive at a fourfold scheme of classification.

The first class—centric and direct—will contain most of the great literature of Europe, which has naturally emerged from, and deals with, the court or the city. Tragedy belongs here (Hamlet's Denmark and Thésée's Athens are part of Renaissance court culture, wherever they are ostensibly situated), and so do most novels. It would be odd if this were not the area in which greatness harboured.

In the second class—provincial-direct—we must put the ballads, which emerge from, and belong to, regional pockets of our culture: the narrative poems of Wordsworth, proudly proclaiming their setting in humble and rustic life; the regional novel; dialect poetry.

The third class—centric-mediated—can take two forms, positive and negative. If positive, then the view of court or city is mediated by longing and respect; it is seen from far as the desirable top where, if we are lucky, there may be room. The archetype of such writing is the Dick Whittington story. If it is negative, we get pastoral satire: denunciation of court by contrasting it with Arcadian simplicity.

Finally, there is provincial-mediated, which is pastoral. This too can be positive or negative. If the poet's need is to escape from the sophisticated corruption of court life into the freshness, simplicity and honesty of an unspoiled countryside, the result is pastoral properly speaking. If, however, he looks at the country, not through the eyes of his wishes, but through those of fear or dislike, if he believes in courtly grace and subtlety and is simply pausing to laugh at rustic boors, we can call the result anti-pastoral.

What would a poem be like which did not strive towards the matter-of-fact gaze of the expert, but deliberately saw nature in terms of an outsider's expectations?—which brought to the countryside emotions and expectations which were not rejected, but which determined the way the poem was written? Would it not be like this?—

> O sweet woods, the delight of solitariness!
> O how much I do like your solitariness!
> Here nor treason is hid, veiled in innocence,
> Nor envy's snaky eye finds any harbour here,
> Nor flatterer's venomous insinuations,
> Nor cunning humourist's puddled opinions,
> Nor courteous ruins of preferred usury,
> Nor time prattled away, cradle of ignorance,
> Nor causeless duty, nor cumber of arrogance,
> Nor trifling title of vanity dazzleth us,
> Nor golden manacles stand for a paradise.
> Here wrong's name is unheard, slander a monster is.
> Keep they spright from abuse; here no abuse doth
>   haunt:
> What man grafts in a tree dissimulation?

> [Sidney, song from *Arcadia* (1598)]

No poem could have a simpler structure than this. It is a plain insistent assertion that the country is free from certain evils. This negative point is the only one it makes. Almost every detail mentioned is a detail, not about the country, but about the court—it is a poem about what the country is *not* like. This gives it a curious kind of strength, a kind that is incompatible with subtlety: a growing passion of indignation and need mounts in its cumulative rhetoric, and its very formality adds to its power, in a way that is only possible in Elizabethan poetry, when men sometimes (especially for emotions like hate and indignation) seem to have thought, and felt, in rhetorical patterns.

Sidney shows us the poetic mechanism we are looking for so clearly that his poem consists entirely of an announce-ment of what kind of poem he is writing. Let us turn to someone who has the same point to make, but spent rather longer in the woods:

> Now my co-mates, and brothers in exile,
> Hath not old custom made this life more sweet
> Than that of painted pomp? Are not these woods
> More free from peril than the envious court?
> Here feel we but the penalty of Adam,
> The season's difference, as the icy fang
> And churlish chiding of the winter's wind,
> Which when it bites, and blows upon my body
> Even till I shrink with cold, I smile, and say
> This is no flattery: these are counsellors
> That feelingly persuade me what I am:
> Sweet are the uses of adversity
> Which like the toad, ugly and venomous,
> Wears yet a precious jewel in his head:
> And this our life, exempt from public haunt,
> Finds tongues in trees, books in the running brooks,
> Sermons in stones, and good in everything.
> I would not change it.

> [*As You Like It* (1599), II i 1-18]

Nothing in this passage is an attempt to see the countryside as it is. One point runs through it all, that the country is not the court. The contrast with 'painted pomp', with 'flattery', with 'public haunt', determines everything. Real toads are not venomous, and carry no jewels, but to the exiled Duke this does not matter, for the toads of Arden are not real.

The next example is also highly conventional: but it is non-dramatic, and of greater verbal complexity than the Duke's lines. It is by the most sophisticated and, probably, the most pastoral of seventeenth-century poets:

> Ametas and Thestylis Making Hay-ropes

> A. Thinkst thou this love can stand,
>   whilst thou still dost say me nay?
>   Love unpaid does soon disband:
>   Love binds love as hay binds hay.
> Th. Thinkst thou that this rope would twine
>   If we both should turn one way?
>   Where both parties so combine,
>   Neither love will twist nor hay.
> A. Thus you vain excuses find,
>   Which yourselve and us delay:
>   And love ties a woman's mind
>   Looser than with ropes of hay.
> Th. What you cannot constant hope
>   Must be taken as you say.
> A. Then let's both lay by our rope,
>   And go kiss within the hay.

> [Marvell (c. 1650)][1]

Marvell is a poet of paradox: not flagrantly, like Donne and Crashaw, but delicately and deeply. The deepest paradox in this poem is both hidden and obvious: it is the contrast between its rustic image and its verbal sophistication. The poem depends utterly on the figure of the hay-ropes, as if the two lovers had no other way of expressing themselves: their dialectic consists in modifying the analogies that can be drawn from this one vehicle. Yet it is not as if they think in images: for the comparison is regularly deployed as a formal simile, and at least in a technical sense the thought exists independently of it. It is a poem in which we can see the rhetorical art, and admire the poet's skill.

Yet as long as we admire the skill, the lovers stay apart: the better they express their feelings, the less they love. This is the paradox, too, of Marvell's 'The Definition of Love', that perfection and fulfilment are incompatible:

> My love is of a birth as rare
> As 'tis for object strange and high;
> It was begotten of Despair
> Upon Impossibility.

The perfect love, that poem says, does not exist: 'Ametas and Thestylis' moves in exactly the opposite direction. Here is a perfect image for love, it says; look how much can be expressed through it. But its lovers, rejecting despair and impossibility, must reject the attempt to express their love. They must lay aside the rope and go kiss within the hay. The poem is over, and the rest is silence.

The sophistication of this poem completely prevents us from seeing haymaking as it really is, and country life is shamelessly subordinated to the poet's wish to turn a polished analogy. And then, in the end, the poem gaily rejects everything it has done. The country folk, showing more good sense than the poem, are going to stop talking about love, and get on with it.

The Renaissance poets were, of course, well aware that their version of the countryside was an illusion. To show this, we can turn to the first and most famous of all, Jacopo Sannazaro, whose *Arcadia,* published in 1502, began a vast literary fashion. In the Epilogue to this work, Sannazaro defends himself for writing pastoral. Addressing his pipe ('sampogna'), he says: 'Do not mind if someone, accustomed perhaps to more exquisite sounds, rebukes your baseness or considers you rude'; nor (the opposite criticism) if they say that you have not followed the laws of shepherds properly, and 'that it is not fitting for anyone to pass further than what belongs to him' ('passar più avanti, che a lui si appartiene'): which seems to refer both to social and stylistic climbing. To this latter criticism Sannazaro replies that he has been the first in this age to

> awaken the sleeping woods, and teach shepherds to
> sing the songs they had forgotten. All the more since
> he who made you out of these reeds came to Arcadia
> not as a rustic shepherd but as a most cultured youth,
> although unknown and a pilgrim of love.

Pastoral poetry, in other words, is the work of courtiers: for that reason, it would be inappropriate to censure it for baseness (it isn't really) or for presumption (why shouldn't he 'passare più avanti', considering who he really is?). Sannazaro is having his oatcake and eating it. Not surpris-

ing, then, that when Selvaggio meets Montano (*Prosa Secunda*) and asks him to sing, he addresses him 'con voce assai umana'. This 'humanist voice' (a modern translation renders it 'in a most courteous phrase') is no doubt a deliberate slip of the tongue, a quiet reminder of how educated these shepherds naturally are.

There is a formal device that corresponds to the fact that the version of the countryside is mediated. The song which Montano sings in reply to Selvaggio's request tells how he found Uranio stretched out sleeping, and woke him, and they then discussed whether to sing. In *Prosa Terzia,* the shepherds go to the feast of Pales, and as they enter the holy temple they see various scenes painted on the gate— nymphs, Apollo guarding Admetus's cattle, Endymion, and so on. When we hear the priest's prayer in the temple, we realise that we are in the same world as these mythological paintings: he prays not to see Diana bathing, or the vengeful nymphs.

What we have in these two examples is the obliqueness of presentation so common in pastoral. The shepherd poet sings only after announcing he is going to sing, or discussing what, or taking part in a contest. Rural or mythological scenes are not described direct, but paintings of them are described. The method is old, and goes back to Virgil, to Theocritus even; and some scholars tell us that it has its origin in the actual shepherd contests of rural Sicily. Whether that is true or not, its place in Renaissance pastoral is surely the opposite—not as a sign of realism, but as a sign of sophistication, a way of removing us from the immediacy of real rustics in real fields.

PASTORAL AND ANTI-PASTORAL:
'AS YOU LIKE IT'

Of course, the same work may hover between positive and negative—as for instance *As You Like It* does. The Duke, we have seen, is a poet of simple pastoral enthusiasm; but the play as a whole sets pastoral and anti-pastoral constantly against each other, and does not encourage us to form a clear preference.

They are set against each other most directly in III ii: the conversation between Corin and Touchstone on the shepherd's life. Each speaks unequivocally for one of the attitudes: courtly trickery against the good sense of Arden, or courtly polish against the slow-witted rustic chewing his straw. It is an old argument, going back at least to the twentieth idyll of Theocritus, in which Eunica despises the neatherd for his coarse smell, and he tells himself indignantly about the neatherds who have been loved by goddesses. Who wins that argument? And who wins this one?

> TOUCH. Hast any philosophy in thee, shepherd?
>
> CORIN. No more, but that I know the more one sickens, the worse at ease he is; and that he that wants money, means and contentment is without three good friends. That the property of rain is to wet, and fire to burn. That a good pasture makes fat sheep; and that a great cause of the night is lack of the sun. That he that hath

learned no wit by nature, nor art, may complain of good breeding, or comes of a very dull kindred.

Touch. Such a one is a natural philosopher.

[III ii 21 ff.]

It is quite wrong to play this scene (as I have seen it done) with a sly Corin winking at the audience, and smiling to see whether Touchstone will take him seriously. If Touchstone believes in courtly wit, as he clearly does, then Corin must be allowed to believe in rustic sense, and not turn into a secondary Touchstone. It is easy to say what each stands for; but it is not so easy to say who has the better of it.

A natural philosopher has no need of artificialities or rhetoric, for he goes directly to what is really important; a 'natural' who philosophises will produce nothing but empty platitudes like these. Touchstone is consciously punning, but which meaning of 'natural' more truly describes Corin? 'The property of rain is to wet', he says—just like the Bachelierus of Molière, who has been taught in medical school the reason why opium makes us sleep:

> A quoi respondeo
> Quia est in eo
> Virtus dormitiva,
> Cuius est natura
> Sensus assoupire.
> Chorus: Bene, bene, bene respondere
> . . .

[*Le Malade Imaginaire,* 3me Intermède]

Isn't Corin, too, offering a tautology as if it were a substantive point? That's what rain is. Or is he? Shakespeare is at his most elusive here. These are the things that a countryman needs to know—not how to kiss hands, but how to look after his sheep, who have to be protected from the elements. In a world of servants, coaches and umbrellas, rain doesn't wet any more.

Of course, it would be wrong for either of them to win clearly in the third act. The balance must continue to the end: a balance between the play's official self and its undercurrents—for, of course, it is officially pastoral, and on the deepest level, I believe, it stays so. Act I is certainly pastoral in its preference. The court is corrupt, as Le Beau admits with a sad gesture towards a happiness that he can locate only by saying it is not to be found here:

> . . .   Sir, fare you well
> Hereinafter in a better world than this,
> I shall desire more love and knowledge of you.

[I ii 272-5]

We have already been told where this better world is. In (surely) one of the most haunting sentences in English—given, with an irony the play can easily handle, to Charles the thug—we have been told of the Duke's banishment:

> They say he is already in the Forest of Arden, and a many merry men with him; and there they live like the

old Robin Hood of England: they say many young gentlemen flock to him every day, and fleet the time carelessly as they did in the golden world.

[I ii 108 ff.]

England and France are casually mixed up because we are in neither England nor France: this Arden is out of space and time. C. S. Lewis has described very well where it is, in his defence of Spenser's shepherds:

> Some readers cannot enjoy the shepherds because they know (or say they know) that real country people are not more happy or more virtuous than anyone else; but it would be tedious to explain to them the many causes (reasons too) that have led humanity to symbolise by rural scenes and occupations a region in the mind which does exist and which should be visited often.[2]

Arden is the world that Le Beau was longing for (though he, alas, never gets there). The visitors to Arden sing its praises in much the same terms as the Duke's simple solemn eulogy:

> Blow, blow, thou winter wind,
> Thou art not so unkind
> As man's ingratitude.
> . . .

[II vii 175-8]

What little action there is mostly confirms this idyllic view. Orlando 'thought that all things had been savage here', but he finds only hospitality and friendship. Above all, Arden is the place of happy lovers: there they find what they could not find at court—leaving, if necessary, their wickedness behind them. To dress Corin up as Hymen is an ingenious way of relating the happy love-stories to the pastoral element—though at a price, since it destroys the atmosphere of mystery, even magic, that seems to be growing at the end.

All this, then, makes *As You Like It* a pure pastoral . . . but: inevitably, there are buts. First, the action. However much the Duke may like Arden, the moment he is offered his kingdom back he forgets the sermons in stones and takes it. He was speaking as exiled dukes no doubt should in Arden; but he did not actually *mean* it.

As we look carefully at them, all the pastoral points grow slightly dubious. Orlando finds kindness in the forest, but at the hands of courtiers, not countrymen. The lovers marry, but then they leave Arden: it is the place for love but not for marriage. And, most important of all, there are Touchstone and Jaques.

The task of these two choric characters is to comment and to mock: to remind us of what the others forgot. Touchstone, as we have already seen, is explicitly anti-pastoral, mocking the Arcadian life as he mocks romantic love—and often both at once:

> . . . I remember when I was in love I broke my sword upon a stone, and bid him take that for coming a-night

to Jane Smile, and I remember the kissing of her batlet, and the cow's dugs that her pretty chopped hands had milked; . . .

[II iv 42 ff.]

Jaques is a more complicated character, and his relation to the pastoral theme is less obvious. He mocks at romantic love more churlishly than Touchstone ('Rosalind is your love's name?': we can hear the sneer); at poetry ('call you 'em stanzas?'); and at the pastoral life:

If it do come to pass
That any man turn ass,
Leaving his wealth and ease
A stubborn will to please,
. . .

[II v 47-50]

He is anti-pastoral from the moment he appears—indeed, before he appears, for the corollary of telling the Duke that he usurps more than his brother (Jaques's first, reported opinion) is that there should not be any people in Arden—or, at any rate, no courtiers. Jacques welcomes Touchstone into the forest along with that un-Arcadian property, a watch; he thinks marriage should obey the proper rules and not be carried out under a bush, like a beggar. In this his morality is centric; and, most interesting of all, he refuses to go along with the others at the end of the play.

Most interesting: for what he is refusing is to go back to court yet this does not make him a pastoral character. He is not staying in Arden either, not even for the rest of the dance. During the brief time remaining to the play, he would rather stay at the abandoned cave, a forest without pastoralists. After that, he will go where he really belongs: to a monastery or hermitage. There his sneers can be sublimated into *contemptus mundi;* in Arden they are merely kill-joy. Pastoral and monasticism are both retreats from the world, but quite different from each other. A monastery is an act of pure withdrawal, and because of this it can be accepted by the community it withdraws from. Retreat is a human need, and the occasional or partial retreats everyone needs are symbolised and reinforced by the existence of groups who have retreated totally. The countryside, however, is accepted by the court, not psychologically, but economically: it represents, not withdrawal, but simply farming. The pastoral poet is therefore exploiting his medium as the hermit is not, turning country life, which is community life, into an occasion for withdrawal from the community. Out of this exploitation can come a fruitful artistic tension, but this tension will be destroyed by anyone who has no interest whatever in the medium, only in withdrawal. That is why Jaques never felt at home in Arden. Touchstone disliked it because it was not the court. Jaques discovers only at the end that his true vocation is that of an old religious man.

Touchstone and Jaques were added by Shakespeare to Lodge's story.[3] This makes it obvious that he has changed

his source by complicating the simple pastoralism into something more ambivalent, where the choruses undermine the official message. It is not surprising that a few other changes mock the pastoral world, or stand tiptoe on the edge of mockery. Thus Shakespeare removed the violence. Lodge's wrestler kills the franklin's sons and is killed by Rosader; Charles breaks their ribs ('that there is little hope of life in them'), and when he is thrown by Orlando, Le Beau reports, 'He cannot speak, my lord' (the line usually gets a laugh), and Charles is then carried out. No actual deaths, but very nearly. Lodge's usurper is killed in battle; but Shakespeare's, though he raises an army, turns out at the last minute to be harmless:

. . .
And to the skirts of this wild wood he came;
Where meeting with an old religious man,
After some question with him, was converted
Both from his enterprise and from the world,
His crown bequeathing to his banished brother
And all their lands restored to them again
That were with him exiled. This to be true
I do engage my life.

[V iv 164-71]

He needs to engage it, the whole story is so gloriously improbable. The outcome reeks gaily of fairy-tale. Having removed the battle, Shakespeare makes fun of what he has done, as if all you have to do, to get rid of the violence, is to wave a happy ending at your story.

The one touch of violence that remains is the wounding of Orlando, which is brought right on stage in the form of the bloody napkin—at sight of which Rosalind forgets her shepherd's role and almost puts an end to the game she has been playing. This is Shakespeare's comment on the tone of his play. 'Look', he has already said, 'no blood.' Now he says, 'See what blood would do to my pastoral; it would spoil everything'.

Notes

1. Marvell's 'Ametas and Thestylis Making Hay-ropes' was published in *Poems* (1681), but written c. 1650.

2. C. S. Lewis, *The Allegory of Love* (London, 1936), ch. 7.

3. Thomas Lodge, *Rosalynde* (1590) is the source of *As You Like It.*

John Barrell and John Bull (essay date 1974)

SOURCE: "The Elizabethan Pastoral," "The Pastoral Drama," and "The Seventeenth-Century Pastoral," in *The Penguin Book of English Pastoral Verse,* introduced and edited by John Barrell and John Bull, Penguin Books, 1974, pp. 13-20; 107-11; 141-48.

[*In the following excerpts, Barrell and Bull trace the development of English pastoral poetry and its relation to*

*the changing social conditions of the Elizabethan and Ja-
cobean periods. The critics examine the relations between
the conventions of the pastoral mode and the actuality of
rural life as well as the evolving historical reality of
gentlemen-poets' connection with the land.*]

THE ELIZABETHAN PASTORAL

During the Dark and Early Middle ages, the Pastoral all
but disappeared in Europe. It did find some form of expression in the troubadour *pastourelles* in France, poems
which reflect the transition from a popular ballad tradition
to a sophisticated court culture—and thus have as their
dominant theme the conflict between the two worlds in the
attempted seduction of a peasant girl by a courtly knight.
But feudal society was too stratified, too static, to allow a
proper consideration of pastoral matters. Interest in the
Pastoral revives in the Renaissance when the feudal idea
of community is first seriously threatened. But the Pastoral
offered more than a nostalgic myth. It is the *Eclogues* of
Virgil that are taken as a model, with the possibilities that
they afforded for a greater sophistication, for didacticism,
and even for religious satire; an apparently humble cloak
for dangerous thought. As the Bible became available in
the sixteenth century in the vernacular, so the links between the Pastoral and Christ the shepherdking were
strengthened, with an emphasis on the nativity and its associations with the pastoral theme of regeneration and the
coming of the new Golden Age. These strands were most
highly developed in Italy—particularly by Petrarch and by
Mantuan, to whom Spenser's *The Shepheardes Calendar*
acknowledges a debt—and it is by way of Italy that the
mainstream of the Pastoral reaches England.

Apart from a few translations, and the 'eglogs' of Barnabe
Googe, the first important attempt to write an English Pastoral is *The Shepheardes Calendar* (1579), a poem in
which the conventions established by a number of pastoral
poets—Theocritus, Virgil, Sannazaro, Mantuan, Marot—
are assimilated and 'English'd' with remarkable success.
Spenser's shepherds—Colin Clout, Hobbinol, Cuddie and
the rest—have almost all been identified with members of
Spenser's circle and correspondence—Colin is Spenser
himself—and most of them reveal a sophistication, a delicacy, and a learning which a number of critics have
thought so uncharacteristic of shepherds as almost to break
in on the 'kind', to be not at all the proper language of the
genre. But these shepherds, at least as courtly as their European predecessors, are equally capable of the bucolic
roughness we find in Theocritus, and Spenser's problem in
this poem, and his success, was a matter of finding a form
in which the sophisticated and the bucolic could coexist.
The essence of this sort of Pastoral, as William Empson
has put it, is the belief that 'you can say everything about
complex people by a complete consideration of simple
people'; but, however you disguise the fact, this is bound
to involve making shepherds more complex than shepherds are expected to be; so that we can suspend our disbelief only in proportion as we can be made to feel that
these are credible shepherds talking.

Unlike Italy and France, England had still to develop a secure and protected literary language when Spenser began
writing, and even the poets most determinedly devoted to
a separation of genres, of 'kinds', by language as well as
by subject-matter, were liable to find their poems being invaded by words obviously inappropriate to the type of
poem they were writing. A properly written eclogue requires an infusion of dialect—Theocritus' peasants had
spoken in Doric, and Spenser half-invented an archaic provincial dialect to put in the mouths of his shepherds, too.
In Italy and France, where the theory of kinds was well
established, the use of dialect was understood easily for
what it was—the conventional attribute of shepherds and
of the kind appropriate to them. It was not the best language, but the *proper* language of the kind, so that the
'low' words didn't so much point to the low things they
described, as make a general point about the humble status
of Pastoral. In England we find Spenser trying to make the
same point, with the help of cumbersome glosses, but in
The Shepheardes Calendar, and in the Pastorals of many
of his successors, this language has a quite different effect
from the one officially intended. The dialect-words or the
low-life words used by Spenser, or by Drayton for example, are by no means as unusual as they ought to seem,
because they are parts of a language quite proper in other
types of English writing. They will not let us see them as
literary curios, or simply as signs of the kind being used—
they point firmly to the things they denote. When Spenser
refers to a 'galage', or when Drayton mentions 'start-ups',
we recognize that this is a possible version of English
Doric, but we visualize also with disarming clarity the
rude action of the rustic pulling on his boots. The artificial
roughness so carefully cultivated by the pastoral poet gives
way for a moment to a genuine roughness which the Pastoral had previously no less carefully excluded; and as the
language points to an image of a contemporary and a recognizable reality, it suggests the possibility that the Pastoral might be used to describe rural life not only in Arcadia,
but in the England of 1580.

It can hardly be said that Colin, Cuddie and the rest are
made to be particularly knowledgeable about sheep—they
know rather more than a well-read townsman of the twentieth century might be expected to know, but not a great
deal more; it doesn't seem, either, that their credibility is
much to do with the archaisms that Spenser finds for them
to speak. But apart from Colin himself, Spenser's shepherds are capable of speaking with a cheerfully colloquial
tone, and a robustness of expression, which represent a far
more serious attempt to find an English Doric than do the
intrusive and well-researched words from provincial and
Middle English. This tone is not the invariable one of
Hobbinol and the others—it disappears and reappears during the course of each eclogue, and alternates with a far
more courtly tone; so that an eclogue will often be introduced by some talk about sheep and some raillery between
the participants in the dialogue, which gives way to a lyrical complaint, or to a more sententious passage written
partly in a 'higher' language, in turn succeeded by a particularly broad piece of shepherd's talk. This causes some

strange disjunctions of level: the roughness of the shepherds' language invites us to believe in them as real shepherds; but when we do, it is their politeness we are asked to admire, so that we cannot help noticing that these are not shepherd-poets, but sometimes shepherds and sometimes poets; that when they make their complaints, they have to employ a different language from that of their usual banter.

In this way the poem obliges us to recognize a variety of social possibilities and identities: we have to distinguish between a set of low-life characters speaking a fairly plausible version of colloquial, rural English; the friends of Spenser masquerading as these shepherds; Colin himself, masquerading as a more conventional shepherd-poet, who because he is unhappy in love has the excuse never to descend from the polite language into the language of his friends; and those friends again, disguising themselves for a second time, this time as more conventional Arcadian shepherds on Colin's level, whenever they have something of real importance to say. The disjunctions, the different levels, the artifices by which Spenser should be able to lead us away from any contemporary reality, instead keep leading us back to it, and invite us to ask what sort of natural simplicity, what sort of Arcadia, could be the product of so much necessary confusion and artifice.

The idea that the Pastoral is masquerade, that the 'shepherd's weeds' are not the natural attributes of the poet, but are perhaps too self-consciously assumed by him, was much exploited by Shakespeare and by other writers who sometimes chose to be satirical at the Pastoral's expense, but it is never far away from Spenser either. It becomes explicit in the passage from the sixth book of *The Faerie Queene,* included in this anthology. Sir Calidore, staying among the shepherds of Arcadia and finding fair Pastorella unimpressed by his 'courteous guize', assumes the dress of a shepherd and then easily wins her love. But in becoming a shepherd he does not cease to be a chivalrous knight; and when Pastorella finds that she does finally prefer Sir Calidore to the shepherd Corydon, it is because his knightly qualities, so unusual and so becoming in a 'shepherd', strike an answering chord in her heart. For she too, although she does not know it, is not really of shepherd-stock, but of altogether higher degree. Sir Calidore has traditionally been identified with Sir Philip Sidney, and whether or not this was Spenser's intention, the figure of the knight dressed as a shepherd is very close to the hardly less fictitious character attributed to Sir Philip by many Elizabethan writers and nostalgic Jacobeans. The mythological Sir Philip embodied all the values of one kind of pastoral vision: he was the most learned and the most chivalrous courtier, at once the most brilliant individual and the most faceless, the most anonymously perfect knight. He was also the shepherd-poet Astrophel, and author of the *Arcadia,* a model Pastoral in prose and verse; and while in the title of Spenser's 'Astrophel', a pastoral elegy on his death, Sidney is described as 'the most noble and valorous knight', in the poem itself he is 'a *gentle* shepherd borne in Arcady'; that is to say, a shepherd, but an exceptionally well-born one.

The court is of course conventionally opposed in Pastoral to the country, but in the figures of Sir Calidore and Sir Philip courtier and shepherd coexist so harmoniously that it becomes hard to distinguish between them, and in this version of Pastoral both combine in their distrust of the court. We can see fairly clearly here the Golden Age being relocated in the myth of a recent feudal past: the courtier or poet represents himself as estranged from the hurly-burly of the Renaissance court, the world of individualism, the struggles for preferment, so that he becomes an old-fashioned courtly poet, or valorous knight, in a court that has left him behind. This first act of masquerade is followed by a second, as the courtier disguises himself next as a shepherd. The world thus created—in *The Faerie Queene,* and in the poems from the *Arcadia*—has far more to do with the dream of an old social order than with that of a pre-historic Golden Age. It is a world in which a 'natural' chivalry and a 'natural' simplicity replace the artful and the politic, and in which such classes of people as the poem admits can meet in an apparently natural social order, accepted by everyone; so that knights can become shepherds, and knights again, just because there is no question of these transformations reflecting any actual social mobility. The shepherds in Spenser's later Pastoral, and in the *Arcadia,* are far more courtly than were those in the more homely passages of *The Shepheardes Calendar;* one could never imagine Sir Philip as Cuddie, complaining that his shoe was stuck to his foot by the cold.

The prevailing tone of this higher kind of Pastoral is nostalgic, and although nostalgia is a permanent conventional feature of earlier Pastoral, it reappears in Sidney's poems particularly as the malaise of the Renaissance, 'wanhope' or 'accidie'. In Sidney's 'Disprayse of a Courtly life', a courtier presents himself as having been, formerly, a shepherd, who tended his sheep with the other shepherds 'lovingly like friends'; but now he lives in the 'servíle Court', where pride and intrigue make him long for the artlessness of the country; he prays that Pan might restore him to his former state; and the poem ends with the moral that 'the meane estate is best'. But this version of pastoral-courtly 'accidie' is more complex than at first appears, for Sidney's nostalgia is implicitly recognized by him as being for an ideal literary world, and not for any real or possible alternative way of life. As such it carries with it the assurance that no return is possible, that there is nothing to return to.

The nostalgia of Sidney becomes still more problematic when we find it expressed by those already inhabiting his Arcadia. A very large number of the poems from the *Arcadia* itself are laments, some to do with disappointments in love but all expressing a generalized despair which sees no chance of a return or a release. The process by which this final refinement of pastoral nostalgia has been reached is complicated enough: the poet, who first imagines himself as a poet or courtier from an earlier time, then imagines himself as a shepherd in a classical Arcadia; but his nostalgia is not removed by these two movements back in time—it stays with him, so that he finds himself still looking back to the Golden Age he apparently already inhabits, or to a Golden Age before the Golden Age. The hopelessness, the impossibility of Arcadia becomes clearer with each fresh artifice and masquerade—the poets of the generation after Sidney look back to the arguably less artificial *Shepheardes Calendar* to discover how the Pastoral might still be written.

Apart from the dramatists, the most remarkable poet of this next generation is Michael Drayton, who in *The Shepheardes Garland* (1593) is clearly impatient with masquerades and searches for Arcadia. There is in Drayton's Pastoral no simple or formal nostalgia for the Golden Age—his shepherds are old, their time has past, they live on to mock the pastoral pretensions of those around them. The few youthful shepherds in these eclogues are quickly relieved of their lyricism and their hopes by their much-lived elders. *The Shepheardes Garland* is centred on the ageing Rowland (presumably the poet) who looks back to a time when life was better, a time before urbanization and the first processes of the manufacturing industries, before the trees were ripped up to reveal the mineral earth beneath them. There is no suggestion of a recoverable pastoral age, for 'the golden age is gone' and 'wishes may not revoke that which is past'. The tone is one of almost unrelieved pessimism. In the final eclogue, Rowland, after half a night lamenting the hopelessness of his past aspirations, retires to bed, 'never a man alive so hard bested'. The future has nothing to offer, and the contemplation of the past brings only despair.

Drayton never really fitted into the court circle to which he looked so unsuccessfully for patronage. In the fourth eclogue, Wynkin bemoans the loss of Sir Philip Sidney, in the shape of Elphin, 'the God of Poesie', and we see not only the pessimistic awareness of the growth of a new kind of urban, not courtly, culture, but an acute sense of the significance for poetry of this change. Drayton's Pastoral, for all its freshness and its brilliance of detail, is a self-conscious turning-back not to some imaginary idealized Arcadia but to a time immediately before he was writing, the great period of Spenser and Sidney; the world those poets had turned away from has become an Arcadia for Drayton. And his despair is the stronger precisely because he can no longer locate the Golden Age in a mythical and a feudal past. In the first eclogue, Rowland, surrounded by all the traditional emblems of a pastoral Spring, remains as an aged shepherd outside the tradition that has produced him, a creature of Winter:

> The heavens with their glorious starry frame,
> Preparde to crowne the sable-vayled night:
> When *Rowland* from this time-consumed stock,
> With stone-colde hart now stalketh towards his flock.

The final line—and especially that sudden change of tense—removes Rowland's despair from the well-rehearsed lines of conventional complaint, and introduces a personal tone that is predominant throughout the rest of the eclogues.

In the eighth eclogue we have the deliberate archaism of Motto's 'worthy rhyme' of Dowsabell, which seems to exist only to indicate its irrelevance in a changed society. The story, with its heavy echoes of Chaucer—and so with the suggestion of an earlier literary 'pastoral' age when it was possible for the poet to prosper—delights the reader with its simple expression of reciprocated love, only to return him inevitably to the sad and unfulfilled reality of the present; just as elsewhere, the love poetry of the young Rowland can be recalled, but only ironically. There was no possibility of a resurrection of an Elphin, for the Elizabethan Golden Age (that of Betta in the third eclogue) had ended. The courtly shepherd with his elaborate series of masks has been replaced in Drayton by the figure of the poet no longer able to rely on court patronage. For the first time in the development of the English Pastoral the poet finds himself quite shut out of his courtly Arcadia. The sense of despair is even stronger in the revised version of the eclogues, produced after the accession of James I, when 'malice denies mee entrance with my sheepe'. In the revised ninth eclogue (which becomes the tenth in the second version) in an image which recalls the end of the original first eclogue, brings Rowland no longer to a restless sleep, but to death; as one who 'as a stone, alreadie seemed dead'.

．．．．．

THE PASTORAL DRAMA

The reaction against the aristocratic Arcadia of Spenser and Sidney was led by the Elizabethan and Jacobean dramatists, and in particular by Shakespeare. Sidney and Spenser were eloquent adherents to a European tradition which saw poetry in terms of different 'kinds' with different subjects appropriate to them; so that kings, lords, military leaders could properly appear only in the Heroic kind, or the Tragic, while Pastoral was concerned with a polite version of low life as it was lived by shepherds. But when Pastoral began to be written in England, there was already a native tradition directly inimical to such a hierarchical idea of literature. Other poets, in other countries of Europe, had achieved in the Pastoral kind a fairly unproblematic synthesis of elements in their native literatures, whether peasant songs or pastoral ballads, with the conventions they had inherited from the ancients; but only in England had a popular drama developed, during the Middle Ages, in which it was not at all unusual for members of the highest and the lowest ranks of society to be represented together on the stage. An example of an English comedy in which courtly and low-life characters are brought together in a version of Pastoral [is] *Sir Clyomon and Clamydes* . . . , and the culmination of the tradition can be seen, of course, in Shakespeare, and perhaps particularly in the relationship between Prince Hal and the riff-raff of the Boar's Head. It is not that social distinctions are done away with in this English tradition; they preoccupy Shakespeare considerably, and their importance is continually reaffirmed by him; but in English drama, and to an extent in the Elizabethan novel, these distinctions can be explored by figures from the nobility and from low-life together. This tradition had begun with the medieval Christian drama, in which differences of rank had receded into unimportance before the long perspectives of purgatory and damnation; and it was well equipped to deal with the social confusions of England in the second half of Elizabeth's reign in a way which the pure Pastoral—with its commitment to deal only with low-life characters, or with courtiers masquerading as shepherds—was not.

In Shakespeare's *As You Like It,* the pretensions of the Pastoral to provide a possible alternative to the struggles of the courtly life are deflated, at the same time as we are still invited to enjoy those pretensions for what they are worth. Shakespeare's technique in this play is to bring together two sorts of shepherd from two literary traditions: Corin and Audrey belong to a native English tradition, the impossibly earthy rustics who had been made fun of in *Sir Clyomon and Clamydes;* Silvius and Phebe are a refined and delicate shepherd and shepherdess from the pages of the *Arcadia.* When the courtly characters Rosalind, Celia and Touchstone first arrive in the forest of Arden, they seem to expect from Corin something of the welcome that Sir Calidore found among the shepherds of *The Faerie Queene;* Corin replies that he wishes he could be of more help, but he is 'shepherd to another man', who is not given to deeds of hospitality. This intrusion of economic realities into the English Arcadia invites us to expect that Shakespeare will go out of his way to point the contrast between Corin and the anachronistic lovers Silvius and Phebe; but in fact almost all the weight of Shakespeare's satire is brought to bear against the genuinely low-life shepherds. For Touchstone, in his conversations with Corin and with Audrey, keeps insisting, and reasonably enough, that if theirs is the pastoral life it is really not more attractive than life at court; the simplicity of the one hardly compensates for the loss of comfort in leaving the other. And this insistence, that there is a pastoral life which is both real and difficult, creates the context in which we can evaluate the pastoral tradition inhabited by Silvius and Phebe, and indeed the pastoral elements in the play as a whole. We are invited to enjoy this courtly Pastoral, but for what it obviously is—a masquerade, a game for the amusement of bored courtiers and not a conceivable alternative to the uncongenial and disorderly reality of life in Elizabeth's court.

In contrast, *The Winter's Tale,* which dates from late in Shakespeare's career, does seem to offer the pastoral life as a serious alternative to that of the court. The play divides naturally into three sections: the court where jealousy and tyranny prevail; the countryside of Bohemia which displays all the virtues of the simple rural life in a naturalistic setting; and finally the court again, improved and softened by its contact with the country. Shakespeare has altered his main source (Greene's *Pandosto,* 1592) in ways which emphasize the *positive* qualities of the pastoral alternative. The old Shepherd who finds the abandoned Perdita thinks naturally of caring for the child before he discovers the treasure left with her, whereas in Greene the baby and the wealth are discovered simultaneously and covetousness is the prime instigation of the action of the shepherd and his wife. Furthermore, Shakespeare's presen-

tation of the lives of the shepherds is much more vivid (as is evident from the extract in this anthology), and the detailed celebration of the natural life has no counterpart either in Greene or in the forest in *As You Like It.* The sheep-shearing feast-scene was frequently played as a separate piece throughout the late eighteenth century, and the removal of this scene from its courtly setting is a fair indication of the nature of its appeal.

However, in spite of the presentation of a court life ameliorated by that of the country, it is evident that the strength of *The Winter's Tale* is essentially that of myth. The court may be infused with the virtues of the country, but there is never a formal fusion. The possibility of an actual, as opposed to a mythic, social mobility, is mocked when (V, 2) the old Shepherd and the Clown are rewarded for their fostering of the King's daughter by being made Gentlemen, and yet still continue to act the role of naïve and gullible rustics. The two finest ornaments of the rural scene are (of course) disguised aristocrats; Perdita is always seen to be as different from her fellow shepherds as was Pastorella in *The Faerie Queene;* and the Prince Florizel has no difficulty in recognizing her aristocratic qualities through her 'unusual weeds'. Indeed her part as Queen of the Feast is a recognition of her implied majesty. Perdita gives to Camillo and the disguised Polixenes flowers worthy of their age, hybrid carnations and gillyflowers, 'which some call Natures bastards', thus affording Polixenes opportunity to discourse on the benefits of a cross-breeding of the 'baser kind' and the 'nobler race', precisely that process which, as it appears, will occur if he consents to the marriage of his son Florizel to the base Perdita. Ironically, it is Perdita who argues against the marriage of the high and the low, court and country. The world of *The Winter's Tale* is ultimately that of the 'Whitsun Pastorals', where, for a short while, the illusion of social mobility can appear, but where in the end the old harmony and the old order will prevail. Shakespeare's court audience always knows that the beautiful and virtuous shepherdess is Perdita, the heir to the throne of Sicily. *The Winter's Tale* may preach on the surface a gospel of cross-breeding, but the final effect is a celebration not of the rural life but, albeit often ambiguously, of that of the court; thus the play both proclaims and precludes the alternative.

Shakespeare's success in the dramatic Pastoral had much to do with his willingness to bring together the conventions of the 'right Pastoral' and those of English low-life comedy; in *As You Like It* he was concerned to distinguish between these two traditions, in *The Winter's Tale* to join them together in a fiction of the pastoral life at once delightful and credible. Ben Jonson, in his play *The Sad Shepherd* (c. 1612), appears to be trying to write as conventional and proper a Pastoral as he can, but one dealing with English and not Arcadian shepherds; the result is a sort of epitaph on the first phase of conventional English Pastoral. Like Corin in *As You Like It,* the shepherds in Jonson's play are quite conscious of the economic realities which have stopped Sherwood Forest from being an English Arcadia. The exchange of speeches on pages 133-5 is an eloquent account of the appearance in Sherwood of a new sort of sheep-farmer, more acquisitive than the old, and puritanical in attitude to the traditional feasts and sports of English shepherds. This theme, or a version of it, will be heard again from time to time throughout the history of the Pastoral in England; and yet it comes more strangely from the mouths of Jonson's shepherds than it had from Shakespeare's Corin. The language Jonson invents for the shepherds in his play has a delightful simplicity which nevertheless belongs quite clearly to the formal, the courtly Pastoral, far more than to the English comic tradition. They complain of their fate in a homelier version of the same sophisticated Arcadian despair we saw in Sidney; and, like Sidney's shepherds, their tone reveals a quite fatalistic acceptance of their obsolescence. And in this way the sense of an old style of shepherd unequipped to deal with the demands of a changing style of agriculture is matched precisely by our sense of the inadequacy of the old pastoral conventions to deal with this sort of intrusion of reality. These shepherds are automata, wound up years ago but still stumbling around the changed landscape; they are trapped by an anachronistic tradition, by the fact that Jonson is not prepared to admit any very thorough mixture of kinds; so that the shepherds can never become genuinely comic in a way that might re-animate them, and make us feel their disappearance is less than inevitable.

. . . . .

THE SEVENTEENTH-CENTURY PASTORAL

'The *Golden-Age* was when the world was yong' for Fulke Greville and his fellow 'Spenserians', but for most poets after about 1610 the pastoral age had not only receded but had disappeared from view. Writers of Pastoral in the years between the accession of James I and the outbreak of the Civil War—where they are to be found—concur in Drayton's location of the Golden Age within the historical development of the English Pastoral. The second book of William Browne's *Britannia's Pastorals* opens with a nostalgic eulogy of Spenser, and the sense of an era having past is prevalent. The dominant model for such writers is the later Spenser, of *The Faerie Queene*. It has been argued that in Browne we have the first evidence of an actual observed English landscape—a move, that is, away from the classical towards the romantic—but, as in works like Phineas Fletcher's *The Purple Island,* it is the formal rehearsal of past artificiality that is most striking. The Golden Age has passed, and as the life of the Court becomes increasingly subjected to external political pressures the possibility of a celebration of a courtly idealism is ever more problematic.

The metaphysical poets were rarely interested in a pastoral tradition—Donne's 'The Baite' is little more than an exercise-piece, one in a long and ever more tedious series of replies to Marlowe's long-dead 'Passionate Sheepheard'. The imagery of the metaphysicals, where it is not concerned with personal salvation, is insistently contemporary, full of references to a new mercantile age, to commerce, exploration, political struggle and conquest. The

poetry is critical of the values of such an age undoubtedly, but the poets no longer see a viable alternative in a world of pastoral innocence. In place of a vision of a simple, harmonized society, the metaphysicals looked for a resolution of contemporary problems in terms of the individual, be it in the area of the religious or the secular. A pastoral tradition which had arisen in reaction to an awakening of an individualist philosophy in the Renaissance had little to offer a writer intent on exploring the new world of scientific rationalism. The poetry of the metaphysical period is largely that of an urban culture which no longer feels sufficient connection with a rural alternative, an alternative which had anyway become ever more an artifice and a way of avoiding the contemporary and the threatening. The poet's problems were to be faced either in their urban context or by a turning inwards; a school of poetry which could call into question the whole manner of discussing human relationships taken over from Petrarch and an Italian tradition would clearly have little use for that other foreign importation, the Pastoral.

Where there is any expression of the pastoral vision it is either from poets looking back (those who looked through Drayton to Spenser) to an aristocratic culture that had all but passed, or . . . as an implicit assumption in urban and court satire. At the same time, however, the seventeenth century sees the emergence of a different kind of pastoral voice, one that expresses no longer a merely idealized view of the countryside surrounding the town which housed the poet, and one which makes for the first time hesitant moves in the direction of 'realism'. The two sonnets of Drummond (another 'Spenserian') that we have included are very similar in theme, both praising an actual retreat from an urban world of politics and commerce. It is a theme that derives chiefly from Horace—Pope's 'Ode to Solitude' is included as a later example of juvenile borrowing from the Horatian—but its origins may also be sought in a non-pastoral area, the essay-form as developed by Montaigne. This turning away from the 'real' world of affairs is very much like the 'turning inwards' of the metaphysicals, and in a writer such as Cowley the two become merged. The country is seen as a place where the individual is free to find himself. What is different about this rural alternative is that it purports to have a specific geographical location—that is, the poet is not wandering around a classical landscape, but is supposedly living in the country with a roof over his head and a plot of land to work for his food. The seventeenth century produced many 'imitations' of Horace's 'Epode, In Praise of a Country Life', and, although space will not permit examples, the opening of that of Jonson will make the point:

> Happie is he, that from all Business cleere,
> As the old race of Mankind were,
> With his owne Oxen tills his Sires left lands,
> And is not in the Usurers bands:
> Nor Souldier-like started with rough alarmes,
> Nor dreads the Seas inraged harmes:
> But flees the Barre and Courts, with the proud bords,
> And waiting Chambers of great Lords.

The group ritual of the older pastoral is replaced by an emphasis on the individual's relationship to his own land—the possession of 'paternal acres' is all-important. The poet never imagines himself living below his own social level, as a shepherd or traditional pastoral figure, so that the fantasy of country property—and fantasy it is, for Jonson like most celebrators of such a retreat possessed not a single field to till—does at least have a solid connection with the poet's life.

What is being celebrated here is more than an imaginative escape from the pressures of urban life; it is also the possibility of economic freedom for the writer. The fantasy is an adaptation of the situation of the pastoral poet to that of his patron, the landowner. What these poems represent is a 'bourgeois' version of the myth, with the poet, no longer cast as shepherd or clown, in the role of gentry-farmer supporting himself single-handedly—or probably with the aid of a buxom country wife—in such a way as to leave ample time for the main business of philosophical reflection. The patronage of the manor house is replaced by the freedom of the self-sufficient small farm.

But if the manor house had meant restriction, it had also meant security. As a microcosm of the larger society it symbolized both power and patronage, and stood in a relationship of mutual dependence with the rural community around it. The values of this world are invoked by Jonson in 'To Penshurst', when however this harmonious relationship is not the rule but the exception. The poet eats, as do the 'farmer and the clowne', the same food as the 'lord and lady', and he is happy to celebrate their munificence. The house which had given birth to the Pastoral—Sidney had lived there—still remains as a final embodiment of the pastoral myth of aristocratic organization; farmers and classical gods walk the same fields. As in Carew's 'To Saxham', the fish, flesh and fowl of the estate queue happily for their turn to be eaten; the humour is deliberate and indicates the ultimate impossibility of the vision. Jonson may express a nostalgia for what Penshurst represents but he is too much the realist not to realize that it is something that has passed.

Herrick's 'The Hock-Cart' is an attempt, from a Cavalier perspective, to deal honestly with the nature of the bond between the landowner and his workers. The union of the two groups is achieved in the ritual of the harvest-feast - a recurrent theme in the Pastoral—when the workers put down their tools to celebrate their master in feast and song. But the relationship is harsher than that; the harvest-feast slurs over the reality. The following morning will see the old order of ruler and ruled re-established, and the brief equality of the feast will cease. Like the oxen that pull their ploughs, the workers will resume their toil;

> And, you must know, your Lords word's true,
> Feed him ye must, whose food fils you.
> And that this pleasure is like raine,
> Not sent ye for to drowne your paine,
> But for to make it spring againe.

This strain, which becomes ever more evident throughout the century, makes it increasingly difficult for the serious perpetuation of this kind of pastoral celebration. Civil strife and the growth of a new landowning class would complete the process. When Pope refers to a vision of a restored 'manor house' community a century later, his appeal is one of political nostalgia. The account of rural organization had always been a mythical one, and the nearer it approaches to 'realism' the more its bones are revealed to all.

This sense of the passing of an age finds its greatest expression in Milton's 'Lycidas' (1637). The poem is a revitalization of an old form—the pastoral elegy—and also, in effect, an elegy for the Pastoral. The poet mourns the death of the young shepherd, Lycidas—Edward King, a young Cambridge scholar—and argues that with his death, the possibility of the traditional Pastoral has ended. Milton had already, in 'L'Allegro' (c. 1631), drawn heavily on the earlier Pastoral. Milton's shepherds are unable to play a pastoral role; the sheep are untended and hungry; the shearers have lost their skills; and the poet disturbs nature in his sorrow, preventing the coming of Spring and a new pastoral cycle. But 'Lycidas' is not just the culmination of the 'idealized' tradition. The world of the traditional Pastoral is opposed by that of the Christian myth, and the poem concludes with a resolution of the two in the resurrection of Lycidas into a heavenly paradise—not the now impossible earthly one—leaving the poet with renewed hope, to wander in 'fresh woods, and pastures new'. Although the poem is full of echoes of the past—the inclusion of anti-clerical satire, for instance, is sanctioned by Spenser's 'Fifth Eclogue'—the tone is not finally one of impossible nostalgia. The world of Lycidas has passed, and the poet, having assimilated the past, must find his own way in the new world. The conclusion is optimistic and indicative of an emergent Protestant consciousness on Milton's part, with the emphasis falling on the individual's break with the tradition.

There is a considerable amount of reference to the world of conventional Pastoral in *Paradise Lost* as well. In Book IX the reader's pastoral expectations are played upon for dramatic effect with the presentation of Satan 'as one who long in populous City pent'; but it is in Book IV that we find a full fusion of the classical and the christian Pastoral. No account of the Garden of Eden could conceivably ignore the pastoral tradition, and it is not too surprising to find 'Universal Pan' walking the same groves as Adam and Eve. In Book IV, Milton leaves the grand epic style for a quieter, pastoral voice. His Paradise is very like Blake's state of 'Innocence' in which the beasts of the earth pose no threat to man, and God's creatures live the 'happiest life (of) simplicitie and spotless innocence'. But Milton does not see Paradise as a pre-Rousseauite home for 'natural-man'. He is concerned to present the Garden as a planted Garden, a creation of the universal architect, and in opposition to the chaos that is the world of Satan and unbridled passion. The pastoral represented an ordered nature for man before the Fall, an environment which offered no threat.

The opposition of created Garden and unspoilt Nature is obviously central to the Pastoral, but it is an opposition that may take many forms. Untamed Nature may be a place of repose from the vexations of the town, or a threat to man in organized society; the Garden may appear as a recognition of the essential harmony of the natural order, or a denial of it. The poet who is most concerned with the ambiguities of this opposition in the seventeenth century is Andrew Marvell. In his 'mower' poems, the cultivated Garden is not an indication—as it is in Milton—of an ordered Universe, but is an urban phenomenon, the product of 'Luxurious Man' after the Fall. It is only in the exotic 'Bermudas' that Marvell's puritan emigrés can find an unaltered paradise, far from the possibility of urban 'knowledge'. 'The Mower against Gardens' suggests the impossibility of harmony between man and his environment, and thus offers a serious threat to the entire pastoral tradition. But there is no simple praise of the natural life, for wild Nature is always threatening. The figure of the innocent but ineffective Shepherd is rejected in favour of the Mower with his destructive relationship to the land, 'depopulating all the ground'. The mower does not respond to the natural, as does the shepherd, but struggles against it, reducing it to order. So that although he is hostile towards the artificiality of cultivation, it is his job precisely to tame Nature, to tailor it more neatly for urban man. This ambiguity of attitude becomes even more complicated when we realize that there is no straightforward identification by Marvell with the mower. In 'Ametas and Thestylis making Hay-Ropes'—a poem whose apparent simplicity is deceptive—the world of urban metaphysical wit is thrown over for the natural rural activity of weaving, in imagery which combines the idea of work, dancing and copulation. Again the sterility of the city is opposed by the natural activities of the country, but activities which have a sense of pattern, of order.

The problems raised by Marvell's poetry are many and complex, and it is in 'The Garden' that he comes nearest to resolving them. The poem contrasts the efforts of ambitious urban man who labours incessantly to win the 'Palm . . . Oke, or Bayes', with a vision of a natural paradise in which the individual, free from society, has the whole of Nature dancing attendance:

> What wond'rous Life in this I lead!
> Ripe Apples drop about my head;
> The Luscious Clusters of the Vine
> Upon my Mouth do crush their Wine.

But—although Marvell clearly conjures with imagery of a sensual Garden of Eden, the poem does not adopt a nostalgic Golden Age tone; nor is Marvell acceding wholly to the Horatian tradition of 'retreat'. He regards the original Eden as an idealized pastoral condition before the demands of human relationships enforced a separation of needs and desires, and considers how to achieve this paradise once more. Thus the Garden is both a place of natural retreat, where the trees 'weave the Garlands of repose' allowing the poet to think in serenity; and a created retreat,

giving evidence of the hand of a gardener. The Garden is a paradise of the imagination, to be found by a turning inwards:

> Mean while the Mind, from pleasure less,
> Withdraws into its happiness;
> The Mind, that Ocean where each kind
> Does streight its own resemblance find;
> Yet it creates, transcending these,
> Far other Worlds, and other Seas;
> Annihilating all that's made
> To a green Thought in a green Shade.

The Garden is a world within the world and not a separation from it; it is a state of individual harmony that has no geographical placement, and is not to be achieved by the labour of men as conventionally understood. The traditional oppositions of the Pastoral are reconciled in Marvell's 'happy Garden-state', and the Golden Age is relocated in the world of puritan individualism.

Louis Adrian Montrose (essay date 1983)

SOURCE: "Of Gentlemen and Shepherds: The Politics of Elizabethan Pastoral Form," in *ELH*, Vol. 50, No. 3, Autumn 1983, pp. 415-59.

[*In the following excerpt, Montrose offers an historical prologue to reading the Elizabethan pastoral, and claims that the pastoral embodies the contradictory values of Elizabethan social life.*]

I SHEPHERDS AND CRITICS

Modern theories of pastoral have a way of turning into theories of literature. Perhaps the most influential of such theories have been those of William Empson and Renato Poggioli. The former isolates the pastoral "process" in verbal strategies for "putting the complex into the simple"; the latter analyzes the pastoral "impulse" as a projective mechanism for the sublimation of civilization's discontents.[1] Such generous definitions have encouraged a transformation of virtually every kind of literary text into yet another version of pastoral. Indeed, the rage for pastoral and pastoralization evident in Anglo-American literary studies during the past quarter century seems in itself to constitute a symptomatic pastoral impulse, an exemplary pastoral process: to write *about* pastoral may be a way of displacing and simplifying the discontents of the latter-day humanist in an increasingly technocratic academy and society; the study of pastoral may have become a metapastoral version of pastoral. The version of pastoral I shall propose here is predicated upon a recognition of the historical and social specificity of literary forms and formal categories—and, indeed, of the very concept of "literature"—an acknowledgment that criticism is a cultural practice that ineluctably constructs the meanings it purports to transcribe. I have not written a comprehensive survey of Elizabethan pastoral literature; on the contrary, I have been highly selective in the use of examples, aiming at suggestive hypotheses rather than exhaustive descriptions.[2] The present essay is intended as a prolegomenon and a provocation to the rereading of Elizabethan pastoral texts.

The historical study of Elizabethan pastoralism cannot confine its inquiry to matters of literary taxonomy and thematics, to what pastorals "are" or what they "mean"; it must also ask what pastorals *do,* and by what operations they perform their cultural work. Such an inquiry may necessitate a transformation of the theoretical assumptions—explicit or implied—upon which much modern criticism of Elizabethan literature has been founded. For example, consider the theoretical assumptions of Laurence Lerner's recent study, *The Uses of Nostalgia,* a book on pastoral that is indebted to the ideas of Empson and Poggioli.[3] With ironic condescension, Lerner writes that "the sixteenth century found no difficulty in knowing what pastoral was: it was a poem about shepherds." Lerner's project is "to set what pastoral really is against what it was supposed to be," even if this requires him "to tamper with history" (39). His book "does not discuss any poems simply because their characters are dressed up as shepherds and shepherdesses" (34); "courtier and shepherd," after all, "are just trappings" (39). There is, we are told, "a good deal of the pastoral impulse in literature that is not pastoral in form—just as there were pastorals in the sixteenth century that observed no more than the mechanics of the tradition" (39). In response, we might ask how a tradition can be separated from its "mechanics," and what a pastoral "impulse" that is not embodied in pastoral *form* might be. What is here objectified as "theme" is itself the critic's own rewriting of the intrinsically *formal* constituents of a text. Merely to pose the question of "what pastoral really is" is to situate oneself within an idealist aesthetics that represses the historical and material determinations in any written discourse, including the critic's own. "What pastoral really is" can only be addressed in terms of what it was, and is, "thought to be." Lerner's work exemplifies a curiously widespread indifference to the possibility that pastoral's merely conventional, formal, or mechanical elements may themselves require (and reward) interpretation. We might do well to reverse Lerner's perspective, to consider pastoral as the manifestation of an impulse to dress up characters as shepherds and shepherdesses. Such a shift might help us to "reproblematize" the significance of pastoral's dominant modal form—"a poem about shepherds"—and to clarify the mode's historical vicissitudes.[4] As far as Elizabethan writers were concerned, pastorals were indeed poems about shepherds, if only figuratively so; for them, it was precisely the shepherdly trappings that made pastorals pastoral.[5] And it is the culture-specific significance of such conventions upon which any historicist criticism must insist.[6]

One of the strengths of Empson's own perspective was its suggestion that pastoral forms may not only embody individual psychological accomodations to the social order (as Poggioli suggests) but may also mediate class differences and ideological contradictions, so as to make a particular version of "the social order" possible:

> The essential trick of the old pastoral, which was felt to imply a beautiful relation between rich and poor, was to make simple people express strong feelings (felt as the most universal subject, something fundamentally true about everybody) in learned and fashionable language (so that you wrote about the best subject in the best way). From seeing the two sorts of people combined like this you thought the better of both; the best parts of both were used. The effect was in some degree to combine in the reader or author the merits of the two sorts; he was made to mirror in himself more completely the effective elements of the society he lived in.
>
> (*Some Versions of Pastoral,* 11-12)

Kenneth Burke, an early advocate of Empson's book, sharpened its implications for an ideological analysis by observing that pastoral deals with "class consciousness" not by emphasizing conflict but by aiming at "a stylistic transcending of conflict" in symbols of communion, thereby contributing "to the 'mystifications' of class."[7] The representative strengths of aristocratic and peasant values and styles are combined—but only for the benefit of the peasant's betters, Empson's "reader" and "author." When, in 1594, a rural laborer in Essex asked rhetorically, "What can rich men do against poor men if poor men rise and hold together?" he was, in effect, demystifying "the beautiful relation between rich and poor" that Empson poses as the pastoral trick.[8]

The element of ideological criticism in the work of Empson and Burke has given sinews to the modern study of pastoral. But the conception of a rigid dichotomy of economic class—the rich and the poor—misrepresents the multiple and overlapping status hierarchies of Elizabethan society, and the connotations of a pastoral "trick" are too crudely conspiratorial to describe the complex mediations through which cultural forms and social relations are reciprocally shaped.[9] Nevertheless, despite its oversimplifications and anachronisms, Empson's perspective does point us toward a more precise characterization of the interplay between Elizabethan pastorals and Elizabethan society. This may be specified as a dialectic between Elizabethan *pastoral forms* and Elizabethan *social categories.* Elizabethan pastoral forms may have worked to mediate differential relationships of power, prestige, and wealth in a variety of social situations, and to have variously marked and obfuscated the hierarchical distinctions—the symbolic boundaries—upon which the Elizabethan social order was predicated. I shall develop this proposition in the succeeding sections of the present essay. Before doing so, however, I should like to consider further the materialist critique of pastoral mystification adumbrated in the writings of Burke.

In *The Country and the City,* Raymond Williams has attacked "the ordinary modern meaning of pastoral" that has been institutionalized by academic criticism.[10] He points out that such an approach is confined to the superstructural elements of texts and traditions, that it fails to confront the social embeddedness of literary discourse. Working from within a countertradition of agrarian radicalism, Williams excavates the complex mediations by which English literature grows from the soil of English society—how poems and novels embody changing modes of production and property relations, the shifting dialectic between rural and urban forms of social life. Williams' study challenges the ideological assumptions of that "English pastoral tradition" which has been shaped by Anglo-American literary criticism. *The Country and the City* is important for the study of Elizabethan works conventionally called "pastoral" even though—in part, perhaps, because—Williams refuses to consider them. He writes that "Virgil, like Hesiod, could raise the most serious questions of life and its purposes in the direct world in which the working year and the pastoral song are still there in their own right" (21). And it is an imitation of this "direct world," an accurate reflection of the material conditions of an agrarian society, that is the focus of Williams' analyses and the touchstone for his judgments:

> The achievement, if it can be called that, of the Renaissance adaption of just these classical modes [i.e., Virgil's eclogues and georgics] is that, step by step, these living tensions are excised, until there is nothing countervailing, and selected images stand as themselves: not in a living but in an enamelled world. . . . What happened in the aristocratic transformation was the reduction of these primary activities to forms, whether the "vaile" of allegory or the fancy dress of court games.
>
> (18, 21)

Here Williams uses "form" as a pejorative term. Yet Virgil, by the very act of writing, also necessarily "reduced" the "primary activities" of herding and planting to "forms"—namely, the eclogue and the georgic. And, in a more fundamental sense, these "primary activities" themselves embody and reproduce culture-specific forms of practical knowledge appropriate to pastoral and agrarian modes of production. When Williams writes of the world of "the working year and the pastoral song" as a *direct* world, his nostalgic vision is tempered by his political commitment.

The Country and the City is a work of powerful and eloquent moral indignation; one that effectively and honestly demonstrates that the politics of literature are inseparable from the politics of criticism. However, in his brief and categorical dismissal of "the Renaissance adaption" of pastoral, Williams uncharacteristically oversimplifies the ideological complexity of a large and heterogeneous corpus of cultural texts. A vulgarization of Williams' perspective on Renaissance pastoral introduces a recent anthology of English pastoral verse: "The pastoral vision is, at base, a false vision, positing a simplistic, unhistorical relationship between the ruling, landowning class—the poet's patrons and often the poet himself—and the workers on the land; as such its function is to mystify and to obscure the harshness of actual social and economic organization."[11] Although I am in sympathy with the thrust of this argument, I find its own formulation to be simplistic and unhistorical. In his more recent work, Williams has explicitly repudiated an outmoded Marxian aesthetic in which cul-

ture is represented as a superstructural reflection of an economic base. This model, which to some degree continues to inform Williams' critical practice in *The Country and the City,* has been succeeded by one in which culture is represented as at once more autonomous in its processes and more material in its means and relations of production.[12] If we construe "culture as the *signifying system* through which necessarily (though among other means) a social order is communicated, reproduced, experienced and explored" (*Culture,* 13), then the making of Renaissance pastoral "forms" may now appear to be not merely a process of "reduction" or simply a "false vision," but rather a "primary activity" in its own right: "forms and conventions in art and literature [are] inalienable elements of a social material process" (*Marxism and Literature,* 133). Thus the transformation of agrarian activity into pastoral form can be construed as an instance of a totalizing cognitive process by which Elizabethan experience was structured, represented, and reproduced. Williams, following Antonio Gramsci, postulates such a "hegemonic" process:

> Hegemony is . . . not only the articulate upper level of "ideology," nor are its forms of control only those ordinarily seen as "manipulation" or "indoctrination." It is a whole body of practices and expectations, over the whole of living. . . . It is a lived system of meanings and values—constitutive and constituting—which as they are experienced as practices appear as reciprocally confirming.
>
> (*Marxism and Literature,* 110)

Elizabethan pastoral discourse is indeed "ideological" (in Williams' narrowed conception of that term) but is not reducible to a particular ideology—which is what Williams seems to imply in *The Country and the City.* My subject is that "aristocratic transformation" of pastoral which Williams has repudiated as the "reduction" of "living tensions" to "an enamelled world." I am not concerned to apologize for this version of pastoral but rather to understand some of the reasons for its cultural vitality and to locate its place within the "lived system" of Elizabethan "meanings and values."

The eclogue was the pastoral genre inherited and imitated by Renaissance poets. But Elizabethan pastoral is characterized by a proliferation into other genres of what Alastair Fowler calls "conscious model innovations" ("The Life and Death of Literary Forms," 214): not only are there eclogues and interpolated pastoral episodes within larger narrative and dramatic forms, but also lyrics, romances, satires, comedies and tragicomedies, erotic Ovidian narratives, pageants and masques, all of which may be wholly or partially pastoral. It is this explosion of pastoral possibilities that makes the last decades of the sixteenth century and the first decades of the seventeenth century the golden age of English pastoral literature. Pastoral pervades the forms and performances of Elizabethan culture. It is ubiquitous not only in established literary and pictorial genres but also in religious, political, and didactic texts and in the figurative discourse of letters, speeches, and recorded conversation. What all of these texts have in common is not a genre, theme, or impulse but rather a nexus of conventional persons, places, animals, objects, activities, and relations. These conventions combine into a symbolic formation which has been selected and abstracted from a whole way of life that is materially pastoral, a world in which animal husbandry is a primary means of production. Thus, the properties of Elizabethan pastoral are *formal* properties, formal properties rooted not only in a literary tradition but also in those conditions of Elizabethan social and economic life to which that tradition continues to be meaningful. Therefore, the logical place to begin studying the social matrix of Elizabethan pastoral form should be in the pastures themselves, where we can observe the material conditions and relations of an agrarian society. But if we are to follow the direction of the pastoral process, we shall find that we must very soon shift our ground from the country to the court. Such is the trajectory of this essay: part two explores the inhibition of relations between agrarian life and pastoral form in terms of an Elizabethan preoccupation with the discriminations of social status. . . .

II Commons and Gentles

Nine out of ten people in Elizabethan England were rural dwellers, and sheep outnumbered people, perhaps by as many as three to one. This was a society dependent upon unreliable sources of agrarian production for its physical survival, and dependent upon sheep for food and fertilizer as well as for wool, the raw material of England's basic industry.[13] Foreign visitors were repeatedly struck by the abundantly pastoral quality of the English landscape, its inhabitation by "countless numbers of sheep." Such travelers' accounts corroborate the opinion of a native: in his *Description of England,* William Harrison maintains that

> Our sheep are very excellent, sith for sweetness of flesh they pass all other. And . . . our wools [are] to be preferred before those of . . . other places.

> Certes this kind of cattle is more cherished in England than standeth well with the commodity of the commons or prosperity of divers towns, whereof some are wholly converted to their feeding; yet such a profitable sweetness is found in their fleece, such necessity in their flesh, and so great a benefit in the manuring of barren soil with their dung and piss that their superfluous numbers are the better borne withal.[14]

For Harrison, the enclosing and engrossing attendant upon large scale sheepfarming were necessary evils, so vital was pastoralism to the Elizabethan way of life. The nation's pastoral life was in fact symbolically enshrined within the Parliament itself: a French ambassador described in his journal the central placement there of "four great mattresses, full of wool and covered in red . . . these are very high and well stuffed; they say that it signified the prosperity of England which comes from wool."[15]

The pervasive importance of agriculture and animal husbandry in Elizabethan society might lead one to expect an open interplay between the features of Elizabethan rural life and those of Elizabethan pastoral form. Yet such an interplay is, in most cases, curiously difficult to locate and describe: it is, at best, tenuous or fragmentary, sublimated or displaced. Most criticism of Elizabethan pastoral literature seems untouched by the issues Raymond Williams has raised; it is content to take the "enamelled world" of pastoral idealization on its own terms. Pastoral literature is usually studied in the context of literary history or thematics, that is, within an apparently autonomous system of literary discourse that has been largely constructed by the criticism that studies it. But if there appear to be no connections between the material and textual domains of Elizabethan life, it is because they have been ruptured or occluded. If Elizabethan rural life seems irrelevant to Elizabethan pastoral literature, that irrelevance is nevertheless *conspicuous.* Indeed, the suppression or marginalization of material pastoralism constitutes an essential feature of Elizabethan literary pastoralism—a feature that demands interpretation.

In the stratified agrarian society of Elizabethan England, the pastoral metaphors of Scripture might emphasize the common creaturely bonds of humankind: lords and commons alike were sheep in Christ's flock. But they could also sanction religious and secular hierarchies: prelates and princes were Christ's vicegerents, shepherds of the human flock. The wide if very uneven distribution of livestock ownership further complicated this pattern of pastoral relations. The dichotomy of "rich and poor" that Empson shares with the laborer from Elizabethan Essex must be specified as a conflicting relationship to real property, the traditional source of wealth, power, and prestige. The pastoral "trick" may have had some point in the Elizabethan countryside because some commoners did in fact own sheep. Substantial yeomen, who were often freeholders, sometimes had great flocks. But poor husbandmen who were copyholders, landless agrarian laborers, and youthful servants in husbandry often kept a few sheep for domestic uses. The shepherds themselves, who were usually contracted laborers with specialized skills, were sometimes paid in livestock allowed to graze on their employers' pastures.[16] Thus landed gentlemen and landless laborers, metaphorical shepherds and literal shepherds, could identify with each other because they shared a benevolent lordship over domesticated creatures that gave bountifully of themselves to the human community.

Such a "beautiful relationship between rich and poor" is operative in the conceit of the lordly shepherd, which occurs in a pastoral poem by the aptly named Richard Barnfield:

> Like a great King he rules a little land,
> Still making Statues, and ordayning Lawes;
> Which if they breake, he beates them with his Wand:
> He doth defend them from the greedy Jawes
> Of ravening Woolves, and Lyons bloudy Pawes.
>   His Field, his Realme, his Subjects are his Sheepe,
>   Which he doth still in due obedience keepe.[17]

Because Empson's analyses tend to be confined to forms of writing within the domain of literature, it may be useful to complement Barnfield's poem by considering an Elizabethan pastoral text that was actually produced within a pastoral environment. Sir Horatio Palavicino signed letters from his Cambridgeshire estate, "being amongst my shepperds clippinge my shepe."[18] Palavicino does not address the shepherds themselves; he self-consciously evokes them in a rhetorical strategy aimed at his correspondent. The epistolary transaction frames and delimits Palavicino's pastoral world and his own place within it. Palavicino was a political agent and a creditor of Queen Elizabeth, an alien who had acquired his English property and become an English gentleman by means of the wealth he had accumulated from his moneylending and commercial ventures. His idyllic gesture suppresses his bitter and protracted dispute with one of his shepherds, as well as his legal battle with his tenants over grazing rights; however, it does hint at his aggressive acquisition of pasturage in order to capitalize on the demand for wool. In Palavicino's valediction, the relationship between master and men is translated into pastoral fraternity. But the evocation of communion and community is contradicted by Palavicino's conspicuous reiteration of the first-person possessive pronoun. The otiose country gentleman is also the calculating businessman whose gold and silver is ewes and rams. In Palavicino's letter, as in Barnfield's poem, the sheep becomes a hierarchy-transcending incarnation of property, a subject of human exploitation uniting or identifying the interests of groups that had profoundly differing proprietary relations to the land itself, to their own labor, and to each other.

It is difficult to imagine Palavicino or any other Elizabethan gentleman signing his letters, "being amongst my ploughmen, tilling my fields." The georgic figure of the ploughman or husbandman is banished from the vast majority of Elizabethan pastoral texts. Barnfield, however, does invoke such agrarian laborers in "The Shepherds Content":

> The painfull Plough-swaine, and the Husband-man
> Rise up each morning by the breake of day,
> Taking what toyle and drudging paines they can,
> And all is for to get a little stay;
> And yet they cannot put their care away:
>   When night is come, their cares begin afresh,
>   Thinking upon the Morrowes busines.

(st. 15)

Although these absent presences are invoked to demonstrate that "Shepherd's life is best," the anomalous stanza generates precisely those "living tensions" (as Williams calls them) that the poem has ostensibly expunged from its "world." By the eighteenth century, poets like Stephen Duck and George Crabbe would turn Barnfield's exclusionary procedure inside out, making such agricultural laborers the victimized heroes of an explicitly antipastoral rural poetry.[19] But in the culture of the literate Elizabethan classes, the omnipresent realities of rural life enter formal discourse almost exclusively in *pastoral* terms. Agriculture and sheepraising were sometimes competing for the same land resources, as the enclosure controversy reminds us.

But they were equally likely to exist together in a symbiotic relationship: "in all areas of mixed farming, the folding of sheep on the arable was a pillar of the farming system"; "in all save the strictly wood-pasture districts, the sheepfold was . . . the mainstay of husbandry. . . . The whole farm was laid out and run to suit the sheep, but only on the strict understanding that they devoted themselves to fertilizing the land for corn and grain."[20] Elizabethan pastoral literature betrays almost no trace of this positive relationship that sheepherding often bore to other agrarian activities. The imaginative ecology of pastoral literature tends to suppress the intimate connection—whether hostile or beneficent—between herding and farming that was in fact typical of the Elizabethan countryside.

The note of ambivalence in William Harrison's already quoted account of Elizabethan sheepfarming registers the fact that pastoralism was the focus of a moral, economic, and ecological controversy that had provoked pamphlets and petitions, riots and rebellions, throughout the sixteenth century; it would remain controversial throughout the following century. In order to capitalize on an expanding market for wool (and also for mutton) Tudor land-owners enclosed common fields and engrossed small, scattered holdings. These and other measures taken to "rationalize" pastoral farming often resulted in the abrogation or erosion of traditional tenant rights and in the disruption or even the destruction of village life in some rural areas.[21] The controversy about this agrarian transformation became acute during the tumultuous spiritual, political, social, and economic upheavals of the mid-sixteenth century. During this period, reform-minded polemicists attacked the causes as well as the consequences of agrarian unrest in a mode of satire and complaint that found its roots in *The Vision of Piers Plowman*. In this literature, the fundamentally opposed interests of Commons and Gentles were metaphorized in the opposition of Ploughman and Shepherd; that is, in terms of the single issue that repeatedly catalyzed agrarian discontent throughout the century.[22]

What is probably the best known expression of the antipastoral attitude in Tudor England actually comes from the pre-Reformation period, from the pen of Thomas More. In part 1 of *Utopia,* Morus makes an impassioned attack on incipient agrarian capitalism:

> Your sheep . . . that used to be so meek and eat so little . . . are becoming so greedy and wild that they devour men themselves, as I hear. They devastate and pillage fields, houses, and towns. For in whatever parts of the land that sheep yield the softest and most expensive wool, there the nobility and gentry, yes, and even some abbots though otherwise holy men, are not content with the old rents which the land yielded to their predecessors. Living in idleness and luxury, without doing any good to society, no longer satisfies them; they have to do positive evil. For they leave no land free for the plow; they enclose every acre for pasture. . . . As if enough of your land were not already wasted on woods and game-preserves, these worthy men turn all human habitations and cultivated fields back to wilderness.[23]

Here pastoralism exemplifies the rapaciousness of spiritual and temporal *lords,* whose whole way of life is inimical to the true practice of Christianity. More's observation of agrarian relations in Tudor society conditions his invention of those in Utopian society. The most remarkable feature of the latter is that "agriculture is the one occupation at which everyone works, men and women alike, with no exceptions" (40). If Utopia is a true commonwealth, while European society is merely "a conspiracy of the rich" (89), it is because More's fiction radically alters the relations of production as well as the relations of distribution. Within the moral ecology of More's Humanism, the regression to wilderness produced by sheepfarming manifests the spiritual regression of England's lordly shepherds. Therefore, idleness—an aristocratic prerogative in Renaissance Europe—must be rigorously excluded from the lives of *all* Utopians. Labor, both manual and intellectual, is at once an acknowledgment of the defective human condition and the means of its repair. The program articulated in More's fiction is to reclaim the wilderness by the joint labors of cultivation and education.[24]

The Christianized georgic mode of More's Erasmian Humanism finds a striking new embodiment a century and a half after *Utopia* in the Puritan Humanism of *Paradise Lost*—not in punitive post-lapsarian labor but in the unalienated labor of Edenic cultivation. In Milton's unorthodox treatment of the unfallen human condition, Adam and Eve "labor still to dress" a luxuriant garden that is "tending to wild" (*PL* 9.205, 212).[25] The Christian revolutionary in Milton shared with the social revolutionaries of the mid-seventeenth century a belief in the original dignity of labor.[26] In the texts of More and Milton, the validation of agricultural labor goes hand in hand with a radical critique of aristocratic values and styles—a critique that is, of course, not proletarian in character but rather religious, intellectual, and bourgeois. The pastoral flowering of late Elizabethan and early Jacobean England, on the other hand, is dominantly aristocratic in values and style—even though the majority of its poets were of relatively humble origins and means. Renaissance pastoral takes the court as its cynosure. Although many of these works direct criticism or hostility against courtly decadence or the inequities of courtly reward, such anti-courtliness tends to measure either the court's distance from its own high ideals or the courtier's distance from the satisfaction of his ambitions. In other words, the element of anticourtliness in Elizabethan pastoral literature is quite unlike the anticourtliness of *Utopia* or *Paradise Lost* in that it is itself an aspect of courtly or aristocratic culture. Indeed, it is one of that culture's characteristic forms—an authorized mode of discontent—rather than a critique made in terms of a consciously articulated oppositional culture.

English literary pastoralism began to flourish in the last quarter of the sixteenth century, in the latter half of Elizabeth's reign—that is, only after the diminution of the bitterly controversial agrarian literature whose subject was precisely those material practices and relations that provided a social matrix for Elizabethan pastoral conventions.

If cultural expropriation followed upon economic expropriation, a period of decontamination was nevertheless necessary before such pastoral forms were fit to embody the changing concerns of writers, patrons, and audiences.[27] In the troubled countryside of earlier Tudor writings, gentlemen abuse their tenants; in the idyllic countryside of Elizabethan pastorals, gentlemen may escape temporarily from the troubles of the court. The readers and writers of Elizabethan pastorals have little discernible interest in defending traditional peasant rights or in acknowledging those agrarian activities that exemplify baseness. On the contrary, Elizabethan poets who oppose pastoral goodness to courtly vice create shepherds who exemplify the ideals of *gentility.* Such a poetry is not concerned to embrace the lot of Elizabethan husbandmen or to advance egalitarian ideas but to recreate an elite community in pastoral form. In such pastorals, ambitious Elizabethan gentlemen who may be alienated or excluded from the courtly society that nevertheless continues to define their existence can create an imaginative space within which virtue and privilege coincide.

Although farming was a poetic subject sanctioned by Virgil's *Georgics,* the Elizabethans banished it to manuals on husbandry. If the georgic mode was fundamentally uncongenial to Elizabethan poets, one reason may have been that the culture of the Elizabethan elite stigmatized the varied tasks of manual labor. Literary celebrations of pastoral otium conventionalize the relative *ease* of the shepherd's labors. Compared to other agrarian tasks, sheepfarming requires very little investment of human resources.[28] The fictional time-space of countless eclogues and other Elizabethan pastorals is structured by the diurnal rhythm of shepherding: driving the flock out to pasture at daybreak and driving them back to fold at dusk. Within this frame, the literary shepherd's day is typically occupied by singing, piping, wooing, and the other quaint indulgences of the pastoral life.

The characteristic condition of such a life was well described by Richard Mulcaster as "great leisure to use liberty where the meaner sort must labor." Mulcaster, however, was writing about the benefits of *gentility:* "Those things gentlemen have, and are much bound to God for them, which may make them prove excellent if they use them well: *great ability* to go through withal where the poorer sort must give over, ere he come to the end; *great leisure* to use liberty where the meaner sort must labor; *all opportunities* at will where the common is restrained."[29] Peter Laslett elaborates upon the material basis for the distinction between gentles and commons:

> The term gentleman marked the exact point at which the traditional social system divided up the population into two extremely unequal sections. About a twenty-fifth, at most a twentieth, of all the people alive in the England of the Tudors and the Stuarts . . . belonged to the gentry and to those above them in the social hierarchy. This tiny minority owned most of the wealth, wielded the power and made all the decisions, political, economic and social for the national whole. . . .

Here was a society which has no devices for the saving of labour. . . . The simplest operation in everyday life needed effort. . . . The working of the land, the labour in the craftsman's shop, were infinitely taxing. . . . Yet the primary characteristic of the gentleman was that he never worked with his hands on necessary, as opposed to leisurely, activities.

The simple fact of leisure dividing off this little society of the privileged—it had to be little at a time when the general resources were so small—is the first step in comprehending the attitude of our forefathers to rank and status.

(*The World We Have Lost*, 27, 29, 30)

Laslett's description implies that the distinction between gentility and baseness was a social marker that became physically inscribed upon the body itself. The conventions of pastoral romance transpose this marker into those refinements of carriage and complexion that manifest the natural superiority of rusticated aristocrats to the coarse and sunburned rustics among whom they sojourn. The amorous and aesthetic pursuits of literary shepherds were cultural luxuries available only to a tiny minority in the society of early modern England—luxuries of the kind prized and enjoyed by Renaissance gentlemen and, in particular, by Renaissance courtiers.

The opposition of gentility and baseness was, then, the most fundamental of Elizabethan social discriminations. Mulcaster put the matter patly: "All the people which be in our country be either *gentlemen* or of the *commonality*" (*Positions*, 162). Elizabethan commentators recognized several gradations within this dichotomy, and there existed other status and interest groups that were either misunderstood or thought unworthy of mention. But this social boundary was universally acknowledged, even when its exact placement was in dispute. The Elizabethan preoccupation with marks of status and with the nature of gentility were themselves symptoms of unprecedented social mobility.[30] As David Cressy has pointed out, Elizabethan commentators had to struggle with social facts that did not fit their received social theories: "Their major difficulty . . . lay in trying to describe a society whose legal system and status system were based on possession of land at a time when non-landed skills, wealth and power were increasingly significant" ("Describing the Social Order of Elizabethan and Stuart England," 29). Sir Thomas Smith wrote that "we in England divide our men commonly into foure sortes, gentlemen, citizens, yeoman artificers, and laborers."[31] The first group encompassed the entire social elite, from the monarch and peers down to simple gentlemen—not only country gentry but wealthy bourgeois social climbers who invested in land, and university educated professionals, clergy, and scholars. Smith concluded—with some contempt—that

gentlemen . . . be made good cheape in England. For whosoever studieth the lawes of the realme, who studieth in the universities, who professeth liberal sciences, and to be shorte, who can live *idly and without manuall labour,* and will beare the port, charge and coun-

tenaunce of a gentleman, he shall be called master . . . and shall be taken for a gentleman.

(*De Republica Anglorum*, 40; italics mine)

Some Elizabethan pastorals explicitly set forth discriminations between gentility and commonality; others function to manifest the gentility—or deny the commonality—of their authors and their audiences. And many more, when put into the context of their production and reception, reveal an implicit or oblique engagement with problems of status. This affinity of pastoral forms for the symbolic mediation of social categories depends primarily upon pastoral conventions of leisure and labor, conventions in which a rich and heterogeneous Renaissance cultural tradition deriving from both biblical and classical sources interacts with the material features of Elizabethan ecology, economy, and society.

In effect, the distinction between gentility and baseness depended upon a *differential* subjection to the penalty of fallen Adam, a selective dispensation from the original injunction that "In the sweat of thy face shalt thou eat bread, til thou returne to the earth: for out of it wast thou taken" (Genesis 3: 19; *Geneva Bible,* 1560 ed.). In Chaucer's time, the Peasants' Revolt epitomized and challenged this social differentiation in a powerfully interrogative proverb: "When Adam dalf and Eve span, / Who was thanne a gentil man?"[32] To the *arrivistes* of the Tudor aristocracy, that question must have been particularly irksome. Not surprisingly, allusions to the proverb declined markedly during the sixteenth century. But some gentlemen remained willing to acknowledge it, if only in order to repudiate it. At the beginning of the sixteenth century, Edmund Dudley maintained that it was the sin of "Arrogancy" that taught the commons that

ye be made of the same metell and mold that the gentiles be made of. Whie then should thei sport and play and you labor and till? He will tell you also that at your birthes and at your deethes your riches be indifferent. Whie should thei have so motche of the prosperite and treasure of this world and ye so lytle? Besydes that, he will tell you that ye be the childeren and righte enheritors to Adam aswell as thei. . . . He will shew also how that christ bought you as derely as the nobles with one maner of price, which was his preciouse Bloude. Whie then should ye be of so poore estate and thei of highe degre? . . . And percase he will enforme you how . . . god creatyd in you one maner of noblenes without any diversitie, and that your soules be as precious to god as theires.[33]

Early in the following century, James Cleland opened a treatise on nobility by invoking the proverb, then answering it with equivocations:

To satisfie then the common objection of the vulgar, who disapprove al inequalitie, in demanding

When Adam delv'd, and Eva span,
Who was then a Noble man?
. . .

I grant that not only in respect of our beginning, but of our ending too, we are all equals without difference or superioritie of degrees, all tending alike to the same earth from whence we sprong. . . . King and subject, noble and ignoble, rich and poore, al are borne and die a like: but in the middle course, betweene our birth and burial, wee are over-runne by our betters, and of necessitite must needs confesse that some excell & are more noble than others.[34]

For Cleland, nobility is not "subject to the mutabilitie of Fortune" but "is permanent in the minde" (4). However, he hastens to add that he does not mean by this "that everie one who lives vertuouslie, and can daunt his affections, is foorthwith a *Noble* or a *Gentleman,* but hee onlie whose Vertue is profitable to the King and Countrie; whom his Majestie esteemes worthie to beare a coate of armes, & to enjoie diverse priveledges for services done to him & His kingdome" (5-6). There is a telling contrast between the emphases of Dudley and Cleland, which measures the success of the Henrician and Elizabethan regimes in establishing the royal court as the source of identity and honor, power and reward.[35] By the beginning of the Stuart dynasty, the focus of the argument has changed from the agrarian relationship between lords and laborers to the courtly relationship between the king and the privileged society of royal dependents who serve him. As I have already suggested, pastoral discourse follows a similar direction during the sixteenth century. Literary pastoralization involves not only a process by which agrarian social relations are inscribed within an ideology of the country but also a process by which that initial inscription is itself appropriated, transformed, and reinscribed within an ideology of the court.

The production of Elizabethan pastoral discourse is characterized by ideological processes of displacement, sublimation, and repression. The aristocratic and courtly culture of the Renaissance cleanses the taint of agrarian labor from pastoral imagery, thus making possible a metaphorical identification between otiose shepherds and leisured gentlemen. Such a process is observable in "The Shepheards Content." Here Barnfield shows how Empson's literary swain actually combines the best parts of the best people:

> He is a Courtier, for he courts his Love:
> He is a Scholler, for he sings sweet Ditties:
> He is a Souldier, for he wounds [i.e., of love] doth
>   prove;
>
> . . .
>
>   He is a Gentleman, because his nature
>   Is kinde and affable to everie Creature.
>
>   (st. 41)

When Bacon notes that Cain and Abel figure the Ploughman and the Pastoralist, his purpose is to emphasize a distinction that is at once social and spiritual: "We see again the favour and election of God went to the shepherd, and not to the tiller of the ground." The relative moral valuations borne by the Ploughman and the Shepherd in an ear-

lier and more critical Tudor literary tradition have been reversed. For Bacon, the Shepherd is an image of the contemplative life, "by reason of his leisure, rest in a place, and living in the view of heaven."[36] Sixteenth-century writers customarily located the initial distinction between nobility and baseness—the origins of inequality—in the moral distinction between Adam's heirs, the superiority of Seth over Cain, and in the postdiluvian world, in the moral distinction between Noah's heirs, the superiority of Shem and Japhet over Cham. Having claimed so much in his *Blazon of Gentrie* (1586), Johne Ferne goes on to assert that "from S[h]em did pursue by the flesh, our Saviour and King Jesus Christ: a Gentleman of bloud, according to his humanitie, Emperour of heaven and earth, according to his deitie, even as his holy Heralds, (the Evangelistes) have out of their infallible recordes testified."[37] Ferne feels it necessary to prove even the Good Shepherd's pedigree to be socially acceptable.

In a celebrated formulation, Lévi-Strauss specifies the social function of mythic narratives as the provision of "a logical model capable of overcoming a contradiction (an impossible achievement if, as it happens, the contradiction is real)."[38] I propose that pastoral form may encode such a function in Renaissance culture—a culture in which a theory of social fixity was contradicted by the evidence of social flux, in which the putative coincidence of virtue, honor, and gentility with lineage, status, and wealth was continually placed in question. The primarily courtly pastoral of the Renaissance puts into play a symbolic strategy, which, by reconstituting the leisured gentleman as the gentle shepherd, obfuscates a fundamental contradiction in the cultural logic: a contradiction between the secular claims of aristocratic prerogative and the religious claims of common origins, shared fallenness, and spiritual equality among men, gentle and base alike. When Adam delved and Eve span, who was then a gentleman? Elizabethan pastoral participates in the ideological process of providing evasive answers to such pointed questions about personal, familial, and collective origins. I am not proposing a monocausal explanation for the ubiquity of pastoral forms in Elizabethan culture; nor am I implying that the mediation of social boundaries was necessarily a conscious motive in the writing of Elizabethan pastorals. The social ambiguities and contradictions to which I have pointed could be encoded in cultural forms and practices other than pastorals. And the range of pastoral significations is not reducible to a single ideological operation. I have sought to draw attention to what seems to me a vital though largely unremarked conjunction of form and function, and to suggest why the fit between them was so good. A social matrix for Elizabethan pastoral forms and practices may be located in the interstices between the categories of baseness and gentility, on that ambiguous social boundary that pastorals symbolically mark and transgress. In Elizabethan culture, the metaphor of the gentle shepherd could enact a variety of strategies in behalf of gentlemen—or would-be gentlemen—who were lineal descendants of Adam and Eve.

Notes

1. William Empson, *Some Versions of Pastoral* (1936; rpt. New York: New Directions, 1968), 23, Renato Poggioli, *The Oaten Flute* (Cambridge: Harvard Univ. Press, 1975), 1.

2. For comprehensive historical surveys of English Renaissance pastoralism, see Walter W. Greg, *Pastoral Drama and Pastoral Poetry* (1906; rpt. New York: Russell & Russell, 1959); Hallett Smith, *Elizabethan Poetry* (1952; rpt. Ann Arbor: Univ. of Michigan Press, 1968), 1-63; Simone Dorangeon, *L'Églogue Anglaise de Spenser à Milton* (Paris: Didier, 1974); Helen Cooper, *Pastoral: Medieval into Renaissance* (Ipswich: D. S. Brewer, 1977), 144-213.

3. Laurence Lerner, *The Uses of Nostalgia* (New York: Schocken, 1972), 39.

4. For the notion of reproblematization, I am indebted to Fredric R. Jameson, "The Symbolic Inference; or, Kenneth Burke and Ideological Analysis," *Critical Inquiry* 4 (1978), 507-23. Jameson suggests that to invoke "ideology" and the ideological is "to reproblematize the entire artistic discourse or formal analysis thereby so designated. The term 'ideology' stands as the sign for a problem yet to be solved, a mental operation which remains to be executed. . . . [I]t is an imperative to re-invent a relationship between the linguistic or aesthetic or conceptual fact in question and its social ground" (510). The present essay is intended as a contribution to the reinvention of a relationship between Elizabethan pastoral and its social ground.

In a recent essay that draws upon the work of William Empson and Kenneth Burke, Paul Alpers writes that "a definition of pastoral must first give a coherent account of its various features—formal, expressive, and thematic—and second, provide for historical continuity or change within the form." He finds the basis of such a definition in the Burkean concept of a "representative anecdote," "a brief and compendious rendering of a certain situation or type of life." For Alpers—as, I believe, for Renaissance poets and critics—"the representative anecdote of pastoral is the lives of shepherds." This means "that pastoral works are representations of shepherds, who are felt to be representative of some other or of all other men. But since all the terms in this definition are subject to modification or re-interpretation, pastoral is historically diversified and transformed." See Alpers, "What Is Pastoral?," *Critical Inquiry* 8 (1982), 437-60; quotations from 441, 448, 449, 456, respectively. The present essay might be thought of as a culture-specific ideological analysis of pastoral's representative anecdote.

Because terminological ambiguity besets so much discussion of pastoral, it may be useful at the outset to note Alastair Fowler's formal distinction between *genre* and *mode:* "By genre I mean a better defined and more external type than mode. Genres each have their own formal structures, whereas modes depend less explicitly on stance, motif, or occasional touches of rhetorical texturing." See Alastair Fowler, "The Life and Death of Literary Forms," *New Literary History* 2 (1971), 199-216; quotation from 202. Thus, "pastoral" as a noun is a modal form, while "pastoral" as an adjective (as, for example, pastoral eclogue, elegy, or romance) is genre-specific.

5. For example: Sidney defends the pastoral, which, "sometimes, under the pretty tales of wolves and sheep, can include the whole considerations of wrong-doing and patience" (*A Defence of Poetry,* in *Miscellaneous Prose of Sir Philip Sidney,* ed. Katherine Duncan-Jones and Jan Van Dorsten [Oxford: Clarendon, 1973], 95). William Webbe writes that *"Eglogues . . . bee commonly Dialogues or speeches framed or supposed betweene Sheepeheardes, Neteheardes, Goteheardes, or such like simple men. . . .* Although the matter they take in hand seemeth commonlie in appearaunce rude and homely, as the usuall talke of simple clownes, yet doo they indeede utter in the same much pleasaunt and profitable delight. For under these personnes, as it were in a cloake of simplicitie, they would eyther sette foorth the prayses of theyr freendes . . . or enveigh against abuses" (*A Discourse of English Poetrie* [1586], in *Elizabethan Critical Essays,* ed. Gregory Smith, [Oxford: Clarendon, 1904], 1: 262). In a preface to the 1619 edition of his pastoral poetry, Michael Drayton writes that "pastorals, as they are a Species of Poesie, signifie fained Dialogues, or other speeches in Verse, fathered upon Heardsmen . . . who are ordinarie persons in this kind of Poeme. . . . The subject of Pastorals, as the language of it ought to be poor, silly, & of the coursest Woofe in appearance. . . . Nevertheless, the most High, and most Noble Matters of the World may be shaddowed in them, and for certaine sometimes are" ("To the Reader of His Pastorals," in *The Works of Michael Drayton,* ed. William Hebel, et al. [Oxford: Shakespeare Head, 1961], 2: 517). The opinions quoted here are representative of Tudor and Jacobean discussions of pastoral; these are surveyed in J. E. Congleton, *Theories of Pastoral Poetry in England 1684-1798* (Gainesville: Univ. of Florida Press, 1952), 37-51. Puttenham's discussion of pastoral is analyzed in detail in part three of the present essay.

6. In his Introduction to a recent collection of studies of "The Forms of Power and the Power of Forms in the Renaissance," Stephen Greenblatt writes that "Renaissance literary works are no longer regarded either as a fixed set of texts that are set apart from all other forms of expression and that contain their own determinate meanings or as a stable set of reflections of historical facts that lie beyond them."

Distinctions "between artistic production and other kinds of social production . . . do in fact exist, but they are not intrinsic to the texts; rather they are made up and constantly redrawn by artists, audiences, and readers. These collective social constructions on the one hand define the range of aesthetic possibilities within a given representational mode and, on the other, link that mode to the complex network of institutions, practices, and beliefs that constitute the culture as a whole" (Introduction, *Genre* 15.1-2 [1982], 4). My only qualification of this admirable formulation is that not only "the range of aesthetic possibilities" but also the very category of the aesthetic is socially constructed.

7. Kenneth Burke, *A Rhetoric of Motives* (1950; rpt. Berkeley: Univ. of California Press, 1969), 123-24. Also see his early reviews of Empson's book, rpt. in *The Philosophy of Literary Form,* 3rd ed., rev. (Berkeley: Univ. of California Press, 1973), 422-26. For a recent appreciation of Empson's work, see Paul Alpers, "Empson on Pastoral," *New Literary History* 10 (1978), 101-23.

8. Quoted in Christopher Hill, *Reformation to Industrial Revolution,* rev. ed. (Harmondsworth: Penguin, 1969), 119.

9. On Elizabethan social structure, see Lawrence Stone, "Social Mobility in England, 1500-1700," *Past & Present,* no. 33 (April 1966), 16-55; Peter Laslett, *The World We Have Lost,* 2nd ed. (New York: Scribner's, 1971), 23-54; David Cressy, "Describing the Social Order of Elizabethan and Stuart England," *Literature and History,* no. 3 (March 1976), 29-44.

10. Raymond Williams, *The Country and the City* (New York: Oxford Univ. Press, 1973).

11. The editors' Introduction, in *A Book of English Pastoral Verse,* ed. John Barrell and John Bull (New York: Oxford Univ. Press, 1975), 4.

12. See Raymond Williams, *Marxism and Literature* (New York: Oxford Univ. Press, 1977); "Base and Superstructure in Marxist Cultural Theory," in *Problems in Materialism and Culture* (London: NLB, 1980), 31-49; *Culture* (London: Fontana, 1981); "Marxism, Structuralism and Literary Analysis," *New Left Review,* no. 129 (Sept.-Oct. 1981), 51-66.

13. See Peter J. Bowden, *The Wool Trade in Tudor and Stuart England* (London: Macmillan, 1962), xv: "Wool was, without question, the most important raw material in the English economic system. . . . Every class in the community, whether landlord, farmer, merchant, industrial capitalist or artisan, had an interest in wool, and it was the subject of endless economic controversy." Material on every aspect of Elizabethan sheepraising and agriculture is to be found in *The Agrarian History of England and*

Wales, Volume IV, 1500-1700, ed. Joan Thirsk (Cambridge: Cambridge Univ. Press, 1967). Future pages references to the *Agrarian History of England and Wales* will be to volume four.

14. William Harrison, *The Description of England* (1577, 1587), ed. Georges Edelen (Ithaca: Cornell Univ. Press, 1968), 308, 310. For the impressions of visitors that England was a land of "countless numbers of sheep," see *England as seen by Foreign Visitors in the Days of Elizabeth and James the First,* ed. William Brenchley Rye (1865; rpt. New York: Benjamin Blom, 1967), 30, 31, 57, 70, 109. On the sheep population of Elizabethan England, see Bowden, *The Wool Trade in Tudor and Stuart England,* 37-38.

15. André Hurault, Sieur de Maisse, *Journal* (1597), trans. and ed. G. B. Harrison and R. A. Jones (Bloomsbury: Nonesuch, 1931), 30.

16. See Alan Everitt, "Farm Labourers," in *Agrarian History of England and Wales,* 414; K. J. Allison, "Flock Management in the Sixteenth and Seventeenth Centuries," *Economic History Review,* 2nd ser., 11 (1958), 98-112; Mildred Campbell, *The English Yeoman Under Elizabeth and the Early Stuarts* (1942; rpt. New York: Barnes & Noble, 1960), 197-205; Ann Kussmaul, *Servants in Husbandry in Early Modern England* (Cambridge: Cambridge Univ. Press, 1981), 25, 39.

17. "The Shepherds Content" (1594), st. 22, in Richard Barnfield, *Poems, 1594-1598,* ed. Edward Arber (1882; rpt. New York: AMS, 1967). I have silently modified obsolete typographical conventions in quotations from this and other editions of Elizabethan texts.

18. Quoted in Lawrence Stone, *An Elizabethan: Sir Horatio Palavicino* (Oxford: Clarendon, 1956), 283. On Palavicino as a rapacious sheepfarmer, see especially 275-76.

19. See, for example, the selections anthologized in *A Book of English Pastoral Verse,* ed. Barrell and Bull, 385-424.

20. Joan Thirsk, "Farming Techniques," in *Agrarian History of England and Wales,* 188; Eric Kerridge, *The Farmers of Old England* (London: George Allen & Unwin, 1973), 20.

21. For balanced discussion of this still controversial subject, see Joan Thirsk, "Enclosing and Engrossing," in *Agrarian History of England and Wales,* 200-55; M. W. Beresford, *The Lost Villages of England* (1954; rpt. London: Lutterworth, 1965); J. A. Yelling, *Common Field and Enclosure in England, 1450-1850* (London: Macmillan, 1977).

22. On the *Piers Plowman* tradition in Tudor satire, see Helen C. White, *Social Criticism in Popular Religious Literature of the Sixteenth Century* (1944; rpt. New York: Octagon Books, 1965), 1-40; Smith, *Elizabethan Poetry,* 194-216. Whitney R. D. Jones,

The Mid-Tudor Crisis (London: Macmillan, 1973), provides a good introduction to the issues of the period.

23. Sir Thomas More, *Utopia* (1516), trans. and ed. Robert M. Adams (New York: Norton, 1975), 14. Further quotations will be from this edition.

24. On the importance of cultivation and education in Utopia, see Wayne A. Rebhorn, "Thomas More's Enclosed Garden: *Utopia* and Renaissance Humanism," *English Literary Renaissance* 6 (1976), 140-55. Two brilliant and complementary studies of Utopian society in the context of More's life and times are J. H. Hexter, *The Vision of Politics on the Eve of the Reformation* (New York: Basic Books, 1973), 19-149; and Stephen Greenblatt, *Renaissance Self-Fashioning* (Chicago: Univ. of Chicago Press, 1980), 11-73.

25. *Paradise Lost* is quoted from John Milton, *Complete Poems and Major Prose,* ed. Merritt Y. Hughes (New York: Odyssey, 1957). On Milton's unorthodox presentation of Eden, see J. M. Evans, *Paradise Lost and the Genesis Tradition* (Oxford: Clarendon, 1968); and Barbara Kiefer Lewalski, "Innocence and Experience in Milton's Eden," in *New Essays on Paradise Lost,* ed. Thomas Kranidas (Berkeley: Univ. of California Press, 1969), 86-117.

26. "Man hath his daily work of body or mind / Appointed, which declares his Dignity" (*PL* 4.618-19). Regarding seventeenth-century ideas about wage labor, see Christopher Hill, *Change and Continuity in Seventeenth-Century England* (London: Weidenfeld & Nicholson, 1974), 219-38; and, for Milton's connections with the radicals, see Hill, *Milton and the English Revolution* (1977; rpt. Harmondsworth: Penguin, 1979), esp. 93-116, 395-96. (It should be noted that Hill tends to overstate his case.)

27. I offer this hypothesis tentatively, and only as a partial explanation of the "cultural lag" between the longstanding importance of sheepfarming in the English economy and the later Elizabethan emergence of pastoral as an important literary mode. In *The Political Unconscious* (Ithaca: Cornell Univ. Press, 1981), Fredric Jameson suggests that "the strategic value of generic concepts for Marxism clearly lies in the mediatory function of the notion of a genre, which allows the coordination of immanent formal analysis of the individual text with the twin diachronic perspectives of the history of forms and the evolution of social life" (105). To seek for direct correlations between socioeconomic and literary change would be to fall into the reductionism of reflection-theory. Any study of the problematic relationship between pastoral farming and pastoral writing must acknowledge the limited autonomy of each and the mediated nature of their relationship.

28. Thomas More recognized this as a cause of underemployment and vagrancy: "One herdsman or shepherd can look after a flock of beasts large enough to stock an area that would require many hands if it were plowed and reaped" (*Utopia,* 15).

29. Richard Mulcaster, *Positions* (1581), ed. Richard L. DeMolen (New York: Teachers College Press, 1971), 157.

30. As Lawrence Stone puts it, in *The Crisis of the Aristocracy 1558-1641* (Oxford: Clarendon, 1965), the dominant ideology and the particular policies that were "designed to freeze the social structure and emphasize the cleavages between one class and another were introduced or reinforced at a time when in fact families were moving up and down in the social and economic scale at a faster rate than at any time before the nineteenth and twentieth centuries. Indeed it was just this mobility which stimulated such intensive propaganda efforts" (36). On the Elizabethan preoccupation with the origins and nature of gentility, see Ruth Kelso, *The Doctrine of the English Gentleman in the Sixteenth Century* (1929; rpt. Gloucester, Ma.: Peter Smith, 1964).

31. Thomas Smith, *De Republica Anglorum* (1583), ed. L. Alston (1906; rpt. Shannon: Irish Univ. Press, 1972), 31.

32. See Albert B. Friedman, "'When Adam Delved . . .': Contexts of an Historic Proverb," in *The Learned and the Lewd: Studies in Chaucer and Medieval Literature,* ed. Larry D. Benson (Cambridge: Harvard Univ. Press, 1974), 213-30. Friedman notes that allusions to the proverb begin to decline in the early sixteenth century.

33. Edmund Dudley, *The Tree of Commonwealth* (1509/10), ed. D. M. Brodie (Cambridge: Cambridge Univ. Press, 1948), 88-89.

34. James Cleland, *The Instruction of a young Noble-man* (Oxford: Joseph Barnes, 1612), 2-3.

35. See Stone, *The Crisis of the Aristocracy;* and Mervyn James, *English Politics and the Concept of Honour 1485-1642* (London: Past & Present Society, 1978).

36. *Of the Advancement of Learning,* book 1, in *The Works of Francis Bacon,* ed. James Spedding, et al. (Boston: Taggard & Thompson, 1860-64), 6: 138.

37. John Ferne, *The Blazon of Gentrie* (1586), facsimile ed. (Amsterdam: Theatrum Orbis Terrarum, 1973), 2-3.

38. "The Structural Study of Myth," in Claude Lévi-Strauss, *Structural Anthropology,* trans. C. Jacobson and B. G. Schoepf (New York: Basic Books, 1963), 1:229. Fredric Jameson reformulates Lévi-Strauss' structuralist theory in the terms of an explicitly Marxist discourse. For Lévi-Strauss' operative narrative unit, the *mythologeme,* Jameson substitutes the concept of the *ideologeme,* "the smallest intelligible unit of the essentially

antagonistic collective discourses of social classes" (*The Political Unconscious,* 76). The ideologeme should be grasped, "not as a mere reflex or reduplication of its situational context, but as the imaginary resolution of the objective contradictions to which it thus constitutes an active response" (118).

Bryan Loughrey (essay date 1984)

SOURCE: Introduction to *The Pastoral Mode: A Casebook,* edited by Bryan Loughrey, Macmillan Publishers Ltd., 1984, pp. 8-17.

[*In the following excerpt, Loughrey discusses the classical European origins of the pastoral form and surveys its embodiment in works by writers of the English Renaissance.*]

Pastoral is a contested term which modern critics have applied to an almost bewildering variety of works. In earlier critical discourse, however, it had a fairly limited and stable sense, describing literature which portrayed, often in an idealised manner, 'the life of shepherds, or of the country'.[1] The genre originated with the Greek poet Theocritus (c. 316-260 BC), who entertained the sophisticated Alexandrian court of Ptolemy with a series of vignettes depicting the countryside and peasantry of his native Sicily. His *Idylls* are not entirely typical of the later tradition, since they contain considerable elements of realism and sometimes dwell on the harsher aspects of the lives led by an entire rural community, consisting not just of shepherds, but of farmers, serfs, goatherds, fishermen, neatherds and housewives. Nevertheless, Theocritus's successors found in the *Idylls* almost all the motifs which later crystallised into the conventions of formal pastoral: herdsmen find leisure to indulge in impromptu song contests or debates; extravagantly praise the beauty of their coy mistresses, or the charms of country life; recount tales derived from classical mythology or regional folklore; and bewail the death or absence of lovers. In many cases, Theocritus provided a model for the form as well as the content of subsequent pastoral verse. Idyll I, for example, in which Thyrsis sings of the death of Daphnis, employs all the machinery of pastoral elegy (invocation to the muse, expression of grief, inquiry into the causes of death, pathetic fallacy, description of the bier and procession, lament, concluding note of consolation) which Milton made use of in 'Lycidas' and an anonymous eighteenth-century critic parodied in 'Recipe for a Pastoral Elegy'.

Vergil based his earliest known works, the *Eclogues,* on Theocritus's *Idylls.* He introduced, however, a number of innovations which decisively influenced almost all later writers of pastoral. In particular, he transferred his herdsmen from Sicily to Arcadia, the now traditional home of the shepherd of literary convention. Arcadia, as Bruno Snell has convincingly argued, represented for Vergil not a humdrum province of Greece, but a poetic landscape whose woods and mountains were haunted by the Olympian Immortals. It was an imaginary topography where 'the currents of myth and empirical reality flow one into another', and gods mingled freely with men. The shepherd inhabitants of this world were similarly etherealised. Despite the topical and political themes introduced into the *Eclogues,* Vergil's herdsmen are consistently portrayed as refined, serious-minded individuals, ruled by tender passions which they express through poetry. It comes as no surprise when Vergil, in Eclogue X, inserts his own friend, the contemporary poet Gallus, into this setting, for shepherd and artist have become virtually indistinguishable. From Vergil onwards, pastoral poetry has been preoccupied with such tensions between reality and the world of the imagination, so that the form is often peculiarly self-conscious of its own aesthetic nature, and concerned far more with exploring the meaning of its conventions than in depicting any actual countryside.

The involvement of pastoral with classical mythology helped forge its association with the myth of the Golden Age, an elegiac lament for a lost age of innocence which shares many of the characteristics of the Christian idea of Eden. It was conceived of as a time at the dawn of history when Saturn and Astraea, the virgin goddess of Justice, ruled in the Garden of the Hesperides, and mankind lived unalienated from either its environment or itself. The season was perpetual spring, which rendered clothing superfluous, and allowed a fecund nature to provide sustenance without toil. Unhindered by the divisive influence of ambition, greed, aggression, or jealousy, men and women lived together in a fellowship based on leisure and love. The most familiar rendering of this myth is contained in Ovid's *Metamorphoses,* translated by Arthur Golding in 1567:

> Then sprang up first the golden age, which of its selfe maintainde,
> The truth and right of every thing unforst and unconstrainde.
> There was no feare of punishment, there was no threatning lawe
> In brazen tables nayled up, to keepe the folke in awe.
> There was no man would crouch or creepe to Judge with cap in hand,
> They lived safe without a Judge in every Realme and lande.
> The loftie Pynetree was not hewen from mountaines where it stood,
> In seeking straunge and forren landes to rove upon the flood.
> Men knew none other countries yet, than were themselves did keepe:
> There was no towne enclosed yet, with walles and ditches deepe.
> No horne nor trumpet was in use, no sword nor helmet worne.
> The worlde was suche, that souldiers helpe might easly be forborne.
> The fertile earth as yet was free, untoucht of spade or plough,
> And yet it yeelded of its selfe of every things inough.
> And men themselves contented well with plaine and simple foode,

That on earth by natures gift without their travell
  stoode,
Did live by Raspis, heppes and hawes, by cornelles,
  plummes and cherries,
By sloes and apples, nuttes and peares, and lothsome
  bramble berries,
And by the acornes dropt on ground from *Joves* brode
  tree in fielde.
The Springtime lasted all the yeare, and *Zephyr* with
  his milde
And gentle blast did cherish things that grew of owne
  accorde.
The ground untilde, all kinde of fruits did plenteously
  avorde.
No mucke nor tillage was bestowde on leane and
  barren land,
To make the corne of better head and ranker for too
  stand.
Then streames ran milke, then streames ran wine, and
  yellow honny flowde
From ech greene tree whereon the rayes of firie
  Phebus glowde.[2]

As the keeping of flocks was deemed to be the original employment of mankind, the life-styles of the denizens of the Golden Age and the shepherds of Arcadia were increasingly equated. This in part encouraged poets to develop the escapist elements of the genre, and indulge in nostalgic dreams of a past happier time. But the myth could also function as a social critique, for, as Harry Levin explains, it can only be defined by the negative formula 'not like now'. Thus many pastoral satires made use of the trope to attack corruptions of State (courtiers are hireling shepherds) or Church (pastors neglect their flocks). Vergil's Eclogue IV stood the myth on its head and celebrated the birth of a child who was to restore the Golden Age in the near future. Its Messianic message, one consistently interpreted as a prophecy of the birth of Christ, is in W. H. Auden's terms Utopian rather than Arcadian, a vision of the future where the 'contradictions of the present . . . have at last been resolved'.

Horace's Epode II is the fountainhead of the third strand of classical pastoral, the great myth of rural retirement:

Happy the man, who far from town's affairs,
The life of old-world mortals shares;
With his own oxen tills his forebears' fields,
Nor thinks of usury and its yields.
No soldier he, by the fierce bugle called,
Nor sailor, at each storm appalled;
He shuns the forum, and the haughty gate
Of nobles stronger than the State.
His business is round poplars tall to twine
The ripe young layers of the vine;
Or in some quiet valley to survey
His lowing heifers as they stray.
Now with his knife the worthless shoots he lops,
Grafting instead for richer crops;
Draws the new honey, in pure jars to keep,
Or shears the timid staggering sheep.
When Autumn, with his mellow fruitage gay,
Doth o'er the fields his head display,
What joy it is the grafted pears to try,

And grapes which with sea-purple vie;
Fit gift, Priapus, choosing for thy hand,
Or Silvan, thine, guard of his land!
What joy, beneath some holm-oak old and grey
Or on thick turf, one's limbs to lay;
While streams past toppling banks roll down their
  flood,
And the birds croon in every wood,
And fountains murmur with their gushing streams
Sounds that shall sooth to sleep and dreams.
Then when the thunderous winter comes again,
Rainstorms and snowdrifts in its train,
This side and that a many hounds he'll set.[3]

The numerous imitations of this piece, such as Katherine Philips's 'A Country-Life', generally ignore Horace's craftily ironic postscript:

Alfius the usurer, when thus he swore
Farmer to be for ever more,
At the mid-month his last transaction ending,
By next new moon is keen for lending.

Alfius the moneylender is a week-end cottager who will soon return to the city despite the charms of the countryside. T. G. Rosenmeyer has objected that the Horatian praise of country life has more in common with *Georgic*, didactic literature on the subject of husbandry, than pastoral. But while it is true that in many cases the shepherd of literary convention does not feature at all in such works, the two traditions are so closely allied that they frequently impinge on one another, for the emotional basis of each is recognisably similar—'God made the country, and man made the town'.[4]

Few pastorals were written during the Middle Ages, but the form survived in such peripheral genres as *Pastourelle* and vernacular *Bergerie*. The revival of classical scholarship in the Renaissance, however, led to a renewal of interest in the mode, and many of the greatest poets of the period experimented with Latin eclogues. Probably the most influential were a set by Mantuan (1448-1516), which directly inspired the first clumsy attempt at formal pastoral in English, Alexander Barclay's five *Eclogues* (c. 1515-21).

The first English work to rival the achievement of the Continental pastoralists was Edmund Spenser's *The Shepheardes Calender* (1579). Spenser modelled his XII eclogues, one for each month of the year, on the bucolics of Theocritus, Vergil and Mantuan, but attempted to naturalise the form by incorporating within the poem considerable elements of a native realism derived from Chaucer. The extraordinary contemporary popularity of *The Shepheardes Calender,* stemming both from its dazzling technical virtuosity and allegoric subtlety, helped create a vogue for pastoral: it is therefore perhaps ironic that A. C. Hamilton should find its overall argument to be 'the rejection of the pastoral life for the truly dedicated life in the world'. The eclogues of Spenser's prolific followers—Drayton, Browne, Wither and Phineas Fletcher—developed in their own distinctive ways the methods of *The Shepheardes*

Calender. But pastoral soon lost its almost exclusive association with the eclogue form, and during the period 1579-1680 came to exercise a pervasive influence, which a short survey such as this can do no more than hint at, over the entire literature and culture of Renaissance England.

Most epics of the period, for example, are studded with pastoral landscapes. Sometimes these take the form of the *locus amoenus,* a set-piece description of an ideal landscape which serves as the backdrop to the development of the plot's romantic interest, but which may, as in the case of Acrasia's Bower of Bliss in Book II of Spenser's *The Faerie Queene* (1596), represent a sensual snare tempting the unwary knight from the path of virtue. On other occasions shepherds are introduced to complicate the value structure of the poem, providing a subversive alternative to the predominant martial and heroic ethos: Calidore's 'truancy' among the herdsmen of Book VI of *The Faerie Queene,* for example, not only allows him to woo fair Pastorella but finally enriches his understanding of the true nature of Courtesy. The popular prose romances of the period, derived from the example of Longus's *Daphnis and Chloe* (c. 350 BC) and Sannazaro's *Arcadia* (1502), also blended the heroic with the bucolic. Sir Philip Sidney's *Arcadia* (1590), for example, intersperses pastoral lyrics within an intricate plot of courtly love and adventure which requires its major protagonists to spend much of their time disguised as shepherds.

Pastoral songs and lyrics not only existed as components of larger works but were popular in their own right. The most famous example, Marlowe's 'The Passionate Shepherd to his Love', was originally published in an anthology of exclusively pastoral verse, *England's Helicon* (1600). Its exploitation of the dissonance between the world of natural simplicity evoked and the artful presentation of the poem itself is characteristic of the genre.

> Come live with mee, and be my love,
> And we will all the pleasures prove,
> That Vallies, groves, hills and fieldes,
> Woods, or steepie mountaine yeeldes.
>
> And wee will sit upon the Rocks,
> Seeing the Sheepheards feede theyr flocks,
> By shallow Rivers, to whose falls,
> Melodious byrds sing Madrigalls.
>
> And I will make thee beds of Roses,
> And a thousand fragrant poesies,
> A cap of flowers, and a kirtle,
> Imbroydred all with leaves of Mirtle.
>
> A gown made of the finest wooll,
> Which from our pretty Lambes we pull,
> Fayre lined slippers for the cold:
> With buckles of the purest gold.
>
> A belt of straw, and Ivie buds,
> With Corall clasps and Amber studs,
> And if these pleasures may thee move,
> Come live with mee, and be my love.

> The Sheepheards Swaines shall daunce and sing,
> For thy delight each May-morning,
> If these delights thy minde may move;
> Then live with mee, and be my love.

The speaker may claim to be a simple swain, but his rhetoric marks him off as a displaced courtier, singing not of cakes and ale but coral clasps and amber studs amidst an environment which promises birds that sing complicated part songs and a workforce only too pleased to put on rustic entertainments for the tourists.

The elements of wish-fulfilment are even more clearly apparent in the numerous libertine seduction poems which celebrate the promiscuous sexual *mores* of the Golden Age:

> Then unconfined each did Tipple
> Wine from the Bunch, Milk from the Nipple.[5]

The doctrine that Man was most innocent when pursuing untrammelled instinctual gratification did not, however, go unchallenged. Milton's Adam and Eve may appear to condone it, since before the Fall the act of love is both totally satisfying and, because divinely ordained, completely innocent. But the happy couple live in a state of married chastity, and Milton is at pains to contrast their lawful pleasures with 'the bought smile / Of harlots, loveless, joyless, unendeared, / Casual fruition'. It is unusual to find such explicit sexuality in the garden literature of the period, which normally celebrated the joys of contemplative retirement. Marvell's 'The Garden' is more typical of this strand of pastoral, with its stress on *otium* and the recuperative powers of nature: ecstasy is attained not through sexual indulgence but through a withdrawal from the world of the senses towards a *hortus conclusus* of repose:

> Mean while the Mind, from pleasure less,
> Withdraws into its happiness:
> . . .
> Annihilating all that's made
> To a green Thought in a green Shade.

It is equally possible, of course, to view the cultivated garden as a symbol of Man's perversion of an unspoilt Nature. It is entirely typical of Marvell's complex pastoral vision that he explored this central ambiguity. His 'Mower' poems wittily contrive to subvert the traditional pastoral harmony between Man and his environment, and demonstrate the ease with which pastoral conventions could become the vehicle for metaphysical speculation.

The country house poems of the period appear to have a more direct relationship with the realities of the English countryside. Ben Jonson's 'To Penshurst', for example, describes the landed estate where Sidney wrote his *Arcadia,* and celebrates its hierarchical yet harmonious social organisation in which farmers and aristocrats meet on terms of an easy familiarity bred of mutual respect and dependency. The Marxist critic Raymond Williams however, demolishes this aristocratic myth by demonstrating the brutally exploitative economic infra-structure which supported such great houses. In his view, the pastoral themes and images in 'To Penshurst' serve to mystify and thus legitimise the true relationship between the landowning classes and their agricultural workers. Similarly, James Turner is concerned to relate the ideology of 'A Country-Life' to the circumstances of its author: 'Katherine Philips's life was the diametric opposite of what she purports to celebrate. The meaning of "A Country-Life" cannot be adequately grasped without relating it to this matrix of contradiction and suppression.'

The problematic relationship between the reality of life in the countryside and the pastoral myth of rural existence is part of Shakespeare's concern in *As You Like It* (1599). The Duke may find life in the forest of Arden 'more sweet / Than that of painted pomp', but Touchstone is there to remind us that it is a good deal more comfortable in Court, and the aristocrats do not hesitate to return there when given the opportunity. In *The Winter's Tale* (c. 1610) the pastoral life does seem to offer a genuine alternative to that of a court dominated by jealousy and tyranny, but the distinction is by no means clear cut. Perdita is nurtured by the shepherds of Bohemia, but she is in fact a lost princess and her native virtue is genetically determined. Few such complexities trouble John Fletcher's *The Faithful Shepherdess* (1608) which introduced the pastoral tragi-comic mode to the English stage. Fletcher derived the mixed generic form largely from the seminal examples of Tasso's *Aminta* (1573) and Guarini's *Il Pastor Fido* (c. 1580) which had developed the inherent dramatic potential of the dialogue format of most eclogues. The play was a failure in the popular theatre, but was successfully revived at court in 1632. Pastoral themes also infiltrated the semi-dramatic court genre of the masque. Both Milton's *Comus* (1634) and Ben Jonson's *The Golden Age Restored* (1616) for example, consciously blend classical and native pastoral imagery. This form of entertainment, however, ended with the Civil War and was not revived after the Restoration.

Even though its heyday was over, pastoral verse remained a popular medium in the early part of the eighteenth century. Pope made his dazzlingly precocious poetic début with a set of *Pastorals* (1704) modelled with neo-classical propriety on Vergil. Ambrose Philips, on the other hand, attempted to inject into his *Pastorals* (1708) details of life in the contemporary English countryside. His talents were unfortunately limited, so that Pope and his fellow Scriblerians had little difficulty in ridiculing the result. The happiest outcome of the ensuing literary war, which Hoyt Trowbridge traces in some detail, is Gay's *The Shepherd's Week* (1714). It is the earliest and probably the best mock-pastoral, which parodies Philips's style by selectively presenting the grosser aspect of rustic life, yet describes country scenes with a vivacity that many have enjoyed for its own sake.

During the course of the century formal pastoral increasingly came to be regarded as a sentimental masquerade, remote from the affairs of everyday. The trivialisation of its images is best symbolised by the inanities of Marie Antoinette's mock dairy farm, *le Petit Trianon*. Anti-pastoral developed as a response to this state of affairs. George Crabbe, for example, indignantly contrasted empty pastoral rhetoric with the drudgery of actual rural labour in *The Village* (1783):

> I grant indeed that fields and flocks have charms
> For him that grazes or for him that farms
> But when amid such pleasing scenes I trace
> The poor laborious natives of the place
> And see the mid-day sun with fervid ray,
> On their bare heads and dewy temples play;
> While some, with feebler heads and fainter hearts,
> Deplore their fortune, yet sustain their parts -
> Then shall I dare these real ills to hide
> In tinsel trappings of poetic pride?
>
> [I, 39-49]

The increasing dominance of the mode of realism meant that serious poetic efforts were directed towards the nature poetry which romantic sensibility found so convivial. Wordsworth termed 'Michael' (1800) a 'Pastoral' but as Michael Squires notes, the union of realism and sublimity it achieves is incompatible with formal pastoral. With Wordsworth the shepherd of literary convention leaves the stage, returning only for occasional appearances in works such as Arnold's *Thyrsis* (1866).

Although formal pastoral poetry had its origins in classical times, pastoral critical theory did not. Renaissance scholars were disturbed to find that, despite the fact that the genre came into being two generations after his death, Aristotle had not classified the characteristics of pastoral! The earliest serious theoretical discussions, Vida's *Ars Poetica* (1527) and Sebillet's *Art Poétique Françoys* (1548), received no contemporary translation and so fall outside the scope of this volume.[6] Their concerns were reflected, however, in the first extensive consideration of pastoral in English, E. K.'s dedicatory Epistle to Spenser's *The Shepheardes Calender* (1579). E. K. (probably Edward Kirke) praises Spenser both for dignifying the language, and for giving his eclogues a native hue. He picks out, for example, Spenser's deliberate archaisms, claiming 'such old and obsolete wordes' fittest for the 'rusticall rudeness of shepheardes', and thus enunciates the principle of generic decorum which was to dominate many later treatises. His other chief concern is with explicating the allegory of the poem, which he believed unfolded 'great matter of argument covertly'.

Sir Philip Sidney's *An Apologie for Poetrie* (c. 1583) defended imaginative literature from the attacks of the Puritans. His discussion of pastoral is brief, for he believed in a hierarchy of literary genres, with epic and tragedy occupying the most exalted positions, and pastoral the humblest. Its value is primarily didactic, teaching both the 'miserie of people under hard Lords or ravening Souldiours', and also 'what blessednesse is derived to them that lye lowest from the goodnesse of them that sit highest'. As Laurence Lerner notes, the potentially radical implications of the first lesson are immediately vitiated by the socially conservative message of the second.[7] George Puttenham's brief discussion of pastoral in his *Arte of English Poesie* (1589) is almost exclusively devoted to the question of its origins. His contention that, although sheep-keeping may have been one of the earliest employments of mankind, pastoral poetry was the product of a later urban culture, is almost universally accepted by modern scholars.

John Fletcher's 'Preface' to his *Faithful Shepherdess* (c. 1609) is a skirmish in the critical war surrounding Guarini's *Il Pastor Fido* (c. 1580). Jason Denores had criticised the latter in his *Discorso* (1587) and thus provoked a lively dispute concerning the legitimacy of such hybrid genres as pastoral tragi-comedy. Ben Jonson also felt constrained to defend his *Sad Shepherd* (c. 1636) from charges of generic mongrelism, and in his 'Prologue' to the play makes a sensible plea for critical flexibility.

Michael Drayton's compact 'To the Reader of his Pastorals' (1619) generally eschews critical squabbles. Drayton leaves such disputes to 'Scaliger and the Nation of Learned Censors', preferring instead to dwell on the well established analogies between Biblical and pastoral themes: 'In the Angels song to Shepheards at our Saviours Nativitie Pastorall Poesie seems consecrated.' He shares with E. K. a concern for decorum and an admiration for Spenser, but displays an empirical bias which leads him to prefer Theocritus's *Idylls,* on account of their realistic detail, to Vergil's *Eclogues.* Thomas Hobbes's 'Answer to the Preface before Gondibert' (1650) is even more frankly empirical, viewing pastoral simply as representation of the countryside. It was the last major critical statement concerning pastoral made before discussion became dominated by the influence of René Rapin (1621-86) and Bernard le Bouvier de Fontenelle (1657-1757).

Notes

1. *OED:* Pastoral, *a.* and *sb.* I, 3.

2. Ovid, *The Metamorphoses,* trans. Arthur Golding (1567): I, 102-31; in W. H. D. Rouse (ed.), *Shakespeare's Ovid* (London, 1961), p. 23.

3. Horace, Epode II trans. J. Marshall (Everyman edition, London, 1911), pp. 113-14.

4. William Cowper, *The Task.*

5. Richard Lovelace, 'Love Made in the First Age'.

6. For details of these and other early theorists, see J. E. Congleton, *Theories of Pastoral Poetry in England, 1684-1798* (Gainesville, Fl., 1952).

7. L. D. Lerner, *The Uses of Nostalgia* (London, 1972), p. 118.

PRINCIPAL FIGURES OF THE ELIZABETHAN PERIOD

E. K. (essay date 1579)

SOURCE: "E. K.," in The Pastoral Mode: A Casebook, edited by Bryan Loughrey, Macmillan Publishers Ltd., 1984, pp. 29-33.

[*In the following dedicatory epistle to Gabriel Harvey, which was originally prefixed to the 1579 edition of Edmund Spenser's* Shepheardes Calender, *the writer "E. K." (probably Edward Kirke) praises Spenser for dignifying the language with the use of archaisms and for giving his eclogues a particularly English hue.*]

Uncouthe unkiste, Sayde the olde famous Poete Chaucer: whom for his excellencie and wonderfull skil in making, his scholler Lidgate, a worthy scholler of so excellent a maister, calleth the Loade-starre of our Language: and whom our Colin [C]lout in his Aeglogue calleth Tityrus the God of shepheards, comparing hym to the worthines of the Roman Tityrus Virgile. Which proverbe . . . as in that good old Poete it served well Pandares purpose, for the bolstering of his baudy brocage, so very well taketh place in this our new Poete, who for that he is uncouthe (as said Chaucer) is unkist, and unknown to most men, is regarded but of few. But I dout not, so soone as his name shall come into the knowledg of men, and his worthines be sounded in the tromp of fame, but that he shall be not onely kiste, but also beloved of all, embraced of the most, and wondred at of the best. No lesse I thinke, deserveth his wittinesse in devising, his pithinesse in uttering, his complaints of love so lovely, his discourses of pleasure so pleasantly, his pastorall rudenesse, his morall wisenesse, his dewe observing of Decorum everye where, in personages, in seasons, in matter, in speach, and generally in al seemely simplycitie of handeling his matter, and framing his words: the which of many things which in him be straunge, I know will seeme the straungest, the words them selves being so auncient, the knitting of them so short and intricate, and the whole Periode and compasse of speache so delightsome for the roundnesse, and so grave for the straungenesse. And firste of the wordes to speake, I graunt they be something hard, and of most men unused, yet both English, and also used of most excellent Authors and most famous Poetes. In whom whenas this our Poet hath bene much traveiled and throughly redd, how could it be, (as that worthy Oratour sayde) but that walking in the sonne although for other cause he walked, yet needes he mought be sunburnt; and having the sound of those auncient Poetes still ringing in his eares, he mought needes in singing hit out some of theyr tunes. But whether he useth them by such casualtye and custome, or of set purpose and choyse, as thinking them fittest for such rusticall rudenesse of shepheards, eyther for that theyr rough sounde would make his rymes more ragged and rustical, or els because such olde and obsolete wordes are most used of country folke, sure I think, and think I think not amisse, that they bring great grace and, as one would say, auctoritie to the verse. For albe amongst many other faultes it specially be obiected of Valla against Livie, and of other against Saluste, that with over much studie they affect antiquitie, as coveting thereby credence and honor of elder yeeres, yet I am of opinion, and eke the best learned are of the lyke, that those auncient solemne wordes are a great ornament both in the one and in the other; the one labouring to set forth in hys worke an eternall image of antiquitie, and the other carefully discoursing matters of gravitie and importaunce. For if my memory fayle not, Tullie in that booke, wherein he endevoureth to set forth the paterne of a perfect Oratour, sayth that ofttimes an auncient worde maketh the style seeme grave, and as it were reverend: no otherwise then we honour and reverence gray heares for a certein religious regard, which we have of old age. Yet nether every where must old words be stuffed in, nor the commen Dialecte and maner of speaking so corrupted therby, that as in old buildings it seme disorderly and ruinous. But all as in most exquisite pictures they use to blaze and portraict not onely the daintie lineaments of beautye, but also rounde about it to shadow the rude thickets and craggy clifts, that by the basenesse of such parts, more excellency may accrew to the principall; for oftimes we fynde ourselves, I knowe not how, singularly delighted with the shewe of such naturall rudenesse, and take great pleasure in that disorderly order. Even so doe those rough and harsh termes enlumine and make more clearly to appeare the brightnesse of brave and glorious words. So oftentimes a dischorde in Musick maketh a comely concordaunce: so great delight tooke the worthy Poete Alceus to behold a blemish in the ioynt of a wel shaped body. But if any will rashly blame such his purpose in choyse of old and unwonted words, him may I more iustly blame and condemne, or of witlesse headinesse in iudging, or of heedelesse hardinesse in condemning for not marking the compasse of hys bent, he wil iudge of the length of his cast. For in my opinion it is one special prayse, of many whych are dew to this Poete, that he hath laboured to restore, as to theyr rightfull heritage such good and naturall English words, as have ben long time out of use and almost cleane disherited. Which is the onely cause, that our Mother tonge, which truely of it self is both ful enough for prose and stately enough for verse, hath long time ben counted most bare and barrein of both. Which default when as some endevoured to salve and recure, they patched up the holes with peces and rags of other languages, borrowing here of the French, there of the Italian, every where of the Latine, not weighing how il, those tongues accorde with themselves, but much worse with ours: So now they have made our English tongue, a gallimaufray or hodgepodge of al other speches. Other some not so wel seene in the English tonge as perhaps in other languages, if they happen to here an olde word albeit very naturall and significant, crye out streight way, that we speak no English, but gibbrish, or rather such, as in old time Evanders mother spake. Whose first shame is, that they are not ashamed, in their own mother tonge straungers to be counted and alienes. The second shame no lesse

then the first, that what so they understand not, they streight way deeme to be sencelesse, and not at all to be understode. Much like to the Mole in sopes fable, that being blynd her selfe, would in no wise be perswaded, that any beast could see. The last more shameful then both, that of their owne country and natural speach, which together with their Nources milk they sucked, they have so base regard and bastard iudgement, that they will not onely themselves not labor to garnish and beautifie it, but also repine, that of other it shold be embellished. Like to the dogge in the maunger, that him selfe can eate no hay, and yet barketh at the hungry bullock, that so faine would feede: whose currish kind though it cannot be kept from barking, yet I conne them thanke that they refrain from byting.

Now for the knitting of sentences, whych they call the ioynts and members thereof, and for al the compasse of the speach, it is round without roughnesse, and learned wythout hardnes, such indeede as may be perceiued of the leaste, understoode of the moste, but iudged onely of the learned. For what in most English wryters useth to be loose, and as it were ungyrt, in this Authour is well grounded, finely framed, and strongly trussed up together. In regard whereof, I scorne and spue out the rakehellye route of our ragged rymers (for so themselves use to hunt the letter) which without learning boste, without iudgement iangle, without reason rage and fome, as if some instinct of Poeticall spirite had newly ravished them above the meanenesse of commen capacitie. And being in the middest of all theyr bravery, sodenly eyther for want of matter, or of ryme, or having forgotten theyr former conceipt, they seeme to be so pained and traveiled in theyr remembrance, as it were a woman in childebirth or as that same Pythia, when the traunce came upon her.

> Os rabidum fera corda domans &c.

Nethelesse let them a Gods name feede on theyr owne folly, so they seeke not to darken the beames of others glory. As for Colin, under whose person the Author selfe is shadowed, how farre he is from such vaunted titles and glorious showes, both him selfe sheweth, where he sayth.

> Of Muses Hobbin. I conne no skill. And,
> Enough is me to paint out my unrest, &c.

And also appeareth by the basenesse of the name, wherein, it semeth, he chose rather to unfold great matter of argument covertly, then professing it, not suffice thereto accordingly. Which moved him rather in glogues, then other wise to write, doubting perhaps his habilitie, which he little needed, or mynding to furnish our tongue with this kinde, wherein it faulteth, or following the example of the best and most auncient Poetes, which devised this kind of wryting, being both so base for the matter, and homely for the manner, at the first to trye theyr habilities: and as young birdes, that be newly crept out of the nest, by little first to prove theyr tender wyngs, before they make a greater flyght. So flew Theocritus, as you may perceive he was all ready full fledged. So flew Virgile, as not yet well feeling his winges. So flew Mantuane, as being not full somd. So Petrarque. So Boccace; So Marot, Sanazarus, and also divers other excellent both Italian and French Poetes, whose foting this Author every where followeth, yet so as few, but they be wel sented can trace him out. So finally flyeth this our new Poete, as a bird, whose principals be scarce growen out, but yet as that in time shall be hable to keepe wing with the best.

Now as touching the generall dryft and purpose of his glogues, I mind not to say much, him selfe labouring to conceale it. Onely this appeareth, that his unstayed yougth had long wandred in the common Labyrinth of Love, in which time to mitigate and allay the heate of his passion, or els to warne (as he sayth) the young shepheards his equalls and companions of his unfortunate folly, he compiled these xij. glogues, which for that they be proportioned to the state of the xij. monethes, he termeth the SHEPHERDS CALENDAR, applying an olde name to a new worke. Hereunto have I added a certain Glosse or scholion for thexposition of old wordes and harder phrases: wich maner of glosing and commenting, well I wote, wil seeme straunge and rare in our tongue: yet for somuch as I knew many excellent and proper devises both in wordes and matter would passe in the speedy course of reading, either as unknowen, or as not marked, and that in this kind, as in other we might be equal to the learned of other nations, I thought good to take the paines upon me, the rather for that by meanes of some familiar acquaintaunce I was made privie to his counsell and secret meaning in them, as also in sundry other works of his. Which albeit I know he nothing so much hateth, as to promulgate, yet thus much have I adventured upon his frendship, him selfe being for long time farre estraunged, hoping that this will the rather occasion him, to put forth divers other excellent works of his, which slepe in silence, as his Dreames, his Legendes, his Court of Cupide, and sondry others; whose commendations to set out, were verye vayne; the thinges though worthy of many, yet being knowen to few. These my present paynes if to any they be pleasurable or profitable, be you iudge, mine own good Maister Harvey, to whom I have both in respect of your worthinesse generally, and otherwyse upon some particular and special considerations voued this my labour, and the maydenhead of this our commen frends Poetrie, himselfe having already in the beginning dedicated it to the Noble and worthy Gentleman, the right worshipfull Ma. Phi. Sidney, a special favourer and maintainer of all kind of learning. Whose cause I pray you Sir, yf Envie shall stur up any wrongful accusasion, defend with your mighty Rhetorick and other your rare gifts of learning, as you can, and shield with your good wil, as you ought, against the malice and outrage of so many enemies, as I know wilbe set on fire with the sparks of his kindled glory. And thus recommending the Author unto you, as unto his most special goodfrend, and my selfe unto you both, as one making singuler account of two so very good and so choise frends, I bid you both most hartely farwel, and commit you and your most commendable studies to the tuicion of the greatest.

Your owne assuredly to
be commaunded E. K.

A. C. Hamilton (essay date 1956)

SOURCE: "The Argument of Spenser's *Shepheardes Calender*," in *ELH*, Vol. 23, No. 3, September 1956, pp. 171-82.

[*In the following essay, Hamilton explores the larger meaning of Edmund Spenser's* Shepheardes Calender—*which he claims is the rejection of the pastoral life for the truly dedicated life in the world—by examining not what the poem has in common with other pastoral poetry, as has been the strategy of other critics, but by looking at what is unique in Spenser's re-creation of the pastoral form.*]

The critical attention given Spenser's *Shepheardes Calender,* apart from praise of the work as a brilliant poetical exercise, has mainly been to identify certain historical allusions. While the poem is deliberately designed, so it would seem, to provoke from the reader E. K.'s delighted response to "a pretty Epanorthosis in these two verses" or "a very Poeticall πέθος," its brilliant rhetorical surface deliberately conceals reference, as E. K. hints many times in his glosses, to certain persons and events. Accordingly, the poem provokes the critic to turn from the display of sheer poetic skill in order to uncover some historical allegory. Yet even a probable identification of Rosalind or Dido or Cuddie does not take one very far into the poem which is read then only as a cipher or intellectual puzzle. The poem was not so read in Spenser's own age. In his *Skialetheia* Guilpin praised "deep Spencer" for "his profound-prickt layes"; to Whetstone, it was "a work of deepe learning, iudgment & witte"; while upon the evidence of the *Calender* alone Nashe upheld "diuine Master *Spencer,* the miracle of wit, to bandie line for line for my life in the honor of *England* gainst *Spaine, France, Italie,* and all the worlde."[1] Unless we dismiss this praise as jingoism, we must allow that the poem has depths of meaning which cannot be probed by removing an allegorical veil. This is to say the obvious, perhaps; yet criticism of the *Shepheardes Calender* has not been much more than footnotes to E. K.'s glosses.

What is so perverse about this effort to identify historical allusions is that Spenser has laboured so carefully to conceal them. Why, then, should the critic turn from what the poet says to what he has left unsaid? Certainly parts of the poem "reflect"—though in no simple one-to-one correspondence—the contemporary historical situation, awareness of which would then provide an added social impact for the contemporary reader; but the poem's substance, its meaning, is not there. Again to say the obvious, Rosalind or Dido or Cuddie is clearly in the poem, while whoever in the age may be doubtfully identified with one of these poetic facts is not, unless we confuse art and life. Spenser conceals private meaning in his poem, it is true; but he does so in order to turn the reader from the particular to the universal. A general moral meaning is dominant throughout the poem: E. K. writes that "the keeping of sheepe . . . is the argument of *all* Aeglogues," and Spenser affirms that his purpose is "to teach the ruder shepheard how to feede his sheepe." Moreover, Spenser insists in the Epilogue that his *Calender* be not confined to any particular historical setting:

> Loe I haue made a Calender for *euery* yeare,
> That steele in strength, and time in durance shall
>   outweare:
> And if I marked well the starres reuolution,
> It shall continewe till the worlds dissolution.

As E. K. paraphrases these lines: "all thinges perish and come to theyr last end, but workes of learned wits and monuments of Poetry abide for euer."[2] Spenser is not writing a history of his time, but prophecy; or rather, as the poet he considers in Sidney's terms not "what is, hath been, or shall be," but ranges "into the diuine consideration of what may be, and should be."[3] That Milton read the *Shepheardes Calender* in this way is evident from his comment upon "that false shepherd Palinode in the eclogue of May, under whom the poet lively personates our prelates, whose whole life is a recantation of their pastoral vow, and whose profession to forsake the world, as they use the matter, bogs them deeper into the world. Those our admired Spenser inveighs against, not without some presage of these reforming times."[4] Spenser's intent in choosing "rather to vnfold great matter of argument couertly, then professing it," is not to set up an historical maze, but to seek the universal level of significance. By his time, the pastoral form had become the vehicle for such higher meaning. Drayton believed that "the most High, and most Noble Matters of the World may bee shaddowed in them," and he held Spenser to be "the prime Pastoralist of England."[5]

My purpose in this paper is to explore the larger meaning of the *Shepheardes Calender*. To state my own position briefly: I believe that the whole poem is integrated through the form of the Calendar; and I shall attempt here to describe the nature of its meaning as a whole, what may be called the poem's argument. It is generally agreed that the poem lacks unity both in form and content;[6] my purpose is to prove otherwise. Only one critic, to my knowledge, treats the poem as a whole. Hallett Smith writes that Elizabethan pastoral poetry illustrates a "pastoral idea" which is "an ideal of the good life, of the state of content and mental self-sufficiency," and that "the pastoral idea, in its various ramifications, *is* the *Calender.*"[7] His understanding of Spenser's poem is directly opposed to mine. When he analyzes the poem he does so through the different kinds of eclogues which he sees illustrating the "pastoral idea" and not in terms of the poem's internal structure or developing pattern through which it may possess its own organic unity. My approach, too, differs: being not through what the poem has in common with Elizabethan pastoral poetry, but through what is unique in Spenser's recreation of the pastoral form. The beginning, then, of my discussion of the poem's argument is Spenser's use of the Calendar.

Spenser's contribution to the pastoral form was the Calendar. Its use may have been suggested through Virgil's Fourth Eclogue which celebrates the return of the Golden Age, and the subsequent linking of the pastoral with the Nativity. "In the Angels Song to Shepheards at our Saviours Nativitie," Drayton writes, "Pastorall Poesie seemes consecrated";[8] and in his "General Argument" E. K. justifies the poem's beginning with the month of January because of its association with the Incarnation of Christ "who as then renewing the state of the decayed world, and returning the compasse of expired yeres to theyr former date and first commencement, left to vs his heires a memoriall of his birth." The year with its cycle of seasons determines the form of the poem. The opening lines announce the poet's Exodus as he "led forth his flock, that had bene long ypent," and in the wilderness of the winter setting he complains of his suffering through the revolution of the seasons. The contest of the seasons suggests the sequence of winter-summer-winter that dominates the January-June-December eclogues, and through them the shape of the whole poem. The form of the Calendar allows Spenser to return to the ritual origins of the pastoral seen in Bion's *Lament for Adonis;* only now the lament for the dying God becomes the lament for himself. The poet is Adonis, the love-wounded God for whom all Nature laments:

> Thou barrein ground, whome winters wrath hath
>   wasted,
> Art made a myrrhour, to behold my plight:
> Whilome thy fresh spring flowrd, and after hasted
> Thy sommer prowde with Daffadillies dight.
> And now is come thy wynters stormy state,
> Thy mantle mard, wherein thou maskedst late.
>
> Such rage as winters, reigneth in my heart,
> My life bloud friesing with vnkindly cold:
> Such stormy stoures do breede my balefull smart,
> As if my yeare were wast, and woxen old.
>
> *(Jan. 19-28)*

The ritual quest for the God becomes the quest for himself, and the poem's major theme is the effort to "find" himself. The association of the Calendar with the Nativity adds the life-death-life sequence, and the mutability of life that brings death within nature is opposed at the end of the poem by the November eclogue where for the first time the pagan mood of despair is supplanted by the full Christian assurance of man's resurrection out of Nature. This assurance, together with the aspiration in October to cast off his shepherd's weeds, brings him to the resolution of the final eclogue when he lays down the oaten pipe and emerges as England's heroic poet. The *Calender* becomes the poet's manifestation, his epiphany to the world. Since the poem is set within the framework of the Nativity, its moment of time is when the pagan world violently confronts the Christian, and the old gods are rejected for the new. The traditional lament, "Pan is dead" is rendered in Spenser's cry: "Perdie god was he none"; and in the final eclogue, the pagan pastoral world gives way to the Christian with the poet's prayer to the greater Pan. Since Christ is the second Adam whose birth returns "the compass of expired yeres to theyr former date and first commencement," the poem is set also in the framework of the Fall which is constantly echoed and retold throughout.

Within the form of the Calendar, the various eclogues are divided by E. K. into "three formes or ranckes": the Recreative, the Moral, and the Plaintive. The relationship of these three distinct kinds of eclogues provides the poem's argument; but first it is necessary to see how they are distinct. The pastoral world which provides the poem's setting is traditionally identified with Arcadia, the state of innocence before the Fall. This "unreal" world, seen in the poem's deliberate artifice with its conventions of the shepherd life, provides the subject of the Recreative eclogues: March with its story of Cupid, April's hymn of praise, and the contest of the shepherds in August. These eclogues exist in the poem as fragments of an earlier pastoral tradition, the idyll, that serve to "test" the poet's skill. In each he seeks to "overgo" the traditional form. When this timeless pastoral world is placed in the order of time given by the Calendar form, it is seen from the perspective of the Fall caught in perpetual mutability. The pastoral world of innocence circumscribed by the "real" world of fallen nature becomes the subject of the moral eclogues with their allegory of the political and religious conditions of England. The simple pastoral life of enjoyable ease must then be rejected for the dedicated life where man does not live according to Nature but seeks escape out of Nature. For this reason the pastoral life is identified with the antagonists in the moral eclogues: Cuddie's "flowring youth" (*Feb.,* 31), Palinode's yearning for "lustihede and wanton meryment" (*May,* 42), the wanton poets singing "rymes of rybaudrye" (*Oct.,* 76), and Morrell upon the hill identified with the Garden of Eden where "vsed shepheards all to feede theyr flocks at will, / Till by his foly one did fall, that all the rest did spill" (*July,* 65-8). The good shepherds of the moral eclogues, such as Thomalin, know that since the Fall "shepheardes bene foresayd from places of delight" (*July,* 69-70). In the moral eclogues the pastoral conventions become radically allegorical; simple lyricism is replaced by satire, irony, and open denunciation. The poet's relation to the simple pastoral world of innocence becomes the subject of the Plaintive eclogues. Within the pastoral world he is the melancholy shepherd dominated by the elusive and faithless Rosalind. While Hobbinoll, the shepherd of the pastoral world, may find Paradise, the poet Colin Clout must journey through a wilderness:

> O happy *Hobbinoll,* I blesse they state,
> That Paradise hast found, whych *Adam* lost.
> Here wander may thy flock early or late,
> Withouten dreade of Wolues to bene ytost:
> Thy louely layes here mayst thou freely boste.
> But I vnhappy man, whom cruell fate,
> And angry Gods pursue from coste to coste,
> Can nowhere fynd, to shroude my lucklesse pate.
>
>   (*June,* 9-16)

(Significantly, the last lines echo Virgil's opening description of Aeneas.) Paradise, tempting man to return to the

life of pleasurable ease, is evil; for life lived merely according to Nature, as portrayed through the device of the Calendar, yields eternal death. For this reason the poet withdraws from the pastoral world, signified in the opening eclogue by the act of breaking the shepherd's pipe, and remains disguised until he may find his rightful place in the real world reflected in the moral eclogues. The mode of the plaintive eclogues is the pastoral elegy with its central theme of death and rebirth: hence at the beginning, middle, and end of the poem the poet laments his present "death" until the climax in December: "winter is come, that blowes the balefull breath, / And after Winter commeth timely death" (149-50). At this moment when the year begins to descend through another cycle of seasons, the poet casts off his pastoral disguise, turns from Pan to address the greater Pan, and frees himself from bondage to the pastoral life:

> Adieu delightes, that lulled me asleepe,
> Adieu my deare, whose loue I bought so deare:
> Adieu my little Lambes and loued sheepe,
> Adieu ye Woodes that oft my witnesse were:
>   Adieu good *Hobbinol,* that was so true,
>   Tell *Rosalind,* her *Colin* bids her adieu.

This sudden and climactic resolution coming with full force only in the final line suggests that the poet's release is achieved through the act of writing the poem.

The kinds of eclogues are carefully juxtaposed: in the first half of the poem there is the movement from the opening plaintive eclogue to the moral eclogue and to the recreative eclogue which is repeated, then returning to the moral and to the plaintive eclogue of June; in the second half, there is the same descent from the plaintive to the moral and to the recreative, then returning as before to the moral eclogue which is repeated and to the final plaintive eclogues which resolve the argument of the whole poem.[9] Within this structure Spenser explores the roles of the poet and pastor in society. The subject of the eclogues alternates from the poet to the pastor regularly (the pair of recreative eclogues March and April being taken as one), until October where the poet aspires to fulfil the pastor's role in society. Thus the eclogues form pairs: what is first treated in terms of the poet is then expanded in religious terms. The patterning of the eclogues, as I seek to establish now, provides the developing argument of the poem.

The two opening eclogues serve as prelude to the poem, even as January and February precede the natural year. In January, the poet as Colin is identified with Nature, being at one with Nature, reflected by and reflecting Nature, as he invokes the Nature God Pan. Brought to despair through his vain love for Rosalind, he may only withdraw and break his pipe: "both pype and Muse, shall sore the while abye. / So broke his oaten pype, and downe dyd lye" (71-2). His complaint, "such rage as winters, reigneth in my heart" is expressed in the following eclogue through Cuddie's lament against "rancke Winters rage"; and in reproof Thenot moralizes upon the mutability of the world which must go "from good to badd, and from badde to worse, /

From worse vnto that is worst of all, / And then returne to his former fall" (12-14). He illustrates the world's mutability through the fable of the Oak that "had bene an auncient tree, / Sacred with many a mysteree" but later is cut down through the complaints of the ambitious Briar. Whatever particular meaning the fable may hold, the "morall and generall" meaning is dominant, as E. K. declares: it stands as an allegory of the dangers of Reformation, the Oak being the Catholic Church which suffers reform by the Established Church under Elizabeth (the Briar with "colours meete to clothe a mayden Queene").[10] Cutting the tree corresponds to breaking the shepherd's pipe: the January eclogue stands, then, as an allegory of the aspirations of the Renaissance poet. It expresses the desire of England's "new Poete," the successor of the old Poet Chaucer, to escape the pastoral form.[11] The poem becomes his "retracciouns" of "many a song and many a leccherous lay"—his Dreams, Legends, Courts of Cupid, and his Dying Pelican—and the record of his dedication to the higher argument of the heroic form.

"The yeare beginneth in March" and "proportioned" to that season is a recreative eclogue describing the pastoral world of Flora who "bids make ready *Maias* bowre" and leads the shepherds to "sporten in delight, / And learne with Lettice to wexe light" (17, 19-20). The fable of the discovery of Cupid whose wound, the shepherd complains, "ranckleth more and more, / And inwardly it festreth sore" (100-1) presents allegorically the state of human nature within the natural world. The eclogue defines the world out of which the poet seeks escape. E. K. writes in the "Epistle" that the poet's purpose in his poem is to warn others against his folly, for "his vnstayed yougth had long wandred in the common Labyrinth of Loue." In the following eclogue the poet as Colin is described as one who "doth forbeare / His wonted songs" for "Loue hath wounded [him] with a deadly darte" (22). This account is juxtaposed to the intensely lyrical hymn of praise to the Queen who appears as Flora attended with her nymphs, being crowned with flowers and surrounded by "this beuie of Ladies bright" (118). She inspires him to song, and he dedicates to her his poetic labours:

> To her will I offer a milkwhite Lamb:
>   She is my goddesse plaine,
>   And I her shepherds swayne,
> Albee forswonck and forswatt I am.

> (96-99)

The counterpart of April is the May eclogue: here Palinode the dedicated shepherd-pastor delivers his hymn of praise to Lady Flora who is a parody of the Virgin Queen, being the companion of "a lusty Tabrere" (22). (The two eclogues are companion pieces on the themes of sacred and profane love.) As the shepherds in March are led by Flora to "sporten in delight," so Palinode lusts after the "great sport" of Lady Flora and her Nymphs. The protagonist, Piers, reproves Palinode's recantation of the dedicated life for "shepheard must walke another way, / Sike worldly souenance he must foresay" (81-2), and denounces

any temporizing between them. Piers' declaration completes the first part of the poem's argument: by withdrawing from the postoral life the poet need not be, as Palinode, a "worldes childe" but may lead a dedicated life within but not of the world. Milton understood that the eclogue shows how one must "learn first to renounce the world and so give himself to God, and not therefore give himself to God, that he may close the better with the world."[12] Hence with June the poet returns to the pastoral setting being now prepared to forsake the pastoral Paradise for a dedicated life. His poetical ambitions are expressed through Hobbinoll's advice to leave the pastoral world for the court. But he dare not as yet aspire to a higher muse, though he hopes to be baptized by Chaucer, and rejects the ambition that would lead him to "presume to *Parnasse* hyll" (70). Thus the first part of the poem treats of the individual self and points forward to the truly dedicated life. There remains the problem treated in the second part, how one may lead the dedicated life within the fallen world. In July, the companion eclogue to June, the same theme of aspiration is given for the shepherd-pastor. Morrell, the proud and ambitious pastor inhabits the hill which is identified with seven different hills (signifying the seven hills of Rome and therefore the fallen world) including Eden and Parnassus. As the poet in June would not climb Parnassus, so the good pastor Thomalin scorns the hill and loves the low degree.

The August eclogue is a recreative interlude displaying the poet's skill through the traditional singing-contest in which the shepherds' praise of love is significantly opposed by his lament upon love. Renwick calls the eclogue an "allegory of the new poetry: the simple swains sing merrily enough, but a grave, elaborate, Italianate song of *Colin's* hushes them in admiration, their simple impromptu is overshadowed."[13] The September and October eclogues conclude the debate upon the role of the poet-pastor in society. In September, the allegorical veil is removed and Diggon denounces openly the corruption of pastors in England. His denunciation summarizes the attacks made previously against the shepherds who "bene ydle and still, / And ledde of theyr sheepe, what way they wyll" (as Palinode), those who "bene false, and full of couetise, / And casten to compasse many wrong emprise" (such as Morrell), and those represented by the Briar who "ne in good nor goodnes taken delight: / But kindle coales of conteck and yre" (80-7). Corrupt pastors ("badde is the best") corrupt the sheep who do not listen to their voice but "wander at wil, and stray at pleasure, / And to theyr foldes yead at their owne leasure" (144-5). October presents a similar complaint against the corrupt age; and at this moment of crisis the poet aspires to become the heroic poet who may fulfil the role of the pastor and through his work move the infected will:

> O what an honor is it, to restraine
> The lust of lawlesse youth with good aduice:
> Or pricke them forth with pleasaunce of thy vaine,
> Whereto thou list their trayned willes entice.

> (21-4)

In the May eclogue Piers upheld the dedicated life within the world; now he advocates the life of service dedicated to the Queen. He urges the poet to "lyft vp thy selfe out of the lowly dust," and Colin is inspired by that love which "lyftes him vp out of the loathsome myre" and may "rayse [his] mynd aboue the starry skie" (92, 4). That man may be lifted out of the lowly dust and raised above the starry sky becomes the theme of the November eclogue which treats the death and resurrection of Dido. E. K.'s claim that this eclogue surpasses all others in the book is a measure of its significance. Here, for the first time, is shown the ultimate defeat of Nature with man's release from the state of mutability. The assurance of resurrection out of the state of Nature resolves, as it does for Milton in *Lycidas,* the problems which led to writing the poem. Then with the return to the pastoral setting in the concluding eclogue, the poet prays to the greater Pan who is Christ: to Him he addresses his complaint against life confined to the state of Nature, and at the end abandons the pastoral world.

The argument of the *Shepheardes Calender* is, then, the rejection of the pastoral life for the truly dedicated life in the world. For Spenser, this life is that of the heroic poet whose high religious calling is to serve the Queen by inspiring her people to all virtuous action. Upon the level of merely private allusion, the poem may refer covertly to Spenser's circle of friends, to local gossip and other topical matters; but such allusion is carefully submerged, being occasional, digressive, and extrinsic to the poem's organic unity. Upon another level, the personal, the poem records Spenser's progress from his apprenticeship to pastoral poetry towards the heroic poem. Like the Red Cross Knight, he is a "clownishe younge man" described in the "Letter to Ralegh" who "rested him on the floore, vnfitte through his rusticity for a better place" until the Faery Queen appoints him his task. (A year after the *Calender* appeared, Spenser started to write *The Faerie Queene.*) This level of meaning is transmuted through the pastoral conventions and the Calender form into an allegory of human life within the order of Nature. Through the device of the Calender, human life is seen in the perspective of the Fall and the Nativity: the one bringing the state of death out of which man must escape through rejecting the pastoral Paradise, the other promising rebirth which he may gain through seeking the truly dedicated life in the world.

Notes

1. *Skialetheia* or, A Shadowe of Truth, 1598, El[r]; *Sir Phillip Sidney,* his honorable life . . . by G. W., 1586, B2[v] Margin; Nashe, Preface to Greene's *Menaphon,* in *Eliz. Crit. Essays* (Ed. G. G. Smith, Oxford, 1904), I, 318.

2. Gloss on December Emblem. All quotations of the poem are from *Spenser's Minor Poems,* Ed. E. De Selincourt, Oxford, 1910.

3. *Apologie for Poetrie* (Ed. J. Churton Collins, Oxford, 1907), p. 11.

4. *Animadversions,* in *The Student's Milton* (Ed. F. Patterson, New York, 1933), p. 500.

5. "To the Reader of his Pastorals" in *Works* (Ed. Hebel, Oxford, 1932), II, 517-8.

6. *The Minor Poems* (Baltimore, 1943), I, 571-655.

7. *Elizabethan Poetry* (Cambridge, Mass., 1952), pp. 2, 46.

8. *Op. cit.,* II, 517.

9. The juxtaposition of the eclogues may be given diagrammatically:

Plaintive	1	6		11–12
Moral	2	5	7	9–10
Recreative	3–4		8	

10. Cf. Greenlaw, in *Minor Poems,* I, 603.

11. The antithesis between the old poet and the new is carefully made in the Epistle: "the new Poete . . . the olde famous Poete Chaucer . . . that good old Poete . . . this our new Poete."

12. *Animadversions,* p. 500.

13. *The Shepherd's Calendar* (London, 1930), p. 206.

Elizabeth Dipple (essay date 1968)

SOURCE: "Harmony and Pastoral in the *Old Arcadia,*" in *ELH,* Vol. 35, No. 3, September 1968, pp. 309-28.

[*In the following essay, Dipple examines Philip Sidney's use of pastoral setting and conventions in the* Old Arcadia, *and argues that Sidney ironically exploits pastoral connotations to dramatize the fall from harmony to disharmony and to illustrate the ultimate impracticability of the idealized pastoral world.*]

I

Arcadia amonge all the Provinces of *Grece* was ever had in singuler reputation, partly for the sweetnes of the Aire and other naturall benefittes: But, principally, for the moderate & well tempered myndes of the people, who, (fynding howe true a Contentation ys gotten by following the Course of Nature, And howe the shyning Title of glory somuche affected by other Nacions, dothe in deede help litle to the happines of lyfe) were the onely people, which as by theire Justice and providence, gave neyther Cause nor hope to theyre Neighboures to annoy them, so were they not stirred with false prayse, to truble others quyett. Thincking yt a smalle Rewarde for the wasting of theire owne lyves in ravening, that theire posterity shoulde longe after saye, they had done so: Eeven the *Muses* seemed to approove theire goode determinacion, by chosing that Contrie as theire cheefest reparing place, and by bestowing theire perfections so largely there, that the very *Shepeardes* them selves had theire fancyes opened to so highe Conceiptes (as the most learned of other nations have been long tyme since content) bothe to borrow theyre names, and imitate their Conning.[1]

Thus in the first words of the *Old Arcadia* Sidney establishes his literary arch-image,[2] advertises his locus and controls his reader's reaction. It appears that the work will be another Renaissance pastoral set in utopian Arcadia and sustained in prose romances by such former models as Sannazaro's *L'Arcadia* or Montemayor's *Diana.* Because of the romance's generic precedents, the reader should expect either the extreme of pastoral melancholy archetypally imaged in Sannazaro's laments, or that of omnipotent joy found in the heart of the pastoral through the ministering of Montemayor's Felicia. It is with some surprise, therefore, that one finds both politico-personal morality and high comedy[3] rapidly ensuing, and the whole romance constituting a kind of literary mélange entirely foreign to its real or imagined models.[4]

Few problems have yet been confronted in Sidney criticism, but fewest of all in studies of the *Old Arcadia,* with its puzzling constitution in spite of a simplistic Terentian five-act structure. The work's often typological overtones, its use of oracular pronouncements, and its final deus-ex-machina denouement through a phony resurrection have all served to confuse rather than aid commentary. Greater than any of these stumbling-blocks, however, and the central issue on those rare occasions when the work is discussed at all, is the question of genre—is it an epic, a pastoral, a play, or merely a charming and "toyfull" recitation which must amuse beyond the ordinary expectation? Because pastoral is, as Professor Hamilton has pointed out, "cool" right now,[5] it is in this area that the work can be most easily victimized—and indeed Sidney's introductory framework would encourage us to do so. By choosing the infinitely weary spiritual landscape of Arcadia, he would lead us down the primrose path to an idyllic pleasaunce or pastoral center where the Freudian imagination is released and where highly stylized peril touches destruction but is, of course, miraculously removed. It is not all wrong to read the work lightly and frivolously as Lanham does, or even to give it a ponderous historical framework as Davis assigns to this aspect of the *New Arcadia,* but both of these approaches[6] dodge the peculiar achievement of the pastoral element of the romance.

The easiest way to begin talking about this Arcadia is to establish its essential polarities as Sidney presents them. In the first place, Arcadia is a much chronicled and sung literary landscape which can be spontaneously represented to the reader who has, of course, seen it all before and often; but it is simultaneously an historical and geographical location. The Renaissance mind would instantly, and probably with some surprise, recognize Sidney's eclectic, ironic copying of Polybius who talks thus of his native land in his *History:*

> And for that the people of *Arcadia* haue a certaine fame and renowne of good men, not onely for their easie kinde of life, and their good dispositions, and great honesty towards all the world, but also for the honour and reuerence they beare vnto the Gods. . . . It is certaine that Musique, (I meane true Musique) is profitable to all the world, and necessary for the *Arcadians.* . . . Neither had the ancient *Arcadians* Musique in so great honour in their Common-wealth, as they not onely caused Children to learne it, but also young men vnto the age of thirty yeares, who otherwise were rude and vnciuil . . . all their life is adicted to this kinde of singing, not so much for the pleasure they take to heare the Musique, as to excite them to sing together. . . . Which things (in my opinion) were wisely inuented by their Ancestors, Not for lasciuiousnesse or delights, but for that they see the continuell toile of the people in manuring the land, with a rudenesse and brutishnesse of life, and moreouer with an austeere kinde of liuing, which proceedes from the coldnesse and roughnesse of the Ayre, to the which of necessity we growe like.[7]

The differences between Sidney and Polybius illustrate the differences between history and literature, between the limits of the historian and the vast freedom of the right poet which Sidney worked out in the *Defence.*[8]

The Arcadia of Sidney's ancient historical source does not have the characteristics of a sympathetic *locus amoenus:* it is not "had in singuler reputation . . . for the sweetnes of the Aire and other naturall benefittes," but is a harsh rural land where the air is cold and rough. In this desolate place, music is essential not as an image of the harmony and peace of the landscape but as an antidote to the base uncivility with which the inhabitants would naturally be afflicted through their environment. Thus the historical view would convey a certain objective realism whereas the literary would lead to an opposite interpretation. Generally, pastoral writers—and here Sannazaro may serve as a generic example—eschewed reality[9] and concentrated on embroidering the utopian literary tradition, and the patina of Sidney's description would suggest that he is following the custom, as in a sense he is. The peace and political stability of the land, the harmonic, well-tempered stability of the Arcadians, the endowment of the Muses and the natural beauty all combine to present a prototype of the perfectly imaged pastoral land. In the prose beginning of the First Eclogues, also, this same pastoral purity can be found, and again the echo of Polybius' classic description is there:

> The maner of the *Arcadian* Shepeardes was when they mett, together, to pass theyre tyme eyther in suche Musick, as theyre Rurall education woulde afforde them, or in exercyse of theyre body, and trynge of Masteryes: But, of all other thinges they did especially delighte in Eglogues, wherein, they woulde, some tyme contend for a pryze of well singing, sometymes lament the unhappy pursuite of theyre afflictions, some tymes ageane under hidden formes, utter suche matter, as otherwyse were not fitt for theyre Delivery. Neyther ys yt to bee marveyled, that they did so muche excell other Natyons in that quality, since from theire Chyldehood, they were brought up unto yt. . . . But the peace wherein they did so notably florish (and specially the sweete enjoyng of theyre peace to so pleasant uses) drew dyvers straungers aswell of greate, as meane bowses.

> (F, 52)

As in the first passage of the romance, this description adds literary overtones to Polybius' data, for here we are presented with a formula for potential allegory "under hidden formes." One side of Sidney's achievement, then, is the presentation of a pastoral milieu, but the telling factor in his modification lies in the ironic subsurface of realism which the Polybian echoes implant in the mind. Under the harmonic tendency of the ancient Arcadians lay the harsh reality of life lived in a very unpleasant place, and as Sidney develops his romance, he will show how, under the harmonic surface of utopia, lies a world of broken laws and moral errors.

Because of this layered structure of meaning, we can very early clear the *Old Arcadia* from any imputation that it is generically in the mainstream of pastoral. As a genre, the pastoral demands a one-dimensional spiritual landscape where allegory may be possible but where realism is not. In this respect, the genre is entirely literary or artificial, and although Sidney begins ironically more or less in this mode, his immediate introduction of Basilius and the whole narrative sequence of the first few pages belie real pastoral intention. There is, in fact, a kind of split between landscape and narrative, for the Arcadian setting prepares us for an idyllic although perhaps melancholy or even bitter tale of shepherds, whereas the narrative instantly presents us with outright, unmasked royalty—the duke Basilius, "a Prince of sufficient skill, to governe so quyett a Contrie," and his oracle.

The polarities consist in the extremes of pastoral setting as opposed to political narrative romance or dramatic sequence, the one illuminating the other, but the accomplishment is maintained at a double level. Because his work is generically multileveled, Sidney is able to scrutinize the viability of pastoral with an eye to both political and comic reality. Arcadia, as both a literary landscape and a real place where adventure is laced with moral meaning and judgments, is no longer a prototypical ideal. Instead of the containment of standard pastoral, this particular mode allows a vision of the impracticability of Arcadia; it takes the myth of a harmonic paradise common to Greek and Christian thought and places it within the norms of action typical of real, post-lapsarian men. The result is a moral exemplum illustrating the ultimate inadequacy of the romance heroes, Pyrocles and Musidorus, who lose themselves in this puzzling world.

In Sidney's work, pastoral perfection is achieved only through the progression of the Eclogues which conclude the first four books, particularly in the third set with the harmony illustrated by the marriage of Kala and Lalus.[10] The reason for this is clear: the unpretentious Arcadian shepherds combined with their greathouse visitors, Klaius, Strephon and especially Philisides, satisfy the personal characteristics of either rustic simplicity or elaborate literary masking demanded by the pastoral genre. These shepherds and quasi-shepherds are generally limited to the eclogues (although the valiant Philisides may join Musidorus in aiding the ladies and Cleophila during the Phagonian uprising at the end of Book II): they are, in other words, contained by their genre, within which they are

able to project the image of virtuous and happy marriage. In their ideal world which can be touched from without by melancholy (as, for example, in Philisides' laments or the universal sorrow at Basilius' death), there is an unblemished, unlapsed quality that separates it from the real world of action and responsibility which is presented in the main body of the *Old Arcadia.*

While the pastoral setting itself is being examined, its connotations lend a major ideological force to the romance narrative. According to literary expectations, Arcadia is the land of peace and harmony which Sidney describes in the two passages quoted above. The harmonic value of the milieu is of central importance, for this locus gives us all the possibilities of world harmony in one arch-image. The three harmonies of Boethius—*musica mundana, musica humana* and *musica instrumentalis*[11]—are co-present in the political peace and justice of the nation, the well-tempered minds of the Arcadians, and their constant practice of instrumental and vocal music. The gods of Arcadia also contribute to the total image: Apollo, the oracular god of the lute and the metaphor for divine harmony,[12] is the god of the royal Arcadians, and Pan, the rustic god with his syrinx, is the god of Dametas and the simple shepherds. Arcadia and harmony, then, are absolute equivalents, and what seems at first to be mere pastoral is translated into a divine neo-platonic idea. Harmony, which commands every level of creation, from the spheres to the nation, to the individual, to the man-made musical instrument, is the major term the Renaissance understood to represent the state of balance and divine perfection: this is the state in which man was created and which he has been re-seeking since his first sin. More significantly for the present argument, this is the starting-point for Sidney's first version of Arcadian romance.

In this respect, too, the pattern of the first few pages of the work provides a model for its construction. In the opening sequences, the prose moves from composition of place to narrative event, and in the process changes from the unity of a perfect world to the fragmentation of that unity. Basilius changes from an adequate ruler to one who abdicates his responsibility and thus threatens the just equanimity of the state, as his vice-regent Philanax immediately sees.[13] The implication is that the unified ideal, when held outside of time in a kind of stasis, is broken at the moment when sequential time and actual human action begin, when man's "infected will"[14] swings into operation. As the story progresses, this pattern is everywhere apparent. The Arcadian state descends from its peace to disharmony and civil war during the Phagonian uprising in Book II, the landscape itself is disrupted with the entrance of the marauding lion and bear at the end of Book I, and the harmonic virtue and self-containment of the leading active characters—Basilius, Gynecia, Pyrocles and Musidorus—is broken by sexual incontinence which reaches its climax at the end of Book III. As this design develops, Sidney even introduces Urania, Muse of Astronomy,[15] the chief of the Muses whose voice subsumes that of all her sisters, thinly disguised as a beautiful shepherdess who had once elevated the minds of Klaius and Strephon who loved her, but who has fled the land, just as all other harmonic perfections leave their fragmented, strife-torn seats.

Most of the ambient *energia* of the *Old Arcadia* is concentrated on this process of fragmentation, and consequently the fall from perfection to destruction or, to be more exact metaphorically, from harmony to disharmony, receives its impetus from an exploitation of the connotations of the work's pastoral basis.

II

As in the case of all ideal landscapes, Sidney's projection of Arcadia has its primitive fascination and can enrapture even active, worldly heroes like Pyrocles and Musidorus. After Pyrocles has fallen in love early in Book I with a picture of Basilius' daughter Philoclea which he has seen in Kerxenes' gallery in Mantinea, the Arcadian capital, he rationalizes his lapse from the pursuit of active and virtuous adventures to the unenchanted Musidorus. His is the vocabulary of dangerous intoxication imaged by "the Cupp of poyson" metaphor which will begin Book II and reach its climax at the moment of Basilius' collapse at the mouth of the cave, Gynecia's golden cup in his hands.

> Doo yow not see how every thinge Conspires together to make this place a heavenly Dwelling? Doo yow not see the grasse, howe in Coloure they excell the Emeraudes every one stryving to passe his fellowe, and yet they are all kept in an equall heighte? And see yow not the rest of all these beutyfull flowers, eche of whiche woulde requyer a mans witt to knowe, and his lyfe to express? Doo not these stately trees seeme to meynteyne theyre florisshing olde age with the onely happynes of theyre seate beeyng clothed with a Continuall springe, bycause no beauty here shoulde ever fade? Dothe not the Ayer breath health whiche the Byrdes, . . . do dayly solempnize with the sweet consent of theyre voyces? Ys not every Eccho here a perfect Musick? and these fresh and delightfull brookes, how slowly they slyde away, as, lothe to leave the Company of so many thinges united in perfection, and with how sweete a Murmer they lament theyre forc[ed] departure: Certeynly, certeynly Cossyn yt must needes bee, that some Goddess this Dezert belonges unto, . . .
>
> (F, 12-13)[16]

But Musidorus is, after all, Duke of Thessalia, where the vale of Tempe with its traditional associations as the *locus amoenus*[17] spreads its enchantment, and his rather stunned answer indicates the interchangeability of Arcadia and Tempe: "I merveyle at the excessive prayses yow give to this Dezart, . . . even *Tempe* in my *Thessalia,* where yow and I to my great happynes were brought up together ys nothing inferior unto yt." (F, 14) Although as classical loci their associations are identical, this particular Arcadia is altered and intensified by the reality of human personality which the princes first apprehend in idealized form. The picture of Philoclea has a transforming and elevating power over her land as she is read as a neo-platonic embodiment of beauty for Pyrocles. Musidorus, temporarily

free, will encounter his moment of enrapturement later, when he is caught by the virtue of Pamela who stubbornly but wisely protests the political and moral folly of her father. In the Arcadian retreat, she silently wears the dual pastoral-theological impresa of "a perfect white Lambe tyed at a stake, with a greate number of Chaynes, as yt yf had been feared leste the silly Creature shoulde do some greate harme," (F, 33) and her charm for the more ruminative Musidorus is largely dependent on her neo-platonic imaging of virtue rather than on the simpler sensuous beauty which characterizes her sister Philoclea. Musidorus too, through his elevated love for her, quickly submits to the specific power of this Arcadia: "*Arcadia, Arcadia* was the place prepared to bee stage of his endles overthrowe. *Arcadia* was, (alas well might I say yt ys) the Charmed Circle where all his spirites shoulde for ever bee enchaunted." (F, 100) The morally hardy prince is enveloped by the peculiar metaphysics of the place, and his intoxication, like Pyrocles', is complete.

Here also, in the interior of the romance and in the middle of the Arcadian land, Sidney uses a system of polarities to illuminate the choices and actions of the princes. The princesses represent an ideal good to their petrarchan lovers, an ideal which could reach its expected zenith of achievement by a pair of virtuous marriages. The princes go into disguises, Pyrocles as an Amazon and Musidorus as a shepherd, in order to pursue this end, but there is an equally strong negative force operating against them—the force represented by Basilius' irresponsibility, his lechery, and his absurd, chaotic tomfoolery. Above all, the heroes are invented to live lofty lives—lofty in active achievement (see their pre-Arcadian experiences as recounted by Histor in the Eclogues), lofty in petrarchan love activity (see their elegant participation in the Eclogues), and lofty in their pursuit of neo-platonic philosophy.[18] They are, in short, heroes of an absolutely literary nature, answering the highest demands of the epic romances, the sonnet sequences, and the Florentine neo-platonic dialogues. They enter an absolutely literary landscape, the pastoral, which in its conventional usage can satisfy all the elaborate artifice of these high Renaissance modes. But here, in keeping with the design of the *Old Arcadia,* their literary perfection is fragmented by the onslaught of psychological realism, illustrated in the character of Basilius and expanded into low comic action through the personality of the shepherd Dametas. This landscape, as Sidney's method illustrated in the beginning of the romance and as it continues to affirm, is one in which literary idealism co-exists with unadorned, quasi-historical realism; the result of this ironic co-existence is explosive, magnificent comedy interlaced with a heavy didacticism which demands that we recognize the seriousness of the romance as well as its gamesomeness.

Instead of achieving the heroic stature they are made for and had once illustrated in their pre-Arcadian lives, the princes are now continually degraded, they stoop to lust and, at the height of their performance in Book V, can only quarrel before Evarchus with frustration and hysterical magnanimity about which of the two more deserves to die in order to save his friend. For heroes so purely framed at their inception, this is indeed a tawdry list of accomplishments. Arcadia in its enchantment has played an unforeseeable trick of inversion, a trick which extends inward in the work itself to the whole, harmonic constitution of character in the young princes and outward toward the reader whose expectations of Arcadian romances are more conventional and stereotyped, and built on less ambivalent definitions and nuances. Just as it was Basilius' fatal error in the narrative to assume his right to know the riddles of the future in spite of a stern reminder that "there ys no thinge so certeyne as oure Continuall uncerteinty" (F, 2), so it would be the reader's preconceived error to suppose that because a tale is set in Arcadia, it would automatically follow the standard, foreseeable progress of all pastoral romances. This seems to me to be the seat of the misreadings and underestimation which have been the lot of the *Old Arcadia* whenever critical attention has been turned to it, and it is certainly the most valid reason for refusing to pull out the scholarly machinery of analogue, operated most recently by Walter Davis' schematizing in his book on the 1593 *New Arcadia*.[19]

III

Because the meaning of Arcadia is expanded by the duality which realism allows it, the reading of the *Old Arcadia* involves a constant process of discovery. The broad, inclusive system of symbolism which the word Arcadia calls to it and which Sidney so subtly exploits gives us the real guide to the mythic resonances of this new place invented by Sidney from the ashes of the conventional pastoral world.

I have already touched on the evoking of images of harmony in the opening of both the main narrative and the Eclogues. According to Sidney's description of Arcadia as well as Polybius' account of that ancient geographical location, harmony is the starting point for any consideration of the land. This condition extends also to the standard literary tradition where singing shepherds, Apollo with his lute, and Pan with his syrinx dominate the pastoral. The real difference between the convention and the present romance is the difference between the static absoluteness of the literary ideal (the changes most poets make are in detail and tone, not in basic interpretation[20]), and the shifting, confusing narrative stream which progressively inverts whatever might seem at first to be firm, conventional or clearly delineated.

At the static moment of the opening of the romance, Arcadia is the perfect pastoral place—harmonic, peaceful, temperate, governed by a sufficiently competent duke. Immediately, however, we are spun from that moment directly into the narrative sequence, the story of Basilius' faulty oracle-seeking and his retirement from his responsibility and the *vita activa,* his retreat to the desert lodges, and his symbolic association with the Dametas family, true shepherds who are treated with a degraded comic scorn. In-

stantly the literary ideal is snapped, for Dametas is not a graceful shepherd or a product of the creative imagination, but a real buffoon. In a world where real issues are not decked by the high mimetic style, Basilius' retreat is seen in its real aspect as a descent from his high romance position to an allegorical identification with Dametas, and all the escapist pastoral glory of his choice of a country landscape is dissolved in this unyielding picture of the realistic results of his folly.

Similarly the two princes are allowed a static literary moment in Kerxenes' garden in Mantinea (it is significant for this theory of stasis that in the *New Arcadia* Kerxenes' name is changed to Kalender), a moment that outlines the almost mystical nature of the Arcadian landscape as a sympathetic image for Philoclea. As in the case of Basilius, this stasis is banished by action and the necessities of the narrative, for the two princes move into disguises which occasion their degradation, as Pyrocles is lowered from man to woman, Musidorus from prince to shepherd. As soon as they have acquiesced to circumstantial demands, they are caught by the inexorable flow of events that has its origin in Basilius' first action of consulting the oracle, and the downward moral direction of the subsequent narrative line pulls them into positions of increasing helplessness. From their original static base of epic heroism and neo-platonic idealism, they are degraded through the dynamic realism of Arcadia to plotting, frustrated young princes whose lives are demanded by a just judge.

The work moves instantaneously from literary stasis to the dynamic flux of realistic examination, from the timeless world of pastoral to the world of hopelessly flawed character and action. The movement has a partial illustration in the fall in Basilius' personal status and in the princes' progressively weakening heroic image, but its ultimate symbolic measure is in the complex, extensive use of images of disharmony as contrasted to the harmony of that first instant in Arcadia and in the lives of the young heroes of the romance. The anagogical overtones are almost oppressively obvious: the fall of all men through one man's (the paternal Basilius') sin, and the fall from a static, timeless, ideal world to a sequential, temporal one where action is necessary but fruitless, where the high intentions of the "erected wit" are stopped by the "infected will," and where neo-platonic virtue stoops to rather low-grade lust. The archetypal resurrection of Basilius can, unfortunately, add much sterility to this kind of reading, but that issue is better skimmed over and the instrumental imagery actually employed given a just examination.

So overwhelming is the use of metaphors of disharmony as a literary vehicle in this partially anti-pastoral work that no major advancement in the plot or meaning is made without calling it into play. As Pyrocles-Cleophila attempts to insinuate himself into the royal Arcadian group, for example, he is discovered by the base Dametas as he sits singing his song of self-separation, "Transformde in shewe, but more transformde in mynde." The shepherd's reaction is splendidly comic and symbolic of the larger metaphoric structure of the romance:

> . . . yt awakened the Shepearde *Dametas,* who at that tyme had layde his sleepy back uppon a sunnye banck, not farr thence, gaping as farr, as his Jawes woulde suffer him. But beeyng trubled oute of his sleepe (the best thinge his lyfe coulde bringe forthe) his dull sences coulde not convey the pleasure of the excellent Musick to his rude mynde, but that hee fell into a notable rage: In so muche, that, taking a hedging bill lay by him, hee guyded him self by the voyce, till hee came to the place, where hee sawe *Cleophila* sitting and wringing her handes, and with some fewe wordes to her self breathing oute to her self part of the vehemency of that passion which shee had not fully declared in her songe. But, no more were his eyes taken with her beauty then his eares with her musick, but beginning to sweare by the pantaple of *Pallas, Venus* wastecoate & suche other Oathes as his rusticall bravery coulde imagyn, leaning his handes uppon his bill and his Chinne uppon his handes, hee fell to mutter such Cursinges and Raylinges ageanst her, as a man mighte well see hee had passed through the discipline of an Alehowse.

> (F, 26)

Leo Spitzer has noted the qualities of sin and fragmentation that belong to the disharmonious man, the man who, like Shylock, has no music in him and cannot understand the organizing celestial harmony of the universe.[21] Dametas, in his inability to recognize either musical harmony or human beauty, is this man and symbolizes the true nature of Sidney's Arcadia. Contrasted to him, Basilius reacts to the harmony of Cleophila's beauty culpably but much differently: his is a sexual perversion of her harmonic potentiality:

> But, *Basilius,* who began to feele the sparckles of those flames, which shortly after burned all other thoughtes oute of his harte, felt suche a musick, as hee thoughte, in her voyce, and such an eye pleasing in her face, that hee thoughte his retyring into this solitary place was well employed, yf yt had bene onely to have mett with such a guest.

> (F, 32)

Not only in the romance's large framework, but also in such reader-conditioning particulars, disharmony is essential in forming the sense of wholeness which has too often led the modern mind to underestimate the excellent simplicity of the work.

In accordance with the *Old Arcadia*'s five-act structure, there are four climactic moments, one at the end of each of the first four books, and before the resolving harmonies of a happy ending. Each one is a repetition, in its own thematic terms, of the primary fall from harmony to disharmony so strikingly shown in the dualities of the opening pages. Through the bold use of this technique of constant thematic repetition, Sidney ensures that we read correctly, and the morality of realistic vision is displayed through the medium of art.

Because Book I must of necessity concentrate so heavily on the establishment of landscape as literary idea, its cli-

mactic disharmonious image must have to do with an act of disruption of this landscape. Early in the narrative, however, the intended concept of Arcadia has been clarified, so here Sidney narrows his scope from the archetypal pastoral country to a small pleasaunce or arbor which is both a *locus amoenus* and an Arcadian *hortus conclusus.* In this pleasaunce the shepherds join with their aristocratic betters for the first pastoral games:

> It was in deede a place of great delighte, for throughe the middest of yt there ranne a sweete brooke, whiche did bothe holde the eye open with her beutyfull streames, and close the eye with the sweete purling noyse yt made upon the pible stones yt rann over. The Meadow yt self yeelding so liberally all sortes of flowers, that yt seemed to norish a Contention betuixt the Coloure and the smell, whether in his kynde were the more delightfull: Rounde aboute the Meadowe (as yf yt had beene to enclose a Theater) grewe all suche sorte of Trees, as eyther excellency of fruite, statelynes of grouthe, continuall greenes, or Poeticall fancyes have made at any tyme famous. In moste parte of which Trees, there had bene framed by Arte, suche plesant Arboures, that yt became a gallery a lofte from one Tree to the other, allmoste rounde aboute, whiche beelowe yeelded a perfect shadowe, in those whott Contryes counted a great pleasure.

> (F, 42)

Eventually this will become the place where the eclogues and games of the shepherds take place, but before this literary pastoral activity, the disruption of its harmonic appearance must be put into terms of both action and symbol.

Every one has gathered to this place except Basilius, "when, sodenly, there came oute of the wood, a monsterus Lyon, with a shee Beare, of litle less fercenes, whiche having been hunted in forrestes farr of had by chaunce come to this place, where suche Beastes had never before bene seene." The fact that the animals (obviously to be glossed as images of human bestiality) are foreign to the landscape indicates that the symbology of the circumstance is a vehicle for the larger metaphor of the work. They plunge into a pleasaunce arranged for the practice of vocal and instrumental harmony, and their immediate prey is the Basilian daughters, Philoclea and Pamela, neoplatonic Beauty and Virtue, who can still be saved by Pyrocles and Musidorus, disguised and degraded though they already are. Throughout the romance, the two sisters maintain their symbolically functional connotations and are ultimately analogous to the Urania of the Fourth Eclogues. The destruction of Beauty and Virtue would embody the absolute failure of the neo-platonic world in which the princes would choose to live, and the whole incident, as the shepherds flee their harmonic, formerly secure garden, prefigures the ideology present in the flight of Urania[22] as well as the very real danger of the future bestiality of Pyrocles and Musidorus, which is followed by the imprisonment of the symbolic sisters. Finally, through the lion and bear episode, the reader can witness the failure of the pleasaunce, the disruption of harmony, and the present bestial hearts of Gynecia and Basilius.

Book II removes the theme of disharmony from landscape to nation, from literary idyll to the harmonic idea of just government. The Phagonian uprising has long been recognized as a bit of political Elizabethiana,[23] but it is equally necessary to regard its adherence to the larger thematic pattern of the romance. In the moral harmony which ought to exist in the state and microcosmically in its ruler, justice is the major of the four necessary virtues (Justice, prudence, fortitude, temperance)[24]—the justice which maintains the contentment of the people. By withdrawing himself and his justice, Basilius had paved the way for ensuing disharmony. The Phagonians had begun lawfully enough with a celebration of Basilius' birthday, but as the wine progressively upset their rationality, they were overcome with a passionate, enraged sense of Basilius' failure toward them. As the harmony of reasonable control in them is drowned, they apprehend more clearly and more indignantly where Basilius has erred, with the result that civil war erupts and Basilius himself, who ought to be the just, harmony-producing head of state, is almost killed.

As the confused tumult of their drunken attack is heard in the enclosed area of the pastoral lodges, vocal and instrumental music is again interrupted. Philisides and Dorus are indulging themselves in a witty competitive eclogue of the traditionally sorrowful-joyous, lover-shepherd type,[25] when they are interrupted and called to do battle to defend the princesses and Basilius. The interruption of their music which, as they sing, almost lulls the reader back to the pastoral norms which the romance has rejected, combined with the civil contention which echoes the failure of the great moral harmony of justice, completes our sense of how far this fictional Arcadia is distanced from a peaceful pastoral place.

Book III is the book of the cave, that reverberating symbol so admirably documented in its Ovidian connotations by Walter Davis.[26] The *Old Arcadia* has moved from exteriors of landscape and nation to the interiors intrinsic to them. The subject matter of the third book deals with libidinous sex in its most indecent (and hence, comic) form—Gynecia's embarrassing, clutching demands that her appetite for Pyrocles be satisfied, and Basilius' eighty-year-old horniness. But much more significant than either of these is the process of fall in the initially harmonic mind of Pyrocles. As Davis suggested in his article, "Actaeon in Arcadia," Pyrocles is forced to recognize the cave as a dark symbol of his own mind, and to understand that the sexual sufferings of Gynecia perfectly and horrifyingly reflect his own:

> O *Venus,* sayde *Cleophila,* who ys this, so well acquaynted with mee, that can make so lyvely a Purtraiture of my myseryes? yt ys surely, the Spirite appoynted to have Care of mee, which dothe now in this darcke place beare parte with the Complayntes of his unhappy Charge: For yf yt bee so, that the Heavens have at all times mesure of theyre wrathfull harmes, surely so many have come to my blissles lott, that the rest of the worlde have too smalle a proportion, to make so waylefull a Lamentatyon. But, (saide shee), what soever thow bee, I will seeks the oute, for thy

> Musick well assures mee wee are at least hande fellowe Prentyzes to one ungracyous Master . . .

> (F, 171)

He can only gasp at the appalling demands and propositions Gynecia then inflicts on him, and try to free himself, to escape through his witty plan of tricking the Arcadian duke and duchess into sleeping with each other in the cave, while he is left at liberty to flee to the chaste Philoclea's arms. His actions indicate that he believes he can also free himself from his just enunciated identification with both Gynecia's lust and the archimagistic connotations of the cave: the scene of his primary recognition is, in other words, not accepted as a place of ultimate self-revelation.

As he pauses at Philoclea's chamber door, he automatically takes up the harmonic metaphor as the necessary way of regarding this neo-platonic heroine. His pure, idealized response to her voice "whiche hee thought yf the Philosophers sayde true of the heavenly sphaered harmony, was by her not onely represented but farr surmounted" (F, 218) is, within the same sentence, contradicted by the incipient sexual degradation of his concept of her beauty. His eyes are "overfilled," his sensuous desire replaces the lofty, neo-platonic, harmonic tone with which he had begun. Her smock is loose and disarranged, and it is quite clear that he is watching her "lefte thighe downe to the foote" with the help of a "Riche Lampe" much more than he is contemplating the divine harmony of her voice. Indeed, he doesn't even notice at first that her voice is complaining against him for his faithlessness, and Sidney is very direct in his description of the real sexual intention which preoccupies him:

> That quyte forgetting hym self, and thincking therein all redy hee was in the best degree of felicity, I thincke hee woulde have lost much of his tyme and with too muche love omitted great fruite of his Love, had not *Philocleas* pityfull accusing of hym, forced hym to bringe his spirites ageane to a newe Byas.

> (F, 218)

As he argues with her and soothes her, he also climbs into her bed, and feasts his eyes on her naked body. The tenor of his sensual vision is handled in high style by Sidney who reverts to a lengthy song imputed to the shepherd Philisides (Sidney himself?), "What Toungue can her perfections tell?" (F, 223-226) The song is very long indeed, one stanza concentrated in Petrarchan style on the adoration of every part of her face and body—and there are many parts. Pyrocles, his mind preoccupied with other things, does not himself take up the task of poetic rhetoric and sing the verses himself: the ironic wit of Sidney's point of view can only be conveyed by his own words:

> But doo not thincke (Fayre Ladyes) his thoughtes had suche Leysure as to ronne over so longe a Ditty: The onely generall fancy of yt came into his mynde fixed uppon the sence of the sweet Subject. Where using the benefitt of the Tyme, and fortifying hym self, with the

Confessing her late faulte, (to make her nowe the sooner yeelde to penance) turning the passed greeffes and unkyndenes, to the excess of all kynde Joyes (as passyon ys apte to slyde into all Contrary) beginning nowe to envy *Argus* thowsand eyes *Brierius* hundred handes, feighting ageanst a Weyke resistance which did stryve to bee overcome; Hee gives mee occasyon to leave hym in so happy a plight . . .

(F, 226-227)

Sidney's wit lends kindness to Pyrocles' fall into sensuality and consummation, but the fall in itself is significant in its distance from the neo-platonic purity of spirit with which he had entered this landscape. His friend, Musidorus, will not follow him into incontinence until he tries to rape the sleeping Pamela in Book IV, but the point of the cave sequences and their result are the fall from ideological harmony to sexual disharmony in the mind of the young heroes.

Probably the greatest disharmonic event in the *Old Arcadia* is the quasi-death of Basilius in Book IV, and all of its ensuing ramifications. Gynecia is forced to see the real horror of her lust and jealousy, the princes must prepare themselves for the subjection to trial and possible death, the state grows increasingly chaotic and disorderly in spite of Philanax's major attempts to maintain national equilibrium. In this book the disharmonic elements of all of the other books are gathered together, and even the lowly shepherds, the creatures of the literary pastoral, are impelled into the major text (see Agelastus' dirge, "Synce wayling ys a budd of Causefull Sorrowe," F, 265-6) and reflect in their songs in the Fourth Ecologues the final disharmony of the world of Arcadia.[27]

To this shambles of a country comes Evarchus, who will restore justice and moral equilibrium by his judgments against all the major players in this peculiar drama. It is at this point that the work could easily lose its realism and non-idealistic awareness, but the justice of Evarchus would have to be overwhelmed with mercy past either expectation or endurance, and the assumption would have to be that Arcadia is returned to the harmonic vision of peace and stasis which the opening paragraph had indicated. Since Sidney's task seems to have involved a realistic examination of the viability of a harmonic, pastoral idyll for men of action, such a conclusion is out of the question. Instead of that, we do in fact have a powerful statement of justice, but it is destructive of all of the people who have played the Arcadian game of either escape or sexual liberty. The only possibility of maintaining realism is the one Sidney employs. The judgments of Evarchus are reversed magically, by the magic potion of Gynecia: Basilius comes to consciousness once again, and the world goes on—not in the sense of the literary stasis of a simple, happy ending, but through the indication of sequence and infinite continuation through time and action, from one generation to another, that the last paragraph of the work indicates:

But the solempnityes of the Marriages with the *Arcadian* pastoralles, full of many *Comicall* adventures hap-

pening to those Rurall Lovers, the straunge story of the fayre Queene *Artaxia* of *Persia* and *Erona* of *Lydia,* with the Prince *Plangus* wonderfull Chaunces whome the later had sent to *Pyrocles,* and the extreme affection *Amasis* kinge of *Egipt* bare unto the former: The Sheperdish Loves of *Menalcas* with *Kalodulus* Daughter, and the pore hopes of *Philisides* in the pursuite of his affections, the strange Countenance of *Claius* and *Strephons* desyre, Lastly the Sonne of *Pyrocles*[28] and *Melidura* the fayre Daughter of *Pamela* by *Musidorus:* who even at theyre byrthe entred into admirable Fortunes may awake some other Spirite to exercyse his Penn in that, wherewith myne ys allredy dulled.

(F, 389)

Part of this is doubtless the creative literary hysteria that makes a novelist so reluctant to leave the characters he has spawned, and much of it is an indication that Sidney will write more or again, but it in no way hinders—it helps rather—the total reading of the first created Arcadian vision which would destroy the false delicacy of literary modes and substitute the kind of viability real action calls for in the time-oriented world of external responsibility that Sidney must have longed for as he rusticated at Wilton.

Notes

1. *Old Arcadia,* p. 1. All quotations from the text, unless otherwise indicated, are from Volume IV of the 1962 reprint of *The Prose Works of Sir Philip Sidney,* ed. Albert Feuillerat, 4 vols. (Cambridge, first printed 1912). Although there is evidently a new edition in progress under the editorship of Mrs. Jean Robertson Bromley, we can, at present, only sigh the lack of a more readable text. In the other extant manuscripts I have looked at, both spelling and punctuation are infinitely better and lend much to the coherence of the narrative which, in its printed state, often looks appallingly illiterate. Generally I must quote Feuillerat, who claimed that he used the Clifford ms. because it was well preserved and the secretarial hand careful and legible. Perhaps so, but secretarial neatness is less important than literary accuracy. When things looked particularly ludicrous, I corrected punctuation according to the sense, but this is all.

2. The term is from the vocabulary set up by Thomas Greene, *The Descent From Heaven* (New Haven, 1963).

3. The *Old Arcadia*'s only recent critic, Richard A. Lanham, *The Old Arcadia* (New Haven, 1965), views the work as a comic drama.

4. Tradition has claimed Sannazaro's *Arcadia* and Montemayor's *Diana* as models for the *Old Arcadia.* John F. Danby in his essay in *Poets on Fortune's Hill* (London, 1952), suggests the late Shakespearian romances as kindred plays.

5. A. C. Hamilton, "Spenser's Pastoral," *ELH,* XXXIII (1966), p. 518.

6. Lanham, *The Old Arcadia.* Walter R. Davis, *A Map of Arcadia* (New Haven, 1965).

7. *The History of Polybivs the Megalopolitan* (London, 1634), Book IV, pp. 185-6.

8. In Feuillerat, Vol. III, p. 8, Sidney says: "so as he goeth hand in hand with nature, not enclosed within the narrow warrant of her gifts, but freely raunging within the Zodiack of his owne wit." On page 10 he describes the power of the right poet thus: "For these third be they which most properly do imitate to teach & delight: and to imitate, borrow nothing of what is, hath bin, or shall be, but range onely reined with learned discretion, into the divine consideration of what may be and should be."

9. The entire landscape in Sannazaro lends the needed atmosphere and mood, but has no place. See the excellent discussion of this literary habit *passim* in David Kalstone, *Sidney's Poetry: Contexts and Interpretations* (Cambridge, Mass., 1965).

10. For an explanatory discussion of this, see my monograph, "The 'Fore Conceit' of Sidney's Eclogues," *Literary Monographs,* I (1967), pp. 33-38.

11. The three musics are explained at length in the *De Musica* of Boethius. See Anitii Manlii Severini Boethi . . . *Opera* (Basiliae, 1546), Lib. I, Cap. II of *De Musica,* p. 1065. Both Leo Spitzer, *Classical and Christian Ideas of World Harmony* (Baltimore, 1963) and John Hollander, *The Untuning of the Sky* (Princeton, 1961), briefly cite Boethius as the expositor of the three harmonies.

12. Spitzer, p. 8.

13. See Philanax's response to Basilius' announcement (F, 4-6), especially p. 4: "These thirty yeares past have yow so governed this Realme, that, neither youre Subjectes have wanted Justice in yow, nor yow obedience in them, and youre Neighboures have founde yow so hurtlesly stronge, that they thought yt better to rest in youre frendship then make nowe tryall of youre enmity: Yf this then have proceeded oute of the good Constitution of your State, and oute of a wyse providence generally to prevent all those thinges, which mighte encomber your happynes, why shoulde yow now seeke newe Courses, since youre owne example comfortes yow to continew on?"

14. This term and its opposite, the "erected wit" are taken from the *Defence* (F, III, p. 9).

15. In the Fourth Eclogues, pp. 307 ff. See also my monograph, pp. 40-47.

16. Notice the imagery of perfection and music intrinsic to Pyrocles' verbalization. The emerald-like grass grows to an even height, the birds sing in "sweete consent," the echo is "a perfect Musick," no beauty fades. What Pyrocles sees is a harmonious world of pastoral stasis, and he sees it because he has first seen a picture of Philoclea who has aroused his neo-platonic instinct for harmonic perfection. Spitzer, p. 61, points out that the tradition is petrarchan: "With Petrarch it is the divine lady who has become the shrine of supernatural harmony; this theory (ancient, troubadour, etc.) required the eyes to be the seat of love. . . ."

17. Ernst Robert Curtius, *European Literature and the Latin Middle Ages,* trans. Willard R. Trask, Bollingen Series XXXVI (New York, 1952), p. 198.

18. Lanham, pp. 245-256, gives a lengthy reproduction of the argumentative speeches of the two princes and briefly mentions their neo-platonic bias. One wonders if one needs to be told, or to have the speeches quoted at such breath-taking, page-filling length.

19. Davis, *A Map of Arcadia.* This is not meant to be as bitchy a statement as it sounds. Davis is talking about the landscape of the *New Arcadia,* and there Arcadia is quite a different place.

20. The stability of tone is generally accepted by theorizers of the pastoral genre, from Snell's essay on Virgil to Davis' book on the *New Arcadia.* See the following for affirmation: W. W. Greg, *Pastoral Poetry and Pastoral Drama* (London, 1906), passim; Bruno Snell, *The Discovery of the Mind,* trans. T. G. Rosenmeyer (Oxford, 1948), pp. 281-310; Renato Poggioli, "The Oaten Flute," *HLB,* XXX (1957), 147-184.

21. Spitzer, pp. 65-66 and 99-102.

22. See footnote 15, above. Also, Lily Bess Campbell, "The Christian Muse," *HLB,* VIII (1935), 29-70 and John M. Steadman, "'Meaning' and 'Name': Some Renaissance Interpretations of Urania," *Neuphilologische Mitteilungen,* LXIV (1963), 209-232.

23. Edwin A. Greenlaw, "Sidney's *Arcadia* as an Example of Elizabethan Allegory," in *Anniversary Papers* by Colleagues and Pupils of George Lyman Kittredge (Boston, 1913), 327-338, and W. D. Briggs, "Political Ideas in Sidney's *Arcadia,*" *SP,* XXVIII (1931), 137-161.

24. Spitzer, pp. 64-66. See also *Les Six Livres de la Republique* de I. Bodin Angeuin (Paris, second edition, 1577), Book VI, Chapt. VI, p. 796.

25. See Feuillerat, pp. 118-119. These are songs which, by virtue of their witty inverting of each other, belong properly in the purer pastoral of the Eclogues.

26. Walter R. Davis, "Actaeon in Arcadia," *SEL,* II (1962), 95-110.

27. See again my monograph, pp. 38-40.

28. The Phillips manuscript in the British Museum changes the wording here, thus enlarging the plan for the future generation. It reads: "Lastly, the son of Pyrocles, named Pirophilus, and Melidura . . ."

James Sambrook (essay date 1983)

SOURCE: "Some Spenserians," in *English Pastoral Poetry,* Twayne Publishers, 1983, pp. 48-58.

[*In the following excerpt, Sambrook surveys the eclogues of courtly writers such as Michael Drayton, Richard Barnfield, George Wither, and William Browne, who took Edmund Spenser as their model, and contends that the work of these later poets lacks the symbolic richness and formal complexity of that of their master.*]

Allegory became a less potent lure as Elizabethan and Jacobean poets moved further away from Italian models. A late Jacobean critic, Michael Drayton, in the address to the reader of his *Pastorals* (1619), admits allegory as a possibility rather than a necessity: "the most High, and most Noble Matters of the World may bee shaddowed in them, and for certaine sometimes are." However, Drayton agrees with his predecessors that among English pastoral poets Spenser stands first: "Master Edmund Spenser had done enough for the immortality of his Name, had he only given us his Shepheards Kalender, a Master-piece if any."[1]

The Shepheardes Calender became the principal model for Elizabethan and Jacobean pastoral eclogue, although English translations from both Theocritus and Virgil appeared in the decade following its publication. *Sixe Idillia, that is, six small, or petty, poems, or aeglogues,* printed at Oxford in 1588 contained translations by an anonymous hand of idylls 8, 11, 16, 18, 20, and 31 attributed to Theocritus. The first four of these were discussed in chapter 1. Idyll 20, wrongly numbered 21 in the 1588 volume, is a pseudo-Theocritean piece in which an oxherd complains about Eunica, a girl in the town, who has rejected his love; he calls his fellow herdsmen to witness that he is handsome and accomplished, and regrets that Eunica is apparently unaware that even goddddesses have loved country lads. Idyll 31 is a whimsical fable, according to which Aphrodite summons the boar which killed her beloved Adonis, and the creature explains that he had intended only to kiss the youth's naked thigh and had gored him by mistake. On this, Aphrodite forgives the boar and makes it one of her followers. The "Argument" prefixed by the translator in the 1588 edition displays that common Elizabethan tendency to impose allegorical interpretations upon classical myth, for it concludes "The Poet's drift is to shew the power of Love, not only in men, but also in brute beasts: although in the last two verses, by the burning of the Boar's amorous teeth, he intimateth that extravagant and unorderly passions are to be restrained by reason."[2]

In 1591 appeared *The Shepherds Starre,* a much amplified "paraphrase upon the third of the Canticles of Theocritus, Dialogue wise" by Thomas Bradshaw; and in 1647 and 1651 translations by Thomas Stanley of idylls 20 and 31, and pieces by Bion and Moschus were published. Clearly, early translators went to the lightest and "prettiest" parts of Theocritus. The publication of a full translation had to wait until Thomas Creech's *Idylliums* (1684).

In the case of Virgil, William Webbe Englished the first and second eclogues in his *Discourse on English Poetry* (1596), and A. F. (possibly Abraham Fraunce) published in 1589 his translation of *The Bucoliks of P. Virgilius Maro . . . with his Georgiks.* Typical of his age, A. F. stressed the allegorical character of Virgil's eclogues: in the dedication he went so far as to claim that the "principall occasion of writing these Pastoralls was the majestie of *Julius Caesar* and *Augustus his sonne.*"

All types of formal elogue represented in *The Shepheardes Calender* are found in the work of Spenser's Elizabethan and Jacobean successors, but love-complaint is the commonest. Virgil's pederastic second eclogue provided a model for the two opening poems of Richard Barnfield's *The Affectionate Shepherd* (1594): "The Tears of an Affectionate Shepheard sicke for Love or The Complaint of Daphnis for the Love of Ganimede," and "The Second Dayes Lamentation of The Affectionate Shepheard." Daphnis's invitation to love is accompanied by an offer of gifts, which include "Straw-berries or Bil-berries . . . Bath'd in a melting Sugar-Candie streame," "A golden Racket, and a Tennis-Ball," "a green Hat and a Feather," a lamb, a goat, a nightingale, green-cheese, nutmeg, ginger, and much else besides. All this goes back, through Virgil, to the less extravagantly miscellaneous catalog of gifts in the eleventh idyll of Theocritus. Theocritus's Polyphemus describes Galatea as "Whiter to look upon than curds, more delicate than a lamb, / Than a young calf more skittish, plumper than ripening grape," (20-21), and leaves it at that; Virgil does not elaborate on the beauty of Alexis which is simply announced in the first word of the eclogue, "formosum"; but Barnfield's Daphnis offers elaborate and luscious descriptions of the beautiful, unloving Ganimede:

> a sweet-fac'd Boy,
> (Whose amber locks trust up in golden tramels
> Dangle adowne his lovely cheekes with joy,
> When pearle and flowers his faire haire enamels). . . .
> His Ivory-white and Alabaster skin
> Is stained throughout with rare Vermillion red,
> Whose twinckling starrie lights do never blin
> To shine on lovely *Venus* (Beauties bed:)
>   But as the Lillie and the blushing Rose,
>   So white and red on him in order growes.[3]
>
>   (7-10, 13-18)

Barnfield's enameled and sugary elaboration of the catalog of gifts, and, more particularly, of the beauties of the reluctant boy clearly show the influence of recent erotic Ovidian mythological narrative poems by Lodge, Marlowe, and Shakespeare.

The third poem in Barnfield's volume, "The Shepherds Content, or The happines of a harmless life," conventionally compares the shepherd's life with the monarch's, courtier's, soldier's, scholar's, merchant's, and husbandman's. Though Barnfield's conception of the shepherd's life is Arcadian, he introduces frolics and well-known songs and dances of the English shepherd who,

> when Night comes drawes homeward to his Coate,
> Singing a Jigge or merry Roundelay;

(For who sings commonly so merry a Noate,
As he that cannot chop or change a groate)
　　And in the winter Nights (his chiefe desire)
　　He turns a Crabbe or Cracknell in the fire.

He leads his Wench a Country Horn-pipe Round,
About a May-pole on a Holy-day;
　　Kissing his lovely Lasse (with Garlands Crownd)
　　With whopping heigh-ho singing Care away.

(188-97)

Typical of Barnfield's eclecticism, this poem finds room for a love lament, an elegy on Sidney, and compliments to Spenser, Drayton, and Watson (or his translator Fraunce), under their pastoral names of Colin, Rowland, and Amintas.

Elizabethan pastoral of courtly compliment readily took up the Spenser-Sidney image of Elizabeth as queen of shepherds and lady of May. A funeral eclogue on Walsingham, *Meliboeus* (1590), translated by Thomas Watson from his own Latin, is by no means the only poem in which she is "Diana matchlesse Queene of Arcadie." In George Peele's thoroughly Spenserian *An Eglogue Gratulatorie* (1589), to "the right honourable and renowned Shepherd of Albions Arcadia," Robert earl of Essex, she is the employer of two swains, Sidney and Essex, who "served, and watch'd, and waited late, / To keep the grim wolf from Eliza's gate." Here the overtones of religious pastoral can be heard, for the grim wolf is not merely Spain but also Roman Catholicism, which threatens the innocent and peaceable flock of a queen who is supreme head of a national church. In 1603 Henry Chettle used eclogues and prose passages after the fashion of Sannazaro to weave a capacious *Englandes Mourning Garment*: "Worne here by plaine Shepheardes; in memorie of their sacred Mistresses, Elizabeth, Queen of Vertue while shee lived, and Theame of Sorrow, being dead. To which is added the true manner of her Emperiall Funerall. After which followeth the Shepheards Spring-Song, for entertainment of King James our most potent Soveraigne. Dedicated to all that loved the deceased Queene, and honor the living King." Some interest attaches to Chettle's mention of contemporary poets under pastoral names, including Shakespeare as Melicert. Also indebted to both Sannazaro and Spenser are the *Piscatorie Eclogs* appended to Phineas Fletcher's *The Purple Island* (1633).

There is bucolic masquerade too in *The Shepheards Hunting* (1615) by the wordy and contentious George Wither (1588-1667). This set of five long eclogues reprints two that had appeared in the previous year as an appendix to William Browne of Tavistock's collection *The Shepheards Pipe*: Browne appears as Willy, and Wither himself as Roget; the principal subject of their discourse is Wither's imprisonment in the Marshalsea, and the "shepherd's hunting" of the title is Wither's career as a satirist which had landed him in prison. Wither's *Fair Virtue* (1622) is a shapeless medley of pastoral description and song which extends to nearly five thousand lines. Wither, like Barnfield, is best in short pieces, such as that delightful evoca-

tion of the undergraduate's salad days, "I loved a lass a fair one," with its idyllic glimpses of the Oxford countryside.

The greatest pastoralist among Spenser's disciples is Michael Drayton (1563-1631). His pastoral name "Rowland of the Rock" was often linked to Colin Clout's in contemporary complimentary verse, and his first pastorals, a set of nine "eglogs" entitled *Idea, the Shepheards Garland* (1593), betray clearly, in structure, subject, language, and meter, the influence of *The Shepheardes Calender*. Thus the first and last eclogues are love laments by Rowland himself, the seventh is a debate between youth and age, and the third is a panegyric upon Elizabeth, here called "Beta" to complement Spenser's praise of Elisa. The fourth in some ways complements Spenser's *Astrophel,* since its central passage is a lament for a dead shepherd who represents Sidney. The only tune in Spenser's poem that finds no echo in Drayton's is the religious and political satire. Drayton ignores allegories of shepherd as Christian pastor in order to concentrate upon the equation between shepherd and poet. His subject is not man's whole life, of which the twelve months of *The Shepheardes Calender* are emblematic, but the poet's craft, as he indicates in his subtitle, "Rowland's Sacrifice to the nine Muses."

The freshest of the eclogues is the eighth, in which the burlesque tone of a mock-romance reminiscent of Chaucer's "Sir Thopas" is offset by affectionate regionalism; for the setting is Drayton's beloved Warwickshire, and the delicious beauty of Dowsabell, heroine of the tale, is defined by reference to good things of the Midland countryside, such as Leominster wool, the grass that grows beside the Derbyshire Dove, and the swan that swims in the Trent (lines 147-52). Dowsabell loves and is loved by a jolly shepherd, and their happy little wooing dialogue acts as a corrective to Rowland's love complaints in other eclogues. The mood and technique of this poem are close to the pastoral ballads found in contemporary broadsides and miscellanies. While in no sense "realistic," it draws some of its vitality from the wooing games of real country people.

English country games crop up unexpectedly in Drayton's *Endimion and Phoebe: Ideas Latmus* (1595) when satyrs on Mount Latmus play barley-break. This poem is one of those Ovidian mythological narratives so fashionable in the 1590s, of which Marlowe's *Hero and Leander* (written 1590) and Shakespeare's *Venus and Adonis* (1593) are best known; but though Drayton borrows from Marlowe and Shakespeare, his treatment of love, in accordance with the myth he has chosen, is Platonic and almost entirely without their eroticism. Endimion is, of course, a shepherd, and his home upon the slopes of Mount Latmus has all the features of the Arcadia described by Sannazaro. *Endimion and Phoebe* was considerably cut and extensively revised when it appeared in Drayton's collected *Poems* (1606) under the title of "The Man in the Moone." Here the myth becomes a tale told by old Rowland at a shepherds' feast in honor of Pan, and is linked to this framework by a satirical passage about misdeeds of shepherds as observed by the man in the moon. The satire, the framework, and the identity of the tale-teller all serve to make the poem something of an oversized eclogue, and to link it with Drayton's *Eglogs* which it immediately follows in the 1606 collection.

These *Eglogs* are a complete rewriting and rearrangement of *The Shepheards Garland* with the substitution of a new ninth eclogue. Drayton's revisions introduce a new note of satirical bitterness. For instance, in the sixth eclogue, a re-handling of the fourth in *The Shepheards Garland,* the deaths of Sidney and Queen Elizabeth (and the accession of the "Northerne" monarch, James I) are made to signify the death of an old order of virtue, poetry, and patronage:

> The Groves, the Mountaynes, and the pleasant Heath,
> That wonted were with Roundelayes to ring,
> Are blasted now with the cold Northerne breath,
> That not a Shepheard takes delight to sing.[4]
>
> (85-88)

Despite such occasional asperity, the dominant mood of this series, as of the earlier series of eclogues, is delight in the poet's art and in the English landscape. The setting of the ninth eclogue is just such a sheep-shearing feast in the Cotswold Hills as the one described in Drayton's *Poly-Olbion,* song 14, and depicted on the map for that song. The songs in the ninth eclogue are marked by such refined and formalized hyperbole as that[5] which represents Sylvia, the moorland maiden, staying the course of nature and defying mutability:

> *Motto.* Why doth the Sunne against his kind,
>   Stay his bright Chariot in the Skies?
> *Perkin.* He pawseth, almost strooken blind,
>   With gazing on her heavenly Eyes . . .
> *Motto.* How come those Flowres to flourish still,
>   Not withering with sharpe Winters breath?
> *Perkin.* Shee hath rob'd Nature of her skill,
>   And comforts all things with her breath.
> *Motto.* Why slide these Brookes so slow away,
>   As swift as the wild Roe that were?
> *Perkin.* O, muse not Shepheard, that they stay,
>   When they her Heavenly voice doe heare.
>
> (149-52, 157-64)

Thus Perkin expresses the timeless quality of his love as well as the excellence of his mistress. The exquisite formality of this song satisfyingly balances the vivid and sympathetic rustic observation in the setting.

Balance is lost in *The Shepheards Sirena* published with *The Battaile of Agincourt* in 1627, but probably written about thirteen years earlier. The lyric, "Neare to the Silver *Trent, Sirena* dwelleth," is one of the finest of its age; the "framework" has shepherds and shepherdesses who sing roundelays and dance "trenchmore," but they also fight to prevent swineherds invading the sheep walks with their hogs and rooting up the pastures. There is an allegory here, which Drayton leaves obscure (and deliberately so if the "Angry Olcon" who encourages these swineherds is

James I, as most commentators believe),[6] but the asperity of this passage is out of key with the rest of the eclogue. This same 1627 volume contains Drayton's exercise in the fashionable minor Jacobean-Caroline genre of fairy poetry: *Nimphidia,* a happy piece of mock-heroic whimsy. Its fairies owe most to art, but something to a still living rustic superstition too:

> These make our Girles their sluttery rue,
> By pinching them both blacke and blew,
> And put a penny in their shue,
>   The house for cleanely sweeping.
>
> (65-68)

Fairy lore and rustic custom find their way together into Drayton's last pastoral *The Muses Elizium* (1630), the eighth "Nimphall" of which is a prothalamion celebrating the wedding of a nymph and a fay. In several nimphalls Elizium is contrasted with the ironically named Felicia, a once paradisal and now wretched region which represents the real world, or specifically England;[7] and in the tenth nimphall Drayton introduces himself, in the character of an aged satyr, fleeing from plague-stricken Felicia and coming to Elizium, that "Paradise on earth," without tempest or winter, where delights never fade, where brooks are decked with lilies, and trees always laden with ripe fruit, where sit "Apolloes prophets," and before them sing the Muses and dance the Graces:

> Decay nor Age there nothing knowes,
> There is continuall Youth,
> As Time on plant or creatures growes,
> So still their strength renewth.
>
> The Poets Paradise this is,
> To which but few can come;
> The Muses only bower of blisse
> Their Deare *Elizium.*
>
> (97-104)

This Paradise is the world of literary art itself, and *The Muses Elizium* as a whole represents Drayton's furthest development in pastoral toward pure aesthetic patterning and the creation of pleasing forms that are freed from any reference to objective reality.

An alternative development of pastoral toward idyllic loco-descriptive poetry may be observed *in extenso* in Drayton's *Poly-Olbion* (part 1, 1612; part 2, 1622), a thirty-thousand-line-long poetical guide book to the rivers, mountains, forests, antiquities, legend, customs, natural resources, and occupations of all the counties of England and Wales. Drayton's address "to the Generall *Reader*" promises him a journey through "delicate embrodered Meadowes, often veined with gentle gliding Brooks; in which thou maist fully view the dainty Nymphes in their simple naked bewties, bathing them in Crystalline streames; which shall lead thee, to most pleasant Downes, where harmlesse Shepheards are, some exercising their pipes, some singing roundelaies, to their gazing flocks"; and the maps that preface each of the thirty songs show a nymph in every stream and a shepherd on every hill. In order to dramatize his catalog of the varied beauties of the English countryside he uses the machinery of classical pastoral, the local deities; thus the nymph of the Irwell boasts of that river's beauty and incidentally paints a familiar picture of the well-being and gaiety of English country folk:

> Yee lustie Lasses then, in *Lancashire* that dwell,
> For Beautie that are sayd to beare away the Bell,
> Your countries Horn-pipe, ye so minsingly that tread,
> As ye the Eg-pye love, and Apple Cherry-red;
> In all your mirthfull Songs, and merry meetings tell,
> That *Erwell* every way doth *Ribble* farre excell.
>
> (65-70)

Allegorical satire in *The Shepheards Sirena* directed against those unidentified bad poets who defile beautiful and sacred old sheep-walks reappears in Drayton's commendatory verses "to his friend the Author" which preface *Britannia's Pastorals, Book I* by William Browne (1690-45?). Drayton welcomes this young pastor to the company of true shepherds who continue the Spenserian tradition; but Browne, like Drayton, diverges further from Spenser the more he writes. *Britannia's Pastorals* (book 1, 1613; book 2, 1616; and a fragment of book 3 written in the 1620s) is a discursive narrative poem founded upon hints from Ovid, Sannazaro, Tasso, Sidney, *The Faerie Queene,* and John Fletcher's pastoral play *The Faithful Shepherdess.* Browne's romantic action finds a place for a varied cast of shepherds and shepherdesses, Olympian Gods, lustful satyrs, Grecian local deities, Devonshire fairies and personifications of Truth, Time, and Riot. Though it is the longest narrative pastoral poem in the language it is technically a series of eclogues because it consists of a succession of songs which are sung by a shepherd to an audience of fellow shepherds. At the end of each song the narrative is broken off, as night falls, or as rain begins, or as a sheep caught in a brake requires the singer's attention. Browne follows the Elizabethan poets' fashion of localizing classical myth, and transporting a whole system of pagan deities, nymphs, and satyrs to the England of their own day: indeed, his true subject is the English countryside and its people. He asks at the opening of book 1, song 1:

> What need I tune the Swaines of *Thessaly?*
> Or, bootlesses, adde to them of *Arcadie? . . .*
> My *Muse* for lofty pitches shall not rome
> And homely pipen of her native home
>
> (9-10, 13-14)[8]

and the complicated romantic action is often relieved by glimpses of the people of Browne's native home, Devonshire, at work in the fields or at play at a May game or rustic wedding. A characteristic passage is the following from book 2, song 1:

> Long on the shore distrest *Marina* lay:
> For he that ope's the pleasant sweets of *May,*
> Beyond the *Noonstead* so farre drove his teame,

> That harvest folkes, with curds and clouted creame,
> With cheese and butter, cakes, and oates ynow,
> That are the *Yeomans,* from the yoke or Cowe,
> On sheaves of corne were at their noonshuns close,
> Whilst by them merrily the *Bagpipe* goes:
> Ere from her hand she lifted up her head,
> Where all the *Graces* then inhabited.
> When casting round her over-drowned eyes,
> (So have I seen a Gemme of mickle price
> Roll in a Scallop-shell with water fild)
> She, on a marble rocke at hand behild,
> In Characters deepe cut with Iron stroke,
> A Shepheards moane, which, read by her, thus spoke:
>   Glide soft, ye silver Floods,
>   And every Spring:
>   Within the shady Woods
>   Let no Bird sing!
> Nor from the Grove a *Turtle-Dove*
> Be seene to couple with her love:
> But silence on each Dale and Mountaine dwell,
> Whilst *Willy* bids his friend and joy *Farewell.*
>
> (225-48)

Heroic action is suspended for a moment as Browne gives the time of day with a reference to harvesters, before he continues, by way of the pearl conceit, to the higher style of his stately lyric. These Devonshire vignettes, or idylls (if we retain the meaning of eidullion, "a little picture"), often appear in the form of extended similes, such as the angler and the squirrel-hunt in book 1, song 5. Such characteristic thumbnail sketches as "A Little Lad set on a banke to shale / The ripened Nuts" (book 2, song 4) have an immediacy and clarity that contrast strikingly with the overall narrative.

The local patriotism that underlies the whole work is proudly declared in book 2, song 3: "Haile, thou my native soile! thou blessed plot / Whose equal all the world affordeth not!" (602-3). Such patriotism is given a specifically pastoral character in book 2, song 4, where an aged shepherd is drawn from his story of Pan and Syrinx into a digression that is unusually distant even for Browne:

> And now, ye Brittish Swains (Whose harmlesse sheepe
> Then all the worlds beside I joy to keepe,
> Which spread on every Plaine and hilly Wold
> Fleeces no lesse esteem'd then that of gold,
> For whose exchange one *Indy Iems* of price,
> The other gives you of her choicest spice.
>
> (933-38)

Britain's exports of wool and woollen goods were to become a well-loved and well-worn theme for the patriotic poets of the following century, but those poets would regard with less equanimity than Browne the foreign luxuries for which wool was exchanged. An anticipation of another favorite eighteenth-century theme occurs when, in book 2, song 3, Browne assures his readers that golden-age shepherds are blessed with natural reason:

> O happy men! you ever did possesse
> No wisedome but was mixt with simplenesse;

So wanting malice and from folly free,
Since reason went with your simplicite.

(426-29)

Drayton, Wither, and Browne presented themselves as a group—using pastoral often to celebrate the friendships of poets. In their work there was a tendency to "naturalize" the pastoral to the English scene; they viewed Elizabethan England retrospectively as a golden age. As late as the 1620s, in an age when poetic fashions inclined either toward "strong lines" or Horatian urbanity, they took Spenser as their model. However, it is the more relaxed, even homely, elements in Spenser that they inherited; the symbolism of *The Shepheardes Calender* was beyond them. Thus beside their master they appear comparatively unserious.

Notes

1. *The Works of Michael Drayton,* ed. J. W. Hebel, 5 vols. (Oxford: Basil Blackwell, 1961), 2:517-18.

2. *Some Longer Elizabethan Poems,* intro. A. H. Bullen, in *An English Garner* (1903; reprint ed., New York: Cooper Square, 1964), p. 145.

3. Quotations from Barnfield are taken from *Some Longer Elizabethan Poems,* intro. Bullen.

4. Quotations from Drayton are taken from *The Works,* ed. Hebel.

5. This song had been published, with slight variations, in *England's Helicon* (1600).

6. See *The Works,* ed. Hebel, 5:206-9, and authorities cited there. Hebel links Drayton's poem with Browne's *The Shepheards Pipe* (1614), Wither's *The Shepheard's Hunting,* and those satires which earned Wither royal displeasure and landed him in prison.

7. The identification of Felicia with England is argued in R. F. Hardin, *Michael Drayton and the passing of Elizabethan England* (Lawrence: University of Kansas Press, 1973), pp. 127-31. Hardin treats Drayton as essentially a poet of nostalgic patriotism.

8. Quotations from Browne are taken from *The Works,* ed. G. Goodwin, 2 vols. (London: Routledge, 1894).

PRINCIPAL FIGURES OF THE LATER RENAISSANCE

Samuel Johnson (essay date 1780)

SOURCE: "On Milton's *Lycidas*," in *The Pastoral Mode: A Casebook,* edited by Bryan Loughrey, Macmillan Publishers Ltd., 1984, pp. 71-3.

[*In the following excerpt, originally published in his* Lives of the English Poets *in 1780, Johnson critcizes what he thinks are the faults of John Milton's poem* Lycidas, *whose pastoral form he finds vulgar and disgusting.*]

. . . One of the poems on which much praise has been bestowed is Lycidas; of which the diction is harsh, the rhymes uncertain, and the numbers unpleasing. What beauty there is, we must therefore seek in the sentiments and images. It is not to be considered as the effusion of real passion; for passion runs not after remote allusions and obscure opinions. Passion plucks no berries from the myrtle and ivy, nor calls upon Arethuse and Mincius, nor tells of rough satyrs, and fauns with cloven heel. Where there is leisure for fiction, there is little grief.

In this poem there is no nature, for there is no truth; there is no art, for there is nothing new. Its form is that of a pastoral—easy, vulgar, and therefore disgusting; whatever images it can supply are long ago exhausted; and its inherent improbability always forces dissatisfaction on the mind. When Cowley tells of Hervey, that they studied together, it is easy to suppose how much he must miss the companion of his labours, and the partner of his discoveries; but what image of tenderness can be excited by these lines?

We drove a field, and both together heard,
What time the grey fly winds her sultry horn,
Battening our flocks with the fresh dews of night.

We know that they never drove a field, and that they had no flocks to batten; and though it be allowed that the representation may be allegorical, the true meaning is so uncertain and remote, that it is never sought, because it cannot be known when it is found.

Among the flocks, and copses, and flowers, appear the heathen deities; Jove and Phbus, Neptune and olus, with a long train of mythological imagery, such as a college easily supplies. Nothing can less display knowledge, or less exercise invention, than to tell how a shepherd has lost his companion, and must now feed his flocks alone, without any judge of his skill in piping; and how one god asks another god what is become of Lycidas, and how neither god can tell. He who thus grieves will excite no sympathy; he who thus praises will confer no honour.

This poem has yet a grosser fault. With these trifling fictions are mingled the most awful and sacred truths, such as ought never to be polluted with such irreverend combinations. The shepherd likewise is now a feeder of sheep, and afterwards an ecclesiastical pastor, a superintendant of a christian flock. Such equivocations are always unskilful; but here they are indecent, and at least approach to impiety; of which, however, I believe the writer not to have been conscious.

Such is the power of reputation justly acquired, that its blaze drives away the eye from nice examination. Surely no man could have fancied that he read Lycidas with pleasure, had he not known the author. . . .

Northrop Frye (essay date 1958)

SOURCE: "Literature as Context: Milton's *Lycidas*," in *The Pastoral Mode: A Casebook*, edited by Bryan Loughrey, Macmillan Publishers Ltd., 1984, pp. 205-15.

[*In the following excerpt, originally delivered as a lecture in 1958 and published in* 20th Century Literary Criticism *in 1972, Frye discusses John Milton's* Lycidas *as a pastoral elegy, noting the four creative principles of convention, genre, archetype, and autonomous form that Milton uses in its composition. The critic also elucidates the poem's classical and Christian mythic dimensions.*]

. . . *Lycidas* . . . is an elegy in the pastoral convention, written to commemorate a young man named Edward King who was drowned at sea. The origins of the pastoral are partly classical, the tradition that runs through Theocritus and Virgil, and partly Biblical, the imagery of the twenty-third Psalm, of Christ as the Good Shepherd, of the metaphors of 'pastor' and 'flock' in the Church. The chief connecting link between the traditions in Milton's day was the Fourth or Messianic Eclogue of Virgil. Hence it is common enough to have pastoral images echoing both traditions at once, and not surprising to find that *Lycidas* is a Christian poem as well as a humanistic one.

In the classical pastoral elegy the subject of the elegy is not treated as an individual but as a representative of a dying spirit of nature. The pastoral elegy seems to have some relation to the ritual of the Adonis lament, and the dead poet Bion, in Moschus's poem, is celebrated with much the same kind of imagery as Bion himself uses in his lament for Adonis. The phrase 'dying god', for such a figure in later pastoral, is not an anachronism: Virgil says of Daphnis, for example, in the Fifth Eclogue: *'deus, deus ille, Menalca'* ['a god, he is a god, Menalca']. Besides, Milton and his learned contemporaries, Selden, for example, or Henry Reynolds, knew at least as much about the symbolism of the 'dying god' as any modern student could get out of *The Golden Bough*, which depends mainly on the same classical sources that were available to them. The notion that twentieth-century poets differ from their predecessors in their understanding or use of myth will not bear much scrutiny. So King is given the pastoral name of Lycidas, which is equivalent to Adonis, and is associated with the cyclical rhythms of nature. Of these three are of particular importance: the daily cycle of the sun across the sky, the yearly cycle of the seasons, and the cycle of water, flowing from wells and fountains through rivers to the sea. Sunset, winter, and the sea are emblems of Lycidas's death; sunrise and spring, of his resurrection. The poem begins in the morning, 'Under the opening eyelids of the morn', and ends with the sun, like Lycidas himself, dropping into the western ocean, yet due to rise again as Lycidas is to do. The imagery of the opening lines, 'Shatter your leaves before the mellowing year', suggests the frosts of autumn killing the flowers, and in the great roll-call of flowers towards the end, most of them early blooming flowers like the 'rathe primrose', the spring returns. Again,

the opening invocation is to the 'Sisters of the sacred well', and the water imagery carries through a great variety of Greek, Italian and English rivers to the sea in which the dead body of Lycidas lies.

Lycidas, then, is the 'archetype' of Edward King. By an archetype I mean a literary symbol, or cluster of symbols, which are used recurrently throughout literature, and thereby become conventional. A poetic use of a flower, by itself, is not necessarily an archetype. But in a poem about the death of a young man it is conventional to associate him with a red or purple flower, usually a spring flower like the hyacinth. The historical origin of the convention may be lost in ritual, but it is a constantly latent one, not only in literature but in life, as the symbolism of the scarlet poppies in World War I shows. Hence in *Lycidas* the 'sanguine flower inscrib'd with woe' is an archetype, a symbol that recurs regularly in many poems of its kind. Similarly Lycidas himself is not only the literary form of Edward King, but a conventional or recurring form, of the same family as Shelley's Adonais, the Daphnis of Theocritus and Virgil, and Milton's own Damon. King was also a clergyman and, for Milton's purposes, a poet, so, having selected the conventional archetype of King as drowned young man, Milton has then to select the conventional archetypes of King as poet and of King as priest. These are, respectively, Orpheus and Peter.

Both Orpheus and Peter have attributes that link them in imagery with Lycidas. Orpheus was also an 'enchanting son' or spirit of nature; he died young, in much the same role as Adonis, and was flung into the water. Peter would have drowned too without the help of Christ; hence Peter is not named directly, but only as 'The Pilot of the Galilean Lake', just as Christ is not named directly, but only as 'Him that walked the waves'. When Orpheus was torn to pieces by the Maenads, his head went floating 'Down the swift Hebrus to the Lesbian shore'. The theme of salvation out of water is connected with the image of the dolphin, a conventional type of Christ, and dolphins are called upon to 'waft the hapless youth' just before the peroration begins.

The body of the poem is arranged in the form ABACA, a main theme repeated twice with two intervening episodes, as in the musical rondo. The main theme is the drowning of Lycidas in the prime of his life; the two episodes, presided over by the figures of Orpheus and Peter, deal with the theme of premature death as it relates to poetry and to the priesthood respectively. In both the same type of image appears: the mechanical instrument of execution that brings about a sudden death, represented by the 'abhorred shears' in the meditation on fame and the 'grim two-handed engine' in the meditation on the corruption of the Church. The most difficult part of the construction is the managing of the transitions from these episodes back to the main theme. The poet does this by alluding to his great forerunners in the pastoral convention, Theocritus of Sicily, Virgil of Mantua, and the legendary Arcadians who preceded both:

> O fountain Arethuse, and thou honour'd flood,
> Smooth-sliding Mincius, crown'd with vocal reeds,
> . . .

and later:

> Return, Alpheus, the dread voice is past
> That shrunk thy streams: return, Sicilian Muse,
> . . .

The allusion has the effect of reminding the reader that this is, after all, a pastoral. But Milton also alludes to the myth of Arethusa and Alpheus, the Arcadian water-spirits who plunged underground and reappeared in Sicily, and this myth not only outlines the history of the pastoral convention, but unites the water imagery with the theme of disappearance and revival.

In pastoral elegy the poet who laments the death is often so closely associated with the dead man as to make him a kind of double or shadow of himself. Similarly Milton represents himself as intimately involved with the death of Lycidas. The theme of premature death is skilfully associated in the opening lines with the conventional apology for a 'harsh and crude' poem; the poet hopes for a similar elegy when he dies, and at the end he accepts the responsibilities of survival and turns 'Tomorrow to fresh woods, and pastures new', bringing the elegy to a full rich *tierce de Picardie* or major chord. By appearing himself at the beginning and end of the poem, Milton presents the poem as, in a sense, contained within the mind of the poet.

Apart from the historical convention of the pastoral, however, there is also the conventional framework of ideas or assumptions which forms the background of the poem. I call it a framework of ideas, and it may also be that, but in poetry it is rather a framework of images. It consists of four levels of existence. First is the order revealed by Christianity, the order of grace and salvation and of eternal life. Second is the order of human nature, the order represented by the Garden of Eden in the Bible and the Golden Age in classical myth, and which man in his fallen state can, up to a point, regain through education, obedience to law and the habit of virtue. Third is the order of physical nature, the world of animals and plants which is morally neutral but theologically 'fallen'. Fourth is the disorder of the unnatural, the sin and death and corruption that entered the world with the Fall.

Lycidas has his connections with all of these orders. In the first place, all the images of death and resurrection are included in and identified with the body of Christ. Christ is the sun of righteousness, the tree of life, the water of life, the dying god who rose again, the saviour from the sea. On this level Lycidas enters the Christian heaven and is greeted by the 'Saints above', 'In solemn troops, and sweet societies', where the language echoes the Book of Revelation. But simultaneously Lycidas achieves another apotheosis as the Genius of the shore, corresponding to the Attendant Spirit in *Comus,* whose habitation is said to be a world above our own, identified, not with the Christian

heaven, but with Spenser's Gardens of Adonis. The third level of physical nature is the world of ordinary experience, where death is simply a loss, and those who mourn the death have to turn to pick up their tasks again. On this level Lycidas is merely absent, 'to our moist vows denied', represented only by the empty bier with its flowers. It is on this level too that the poem is contained within the mind of the surviving poet, as on the Christian level it is contained within the body of Christ. Finally, the world of death and corruption holds the drowned corpse of Lycidas, which will soon come to the surface and 'welter to the parching wind'. This last is an unpleasant and distressing image, and Milton touches it very lightly, picking it up again in an appropriate context:

> But swoln with wind and the rank mist they draw,
> Rot inwardly, . . .

In the writing of *Lycidas* there are four creative principles of particular importance. To say that there are four does not mean, of course, that they are separable. One is convention, the reshaping of the poetic material which is appropriate to this subject. Another is genre, the choosing of the appropriate form. A third is archetype, the use of appropriate, and therefore recurrently employed, images and symbols. The fourth, for which there is no name, is the fact that the forms of literature are autonomous: that is, they do not exist outside literature. Milton is not writing an obituary: he does not start with Edward King and his life and times, but with the conventions and archetypes that poetry requires for such a theme.

Of the critical principles illustrated by this analysis, one will be no surprise . . . *Lycidas* owes quite as much to Hebrew, Greek, Latin and Italian traditions as it does to English. Even the diction, of which I have no space to speak, shows strong Italian influence. Milton was of course a learned poet, but there is no poet whose literary influences are entirely confined to his own language. Thus every problem in literary criticism is a problem in comparative literature, or simply of literature itself.

The next principle is that the provisional hypothesis which we must adopt for the study of every poem is that that poem is a unity. If, after careful and repeated testing, we are forced to conclude that it is not a unity, then we must abandon the hypothesis and look for the reasons why it is not. A good deal of bad criticism of *Lycidas* has resulted from not making enough initial effort to understand the unity of the poem. To talk of 'digressions' in *Lycidas* is a typical consequence of a mistaken critical method, of backing into the poem the wrong way round. If, instead of starting with the poem, we start with a handful of peripheral facts about the poem, Milton's casual knowledge of King, his ambitions as a poet, his bitterness against the episcopacy, then of course the poem will break down into pieces corresponding precisely to those fragments of knowledge. *Lycidas* illustrates, on a small scale, what has happened on a much bigger scale in, for example, the criticism of Homer. Critics knowing something about the fragmentary nature of heroic lays and ballads approached the *Iliad* and the *Odyssey* with this knowledge in mind, and the poems obediently split up into the pieces that they wished to isolate. Other critics came along and treated the poems as imaginative unities, and today everyone knows that the second group were more convincing.

The same thing happens when our approach to 'sources' becomes fragmented or piecemeal. *Lycidas* is a dense mass of echoes from previous literature, chiefly pastoral literature. Reading through Virgil's Eclogues with *Lycidas* in mind, we can see that Milton had not simply read or studied these poems: he possessed them; they were part of the material he was shaping. The passage about the hungry sheep reminds us of at least three other passages: one in Dante's *Paradiso,* one in the Book of Ezekiel, and one near the beginning of Hesiod's *Theogony*. There are also echoes of Mantuan and Spenser, of the Gospel of John, and it is quite possible that there are even more striking parallels with poems that Milton had not read. In such cases there is not *a* source at all, no one place that the passage 'comes from', or, as we say with such stupefying presumption, that the poet 'had in mind'. There are only archetypes, or recurring themes of literary expression, which *Lycidas* has recreated, and therefore re-echoed, yet once more.

The next principle is that the important problems of literary criticism lie within the study of literature. We notice that a law of diminishing returns sets in as soon as we move away from the poem itself. If we ask, who is Lycidas? the answer is that he is a member of the same family as Theocritus's Daphnis, Bion's Adonis, the Old Testament Abel, and so on. The answer goes on building up a wider comprehension of literature and a deeper knowledge of its structural principles and recurring themes. But if we ask, who was Edward King? What was his relation to Milton? How good a poet was he? we find ourselves moving dimly in the intense inane. The same is true of minor points. If we ask, why is the image of the two-handed engine in *Lycidas*? we can give an answer, along the lines suggested above, that illustrates how carefully the poem has been constructed. If we ask, what is the two-handed engine? there are forty-odd answers, none of them completely satisfactory; yet the fact that they are not wholly satisfactory hardly seems to be important.

Another form of the same kind of fallacy is the confusion between personal sincerity and literary sincerity. If we start with the facts that *Lycidas* is highly conventional and that Milton knew King only slightly, we may see in *Lycidas* an 'artificial' poem without 'real feeling' in it. This red herring, though more common among third-rate romantics, was dragged across the study of *Lycidas* by Samuel Johnson. Johnson knew better, but he happened to feel perverse about this particular poem, and so deliberately raised false issues. It would not have occurred to him, for example, to question the conventional use of Horace in the satires of Pope, or of Juvenal in his own. Personal sincerity has no place in literature, because personal sincerity as

such is inarticulate. One may burst into tears at the news of a friend's death, but one can never spontaneously burst into song, however doleful a lay. *Lycidas* is a passionately sincere poem, because Milton was deeply interested in the structure and symbolism of funeral elegies, and had been practising since adolescence on every fresh corpse in sight, from the university beadle to the fair infant dying of a cough.

If we ask what inspires a poet, there are always two answers. An occasion, an experience, an event, may inspire the impulse to write. But the impulse to write can only come from previous contact with literature, and the formal inspiration, the poetic structure that crystallises around the new event, can only be derived from other poems. Hence while every new poem is a new and unique creation, it is also a reshaping of familiar conventions of literature, otherwise it would not be recognisable as literature at all. Literature often gives us the illusion of turning from books to life, from second-hand to direct experience, and thereby discovering new literary principles in the world outside. But this is never quite what happens. No matter how tightly Wordsworth may close the barren leaves of art and let nature be his teacher, his literary forms will be as conventional as ever, although they may echo an unaccustomed set of conventions, such as the ballad or the broadside. The pretence of personal sincerity is itself a literary convention, and Wordsworth makes many of the flat simple statements which represent, in literature, the inarticulateness of personal sincerity:

> No motion has she now, no force:
>   She neither hears nor sees;
> . . .

But as soon as a death becomes a poetic image, that image is assimilated to other poetic images of death in nature, and hence Lucy inevitably becomes a Proserpine figure, just as King becomes an Adonis:

> Rolled round in earth's diurnal course
>   With rocks, and stones, and trees.

In Whitman we have an even more extreme example than Wordsworth of a cult of personal statement and an avoidance of learned conventions. It is therefore instructive to see what happens in *When Lilacs Last in Dooryard Bloomed*. The dead man is not called by a pastoral name, but neither is he called by his historical name. He is in a coffin which is carried the length and breadth of the land; he is identified with a 'powerful western fallen star'; he is the beloved comrade of the poet, who throws the purple flower of the lilac on his coffin; a singing bird laments the death, just as the woods and caves do in *Lycidas*. Convention, genre, archetype and the autonomy of forms are all illustrated as clearly in Whitman as they are in Milton.

Lycidas is an occasional poem, called forth by a specific event. It seems, therefore, to be a poem with a strong external reference. Critics who cannot approach a poem except as a personal statement of the poet's thus feel that if it says little about King, it must say a good deal about Milton. So, they reason, *Lycidas* is really autobiographical, concerned with Milton's own preoccupations, including his fear of death. There can be no objection to this unless Milton's conventional involving himself with the poem is misinterpreted as a personal intrusion into it.

For Milton was even by seventeenth-century standards an unusually professional and impersonal poet. Of all Milton's poems, the one obvious failure is the poem called *The Passion,* and if we look at the imagery of that poem we can see why. It is the only poem of Milton's in which he is preoccupied with himself in the process of writing it. 'My muse', 'my song', 'my harp', 'my roving verse', 'my Phoebus', and so on for eight stanzas until Milton abandons the poem in disgust. It is not a coincidence that Milton's one self-conscious poem should be the one that never gets off the ground. There is nothing like this in *Lycidas:* the 'I' of that poem is a professional poet in his conventional shepherd disguise, and to think of him as a personal 'I' is to bring *Lycidas* down to the level of *The Passion,* to make it a poem that has to be studied primarily as a biographical document rather than for its own sake. Such an approach to *Lycidas* is apt to look most plausible to those who dislike Milton, and want to see him cut down to size.

One more critical principle, and the one that I have written this paper to enunciate, seems to me to follow inevitably from the previous ones. Every poem must be examined as a unity, but no poem is an isolatable unity. Every poem is inherently connected with other poems of its kind, whether explicitly, as *Lycidas* is with Theocritus and Virgil, or implicitly, as Whitman is with the same tradition, or by anticipation, as *Lycidas* is with later pastoral elegies. And, of course, the kinds or genres of literature are not separable either, like the orders of pre-Darwinian biology. Everyone who has seriously studied literature knows that he is not simply moving from poem to poem, or from one aesthetic experience to another: he is also entering into a coherent and progressive discipline. For literature is not simply an aggregate of books and poems and plays: it is an order of words. And our total literary experience, at any given time, is not a discrete series of memories or impressions of what we have read, but an imaginatively coherent body of experience.

It is literature as an order of words, therefore, which forms the primary context of any given work of literary art. All other contexts—the place of *Lycidas* in Milton's development; its place in the history of English poetry; its place in seventeenth-century thought or history—are secondary and derivative contexts. Within the total literary order certain structural and generic principles, certain configurations of narrative and imagery, certain conventions and devices and *topoi,* occur over and over again. In every new work of literature some of these principles are reshaped.

Lycidas, we found, is informed by such a recurring structural principle. The short, simple, and accurate name for this principle is myth. The Adonis myth is what makes *Ly-*

cidas both distinctive and traditional. Of course if we think of the Adonis myth as some kind of Platonic idea existing by itself, we shall not get far with it as a critical conception. But it is only incompetence that tries to reduce or assimilate a poem to a myth. The Adonis myth in *Lycidas* is the structure of *Lycidas.* It is in *Lycidas* in much the same way that the sonata form is in the first movement of a Mozart symphony. It is the connecting link between what makes *Lycidas* the poem it is and what unites it to other forms of poetic experience. If we attend only to the uniqueness of *Lycidas,* and analyse the ambiguities and subtleties of its diction, our method, however useful in itself, soon reaches a point of no return to the poem. If we attend only to the conventional element, our method will turn it into a scissors-and-paste collection of allusive tags. One method reduces the poem to a jangle of echoes of itself, the other to a jangle of echoes from other poets. If we have a unifying principle that holds these two tendencies together from the start, neither will get out of hand.

Myths, it is true, turn up in other disciplines, in anthropology, in psychology, in comparative religion. But the primary business of the critic is with myth as the shaping principle of a work of literature. Thus for him myth becomes much the same thing as Aristotle's *mythos,* narrative or plot, the moving formal cause which is what Aristotle called the 'soul' of the work and assimilates all details in the realising of its unity.

In its simplest English meaning a myth is a story about a god, and Lycidas is, poetically speaking, a god or spirit of nature, who eventually becomes a saint in heaven, which is as near as one can get to godhead in ordinary Christianity. The reason for treating Lycidas mythically, in this sense, is conventional, but the convention is not arbitrary or accidental. It arises from the metaphorical nature of poetic speech. We are not told simply that Lycidas has left the woods and caves, but that the woods and caves and all their echoes mourn his loss. This is the language of that curious identification of subject and object, of personality and thing, which the poet has in common with the lunatic and the lover. It is the language of metaphor, recognised by Aristotle as the distinctive language of poetry. And, as we can see in such phrases as sun-god and tree-god, the language of metaphor is interdependent with the language of myth.

I have said that all problems of criticism are problems of comparative literature. But where there is comparison there must be some standard by which we can distinguish what is actually comparable from what is merely analogous. The scientists discovered long ago that to make valid comparisons you have to know what your real categories are. If you're studying natural history, for instance, no matter how fascinated you may be by anything that has eight legs, you can't just lump together an octopus and a spider and a string quartet. In science the difference between a scientific and a pseudo-scientific procedure can usually be spotted fairly soon. I wonder if literary criticism has any standards of this kind. It seems to me that a critic practically has to maintain that the Earl of Oxford wrote the plays of Shakespeare before he can be clearly recognised as making pseudo-critical statements. I have read some critics on Milton who appeared to be confusing Milton with their phallic fathers, if that is the right phrase. I could call them pseudo-critics; others call them neo-classicists. How is one to know? There is such a variety of even legitimate critics. There are critics who can find things in the Public Records Office, and there are critics who, like myself, could not find the Public Records Office. Not all critical statements or procedures can be equally valid.

The first step, I think, is to recognise the dependence of value judgements on scholarship. Scholarship, or the knowledge of literature, constantly expands and increases; value judgements are produced by a skill based on the knowledge we already have. Thus scholarship has both priority to value judgements and the power of veto over them. The second step is to recognise the dependence of scholarship on a co-ordinated view of literature. A good deal of critical taxonomy lies ahead of us. We need to know much more than we do about the structural principles of literature, about myth and metaphor, conventions and genres, before we can distinguish with any authority a real from an imaginary line of influence, an illuminating from a misleading analogy, a poet's original source from his last resource. The basis of this central critical activity that gives direction to scholarship is the simple fact that every poem is a member of the class of things called poems. Some poems, including *Lycidas,* proclaim that they are conventional, in other words that their primary context is in literature. Other poems leave this inference to the critic, with an appealing if often misplaced confidence.

Jay A. Gertzman (essay date 1974)

SOURCE: "Robert Herrick's Recreative Pastoral," in *Genre,* Vol. VII, No. 2, June 1974, pp. 183-95.

[*In the following essay, Gertzman illustrates Robert Herrick's "recreative" (as opposed to didactic) pastoral in several poems in his* Hesperides, *noting that the "cleanly wanton" poems are marked by playful humor, fancy, naive enthusiasm, and genial humility.*]

The pastoral poetry of the Renaissance has received a great deal of critical attention in recent years. Of special interest have been the uses to which great poets such as Spenser, Milton and Marvell have put the genre. The moral and spiritual depths beneath the physically delightful surface have been well documented. But the attractiveness of pastoral for some minor poets, especially lyric poets, has been less fully considered. Of these poets Robert Herrick is an interesting example, especially because of his *Hesperides,* in which we find a very definite pastoral sensibility, but one in which mood predominates over didactic intent, and in which Christian ceremonies are used to suggest the goodness of sensual pleasure. This kind of recreative

pastoral is very different from that which aims at speaking covertly of postlapsarian realities, or of Arcadian retirement as a way of refreshing the will for a renewed struggle against the fallen world.[1]

Herrick obviously thought the pastoral concept to be intrinsic to *Hesperides.* Its introductory poems place before the reader flowers, streams, birds, shepherds, cottages, "budding boys and girls," and love and song. These emblems, and the pastoral genre itself, imply attitudes especially congenial to Herrick's pastoral sensibility. To specify the kinds of attitudes these were, let us consider the congeries of ideas and moods inherent in the concepts of the Golden Age, and the *locus amoenus,* or pleasant place. Herrick fancies his book itself to be one of these.

Our poet's idea of the Golden Age (the most renowned "pleasant place") may have come from Homer, Hesiod, Ovid, Virgil, Pindar, Horace, or, of course, from any number of contemporary writers. However, the whole concept is so pervasive that Herrick's acquaintance with it need not have come from his reading at all. He could have found the Gardens of the Hesperides associated with the Golden Age and Elysium in Hesiod, or in Renaissance dictionaries of antiquities.[2] Hesiod associates the Golden Age with the "Isles of the Blessed" (*Works and Days,* 167-69), which, as is Homer's Elysium, is at the world's end.[3] Later, he "touches upon another place which later became the site of a Golden Age existence—the Hesperides. He tells of their creation 'beyond glorious Ocean' in *Theogony* 215-16, thus locating them in the same place as Homer's Elysium, and his own Islands of the Blessed."[4] Contrary to the opinion of Starnes and Talbert, therefore, there is precedent in classical poetry for the association of the Hesperides, the western gardens wherein were planted the golden apples which Gea gave Juno as a wedding present, with earthly paradise. Starnes and Talbert find this equation made in the *Dictionarium* of Charles Stephanus,[5] one of the handbooks of classical antiquities which they (and R. H. Deming) convincingly show to have been a part of school curricula, and of much value to Renaissance poets. Stephanus says: "Pliny and Solinus report that there was an inlet of the sea, with a winding course in the form of a dragon, which encompassed the gardens of the Hesperides."[6] A cross-reference cites the *Atlanticae Insulae,* which are identified as the isles of the blessed, and associated with Homer's Elysian fields. "Pliny seems to call these isles the Hesperides,"[7] says Stephanus, and goes on to describe the "rare and gentle" showers, "dewbearing" and temperate winds, "the fertile soil, cultivated without human effort, [which] produces delicious fruit for the carefree people."[8]

The characteristics of the *locus amoenus* which Herrick most richly exploited are the fertility and loveliness of the place itself, and the soft primitivism of its inhabitants. The Hesperidean fruits and flowers, west wind, and eternal spring are evidence of pleasant place fertility—Homer's Gardens of Alcinous are one *locus classicus.* Fertile nature, out of perfect love and sympathy for man, provides him with all he needs. *Amoenus* (lovely, pleasant) is "Virgil's constant epithet for 'beautiful' nature (e.g., *Aeneid* V, 734 and VII, 30)."[9] Servius' commentary associates "amoenus" with "amor," because these pleasant places are not associated with usefulness, but exist only to bring man to the state of fulfillment known as *otium*.[10] This kind of existence in perfect sympathy with nature is known as "soft primitivism"; it is characterized by familial and sexual love, sinless enjoyment of beauty, constant song and fertility. Marital or property laws are needless, as are guilty consciences.[11] In Curtius' words, "the shepherd's world is linked to nature and to love."[12] Curtius was speaking of Arcadia as a microcosm embracing erotic motifs, among others. But the remark suggests to me some of the broader implications of love in the *locus amoenus*—nature's own love for the shepherd, and the shepherd's love for his fellow creatures in imitation of nature's behavior.[13] Because of the shepherd's satisfaction, psychic harmony, and sense of self sufficiency, he is a fit inhabitant for the garden, which embodies all the sweetness of the Hesiodic Golden Age, and in which moralistic sobriety has no place.

We need to show how *Hesperides* might be considered as a kind of *locus amoenus*: a repository of golden age, soft primitive sentiments, and thus a congenial place for delineation of a recreative, not didactic, pastoral behavior. Let us start with the title. It could refer not only to the Hesperidean garden, but to the nymphs who guard it (the poems equalling these nymphs), to the evening star (the collection having appeared late in life and the poems being children of Herrick's old age as the nymphs were daughters of old Hesperus), or to the golden apples of the garden (the poems as fruits of Devonshire, comprising a garden of poetry). The meanings of the title are further clarified by the engraved frontispiece, which sets a bust of Herrick against Parnassus, the spring of Helicon, Pegasus, and the nine muses. Two of these are about to crown Herrick with flowers from the garden, five others dance beneath the largest tree, and the other two point to a poem on the base of the bust which suggests the "peaceful olive" should be placed on Herrick's brow, for "arms are banished" from his verses, and "young and old, mother and maid" may enjoy them.[14] The golden age pleasant place is implied in all these references—beautiful nymphs, the west wind, peace, song, golden fruits, and children. Whichever meaning is uppermost, they all imply spontaneous, genial delight—the recreative impulse inherent in a golden age, *locus amoenus* of soft primitivism.

I wish to illustrate recreative pastoral in several representative poems in *Hesperides*. These poems are marked by benevolence, geniality, and spontaneity; they unite man and nature via the pathetic fallacy; finally, they delineate "cleanly-*Wantonnesse*." These various characteristics are common to all the poems I will discuss. To speak of the characteristic mood of some, the relation of man and nature in others, and the cleanly wanton strategy for living the good life in still others would be to oversimplify the kind of experience communicated in any one poem. I intend, instead, to discuss, first, poems in which Hesperides

is spoken of as a pastoral realm, and second, poems using specific topoi relating to the Golden Age. To conclude, I will call attention to Herrick's uses of pastoral in a few lyrics on such favorite topics of his as weddings, flowers, and Julia.

One of Herrick's most anthologized poems is the introductory "Argument of his Book" (5.1).[15] One can easily find pastoral notions. He states his subjects: nature's bounty (flowers, dew, birds) and mysteries (twilight, fairies, how roses come red), "times transhifting" (the cyclically progressing seasons and ages of man) and ways of interpreting it through festivals and ceremonial objects (balm, oil, spices); finally, heaven and hell. The speaker is especially aware of nature's fertility, and its association with deity (dew, rain, the four sweet months, youth, love, fairies, festivals). The life of man has the same cyclical configuration as has nature's, and, as the assured, direct tone of the poem suggests, the speaker at least is perfectly content with this. His *otium* is connoted by the references to participation in ceremony, understanding of nature's secrets, assurance of heaven, acquaintance with Faerie. There is no wish to dominate, impose one's will upon, or transcend fate, nature, or the human condition. Winter, age, death are suggested, but cause no alarm—nothing painful or evil is associated with them. They are part of nature; there is no sense of unfulfilled longing or tragic incompleteness. Although Herrick uses no specific golden age topoi (such as nature's spontaneous production, eternal spring, absence of law, natural harmony of plants, animals and man), the general emotional ambience of the pleasant place and the sense of contentment and sensual fulfillment is strong. The speaker's attitude is paramount factor, golden age topoi or no.

The distinctiveness of this attitude lies in its cleanly-wanton flavor. Briefly to suggest some of the implications of this oxymoron is in order. It embodies what Kenneth Burke would call a "strategy for living." Its salient characteristic is a carefree unconcern for the kind of behavior desirable in confronting "seriously" the real world. Cleanly-wantonness postulates a decorous sensual indulgence which refines away feral impulse and allows man to enjoy nature and his appetites "wantonly," in an unashamed, unselfconscious and sinless (i.e., cleanly) way. The natural world Herrick describes is kept "cleanly" by images which fancifully veil facts like age and winter with gay and vigorous movement, and by personifications which show nature behaving with spontaneity and innocence. Sometimes, the sensuality is "cleanly" because the desire is artfully prolonged, not violently satiated. At other times, cleanly-wantonness involves the use of sentiment, fancy, or humor, or all three, to veil harsh realities. Although a lyric's ostensible subject may be *carpe diem,* unrequited love, or death, the mood of the poem is often at odds with, and takes precedence over, the didactic content.

"The Argument" introduces the cleanly-wanton attitude quite fully. The ceremonies and festivities described celebrate a decorous manner of interpreting and accepting natural flux, or remaining calm and content, of restraining despair and anger, of prolonging happiness and general good feeling. The attitude contingent upon these strategies is reflected in the relaxed, direct, calm assuredness of the tone. Cleanly wantonness is especially reflected in the character of the speaker-poet, who avoids harsh reality by unselfconsciously singing of spring, youth, love, and festival, and by relegating death and sadness to the background. Heaven and hell are mentioned, but rather offhandedly, at the end of the poem, as if to suggest that the persona is more interested in mood and enjoyment (and perhaps advertising the completeness of his book) than in intellectual acuteness, and that he is not even above a little fibbing. He may be thinking of *Hesperides'* companion volume, the *Noble Numbers*. But nothing is advertised about the blunt, often ugly realities of the epigrams and verse epistles which appear in the former volume. The poet is either fibbing, or unwilling to face unsettling reality.

Herrick has several other poems about his "booke," which project the same cleanly wanton innocence described above. In the second poem in the collection, "To His Muse" (5.2), lines 6-18 refer to beneficent nature as a place of song, love, *otium:*

> There with the Reed, thou mayst expresse
> The Shepherds Fleecie happinesse:
> And with thy *Eclogues* intermixe
> Some smooth, and harmlesse *Beucolicks.*
> There on a Hillock thou mayst sing
> Unto a handsom Shephardling;
> Or to a Girle (that keeps the Neat)
> With breath more sweet then Violet.
> There, there, (perhaps) such Lines as These
> May take the simple *Villages.*
> But for the Court, the Country wit
> Is despicable unto it.

These lines celebrate "Fleecie Happinesse"—the peaceful life close to nature and the sheep one cares for. The poet's muse is efficacious with simple country folk, who are immersed in song, love, and nature's bounty. The speaker pleads with her to control her desire to seek fame and fortune. The strongly felt fatherly affection of the speaker for his *"Mad maiden"* (imagine Virgil or Spenser, or even Horace, so invoking the exalted goddess to whom they owe the inspiration for prophetic utterance!) dramatizes the kind of cleanly existence she can enjoy "at home." In typical "cleanly wanton" fashion, attention is shifted away from mankind's potentially self-destructive exploratory urges, and mundane contingency in general, in favor of filial affection. The lively, engaging *icon* of the sweetly scented Muse sitting on a hill singing for the "handsome Shepherling" or shepherdess vividly depicts the cleanly wantonness of the pastoral life as a spontaneous burst of humble affection and self-fulfillment—just as the fatherly love of the speaker is.

In his occasional verses to the royal family, Herrick also speaks of his book as a realm of recreative pastoral. Two of these suggest in some details the return of the Golden Age effected by the messianic hero—in one case King Charles (25.2), in the other the Duke of York (108.1). These poems emphasize the recreative congeniality of the *locus amoenus* by giving a delightful turn to the commonplace dichotomy between court and country, king and shepherd. The speaker fancies that royalty not only complements the beauty of the pastoral realm (the country, or *Hesperides, "This Sacred Grove"* [107.2]) with its proper beneficence, but that the King or Prince is himself responsible for the Arcadian felicity.

> May his soft foot, where it treads,
> Gardens thence produce and Meads:
> And those Meddowes full be set
> With the Rose and Violet.

> (108.1 11. 13-18).

The prince's goodness makes that of the pastoral realm possible. The king or prince's beneficence is therefore equated with that of the Hesperidean gardens, at least in the mind of the speaker, who, as an unsophisticated creature of his environment, can see even royal virtue only in terms of his own experience. The prince is a "Chick of *Jove,*" a "Rose of *Jerico,*" a cleanly wanton creature himself. The King also becomes one when he is fancied to be the West's Genius whom nature welcomes as a blushing bride would her groom after a long, mourning widowhood (25.2), or, as the queen does when she is imagined to become *Lady of the Spring* and queen of the Hesperidean garden (107.2).

A second set of poems that illustrate recreative pastoral are those which contain specific references to the golden age. Two of these are "The Apparition of his Mistress calling him to Elysium" (205.5) and *"To Phyllis, to love, and live with him"* (192.1). In the former, the only one which makes comprehensive use of them, a ceremonial, cleanly atmosphere of refined and prolonged sensual beauty is created by classical ceremonial and Biblical references, and by gorgeously artificial imagery (gilding, purfling, enameling, tinselling). In this atmosphere appropriate for Elysium, the artificial reworking of nature is sinless, as is the wanton reveling of the inhabitants. The poem is pervaded with dancing, drinking, games, love, shining color and sound. Equally indigenous to Elysium are the speaker's fancy (the gilded and enameled nature, Anacreon, "Besmear'd with Grapes," reciting Herrick's own poetry as they "rage . . . drink and dance together," Beaumont and Fletcher as "Swans" and "Sirens," Jonson in "a Globe of Radiant fire") and his homely, genial wit (Jonson, enthroned as he is, is simply "our chiefe," the cock is "Bellman of the night"). The poem has been called "an invitation to die rather than to live."[16] It seems rather to be a dream vision, dispelled by the coming of the dawn. Besides, death has no place in the poem; its strategy is wholly conceived to celebrate vibrant and sinless life.

In the invitation poem, a cleanly wanton nature, personified as blessing Phyllis and "melting" her into dreams, replete with "blushing" and "simp'ring" fruit, is a perfect setting for the lovely, generous and protective shepherd-esses who attend the girl as their queen, singing, dancing, and bearing gifts. Golden age nature and innocent man are in complete harmony. Phyllis as queen, like the Queen of England, is not really a part of this, but her beauty, like the Queen's, complements it and inspires the undiscriminating, innocent, cleanly-wanton shepherds to give her a distinctive place.

A final poem which contains Golden Age topoi is "Corinna's *going a Maying.*" Man becomes part of nature ("budding girls and boys," clothes as "Foliage"), nature (the sun, the morning, the dawn) cares for and protects man, love and delight are freely enjoyed as "harmless follie" sanctioned by nature itself, and the deities (Flora, Apollo, Titan) who inhabit it bless it with sun, dew and flowers. The humor, spontaneous energy, sensuality, and childlike directness of the poem provide the cleanly wantonness which is inseparable in Herrick from the benevolence, generosity and fertility of the *locus amoenus,* and which the final inevitability of death cannot negate but only sanctify—which is, indeed, all the more reason for taking the "harmlesse follie of the time."

Before closing, I should like to refer to a few additional poems which incorporate recreative pastoral most successfully, and therefore show its pervasiveness in *Hesperides.* In "A Nuptial Song . . ." (112.3) the reader is simultaneously aware of the ennobling spiritual power of love, and of its wildly sensual side. The juxtaposition of fanciful idealism and humor is also cleanly-wanton strategy, aiming in this poem at celebration of an event of intense, idealized, but still human happiness. This is not done with solemn pietistic intensity but with playful, subtle wit suggested in the complex rhythms of each stanza, the lines of which are visually as well as aurally meandering. They range from two to five syllables, and at one point a dimeter line is forced to rime with a pentameter one, perhaps to suggest the forced but felicitous coupling the poem is all about. We are constantly pulled back from the ethereal and intensely sensual to the very real world. For example, a "smirk Butler" and a "Codled Cook" (exiting from his "Torrid Zone") run to see their new mistress; the guests wish the couple to multiply "like fish." Herrick keeps sensual impulse strongly in mind. The bridegroom is like Jove as he wildly tears up "like flakes of snow" the sheet in which his bride has been sewn. In stanza [Illegible Text], the bed itself is the subject:

> And to your more bewitching, see, the proud
> Plumpe Bed beare up, and swelling like a cloud,
> 　Tempting the too too modest; can
> 　　Yee see it brusle like a Swan,
> 　　　And you be cold
> To meet it, when it woo's and seemes to fold
> 　The Armes to hugge it? throw, throw
> Your selves into the mighty over-flow
> 　　　　Of that white Pride, and Drowne
> 　The night, with you, in floods of Downe.

The conceit is full of the kind of wit we have been discussing as one characteristic of Herrick's pastoral persona.

The speaker is innocent of appearing ridiculous in expressing the full vitality of his good humor, or the exuberance of his imagination, and in this he imitates (or perhaps excites) the exuberant mood of the bridal couple. This mood in the speaker is extended into the external world, in this case the bed itself; proud, plump, swelling, tempting, it is in its own way vital and genial. It seems to flirt with the couple, plumping itself up, bristling its feathers. Because this is amusing, it is cleanly-wanton, and in that the speaker sees the environment (even the conjugal bed) as benevolent and generous, he has a pastoral attitude. Herrick's cleanly wanton strategy has strong affinities with his pastoral strategy in that they both delineate the (poetic) experience of a comfortable, sinless, spiritually and sensually gratifying life of ease, contentment, freedom and love such as the "shadows of Elizium" have enjoyed from Homer to Drayton.

Many of Herrick's short poems on flowers also reveal his pastoral stance. Many of these are about transiency, or unrequited love, and the element of pathos is strong. But sentiment, fancy, even humor transform sadness into sweetness unconnected with tragic realities. "To the Willow Tree" (106.2) is about unrequited love—boy and girl weep all night under it, and wear willow garlands "Bedew'd with Teares," when the "Lovers Rose" is "laid aside forlorne." But loneliness and disappointment are not part of the experience of the poem. Rather we see the weeping, weary, neglected "Love-spent Youth, and love-sick Maid," and the cooling, protective, solicitous tree— "the only true plant." Not only the tree itself, but the speaker and even the neglected boy and girl behave in a cleanly-wanton and pastoral manner. The speaker shares the lovers' uninhibited spontaneity, although his own benevolence and concern, like the Willow's, softens the sadness, and helps heal the wound by giving the victims something to lean on, thus relieving the lover's despair, and focusing not on that but rather on the soothing concern of speaker and tree. Nature is seen as a source of rich enjoyment and love. Even though the vulnerability of human happiness is basic to the poem's intentions, the behavior of tree, speaker, and even the lovers (since they are like protected and comforted children) draws attention away from the fact and creates a relaxed, comforting attitude, which allows the reader (as well as the lovers) to indulge in cleanly sentiment.

The poem and its effects are typical of its kind. In many poems about flowers, the speaker's candid, full-hearted benevolence brings him so close to them that they can be described as a "sisterhood" of smiling virgins,[17] "Maiden Posies," "Poore Girls,"[18] "sweet Babes," "whimp-ring Younglings."[19] With the distance between man and nature so shortened, and because of the sensual as well as emotional sweetness, the poems project a cleanly and recreative experience. The speaker, as well as the reader, remains genial and relaxed, content with a fanciful and sentimental restatement of old truths playfully recast so as to lose any unsettling facets.

In a few of the Julia poems the girl is co-existent with the flowers as a creature of nature. The flowers sit in parliament in Julia's bosom, under a "Lawne" canopy, and vote the Rose the queen of flowers.[20] The rose, violet and primrose hang down their heads when Julia is sick, and are resurrected when she recovers.[21] Roses nestle, snuggle and blush in Julia's breast as in a nunnery.[22] The flowers themselves behave with geniality, spontaneity and benevolence, and Julia herself, as pastoral nature itself, is generous and fertile. The speaker's excitement and sense of ingenuous wonder in these poems reinforces the sensual vividness of the fanciful conceit itself, and points up further the innocent love, generosity and empathy with nature which marks a pastoral sensibility.

I think we have said enough to illustrate the kind of pastoral Herrick writes. He uses the characteristics of the "pleasant place"—nature's fertility, benevolence, and generosity, and soft primitive *otium*. He does not reflect systematically the full range of values associated with this concept—there is nothing specifically about Astrea dwelling with men, nature's spontaneous self-generation, or natural law. But *Hesperides,* or, at least, the variety of cleanly wanton verses we have looked at, does definitely project pastoral values. The characteristics of nature in the pleasant place are those which would cause its inhabitants to behave in a cleanly-wanton manner, to indulge in spontaneous, child-like acts which, within the confines of an *Hesperides,* are innocent. If we consider that seventeenth century definitions for "cleanly" (as the *O.E.D.* shows) would include *innocent, unstained, chaste, void of moral stain, graceful, well fashioned,* we can see how, in *Hesperides,* this kind of cleanliness would counteract such pejorative connotations of "wantonness" as *lewdness, cruelty, violence,* and combine with concepts such as *frivolous, giddy, luxuriant, robust, sportive* and *frolicsome.*

Herrick's pastoral cannot be discussed in terms of the figuring forth of "greater matters," or by isolating plaintive or moral intentions. Nor does it help to look for Empsonian double perspectives by which the urbane reader's values and responsibilities are seen as nobler, as well as more difficult to fulfill, than the Arcadian's. Herrick's Arcadia is "merely" a place of playful humor, fancy, and delicate sentiment. His pastoral personae respond to experience as do creatures of the Golden Age—with genial humility and buoyant, naive enthusiasm. They thus mirror the benevolence of the pleasant place—be it called Elysium, the fortunate isles, or Hesperides. Their behavior is characterized by passive contentment, child-like spontaneity, and faith and trust in one's fellow man, animals, and flowers. Although death and misfortune in love make them sad, the sentiment is a delicate and tender reflection of their sweetness and innocence. Their behavior is cleanly, that is, genial, spontaneous, and unsophisticated. Refined of destructive instincts, it is wanton in its simple immediacy. This kind of cleanly wanton behavior is naive, child-like, sometimes funny, but there is no suggestion that the sophisticated reader is better off. Given its golden age affinities, there is no possibility of this kind of conduct being available to Herrick's contemporaries. It is completely a clever and recreative fiction.

Certain key strategies guide this kind of cleanly wanton pastoralism. Mood is predominant over didactic intention. Christian ceremonies are used to suggest the goodness of sensual pleasure and the purity of female beauty, when destructive impulses are disciplined and pleasurable sensation artfully, decorously prolonged. Didactic topoi can be used, but the cleanly wanton mood is predominant and somber warning is absent; it just does not have a place in the Hesperidean emotional ambience. Nor does royal or civic virtue of the postlapsarian world, and kings and civic dignitaries are praised by being fancied to partake of the cleanly-wanton vision. Herrick's *Hesperides,* although it may not take us very far toward understanding all that is going on in Spenser's eclogues, Milton's elegies, or Marvell's lyrics, does characterize rather richly and fully one kind of pastoral sensibility.

Notes

1. The malleability of classical pastoral to Christian moral themes is analyzed in E. W. Tayler, *Nature and Art in Renaissance Literature* (New York: Columbia U. Press, 1964). For Renaissance didactic pastoral's use of prosody, "low" diction, classical allusion and periphrasis, see Dorothy McCoy, *Tradition and Convention: A Study of Periphrasis in English Pastoral Poetry 1557-1715,* Studies in English Literature, Vol. 5 (The Hague: Moulton, 1965), and Bernard Groom, *The Diction of Poetry from Spenser to Bridges* (Toronto: U. of Toronto Press, 1955). A number of scholars have worked with the manner in which statements about the fall, ambition, political corruption, mutability, and grace are adapted to the pastoral mode: Northrop Frye, "The Structure of Imagery in *The Faerie Queene,*" *Fables of Identity* (New York: Harcourt, Brace & World, 1963), Hallett Smith, *Elizabethan Poetry* (Cambridge: Harvard U. Press, 1952), Rosemund Tuve, *Images and Themes in Five Poems by Milton* (Cambridge: Harvard U. Press, 1957), Donald M. Friedman, *Marvell's Pastoral Art* (Berkeley: U. of California Press, 1970), and Patrick Cullen, *Spenser, Marvell and Renaissance Pastoral* (Cambridge: Harvard U. Press, 1970). Cullen makes interesting distinctions between "Mantuanesque" and "Arcadian" pastoral. The former is for purposes of Christian polemic; the latter concerns itself with the ease and contentment of the *pastor felix.*

The recreative intentions of pastoral are delineated by Renato Poggioli ("The Oaten Flute," *Harvard Library Bulletin,* II [1957], 148-84), and Bruno Snell ("Arcadia," *The Discovery of the Mind* [1953; rpt. New York: Harper's, 1960]). These men show that Arcadia is a place of pathos, fancy, and dream, replete with wish fulfillment, sentimentality, and solitary communion with nature. Charles W. Hiatt speaks of sentimentality and self-indulgent lyricism as characteristic of Virgilian pastoral; see "The

Integrity of Pastoral: A Basis for Definition," *Genre,* 5 (1972), pp. 1-30. In an essay entitled "The Renaissance Perversion of Pastoral" (*J.H.I.,* 22 [1961], 254-61), S. K. Heninger, Jr. suggests that Renaissance pastoral's didactic intentions are a "perversion" of the genre's pristine focus on an ideal order and simplicity. This kind of judgement, it seems to me, is unfair. To say that "pure" pastoral should provide a therapeutic escape from the mundane world, and should not be used to "glance at greater matters" *via* satire, moral allegory and Christian iconography is to disparage the complex effects of which Renaissance pastoral is capable in the hands of poets such as Spenser, Milton, Sidney, Drayton, and Marvell.

2. R.H. Deming, "The Classical Ceremonial in the Poetry of Robert Herrick," Diss. Univ. of Wisconsin, 1965, Chapter 1; DeWitt Starnes and E.W. Talbert, *Classical Myth and Legend in Renaissance Dictionaries* (Chapel Hill: U. of North Carolina Press, 1955), pp. 308-16.

3. A. Bartlett Giamatti, *The Earthly Paradise and the Renaissance Epic* (Princeton, New Jersey: Princeton University Press, 1966), pp. 18-19.

4. Ibid., p. 19.

5. Starnes and Talbert, *Classical Myth,* p. 310.

6. Ibid., p. 309.

7. Ibid., p. 310.

8. Ibid.

9. Ernst Curtius, *European Literature and the Latin Middle Ages,* trans. Willard R. Trask (1953; rpt. New York: Harper and Row, 1963), p. 192.

10. Ibid.

11. Arthur O. Lovejoy and George Boas, *Primitivism and Related Ideas in Antiquity* (1925; rpt. New York: Octagon Books, 1965), pp. 14-15.

12. Curtius, *European Literature,* p. 87.

13. As is the case with the Golden Age topoi, that of the *locus amoenus* could be used for a variety of purposes with which I am not concerned. See David Evett, "Paradise's Only Map: *The Topus* of the *Locus Amoenus* and the Structure of Marvell's *Appleton House,*" *PMLA,* 85 (1970), pp. 504-13. This essay shows instances where "the full expressive force of the *topos* is exerted toward achieving some kind of moral seriousness (p. 506). It also shows that the *topos* could serve as an illusory "refuge from the processes of time and mortality" (p. 507).

14. F. W. Moorman, *Robert Herrick* (London: John Lane, 1910), p. 110; J. Max Patrick, ed., *The Complete Poetry of Robert Herrick* (New York: Doubleday, 1963), p. 5; G. L. M. Smith, "Herrick's *Hesperides,*" *MLR,* 9 (1914), pp. 373-74.

15. The definitive edition of Herrick is L. C. Martin, ed., *Robert Herrick's Poetic Works* (Oxford: Clarendon Press, 1956). Hereafter cited as *Works.* Poems are identified by page number, and the number of the poem on the page (i.e., *Works* 5.2=page 5, second poem).

16. R. S. Forsythe, "'The Passionate Shepherd' and English Poetry," *PMLA,* 40 (1925), 705.

17. "To a Bed of Tulips," *Works,* p. 184.1.

18. "To Violets," *Works,* p. 83.

19. "To Primroses fill'd with morning-dew," *Works,* 104.1.

20. "The Parliament of Roses to Julia," *Works,* 8.2.

21. "Upon Julia's Recovery," *Works,* 7.4.

22. "Upon Roses," *Works,* 25.3.

Barry Weller (essay date 1999)

SOURCE: "The Epic as Pastoral: Milton, Marvell, and the Plurality of Genre," in *New Literary History,* Vol. 30, No. 1, 1999, pp. 143-57.

[*In the following essay, Weller maintains that Andrew Marvell's poetry rehearses the pastoral motifs that inform John Milton's epic poem* Paradise Lost, *and he examines how the lyric mode is used in the expansive form of the epic.*]

When Milton begins *Paradise Regained* by defining himself as "I who erewhile the happy garden sung,"[1] he is echoing the lines—possibly discarded by Virgil, possibly even non-Virgilian—which prefaced Renaissance editions of *The Aeneid:*

> Ille ego, qui quondam gracili modulatus avena
> carmen, et egressus silvis vicina coegi
> ut quamvis avido parerent arva colono,
> gratum opus agricolis; at nunc horrentia Martis
>
> [I am he who once tuned my song on a slender reed,
> then, leaving the woodland, constrained the neighbouring
> fields to serve the husbandman, however grasping—a work
> welcome to farmers; but now of Mars' bristling (arms and the man I sing)][2]

Virgil here is of course defining the shape of a canonical poetic career, moving from pastoral to georgic to epic, which his own works established. Later poets imitated both this progress of poetic ambition and these lines. Spenser's version of this gesture is the most familiar:

> Lo I the man, whose Muse whilome did maske,
>   As time her taught, in lowly Shepheards weeds,
>   Am now enforst a far vnfitter taske,
>   For trumpets sterne to chaunge mine Oaten reeds,
>   And sing of Knights and Ladies gentle deeds.[3]

The remarkable thing about Milton's use of these lines is that he retrospectively identifies *Paradise Lost* as a pastoral, a poem about "the happy garden"—as opposed to the *true* epic, *Paradise Regained,* which he is about to write. No one familiar with Milton's aggressive approach to inherited literary traditions will be surprised by such metageneric discourse. Nevertheless, few of Milton's critics have followed this cue; even Empson, in his enterprising pursuit of the pastoral mode's transformations, apparently hesitated to regard all of *Paradise Lost* as a pastoral. Moreover, the allusive gesture raises other perplexities about how Milton regarded the shape of his own career. Once again, even critics who have noted the Virgilian signature (for example, Lawrence Lipking)[4] have declined to explore its implications for Milton's self-understanding. Is there a Miltonic georgic, or does *Paradise Lost* occupy the place of both pastoral and georgic in preparation for Milton's efforts to sing the better, but unspectacular "fortitude / Of patience and heroic martyrdom" (*PL* 9.31-32) (unspectacular, because even *Paradise Regained* gives us only the private version of Christ's abstinence from asserting His own will as separate from that of the Father). Perhaps it is the political writings which dominated the middle part of Milton's life and career that should be regarded as his georgic: plowing the fields of the commonwealth and sowing the seeds of a new political order to come. That is a speculation for a different kind of essay, of the more innocent genre, is an indispensable topic for Milton's poetic enterprise—or, indeed, as Anthony Low has shown in *The Georgic Revolution,* for the generic and political bearings of seventeenth-century poetry in general.[5]

Low takes account of the opening lines of *Paradise Regained,* but directs his attention less toward Milton's retrospective redefinition of *Paradise Lost* than toward the ways in which georgic elements reshape the conception of heroic action in *Paradise Regained:* "Like the *Georgics, Paradise Regained* does not describe a pastoral retreat from responsibility but instead dwells on small, recurrent actions, often trivial or inglorious in themselves, that nevertheless converge towards a turning-point in the world's history." He reaches the strong and suggestive conclusion that "Milton chose in effect to write his *Aeneid* first and then his *Georgics,* and thereby to reverse the usual priorities."[6] Such a reconfiguration of generic hierarchies seems entirely within the scope of Milton's engagement with tradition, but in exploring the generic status of *Paradise Regained* Low leaves in place the assumption that *Paradise Lost* is indeed "epic"—"his *Aeneid*"—despite Milton's provocative hints to the contrary.

Low's emphasis on the significance for Milton of "small, recurrent actions, often trivial or inglorious in themselves" is also helpful (though its immediate application invites comparison with Stanley Fish's descriptions of *Paradise Regained* as an epic of *inaction*).[7] Do such actions, however, belong exclusively to the world of georgic, rather than pastoral, poetry? The large-scale argument and ethical drive of Law's book strongly opposes pastoral *otium* ("as pastoral retreat from responsibility") to the georgic's higher valuation of labor, but Milton's most explicitly pastoral poems, *Lycidas* and *Epitaphium Damonis,* foreground

the *duties,* not the leisure, of both the literal and metaphorical shepherd, even if his will to fulfill such obligations, to continue his work, is temporarily suspended by grief or a sense of futility. The plaintive refrain of *Epitaphium Damonis—Ite domum impasti, domino iam non vacat, agni;* "Go home unfed, my lambs, your troubled master is not free to tend you"—gives formal expression to the recurrent demands of pastoral labor (II. 18, 26, 35, and so on). This periodic rhythm, in which the shepherd participates no less than the agricultural laborer of the georgic, is essential to the contrast between epic and pastoral temporality which this essay seeks to explore—and which may partially explain Milton's implied classification of *Paradise Lost* as pastoral. As for "actions trivial and inglorious in themselves" which nevertheless "converge toward a turning-point in the world's history," it is hardly necessary to note that the central event of *Paradise Lost,* considered simply as an action, is the plucking of a fruit.

If the allusion with which Milton opens *Paradise Regained* redirects the reader's attention to pastoral, one way of considering what status and force that genre might have had for him by the second half of the seventeenth century is to revisit the work of Andrew Marvell, the contemporary writer who might have been best equipped to ponder Milton's challenging evocation of pastoral. Marvell is arguably the century's most distinguished exponent of the genre. As Paul Alpers comments, "Marvell's unusual self-consciousness about pastoral fictions and conventions makes him not just a poet to study, but a collaborator in critical analysis and definition."[8] Anthony Low observes Marvell's affinities with the georgic enterprise of revaluing agricultural labor—his central pastoral figure, after all, is not a shepherd but a mower—but stops short of claiming Marvell for georgic poetry, assigning him rather a place "among the most subtle of English *pastoralists.*"[9]

Marvell is in any case a contemporary poet in whom Milton certainly took an interest. Milton had known him at least as early as 1653, when he recommended him to the Council of State as Assistant Latin Secretary; even though this initial recommendation failed to gain Marvell the appointment, he eventually succeeded to Milton's own position as Latin Secretary in 1657, and his and Milton's paths continued to cross as servants of the Commonwealth. Although Marvell's lyrics went unpublished until 1681, after his death, the complex of personal and political relationships between Milton and Marvell strengthens the surmise that the older poet would have read Marvell's major lyrics, dating from the 1650s, in manuscript form. The relations between Milton and Marvell have been sensitively and astutely explored by Judith Herz. Herz, however, focuses primarily on the influence of Milton's early poems on Marvell's lyrics, and she concludes that "in *Paradise Lost* one does not find too many clear traces of Milton's reading of Marvell."[10]

While there are perspectives from which this last assertion might be disputed, the positive and historical connections between the two poets matter less than the opportunity their works offer to consider the lyric and epic embodiments—face-to-face, as it were—of a shared set of narrative and even theological possibilities. Surprisingly, Marvell, especially in his mower poems, rehearses in a pastoral, quintessentially lyric mode the motifs which will inform *Paradise Lost;* and it is tempting to take the opening of *Paradise Regained* as testimony that Milton saw and acknowledged such a connection; that is, that he understood that such topics as enclosure and freedom, lost innocence and the consciousness of mortality, errancy and the longing to find a "home" in the world might belong to the province of pastoral and georgic as well as epic. If Milton tacitly claims that his sprawling, ambitious storytelling may best be understood as pastoral, Marvell explores the question of what narrative—arguably the narrative which sets the terms of human history—looks like when distilled and compressed into the more traditional dimensions of pastoral lyric. How does narrative possibility, deliberately circumscribed and held in check, inflect the shape and mood of a lyric? What claims can lyric make for itself as a narrative medium against the hectoring expansiveness of epic poetry?

If this description of the epic seems prematurely to load the dice, it echoes the rhetoric of Marvell's own lyrics which always imply awareness of the potential grandiosity of their topics. At the threshold of *Upon Appleton House* (ironically, perhaps, the longest of his poems) he announces the ideology of lyric; ostensibly describing the "sober frame" of Nun-Appleton House, the language implicitly endorses its own style and sense of proportion:

> Humility alone designs
> Those short but admirable lines,
> By which, ungirt and unconstrained,
> Things greater are in less contained.[11]

I call such language the ideology of lyric because Marvell already echoes Donne's distaste for "chronicle" and "half-acre tombs" and his preference for building "pretty rooms" or stanzas in the unassuming but wholly adequate space of songs and sonnets. At the same time *Upon Appleton House* makes the alignment of genre with length less literal or quantifiable. Despite the scope of its argument and its seven hundred seventy-six lines—approximately the size of a book of *Paradise Lost*—*Upon Appleton House* arguably retains the sensibility of a lyric: that is, each of its conceits or images is developed with a concentrated wit that is serenely indifferent to the poem's forward movement. In discussing the "precision and symbolic secrecy" of Marvell's emblematic images, Rosalie Colie speaks of "the actual and conceptual space around each of [their] elements"[12] which forces the reader to supply missing connections and applications. The emblematic seems the most spatialized, the least narrative of poetry's representational possibilities. Does it also require something like pastoral leisure—a leisure antithetical to narrative momentum and linearity—to unravel such enigmatic significances?

Colie entitles her chapter devoted to emblems and emblematic poetic practice "Small Forms: *Multo in Parvo*,"

and the Latin phrase encapsulates the peculiar densities of seventeenth-century lyric. (For a non-Marvellian example, consider the political content of Lovelace's "The Grasshopper," as expounded by Don Cameron Allen.)[13] Marvell appears consciously, even aggressively, to avoid the heroic mode of narration in both *Upon Appleton House* and "An Horatian Ode upon Cromwell's Return from Ireland." If the potentially epic or public content of these poems threatens to burst the boundaries of lyric discourse (like the "three-forked lightning" of Cromwell dividing his "fiery way" through his own allies ["An Horatian Ode" 13, 16]), the poet has nevertheless refrained from claiming on his own behalf the position of epic bard. Marvell has always been discussed as a self-consciously "minor" poet, cowed perhaps by his distinguished contemporary's achievement of his "vast design" ("On Mr. Milton's *Paradise Lost*" 2). Nevertheless the firm and repeated engagement of his lyrics with the imaginative terrain of the epic suggests a more sustained argument about the virtues of *multum in parvo* and a firm, not necessarily modest, assertion about the narrative efficacy of lyric—as though the potency of plot might be experienced even more intensely in the narrative kernel than in its discursive full expansion. A cultural politics—more ramified and elusive than the question of party adherences—may have strengthened his reluctance to assume the prerogatives of an epic stance. Recent criticism has foregrounded the linkage between gender and genre, but this line of inquiry might be supplemented by further consideration of the ways in which Donne, Marvell and other seventeenth-century lyric poets, though male, perceived themselves as socially marginal. (Marvell may have felt estranged from masculine privilege for other reasons too.)[14] The motives—political, esthetic, even psychological—for repudiating the authority and putative centrality of "public," large-scale forms such as epic narrative were clearly multiple, and this essay returns, at least briefly, to such questions in its conclusion.

Marvell's general address to the aesthetics of scale may be clarified by examination of a poem which supplies a particular instance of "Things greater . . . in less contained" and suggests emergent intimacies between Marvell's lyrics and Milton's epic (*Upon Appleton House* 44). If "The Mower to the Glowworms" were read without its title, it would be a kind of riddle poem, since it is not until the third stanza, midway through the poem, that "Ye living lamps" and "Ye country comets" are finally named as "glowworms," and the suspended identification solicits the cosmic and political contexts which the evocation of glowworms will deflate:

> Ye living lamps, by whose dear light
> The nightingale does sit so late,
> And studying all the summer night,
> Her matchless songs does meditate;
>
> Ye country comets, that portend
> No war, nor prince's funeral,
> Shining unto no higher end
> Than to presage the grass's fall;

> ("The Mower to the Glowworms" 1-8)

In the high style of seventeenth-century verse (the Miltonic style, for example) "ye living lamps" might well be the stars and planets or the angelic intelligences that animate them; "Ye country comets" extends the astronomical discourse but, with a parodic stance of bumpkin bashfulness, disowns the national consequences of light which "portend[s] / No war, prince's funeral." However, the disavowal contains a sly kicker: if these comets shine to "no higher end / Than to presage the grass's fall," they shine for the most inclusive end of all, for "All flesh is grass," and as "The Mower's Song" declares, "flow'rs, and grass, and I and all, / Will in one common ruin fall" (21-22). Indeed, the fall occurs over and over again throughout Marvell's pastoral poems: Damon the Mower cuts his own ankle, and "there among the grass fell down, / By his own scythe, the Mower mown" and the speaker of "The Garden" "Stumbling on melons . . . Ensnared with flowers" falls "on grass" ("Damon the Mower" 79-80; "The Garden" 39-40). The fact that these recurrent falls are pratfalls, comic rather than tragic events, makes its own comment on the lofty import of *the* Fall; falling, in a natural setting, Marvell seems to say, is too endemic to the clumsy, perishable stuff of human flesh to evoke either surprise or lasting regret. Where the narrative of epic may differ from that of lyric is in the epic premise of one-time, irrevocable events which shape and enchain sequential history.

The third stanza of Marvell's poem moves even closer to the world (and words) of *Paradise Lost:*

> Ye glowworms, whose officious flame
> To wandering mowers shows the way,
> That in the night have lost their aim,
> And after foolish fires do stray.
>
> ("The Mower to the Glowworms" 9-12)

The "officious flame" of the glowworms will become, in an epic frame, Raphael's description of the stars and planets as "those bright luminaries / Officious" (*PL* 8.98-99; in both instances it seems possible to hear the modern sense of "officious" intruding upon the more seventeenth-century sense of "serviceable"). It is perhaps at this moment, too, that Milton offers his response to Marvell's argument that "small is beautiful"; when Adam seems shocked at the wastefulness of the "great architect"'s design, Raphael says,

>   let it speak
> The maker's high magnificence, wh built
> So spacious, and his line stretched out so far;
> That man may know he dwells not in his own
>
> (*PL* 8.100-3)

"The wandering mowers" to whom the glowworm's light "shows the way" are Marvell's pastoral equivalent of a postlapsarian Adam and Eve; the conjunction of "way" and "wandering" in the final lines of the epic is almost too familiar to need citation ("They hand in hand with wandering steps and slow, / Through Eden took their solitary way" [*PL* 12.648-49]), although, notoriously, wandering

and errancy mark the reader's apprehension of Milton's Eden even before its inhabitants have incurred expulsion.

The "foolish fires" of the next lines anticipate one of *Paradise Lost*'s most famous similes, comparing Satan to a will-o'-the-wisp (or "wandering fire") as he leads Eve to the forbidden fruit (*PL* 9.634-43). Epic simile is, in effect, abbreviated lyric, often expressing a yearning for the pastoral world its own events disrupt or displace—only one of the ways in which epic narrative thematizes homecoming and its opposite. Marvell's lyric also encapsulates its plot as loss ("That I shall never find my home"), and describes this loss in terms which resonate for *Paradise Lost* ("For she my mind hath so displaced" ["The Mower to the Glowworms" 16, 15]). *Paradise Lost* narrates the mind's dis-placement not so much in terms of self-alienation as in terms of its unmooring from a particular place, from an origin to which its identity is referable; what remains is to discover that the mind is its own place and that the renunciation of Eden will produce a "paradise within thee, happier far" (*PL* 12.587). In this sense *Paradise Lost* is as much an epic of subjectivity as its Romantic or post-Romantic successors, and it may be this investment in subjective experience which encourages Milton to claim alliance with the lyric at least through its specifically pastoral embodiments.

"Damon the Mower" and "The Garden" have already been mentioned in the context of the Fall as pratfall, but troping the fall—and compressing its tragic and comic possibilities into a single image—is only one example of how Marvell's pastoral poems incorporate the narrative possibilities and concerns with human freedom and agency that are writ large in *Paradise Lost*. The speaker of "The Mower against Gardens" might be inveighing against the divine gardener Himself when he complains that the gardener enclosed

> A dead and standing pool of air
> And a more luscious earth for them did knead,
> Which stupified them while it fed.
>
> (6-8)

Enclosure in itself precipitates the fall, fostering a longing for the "wild and fragrant innocence" of "the sweet fields"; without this fortunate fall, Eden would be a tyrant's "green seraglio," inhabited by "eunuchs" of the human will (34, 32, 27). "The Mower against Gardens" does not enact the narrative of transgression which would break the garden's protective but suffocating limits, but it does suggest the necessity of this plot.

"The Garden," on the other hand, has a more complicated and ambivalent relation to the enclosed space of both garden and lyric—in punning terms, the lyric plot. If the formality and boundedness of the garden represent the space of lyric utterance, "The Garden" offers two ways of imagining the relation of lyric to the more indefinite duration and extension of narrative (including, of course, the narrative of epic): it is, on the one hand, exempt from the mystifications, the vain amazements, of the public spaces in which the linear entailments of historical narrative unfold, but it also supplies the space in which engagements with a more strenuous world of political and erotic imperatives may be rehearsed. At least initially, "The Garden" suggests that gardens are places where narrative is preempted:

> How vainly men themselves amaze
> To win the palm, the oak, or bays
> And their uncessant labours see
> Crowned from single herb or tree,
> Whose short and narrow verged shade
> Does prudently their toils upbraid,
> While all flow'rs and all trees do close
> To weave the garlands of repose.
> . . .
> No white nor red was ever seen
> So am'rous as this lovely green.
>
> (1-8, 17-18)

The plots of erotic love, statesmanship, sainthood, and athletic or military prowess are already anticipated within the garden, but the verb "close" ("all flow'rs and all trees do close") has ominous undertones that warn against a premature resolution which depends, among other things, upon the exile of other human bodies:

> Such was that happy garden-state,
> While man there walked without a mate:
> . . .
> Two paradises 'twere in one
> To live in paradise alone.
>
> (57-58, 63-64)

"The Garden" cannot unequivocally embrace this image of self-sufficiency, and the verdant withdrawal of the mind, "from pleasures less," finds less a supplement than a counterpoise in the image of the bird who "sits,

and sings . . . till prepared for longer flight" (41, 53, 55); the solitude and repose of the garden do not foreclose but enable—enable, for example, a transcendence of (even an escape from) their own forms of transcendence.

Thus, whether "The Garden" aborts potential narratives, proleptically assimilates them, or presents lyric as narrative's point of departure, it seems questionable to reserve the term "narrative" for events which occur in public spaces. If lyric is a figuration of experience outside of history—an improbable transcendence, unless lyrics themselves have no determinate origins—what status do we accord to its internal movement? It is of course possible to insist on a strong separation between history and other manifestations of temporality, but the term "narrative," which encodes no such distinction, threatens this notional boundary. The sequence of moments within a poem always produces not only a single but a double narrative: the possibly illusory trace of a movement of intellect and feeling to be derived from the poem, and the successive stages of making meaning and connection which the reader's progress through the poem enacts (and it is the spe-

cific contribution of reader-response criticism, at its most rigorous, to model this second kind of narrative). Pastoral, in any case, provides a middle term between a critical definition of lyric which emphasizes its capacity to arrest, freeze, and remove its happening from the flux of history (to paraphrase Sharon Cameron in *Lyric Time*[15]) and an account of narrative which foregrounds its mimesis of historical events. Things clearly happen in the pastoral: ploughing, sowing, harvesting and gleaning, the breeding, herding, and slaughter of livestock, birth and dying—not to mention the gratuitous embellishment and celebration of these compulsive rhythms by song, dance, and festival. To deny these repetitive sequences a place in history—or to declare them non-narrative because they *are* repetitive—would be to make political history the only history that matters. Moreover, it is in relation to the cyclical character of pastoral narrative that Milton's identification of *Paradise Lost* is, theologically at least, most significant. While the events of *Paradise Lost* seem to constitute a singular narrative, and are thus far epic, it is by no means necessary—perhaps even spiritually myopic—to suppose that they have occurred once and for all. The archangel Michael, prompting Adam and Eve to rebuild their paradise within, surely implies that rebellion, fall, repentance, regeneration, the loss and recovery of heaven or of Eden are narrative potentialities of individual lives. By seeing the epic as pastoral, Milton incorporates human cycles of spiritual struggle into the epic dimensions of Christian narrative. The incidents of Christian history are always figural, always atemporally available to the believer; if epic imitates events which are locked into a particular sequence of imperial emergence or decay, spiritually significant events will escape the confines of its narrative. Not surprisingly, Milton uses the pastoral mode for his "Ode on the Morning of Christ's Nativity" which shatters the unidirectional linearity of history by urging his poem—and the reader—to get to the stable before the wise men do.

Upon Appleton House likewise enacts the sense that history can be entered, or reentered, at multiple moments as the "tawny mowers" move through the high grain of the estate like the "Israelites . . . Walking on foot through a green sea" (389-90). Miltonic similes offer comparable experiences of transhistorical montage as the image of rebel angels, swept by waves of hellfire, fades into the (ahistorical? contemporary?) image of fallen leaves in an Umbrian vale (or is Vallombrosa the valley of the shadow of death?), which yields in turn to a view of Pharaoh's army overwhelmed by the Red Sea—only to reinstate the visual rhyme of Lucifer's fallen followers (*PL* 1.301-2). Historical boundaries are not the only ones to dissolve in *Upon Appleton House;* the farmworker Thestylis (herself a surrogate for the poet, as Alpers notes [*WP* 243]) *knows* that the poet has compared the mowers to the Jews leaving Egypt:

> 'He called us Israelites;
> But now, to make his saying true,
> Rails rain for quails, for manna dew.'
>
> (406-8)

Is Thestylis outside or inside the poet's consciousness? Has the poet verified his comparison by deploying the narrative to *make* it true? Does the distinction between the figural and the empirical matter?

Significantly, the pastoral freedom of the imagination is seen as requiring a georgic preparation, a clearing of the ground; the labor of mowing produces

> A new and empty face of things,
> A levelled space, as smooth and plain
> As cloths for Lely stretched to stain.

> (442-44)

Not only does "stain" suggest that Lely's canvas may be most valuable when blank, but even God's handiwork seems most potent at the threshold of realization: "The world when first created sure / Was such a table rase and pure" (445-46). In this context the political project of the Levellers ("this naked equal flat / Which Levellers take pattern at" [449-50]) appears creative as well as destructive, and the following stanzas associate the close-cropped surface of "polished grass" with the mirrors of art ("A landskip drawn in looking-glass") and science ("multiplying glasses," i.e., microscopes)—media of reflection and knowledge (457, 458, 462). In "Damon the Mower" the title figure also stakes the value of his labor on its power to expose: "This scythe of mine discovers wide / More ground than all his [the shepherd's] sheep do hide" (51-52). Perhaps it is not surprising that the poet who could envision the spiritual achievement of "Annihilating all that's made / To a green thought in a green shade" ("The Garden" 47-48) would devote so much attention to the mind's powers to undo the world as part of its (re)making, but it is a conception of work, both intellectual and imaginative, which unexpectedly links Marvell's poetics to the projects of twentieth-century philosophy.

Inevitably the mower's georgic labor links him to the ultimate figure of erasure: "For Death thou art a Mower too" (Damon the Mower" 88). The ground which the mower's work—and the georgic work of art—reveals is mortality. If Marvell tropes the pastoral tradition by substituting a mower for a shepherd, it has less to do with the cultural politics surrounding the contemporary status of labor than with a desire to strengthen the dignity of pastoral—to supply the weight of labor to its almost weightless sense of freedom and to deepen the consciousness of mortality that pervades the lives of shepherds, farmers and, for that matter, poets. Pastoral conventionally concedes that its world is not exempt from death—*Et in Arcadia ego*[16]—but that acknowledgment might well be regarded as too insouciant or perfunctory. Even in Marvell's poetic world, the sense of threat is muted: Damon brings Juliana "the harmless snake . . . Disarmèd of its teeth and sting," but the reason that Juliana prefers the shepherd is surely not that his gifts are superior or that he sweats less, but that tending flocks evokes less awareness of death than the sharp strokes of Damon's scythe which cause the grass to wither ("Damon the Mower" 35-36).[17]

Although the mower participates in a cycle of agricultural activity, the stages of this cycle, from sowing to harvest, provide a sharper temporal punctuation than the ebb and flow of herders' activity. The georgic, in other words, supplies a middle term between the presumptive linearity and the irreversibility of secular history (on which epic narrative putatively models itself) and the relaxed, repetitive eddies of pastoral's extrahistorical events. Marvell does not compromise the meditative space of pastoral by anchoring it in the georgic's less open-ended temporality but displays the wit, for which T. S. Eliot famously praised him, of recognizing, as "implicit in the expression of every experience, . . . other kinds of experience which are possible."[18] One might argue that in this instance the wit is redundant: that the pastoral already knows what kinds of experience it tacitly defers or holds at bay—just as the reply of Ralegh's skeptical nymph to the plea of Marlowe's ardent shepherd (both wholly permissible expressions of the pastoral mode) can seem a trifle literal-minded. However, in the context of this essay, the more important aspect of Marvell's pastoral practice is not that it recognizes that "flowers do fade" and "wayward winter" beckons but that without renouncing its own particularity it opens onto other genres: rehearsing the potential elements of large-scale, even epic narrative, and incorporating the gravity of georgic's rural vision. Eliot's definition of wit, if extended to mode or genre, either dissolves the very idea of such species or insists on their necessary complementarity, even interpenetration. As they follow their strikingly different poetic talents and inclinations, both Milton and Marvell discover in the always controvertible rules of genre new opportunities to debate the very stakes of literary representation.

Needless to say, if Milton invites readers to revisit *Paradise Lost* as a kind of pastoral, he does not suppose that pastoral involves an evasion of that "mortal taste" on which the poem's opening lines insist. As Book IX of *Paradise Lost* had begun with a critique of epic presuppositions, the beginning of *Paradise Regained* invokes Virgil to comment aggressively on the post-Virgilian, and non-Christian, hierarchy of genres, but these lines also prompt a particular rereading of *Paradise Lost,* in which its events belong not to the "absolute past" of traditional epic (see Bakhtin, elaborating Goethe[19]) but to an immediate and renewable present of spiritual experience, a pastoral of the soul. Still, a pastoral *Paradise Lost* is only one of the generically plural possibilities of reading that the poem generates; just as Christian history is both atemporal *and* linear—in the epic sweep from first Adam to second, from creation to apocalypse—its poetic representation must fulfill as well as resist a chronologically structured narrative pattern.

Reading a book, especially in the age of print, is the very pattern of a spiritual experience. There is no place in which it necessarily occurs ("To teach thee that God attributes to place / No sanctity, if none be thither brought" [*PL* 9.836-37]); its events occur in an eternal present, as conventions of critical discourse corroborate; and it cannot supply something which the supplicant for grace or understanding does not already possess:

> who reads
> Incessantly, and to his reading brings not
> A spirit and judgment equal or superior . . .
> Uncertain and unsettled still remains,
> Deep-versed in books and shallow in himself
>
> (*PR* 4.322-24, 325-26)

Could a radical practice, such as Milton's, of reading or of spiritual freedom—they are virtually the same—accept a prescriptive or normative account of the values which an epic promulgates? E. M. W. Tillyard defines the epic poet as "the mouthpiece of the age," who "must be centered in the normal, he must measure the crooked by the straight, he must exemplify that sanity which has been claimed for true genius. No pronounced homosexual, for instance, could succeed in the epic, not so much for being one as for what his being one cuts him off from."[20] If Marvell and other seventeenth-century poets did shy away from the pretensions of epic, it may well have been from such hegemonic complacencies that they recoiled. Other critics, including Bakhtin and Lukacs, have expressed, less repulsively than Tillyard, the sense that epic narrative entails a unanimous evaluation of events from an "absolute past." But when the epic narrates sacred events, it seems theologically impossible for a believer to regard them as "absolutely past"; that spiritual contemporaneity has a secular double in the present tense of the reader's subjectivity—that is, the moment in which the reading occurs. It is debatable whether the critics who have been mentioned articulate even the implied ideology of epic, but the *experience* of epic has always been more diverse. *The Aeneid,* for example, mourns the victims, or incidental casualties, of the Roman empire's inception far more than it celebrates its sober, stricken founder—even St. Augustine wept for Dido—and *Paradise Lost,* like all of Milton's poetry, is saturated in nostalgia for non-Christian realms of imaginative experience. The religious and literary motives for preserving a reader's freedom mesh with one another, and that freedom includes the prerogative of reading the epic narrative with a sense of its plural generic possibilities—to read it, for example, as lyric, as elegy, as pastoral, as georgic, and not as the triumphalist voice of a patriarchal culture. The allusive gesture with which Milton opens *Paradise Regained* does not so much diminish, as enrich, *Paradise Lost,* with a nod not only to the varied world of poetic pastoralism (and perhaps to Marvell as its contemporary exponent) but to the generic pluralism of epic itself.

Notes

I wish to thank Jane Hedley for the opportunity to present an initial version of this essay on a panel of the 1997 Modern Language Association Convention; Kathryn Stockton and Karen Brennan for their encouragement to develop the talk into an essay; and Robert Caserio and Herbert Tucker for their perceptive suggestions for revision.

1. John Milton, *Paradise Regained, John Milton,* ed. Stephen Orgel and Jonathan Goldberg (Oxford, 1991); references to Milton's poems will be to this edition and cited in text by poem, book, and/or line number.

2. Virgil, *Eclogues, Georgics, Aeneid I-VI,* with tr. H. Rushton Fairclough (Cambridge, Mass., 1935), pp. 240-41.

3. Edmund Spenser, *The Faerie Queene,* bk. 1, Proem, st. 1, II. 1-5, ed. A. C. Hamilton (London, 1977), p. 27.

4. Lawrence Lipking, *The Life of the Poet: Beginning and Ending Poetic Careers* (Chicago, 1981), p. 69.

5. Anthony Low, *The Georgic Revolution* (Princeton, 1985).

6. Low, *Georgic Revolution,* p. 351. Low presumably is using "priorities" in both a temporal and a moral sense.

7. Stanley Fish, "The Temptation to Action in Milton's Poetry," *ELH,* 48 (1981), 516-31, and "Things and Actions Indifferent: The Temptation to Plot in *Paradise Regained,*" *Milton Studies,* 17 (1983), 163-85.

8. Paul Alpers, *What Is Pastoral?* (Chicago, 1996), p. 66; hereafter cited in text as *WP.*

9. Low, *Georgic Revolution,* p. 274; italics mine.

10. Judith Herz, "Milton and Marvell: The Poet as Fit Reader," *Modern Language Quarterly,* 39 (1978), 262.

11. Andrew Marvell, *Upon Appleton House,* II. 41-44, in *The Complete Poems,* ed. Elizabeth Stony Donno (Harmondsworth, 1976); references to Marvell's poems will be to this edition and cited in text by poem and/or line number.

12. Rosalie L. Colie, "Small Forms: Multo in Parvo," in *The Resources of Kind: Genre-Theory in the Renaissance,* ed. Barbara K. Lewalski (Berkeley, 1973), pp. 48, 41.

13. Don Cameron Allen, "A Reading of Lovelace's 'The Grasshopper,'" in *Image and Meaning: Metaphoric Traditions in Renaissance Poetry* (Baltimore, 1960), pp. 80-92.

14. For a compact summary of critical speculations on this topic, see John Rogers, *The Matter of Revolution: Science, Poetry and Politics in the Age of Milton* (Ithaca, 1996), pp. 91-92n.

15. Sharon Cameron, *Lyric Time: Dickinson and the Limits of Genre* (Baltimore, 1979).

16. Erwin Panofsky, "*Et in Arcadia Ego:* Poussin and the Elegiac Tradition," in his *Meaning in the Visual Arts* (Garden City, NY, 1955), pp. 295-320.

17. Ironically, it is Juliana rather than the mower who is the bearer of mortality. In "Damon the Mower" the only sting in the meadows belongs to Juliana—"Hark how the Mower Damon sung, / With love of Juliana stung"—and "The Mower's Song"

frankly laments, "she / What I do to the grass, does to my thoughts and me" [1-2; 5-6]. On the connection between desire and the apprehension of death, and the gynephobic tradition which derives from it, see Henry Staten's *Eros in Mourning: Homer to Lacan* (Baltimore, 1995).

18. T. S. Eliot, "Marvell" (1921) in his *Selected Essays* (New York, 1964), p. 262.

19. M. M. Bakhtin, "Epic and Novel" in *The Dialogic Imagination,* tr. Caryl Emerson and Michael Holquist (Austin, 1981), pp. 13-16.

20. E. M. W. Tillyard, "The Nature of the Epic" in *Parnassus Revisited: Modern Critical Essays on the Epic Tradition,* ed. Anthony C. Yu (Chicago, 1973), pp. 51, 480.

PASTORAL DRAMA

Ashley H. Thorndike (essay date 1899)

SOURCE: "The Pastoral Element in the English Drama Before 1605," in *Modern Language Notes,* Vol. 14, No. 4, April 1899, pp. 114-23.

[*In the following essay, Thorndike examines the development of the English pastoral drama, noting the introduction of particularly English elements—such as the appearance of comic characters and the satyr type—into the literary form.*]

Most accounts of the English pastoral drama have begun with Fletcher's *Faithful Shepherdess* or Daniel's *Queen's Arcadia.* There have been references, of course, to some of Lyly's plays, Peele's *Arraignment of Paris* and Sidney's *May Lady,* but there has been no recognition of a continuous and considerable development of the pastoral drama before Daniel and Fletcher introduced the genre already highly developed by Tasso and Guarini.

It is the purpose of this paper to present evidence of such a development before 1605, the date of Daniel's *Arcadia;* and this evidence will fall naturally into two divisions. First, we shall consider evidence of a pastoral element in entertainments and shows presented to the queen; and secondly, we shall consider plays and allusions to plays which show that pastorals were not uncommon on the London stage. The evidence under the first head has for the most part not been presented before, and that under the second has not all been previously utilized.

Taken altogether, this evidence will be enough to throw some light on many questions concerning the origin and development of English pastoral drama. The important and direct influence of the Italian drama on Fletcher and Daniel is well known, but the existence of an English pastoral drama prior to their plays at once suggests that they may have been influenced by it, as well as by the Italian forms. The extent and character of Italian influence on this early English development offers another subject for investigation. While the existence of such Italian influence is undoubted, the existence of a characteristic English development apart from foreign influence is equally to be expected. In the main, we shall leave to one side the question of Italian influence, and point only to such conclusions in regard to the characteristics of the drama as the evidence seems prima facie to warrant. In fact we shall try to do little more than to present the evidence.

I. The Pastoral Element in Royal Entertainments Before 1605

The theory of Rossi[1] that the Italian pastoral drama was developed from the eclogue through the medium of public pageants in honor of noble families, at once suggests the possibility of a similar development in England. The pastoral idea, in general, was a fashionable cult of the court: and the pastoral plays of Lyly, Peele, and Daniel, were all court entertainments. In the royal shows, then, if anywhere, we might expect to find germs of the finished form. I have, therefore, examined the accounts of the entertainments presented to Queen Elizabeth on her various progresses in order to discover whether or not they contain any elements such as afterwards appear more highly developed in the pastoral plays of Fletcher and Jonson. Such elements do appear, and will be briefly enumerated.

A word may first be prefaced in regard to the character of these royal entertainments. Wherever the queen made a journey she was greeted with an oration or show, and often with an elaborate entertainment, highly spectacular, and more or less dramatic. Sometimes the village schoolmaster, or some local functionary prepared the show; sometimes a court favorite like Gascoigne, or a great gentleman like Sidney, devised the entertainments. Hence their artistic quality varies widely. Some of them, doubtless, suggested Shakspere's burlesque in the pageants of Holofernes and Bottom, the weaver; and, on the other hand, some of them with their songs and fairies may possibly have suggested the beautiful conception of *Midsummer Night's Dream.* They also vary widely in their subject matter. Some with their allegorical characters are like the old moralities, some have deities and scenes from classical mythology, some fairies and bits of folk lore, some are satirical, some deal with romance and chivalry, and some have pastoral elements such as shepherds and satyrs. Often the performance contained a mixture of several of these varieties, and the only invariable point of similarity was the fulsome panegyric to the virgin queen.

In considering the pastoral elements I shall give a broad meaning to the phrase and take account of everything which can have had any relation to the pure pastoral drama. It must be remembered, too, that the accounts which we have of these entertainments before the queen are few compared with the number actually presented, and that we have no records at all of the many given before private persons. A single representation which has been preserved may, therefore, be taken as typical of a considerable number; and the existence of any pastoral elements may fairly be considered proof that such elements were not uncommon.

The first indication of anything at all pastoral is a reference to "a mask of wild men" performed at Greenwich in 1573.[2] The mask is lost. The connection between wild men and satyrs will appear later.

In 1575, at Kenilworth,[3] George Gascoigne prepared several devices to add to the interest of Leicester's entertainment. One evening as the queen was returning from the chase, she was greeted by a "Humbre Salvagio," "with an oaken plant pluct up by the roots in his hands, himself foregrone all in moss and ivy." At the end of his speech he called on "his familiars and companions, fawns, satyrs, nymphs, dryads, and hamadryads." None answered but echo; and then ensued a long dialogue between the wild man and echo. Here, then, we have a representative of the satyr type and the device of the echo dialogue, both elements of the pastoral drama.

This show seems to have been favorably received, for a similar exhibition[4] was at once prepared, but for some reason not presented. In the midst of an entertainment presenting Diana and her nymphs, a man clad all in moss comes in and announces that he is the son of the "humbre salvagio" and has a similar dialogue with echo.

On another day,[5] as the queen was going hunting, she was meet by Gascoigue, "dressed as Sylvanus, god of the woods." He made a long speech, running along by her horse, and led her to a bush, whence "deep desire" was heard speaking. This business of a voice from a bush or tree is repeated in other entertainments, and also in *Pastor Fido* (i, 4), where we have "a shrill voice from riv'd beech." In Gascoigne's device, Pan, Diana, and her nymphs also appear.

These three Kenilworth devices show that the introduction into English drama of Diana and her nymphs, and wilder denizens of the woods, such as Pan, Silvanus, and the satyr tribe, goes back at least to 1575. As in later representations, it is the hunting horns which disturb these wood-dwellers. It seems certain that Gascoigne borrowed most of this pastoral material directly from similar Italian performances.

In 1578, at Wanstead, the Contention of a Forester and a Shepherd for a May Lady, by Sir Philip Sidney, was presented before the queen. Here for the first time we find shepherds and a distinct pastoral setting. The old shepherd,afterwards a favorite character,makes his first English appearance; the chorus of foresters and shepherds reminds us of the chorus of huntsmen and shepherds in *Pastor Fido* (iv, 6); and Therion, the hunter, who is rude and

sometimes strikes the lady, and his rival Espiles, who is mild and gentle, are rudimentary types not unlike the contrasted Silvio and Mirtillo. The singing match is also a bit of dramatized eclogue; but, on the other hand, the burlesque schoolmaster, and the lady, dressed like "an honest man's wife of the country," are English elements quite foreign to the conventional pastoral genre.

I have found no other traces of a pastoral element in the accounts of the queen's progresses until 1591. At Cowdray in that year, a wild man awaited the queen by a tree and made a speech.

In 1592 at Bissam,[6] on the queen's arrival at the top of the hill, she was again met by a wild man who made a speech full of references to Pan, Sylvanus, and Echo.[7] At the middle of the hill, "sate Pan and two virgins keeping sheep and sewing in their samplers." Pan made love to the shepherdesses, and a long dialogue ensued, the subject of which may be well enough described in two phrases of the virgins—"the follies of the gods who became beasts for their affections; the honour of virgins who became goddesses for their chastity." At the bottom of the hill, Ceres and her nymphs completed the show. Here, then, we have again the satyr element both in the wild man and Pan, who woos the virgins with presents of chestnuts; and the chastity motive, so highly developed in later drama.

In the same year at Sudely,[8] an old shepherd greeted her majesty in a pastoral strain, praising the country as a very Arcadia where "we carry our hearts at our tongues' ends, being as far from dissembling as our sheep from fierceness;" and presenting her with a lock of wool "in which nothing is to be esteemed but the whiteness, virginity's color; nor to be expected but duty, the shepherd's religion.

On a Sunday, at the same place, there was a performance in which Apollo appeared running after Daphne, while a shepherd followed lamenting the loss of his nymph. Apollo turned Daphne into a tree, "and on one side of the tree appeared one who sung; and on the other, one who played." After the song the tree rived; Daphne appeared; and upon being pursued by Apollo, fled to her majesty," uttering this—"for whither should chastity fly for succour but to the queen of chastity?"—and so on, in a long panegyric on chastity and the virgin queen.

On another day at the same place,[9] there was a speech by one "cloked in a sheep's skin, face and all." Then her majesty was brought among shepherds, among whom was a queen and king to be chosen. Melibaeus and Nisa appeared as shepherds, also the Cutter of Cootsholde, a comic and not a pastoral personage.

In these entertainments we find again the pastoral setting, the exploitation of chastity, and the mixture of mythological and English country characters. These entertainments also warrant us in concluding that the representation of shepherds and nymphs and wild men, was not uncommon in such pageants. Pastoralism was certainly popular in the literature of the day, and played a considerable part in these theatrical shows, even when the pieces were not pastoral in theme or character. This prevalence of the pastoral may be illustrated by a few lines from a masque of knights and ladies,[10] in which the queen of fairies had a part. The lines are, I think, fairly typical of many similar songs and pastoral allusions.

> Of our new destiny
> Echo, echo, certify,
> Farewell all in woods that dwell,
> Farewell Satyrs, nymphs farewell,
> Adieu desires, fancies die,
> Farewell all inconstancy.

From 1592 on, the queen's progresses were very infrequent, and only one other pastoral entertainment appears. In 1600-1 a "Dialogue between two shepherds, Thenot and Piers, in praise of Astrea," was recited at the home of the author, the Countess of Pembroke. It is simply an eclogue.

One of the first entertainments offered to Queen Anne must be added to complete our list. In her progress to her coronation (1603), she was entertained at Althorpe with a kind of masque written by Ben Jonson, and entitled "The Complaint of the Satyrs against the Nymphs." A satyr was lodged in a spinet (little wood), by which her majesty and the prince were to come, and advancing his head above the top of the wood, he began:

> Here! there! and everywhere!
> Some solemnities are near
> That these changes strike my ear,
> My pipe and I a part shall bear, etc.

After piping a strain he ran out and welcomed the queen. Then a bevy of fairies, headed by Queen Mab, tripped out and began to dance and sing. Thereupon the satyr

"came hopping forth, and mixing himself with the fairies, skipped in, out, and about their circle, while they made offers to catch him."

He mocked them in a long song, of which a few lines will indicate the tenor:

> This is she that empties cradles
> Takes out children, puts in ladles,
> Trains forth midwives in their slumber
> With a sieve the holes to number
> And then leads them from her burrows
> Home through ponds and water furrows.

The fairies declared to Queen Mab,

> This is only spite
> For you would not yester night
> Kiss him in the cock shut light.

Then they caught him and pinched him black and blue. The satyr ran away, but later reappeared, and in a long speech to Queen Anne, closed the ceremony.

So far as I know, the foregoing are the only bits of pastoral pageants before 1605 which have been preserved. Meagre as they are, they may be fairly taken, I think, to indicate that Daniel and Fletcher did not work in an altogether untried field. Even apart from the plays of Lyly and Peele, and the masques of Sidney and Jonson, the entertainments of the queen's progresses show a considerable amount of the pastoral element. Before 1600 the chastity motive, the setting of shepherds and hunters, the story of unrequited love, the singing contest, the hunting party with sounding horns—all these had become material of the pastoral drama. Some characters, too, such as the satyr type, the rude forester, and the venerable shepherd, were pretty familiar. That, after all, this is a small contribution, that Daniel and Fletcher are to be credited with creative work, goes without saying; but in the light of these earlier pastoral dramatic attempts, it hardly seems possible that their work could have seemed absolutely new either to themselves or the Elizabethan public.

How far Italian influence can be traced in these early pastoral exhibitions cannot probably be definitely determined. I find no sure indications of the influence of either *Aminta* or *Pastor Fido*. These plays may have had an effect in increasing the prevalence of pastoral exhibitions after 1580; but, on the other hand, this prevalence must in a considerable measure have resulted from the popularity of pastoral poetry in general. Most of the pastoral entertainments might have well enough been suggested by the pastoral eclogues and romances. At the same time, there can be no doubt that the use of the pastoral in royal entertainments was at least suggested in the cases of Gascoigne and Sidney by similar pastoral entertainments in Italy.

The mixture of pastoral with mythological elements is only natural, both being taken from classical sources; and is, in fact, to be found in nearly all pastoral drama. The mixture of pastoral with native comic characters is, perhaps, more distinctively an English development. It may, indeed, possibly be taken as an evidence of the influence of contemporary public plays, though to some extent this mixture was anticipated in Spenser's and Barclay's eclogues. Pastoral poetry, at any rate, anticipated the pastoral drama in the introduction of contemporary satire. However, the honest country woman and the pedant Rombus of Sidney's *May Lady,* and the Cutter of Cootsholde at Sudeley, are worth noting, since they precede Daniel's use of contemporary satire, and Shakspere's introduction of English rustics, in the Arcadia of *As You Like It.*

More notable as an English variation is the development of the satyr type. Just what connection or difference existed between the wild man of the woods and the satyr, would probably have puzzled both spectators and authors to explain. How dim their ideas may have been, can be surmised from a contemporary description of a stone figure at Hamstead. Nichols[11] points out its resemblance to Gascoigne's "Humbre Salvagio"—"all his limbs being covered with thick hair and his loins surrounded with a girdle of foliage;" and from the illustration, it certainly appears to have been intended for a wild man. The contemporary account, however, calls it a "figure of Hercules with his club."

The wild man of the earliest entertainments is covered with moss, dwells in the woods, and is the companion of satyrs and nymphs. This wild man is differentiated from Silvanus, the god of the woods; but the two look much alike. Later the wild man appears with Pan who woos a shepherdess. Wild man, Humbre Salvagio, Silvanus, or Pan; the personage is the same from a theatrical point of view. So far as we can determine the characteristics with which he is endowed, he is a simple, wild animal, who lives like a squirrel, who ordinarily frolics with the nymphs, and plays his pipe in peace, but who comes forth in wonderment to see the queen.

There is nothing of the classical satyr's lasciviousness in this,[12] nothing of the rude lust of the satyr of the Italian pastoral drama. The satyr kind of the pageants certainly owed nothing to the elaborate development of the satyr in the Italian drama. In Ben Jonson's masque the difference is even greater. The satyr, there so-named, is introduced as the companion of Queen Mab and her fairies. He is a creature not of Arcadia but of fairy land. He is a singer, a piper, a merry fellow, and in addition serves as a messenger and a sort of chorus. This satyr, however, in his appearance from a bush, his wonderment at the queen's appearance, his long address, his introduction of the host, serves in the same situations and performs the same duties as the wild man. Here, then, we possibly have a direct contribution to the pastoral drama. From the wild man to Jonson's satyr is only a short step, and from Jonson's satyr to Fletcher's is an equally short step. The satyr in the *Faithful Shepherdess* is far removed from the lustful satyrs of *Sacrificio, Aminta,* or *Pastor Fido;* he again is an artless creature near related to the fairies, and serves as messenger and chorus. He gains of course in refinement from the delicacy of the verse, and the moral element elaborated in his adoration of chastity. This spontaneous reverence for chastity, however, also appeared in the wild men and Pan, when they encountered Elizabeth. From the wild men to Fletcher's satyr, then, we have what looks like a development peculiar to English soil; and, in this connection,it is worth noting that as theatrical parts, these are points of similarity between Fletcher's satyr and Shakspere's Ariel.

II. THE PASTORAL ELEMENT IN PUBLIC THEATER BEFORE 1605.

In tracing the pastoral element in the public drama, we shall first examine the extant plays, and then note the references to pastoral plays, that are not extant. None of the extant plays are pure pastorals like *Pastor Fido* or the *Faithful Shepherdess.* In the extent of their use of mythological characters and stories, they rather resemble such an early pastoral drama as Politian's *Orfeo.* Some of their mythological material, however, as for example, Lyly's use of a miraculous transformation, of an oracle, of a festival to some God, or of the tracing of divine descent, may

fairly be called the common property of all pastoral plays. More distinctly pastoral elements, such as shepherds, song contests, and the story of unrequited love also appear.

The Arraignment of Paris, by Geoge Peele. First quarto 1584. Probably acted about 1508.

The main part of the play deals with classical mythology; but here, as in some of the entertainments, Diana and her nymphs are brought in close connection with shepherds. The chorus of shepherds also appears, and in the first act a shepherd is contrasted with a hunter. The story of Colin's unrequited love and the talk of his fellow shepherds Hobbinol, Thenot, and Diggon, follow the *Shepherd's Calendar.* The probability of Italian influence is also apparent from an Italian song of twelve lines[13] which is incorporated in the text. Oenone appears as a nymph among the shepherds, and Paris is alluded to as "Amyntas' lovely boy," probably a reference to Watson's *Amyntas.*[14]

Gallathea, by John Lyly. Entered S. R. 1585. First quarto 1587, Written about 1580.[15]

The sacrifice of a virgin to Neptune forms the basis of the plot as in *Pastor Fido.* Melibeus and Tyterus are shepherds; Gallathea and Phyllida are their daughters, who assume boys clothing to avoid the sacrifice. Diana's nymphs again appear in connection with the shepherds; each of the nymphs, in fact, falls in love with a shepherd. With their loves, and the love which springs up between Gallathea and Phyllida, there is a complication of love affairs something like that of the later pastoral drama. Besides this pastoral story, the play has a large mythological element, a ship-wreck, and a good deal of contemporary satire. The pastoral element, however, is quite distinct and brings us nearer than any previous play to the later forms of Daniel and Fletcher.

Love's Metamorphosis by John Lyly. First quarto 1601. Acted, probably, about 1580. Revived (see title page) 1597-1600.

The title page of the first quarto describes the play as "a wittie and wurthy pastorall," and the scene is given Arcadia. Nisa, Celia, Niobe, and Tirtena appear as nymphs of Ceres, and the first three have importunate lovers in Ramis, Montanus, and Silvestris. These last are spoken of as amorous foresters and huntsmen;[16] neither shepherds nor sheep are mentioned. In content, however, the play is, perhaps, nearer to the developed pastoral form than any other of Lyly's. Each of the foresters woos a nymph, and each nymph refuses very persistently, so there is an opportunity for a good many love dialogues,[17] and much bemoaning of unrequited love. There is also a good deal of praise of chastity and talk of "gods amorous and virgins immortal, goddesses full of crueltie, and men of unhappinesse." [V. 1.)

There are a few other distinct pastoral elements; for example, the writing of verses on the trees (i. 1), the nymphs celebrating the festival (i. 2), and Fidelias who "chased with a Satyre, by prayer to the gods became turned to a tree" (i. 2).

The title page shows that the play was intended for a pastoral, hence we may assume that a story of unrequited love was definitely recognized as the proper content of a pastoral.

Midas by John Lyly. Entered S. R. 1591. First quarto 1592. Acted 1590(?).

The pastoral element is very slight, but Apollo, Pan, and nymphs appear in conjunction with five shepherds, Menaleus, Coryn, Celthus, Draipon, and Amyntas. There occurs, too, a long dispute between a huntsman and other servants, on the merits of hunting (iv, 3). Furthermore, in the prologue, spoken in Pauls, there is an allusion which seems to show that plays called pastorals were common on the stage.

> At our exercises, souldiers call for tragedies, their object is blood: courtiers for comedies, their subject is love; countrimen for pastorals, sheepheards are their saints.

In this connection, Polonius' words to Hamlet may be recalled.—"The best actors in the world, either for . . . pastoral, pastoral-comical, historical-pastoral—," etc. Lyly's prologue seems to show that even by 1590 the pastoral was recognized to be a distinct kind of drama, just like tragedy, comedy, or history.

Amphrisa, the Forsaken Shepherdess, or Pelopoea and Alope by Thomas Heywood. First printed in *Dialogues and Dramas*, 1636. Identified by Mr. Fleay[18] with one of the *Five Plays in One* acted at the Rose, 1597. This identification is plausible, but by no means certain, so this play may have been written after 1605.

This is a pure pastoral but is very brief, occupying only eleven quarto pages. Pelopoea and Alope, two shepherdesses, appear and speak of Amphrisa's false lover who has forsaken her. Amphrisa then enters; and a long conversation ensues, which results in the conclusion that the only remedy for injuries is patience. The queen of the country, with her nymphs, now enters. They have been chasing the stag and after telling of their exploits, listen in hiding, to the talk of the Arcadian girls, and are charmed by it. Amphrisa meanwhile is presented with a willow garland so that:

> All th' Arcadian swains and nymphs that see
> Your brows ingirt with this forsaken wreath
> Will take note of his falsehood and your faith;
> Your innocence and his inconstancie.

The queen finally discovers herself, compliments the shepherdesses; and several songs and dances close the entertainment.

The Woman in the Moon: by John Lyly. Entered S. R. 1595. First quarto 1597. Probably written between 1590-5.

As often in Lyly's plays, the main action depends on transformation, and there are plenty of mythological personages: the pastoral element, however, is considerable.

Four "Utopian shepherds," "all clad in skins" appear, ask for a female companion, and sing a roundelay. Pandora is given them, and throughout the play they appear as suitors; Stesias in particular, filling the part of the forsaken, scorned, and love-sick swain. To settle their contention, she sends them:

> to slay the savage boar
> Which roaring up and down with ceaseless rage
> Destroyes the fruit of our Utopian fields
> And he that first presents us with his head
> Shall wear my glove in favour of the deed.
>
> (ii, 1.)

Later, the shepherds dispute who had the largest share in slaying the boar. The passage suggests the incident of Silvio's victory over the boar in *Pastor Fido* (iv, 3). There seems, indeed, to be a similarity in phrasing. The *Pastor Fido* is also suggested by another incident, when Pandora's servant tells her: "Mistress, my mayster is in this cave, thinking to meet you, and search us here." (iv, 1.) Still further, we find a trace of the Satyr motive. Pandora, who becomes light and wanton through Venus' agency (iii, 2.), enters in company with Joculo, and the following dialogue ensues.

> P. Prethee be quiet, wherefore should I daunce?
> J. Thus daunce the Satyrs on the even lawnes.
> P. Thus, pretty Satyr, will Pandora daunce.
> Cupid. And thus will Cupid make her melody.
> J. Were I a man I would love thee.
> P. I am a mayden, wilt thou have me?
> J. But Stesias says thou art not.
> P. What then? I care not.
>
> (iii, 2.)

Joculs thus appears to be a sort of satyr; he does not come on the stage again. "Utopian" is rather curious for Arcadian, but the two seem to be the same as far as the nature of the scene is concerned. The setting of shepherds and an Arcadian-like country, and the story of unrequited love appear again, and the satyr element appears for the first time, I believe, in the regular drama.

The Maid's Metamorphosis; anonymous. First quarto 1600.

Whether this was an old play (as early as 1590) revived, or was written shortly before publication, are questions which do not especially concern us; nor does the question of authorship, although we may note that it has been attributed to Lyly, and is thought by Mr. Fleay to have been written by Lyly and Daniel.

The play is a medley in which Apollo and the muses, a magician, fairies, court people, clowns, shepherds, and foresters, all appear; and the main action deals with the transformation of the heroine into a boy and back again. If the author be not Lyly, his indebtedness to Lyly is manifest; and his indebtedness to the *Fairy Queen* is also marked. The pastoral element, however, follows dramatic conventions that were earlier instituted.

The heroine, Eurymine, is saved from death, but banished from court. She wanders in a forest, where she meets with Silvio, "a ranger," and Genulo, a shepherd, who at first, take her for a nymph or goddess and immediately become rivals for her love. Then ensues a long poetical contention as to whose house she shall be taken, in which forester and shepherd proclaim the merits of their respective callings in genuine pastoral style. This contention ends in rival songs by a chorus of shepherds and a chorus of woodmen. Eurymine settles the dispute by accepting a cottage from the forester and a flock from the shepherd. The whole scene at once recalls Sidney's *May Lady,* and was very likely suggested by that entertainment. In this scene, in the rivalry of the forester and shepherd throughout the play, and in the choruses of woodmen and shepherds, we are still further reminded of the *Pastor Fido.* If the play was written as late as 1600, I should think there could be little question of the influence of Guarini; this influence, however, seems general, rather than specific; the direct indebtedness seems to be to Sidney.

Eurymine is now established as a shepherdess; her lover Ascanio seeks her in vain; the rivals woo her in another eclogue, and Apollo, whose advances are repulsed, transforms her into a boy.

Among the distinct pastoral elements, we have an elaborate echo dialogue, in form exactly like that of Gascoigne's; and the rival song contest of shepherd and forester when they serenade Eurymine. The comic dialogues of the clowns—Joculo, the court clown, Frisco, the forester's boy, and Mopso, the shepherd's boy—furnish in addition some bits of real English rusticity. Throughout, moreover, there are many pastoral references, and the forest is obviously Arcadian.

In short, we have the pastoral element so well developed that it suggests Guarini, but on the other hand, the mythological and transformation and comic dialogue scenes, show at least a direct imitation of Lyly. The pastoral scenes, too, follow Sidney and Gascoigne, and are not very different from Lyly's. At all events, the play adds definite evidence of the use of pastoral elements in the drama, and takes its place in the development from the early forms of Gascoigne and Sidney. It shows, too, a pretty highly developed pastoral play at least five years before the *Queen's Arcadia.*

As You Like It: Shakspere. Entered S.R. 1602. Probably first acted in later half 1599.

Arden is a sort of Arcadia, inhabited by pastoral shepherds and court ladies in pastoral disguise. The disguised shepherdess appears also, it will be remembered, in the *Maid's Metamorphosis.* In the unrequited love of Silvius for Phoebe, in his laments and her rebuffs, we find again a distinct pastoral element. Shakspere took practically the whole of this pastoral element from Lodge's *Rosalynde.* Just as the *Shepherd's Calendar,* and the *Fairy Queen,* and doubtless Sidney's *Arcadia,* influenced the stage pastoral, so here a pastoral novel receives dramatization. Moreover, the dramatized pastoral and, in particular, the presentation of the pastoral story of unrequited love, must have already been familiar on the stage.

We shall now consider some evidences of the existence of other pastoral plays not extant, and then enumerate in chronological order all the entertainments or plays before 1605, containing pastoral elements.

Phyllida and *Covin,* presented at court by the Queen's men, Dec. 26, 1584.[19]

A Pastoral Tragedy; by George Chapman. He received £2 in earnest of a tragedy by this name from Henslow, July 17, 1599.

The Arcadian Virgin; by Chettle and Haughton. From Henslow's diary, we learn that the authors were advanced money on this play, Dec. 13, and 17, 1599.

Still further evidence of the existence of pastoral plays is found in Henslow's inventory of stage properties, 1598, where there is mention of "two white shepherds coats." Apart from this, there is no evidence of any pastoral play, or play with shepherds in it, performed by his company before 1598.

In *Mucedorus* (earliest known quarto 1598, but play certainly older) there is mention of "a mask of shepherds, presented by Lord Jules" (i, 1). Mr. Fleay says this mention is an addition of the 1606 quarto, and identifies it with the shepherds mask of the time of James I, but this latter he elsewhere says is Jonson's *Pan's Anniversary,* of June 16, 1623.[20] At all events the mask alluded to was probably acted before 1605.

LIST OF ENTERTAINMENTS AND PLAYS,
CONTAINING PASTORAL ELEMENTS BEFORE 1605

1573. *A Mask of Wild Men* at Greenwich. Fleay, *Chr.* ii, 341.

1575. *Entertainments to the Queen* at Kenilworth, Gascoigne. Nichols i, 436, 503, 575.

1578. *May Lady* at Wanstead. Sidney.

1581. (Before 84) *Arraignment of Paris* at court. Peele.

1582. (Before 85) *Gallathea,* at court. Lyly.

1582. (Before 1600) *Love's Metamorphosis.* Lyly.

1584. *Phyllida and Corin,* at court. Anonymous.

1590. (Before 1592) *Midas,* at court and in public (most of those court plays were probably also acted on public stage by children's companies). Lyly.

1591. *Wild Man* at Cowdray.

1592. *Entertainment to the Queen* at Bossans. Nichols iii, 135 seq.

1592. *Two Entertainments* at Sudeley. Nichols iii, 137 seq.

1590-95. *A Woman in the Moon,* at court. Lyly.

1597 (?) (Before 1631). Amphrisa, the forsaken shepherdess. Heywood.

Before 1598. Some play by Henslow's company with two shepherds in it.

1599. *A Pastoral Tragedy,* public. Chapman.

1599. *The Arcadian virgin,* public. Chettle and Haughton.

1599. *As You Like It,* public. Shakspere.

1597-99. Revival of *Love's Metamorphosis* and probably other of Lyly's plays.

In or before 1600. *Maid's Metamorphosis,* public. Anonymous.

1600-1. *A Dialogue between two shepherds. Entertainment to the queen.* Countess of Pembroke.

1603. *A Complaint of Satyrs against Nymphs. Entertainment to Queen Anne.* Ben Jonson.

Before 1605. *Mucedorus,* with the mask of shepherds.

Before 1606. *Pastor Fido,* performed at Cambridge University. Nichols. Progresses of James I, vol. i, p. 553.

This list is enough to convince one that the pastoral had wide vogue as a dramatic form. From 1573 on, it played a part in pageants; and from 1580 on, it played a part on the London stage. In London it was represented by at least three companies, the Paul's boys and their successors, Henslow's company and Shakspere's. Indeed, we can hardly doubt that if we had the evidence of the other companies which we have of Henslow's, we should have still further proof of the prevalence of the pastoral drama.

One other important fact is brought out by this list, the popularity of the pastoral plays 1597-1600. During this period Lyly's *Love's Metamorphosis,* and probably others of his plays, were revived by the children of the chapel. At Henslow's theatres, there were several pastoral plays, and at the Globe, *As You Like It.*

The pastoral play was, then, certainly common and popular, though not completely developed. Our evidence is, however, sufficient to enable us to define the general type with some exactness.

The scene is in Arcadia, sometimes explicitly stated as in *Gallathea* and *Love's Matamorphosis* and sometimes only implied. In all cases, however, the action takes place in a forest and its environs. Shepherds and sometimes shepherdesses appear as inhabitants of this Arcadia; sometimes these are of Arcadian origin, sometimes as in *Maid's Metamorphosis* and *As You Like It,* people of the court also appear in shepherd's guise. Foresters, usually in rivalry with the shepherds, nymphs, magicians, and various gods and godesses also appear among the dramatis personae.

The main story of the pastoral portion of the play is always one of unrequited love. The importunate suitor and the cruel or indifferent maid appear over and again. Sometimes the complication of love affairs results, as in *Gallathea* and *As You Like It,* in something like the love-chain of the later pastoral.

The chastity motive is rarely absent. The chastity of maids in resisting the overtures of amorous gods, the rejection of lovers because of a preference for the virgin state, the divine nature of this virginity—these are favorite subjects.

Among the scenes and situations used we have found hunting scenes, echo dialogues, song contests, rival discussions of a hunter's and a shepherd's lives; writing verses on a tree, the celebration of a festival by the nymphs, the proposed sacrifice of a virgin, the transformation of a maiden to a tree, most of which have been used more than once in the plays discussed. In these scenes, then, the pastoral drama of Daniel and Fletcher was surely forestalled in the use of much of its material.

The satyr appears only once in the plays and is then a merry fellow, Joculo, not far removed from the faun-like satyr of the entertainments. The motive of crude, ungoverned lust hardly appears at all except in the pursuer of Fidelias in *Love's Metamorphosis* and in the amours of the gods.

Thus pastoral drama is interwoven with a sort of mythological spectacle. Many of the mythological scenes as the transformation scenes, the embassy to an oracle, and the presence of Diana, Pan, Apollo, and nymphs, are closely connected with the pastoral scenes. In general, however, anything from classical mythology seems to have been thought a fit companion for the pastoral. On the other hand, contemporary satire and bits of native comedy, were often introduced into the Utopian Arcadia.

So much for the characteristics of the pastoral drama before 1605; that it owed much to the Italian drama cannot be doubted, but the exact nature of its indebtedness is a question I cannot pretend to discuss. It was also directly influenced by the non-dramatic English pastorals. The influence of the *Shepherd's Calender,* the *Faery Queen,* and Lodge's *Rosalynde* have been noted; and Sidney's *Arcadia* doubtless served to increase the vogue of the dramatic pastoral. That the influence of the Italian drama was equally direct is possible enough; but as in the entertainments, so in the plays, there is no sure evidence of a use of *Aminta* or *Pasto Fido.*

The inter-influence of the entertainments and stage-plays can hardly be determined from the meagre evidence we have, but taking the two together, there is certainly evidence of a direct dramatic influence on Daniel and Fletcher. Even before their time, Chettle and Haughton, Henslow's hacks, must have gone to work to compose their *Arcadian Virgin* on lines already definitely laid down by theatrical precedent. In 1599, too, when Shakespeare dramatized Lodge's novel, he must have been conscious of preparing for the stage material, already familiar there in the work of other dramatists. Surely when Daniel prepared his pastoral, he can hardly have seemed wholly an innovator; and when Fletcher brought out his *Faithful Shepherdess* on the London stage, he was only presenting in a more elaborate form a dramatic genre already well naturalized.

Notes

1. Battista Guarini, ed Il Pastor Fido, 1886. Part ii, Chap. 1.

2. F. G. Fleay, *A Chronicle of the English Drama,* 1559-1142, ii, 341.

3. Nichols, *Progresses of Elizabeth.* Vol. i. p. 436.

4. Nichols i, 503.

5. Nichols i, 575.

6. Nichols iii, 135.

7. Nichols iii, 137.

8. Nichols iii, 137.

9. Nichols iii, 142.

10. Nichols iii, 202.

11. Nichols ii, p. 121.

12. So far as the wild man is classical, he is clearly a faun rather than a satyr; and so indeed are Fletcher and Jonson's satyrs. The Elizabethans seem to have confused the two.

13. Act ii, p. 350, Routledge Edition.

14. Act iii, p. 360; also cf. p. 584, note.

15. Cf. *Endymion,* Ed. by G. P. Baker, 1894. Introduction.

16. Act i, sc. 2.

17. Cf. act i, sc. 1 act iii, sc, 1; act v, sc. 2.

18. *Chronicle of Drama,* vol. i, p. 286.

19. F. G. Fleay, *Chronicle of Drama,* vol. ii, p. 297.

20. Cf. *Cronicle of Drama,* vol. ii, p. 344; and vol. ii, p. 14.

Walter W. Greg (essay date 1906)

SOURCE: "The Three Masterpieces," in *Pastoral Poetry and Pastoral Drama,* A. H. Bullen, 1906, pp. 264-316.

[*In the following excerpt, Greg examines what he judges the two greatest English dramatic pastoral romances, John Fletcher's* Faithful Shepherdess *and Ben Jonson's* Sad Shepherd. *He notes Fletcher's greater indebtedness to Italian pastoral dramas than to English courtly-chivalric pieces and finds Jonson's work—the first truly English pastoral—to be a fine achievement despite its several weaknesses. Greg compares these two pieces to Thomas Randolph's* Amyntas, *a work that, despite its "inferior" merit, shares with the other dramas certain characteristics of form.*]

I

Among English pastorals there are two plays, and two only, that can be said to stand in the front rank of the romantic drama as a whole. The first of these is, of course, Fletcher's *Faithful Shepherdess.* In the case of the second the statement would perhaps be more correctly put in the conditional mood, for whatever might have been its importance had it reached completion, the fragmentary state of Jonson's *Sad Shepherd* has prevented its taking the place it deserves in the history of dramatic literature. With these two productions may for the purposes of criticism be classed Thomas Randolph's *Amyntas,* which, however inferior to the others in poetic merit, yet like them stands apart in certain matters of intention and origin from the general run of pastorals, and may, moreover, well support a claim to be considered one of the three chief English examples of the kind.

These three plays embrace a period of some thirty years, before, during, and after which a considerable number of dramatic productions, more or less pastoral in character, appeared. The chief feature in which the three plays we are about to consider are distinguished from these is a certain direct and conscious, though in no case subservient, relation they bear to the drama of the Italians; while at the same time we are struck with the absence of any influence of subsidiary or semipastoral tradition, of the mythological drama, or the courtly-chivalric romance. We shall therefore gain more by considering them in connexion with each other than we shall lose by abandoning strict chronological sequence.

When Fletcher's play was produced, probably in the winter of 1608-9, it proved a complete failure[1]. An edition appeared without date, but before May, 1610, to which were prefixed verses by Field, Beaumont, Chapman, and Jonson. If, as some have supposed, the last named already had at the time a pastoral play of his own in contemplation, the reception accorded to his friend's venture can hardly have been encouraging, and may have led to the postponement of the plan; as we shall see, there is no reason to believe that the *Sad Shepherd* was taken in hand for another quarter of a century almost. The *Faithful Shepherdess* was revived long after Fletcher's death, at a court performance in 1633-4, and shone by comparison with Montagu's *Shepherds' Paradise* acted the year before. It was then again placed on the public boards at the Blackfriars, where it met with some measure of success.

The *Faithful Shepherdess* was the earliest, and long remained the only, deliberate attempt to acclimatize upon the popular stage in England a pastoral drama which should occupy a position corresponding to that of Tasso and Guarini in Italy. It was no crude attempt at transplantation, no mere imitation of definite models, as was the case with Daniel's work, but a deliberate act of creative genius inspired by an ambitious rivalry. Its author might be supposed well fitted for his task. Although it was one of his earliest, if not actually his very earliest work, it is clear that he must have already possessed an adequate and practical knowledge of stagecraft, and have been familiar with the temper of London audiences. He further possessed poetical powers of no mean order, in particular a lyrical gift almost unsurpassed among his fellows for grace and sweetness, howbeit somewhat lacking in the qualities of refinement and power. That he should have failed so signally is a fact worth attention. For fail he did. His friends, it is true, endeavoured as usual to explain the fiasco of the first performance by the ignorance and incompetence of the spectators, but we shall, I think, see reason to come ourselves to a scarcely less unfavourable conclusion. Nor is this failure to be explained by the inherent disadvantage at which the sentimental and lyrical pastoral stood when brought face to face with the wider and stronger interest of the romantic drama. Such considerations may to some extent account for the attitude of the contemporary audience; they cannot be supposed seriously to affect the critical verdict of posterity. We must trust to analysis to show wherein lay the weakness of the piece; later we may be able to suggest some cause for Fletcher's failure.

In the first place we may consider for a moment Fletcher's indebtedness to Tasso and Guarini, a question on which very different views have been held. As to the source of his inspiration, there can be no reasonable doubt, though it has been observed with truth by more than one critic, that the *Faithful Shepherdess* may more properly be regarded as written in rivalry, than in imitation, of the Italians. In any case, but for the *Aminta* and *Pastor fido,* the *Faithful Shepherdess* would never have come into being; as a type it reveals neither original invention nor literary evolution, but is a conscious attempt to adapt the Italian pastoral to the requirements of the English stage. As an individual piece, on the other hand, it is for the most part original and independent, little direct influence of the Italians being traceable in the plot, whether in general construction or in single incidents and characters. A certain resemblance has indeed been discovered between Guarini's Corisca and Fletcher's Cloe, but the fact chiefly shows the superficiality of the comparison upon which critics have relied, since if Corisca suggested some traits of Cloe, she may be held

responsible for far more of Amarillis. Where Guarini depicted a courtesan, Fletcher has painted a yahoo. Corisca, wanton and cynical, plays, like Amarillis, the part of mischief-maker and deceiver, and, so far from seeking, like her successfully eludes the embraces of the shepherd-satyr. On the other hand, a clear difference between Fletcher's work and that of the Italians may be seen in the respective use made of supernatural agencies. From these the southern drama is comparatively free. A somewhat ultra-medicinal power of herbs, the introduction of an oracle in the preliminary history and of a wholly superfluous seer in the *dénoûment* make up the whole sum so far as the *Pastor fido* is concerned, while the *Aminta* cannot even show as much as this. In the *Faithful Shepherdess* we find not only the potent herbs, holy water, and magic taper of Clorin's bower, but the wonder-working well and the actual presence of the river-god, who rises, not to pay courtly compliments in the prologue, but to take an actual part in the plot[2]. Alike in its positive and negative aspects Fletcher's relation to the Italian masters was conscious and acknowledged. Far from feigning ignorance, he boldly challenged comparison with his predecessors by imitating the very title of Guarini's play, or yet closer, had he known it, that of Contarini's *Fida ninfa*[3].

A glance at the dramatis personae reveals a curious artificial symmetry which, as we shall shortly see, is significant of the spirit in which Fletcher approached the composition of his play. In Clorin we have a nymph vowed to perpetual virginity, an anchorite at the tomb of her dead lover; in Thenot a worshipper of her constancy, whose love she cures by feigning a return. In Perigot and Amoret are represented a pair of ideal lovers—so Fletcher gives us to understand—in whose chaste bosoms dwell no looser flames. Amarillis is genuinely enamoured of Perigot, with a love that bids modesty farewell, and will dare even crime and dishonour for its attainment; Cloe, as already said, is a study in erotic pathology. She is the female counterpart of the Sullen Shepherd, who inherits the traditional nature of the satyr, that monster having been transformed into the gentle minister of the cloistral Clorin. So, again, the character of Amarillis finds its counterpart in that of Alexis, whose love for Cloe is at least human; while Daphnis, who meets Cloe's desperate advances with a shy innocence, is in effect, whatever he may have been in intention, hardly other than a comic character. The river-god and the satyr, the priest of Pan and his attendant Old Shepherd, who themselves stand outside the circle of amorous intrigue, complete the list of personae.

The action which centres round these characters cannot be regarded as forming a plot in any strict sense of the term, though Fletcher has reaped a little praise here and there for his construction of one. It is hardly too much to say that the various complications arise and are solved, leaving the situation at the end precisely as it was at the beginning. Even so may the mailed figures in some ancestral hall start into life at the stroke of midnight, and hold high revel with the fair dames and damsels from out the gilt frames upon the walls, content to range themselves once more and pose in their former attitudes as soon as the first grey light of morning shimmers through the mullioned windows. Perigot and Amoret come through the trials of the night with their love unshaken, but apparently no nearer its fulfilment; Thenot's love for Clorin is cured for the moment, but is in danger of breaking out anew when he shall discover that she is after all constant to her vow; Cloe recovers from her amorous possession; the vagrant desires of Amarillis and Alexis are dispelled by the 'sage precepts' of the priest and Clorin; Daphnis' innocence is seemingly unstained by the hours he has spent with Cloe in the hollow tree; while the Sullen Shepherd, unregenerate and defiant, is banished the confines of pastoral Thessaly. What we have witnessed was no more than the comedy of errors of a midsummer night.

The play, nevertheless, possesses merits which it would be unfair to neglect. Narrative is, in the first place, entirely dispensed with in favour of actual representation, though the result, it must be admitted, is somewhat kaleidoscopic. Next, the action is complete within itself, and needs no previous history to explain it; no slight advantage for stage representation. As a result the interest is kept constantly whetted, the movement is brisk and varied, and with the help of the verse goes far towards carrying off the many imperfections of the piece.

It will have been already noticed that the characters fall into certain distinct groups which may be regarded as exemplifying certain aspects of love. Supersensuous sentiment, chaste and honourable regard, too colourless almost to deserve the name of love, natural and unrestrained desire, and violent lust, all these are clearly typified. What we fail to find is the presentment of a love which shall reveal men and women neither as beasts of instinct nor as carved figures of alabaster fit only to adorn a tomb. This typical nature of the characters has given rise to a theory recently propounded that the play should be regarded as an allegory illustrative of certain aspects of love[4]. So regarded much of the absurdity, alike of the characters and of the action, is said to disappear. This may be so, but does it really mean anything more than that abstractions not being in fact possessed of character at all, and being as ideals unfettered by any demands of probability, absurdities pass unnoticed in their case which at the touchstone of actuality at once start into glaring prominence? Moreover, though the *Faithful Shepherdess* was among the first fruits of its author's genius, and though it may be contended that he never gained a complete mastery over the difficult art of dramatic construction, Fletcher early proved his familiarity with the popular demands of the romantic stage, and was far too practical a craftsman to be likely to add the dead-weight of a moral allegory to the already dangerous form of the Arcadian pastoral. The theory does not in reality bring the problem presented by Fletcher's play any nearer solution; since, if the characters are regarded solely as representing abstract ideas, such as chastity, desire, lust, they strip themselves of every shred of dramatic interest, and could not, as Fletcher must have known, stand the least chance upon the stage; while if they take to cover

their nakedness however diaphanous a veil of dramatic personality, the absurdities of character and plot at once become apparent.

What truth there may be underlying this theory will, I think, be best explained upon a different hypothesis. Let us in the first place endeavour, so far as may be possible after the lapse of nearly three centuries, to realize the mental attitude of the author in approaching the composition of his play. In order to do this a closer analysis of the piece will be necessary.

The first point of importance for the interpretation of Fletcher's pastoralism is to be found in the quaintly self-confident preface which he prefixed to the printed edition. Throughout our inquiry we have observed two main types of pastoral, to one or other of which all work in this kind approaches; that, namely, in which the interest depends upon some allegorical or topical meaning lying beneath and beyond the apparent form, and that in which it is confined to the actual and obvious presentment itself. Of the former type Drayton wrote in the preface to his Pastorals: 'The subject of Pastorals, as the language of it, ought to be poor, silly, and of the coursest Woofe in appearance. Neverthelesse, the most High and most Noble Matters of the World may bee shaddowed in them, and for certaine sometimes are[5].' In his preface to the *Faithful Shepherdess* the author adopts the opposite position, as Daniel, in the prologue to the *Queen's Arcadia,* and in spite of the strongly topical nature of that piece, had done before him. Fletcher in an oftenquoted passage writes: 'Understand, therefore, a pastoral to be a representation of shepherds and shepherdesses with their actions and passions, which must be such as may agree with their natures, at least not exceeding former fictions and vulgar traditions; they are not to be adorned with any art, but such improper [i. e. common] ones as nature is said to bestow, as singing and poetry; or such as experience may teach them, as the virtues of herbs and fountains, the ordinary course of the sun, moon, and stars, and such like.' His interest would, then, appear to lie in a more or less realistic representation, and he appears more concerned to enforce a reasonable propriety of character than to discover deep matters of philosophy and state. This passage alone would, therefore, make the theory we glanced at above improbable. Fletcher next proceeds, in a passage of some interest in the history of criticism: 'A tragi-comedy is not so called in respect of mirth and killing, but in respect it wants deaths, which is enough to make it no tragedy, yet brings some near it, which is enough to make it no comedy, which must be a representation of familiar people, with such kind of trouble as no life be questioned; so that a god is as lawful in this as in a tragedy, and mean people as in a comedy.' One would hardly have supposed it necessary to define tragi-comedy to the English public in 1610, and even had it been necessary, this could hardly be accepted as a very satisfactory definition. The audience, 'having ever had a singular gift in defining,' as the author sarcastically remarks, concluded a pastoral tragi-comedy 'to be a play of country hired shepherds in gray cloaks, with curtailed

dogs in strings, sometimes laughing together, and sometimes killing one another'; and after all, so far as tragi-
comedy is concerned, their belief was not unreasonable.
Fletcher's definition is obviously borrowed from the academic criticism of the renaissance, and bears no relation to
the living tradition of the English stage: since his play
suggests acquaintance with Guarini's *Pastor fido,* it is perhaps not fantastic to imagine that in his preface he was indebted to the same author's *Compendio della poesia tragi-
comica.* What is important to note is Fletcher's concern at
this point with critical theory.

Without seeking to dogmatize as to the exact extent of
Fletcher's debt to individual Italian sources, it may safely
be maintained that he was familiar with the writings of the
masters of pastoral, and worked with his eyes open: whatever modifications he introduced into traditional characters
were the result of deliberate intention. In general, two
types of love may be traced in the Italian pastoral, namely
the honest human desire of such characters as Mirtillo and
Amarillis, Dorinda, Aminta, and the more or less close approach to mere sensuality found in Corisca and the satyrs.
We nowhere find any approach to supersensuous passion,
indifferent to its own consummation; Silvia and Silvio are
either entirely careless, or else touched with a genuine human love. Nor are the more tumultuous sides of human
passion represented, for it is impossible so to regard
Corisca's love for Mirtillo, which is at bottom nothing but
the cynical caprice of the courtesan, who regards her lovers merely as so many changes of garment—

    Molti averne, uno goderne, e cangiar spesso.

Fletcher appears to have thought that success might lie in
extending and refining upon the gamut of love. He possessed, when he set to work, no plot ready to hand capable
of determining his characters, but appears to have selected
what he considered a suitable variety of types to fill a pastoral stage, not because he desired to be in any way allegorical, but because in such a case it was the abstract relationship among the characters which alone could determine
his choice. Having selected his characters, he further seems
to have left them free to evolve a plot for themselves, a
thing they signally failed to do. Thus there may be a certain truth underlying the theory with which we started, inasmuch as the characters appear to have been chosen, not
for any particular dramatic business, but for certain abstract qualities, and some trace of their origin may yet
cling about them in the accomplished work; but that
Fletcher deliberately intended to illustrate a set of psychological conditions, not by dramatic presentation, but by the
use of types and abstractions, is to my mind incredible. In
the composition of his later plays he had the necessities of
a given plot, incidents, or other fashioning cause, to determine the characters which it was in its turn to illustrate,
and here he showed resourceful craftsmanship. In the case
of the present play he had to fashion characters *in vacuo*
and then weave them into such a plot as they might be capable of sustaining. In other words, he reversed the normal
order of artistic creation, and attempted to make the ab-

stract generate the concrete, instead of making the individual example imply, while being informed by, the fundamental idea.

So much for the formal and theoretic side of the question.
A few words as to the general tone and purpose of the
play. For some reason unexplained, having selected his
characters, which one may almost say exhibit every form
of love except a wholesome and a human one, the author
deemed it necessary that the whole should redound to the
praise and credit of cloistral virginity and glozing 'honour,'
and whatever else of unreal sentiment the cynicism of the
renaissance had grafted on the superstition of the middle
age. Again comparing the *Faithful Shepherdess* with
Fletcher's other work, we find that when he is dealing
with actual men and women in his romantic plays he
troubles himself little concerning the moral which it may
be possible to extract from his plot; he is rightly conscious
that that at all events is not the business of art; but when
he comes to create *in vacuo* he is at once obsessed by
some Platonic theory regarding the ethical aim of the poet.
The victory, therefore, shall be with the powers of good,
purity and vestal maidenhood shall triumph and undergo
apotheosis at his hands, the world shall see how fair a
monument of stainless womanhood he can erect in melo-
dious verse. Well and good; for this is indeed an object to
which no self-respecting person can take exception. There
was, however, one point the importance of which the author failed to realize, namely, that this ideal which he
sought to honour was one with which he was himself
wholly out of sympathy. Consequently, in place of the supreme picture of womanly purity he intended, he produced
what is no better than a grotesque caricature. His cynical
indifference is not only evident from many of his other
works, but constantly forces itself upon our attention even
in the present play. The falsity of his whole position appears in the unconvincing conventionality of the patterns
of chastity themselves, and in the unreality of the characters which serve them as foils—Cloe being utterly preposterous except as a study in pathology, and Amarillis essentially a tragic figure who can only be tolerated on condition
of her real character being carefully veiled. It appears
again in the utterly irrational conversion and purification
of these characters, and we may further trace it in the profound cynicism, all the more terrible because apparently
unconscious, with which the author is content to dismiss
Thenot, cured of his altruistic devotion by the shattering at
one blow of all that he held most sacred in woman.

In this antagonism between Fletcher's own sympathies and
the ideal he set before him seems to me to lie the key to
the enigma of his play. Only one other rational solution is
possible, namely that he intended the whole as an elaborate satire on all ideas of chastity whatever. It is hardly
surprising, under the circumstances, that one of the most
persistent false notes in the piece is that indelicacy of self-
conscious virtue which we have before observed in the
case of Tasso. If on the other hand we have to pronounce
Fletcher free of any taint of seductive sentiment, we must
nevertheless charge him with a considerable increase in

that cynicism with regard to womankind in general which had by now become characteristic of the pastoral drama. We have already noticed it in the case of Tasso's 'Or, non sai tu com' è fatta la donna?' and of the words in which Corisca describes her changes of lovers, to say nothing of its appearance at the close of the *Orfeo.* In English poetry we find Daniel writing:

> Light are their waving vailes, light their attires,
> Light are their heads, and lighter their desires;
>
> > *(Queen's Arcadia,* II. iii.)

while with Fletcher the charge becomes yet more bitter. Thenot, contemplating the constancy of Clorin, is amazed

> that such virtue can
> Be resident in lesser than a man,
>
> > (II. ii. 83.)

or that any should be found capable of mastering the suggestions of caprice

> And that great god of women, appetite.
>
> > (ib. 146.)

Amarillis, courting Perigot, asks in scorn:

> Still think'st thou such a thing as chastity
> Is amongst women?
>
> > (III. i. 297.)

The Sullen Shepherd declares of the wounded Amoret:

> Thou wert not meant,
> Sure, for a woman, thou art so innocent;
>
> > (ib. 358.)

and sums up his opinion of the sex in the words:

> Women love only opportunity
> And not the man.
>
> > (ib. 127.)

So Fletcher wrote, and in the same mood the arch-cynic of a later age exclaimed:

> ev'ry Woman is at heart a Rake!

But it is high time to inquire how it is, supposing the objections we have been considering to be justly chargeable against the *Faithful Shepherdess,* that it should ever have come to be regarded as a classic of the language, that it should be by far the most widely known of its author's works, and that we should find ourselves turning to it again and again with ever-fresh delight. The reader has doubtless already answered the question. Fletcher brought to the composition of his play a gift of easy lyric versification, a command of varied rhythm, and a felicity of phrase, allusion, recollection, and echo, such as have seldom been surpassed. The wealth of pure poetry overflow-

ing in every scene is of power to make us readily forget the host of objections which serious criticism must raise, and revel with mere delight in the verbal melody. The play is literally crowded with incidental sketches of exquisite beauty which suggest comparison with the more set descriptions of Tasso, and flash past on the speed of the verse as the flowers of the roadside and glimpses of the distant landscape through breaks in the hedge flash for an instant on the gaze of the rider[6].

Before passing on, and in spite of the fact that the play must be familiar to most readers, I here transcribe a few of its most fascinating passages as the best defence Fletcher has to oppose to the objections of his critics. It is in truth no lame one[7].

In the opening scene Clorin, who has vowed herself to a life of chastity at the grave of her lover, is met by the satyr, who at once bows in worship of her beauty. He has been sent by Pan to fetch fruits for the entertainment of 'His paramour the Syrinx bright.' 'But behold a fairer sight!' he exclaims on seeing Clorin:

> By that heavenly form of thine,
> Brightest fair, thou art divine,
> Sprung from great immortal race
> Of the gods, for in thy face
> Shines more awful majesty
> Than dull weak mortality
> Dare with misty eyes behold
> And live. Therefore on this mould
> Lowly do I bend my knee
> In worship of thy deity[8].
>
> > (I. i. 58.)

The next scene takes place in the neighbourhood of the village. At the conclusion of a festival we find the priest pronouncing blessing upon the assembled people and purging them with holy water[9], after which they disperse with a song. As they are going, Perigot stays Amoret, begging her to lend an ear to his suit. He addresses her:

> Oh you are fairer far
> Than the chaste blushing morn, or that fair star
> That guides the wandering seaman through the deep,
> Straighter than straightest pine upon the steep
> Head of an agèd mountain, and more white
> Than the new milk we strip before day-light
> From the full-freighted bags of our fair flocks,
> Your hair more beauteous than those hanging locks
> Of young Apollo!
>
> > (I. ii. 60.)

They agree to meet by night in the neighbouring wood, there to bind their love with mutual vows. The tryst is set where

> to that holy wood is consecrate
> A virtuous well, about whose flowery banks
> The nimble-footed fairies dance their rounds
> By the pale moonshine, dipping oftentimes
> Their stolen children, so to make them free

From dying flesh and dull mortality.
By this fair fount hath many a shepherd sworn,
And given away his freedom, many a troth
Been plight, which neither envy nor old time
Could ever break, with many a chaste kiss given
In hope of coming happiness.
By this fresh fountain many a blushing maid
Hath crown'd the head of her long-lovèd shepherd
With gaudy flowers, whilst he happy sung
Lays of his love and dear captivity.

(I. ii. 99.)

Cloe, repulsed by Thenot, sings her roguishly wanton carol:

Come, shepherds, come!
    Come away
    Without delay,
Whilst the gentle time doth stay.
    Green woods are dumb,
And will never tell to any
Those dear kisses, and those many
Sweet embraces, that are given;
Dainty pleasures, that would even
Raise in coldest age a fire
And give virgin blood desire
    Then if ever,
    Now or never,
  Come and have it;
    Think not I
    Dare deny
If you crave it.

(I. iii. 71.)

Her fortune with the modest Daphnis is scarcely better, and she is just lamenting the coldness of men when Alexis enters and forthwith accosts her with his fervent suit. She agrees, with a pretty show of yielding modesty:

        lend me all thy red,
Thou shame-fac'd Morning, when from Tithon's bed
Thou risest ever maiden!

(ib. 176.)

The second act opens with the exquisite evensong of the priest:

Shepherds all and maidens fair,
Fold your flocks up, for the air
'Gins to thicken, and the sun
Already his great course hath run.
See the dew-drops how they kiss
Every little flower that is,
Hanging on their velvet heads
Like a rope of crystal beads;
See the heavy clouds low falling,
And bright Hesperus down calling
The dead night from under ground,
At whose rising mists unsound,
Damps and vapours fly apace,
Hovering o'er the wanton face
Of these pastures, where they come
Striking dead both bud and bloom.

(II. i. 1.)

In the following scene Thenot declares to Clorin his singular passion, founded upon admiration of her constancy to her dead lover. He too can plead his love in verse of no ordinary strain:

        'Tis not the white or red
Inhabits in your cheek that thus can wed
My mind to adoration, nor your eye,
Though it be full and fair, your forehead high
And smooth as Pelops' shoulder; not the smile
Lies watching in those dimples to beguile
The easy soul, your hands and fingers long
With veins enamell'd richly, nor your tongue,
Though it spoke sweeter than Arion's harp;
Your hair woven in many a curious warp,
Able in endless error to enfold
The wandering soul; not the true perfect mould
Of all your body, which as pure doth shew
In maiden whiteness as the Alpen snow:
All these, were but your constancy away,
Would please me less than the black stormy day
The wretched seaman toiling through the deep.
But, whilst this honour'd strictness you do keep,
Though all the plagues that e'er begotten were
In the great womb of air were settled here,
In opposition, I would, like the tree,
Shake off those drops of weakness, and be free
Even in the arm of danger.

(II. ii. 116.)

The last lines, however fine in themselves, are utterly out of place in the mouth of this morbid sentimentalist. They breath the brave spirit of Chapman's outburst:

Give me a spirit that on this life's rough sea
Loves t'have his sails fill'd with a lusty wind,
Even till his sail-yards tremble, his masts crack,
And his rapt ship run on her side so low
That she drinks water and her keel plows air.

(*Byron's Conspiracy,* III. i.)

Into the details of the night's adventures there is no call for us to enter; it will be sufficient to detach a few passages from their setting, which can usually be done without material injury. The whole scenery of the wood, in the densest thicket of which Pan is feasting with his mistress, while about their close retreat the satyr keeps watch and ward, mingling now and again in the action of the mortals, is strongly reminiscent of the *Midsummer Night's Dream.* The wild-wood minister thus describes his charge in the octosyllabic couplets which constitute such a characteristic of the play:

Now, whilst the moon doth rule the sky,
And the stars, whose feeble light
Give a pale shadow to the night,
Are up, great Pan commanded me
To walk this grove about, whilst he,
In a corner of the wood
Where never mortal foot hath stood,
Keeps dancing, music and a feast
To entertain a lovely guest;
Where he gives her many a rose

Sweeter than the breath that blows
The leaves, grapes, berries of the best;
I never saw so great a feast.
But to my charge. Here must I stay
To see what mortals lose their way,
And by a false fire, seeming-bright,
Train them in and leave them right.

(III. i. 167.)

Perigot's musing when he meets Amoret and supposes her to be the transformed Amarillis is well conceived; he greets her:

What art thou dare
Tread these forbidden paths, where death and care
Dwell on the face of darkness?

(IV. iv. 15.)

while not less admirable is the pathos of Amoret's pleading; how she had

lov'd thee dearer than mine eyes, or that
Which we esteem our honour, virgin state;
Dearer than swallows love the early morn,
Or dogs of chase the sound of merry horn;
Dearer than thou canst love thy new love, if thou hast
Another, and far dearer than the last;
Dearer than thou canst love thyself, though all
The self-love were within thee that did fall
With that coy swain that now is made a flower,
For whose dear sake Echo weeps many a shower!
. . .
Come, thou forsaken willow, wind my head,
And noise it to the world, my love is dead!

(ib. 102.)

Then again we have the lines in which the satyr heralds the early dawn:

See, the day begins to break,
And the light shoots like a streak
Of subtle fire; the wind blows cold
Whilst the morning doth unfold.
Now the birds begin to rouse,
And the squirrel from the boughs
Leaps to get him nuts and fruit;
The early lark, that erst was mute,
Carols to the rising day
Many a note and many a lay.

(ib. 165.)

The last act, with its obligation to wind up such loose threads of action as have been spun in the course of the play, is perhaps somewhat lacking in passages of particular beauty, but it yields us Amarillis' prayer as she flies from the Sullen Shepherd, and the final speech of the satyr. However out of keeping with character the former of these may be, it is in itself unsurpassed:

If there be
Ever a neighbour-brook or hollow tree,
Receive my body, close me up from lust
That follows at my heels! Be ever just,

Thou god of shepherds, Pan, for her dear sake
That loves the rivers' brinks, and still doth shake
In cold remembrance of thy quick pursuit;
Let me be made a reed, and, ever mute,
Nod to the waters' fall, whilst every blast
Sings through my slender leaves that I was chaste!

(V. iii. 79.)

Lastly, we have the satyr's farewell to Clorin:

Thou divinest, fairest, brightest,
Thou most powerful maid and whitest,
Thou most virtuous and most blessèd,
Eyes of stars, and golden-tressèd
Like Apollo; tell me, sweetest,
What new service now is meetest
For the satyr? Shall I stray
In the middle air, and stay
The sailing rack, or nimbly take
Hold by the moon, and gently make
Suit to the pale queen of night
For a beam to give thee light?
Shall I dive into the sea
And bring thee coral, making way
Through the rising waves that fall
In snowy fleeces? Dearest, shall
I catch thee wanton fawns, or flies
Whose woven wings the summer dyes
Of many colours? get thee fruit,
Or steal from heaven old Orpheus' lute?
All these I'll venture for, and more,
To do her service all these woods adore.
. . .
So I take my leave and pray
All the comforts of the day,
Such as Phoebus' heat doth send
On the earth, may still befriend
Thee and this arbour!
Clorin.   And to thee,
All thy master's love be free!

(V. v. 238 and 268.)

Such then is Fletcher's play. It is in the main original so far as its own individuality is concerned, and apart from the general tradition which it follows. Its direct debt to Guarini is confined to the title and certain traits in the characters of Cloe and Amarillis. Further indebtedness has, it is true, been found to Spenser, but some hint of the transformation of Amarillis, a few names and an occasional reminiscence, make up the sum total of specific obligations. Endowed with a poetic gift which far surpassed the imitative facility of Guarini and approached the consummate art of Tasso himself, Fletcher attempted to rival the Arcadian drama of the Italians. Not content, as Daniel had been, merely to reproduce upon accepted models, he realized that some fundamental innovation was necessary. But while he adopted and justified the greater licence and range of effect allowed upon the English stage, thereby altering the form from pseudo-classical to wholly romantic, he failed in any way to touch or vitalize the inner spirit of the kind, trusting merely to lively action and lyrical jewellery to hold the attention of his audience. He failed, and it was not till some years after his death that the play, having been stamped with the approbation of the court, won a tardy recognition from the general public; and even when, after the restoration, Pepys records a successful revival in 1663, he adds that it was 'much thronged after for the scene's sake[10].'

II

Randolph's play, entitled 'Amyntas, or the Impossible Dowry,' belongs no doubt to the few years that intervened between the author's exchanging the academic quiet of Cambridge and the courts of Trinity, of which college he was a fellow, for the life and bustle of theatre and tavern in London about 1632, and his premature death which took place in March, 1635, before he had completed his thirtieth year. It is tempting to imagine that the revival of Fletcher's play on Twelfth Night, 1633-4, may possibly have occasioned Randolph's attempt, in which case the play must belong to the very last year of his life; but though there is nothing to make this supposition improbable, pastoral representations were far too general at that date for it to be necessary to look for any specific suggestion. The play first appeared in print in the collected edition of the author's poems edited by his brother in 1638.

Like Fletcher's play, the *Amyntas* is a conscious attempt at so altering the accepted type of the Arcadian pastoral as to fit it for representation on the popular stage, for though acted, as the title-page informs us, before their Majesties at Whitehall, it was probably also performed and intended by the author for performance on the public boards[11]. Yet the two experiments differ widely. Fletcher, as we have seen, while completing the romanticizing of the pastoral by employing the machinery and conventions of the English instead of the classical stage, nevertheless introduced into his play none of the diversity and breadth of interest commonly found in the romantic drama proper, and indeed the *Faithful Shepherdess* lacks almost entirely even that elaboration and firmness of plot which we find in the *Pastor fido*. Randolph, on the other hand, chose a plot closely resembling Guarini's in structure, and even retained much of the scenic arrangement of the Italian theatre. But in the complexity of action and multiplicity of incident, in the comedy of certain scenes and the substratum of pure farce in others, he introduced elements of the popular drama of a nature powerfully to affect the essence of his production. Where Fletcher substituted for a theoretic classicism an academic romanticism, Randolph insisted on treating the venerable proprieties of the pastoral according to the traditions of English melodrama. . . .

[I maintain] that the *Amyntas* is one of the most interesting and important of the experiments which English writers made in the pastoral drama, that it possesses dramatic qualities to which few of its kind can pretend, and that pervading and transforming the whole is the genial humour and the sparkling wit of its brilliant and short-lived author. His pastoral muse was a hearty buxom lass, and kind withal, not overburdened with modesty, yet wholesome and cleanly, and if at times her laugh rings out where

the subject passes the natural enjoyment of kind, it is even then careless and merry, and there is often a ground of real fun in the jest. Her finest qualities are a sharp and ready wit and a wealth of imaginative pathos, alike pervaded by her bubbling humour; on the other hand there are moments, if rare, when in an ill-considered attempt to assume the buskin tread she reveals in her paste-board fustian somewhat of the unregeneracy of the plebian trull. The time may yet come when Randolph's reputation, based upon his other works—the *Jealous Lovers,* a Plautine comedy, clever, but preposterous in more ways than one, the *Muses' Looking Glass,* a perfectly undramatic morality of humours, and the poems, generally witty, occasionally graceful, and more than occasionally improper—will be enhanced by the recognition of the fact that he came nearer than any other writer to reconciling a kind of pastoral with the temper of the English stage. It was at least in part due to a constitutional indifference on the part of the London public to the loves and sorrows of imaginary swains and nymphs, that Randolph's play failed to leave any appreciable mark upon our dramatic literature[12].

III

In Jonson's *Sad Shepherd* we find ourselves once again considering a work which is not only one of very great interest in the history of pastoral, but which at the same time raises important questions of literary criticism. So far the most interesting compositions we have had to consider— Daniel's *Hymen's Triumph,* Fletcher's *Faithful Shepherdess,* Randolph's *Amyntas*—have been attempts either to transplant the Italian pastoral as it stood, or else so to modify and adapt as to fit it to the very different conditions of the English stage. Jonson, on the other hand, aimed at nothing less than the creation of an English pastoral drama. Except for such comparatively unimportant works as *Gallathea* and the *Converted Robber*[13], the spectators found themselves, for the first time, on English soil. In spite of the occasional reminiscences of Theocritus and the Arcadian erudition concerning the 'Lovers Scriptures,' the nature of the characters is largely English. The names are not those of pastoral tradition, but rather of the popular romance, Aeglamour, Lionel, Clarion, Mellifleur, Amie, or more homely, yet without Spenser's rusticity, Alken; while the one name of learned origin is a coining of Jonson's own, Earine, the spirit of the spring. The silvan element, which had been variously present since Tasso styled his play *favola boschereccia,* was used by Jonson to admirable purpose in the introduction of Robin Hood and his crew. A new departure was made in the conjoining of the rustic and burlesque elements with the supernatural, in the persons of the witch Maudlin, her familiar Puck-hairy, her son the rude swineherd Lorel, and her daughter Douce the proud. In every case Jonson appropriated and adapted an already familiar element, but he did so in a manner to fashion out of the thumbed conventions of a hackneyed tradition something fresh and original and new.

Unfortunately the play is but half finished, or, at any rate, but half is at present extant. The fragment, as we have it, was first published, some years after the author's death, in the second volume of the folio of 1640, and the questions as to whether it was ever finished and to what date the composition should be assigned are too intricate to be entered upon here. Suffice it to say that no conclusive arguments exist for supposing that more of the play ever existed than what we now possess, nor that what exists was written very long before the author's death. It is conceivable that the play may contain embedded in it fragments of earlier pastoral work, but the attempt to identify it with the lost *May Lord* has little to recommend it[14]. Seeing that the play is far from being as generally familiar as its poetic merit deserves, I may be allowed to give a more or less detailed analysis of it in this place[15].

After a prologue in which Jonson gives his views on pastoral with characteristic self-confidence, the Sad Shepherd, Aeglamour, appears, lamenting in a brief monologue the loss of his love Earine, who is supposed to have been drowned in the Trent.

> Here she was wont to goe! and here! and here!
> Just where those Daisies, Pincks, and Violets grow:
> The world may find the Spring by following her;
> For other print her aerie steps neere left.

(I. i.)

He retires at the approach of Marian and the huntsmen, who are about to fetch of the king's venison for the feast at which Robin Hood is to entertain the shepherds of the vale of Belvoir. When they have left the stage Aeglamour comes forward and resumes his lament in a strain of melancholic madness. He is again interrupted by the approach of Robin Hood, who enters at the head of the assembled shepherds and country maidens. Robin welcomes his guests, and his praise of rustic sports calls forth from Friar Tuck the well-known diatribe against the 'sourer sort of shepherds,' in which Jonson vented his bitterness against the hypocritical pretensions of the puritan reformers—a passage which yields, in biting satire, neither to his own presentation in the *Alchemist* nor to Quarles' scathing burlesque quoted on an earlier page. As they discourse they become aware of Aeglamour sitting moodily apart, unheeding them. He talks to himself like a madman.

> It will be rare, rare, rare!
> An exquisite revenge: but peace, no words!
> Not for the fairest fleece of all the Flock:
> If it be knowne afore, 'tis all worth nothing!
> Ile carve it on the trees, and in the turfe,
> On every greene sworth, and in every path,
> Just to the Margin of the cruell Trent;
> There will I knock the story in the ground,
> In smooth great peble, and mosse fill it round,
> Till the whole Countrey read how she was drown'd;
> And with the plenty of salt teares there shed,
> Quite alter the complexion of the Spring.
> Or I will get some old, old Grandam thither,
> Whose rigid foot but dip'd into the water,
> Shall strike that sharp and suddaine cold throughout,
> As it shall loose all vertue; and those Nimphs,
> Those treacherous Nimphs pull'd in Earine;

> Shall stand curl'd up, like Images of Ice;
> And never thaw! marke, never! a sharpe Justice.
> Or stay, a better! when the yeares at hottest,
> And that the Dog-starre fomes, and the streame boiles,
> And curles, and workes, and swells ready to sparkle;
> To fling a fellow with a Fever in,
> To set it all on fire, till it burne,
> Blew as Scamander, 'fore the walls of Troy,
> When Vulcan leap'd in to him, to consume him.

(I. v.)

Robin now accosts him, hoping, since his vengeance is so complete, that he will consent to join his fellows in honouring the spring. At this his distracted fancy breaks out afresh:

> A Spring, now she is dead: of what, of thornes?
> Briars, and Brambles? Thistles? Burs, and Docks?
> Cold Hemlock? Yewgh? the Mandrake, or the Boxe?
> These may grow still; but what can spring betide?
> Did not the whole Earth sicken, when she died?
> As if there since did fall one drop of dew,
> But what was wept for her! or any stalke
> Did beare a Flower! or any branch a bloome,
> After her wreath was made. In faith, in faith,
> You doe not faire, to put these things upon me,
> Which can in no sort be: Earine,
> Who had her very being, and her name,
> With the first knots, or buddings of the Spring,
> Borne with the Primrose, and the Violet,
> Or earlicst Roses bluwne: when Cupid smil'd,
> And Venus led the Graces out to dance,
> And all the Flowers, and Sweets in Natures lap,
> Leap'd out, and made their solemne Conjuration,
> To last, but while shee liv'd. Doe not I know,
> How the Vale wither'd the same Day? . . . that since,
> No Sun, or Moone, or other cheerfull Starre
> Look'd out of heaven! but all the Cope was darke,
> As it were hung so for her Exequies!
> And not a voice or sound, to ring her knell,
> But of that dismall paire, the scritching Owle,
> And buzzing Hornet! harke, harke, harke, the foule
> Bird! how shee flutters with her wicker wings!
> Peace, you shall heare her scritch.

(ib.)

To distract him Karoline sings a song. But after all he is but mad north-north-wcst, and though he would study the singer's conceits 'as a new philosophy,' he also thinks to pay the singer.

> Some of these Nimphs here will reward you; this,
> This pretty Maid, although but with a kisse;
>   [*Forces Amie to kiss Karolin.*
> Liv'd my Earine, you should have twenty,
> For every line here, one; I would allow 'hem
> From mine owne store, the treasure I had in her:
> Now I am poore as you.

(ib.)

There follows a charming scene in which Marian, returning with the quarry, relates the fortunes of the chase, and proceeds, amid Robin's interruptions, to tell how 'at his fall there hapt a chance worth mark.'

Robin. I! what was that, sweet Marian?

                              [*Kisses her.*

Marian.   You'll not heare?

Rob.   I love these interruptions in a Story;

                           [*Kisses her again.*

        They make it sweeter.

Mar.   You doe know, as soone

As the Assay is taken—   [*Kisses her again.*

Rob.   On, my Marian.

I did but take the Assay.

                                (I. vi.)

To cut the story short, while the deer was breaking up, there

                    sate a Raven

On a sere bough! a growne great Bird! and Hoarse!

crying for its bone with such persistence that the superstitious huntsmen swore it was none other than the witch, an opinion confirmed by Scathlock's having since beheld old Maudlin in the chimney corner, broiling the very piece that had been thrown to the raven. Marian now proposes to the shepherdesses to go and view the deer, whereupon Amie complains that she is not well, 'sick,' as her brother Lionel jestingly explains, 'of the young shepherd that bekiss'd her.' They go off the stage, and the huntsmen and shepherds still argue for a while of the strange chance, when Marian reappears, seemingly in ill-humour, insults Robin and his guests, orders Scathlock to carry the deer as a gift to Mother Maudlin, and departs, leaving all in amazement. In the next act Maudlin relates to her daughter Douce how it was she who, in the guise of Marian, thus gulled Robin and his guests out of their venison and brought discord into their feast. Douce is clad in the dress of Earine, who, it now appears, was not drowned, but is imprisoned by the witch in a hollow tree, and destined by her as her son Lorel's mistress. The swineherd now enters with the object of wooing the imprisoned damsel, whom he releases from the tree, Maudlin and Douce retiring the while to watch his success, which is small. Baffled, he again shuts the girl up in her natural cell, and his mother, coming forward, rates him soundly for his clownish ways, reading him a lecture for his guidance in his intercourse with women, in which she seems little concerned by the presence of her daughter. This latter, so far as it is possible to judge from the few speeches assigned to her in the fragment, appears to be of a more agreeable nature than one might, under the circumstances, have expected. Jonson sought, it would appear, to invest her with a certain pathos, presenting a character of natural good feeling, but in which no moral instinct has ever been awakened; and it is by no means improbable that he may have intended to dissociate her from her surroundings in order to balance the numbers of his nymphs and swains[16]. After Lorel has left them, Maudlin shows Douce the magic girdle, by virtue of which she effects her transformations, and by which she may always be recognized through her disguises. In the next scene we find Amie suffering from the effect of Karol's kiss. She is ill at ease, she knows not why, and the

innocent description of her love-pain possesses, in spite of its quaint artificiality, something of the *naïveté* of *Daphnis and Chloe.*

> How often, when the Sun, heavens brightest birth,
> Hath with his burning fervour cleft the earth,
> Under a spreading Elme, or Oake, hard by
> A coole cleare fountaine, could I sleeping lie,
> Safe from the heate? but now, no shadie tree,
> Nor purling brook, can my refreshing bee?
> Oft when the medowes were growne rough with frost,
> The rivers ice-bound, and their currents lost,
> My thick warme fleece, I wore, was my defence,
> Or large good fires, I made, drave winter thence.
> But now, my whole flocks fells, nor this thick grove,
> Enflam'd to ashes, can my cold remove;
> It is a cold and heat, that doth out-goe
> All sense of Winters, and of Summers so.

                                (II. iv.)

To the shepherdesses enters Robin, who upbraids Marian for her late conduct towards him and his guests. She of course protests ignorance of the whole affair, bids Scathlock fetch again the venison, and remains unconvinced of Robin's being in earnest, till Maudlin herself comes to thank her for the gift. Marian endeavours to treat with the witch, and begs her to return the venison sent through some mistake, but Maudlin declares that she has already departed it among her poor neighbours. At this moment, however, Scathlock returns with the deer on his shoulders, to the discomfiture of the witch, who curses the feast, and after tormenting poor Amie, who between sleeping and waking betrays the origin of her disease, departs in an evil humour. The scene is noteworthy for its delicate comedy and pathos.

Amie [*asleep*]. O Karol, Karol, call him back againe . . .

    O', ô.

Marian. How is't Amie?

Melifleur.   Wherefore start you?

Amie. O' Karol, he is faire, and sweet.

Maud.   What then?

Are there not flowers as sweet, and faire, as men?

The Lillie is faire! and Rose is sweet!

Amie.   I', so!

Let all the Roses, and the Lillies goe:

Karol is only faire to mee!

Mar.   And why?

Amie. Alas, for Karol, Marian, I could die.

Karol he singeth sweetly too!

Maud.   What then?

Are there not Birds sing sweeter farre, then Men?

Amie. I grant the Linet, Larke, and Bul-finch sing,

But best, the deare, good Angell of the Spring,

The Nightingale.

Maud.   Then why? then why, alone,

Should his notes please you?

Amie. This verie morning, but—I did bestow—

It was a little 'gainst my will, I know—

A single kisse, upon the seelie Swaine,

And now I wish that verie kisse againe.

His lip is softer, sweeter then the Rose,

His mouth, and tongue with dropping honey flowes;

The relish of it was a pleasing thing.

Maud. Yet like the Bees it had a little sting.
Amie. And sunke, and sticks yet in my marrow deepe
And what doth hurt me, I now wish to keepe.

(II. vi.)

After this exhibition of her malice the shepherds and hunts-men no longer doubt that it was Maudlin herself who de-ceived them in the shape of Marian, and they determine to pursue her through the forest. The wise shepherd, Alken, undertakes the direction of this novel 'blast of venerie,' and thus discourses of her unhallowed haunts:

Within a gloomie dimble shee doth dwell,
Downe in a pitt, ore-growne with brakes and briars,
Close by the ruines of a shaken Abbey
Torne, with an Earth-quake, down unto the ground;
'Mongst graves, and grotts, neare an old Charnell house,
Where you shall find her sitting in her fourme,
As fearfull, and melancholique, as that
Shee is about; with Caterpillers kells,
And knottie Cobwebs, rounded in with spells.
Thence shee steales forth to relief, in the foggs,
And rotten Mistes, upon the fens, and boggs,
Downe to the drowned Lands of Lincolneshire.
. . . [There] the sad Mandrake growes,
Whose grones are deathfull! the dead-numming Night-shade!
The stupifying Hemlock! Adders tongue!
And Martagan! the shreikes of lucklesse Owles,
Wee heare! and croaking Night-Crowes in the aire!
Greene-bellied Snakes! blew fire-drakes in the skie!
And giddie Flitter-mice, with lether wings!
The scalie Beetles, with their habergeons,
That make a humming Murmur as they flie!
There, in the stocks of trees, white Faies doe dwell,
And span-long Elves, that dance about a poole,
With each a little Changeling, in their armes!
The airie spirits play with falling starres,
And mount the Sphere of fire, to kisse the Moone!
While, shee sitts reading by the Glow-wormes light,
Or rotten wood, o're which the worme hath crept,
The banefull scedule of her nocent charmes.

(II. viii.)

In the third act we are introduced to Puck-hairy, who la-ments his lot as the familiar of the malignant witch in whose service he has now to 'firk it like a goblin' about the woods. Meanwhile Karol meets Douce in the dress of Earine, who, however, runs off on the approach of Ae-glamour. The latter fancies she is the ghost of his drowned love, and falls into a 'superstitious commendation' of her. His delusions are conceived in a vein no less happy and more distinctly poetical than those of Amyntas.

But shee, as chaste as was her name, Earine,
Dy'd undeflowr'd: and now her sweet soule hovers,
Here, in the Aire, above us; and doth haste
To get up to the Moone, and Mercury;
And whisper Venus in her Orbe; then spring
Up to old Saturne, and come downe by Mars,
Consulting Jupiter; and seate her selfe
Just in the midst with Phoebus, tempring all

The jarring Spheeres, and giving to the World
Againe, his first and tunefull planetting!
O' what an age will here be of new concords!
Delightfull harmonie! to rock old Sages,
Twice infants, in the Cradle o' Speculation,
And throw a silence upon all the creatures! . . .
The loudest Seas, and most enraged Windes
Shall lose their clangor; Tempest shall grow hoarse;
Loud Thunder dumbe; and every speece of storme
Laid in the lap of listning Nature, husht,
To heare the changed chime of this eighth spheere!

(III. ii.)

After this Lionel appears in search of Karol, who is in req-uisition for the distressed Amie. They are about to go off together when Maudlin again appears in the shape of Mar-ian, with the news that Amie is recovered and their pres-ence no longer required. At this moment, however, Robin appears, and suspecting the witch, who tries to escape, seizes her by the girdle and runs off the stage with her. The girdle breaks, and Robin returns with it in his hand, followed by the witch in her own shape. Robin and the shepherds go off with the prize, while Maudlin summons Puck to her aid and sets to plotting revenge. Lorel also ap-pears for the purpose of again addressing himself to his imprisoned mistress, and, if necessary, putting his moth-er's precepts into practice. With the words of the witch:

Gang thy gait, and try
Thy turnes with better luck, or hang thy sel';

the fragment breaks off abruptly. From the Argument pre-fixed to Act III we know that Lorel's purpose with Earine was interrupted by the entrance of Clarion and Aeglamour, and her discovery was only prevented by a sudden mist called up by Maudlin. The witch then set about the recov-ery of her girdle, was tracked by the huntsmen as she wove her spells, but escaped by the help of her goblin and through the over-eagerness of her pursuers. . . .

Subject to [some] reservations it appears to me that the characters and general tone of Jonson's pastoral are per-fectly harmonious and congruent. The shepherds are far removed from the types of Arcadian convention, and may more properly be regarded as idealizations from the actual country lads and lasses of merry England. Their names are borrowed from popular romance, which, if somewhat French in its tone, was certainly in no way antagonistic to the legends of Sherwood nor to the agency of witchcraft and fairy lore[17]. Even Alken, in spite of his didactic bent, is as far as possible from being the conventional 'wise shepherd,' and certainly no Arcadian ever displayed such knowledge as he of the noble art, while his lecture on the blast of hag-hunting, though savouring somewhat of bur-lesque, contains perhaps the most thoroughly charming and romantic lines that ever flowed from the pen of the great exponent of classical tradition. That the characters owe nothing to Arcadian tradition is not contended, nor do I know that it would be desirable that they should not, since that tradition forms at least a convenient, if not an altogether necessary, precedent for such pastoral idealization; but even if it is going rather far to say that they 'belong to a definite age and country,' they have yet sufficient individuality and community of human nature to be wholly fitting companions for the gallant Robin and his fair lady. Jonson, it would appear, consciously adopted the pastoral method, if hardly the pastoral mood, of Theocritus, in contradistinction to that of the courtly poets in Italy. It will be noticed that he has not forborne to introduce references to sheepcraft, but the fact that these enter more or less naturally into the discourse, and are not, as in Fletcher's pastoral, introduced in the vain hope of giving local colour to wholly uncolourable characters, saves them from having the same stilted effect, and is at the same time evidence of the greater reality of Jonson's personae. It is also noteworthy that Jonson has even ventured upon allegorical matter in one passage at least, but has succeeded in doing so in a manner in no wise incongruous with the nature of actual rustics, though the collocation of Robin Hood and the rise of Puritanism must be admitted to be historically something of an anachronism.

Robin and Maid Marian are, of course, characters no whit less idealized than the shepherds, though the process was largely effected by popular tradition instead of by the author. But this being so, such characters as Much and Scathlock must be no less incongruous with Robin and Marian than with Karol and Amie—a proportion which those who love the old Sherwood tradition would be loath to admit. In any case the incongruity, if it exists, is not of Jonson's devising, but consecrated for ages in the popular mind. The truth is, however, that Much and Little John, Scathlock and Scarlet are, in spite of their more homely speech and humour, scarcely less idealized than any of the other characters I have mentioned. That Jonson has even sought to tone down such harshness of contrast as he found is noticeable in his treatment of a recognized figure of burlesque like Friar Tuck, who is throughout portrayed with decorum and respect.

Lastly, to come to the third group of characters. If it was impossible for an English audience to regard as burlesque such popular and sympathetic characters as Robin and his merry men, so a malignant witch and a mischievous elf were far too serious agents of ill to be treated in this light either. Characters whose unholy powers would have fitted them for death at the stake can scarcely have been regarded even by the rude audiences of pre-restoration London as fitting subjects of farce, while there is nothing to lead us to suppose that Jonson, whatever his private opinion on the subject may have been, sought in the present instance to cast ridicule upon the belief in witches, but rather it is evident that he laid hands upon everything that could give colour to their sinister reputation. On the other hand, he has treated the whole subject with an imaginative touch which relieves us of all tragic or moral apprehension, removes all the squalid and unblessed surroundings into the region of romantic art, and makes it impossible to regard the characters as less idealized than those of the shepherds and huntsmen. I cannot myself but regard the elements of witchcraft and fairy employed by Jonson as

far more in harmony not only with Robin Hood and his men, but also with the shepherds of Belvoir vale, than would have been the oracles, satyrs, and other outworn machinery of regular pastoral tradition.

There remains the rusticity of language which distinguishes some of the ruder characters from others more refined. That some contrast between the groups was intended is indisputable, that the contrast is rather harsher than the author intended may be plausibly maintained. There is, on the whole, a lack of graduation. Into the question of dialectism in general it is needless to enter. The speech employed would be inoffensive, were it not that it is, and is felt to be, no genuine dialect at all, but a mere literary convention, a mixture of broad Yorkshire and Lothian Scots, not only utterly out of place in Sherwood forest, but such as can never have been spoken by any sane rustic. Still more than of Spenser is Ben's dictum true of himself, that where he departed from the cultivated English of his day, whether in imitation of the ancients or of provincial dialect matters not, he failed to write any language at all. Yet here, if anywhere, we should be justified in arguing that it is unfair to judge an unrevised fragment as if it were a completed work in the form in which the author decided to give it to the world. Jonson, as his *English Grammar* shows, was not without a knowledge of the antiquities at least of our tongue, and it is reasonable to suppose that, had he lived to publish his pastoral himself, he would have removed some of the more glaring enormities of language, along with certain other improprieties which could hardly have escaped his critical eye.

Jonson then, as it seems to me, setting aside a few points of minor importance, successfully combined what he found suited to his purpose in previous pastoral tradition, with what was most romantic and attractive in popular legend and a genuine idealization from actual types, to produce a veritable English pastoral, which failed of success only in that it remained unfinished at the death of its author.

Notes

1. Fleay considers the *Faithful Shepherdess* a joint production of Beaumont and Fletcher. The only external evidence in favour of this theory is a remark of Jonson's reported by Drummond: 'Flesher and Beaumont, ten yeers since, hath [*sic*] written the Faithful Shipheardesse, a Tragicomedie, well done.' Considering that the same authority makes Jonson ascribe the *Inner Temple Masque* to Fletcher, his statement as to the *Faithful Shepherdess* cannot be allowed much weight, while I hardly think that the fact of Beaumont having prefixed commendatory verses to Fletcher in the original edition can be set aside as lightly as Fleay appears to think. He relies chiefly upon internal evidence, but in his *Biographical Chronicle,* at any rate, does not venture upon a detailed division. For myself, I can only discover one hand in the play, and that hand Fletcher's. Fleay places the date of representation before July, 1608, on account of an outbreak of the

plague lasting from then to Nov. 1609, but A. H. Thorndike (*The Influence of Beaumont and Fletcher on Shakspere,* Worcester, Mass., 1901, p. 14) has shown good reason for believing that dramatic performances were much less interfered with by the plague than Fleay imagined.

2. Most of these, it may be remarked, as well as the character of Thenot and the unconventional rôle of the satyr, find parallels in the earlier stages of the Italian pastoral. The transformation-well recalls the enchanted lake of the *Sacrifizio;* the introduction of a supernatural agent in the plot reminds us of the same play, as well as of Epicuro's *Mirzia;* the friendly satyr, of this latter, which may be, in its turn, indebted to the revised version of the *Orfeo;* the character of Thenot is anticipated in the *Sfortunato.* I give the resemblances for what they are worth, which is perhaps not much; it is unlikely that Fletcher should have been acquainted with any of the plays in question, though of course not impossible. The magic taper appears to be a native superstition, a survival of the ordeal by fire.

3. Certain critics have suggested that the *Pastor fido* might more appropriately have borne the title of Fletcher's play. This is absurd, since it would mean giving the title-rôle to the wholly secondary Dorinda. Perhaps they failed to perceive that Mirtillo and not Silvio is the hero. With Fletcher's play the case stands otherwise. There is absolutely nothing to show whether the title refers to the presiding genius of the piece, Clorin, faithful to the memory of the dead, or to the central character, Amoret, faithful in spite of himself to her beloved Perigot. I incline to believe that it is the latter that is the 'faithful shepherdess,' since it might be contended that, in the conventional language of pastoral, Clorin would be more properly described as the 'constant shepherdess.' (Cf. II. ii. 130.)

4. See Homer Smith's paper on *Pastoral Influence in the English Drama.* His theory concerning the *Faithful Shepherdess* will be found on p. 407. Whatever plausibility there may be in the general idea, the detailed application there put forward would appear to be a singular instance of misapplied ingenuity in pursuance of a preconceived idea.

5. 'Poems' [1619], p. 433. Compare Boccaccio's account of pastoral poetry already quoted, p. 18, note.

6. One fault, which even the beauty of the verse fails to conceal, is the introduction of all sorts of stilted and otiose allusions to sheepcraft, which only serve to render yet more apparent the inherent absurdity of the artificial pastoral. These Tasso and Guarini had had the good taste to avoid, but we have already had occasion to notice them in the case of Bonarelli. Daniel is likewise open to censure on this score.

7. I quote, of course, from Dyce's text, but have for convenience added the line numbers from F. W. Moorman's edition in the 'Temple Dramatists.'

8. The officious critic must be forgiven for remarking that the satyr is not, as might be supposed from this speech, suddenly tamed by Clorin's beauty and virtue, but shows himself throughout as of a naturally gentle disposition. Consequently Clorin's argument that it is the mysterious power of virginity that has guarded her from attack and subdued his savage nature appears a little fatuous.

9. Specifically from 'wanton quick desires' and 'lustful heat.' One is almost tempted to imagine that the author is laughing in his sleeve when we discover of what little avail the solemn ceremony has been.

10. In 1658 there appeared a Latin translation, under the title of *La Fida pastora,* by 'FF. Anglo-Britannus,' namely, Sir Richard Fanshawe, as appears from an engraved monogram on the title-page.

11. As Fleay points out, the prologue and epilogue are not suited to court representation.

12. The fact that the play was never published as a separate work makes it difficult to estimate its popularity with the reading public. The whole collection was frequently reprinted, 1638, 1640, 1643, 1652, 1664 and 1668 twice. In 1703 appeared the *Fickle Shepherdess,* 'As it is Acted in the New Theatre in Lincolns-Inn Fields. By Her Majesties Servants. Play'd all by Women.' This piece is said in the epistle dedicatory to Lady Gower to be 'abreviated from an Author famous in his Time.' It is in fact a prose rendering, much compressed, of the main action of Randolph's play, the language being for the most part just sufficiently altered to turn good verse into bad prose.

13. Vide post, p. 382.

14. For a detailed discussion of the evidence I must refer the reader to the Introduction to my reprint of the play in the *Materialien zur Kunde des älteren Englischen Dramas* (vol. xi, 1905). The following summary may be quoted. '(i) There is no ground for supposing that there ever existed more of the *Sad Shepherd* than we at present possess. (ii) The theory of the substantial identity of the *Sad Shepherd* and the *May Lord* must be rejected, there being no reason to suppose that the latter was dramatic at all. (iii) The two works may, however, have been to some extent connected in subject, and fragments of the one may survive embedded in the other. (iv) The *May Lord* was most probably written in the autumn of 1613. (v) The date of the *Sad Shepherd* cannot be fixed with certainty; but there is no definite evidence to oppose to the first line of the prologue and the allusion in Falkland's elegy [in *Jonsonus Virbius*], which agree in placing it in the few years preceding Jonson's death.'

15. The play has no doubt been somewhat lost in the big collected editions of the author's works, and has

also suffered from its fragmentary state. Previous to my own reprint it had only once been issued as a separate publication, namely, by F. G. Waldron, whose edition, with continuation, appeared in 1783. One of the best passages, however (II. viii), was given in Lamb's *Specimens*. In quoting from the play I have preferred to follow the original of 1640, as in my own reprint, merely correcting certain obvious errors, rather than Gifford's edition, in which wholly unwarrantable liberties are taken with the text.

16. Waldron, in his continuation, matches her with Clarion.

17. It has recently been argued with much ingenuity that Marian is originally none other than the familiar figure of French *pastourelles*. However this may be, it is a question with which I am not here concerned. It was the English Robin Hood tradition that formed part of Jonson's rough material. See E. K. Chambers, *The Mediaeval Stage,* i. p. 175.

Carol Gesner (essay date 1959)

SOURCE: *"The Tempest* as Pastoral Romance," in *Shakespeare Quarterly,* Vol. 10, No. 4, Autumn 1959, pp. 531-39.

[*In the following essay, Gesner argues that William Shakespeare's* The Tempest *is primarily a pastoral play, and that in composing the work Shakespeare used the Greek pastoralist Longus's* Daphnis and Chloe *as an immediate source.*]

The problem of the source of *The Tempest* has long intrigued scholars, because a single entirely satisfactory work has never been uncovered to account for its origin. Many significant contributions to the solution of the problem have, however, been offered. In 1817 Ludwig Tieck pointed to *Die schöne Sidea,* a play by Jacob Ayrer, as a source or close analogue. Its plot parallels *The Tempest* in that it centers on a prince-magician, served by a spirit, father of a daughter whose hand is won when the son of an enemy carries logs. *Die schöne Sidea* was surely written before 1605, the date of Ayrer's death, but since it went unpublished until 1618, seven years after the composition of *The Tempest,* a common ancestor is conjectured for the two.[1] The Italian *commedia dell' arte,* a form of entertainment very popular in Shakespeare's England, is also thought to have been a suggestive force for *The Tempest.* Several of the comedies dealt with the theme of men shipwrecked on an island ruled by a "Mago". Love intrigues between the crew and the natives formed the plot materials, and often the greed of the sailors provided the comic situation.[2] A possible source for the political intrigue which resulted in Prospero's banishment has been found in William Thomas' *History of Italy.*[3] The plot has also been linked to the Spanish *Noches des Invierno* of Antonio Eslava, in which a dethroned king raises a magic castle in mid-ocean, where he lives with his daughter until, also by magic, he brings about a marriage between her and the son of an enemy.[4] The *AEneid* of Virgil is credited with inspiring both the storm and the meeting of the lovers.[5] Many contemporary accounts of storms and shipwrecks have also been offered as sources for the storm of the first act, and in many there can be found a few similarities to the storm of the play.[6]

Even after careful study of all these suggested influences, different as each may be, none seems to rule out another, for the prime factor in Shakespeare's art is its marvelous composite quality. Indeed, a realization of its composite nature is the essential key to the understanding of his genius; thus, it is without questioning the value of these recognized sources or analogues that Longus' romance of *Daphnis and Chloe* is suggested as another important influence on the genesis of the play.

As early as 1916 Edwin Greenlaw showed clearly that *Daphnis and Chloe* was the ultimate parent of the chief elements in the plot of a type of pastoral which was used by Sidney, Spenser, and Shakespeare.[7] From a study of these sources he singled out what he described as a composite pastoral plot, the essentials of which are as follows:

> (1) A child of unknown parentage, usually a girl, is brought up by shepherds. As a variant, the heroine may be living in seclusion among shepherds.

> (2) A lover is introduced. He may be a foundling or a man of high birth in guise of a shepherd or forester.

> (3) The love story is complicated by a rival shepherd, usually a rude, bumbling, or cowardly person. He functions as a foil to the hero and supplies the comic element.

> (4) Melodramatic incidents—the attack of a lioo or a bear—give the hero opportunity to prove his prowess.

> (5) A captivity episode is usually introduced. The heroine is abducted; the hero comes to the rescue.

> (6) It finally develops that the heroine is of high birth and may marry the hero.

> (7) A malcontent or melancholy shepherd is introduced to the plot from Italian or Spanish sources.

The presence of some of these stock pastoral elements, Greenlaw clearly demonstrates in the plots of *As You Like It, Cymbeline,* and *The Winter's Tale,* but always with the accurate implication that Shakespeare was depending on the established pastoral tradition, derived ultimately from Longus, rather than on Longus as an immediate source. That *The Tempest* is primarily a pastoral play, the plot of which fits easily into the stock framework, Greenlaw does not recognize, but this may be readily demonstrated:

> (1) Miranda, unaware that she is the daughter of the rightful Duke of Milan, is reared in pastoral seclusion on a desert island.

> (2) Ferdinand appears in the role of her lover and undertakes pastoral labors to win her. (Carries logs.)

(3) Caliban replaces the blundering shepherd. Before the play opens he has made an attempt against Miranda's honor:

> [Prospero to Caliban] . . . I have us'd thee,
> Filth as thou art, with human care; and lodg'd thee
> In mine own cell, till thou didst seek to violate
> The honour of my child.
>
> (I. ii. 345-348)[8]

The comedy scenes between Caliban and the crew members, Trinculo and Stephano, provide humor and reveal Caliban as a bumbling coward. He is, however, the foil to Ariel rather than to the hero.

(4) The traditional melodramatic elements supplied by an attack of a lion or a bear are omitted, unless the storm be designated melodrama.

(5) The captivity episode is represented by the plot of Caliban, Trinculo, and Stephano to kidnap Miranda. The plot is not successful, but the captivity motif is present.

(6) When the identity of Miranda and her father is revealed to the strangers, a reconciliation is effected and the lovers make plans for marriage.

The seventh element of the stock pastoral plot, the melancholic or philosophic shepherd—represented by Jacques in *As You Like It,* Philisides in Sidney's *Arcadia*—is not obviously present; for this Renaissance tradition of melancholy or discontent has been passed over and the thoughtful character, represented in *The Tempest* by Prospero, reverts to the earlier purely philosophic type as represented by the shepherd Philetas in *Daphnis and Chloe.* But significantly present in *The Tempest* is another important feature of the *Daphnis and Chloe* plot, supernatural direction, a feature which was not included in the stock pastoral as it developed during the Renaissance. In *Daphnis and Chloe,* Pan and the nymphs handle the problem of motivation and preside over the peripeties, while Eros personally conducts the love story. In *The Tempest* the supernatural control is in the hands of Prospero, but is executed by Ariel.

If it is agreed that *The Tempest* embodies elements of the Longus romance which were the typical pastoral material of the Renaissance, the problem now becomes one of determining just how direct the influence of Longus is on the play. The stock features as outlined could have been derived from almost any pastoral composition of the period. The omission of any melancholy or malcontent element in Prospero's characterization—the so-called Italian or Spanish feature of the stock plot—and the addition of the supernatural machinery point directly to Longus rather than to an intermediary source, except that omission can not be a conclusive argument, and supernatural direction abounds in classical literature. Other close parallels with Longus do, however, exist, and these, coupled with the Greek features of the plot, lead one to suggest that Shakespeare was familiar with *Daphnis and Chloe* before he wrote *The Tempest,* an idea bolstered by Samuel Lee Wolff's recogni-

tion of *Daphnis and Chloe* as a primary source of the pastoral sections of *The Winter's Tale.*[9]

But first, an examination of the bibliographic accessibility of *Daphnis and Chloe* to Shakespeare. In 1559 Jacques Amyot brought the romance into the Renaissance orbit by the publication of a French translation at Paris. This was reissued in 1594, 1596, and 1609. Rome in 1569 and again in 1581 saw the publication of the *Expositorum ex Longo libri IV* of Laurentius Gambara. A second French translation of the romance was published by "L. L. L." at Paris in 1578. In 1587 Angel Day published his English translation: *Daphnis and Chloe excellently describing the weight of affection, the simplicity of love, the purport of honest meaning, the resolution of men, and disposition of Fate, finished in Pastorall, etc.* A Greek and Latin text prepared by Raphaelis Columbanius was issued in 1598 at Florence. Another prepared by the scholarly Juda and Nicolae Bonnuitius was published in 1601 at Heidelberg, and in 1605 appeared at Hanover another such edition by Gothofredus Jungermannus.[10] *The Tempest* is almost always dated 1611[11]; thus any of these publications presumably were accessible to Shakespeare, although the French translation of Amyot and the English translation of Day would seem to be the sources which could be most readily utilized.

But to turn to an examination of the romance and the play: First, there is a general parallel in theme and setting. Both *Daphnis and Chloe* and *The Tempest* take as their central topic the idea of celebrating the innocence of youth. Miranda and Ferdinand, Daphnis and Chloe are blessed innocents as lovers. Further, both works are island stories: in each the locale of the action is a sea-surrounded paradise. Nature plays a significant part in the background and becomes a part of the intangible atmosphere in both novel and play. The characters refer frequently to nature and seem to be aware of it as a kind of presence.[12]

Second, there is a general correspondence in the characters. Daphnis and Ferdinand are both pretty youths who engage in pastoral labors, and, although Daphnis is country bred and Ferdinand court bred, both approach the heroines with innocent and reverent love. There is no more trivial sophistication in the love of Ferdinand for Miranda than in the pasture-bred love of Daphnis for Chloe. Further, Daphnis is led to Chloe by the supernatural agency of Eros:

> So nowe haue I [Eros] . . . in . . . charge . . . Daphnis and Chloe, . . . this morning [I] brought them together vnto the downes.[13]

And Ferdinand is led to Miranda by the supernatural agency of Ariel:

> *Re-enter* ARIEL *invisible, playing and singing;* FERDINAND *following*

Ariel literally sings Ferdinand to his bride!

Chloe and Miranda are both reared in pastoral seclusion, ignorant of their high births. Both are characterized as innocent of the world and of love—Miranda has seen no man but her father and the semi-man Caliban before she beholds Ferdinand. Chloe does not understand her emotions which are aroused by the sight of Daphnis in his bath. Chloe helps with Daphnis' herds; Miranda begs to carry logs for Ferdinand. Both have a high regard for their pastoral rearing. At the end of the novel, Chloe's city-born aristocratic background has been established; nevertheless, she and Daphnis return to the country for their wedding and settle there for a long life of pastoral delight. When Miranda hears of her former high estate, she says to her father:

> What foul play had we that we came from thence?
> Or blessed was't we did?
>
> (I.ii.60f.)

Philetas of the novel and Prospero of the play generally coincide. Philetas is a philosophic shepherd who supervises the love affair of Daphnis and Chloe and acts as judge when Daphnis is tried for trouble created by city gallants. He is generally respected and is a kind of presiding patriarch of his island home. Prospero is also a philosopher, although he combines the philosophy with magic. By magic he instigates the love affair of Miranda and Ferdinand. At the end of the play he serves in a judge-like capacity when all identities are revealed and the knots of the plot are untied. He, like Philetas, is the deeply respected patriarch of an island.

Eros is the supernatural instigator and director of the loves of Daphnis and Chloe; Philetas only supervises and instructs. Invisible to the lovers, Eros leads them together. He is associated with gardens, sunlight, laughter:

> . . . there is no nightingale, thrush, or other kinde of bird whatsoeuer, that haunteth either woods or hedgerowes, that euer gaue foorth the like, or carried in hir tunes, so delightfull a melodie.
>
> (p. 57)

In the novel Eros is a semi-allegorical character. His presence is felt; his work is recognized; but he is invisible to all except Philetas. Matching him in *The Tempest* is Ariel, the supernatural sprite who leads Miranda and Ferdinand together. Prospero instigates the plans for this love, but Ariel executes them. Thus, the roles are reversed. Like Eros, Ariel is associated with the pleasant and sunny aspects of nature. His coming seems to create music. He is at will invisible to all but Prospero, but others feel his presence and seem to be aware of his influence. The actual derivation of his name is from the Hebrew Cabala, where he is the Prince of the Angels,[14] yet the verbal correspondence between *Ariel* and *Eros* is suggestive.

An incidental correspondence between *Daphnis and Chloe* and *The Tempest* may rest in Prospero's command to Ariel: "Go make thyself like a nymph of the sea" (I. ii. 301). The reason for the command has been questioned, since there is no obvious advantage presented in the play by the proposed transformation.[15] But nymphs figure in *Daphnis and Chloe* as the guardians of the heroine, and they play an important role in the supernatural machinery of the novel. On the supposition that Shakespeare was familiar with the pastoral traditions established by Longus, it is here suggested that Ariel in the role of a nymph simply suggested itself, since he was to be the supernatural agent to accomplish in *The Tempest* much of what the nymphs accomplish in *Daphnis and Chloe*.

Dorco functions in the novel as the rude, bumbling shepherd, the rival of Daphnis, who supplies the comedy in his uncouth efforts to win Chloe. As part of his suit he supplies her with abundance of country gifts (p. 23). When these fail to win her, he disguises himself in a wolf skin and attempts rape. Caliban corresponds closely with Dorco, except that his "wolf skin" is a part of his nature. He is a kind of half-man, half-beast, frequently represented on the stage dressed in an animal skin. In the play he is referred to variously as a cat, puppy-head, fish, or tortoise. Thus, he can be interpreted as any animal-like man-monster, or as a very uncouth man. Before the play opens he has tried to rape Miranda; he functions in the comic scenes with Trinculo and Stephano, and to win their friendship offers them a profusion of country gifts.[16]

There are a few incidental correspondences between novel and play which suggest that the pastoral influence on *The Tempest* might have had its source in Longus. An incursion of foreigners occurs in both, and in both instances is associated with a great storm at sea. In *Danhnis and Chloe*, gallants of Mytilene come to the island to hunt. They make trouble, are punished, and in revenge kidnap Chloe. At this, Pan deliberately creates a fearful storm and commotion at sea. Angel Day translates the storm passage thus:

> . . . *it seemed at night in the middest of their banqueting*, that *all the land about them was on fire*, and a sodaine *noise arose in their hearing as of a great fleete, and armed nauie for the seas, approching towardes them*. The sound whereof and dreadfull sight, made some of the to crie *Arme Arme*, and others to gather together their companies & weapons. One thought his fellowe next him was hurt, an other feared the shot that he heard ratling in his eares, this man thought his companion slaine hard by his side, an other seemed to *stumble on dead carcasses*. In briefe, the *hurrie and tumult was so wonderfull and straunge, as they almost were at their wittes endes*. . . . *A dreadful noise was heard from the rocks*, not as the sound of any naturall trumpets, but far more shril and hideous, . . . about the middest of the day, . . . Pan himself in a vision stoode right before him, and beeing as he was in the shape vnder the *Pine* before described, [orders him to return Chloe] . . . The Captaine . . . caused present serch to be made for Chloe . . . and shee being found with a chapelet of the *Pine* tree leaues vpon her head, hee declared vnto them the expresse commaundement and direction of the god: . . . Chloe was no sooner parted out of the vessel where shee was, but they heard from the *hie rockes a sound againe*, but nothing dreadfull as the other, but rather *much sweete, melodious, and pleas-*

ing, such as the most cunning sheepheards use before their flockes and heards,[17]

In *The Tempest,* Neapolitan and Milanese noblemen and their retainers come ashore on the island as the result of a great storm created by the supernatural direction of Prospero and executed by the supernatural agency of Ariel. The storm is described as follows:

> [Miranda] The sky, it seems, would pour down
>   stinking pitch,
> But that the sea, mounting to th' welkin's cheek,
> Dashes the *fire* out.
>
> (I. ii. 3ff)

> [Ariel] I boarded the king's ship; now on the beak,
> Now in the waist, the deck, in every cabin,
> *I flam'd amazement:* sometime I'd divide
> And *burn in many places;* on the topmast,
> The yards, and boresprit, would I *flame distinctly*
> Then meet, and join: *Jove's lightnings,* the precursors
> O' the *dreadful thunder-claps,* more momentary
> And sight-outrunning were not: the fire and cracks
> Of sulphurous roaring the most *mighty Neptune*
> Seem to besiege and make his bold waves tremble,
> Yea, his dread trident shake.
>   . . .
>   *Not a soul*
> *But felt a fever of the mad and play'd*
> *Some tricks of desperation.* All but mariners,
> Plunged in the foaming brine and quit the vessel,
> Then *all a-fire* with me: the king's son, Ferdinand,
> With hair up-staring,—then like reeds, not hair,—
> Was the first man that leap'd, cried, 'Hell is empty,
> And all the devils are here.'
>
> (I. ii. 196-206, 208-215)

> *Fer.* [dinand] Where should *this music* be? i' th' air,
>   or th' earth?
> It sounds no more;—and sure, it waits upon
> Some god o' th' island. Sitting on a bank,
> Weeping again the king my father's wrack,
> *This music crept by me upon the waters,*
> Allaying both their fury, and my passion,
> *With its sweet air:* thence I have follow'd it,—
>
> (I. ii. 385-391)

> [Prospero]   *—I have bedimm'd*
> *The noontide sun,* call'd forth the mutinous winds,
> And 'twixt the green sea and the azur'd vault
> *Set roaring war: to the dread-rattling thunder*
> *Have I given fire* and rifted Jove's stout oak
> With his own holt: the strong-bas'd *promontory*
> Have I made shake; and by the spurs pluck'd up
> The *pine* and cedar: *graves at my command*
> *Have wak'd their sleepers, op'd, and let them forth*
> By my so potent art.
>
> (V. i. 41-50)[18]

Thus do the situations parallel: an incursion of foreigners to a sea island is associated with a supernaturally created storm. The storms are accompanied by darkness during daylight hours, illusions of fire, supernatural visions of dead men, and desperate behavior on the part of those trapped in the fray. Both tumults are compared to war, and both end on a strain of sweet music. Ultimately it is found that no harm has occurred to the unfortunates involved in them. The parallels in the descriptions of the storm are indicated by italics, but to assert that the Day version of Longus contributed to Shakespeare's thinking is unsound, for Amyot's French translation is equally suggestive:

> . . . soubdainement advis que toute la terre devint en feu, & entendirent de loing tel que seroit le flot d'une grosse armée de mer, qui fust venuë contre eulx: l'un cryoit à l'arme, l'autre appelloit ses compagnons, l'un pensoit estre jà blessé, l'autre cuydoit veoir un homme mort gisant devant luy; . . . & entendoit-on le son d'une trompe du dessus d'une roche haulte & droicte, estant à la crime de l'escueil, [*promontory* or *cliff*] au pied duquel ilz estoyent à l'abryt; mais ce son n'estoit point plaisant à oüyr, comme seroit le son d'une trompette ordinaire, ains effroyoit ceux qui l'entendoyent, ne plus ne moins que le son d'une tromperte de guerre là nuict: . . . que l'on entendit derechef le son de la trompe dedans le rocher, mais non plus effroyable ne maniere de l'alarme, ains tel que les bergers ont accoustumé de sonner quand ilz menent leurs bestes aux champs.[19]

If one accept these passages as evidence that Shakespeare knew Longus, it would be impossible to decide whether from Day or Amyot. Certainly the French version was the more accessible of the two, for although Day's would be the easier to read, Amyot's had gone through four editions between 1559 and 1609, while the English version appeared but once in 1587. The 1578 French translation of "L. L. L." was also buried in one edition.[20] There is, however, evidence in the marriage festivities that if Shakespeare was influenced by *Daphnis and Chloe* when writing *The Tempest,* he probably had read a version other than Day's, or had read Day's as well as another.

Whatever may have been the contemporary reason for interrupting the action of *The Tempest* with the marriage masque of Act IV, its appropriateness to the play cannot be denied, for the masque was a major attraction at many wedding festivities involving people of royal or noble rank during the Elizabethan period, and it serves in the play to elucidate the pastoral nature of the love of Miranda and Ferdinand, and to give a kind of pastoral blessing to their projected union. First Ceres, "most bounteous lady . . . Of wheat, rye, barley, vetches, oats, and peas (IV. i. 60f.)" is called in by Iris, "Who with . . . saffron wings . . . Diffusest honey-drops, refreshing showers (IV. i. 78f)" to Ceres' "bosky acres (IV. i. 81)". Then Juno enters and with Ceres sings a wedding song to Miranda and Ferdinand.[21] Next the nymphs "of the wandring brooks" (IV. i. 128) are called. They enter, followed by "sun-burn'd sicklemen, of August weary" (IV. i. 134). The nymphs and reapers join together in a dance just before the masque vanishes.

Nothing else in the play proclaims its essential pastoral nature so positively as does the masque. The structure of the stock pastoral plot is nearly perfect, but it is hidden from the unobservant behind the conventional romance of the situation and the elements of magic in Prospero's characterization. The same air of magic tends to conceal the pastoral quality of the island setting. It is as though Shakespeare saw this and would loudly and clearly proclaim the play pastoral by the device of the masque.

The pastoral blessing on the marriage of Miranda and Ferdinand may have been suggested by the country wedding of Daphnis and Chloe:

> . . . Her father gave Chloe away in the presence of the Nymphs, . . . and regaled [the villagers] . . . luxuriously. . . . the entertainment was all of a rustic and pastoral kind. One sang the song the reapers sing, another cracked the jokes the vintagers crack.
>
> (p. 97)

Day, perhaps tired when he reached the final page, omits the wedding from his translation, but Amyot (p. 156 f.) follows his source more closely.

Thus it can be seen that if the nymphs and reapers dancing in Shakespeare's bucolic marriage masque were suggested by the nymphs and reapers of Daphnis and Chloe's wedding, they probably derive from Amyot. Of course the Greek editions would not have been beyond Shakespeare's reach, but they certainly are less obvious considerations.

The conclusion that Longus is an ultimate influence on *The Tempest* is based on the presence of the elements of the stock pastoral plot, from which it deviates in only one instance. The conclusion that Longus is a direct, a primary influence, is not so surely established, but the coincidences of the chief characters, the striking coincidences in the storms, and the similarities in the wedding festivities certainly suggest that Shakespeare was familiar with Longus at first hand. In connection with this it is well to recall Wolff's conclusion that Longus is a primary source of *The Winter's Tale*, a play written probably no more than a year before the composition of *The Tempest*.[22]

Notes

1. See *A New Variorum Edition of Shakespeare: The Tempest*, ed. H. H. Furness (Philadelphia, 1920), pp. 324-341, for a discussion of the coincidences and a reprint of Ayrer's play.

2. E. K. Chambers, *William Shakespeare: A Study of Facts and Problems* (Oxford, 1930), I, 493f., reviews the theory.

3. J. M. Nosworthy, "The Narrative Sources of *The Tempest*", *RES*, XXIV (1948), 282.

4. Nosworthy, pp. 383f.

5. Nosworthy, pp. 287-293.

6. Reviewed in the Variorum *Tempest*, pp. 308-315, 320-324.

7. "Shakespeare's Pastorals", *SP*, XIII (1916), 122-154.

8. *The Complete Works of William Shakespeare*, ed. W. J. Craig (London, 1947). All further citations of Shakespeare are from this edition.

9. S. L. Wolff, *The Greek Romances in Elizabethan Prose Fiction* (New York, 1912), pp. 447-455.

10. The Renaissance bibliography of Longus is cited in detail in my *Greek Romance Materials in the Plays of Shakespeare* (University Microfilms, 1956), pp. 333f.

11. See Robert Adger Law, "On the Dating of Shakspere's Plays", *Shakespeare Association Bulletin*, XI (1935), 46-51. Law publishes a convenient tabulation of the conclusions of J. Q. Adams, R. M. Alden, T. Brooke, O. J. Campbell, H. Craig, and T. M. Parrott as to the dating of Shakespeare's plays.

12. For example, see Longus, "Daphnis and Chloe", *Three Greek Romances,* tr. Moses Hadas (New York, 1953), pp. 21, 30, 36, 58f; and *The Tempest,* ed. Craig, I. ii. 336ff; II. i. 49-52, 55f; II. ii. 173f; III. ii. 147-150. All quotations are from this edition.

13. Longus, *Daphnis and Chloe: The Elizabethan Version from Amyot's Translations by Angel [Illegible Text] Reprinted from the Unique Original,* ed. Joseph Jacobs (London, 1890), p. 58. Quotations are from this edition.

14. See Nelson Sherman Bushnell, "Natural Supernaturalism in *The Tempest*", *PMLA,* XLVII (1932), 690, and W. S. Johnson, "The Genesis of Ariel", *SQ,* II, 205-210.

15. *The Tempest,* ed. Furness, p. 64, reviews the question. See also Irwin Smith, "Ariel as Ceres", *SQ,* IV, 430-432.

16. See II. ii. 173f, 180-185.

17. Day, pp. 74-77. My italics except "*Arme Arme.*"

18. My italics except "*Fer.*"

19. Longus, *Les Amours Pastorales de Daphnis et Chloé,* tr. Jacques Amyot. (n.p., 1731), pp. 61-64.

20. I have been unable to obtain this edition for examination.

21. See IV. i. 110-117.

22. Law dates *The Winter's Tale* between 1610 and 1611.

Jerry H. Bryant (essay date 1963)

SOURCE: "The Winter's Tale and the Pastoral Tradition," in *Shakespeare Quarterly,* Vol. 14, No. 4, Autumn 1963, pp. 537-98.

[*In the following essay, Bryant notes the indebtedness of William Shakespeare's* The Winter's Tale *to the classical European and English pastoral traditions and argues that with this subtle dramatized commentary on appearance and reality Shakespeare brought freshness to the pastoral mode and transformed its hackneyed conventions.*]

It is curious that no appraiser or appreciator seems to have puzzled over the kinship of *The Winter's Tale* with the pastoral tradition. Most commentators tacitly assume the connection, then abandon it to court other features. Some explain the drama as tragicomedy, some as one of the "last plays". Others see it against the background of Elizabethan thought. Still others, lately, have examined the grammar, the vocabulary, and the reverberations of the imagery. All these approaches are good, cogent, helpful; but the pastoral element has gone begging for an analyst. For that matter, Sir Walter Greg once went so far as to say that "it is characteristic of the shepherd scenes in that play, written in the full maturity of Shakespeare's genius, that, in spite of their origins in Greene's romance of *Pandosto,* they owe nothing of their treatment to pastoral tradition, nothing to convention, nothing to aught save life. . . ."[1] This persistent neglect of an important historical precedent deserves correction. I should like, therefore, first to try to show that Shakespeare is in fact very much a part of the pastoral tradition and that *The Winter's Tale* can be seen as an example of the English pastoral drama, which has roots in classical, Italian, and English literature. Then I should like to go on to a consideration of the freshness and vitality which Shakespeare brings to the tradition, showing how he transforms the hackneyed conventions of the pastoral into an involved and subtle commentary on appearance and reality.

The most indirect influence upon the English pastoral drama and hence upon *The Winter's Tale* is the classical one. First of all there was the pastoral eclogue, given most of its forms and themes by Theocritus. His shepherds were isolated in the hills of Sicily where they were safe from the fever of the city and court. They piped to their flocks, contested in song with their companions, wooed their nymphs, complained of unrequited love. They spoke of milk-white lambs, pretty shepherdesses, and gifts of red apples. Theocritus' pastoral world was also a place where gods and goddesses rubbed shoulders with human Sicilians. But even the mythological deities were drawn with an exactness and a benign humor which have given the Theocritan idyls their hallmark of refreshing and delightful realism.

The Greek pastoral idyl was extended into the Roman world by Virgil, who imitated Theocritus. In the exchange, something of the original freshness was lost. Virgil's mind was largely upon either his own problems or those of the world, and he used the eclogue to disguise contemporary allusion or direct satire upon the shortcomings of the civilized world.[2] Thus, though the complaints, the singing contests, the talk of love remained, they were included for something more than the simple delight they in themselves could bring. And so we get a noble prophecy of Astrea's return, some waspish complaining about the politics which caused Virgil trouble with his farm, and Silenus' philosophical song describing the progress of earth's creation.

The other aspect of the classical influence upon the English pastoral drama is the Greek romance. The long prose tales of Heliodorus and Achilles Tatius, in particular, received enthusiastic audience during the Renaissance for the endless adventuring to exotic shores contained in them. Unlike the stories of chivalry, which spotlighted the activities of a single knight, the Greek romance focused upon two protagonists, a boy and a girl. The typical tale begins with their falling in love. But before the two youths are able to consummate their passion, the gods send down on their heads every conceivable kind of adversity. They are kidnapped, singly or in pair; they are captured by pirates, separated, sold into slavery; re-united, they are cast adrift in a violent storm. The reader follows these exciting characters from one end of the world to the other. Other things keep the lovers apart. In the *thiopica* of Heliodorus, the hero cannot marry the heroine because of her inferior origins. But after the two have been tossed about the world's seas, she is discovered to be the daughter of the Ethiopian king. The disparity resolved, the two marry amidst much rejoicing.

The eclogue and the Greek romance went pretty much underground during the period of the Middle Ages. But they both reappeared in the Renaissance with considerable force. Virgil's pastoralism was adopted by Boccaccio, Petrarch, Mantuan, Tasso, Marot, and Spenser. Latin and vernacular eclogues sprang abundantly from these writers' pens. The artificiality which was incipient in Virgil's pastorals became the identifying trait of the Renaissance ecloguists' work. The pastoral scene is used to disguise hyperbolic praise of patrons or monarchs, to mask satire upon the sham and hypocrisy of contemporary society, to cover up discussions of religious and political issues. Since the aim of these writers was not to recreate an accurate picture of the shepherd's life, the scene became idealized and stereotyped, a quality which we always associate today with the pastoral as a form, ignoring the realistic beginnings of the tradition. Nevertheless, this genre was extremely popular and it is important to the pastoral drama.

The first direct influence upon the English stage which I want to examine is the Italian pastoral drama. It is Greg's thesis that this drama grew out of the pastoral eclogues discussed above, which were read with enthusiasm at the court of Ferrara.[3] The plays which came to be written to meet the demand for more drama than the mere eclogue provided contained echoes of the Greek romance. The best examples of the Italian pastoral drama are Tasso's *Aminta,* first acted at Ferrara in 1573 and translated into English in 1591, and Guarini's *Il Pastor Fido,* performed at Ferrara in 1585 and translated in 1602. Aminta, in Tasso's play, is unsuccessful in his suit to the huntress Silvia. When Aminta rescues his love from the clutches of a rude satyr who has bound her to a tree, Silvia, with rather questionable modesty, runs away into the forest. Later it is thought that she has been devoured by a wild beast. In despair Aminta leaps off a cliff. But Silvia has not been killed and she returns from the forest. Upon being informed of the results of her hard-heartedness and Aminta's great love and fidelity, she goes to recover his body. Luckily, Aminta was not killed when he jumped, and the two join their loves.[4]

Il Pastor Fido is longer and more complicated than the *Aminta* and has more resemblances to the Greek romance. Mirtillo, the faithful shepherd, cannot marry his Amarillis because of his low birth. The oracle has assured the country that it will not be delivered from a certain curse until

> two of heavens issue love unite
> And for the auncient fault of that false wight,
> A faithful Shepherds pittie make amends.[5]

Mirtillo, doggedly faithful throughout, turns out to be the shepherd spoken of in the prophecy, for his fidelity "makes amends". And at the auspicious moment, he is also found to be of "heavens issue", i.e. of royal shepherd birth. These brief synopses show that the dominating interest in the Italian pastoral drama is the youthful love affair, as it was in the Greek romance. They also show that fidelity and honor can overcome any impediment to the realization of love. What they do not reveal are the rich appendages to the main action: the lustful satyrs, the wanton shepherds and shepherdesses, the disguise, the mistaken identities—in short, any of the dramatic devices which provide conflict by threatening the chastity, honor, and fidelity of the hero or heroine. The more obstacles to overcome the better, but fidelity always wins out; maidenheads are retained; chaste Jack gets his chaste Jill.

The other direct influence upon the English pastoral drama is the pastoral prose romance. Sidney's *Arcadia,* Greene's *Menaphon* and *Pandosto,* Lodge's *Rosalynde*—all eventually were acted, in one form or another, upon the stage. Like the Italian pastoral drama, the romance has roots in classical literature, that is, the Greek romance; all three genres, in fact, share several features. All are preoccupied with the honor of the heroine, an honor kept intact so long as she remains a virgin. All produce conflict by throwing up obstacles in the course of true love. And the theme of fidelity in love is central in all three forms. Finally, all rely extensively upon mistaken identity or disguise. In the pastoral romance a maiden of royal birth is for various reasons, usually parental dissatisfaction, sent into the wilds where she is raised by shepherds. Variations have the abandoned person a child, either male or female. Then, the banished character's lineage unknown, he woos a princess (who might be disguised as a shepherd); or she is wooed by a prince.[6] The disguise motif is carried out in a variety of ways—change of clothing, magical transformation, or confusions surrounding the birth of the hero or heroine. These disguises, however, are no match for the protagonists' powerful love. The heroes' passion sweeps away appearances; a prince's love will be drawn to a princess in spite of the fact that she is dressed in shepherd's weeds. All of this suggests a further contribution of the pastoral romance: the court element, for the pastoral episode usually is presented within a frame of action which begins and ends in the court. With the ejection of one or more characters from court the action is set in motion, and the resolution is made when those characters are accepted back into the active life after finding the necessary answers in a pastoral setting.

Examples of the English pastoral drama show a wide range of borrowing from all of these traditions. George Peele's *The Arraignment of Paris,* an odd, masque-like little play, is very much like a pastoral eclogue. On the other hand, Fletcher's *The Faithful Shepherdess* begins a large debt to the Italian pastoral drama with its title. A composite of the Greek romance, the Italian pastoral drama, and the pastoral romance occurs in *The Maydes Metamorphasis,* which contains the court frame, features dancing and singing, and peoples itself with mythological deities, shepherds, nymphs, princes, and princesses. It also uses the oracle. Love and fidelity, impeded by the forces of disguise and lust, form the main plot motives. A companion piece to *The Maydes Metamorphosis* is *The Thracian Wonder,* an incredibly complicated dramatization of Greene's incredibly complicated romance *Menaphon.*[7] This play deals not only with several sets of lovers, but several generations of them.

The debt of *The Winter's Tale* to the pastoral tradition which I have sketched can be made clear through some specific citations. For instance, the humor and realism in the fourth act have been cited as examples of Shakespeare's freedom from the pastoral tradition. The fact is that the tradition began in a humorous spirit with Theocritus. In Idly IV[8] two herdsmen gossip about the state of local herds and flocks, a neighbor's journey to the Olympics, the death of Amaryllis, and the fact that their cows are grazing in the wrong place. Battus gets a thorn in his foot. The talk turns to the pursuit of a young girl by an old man, who is apparently successful. In the next Idyl a goatherd and a shepherd hotly accuse each other of robbery. They resolve their argument through a singing contest. Thievery, thorns in a shepherd's foot, cows grazing in the wrong place—Theocritus is amusingly frank and quite realistic.

Perhaps the humor which was potential in the pastoral was smothered by the serious purposes of Virgil and his imitators, but clearly Theocritus' impulse was valid. The low characters which the poet must treat make the form ripe for comedy. Even Guarini sees the comic possibilities. In Act I, Scene v, of *Il Pastor Fido,* a satyr embarks upon an amusing discourse concerning the artifice of women in decorating their faces with make-up and plucking their eyebrows. There is also a pretty scene in which Dorinda, a determined shepherdess in pursuit of the young bachelor hunter Silvio, withholds the boy's hunting dog until he gives her a kiss.

Comic realism abounds in much of the English pastoral drama. *The Maydes Metamorphosis* contains three comic characters who are the ancestors of Autolycus. Joculo, Mopsa, and Frisco are a spry lot, rogues and singers. In one of the longest acts of the play the three comics enter

tempts the chastity of Fawnia, whom, of course, he does not recognize. Egistus, discovering the whereabouts of his son and his son's paramour, requests Pandosto to execute them. At the last moment, however, Fawnia's foster father appears and reveals her true identity. The shock is so great for Pandosto that he commits suicide. Dorastus and Fawnia are left occupying the stage, prototypes of pastoral romantic lovers. The goal of the book is the happiness of Dorastus and Fawnia, and it is achieved through a stereotyped fidelity.

Shakespeare makes many changes, but the most significant one is the departure from the usual handling of the fidelity theme. Instead of making the inviolable love between Florizel and Perdita the center of the action, he uses it for the examination of a larger problem—the nature of truth. The fact that Hermione remains alive and steals the last scene from her daughter throws the dramatic weight upon the story of herself and Leontes. Greene exploits the conventional courtly romance between Dorastus and Fawnia, playing upon their falling in love, and the obstacles to consummating that love, for the sake of sentimental chills. Shakespeare is not interested in that. By shifting the focus, he anatomizes an infected king whose disease is an inability to see the truth. Leontes' disease is developed through contrast with other examples of the apprehension of truth and reality. Shakespeare, in submitting to certain superficial aspects of the pastoral tradition, transforms them into devices for commenting seriously upon the theme of reality and experience and its importance to the conduct of a king.

The serious commentary begins with Leontes' misapprehension of actuality. Suddenly, without warning, he is seized by an unreasoning, unfounded certainty of his wife's infidelity. His infected mind "[does] make possible things not so held" (I. ii. 139). He deludes himself into believing the raging fancies of his own dreams, fancies derived from the most tenuous appearances. Camillo shows that nothing is going on between Hermione and Leontes' childhood friend Polixenes by having to ask whom Leontes suspects Hermione of being unfaithful with (I. ii. 307). Both chastity and fidelity are issues here, as the conventions demand, but they are not the main issues. The main one is the awfulness of Leontes' burning mind, fabricating at will: "Is whispering nothing? Is leaning cheek to cheek? Is meeting noses? Kissing with inside lip?" (I. ii. 284-286). To this Camillo replies, "Good my lord, be cur'd." Camillo cannot verify Leontes' suspicions because there is nothing to be verified. Fearing for his own life and unable any longer to support Leontes' imaginings, Camillo defects to Polixenes with the information about Leontes' plot upon the life of the Bohemian king. Hard upon this, Leontes' Sicilian courtiers, for whom we have no reason to feel anything other than respect and trust, deny Leontes' accusations against Hermione and Polixenes. Finally, divinely pointing up the phantoms of Leontes' mind, the oracle clears Hermione in every eye but Leontes'.

This jealousy, this humour, brings Leontes near to madness—"Dost think I am so muddy, so unsettled, / To appoint myself in this vexation . . ." (I. ii. 325-326). Paulina declares that she is "no less honest than you are mad" (II. iii. 70-71), and "These dangerous unsafe lunes I' th' King, beshrew them" (II. ii. 30). In this humour Leontes betrays the obligations of a good king. He becomes cruel and peremptory. He refuses the counsel of his nobles. He commits himself, without moderation, to his own passion. The results of this are serious. He loses a friend, a son, a daughter, and a wife. But the consequences are not confined to the personal sphere. A ruler who treats the truth as something of his own making must eventually unhinge his state. The repercussions of his irresponsible suspicions, so firm in his mind that they create a world which he actually sees and feels (II. i. 152), are potentially cataclysmic. An apprehension of what is and what should be are principal requirements for the good ruler; Leontes attempts to shape reality to his own fantasies.

The psychological implications of Leontes' anger are a good deal deeper than those present in similar situations in other examples of the pastoral drama. In part this derives from Greene. But Pandosto's jealousy is brought about gradually; he at least makes a feint at examining what might be only appearances, Shakespeare treats the situation with more daring. Because he provides no real motives for Leontes' jealousy, the irrationality of his fancies is dramatically emphasized. In *The Maydes Metamorphosis* the Duke banishes Eurymine because his son loves her. He does not, however, merely imagine that that love exists; he has it from his son's own testimony. He is legitimately angered because he does not and cannot know Eurymine's birth, and so attempts to save his son from an inferior match. Radagon, in *The Thracian Wonder*, disguises himself to woo Ariadne, the daughter of the Thracian king. She submits and when she becomes pregnant, unmistakably by Radagon, her father sends the two lovers and the child to sea in little boats. The actions of these two rulers might not have been "right", but the men knew what they saw. The only disguises in these plays were physical disguises which really did mask the identity of those involved. But the disguise in the first three acts of *The Winter's Tale* is of Leontes' own making and is intimately connected with psychological truth and observable reality. Some ten years after the production of *The Winter's Tale* Bacon, speaking in another context, will state a generality which embraces Leontes' problem: ". . . everyone . . . has a cave or den of his own, which refracts and discolours the light of nature. . . ."[18]

Shakespeare cures Leontes' infected mind through the pastoral, and, as we have seen, that episode contains almost all of the conventions of the genre. The devices of disguise and mistaken identity are again put to the task of exploring the reality and appearance theme. But more than that, Shakespeare uses them to point up Leontes' shortcomings. In contrast to his distortion of reality according to his own "den", the characters in Act IV are confronted with tangible costume disguises and mistaken identities which make their inability to see the truth quite justifiable. Polixenes, in other words, like the Duke in *The Maydes*

Metamorphosis, cannot be blamed too severely for not wanting his royal son to marry what appears to be a mere shepherd girl. The reprehensibility of Leontes' unjustifiable delusions, however, is most effectively emphasized by Florizel and Autolycus.

Florizel is the fairy prince who does not concern himself with the mere appearance of outward trappings. Through infallible intuition and the highest integrity he pierces externals to discover the emotional truth of Perdita's real quality. The clarity of his vision, which sees through the physical disguise, throws into relief the blindness of Leontes, who had no such impediment to overcome. Indeed, the truth was clear to all but him. In Act IV the truth is clear only to the faithful Florizel. Shakespeare heightens the effectiveness of this contrast by ennobling the relationship between Florizel and Perdita, another example of his transformation of hackneyed conventions into living situations. In former pastorals, love was a matter of sex and it was expressed through chastity. Shakespeare does not avoid or reject the virtue; he simply does not use it as the foundation of real love. Perdita is too charming for chastity even to be an issue. Without the priggishness of her pastoral forebears, she declares her heart with disarming candor. She is like her mother and Florizel discerns her worth under her apparent identity. This innocent love, in other pastorals valuable only in itself, becomes the means of restoring a civic body to health.

The other main contrast to Leontes' behavior comes in Autolycus. He suffers from no delusions. He may be a thief, a cozener, a sharp salesman, but he is thoroughly truthful with himself, and he has taken full measure of the reality about him. The most interesting comments on the nature of truth and appearance and reality are made through Autolycus. First of all, his constant changing of costumes reflects truth—it is first one thing and then another. Secondly, the word truth is bandied about during the ballad-selling, and Autolycus, knowing the truth, is several jumps ahead of his coneys. Mopsa, in her country innocence, says, "I love a ballad in print o' life, for then we are sure they are true" (IV. iv. 263). How slenderly people go about learning the truth, as though print could create it. The silly shepherds, mouths hanging open in awe, take the pedlar's word for truth that a usurer's wife actually bore "twenty money-bags at a burden", and that a fish high above the water sang a "ballad against the sad hearts of maids". The truth is disguised under many robes, but Mopsa's gullibility is no more grotesque and certainly less consequential than Leontes', who believed something worse upon less provocation.

Later, when Autolycus switches clothes with Florizel, his shrewd eye detects "a piece of iniquity" in the prince's actions. But instead of performing his duty to his sovereign like a good subject, he decides to conceal his knowledge about Florizel's actions because such concealment is the "more knavery". Under different circumstances such a commitment to knavery would seem sinister, as it does with Richard III. But Shakespeare's use of irony saves Au-

tolycus for comedy and strengthens his effectiveness as a foil to Leontes. It is ironical that Autolycus should use such a clear grasp of reality to achieve knavery, while a king, lacking that grasp, threatened a whole realm. But, to enrich the irony, dramatically it is not knavery at all for it works a better end, since it allows Florizel's escape and sets up the happy conclusion. The escape of the lovers is served by a knave, when two kings almost destroyed the youngsters through varying degrees of blindness.

The final comment upon Leontes' inability to distinguish between reality and appearance comes in Act V. The Clown and the Old Shepherd, now known to be the foster relatives of Perdita, confront Autolycus with their new-made fineries. The Clown forces from him the acknowledgment that the two shepherds are "gentlemen born". It is characteristic of Autolycus' astute acceptance of circumstances that he meekly, without the old loquacity, surrenders: "I know you are now, sir, a gentleman born" (V. ii. 146). The Clown will never know the difference between the truth and mere appearances. Autolycus has always known, and has laughed. The Clown is a generous fellow and when Autolycus declares that he is going to mend his ways, the Clown insists that he "will swear to the Prince thou art as honest a true fellow as any in Bohemia" (168). This swearing disturbs the Old Shepherd, who asks, "How if it be false, son?" The Clown replies, "If it be ne'er so false, a true gentleman may swear it in the behalf of his friend" (176). A gentleman, in short, may swear the truth into existence; just as a ballad in print, for Mopsa, might declare absurdities true; and just as Leontes' fancies might "make possible things not so held". These distortions of truth are all of the same class. Leontes' delusions, serious as they are, are made ridiculous when they are paralleled with those of Mopsa and the Clown.

The Clown gets in the last word with Autolycus, and as though to emphasize the pertinence of his remarks to the Leontes episode, he opens the curtains for the final scene when he announces the entrance of the royal entourage on its way to see the "Queen's picture". And so the action shifts and we are shown the final prodigy. Hermione, appearing to be a statue, returns to life. Appearances are swept away and reality is restored. Theodore Spencer has said that in the last plays appearance is evil and reality is good.[19] In *The Winter's Tale,* the evil lies not in appearance itself but in the royal mind which insists that appearance is reality. To explore this premise, Shakespeare converts the stereotyped conventions of the pastoral drama into highly original instruments which combine to form one of the best of his last plays.

Notes

1. W. W. Greg, *Pastoral Poetry and the Pastoral Drama* (London, 1906), p. 411.

2. Greg, p. 7.

3. Greg, p. 169.

4. All references are to Torquato Tasso, *Aminta,* ed. Louis E. Lord (London, 1931).

5. Giovanni Baptista Guarini, *Il Pastor Fido,* printed for Simon Waterford, 1602, sig. C2.

6. For an extensive list of plot conventions see Edwin Greenlaw, "Shakespeare's Pastorals", *SP,* XII (1916), 123.

7. Cf. J. Q. Adams, "*Menaphon* and *The Thracian Wonder*", *MP,* III (1906), 317-318.

8. All references to the Idyls are from *Theocritus, Bion, and Moschus,* ed. A. Lang (London, 1918).

9. *The Maydes Metamorphosis,* in *Old Plays,* ed. A. H. Bullen (London, 1882), p. 136.

10. *Il Pastor Fido,* sig. N4.

11. *The Maydes Metamorphosis,* p. 138.

12. George Peele, *The Arraignment of Paris,* eds. Charles Read Baskervill, Virgil B. Heltzel, and Arthur H. Nethercot (New York, 1934), p. 211.

13. John Webster, *The Thracian Wonder,* printed by Tho. Johnson, 1661.

14. G. Wilson Knight, *The Crown of Life* (New York, 1947), p. 98.

15. John Fletcher, *The Faithful Shepherdess* in *Beaumont and Fletcher,* ed. J. St. Loe Strachey, vol. II (New York, 1950).

16. Greg, p. 190.

17. Robert Greene, *Pandosto,* ed. P. G. Thomas (London, 1907).

18. Sir Francis Bacon, *Novum Organum,* in *Selected Writings,* ed. Hugh G. Dick (New York, 1955), p. 470.

19. Theodore Spencer, "Appearance and Reality in Shakespeare's Last Plays", *MP,* XXXIX (1942), 269.

FURTHER READING

Criticism

Alpers, Paul. "Pastoral and the Domain of Lyric in Spenser's *Shepheardes Calender." Representations* 12 (Autumn 1985): 83-100.

> Discusses the influence of Spenser's *Shepheardes Calender* on English poetry, arguing that in composing the first set of English pastorals in the European tradition Spenser helped himself—and English poetry in general—to overcome the difficulties of writing lyric verse.

Bernard, John D. "Spenserian Pastoral and the *Amoretti." ELH* 47, No. 3 (Autumn 1980): 419-32.

> Argues that the pastoral is a major factor that shapes Edmund Spenser's conception of his subject in the love poems of the *Amoretti.*

Blanchard, J. Marc. "The Tree and the Garden: Pastoral Poetics and Milton's Rhetoric of Desire." *Modern Language Notes* 91, No. 6 (1976): 1540-68.

> Examines "Comus" and *Paradise Lost* in the context of the pastoral and the masque, and seeks to understand the relationship of mimesis, or literary imitation, to language and desire.

Buxton, John. "Michael Drayton." *In A Tradition of Poetry.* London: Macmillan, 1967.

> Examination of Drayton's work, emphasizing his interest in pastoral themes.

Cheney, Patrick. "Career Rivalry and the Writing of Counter-Nationhood: Ovid, Spenser, and Philomela in Marlowe's 'The Passionate Shepherd to His Love.'" *ELH* 65, No. 3 (1998): 523-55.

> Claims that Marlowe's famous pastoral poem is as an amatory lyric in the style of the Greek poet Ovid.

Cooper, Helen. *Pastoral: Mediaeval into Renaissance.* Totowa, N.J.: Rowman and Littlefield, 1977, 257 p.

> Discussion of medieval pastoral literature and its influence on Renaissance pastoralism.

Cory, Herbert E. "The Golden Age of the Spenserian Pastoral." *PMLA* 25 (1910): 241-67.

> Survey of the pastoralists who followed Spenser, including Greene, Drayton, Browne, and Fletcher.

Cullen, P. Spenser. *Marvell and Renaissance Pastoral.* Cambridge, Mass.: Harvard University Press, 1970, 212 p.

> Discusses the flexibility and variety of the pastoral form by comparing the works of Spenser and Marvell.

Empson, William. *Some Versions of Pastoral.* London: Chatto and Windus, 1935, 298 p.

> Landmark study that tries to show the ways in which the pastoral process and its resulting social ideas have been used in English literature. Includes chapters on Shakespeare, Marvell, and Milton.

Friedman, Donald M. *Marvell's Pastoral Art.* Berkeley: University of California Press, 1970, 300 p.

> Comprehsive study of Marvell's wide-ranging use of pastoral themes in his poetry.

Greenlaw, E. "Shakespeare's Pastorals." *Studies in Philology* XIII (1916): 122-54.

> Detailed analysis of Shakespeare's pastoral plays in the context of the genre of pastoral romance.

Greg, Walter W. *Pastoral Poetry and Pastoral Drama.* London: A. H. Bullen, 1906, 464 p.

> Important early study that focuses on the pastoral drama in Elizabethan literature; includes discussions of dozens of plays and offers chapters devoted to the principal dramatists of the form.

Grundy, Joan. *The Spenserian Poets: A Study in Elizabethan and Jacobean Poetry.* London: Edward Arnold, 1969, 224 p.

Argues that pastoral poets Drayton, Browne, and Wither were conservative and backward-looking.

Haber, Judith. *Pastoral and the Poetics of Self-Contradiction.* Cambridge: Cambridge University Press, 1994, 218 p.

Study that seeks to account for the persistence of the "antipastoral" in pastoral poetry.

Hanford, J. H. "The Pastoral Elegy and Milton's *Lycidas.*" *PMLA* 25 (1910): 403-07.

Explores the relationship of Greek elegy to Milton's poem.

Jones, Ann Rosalind and Peter Stallybrass. "The Politics of *Astrophel and Stella,*" *Studies in English Literature, 1500-1900* 24 (Winter 1984): 53-68.

Suggests that the poems in Sidney's *Astrophel and Stella* function as a complex displacement of the ideological pressures of the court.

Kermode, Frank. "Introduction." In *The Tempest* (Arden Edition). London: Arden, 1958.

Analysis of the tension between nature and art in Shakespeare's play.

Kronenfeld, Judy Z. "Social Rank and the Pastoral Ideals in *As You Like It.*" *Shakespeare Quarterly* 29, No. 3 (Summer 1978): 333-48.

Argues that in *As You Like It* Shakespeare calls into question the pastoral idealizations of the relationship between the high and the low, or the Christian and the courtly.

Levin, Harry. *The Myth of the Golden Age in the Renaissance.* Bloomington: Indiana University Press, 1969, 231 p.

Detailed examination of the idea of the Golden Age as manifested in literary and artistic works of the Renaissance.

Mallette, Richard. *Spenser, Milton and the Renaissance Pastoral.* East Brunswick, N.J.: Associated University Presses, 1981, 224 p.

Notes the correspondences between Spenser and Milton and examines how both poets employed pastoral conventions in unique ways to understand, promote, and evaluate the enterprise of poetry.

Marinelli, Peter V. *Pastoral.* London: Methuen & Co. Ltd., 1971, 90 p.

Explores the nature of the pastoral from its beginnings to the twentieth century, concentrating on Renaissance pastoralists.

Orgel, S. K. "Sidney's Experiment in Pastoral: *The Lady of May.*" In *Essential Articles for the Study of Sir Philip Sidney,* pp. 61-71. Hamden: Archon Books, 1986.

Argues that Sidney's mixed-mode court masque about the contemplative life, *The Lady of May,* provides us with a "brief and excellent example of the way his mind worked."

Patrides, A. ed. *Milton's "Lycidas": The Tradition and the Poem.* Columbia: University of Missouri Press, 1983, 270 p.

Collection of the major critical writings on Milton's pastoral poem.

Poggioli, Renato. *The Oaten Flute: Essays on Pastoral Poetry and the Bucolic Ideal.* Cambridge, Mass.: Harvard University Press, 1975, 340 p.

Reconstruction and reinterpretion of the bucolic ideal as presented in idyllic literature from the early Renaissance to the twentieth century, emphasizing the pyschology of the genre.

Sambrook, James. *English Pastoral Poetry.* Boston: Twayne Publishers, 1983, 160 p.

Short, descriptive history of general tendencies and individual achievements in English nondramatic pastoral poetry from the sixteenth to the beginning of the nineteenth century.

Schenk, Celeste Marguerite. *Mourning and Panegyric: The Poetics of Pastoral Ceremony.* University Park: The Pennsylvania State University Press, 1988, 228 p.

Offers a poetics of pastoral ceremony, beginning with classical elegies and ending with Romantic and modern ceremonial lyrics.

Schwenger, Peter. "Herrick's Fairy State." *ELH* 46, No. 1 (Spring 1979): 335-55.

Examine's Herrick's bucolic fairy poems "Oberon's Feast" and "Oberon's Palace" as a single unit.

Stillman, Robert E. "The Politics of Sidney's Pastoral: Mystification and Mythology in the *Old Arcadia.*" *ELH* 52, No. 2 (Winter 1985): 795-814.

Analyzes the *Old Arcadia* as myth, arguing that this makes it possible to understand the "double sense" of the text—its remoteness from the historical world and its desire to make contact with it.

The Slave Trade in British and American Literature

INTRODUCTION

Literature written about the Atlantic trade in African slaves by white British and American authors and by former captives contributed to the debate about slavery and eventual abolition of the institution.

The era of the Atlantic slave trade began under the Portuguese in the 1490s and continued until the 1870s. During that time, between 10 and 12 million Africans were enslaved in order to support European and American commercial interests. Africans were taken by ship to European- and American-controlled ports to work on sugar, coffee, cocoa, and cotton plantations; in gold and silver mines; in rice fields; and as house servants. At the height of the traffic in the 1780s, European and American slaving vessels carried some forty thousand captive human beings a year from their native countries to a world of which they had no previous knowledge where they would be owned as property. The "triangular" trade system used by the slavers was so named because ships embarked from European ports, stopped in Africa to gather captives, set out for the New World to deliver their human cargo, and returned to ports of origin. The notorious "Middle Passage" was that leg of the slave trade triangle that brought slaves from West Africa to North America, South America, and the Caribbean. Accounts of the Atlantic trade in human lives date from the early sixteenth century, and European writers began introducing descriptions of Africans into their literature by the 1550s. The height of literary interest in the slave trade coincides with the period of greatest activity in the trade itself, and the later eighteenth century in Britain and the United States saw a proliferation of poems, novels, lectures, pamphlets, traveller's narratives, and non-fiction works about the immorality and horror of African chattel slavery.

African characters figured in numerous fictional works of the sixteenth and seventeenth centuries, including, most famously, Shakespeare's *Othello,* but the first British work of imaginative literature written specifically about slavery and the slave trade was Aphra Behn's *Oroonoko; Or The Royall Slave* (1688). The mid-1660s setting of Behn's fictional account about a slave of royal lineage from the Gold Coast who is killed after leading a slave revolt in Surinam—where Behn had lived as a child—roughly corresponds with Britian's initial participation in the slave trade. *Oroonoko* has been seen by many critics as a pionerring antislavery work, although some commentators such as Anne Fogarty claim that the work is as much about insurmountable barriers between its white and black characters as it is about the evils of slavery. *Oroonoko* was

adapted for the stage several times in the late 1600s and throughout the 1700s, and proved immensely popular to British audiences. After *Oronooko,* depictions of or comments on slavery and the slave trade appeared at least incidentally in the works of many major British writers of the eighteenth century, including Samuel Johnson, William Cowper, and Samuel Taylor Coleridge, all of whom denounced slavery. Less well-known British opponents of slavery include the poets James Thomson, William Roscoe, and Richard Savage. Many well-meaning and liberal writers who wrote about the slave experience presented sentimental portraits of Africans and in many instances made clear their beliefs about the fundamental differences between blacks and whites. But these writers were generally driven by their humanitarian concern—as they pointed out the hypocrisy inherent in the practice of enslaving human beings conducted by citizens of a nation that prided itself on its high civilization and devotion to the principles of liberty—and antislavery works laid the foundation for the abolitionist movement by opening up public debate about the morality of slavery. Not all white British authors, of course, opposed slavery, and many travel narratives by participants in the trade and writings of virulently racist thinkers such as Edward Long were used to buttress public support for the slave trade. However, the intellectual and social climate created by British antislavery writers in the 1700s did a great deal to make possible the abolition of slavery in Britiain in the early nineteenth century.

The slave trade was made illegal in the United States in the early part of the nineetenth century also, but slavery as an institution was not outlawed there until more than half a century later. White American writers in the seventeenth and eighteenth centuries were far less inclined to speak against slavery than were their British counterparts, although antislavery literature, especially in the form of pamphlets, did begin to proliferate during the Revolutionary years. However, even writers who advocated freedom for blacks, including Thomas Jefferson, stressed what they thought to be their "natural inferiority." But as in Britain, white antislavery writers in the United States in the eighteenth century set the stage for the great antislavery debates and abolitionist movement of the next century.

For many years readers and critics focused on white responses to the "slavery problem" and overlooked the profound impact of African literary figures on the slavery debate and subsequent abolitionist movement. Accounts about the slave trade and slavery by former captives are not as abundant as those by white authors, but those that are available offer invaluable, first-hand insight and unique perspectives on the horrors of slavery and its effect on Africans' sense of identity. The first African to speak out against slavery was Ignatius Sancho, who was born on a slave ship and brought to England after some years spent in Grenada. Sancho's *Letters* (1782) are written in the sentimental style of his white British contemporaries, but beneath his sentimental rhetoric he speaks urgently for the freedom of his fellow Africans and against the brutalities of the slave trade. Perhaps the most original and articulate critic of the slave trade was Olaudah Equiano, a Nigerian who had been captured and sold into slavery when he was ten years old. *The Interesting Narrative of Olaudah Equiano, or Gustavus Vassa, the African* (1789) recounts not only the details of Equiano's travels and life as a slave, but expresses his position on important issues such as religion and the treatment of women, black indentity, and the nature of oppression. Equiano's friend Ottobah Cugoano was also an important voice in the antislavery campaign in Britain, and with his book *Thoughts and Sentiments on the Evil of Slavery* (1787) and involvement in British politics sought to better the situation of blacks in England. All three of these brilliant men had a profound impact on the abolitionist movement in Britain not only by contributing to the intellectual debate but by overturning standard, negative stereotypes of Africans. African American writers of the eighteenth century did not have the same impact on the slavery debate as did these British ex-slaves. The two best-known African American writers of the eighteenth century, the poets Jupiter Hammon and Phillis Wheatley, wrote about slavery but tended to stress freedom in the afterlife over the call for human liberty. Lesser-known African American writers of the eighteenth century who bring interesting perspectives into discussions about slavery are Briton Hammon and John Marrant. Critics have not investigated their works in any detail, and it remains to be shown to what extent the lives and works of these and numerous other Africans affected public perceptions of slavery and contributed to the strength of the abolitionists' cause.

REPRESENTATIVE WORKS

Aphra Behn
Oroonoko; Or, The Royall Slave (novel) 1688

Samuel Taylor Coleridge
"Ode on the Slave Trade" (poem) 1792
A Lecture on the Slave Trade and the Duties that Result from its Continuance (lecture) 1795

Ottobah Cugoano
Thoughts and Sentiments on the Evils of Slavery (narrative) 1787

William Cowper
The Task (poems) 1785
"The Negro's Complaint" (poem) 1788
"The Morning Dream" (poem) 1788
"Sweet Meat Has Sour Sauce" (poem) 1785

Olauda Equiano
The Interesting Narrative of Olaudah Equiano, or Gustavus Vassa, the African (autobiography) 1789

Alexander Falconbridge
An Account of the Slave Trade on the Coast of Africa (travel narrative) 1788

Jupiter Hammon
An Evening Thought; Salvation by Christ with Penentential Cries (poem) 1760
"A Dialogue Entitled the Kind Master and the Dutiful Servant" (poem) date unknown
An Address to the Negroes of the State of New York (lecture) 1760

Ignatius Sancho
The Letters of Ignatius Sancho, An African to which are Prefixed Memoirs of His Life by Joseph Jekyll (letters) 1782

William Snelgrave
A New Account of Guinea and the Slave Trade (travel narrative) 1744

James Thomson
Seasons (poems) 1730

Phillis Wheatley
Poems on Various Subjects, Religious and Moral (poems) 1773

OVERVIEWS AND GENERAL STUDIES

Geneviève Fabre (essay date 1999)

SOURCE: "The Slave Ship Dance," in *Black Imagination and the Middle Passage,* edited by Maria Diedrich, Henry Louis Gates, Jr., and Carl Pedersen, Oxford University Press, 1999, pp. 33-46.

[*In the following essay, Fabre discusses the dances performed on board slave ships headed for the New World as they are variously represented in accounts from ships' logs, observers travelling on the ships, and the captives themselves. She then explores the forced dances' dual relation to the realities of the Middle Passage and to an African heritage.*]

We are almost a nation of dancers, musicians and poets.

Olaudah Equiano (1789)

Dance is for the African "the fullest expression of art."

Lee Warren, *The Dance of Africa* (1972)

The central importance of dance in West and Central Africa has been often emphasized by historians, anthropologists, and Africans themselves. A communal activity, dance was also a crucial element in ceremonial life and created special bondings among all celebrants, thus united by certain beliefs and practices. In the cults honoring the gods or the ancestors, dance was a way of mediating between the godly and the human, the living and the dead. Deities were praised, called upon through a dance designed to invoke special features, proprieties, or abilities. Dance was thus used to solicit intercession, to thwart wrath or punishment that human action might have incurred, to flatter, or to appease. Dancers not only communicated with the spirits but also impersonated them through specific body movements, rhythms, or masks and became possessed themselves.

From a more worldly perspective, festive dancing could represent a feat, a battle, a victory, a particular domestic event; dramatize a crisis or a confrontation; or become a vehicle for comment, satire, or parody.[1] As a much valued art form, it required skills one learned. Dancers were honored, and officials were supposed to be good dancers; any deficiencies could threaten their status, whereas competence enhanced their aura. The characteristics of the dances could vary greatly from one society to the other—each boasting the best dancers and unique styles,[2] yet dance received in each the same consideration and was used for similar functions. Ceremonial or celebratory, dramatic or theatrical, parodic or satiric, it was pervasive everywhere.

In this chapter, I examine the first recorded dance on the way to the New World, when African captives were encouraged or forced to dance and sometimes "whipped into cheerfulness." It is highly symbolic and ironic that these performances should occur under the eye and whip of the slavers and their crew and on the deck of the slave ship. I shall therefore examine these dances' dual relation to the realities of the Middle Passage and to an African heritage. I question whether the slave ship dance constituted a definite assault on the captives' cultures and a dramatic break with former beliefs and practices, or whether it was a step toward the creation of a new culture in which still vivid memories of African dance could help bring shape and meaning to the experience of enslavement.

The slave ship dance had a wide range of witnesses and was often briefly mentioned in accounts and reports published on the slave trade. One of the first mentions occurs in the log of the English slave ship *Hannibal* in 1664: "Africans linked together were made to jump and dance for an hour or two. If they go about it reluctantly or do not move with agility, they are flogged."[3] The practice seems to have been widespread and was kept long after the abolition of the trade. The last record dates from 1860 when a slave ship, *Wildfire,* with 150 Africans from the River Congo, was taken in tow by an American ship in sight of Cuba and brought to Key West, Florida.[4]

Documents on the dance come essentially from three sources: slavers and captains who allude to them in logs or journals; observers who traveled on the ships as surgeons, guests, or visitors; the captives themselves, who endured the Middle Passage and mentioned their experience in their memoirs or autobiographies. From all these fragmented and scattered descriptions, one may grasp the scope of these dances, their significance and functions for the parties involved, and their underlying meanings for the "performers" themselves. Accounts by the slavers and captains present the dances as necessary, healthy forms of exercise; they emphasize the lightheartedness of the dancers inclined to "amuse themselves with dancing" and proclaim the captain's intentions to take good care of the captives and promote their happiness. Thus, James Barbot, owner of the *Albion* that voyaged the coast of Guinea near the Calabar River in the late seventeenth century, insists in his account on the good care the slaves received during the passage and describes the dancing as a happy pastime "full of jollity and good humor that afforded an abundance of recreation."[5] Practiced as a regular activity necessary for the health of the cargoes (we are told slaves "jumped into their irons for exercise"), dancing had a healing effect on slaves' suicidal melancholy. There was a common belief that if "not kept amused" and in motion slaves would die: these pleasant exercises were keeping the slavers' stock "in good condition" and "enhancing [their] prospects of making a profitable journey." Keeping the slaves in good shape was a major concern in the general economy of the trade at a time when losses in human lives through disease, epidemics, or suicide were high and caused much alarm. Captains had to commit themselves to carry the captives safe, whole, and fit for sale. When in the 1780s the slave trade came under attack and closer scrutiny, captains were requested to answer inquiries concerning the load, space, and provisions allotted on their ships, and laws were passed in 1788 to enforce stricter regulations, stipulating the load of each cargo. When called before Parliament, captains protested against the bill, declared it superfluous, and often referred to the dances as evidence of their goodwill and of the pleasant atmosphere that reigned on their vessels.

Opponents to the trade sent petitions for its abolition and tried to gather evidence that would question the captains' proclamations of innocence. Thus, in a publication that became famous, Thomas Clarkson collected testimonies from less biased witnesses.[6] Their observations offer a very different picture of the dance scene. The captives are described as "compelled to dance by the cat" or jump to the lash—this "jumping" termed "dancing."[7] A surgeon, Thomas Trotter, who traveled on the *Brookes* in 1783, sees the dance as a joyless ceremony that he called "dancing the slave." "Crew members paraded on deck with whip and cat o' nine tails."[8] Captives danced in shackles (except women and children) and on crowded decks. Dancing by the cat was perceived as a violent and painful exercise: "the parts . . . on which their shackles are fastened are often excoriated."[9] Physically damaging, the dances were also often humiliating. Captives left the hold for another kind of confinement: hampered by their shackles, the once free and expert dancers of Africa became the butt of mockery. Observers thus often emphasized surveillance and co-ercion and noted that slavers, who rarely mentioned the use of whips, ignored the complaints of the dancers.

The strict control or even violence were exerted to prevent any carry-over of indigenous practices. Fear was great indeed that the enslaved would use these exercises to develop some kind of secret coding and prepare a mutiny: the ships' guns were sometimes aimed at the dancers to intimidate them, and constant watch was secured. Whip and gun were used to set the limits and avoid transgression. "Dancing the slave" was part of a deliberate scheme to ensure subordination by destroying former practices, to curb any attempt at recovering freedom of movement, action, or thought.

Slave ship dances were also used to entertain captains, their crews, and their guests. These amusements were slightly more formal; musicians were requested (and the great number of advertisements asking for musicians attest to the importance of such shows). If no professional musician were available, a sailor would play the fiddle or bagpipe, or a captive would be designated to play a European instrument or to improvise on a broken drum or banjo. He could also use whatever was available: utensils, ship equipment, or kettles. The captives often brought with them instruments that they were sometimes allowed to play.[10] Meant to enliven the journey, some dances could turn into "wild, lewd parties" in a parody of primitive naked rejoicing.[11] After the trade was abolished, illegal slavers were careful not to attract attention of patrol ships or pirates. Yet in spite of the high risk, they were unwilling to relinquish a practice that was a source of profit and amusement. Dances continued but were carefully planned, either at night—a device that slaves would later use once ashore to escape surveillance—or by summoning only a portion of the captives at a time.

Rewards or liquor were also offered to the best performers. This practice can be seen either as a way of acknowledging and encouraging skill or as a means of buying talent and disarming resistance. This system introduced a hierarchical order and encouraged competitiveness among dancers. The rewards the best dancers received designated them as an elite, leaders who could perhaps be used to control others, who could organize or curb revolt. One needs to determine whether the best performers selected by the "rulers" were the same the captives tacitly chose and managed to impose. Performing skills were quickly singled out and endowed some slaves with a form of power that had to be promptly rechanneled.

All these strategies devised by whites prefigure many of the methods used in the "management" of plantations—ranging from intimidation to reward and privileges. Dancing the slave may seem to have been confined to the slave ship journey, but it endured under many other forms. Slaves may not have had to dance under the lash, yet the whip was always present physically or symbolically, conceived as the best instrument to punish insubordination or

to "fix and season" independent-minded Africans. Significantly, lash and fiddle were used in coffles in the same manner as they had been on the ships, this time to urge chained "niggers" to march on and accept this other passage to another unknown destination, sale, and uncertain fate.[12]

On the other hand, slave ship "entertainments" prefigure these performances when slaves' musical and dancing skills would be appreciated, and used. Captains and plantation owners took the same pride in showing how talented the captives were, and these plantation dances did not escape the attention of those who organized the first traveling minstrel shows in the 1830s.

Thus, even before the ships' arrival into the New World, performance was an important stake, essential in many cultural events but also determinant in white and black relations, with its web of ambivalent feelings: hatred and attraction, contempt or praise, condescension or respect. It created secret bonds and interdependence. Performance was at the same time a well-planned necessary event, a duty and an artistic accomplishment that could be rewarded.

If dancing the slave involved many strategies and much scheming on the part of the slavers, one may surmise that the captives responded with equally elaborate devices to develop—secretly but purposefully—a form of dancing that could escape control and manipulation.

The slaves' point of view is rarely mentioned in the accounts and was no concern to slavers except when they suspected plotting and mutiny; the grief, indignation, or resignation, the aspirations or strivings the dance might have expressed, were ignored or denied. Only a few perceptive observers—mostly, as we saw, the surgeons—were attentive to the moods of the performers. Occasionally a document hints at this hidden dimension of experience, such as this short poem, "The Sorrow of Yomba" (1790):

> At the savage Captain's beck,
> Now like brutes they make us prance:
> Smack the Cat about the Deck,
> and in scorn they bid us dance.[13]

Fear seems to have prevailed. Testimonies of African slaves to the Select Committee of the House of Lords[14] or early narratives—like that of Olaudah Equiano, who, as an Ibo boy of eleven, boarded a slave ship in 1756—underscore the terror and horror. If slaves near the coast were familiar with the trade, those who came from the interior had no notion of their captors' intentions. After the trauma of capture, the long march on land or water to the sea, they boarded the ships in unspeakable terror. Many preferred suicide to the brutalities they would endure at the hands of voracious traders. Their "imagination ran wild" as Equiano says; rumors, reinforced by sailors or interpreters who sought to exploit the captives' fear, spread from Senegambia to Angola that the slavers, whose appetite for human cargo had become prodigious, were insatiable cannibals (in a strange reversal of the stereotype ascribed to Africans). Equiano tells us that when he saw "a multitude of black people of every description chained together" near a "large furnace of copper boiling," "every one of their countenances expressing dejection and sorrow," he was convinced they were about to be eaten; and many Africans thought that the captives who never returned had been eaten or murdered.[15] Another slave, Augustino, recalls that when the younger ones were allowed to come on deck, several jumped overboard in fear they might be fattened to be eaten.[16] The white man's cannibalism explained his hunger for slaves and hence the trade. It was not uncommon among Africans to express such suspicions toward the neighboring peoples they distrusted. It is therefore not surprising that they ascribed the same features to white traders, who were stranger to them, and saw themselves as the new sacrificial victims. Furthermore, many slaves who were familiar with canoes on rivers, but had never seen a ship, imagined that it was some object of worship or magic brought to their shores by the white man for a general slaughter. The fear and horror persisted and led not only to acts of despair but also to murderous revolt. Fright remained, says Equiano, until they reached the West Indies and bitter cries could be heard through the nights. Historians tell us that the *Amistad* rebellion off the Cuban coast in 1839 occurred because the captain's slave informed the captives that they were about to be eaten. "Desperate, they rose in revolt, murdering most of the crew, saving only a few to navigate the ship back to Africa"[17]

Thus, one can understand how the idea and image of death informed the slave ship dance and brought with it a whole train of associations. For the captives who identified with the roaming and restless spirits of the dead, beliefs about death and the journey to the other world could help them negotiate this unfamiliar voyage to unknown shores. Death was less feared than enslavement. And if it meant the only possible reunion with those who had been left behind—ancestors, friends, and kin—and with the home country, this "journey back" could be ceremonially performed or physically accomplished. The dance was the symbolic enactment of a whole system of beliefs, reinforcing worship rites and calling forth the gods, or the dead, or supernatural forces that could perhaps counteract white schemes. Or it could be the prelude to action: the collective meeting with death or revolt against the slavers. Death should be self-willed and not inflicted by others. And it was not merely an escape, a relief from hardships; it was seen as the only path to resistance that could wreck the slavers' project and challenge their power.

Beliefs associated with death, and the attitudes they engendered, accompanied the slaves through their journey and their New World odyssey—just as they later shaped their burial and death rituals. The African heritage was thus very much present on the slave ship—a heritage consisting of a set of beliefs and practices but also of a body of knowledge that could serve as tools to help them out of their present predicament.

Significantly, the dance was informed by certain frames of mind and occasionally signaled appropriate moments for action. The torpor of some of its movements featured death itself; the twists and contortions of body and limb figured the anxiety and the pain; the sudden clapping of hands and stomping of feet, the jumping and leaping, contrasting with the swaying of bodies and slow shuffle, evoked the possibility of escape or of greater freedom. The dance thus stages the various moods and moments of the slave ship experience—the temptation to surrender and despair, the suffering and humiliations, the awakening of energies, the call for daring or insurgent acts. Improvised, and yet purposeful, the dance is both an experiment with, and a rehearsal of, all possible forms of "escapes." All moods, emotions, and ideas are made physically present through the body in carefully orchestrated gestures that, as they express and try to make sense of the plight, suggest certain basic African rhythms; the body, that was so central to the lived and felt Middle Passage experience, is entrusted with the task of representation and figuration, just as it also must perform the actual acts the dance may induce.

Also important were the sound and vocal structure of the dance—the humming and whispering that burst into outcries of pain or jubilant shouting, the way emotions broke into moaning and singing, the language of voice and song and the tunes brought from Africa, the use of African tongues often mentioned by witnesses and of "talking drums" whenever they were allowed as well as all the substitutes found to replace them, and the devices sought to deaden the sound and disguise its meaning. The possibility of recreating familiar tunes with whatever was available enabled the captives to keep their musical tradition alive, its beats and rhythms, the subtle combination of vocal and instrumental effects.

Codes of silence were also developed. Silence was another answer to the humiliations suffered, alternating with moments of extreme vocal expression and shrieks of grief. The silence of "sealed lips" (that is evoked in a Yoruba sculpture) accompanied the silence of the drum—often described as "an instrument of significant silence" all the more powerful when it was suppressed[18]—and it became a critique of the cruelty and violence inflicted. Silence was also a bond cementing solidarity between captives who would not betray one another. This tacit pact agreed upon on the slave ship endured; it became a crucial code of behavior, severely punished when it was broken.

In the slave ship dance, the basic principles of many performances to come were set: the blending and interplay of dance, song, and music; the call-and-response pattern between dance and music, between voice and instrument, body and song, and mostly between leader-caller and the assembly of dancers (later called celebrants or worshippers when the "performance" would be conceived more as a ceremony); the gift for improvisation; the combination of spiritual and practical purposes; the implicit reference to the spirit world; the emphasis on communication, on the sharing of information and meaning as well as on the necessity to disguise any signal or message; the techniques of deceit to avoid surveillance, to conceal one's mood or designs. These skills and devices, found among all generations of captives, were passed on and improved upon by slaves through several decades.

Codes of kinship and loyalties were also asserted in which slaves acknowledged their common origin, thus reacting against the brutal exigencies of the trade, the cruel separations already experienced on the coast and in the pens, the deliberate destruction of their culture. African identity had to be proclaimed when it was most threatened. It became a mooring that could ensure survival, a thing to remember, a structure around which to create strong bonds in anticipation of other partings and bereavements.

Shipmates and countrymen took silent vows either to find a way back home—a constant preoccupation for early Africans—or to cultivate ties to sustain new communities. Later, after their arrival in the New World, these shipmates' groupings would assume a more official existence, be organized into "societies" that held multiple functions; inaugurated by a formal ceremony, they invented their own rituals, among which oaths of allegiance and mutual assistance figured prominently, and had their feasts, pageants, and marches.[19] In these ceremonial events celebrating the endurance and survival from the soul-destroying slave ship experience, the Middle Passage was symbolically evoked in its three moments: violent displacement, rebirth, and reunion, the memory kept and reactivated in order to cement the new communities.

In a sort of antithesis of the passage, some ceremonies, oriented in time and space toward Africa, symbolically staged the reunion with countrymen, the travel back to the motherland and home of the ancestors. This return is accomplished even more powerfully by spiritually potent Africans who could fly back to Africa, whose feats are reported or sung in that other ceremonial space, the storytelling session.

It is interesting to note that in the New World, many images antithetic to the slave ship journey were to emerge. Some were generated by the exegesis and reinterpretation of the biblical text inspired by the Evangelical movement. The cruel Middle Passage was opposed by the triumphant return similar to the crossing of the Red Sea by the children of Israel. The experience of conversion was pictured as a rebirth after a long journey through hell; the black church itself was conceived as a ship where "storm-tossed" people can assemble, worship, and "labor the spirit."[20] Ironically, the dreaded ship becomes the instrument of salvation in a religious and a practical sense. In a totally different mood, insurrectionary New World slaves saw slave ships as potential instruments of their liberation: they would use whatever ship they could capture to prepare a revolt. The mere sight of a ship inspired them to action. Thus, at the time of the Montserrat insurrection of 1768 in the Leeward Islands, slaves took advantage of the presence of three Dutch vessels offshore to prepare a mass es-

cape by seizing the ships and sailing off perhaps to Puerto Rico, and they improvised a "Fire on the Mountain" song for the occasion.[21] In another inversion, slaves mastered their former fear of white cannibalism by inventing drinking toasts in calypso fashion at elaborate dancing feasts in Port-of-Spain and, playing on elements of the Catholic communion, made a song (often sung by market women): "The flesh of white people is our bread, their blood our wine."[22] One could find many other instances of inversion; one of the most intriguing is perhaps the famous Jonkonnu carnival in Jamaica and North Carolina that stilled the fright inspired by white traders by celebrating, in song, mask, and dance, a powerful African middleman and a major slaving place on the Guinea Coast.[23]

The slave ship experience itself, encapsulated in the dance, became a site of memory that informed many performatory or ceremonial events. I would like to dwell on one such event that probably has the strongest connection with the Middle Passage dance. It offers in a different setting a reinterpretation of that scene and introduces a new dynamic of time and space that highlights its symbolic significance.

In Caribbean cultures the slave ship dance received a name that is both specific and generic, "limbo," and became the prototype for other dances still practiced today. The limbo dance begins precisely on the slave ship, on the cramped deck where slaves were summoned, and is informed with this primal scene. Suddenly emerging from the ship's bowels, the figures of the shackled dancers of the limbo dance suggest a play with contrasts. The posture of the slaves in "limbo," hampered by their chains, trying to set their bodies in motion first, evokes what Wilson Harris has called in an insightful essay, "the eclipse of the resources of sensibility."[24] But the dance also asserts the possibility of movement: it sets body and limb in motion and arouses the senses. The disabled bodies are able to perform a dance that is potentially the dance of life, a dance that can imaginatively break the chains and defy traders or captains and their crew. Thus, dancers translated the blunt order to instil life in their numbed and prostrated bodies into a secret call to be born again; they assembled all their energies to transcend the agony and pain. The healthy exercise that the chains turn into a grotesque pantomime that reinforces images of inferiority becomes a ritual of rebirth. The dance to ensure that the cargo of living flesh will arrive safe on the other shore is channeled to other ends. Neither mind nor limb will be so easily manipulated and conquered, and the survival will serve other purposes.

In the limbo dance, the possibility of renascence is evoked through metamorphosis: the dancer moves under a bar that is gradually lowered "until a mere slit of space remains through which with spreadeagled wings he passes like a spider."[25] In this symbolic reenactment of the slave ship dance, the leap to freedom is dramatized, visualized, and narrated. The spider image connects this choreography with another form of performance, storytelling, and with the animal trickster tales of West Indian and African folklore. Inadvertently and ironically, the rulers who order the dance provide an occasion for escape; the performer finds a way out of a desperate situation. This trickster's device announces and prefigures many other tricks and strategies, such as "stealing away," that slaves would later use to find a more appropriate space for their gatherings, dances, frolics, or worship. Onlookers on the ship would pay no more attention to a spider sneaking out through a slit of space than they did to the slaves' real "performance"; the meaning of the dance eluded them.

Invisible or perceived only as bodies and commodities that were shipped away, the enslaved would turn this liability—their invisibility as human beings and as magnificent and crafted performers—into an asset and proclaim with vehemence of limb and voice their humanity and vitality, as well as their capacity to outwit and "put on massa." They developed performatory skills to communicate in explicit or secret codes their grievances and strivings.

The slave ship dance was therefore not simply an atavistic spectacle or a meaningless, grotesque dance "under the whip" but a creative phenomenon of importance for the newly enslaved. Haunted by memories of Africa, beset by the slave trade whose laws and economic proscriptions violate their inner beings, the dancers perform an epic drama that announces the emergence of the New World Negro. Many elements in the slave ship setting supply figurative meaning. On one level, the dance expresses the predicament of the captives, caught in the prison of history, the vessel or the trade born of the inordinate ambition of the slavers. In an age of violence and despair, Africans experience the soul-destroying effect of the Middle Passage: their country irretrievably lost, the New World still unknown and forbidding. On another level, a craving for meaning enables them to deal with their dilemma symbolically; the "limbo imagination," as Wilson Harris calls it, "points to new horizons"[26] and announces the necessity of a new drama. As the dance reenacts the tragedy of dismemberment and dislocation, it stages the possibility of transformation through recollection, reassembly and movement. This inarticulate, obscure desire to be born again infuses the performance with mental design, with a sense of time and space.

This dance born on the slave ship found its way into many other performances: in feasts where the limbo is performed, in carnivals where its ironic replica appears: the dancing on high stilts evoking elongated limbs and the ability to confer with superior creatures or the gods. Slaves were thus encouraged to deliberately seek occasions to assemble; devise counterperformances that would magnify all the movements, gestures, and voices confined or repressed on the ship; and express more freely their feelings and emotions. In the words lent to a slave, if "slaves' bodies were owned by the masters in their dances, slaves skip about as if their heels were their own."[27]

The slave ship scene also prefigures a form of gathering essential to all performances, creating new bonds and solidarity to be translated in the image of a circle or ring: the chaotic heaping of bodies would be reordered into a different pattern or architecture.

Exploring other essential forms of performance in worship, or what Raboteau has called "danced and sung religion,"[28] would be interesting. In praise and hymn singing, the worshippers performed songs that seem to resonate within the slave ship experience, with frequent references to the belly of the whale or "the fiery furnace" from which singers ask to be delivered, as in the song "O Lord give me the Eagle's Wing."[29] Significantly, the ring shout appears as an ironic duplication of the steps of the slave ship dance, a further stylization of which the worshippers have reached fuller command: the slow movement of heel and toe, the double shuffle, the low sound, the sudden bursting of voice and motion.

Performance brought into play many recreative capacities, as a response to harsh realities—dislocations, dismemberment, violations. Born of many interactions, it also created new bridges connecting continents and expanding boundaries. On the slave ship the enslaved were exposed to discrete African cultures whose singularity was assessed, as well as to the culture of the traders. The captain forcing them to dance to the music of some European instrument became the unexpected agent of a form of acculturation. In this "gateway to the New World," the process from destruction to creation, begun through a complex blending of legacies, transformed into new configurations.

In new settings after the Middle Passage, African Americans actively sought places and moments that would offer occasions to perform their new culture. Many artistic strategies of concealment were devised to avoid interference, censorship, or punishment and to resist "seasoning" and manipulation. They reaffirmed that, even if control were exerted, the imagination is free. Performance became a site for acts of resistance and liberation. The rehearsal of freedom took place at different levels: as a quest for space and movement, as freedom to summon gatherings, as freedom from bondage in fixed roles and representations, freedom to play with and transgress imposed forms and conventions. It spelled out a new grammar of social behavior. Thus imaginatively enacted, the ideal of freedom was made visible; its advent became more urgent.

As the first New World performance, the slave ship dance established an interesting relation and dramatic tension between history and memory, between past and future. It asserted at the same time the will to remember and to reconstruct, however painfully, a chain of memories and simultaneously forget in order to invent a future, later acted out on casual and improvised stages. Most important, it created a fleeting relationship between gesture and vision, whether, as Herbert Blau writes, "you make the gesture to have the vision or you have the vision so that the gesture can be made."[30] The slave ship performance was a creative and daring act that proclaimed, with the sovereignty of the body, the vibrant intensity of one's imagining power.

Notes

1. On African dance: Michel Huet, *The Dance, Art and Ritual of Africa* (New York: Pantheon Books, 1978); John Miller Chernoff, *African Rhythm and African Sensibility* (Chicago: University Press of Chicago, 1979); Sterling Stuckey, *Slave Culture* (New York: Oxford University Press, 1987); Dena Epstein, *Sinful Tunes and Spirituals* (Urbana: University of Illinois Press, 1977); Robert Farris Thompson, *African Art in Motion* (Los Angeles: University of California Press, 1974); Katrina Hazzard-Gordon, *Jookin': The Rise of Social Dance Formation in African American Culture* (Philadelphia: Temple University Press, 1990); *The Interesting Narrative of the Life of Olaudah Equiano, or Gustavus Vassa, the African* [London: 1789], in Ama Bontemps, ed., *Great Slave Narratives* (Boston: Beacon Press, 1969), 1-192.

2. Thus, Equiano claims that the dances in the kingdom of Benin had "a spirit and variety which [he] had scarcely seen elsewhere." Bontemps, 7.

3. Quoted in *The Art of Exclusion,* the account was published in England in 1788.

4. The dance was meant "to keep the cargo alive long enough to reach the market." Epstein, 14.

5. George Francis Dow, *Slave Ships and Slaving* (Westport, Conn.: Grayson & Grayson, 1933), 84-85.

6. *An Abstract of the Evidence Delivered Before a Selected Committee of The House of Commons in the years 1790 and 1791 on the Part of the Petitioners for the Abolition of the Slave Trade* (London: James Phillips & George Yard, 1791), 37. Clarkson also wrote a *History of the Rise, Progress and Accomplishment of the African Slave Trade by the Parliament* (London: John W. Parker, 1839). On the trade, see Philip D. Curtin, *The Atlantic Slave Trade: A Census* (Madison: University of Wisconsin Press, 1969); W. E. B. Du Bois, *The Suppression of the Slave Trade to the United States of America* (reprint: New York: Dover, 1971); Daniel P. Mannix and Malcolm Cowley, *Black Cargoes* (New York: Viking, 1962); Edmund B. D'Auvergne, *Human Livestock* (London: Grayson & Grayson, 1933); E. Donnan, ed., *Documents Illustrative of the Slave Trade to America,* 4 vols. (Washington, D.C.: 1930-1935).

7. Clarkson, *History,* 304-305.

8. See George Howe, "The Last Slave Ship," *Scribner's Magazine,* July 1890, 114, 123-24.

9. Ecroide Claxton, surgeon, who sailed on the slave ship, *Young Hero,* in 1788. In Clarkson, *History,* 304-305.

10. Some Africans were enticed on board the slave ships and offered rewards to perform tribal dances. When the dancing was over, they were taken below, and given intoxicating drinks. When they awoke, they were far out at sea. See Edward Thorpe, *Black Dance* (Woodstock, N.Y.: Overlook Press, 1990), 10.

11. A surgeon on a Brazilian ship *Georgia* witnessed such a scene around 1827: members of the crew "stripped themselves and danced with black wenches . . . rum and lewdness reigned supreme," in Dowe, 241.

12. When slaves were transported from Virginia to the better markets of the cotton territories, they marched, "their feet heavily loaded with irons," to the sound of a fiddler who was supposed to enliven their spirit. Among the songs they sung was the famous "song of the coffle gang": "We came to be stolen and sold to Georgia" (quoted in George W. Clark, *Liberty Minstrel,* 5th ed. [New York: published by author, 1846]).

13. Rare Book Collection, Cornell University, Ithaca, N.Y.

14. "Report of the Select Committee of the House Of Lords, Appointed to Consider the Best Means Which Great Britain Can Adopt for the Final Extinction of the African Slave Trade: Session 1849," London, 1849.

15. In Bontemps, 47.

16. "Report of the Select Committee," 1849, 163. For more detailed analysis of the belief in white cannibalism: W. D. Piersen, *Black Legacy: America's Hidden Heritage* (Amherst: University of Massachusetts Press, 1993), chap. 1, 1-34; Michael Mullin, *Africa in America. Slave Resistance in the American South and the British Caribbean 1736-1831* (Urbana: Illinois University Press, 1992), 35.

17. Edwin P. Hoyt, *The Amistad Affair* (New York: 1970), 37.

18. Robert Farris Thompson, *Flash of the Spirit* (New York: Random House, 1983), 327.

19. Mullin, 15, 32, 35.

20. Joseph M. Murphy, *Working the Spirit. Ceremonies of the African Diaspora* (Boston: Beacon Press, 1994), 172.

21. Mullin, 219.

22. Mullin, 223.

23. See Geneviève Fabre, "Festive Moments in Antebellum African American Culture," in Werner Sollors and Maria Diedrich, eds., *The Black Columbiad* (Cambridge, Mass.: Harvard University Press, 1994), 42-53.

24. "History, Fable and Myth in the Caribbean and Guianas" (first published in Georgetown: National History and Arts Council, 1970), revised in *Explorations* (Mundelstrup: Dangaroo Press, 1981), 20-42. Reprinted in: *Selected Essays of Wilson*

Harris, ed. Andrew Bundy (New York: Routledge, 1999), 152-166

25. Harris, 159.

26. Harris, 159.

27. In an imaginary dialogue between a slave and his master, in *Friendly Advice to the Gentlemen Planters of the East and West Indies by Philotheos Physiologus* (London: A. Sowle, 1634), 146-148.

28. Albert J. Raboteau, *Slave Religion* (New York: Oxford University Press, 1978).

29. These songs found echoes in the jubilant or mournful hollers and tunes of firemen and regiment marchers observed in 1862 by Thomas Wentworth Higginson in his *Army Life in a Black Regiment* (Boston: Fields, Osgood, 1870), 23-24.

30. *The Eye of Prey* (Bloomington: Indiana University Press, 1987), 178.

DEPICTIONS BY WHITE WRITERS

William Heffernan (essay date 1973)

SOURCE: "The Slave Trade and Abolition in Travel Literature," in *Journal of the History of Ideas,* Vol. 34, No. 2, April-June 1973, pp. 185-208.

[*In the following essay, Heffernan surveys the depiction of the slave trade in travel literature by eighteenth-century white authors, which he argues provides greater insight into public opinion than does imaginative writing of the same period. Travel writing about Africa, he maintains, was a genre that shaped white attitudes toward blacks and provided the substance for pro- and anti-abolitionist arguments.*]

Much has been written about the relationship between the anti-slavery poems, plays, and novels that appeared with extraordinary profusion in the last two decades of the eighteenth century and the abolition movement. Thomas Clarkson's history of the abolition movement contains a long bibliography of imaginative literature which aided the cause of abolition, and modern studies by Wylie Sypher, Hoxie Neal Fairchild, Eva Beatrice Dykes, N. Verle McCullough, and Richard M. Kain have unearthed, and studied in detail, all such examples of imaginative literature from the eighteenth and early nineteenth centuries.[1]

Only passing attention, however, has been paid the relationship between travel literature and the arguments both for and against abolition of the slave trade. Even a cursory survey of the travel literature reveals that much of the evidence used to support both sides of this controversy was drawn from travellers to Africa. Clarkson, himself, records in exacting detail the number of copies of travellers' accounts published by the Committee for the Abolition of the Slave Trade. He notes, for example, that between January and February 1788, the Committee published three thousand copies each of Alexander Falconbridge's *An Account of the Slave Trade on the Coast of Africa* (London, 1788) and John Newton's *Thoughts on the Slave Trade* (London, 1788).[2]

Clarkson also watched with great avidity for the arrival of travellers fresh from Africa, and employed many of them in giving evidence on the abolitionist side. Two Swedish travellers, one of whom was to play a prominent part in the Sierra Leone expedition, and both of whom were later to publish their travels, were sought out by Clarkson upon their arrival in England from Africa late in January 1788. Employed by the King of Sweden to go on a scientific expedition, Dr. Andrew Sparrman (professor of physics and inspector of the Royal Academy of Stockholm) and C. B. Wadstrom (chief director of the assay-office in Stockholm, and later author of an influential essay proposing the colonization of Sierra Leone) agreed to give testimony for Clarkson; Sparrman to do so before the privy council, Wadstrom before the privy council and the Commons. Chiefly, they aided him in proving the existence of a productive society in Africa, thus countering the claim of the slavers that the natives were mercifully being removed from a barbaric unproductive society, and were being civilized and made productive in the West Indies. Their contribution to abolition was summarized by Clarkson who wrote:

> I had not long been with them before I perceived the great treasure I had found. They [Wadstrom and Sparrman] gave me many beautiful specimens of African produce. They showed me their journals, which they had regularly kept from day to day. In these I had the pleasure of seeing a number of circumstances minuted down, all relating to the Slave-trade, and even drawings on the same subject. I obtained a more accurate and satisfactory knowledge of the manners and customs of the Africans from these, than from all the persons put together whom I had yet seen. I was anxious, therefore, to take them before the committee of council, to which they were pleased to consent; and as Dr. Sparrman was to leave London in a few days, I procured him an introduction first. His evidence went to show, that the natives of Africa lived in a fruitful and luxuriant country, which supplied all their wants, and that they would be a happy people if it were not for the existence of the Slave-trade.[3]

Alexander Falconbridge's account of the slave trade was directly solicited by Clarkson. While gathering evidence for the abolitionists in Bristol, Clarkson had met Falconbridge, a ship's surgeon who had been on four voyages aboard a slaver on the coast of Africa; when asked by Clarkson to contribute information in support of abolition, Falconbridge readily agreed. Clarkson asked Falconbridge to accompany him on what might be called a fact-finding mission to Liverpool, the center of the slave trade in England, where Clarkson hoped to gain further evidence against the trade. Falconbridge, whom Clarkson describes as "an athletic-looking man,"[4] not only acted as Clarkson's bodyguard, for Clarkson was threatened and insulted everywhere he went, but also supplied Clarkson with first-hand evidence against those who drew Clarkson into arguments about the trade. Falconbridge was persuaded by the Committee of the Abolition Society to write his account of the slave trade because "the facts and circumstances, which had taken place but a little time ago, were less liable to objections (inasmuch as they proved the present state of things) than those which had happened in earlier times."[5]

Not all the travellers, however, were as cooperative as Falconbridge. Others appeared in behalf of the other side; among the travellers who appeared before the privy council or the Commons to give testimony in support of the slave trade were three whose accounts were published between 1780 and 1800: Robert Norris, a former captain in the trade whose *Memoirs of the Reign of Bossa Ahádee* (London, 1789) was the most damaging book to the abolitionist cause; John Matthews, a former lieutenant in the Royal Navy turned slave trader whose *A Voyage to the River Sierra-Leone* (London, 1788) contained, in addition to a description of that country based on information gathered during his residence there between 1783-87, an essay defending the slave trade; and Archibald Dalzel whose *The History of Dahomey, An Inland Kingdom of Africa* (London, 1793) was largely a compilation of materials from other sources chiefly Norris' travels, early works by Captain William Snelgrave, *A New Account of Guinea and the Slave Trade* (London, 1754), William Smith, *A New Voyage to Guinea* (London, 1744), and an account written for Dalzel by Lionel Abson, Governor of Ouidah.[6] While Dalzel's work is hostile to the Negro, and is an anti-abolition work, ironically it is the first history of a Negro nation; and, in this respect, is enlightened, recognizing as it does that African states do have histories.

Matthews and Norris appeared before the privy council as delegates from Liverpool in support of the slave trade; and, with Dalzel, the latter reappeared before the Commons. Norris' testimony was particularly irksome to Clarkson, not only because his book had created such a stir with its pictures of African brutality and cannibalism, but because Clarkson had met him in Liverpool shortly after Norris had finished his travels, had interviewed him five or six times "at his own house," had read his travels, and had received evidence from him in support of abolition. Clarkson was so convinced from these interviews that Norris would give testimony for the abolitionists that he tried to persuade William Pitt, the prime minister, to summon him before the privy council then meeting to consider the effects of abolition. Discovering Norris was in London, Clarkson sought him out, only to receive a letter from Norris "full of flattery" which, while recognizing "the general force of [the abolitionists'] arguments," and that "justice and humanity" were on the abolitionists' side, admitted that "he had found occasion to differ from me, since we had last parted, on particular points, and that he had

therefore less reluctantly yielded to the call of becoming a delegate,—though notwithstanding he would gladly have declined the office if he could have done it with propriety."[7] Pitt, who by now had been persuaded to take the abolitionists' side, tried to weaken the force of Norris' testimony by spreading word that he had formerly given evidence for the abolitionists, so that when Norris later appeared again before the Commons, Clarkson records he could scarcely hold up his head, or look the abolitionists in the eye.

In content, African travel books include not only lurid descriptions of the conditions of the trade—the brutality of the slave ship, mortality among slaves and seamen, the debilitating effects of the trade on the morality of blacks and whites—but also discussions of such broader subjects as the character of the Negro, the nature of racial and cultural differences, and the concepts of primitivism and progressivism as they relate to different societies. The conditions aboard the slave ships, however, were cited by abolitionists more frequently than any other evil of the trade, since these obviously would excite public outrage against the conditions of the trade. Both Newton and Falconbridge had first-hand experience on the slave ships, and Clarkson had visited many of them. Yet the charges of these writers were denied in travel books written by such supporters of the trade as Robert Norris and William Snelgrave. Norris denounced such abolitionist authors as Newton and Falconbridge as "hireling scriblers, profligate common sailors, and the scum of the people";[8] and Norris called the publications of the abolitionists "gross mistatements of facts, and misrepresentation of characters."[9]

The descriptions of the slave ships in abolitionist travel literature were also used to corroborate the abolitionists' testimony before the privy council and Commons. Clarkson described two ships' holds which he had seen and in which slaves were stacked in tiers on platforms allowing just three or four square feet for each slave.[10] Clarkson's cross-examination of hostile witnesses revealed, "the height from the floor to the ceiling, within which space the bodies on the floor and those on the platforms lay, seldom exceeded five feet eight inches, and in some cases it did not exceed four feet."[11] The single most effective piece of propaganda released by the Committee for Abolition was a print of the design of a slave ship which made "an instantaneous impression of horror upon all who saw it."[12] Clarkson records that the Bishop of Chartes once told him that he doubted the truth of the abolitionists' accounts of the horrors of the slave trade until he saw the print, after which "there was nothing so barbarous which might not readily be believed."[13]

Falconbridge's travels confirm Clarkson's testimony and add to it an account of the physical suffering of the Negroes as seen by a medical man aboard the slave ships. Falconbridge complained that eight foot high barricades, erected around the ship to prevent suicides and to protect against the frequent rebellion of the slaves, excluded fresh air from the holds making the rooms intolerably hot. "The confined air, rendered noxious by the effluvia exhaled from their bodies, and by being repeatedly breathed, soon produces fevers and fluxes, which generally carries off great numbers of them."[14] Due to a lack of sanitary facilities in the holds, Falconbridge recorded "the deck, that is, the floor of their rooms, was so covered with the blood and mucus which had proceeded from them in consequence of the flux, that it resembled a slaughter house."[15] Nor were these the only horrors of the scenes below the deck. As the ship rolled and pitched in the sea those Negroes lying on the floor

> frequently have their skin, and even their flesh entirely rubbed off, by the motion of the ship, from the prominent parts of the shoulders, elbows, and hips, so as to render the bones in those parts quite bare. And some of them, by constantly lying in the blood and mucus, that had flowed from those afflicted with the flux . . . have their flesh much sooner rubbed off, than those who have only to contend with the mere friction of the ship. The excruciating pain which the poor sufferers feel from being obliged to continue in such a dreadful situation, frequently for several weeks, in case they happen to live so long, is not to be conceived or described. Few, indeed, are ever able to withstand the fatal effects of it. The utmost skill of the surgeon is here ineffectual.[16]

The abolitionists produced mortality figures to document their case against the unhealthy conditions on the slavers. Falconbridge cited one voyage during which 105 out of 380 died in the middle passage, a proportion which was not uncommon since sometimes "one half [to] two thirds and even beyond that have been known to perish."[17] Others confirmed Falconbridge's claim. A Captain Harry Gandy of Bristol claimed to have been aboard a slave ship in 1740 on which 90 of 190 slaves were killed during a mutiny, or thrown overboard afterwards. Captain Newton lost 62 of 218 slaves on a voyage to South Carolina. Anthony Benezet, the American abolitionist whose writings stirred Clarkson's interest in abolition, claimed that 30,000 slaves died annually among the British, either in the middle passage, or in the seasoning in the West Indies. In the Barbadoes alone, Benezet claimed that of the 35,000 slaves brought there annually, 12,000 died. Captains of slavers who had turned against the trade volunteered statistics: a Captain Morley lost 313 of 1325; a Captain Town 115 of 630; a Captain Claxton 132 of 250; and a Captain Withers lost 360 slaves or more than half his "cargo" from the smallpox. Clarkson set the mortality figures more conservatively at less than 12½ per cent on the middle passage, and 4½ per cent in the harbors, but computed that within two years not half survived the seasoning.[18]

Falconbridge's portrait of the slave ship describes other kinds of cruelty, confirmed by other abolitionist writers, which was inflicted on the Negroes. His description of the shackles placed on the Negroes and used to confine them in groups of fifty or sixty is confirmed by Dr. Trotter's testimony before the Commons, which described the men being secured on deck by a large chain "run through a ring in their shackles,"[19] and being forced to jump in their chain

for exercise, a practice called "dancing" by the slaves. The practice of chaining the slaves was so odious to John Newton that he later, in his autobiography, *An Authentic Narrative* (London, 1764), described himself as "a sort of gaoler or turnkey and I was sometimes shocked with an employment that was perpetually conversant with chains, bolts and shackles."[20]

Falconbridge's claim that aboard some ships "common sailors are allowed to have intercourse with such of the black women whose consent they can procure," and that "officers are permitted to indulge their passions among them at pleasure,"[21] is corroborated by an entry dated January 31, 1753 in Newton's journal kept aboard the slave ship *African,* an entry which demonstrates, paradoxically, both Newton's humanity, and, in its concluding remark, his gradual brutalization by the trade:

> William Cooney seduced a woman slave down into the room and lay with her brutelike in view of the whole quarter deck, for which I put him in irons. I hope this has been the first affair of the kind on board and I am determined to keep them quiet if possible. If anything happens to the woman I shall impute it to him, for she was big with child. Her number is 83. . . .[22]

Most of the charges of cruelty were denied by the anti-abolitionist writers. They claimed that neither the Captain of a slaver nor a West Indian planter was likely to risk the destruction of his own property by acts of cruelty. Snelgrave's account of the slave ship admitted frequent mutinies occasioned by "ill usage" from the sailors, but he argued it was more often due to the Negroes' fear of being eaten by the white men who had bought them. Once out of sight of land where the danger of mutiny was lessened, aboard Snelgrave's ship the Negroes' chains were removed and they were allowed on deck from morning until sundown.[23]

Norris, on the other hand, admitted none of the atrocities the abolitionists described. His travel book, with its appendaged defense of slavery, scarcely mentions the details of the slave ship, except to claim that the ships employed in the trade were specially constructed "for the accommodations of the Negroes," and that "every possible attention [was] paid to their health, cleanliness and convenience," even making the captain's cabin available to the sick.[24] Clarkson recorded Norris' testimony before the privy council and Commons in which, according to Clarkson, Norris "painted the accommodations on board a slave-ship in the most glowing colours." Their rooms were "luxurious, . . . fitted up as advantageously as circumstances could possible admit," and their "apartments were perfumed [daily] with frankincense and lime-juice."[25] In his travels, Norris denied that the punishment meted out to slaves was not justifiable. "If a Negro is slothful or flagitious," Norris wrote, "he is like rascals and drones of society in every well regulated community, poor and miserable; and subject to correction, as a punishment for his own vices, and for the instruction of others."[26]

The anti-abolitionists did not content themselves merely with answering these charges about the conditions of the trade; rather they sought to justify the trade and the reported high mortality rates among the slaves by positive arguments. For example, they contended that the slave ships acted as a nursery for English seamen,[27] and thereby insured the continuance of British supremacy on the seas. It was argued that abolition would weaken both the strength of the navy and the mercantile interests of the nation which depended on trained seamen.

However, this claim was challenged by the abolitionists who proved conclusively that the mortality rates among British seamen was so high that England was actually losing trained seamen as a result of the trade. When Archibald Dalzel claimed in his testimony that mortality among seamen was not high, he was publicly embarrassed in cross-examination by Thomas Clarkson who had checked the muster-rolls of Dalzel's and other ships. "He confessed with trembling, that he had lost a third of his sailors in his last voyage."[28]

Clarkson's examination of the muster-rolls of slave ships leaving British ports revealed that half the seamen who went out failed to return, and that one-fifth of the crews died during the voyage, a figure which was repeated by John Newton.[29] Between 1784 and 1790, 350 slave vessels carrying 12,263 seamen left British ports. Of these crews, 2,643 died during the voyages and only 5,760 seamen returned to their home ports.[30] Falconbridge, who noted the absence of apprentices on the ships, wrote that many ships were unable to leave the West Indies for want of crew members, and concluded, "this trade may justly be denominated the grave of seamen."[31] So widely publicized were these mortality figures, that the image of Africa as "the white man's grave," with its unhealthy climate, began to emerge during the abolitionist controversy.

The chief claim of the pro-slavery faction was that slavery was a merciful act, removing the Negro, as it did, from barbarism, and introducing him to Christianity and an enlightened way of life. Since it was an accepted myth that the unhealthy tropical environment made labor impossible for whites, but not for Negroes, the argument from necessity was used to prove that slavery was part of a divine plan for the conversion of Africans to Christianity. Archibald Dalzel wrote that, "Asiatic pomp, and European necessity for labourers enured to a tropical sun, appear to have been the only effectual instruments of mercy, the only means whereby the lives of many of those unfortunate people have been saved."[32] Furthermore, slaves, so the argument went, were happier in the state of slavery in the West Indies than with freedom in their native lands, and as proof, pro-slavery advocates reported that planters often effectively threatened unmanageable Negroes with return to Africa.[33]

Slavery was merciful in other respects as well. Oddly the current of benevolence in England was appealed to when it was claimed that slavery rescued the inhabitants from tyrannical rulers who not only exercised despotic powers over the Africans, but who often wantonly killed them; in-stead, slavery delivered them into the "cherishing hands of Christian masters."[34] Also, slavery prevented overpopulation and ultimate starvation in Africa. While in Jaqueen in 1727, Captain William Snelgrave records receiving a letter from a Captain Dagge of the slave ship *Italian,* who wrote Snelgrave of his success in obtaining slaves in Ouidah where "the People being in a starving Condition, [are] obliged to sell their Servants and Children for Money and Goods to buy Food."[35] This last argument was based on the notion that polygamy was responsible for Africa's populousness, and that Africa could, "not only continue supplying all the demands that offer for her surplus inhabitants, in the quantities it has hitherto done, but, if necessity required it, could spare thousands, nay millions more, to the end of time, all of whom may be considered as rescued by this means from that certain death, which awaited them in their own country."[36] Clarkson answered the argument that slavery was merciful with an ironic question, "How many have pined to death, that, even at the expence of their lives, they might fly from your benevolence?"[37] John Atkins, who had seen conditions both in Africa and the West Indies, also rejected the argument. He found the conditions in the West Indies worse than those from which Africans had been transported, for in Africa, "they get Ease with their spare diet," but in the West Indies, "they get the brown Bread without the Gospel."[38]

As part of the argument from benevolence, claims and counter-claims about the methods of obtaining slaves were made. Snelgrave listed four ways in which a freeborn Negro might become a slave: by being made a prisoner of war, as punishment for a crime, as a result of debt, or by being sold into slavery by one's parents. Anti-abolitionists claimed that most slaves were prisoners of war, and that slavery rescued them from certain execution at the hands of their blood-thirsty captors: Norris in his *Memoirs of the Reign of Bossa Ahádee* drew a picture of the kinds of mass-executions and bloody human sacrifices from which slavery reprieved captured Africans. His description of these sacrifices, resulting from the conquest of Ouidah ("Whydah") by Dahomey challenged Atkin's claim that the Dahomian king wished to put an end to the slave trade; instead Norris' description concludes, "the conquest of it [Ouidah], by the king of Dahomey, has diminished the traffic in slaves; not by the substitution of one more innocent, but by a carnage, and depopulation, the most horrible that ever occurred, perhaps, in the history of mankind."[39] When Norris repeated his narration before the privy council, Clarkson described his testimony as "most frightful."[40]

The most conclusive argument that such prisoners would be executed, were it not for the slave trade, was offered in Archibald Dalzel's *History of Dahomey* in which he related a speech by Adahoonzou, who became king of Dahomey after 1774, to Lionel Abson, then governor of Ouidah; the speech answers the charge made by abolitionists that such wars were incited by Europeans for the purpose of procuring slaves. The abolitionists, for example, had called such wars "a monster of British growth, transported thither by avarice."[41] Benezet wrote that white slave traders furnished Negroes with "prodigious quantities of ammunition and arms," and have thereby "incited them to make war one upon another";[42] and Alexander Falconbridge observed that enmity among Negroes had been fostered by white men, and "all social intercourse destroyed,"[43] in order to procure slaves. But the speech of Adahoonzou laid to rest these arguments for most of the British public. "In the name of my ancestors and myself," the king swore,

> no Dahomian ever embarked in war merely for the sake of procuring wherewithal to purchase your commodities. I, who have not been long master of this country, have without thinking of the market, killed many thousands, and I shall kill many thousands more. When policy or justice required that men be put to death, neither silk, nor coral, nor brandy, nor cowries, can be accepted as substitutes for the blood that ought to be spilt for example sake. Besides, if white men chuse to remain at home, and no longer visit this country for the same purpose that has usually brought them hither, will black men cease to make war? I answer, by no means. And if there be no ships to receive their captives, what will become of them? I answer for you, they will be put to death.[44]

After reading this speech, the reviewer in the *Gentleman's Magazine* for January 1796 predicted that "If the speech of King Aduhoonzon [sic] to the present governor of Whydah does not exculpate Europeans from the horrid charge of exciting war to get slaves, we despair of convincing the advocates for the abolition of the slave trade."[45] However, Falconbridge's travels offered proof to contradict Norris. At Bonny on the West Coast, Falconbridge had observed that during a three year suspension of the trade, when England was at war with France, the only bad effect of the suspension was the poverty of black traders. "It was a very bad thing," one black merchant had complained to Falconbridge, for the temporary suspension of the trade was "making us traders poorer, and obliging us to work for our maintenance."[46]

The legal case for slavery resulting from war was based on Locke's notion of a just war. "Captives taken in a just and lawful war," Locke had written, "are subject to a despotical power";[47] thus, the despotic King of Dahomey was free to sell his captives to the English. Benezet rejected the applicability of Locke's ideas to African slavery on two grounds: first, Africans participated in war involuntarily, following their commander under pain of death; secondly, even in a just war, once the war was over, the conqueror had no right to deprive prisoners of their liberty, or "sell them for Slaves for Life."[48] In *Oroonoko,* Aphra Behn has Oroonoko, or as he is called in the West Indies, Caesar, deliver an impassioned speech to his fellow slaves against slavery, since those who are now their masters were not their conquerors: "And why," said he, "my dear friends and fellow-sufferers, would we be slaves to an unknown people? Have they vanquished us nobly in fight? Have they won us in honourable battle? And are we by the chance of war become their slaves? This would not anger a noble heart; this would not animate a soldier's soul. No, but we are bought and sold like apes or monkeys, to be the sport of women, fools and cowards."[49]

Most abolitionists rejected out of hand their opponents' contention that the bulk of slaves purchased were prisoners of war; rather they contended that most slaves had been kidnapped either by marauding black traders, or were "panyared," i.e. forcibly taken aboard a Guineaman, by some unscrupulous captain. Falconbridge, as surgeon of a slave ship, did not observe among those who it was claimed were prisoners of war, the least sign of any one's having been recently wounded,[50] and Nicholas Owen, an Irish sailor who settled near Sierra Leone as an independent trader from 1757 until his death in 1759, recorded in his daily journal instances of kidnapping along this section of the Guinea Coast.[51]

Another strong argument for the continuance of the slave trade was based on its commercial value. Norris, for example, pointed out that Britain's economic well-being depended on the continuance of the slave trade. He assessed the annual value of slave labor in the West Indies at five million pounds annually, of which one and one-half million formed part of England's annual revenue. One thousand ships and fifteen thousand sailors were involved in the African trade, while Africa and the West Indies consumed the value of three million in domestic manufactures. Norris warned of the "fatal consequences that would inevitably ensue from a check given to this extensive commerce."[52]

But Clarkson had carefully examined the dock duties at Liverpool, and he had found that in 1772 when a hundred vessels sailed for the coast of Africa, the duties amounted to £4552, and that in 1779 during a war when only eleven vessels were engaged in the slave trade, the duties rose to £4957. He concluded that neither the West Indies, nor Liverpool had been affected by what he termed "a practical experiment with respect to abolition."[53] Both David Hume and Adam Smith also rejected the idea that slavery was economically beneficial. Both argued that free labor would always be more productive than slave labor, because free men were always more ambitious.[54]

It did not require special training in economics to see that the South Atlantic system of transporting slaves was wasteful; consequently, there was a great deal of discussion, in the final decades of the century, about establishing plantations in Africa itself as a way of stimulating an effective economy in Africa. There had been some minor experimentation along these lines already, in the late seventeenth and early eighteenth centuries, with the growing of indigo on Bence Island near Sierra Leone and of corn on the Gold Coast for the supply of slave ships.

Joseph Corry's scheme for colonizing the interior of Africa combined both the new theory of economic development and the idea that Africa could develop its own plantations. Corry's aims were threefold: 1) to maintain England's ascendancy in Africa; 2) to extend her commerce by drawing upon the resources of the interior of Africa; 3) to improve the natives. While Corry claimed to be a "zealous advocate of the radical abolition of the slavery of mankind,"[55] he was opposed to any legislative act which would immediately abolish slavery. Corry accepted the notion that great bloodshed in Africa would follow such abolition, and to avoid this, "the intellectual powers of the people [must be] improved by civilization."[56]

Corry proposed establishing a colony on the West Coast of Africa, preferably at Bence Island, to be worked by slave labor brought from the interior. Corry accepted the myth that laborious work was harmful to whites in a tropical environment, but not to natives. He suggested that children aged 5-7 be purchased and given an education which would include "letters, religion and science [and would be] adapted to the useful purposes of life."[57] Upon completion of their education, they were to be returned to their countries and "employed as agents"[58] to disseminate the values of civilization. Corry foresaw that the end of the slave trade was imminent, and concerned about French influence in Africa, he warned his English contemporaries that the fate of "one-fourth of the habitable globe and its infinite resources"[59] hung in the balance. "Let example first encite their admiration," Corry wrote, "and their barbarism will bow before the arts of civilization, and slavery will be gradually abolished."[60]

Even the most rabid anti-abolitionists accepted the idea of the civilizing influence of commerce on the African. Norris wrote of Ouidah and other "maritime states," that "in proportion as these states became improved in civilization, and addicted to agriculture and trade, they declined from their ancient ferocity of temper: they had grown voluptuous and effeminate, and lost every spark of martial fire."[61] There is, paradoxically, in Norris and other travel writers a recognition of a loss of something in civilizing the natives—a simultaneous progressive view of history, seen in the assumed superiority of European culture, and a primitivism evident in the acknowledgement of the corrupting influence of luxury. The same ambivalence is evident forty years earlier in the travels of John Lindsay. Lindsay, writing early in the century when Africa still allured travellers with prospects of abundant gold mines in the interior, believed that the most effectual way of getting gold out of the mines was through trade which would civilize the natives. Lindsay could not help but acknowledge "an unfairness in endeavouring to debauch a hardy people with effeminacy."[62] Copying the English and learning to desire conveniences "they knew not before, they must of course grow more polish'd,"[63] and must work harder to get more gold; thus, inevitably, the gold mines would be opened to Europeans.

It is rather obvious then that the abolition question and conflicting opinions about Africans in travel books raised important questions about the place of the African in the scheme of nature: was he a noble savage, or a cruel barbarian? What was the origin and significance of his color? Was his character distinct from that of the European, and if such differences existed, were they caused by his environment, or were they essential to his race? Answers to these and other questions like them could, of course, only

be theoretical, but travel literature helped give these answers an empirical base, and a pretext for claiming a pseudo-scientific authority. Throughout most of the century, however, an open-mindedness prevailed, i.e., until the decades of the abolition controversy when self-interest and positiveness led to biased reports and these, in turn, to the beginnings of racial prejudice at home.

At one extreme, some thought the Negro to be a noble savage, but as both Hoxie Fairchild and Wylie Sypher have pointed out, this belief was not at first accepted. Sir John Hawkins and other early explorers thought nothing of selling Negro slaves in the West Indies, while at the same time considering the Indians as ennobled creatures. It is only afterward, toward the close of the seventeenth, and in the early eighteenth centuries, that the Negro came to be regarded as a noble savage according to Fairchild's definition of the term: "any free and wild being who draws directly from nature virtues which raise doubts as to the value of civilization."[64] At first, however, this ennobling of the Negro was largely due to confusion about the identity of Negroes and Indians. Pope's often cited couplets from "Windsor Forest" on slavery: "O stretch thy reign, fair Peace! from shore to shore, / Till Conquest cease, and slavery be no more; / Till the free Indians in their native groves / Reap their own fruits, and woo their sable loves" (407-10), illustrate this confusion, as does a passage in Aphra Behn's *Oroonoko* in which a humane planter describes the virtues of modesty and innocence in the Negro:

> And though they are all thus naked, if one lives for ever among 'em, there is not to be seen an undecent action, or glance: and being continually us'd to see one another so unadorn'd, so like our first parents before the fall, it seems as if they had no wishes, there being nothing to heighten curiosity; but all of you can see, you see at once, and every moment see; and where there is no novelty, there can be no curiosity. Not but I have seen a handsome young Indian, dying for love of a very beautiful young Indian maid; but all his courtship was, to fold his arms, pursue her with his eyes, and sighs were all his language: whilst she, as if no such lover were present, or rather as if she desired none such, carefully guarded her eyes from beholding him; and never approach'd him, but she look'd down with all the blushing modesty I have seen in the most severe and cautious of our world. And these people represented to me an absolute idea of the first state of innocence, before man knew how to sin.[65]

Benezet thought the confusion in racial identity between the Negro and the Indian degrading to the Negro. Using the accepted means of evaluating societies, he argued that Indians were nomadic, hence inferior and less capable of being civilized than Negroes who lived in an agrarian society. "The Natural Disposition of the Generality of the Negroes," he concluded, "is widely different from the roving Dispositions of our Indians." Clarkson, too, noted the Indians' "unbending ferocity," in contrast to the Negro's "softness, and plasticity, and pliability."[66]

From favorable reports of travellers, certain stock Negro traits began to emerge, particularly as these reports were absorbed and interpreted by philosophers and other men of letters; such characteristics, for example, as courage, hospitality, stoicism, respect for the aged, compassion for the unfortunate, filial reverence, benevolence, and love[67] helped eulogize the Negro as a noble savage. William Smith's travels, for example, presented the proposition upon which much of this noble savagery was based. Citing the superiority of natural law over human law, Smith wrote: "Whether it is better to be a Negro in Morality or a European with me is easily decided. A Guinean by treading in the Paths prescrib'd him by his Ancestors, Paths natural, pleasant and diverting, is in the plain Road to be a good and happy Man; but the European has sought so many Inventions, and has endeavour'd to put so many Restrictions upon Nature, that it would be next to a Miracle if he were either happy or good."[68]

At the other extreme, however, were the anti-abolitionist travel books which recorded only the barbarism of the Negro. The most graphic accounts of African barbarity came from those who wrote about the kingdom of Dahomey, viz., Norris, Dalzel, and Snelgrave. Each focused his attention on the destructive wars, on the extensive human sacrifice, and on reported cannibalism, although none of these travellers actually witnessed cannibalism being practiced. Snelgrave who visited the country of Ouidah in 1727, shortly after its conquest by the Dahomians, described the fields being strewn with the bones of the slaughtered prisoners of war. Both Norris and Dalzel, who it will be remembered argued that slavery rescued such prisoners from certain death, contended that as a result of this war the traffic in slaves amounted to less than a fourth of what it had been.[69] Norris, borrowing his description of the formerly prosperous and populous maritime kingdom of Ardrah from Smith's travels, and the account by Dutch traveller William Bosman, contrasted the kingdom's industriousness in the past with its present desolateness after the destructive war with Dahomey: "The elysium had vanished; the fields lay uncultured, overrun with weeds, and strewed with human skeletons; and the very air of the place was impoisoned with exhalations pestiferous to the lives of European visitors."[70] The final impression left by these travellers was one of a barbaric despot triumphing over an African civilization enlightened by contact with Europeans. Such a description rejected the abolitionists' contention that the barbarism of the Negro was a result of the slave trade; rather, the civilization of Ardrah, Norris implied, was built upon the slave trade, and was destroyed by a naturally barbarous people who had no former contact with the trade.

Norris visited the Dahomian king, Bossa Ahádee, in 1772 and 1773 at a time when annual ritualistic sacrifices were being performed in honor of their ancestors, sacrifices which Norris contended involved not only the murder of humans, but also cannibalism. His descriptions of the king's palace and of the ceremonies helped contribute to the hardening of reaction against abolition in the 90's. Like Snelgrave before him, he was shocked to find the numbers of human skulls placed atop stakes and used to

adorn the palace; at the door itself, he noted on each side "a human head, recently cut off, lying on a flat stone, with the face down, and the bloody end of the neck toward the entrance."[71] Snelgrave had recorded heaps of human skulls gathered to build a monument, and palace guards adorned with long necklaces of human teeth.

Such shocking details were repeated on page after page, as Norris sought to rebut point for point the abolitionists' contention that the debasement of the African was the result of the conditions of the slave ship and West Indian plantation life. Norris was overwhelmed by "an insupportable stench" from the bodies of those who had been sacrificed earlier; he describes the air thick with flies, vultures eating the carcasses, and mutilated bodies hanging from gibbets.[72]

But the stories which outraged the eighteenth-century audiences most were the tales of cannibalism. Norris described the conclusion of the Dahomian ceremonies which, he was careful to explain, was never witnessed by the whites. The ceremony consisted of throwing from a stage into a crowd "a man tied neck and heels, an alligator muzzled, and a couple of pigeons," which were then torn to pieces by the crowd. Whoever carried off the heads of the victims was rewarded. "If report may be credited," Norris concluded, "the carcase of the human victim is almost wholly devoured, as all the mob below will have a taste of it."[73]

Snelgrave described a similar ceremony in which "the Head of the Victim was for the King; the Blood for the Fetiche [Fetish], or God; and the Body for the common People."[74] While Snelgrave admitted depending upon the king's translator for proof that the common people took away the sacrificed bodies and "boiled and feasted on them, as holy Food," he asserted with assurance the truth of an anecdote he had from a surgeon aboard a slave ship, that he had seen "human Flesh sold publicly in the great Marketplace [in Ouidah]."[75] That these anecdotes must have been generally accepted as true in England, is attested to by James Bruce, normally skeptical of African anecdotes, who repeated with confidence that cannibalism and devil worship were widely practiced over Africa until the beginning of the slave trade.[76]

The only traveller who recorded serious doubts about cannibalism was John Atkins who claimed, "this Man-Eating must be an Imposition on the Credulity of the Whites."[77] Atkins neither accepted Snelgrave's argument that human sacrifices were barbaric, nor acknowledged that such sacrifices inevitably led to cannibalism; Atkins cited the practice of human sacrifice recorded in scripture to refute the charge of barbarism; and noted, furthermore, that cannibalism was not practiced on Bullfinch Lambe, an Englishman who was a captive of the Dahomians. Atkins concluded that "the [only] true Anthropophagi are the diverse Insects infesting us in diverse countries."[78] With amusement, Atkins dismissed most stories of cannibalism with an anecdote from a French travel book which boasted, with a strange kind of chauvinism, that Indians living on the American-Canadian border were partial to "the Flesh of a Frenchman as of finer Taste than that of an Englishman."[79]

While Atkins dismissed Snelgrave's and other traders' reports as biased, asserting that he doubted if such a practice as cannibalism existed "on the face of the Earth," he did acknowledge belief in ritualistic cannibalism, as an expression of "intense Malice against a particular Enemy, and *in terrorem,*" or as a way to conclude "with a Bond of Secrecy some very wicked Societies of Men." Snelgrave, himself, had attested to the extreme terror the idea of being eaten held for the Dahomians' enemies.[80]

Dalzel's history began where Norris' had left off. He described the continuation of similar practices into the reign of Bossa Ahádee's son, Adahoonzou. Dalzel's narrative included one scene where Adahoonzou displayed with pleasure the shrunken head of an enemy, and another in which Adahoonzou demonstrated, for the benefit of his executioners, the proper methods of cutting off prisoners' heads.[81] All this, Dalzel pointed out, was the more surprising because prior to coming to power, Adahoonzou had shown some revulsion toward the cruel practices of his father.

The cumulative effect of the horrid details narrated by Norris and Dalzel was to leave in their readers' minds no doubt about the Negro's barbarism; and ultimately, of course, to condone enslaving those who did not feel the loss of liberty. This last point, which denied any sensibility to the Negro, was emphasized by Norris and repeated by Anna Maria Falconbridge.[82] The reputed benevolence of the Negro toward the white man was also dismissed as mere self-interest, and the virtue of strong filial attachments, for which the Negro was noted, was challenged[83] by Norris who claimed that principles of state in Dahomey required mothers to give up their children to be raised by others, so children would know no other attachment than to the king. While there was no attempt, in these travel books which were hostile to Negroes, to assert that the Negro was not fully a human being, his customs which broke many European social taboos, marked him as different, as barbaric. The Negro, himself, was made to condemn any attempt to impose European standards on his behavior. Dalzel recorded a speech of Adahoonzou's which claimed that humanitarian whites did not understand "blacks, whose disposition differs as much from that of the whites, as their colour. The same Great Being formed both; and since it hath seemed convenient for him to distinguish mankind by opposite complections, it is a fair conclusion to presume, that there may be as great a disagreement in the qualities of their minds."[84]

While the anti-abolitionists were denying that the Negro had any sensibility, abolitionists were making him into a genuine man of feeling. Both the Negro's sense of pity and his benevolence toward others, as well as his ability to feel pain, were documented not only to show he was the moral and intellectual equal of the white man, but also to show his sensitivity to slavery. Thus Benezet both asserted that the Negro had "the same natural affections" as well as the same susceptibility to "pain and grief" as whites.[85] African poetry was often printed in magazines to prove the former.[86] Clarkson, for example, pointed to the writings of Phillis Wheatly and Ignatius Sancho as examples of Negro sensibility.[87] Defoe characterized the Negro as a man of feeling in *Robert Drury's Journal,* a portrait probably drawn from many such examples in African travel books:

> the best character I could give myself to recommend me to my wife's mother was, that I had as tender a heart as a black; for they certainly treat one another with more humanity than we do. Here is no one miserable, if it is in the power of his neighbours to help him. Here is love, tenderness, and generosity which might shame us; and moral honesty too.[88]

Of the latter, the Negro's ability to feel the pains of slavery, there are numerous instances in Alexander Falconbridge's travels. He records the frequency of suicide among the Negroes, and mentions incidents in which Negroes went insane when they realized they were being sold. He saw, for example, a woman chained to a post outside a trader's door "in a state of furious insanity," and described another young woman "chained to the deck, who had lost her senses soon after she was purchased."[89] The point of these examples was, of course, that the Negro could scarcely lose what his detractors claimed he never had.

In their attempts to defend the Negro from racial prejudice, abolitionists drew upon contradictory systems of thought. As primitivists, they argued that the Negro was the intellectual equal, and perhaps the moral superior of the white man, but, as progressivists, they acknowledged that he had been denied the advantages of enlightenment. The most often cited explanation for African barbarism, for example, contended that the African "barbarian" was similar to the Anglo-Saxon barbarian; that is, due to geographic isolation, wars, and climate, Africa's development had been retarded, and the African, rather than being inherently inferior, was simply representative of an earlier culture. Such a view drew upon two basic presumptions of eighteenth-century thought, viz., that all men are everywhere essentially the same, and that the history of nations can be viewed as a progression upward. Thus, in his speech for abolition before the Commons, Pitt offered his analysis of African "backwardness":

> We were once as obscure among the nations of the earth, as savage in our manners, as debased in our morals, as degraded in our understandings, as these unhappy Africans. But in the lapse of a long series of years, by a progression slow, and for a time almost imperceptible, we had become rich in a variety of acquirements.[90]

And, a contributor to the *Universal Magazine* in 1781 wrote: ". . . the Goths and Vandals, from whom we boast our high descent? Uninformed barbarians, in a state of nature, with scarce one beam of reason or of virtue."[91] Bringing commerce and Christianity to Africa would close the gap existing between Europe's and Africa's progress. Implied in all these judgments about Europe's relative superiority was, of course, a technological standard of excellence.

Those who found the progressive view of history unacceptable could still argue about African equality from the degenerationist point of view. The editor of *The Bee* wrote in 1791, that while "Europe shall sink into the abyss which luxury at length prepares for all mankind, then may Africa prove an asylum to the virtuous part of mankind; and after an interval of ages, she may once more, as she has already done, diffuse the light of knowledge upon Europe."[92] And traveller John Atkins wrote that as the glory of Greek and Turkish civilizations had once been great, perhaps the "Revolution of as many ages would raise it again, or carry it to the Negroes and Hottentots, and the present possessors be debased."[93]

Despite their efforts, however, abolitionists knew that racial prejudice was beginning to grow in England and America; in England a generation was being raised that judged the Negro on the basis of the effects of slavery. As Clarkson observed, "They judged only from what they saw; they believed the *appearances* to be *real*."[94] Clarkson was calling attention to the public's association of the physical features of the African, especially his color, with the slave trade's debasing effects, the inferior status of slaves, and the African way of life. That such color consciousness was becoming widespread in the eighteenth century can be seen in the frequent references to color in the autobiography of Olaudah Equiano or, as he was known by his Christian name, Gustavus Vassa, an African living in England. In one instance, for example, Equiano recalls growing up among white children, and being made to feel ashamed of his complexion as compared with that of a white playmate.

> I had often observed that when her mother washed her face it looked very rosy; but when she washed mine it did not look so: I therefore tried oftentimes myself if I could not by washing make my face of the same colour as my little play-mate (Mary), but it was all in vain; and I now began to be mortified at the difference in our complexions.[95]

It followed, of course, that if black races were inferior, then white races were superior. In *Robert Drury's Journal,* one of Defoe's characters says that since God has not created us equal, "He is pleased to distinguish those whom he designs for the government of mankind, by making them in such . . . colour that no man can be ignorant of their superiority."[96] Anatomist J. F. Blumenbach's theory of three primary races—Caucasian, Ethiopian, and Mongolian—left disagreement as to their ranking, until biologists used color as the sole factor in ranking races, whiteness of skin marking the highest race, and gradations of darker skin marking orders of inferiority.[97] Such racist theories were easily squared with other concepts, notably the climatic theory of national behavior and the great chain of

being. Climatic theorists who accepted the notion that the further south one went the greater the national inferiority, also ranked the Negro at the bottom of the chain of being.

Since color was solely the accident of climate, it followed that color could be reversed in either direction by a change in climate. George Roberts, for example, wrote that "if a white man and woman were to come and live with them [Africans], and go naked, and exposed to the scorching sun, as they were, perhaps, their Posterity, in three or four Generations, might be changed to their Complexion";[98] and conversely, Thomas Salmon wrote that "Blacks, in a few generations, would become white, if brought over hither."[99] Clarkson failed to see miscegenation as the obvious cause of lightening skin tone in successive generations of Negroes, and instead quoted Abbé Raynall who wrote:

> The children which the *Africans* procreate in *America,* are not so black as their parents were. After each generation the difference becomes more palpable. It is possible, that after a numerous succession of generations, the men come from *Africa* would not be distinguished from those of the country, into which they may have been transplanted.[100]

Although theologically unorthodox, polygenesis was the most generally accepted theory of racial origins. According to this theory black and white men were created separately, and therefore comprised separate species. Atkins, for example, wrote that black Africans would not lighten by a mere change in climate for "tho' it be a little Heterodox, I am persuaded the black and white Race have, *ab origine,* sprung from different-coloured first Parents."[101] This theory appealed to the diversitarianism of the age, which focused on differences between men, rather than their similarities, and the theory could also be easily adapted to the great chain of being, where as a result of Buffon's work in comparative anatomy, the missing link between men and apes was being sought. While monogenesis resulted in ranking the races, it was less unfavorable than polygenesis to Africans, and other "degenerate" races, for they were all included in humanity, and even the most "degenerate" were capable of improvement; but polygenesis established a permanent distinction between the sons of Adam and other races.[102]

Travel literature on Africa proved to be an important source of information for both abolitionists and anti-abolitionists in the final decades of the eighteenth century. Since travel literature enjoyed such popularity during this time, and since the statistics supplied by travellers make their way into periodical literature, it is safe to conclude that African travel literature greatly influenced popular thinking about abolition, and, through its creation of myths, helped shape racial and imperialistic attitudes for the next century.

African travel books both fed already existing myths, and created new ones. The myth of Africa as the dark continent—a phrase which described Europe's lack of information about the continent as well as the barbarism of its inhabitants—was confirmed by eighteenth-century travellers who were shocked at the cultural dissimilarity of European and African. Early in the century barbarism did not necessarily imply racial inferiority; however, myths of racial inferiority grew out of the travel literature related to the abolition movement of the 1790's. Conversely, abolitionists tended to depict the African in terms of another myth, the myth of the noble savage.

The contradictory image of the African as cruel barbarian, or noble savage, is only one example of many contradictory myths about Africa which found their way into the travel literature. In West Africa, for example, the myth of tropical exuberance conflicted with the myth of the "white man's grave." Some travellers depicted West Africa as an Edenic land where food was provided without the necessity of work; others depicted West Africa as a disease-ridden land where white men could scarcely set foot with impunity. Some saw in Africa confirmation of the unity of the chain of being; the variety of species extended even to mankind when men could be found in different colors; others emphasized the separateness of the links in the chain. In West Africa, progressivists saw a land of potential, a land ready for proselytizing and uplifting; degenerationists saw in Africa confirmation of the cycles of history: once great states had, following the inevitable cycles of history, fallen into a state of degeneracy.

In studying the history of the abolition movement in the late eighteenth century, scholars, it would seem, have misspent their efforts for, having attributed undue importance to imaginative literature as a barometer of public opinion on abolition, they have inadvertently neglected travel literature; African travel books are at once a widely read genre, and, as I have shown, a genre which shaped the attitudes toward Africa and Africans, while providing the substance of the arguments for and against abolition.

Notes

1. Thomas Clarkson, *The History of the Rise, Progress, and Accomplishment of the Abolition of the Slave Trade by the British Parliament,* 2 vols. (London, 1808); Wylie Sypher, *Guinea's Captive Kings: British Anti-Slavery Literature of the XVIIIth Century* (Chapel Hill, 1942); Hoxie Neale Fairchild, *The Noble Savage: A Study in Romantic Naturalism* (New York, 1928); Eva Beatrice Dykes, *The Negro in English Romantic Thought* (Washington, D.C., 1942); N. Verle McCullough, *The Negro in English Literature* (Devon, 1962); and Richard M. Kain, "The Problem of Civilization in English Abolition Literature, 1772-1808," *Philological Quarterly,* 15 (Jan. 1936), 105-25.

2. Clarkson, I, 463.

3. *Ibid.,* I, 489-90.

4. *Ibid.,* I, 388.

5. *Ibid.,* I, 459-60.

6. Archibald Dalzel, *The History of Dahomey. An Inland Kingdom of Africa* (London, 1793), Preface, v-vii.

7. Clarkson, I, 478-79.

8. Robert Norris, *Memoirs of the Reign of Bossa Ahádee* (London, 1789), 181.

9. *Ibid.,* 169.

10. Clarkson, I, 327-29.

11. *Ibid.,* I, 537-38.

12. *Ibid.,* III, 111. The print is reproduced facing this page.

13. *Ibid.,* II, 152-53.

14. Alexander Falconbridge, *An Account of the Slave Trade on the Coast of Africa* (London, 1788), 24.

15. *Ibid.,* 25.

16. *Ibid.,* 27-28.

17. *Ibid.,* 28.

18. For mortality figures among the slaves see Falconbridge, 29; Anthony Benezet, *Some Historical Account of Guinea,* 126-29; *A Caution to Great Britain and Her Colonies* (Philadelphia, 1785), 39-40; *A Short Account of that Part of Africa, Inhabited by the Negroes,* 2nd ed. (Philadelphia, 1762), 48; and *A Short Address Originally Written to the People of Scotland, on the Subject of the Slave Trade* (Shrewsbury, 1792), 14-15; Clarkson, *History,* II, 59, and *An Essay on the Slavery and Commerce of the Human Species* (London, 1786), 140.

19. *A Short Address,* 15.

20. Quoted in John Newton, *The Journal of a Slave Trader 1750-1754,* ed. by Bernard Martin and Mark Spurrell (London, 1962), 95.

21. Falconbridge, 23-24.

22. Newton, *The Journal of a Slave Trader 1750-1754,* 75.

23. William Snelgrave, *A New Account of Guinea, And the Slave Trade* (London, 1754), 162-64.

24. Norris, 170-72.

25. Clarkson, *History,* II, 48-49.

26. Norris, 176.

27. *Ibid.,* 170.

28. Clarkson, *History,* I, 541-43.

29. *Ibid.,* I, 247-48; Newton, 102.

30. For the annual figures see *A Short Address,* 29.

31. Falconbridge, 11.

32. Dalzel, 24.

33. See Norris, 179-80.

34. Anna M. Falconbridge, *Narrative of Two Voyages to the River Sierra Leone during the Years 1791-1793,* 2nd ed. (London, 1802), 236; 1st ed. 1794.

35. Snelgrave, 86.

36. Norris, 156-57.

37. Clarkson, *Essay,* 113.

38. John Atkins, *Voyage to Guinea, Brasil, and the West-Indies,* 2nd ed. (London, 1737), 62; 1st ed. 1735.

39. Norris, 147.

40. Clarkson, *History,* I, 480.

41. *A Short Address,* 5.

42. Benezet, *Some Historical Account,* 82.

43. Alexander Falconbridge, 14.

44. Dalzel, 218.

45. Quoted in Sypher, 23.

46. Alexander Falconbridge, 9-10.

47. John Locke, *Two Treatises of Government,* in *Works* (London, 1823), V, 442. Although Locke was against slavery ("Slavery is so vile and miserable an estate of man, and so directly opposite to the generous temper and courage of our nation, that it is hardly to be conceived that an Englishman, much less a gentleman, should plead for it." *Ibid.,* V, 212), nevertheless, in his exposition of the limited power of a conqueror over the rights of a conquered people, Locke (arguing inconsistently) supported slavery which resulted from a "just war."

48. Benezet, *A Short Account,* 44-45.

49. Aphra Behn, *Two Tales: The Royal Slave and The Fair Jilt* (Cambridge, 1953), 63.

50. Alexander Falconbridge, 16.

51. Nicholas Owen, *Journal of a Slave Dealer,* ed. Eveline Martin (London, 1930), 37-38.

52. Norris, 164-65. Historian Philip D. Curtin lists the value of British goods sold in Africa itself at £69,000, and income from the sale of slaves alone at £1,000,000 (Philip D. Curtin, *The Image of Africa: British Ideas and Action 1780-1850* [Madison, 1964], 6).

53. Clarkson, I, 374-75.

54. Hume, *Essays, Moral, Political, and Literary,* ed. T. H. Green and T. H. Grose (London, 1875), I, 390, n. 2; Adam Smith, *An Enquiry into the Nature and Causes of the Wealth of Nations* (London, 1826), 363.

55. Corry, *Observations upon the Windward Coast of Africa* (London, 1807), 53.

56. *Ibid.,* 71.

57. *Ibid.,* 81.

58. *Ibid.,* 82.

59. *Ibid.,* 89.

60. *Ibid.,* 100.

61. Norris, 130.

62. Lindsay, *A Voyage to the Coast of Africa in 1758* (London, 1759), 101.

63. *Ibid.,* 104.

64. Fairchild, 2.

65. Behn, 3.

66. Benezet, *A Short Account,* 72; Clarkson, *Thoughts on the Necessity of Improving the Condition of the Slaves in the British Colonies* (London, 1823), 21.

67. McCullough, 65-66.

68. William Smith, *A New Voyage to Guinea* (London, 1744), 249-50. See R. W. Frantz, "The English Traveller and the Movement of Ideas 1660-1732," *The University Studies of the University of Nebraska,* 32-33, 1932-33 (Lincoln, 1934) for the persistence of this primitivism in travel literature of the Restoration and early eighteenth century. Frantz concludes: "This belief in the existence of a fixed moral law known to all peoples who remain unspoiled by corrupting traditions led many a voyager painstakingly to record those virtues which he considered to be natural to man" (106).

69. Norris, x-xi; Dalzel, 26-27.

70. Norris, 142-44.

71. *Ibid.,* 94; Snelgrave, 31-38.

72. *Ibid.,* 100-01.

73. *Ibid.,* 125-26.

74. Snelgrave, 44.

75. *Ibid.,* 52-53.

76. James Bruce, *Travels to Discover the Source of the Nile, In the Years 1768, 1769, 1770, 1771, 1772, and 1773* (Edinburgh, 1790), I, 393-94.

77. Atkins, 129.

78. *Ibid.,* xxv.

79. *Ibid.,* xxiv-xxv.

80. *Ibid.,* 123-24; Snelgrave, 42.

81. Dalzel, 154-55, 172-73.

82. Norris, 159; Anna M. Falconbridge, 238-39.

83. Smith, 22; Norris, 88-89.

84. Dalzel, 217.

85. Benezet, *A Short Account,* 78.

86. Kain, 107, n. 13.

87. Clarkson, *Essay,* 175-76.

88. Daniel Defoe, *Madagascar, or Robert Drury's Journal, During Fifteen Years' Captivity on that Island,* ed. Captain Pasfield Oliver (London, 1890), 172-73; 1st ed. 1729. For references to Defoe's disputed authorship of the *Journal* see Oliver's introduction; William P. Trent, *Daniel Defoe: How to Know Him* (Indianapolis, 1916), 262-64; Arthur W. Secord, *Studies in the Narrative Method of*

Defoe (New York, 1963), 207; John Robert Moore, *Daniel Defoe: Citizen of the Modern World* (Chicago, 1958), 343, 354.

89. Alexander Falconbridge, 31-32.

90. Clarkson, *History,* II, 444-45.

91. Quoted in Kain, 115.

92. Quoted in Kain, 119.

93. Atkins, xviii.

94. Clarkson, *Essay,* 23.

95. Equiano, *The Interesting Narrative of the Life of Olaudah Equiano, or Gustavus Vassa, the African,* 2nd ed. (London, 1789), I, 109.

96. Defoe, 156.

97. For the discussion of Blumenbach's work and related racial theories see Curtin, 37-46, and Sypher, 54-58.

98. George Roberts, *The Four Years' Voyage of Captain George Roberts* (London, 1726). Reprinted in Thomas Astley, *A New General Collection of Voyages and Travels* (London, 1745), I, 599-627; citation is from *A New General Collection of Voyages and Travels,* ed. Thomas Astley, 4 vols. (London, 1745), I, 619. Some think Roberts' *Voyage* is by Defoe. See E. G. Cox, *A Reference Guide to the Literature of Travel* (Seattle, 1935-38), I, 370.

99. Thomas Salmon, *Modern History: or, the Present State of All Nations,* 3rd ed. (London, 1746), III, 59.

100. Clarkson, *Essay,* 202.

101. Atkins, 39.

102. The best account of the monogenetic and polygenetic theories of the origin of race can be found in Curtin, 40-43.

Keith A. Sandiford (essay date 1988)

SOURCE: "The Intellectual Milieu: Contexts for Black Writing," in *Measuring the Moment: Strategies of Protest in Eighteenth-Century Afro-English Writing,* Associated University Presses, 1988, pp. 43-72.

[*In the following excerpt, Sandiford provides an overview of white authors' writings on slavery and the slave trade in Britain from the 1680s to the end of the eighteenth century, and argues that the convergence of ideological currents during this time created a more favorable climate in which blacks could live and write.*]

The antislavery movement did not win the concerted advocacy of belletristic writers until the last three decades of the eighteenth century. The slow response was due to the following three factors. The first was the die-hard persistence of legalistic doctrines about slavery that helped to shield the institution from criticism for a long time. The second was that before the formation of the Abolition Society accelerated the course of antislavery, literary figures were likely to be as uninformed about the true nature of the slave trade as ordinary citizens. The third reason was the relation of such figures to the temper of their times. Like the parliamentarians, the philosophers, and the churchmen, they found it hard to escape the prejudices of their age: some could accept the idea of Black people's humanity only with reservation; others might concede kindred humanity but found the thought of the Black's social equality unpalatable.[1] It is not surprising, therefore, that the earliest appearance of the African in English literature was as an abstract literary idealization rather than as a figure of unquestionable human identity.

The idealized figure of the "Noble Negro," which begins to appear in late seventeenth-century literature, bears little resemblance to the common plantation slave who became the consuming preoccupation of abolitionist writers. The "Noble Negro" is princely, heroic. He is endowed with all the natural virtues of courage and moral incorruptibility that European primitivists liked to imagine were the distinctive marks of primitive humanity. This literary ideal clearly informs the vision of Mrs. Aphra Behn's celebrated work, *Oroonoko* (1688).

The hero of that work, Oroonoko, is high-born and high-minded; his physical features are more Roman-patrician than negroid. Oroonoko is fearless in the face of his masters' torture and treachery, and faithful in love to the beautiful Imoinda. Altogether, the lineaments of his origin and character serve to set him apart from the much maligned, downtrodden slave. Mrs. Behn's fictional portrait conformed more nearly to the artificial models of conventional heroic tragedy, as exemplified by Dryden, than to the actual particulars of slavery that a Ramsay or Raynal described for definite humanitarian purposes. Wylie Sypher strongly denies any genuine antislavery design in Oroonoko: "Mrs. Behn is not repelled by slavery," he perceives, "but by the enslaving of a prince."[2]

Mrs. Behn's *Oroonoko* went through many editions, translations, and adaptations. In 1696 Thomas Southerne dramatized *Oroonoko,* and the subsequent stage history of that production was nothing short of phenomenal; the play was performed at least once every season until 1801. The relation of the Oroonoko legend to antislavery, however, rests more in the metamorphosis wrought through changing audience interpretation over the years than in what its original authors proposed. It established the tradition of the "Noble Negro," an image that, although highly sentimentalized and unrealistic, stirred most English citizens' consciousnesses to consider more seriously the plight of the African and the ineluctable proofs of Britain's complicity in crimes against humanity.

That Mrs. Behn and Southerne lacked genuine humanitarian commitment in their work must be attributed to the pervasive ambivalences of their age. The Augustans could shed the tear of social sympathy with one eye while winking at injustice with the other. In general, they were too sensible of the inequities on which their Golden Age of progress and stability was built to make any unequivocal stand for enlightened egalitarianism. That had to wait until the next century.

Daniel Defoe was a case in point. In *Reformation of Manners* (1702), a satirical work ranging widely over a multitude of evils, he denounced the slave trade. But fourteen years earlier he had supported the same trade in his *Essay on Projects* (1688). Forty years after *Reformation* we find him urging the continued growth of the slave trade in his *Plan of the English Commerce*. This inconsistency is a consistent reflection of Defoe's tradesman's mentality. His was an unremitting voice for the vigorous promotion of free trade all over the world; his glowing paeans to the virtues of an enlightened commerce are identical with the spirit of proslavery panegyrics appearing later in the century.

Richard Savage, on the other hand, conceived of a colonial enterprise that would yield the best of both worlds—prosperity for the Englishman and liberty for the African. He recognized the value of the plantations to the British economy and supported their development, but he discountenanced the subjugation and enslavement of the Africans:

> Why must I Afric sable children see
> Vender for slaves though formed by nature free,
> The nameless tortures cruel minds invent,
> Those to subject whom nature equal meant.
>
> ("Of Public Spirit" [1737], 141)

Savage was probably the first English poet of mark to devote more than passing attention to the moral implications of colonialism and to plead for compassion for the Black slave. Samuel Johnson, in his *Lives of the English Poets,* particularly praised the tenderness and sympathy Savage displayed in this poem and commended his courage in asserting "the natural equality of mankind" at a time when such ideas were still subject to suspicion.[3]

By midcentury Johnson was stating his own opposition to slavery on the basis of natural rights. He was particularly critical of the Europeans' motives for undertaking voyages of exploration: "The Europeans have scarcely visited any coast, but to gratify avarice, and extend corruption; to arrogate dominion without right, and practice cruelty without incentive."[4] In the same place, he decried the wanton brutality of the Portuguese in firing on the bewildered Africans during their first contacts on the African coast: "We are openly told that they had less scruple concerning their treatment of the savage people, because they scracely considered them as distinct from beasts."[5]

Johnson's biographer, James Boswell, relates that Johnson always hated slavery with a passion, and that on one occasion at Oxford, he made a toast "to the next insurrection of the negroes in the West Indies."[6] Johnson recognized the flagrant irony in the American colonists' revolt against British rule: "How is it," he asked, "that we hear the loudest yelps for liberty among the drivers of negroes?" Johnson's championship of the Black cause is remarkable, for he was a Tory in politics and fundamentally conservative in most things. It was undoubtedly his deeply humane spirit that set his face so firmly against the unjust institution of slavery.

But Boswell was not convinced. He thought Johnson's opinions were the result of "prejudice and imperfect or false imformation." True Whig that he was, Boswell fully appreciated the extensive profits that accrued to the nation from the slave trade and the slave colonies, and so he could muster nothing better than this specious attempt to justify slavery, a claim that it benefited both Englishmen and Africans: "To abolish a status which in all ages God has sanctioned, and man has continued, would not only be robbery to an innumerable class of our fellow subjects; but it would be extreme cruelty to the African Savages, a portion of whom it saves from massacre, or intolerable bondage in their own country, and introduces into a much happier state of life."[7]

And that idyll of slavery would gain credibility as long as the public remained ignorant of the harsh truth. James Thomson, although more enraptured with the pride and beauty of the African wilderness than with the human value of the Africans themselves, pitied the hapless slaves who were unceremoniously uprooted and loaded on to ships bound for strange lands. He provided for the English readers one of the first pictures of the horrors that attended the Middle Passage. Lured by the scent of rotting flesh and jettisoned corpses, a shark stalks the slave ship:

> Behold he rushing cuts the briny flood,
> Swift as the gale can bear the ship along;
> And from the partners of that cruel trade
> Which spoils unhappy Guinea of her sons
> Demands his share of prey—demands themselves.
>
> ("Summer," from *The Seasons,* 1016-21)

That was in 1727. As yet, writers still contrived to subsume their antipathy to the slave system beneath the formal literary ornaments of euphemism and periphrasis. Even James Grainger, who became known as the bard of the sugar cane, was apt to romanticize the West Indian neighorhood and sentimentalize the lot of the slave in his georgic to plantation society, *The Sugar Cane* (1764). His effusions were of this order:

> Nor Negro, at thy destiny repine
> Though doom'd to toil from dawn to setting sun
> How far more pleasant is thy rural task,
> Than theirs who sweat, sequester'd from the day
> In dark tartarean caves, sunk far beneath
> The Earth's surface.
>
> (4, 165-70)

Grainger typified many other Englishmen of his day who, as men of sense, regretted the slaves' suffering, but as men of property could not bring themselves to dismantle the system that inflicted that suffering.[8] Grainger owned slaves on his Saint Kitts estates. His familiarity with African character and manners lends veracity to his delineations of the different tribal types that were to be found in the West Indies. The slave for him always remains a feeling human, albeit an unfortunate one:

> Howe'er insensate some may deem their slaves,
> Nor 'bove the bestial rank; far other thoughts
> The Muse, soft daughter of Humanity!
> Will ever entertain.—The Ethiop knows,
> The Ethiop feels, when treated like a man.
>
>   (4, 421-25)

The poetry is not fashioned to serve the ends of truth, nor can it accommodate itself to the urgency of a political moment; but it has benevolism and, as we have seen, this was a necessary antecedent to the more practical humanitarianism of the last years of the century.

Nearly one hundred years after *Oroonoko* was first published, the literary successors of Aphra Behn and Thomas Southerne began transforming the original idealized hero of European myth making into a distinctly political symbol. The "Noble Negro" was not only an enslaved prince, exhibiting the classical qualities of terror and fear and defying his enemies with an indomitable spirit, but he was now being presented as a man of feeling, a benevolist whom slavery scarred and demoralized. In this figure, he was supposed to represent the human virtues of all African slaves, not the overdrawn excellences of a primitivistic ideal. The capacity for feeling, for compassion, and for generosity established the Black's claim to equality with the white. It was the abundance and legitimacy of these virtues that commended the African as a literary figure and Sancho as a literary artist to the reading public. "Beyond any doubt," Philip Curtin observes, "the use of the savage hero as a literary device helped to create a much more favorable emotional climate for Africans than they would otherwise have enjoyed."[9]

Nowhere is the literary myth of the "Noble Negro" more strikingly transfigured than in that minor poetic genre commonly known as the "Dying Negro Poems." Thomas Day was its most worshipful exponent; his poem, "The Dying Negro," its immortal prototype. Although Day has traditionally been given credit for its authorship, the poem was actually a collaborative effort between him and his friend, John Bicknell. The poem is a tragic tale of heroism and natural passion. It seems to have been occasioned by the report of a slave who had escaped his master's custody and planned to receive baptism as a preliminary to marrying a white woman. His master got wind of his plan, recaptured him, and placed him on a ship bound for America. The slave killed himself rather than accept renewed bondage. The sentiments of the poem are noble and the tone high-serious. Day emphasizes the native worth of the African by pointing to his devaluation by European slavery:

> Fallen are my trophies, blasted my fame,

> Myself become a thing without a name
> The sport of haughty lords, and even of slaves the
>   shame.

He makes the Black slave's love for his white bride-to-be as strong as any classical or romantic hero's and certainly superior to any passion of the oppressing antagonists.

> And I have loved thee with as pure a fire
> As man e'er felt, or woman could inspire
> No pangs like these my pallid tyrants know,
> Not such their transports, and not such their woe.
> Their softer frames a feeble soul conceal,
>   a Soul unus'd to pity or to feel;
> Damped by base lucre and repelled by fear,
> Each noble passion faintly blazes there.

The hero dies in the hope that Africa will one day triumph over her enemies. He thunders an apocalyptic vision of conquest and revenge. His final utterance is a gesture of triumph and defiance:

> Receive me falling, and your suppliant hear
> To you this unpolluted blood I pour,
> To you that spirit which ye gave restore.

The final two lines were to become the epitome of the Black's unquenchable spirit in "Noble Negro" mythology. They were some of the most frequently quoted lines in abolitionist writing.

Day's poem had its objective equivalent not only in an actual suicide but also in the famous case of James Somerset, the determination of which was to be a milestone in the abolitionists' struggle. Somerset's victory was to furnish the legal precedent on which Blacks in England could thereafter stake their claim to self-possession and resist forcible constraint by slave agents.

Somerset had accompanied his master James Stewart from Virginia to England in 1769 and deserted him there in 1771. Stewart had him recaptured and placed on a ship, intending to sell him into slavery in Jamaica. Granville Sharp and other African sympathizers procured a writ of *habeas corpus* and had Somerset released. They sought to have this case resolved on the principle of the individual's right to personal liberty and to declare that no man could be a slave in England. Much tactical stalling and many procedural complications delayed the course of justice, some of them expressly in the interests of the slave lobby. Finally in June 1772, Chief Justice Mansfield gave his judgment that a slave owner could not forcibly remove a slave from England. Although Mansfield adeptly circumvented the pivotal issue of slavery's legality, his decision was widely interpreted as conferring absolute freedom on slaves in England, and that assumption further intensified literary protest in the decade following the publication of Day's poem.

The Abolition Committee gave active support to writers of antislavery verse, and it devised a thoroughly effective machinery for the dissemination thereof. One of the first productions that was given to the public under the committee's aegis was William Roscoe's poem, "The Wrongs of Africa" (1787-88). Roscoe's poem paints Africans sympathetically and upbraids Britain, the champion of liberty, for its rapacious greed and cruelty in the slavery business. Roscoe's hero, Cymbello, is, like Day's, a fierce, spirited, apocalyptic figure; his deeds presage the imminent collapse of the West Indian system.

The committee was also instrumental in influencing England's most popular poet of the last two decades of the century to wield his pen in the service of the slaves' cause. William Cowper, that poet, was neither by temperament nor by inclination fitted for political movements, but he was a truehearted humanitarian and an intense Evangelical. He found slavery indefensible and censured the ruthlessness of Britain's commercial and imperialistic designs upon African and other primitive peoples.[10] Cowper believed in the equal brotherhood of all men under the fatherhood of God. He also believed that Africans, like all primitive peoples, possessed souls that made them just as worthy of freedom as "civilized" Europeans.

Cowper's earliest attacks on slavery came in "Charity" (1782). There he characterized the slave trade as loathsome and deplored its destruction of the social bonds that knit humankind together as a single race. In *The Task* (1785) he expressed an equally vehement distaste for the idea of slaves as personal property:

> I would not have a slave to till my ground,
> To carry me, to fan me while I sleep,
> And tremble when I wake, for all the wealth
> That sinews bought and gold have earned.
>
> (29-32)

Cowper became an unwitting propagandist for the abolitionist campaign when the committee distributed thousands of copies of his poem "The Negro's Complaint" (1788) all over England. The verses of this poem, along with those of two other Cowper pieces, "The Morning Dream" (1788) and "Sweet Meat Has Sour Sauce" (1788), were set to music and sung as popular ballads in the streets. "The Morning Dream" proclaimed a vision of Liberty, a female figure, sailing to the West Indies to free the slaves. Oppression is vanquished at her sight and thousands of Black voices raise shouts of joy at their release from enslavement.

Among the eminent literary figures of the eighteenth century, Cowper undoubtedly holds first place for the volume of his work specifically addressed to slavery and the impact that it had on the popularization of antislavery. As the wave of abolitionist writing crested in the 1790s, other major poets raised their voices too. The Romantics paid tribute to the humanitarian revolution in modest but memorable tokens.

Coleridge won the Browne Gold Medal at Cambridge University for his "Ode on the Slave Trade" (1792), and he lectured at Bristol on the slave trade in 1795. Southey wrote a series of "Slave Trade Sonnets" (1794) condemning the slave traders and invoking the injured Africans to drive the European intruders out of their country with all their native strength. Wordsworth's enthusiasm was hesitant and belated. He had been disillusioned by the sorry turn in the tide of French revolutionary affairs, after he had thrown his full moral support behind its high ideals at the outset in 1789. In 1792 he confessed a deepening disenchantment with political movements, as the reign of terror and orgiastic bloodshed gripped France. But with the abolition bill bidding fair for passage in Parliament, he wrote a sonnet to Thomas Clarkson (1807) and another to Toussaint L'Ouverture, the black Haitian revolutionary (1807).

As might be expected, the saturation of the mass media with antislavery propaganda satiated the public mind. As enthusiasm for the original ideals of the French Revolution began to flag with the coming into leadership of extremists, so too in the 1790s abolition showed a decline, as slave uprisings in the West Indies, some of them bloody and terrifying to white supremacists, occurred with increasing frequency. Anna Letitia Barbauld, an uncommonly gifted woman and an earnest campaigner for antislavery, complained in her "Epistle to Wilberforce" (1791) that the country had grown impervious and deceitful through its love of ease and pleasure:

> Each flimsy sophistry by turns they try;
> The plausive argument, the daring lie,
> The artful gloss, the moral sense confounds,
> The acknowledged thirst of gain that honour wounds.
>
> (25-30)

Thomas Campbell's "Pleasures of Hope" (1799) reflects the waning of the "Noble Negro" sentimental fashion. No longer is the sad plight of the enslaved African the burden of poetic song; that theme has diminished to mere allusions. Campbell strains more toward a vision of universal improvement as the source of healing for a troubled and imperfect world:

> Where barbarous hordes on Scythian mountains roam,
> Truth, Mercy, Freedom, yet shall find a home;
> Where'er degraded Nature bleeds and pines
> From Guinea's coasts to Sibir's dreary mines
> Truth shall pervade the unfathom'd darkness there,
> And light the dreadful features of despair.
>
> (1, 350-55)

Only James Montgomery seemed not to have lost the old fervor, the revolutionary optimism that characterized abolitionists of the two preceding decades. Montgomery had long been an uncompromising foe of slavery and a friend of the Africans. His poem, "The West Indies" (1807), depicts Africans in their familiar surroundings as industrious, peaceful, and hospitable. Montgomery never doubted the human identity of his subjects:

> Is he not man by sin and suffering tried?
> Is he not man, for whom the Saviour died?

Believe the Negro's powers:—in headlong will,
Christian! thy brother thou shalt prove him still;
Belie his virtues; since his wrongs began,
His follies and his crimes have stampt him Man.

(2, 107-12)

But even Montgomery, for all his ardor, was forced to acknowledge the declining enthusiasm for antislavery at this time. He observed that "Public feeling had been wearied into insensibility by the agony of interest which the question of the African slave trade excited during three and twenty years of intense and almost incessant discussion."[11] Now in the first decade of the new century, other causes and other issues were claiming priority in politics and literature. The antislavery movement had not died, but it was obviously cooling. The forces of reaction had started to brand abolitionists as anarchists, levellers, whose principles, they feared, would bring on Britain the same political instability and social unrest that were currently rife in France.

It only remains now to consider the role played by periodical literature specifically, in spreading abolitionist ideas, and also generally, in stimulating public awareness about the condition of the African. The eighteenth century saw the rise and flourishing of periodicals and literary magazines. And just as the older literary genres turned increasingly to the defence of common humanity and human integrity, the periodicals likewise reflected the widespread discussion of the problem of slavery. In general, the last three decades of the century saw the same intense agitation and debate in the periodicals as in verse, drama, and fiction.

In no journal were the twin issues of slavery and the slave trade debated with greater animation than in the *Gentleman's Magazine*. Undoubtedly one of the most widely circulated magazines of the day, this journal began noticing the Black presence in 1764. Between 1770 and 1780, as antislavery protest mounted, the magazine's pages resonated with the claims and counterclaims of spokesmen on either side of the debate. When later on, the African became a figure of sentimentality and heroic romance, the *Gentleman's Magazine* also reflected the fashion by printing dozens of the "Noble Negro" poems. The delineations of this idealized African were not significantly different from those described above, but the *Gentleman's* verses seemed to emphasize the idyll of an illustrious past. Snatched from the clinging arms of wife and children, the noble African, who had spent his early years in feats of bravery and adventure, is now dragged away to sea, to a life of fear and coercion:

Everything I see affright me
Nothing I can understand,
With the scourges white man fight me,
None of this is Negro land.

("The African's Complaint on-Board a Slave Ship," *The Gentleman's Magazine* 63 [1793]: 749)

The periodicals popularized the image of the African as a child of Nature who felt deeply the pangs of separation from his pastoral haunts, who pined for the felicities of hearth and home, who practiced hospitality to strangers, and whose generosity and innocence were nearly always betrayed by the white man's guile. Thomas Adney's "The Slave," which appeared in the *European Magazine* (July-December 1792), vilifies the European by its ironic compliments and humanizes the African slave by underscoring his moral virtues:

What tho' no flush adorn my face,
Nor silken tresses deck my hair,
Altho' debarr'd of polish'd grace
And scorn'd by those more haply fair;
Yet in my veins does honour roll,
Tho' subject to a tyrant's call;
Heav'n gave to man a noble soul,
And not to seek a Brother's fall.

(160-68)

Natural goodness was but one of the Black person's virtues celebrated in the pathetic verses of the popular journals. Mungo, a stock symbol of the suffering, abused African, was also capable of feeling:

I am a slave when all things else are free.
Yet I was born, as you are, no man's slave
An heir to all that lib'ral nature gave:
My thoughts can reason, and my limbs can move
The same as yours; like yours my heart can love.[12]

("Mungo's Address," 10-14)

By taking the rhetoric of their cause to the pages of the periodical press, the abolitionist agents ensured that their ideas received optimal exposure through the frequent publication and mass circulation of the popular journals. In this way, favorable notions about African character were disseminated and became fixed in the public mind, eventually transforming themselves into myths useful to abolitionist propaganda. The soul of the dead slave, for instance, always returned to its native Africa where it was welcomed in ceremonies befitting a hero. The daring hope of a revitalized Africa, rising up to visit revenge on her foes and to restore the arts of liberty and peace to the land, remained a cherished vision in these poems until as late as 1809:

Now Christian, now, in wild dismay,
Of Afric's proud revenge the prey,
Go roam the affrighted wood;
Transformed to tigers fierce and fell
Thy race shall prowl with savage yell;
And glut their rage for blood.

("Ode on Seeing a Negro Funeral," 31-36)

The *Edinburgh Review,* in the liberal tradition of the Scottish Enlightenment, lost no opportunity to come to the defense of Blacks, traduced as they often were by proslavery polemicists. One contributor to the *Review* stoutly controverted the claims of a detracting work, in which Africans were stigmatized as foul-smelling, ill-favored and "only one step removed from the state of beasts." The reviewer maintained that Africans, as part of mankind, were capable of improvement like all other members of the human family. He pointed to the Blacks' successful strategy and execution of the Saint Domingue revolt (1791) as compelling evidence of their superior capabilities.[13]

The foregoing survey of the broad intellectual background to abolition illustrates a timely convergence of powerful ideological currents that created a more favorable climate for Blacks to live in and a more receptive audience for Black literary expression than would otherwise have prevailed in eighteenth-century Britain. The cult of benevolism established the principle that all human beings were capable of sensations of pleasure and pain and urged the desirability of working for the increase of the one and the avoidance of the other, particularly on behalf of one's fellow creatures. It forced people to reexamine the proslavery polemicists' rationalization that Blacks were suited to slavery because they were incapable of feeling its rigors. As the Enlightenment promoted the systematic study of humanity and human socieites, Europeans began to reconcile themselves to the idea that the African was a legitimate member of the human race and that it would be highly beneficial to universal progress to accept Africa into the community of nations.

Gradually, the pronouncements of leading humanitarians rejected the assumption of Black inferiority and asserted the moral and intellectual equality of the Black slave with the white master. The result was bound to undermine the philosophical foundations on which the colonial slave system was established. For some, the African slave became humanized. Once it was acknowledged that Blacks had a moral nature and intellectual capacity, it was reasonable to believe that they could attain the humanistic ideal of perfectibility.

Enthusiastic negrophiles were fascinated by the thought that the pure blood and robust strength of the African could serve as a potent force in the shaping of a new civilization, the image of which was often mirrored in the mythology of "Noble Negro" poems.[14] Some abolitionist visionaries went further and predicted that European civilization would be eclipsed and eventually supplanted by an Africa revivified and restored to become the center of universal culture and progress. But a great number of abolitionists—and progressivists generally—shared the optimistic view of continuing progress for Africa as well as for Europe. They envisioned the replacement of the lopsided, antihumanitarian trade in slaves by a flourishing trade in more conventional material goods, a system of enlightened commercial relationships and cultural exchange that would ideally yield equal benefits for both Africans and Europeans. . . .

Notes

1. For a discussion of this ignorance and the consequences for literature, see Sypher, *Guinea's Captive Kings,* 29.

2. Sypher, *Guinea's Captive Kings,* 110.

3. *The Works of Samuel Johnson* (London, 1810), 10:315, 356-59.

4. Johnson, *The World Display'd* (London, 1759), in *Works* 2:276.

5. Johnson, *The World Display'd,* 274.

6. Boswell, *Life of Johnson* 2:154.

7. Boswell, *Life of Johnson* 2:156.

8. Sypher recognizes this inconsistency in eighteenth-century publicists: the posture they adopted in their literary opinions was often quite radically different from that of their practical and political life.

9. Curtin, *Image of Africa,* 49.

10. Perhaps the most balanced appraisal of Cowper's life and work in a humanitarian light is Lodwick Hartley's *William Cowper, Humanitarian* (Chapel Hill: The University of North Carolina Press, 1938).

11. James Montgomery and James Grahame, *Poems of the Abolition of the Slave Trade* (London, 1809), ii.

12. *The Bee* (Feburary 1793): 215-16.

13. *Gentleman's Magazine* 79 (1809): 1149.

14. *Edinburgh Review* 6 (1805): 326-50. The following is a selection of further periodical contributions to antislavery: Robert Burns, "The Slave's Lament" (1792); Samuel Rogers, "The Pleasures of Memory" (1792); Robert Southey, "To the Genius of Africa" (1795), "The Sailor in the Slave Trade" (1798); William Bowles, "The Dying Slave" (1798); Thomas Campbell, "The Pleasures of Hope" (1799); Leigh Hunt, "The Negro Boy" (1802); Amelia Opie, "The Negro Boy's Tale" (1802), "The Lucayan's Song" (1808). After Sypher's book, the single most scholarly attempt to relate abolition literature to the wider history of ideas is undoubtedly Richard Kain's article, "The Problem of Civilization in English Abolition Literature 1772-1808," *Philosophical Quarterly* 15 (1936): 103-25. I am in Professor Kain's debt for some of the major insights and bibliographical resources that went into planning this chapter.

Deidre Coleman (essay date 1994)

SOURCE: "Conspicuous Consumption: White Abolitionism and English Women's Protest Writing in the 1780s," in *ELH,* Vol. 61, No. 2, Summer 1994, pp. 341-62.

[*In the following essay, Coleman examines late eighteenth-century British texts discussing slavery and women's rights, and notes that even liberal-minded white writers sought to preserve what they viewed as the essential boundaries between whites and blacks.*]

In this paper I wish to examine two overlapping areas of middle-class polemic from the 1790s: white abolitionism and English women's protest writing. A certain polarization has crept into recent discussions of abolitionism, with some critics arguing that a relatively benign "cultural racism" in the eighteenth century came to be supplanted by a more aggressive biological racism.[1] Patrick Brantlinger, for instance, characterizes late eighteenth-century abolitionist writing as more "positive" and "open-minded" about Africa and Africans than the racist and evolutionary accounts that were to follow in the wake of Victorian social science; in his view, the Victorians must bear responsibility for inventing the myth of Africa as the Dark Continent.[2] But while abolitionism may have taken its roots in philanthropy and a new-found enthusiasm for the universal rights of man, the many tracts it spawned contradict such a clear-cut distinction between the earlier and later periods. In its luridness and violence, late eighteenth-century anti-slavery rhetoric points directly, for instance, to the systematic colonization of Africa; it is also rich in the sorts of phobias and bogeys more commonly associated with the later nineteenth century, such as miscegenation, cannibalism, and an essentialist stereotyping of sex and race, such as the perception of white woman's sexuality as a form of degenerate black sexuality.

The close association of woman in this earlier period with slavery, luxury, sexual license, and violent cruelty intersects problematically with the second area of oppositional rhetoric I wish to examine: women's protest writing. In seeking to capitalize upon fashionable anti-slavery rhetoric for their own political objectives, women only increased the general murkiness of abolitionist rhetoric, an effect most evident in their employment of the emotive but clichéed analogy between their own disenfranchised lot and the plight of enslaved Africans. While these late eighteenth century women both anticipate and confirm Frederick Douglass's claim, in mid nineteenth-century America, that "the cause of the slave has been peculiarly woman's cause," their writings also reveal clearly why any political link between white women and black people was doomed to be a bitter misalliance.[3] As bell hooks has argued, in an essay on the history of racism and feminism in America, the analogy between white women and blacks is a deeply conservative one, concerned to uphold and maintain the racial hierarchy that grants white women a higher status than black people.[4]

My first text is a lecture Coleridge delivered in Bristol in 1795, advertised in the *Bristol Mercury* as "A Lecture on the Slave Trade, and the duties that result from its continuance."[5] Although the fight for abolition of the trade had not yet been decisively lost, the impetus had slowed markedly from the heyday of protest in the period 1789-1792. That heyday is probably best illustrated by the immense popularity and circulation of Wedgwood's design of the manacled and supplicating slave, doubly captured by chains and by discourse, with the ventriloquized Christian motto floating above his head: "Am I not a man and a brother." Janus-faced, the motto stands curiously open to a positive or negative response, a reflection perhaps of the white racist spectre that often underlies sentimental ideals of equality between white and black: the spectre of too close a blood kinship, the term "brother" reading literally rather than figuratively in a nightmare confusion of the races through interracial sex.[6] Nevertheless, thousands of seals and cameos with this design were sold or given away gratis; women wore it as pins in their hair, men sported the design on rings, on shirt-pins, or coat-buttons.

The waning of enthusiasm in the mid 1790s was principally caused by the reactionary climate of suspicion and fear generated by the Pitt government. By the time Coleridge made his somewhat belated contribution, abolitionism had begun to lose its respectability, and in some quarters, was even associated with jacobinism. In a daring jest at the end of his lecture, Coleridge flirts with that association between anti-slavery and revolutionism by enjoying, rhetorically, the dangers of the pro-slavers' too easy identification of England's labouring poor with the West Indian slaves. Although he does not mention the recent and bloody revolts on Santo Domingo and other West Indian islands, they clearly form the back-drop to his joking:

> I have heard another argument in favor of the Slave Trade, namely, that the Slaves are as well off as the Peasantry in England! Now this argument I have [seen] in publications on the Subject—and were I the attorney General, I should *certainly* have prosecuted the author for sedition & treasonable Writings. For I appeal to common sense whether to affirm that the Slaves are as well off as our Peasantry, be not the same as to assert that our Peasantry are as bad off as Negro Slaves—and whether if the Peasantry believed it there is a man amongst them who [would] not rebel? and be justified in Rebellion? (*LST*, 250-51)

Daring though this was in 1795, if we return to the title of Coleridge's lecture, we note that this is a lecture "on" and not against the trade, a formulation that might reflect some acquiescence in the current status quo—as might his allusion to "the duties" that must follow from the continuance of the planters' rights: namely, the moral duties of boycotting two West Indian commodities, sugar and its by-product rum, the one "useless," the other, "pernicious" (*LST*, 248). But the duties that result from the continuation of the trade are not just the moral ones of abstinence. Duties are also economic, and it is likely that the pun served to remind his audience that the very high price of sugar reflected the import duties that formed such a large part of the Government's revenue. At the height of the boycotting campaign, Thomas Clarkson boasted that the Government's sugar revenue had fallen by £200,000 in the last quarter of the year 1791.[7] There were also the unequal sugar duties that, by providing artificial protection to West Indian sugar, prevented free trade and more competitive pricing. Thus the high cost in moral terms was also a high economic cost to the consumer in the form of taxes, and it is perhaps not too far-fetched to see in Coleridge's pun on "duties" the economic challenge to the old protectionist, plantocratic economy that must always be seen to go hand in hand with the moral and humanitarian grounds for abolition.

Broadly speaking there is a gender to the items Coleridge singles out for boycotting. Sugar and its sweetness tend to be associated with women and that quintessentially feminine pastime, tea-drinking; rum, with men—in particular the British sailors, for whom rum was almost a munition of war.[8] Sugar, the primary substance, interests Coleridge more than rum, partly because of its gender and partly because it was such a mobile signifier. Once the possession of a rich minority, an indicator of status and rank, by the end of the eighteenth century sugar was downwardly mobile, as was tea, the beverage it sweetened (the duties on tea were lifted in 1784). Nevertheless, despite the fall in prestige that accompanied the democratization of its consumption, sugar still retained something of its former status as a luxury item. It was, after all, a tropical import; it was also, as Coleridge argued, useless—a superfluity rather than a food, an additive rather than something sustaining, enjoyed in periods of leisure, such as the work break or, less innocently, enjoyed at the feminine, gossippy, trivial tea-table—diverting "the pains of Vacancy by the pestilent inventions of Luxury" (*LST,* 236). The association of women with brutal colonization and with the leisured consumption of luxury imports is, of course, well established by the end of the eighteenth century.[9] Punning in another 1795 lecture on the connection between Britain's "commercial Intercourse" and death, Coleridge argues that the trade in the East Indies had cost 8 million lives—"in return for which most foul and heart-inslaving Guilt we receive gold, diamonds, silks, muslins & callicoes for fine Ladies and Prostitutes. Tea to make a pernicious Beverage, Porcelain to drink it from, and salt-petre for the making of gunpowder with which we may murder the poor Inhabitants who supply all these things."[10]

It is easy enough to show that Coleridge's imagination was haunted by the horrors of slavery. The diseased bodies that rot the ships' planks during the middle passage—a detail mentioned twice in this lecture—pass into *The Rime of the Ancient Mariner*: "I looked upon the rotting sea, / And drew my eyes away; / I looked upon the rotting deck, / And there the dead men lay."[11] At the same time, however, the contradictions embedded in his oppositional rhetoric give credence to the claim that the ideology of anti-slavery is closely allied to that of colonization and imperialism. Principally I would draw attention to the lecture's uneasy slide between identity and difference, between outraged sympathy and identification with the oppressed slaves, and uneasy notions of African otherness. The desire to naturalize and recuperate the other co-exists with a sharp sense of cultural difference as savagery; at the same time his text remains imprisoned within what Frantz Fanon has described as "manichean delirium," a pathological colonial relation whereby the world is radically divided into paired oppositions—white/black, good/evil, superior/inferior—in which the primary sign is the privileged one. Issues of gender and class raise the temperature of this delirium even higher. In the end, despite the axiom in morality promulgated in his lecture, "That Wickedness may be multiplied but cannot be divided and that the Guilt of all attaches to each one who is knowingly an accomplice,"

Coleridge the Unitarian ultimately deflects the blame for the trade away from himself and onto a variety of others: onto eucharistic worshippers, atheists and deists, novel-reading, tea-drinking ladies and, last but not least, the African victims themselves (*LST,* 247).[12]

As an instance of identification—idealized and nostalgic—take the following sentimental vignette, put forward by Coleridge's lecture in rebuttal of the argument that Africans were better off in the plantations than in their own native country:

> The Africans, who are situated beyond the contagion of European vice—are innocent and happy—the peaceful inhabitants of a fertile soil, they cultivate their fields in common and reap the crop as the common property of all. Each family like the peasants in some parts of Europe, spins weaves, sews, hunts, fishes and makes basket fishing tackle & the implements of agriculture, and this variety of employment gives an acuteness of intellect to the negro which the mechanic whom the division of Labour condemns to one simple operation is precluded from attaining. (*LST,* 240)

The confrontation appears to be between two antagonistic modes of production—that of the self-subsisting, Pantisocratic Africans, unsullied by commerce, and that of the metropolitan, capitalist center. Ironically, the text from which this vignette is taken is Carl Wadstrom's *Essay on Colonization* (1794).[13] A Swedish abolitionist and naturalist who advertised himself as "a zealous friend to the Africans," Wadstrom devotes his hefty tome to elaborating upon his enthusiastic proposition that "the colonization of Africa is not only practicable, but, in a commercial view, highly prudent and adviseable" (*EC,* iii). Wadstrom may fulminate against the barbarities of the slave trade and the uprooting of Africans from their lives of agricultural innocence, but he does so because the horrors of the middle passage seemed so unnecessary; why not transform all of Africa into one happy plantation managed by Europeans for European advantage? It was "surely somewhat preposterous" Wadstrom argued,

> to drag the Africans to the West Indies, there to drudge amidst whips and chains, in cultivating a commodity which, had they been prudently and humanely dealt with, they might have been induced to raise, as an article of commerce, upon their own soil, and that much nearer to the European markets than the nearest of the West Indian islands. (*EC,* 4)

The pastoral idyll excerpted by Coleridge reads very differently when read back into its context, for it actually forms part of Wadstrom's complaint that the Africans, laboring solely for their "natural necessities," currently "do every thing in a solitary, desultory manner." In order to establish a labor pool and rationalize production, all the white colonizer need do is to excite in the Africans "innocent artificial wants" and then organize them so that they labor "in concert" and upon a system. "Refined nations form systems, and rise to generals," he writes; "unpolished tribes dwell on detail, and trifle in particulars." The colonizers must acquaint the Africans "with the dexterity and dispatch arising from the division of labour, and with the numerous advantages of combined exertions systematically conducted" (*EC,* 14-16). With its chapters on exploration, natural history, and native customs, Wadstrom's text exemplifies perfectly that would-be harmless confluence of scientific and commercial interests, which Mary Louise Pratt has designated "anti-conquest": "The strategies of representation whereby European bourgeois subjects seek to secure their innocence in the same moment as they assert European hegemony."[14] Small wonder that the West Indian planters and monopolists, with their exhausted estates, vigorously opposed "free" settlements like Sierra Leone, the West African colony inaugurated by British abolitionists in the mid 1780s. For Wadstrom, however, who was a keen supporter of the Sierra Leone project, competition between the two systems was quite unnecessary; instead, he urged his fellow colonizers to teach the Africans

> to avenge themselves on the blind and sordid men who purchase them, only by becoming more useful to them as free-men, than ever they have been, or can be, as slaves. Thus, on the wreck of tyranny, let us build altars to humanity, and prove to the negroes that the Europeans, become just from sound policy, and generous from a sense of their true interests, are at last disposed to make some atonement for the irreparable mischiefs their perverted system of commerce has occasioned in Africa. (*EC,* 23-24)

From the ashes of the slave trade rises the phoenix of systematic commercial colonization. Ignatius Sancho, an eighteenth century Anglo/African writer whose letters were published in England in 1782, was perfectly correct in saying of his times that "the Grand object of all Christian navigators is money—money—money."[15]

The second instance of identification with the African is Coleridge's Eurocentric conflation of the British slave merchants' two quite different sets of victims—on the one hand, press-ganged British seamen, on the other, enslaved Africans. As in the preceding instance, he draws heavily on someone else's text—this time, Thomas Clarkson's *Essay on the Impolicy of the African Slave Trade* (1788), borrowed the day before from the Bristol Library, together with Wadstrom's *Essay on Colonization.* In using Clarkson's "Impolicy" essay, rather than his earlier *Essay on the Slavery and Commerce of the Human Species* (1786), Coleridge reverses the order of Clarkson's priorities, which had been to present the inhumanity of the trade first, then the more pragmatic considerations of its economic impolicy. There are two points I want to make here. The first is that Clarkson's *Impolicy* essay fits well with Wadstrom, because Clarkson centers his *Impolicy* argument around the belief that it would be far preferable to colonize and commercialize Africa for commodities like sugar and cotton than to export enslaved Africans to the West Indies for the same purpose; to press the point home, Clarkson's gifts of the *Impolicy* essay to Prime Minister Pitt and Louis XVI were accompanied by specimens of African native

produce and manufactures.[16] My second point is that, while it was important to reiterate the charge that Africa was a grave rather than a "nursery" for British seamen (as claimed by the pro-slavers), Coleridge goes so far as to detach the familiar narrative of enslavement from the enslaved, reserving it instead for the enslavers. Because the burden of his concern is for the evil effects of slavery upon his countrymen rather than upon Africans, he narrates (via Clarkson), how the British sailors are captured through a method of false purchasing involving both trickery and force; they suffer savage punishments on the sea journey, the numerical losses are high, and in general, the means by which the trade is carried on is "so destructive and iniquitous as to brand with ignominy every nation that tolerates it" (*LST,* 239).[17] Britain, here projected as a nation self-enslaved, self-branded, self-injured, seems to mirror the Africa of the pro-slavers, a country whose inhabitants were already enslaved before the advent of the European trade. It is even just possible that the entire Western system of "buying, selling and torturing human flesh" is encoded by Coleridge as a primitive art, practised to perfection in Africa and transmitted to the civilized world.

In support of that last point I want now to direct attention to the most conspicuous oppositional strategy of Coleridge's essay, which is to effect a reversal so that England is black not white, savage rather than civilized, superstitious rather than rational. While an Anglo-African contemporary of Coleridge's, the ex-slave Olaudah Equiano, was making this reversal real by describing in his autobiography his terrible fear that the white English sailors, with their "horrible looks, red faces, and long hair," were going to eat him, Coleridge's strategy is a rhetorical one, centering on his extended pun on cannibalism and the eucharistic rites, a conflation supposedly designed to dismantle the ideological basis of European colonialism and racism.[18] To the Christian who calls down blessings on the food he is about to eat, Coleridge scoffs:

> Gracious Heaven! . . . A part of that Food among most of you is sweetened with the Blood of the Murdered . . . O Blasphemy! Did God give Food mingled with Brothers blood! Will the Father of all men bless the Food of Cannibals—the food which is polluted with the blood of his own innocent Children? (*LST,* 248)

This type of lurid rhetoric was common enough in the many dissenting tracts urging readers to give up sugar. In the tenth edition of one such pamphlet, the author William Fox imaged sugar as a "loathsome poison," a host held to the lips but "steeped in the blood of our fellow creatures"; minute calculations were also performed: "In every pound of sugar used . . . we may be considered as consuming two ounces of human flesh."[19] Since one of the problems with slavery was that it tended to be, for most British people, "out of sight, out of mind," abolitionists like Fox and Coleridge purposefully link the two worlds of black and white, the colony and the metropolis, the site of production and the site of consumption. In Coleridge's words, his aim is to convert "the produce into the things producing, the occasioned into the things occasioning" by means of his truth-painting imagination (*LST,* 248). Seeking to destabilize the categories of white and black, the "civilized" and the "primitive," so that, satirically, the European consumer becomes the "true" savage, Coleridge disavows otherness, but the disavowal tips over into violence. Instead of collapsing the opposition between Europe and Africa, the pun on cannibalism and eucharistic rites has the opposite effect of reinforcing the boundaries. The very introduction of the topic of cannibalism—that ultimate boundary marker between self and other—was a sure way of putting his listeners in mind of the chief arguments for justifying slavery—the unspeakable savagery of Africa and the Africans.

The blasphemous eucharistic feast is anticipated by a number of eating metaphors—no doubt intended as food for thought, what Coleridge sarcastically terms at the beginning of his talk, "intellectual aliment" (*LST,* 235). First there is the "seasoning" of the African slave, a two to three year period of acclimatization and "light" labor before the rigors of the cane-fields. Following the seasoning one could apply a range of European culinary practices, such as roasting alive (Coleridge cites one such incident [*LST,* 243]); or there was boiling, a "common punishment" according to the evidence presented by abolitionists before the House of Commons in 1790 and 1791.[20] . . . [In James Gilray's] 1791 abolitionist cartoon, entitled "Barbarities in the West Indias", boiling literalizes the metaphor of sugar-eating Europeans ingesting African flesh and blood. The drowning African melts in the huge cauldron of boiling sugar juice; he or she passes invisibly but materially into the substance of refined white sugar, which then circulates around the tea-tables of the West. In this diabolic inversion of the Eucharist, the black African is a type of crucified Christ, the eating of whose body brings damnation rather than salvation. Blackness is consubstantial with whiteness.

Such a radical internalization of black within white might, however, suggest more than the violence of an inhuman labor system. It could also be argued that the huge sugar cauldron represents the melting pot of miscegenation, the threat of black men with white women, the reality of white men with slave women and the large mulatto populations to which this most common form of sexual exploitation gave rise.[21] While interracial sex was firmly established as a way of life in the West Indies, mulatto populations undermined the logic of slavery by confusing the essential distinction between the races. Hence the West Indian obsession with racial purity, as can be seen in the development of an elaborate system of nomenclature for classifying colored offspring, with the Quinterones indistinguishable, in the end, from whites. There was also a growing fear of large mulatto populations, and the slave rebellions they might precipitate; the bloodshed and anarchy of Santo Domingo, for instance, was widely construed as the result of tension between the colonial *grands blancs* and the free *gens de couleur,* or free coloreds. In the light of these last two points, then, the melting pot of miscege-

nation might also embody the white supremacist's fantasy of assimilation leading to racial extinction, the stain of blackness removed by repeated incest, a process tried and proved in the West Indies and commonly known as "washing a man's self white" through several generations of daughters.[22] To many, though, the hoped-for invisibility of blackness through racial amalgamation offered little comfort; the stain of racial pollution would always be ineradicable, always likely to re-surface, like the return and revenge of the repressed, in the coal-black baby.

Fanon, in analyzing the structure of white negrophobia, argued that "it is in his corporeality that the Negro is attacked . . . the Negro is only biological . . . [he] symbolises the biological."[23] The same might also be said of woman; in fact, recent feminist analyses, such as that of Marianna Torgovnick, establish convincingly the sort of circularity that exists (and has always existed) between concepts such as the "female" and the "primitive."[24] Somewhat ironically, then, from the first settlement of the British West Indies, we see feminist writers opening out their anti-slavery analogies from the seraglios of the east to the sugar plantations of the west, a new direction that only intensifies throughout the eighteenth century, culminating in a lively debate about the links between the oppression of black Africans and women's legal and domestic subordination (especially within marriage, under the common law doctrine of coverture).[25]

It is possible that the scapegoating of the white Lady at the end of Coleridge's lecture represents a reaction to the fillip given to feminism by abolitionist rhetoric. Setting the white woman in opposition rather than alongside her black African counterpart, Coleridge sneers:

> Sensibility indeed we have to spare—what novel-reading Lady does not over flow with it to the great annoyance of her Friends and Family—Her own sorrows like the Princes of Hell in Milton's Pandemonium sit enthroned bulky and vast—while the miseries of our fellow creatures dwindle into pigmy forms, and are crowded, an unnumbered multitude, into some dark corner of the Heart where the eye of sensibility gleams faintly on them at long Intervals—(*LST,* 249)

Of course I say "in opposition" (the white woman is a "savage" to the African), but it will be obvious that Coleridge is also identifying the landscape of Africa and its inhabitants (the "pigmy forms") with the body of this atavistic woman, particularly with the fathomless depths of her heart of darkness—a nice anticipation, this, of Freud's description of adult female sexuality as the "dark continent" of psychology.[26] Voraciously carnal, in her violence and savagery Coleridge's English woman *is* Africa and all Africans. Her heart is the grave of Africa, and her consumption a consummation, a pun on eating and sexuality anticipated by Coleridge in his earlier desire for the "consummation" of abolition, now that "nine millions of Slaves have been consumed by the Europeans" (*LST,* 246). This conflation of femininity and negritude, of sexual license and violent cruelty, anticipates later medical and scientific research on the pathology of the sexualized female. Once we place Coleridge's white woman within a racialized category, we have no trouble recognizing her for what she really is beneath her civilized exterior; the dark corner of her heart is the black hidden within, the primitive whose unbridled sexuality is allied to degeneracy and madness.[27] She is the prototype of Charlotte Bronte's white Creole heiress, Bertha Mason, the suspicion of whose impure race becomes absurdly visible in the "blackened inflation" of her "savage face," her "pigmy intellect" and "giant propensities."[28]

Although Coleridge's editors cite the work of his friend Benjamin Flower, *The French Constitution* (1792), as the source for his novel-reading Lady (*LST*, 248-49n), an equally strong case could be made for the following passage from Mary Wollstonecraft's *Vindication of the Rights of Men* (1790):

> Where is the dignity, the infallibility of sensibility, in the fair ladies, whom, if the voice of rumour is to be credited, the captive negroes curse in all the agony of bodily pain, for the unheard of tortures they invent? It is probable that some of them, after the sight of a flagellation, compose their ruffled spirits and exercise their tender feelings by the perusal of the last imported novel.[29]

The source of the rumor was the evidence currently being heard before the House of Commons, some of which detailed highly sensational stories of the cruelties of planters' wives and daughters. While the purpose of this evidence was designed to show how even "those most disposed to benevolence and compassion" could be corrupted by the iniquity of slavery, Wollstonecraft's purpose in citing this material is twofold and quite specific; she is concerned to overturn Burke's influential gendering of aesthetic categories in *A Philosophical Enquiry into the Origin of our Ideas of the Sublime and Beautiful* (1757), and also to respond to certain hysterical features of his *Reflections on the Revolution in France* (1790).[30] The two aims, in fact, are linked: the attack on the rigidity of Burke's gender distinctions licenses Wollstonecraft to play gleefully upon his deepest fears about how these distinctions might become vulnerable to revolutionary violations. These fears surface most conspicuously in the spectacle he paints of those "furies of hell," the "ferocious" fish-women who forced the royal family back to Paris in October, 1789. Instead of the triumph of a civilized martial nation, the march resembled nothing more than "a procession of American savages."[31] Nor were Burke's fears about women confined to those of the lower orders; even the queen herself, the focus of so much of his sentimental and flowery rhetoric, when once stripped of the "pleasing illusions" and "decent drapery of life," descends to an animal, "And an animal not of the highest order."[32]

While the point of Wollstonecraft's passage is anti-Burke rather than anti-slavery, it nevertheless strengthens the association I mentioned earlier between the brutality of slavery and colonization, and the degenerate, depraved, de-

vouring woman. Another instance of this association can be seen in Mrs Barbauld's verse *Epistle to William Wilberforce*. No doubt mindful, like Wollstonecraft, of the horrific case against women unravelling before Parliament, she writes:

> Lo! where reclined, pale Beauty courts the breeze,
> Diffused on sofas of voluptuous ease;
> With anxious awe her menial train around
> Catch her faint whispers of half-uttered sound;
> See her, in monstrous fellowship, unite
> At once the Scythian and the Sybarite!
> Blending repugnant vices, misallied,
> Which frugal nature purposed to divide;
> See her, with indolence to fierceness joined,
> Of body delicate, infirm of mind,
> With languid tones imperious mandates urge;
> With arm recumbent wield the household scourge;
> And with unruffled mien, and placid sounds,
> Contriving torture, and inflicting wounds.[33]

According to Hannah More, herself the author of a poem addressed to Wilberforce, no passage in Barbauld's epistle pleased the leading parliamentary abolitionist more than this description of the "union of barbarity and voluptuousness in the West Indian woman."[34] Seen in this context, the prominence of the sofa in *Mansfield Park*, upon which the languid and indolent Lady Bertram lolls with her pug, is no accident but a reminder to the reader of the somewhat tainted source of Sir Thomas's wealth, the slave trade that underpins his English "plantations" at Mansfield Park.[35]

If Lady Bertram is a kind of hybrid, an English woman with some features of the West Indian plantation-owner's wife, the English woman proper forms the subject of one of Hannah More's numerous interventions in the slavery debate, a rather grotesque jeu d'esprit entitled *The White Slave Trade. Hints towards framing a Bill for the Abolition of the White Female Slave Trade, in the cities of London and Westminster* (1792). In this prose tract More asks those working for West Indian abolition to consider "the abolition of slavery at *home*—a slavery the more interesting," she argues, in that it may be found to involve "the wives, daughters, nieces, aunts, cousins, mothers, and grandmothers even of these very zealous abolitionists themselves."[36] This slavery is personified by Fashion, a tyrant presented by More as crueller than any West Indian slave-driver. Jokily modeling her feminist case on the two abolitionist grounds of the inhumanity and impolicy of the trade, More's target is the marriage market with its "coming out" season(ing) and sale of sweet fair English flesh.[37] Arguing that the young English woman is a greater sufferer than the African, More likens her obligatory appearance in overcrowded rooms to the cramming of slaves in ship-holds; worse still, the young debutante's enforced absence from the safety of family life is compared to one of the most brutal features of slavery: the forcible separation of African families upon captivity or at auction. Although in jest, More's thoroughgoing application of every aspect of her analogy strikes us as obscene; and of course the joke has its all too serious counterpart in the protest writings of other contemporary women. Mary Ann Radcliffe, for instance, rebuked the abolitionists for callously putting the cause of illiterate slaves before that of their own country-women. In a short pamphlet pleading for greater employment opportunities for middle-class women, Radcliffe appeals to her white male audience in the name of racial solidarity: "What are the untutored, wild imaginations of a slave, when put in the balance with the distressing sensations of a British female, who has received a refined, if not a classical, education, and is capable of the finest feelings the human heart is susceptible of?"[38] The same point is made, albeit with more delicacy, in Jane Austen's *Emma*. While for propriety's sake Jane Fairfax denies making any strict equation between the moral enormity of the slave-trade and "governess-trade," her bitter conjunction of the two ("the sale—not quite of human flesh—but of human intellect") leads her to insinuate that of the two sets of victims, it is the governesses who bear the "greater misery."[39]

Flower's *French Constitution,* which, as I have already mentioned, is cited by Coleridge's editors as the source of his vision of feminine barbarity, brings into collision the two worlds of the white English and the West Indian woman. Mindful of the evidence before the House, and keen to publicize two recently published abolitionist tracts, Flower indulges himself in the rhetoric of feminine sensibility that Wollstonecraft so deplored:

> I wish to recommend these tracts more particularly to the attention of those whose influence and example in society can effect any thing they please—I mean *THE LADIES.* They are formed to feel, more than the men are; and if there ever was a subject which ought in a peculiar manner to call forth their feelings, it must be that of the Slave Trade. When they read the abstract of the evidence repeatedly laid before the public—When they attend to the conduct of some of the West Indian Ladies towards their slaves—With what horror and anguish must they behold a system which divests the sex of their peculiar glory, their amiableness, their sensibility; a system which transforms the loveliest part of God's creation into savages and brutes! Let them, if they can, when reflecting on this subject, continue morning and evening, to sweeten their tea, and the tea of their families and visitors, with the blood of their fellow creatures: but should they continue such a practice, they must not be surprised, if some persons should presume to think, that the pretensions of the present age to exalted sentiments, refined feelings, and exquisite sensibility, are little more than pretensions; and that pure sterling excellence and goodness are not so often found in real life, as in the imagination of the poet and novelist.[40]

Beneath the chivalry—the standard appeal to woman as a creature of superior moral refinement—we see emerging those inexplicable and irrational connections between female sexuality, race, and versions of the primitive. To the extent that Flower's woman drinks blood, "a diet only fit for savages," she is, like Bertha Mason, both cannibal and vampire.[41] She needs the abolitionist tracts more than her male counterpart because ultimately she is the real savage. She becomes what she eats, one of those "savages and brutes," then dangerously serves up to others the food she has polluted, disguised as sweetness. When reading the tales of the inhuman cruelty of the planters' wives and daughters, the English woman is advised to look into the mirror of her own barbarity.

Every passage alluding to the evidence before the House of Commons effaces what a reading of that evidence makes quite clear. White woman's cruelty was not random and indiscriminate; for the most part it was aimed at women slaves, for sexual reasons, such as "*being found pregnant,*" or "*for jealousy.*"[42] John Stedman, a British mercenary to the West Indies, noting in 1790 the white men's preference for African rather than creole women, remarked that it was small wonder "the poor ill treated Ladies should be Jealous of their Spouses and so bitterly take revenge on the cause of their disgrace—the negro and Mulatto Girls whom they persecute with the greatest bitterness and most barbarous tyranny."[43] So what the English woman sees when she reads these tales of female ferocity is no general spectacle of depravity but the terrible image of the workings of patriarchal right, in particular as this is manifested in the holding of property in women, what Robert Wedderburn denounced as "this dreadful species of female *property.*"[44] The slave-master husband who has right of sexual access to his wife also has right of sexual access to his slaves; thus it comes about that oppressed white women victimize their even more oppressed women slaves.

The sexual and racial oppression that we see in the evidence before the House of Commons—white master with black woman slave—is not, however, as close to the surface of Flower's passage as that most taboo form of interracial sex: white woman with black man. In drinking the African's blood, the white English woman not only becomes black in a moral sense; the mingling of black and white blood is clearly a metaphor for sexual intercourse. Here the violence of slavery as a labor system merges with the gothic horror of slavery as a sexual system. Under slavery, the torture and murder of blacks stains with sin the blood of the national community, but with emancipation the purity and integrity of English blood seems suddenly at risk of sexual pollution. As soon as public opinion appeared to be turning against the trade from the 1770s onwards, pro-slavery writers moved quickly to play upon the spectre of a Britain overrun with freed black men. To an absurd degree, the fears associated with mulatto populations in the West Indies began, in some quarters, to be matched by fears about the impact of abolition on race relations in Britain. Edward Long, planter, polemicist, and chief caricaturist of black sexuality, provides us with the best known statement of its kind. In his *Candid Reflections* (1772) we read:

> The lower class of women in England are remarkably fond of the blacks; for reasons too brutal to mention they would connect themselves with horses and asses if the laws permitted them. By these ladies they [the blacks] generally have a numerous brood. Thus, in the course of a few generations more, the English blood will become . . . contaminated with this mixture . . .

this alloy may spread so extensively as even to reach the middle, and then the higher orders of the people, till the whole nation resembles the *Portuguese* and *Moriscos* in complexion of skin and baseness of mind. This is a venomous and dangerous ulcer, that threatens to disperse its malignancy far and wide, until every family catches infection from it.[45]

Thirteen years later James Tobin, plantation owner and father of one of Wordsworth and Coleridge's close Bristol friends, echoed Long's dire predictions, warning that "great numbers of negroes at present in England, the strange partiality shewn for them by the lower orders of women, and the rapid increase of a dark and contaminated breed, are evils which have long been complained of and call every day more loudly for enquiry and redress." Once again we see the convergence of woman and blackness, the mythical sexual promiscuity of black man finding a fitting mate in the lower ranks of the so-called higher species, with the result that "in almost every village are to be seen a little race of mulattoes, mischievous as monkeys and infinitely more dangerous."[46] So thin was the line between the black African and the degraded white female that, in the same year Flower published his *French Constitution,* Clara Reeve was arguing that, with abolition, the Africans "will flock hither from all parts, mix with the *natives,* and spoil the breed of the common people," producing "a vile mongrel race of people, such as no friend to Britain can ever wish to inhabit it."[47]

Whereas slavery formalized relations between blacks and whites, emancipation would clearly have the opposite effect, making the question of maintaining the rigid boundaries of race all the more urgent and important. The spectre of an England overrun with blacks and mulattoes, the slow but sure extinction of the white race: these fears were not held exclusively by planters and other pro-slavers. Abolitionists were also alarmed by the growing black population, especially when the end of the American War of Independence brought many ex-slaves to London, swelling the numbers of black poor already living in ghettoes. The disastrous Sierra Leone scheme, drawn up by leading abolitionists like Granville Sharp and Clarkson in the mid to late 1780s, was clearly designed to rid London of its surplus blacks. Although masquerading as a relief effort, the scheme was nothing more than enforced transportation; and there seems no doubt that fear of interracial sex was one of the prime motives. Jonas Hanway, philanthropist, abolitionist, and chief mover of the new settlement, was known for his intense dislike of "unnatural connections between black persons and white; the disagreeable consequences of which make their appearance but too frequently in our streets."[48] At exactly the same time in America, in 1787, Thomas Jefferson was arguing the necessity of both emancipation and removal; once freed, the black "is to be removed beyond the reach of mixture." To those who argued for assimilation, he listed the following objections: "Deep rooted prejudices entertained by the whites; ten thousand recollections, by the blacks, of the injuries they have sustained; new provocations; the real distinctions which nature has made."[49] And first in order of

importance amongst those "real distinctions" is color: the physical inferiority of the negro, and his inevitable desire to join himself to the "superior beauty" of white woman. For Jefferson such a preference was as predictable as "the preference of the Oran-ootan for the black women over those of his own species." Equality for the black male, in so far as that meant equal access with white men to white women, led Jefferson to fear social anarchy, even "the extermination of the one or the other race."[50]

Ten years after his lecture on the slave trade, Coleridge noted in his diary a curious fact related to him by a traveler from the West Indies: that when it came to whipping, "the Negroes often console themselves in their cruel punishments, that their wounds will become *white.*" In spite of their abhorrence of the cruelty of white men, they look on this whitening "as a grand Progression in their rank of Nature." The longing to be free is perceived as a longing to transgress the boundary of color, a transcending of self through disfigurement, pain and abjection. Coleridge's note continues:

> Their Love of *white,* their belief that superior Beings are white, even in the inmost parts of Africa where they have seen no White men/ it is a color beloved by their good Deities & by the Supreme of all, the Immense, to whom they do not pray, but whose existence they confess. This among so many others in favor of permanent Principles of Beauty as distinguishable from Association or the Agreeable/[51]

The conviction of an ordered ranking and hierarchy in nature is similar to that held by Jefferson, as is the application of neoclassical notions of beauty to underpin the racist fantasy of an inevitable gravitation of black towards white, black longing to enter and be merged with white. The belief in a common humanity, the sentimental identification of the African as brother: these recuperative features of abolitionism always coexist with a panicky and contradictory need to preserve essential boundaries and distinctions. Thus it comes about that the miscegenation that makes a mockery of the "real distinctions" underpinning slavery assumes grotesque proportions within the context of emancipation. At the level of white fantasy, abolition would appear to usher in a shocking reversal— one that involves freed black men with white women rather than white masters with black slaves. Accepting the black man as an equal and as a brother, as the Wedgwood seal invites us to do, is essential for ending the violent bloodletting of slavery; the fear remains, however, of the perilous intimacies abolition will bring, the fear of a blood disseminated.

Notes

1. Catherine Hall, in a recently published collection of her essays, asks: "How did the respectable middle-class orthodoxy of emancipation, the conviction that blacks were men and brothers, women and sisters, become the new racism of the late 1860s, confident in its assumption that blacks were a different species, born to be mastered?"

White, Male and Middle-Class: Explorations in Feminism and History (Cambridge: Polity Press, 1992), 26.

2. Patrick Brantlinger, "Victorians and Africans: The Genealogy of the Myth of the Dark Continent," *"Race," Writing and Difference,* ed. Henry Louis Gates, Jr. (Chicago: Univ. of Chicago Press, 1986), 189, 185, 217.

3. Catharine Stimpson, "'Thy Neighbor's Wife, Thy Neighbor's Servants': Women's Liberation and Black Civil Rights," *Woman in Sexist Society: Studies in Power and Powerlessness,* ed. V. Gornick and B. Moran (New York: Basic Books, 1971), 455.

4. bell hooks, "Racism and Feminism," *Ain't I A Woman: Black Women and Feminism* (Boston: South End Press, 1981), 144.

5. Samuel Taylor Coleridge, "Lecture on the Slave Trade," in *Lectures 1795: On Politics and Religion,* ed. L. Patton and P. Mann (Princeton: Routledge and Princeton Univ. Press, 1971), 235-51. Hereafter, cited parenthetically in the text and abbreviated *LST.*

6. Playing upon the literal interpretation of the abolitionists' slogan, Robert Wedderburn, the mulatto preacher and insurrectionist, publicly taunted his white half-brother with the words "BROTHER OR NO BROTHER—'THAT IS THE QUESTION?'"; see *The Horrors of Slavery and other Writings by Robert Wedderburn,* ed. Iain McCalman (Edinburgh: Edinburgh Univ. Press, 1991), 51, 55.

7. See the *Correspondence of Josiah Wedgwood 1781-1794* (London: The Women's Printing Society, 1906), 186.

8. For the importance of rum as a West Indian commodity, see Richard Pares's story of the Pinneys of Bristol, *A West-India Fortune* (London: Longmans, Green & Co, 1950), 193.

9. Two recent articles dealing with this subject are Laura Mandell, "Bawds and Merchants: Engendering Capitalist Desires," *ELH* 59 (1992): 107-23, and Laura Brown, "Reading Race and Gender: Jonathan Swift," *Eighteenth-Century Studies* 23 (1990): 425-43.

10. Samuel Taylor Coleridge, "Lectures on Revealed Religion," in *Lectures 1795: On Politics and Religion* (note 5), 226.

11. Samuel Taylor Coleridge, *The Rime of the Ancient Mariner,* in *Samuel Taylor Coleridge,* ed. H. J. Jackson (Oxford: Oxford Univ. Press, 1985), 54.

12. The same claim of shared guilt is made in the much reprinted tract of William Fox, *An Address to the People of Great Britain, on the Propriety of Abstaining from West India Sugar and Rum,* 10th ed. with additions (1792; Philadelphia: Daniel Lawrence, 1792), 8-9.

13. C. B. Wadstrom, *An Essay on Colonization, particularly applied to the Western Coast of Africa,* with some free thoughts on Cultivation and Commerce; also Brief Descriptions of the colonies already formed, or attempted, in Africa, including those of Sierra Leona and Bulama (London: Darton and Harvey, 1794). Hereafter, cited parenthetically in the text and abbreviated *EC.*

14. Mary Louise Pratt, *Imperial Eyes: Travel Writing and Transculturation* (New York: Routledge, 1992), 7.

15. Quoted from Keith A. Sandiford, *Measuring the Moment: Strategies of Protest in Eighteenth-Century Afro-English Writing* (Selinsgrove, PA: Susquehanna Univ. Press; 1988), 90.

16. See E. L. Griggs, *Thomas Clarkson: The Friend of Slaves* (1936; reprint, Westport, CT: Negro Universities Press, 1970), 45, 53.

17. For an influential, much quoted account of the brutal treatment of English sailors, see Alexander Falconbridge, late surgeon in the African Trade, *An Account of the Slave Trade on the Coast of Africa* (London: J. Phillips, 1788).

18. See *The Life of Olaudah Equiano, or Gustavus Vassa The African. Written by Himself* (1789; reprint, New York: Negro Universities Press, 1969), 44. White man's cannibalism seems to have been a common fear; Robert Wedderburn's poem, "The Africans Complaint on board a Slave Ship," contains the following lines: "Here de white man beat de black man, / 'Till he's sick and cannot stand, / Sure de black be eat by white man, / Will not go to white man's land" ([note 6], 95).

19. Fox (note 12), 4, 5.

20. See *An Abstract of the Evidence delivered before a Select Committee of the House of Commons in the years 1790, and 1791; on the part of the Petitioners for the Abolition of the Slave-Trade* (London: James Phillips, 1791), 72.

21. The recently edited diaries of the Jamaican slaveholder Thomas Thistlewood give a chillingly graphic account of such exploitation; see *In Miserable Slavery. Thomas Thistlewood in Jamaica, 1750-86,* ed. D. Hall (London: Macmillan, 1989).

22. For an instance of this, see the anonymous novel *Adventures of Jonathan Corncob, Loyal American Refugee. Written by himself* (1787; reprint, Boston: Godine Publishers, 1976), 73.

23. Frantz Fanon, *Black Skin: White Masks,* trans. C. L. Markmann (1952; London: Pluto Press, 1986), 163-67.

24. Marianna Torgovnick, *Gone Primitive: Savage Intellects, Modern Lives* (Chicago: Chicago Univ. Press, 1990).

25. See Vivien Jones, ed., *Women in the Eighteenth Century: Constructions of Femininity* (New York: Routledge, 1990), 154, 210.

26. This notorious reference is to be found in his 1926 essay, "The Question of Lay Analysis," *The Essentials of Psycho-Analysis,* ed. Anna Freud, trans. J. Strachey (London: Hogarth Press, 1986), 32.

27. See Sander L. Gilman's essay, "The Hottentot and the Prostitute: Toward an Iconography of Female Sexuality," in *Difference and Pathology: Stereotypes of Sexuality, Race, and Madness* (Ithaca: Cornell Univ. Press, 1985), 76-108.

28. Charlotte Bronte, *Jane Eyre* (1847; rpt., Oxford: Oxford Univ. Press, 1980), 286, 310.

29. *The Works of Mary Wollstonecraft,* ed. J. Todd and M. Butler, 7 vols. (London: William Pickering, 1989), 5:45.

30. The evidence heard before the House is found in *An Abstract* (note 20), 73n.

31. Edmund Burke, *Reflections on the Revolution in France* (1790; reprint, Harmondsworth: Penguin, 1969), 165, 159.

32. Burke (note 31), 171.

33. *The Works of Anna Laetitia Barbauld. With a Memoir by Lucy Aikin,* 2 vols. (London: Longman, 1825), 1:176-77.

34. See Betsy Rodgers, *Georgian Chronicle: Mrs Barbauld and her Family* (London: Methuen, 1958), 112.

35. Jane Austen, *Mansfield Park,* in *The Novels of Jane Austen,* ed. R. W. Chapman, 5 vols. (Oxford: Oxford Univ. Press, 1923), 3:190, 432. For a reading of Fanny as a slave sent to her uncle's English "plantations" see Yasmine Gooneratne's article in *Sensibilities: The Jane Austen Society of Australia* (Sydney: The Jane Austen Society, 1992), 2-16; also, Claudia L. Johnson, *Jane Austen: Women, Politics and the Novel* (Chicago: Univ. of Chicago Press, 1988), 106-7.

36. *The Works of Hannah More,* 11 vols. (London: T. Cadell, 1830), 3:385.

37. Similarly, in *Mansfield Park* (note 35), Austen's reference to the "trade of *coming out*" for young women is yet another of that novel's many slavery allusions (3:267).

38. Mary Ann Radcliffe, *The Female Advocate Or an Attempt to Recover the Rights of Women from Male Usurpation* (1792) (1799; reprint, New York: Garland Publishing, 1974), 469.

39. Jane Austen, *Emma,* in *The Novels of Jane Austen* (note 35), 4:300-301. For another uneasy conjunction of feminism and anti-abolitionism, see Anna Maria Falconbridge's *Narrative of Two Voyages to the River Sierra Leone* (1802; reprint, London: Frank Cass, 1967) and Pratt's (note 14) discussion of Falconbridge (102-7).

40. Benjamin Flower, *The French Constitution,* 2nd ed. (London: G. G. J. & J. Robinson, 1792), 452-53.

41. See Catharine Macaulay, *Letters on Education, with Observations on Religious and Metaphysical Subjects* (1790; reprint, New York: Garland Publishing, 1974), 39.

42. *An Abstract* (note 20), 76.

43. John Gabriel Stedman, *Narrative of a Five Years Expedition against the Revolted Negroes of Surinam,* ed. R. and S. Price (1790; reprint, Baltimore: Johns Hopkins Univ. Press, 1988), 49.

44. See Wedderburn (note 6), 55.

45. Quoted from Peter Fryer, *Staying Power: The History of Black People in Britain* (London: Pluto Press, 1984), 157-58.

46. Quoted from Fryer (note 45), 161-62. Olaudah Equiano wrote a brilliant letter in reply to Tobin, published in *The Public Advertiser,* 28 January 1788. Dismissing "the mixture of colour" as of "no consequence," he goes on to attribute to this warped prohibition on interracial marriage the hideous oppression of black women by white planters; the letter has been reprinted in *Black Writers in Britain, 1760-1890,* ed. P. Edwards and D. Dabydeen (Edinburgh: Edinburgh Univ. Press, 1991), 74-77.

47. Clara Reeve, *Plans of Education, with Remarks on the Systems of Other Writers. In a Series of Letters between Mrs. Darnford and her Friends* (1792; reprint, New York: Garland Publishing, 1974), 90-91; emphasis added.

48. Quoted from Fryer (note 45), 196.

49. Thomas Jefferson, *Notes on the State of Virginia,* ed. W. Peden (1787; reprint, New York: W. W. Norton & Co., 1982), 143, 138.

50. Jefferson (note 49), 138.

51. *The Notebooks of Samuel Taylor Coleridge,* 4 vols., ed K. Coburn (London: Routledge, 1957-), 2:2604.

Ann Fogarty (essay date 1994)

SOURCE: "Looks That Kill: Violence and Representation in Aphra Behn's *Oroonoko*," in *The Discourse of Slavery: Aphra Behn to Toni Morrison,* edited by Carl Plasa and Betty J. Ring, Routledge, 1994, pp. 1-17.

[*In the following essay, Fogarty offers a new reading of Aphra Behn's 1688 novel* Oroonoko, *arguing that the novel does not reveal parallelisms bewteen slavery and the subjugation of women as has generally been held, but rather emphasizes that a harmonious co-existence between the black slave and his white female friend is an impossibility.*]

Aphra Behn's novella with its violent account of the execution of an African slave who was once a king was published—significantly—in 1688, the year that saw the bloodless deposition of King James II in England.[1] The social unrest that led to the dismemberment of the slave-king in Behn's fiction is matched by a similar discord in late-seventeenth-century England that issued in the ousting of the final Stuart king from his throne. Reality and fiction seem to mimic each other yet, as this chapter will show, the symmetries that *Oroonoko* suggests are ultimately spurious ones. In this reading of the intricacies of *Oroonoko,* I shall argue that Behn utilizes the ambiguity and eccentric vision of the woman writer in order to indicate that a confluence of perspectives between the black slave Oroonoko and his sympathetic white female friend is an impossibility. The partisan and divisive nature of political and ethnic identity, as of sexual desire, ultimately prevents the harmonious and non-exploitative co-existence of different races. This reading of *Oroonoko* consequently runs counter to many recent interpretations that celebrate it as an unproblematic and pioneering document in the history of anti-slavery literature. In particular, it contests the finding frequently proposed as a key to Behn's liberalism—namely the belief that slavery functions in *Oroonoko* as a means of tracing a parallelism between the subjugation of other races and the oppression of women. This view holds that Behn's narrator identifies with the fate of a black slave because she sees his powerlessness as homologous with her own.

Such a reading of *Oroonoko* ignores patent tensions and contradictions in the text: Behn's novella is built around a series of disjunctions and displacements as well as a set of identifications. The narrator is torn between her fascination with other cultures and an unremitting ethnocentrism. In addition, she is divided between her admiration for the central male protagonist and a regard for female virtue and courage as represented by Imoinda. Such, moreover, is the ambivalence and complexity of Behn's political allegory that all the central figures in her drama of colonial unrest may be seen in diametrically opposed ways. Oroonoko, the oxymoron embedded in the subtitle reminds us, is a "Royal Slave"; he is simultaneously at the bottom of the social scale and at its pinnacle. Conforming to two shifting and conflicting registers of meaning, Oroonoko is both a renegade and a falsely deposed sovereign. Paradoxically, he acts as an allegory both of royal power and of social anarchy. Similarly, Imoinda, Oroonoko's wife, plays a double part in Behn's multilayered allegory. She is at once an image of female oppression and a sign of otherness, simultaneously representing—like Oroonoko himself—moral order and savagery. While she has a civilizing effect on the world around her, she is also the cause of a family feud in Coramantien and the instigator of the slave-revolt in Surinam.

In analysing the pivotal function of these contradictions in Behn's text, I shall make the case that *Oroonoko* is ultimately fractured by the twofold political causes that Behn espouses. Her lifelong support of royalism is at odds with her passionate defence of the rights of women. The conflicting allegories and shifting viewpoints of her novella and its repeated questioning of the boundaries between reality and fiction map out the dissonances and discontinui-ties in Behn's attempt to write an account of history from the perspective of those who remain outside it. The permanent dilemma for the author is that she discovers not only that there is a lack of congruence between the needs and desires of women and slaves as marginalized subjects in the colonial world of Surinam, but that these two groups are also often dismayingly at odds. Far from making common cause, women and slaves seem forced into positions of conflict.

The reception of *Oroonoko* has been a peculiarly troubled one. Indeed, the heated debate that this text generated throughout the twentieth century has until recently ignored Behn's representations of ethnic otherness and concentrated instead on questioning the authenticity of the female author. Tellingly, the issue of gender was allowed to displace that of race in analyses of the text. The problem of misrecognition which is such a prominent theme of Behn's novella (whereby the viewpoint of one particular social group occludes that of another) seems to be amply illustrated by the critical misreadings that the text has spawned. By tracing the interpretative battles which *Oroonoko* has instigated, I want both to give an account of the multifarious critical responses to this work and to pinpoint their elisions and shortcomings. However, in the crosscomparison of the many analyses of Behn's narrative, the objective is not to formulate a reading that will act as a corrective to previous interpretations; rather, I shall suggest that this tale of romance and injustice brings its audience face to face with the problem of representativity. *Oroonoko* is predicated on a crisis in authority. Those interpretations that attempt to stabilize the text by defining it as the mouthpiece of one particular ideology—be it colonialism, royalism, or some embryonic version of feminism or abolitionism—cancel out the hesitancies and contradictions that are integral to its workings.

In her dedicatory epistle and introduction to the tale itself, Behn is insistent that the story she is about to relate is not a fictive invention but rather a truthful and accurate reconstruction of historical events. Those aspects of the narrative that strike us as "new and strange" are a measure not of the writer's fertile imagination but of the distance that separates us from the exotic world she is depicting.[2] In this manner, Behn attempts to defuse the otherness of *Oroonoko* by insisting on its factuality. The most vociferous of Behn's detractors refuse, however, to recognize the subtlety of her framing devices which have the function of protecting both author and text. Instead, they query the authenticity of her descriptions and sometimes even go so far as to call her very existence into question.[3] Ernest Bernbaum discovers many inconsistencies in Behn's biography which he feels prove that she never visited Surinam at all. In addition, he accuses her of plagiarism and comes to the damning conclusion that in writing *Oroonoko* she "deliberately and circumstantially lied."[4] For him the likelihood that Behn used George Warren's *Impartial Description of Surinam* (1667) as a source for many of her vivid renderings of Surinam entirely invalidates her work. His debunking of the novella bears out Behn's own fears that a text written by a woman and centring on the plight of a slave will never be given credence by the world. The circularity of his reasoning is further indicative of the plight of the female writer. Bernbaum dismisses *Oroonoko* because it does not correspond with his version of Behn's biography. By questioning the facts of her existence he simultaneously casts doubt on the facts of the story she produced. Both her life and her work are shown to be equally fictive and hence equally dubious. His reading is, effectively, a double erasure: by denying that Behn could have had experience of other cultures, he not only discredits her but also obscures the colonial history that she commemorates.

Bernbaum's ill-founded and cantankerous attack on *Oroonoko* has long been refuted. In particular, Behn's biographers have succeeded in dispelling many of the doubts about the nature and the extent of her travels.[5] It has now been established that, no matter how clouded the evidence, she did indeed spend a short period in Surinam and that moreover her portrayal of this country and of Oroonoko's African homeland is precise and informed rather than fanciful.[6] Other critics, including most prominently B.G. MacCarthy, demonstrate that Bernbaum's concept of realism is so narrowly defined that he inevitably fails to appreciate the complexity of Behn's mode of romantic verisimilitude.[7] However, all the many attempts to rehabilitate this text still insist, problematically, on invoking criteria of truth and accuracy as a means of legitimating Behn's work. Where once her biography and her gender were utilized as weapons to invalidate her writing, it now frequently appears to be the case that her life-story and perspective as a woman are the very things that act as a warranty for the history she records. Critics rising to Behn's defence set out to prove either the realism of her writing or the purity and coherence of her vision.

Early feminist accounts of her work have been especially guilty of such simplifications. Behn is championed, for example, by both Virginia Woolf and Vita Sackville-West as the first professional woman writer. For them, Behn's texts have an automatic resonance because they represent for the first time in English literature a female perspective on the world. Woolf famously declared that "all women together ought to let flowers fall upon the tomb of Aphra Behn," while Sackville-West pronounced with equal insouciance that Behn's having written at all is "much more important than the quality of what she wrote."[8] Much later appraisals of Behn continue to echo this euphoric celebration of her work as establishing a representative female voice in English literature. Dale Spender awards her a prominent ranking in her list of the forgotten mothers of the English novel. Behn's writing deserves special praise because it measures men by women's standards.[9] Spender assumes that the particular merit of these standards lies in their seemingly pre-given moral superiority, finding in Behn not just a singularly female point of view but an ability to sympathize with the political oppression of others. In Spender's reading of *Oroonoko,* therefore, the expansiveness and openness of the woman writer explain Behn's exaltation of the black hero. For all his flaws and

contradictions, not least among these being the fact that he too trades in slaves, Oroonoko is shown to possess a nobility lacking in his white counterparts. Elaine Campbell makes a similar case in defence of *Oroonoko.* For her the vigour and breadth of Behn's imagination is of a piece with her ability to empathize with the problems of people outside her own culture. Behn's work, she declares, is fuelled by a "transcendental quality of compassion."[10]

More recent readings of Behn have attempted to question the all-too-ready assumption that speaking as a marginalized white woman is equivalent to or compatible with speaking for a black African slave. Vron Ware points out, for instance, that an anti-slavery politics should not be equated with a challenging of ideologies of racial domination.[11] Laura Brown and Moira Ferguson are more far-reaching still in their contestations of the view that Behn's assertion of women's right to write and express themselves freely naturally feeds into a desire for the emancipation of slaves. For Brown, the very instability of the narrator in *Oroonoko* ensures that she act as a vehicle for colonial ideology. Notwithstanding her sympathetic insights into the life both of African slaves and of Surinamese Indians, the narrator nevertheless cements the exploitative connections between the colonizing English and native cultures by acting as a mediator between them.[12] Moreover, Brown feels that Behn celebrates her hero more on the grounds of his royal status than on those of his enslavement. Oroonoko is a tragic figure because he is a dispossessed king—not because he is a man denied his freedom. Ferguson, in a similarly trenchant revisionist reading of *Oroonoko,* contends that Behn sets out to attack not the institution of slavery but the inequities and inefficiencies in the running of the colony of Surinam.[13] While she notes the many equivocations in the text, she is nevertheless of the opinion that to see it as an argument in favour of the abolition of slavery is a misreading. Heidi Hutner similarly redresses the anachronistic accounts of Behn's liberal politics that have influenced interpretations of *Oroonoko* until recently.[14] She maintains that Behn indicts not slavery as the source of human oppression but the violence and savagery of colonial expansionism.

From being a paradigmatic text in the history of women's literature and politics and a representative early female voice in the battle against social oppression, *Oroonoko* has become symptomatic of the blind spots and omissions in feminism itself. It is now, it transpires, a prescient narrative because it mirrors the failure of western feminism adequately to address the problem of racism and to recognize the way in which white women themselves play the role of oppressor with regard especially to their black counterparts.[15] Indeed, Ros Ballaster points out, in her persuasive analysis of the politics underlying feminist interpretations of *Oroonoko,* that, perhaps in keeping with Behn's own disengagement with this figure, critics have tended to disregard the role of the black female slave in the text.[16] It is Imoinda and not Oroonoko who acts finally as a figure of alterity in Behn's story of slave-rebellion. Where Oroonoko is Europeanized and depicted as alluring and eloquent, she remains alien, remote and largely silent. Doubly oppressed, Imoinda is an emblem of both sexual and racial otherness. Her physical presence, at once commemorated and yet held at a distance by the narrator, is symbolic of the material existence of the "other woman" who, as Gayatri Spivak argues, western feminism is so much at pains to disavow.[17]

The original feminist reception of *Oroonoko* is now surprisingly reversed. Where once this text was emblematic of the optimism and utopianism of feminist politics, it currently is seen by many critics as a register of the shortcomings and mistaken goals of the fight for women's liberation. Uncomfortably, too, the rereading of the historical contexts of Behn's writing and the concomitant insistence on the political embeddedness of her work seem to indicate that the woman writer is more entrenched in the ideologies of her day than are even her male contemporaries.[18] Her marginalization appears to restrict her vision rather than to allow her a more unblinkered view of the world. The myth of Behn the revolutionary champion of women and slaves has now been scotched by the sobering discovery of her royalist sympathies and seemingly ineradicable racist attitudes. Indeed, it appears to be the case that studies of Behn have come full circle. The earlier sexist denunciations of her deficiencies as a woman writer have now given way to feminist pronouncements on the limitations of *Oroonoko* as a narrative purportedly written in defence of an African slave. The one-time complaint that Behn's writing is false and inauthentic has been replaced by the finding that it is biased and contradictory.

This re-adjusted account of Behn's text runs the risk, I would suggest, of furthering an overly narrow view of her novella and its import. By simply swapping Behn the feminist for Behn the racist we fail to do justice to the complexity of her work. Moreover, in accepting historicist readings of her text that see it as irrevocably rooted in the political beliefs of her day, we fall into the trap of assuming that ideologies are monolithic and pre-empt all critique. In the interpretation of *Oroonoko* that occupies the latter half of this chapter, I want to analyse the tensions and anxieties around which it is built. Moreover, I shall argue that the excessive violence that forces itself upon our attention at the end of the text in the two scenes describing the punishment and killing of Oroonoko is an indication of those racial and sexual conflicts that the writer cannot succeed in resolving. It will be demonstrated that Behn's narrative centres on the problems of authority and representativity.[19] Her text is woven around the rival voices of the woman writer and the slave-king. The story of a dispossessed African king sanctions her presumption in daring to write in the first place. Also, in telling us about the fate of Oroonoko she is afforded the opportunity of depicting her own life, albeit indirectly and allusively. The need to relate the story of the wronged king cancels the impropriety involved in assuming a command of language as a woman. However, at the same time Behn is aware of the danger of her position. In the most frequently cited passage in the text she points to the incongruity of her celebration of Oroonoko:

I ought to tell you, that the Christians never buy any slaves but they give 'em some name of their own, their native ones being likely very barbarous, and hard to pronounce; so that Mr. Trefry gave Oroonoko that of Caesar; which name will live in that country as long as that (scarce more) glorious one of the great Roman: for 'tis most evident he wanted no part of the personal courage of that Caesar, and acted things as memorable, had they been done in some part of the world replenished with people and historians that might have given him his due. But his misfortune was, to fall in an obscure world, that afforded only a female pen to celebrate his fame.

(63-4)

The chronicle of the life of Oroonoko is an equivocal one. Aiming to be a story of heroism, it turns into a register of loss. Oroonoko, the narrator indicates, is demeaned by the fact that his biographer is female. The oddity of her perspective as a woman means that she is incapable of relating the epic tale of courageous exploit required by her central subject as a fitting tribute. However, at the same time, the narrator suggests it is not just incapacity that prevents the woman writer from producing a record consonant with the male view of history as a chain of heroic deeds. Instead, the account of Oroonoko is one of power-conflicts between men and women and slaves and slave-owners. The heroicizing testimonial to Oroonoko that the putative male historian might have produced would have glossed over and suppressed such conflicts. By contrast, the decentred vision of a woman facilitates the narration of a double story. In her version, Oroonoko has both his native African name and his European title. Unlike the male pen, the female does not deny otherness or shirk the reality of the racial, sexual and colonial conflicts which link the English community with that of the black slave. Yet Behn does not suggest that a feminization of history allows us a more balanced and inclusive account of events. Indeed, the problem for the narrator is that by assuming the role of historian she must also admit to her collusion with male coercive force. The text does violence to Oroonoko because it obliterates rather than celebrates him, making the narrator also part of the process whereby the African prince is transformed into the mutilated body of a European slave. Moreover, in presuming to write at all it seems as if the female pen produces rather than questions the horror of this atrocity. Her very powerlessness makes her personal responsibility for his death all the more shocking. The averted gaze of the narrator who is absent, she informs us, from the scene of Oroonoko's execution, nevertheless partakes in this spectacle of violence.

Julia Kristeva has made the point that the presence of the foreigner in our society turns the pronoun "we" into an impossibility.[20] *Oroonoko,* I would argue, registers this dilemma. The narrator is torn between giving an account in the first-person singular of her experiences abroad—thus emphasizing the private intensity of her connection with Oroonoko—and producing a narrative in the first-person plural that stresses membership of the community of white female colonists in Surinam. On the one hand, her relationship with Oroonoko is personal and sympathetic, while on the other her admiring but distancing view of him is part of the collective response of a colonizing society to those it views as foreign. The initial passages of the story map out a conflict between a use of "I" and "we" in describing the fate and personality of the hero. The narrator depicts herself as having an independent point of view: "I was my self an eye-witness to a great part of what you will find here set down." Yet she also indicates that such freedom of vision is compromised and mediated by the English view of racial others. She confides to us that "we who were perfectly charm'd with the character of this great man, were curious to gather every circumstance of his life" (27). Where her statement made in first-person singular suggests a positive interaction with her African friend, the declaration made in first-person plural reminds us of her complicity with the violently dismembering vision which turns the ethnic other into a curiosity and a dreadful spectacle.

Oroonoko may indeed be interpreted as the tragic story of the "looking relations" that structure the interaction between different cultures.[21] Initially, Behn tries to construct a picture of the mutual and noncompeting gazes that symbolize the harmonious co-existence of the various communities living in Surinam and inhabiting the imaginative space of the narrative. In describing the customs of the Surinamese Indians and the life led by Oroonoko prior to his enslavement, Behn fleetingly manages to envisage societies where looking has nothing to do with violence and domination. In addition, by presenting us with positive accounts of these other ways of seeing, she attempts to dissociate herself from the destructive and appropriative gaze that the colonizer brings to bear on other societies.[22] She describes the natural innocence of South American Indians who live in a blameless sphere of purity, where nakedness is not a reminder of dangerous desires:

> And though they are all thus naked, if one lives for ever among 'em, there is not to be seen an undecent action, or glance: and being continually us'd to see one another so unadorn'd, so like our first parents before the fall, it seems as if they had no wishes, there being nothing to heighten curiosity; but all you can see, you see at once, and every moment see.
>
> (29)

In the prelapsarian world of this native culture there is no place for the commandeering "curiosity" that is a feature of English ways of looking. Moreover, in a comic reversal of positions, it is the English traveller who is turned into a sight when the narrator and her friends undertake a trip to visit the local tribes. She describes the consternation that the Indians feel when they first catch sight of the English and the disproportionate exuberance of their attire:

> They had no sooner spy'd us, but they set up a loud cry, that frighted us at first; we thought it had been for those that should kill us, but it seems it was of wonder and amazement. They were all naked; and we were dress'd, so as is most commode for the hot countries, very glittering and rich; so that we appear'd extremely fine: my own hair was cut short, and I had a taffety cap with black feathers on my head; my brother was in a stuff-suit, with silver loops and buttons, and abundance of green ribbon. This was all infinitely surprizing to them.
>
> (78)

Here, it is the colonizers and not the natives who are qualified by their visibility and difference.

In her description of the amorous relationship between Imoinda and Oroonoko in Africa, Behn similarly imagines ways of looking that are the result of the desire for mutuality rather then domination. The exchange of gazes, "the parley of the eyes" (45) between these two lovers, is symbolic of the powerful attraction they feel for one another and the ease with which they can circumvent the obstacles that separate them. Above all, the ideal harmony of the love between Imoinda and Oroonoko is located beyond the divisive sphere of language. Their looks of love constitute an alternative mode of expression which heals all divisions:

> But as soon as the King was busy'd in looking on some fine thing of Imoinda's making, she had time to tell the Prince, with her angry, but love-darting eyes, that she resented his coldness, and bemoan'd her own miserable captivity. Nor were his eyes silent, but answer'd hers again, as much as eyes cou'd do, instructed by the most tender and most passionate heart that ever lov'd: and they spoke so well, and so effectually, as Imoinda no longer doubted but she was the only delight and darling of that soul she found pleading in 'em its right of love, which none was more willing to resign than she.
>
> (41-2)

The narrator tries to recreate this affirmative mode of seeing in her admiring descriptions of Oroonoko. She depicts him as someone visually familiar and attractive yet also strange and exotic. She both acknowledges his cultural difference and attempts to reduce his otherness. Although she Europeanizes his appearance, at the same time she insists that his colour cannot be ignored:

> His nose was rising and Roman, instead of African and flat. His mouth the finest shaped that could be seen; far from those great turn'd lips, which are so natural to the rest of the Negroes. The whole proportion and air of his face was so nobly and exactly form'd, that bating his colour, there could be nothing in nature more beautiful, agreeable and handsome.
>
> (33)

However, the gaze of "surprize and wonder" (32) which the narrator centres on Oroonoko throughout the text can never escape the social differences and power-structures that contour their relationship. Her admiration for him, lingering on his physical beauty as it does, sexualizes and commodifies him. Despite the insistence that she is a nonpartisan observer, the narrator nevertheless uses the fetishizing language of the colonizer in order to control Oroonoko. Similarly, she Europeanizes him not so much to indicate a shared sphere of interests as to cancel and deny ethnic difference. Oroonoko acts as a surface onto which the narrator projects her own political and religious convictions. She tells us that he laments "the deplorable death of our great monarch" (33) and also that her conversations with him are motivated in part by a desire to convert him.

Paradoxically, however, the more she endeavours to erase Oroonoko's difference, the more prominent it becomes. It is not just his colour that refuses to disappear but also his sexuality and masculinity. The narrator's attempt to domesticate her hero underlines his otherness. The power that she wields over him is a phantom one. Oroonoko may call her "great mistress" but in the end is divided from her because of his ethnic otherness and gender difference. Indeed, while the narrator's insistence on the sexuality and physicality of Oroonoko is certainly a means by which she asserts the racial superiority of the white woman over the black native, it simultaneously functions as an index of her own lack of presence and power.[23] His visibility and threatening potency underscore her powerlessness and vulnerability. Momentarily, she co-opts Oroonoko to an ideal female domain of shared feeling and mutual concern. She declares that he "liked the company of us women much above the men" (69). Yet when Oroonoko rebels and delivers his speech exhorting his fellow slaves to revolt it is precisely the feminized sphere to which he is consigned that he cites as the ultimate sign of his social degradation: thus, he upbraids the other slaves by pointing out that they "are bought and sold like apes or monkeys, to be the sport of women, fools and cowards" (83).

At the end of the story, even the ideal love between Imoinda and Oroonoko becomes symbolic of the inequity of the power-relations between men and women. In order to protect her from possible assault, Oroonoko kills Imoinda in advance of leading an attack on his white enemies. His sexual ownership of her justifies the sacrificial mutilation of her body:

> the lovely, young and ador'd victim lays her self down before the sacrificer; while he, with a hand resolved, and a heart-breaking within, gave the fatal stroke, first cutting her throat, and then severing her yet smiling face from that delicate body, pregnant as it was with the fruits of tenderest love.
>
> (94)

Oroonoko is physically transformed by this ritual killing. The narrator views him not from the intimate perspective of friendship but through the horrified eyes of her community:

> We ran all to see him; and, if before we thought him so beautiful a sight, he was now so alter'd, that his face was like a death's-head black'd over, nothing but teeth and eye-holes.
>
> (97)

It is significant that Oroonoko in the closing moments of the narrative is no longer seen as desirable. Instead, he has become an image of abjection and horror. His body is now a sign not of exotic otherness but of savagery. Far from finding him alluring the narrator informs us that she is repelled by his "earthy smell." Yet her attempt to dissociate herself from him only links them all the more. Oroonoko's debilitated condition is mirrored by her own melancholic illness. In addition, her decision to leave the place for some time seems to provoke the final attack on Oroonoko by Banister, "a wild Irish man" (98). The "frightful spectacles" of Oroonoko's execution dominate the ending of the text:

> He had learn'd to take tobacco; and when he was assur'd he should die, he desir'd they would give him a pipe in his mouth, ready lighted; which they did: and the executioner came, and first cut off his members, and threw them into the fire; after that, with an ill-favour'd knife, they cut off his ears and his nose, and burn'd them; he still smoked on, as if nothing had touch'd him; then they hack'd off one of his arms, and still he bore up, and held his pipe; but at the cutting off the other arm, his head sunk, and his pipe dropt and he gave up the ghost, without a groan, or a reproach. My mother and sister were by him all the while, but not suffer'd to save him.
>
> (98-9)

The grotesque and harrowing account of the pipe-smoking Oroonoko being slowly hacked to death acts as a final and lasting reminder of the gulf separating white women and slaves in a colonial society. The bizarre comfort that he draws from tobacco becomes a mocking commentary on the nature of colonial trade. The sadistic excess involved in the slaughtering of Oroonoko and his apparent imperviousness to physical pain once again emphasize his ethnic otherness and archetypally masculine courage. Disturbingly, too, the narrator's mother and sister seem by their very inactivity to collude in this savage killing. Oroonoko's dismemberment appears in part to be a retribution for his role as the object of female desire and fear throughout the text.

Indeed, the ambivalence of Behn's parting description of Oroonoko suggests that the white colonial woman and the black male slave are trapped in an unavoidable pattern of reversal and betrayal. In asserting his masculinity and disaffection with the English colonial regime Oroonoko breaks the bonds of sympathy that linked him with the narrator, thus assuring his downfall. Likewise, the narrator's collapse into female melancholia and sudden expression of fear of the alien world in which she is living render her complicit with the inhuman massacre of the black slave once held to be her friend. The things that link these figures are one and the same with those that pit them against each other. In particular, the experience of slavery both unites and divides the central personae. As a consequence, the final sentence of *Oroonoko* is circular and inconclusive:

> Thus died this great man, worthy of a better fate, and a more sublime wit than mine to write his praise: yet, I

hope, the reputation of my pen is considerable enough to make his glorious name to survive to all ages, with that of the brave, the beautiful, and the constant Imoinda.

(99)

The text ends with an acknowledgement of the separate and disparate nature of its chief protagonists, the narrator, Oroonoko and Imoinda, and with a recognition that because of the different political positions of these individuals the tale that we have read has fallen short of its purpose. Behn succeeds neither in attacking slavery nor in proving that marginalized groups such as women and slaves have a shared experience of the world. The figure of the heroic black slave cannot act as a unifying metaphor for the specific injustices done to kings, women, oppressed ethnic groups and colonized peoples. Fittingly, *Oroonoko* concludes with a desire to circle back on itself and make good its omissions and inconsistencies. Finally and helplessly it gestures at the stories which it can never relate and the list of political causes—those of dispossessed kings, aspiring women writers and black women among them—it can never hope fully to interweave. It seems appropriate that the final name in this catalogue of disparate and incommensurate personae should be that of the black woman slave, Imoinda. Her name remains as a final, lingering reminder of the guilty complicities and contradictions in Behn's attempt to celebrate those forgotten by history. By using the figure of the black slave as a metaphor for the oppression of white political leaders and white women she has been guilty of a double erasure. Imoinda represents the point at which Behn's conflicting beliefs in the rights of colonizing sovereigns and of marginalized women are called most fully into question.

Notes

1. For an account of the revolution of 1688 see J. R. Jones, *Country and Court: England 1658-1714,* London, Edward Arnold, 1978, 234-55.

2. A. Behn, *Oroonoko and Other Stories,* ed. M. Duffy, London, Methuen, 1986, 25, 27 (cited hereafter by page number only in parenthesis).

3. A. Goreau provides an account of the many disputes about the details of Behn's life, also noting the attempts made by Behn's "debiographers" to discredit her. See *Reconstructing Aphra: A Social Biography of Aphra Behn,* Oxford, Oxford University Press, 1980.

4. E. Bernbaum, "Mrs. Behn's Biography a Fiction," *PMLA* 28 (1913) 432-53. The phrase occurs on 434.

5. See M. Duffy, *The Passionate Shepherdess: Aphra Behn 1640-89,* London, Jonathan Cape, 1977, and Goreau, *Reconstructing Aphra.*

6. For evidence of Behn's accuracy in her account of both West African and South American culture see E. Campbell, "Aphra Behn's Surinam Interlude," *Kunapipi* 7: 2-3 (1985) 25-35, B. Dhuicq, "Further Evidence on Aphra Behn's Stay in Surinam," *Notes*

and Queries 224 (1979) 524-6, H. G. Platt, Jr., "Astrea and Celadon: An Untouched Portrait of Aphra Behn," *PMLA* 49 (1934) 544-59, J. A. Ramsaran, "*Oroonoko:* A Study of the Factual Elements," *NQ* 205 (1960) 142-5, K. M. Rogers, "Fact and Fiction in Aphra Behn's *Oroonoko,*" *Studies in the Novel* 20 (Spring 1988) 1-15, and W. Sypher, "A Note on the Realism of Mrs. Behn's *Oroonoko,*" *Modern Language Quarterly* 3 (1942) 401-5.

7. B. G. MacCarthy, *Women Writers: Their Contribution to the English Novel, 1621-1744,* Cork, Cork University Press, 1944, 148-88.

8. V. Woolf, *A Room of One's Own* and *Three Guineas,* ed. Morag Shiach, Oxford and New York, Oxford University Press, 1992, 85, and V. Sackville-West, *Aphra Behn: The Incomparable Astrea,* London, Gerald Howe, 1927, 12.

9. D. Spender, *Mothers of the Novel: 100 Good Women Writers before Jane Austen,* London, Pandora Press, 1986, 47-66.

10. See Campbell, "Aphra Behn's Surinam Interlude," 33.

11. V. Ware, *Beyond the Pale: White Women, Racism and History,* London, Verso, 1992, 50-3.

12. L. Brown, "The Romance of Empire: *Oroonoko* and the Trade in Slaves," in F. Nussbaum and L. Brown, eds, *The New Eighteenth Century: Theory, Politics, English Literature,* New York and London, Methuen, 1987, 41-61.

13. M. Ferguson, "*Oroonoko:* Birth of a Paradigm," *New Literary History* 23 (1992) 339-59.

14. H. Hutner, "Aphra Behn's *Oroonoko:* The Politics of Gender, Race, and Class," in D. Spender, ed., *Living by the Pen: Early British Women Writers,* New York, Teachers College Press, 1992, 39-51.

15. The failure of feminism to reflect upon its unspoken acceptance of white privilege has become a vital area of debate in recent political writing. See especially b. hooks, *Ain't I a Woman? Black Women and Feminism,* London, Pluto Press, 1982, and E. V. Spelman, *Inessential Woman: Problems of Exclusion in Feminist Thought,* Boston, Beacon Press, 1988.

16. R. Ballaster, "New Hystericism: Aphra Behn's *Oroonoko:* The Body, the Text and the Feminist Critic," in I. Armstrong, ed., *New Feminist Discourses: Critical Essays on Theories and Texts,* London, Routledge, 1992, 283-95.

17. G. C. Spivak, "French Feminism in an International Frame," in *In Other Worlds: Essays in Cultural Politics,* New York, Methuen, 1987, 134-53.

18. For discussion of the royalist politics of many seventeenth-century women writers see C. Gallagher, "Embracing the Absolute: The Politics of the Female Subject in Seventeenth-Century England," *Genders* 1 (March 1988) 24-9.

19. For an analysis of the problem of representativity and the difficulty involved in the assumption that a woman writer can speak on behalf of everyone who is marginalized and oppressed see N. K. Miller, *Getting Personal: Feminist Occasions and Other Autobiographical Acts,* London, Routledge, 1991, 72-100.

20. J. Kristeva, *Strangers to Ourselves,* trans. L. S. Roudiez, Hemel Hempstead, Harvester, 1991.

21. As J. Gaines points out, the insistence on normative white ways of looking is a typical feature of racial discrimination. See "White Privilege and Looking Relations: Race and Gender in Feminist Film Theory," *Cultural Critique* 4 (Fall 1986) 59-79.

22. H. K. Bhabha analyses the way in which colonial regimes use a fetishizing gaze in order to insist on the inferiority of other races and cultures and justify the domination of them. See "The Other Question: Difference, Discrimination and the Discourse of Colonialism," in F. Barker, P. Hulme, M. Iversen and D. Loxley, eds, *Literature, Politics and Theory: Papers from the Essex Conference 1976-84,* London and New York, Methuen, 1986, 148-72.

23. F. Fanon shows that white culture links blackness with sexual excess, corporeality and hypervisibility. See *Black Skin, White Masks,* trans. C. Lam Markmann, London, Pluto Press, 1986.

Joyce Green MacDonald (essay date 1999)

SOURCE: "The Disappearing African Woman: Imoinda in *Oroonoko* After Behn," in *ELH,* Vol. 66, No. 1, 1999, pp. 71-86.

[*In the following essay, MacDonald discusses why the character of Oronooko's black African wife, Imoinda, in Aphra Behn's novel* Oroonoko *is depicted as white in later adaptations of the work. The critic claims that Imoinda's whiteness is used to suppress the facts of racial and gender conflict and to confer racial authority on white women.*]

At the climax of a mid-eighteenth-century heroic tragedy, the black hero, discovered in a private chamber with the dead body of his white wife, urges the white men who come upon the sight to "Put up your Swords, and let not civil Broils" involve them in his own desperate fate.[1] The play in question is not a version of *Othello,* as the remark about (bright?) swords and civil broils might at first suggest, but rather John Hawkesworth's 1759 *Oroonoko.* Clearly, as Hawkesworth refashions Thomas Southerne's 1696 dramatization of Aphra Behn's 1688 novella so as most readily and rightfully to fix "Attention . . . upon the two principal Characters, *Oroonoko* and *Imoinda,* who are so connected as to make but one Object, in which all the Passions of the Audience, moved by the most tender and exquisite Distress, are concentrated" (*H,* A2v), he has *Othello*—a dignified, pathetic, mid-eighteenth-century kind of

Othello—in mind. The kind of transaction he conducts with the Shakespearean tragedy, however, ranges beyond establishing similarities of tone. What this revision of Southerne (and beyond him, of Behn) also appropriates is a ready theatrical language for regularizing both Shakespeare's wild passions and the radical racial and sexual illease occasioned by *Oroonoko.* Audiences, it would seem, had a ready-made sentimental frame of reference for a miscegenous *Oroonoko,* but not for one whose enslaved lovers were of the same race.

Hawkesworth's play is only one part of a remarkable constellation of texts originating from Behn's novella as it entered its eighteenth-century afterlife. In Behn, Imoinda is black like Oroonoko. In Hawkesworth and every other text following Behn, she is white. Only recently has this racial transformation become a subject for extended discussion in the work of postcolonial and feminist critics, primarily in relation to Southerne's play, where it first occurs.[2] Yet there are several other white Imoindas after Behn, and I would like to direct my own inquiries into some of them, rather than solely into Southerne, whose play seems to me so radical a revision and literalizing of the sexual and economic implications of Behn as to require a separate discussion of its own.

Behn's *Oroonoko,* of course, poses the most obvious exception to Lynda Boose's assertion of the "unrepresentability" of African women in early modern texts.[3] Following Janet Adelman's psychological analysis of masculine fear of women's reproductive power in Shakespeare, Boose argues that the reason for the virtual absence of black female characters from this discourse is the white and masculine fear that the blackness of black female characters visibly marks them as the location of that dark place through which men must pass in order to be born as men: "The mother's part in him threatens the fantasy of perfect self-replication that would preserve the father in the son."[4] I follow Boose, but consider the possibility that a denial of representation to African women has other rationales than the psychic; or rather, that the psychic is supplemented and articulated by the material practices of racism. The racial revisions eighteenth-century authors make in Behn—revisions which extend beyond the color of the heroine's skin to include Behn's constructions of character and gender identity—are worth examining for what they reveal about the relationships the period established between the social and sexual values and meanings implied by white and black skins, and by white and black sexual bodies.

Historians of Atlantic slavery have only begun recovering the experiences of enslaved African women, detailing how their experiences in bondage differed from and overlapped with those of male slaves.[5] In the interest of extracting as much agricultural work from as many physically able slaves as possible, slave owners in the American colonies and the Caribbean made no distinction between male and female, putting women to work at the most difficult jobs alongside men: harnessing mules or oxen to steer crude wooden plows, cutting logs, hoeing and picking cotton, or chopping and milling sugar cane. Female slaves mined coal, dug canals, and built railroads, although they seem not to have performed much skilled artisanal or mechanical work; the cost of training a slave whose labor power was needed elsewhere and whose availability for skilled jobs could be interrupted by childbirth and nursing was too high. Put to perform men's work, female slaves were frequently regarded as somehow masculinized, as the reports of many observers of American slavery suggest.[6] While gender was thus not always relevant in distinguishing the work of slaves and masters, slave women's field work did become a means of racing the female gender. One historian notes that in Barbados after about 1660, black female slaves began to replace indentured white women as workers in the sugar cane fields in a "racially-inspired labour policy" aimed at establishing "the ideology of white racial superiority . . . a long-term attempt to elevate white women and degrade black women."[7]

That the labor and social history of African women's enslavement has, until recently, been scanted in the interpretive record speaks to the requirements of an older historiography of slavery in the Americas—exemplified by the work of Eugene Genovese—which implicitly modeled its understanding of the structure of slave families on that of slaveholding families, which were held to be at least notionally structured around a benevolent patriarchalism.[8] This domestic historiography of slavery paid small attention to the economic and social roles played by African women in slave communities, but—most crucially, for my interests here—it also contributed to the suppression of knowledge of the extent of female slaves' sexual exploitation and abuse by the men of their masters' families, fearful knowledge which emphasizes the interplay of race, gender, and sexuality in the institutional maintenance of slavery, and the inadequacy of family as a structuring framework for understanding it.[9] As early as 1662, the Virginia colony had passed a law which held that all children born within the colony would follow the condition of the mother, in a departure from English common law which held that children followed the condition of their fathers (or of their mothers' husbands). Such a law implicitly excused white men from paternal responsibility toward their children born of slave mothers, rendering sexual connection with and sex crimes against slave women legally invisible. Indeed, a contemporary feminist analysis of sexuality and slavery suggests that a self-imposed response of concealment and denial to the continuous experience of sexual assault resulted in a kind of self-silencing by slave women, a self-silencing which may be crucial in their absence from the historical record.[10] What was not rendered socially invisible was the frustration and anger of the slave owners' wives, who often reacted against the black women in bondage in their households with rage: "Under slavery we live surrounded by prostitutes, like patriarchs of old, our men lie in one house with their wives and concubines."[11]

In Behn's Surinam, the links between whites' racial authority, black women's sexuality, and white women's so-cial repression were even more explicitly institutionalized. John Stedman, a debt-ridden young Englishman, arrived in Surinam in 1773 as a volunteer for military service on behalf of Surinam's planters, who were engaged in trying to fight back against the ongoing guerilla attacks staged by bands of maroons, or escaped slaves. Composing a *Narrative of a Five Years Expedition Against the Revolted Negroes of Suriname* some years after he had settled his debts and returned to England to marry and raise a family, Stedman writes that he is sorry to have to describe a custom which he is "convinced will be highly censured by the Sedate European Matrons," the so-called "Suriname marriage." The practice, "as common as it is almost necessary to the batchelors who live in this climate," involves having

> a female Slave / mostly a creole / in their keeping who preserves their linnens clean and decent, dresses their Victuals with Skill, carefully attends them / they being most excellent nurses / during the frequent illnesses to which Europeans are exposed in this Country, prevents them from keeping late Hours knits for them, sows for them &c—while these Girls who are sometimes Indians sometime Mulattos and often negroes, naturally pride themselves in living with an European whom they serve with as much tenderness, and to whom they are Generally as faithfull as if he were their lawfull Husband to the great Shame of so many fair Ladies, who break through ties more sacred, and indeed bound with more Solemnity, nor can the above young women be married in any other way, being by their state of Servitude entirely debard from every Christian privilege and Ceremony, which makes it perfectly lawfull on *their* Side, while they hesitate not to pronounce as Harlots, who do not follow them / if they can / in this laudable Example in which they are encouraged as I have said by their nearest Relations and Friends.[12]

The differences between Stedman's existing accounts of "Surinam marriage" provide an example of how the tropes of sentiment could be employed to represent the harsh sexual exigencies of life in a slave society. The manuscript of the *Narrative* and the personal diary Stedman kept in Surinam are full of accounts of his own and others' casual sexual encounters with slave women; eighteenth-century British observers are repeatedly shocked at the offhand brutality with which colonial planters expressed their sexual ownership of their slaves.[13] Stedman himself was involved in a "Surinam marriage" with a slave named Joanna for virtually the entire length of his stay in the country, its financial terms agreed on in advance with Joanna's mother. Such concubinage, as well as the widespread prostitution of slave women by their owners during sugar's fallow season, were common practice throughout the Caribbean. For the reading of "Sedate" (*P,* 47) European women, however, Stedman censored many invidious comparisons between white women of the colony and its Indian and slave women, to whom he is much more attracted because of their "remarkable Cleanliness and youthfull vigour" (*P,* 49). Such censorship points to ways in which slavery was ideologically reproduced for the consumption of an audience of European women, cleansed of the sexual coercion and the depersonalized sexual contacts which formed the fabric of its daily experience for both slaves and masters. The achievement of a new social and economic status for planters' wives and daughters in the colonies occured within this social immersion in a commodified sexuality. Slavery threw white and black women together in a violent, and violently sexualized, intimacy which mocked any idea of the sanctity of home and hearth.[14]

And yet, it is the familial, the domestic, and the private, which figure so significantly in the transformed *Oroonoko*s of the eighteenth century. A white heroine in these eighteenth-century dramas of pathos and sensibility affirms a new means of socially and culturally producing white Englishwomen as part of the reading and theater-going public and in the growing abolitionist movement during which these plays were performed or otherwise circulated.[15] For the consumption of a theatrical audience in which women of leisure were present in increasing numbers in a Britain first entering into the full scope of an imperial expansion crucially supported by Atlantic slavery, a white Imoinda also performs acts of cultural forgetting, organized around tropes of white womanhood and its domestic realm. Those acts of cultural forgetting facilitate the erasure of African women from *Oroonoko* and colonial cultures deeply troubled by the sexual implications of white men's supremacy for the social welfare of white women.[16]

Dramatic adaptations of Behn's *Oroonoko* include those by Thomas Southerne, John Hawkesworth, Francis Gentleman (1760), John Ferriar (1788), and at least one anonymous author (*The Royal Captive,* 1767). As they remade Behn, Ferriar, Gentleman, and Hawkesworth were all explicitly motivated, at least in part, by the impulse to correct the "disgusting extravagances" of Southerne's double plot—one strand of which dealt with the tragedy of Behn's characters Oroonoko and Imoinda, the other with the cross-dressed machinations of a London woman aimed at securing rich husbands for herself and her sister on the colonial frontier.[17] Shakespeare's *Othello* also underwent a striking series of editorial and performative interventions resulting in a play which paradoxically raised white audiences' awareness of its concern with crossing sexualized racial barriers at the same time as it insisted on new decorums of language and gesture.[18]

Like the eighteenth-century *Othello, Oroonoko* in the period was also produced and understood as a drama of sensibility and pathos. Like *Othello,* it was also known to audiences from Southerne's time and afterwards through a long record of eighteenth-century performance as a drama centering on a miscegenous love affair between a black African man and a white woman. Here, I argue that the whiteness of Imoinda in *Oroonoko* after Behn is the product of a cult of sensibility as it confronted that most ungenteel of human institutions, slavery.[19] Imoinda's whitening permits a broader whitening and patriarchalizing of Behn's text and all its ambivalences about the roles of white women, black women, and black men within slavery

and the colonial relations it drove. Slavery in the *Oroonoko* plays is both domesticated and universalized, mystified through the employment of white womanhood so as to erode its historical specificity within Behn's Surinam and in the eighteenth-century Atlantic slave trade. The revisions show their Restoration roots in Behn by their preoccupation with the aristocratic value of personal honor, an ideological concept which, by the time of their performance, had been culturally eclipsed and absorbed by the bourgeois principle of individualism and self-reliance. Both ideologies, the elite and the popular, are deployed here in the service of naturalizing colonialism and its economic reliance on the slave trade.[20]

Before proceeding with my main argument, I would like to sketch in some terms under which we can speak of an African woman's presence in Behn's text. Imoinda in fact appears there only flickeringly, and largely as a focus and a product of others' sexuality. Although we are assured she is so beautiful as to be the perfect match for Oroonoko's princely bearing. "the beautiful Black Venus to our young Mars," she remains for the most part a mysterious and passive object of others' passions.[21] She only assumes "all her additions to beauty" after Oroonoko silently communicates his attraction to her (*O,* 13), but even so she exercises a powerful sexual attraction over Oroonoko's grandfather in Coromantien as well as over "an hundred white men sighing after her and making a thousand vows at her feet" in Surinam (*O,* 12). She comes to Oroonoko out of his grandfather's harem, in an appropriation of sub-saharan Africa and Africans to the discourse of orientalism and of orientalist notions of non-European women's sexuality.[22] In captivity, she becomes a commercial as well as a sexual object. In contrast to the white narrator, who removes herself from the climactic scene of Oroonoko's scourging, presumably because of her tender sensibilities, the heavily pregnant Imoinda is carried away "not in kindness to her, but for fear she should die with the sight, or miscarry, and then they should lose a young slave, and perhaps the mother" (*O,* 64). Despite the sexual allure she exercises almost involuntarily, she also always yields herself to the patriarchal logic which governs familial and sexual relations in Coromantien. When she and Oroonoko agree to marry, they decide "on both sides that, in obedience to him, the grandfather was to be first made acquainted with the design, for they pay a most absolute resignation to the monarch, especially when he is a parent also" (*O,* 14). She accepts the necessity of her death at her husband's hands because in Coromantien, "wives have a respect for their husbands equal to what other people pay a deity; and when a man finds occasion to quit his wife, if he loves her, she dies by his hand" (*O,* 68).

In the first Oroonoko and Imoinda we can thus trace an example of what Homi Bhabha has called "mimicry" in the colonialist text: their black skins and the signs of cultural alterity which literally mark their bodies (the narrator somewhat fancifully compares their facial scarifications to the body painting of the Picts) come to signify primarily as touches of exoticism within the determinedly patriarchal story of gender identity being written for them.[23] And yet even within this absorption of black Africans by a white European narrative of slavery and the sexual and racial relations it dictates, Behn's Imoinda somehow confounds the construction of a seamless account. Her facial scarification is both more extensive and more elaborate than Oroonoko's, "her extraordinary prettiness" augmented rather than lessened by "her being carved in fine flowers and birds all over her body" (*O*, 44). Behn's pregnant Imoinda initially resembles, but ultimately diverges from, the ideal of the English mother whose employment in discourses of eighteenth-century colonialism has been so brilliantly traced by Felicity Nussbaum.[24] Her sexual history and her status as a sexually desiring subject, the active role she takes in fighting for her freedom by her husband's side, and the alien origin traced in her very skin, all mark Behn's production of her as finally—and only—Other than the white woman who tells her story.

Imoinda's status as breeding stock in the minds of the planters is a literal exhibition of how, for women in this period, reproduction has become the only means of production. What is missing from Behn's portrait of an African woman, however, is an acknowledgement of the material bases of differences between women which slavery threw into such sharp relief. Behn recognizes gender difference within her representation of Africans, and also acknowledges the operations of gender within whiteness. As a white *woman,* Behn's narrator responds to the beauty and honorable qualities of Oroonoko and his African bride, Imoinda, and is curiously powerless to intervene in the public crisis of Oroonoko's capture and final, horrible public mutilation. As a *white* woman, she sails upriver and delights in displaying her undergarments to the uncomprehending Indians who inhabit Surinam's interior. But, in flattening all Imoinda's labor into sexual labor, the white narrator declines to recognize how work—sexual and otherwise—distinguished black women from white ones, resulting in her reproduction of an African woman in terms of the emerging social definitions of women of her own race.

A test case for my contention that white womanhood is invoked by post-Behn *Oroonoko* to naturalize the collusion of patriarchy with slavery may be provided by John Ferriar's *Prince of Angola,* distinguished within this series of texts by its avowedly abolitionist purpose. In his preface, Ferriar announces that he is writing his version of Behn in order to shock white people out of their insensitivity to the evils of slavery: "We talk of the destruction of millions, with as little emotion, and as little accuracy of comprehension, as of the distances of the Planets" (*F*, i). To that end, his play, he tells us, will correct both Southerne's structural irregularity and Hawkesworth's inappropriate sentimentality. In Hawkesworth, he tells us, the hero is so passionately swept away by love for his Imoinda that he is incapable of "making any rational reflexions on his condition" (*F*, vi)—that is, of responding to the fact of his enslavement with rage against the slaveholders. Here, Ferriar implies, matters will be conducted differently; romance

will be more carefully segregated from tragedy, and proslavery arguments will in no way be allowed to stand unchallenged.

Ferriar's abolitionist fervor, however, is modulated through gender both in his preface and in his play proper. He addresses a section of his Prologue to "The Ladies of Manchester," who "have distinguished themselves very honorably" in the cause of abolition:

> Here Pity lives in ev'ry gentle Breast.
> Folly may scoff, or Avarice may hate,
> Since Beauty comes the Negroe's Advocate.
> Let others boast in Fashion's Pride to glow,
> To lure the Lover, or attract the Beau;
> You check Oppression's Lash, protect the Slave,
> And, first to charm, are still the first to save.
>
>   (*F*, 2)

The advocacy of the Negroes to which Ferriar alludes here emerges as an aspect of the Manchester ladies' "charm."[25] His appeal to antislavery women may in fact not be based on their feelings toward Africans at all. In his view, one of the things wrong with Southerne's play is that its hero is shown kissing the ground and asking to be allowed to worship the disguised white Imoinda, a ludicrous improbability that "will not be easily understood, by those who know, that an African's highest religious mystery is the Mumbo Jumbo" (*F*, v). Englishwomen's capacity to feel matters more than what they may feel about slaves.

White women are written into *Oroonoko* just as they were thus written into eighteenth-century debates on the slave trade and into wider representations of the gendered prerogatives of empire. Just as the Manchester ladies' femininity is essentialized into a force capable of saving slaves, presumably through the exercise of charm, so too is the femininity of Ferriar's white Imoinda, whose anxieties as a wife entirely dictate her courses of action. She wants nothing more than to belong uninterruptedly to her husband, Oroonoko, asserting that she would rather die than be left to "the wild passions" (*F*, 51) of the lecherous and deceitful lieutenant governor. Ferriar's Oroonoko is at first reluctant to lead the rebellion against the slaveholders as his own former slave Aboan begs him to, but he is finally persuaded to do so by the argument that slavery's worst degradations stem from its denial of male slaves' patriarchal right within the family. One day, Aboan reminds him, he might be sold to a master "Who, proud perhaps to own a Royal Slave, / May suffer you to get young Princes for him" (*F*, 31). Thus moved by the possibility of having the sanctity of his bloodline denied and his reproductive capacity turned to the economic benefit of another man, Oroonoko in his turn convinces the other male slaves to rebel against their owners by arguing that slavery profanes the marriage bond when it denies a husband's right to possess his wife exclusively. He reminds them of the countless times when male slaves have been forced to stand impotently by "When, in the tort'rer's hands, a wretched wife, / Has scream'd for mercy, has implored your aid, / While your distraction made the Christian sport" (*F*, 32).

My point here is not that slavery did not degrade intimate relations between men and women, but rather that Ferriar's fearful white Imoinda experiences her sexual danger as virtually divorced from the fact of her enslavement; in Behn, remember, Imoinda fights at her husband's side in the revolt against the planters, wounding the lieutenant governor with a poisoned arrow. Hawkesworth's Imoinda is even more explicitly exposed to sexual danger than Ferriar's, as the attempted rape is sensationally brought on-stage. After unsuccessfully begging her husband to kill her in order to preserve her virtue, she finally takes the knife and stabs herself: "where I liv'd, I die in these lov'd arms" (*H,* 62). In the process of re-presenting slavery and the colonial enterprise it supported, a white Imoinda who actively seeks death, rather than merely accepting it as does Behn's character, creates a place for middle-class women's complicity with the aims of empire, a complicity which writes them primarily as monogamous, sensitive and maternal—all the things out of which a portrait of a savage African woman would emerge.

In Ferriar, the whitening of Imoinda is accompanied by a broader dissociation of slavery from skin color; the first revolt in the play is actually led by angry Indians, who are never heard from again. The lieutenant governor fears that the black slaves will be drawn into fighting against their white masters and so orders Oroonoko to be chained; as for "the white slaves," he casually remarks, "they'll not stir" (*F,* 18). While these mysterious white slaves are so docile or so demoralized that they are incapable of or uninterested in rebellion, Oroonoko gallantly fights "at the Head of the Planters" (*F,* 19) to thwart the Indians' attempt to carry off African slaves as spoils of their war against the white slaveholders.[26] Just as the moral Blandford has earlier been moved by Oroonoko's dignity even in chains to declare that he "will attend, and serve" (*F,* 9) him, Oroonoko is moved to fight on the planters' behalf after Blandford proves his decency by refusing to have him chained when the Indians' rebellion breaks out. In Ferriar, courage, character, and the right to monogamous love bind men together more than slavery can separate them; or at least, these things unite good men. Blandford bemoans the "cursed" hour that first drove Europe's "cruel sons to visit Afric's shore" and assures Oroonoko that he "must not think" himself to be a slave—without, however, manumitting him (*F,* 23, 25). As the play mounts toward its climax, Blandford sets out to rescue Oroonoko and Imoinda from danger and help them escape, asserting that he wishes he could extend the same "Relief to ev'ry drooping African / That now must envy their deliverance!" (*F,* 46). That he cannot, or at least does not, attempt to end a condition he finds so repugnant is never examined.

Capable of admiring Oroonoko's individual nobility, yet claiming to be helpless before the operations of slavery, the dramatic Blandford in effect occupies the white woman's role laid down in Behn's novella. In Behn, the white narrator and her female friends possess the kind of moral sensitivity which will allow them, as women, to be shocked and troubled by the suffering of slaves; as women,

they will also be powerless to stop their men from conducting and profiting from the slave trade. Yet the difference between genders which Behn's narrative communicates by absence—her female narrator's disappearances from the action during the slave revolt; Oroonoko's execution of Imoinda; and the public torturing of Oroonoko to death—is here articulated as a difference within genders. In Ferriar, there are good white men who are shocked by the "insolence" of cruel slaveowners who will "strip the injur'd negro / Of his last privilege, the rank of man," (*F,* 42) and there are bad white men like the lieutenant governor, motivated only by lust and cruelty. Oroonoko's black skin and Imoinda's white one signify here primarily in relation to the slaveowners' possession (or lack) of finer feelings. Slavery, which, the play points out existed in Africa as well as in the New World and which binds white people as well as blacks in Surinam, has less to do with the color of the couple's skins than with the fact that they are both subject to the whim of an evil man, and denied the privileges of the liberal individualism on which Ferriar's abolitionism is based. Hence, the dying Aboan wishes for a better world in which he will allowed to be Oroonoko's "faithful slave again" (*F,* 48).

If Ferriar's *Prince* comes as close as it can to delivering a slavery under whose terms Africans are no more significant than anyone else, returning to Hawkesworth demonstrates the degree to which romantic sentiment is employed in post-Behn *Oroonoko* to fill the space left by the evacuation of racial difference, and the spectre of conflict it raised, from the text. Confronted by white planters determined to quash the slaves' rebellion, Behn's Oroonoko demonstrates his moral indifference to their power over him by stoically enduring his public dismemberment. The body of the wife he loved and executed decomposes in the rainforest, as Oroonoko's searchers are led to it by the the smell of its decay—"a stink that almost struck them dead" (*O,* 70). In contrast to these haunting bodily spectacles, Hawkesworth's slaves enclose themselves within a culture of pathos and sensibility. After a scene in which the evil lieutenant governor tries to rape Imoinda, for instance, in a portrayal of the sexual horror which drives Ferriar's Oroonoko to rebellion, Hawkesworth contains and disciplines the rage that this sexual danger to Imoinda inspired in Behn and Ferriar with a musical interlude where male and female slaves sing that "Love, Love and Joy must both be free, / They live not but with Liberty" (*H,* 25). Hawkesworth's Oroonoko is even more reluctantly persuaded to lead the rebellion than Ferriar's. Not only was he a slaveholder in Africa, but his present enslavement is not all that unbearable: he is, after all, "Favour'd in my own Person, in my Friends,; / Indulg'd in all that can concern my care, / In my Imoinda's soft society" (*F,* 35). Finally convinced to rebel by the thought that the evil lieutenant governor will probably want Imoinda for himself, he is careful to specify that the rebellion be nonviolent: "The Means that lead us to our Liberty / Must not be bloody . . . / Whate'er the Rage of Passion may suggest" (*F,* 37). In fact, if the slaves can take the slave ship still moored in the harbor by surprise, they can sail back to Africa and out of Europeans' troubled comprehension altogether, thus achieving "triumph without Conflict" (*F,* 43).

The suppression of conflict—racial conflict, as well as the gender conflict between white men and white women played out through the bodies of black women—was, I think, a large part of why the black Imoinda was made to disappear from *Oroonoko.* The beginnings of this suppression are perhaps visible in Behn, where Imoinda's decapitation and Oroonoko's dismemberment render as more easily assimilable fragments the black bodies which, whole, pose painful questions about how they should or can be smoothly incorporated within the sexual and racial processes of slavery.[27] The whiteness of Imoinda after Behn becomes the price of the ticket for white women's admission to a kind of racial authority. A survey of some versions of *Oroonoko* suggests that what mattered in this extension of racial privilege to Englishwomen was the new Imoinda's performance of a kind of gender sacrifice to the inexorable operation of a slave economy: a loving wife and mother, she allows herself to be sacrificed—or even sacrifices herself—to a higher cause. When the African woman is made to disappear—triumphally, without conflict—from *Oroonoko,* a European woman constructed in careful conformity with the interests of a society deeply invested in her chastity and her silence, and requiring her collusion with its new fictions of race, emerges.

Notes

1. John Hawkesworth, *Oroonoko, A Tragedy, As it is now Acted at the Theatre-Royal in Drury-Lane . . . By Thomas Southern. With Alterations* (Dublin: G. Faulkner, P. Wilson, and M. Williamson, 1760), 62. Hereafter cited parenthetically in the text by page number and abbreviated *H.*

2. See Ros Ballaster, "New Hystericism: Aphra Behn's *Oroonoko,* the Body, the Text, and the Feminist Critic," in *New Feminist Discourses: Critical Essays on Theories and Texts,* ed. Isobel Armstrong (London: Routledge, 1992), esp. 288-90; Margaret Ferguson, "Juggling the Categories of Race, Class, and Gender: Aphra Behn's *Oroonoko,*" in *Women, 'Race,' and Writing in the Early Modern Period,* ed. Margo Hendricks and Patricia Parker (London: Routledge, 1994), esp. 218-24; and Stephanie Athey and Daniel Cooper Alarcón, "*Oroonoko*'s Gendered Economies of Honor/Horror: Reframing Colonial Discourse Studies in the Americas," *American Literature* 65 (1993): 415-43.

3. Lynda Boose, "'The Getting of a Lawful Race': Racial Discourse in Early Modern England and the 'Unrepresentable' Black Woman," in *Women, 'Race,' and Writing,* 35-54.

4. Adelman, *Suffocating Mothers: Fantasies of Maternal Origin in Shakespeare, 'Hamlet' to 'The Tempest'* (New York: Routledge, 1992), 107; see also Boose, 45.

5. See, for example, Barbara Bush, *Slave Women in Caribbean Society, 1650-1838* (Bloomington:

Indiana Univ. Press, 1990); James Walvin, *Black Ivory: A History of British Slavery* (Washington: Howard Univ. Press, 1992), 119-34; Marietta Morrissey, *Slave Women in the New World: Gender Stratification in the Caribbean* (Lawrence: Univ. of Kansas Press, 1989); and Hilary Beckles, *Natural Rebels: A Social History of Enslaved Black Women in Barbados* (New Brunswick: Rutgers Univ. Press, 1989).

6. Jacqueline Jones reports that one Texas farmer put his female slaves in breeches while they were out doing men's work, "thus minimizing outward differences between the sexes" ("'My Mother Was Much of a Woman': Black Women, Work, and the Family Under Slavery," *Feminist Studies* 8 [1982]: 242). On the gender divisions which did maintain in slave societies despite this erosion of gender distinction in slaves' labor, also see Susan A. Mann, "Slavery, Sharecropping, and Sexual Inequality," in *Black Women in America: Social Science Perspectives,* ed. Micheline Malson, Elisabeth Mudimbe-Boyi, Jean F. O'Barr, and Mary Wyer (Chicago: Univ. of Chicago Press, 1988), 133-57; and Angela Davis, *Women, Race and Class* (New York: Vintage Books, 1983), 5-11.

7. Beckles, *Natural Rebels,* 29. On the implications of race for the gendering of women and their work, see also Davis, *Women, Race, and Class.* She writes, "As the ideology of femininity—a by-product of industrialization—was popularized and disseminated through the new ladies' magazines and romantic novels, white women came to be seen as inhabitants of a sphere totally severed from the realm of productive work" (12).

8. Eugene Genovese, *Roll, Jordan, Roll: The World the Slaves Made* (New York: Pantheon Books, 1974). Genovese's book has as its central thesis that the paternalistic structure of white slaveowning families extended to their black slaves, and that blacks eagerly sought to replicate this male-dominated structure for themselves. For a valuable review of the emergence of a feminist history of women, sexuality, and gender in writings about American slavery see Patricia Morton's introduction to *Discovering the Women in Slavery: Emancipating Perspectives on the American Past,* ed. with an introduction by Morton (Athens: Univ. of Georgia Press, 1996), 1-26.

9. In "Behind the Mask: Ex-Slave Women and Interracial Sexual Relations" (in *Discovering the Women in Slavery,* 260-277), Hélène Lecaudey emphasizes the degree to which the rape and sexual exploitation of slave women has been represented as miscegenation in much historiography of slavery. In part, she is responding to Genovese, whose interest in recuperating the patriarchal family as a benevolent model for understanding social relations within slavery leads him to view sexual relations between white men and black women primarily as

examples of miscegenation and not as examples of overt or covert force: "Many white men who began by taking a slave girl in an act of sexual exploitation ended by loving her and the children she bore. . . . The tragedy of miscegenation lay not in its collapse into lust and sexual exploitation, but in the terrible pressure to deny the delight, affection, and love that grew from tawdry beginnings" (*Roll, Jordan, Roll,* 415). In *Women, Race and Class,* Davis quotes Genovese and emphasizes that "there could hardly be a basis for 'delight, affection and love' as long as white men, by virtue of their economic position, had unlimited access to black women's bodies" (25-26). See her discussion, 19-29. Bell hooks has also characterized the rape and prostitution of slave women as instruments of sexual terror. On the passage from Africa into New World slavery, she writes, "African females received the brunt of this mass brutalization and terrorization not only because they could be victimized via their sexuality but also because they were more likely to work intimately with white families than with black males" (*Ain't I A Woman?: Black Women and Feminism* [Boston: South End Press, 1982], 20).

10. Darlene Clark Hine, "Rape and the Inner Lives of Southern Black Women: Thoughts on the Culture of Dissemblance," in *Southern Women: Histories and Identities,* ed. Virginia Bernhard, Betty Brandon, Elizabeth Fox-Genovese, and Theda Perdue (Columbia: Univ. of Missouri Press, 1992), 177-89.

11. Mary Boykin Chesnut, quoted in Erlene Stetson, "Studying Slavery: Some Literary and Pedagogical Considerations on the Black Female Slave," in *All the Women Are White, All the Blacks Are Men, But Some of Us Are Brave: Black Women's Studies,* ed. Gloria T. Hull, Patricia Bell Scott, and Barbara Smith (Old Westbury, N. Y.: Feminist Press, 1982), 77.

12. Stedman's narrative, one of the most extensive eyewitness accounts by a European of life in an American slave society, exists in two versions: the manuscript he completed in 1790, and the first published edition of 1796. The 1796 narrative has been reprinted in an edition by R. A. J. Van Lier (Amherst: Univ. of Massachusetts, 1972), while Richard Price and Sally Price have produced a full edition transcribed from the 1790 manuscript (Baltimore: The Johns Hopkins Univ. Press, 1988), and an abridged *Stedman's Surinam: Life in an Eighteenth-Century Slave Society* (Baltimore: The Johns Hopkins Univ. Press, 1992), also based on the 1790 manuscript. In addition, Stedman kept a personal journal during his stay in Surinam. The 1988 edition discusses the 1796 edition's suppression of the 1790 edition and the personal journal's sexual and racial detail, much of which communicates Stedman's and other Europeans' attraction to slave women, lix-lxvi. Here, I quote the 1988 Price edition, 47-48. All subsequent references to Stedman are to the Price edition, cited parenthetically by page number and abbreviated *P.*

13. Beckles reports on a British Army Major Wyvill who was shocked to see a white woman in Bridgetown, Barbados' capital, examine the genitals of a male slave for sale 'with all possible indelicacy' (*Natural Rebels,* 141). The 1790 *Narrative* observes that "Luxury and dissipation in this Country are carried to the extreme and in my opinion must send Thousands to the Grave, the Men are generally a set of poor wither'd mortals—as dry and sapless as a squeesed lemon—owing to their intemperate way of living such as late hours—hard drinking—and particularly their too frequent intercourse with the negro and mulatto female sex, to whom they generally give the preference before the creole Ladies" (*P,* 49). Compare Van Lier's 1972 edition of the 1796 *Narrative,* where the last sentence of this passage reads that the planters are men who "have indulged themselves in intemperance and other sensual gratifications, and who appear withered and enervated in the extreme" (19).

14. This is the thesis of Elizabeth Fox-Genovese in *Within the Plantation Household: Black and White Women of the Old South* (Chapel Hill: Univ. of North Carolina Press, 1988). On the uneasy coexistence of white women and female slaves in U. S. slavery, see Stetson, "Studying Slavery," esp. 75-78. The 1790 *Narrative* is not surprised that "the poor illtreated Ladies should be jealous of their Spouses and . . . bitterly take revenge on the causes of their disgrace—the negro and Mulatto Girls whom they persecute with the greatess bitterness and the most barbarous tyranny," and notes that white women in the colony are so competitive for husbands that "it was even publickly reported that two of them had fought a *Duel* on account of one of our Officers" (*P,* 49).

15. Felicity Nussbaum points to the eighteenth-century shift from home-based cottage industry to wage labor taking place outside the home as a moment of women's loss of economic authority, and argues the concomitant rise of "[n]ew ideologies of maternal affection and sentiment between mothers and children" which glorified European women's relegation to the home under eighteenth-century colonialism (*Torrid Zones: Maternity, Sexuality, and Empire in Eighteenth-Century English Narratives* [Baltimore: The Johns Hopkins Univ. Press, 1995], 24). On the social circumstances surrounding women's new prominence in the early modern theater audience, see David Roberts, *The Ladies: Female Patronage of Restoration Drama, 1660-1700* (Oxford: Clarendon Press, 1989). Moira Ferguson's *Subject To Others: British Women Writers and Colonial Slavery, 1670-1834* (London: Routledge, 1992) is the most comprehensive study of Englishwomen and abolitionist discourse.

16. My phrase "cultural forgetting" resembles the "historical amnesia" that Valerie Amos and Pratibha Parmar write that white feminists suffer as they repeat the assumptions of "white male historians" by ignoring "the fundamental ways in which white women have benefitted from the oppression of black people" ("Challenging Imperial Feminism," *Feminist Review* 17 [1984]: 5). As the first major feminist discussion of the interplay of race and gender in Behn's *Oroonoko,* Laura Brown's "The Romance of Empire: *Oroonoko* and the Trade in Slaves" (in *The New Eighteenth Century: Theory, Politics, English Literature,* ed. Felicity Nussbaum and Laura Brown [New York: Methuen, 1987], 41-61) exhibits this shortcoming to the degree it fails to address how this interplay might also involve Imoinda; the only woman she considers is the white narrator. In *Spectacular Politics: Theatrical Power and Mass Culture in Early Modern England* (Baltimore: The Johns Hopkins Univ. Press, 1993), Paula Backscheider, is perhaps so committed to the project of recovering Behn's discursive authority that she argues that *Oroonoko*'s portrait of the relationship between Imoinda and the narrator demonstrates that in Behn's fictions, "all but the worst women appreciate the good and make loyal friends to other women" (95). Brown and Backscheider are usefully supplemented by the discussions of race and cultural difference in Susan Z. Andrade, "White Skin, Black Masks: Colonialism and the Sexual Politics of *Oroonoko,*" *Cultural Critique* 27 (1994): 189-214; and Isobel Grundy, "'The barbarous character we give them': White Women Travellers Report on Other Races," *Studies in Eighteenth Century Culture* 22 (1992): 73-86.

17. John Ferriar, *The Prince of Angola, A Tragedy, Altered from the Play of Oroonoko, and Adapted to the Circumstances of the Present Times* (Manchester: J. Harrop, 1788), viii. Hereafter cited parenthetically in the text by page number and abbreviated *F.*

18. See Michael Neill, "Unproper Beds: Race, Adultery, and the Hideous in *Othello,*" *Shakespeare Quarterly* 41 (1989): 383-414; and Paul H. D. Kaplan, "The Earliest Images of *Othello,*" *Shakespeare Quarterly* 39 (1988): 171-188.

19. G. A. Starr discusses the character of Oroonoko—but not Imoinda—as it is developed within the discourse of sensibility ("Aphra Behn and the Genealogy of the Man of Feeling," *Modern Philology* 89 [1990]: 362-72), while J. R. Oldfield discusses some of the *Oroonoko* plays in light of growing abolitionist sympathies but does not pay particular attention to women or to women's races ("'The Ties of soft Humanity': Slavery and Race in British Drama," *Huntington Library Quarterly* 56 [1993]: 1-14).

20. J. Douglas Canfield discusses eighteenth-century drama in terms of these epistemic shifts, in which rhetorics of meritocracy and "neostoic exemplary morality mask[s] upper middle-class male dominance over gender, class, and even race." See his "Shifting Tropes of Ideology in English Serious Drama, Late Stuart to Early Georgian," *Cultural Readings of Restoration and Eighteenth-Century English Theater,* ed. J. Douglas Canfield and Deborah C. Payne (Athens: Univ. of Georgia Press, 1995), 196. In discussing a group of heroic tragedies with settings in New World slavery, I am not as surprised as Canfield is that bourgeois dominance dictates the ways in which race can be performed.

21. Aphra Behn, *'Oroonoko' and Other Works,* ed. Paul Salzman (Oxford: Oxford Univ. Press, 1994), 12. Hereafter cited parenthetically in the text by page number and abbreviated *O.*

22. On orientalism in *Oroonoko*'s descriptions of Imoinda, see Diane Roberts, *The Myth of Aunt Jemima: Representations of Race and Region* (London: Routledge, 1994), 15; on the place of the exotic in the narrative generally, see Moira Ferguson, "*Oroonoko:* Birth of a Paradigm," *New Literary History* 23 (1992): 347 (an earlier version of her discussion in *Subject To Others*); and Brown, "Romance of Empire," 44-45 and 51-52.

23. See, for example, Homi Bhabha, "Of Mimicry and Man: The Ambivalence of Colonial Discourse," *October* 28 (1984): 125-133. And yet Bhabha has also claimed that developing a psychological discussion about the positions of non-white women within colonialist discourse would require "a very specific form of attention and articulation" he is not yet able to summon ("The Other Question," *Screen* 24:6 [1983]: 18, n. 1). Gwen Bergner's "Who Is That Masked Woman? or, The Role of Gender in Fanon's *Black Skin, White Masks*" (*PMLA* 110 [1995]: 75-88) takes up Bhabha's proposal. Ann DuCille's "The Occult of True Womanhood: Critical Demeanor and Black Feminist Studies" (*Signs* 19 [1994]: 591-629) addresses the invisibility enforced on black women and black women's scholarship in the academy.

24. See especially Nussbaum's discussion of polygamy and Richardson's *Pamela,* in her *Torrid Zones,* 73-94.

25. The dedicatory poem to Francis Gentleman's revision (Glasgow, 1760) also implies a special connection between women in the audience and the fate of Oroonoko:

Ye CALEDONIAN Fair, in whom we find,
Each charm of person, and each grace of mind;
For virtue's sake, a feeble genius spare,
The cause of virtue's your peculiar care;
In you it lies to censure, or to save;
To your protection take the ROYAL SLAVE. (8).

The ladies of Edinburgh, where Gentleman's play was first performed, are not explicitly addressed as abolitionists, but, as designated champions of "virtue," they hold the power of life and death over the success of this sentimental heroic drama. The "royal Slave" will thrive or perish according to the degree of patronage the ladies extend to him, and to his author.

26. A similar racial displacement occurs in Gentleman's *Oroonoko,* where the slave rebellion is betrayed to the planters through the machinations of one Massingano, now a slave, who had been Oroonoko's enemy and rival in Africa. Gentleman's invention of Massingano's active scheming against Oroonoko works both to move slavery farther from the center of the plot—another African is as instrumental in causing the hero to lead the revolt as is Oroonoko's fear that Imoinda will be sexually abused by a white man—and to deny that race matters to slavery, since the black African Massingano is as malicious as the white lieutenant governor.

27. Sander Gilman suggests that nineteenth-century Parisians could achieve psychic access to the sexuality of their women only through the degraded and dismembered spectacle of a black woman's body ("Black Bodies, White Bodies: Toward an Iconography of Female Sexuality in Late Nineteenth Century Art, Medicine, and Literature," in *'Race,' Writing, and Difference,* ed. Henry Louis Gates, Jr. [Chicago: Univ. of Chicago Press, 1985], 223-61). Bell hooks notes that as valuable as Gilman's discussion is, it still cloaks the particular black woman in question—Sarah Bettman, the "Hottentot Venus"—in absence, since it neither includes, nor remarks on its omission of, her own thoughts on being exhibited (*Black Looks: Race and Representation* [Boston: South End Press, 1992], 62-64).

DEPICTIONS BY FORMER SLAVES

Bernard W. Bell (essay date 1977)

SOURCE: "African-American Writers," in *American Literature 1764-1789: The Revolutionary Years,* edited by Everett Emerson, The University of Wisconsin Press, 1977, pp. 171-93.

[*In the following essay, Bell discusses the careers of ex-slaves Jupiter Hammon, Phillis Wheatley, and Olaudah Equiano, which he claims demonstrate how a hostile white literate society fostered the "twoness" of early black identity in the United States.*]

Because of the distinctive history and acculturation of Africans in the English colonies during the revolutionary pe-riod, their literary gifts are most meaningfully assessed when viewed in the context of the tension between African-American attitudes toward integration and separatism on the one hand and the oral and literate cultural heritages on the other. Most modern historians accept the fact that American slaves were the descendants of peoples with a history and culture. Since culture is basically the symbolic and material resources developed in the process of interaction between the individual, his society, and his environment, it is neither acquired nor lost overnight, whether as the result of conditions imposed by the slave system or by the urban ghettoes. That the African slave's way of life did change radically with his introduction to a new environment and social system goes without saying. But the change was seldom rapid, never uniform, and generally accretive and syncretic rather than a sloughing off of Old World values and survival techniques with the adoption of New World values.

Too many students of American character and culture overlook the fact that the first blacks did not arrive in the colonies with a group identity as "neegars" but with specific African identities. The majority were Ibo, Ewe, Biafada, Bakongo, Wolof, Bambara, Ibibio, Serer, and Arada. Unlike the first white immigrants, they were the only involuntary servants brought to seventeenth-century Virginia in chains and systematically deprived of their Old World cultural heritage and social systems in order to transform them into better slaves. This development was the result of the interaction between slavery and racism, for the increasing demand for cheap labor led to political acts and a social ideology that severely restricted the rights of blacks. Prior to the end of the seventeenth-century free blacks in Virginia could acquire property, vote, and even intermarry with whites. But with the growth of slavery the black codes of the eighteenth century reduced them to a quasi-free lower caste. Christian principles prevented neither southerners nor northerners from arrogating to themselves supreme power over other human beings, yet in practice Africans in the non-slave-based economies of the North fared better than their southern brothers. Many colonial slaves and free blacks in New England, for example, were taught to read and write in order to make them better Christians and more efficient porters, clerks, and messengers. It is also important to remember that the names of such eighteenth-century organizations as the African Society (1787), the New York African Free School (1787), the African Mason Lodge (1787), and the African Methodist Episcopal Church (1794) established the first formal self-conscious group identity of free blacks as African.

While Egyptian, Ethiopian, and Arabic script were known in parts of Africa for centuries, eighteenth-century Africa was basically an oral culture. As Olaudah Equiano, the European-African abolitionist, tells us in his classic slave narrative, the spoken word, music, and dance were at the center of a communal, profoundly religious way of life. In contrast, industrialized Europe and England had moved beyond the oral stage and medieval thinking to a reverence for print and man. The literary tradition and its attendant values, especially reading and writing, were cherished as the exclusive heritage of civilized man. Until the twentieth century these two modes of perceiving, organizing, and communicating experience were believed by Europeans to be related to different stages of development of the mind. But as Claude Lévi Strauss notes, these alternative approaches are actually "two strategic levels at which nature is accessible to scientific enquiry: one roughly adapted to that of perception and imagination: the other at a remove from it . . . one very close to, and the other at a remove from sensible intuition." Each has its own advantages. While a literate orientation heralds the advancement of technology and abstract learning, an oral orientation reinforces the primacy of events and disciplined yet improvisational acts of a group nature. One culture conceives of man as the measure of all things; the other conceives of him as a deeply religious being, living in harmony with a mystical, organic universe.

By 1764 the institution of slavery had been established in the colonies for more than a hundred years, and by 1789 the compulsion of whites to remake blacks into harmless, civilized Christians was a matter of record. As Vernon Loggins observes, Cotton Mather's *Rules for the Societies of Negroes,* written in 1693, was typical of the general attitude of the Puritan and Anglican divines, whose interest in Christianizing blacks was to make them more honest, useful servants. Freedom in the form of manumission or a privileged status was the reward for those considered acceptably acculturated. The deprivation of educational, economic, and political opportunities for the majority of blacks, however, made cultural assimilation the prize of precious few. In addition, the process of adopting the dominant, racist Anglo-Saxon cultural pattern of the revolutionary period resulted in the ethnic double-consciousness that W. E. B. Du Bois eloquently described in *The Souls of Black Folk:* (1903) "it is a peculiar sensation, this double-consciousness, this sense of always looking at one's self through the eyes of others, of measuring one's soul by the tape of a world that looks on in amused contempt and pity. One ever feels his twoness,—an American, a Negro; two souls, two thoughts, two unreconciled strivings; two warring ideals in one dark body, whose dogged strength alone keeps it from being torn asunder." African-Americans were both people of African descent and nonpeople to the majority of whites; they were part of the society yet alienated from it; they were among the first colonists to build the nation, but the nation has yet to grant them first-class citizenship. African-Americans were therefore destined to function on two levels of reality, and their attitudes toward integration and separatism were largely determined by the degree of alienation from or faith in the principles of the dominant white Anglo-Saxon Protestant society.

Integration may be defined as the dual processes of cultural and social assimilation. While cultural assimilation during the revolutionary era involved essentially learning the English language, the Bible, the classics, the popular English and neoclassical writers, and colonial behavior patterns, social assimilation meant full participation in the organizations and institutions of the emerging nation. Fear for their physical and psychological security led white colonists to redefine Africans as a distinctive group of sub-humans who ought to be culturally but not socially assimilated, especially in southern colonies where their numbers were a cause of alarm. This was particularly true of Virginia where there were only 300 blacks in the mid-seventeenth century but 120,156 blacks and 173,316 whites by the mid-eighteenth. Consequently, in 1662 the colony imposed a fine for interracial fornication; in 1691 it banned interracial marriages; and in 1723 it deprived free blacks of the right to vote. In seventeenth-century New England, where the black population was never more than 20,000, blacks were excluded from the militia; nevertheless, from the French and Indian wars to the Battle of Bunker Hill slaves and free blacks alike took up arms in the struggle for American independence.

Although confrontations with British soldiers like that of Crispus Attucks, the fugitive slave and New England seaman who was among the five colonists killed in the Boston Massacre, may be interpreted as integrationist acts of patriotism, the early petitions of slaves for permission to purchase their freedom and to return to Africa have the ring of separatism. In truth, however, the major loyalty of colonial blacks was not so much to a place or a people as it was to the principle of freedom, the principle the white colonists themselves expressed in terms of the natural rights of man as they laid the philosophical foundation for their separation from England. At least three petitions from New England slaves in 1773 sounded a similar note. The first was in January to Governor Hutchinson and the general court from "many slaves, living in the Town of Boston, and other Towns in the Province . . . who have had every Day of their Lives imbittered with this most intollerable Reflection, That, let their Behavior be what it will, nor their Children to all Generations, shall ever be able to do, or to possess and enjoy any Thing, no not even *Life itself,* but in a Manner as the *Beasts that perish.* We have no Property! We have no Wives! No Children! We have no City! No Country. . . ." The second, a letter addressed to delegates to the House of Representatives by four slaves—Peter Bestes, Sambo Freeman, Felix Holbrook, and Chester Joie—"in behalf of our fellow slaves in this province and by order of their Committee," came in April. After expressing "a high degree of satisfaction" with the legislative efforts of the colony "to free themselves from slavery," the letter boldly asserts: "We expect great things from men who have made such a noble stand against the designs of their *fellow-men* to enslave them" and goes on to request "one day in a week to work for themselves, to enable them to earn money to purchase the residue of their time. . . ." Seeing no relief from degrading prejudice and discrimination in America, they were willing to submit to the law "until we leave the province . . . as soon as we can from our joynt labours procure money to transport ourselves to some part of the coast of Africa, where we propose a settlement." The third petition addressed to Governor Hutchinson arrived in June and echoes the sentiments of James Otis's 1764 protest in the

Rights of the British Colonies: "Your Petitioners appre-hend they have in common with other men a natural right to be free and without molestation to injoy such property as they may acquire by their industry, or by any other means not detrimental to their fellow men. . . ." None of these petitioners was granted relief by the courts, the legis-lature, or the governor.

Perhaps the most historically revealing petition for free-dom was dated May 25, 1774—less than a week before the British blockaded the Port of Boston in retaliation for the Boston Tea Party of December 1773—and addressed to Governor Thomas Gage and the General Court of Mas-sachusetts by "a Grate Number of Blacks of the Province . . . held in a state of Slavery within the bowels of a free and Christian Country." This moving document, which speaks volumes about the priority given by blacks to the forging of personal identities on the basis of their common condition and the evolving consciousness of a people in transition from an oral to a literate culture, reads:

> That your Petitioners apprehind we have in common with all other men a natural right to our freedoms with-out Being depriv'd of them by our fellow men we are a freeborn Pepel and have never forfeited this Blessing by aney compact or agreement whatever. But we were unjustly dragged by the cruel hand of power from our dearest frinds and sum of us stolen from the bosoms of our tender Parents and from a Populous Pleasant and plentiful country and Brought hither to be made slaves for Life in a Christian land. . . . How can the master be said to Beare my Borden when he Beares me down whith the Have chanes of Slavery and operson. . . . Nither can we reap an equal benefet from the laws of the Land which doth not justifi but condemns Slavery or if there had bin aney Law to hold us in Bondage we are Humbely of the Opinion ther never was aney to in-slave our children for life when Born in a free Country. We therefore Bage your Excellency and Honours will give this its deer weight and consideration and that you will accordingly cause an act of the legislative to be pessed that we may obtain our Natural right our free-doms and our children be set at lebety at the yeare of twenty one. . . .[1]

As in the past, the legislature voted to let the question "subside"—did they find the petition unintelligible? unac-ceptable? inexpedient?—but subside it did not.

Despite the scores of antislavery petitions by blacks—some in the eloquent prose of the period, others accept-able, all intelligible—Quakers, and other groups, the Founding Fathers chose political expediency over prin-ciple when they deleted all reference to slavery from the final draft of the Declaration of Independence. According to Jefferson, the condemnation of slavery was deleted in deference to the economic interests of Georgia and South Carolina, who argued for the continuation of the slave trade. To compound this fracture between principle and practice, between the emerging national belief in the in-alienable rights of man and colonial laws, between the an-tislavery, industrial North and the proslavery, agrarian

South, the Constitutional Convention of 1787 gave explicit sanction to slavery by providing that representation in Congress and taxes were to be determined by the numbers of free persons in each state "and excluding Indians not taxed, three fifths of all other persons." In addition, the slave trade was extended for twenty years and fugitive slaves were to be surrendered to their owners. If it is true that the fathers of the Constitution were dedicated to the principle of freedom, it is no less true, as John Hope Fran-klin points out in *From Slavery to Freedom,* that they were even more dedicated to the ethnocentric, socioeconomic proposition that "government should rest upon the domin-ion of property."

Although the antislavery movement was set back by the Three-fifths Compromise of the ruling class and its politi-cal repudiation of the natural rights of blacks, many African-Americans felt that the preamble to the Declara-tion of Independence still held out the promise of "Life, Liberty and the pursuit of Happiness" for them as well as whites. For them the Revolutionary War had been a struggle more for personal freedom than for political inde-pendence. And at the end of the war, hundreds of the 5,000 blacks who fought for the patriots were freed by the states even though some masters contested the promises of manu-mission. By 1790 there were nearly 4,000,000 whites and slightly more than 750,000 blacks in the United States. In the southern states there were 641,691 slaves and 32,048 free blacks. The mid-Atlantic states had approximately 36,000 slaves and 14,000 free blacks. In contrast, New England had only 3,700 slaves in a black population of more than 13,000. While Vermont and Massachusetts re-ported no slaves at all, Connecticut had 2,600. The only city able to boast no slaves was Boston. Her 761 blacks were free.

By virtue of his unique situation as a slave or quasifree person in a society that was growing painfully aware of its paradoxical role as the oppressed and the oppressor, the African-American writer's struggle for independence pro-vides a classic metaphor for the psychological and politi-cal schism of the new nation. Even more than the slave petitions for freedom, the writings of two African-Americans and a European-African reveal how individual processes of cultural and social assimilation in a basically hostile white Anglo-Saxon literate society fostered the twoness of early black identity. For Jupiter Hammon, Phil-lis Wheatley, and Olaudah Equiano, the necessity of func-tioning on two planes of reality was a challenge that each met in terms of his own unique situation and gifts.

I

In the case of Jupiter Hammon, we see the influence of the Bible and slavery in shaping an otherworldly view of lib-erty and equality that distorted his social vision. What little is known about his life is found in scraps of informa-tion in letters and in the poetry and prose itself. Born a slave on October 17, 1711, Hammon was owned by the Lloyds, a merchant family of Long Island. A dutiful, intelligent servant, he was apparently encouraged in his efforts to read and write by Henry Lloyd, his first master, for in one of his discourses he refers to the English divines, Burkitt and Beveridge, whose works were in Lloyd's library. In 1733 he purchased a Bible from his master for seven shillings and six pence, an indication of the depth of his religious commitment, his thriftiness, and the nature of his master's benevolence. Since he was well-read in the Bible and considered an exemplary slave, and since there were black and Indian churches on Long Island and in Connecticut during this era, it is highly possible that Hammon was a slave exhorter. In 1760 he became the first black American to publish a poem in the colonies. Apparently this distinction and the prestige it brought his owner contributed to the poet not being freed upon the elder Lloyd's death in 1763. Instead, he was inherited by Joseph, one of four sons. After Joseph's death during the Revolutionary War, the family retainer was passed on to John Lloyd, Jr., a grandson. With the British takeover of Long Island, the patriotic Lloyd family took their talented, faithful servant with them to Hartford, Connecticut, where he is believed to have died a slave around 1800, even though slavery was abolished in the state in 1784 and the Revolutionary War ended in 1783.

Hammon's first broadside poem was titled *An Evening Thought. Salvation by Christ, with Penetential Cries: Composed by Jupiter Hammon, a Negro belonging to Mr. Lloyd of Queen's Village, on Long Island, the 25th of December, 1760.* Lacking the originality, ironic tension, graphic imagery, and call and response pattern of black American spirituals, the poem reveals Hammon's personal resignation to slavery and the inspiration of the Psalms and Methodist hymnals:

> Lord, hear our penetential Cry:
>   Salvation from above;
> It is the Lord that doth supply,
>   With his redeeming Love.[2]

The repetition of "Salvation" in twenty-three of the poem's eighty-eight lines does not significantly elevate the prosaic quality of the verse. The next broadside was *An Address to Miss Phillis Wheatly, Ethiopian Poetess, in Boston, who came from Africa at eight years of age, and soon became acquainted with the gospel of Jesus Christ.* Published in Hartford on August 4, 1778, this twenty-one stanza poem celebrates the salvation of his more famous and youthful contemporary from "heathen" Africa:

> Thou hast left the heathen shore;
>   Through mercy of the Lord,
> Among the heathen live no more,
>   Come magnify thy God.
>   . . .
> Thou, Phillis, when thou hunger hast,
>   Or pantest for thy God,
> Jesus Christ is thy relief
>   Thou hast the holy word.

As usual, the poet reminds his reader that ultimate freedom and joy is not earthly but heavenly:

> While thousands muse with earthly toys,
>   And rage about the street,
> Dear Phillis, seek for heaven's joys,
>   Where we do hope to meet.

Contrary to the poet's view, Phillis Wheatley was more capable of coping with and giving poetic form to the two planes of reality than he. A third poem, *An Essay on the Ten Virgins,* was printed in 1779 and advertised in the *Connecticut Courant* on December 14, 1779, but no copy has been preserved. Hammon's unimaginative use of the meter, rhyme, diction, and stanzaic pattern of the Methodist hymnal combined with the negative image of Africa and conciliatory tone of these early poems reveal the poet's limitations and the costly sociopsychological price he paid for the mere semblance of cultural assimilation.

As his first published sermon indicates, Hammon was under fire from his black brothers and sisters for his otherworldly view of freedom. *A Winter Piece: Being a Serious Exhortation with a Call to the Unconverted: and a Short Contemplation on the Death of Jesus Christ,* published in Hartford in 1782, attempts to explain his ostensible betrayal of his people's struggle for freedom in this life:

> My dear Brethren, as it hath been reported that I had petitioned to the court of Hartford against freedom, I now solemnly declare that I never have said, nor done any thing, neither directly nor indirectly, to promote or to prevent freedom; but my answer hath always been I am a stranger here and I do not care to be concerned or to meddle with public affairs, and by this declaration I hope my friends will be satisfied, and all prejudice removed, Let us all strive to be united together in love, and to become new creatures. (p. 174[3])

The lessons of the Bible and slavery had taught him that for body and soul, black and white, individual and nation, freedom was God's alone to grant:

> Come my dear fellow servants and brothers, Africans by nation, we are all invited to come, Acts x, 34. Then Peter opened his mouth and said, of a truth I perceive that God is no respecter of persons, verse 35. But in every nation he that feareth him is accepted of him. My Brethren, many of us are seeking a temporal freedom, and I wish you may obtain it; remember that all power in heaven and earth belongs to God; if we are slaves it is by the permission of God, if we are free it must be by the power of the most high God. Stand still and see the salvation of God, cannot that same power that divided the waters from the waters for the children of Israel to pass through, make way for your freedom. (p. 175)

Hammon's reference to himself and his people as "Africans by nation" reflects his awareness of the duality of his identity, a duality he unfortunately sought to transcend rather than synthesize through religiosity. Appended to the sermon is the seventeen quatrain "Poem for Children with Thoughts of Death" as further testimony to the poet's piety.

The sermon and poem believed to have been written soon after *A Winter Piece* contain references to "the Present

War." In *An Evening's Improvement. Shewing the Necessity of beholding the Lamb of God . . .* Hammon is true to his apolitical, religious philosophy of life:

> And now my brethren, I am to remind you of a most melancholy scene of Providence; it hath pleased the most high God, in his wise providence, to permit a cruel and unnatural war to be commenced. . . . Have we not great cause to think this is the just deserving of our sins. . . . Here we see that we ought to pray, that God may hasten the time when the people shall beat their swords into a ploughshares and their spears into pruning-hooks, and nations shall learn war no more. (pp. 175-76)

And in the second half of "A Dialogue Intitled the Kind Master and the Dutiful Servant," the two-page poem concluding the sermon, the poet stands above the battle praying for peace:

> Servant
> Dear Master, now it is a time,
>   A time for great distress;
> We'll follow after things divine,
>   And pray for happiness.
> Master
> Then will the happy day appear,
>   That virtue shall increase;
> Lay up the sword and drop the spear,
>   And Nations seek for peace.

Banal, bloodless, unoriginal, and nonracial, these lines on Christian virtue tell us as much about the theology whites imposed on colonial blacks as they do about Hammon's warped sense of identity and poetry.

The most decisive evidence of the poet-preacher's exploitation by those who found his religious convictions a model for African-American character and behavior is found in Hammon's final discourse, *An Address to the Negroes of the State of New York*. Dedicated to the African Society of New York in 1786, the *Address* was published two years after slavery was outlawed in the state and a year before it became the eleventh state to ratify the Constitution. Since Hammon was seventy-six at the time, he sincerely intended this discourse to be the "last . . . dying advice, of an old man." With an uncommon if not unnatural faith in God and white people, whose sinful habits, he believed, did not in God's eyes and his own condone the slaves', Hammon preaches against the sins of disobedience, stealing, lying, swearing, and idleness. Consciousness of the irony of his people's oppression by those who had waged a costly and bloody war to end their own oppression is expressed but quickly suppressed by personal resignation to slavery and otherworldliness:

> Now I acknowledge that liberty is a great thing, and worth seeking for, if we can get it honestly, and by our good conduct prevail on our masters to set us free. Though for my own part I do not wish to be free: yet I should be glad, if others, especially the young negroes were to be free, for many of us who are grown up slaves, and have always had masters to take care of us,

should hardly know how to take care of ourselves; and it may be more for our own comfort to remain as we are. That liberty is a great thing we may know from our own feelings, and we may likewise judge so from the conduct of the white people, in the late war. How much money has been spent, and how many lives have been lost to defend their liberty. I must say that I have hoped that God would open their eyes, when they were so much engaged for liberty, to think of the state of the poor blacks and to pity us. . . . But this, my dear brethren, is by no means, the greatest thing we have to be concerned about. Getting our liberty in this world is nothing to having the liberty of the children of God.[4]

Jupiter Hammon's importance as a poet is essentially historical and sociological, for his blind faith in the benevolence of whites and the kingdom of heaven is a vivid illustration of the ambiguous political role of too many early African-American integrationist writers and preachers whose double-consciousness was both a blessing and a curse in the struggle of blacks for independence.

II

In contrast to Jupiter Hammon, several eighteenth-century black ministers asserted their right to be free of prejudice and to run their own affairs by breaking off from the established white churches and organizing their own separate institutions. Although the dates and themes of their miscellaneous writings do not fall within the scope of this book, their struggle for freedom of worship paradoxically has much in common with one of the ultimate goals of the Revolution. David George, a slave, started the first black Baptist church among the slaves in the colonies in Silver Bluff, South Carolina, between 1773 and 1775. In 1788 Andrew Bryan, another slave exhorter whose master encouraged his preaching because he believed it had a salutary influence on other slaves, established the First African Baptist Church in Savannah, Georgia. But the most celebrated black church fathers are ex-slaves Richard Allen and Absalom Jones. Dragged from their knees while praying in St. George's Methodist Episcopal Church of Philadelphia, these two ministers and the other blacks attending service "all went out of the church in a body, and they were no more plagued with us in the church." In Reverend Allen's words, "we were determined to seek out for ourselves, the Lord being our helper." Thus in 1794 Allen founded the Bethel African Methodist Episcopal Church and fought for many years to protect his church and congregation from the hostility of white Methodist preachers and trustees. During the same year Jones, who had earlier accepted an Episcopalian pastorate, dedicated the St. Thomas African Episcopal Church of Philadelphia. Less assertive but no less pious nor significant is Phillis Wheatley.

As the first slave and second woman writer in America to publish a book of poems, Phillis Wheatley's literary achievement was considered an extraordinary development on both sides of the Atlantic. To many of her contemporaries her poetry was indisputable evidence of the mental equality of blacks. But Moses Coit Tyler's observation in

The Literary History of the American Revolution (1897) that "her career belongs rather to the domain of anthropology, or of hagiology, than to that of poetry—whether American or African" is more useful as an example of the tenacity of eighteenth-century prejudices and the limitations of nineteenth-century American scholarship than as a just assessment of the literary gifts of "Afric's muse," as she calls herself in "Hymn to Humanity." Like Jefferson, Tyler believed her poetry "below the dignity of criticism." But as Julian Mason, Jr., rightly observes in the authoritative edition of the poet's complete works: "Her poems are certainly as good or better than those of most of the poets usually included and afforded fair treatment in a discussion of American poetry before 1800, and this same evaluation holds true when she is compared with most of the minor English poets of the eighteenth century who wrote in the neoclassical tradition."

A frail, precocious African child of seven, Phillis Wheatley was brought to Boston on a slave ship from Senegambia, the territory known in modern Africa as Senegal and Gambia, in 1761. She was purchased by John Wheatley, a prosperous tailor and owner of several household slaves, as a special servant for his wife, Suzanna Wheatley. The Wheatleys were dedicated to missionary work among Indians and blacks; their home was a well-known meeting place for Boston's cultured society. Once Mrs. Wheatley and her daughter Mary discovered Phillis Wheatley's quickness of mind, their humanitarian impulse to provide her with the proper cultivation was irresistible. In a letter to her London publisher in 1772, Mr. Wheatley wrote: "Without any assistance from School Education, and by only what she was taught in the Family, she, in sixteen Months Time from her Arrival, attained the English Language. to which she was an utter stranger before, to such a Degree, as to read any, the most difficult parts of the Sacred Writings, to the great Astonishment of all who heard her." Thanks mainly to Mary Wheatley's teaching, as Benjamin Brawley points out in *The Negro in Literature and Art,* Wheatley soon learned "a little astronomy, some ancient and modern geography, a little ancient history, a fair knowledge of the Bible, and a thoroughly appreciative acquaintance with the most important Latin classics, especially the works of Virgil and Ovid." She took pride in Terence's African heritage, became proficient in grammar, and favored Pope's translations of Homer among the English classics. Mrs. Wheatley's favorite, the young poet was not allowed to associate with the other domestics nor do hard work. Her memory of Africa was vague, and her only recollection of her mother was that she poured out water before the rising sun. Gradually her frail health and literary genius earned her privileged treatment as a companion to her mistress and an adopted member of the family. "I was treated by her more like her child then her servant," Wheatley wrote in 1774 to her African friend, Obour Tanner; "no opportunity was left unimproved of giving me the best of advice; but in terms how tender! how engaging!"

Eager to write, "she learnt in so short a Time, that in the Year 1765, she wrote a Letter to the Rev. Mr. Occum, the Indian Minister," who later published a hymnal for his people. In 1767, when she was only only fourteen, Wheatley wrote her first poem, "To the University of Cambridge, in New England," in blank verse. Bearing witness to the success of Mrs. Wheatley's missionary efforts, the first stanza of the original manuscript reads:

> While an intrinsic ardor bids me write
> The muse doth promise to assist my pen.
> 'Twas but e'en now I left my native shore
> The sable Land of error's darkest night.
> There, sacred Nine! for you no place was found.
> Parent of mercy, 'twas thy Powerful hand
> Brought me in safety from the dark abode.[5]

With the restrained moral fervor of a young New England convert, she admonishes the Harvard students:

> Let hateful vice so baneful to the Soul,
> Be still avoided with becoming care;
> Suppress the sable monster in its growth,
> Ye blooming plants of human race, divine
> An Ethiop tells you, tis your greatest foe
> Its transient sweetness turns to endless pain,
> And bring eternal ruin on the Soul.

Six years later in the first edition of her work, she significantly revised the poem, compressing it from thirty-two to thirty lines, and changing "The sable Land of error's darkest night" to "The land of errors, and *Egyptian* gloom" and "the sable monster" to "the deadly serpent." Unlike Jupiter Hammon, maturity, success, and travel brought increasing artistic and ethnic pride to the young black woman who became a kind of poet laureate for what was then the literary capital of America.

Between 1768 and 1769 the young poet wrote at least three more poems. The first, "To the King's Most Excellent Majesty. 1768," praises King George III for his last favor to the colonies, the repeal of the Stamp Act, and wishes him God's blessings so that he may give further evidence to "his subjects" of his concern for peace and freedom. The second, "On the Death of the Rev. Dr. Sewell, 1769," was the first of several occasional poems celebrating or lamenting the birth or death of Boston's elite. The Reverend Doctor Joseph Sewall (son of Chief Justice Samuel Sewall, who was both presiding judge at the Salem witch trials and the author of the first New England antislavery tract) was pastor for fifty-six years at Boston's famous old South Church where Wheatley became the first of her race to be baptized in 1771. The third poem, "On Being Brought from Africa to America," is the earliest effort of the fifteen-year-old poet to come to grips with the dual nature of her identity. Her shortest poem, it reads:

> 'Twas mercy brought me from my *Pagan* land,
> Taught my benighted soul to understand
> That there's a God, that there's a *Saviour* too:
> Once I redemption neither sought nor knew.
> Some view our sable race with scornful eye,
> "Their colour is a diabolic die."

Remember, *Christians, Negroes,* black as *Cain,*
May be refin'd, and join th' angelic train.

As in the original poem to the Harvard students, the poet accepts the social prejudices and religious mythology of the revolutionary period and considers herself fortunate to have been redeemed by Christ and "refin'd" by the Wheatleys. At the same time, the closing couplet boldly and ingeniously reminds Christians who look on her people with "scornful eye" that it is their duty to cultivate the moral and intellectual capacities of "Negroes" so that they, too, may enjoy spiritual if not social equality. Circulated among the Wheatleys and their friends, these poems soon won a local reputation for the young poet. "The Wheatleys had adopted her," writes J. Saunders Redding in *To Make A Poet Black,* (1939) "but she had adopted their terrific New England conscience."

From her first appearance in print with the elegy *An Elegaic Poem, on George Whitfield* (1770) to the London publication of her first edition of *Poems on Various Subjects, Religious and Moral* in 1773, Wheatley became the object of curiosity and admiration. Her poems and her person were used as evidence in the debate over the intellectual equality of blacks. Reprinted in Boston, Newport, New York, Philadelphia, and England, the elegiac broadside, addressed primarily to the Countess of Huntingdon, philanthropist and Whitefield's patron, immediately extended the poet's reputation. The lines "Great Countess, we Americans revere / Thy name, and mingle in thy grief sincere" allude to the Countess of Huntingdon's philanthropic work and the poet's sense of identity as an American. But her silence about the Boston Massacre, especially the death of the fugitive slave Crispus Attucks, which occurred a few blocks from the Wheatley house in the same year as Whitefield's death, is curious. The circumstances of her privileged position in the Wheatley household seem to have vitiated the poet's sense of ethnic and national identity.

In Boston Wheatley was frequently invited to the homes of people in Mrs. Wheatley's social and missionary circle, where she was regarded with "peculiar interest and esteem." Her trip to England with Nathaniel Wheatley in May 1773, we now know from the recent discovery of new letters by the poet, was not merely for reasons of health but also for an introduction to British missionary circles during a politically volatile time. For in April Parliament had passed the Tea Act and sparked yet another chain of events destined to culminate in the Revolution. Against this backdrop, Wheatley's new admirer and patron, Selina, Countess of Huntingdon, to whom the poet's first edition was dedicated, introduced her to British society, where her exceptional talent and tact as a conversationalist apparently steered her clear of political subjects and won her praise and presents, including a copy of the 1770 Glasgow folio edition of *Paradise Lost* from the lord mayor of London. Mrs. Wheatley's illness and request for her prevented the poet from accepting an invitation to stay in England for presentation at the court of George III. In October Wheatley, little improved in health but much in reputation, was back in Boston. Before she left London, however, she participated in arrangements for the publication of her first volume of poetry.

The first edition of *Poems on Various Subjects, Religious and Moral* contains Wheatley's best poetry. Critics have noted the influence of English writers on her poetry, especially the debt to Milton for "An Hymn to the Morning" and "An Hymn to the Evening," to Gray for the Whitefield elegy, and to Addison and Watts for "Ode to Neptune" and "Hymn to Humanity." But the greatest influence on the volume of thirty-nine poems was religion and neoclassicism. Her Christian convictions and the influence of the Bible are most clearly seen in the inventive use of biblical narrative in "Goliath of Gath," one of her longest poems, and "Isaiah lxiii. 1-8." In the tradition of New England colonial writers, she freely embellishes the biblical account of David and Goliath—a convention that became even more distinctively employed in the African-American tradition. She casts the poems, however, in the neoclassical mode of iambic pentameter couplets, invocation to the muse, elevated language, classical allusions, and panoramic scope. Here—particularly in her precision of meter, use of heroic couplet, and stilted diction—her models were Alexander Pope and the Latin writers themselves. The mixture of Christian and classical references in *Poems on Various Subjects* impressed some of her contemporaries with her genius and acculturation. Others were more fascinated by her youth, sex, race, or class.

Wheatley was certainly aware of the twoness of her identity and reception. Her pride in and exploitation of her African identity is apparent in the reference to Terence in "To Maecenas" and in her self-image in several poems as "Ethiop," "Afric's muse," and "vent'rous Afric." The degree to which she is also conscious of the larger society's Manichean image of Africa and her descendants is obvious in "On Being Brought from Africa to America," "To the University of Cambridge, in New England," and "To the Right Honourable William, Earl of Dartmouth, His Majesty's Principal Secretary of State for North America, etc." In the last poem, written in 1772 upon the Earl of Dartmouth's appointment, with the hope of encouraging him to use his new power to support the colonies' struggle for freedom, we see the skillful manner in which the nineteen-year-old poet gives poetic form to her double vision:

> Should you, my lord, while you peruse my song
> Wonder from whence my love of *Freedom* sprung,
> Whence flow these wishes for the common good,
> By feeling hearts alone best understood,
> I, young in life, by seeming cruel fate
> Was snatch'd from *Afric's* fancy'd happy seat:
> What pangs excruciating must molest,
> What sorrows labour in my parent's breast?
> Steel'd was that soul and by no misery mov'd
> That from a father seiz'd his babe belov'd:
> Such, such my case. And can I then but pray
> Others may never feel tyrannic sway?

Wheatley, as these lines indicate, was more conscious of her African heritage and sophisticated in her craftsmanship than Jupiter Hammon, but her religious indoctrination and unique status in the Wheatley family dictated against the expression of more positive, unequivocal sentiments about her African past.

The poet's visit to England was the high point in her brief career and a test of her piety. In London she was received as a "most surprising genius," but a very important friend of the American missionary movement, John Thornton, believed such praise a worldly snare and cautioned her against pride in her intellectual gifts. Thornton, merchant, philanthropist, and Calvinistic Anglican, and the Countess of Huntingdon, who as the patron of John Marrant, another colonial black writer, persuaded him in 1785 to go to Nova Scotia as a missionary, supported Eleazer Wheelock's Indian Charity School in New Hampsire. Both philanthropists, we learn from a recent critic, kept in close contact with the Wheatleys, who "disbursed the funds Thornton donated to Indian missionary work, posted him on its progress, and sent their son to him for improvement." Thornton was particularly interested in hearing about the progress of Wheelock's famous pupil, the Monhegan Indian preacher Samson Occom. It was to Occom, of course, that eleven-year-old Phillis wrote her first letter. Occom and Thornton both considered the young poet a potential missionary and encouraged her to become "a Female Preacher to her kindred." But in writing to Thornton in 1774 she respectfully declined this role, considering it "too hazardous" and herself "not sufficiently Eligible." Moreover, she did not want to leave her "British & American Friends" and confessed that she was no longer an African but an African-American: "how like a Barbarian should I look to the Natives; I can promise that my tongue shall be quiet for a strong reason indeed being an utter stranger to the Language of Anamaboe . . ." In this manner the poet tactfully responded to Thornton's view that "silent wonder and adoration of the wisdom and goodness of God" more becomes faith than does the ability to "talk excellently of divine things, even so as to raise the admiration of others." In the same letter the poet informs Thornton of Mr. Wheatley's "generous behaviour in granting me my freedom . . . about 3 months before the death of my dear mistress & at her desire, as well as his own humanity. . . ."

Mrs. Wheatley's death on March 3, 1774, and Wheatley's personal hardships over the next decade were to test her faith even more. Writing to her friend Obour Tanner on March 21, she expresses the depth of the loss of her best friend: "I have lately met with a great trial in the death of my mistress; let us imagine the loss of a parent, sister or brother, the tenderness of all were united in her." Despite this loss, the poet continues to invoke her muse for occasional poems such as the 1775 encomium "To His Excellency General Washington." Washington was so pleased by the poem that he invited Wheatley to visit him at Cambridge, an invitation she gladly accepted in 1776. In that poem, *Liberty and Peace,* and "On the Capture of General Lee," the poet coined the term *Columbia* to refer to America. With the death of Mr. Wheatley on March 12,

1778, the family household broke up, and the next month Wheatley married John Peters. Legend has it that her husband was a respectable but excessively proud black man who tried his hand as a baker, grocer, doctor, and lawyer without much success. The marriage resulted in estrangement from her former white friends and a life of poverty. Yet on October 30, 1779, the *Evening Post and General Advertiser* outlined her "Proposals" for publishing by subscription a new volume of "Poems & Letters on various subjects, dedicated to the Right Hon. Benjamin Franklin Esq: One of the Ambassadors of the United States at the Court of France." Since the treaty ending the war was not signed until 1783, she was unable to secure enough subscribers and the book was not published. Misfortunes began to multiply. Her husband was jailed for debt; two of her children died between 1783 and 1784; and she was reduced to working in a cheap lodging house. On December 5, 1784, Phillis Peters died and was buried with her third child, who had died soon after his mother. Her husband disappeared with the unpublished manuscript of her second book. Two years later her first and only book was republished in America.

A vivid example of cultural and ethnic divisions during the revolutionary era is the manner in which Wheatley's genius and poetic talents were praised in the beginning by General Washington in 1776 and dismissed at the end by Thomas Jefferson in 1784. In different degrees and under different circumstances, both Washington and Jefferson were Virginia slaveholders who believed that slavery ought to be abolished by law; that blacks were inferior to whites; and that blacks and whites should be separated. Of the two, however, Jefferson seems to have held the stronger convictions. In response to the letter and poem sent to him by the poet, Washington wrote to "Miss Phillis":

> I thank you most sincerely for your polite notice of me in the elegant lines you enclosed; and however undeserving I may be of such encomium and panegyric, the style and manner exhibit a striking proof of your poetical talents; in honor of which, and as a tribute justly due you, I would have published the poem, had I not been apprehensive that, while I only meant to give the world this new instance of your genius, I might have incurred the imputation of vanity. This, and nothing else, determined me not to give it a place in the public prints.
>
> If you ever come to Cambridge, or near head-quarters, I shall be happy to see a person so favored by the Muses, and to who nature has been so liberal and beneficient in her dispensations.[6]

The sincerity of these sentiments take on a different color in the light of a letter written a few weeks earlier to his former secretary in which Washington says: "I recollect nothing else worth giving you the trouble of, unless you can be amused by reading a letter and poem addressed to me by Miss Phillis Wheatley." In contrast to Washington's amused benevolence, Jefferson's "suspicion" that "the blacks are inferior to the whites in the endowments both of body and mind" sounds more like a conviction when we read the following remarks in *Notes on Virginia:*

Misery is often the parent of the most affecting touches in poetry. Among the blacks is misery enough, God knows, but no poetry. Love is the peculiar oestrum of the poet. Their love is ardent, but it kindles the senses only, not the imagination. Religion, indeed, has produced a Phillis Whately; but it could not produce a poet. The compositions published under her name are below the dignity of criticism. The heroes of the Dunciad are to her, as Hercules to the author of that poem.[7]

No African-American writer during the revolutionary period was more integrated in her society than Wheatley, yet when she was not the object of paternalistic indulgence from admirers, she was the object of intellectual derision for detractors. In either case, the genius and piety that inform her double-consciousness and love of liberty commanded the attention of the age and the ages to follow.

III

Five years after Phillis Wheatley's death, Olaudah Equiano published in London *The Interesting Narrative of the Life of Olaudah Equiano, or Gustavus Vassa, the African* and became the new celebrated black writer of the period. While Wheatley's memories of Africa were vague and essentially religious, those of Equiano are unquestionably the earliest, most detailed description of the nature of bondage and freedom in Africa, the Caribbean, and colonial America from a black perspective. The *Narrative* is the first major slave narrative, a genre that became popular during the abolition movement of the nineteenth century and remains a literary testament to the will of an oppressed people to be free. Completed in 1788, it was first published in America in 1791 and by 1794 had gone into its eighth edition in London.

Neither a black American nor a black Englishmen, Equiano was born in 1745, spent his early childhood in Benin, now a part of southern Nigeria, and his mature years in antislavery work in England. But, as Arna Bontemps notes, his slavery in Virginia and years in the service of a Philadelphia Quaker merchant, who saw to his education and put him to work on small trading vessels in the Caribbean, were the years that shaped his consciousness and provided the frame of reference for his *Narrative*. In addition, bibliophiles and students of American cultural history generally consider Equiano's *Narrative* the most influential of the eighteenth-century black autobiographies. Two others are Briton Hammon's fourteen-page *A Narrative of the Uncommon Sufferings and Surprising Deliverance of Briton Hammon, a Negro Man,* published in Boston in 1760, and John Marrant's more popular *A Narrative of the Lord's Wonderful Dealings with J. Marrant . . . Taken Down from His Own Relation,* published in London in 1785.

Living in the fertile province of "Essaka," some distance from the capital of Benin and the sea, Equiano "had never heard of white men or Europeans, nor of the sea; and our subjection to the king of Benin was little more than nominal, for every transaction of the government . . . was conducted by the chief of elders." His father was an elder who with other "chief men, decided disputes and punished crimes." In most cases, the trial was short and "the law of retaliation prevailed."

The youngest and favorite of seven children, Equiano lived for his first eleven years in a collective, agrarian, religious society whose basic modes of expression were oral. "We are almost a nation of dancers, musicians and poets," he says. "Thus every great event such as a triumphant return from battle or other cause of public rejoicing is celebrated in public dances, which are accompanied with songs and music suited to the occasion." To improve the blessing of an uncommonly rich and fruitful land, agriculture was his people's chief industry; "and everyone, even the children and women are engaged in it. . . . Everyone contributes something to the common stock; and, as we are unacquainted with idleness, we have no beggars." As for religion, Equiano—revealing his European acculturation by assuming a third person voice—writes:

> the natives believe that there is one Creator of all things, and that he lives in the sun, and is girted round with a belt; that he may never eat or drink, but, according to some, he smokes a pipe, which is our own favorite luxury. They believe he governs events, especially our deaths or captivity; but, as for the doctrine of eternity, I do not remember to have ever heard of it; some, however, believe in the transmigration of souls in a certain degree. Those spirits which were not transmigrated, such as their dear friends or relations, they believe always attend them, and guard them from the bad spirits of their foes. For this reason they always, before eating as I have observed, put some small portion of the meat, and pour some of their drink, on the ground for them; and they often make oblations of the blood of beasts or fowls at their graves. (pp. 12-13[8])

In contrast to Phillis Wheatley, Christianity altered but by no means destroyed Equiano's respect for the holistic culture and tribal religion of his people and their reverence for priests, magicians, and wise men.

Despite obvious differences in color and culture between Europeans and Africans, Equiano does not accept the absurd correlations between the color of one's skin and the content of one's mind that characterizes Thomas Jefferson's *Notes on Virginia.* "Are there not causes enough to which the apparent inferiority of an African may be ascribed," Equiano observes, "without limiting the goodness of God, and supposing he forebore to stamp understanding on certainly his own image, because 'carved in ebony.' Might it not naturally be ascribed to their situation. . . . Does not slavery itself depress the mind, and extinguish all its fire and every noble sentiment. . . . Let the polished and haughty European recollect that his ancestors were once, like the Africans, uncivilized, and even barbarous. Did Nature make *them* inferior to their sons? and should *they too* have been made slaves?" In short, inferiority to an acculturated yet proud African writer of the eighteenth century was not an innate, racial constant for nonwhites but the result of different historical and social circumstances.

Regarding slavery in Africa, he confesses that sometimes his nation sold slaves to traders, "but they were only prisoners of war, or such among us as had been convicted of kidnapping, or adultery, and some other crimes which we esteemed heinous." Although his nation and family kept slaves, the difference between the system of slavery in Africa and the New World was crucial:

> With us, they do no more work than other members of the community, even their master; their food, clothing, and lodging were nearly the same as theirs (except that they were not permitted to eat with those who were free-born); and there was scarce any other difference between them, than a superior degree of importance which the head of a family possesses in our state, and that authority which, as such, he exercises over every part of his household. Some of these slaves have even slaves under them as their own property, and for their own use. (p. 12)

When he was eleven, Olaudah Equiano and his sister were kidnapped by native traders, and during his manhood he saw first-hand the difference in slavery in Africa, America, and the Caribbean.

After the wonder of seeing the sea for the first time and the mysterious movement of slave ships as well as the terrors of the middle passage and the dread that "we should be eaten by these ugly men," the narrator was sold to a Virginia planter. He received his most indelible impression of the treatment of slaves in Virginia when he was called to his master's house to fan him and saw a black woman cooking with an iron muzzle locked on her head so that she could neither speak, eat, nor drink. Equiano was sold after "some time" to the captain of a merchant ship and lieutenant in the royal navy, who renamed him Gustavus Vassa and took him to England. In two or three years he not only spoke English and felt "quite easy with these new country-men, but relished their society and manners. I no longer looked upon them as spirits, but as men superior to us; and therefore I had the stronger desire to resemble them, to imbibe their spirit, and imitate their manners." The next step in adopting his new culture was to persuade his mistress in 1759 to have him baptized. He did not become "a first-rate Christian" and missionary, however, until much later after he had searched in vain for the key to salvation among the Quakers, the Roman Catholics, the Jews, and the Turks. He ultimately found the key in Methodism and sought unsuccessfully to be ordained for missionary work "among his countrymen" in Africa.

In 1763 he was sold to Robert King, a Quaker merchant in the West Indies. While working on his master's boats, Equiano witnessed the general practice of white men brutally raping female slaves, including "females not ten years old." He also observed how the system of absentee landlords left many island estates in the hands of managerial incompetents and human butchers. As in America, the Caribbean had its instruments of torture. "The iron muzzle, thumb-screws, &c., are so well known as not to need a description, and were sometimes applied for the slightest

faults." The inhumanity of slavery made him "determined to make every exertion to obtain my freedom and to return to Old England."

In 1766 while the colonists were stiffening their resistance to the Stamp Act, Equiano finally accumulated enough money by trading goods to buy his freedom from King but agreed to continue working for him as a free "ablebodied sailor at thirty-six shillings per month." In this capacity he made several trips to America and experienced the precarious existence of a free black in the colonies. In Savannah, Georgia, for instance, he was severely beaten one night and left for dead by white men. The next morning he was carted off to jail. A similar fate occurred to a free black carpenter he knew, "who, for asking a gentleman that he worked for for the money he had earned, was put into gaol; and afterwards this oppressed man was sent from Georgia, with false accusations, of an intention to set the gentleman's house on fire, and run away with his slaves." On another occasion only his intelligence, facility in English, and independent spirit prevented his kidnapping by "white ruffians." As a free, acculturated black (he became a hairdresser, played the French horn, and went to night school), Equiano was a restless man who continued to respond to the call of the sea and different cultures: Madeira, Jamaica, Barbados, Smyrna, Genoa, Portugal, Spain, Honduras, and Nicaragua. In the 1780s he became London's most celebrated black abolitionist, culminating his fight against oppression with the first publication of the *Narrative* in 1789, the same year that George Washington was inaugurated first president of the United States. Until his death on April 31, 1797, Olaudah Equiano's vision of himself and the world was that of a European-African Christian convert.

IV

In the beginning of *A History of American Literature* (1878), Moses Coit Tyler writes: "The American people, starting into life in the early part of the seventeenth century, have been busy ever since in recording their intellectual history in laws, manners, institutions, in battles with man and beast and nature, in highways, excavations, edifices, in pictures, in statues, in written words. It is in written words that this people, from the very beginning, have made the most confidential and explicit record of their minds." In contrast, as descendants of Africa and bearers of the legacy of an oral tradition, black petitioners for freedom, Jupiter Hammon, Phillis Wheatley, and Olaudah Equiano were more attuned to the power of the spoken word and the wonder of man as a child of God. Confronted by the paradox of their situation as slaves in a largely white Anglo-Saxon Protestant society that had waged a war to realize its belief in the equality and inalienable rights of man, colonial African-American writers, with the exception of Hammon, were more interested in struggling for physical and spiritual freedom than political and economic independence. Their introduction to the written word was primarily to make them better servants, yet they used their acquired knowledge of reading and writing to solicit the good will of the larger white society. Since it was the Bible that served as the principal tool of cultural assimilation and the Protestant church that allowed partial social assimilation, the most striking quality of the writings of African-Americans between 1764 and 1789 is their Christian piety, faith in the philosophy of natural rights as expressed in the Declaration of Independence, and dual vision of the writers themselves as African-Americans.

In the colonial African-American writer's efforts to resolve his double-consciousness and attain recognition of his freedom and human rights, he did not, as many black writers of the 1960s sought to do, voluntarily seek to reject either aspect of his identity. In the words of Du Bois, "he would not Africanize America, for America has too much to teach the world and Africa. He would not bleach his Negro soul in a flood of white Americanism, for he knows that Negro blood has a message for the world." He wanted simply "to make it possible for a man to be both a Negro and an American, without being cursed and spit upon by his fellows, without having the doors of Opportunity closed roughly in his face." Of early white American writings, Tyler says: "Literature as a fine art, literature as the voice and the ministress of aesthetic delight, they had perhaps little regard for; but literature as an instrument of humane and immediate utility, they honored, and at this wrought with all the earnestness that was born in their blood." No less is true of the writings of early black Americans.

Notes

1. Herbert Aptheker, ed., *A Documentary History of the Negro People in the United States*, pp. 7-9.

2. Quotations are from Oscar Wegelin's edition of *Jupiter Hammon, American Negro Poet.*

3. Unless otherwise noted, quotations from Hammon's prose are from Sidney Kaplan's *The Black Presence in the Era of the American Revolution.*

4. William H. Robinson, Jr., ed., *Early Black American Prose*, p. 42.

5. Quotations from Phillis Wheatley are from Julian D. Mason, Jr.'s, edition of *The Poems of Phillis Wheatley.*

6. George Washington, *Writings,* ed. John C. Fitzpatrick, 39 vols. (Washington, D.C.: U.S. Government Printing Office, 1931-44) 4: 360-61.

7. Thomas Jefferson, *Notes on the State of Virginia,* ed. William Peden (Chapel Hill: University of North Carolina Press, 1955), p. 140.

8. Quotations are from Arna Bontemps's edition of Equiano's *Narrative* in *Great Slave Narratives.*

Wilfred D. Samuels (essay date 1985)

SOURCE: "Disguised Voice in *The Interesting Narrative of Olaudah Equiano, or Gustavus Vassa, the African,*" in *Black American Literature Forum,* Vol. 19, No. 2, Summer 1985, pp. 64-9.

[*In the following essay, Samuels contends that Olaudah Equiano's intention in his* Narrative, *which is to point out the miseries of the slave trade, is enhanced by the use of a disguised voice, through which the author takes control of his audience and holds their attention, outwitting and flattering his white readers while simultaneously revealing that they are unscrupulous and uncaring.*]

I.

The author of the slave narrative confronted the difficult task of reporting his lived experiences during slavery to an audience which did not recognize him as a member of its society and, in fact, viewed him "as an alien whose assertion of common humanity and civil rights conflicted with some of its basic beliefs," including the institutionalization of theories of the racial superiority of whites and the inferiority of African slaves.[1] This difficulty was further compounded in certain cases by the former slave, who addressed the question of abolishing slavery, an institution to which members of his audience were often inextricably bound, because, economically speaking, their prosperity was ensured by the slave trade. Consequently, although the narrator often sought, on the one hand, to garner support and sympathy for the abolition of slavery, he recognized, on the other hand, that the very act of writing his narrative or the simplest error on his part could not only be viewed as insolence, but could alienate the very audience that he needed if he were to accomplish his goal.

The already difficult task of not alienating the audience became especially complex for Olaudah Equiano, an Ibo who, after being kidnapped at age eleven and experiencing ten years of slavery, published his two-volume narrative *The Interesting Narrative of the Life of Olaudah Equiano, or Gustavus Vassa, the African, Written by Himself* in 1789.[2] To be sure, the condescending tone of the review which appeared in *The Gentleman's Magazine* reveals the dilemma of the slave narrator in general and specifically of Equiano. According to the reviewer, "These memoirs, written in very unequal style, place the writer on a par with the general mass of men in the *subordinate stations of civilized society,* and so prove that there is no general rule without an exception."[3]

That Equiano had in the foreground of his interest the objective of attracting an audience whose power and voice could, if it decided to act, strike a meaningful blow against the slave trade and slavery is, I believe, suggested in the overtly stated purpose which Equiano couches in the humblest language and tone at the beginning of Chapter I:

> I am not so foolishly vain as to expect from it [his narrative] either immortality or literary reputation. If it affords any satisfaction to my numerous friends, at whose request it has been written, or in the smallest degree promotes the interest of humanity, the ends for which it was undertaken will be fully attained, and every wish of my heart gratified. (1:8)

Equiano further reveals his anticipation of some negative response as well as his awareness of the importance of audience when he declares that, in order to avoid censure, he has chosen not to "aspire to praise" (1:8). In fact, Equiano, one might argue, purposely designs a narrative that is as much about travel in the Mediterranean as it is about slavery in the New World to assure his audience that his purpose throughout is not to offend or alienate.[4]

Yet a common error is made by the critic who, taking Equiano's announced purpose at face value, fails to see his creation of a self whose muted voice veils covert intentions that lie hidden behind the facade—the mask, with which he disguises himself from the very opening lines of the work. For example, Frances Foster Smith incorrectly concludes that "Equiano rarely alters the dispassionate and modest tone of his prefatory remarks. . . . His denial of personal involvement beyond the desire to please friends and to make a small contribution to 'the interest of humanity' is in accordance with accepted standards of gentlemanly humanitarianism."[5]

Although it is indeed correct that Equiano was interested in "gentlemanly humanitarianism," it can be argued that Equiano's posture here allows us to see the control that he seeks to establish over his narrative from the beginning, for as Robert Stepto tells us, the letters, introductions, prefaces, appendices, and other such documents that formed authenticating auxiliary voices in the slave narratives dictated who, in the final analysis, had control: the former slave or his white guarantor.[6]

Thus, more important than Equiano's announced purpose in Chapter I, one might argue, is the significance of an introductory document, in the form of a letter written by him, which begins the narrative. In it, Equiano's voice emerges, cogently though humbly, to address "the Lords Spiritual and Temporal, the Commons of the Parliament of Great Britain":

My Lords and Gentlemen,

Permit me, with the greatest deference and respect to lay at your feet the following genuine Narrative, the chief design of which is to excite in your august assemblies a sense of compassion for the miseries which the Slave-Trade has entailed on my unfortunate countrymen. By the horrors of that trade was I first torn away from all the tender connexions that were naturally dear to my heart; but these, through the mysterious ways of Providence, I ought regard as infinitely more than compensated by the introduction I have thence obtained to the knowledge of the Christian religion, and of a nation which, by its liberal sentiments, its humanity, the glorious freedom of its government, and its proficiency in arts and sciences, has exalted the dignity of human nature.

I am sensible I ought to entreat your pardon for addressing to you a work so wholly devoid of literary merit; but, as the production of an unlettered African, who is actuated by the hope of becoming an instrument towards the relief of his suffering countrymen, I trust that *such a man,* pleading in *such a cause,* will be acquitted of boldness and presumption.

May the God of heaven inspire your heart with peculiar benevolence on that important day when the question of Abolition is to be discussed, when thousands in consequence of your Determination, are to look for Happiness or Misery!

I am,
My Lords and Gentlemen,
Your most obedient,
And devoted humble Servant,
OLAUDAH EQUIANO
or
GUSTAVUS VASSA (I:iii-v)

Clearly, Equiano, in his introductory letter, takes an overt posture that someone interested in operating from a basic logic of humility would assume. He accomplishes this with such carefully chosen phrases as "greatest deference," "respect," and "august assemblies"; and by his flattering description of Great Britain as "liberal" and humane and as a nation whose government knew "glorious freedom." Although the "chief design" of his narrative might not be obvious, the result is; for with this stance, Equiano—a Black and a former slave, by definition a pariah to some of his eighteenth-century readers[7]—captures the attention of his white audience. He succeeds in establishing what Mary Louis Pratt calls an "affective relation" with his audience, one that reduces hostility and gets attention without being offensive.[8] Simultaneously, he gains the upper hand, and from the beginning he succeeds in establishing a power relation in which he takes control. Like a champion chess player who, after making certain instrumental moves, castles his king for safeguarding while he uses his queen to wreak havoc on his opponent, Equiano, by assuming this position, is able to race across the pages of his narrative like a powerful monarch in a "game" that sees him overtly genuflecting and groveling but covertly, and primarily through language, slashing away at his oppressors. Indeed, his use of irony in his opening letter reveals this, for how can a nation known for its liberal sentiments, humanity, and the glorious freedom of its government directly or indirectly justify its involvement in a slave trade that, in its horror, would tear an individual, especially a child, "from all the tender connexions that were naturally dear to [his] heart"?

Equiano's letter, coupled with a frontispiece that features him poised with Bible in hand, pages of errata, and a table of contents, listing exciting chapter-by-chapter captions of the author's adventures, served to present the author's point of view as that of an inoffensive African who wishes to describe his "interesting" experiences to his reading audience. Moreover, his inclusion of an impressive list of subscribers—headed by the Prince of Wales and the Duke of York, but also including the names of England's top dignitaries, Members of Parliament, esquires, barristers, and clergymen, from the Duke of Bedford and the Bishop of Banghor to the Duke of Northumberland and Lord Mulgrave, Granville Sharp, Esq., and the Reverend Mr. John

Wesley—serve only to crystallize this idea for his audience.[9] Also, by publishing his narrative on August first, the "Queen's Birthday," Equiano enhances this perception, for the sacred manner with which her subjects view the Queen would have led them to see the *Narrative*'s appearance as an activity in her honor.[10] Finally, that Equiano's portrait was engraved by Daniel Orme, who, as Historical Engraver to the Prince of Wales, was responsible for engraving the chief heroes of the time,[11] only served to further reduce any possibly negative perception by his audience.

Thus, from the beginning, Equaino's intentions are enhanced by his disguises. With his posture, Equiano catches the interest and imagination of the populace; and with an impressive list of subscribers, which not only suggested that these individuals contributed financially by purchasing copies (some as many as six), but also that they supported and approved of the work, he is able to ensure himself of an audience. Equiano's success in this regard is suggested in the review his narrative received in the prestigious *Monthly Review; or, Literary Journal,* in which, ironically, the reviewer claims that "the narrative wears an honest face."[12]

In presenting these images of himself, Equiano reminds us of the African folk trickster hero Anansi. For like Anansi, who, though small, is able to outwit and overpower the larger animals, often leading to their destruction,[13] Equiano, the powerless former slave, outsmarts, with his tricks, his British audience. By donning the mask of the docile slave, he outwits his audience and simultaneously reveals that its members are unscrupulous and uncaring.

What remains important, however, is that each factor comes together to solidify the control which Equiano maintains from the beginning over his two-volume work: There are no auxiliary voices, no mitigating voices stealing the thrust of his words. Equiano organizes, coordinates, lays out, writes, and publishes his narrative, regardless of who else might assist. What we are left with, then, is what for Pierre Macherey is a "literary production,"[14] for we can see that Equiano is conscious of his purpose and the power of the written word.

II.

Because we are able to find in the narrative's structure the author's strong association with Africa, both suggested and stated, it is possible to argue that Equiano's muted voice camouflages what one might deem the single most important purpose of his narrative: the recreation of a "single self" which is related to an idealized African identity that Equiano wishes to claim as his legacy.

In the light of my contention, Equiano's narrative can be best understood if we make a distinction between the actual sequence of events of the text (*l'histoire*) and the presentation of these events (*recit*).[15] I don't mean to suggest here, of course, that Equiano, at forty-five years of age, was not interested in historicity, in the events that identi-

fied his outer self. His interest in the dynamics of his early life in Africa, ten years of slavery in the New World, maritime experiences which included participation in the Seven Years' War and travel to the Arctic, involvement in British culture during the eighteenth century, in the Abolitionist Movement and the colonization of Sierra Leone—historical events in which he participated actively or inactively—is clear. However, it becomes equally clear that what concerns him more than *what* he has done is who he has or has not become as a result of these events. In short, his feelings and thoughts, the "inner man," remain salient to him. In what must be viewed as his careful self-study, Equiano in his *Interesting Narrative of the Life* seems anxious to know, in the words of Carlyle: "In God's name, what *art* thou?"[16] Consequently, what ultimately concerns us here is related to a question of intentionality: What, in the final analysis, did Equiano intend?

It is in the interpretation or "the construction of textual meaning," to borrow a phrase from E. D. Hirsch, that one might find deeper insights into the meaning of Equiano's text. For Hirsch the critic's first task is the construction of textual meaning: One must interpret the text correctly. This is to be done, he further argues, by identifying the "Intentional Object" of the narrator's awareness as well as the "Intentional Act," the mode by which the narrator becomes aware of the object. Through these, the critic can ascertain the verbal meaning of the text and gain insight into its explicit meaning, which is shared by all. Furthermore, to distinguish what a text implies from what it does not imply, Hirsch argues, the critic must posit, insofar as it is possible, the "horizon" of the text, or "a system of typical expectations and probabilities," to unravel its total meaning. And to specify horizon, the interpreter must familiarize him- or herself with the "typical meaning of the author's mental and experiential world."[17] In spite of what must be clearly designated the inaccessibility of the author's intention, Hirsch's argument is particularly useful.

From what I have suggested thus far, it is possible to conclude that Equiano's narrative is the "intentional act" through which he becomes aware of his intentional object: slavery. However, in the prefatory remarks of Chapter II, Equiano lists an implied and perhaps more important intentional object, one that—because he wishes to avoid censure, as he tells us at the beginning of Chapter I—he subverts with the question of slavery. Apologizing for what some might have considered boldness on his part in sharing with his readers in Chapter I an account of the manners and customs of his African community, Equiano declares that ". . . whether the love of one[']s country be real or imaginary, or a lesson or reason, or an instinct of nature, *I still look back with pleasure on the first scenes of my life, though that pleasure has been for the most part mingled with sorrow*" (I:30; my emphasis). Equiano's use of the present tense here is important, for it connotes a contemporaneous act; there is, in other words, a sense of "now-ness" to his act of "looking back with pleasure" over his earlier life; and there are further implications that the desire to do so is continuous. In the present tense verb *look* is found Equiano's point of view, which embodies implications and irony, for his discourse conceals his simultaneous activity: He will not only be relating his experiences in slavery, whose abolition would enhance, as he says, "the interest of humanity," but concurrently recalling a past life which remains, without a doubt, more meaningful to him with each passing day.[18]

We can better understand the development, discovery, and creation of identity, which for Equiano remains salient, as well as come to grips with his experiences as a slave, which came in direct conflict with this identity, by adopting Hirsch's hermeneutics, which would lead us to unravel the meaning of the text in what we might call the "horizon" of Equiano's experiences. Interestingly enough, the very images that lead us to perceive Equiano as a subservient and passive former slave also embody the very complex characterization of him that we find in the narrative. Perhaps no other image offers a clearer example than the one that emerges from his treatment of his participation in the Seven Years' War.

III.

In 1757, when Equiano arrived in England with Captain Michael Henry Pascal, his master, Great Britain was engaged in a full-fledged war with her colonial rival, France, which she then faced in North America, the West Indies, India, and Africa in an encounter that would lead to her first imperial war. Although the war had been informally in progress since 1748, the escalation which took place in 1756 had brought Great Britain serious defeats, preeminently the loss of Minorca; international embarassment, with the retreat of Admiral John Byng; and personal disgust and despair, with the news of the "Black Hole" deaths in Calcutta. But from a despair that led Horace Walpole to declare that England should "slip her own cables, and float away into some unknown ocean,"[19] Great Britain went on to be victorious in what many historians and critics consider "the most rousing war" in her history. By 1757, under the able leadership of the "Great Commoner," William Pitt, who reluctantly had been appointed to the cabinet by King George II as Secretary of War, the British forces were carefully reorganized, and England succeeded in turning around the events of war in such a manner that 1759 was deemed a "Year of Victories."[20]

Ironically, in this very war that was fought to gain dominance over a part of West Africa that was not very far from his own homeland, and to control such "commodities" as sugar, tobacco, indigo, and Black African slaves, Equiano found an avenue for rising above the "blood-stained gates of slavery," to find meaning, dignity, and honor while still enslaved. Equiano wants his readers to believe that he was able to find in the Seven Years' War an avenue for regaining the power, valor, honor, and respect—in short, the humanity—of which he had been robbed by his abduction into slavery.

In the same manner that his documentations throughout the narrative are more than random inclusions of unrelated voices, the lengthy descriptions of Equiano's experiences at sea contain more than scattered and isolated incidents for the sake of rambling. They, too, reveal an Equiano who in his own tale successfully fashions himself as a protagonist who, in his traditional African experiences, could easily have risen to heroic stature. If, as he seems to suggest throughout his narrative, traditional African communal life must be associated with that which is heroic and ideal, then the Equiano we see in his implied characterization epitomizes the traditional African man, who would manifestly have been the great traditional warrior and title bearer. Consequently, the enigma that characterizes his narrative must be carefully examined when found in his tales about his experiences at sea with his master, Captain Pascal of the Royal Navy, especially those involving Pascal's service under Admiral Boscawen during the Seven Years' War.

On the surface, in his narration of the war Equiano serves as an eyewitness—as an on-the-scene correspondent, reporting with precision the land and sea engagements between the British and the French. But he seems especially aware of those battles in which Boscawen's gallant feats were accomplished when the *Namur,* the vessel on which Equiano along with his master-captain is sailing, is Boscawen's flagship. Perhaps no battle was more important to Boscawen (and, indeed, to Equiano) than the one at Gibraltar in August 1759. A firsthand eyewitness and participant, Equiano carefully details the events of the encounter. He dramatically and suspensefuly reports the August battle:

> The engagement now commenced with great fury on both sides. The *Ocean* immediately returned our fire, and we continued engaged with each other for some time, during which I was frequently stunned with the thundering of the great guns, whose dreadful contents hurried many of my companions into awful eternity. At last the French line was entirely broken, and we obtained the victory, which was immediately proclaimed with loud huzzas and acclamations. We took three prizes, *La Modeste,* of sixty-four guns, and *Le Temeraire* and *Centair,* of seventy-four guns each. The rest of the French ships took to flight with all the sail they could crowd. (I:83-84)

To be sure, Equiano, by creating an image of the war, is able to catch the unique moment in history and to reproduce it for his British audience, who must have been dazzled by the former slave's careful and detailed reporting, his enviable knowledge of naval vessels, and his apparent sense of nationalism.

Although his tale of the engagement ends, Equiano continues by explaining to the reader his assigned role during the battle, making it clear that his role as active participant cannot be gainsaid. Indeed, unlike Robinson Crusoe's Friday or the servant in the plantation literature of Thomas Page, who goes to war with his master to polish his boots and care for his horse, Equiano reveals that he functioned as more than a personal servant during the engagement. He was a fighter:

My station during the engagement was on the middle deck, where I was quartered with another boy, to bring powder to the aftermost gun; and here I was witness of the dreadful fate of many of my companions, who, in the twinkling of an eye, were dashed in pieces, and launched into eternity. Happily I escaped unhurt, though the shot and splinters flew thick about me during the whole fight. Towards the latter part of it, my master was wounded, and I saw him carried down to the surgeon; but though I was much alarmed for him, and wished to assist him, I dared not leave my post. At this station, my gun-mate (a partner in bringing powder for the same gun) and I ran a very risk, for more than half an hour, of blowing up the ship. For, when we had taken the cartridges out of the boxes, the bottoms of many of them proving rotten, the powder ran all about the deck, near the match tub; we scarcely had water enough at the last to throw on it. We were also, from our employment, very much exposed to the enemy's shots; for we had to go through nearly the whole length of the ship to bring the powder. I expected, therefore, every minute to be my last especially when I saw our men fall so thick about me; but, wishing to guard as much against the dangers as possible, at first I thought would be safest not to go for the powder till the Frenchmen had fired their broadside. . . . But immediately afterwards I thought this caution was fruitless; and cheering myself with the reflection that there was time allotted for me to die, as well as to be born, I instantly cast off all fear or thought whatever of death, and went through the whole of my duty with alacrity. (I:84-85)

Here Equiano again resembles the African folk trickster Anansi, who is sometimes caught in the traps that he sets for others, for although he undoubtedly is aware of the possibly indignant reaction of his audience to his work were they to conclude that he had overstepped the bounds of his assured social role, Equiano can be found unmasked for a brief moment when we peer behind the facade. We find in the above passage not the subservient or passive slave, but instead an Equiano who has covertly assumed the role of the chivalrous warrior from the very beginning. And, again, we are made aware that Equiano is saying more in his discourse than what immediately stands before us.

Unlike Admiral Byng, whose retreat jeopardized Great Britain's safety and cost him his life, Equiano, a man of action, "casts off all fear" and rises to the occasion. Though his human instincts cause him to be slow in reacting at first, he, responding with bravery, answers the call of duty nevertheless. Indeed, by telling us that he fearlessly carried the gun powder that was used to send the solid cannon balls splitting over the vast ocean, in spite of the immediate danger, Equiano, one might even be led to conclude, wants his reader to believe that this historical battle could not have been won without the brave Ibo's role and the chivalrous manner in which he met his duties during these pre-armored-warship days when Britain's wooden naval vessels gained control of the ocean.

One cannot help but notice that the humility with which Equiano generally garbs himself seems to have been completely stripped away here, as he calls attention to his heroic performance, and the shift from the observing eye in the "I" of the narration to the "I" of the action becomes important because it moves the focus inward, taking Equiano beyond the explicit meaning that his activities may have conveyed to his British audience. Equiano is in fact saying, I believe: This is not only a world that I objectively experienced, but one that I, through my intrepid acts, helped to create.

To be sure, through his exciting narration and careful choice of words of action and through his functional use of the first-person plural "we," he allows his British readers to participate in the battle, and he gives them a reason for celebration. Here in his narrative they could find yet another record of their undaunting strength and power; here they could find yet another testimony to the masterful skills of their beloved Admiral Boscawen; and here they had evidence of their ability to overcome the enemy, France. Thus, at the explicit level of his narrative, he succeeds in giving his audience both the romance and the drama that it might have associated with naval battle and encounter, a fact that was undoubtedly heightened by the knowledge that this was "Pitt's War," and he boosted their pride in their maritime war for maritime empire, providing rejuvenation after the universal disgrace they had suffered with Byng's defeat.

Equally important, however, is what might be perceived as Equiano's effort to guide his readers' response towards his abolitionist concerns, for with his description and powerful rhetoric he indirectly forces his audience to confront the question of the injustice of slavery and, indeed, to find validation in his argument against this inhuman system that had enslaved an individual of his caliber, one whose personal qualities, dignity, and values represented the highest ideals of British culture. His audience, one might even believe, might somehow have become infuriated by their own participation, direct or indirect, in this heinous system, and with Equiano, they might have concluded that slavery "depresses the mind and extinguishes all its fire and every noble sentiment" (I:29). Equiano's success in capturing and controlling his audience, and his personal account of one of England's finest hours, undoubtedly contributed to the popularity of his narrative, which was to undergo more than fifteen editions.

What remains of paramount importance, however, are the implications of Equiano's text, because throughout his reported acts he places himself firmly in the middle of this "world wide struggle in which the main lines of the British Empire were finally laid down."[21] Rather than hide, escape, or skirt responsibilities, although armorless, Equiano, the African, girds his loins and resolves to meet head on his task, no matter what the required sacrifice, danger, or outcome. A mere lad of fourteen at the time of the battle, he here assumes, he wants us to believe, the role of leader. Overcoming his initial fears and showing tremendous discipline, Equiano in the final analysis emerges as one who had risen to the status that would have been his in Essaka, where the male youth's self-understanding was firmly grounded in the conceptual metaphor "man is warrior" and "warrior is a person of honour, action, and bravery." Consequently, the horizon of Equiano's experience, the conscious and unconscious meanings that are present in his discourse, must be unraveled before the full meaning of his text can be ascertained. The horizon would inevitably include his African past.

The son of a village elder, Equiano retrospectively views his childhood in Africa as his "former happy state," during which he basked in the warmth of his mother's love, was cradled in an awareness of his aristocratic father's wealth and prestige, and was nourished by the knowledge that his parents were committed to securing for him a place within their community through which he, too, would gain the mark of grandeur and distinction that was borne by his father and brother. In preparing him for his *destined* role as a communal leader, Equiano's mother, unaware, of course, of the tragic future that awaited her favorite child, dressed him "with the emblems, after the manner of our greatest warrior." He tells us that, before being kidnapped, he was "trained up in the earliest years in the art of war: my daily exercise was shooting and throwing javelins" (I:31).

Implied in Equiano's text here is the suggestion that the personal history of a pariah, which had been carved out in the wasteland of Western slavery and culture, is not his sole interest. Present also is the notion that the Ibo wants to confront questions related to the loss of personal legacy that this history has wrought. He tells us that slavery did not divert him from the course on which he had been set by a mother who dressed him after the manner of the great Ibo warriors. In fact, in his own traditional world, he would have crossed the threshold into manhood after such dauntless actions, and, indeed, he could have danced to the drum beat reserved for the great warriors.

Finding no warrior's circle in which to dance proudly, finding no marketplace in which to display his war trophies, although he had brought home the "enemies'" head in the form of the ships taken as prizes, Equiano finds, in his narrative-autobiography, not only an avenue for celebrating his valorous act, but also a means of claiming the achievement of his identity and thereby assuming the social role that was rightfully his as an Ibo, Essakan, and African. Equiano thus weaves into his narrative an important "metaphor of self," which, as James Olney tells us, is used by the autobiographer to grasp and understand the unique self that he is—"to grasp the unknown for the known."[22] Equiano's "metaphor of self" is one that makes him the African traditional warrior-man.

Given Hume's contention that the mind is a theater which "parades a variety of posture and situation," one finds it difficult not to agree with Sir Victor Pritchett, who claimed that what the autobiographer is faced with in the final analysis is a decision of "what play [he is] putting on, what its theme is and what postures fit into it." Pritchett tells us: "The play is not '*the* truth' but '*a* truth' of '*our*

truth.'"[23] In other words, it is possible to argue that the historicity and veracity of Equiano's tale about his role in the Seven Years' War is, in a sense, unimportant. What ultimately *is* important is the metaphor of self that he has chosen in relating the events. Thus, although the explicit "posture" he assumes for his audience, that of the abolitionist, is one that we continuously see, it is the implicit posture, grounded in the signification of warriorhood to his traditional African community, that eventually presents the represented self that he has chosen to amplify in the hidden purpose of his narrative.

Consequently, although he succeeds through narration and description in recreating for his readers a sense of the slave trade during the eighteenth century, Equiano ends up recreating what Roy Pascal, in a related context, terms "a part of [his] life in the actual circumstance in which it was lived." In the final analysis, what we get is closer to autobiography, in which, as Pascal tells us, "The centre of interest is the self, not the outside world, though necessarily the outside world must appear so that the personality can find its particular shape."[24]

What we learn from Equiano's autobiographical acts, I believe, is that he can only find in his retrospective assessment of slavery an excruciating severance and senseless extirpation: As he came to realize, slavery meant physical separation from the community and culture which offered reciprocity during the first eleven years of his life. Whereas Essaka meant bonding, security, and aggregation, slavery meant separation, alienation, and liminality. It was for him a void to be transcended, an overpowering force that threatened to dash him into a world of eternal meaninglessness, an experience from which, through the narrative, he would seek a sense of wholeness and being.

Deeply embedded in Equiano's discourse, specifically in its ironics and implications, is the conflict which resulted from conflict between the idealized African self, which he as a member of his Essakan community and as an Ibo accepts as his legacy, and the harsh reality that, having served as a slave in a foreign land, away from family and culture, he had not been able fully to realize this self. The act of writing the narrative becomes not only a process, then, of taking a retrospective glance over the primary experiences that served to form Equiano's historical self, but perhaps more importantly, it functions as praxis, for it allows him to explore his life and at the same time create, develop, and extract from it the meaning which to him remains important. Equiano's self-portraiture contains ironic and metaphoric values which upon examination reveal the dual nature of the thematics and characterization of his narrative. Fundamentally, it reveals that in his efforts to build subjectivity in a world of reification, Equiano reclaims his voice by masking and disguising it. Indirectly, he teaches us to not only listen to the explicit voice of Gustavus Vassa, the person created by the Western enslavers who gave him this name, but also to the voice of Olaudah Equiano, the would-be warrior, whose name means 'fortunate' and 'favored.'

Notes

1. Frances Smith Foster, *Witnessing Slavery: The Development of Antebellum Slave Narratives* (Westport, CT: Greenwood Press, 1979), p. 6.

2. Olaudah Equiano, *The Interesting Narrative of the Life of Olaudah Equiano, or Gustavus Vassa, the African, Written by Himself*, 2 vols. (London: Entered at Stationer's Hall, 1789). Specific references will be to this edition and will appear in the text.

3. *The Gentleman's Magazine*, 59 (1789), 539.

4. Equiano's eighteenth-century British world treasured travel and adventure narratives whose appeal, as Louis B. Wright tells us, cut across class and group (see *Middle Class Culture in Elizabethan England* [Chapel Hill: Univ. of North Carolina Press, 1958], p. 508).

5. *Witnessing Slavery*, p. 18.

6. *From Behind the Veil: A Study of Afro-American Narrative* (Urbana: Univ. of Illinois Press, 1979), pp. 3-31.

7. For the eighteenth-century European views of Blacks, see Winthrop D. Jordan, *White Over Black: American Attitudes Toward the Negro 1550-1812* (Baltimore: Penguin Books, 1969), pp. 3-43.

8. "Ideology of Speech Act Theory," *Century Series*, I (1981), 5-18.

9. That Equiano was conscious of the importance of his list of subscribers is suggested by his careful changing of each list with each new edition. Regional editions bore names of importance to that region. For example, the Dublin edition has a list of Irish subscribers.

10. This is the legal holiday on which the British celebrate the Queen's birthday. It was a common practice to introduce new and important social items, for example fashions, on this day. This was viewed as a form of loyalty. (See Anne Beck, *Dress in 18th Century England* [New York: Holmes & Meier, 1979].)

11. *Print Collector's Quarterly*, July 1927, p. 250.

12. 80 (Jan.-June 1789), 551.

13. See Harold Courlander, *A Treasure of African Folklore* (New York: Crown, 1975), pp. 135-36.

14. *A Theory of Literary Production*, trans. Geoffrey Wall (London: Routledge & Kegan Paul, 1978), pp. 66-78.

15. Jonathan Culler, *The Pursuit of Signs* (Ithaca, NY: Cornell Univ. Press, 1980), pp. 170-71; see also Girard Genette, *Narrative Discourse: An Essay in Method* (Ithaca, NY: Cornell Univ. Press, 1972), passim.

16. Quoted in Wayne Schumaker, *English Autobiography: Its Emergence, Materials and Forms* (Berkeley: Univ. of California Press, 1954), p. 58.

17. "Objective Interpretation," in *Validity in Interpretation* (New Haven: Yale Univ. Press, 1967), pp. 209-44.

18. See Robin Lakoff, "Tense and Its Relation to Participant," *Language,* 46 (1979), 841. According to Lakoff, "the choice of tense is based in part on the subjective factor or how the speaker feels himself related to the event."

19. W. E. Lunt, *History of England,* 4th ed. (New York: Random House, 1956), p. 521.

20. For a thorough discussion of England's role in the war, see Julian S. Corbett, *England and the Seven Years War* (London: Longman, Green and Company, 1918), vols. I-II. See also Walter L. Dorn, *Competition for Empire. 1740-1763* (New York: Harper & Brothers, 1940), passim; and Lunt, pp. 485-550.

21. Corbet, I: 7.

22. *Metaphors of Self: The Meaning of Autobiography* (Princeton: Princeton Univ. Press, 1972), pp. 3-50.

23. *Autobiography* (London: The English Association, 1977), p. 4.

24. *Design and Truth in the Autobiography* (London: Routledge & Kegan Paul, 1960), pp. 8, 9.

Keith A. Sandiford (essay date 1988)

SOURCE: "The Black Presence," in *Measuring the Moment: Strategies of Protest in Eighteenth-Century Afro-English Writing,* Associated University Presses, 1988, pp. 17-42.

[*In the following excerpt, Sandiford examines the social and cultural situation of blacks in England before 1800 and discusses the lives and works of prominent black writers and intellectuals—including Ignatio Sancho, Ottobah Cugoano, Olaudah Equiano, Phillis Wheatley, and Job Ben Solomon—whose works would spur literary reactions and philosophical debates about blacks and the institution of slavery.*]

Ignatius Sancho, Ottobah Cugoano, and Olaudah Equiano were undoubtedly the three best-known Africans in eighteenth-century England. But it is important to establish at the outset that they were also members of a considerable Black community that grew up in England as a direct consequence of that country's participation in the slave trade. The fact that several thousand Africans made their home in England during this period is not yet as fully appreciated as it might be, mainly because standard histories have tended either to minimize or to ignore altogether the significance of the African presence at this early time in Europe as a whole.

This chapter will delineate the social environment created for Blacks by the special conditions of slavery and by their own racial identity. For the literary achievement of Sancho, Cugoano, and Equiano can be properly understood only in relation to those specific conditions and within the wider context of the Black community's group experiences. One of the major propositions of this study is that these three writers were highly conscious of their social responsibility as literate members of that community. This chapter will show specifically that their sense of racial awareness was deeply rooted in a longer tradition of literacy and learning begun by earlier African scholars and personalities who were exposed to European culture and education. Sancho, Cugoano, and Equiano were distinctive as the first to transfigure Black awareness into a literary form, celebrating the validity of their common racial origin and advocating the liberation of their fellow Africans from the disabilities that circumscribed their lives and actions, both on the plantations of the West Indies and within the bounds of freedom-loving Britannia itself. . . .

Yet, the very image of Blacks and the assumptions that defined their relationships with the white colonial and metropolitan society were in large measure a legacy of history, with foundations anterior to the period of slavery. To the older myths about the darkness of Africa and the barbarism of her peoples were added new arguments calculated to promote the expediency of a new economic order. Thus, a complex of attitudes was evolved that justified the commerce in Black human flesh in the West Indies and in England alike and relegated Blacks to a status of degradation which they were to endure until legal redress was finally won in the nineteenth century.

The earliest history of African peoples in Britain predates the period of this study. Latin chroniclers of the Roman conquest record the presence of dark-skinned inhabitants among the primitive tribes of the island. In his account of Britain under Agricola's governorship, Tacitus describes a people of "swarthy complexion and curled hair" coexisting alongside the ruddy-haired, large-limbed Caledonians.[1] The Afro-American ethnologist and historian, J. A. Rogers, states that these people were undeniably of African extraction.[2] More recent commentators suggest that the Romans may have had Black soldiers among their legions in Britain.[3] This view is usually based on the following incident from the life of Severus, the Roman emperor:

> On another occasion when he [Severus] was returning to his nearest quarters from an inspection of the wall at Luguvallum in Britain, at a time when he had not only proved victorious, but had concluded a perpetual peace, just as he was wondering what omen would present itself, an Ethiopian soldier, who was famous among buffoons and always a notable jester, met him with a garland of cypress boughs.[4]

Severus is reported to have been enraged and frightened by the soldier's "ominous" skin color and the color of the garland. It seems clear that the emperor was reacting to the traditional equation of black with evil. The term "Ethiopian," used in antiquity as a generic denotation for all Africans, is the most definite evidence here of the African presence in early Britain. Archaeological excavation on the site of a Romano-British cemetery in use at Trentholme, York, between A.D. 140 and the end of the fourth century, provides further, if not entirely conclusive, evidence for the African claim. Several of the human remains have been identified as approximating the physical features of negroid peoples.[5]

In Tudor and Stuart times Africans continue to appear in the literary and official documents under the designation of "moors" and "blackamoors." Descriptions of Elizabethan and Jacobean court entertainments and public ceremonies attest to the participation of authentic African characters—not white faces painted black.[6]

The English entered the slave trade in 1562 as interlopers in a market monopolized by the Portuguese. Thereafter the gentlemen and merchant adventurers of the trade supplied slaves not only to the Spanish colonies of the New World, but also to the households of the rich and titled of England. Queen Elizabeth herself retained a Black page and a Black entertainer at court.[7] Still, the influx of Africans into the realm in the closing years of the sixteenth century, although as yet comparatively small, was considerable enough to incur the royal displeasure.

In a letter to her Privy Council, dated 11 July 1596, Elizabeth adverted to "divers blackamoores brought into this realm of which kinde of people there are already too manie." Seven days later, the queen issued a license to have several newly arrived Blacks deported.[8] Elizabeth's was the first official measure designed to forestall the potential competition such Africans offered to native English subjects as household servants. Her complaint was to be reiterated with greater urgency and alarm by several observers in the middle of the eighteenth century, when the Black population in England reached twenty thousand.

In the seventeenth century, the number of Blacks in England grew in proportion to England's commercial excursions on the slave coast of Guinea. These were at best spasmodic and generally unofficial. But in 1662, Charles II rationalized the haphazard slaving practices of Englishmen on the Guinea coast by granting a monopoly to the Company of Royal Adventurers.[9] By this gesture, and with the financial backing of other members of the royal family, the country committed itself to full partnership in the "curious" institutions of slavery and the slave trade. Hereafter, Blacks came to be defined as merchandise, commodities to be bought and sold, like horses or fine wines—and were traded as such. Inevitably, as the merchants did a brisk trade in human cargo at the port towns of London, Bristol, and Liverpool, citizens of substance came increasingly to staff their households with Black servants. Captains of slaving ships and government officials returning from colonial outposts all followed the fashion of appearing in public attended by Black body servants to signify their rank and opulence.

Sailors smuggled into England Africans stolen on the slave coast and sold them to willing buyers. Again, literary sources and the public press provide the clearest reflection of the growing vogue for Black servants and of the newcomers' impact on English life. Samuel Pepys records having seen a little Turk and a Black boy in the home of a friend and notes that the two were being kept as pages for his host's daughters. Seven years later, we find that Pepys himself occasionally hired "a black moor of Mrs. Betelier's who dresses meat mighty well. . . ."[10] African serving boys were to be found in several households, and ladies of quality appeared in public with their lap-dogs on leash and their blackamoors in tow.

Advertisements for the sale of Black servants and for the recovery of runaways were common.[11] The following is typical: "On Monday last, a Negroe Boy, about 14 Years old, of a good Complexion, indifferent Tall, speaks good English, with a Drugget Coat, silk waistcoat, with red and yellow stripes, run away. . . ."[12]

By the year 1700, the English had sent some 200,000 slaves to the colonies. In 1713, the Treaty of Utrecht gave Britain the right to transport slaves to the Spanish colonies. Her participation in the slave trade was now legally and internationally recognized. The way was paved for plantation slavery to flourish into a mature economic system.[13]

As could be expected, this intensification of Britain's role in the trade swelled the numbers of Africans within her own shores. The new century saw a diverse collection of these uprooted people settling in England for different reasons; their influence on England's social and economic life became fully visible and often worrying. In the key ports of the trade, London, Bristol, and Liverpool, slaves were being landed by the hundreds to be sold at auction.[14] Some were stowaways who quickly vanished into enclaves already established by their fellow Africans near the docks and rivers. Others were servants destined for wealthy households. It was in this wave of Black humanity that Sancho, Cugoano, and Equiano came to England.

It is convenient at this point to classify and describe the various conditions of Blacks to be found in England during this time. They may be divided into three main groups: (1) those brought to England by returning planters and colonial officials; (2) those brought by merchants and traders for sale or personal use; and (3) those African youths, usually sons of local chiefs and officials, studying in England, either on the initiative of their fathers or under the sponsorship of English philanthropic organizations.[15]

Servants accounted for the majority of the first group. Until their status became the subject of legal debate later in the century, their masters treated them as chattels, to be retained or disposed of as the masters pleased. They were not usually paid wages but were maintained in food and clothing. In the household, they performed the duties of valets, servingboys, and stable lads. In public they were paraded in colorful liveries, their necks girded by metal collars inscribed with their owners' initials. Both of these insignia identified Blacks as slaves and exemplified their masters' affluence and prestige.

It appears that younger Africans were commonly kept as pets. Some became the playmates and companions of their owners' children; others were the favorite pages of noble ladies. Almost all were saddled with pompous names of oriental and classical origin. Sultan, Socrates, Pompey, and Caesar were not uncommon appellations. The many Black pages retained at Knole by the earls and dukes of Dorset were all styled "John of Morocco."[16] Ignatius Sancho got his own name as a token of his owners' partiality for Don Quixote's famous squire.

The second group was composed of those slaves who were brought to England by merchants and captains of the Guinea trade. On the slave ships, they were manifested as common cargo. Landed in England, they were set up for sale on the steps of popular coffeehouses, in public squares, and even in the custom-house. According to one historical account, "The personal traffic in slaves resident in England had been as public and authorised in London as in any of our West Indian possessions. . . ."[17]

The third group was the smallest, but its members, by virtue of their social rank in Africa, enjoyed privileged treatment and high visibility in England. They were usually the sons of chiefs, sent to England (as well as to other parts of Europe) to be educated in Western languages, diplomacy, and commerce. Perhaps the most distinguished members of this group were Anthony William Amo and Philip Quaque, both natives of the Gold Coast.[18] Together with other European-educated African scholars, they vindicated the moral and intellectual capabilities of Blacks in a century when it was convenient to deny these in the interest of economic expediency. Their academic achievements were celebrated in Europe and will be discussed later in this chapter. It will be shown that the precedence of their literacy and the excellence of their academic achievements cooperated with other factors to lend credibility to Sancho, Cugoano, and Equiano and, ultimately, to facilitate the movement toward emancipation of the slaves.

It ought not be supposed, however, that the fundamental tools of literacy were reserved only for this small and exclusive group. While there was no concerted attempt to educate even lower-class Englishmen until the later part of the century, and education for slaves was stoutly resisted and prohibited by law in the colonies, it suited the peculiar needs of English employers at home to provide their Black servants with limited instruction in the rudiments of English.[19] In 1734, the duke of Marlborough paid some £10 15s. for the books and tuition of two blacks in his service.[20] Both Colonel Bathurst, father of Samuel Johnson's associate, and Johnson himself supported the well-known manservant, Francis Barber, in acquiring a rather sound education.[21] Although Sancho's early education was neglected through the narrow-mindedness of his first guardians—they feared that with learning he might forget his place and prove intractable—the duke of Montagu, his first patron, encouraged his avid interest in books by sup-plying his needs from his library. Cugoano relates that he was taught to read and write by the gentleman who res-cued him from slavery in the West Indies. Equiano re-ceived regular instruction from the very beginning of his life as a slave; first he was sent to school by his mistress, Miss Guerin, and later, in his seafaring days, he was fre-quently provided with books and tutors. Thus, Black slaves and servants in England came to acquire skills that were essential for smooth communication with their masters and for their functional intercourse with the society at large.

The picture of Blacks in eighteenth-century England would be incomplete without some reference to those who were not restricted by bonds of servitude or protected by indul-gent patrons. Some free Blacks made their living as musi-cians, entertainers, actors, apprentices, and sailors in the slave trade.

From all accounts, Black performing artists were extremely popular with English audiences.[22] A Black woman played the part of Polly in *The Beggar's Opera,* according to John Jackson's *History of the English Stage.* Another Black is reported to have appeared on stage as early as 1770 at the Smock Alley Theatre in Dublin.[23]

It appears that many Blacks were taught to play musical instruments out of a curious myth that they were pos-sessed of an extraordinary racial aptitude for music. Afri-can drummers and trumpeters became popular figures in military bands and ceremonial parades, penetrating even the elite ranks of the Life Guards, the Grenadiers, and the Cold Stream Guards.

Such Blacks lived largely independent and transient lives; their greater mobility was a powerful magnet to others, who had escaped from service or servitude either in the West Indies or in England itself, and to those who were unable to find employment. For this latter element the specter of poverty and hardship was no less haunting than it was for those derelicts of white society whose abject misery and despair William Hogarth depicted in "Gin Lane" and "Calais Gate."[24] Many undoubtedly took to stealing, gambling, and other illicit activities; some were recommitted to slavery in the West Indies. On the whole, their freedom was precarious, if not illusory.[25]

The English showed warm appreciation for artistically tal-ented Blacks by providing avenues for their gainful em-ployment; they were not so ready, however, to encourage those who were skilled in manual crafts and mechanical trades. The traditional conservatism of the guilds institu-tionalized this discrimination into an almost impregnable barrier. Still, some youths managed to find apprenticeships as artisans, but it was costly to train them, and sponsors were reluctant to invest in members of a group that was growing restive for freedom and making increasing de-mands for social equality. The fears of the establishment were formally expressed in an ordinance, passed by the lord mayor and aldermen of the city of London in 1731, prohibiting the admission of Blacks into trade apprentice-ships.[26]

Another group of Africans, who were at least part-time residents of London, was made up of those who found employment as sailors on ships plying the slave coast. They were usually taken on by the trading companies and taught English in order to assist the English crews in the management of their human cargoes. When not on the sea, their home ports were London, Bristol, and Liverpool. But the very nature of their life made them a highly transient, though not invisible, group.

"Hundreds" of American ex-slaves were among the Loyal-ists who returned to England in 1783 with the British forces after the revolutionary war ended.[27] Fired by the prospect of freedom, they had thrown in their lot with the supporters of the king, who in turn promised to compen-sate them with land and provisions. Now they were sud-denly transplanted to a strange country, with different laws and unfamiliar customs. Their adjustment was all the more problematic because the commission appointed to examine their claims proved generally unsympathetic. Only a small number secured compensation. A few found jobs, but the great majority were reduced to vagrancy and destitution. White poverty was already a dire social problem; now this new wave of Black immigrants, together with their previ-ously settled brothers and sisters, aggravated the situation. At the best of times, the English attitude to the poor was one of fear and distrust: they considered them as a class of shiftless, improvident (and therefore disloyal) citizens. The presence of this alien community of Blacks was, accord-ingly, calculated to exacerbate these traditional tensions and sensitivities to the point of xenophobia.

For some time now in the eighteenth century, the total Black population of England had become the subject of wild and widely varying speculation, especially among in-dividuals espousing what they claimed to be the national interest. In 1764, the *Gentleman's Magazine* estimated the number of Blacks living in London to be 20,000 and grow-ing.[28] One year later, the *Morning Chronicle* raised that number to 30,000. The latter figure was patently unreli-able. It was only during the celebrated Somerset trial (1772) that the Lord Chief Justice Mansfield adopted an official estimate of 15,000. Granville Sharp, that tireless champion of the Black cause, himself placed the figure at 20,000 for all England.[29] Even the best contemporary sources are inexact, but in view of Sharp's association with the Black community through political and humani-tarian activism, his estimate seems the most acceptable.

In the face of growing hostility from their English hosts, therefore, the Black community was forced to pool its own resources and devise strategies for the group's protection and survival. Contemporary sources all concur in their tes-timony that the community was a tightly knit, cohesive body, supporting its members in a variety of ways. The lit-erature of Sancho, Cugoano, and Equiano often reflects those writers' sensitivity to their people's plight and shares something of the solidarity that was to become part of the ethos of Black community life in England.

Sancho's effusive sympathy for human suffering moved him to intercede with his privileged connections on behalf of the needy. In Letter 25, he appealed to Mr. B—to take a fellow Black into service.[30] Evidence from other letters suggests that he made similar appeals regularly, although he kept his representations on a private level.[31] His distaste for overt political action did not, however, diminish in his eyes the several public philanthropic organizations working for the improvement of conditions among the plantation slaves and London's Black poor.

Cugoano planned to use the proceeds from the sale of his book to start a school for Blacks in London. He was deeply concerned that conditions there were fast driving his brothers into a state of mental torpor and moral decadence. He wrote: "Nothing engages my Desire so much as the Descendants of my Countrymen, so as to have them educated in the Duties and knowledge of that Religion which all good Christian people enjoy . . ." (*Thoughts and Sentiments,* introduction, xiii).[32]

Of the three, Equiano was the most instrumental—because the most personally involved—in the struggle to win freedom and human dignity for the Blacks in England. Unprincipled white masters and their marauding slave hunters were in the habit of recapturing freed Blacks and placing them under constraint in England or shipping them back to slavery in the West Indies.[33] In the spring of 1774, Equiano found a job for another black, John Annis, as a cook on board the ship in which he was then sailing. Two months later, Annis was illegally apprehended by his former master. Equiano intervened personally on his behalf and himself initiated some of the legal proceedings, meanwhile drawing on the more expert assistance of Granville Sharp in an abortive attempt to secure the man's release.[34] "I proved the only friend he had who attempted to regain him his liberty if possible, having known the want of liberty myself," Equiano wrote (*Narrative* 2: 121).[35] It was Equiano also who brought to Sharp's notice the shocking details of the "Zong Case," in which 132 Africans were willfully drowned at sea in 1783. Later he was to serve on the London Committee for the Black Poor, and in 1786 he was appointed Commissary of Stores for the Sierra Leone expedition, organized to resettle destitute London Blacks. Equiano's energetic activism was a prime force in shaping the literary character of his *Narrative.* . . .

Sancho, Cugoano, and Equiano were exceptional in possessing a higher level of literacy than most Blacks in their time. Their special relationships with the privileged classes and with influential humanitarians were decided personal advantages. But for the faceless masses who could claim no such connections, the evidence shows that their greatest security lay in a strong sense of racial identity and in a social cohesiveness forged by the legal uncertainty of their status in a society that was growing progressively resentful of their presence.

Proslavery interests consistently abused and vilified Blacks. They exploited the English people's ordinary distrust of strangers by denouncing the Black community as a refuge for criminal escapees from abroad. They also promoted the idea that Blacks were displacing English workers. The hard facts of poverty and distress shared by Black and white masses alike scarcely supported these fears: "Life was so hard and enjoyments so few, it could scarcely be claimed that immigrant Blacks were taking anything from the whites; there was nothing to take in the first place."[36] Despite some antipathy whipped up by racist foes, Blacks in general seemed to have continued popular both with the masters they served and with the English lower classes among whom they lived. This considerable harmony that prevailed in the latter case was nowhere more evident than in specific demonstrations of solidarity and in the high incidence of interracial marriage.[37]

Fugitive slaves and Black victims of injustice often found aid and comfort among white working-class communities. Bands of sympathetic whites regularly wrested Blacks from the hands of their captors or kept such captors at bay with threats of mass violence.[38] Kenneth Little suggests that without the spirit of friendship at this level and the support of the liberal classes higher up, the Black poor could hardly have survived.[39]

Lower-class white women showed a strong partiality for Black mates. The story is told of a female haymaker who followed Frank Barber all the way from Lincolnshire to London. The romantic appeal Barber held for this and other white female admirers was not lost on his master Johnson: "Frank carried the Empire of Cupid further than most men," Johnson told his friends.[40] Naturally, such liaisons provoked widespread anxiety and exacerbated tensions in the minds of the conservative middle class.[41]

The specter of miscegenation was horrifying to the orthodox English imagination. The fear that sexual commingling would be an inescapable consequence of Black immigration was the foremost ground for objection to the Black presence from the very beginning. Perhaps Elizabeth I, that supreme symbol of English purity, beauty, and virtue, ever watchful of the national interest, intended to forestall "contamination" of the pure English genetic strain by deporting the blackamoors in her 1596 decree.[42] Thereafter critics of the Black presence followed her lead in yoking together fears of over-crowding with insinuations about the supposed deleterious effects of Black-white unions. In the eighteenth century, plantocratic interests often veiled their fear of the greater "evil" of interracial marriage beneath the more credible, if specious, objection that Blacks were displacing too many whites in domestic service. A letter in the *London Chronicle* clearly illustrates the typical conjunction of these two attitudes:

> Was a full enquiry to be made, it would appear that their [the Blacks'] numbers now in this kingdom amount to many thousands, and as they fill the places of so many whites, we are by this means depriving so many [Englishmen] of the means of getting their bread, and thereby decreasing our native population in favour of a race whose mixture with us is disgraceful, and whose uses cannot be so various and essential as those of white people.[43]

That most implacable detractor of the African race, Edward Long, in an alarming opinion typical of his racist reactionism, denounced miscegenation as "a venomous and dangerous ulcer that threatens to disperce [*sic*] its malignity far and wide until every family catches the infection from it."[44]

However, such strictures did little to discourage Black-white unions. Circumstances made them inevitable. The numerical predominance of African males over females, arising from the peculiar needs of plantation economy, ensured that the former would turn to native English women for companionship. Even individuals as proud of their racial identity as Cugoano and Equiano married English wives. The products of such unions drew responses ranging from gaping curiosity to irrational fear. The sensation created by the "Spotted Negro Boy," "a fanciful child of nature formed in her most playful mood," was the subject of gossip columns for many a month. The hapless child was at various times set up for public viewing and depicted in several art forms.[45]

James Tobin, a planter who lived in Saint Kitts, saw the proliferation of this "dark and contaminated breed" as an "evil" requiring urgent redress.[46] And Philip Thicknesse, a former governor of the West Indies who was captious about many things in his travels, noticed on his return to England, "in almost every village, a little race of mulattoes, mischievous as monkeys, and infinitely more dangerous."[47]

For all the prejudice and emotion with which these observations are charged, it is significant that they had little effect in mobilizing anything like mass hostility against Blacks. Historians analyzing the general public attitude towards the immigrants are in broad agreement that virulent racism of the kind proclaimed by vested interests like Tobin and Long was not widespread.[48] The unintended effect of extremist reactions was to bind the Black community closer together. The same mixed unions that race purists were opposing became one of the specific recourses Blacks used to strengthen their foothold in Britain.

Sensitive to at least the antipathy of the English middle and upper classes, Blacks therefore formed societies to protect their interests and to promote the welfare of their fellows. The functions of these societies seem curiously to approximate those of modern social service and counseling agencies. In particular, they encouraged servants to desert their masters and contract marriage as soon as possible after their arrival in the country. The notion prevailed within the Black community that marriage conferred automatic freedom on slaves. Sir John Fielding, a noted jurist of the period, described what seemed to have been the regular pattern:

> Many of these gentlemen [merchants and absentee planters] have either at a vast expense caused some of their blacks to be instructed in the necessary qualifications of a domestic servant, or have purchased them after they have been instructed; they then bring them to

England as cheap servants having no right to wages; they no sooner arrive here than they put themselves on a footing with other servants, become intoxicated with liberty, grow refractory, and either by persuasion of others or from their own inclinations, begin to expect wages according to their own opinion of their merits; and as there are already a great number of black men and women who made themselves troublesome and dangerous to the families who have brought them over as to get themselves discharged, these enter into societies and make it their business to corrupt and dissatisfy the mind of every black servant that comes to England; first by getting them christened or married, which, they inform them, makes them free (tho' it has been adjudged by our most able lawyers, that neither of these circumstances alter the master's property in a slave).[49]

A further index of the high level of organization within the Black community is the solidarity it showed to those of its members who from time to time were caught in the clutches of an uneven justice. During the celebrated Somerset case of 1772, a delegation of Blacks attended the courtroom daily, and when on 22 June 1772 Chief Justice Mansfield delivered his final judgment, they made visible and vocal demonstration of their approval. The report in the *London Chronicle* reads:

> Several [Africans] were in Court to hear the event of the above cause so interesting to their tribe, and after the judgment of the court was known, bowed with profound respect to the Judges, and shaking each other by the hand, congratulated themselves upon the recovery of the rights of human nature, and their happy lot that permitted them to breathe the free air of England. No sight could be more pleasingly affecting to the mind, than the joy which shone at that instant in these poor men's countenances.[50]

In a similar expression of fraternalism, London Blacks came to the aid of two men committed to Bridewell for begging in 1773. Some three hundred visited them and the whole community subscribed to their support while they remained in prison.[51]

There is strong evidence that members of the servant class formed the organizing nucleus for such social and political causes. Their leadership and modus operandi have already been referred to in the foregoing citation from Fielding. Philip Thicknesse was piqued by their astuteness: "London abounds with an incredible number of these black men, who have clubs to support those who are out of place," he squirmed.[52] That they were able to respond so successfully and function so effectively is certainly a tribute to their organizing ability and an indication that they had developed their network of clubs and societies to a high order of efficiency.

Through these agencies they developed a social life distinct from that of the dominant culture and marked by a style that has been closely identified with the universal Black experience across the ages. Numerous notices reflect the fact that they celebrated the occasions of communal life in a manner that was uniquely their own and under circumstances calculated to emphasize their cohesiveness and separate racial identity. One of their "fashionable routs," held in 1764, was described thus: "On Wednesday last, no less than fifty-seven of them, men and women, supped, drank, and entertained themselves with dancing and music, consisting of violins, French horns, and other instruments, at a public house on Fleet Street, till four in the morning. No whites were allowed to be present, for all the performers were black."[53] Servants visited each other in their masters' homes, where they held parties and "assemblies." Francis Barber was invited by the servants of the Thrale household to their annual party, and he reciprocated by having his friends over to Johnson's.[54] After the Mansfield decision, the Blacks celebrated the triumph of their cause in a Westminster tavern. Tickets for admission were five shillings each.[55] Although the commentator in the following record seems to praise with faint damns and damn with faint praise, there is no mistaking the characteristic quality of Black festive culture in his description of the christening:

> 1st came the reputed Father, a Guiney Black, a very clever well-drest Fellow, and another Black who was to be the Godfather. 2ndly, the Midwife or rather her deputy, a White Woman, carrying the little sooty Pagan, who was to be metamorphos'd into a Christian. 3rdly, the Mother, who was also a Black, but not of the Guiny Breed, a well shaped well dress'd woman. 4thly, the Two intended Godmothers, attended by 6 or 8 more, all Guiney Blacks, as pretty, genteel Girls, as could be girt with a girdle, and setting aside the Complexion, enough to tempt an old frozen Anchorite to have crack'd a commandment with any of them.[56]

Together with weddings and funerals, such occasions helped to transmit and preserve the communal nature of their past lives in Africa.[57] No doubt these experiences laid the groundwork for that solid sense of community which saw its full maturity in the writings of Cugoano and Equiano.

So far, this discussion has illustrated how the lower orders of Blacks in eighteenth-century England used their artistic talents, the expedient of marriage, and the common bond of racial affinity to legitimize their human validity in English eyes. These were necessary survival measures in a legal environment more inclined to maintain the status quo of a thriving economic system than to extend to these uprooted strangers the basic human rights and freedoms enshrined in English law.

But there was a class of Africans whom the English (and the Europeans at large) accorded unreserved equality at the highest levels of social and intellectual life. This privileged group consisted of African protégés of European nobility, youths sponsored by philanthropic organizations, and individual sons and relations of African officials. Their credentials were those of intellect—proven or promised—and such other personal qualifications as served to extenuate the facts of their race and color. This group of Blacks is important as a contextual factor in this study because

the tradition of its members' moral and intellectual qualities helped to facilitate the acceptance of Sancho, Cugoano, and Equiano when they came to propose themselves as serious exemplars of Black intelligence and as credible spokesmen for the ultimate vindication of African selfhood.

A tradition of African literacy and learning was established in Europe at the height of the Spanish Renaissance. While the West might persist, through blindness and deceit, in denying to African peoples any significant achievements in science, arts, or letters, it could hardly controvert the educability of the African, exposed to the influences of its own intellectual systems. The achievement of the sixteenth-century Black, Juan Latino, is eloquent testimony to the intellectual equality of his race.[58]

Juan Latino was born in Guinea in 1516. At the age of twelve, he was brought with his mother to Spain, where they both became the slaves of Dona Elvira Fernandez, daughter of the distinguished general, Gonzalo Fernandez. Latino's duties were to attend a young master, Dona Elvira's son, to school and to carry his books. In due course, his inquiring mind prompted him to read them also. Within a short time, he was admitted to the Cathedral School of Granada, where he studied alongside his master. Later, he proceeded to the University of Granada, where he excelled in Latin. It was to mark this excellence that he changed his original slave name, Juan de Sessa, to Juan Latino. He took his bachelor's degree in 1546. His career from then on was one of distinguished scholarship and teaching in Latin Grammar and Humane Letters. In 1556 he was appointed to the chair of Latin in his alma mater, with the full concurrence of the *claustro* (faculty). It was his good fortune and crowning honor to be invited to give the Latin address for the opening of the academic year in 1565.

Juan Latino's most celebrated work is the *Austrias* (1573), a Latin eulogy to Don Juan, victor of Lepanto, whom he had met and played cards with in 1569. Latino wrote another work, the *Translatione,* under royal commission, to mark Philip II's solemn ingathering of his ancestors' remains from their original resting places to a mausoleum in the monumental Escorial, then only recently completed. The six-hundred-line poem, finished in 1574, was dedicated to the king and extolled his virtue and filial piety.

Latino was widely acclaimed both in and after his own time. His lecture halls were filled with students from every social class. They came with fervid enthusiasm for the fruits of the New Learning that he dispensed with generosity and zeal. Cervantes himself recognized Latino's excellence by naming him alongside other illustrious figures in the invocatory verses of the *Quixote*. Diego Jimenez de Enciso immortalized him in *The Famous Drama of Juan Latino,* a play based on Latino's life. Latino's contribution to the revival of classical learning in Renaissance Spain was a labor of love for humane scholarship: Miguel Gutierrez paid tribute to that devotion by describing him as "a Negro who spoke in the ex-court of the Moors the language of Virgil with the purity of Horace, and expounded profound doctrines in the Royal and Pontifical University created by Charles V, the Emperor."

Juan Latino lived and made his mark during the grandest epoch of Spanish history—from the accession of Charles V until after the defeat of Philip II's armada. There is some uncertainty about the exact date of Latino's death, but it is believed he lived to a ripe old age and died some time between 1594 and 1597.

Although we cannot claim that Sancho, Cugoano, or Equiano knew Latino or that his work influenced theirs, it is important to elucidate Latino's achievement so that eighteenth-century Black writers can be seen in the light of his precedence. It must be more than a coincidence that Latino's works demonstrate that pervasive conflict between Black self-awareness and Western acculturation which is to be found prominently in the three writers of this study. Herein lies a crucial affinity. In it, a kinship of common blood is bound up with a kinship of common experience, notwithstanding a distance of two hundred years that separated the Renaissance man on the one hand from the Enlightenment trio on the other. The persistence of that shared consciousness transcends time and local experiences to create an independent text or a single *oeuvre*. This might well be the subject of another inquiry.

Two other African scholars, more nearly coeval to the subjects of the present inquiry, continued the tradition of black learning in Europe by acquitting themselves with distinction in academic study and scholarship. The first was Anthony William Amo.[59] Like Latino, he was born on the Guinea Coast, at Axim in Ghana. He was brought to Europe in 1707, when he was four years old, and educated under the patronage of the duke of Brunswick-Wolfenbüttel. His outstanding career started at the University of Halle about 1726. In 1729 he made the public defence of his dissertation, "De Jure Maurorum in Europa." In it he argued that, through royal patents granted by the Roman Emperor Justinian, Africans were entitled to legal exemption from enslavement by Christian Europe. From Halle, Amo went on to the University of Wittenberg where he became Master of Philosophy (Kant was yet a boy) in 1734. His dissertation on this occasion was entitled "Dissertatio Inauguralis Philosophica de humanae mentis . . . ,"[60] an inquiry concerning the presence of sensations in the body and their absence in the mind. According to report, some of his conclusions were quite in advance of his time. He could not accept that ideas of perception existed in the mind. He found self-contradictory the proposition that the mind was both active and passive. Amo's philosophical critiques bear closely on the rationalism of Leibnitz, whom he met at the duke of Brunswick's. Also in 1734, he published another work on a related subject: the distinctions between the operations of the mind and the operations of the senses.

In 1738 Amo published his masterpiece, a work on logic, theory of knowledge, and metaphysics. One year later, he took up a teaching post at the University of Jena.

Highly respected in the German academic community, Amo was proficient in the classical languages—Hebrew, Greek, and Latin—as well as in the three main European languages—Dutch, French, and German. The great measure of respect accorded his scholarship was echoed by the president of the University of Wittenberg who declared that Amo's dissertation "underwent no change, because it was well executed."

Evidently, Amo prosecuted his intellectual convictions in the traditional spirit of academic freedom. He could hardly have felt any fear or reservations on account of those disabilities which traditionally limited the actions of his fellow Africans in diaspora. For, in defiance of an official edict made by Frederick of Prussia against the works of Christian von Wolff, he asserted his intellectual independence by lecturing on Wolff's political ideas at the University of Halle.

The chairman of the faculty commended Amo's entire achievement in this encomium: "Having examined the system of the ancients and moderns, he selected all that was best of them." And as an example of that fine eclecticism, Amo chose this maxim of Epictetus as his motto: "He that accommodates himself to necessity is a wise man, and he has an inkling of things divine."

Amo was equally well recognized in public life. In 1733 he was chosen to lead the procession during the visit to Halle of Frederick of Prussia. He was later to be nominated as Counselor to the Court of Berlin.

The second African scholar and writer of this period was Jacobus Eliza Capitein.[61] He was born in Africa—the exact place is unknown—in 1717. At about age seven, he was sold to Arnold Steinhart, a ship's captain, who took him to Holland and gave him to a friend, Jacobus van Goch. First, Capitein applied himself to the study of painting and later to the disciplines of Latin, Greek, Hebrew, and Dutch at the Hague.

In 1737 he entered the Divinity School of the University of Leyden, after completing his classical training in rhetoric, logic, and catechism at the Hague Latin School. On 10 March 1742 he had the signal honor, not unlike Juan Latino at Granada, of delivering a public oration at Leyden. Ironically, it was a dissertation defending slavery. Capitein contended that there was no specific biblical injunction against slavery and that the state did not preclude Christian freedom.[62]

Capitein was ordained to the sacred ministry on 17 May 1742 in Amsterdam. Later that same year, he was appointed to the position of preacher and school teacher at the Dutch trading post of Elmina on the Gold Coast (Ghana). There he taught mulatto children the rudiments of reading and writing. He was one of the earliest native pioneer scholars to commit African vernacular languages to writing. His vernacular translations of the Lord's Prayer, the Twelve Articles of Belief, and the Ten Commandments were published in Holland in 1744. His more extensive and better known scholarly works are *De Vocatione Ethnicorum,* which reached three editions, and a book of sermons in Dutch.

Probably about the same time Amo and Capitein were starting their university careers on the Continent, a free Black from the West Indies was studying Latin, literature, and mathematics at Cambridge University in England. Francis Williams was born in 1702 in Jamaica. There the duke of Montagu (later Sancho's patron) took a fancy to him and decided to have him educated.[63] The duke's motive was "to see whether a black boy taken and trained at an English school and then at a university, could not equal in intellectual attainments a white youth similarly educated." Williams went down from Cambridge with his bachelor's degree and moved immediately into the fashionable circles of Georgian society. He soon tired of that leisured life, however, and returned sometime between 1738 and 1748 to his native Jamaica.[64] The duke, eager to follow through with his experiment, nominated him to sit on the Council of the island. That prospect was, however, denied him on strong objections from the conservative Governor Trelawny.[65]

Unfortunately, the most extensive account of Williams's life was written by a prejudiced witness, Edward Long. Out of Long's fabric of distortion and innuendo, one may extricate a few substantive facts about Williams's personality and achievements. By the time of his return, Williams had attained a standard of education equal to that of most Cambridge graduates of his day. He opened a school in Spanish Town, where he taught reading, writing, Latin, and elements of mathematics to the children of local planters.

Williams mastered the formal features of conventional eighteenth-century verse, even if his productions are markedly imitative. He found the ode congenial to [his] abilities and wrote several occasional poems in this manner to mark successive inaugurations of the island's governors. One of the odes, "Integerrimo et Fortissimo Viro . . . ," was addressed to George Haldane,[66] who became governor in 1758. It is written in the balanced, stately manner of neoclassical poetry. The sentiment is high and the images are drawn from the well of Greek and Roman antiquity. Although the distinctive qualities of poise, order, and optimism associated with the spirit of neoclassical poetry predominate in Williams's verses, these beauties do not conceal the ambivalence and tension he felt about his status as an educated Black in slave society. The diffidence and self-abasement evident in the following lines are more a reflection of inner confusion than of the usual rhetorical convention of modesty:

> Yet may you deign to accept this humble song,
> Tho' wrapt in gloom and from a faltr'ing tongue;
> Tho' dark the stream on which the tribute flows,
> Not from the skin, but from the heart it rose.

> ("Integerrimo et Fortissimo Viro . . . ," trans. Long)[67]

Long considered this poem highly labored, artificial, and derivative but conceded grudgingly that it showed some imagination and skill.[68] He thought that Cambridge ought to have produced greater excellence, but the truth is that Williams was no better and no worse than scores of versifiers who were to be found pleading the virtues of their pedestrian verses around the fashionable coffee house of London. David Hume, another critic of Black intellect, refused to pay Williams even a modest compliment: "Tis likely he is admired for very slender accomplishments, like a parrot who speaks a few words plainly."[69]

Two other commentators of more reasonable persuasion (and one, more eminently qualified than either Long or Hume) were better disposed toward the West Indian's poetry. The Reverend Robert Boucher Nicholls, dean of Middleham, gave the lie to narrow-minded colonists like Long who were in the habit of ranking Blacks physically and intellectually with apes. Nicholls objected: "I have never heard that an orang outang composed an ode. Among the defenders of slavery we do not find one half of the literary merit of Francis Williams."[70]

James Ramsay, whose observations on the African in the West Indies were the antithesis of the slavocrats' malicious calumnies, saw Williams's poems in a vastly different light:

> Though his verses bear no great marks of genius, yet, there have been bred at the same university a hundred white masters of arts, and many doctors, who could not improve them and, therefore, his particular success in the field of science cannot operate against the natural abilities of those of his colour, till it be proved, that every white man bred there outstripped him. But allowance is to be made for his being a solitary assay, and the possibility of a wrong choice having been made of him.[71]

While Long painted Williams as a pompous, self-opinionated "white man acting under a black skin," scornful of other Blacks and conceited in his learning, Ramsay reported that "other gentlemen of Jamaica speak highly of [his] abilities and of the favour they procured for him."[72]

Whatever the truth of these opinions, the importance of Francis Williams as one of the first Blacks from the West Indies to excel academically ought not to be overlooked. His attainments attested, both to the curious patrons of African intelligence and to the unremitting denigrators of the slaves, that the Black was after all an intelligent being, capable of cultivation and improvement. As we will see later, Sancho, Cugoano, and Equiano each personified these assumptions, and each was conscious that to vindicate them was one of the critical imperatives of black literary expression in the eighteenth century.

A considerable portion of Black scholarship has demonstrated that it is well nigh impossible to reconstruct the truth of the Black past without resorting to a certain amount of stridency and exaggeration. This is perhaps pardonable, if not entirely desirable, because the scholar labors always against a formidable historical structure of systematic negation, vicious calumnies, grudging concessions, artful diminishing, and downright denial of everything that was reputable in the African past. He inherits a critical tradition that is by necessity and definition corrective. It is a severe duty whose object must be to retrieve and repair the image of Africa and her peoples, so that their achievements can be irremovably established among the legitimate acts of human civilization.

Were it possible to reverse history, it might be possible not to have to mention Francis Williams in the same breath as another, more gifted Black poet of the last quarter of the century, Phillis Wheatley. For when all is said and done, Williams, despite his enviable qualifications, was only a minor versifier. Miss Wheatley, on the other hand, was a prodigy for her time and social condition.[73]

The little girl who was later to be named Phillis Wheatley landed in Boston on a slave ship, probably in July 1761. She was bought by Susannah Wheatley, wife of John Wheatley, a respectable Boston tailor. She was then little more than seven years old, frail and sparsely clad, but was destined to become the darling of the Wheatley family. Mary, one of the Wheatley girls, took her in hand and supervised her early education. Her initial mental growth was exceptional: from an untutored Senegalese girlhood, she emerged with a competence in reading, writing, grammar, history, geography, and Latin, uncommon even among white Bostonians of her age. Her favorite reading was the Bible, Virgil, Ovid, and Pope's translation of Homer. Her own essays in verse writing followed naturally from these influences and quickly superseded the original purpose for which Mrs. Wheatley had bought her; namely, to be her personal attendant. Phillis was given access to some of the best libraries and introduced into the circle of Boston literati.

In 1771, Phillis was baptized in the Old South Meeting House in Boston. In that year, too, her childhood friend and tutor, Mary Wheatley, left home to be the wife of the Reverend John Lathrop. New England winters impaired Phillis's health, and her doctor recommended a sea voyage for her convalescence.

Phillis sailed for England in May of 1773 aboard the Wheatley ship, *London,* accompanied by Nathaniel Wheatley. Mrs. Wheatley had announced her arrival in advance in a letter she wrote to the countess of Huntingdon on 30 April 1773. The countess was a patroness of the Calvinist Evangelicals, George Whitefield's sect of Methodism.[74] Phillis's earliest biographers all state that she met the countess on this occasion, but evidence subsequently advanced shows that the countess was in Wales at the time.[75] It is not unlikely, however, that the noble lady was instrumental in getting Phillis introduced into the most fashionable circles of London society.

The notables Phillis met in England treated her with great deference and hospitality. Brook Watson, afterwards lord mayor of London, presented her with a copy of the 1770 Glasgow folio edition of *Paradise Lost* and a copy of Smollett's translation (1770) of the *Quixote.* Lord Dartmouth and other English nobility entertained her royally, and she would have been presented to King George III, had Mrs. Wheatley's illness not occasioned her hasty return to Boston.[76]

Phillis Wheatley's visit to England was not only a rare personal triumph, but also a landmark in the history of Black literature. Her volume, *Poems on Various Subjects, Religious and Moral,* published in London in 1773, was not only the first volume of poetry to be published by a Black American, but it was very likely the first published work of any Black writer in England.[77] Yet Phillis's fame had been made in England before 1773. She had composed an elegy on the death of George Whitefield in 1770, with a dedication to the countess of Huntingdon, and at least four poems later included in the 1773 volume had been printed previously.[78]

The 1773 volume, then, established her reputation and counterposed a solid, coherent collection of literary works written by a Black poet to the strictures of biased negrophobes. Eighteen of Boston's most respected citizens vouched for the authenticity of her poems by signing a testimonial letter that was appended to the collection. Among them were Thomas Hutchinson, governor of Massachusetts; the Honorable Andrew Oliver, lieutenant-governor; John Hancock, signatory of the Declaration of Independence; the Reverend Matthew Byles, Tory poet; and Phillis's master, John Wheatley.

Phillis Wheatley wrote almost exclusively in the formal manner of neoclassical poetry. Influenced primarily by Alexander Pope, her verses reflect the strictest attention to those features of felicitous diction, regular rhythmic patterns, and decorous sentiments that are characteristic of Pope and his school. Her allusions are abundant, drawn from biblical and classical lore; the feelings are controlled, and the presiding consciousness is one of moderation, remarking the general rather than the particular in the whole universe of experience:

> Creation smiles in various beauty gay,
> While day to night, and night succeeds to day:
> That Wisdom, which attends Jehovah's ways
> Shines most conspicuous in the solar rays:
> Without them, destitute of heat and light,
> This world would be the reign of endless night.
>
> ("Thoughts on the Works of Providence," 1773)

Critical opinion has been as sharply divided over Phillis's claim to poetic merit as over her identity as a Black poet. Her most generous critics were those who marveled at her high aspirations in relation to her tender years, the fact that she was a woman, and that she was an African by origin. All through the eighteenth and nineteenth centuries, her poetry was widely reviewed both in England and America, particularly at the height of the abolitionist movement.[79]

The reviewer in the *London Magazine* for 1773 wrote: "These poems display no astonishing power of genius; but when we consider them as the production of a young untutored African, who wrote them after six [*sic*] months casual study of the English language and of writing, we cannot suppress our admiration of talents so vigorous and lively." Sancho, whom she preceded in publication by seven years, praised the truth of nature and the genius he found in her poetry.[80] Peter Peckard did not think her a poet of the first water but still considered her poems of "great and uncommon merit."[81] Thomas Clarkson included some of her verses in his *Slavery and Commerce of the Human Species* and pointed to her achievement as an index of the potentiality of the African mind when given full scope for development.[82] Joseph Snelling, reviewing her *Memoir and Poems* for the *Christian Examiner* in 1834, devoted over three pages to a fair, balanced commentary. He allowed for Phillis's limitations, while at the same time affirming her superiority over poetasters who had been acclaimed for much less. "What proportion of the rhymesters who enrich our newspapers and magazines with their effusions, can write half so well as Phillis Wheatley? She had no assistance. . . . Accordingly we find some ill-constructed and harsh and prosaic lines, but not so many by half as in the verses of most of her contemporary American poets," Snelling wrote.[83]

Critics from Thomas Jefferson to Imamu Baraka (Leroi Jones) have been severe about her faults, although with diverse motivation. Jefferson could not disavow his habitual bigotry towards Blacks to discover anything of merit in her poetry. He wrote: "Religion, indeed, has produced a Phillis Wheatley but it could not produce a poet. The compositions published under her name are below the dignity of criticism."[84] A scurrilous, satirical piece, entitled "Dreadful Riot on Negro Hill . . ." and written anonymously in New York in 1828, attempts to ridicule Phillis's image as a Black poet by identifying her with the dialectal speech of her illiterate brethren.

Adverse critical reaction from black critics has mainly concerned itself with the absence of any strong racial themes or any militant protest against slavery in Phillis's work. Addison Gayle claims that she could have adapted neoclassical forms "to call a new nation into being." "Oblivious of the lot of her fellow blacks," he continues, "she sings not of a separate nation, but of a Christian Eden."[85] Baraka dispraises her imitation and, in an ill-considered judgment, rates her as only mediocre when placed alongside other Black practitioners of formal literature.[86]

To judge Phillis Wheatley by any kind of absolute criterion, applicable either to her own time or to ours, is to disregard the ambiguities with which she, like Sancho, Cugoano, and Equiano, lived and wrote. Too many modern commentators, blinded by a curious habit of reading history backwards, pass sentence on these early writers from the safety of a world vastly different from the world Blacks knew in eighteenth-century England and America. They forget that in those times Blacks exercised literacy only at the sufferance of a few benevolent whites and often under risk of prosecution. They discount the fact that even those whites who supported abolition often drew the line at universal equality. They protest the absence of vehement denunciation of social and political inequalities as though they think that Blacks then owned or controlled the organs of communication. Because they overlook these things, their impatience with what appears superficially as a weak, compliant rhetoric blinds them to the finer levels of subtlety and ambivalence that recent critics are uncovering through harder, more perceptive scrutiny.[87] This study will reveal similar subsurface meanings, particularly in Sancho's letters.

In appraising the social and political consciousness of both Phillis Wheatley and Ignatius Sancho, critics will have to turn more diligently to what might be called a quality of immanence if they are to discover the assertiveness they say they miss. Sancho was quick to recognize that Phillis's power lay in her immanent condemnation of society through emphasis on moral values; for it was through that seemingly harmless manifesto that he too expressed the tensions he felt about the status of Blacks. He must have recognized, in her emphasis on Christianity and other subjects of general morality, affinities and intentions kindred to his own emphasis on benevolence and virtue; for such appeals were the only form of remonstrance white audiences found palatable issuing from Black voices.

To complete this description of the main categories of educated Africans whose demonstrated mental abilities helped to ameliorate English attitudes to Blacks, it remains only to refer to the "student princes."[88] These were the sons of African royalty, chiefly those living in close proximity to European trading forts, who were traditionally sent abroad to learn the "white man's book."[89] Their parents hoped that their exposure to Western civilization would prepare them for wise and enlightened leadership as well as equip them to handle commercial transactions with Europeans more efficiently in their own interest. The Europeans, on their part, found it sound policy actively to encourage African chiefs to send their sons away in the charge of ships' captains or under sponsorship of organizations like the African Committee and the Company of Merchants Trading to Africa. The young boys thus became the means by which governments and their agents cemented their relations with Africa. Sometimes the princes also became hostages and were held in Europe or at European forts in Africa, while their chieftain fathers worked out their disagreements with the foreigner. Kidnapping was not unknown, especially in cases where persuasion failed. Cases have been documented of merchants violating the trust of African chiefs by detaining their sons in England, France, and Spain or even selling the African youths into slavery.[90]

Philip Quaque, son of Birempon Cudjo, a Gold Coast district chief, was one of the most widely noticed of these students.[91] He arrived in England in 1754, when he was thirteen years old, along with two other African youths, Thomas Caboro and William Cudjo. The three boys were sponsored by the Society for the Propagation of the Gospel and entered a school in Islington, where they were instructed by a Mr. Hickman, the headmaster. Their early lessons were in preparation for Christian baptism, and, after satisfying an examining committee of their knowledge of the Creed, the Lord's Prayer, and the Catechism, they were baptized in Islington Parish Church on 17 January 1759.

Shortly thereafter, the students were put in the care of the Reverend John Moore, a member of the society and curate-lecturer of Saint Sepulchre's Church. Philip Quaque's African schoolfellows did not survive their training in England. Thomas Caboro died of consumption in 1758, and William Cudjo of a mental breakdown in 1764.

Philip Quaque probably received the kind of education typical for students of this group who studied in or near London.[92] Religious instruction, Latin, and other classical subjects were almost certainly the main subjects in their curriculum. In March 1765 he was ordained deacon by the Bishop of Exeter in the Chapel Royal of Saint James's Palace, and in May he was elevated to the priesthood by the bishop of London.[93] That same month he was also married to Catherine Blunt, an Englishwoman. In May 1765, Quaque was appointed catechist, missionary, and schoolmaster to the natives of the Gold Coast.

He returned to that region in 1765 and opened a school for mulatto children. "The rougher sort" were admitted later. Both his educational and pastoral activities were beset by intractable problems. Quaque was himself an enigma to the very people he endeavored to serve: he had forgotten his native language and had to speak through an interpreter, and the fact that his wife was a white foreigner further alienated him from the Africans' support. He was ridiculed by certain governors and European officials at the fort, who refused to attend services conducted by a Black man.

Philip Quaque's importance lies more in his contribution to the idea of African educability than in any exceptional learned attainments. While he does not rank with Amo and Capitein because he was not as extensively trained, he was one of the first Africans to be ordained to the priesthood in England and, like Capitein, was a pioneer both in the missionary and educational fields. To Quaque's early work as a teacher may be traced the earliest foundations of modern Ghanian education.

The last royal visitor who will be described here was perhaps the best known and certainly the most highly born and learned of this group. Job Ben Solomon was born in 1701, the son of Solomon Diallo, the Moslem high priest of Boonda, in Gambia.[94] In February 1730, while on an errand to sell two Africans for his father, Job was captured by Mandingoes and sold to the captain of an English ship. Conscious that his new state was incongruous with his princely rank, he asked leave to send word to his father for his release. The message took some fifteen days to reach his home-town, during which time the ship sailed for Maryland where Job was handed over to Mr. Vachell Dunton, the ship's agent there.

In Maryland, Job was sold to Alexander Tolsey. He was put to work first in the tobacco fields and later to tend cattle, but his background as an assistant priest to his father and as a serious student of Islamic learning unfitted him for both of these occupations, and he soon ran away to Kent County on the Delaware. There he was seen by Thomas Bluett (who was later to become his English teacher and biographer), a clergyman with the mission of the Society for the Propagation of the Gospel. Bluett discerned immediately that Job was no ordinary slave, and, after further signs and the interpretations of a Jolof slave, Job was returned to his master.

Two distinctive features identified Job to his white masters as a special person. He had been noticed regularly to withdraw for private prayer, and he could write Arabic. Indeed it was a letter he wrote to his father in Arabic that turned the tide of his fortunes for the better. That letter came to the attention of James Oglethorpe, then a member of Parliament and deputy governor of the Royal African Company.[95] Oglethorpe sent the letter to Oxford for translation and entered into a bond to purchase Job. In March 1733, the young African sailed for England, but owing to a delay, he missed Oglethorpe, who had by this time sailed for Georgia. Arrangements were made to have Job placed in the care of the Royal African Company.

Unlike his princely counterparts, Job did not come to England to receive formal education; instead, he became the source through which an eager audience of English hosts was enlightened concerning the highest potentialities of the African. Thomas Bluett, who had traveled on the ship with him from Maryland, introduced him into a circle of intelligent and cultivated persons at Cheshunt, where the gentry "were mightily pleased with his Company, and concerned for his misfortunes."[96] Job's English was, understandably, halting at first, but he improved with time and practice, his conversations providing a wealth of new knowledge about the flora and fauna, the customs and the peoples, the agriculture, morality, and religion of his native Africa.

The English marveled at Job's remarkable qualities of mind and his demonstrated capability for superior reasoning. He was found to have a prodigious memory and was puzzled that forgetting seemed so common among his new acquaintances: Bluett said "he hardly forgot Anything in his life, and wondered that anybody ever should."[97]

The news of this extraordinary personage reached Sir Hans Sloane, celebrated botanist and antiquary. Sir Hans was then physician to Queen Caroline and introduced Job to George II and other members of the royal family. Job's extensive erudition in those Arabic texts that then constituted the corpus of knowledge in the Islamic world impressed Sir Hans and his circle of learned associates. He became an invaluable assistant to scholars and virtuosi interested in matters oriental and was elected to the Gentlemen's Society of Spalding on 6 June 1734. That society numbered among its members many distinguished scholars, antiquaries, scientists, and men of letters, three of the best known being Alexander Pope, Sir Isaac Newton, and Sir Hans Sloane himself.

In his house at Bloomsbury, Sloane kept a large collection of birds, stones, Egyptian and Roman antiquities, coins, medals, and some forty-two thousand books and manuscripts. Job most probably assisted Sir Hans in translating some Arabic texts and inscriptions. Sir Hans's collection later became the nucleus of the British Museum.[98]

Job's profound knowledge of the Koran and his unwavering faith in the precepts of Islam recommended him to his English hosts as a remarkably devout and moral person. Bluett states in his biographical account that Job could recite the entire Koran before he was fifteen, and that, while he was in England, he made three copies of that book without any reference to a text.[99] Job engaged his hosts freely in discussions of religious doctrine and belief, although (perhaps to the dismay of his evangelical friends like Bluett) he could not bring himself to accept the idea of the Trinity.

Moving freely as he did among the great and powerful, Job did not fail to extract some tangible advantages from them on behalf of his fellow Moslems in Gambia. He secured from the Royal African Company an undertaking that they would release any Moslems sold to them in Gambia in exchange for two other non-Moslem Africans. The company duly instructed their agents on the Coast to honor the terms of that agreement.[100]

There is a strange irony in Job's relationship with the company. Throughout the entire fourteen months he spent in England, he remained technically their legal property. For some time, his friends feared for his safety, suspicious that he might be resold into slavery after all. Yet the company, on its part, spared no effort to see that he was properly accommodated while he remained in its custody. Although his final departure was long delayed—the fitting out and provisioning of a ship for Gambia was a complicated operation—they seem to have sent him home as soon as they could. When Job finally sailed on 15 July 1734, he took with him many gifts and tokens of his English hosts' appreciation. The company gave specific instructions that he be treated with all deference and hospitality during the voyage. They were anxious that the bond of friendship they had formed with Job should enhance their commercial and trading interests in his country.

The presence of a person of such excellent moral and intellectual qualities could not but transform the climate of English opinion about Africa and her sons. Job Ben Solomon consciously disabused the English of many of their prejudices and misconceptions; unconsciously his gifts of mind and person added to the tradition of Black learning that this chapter has aimed to illuminate. His noble character and irreproachable manners helped pave the way for the more radical revaluation of African humanity that Sancho, Cugoano, and Equiano were later to vindicate in literary terms. Job was a living antislavery document; he was perhaps the nearest human equivalent to the intellectualized image of the "noble Negro" that was to be used so forcefully by antislavery writers in the coming years of abolitionist agitation.

The Black presence in eighteenth-century England, then, spurred a literary reaction that was at once dual and complementary: it generated a species of writing from sources within and without itself whose impact was part favorable and part unfavorable. Each point of view attracted an audience sympathetic to its particular premises and tendencies; together both points of view set in train a philosophical debate about the Black man and slavery that was to give these two subjects a place in the broader domain of the history of ideas.

As we have seen, the English public did not accord Blacks automatic human value on their first appearance among them as a group; the Blacks themselves were forced to contrive forms and expedients that would ensure their survival as individuals and solidify them as a nation in exile. The strategies they adopted were dictated by impulses that are in fact cognate with the most primordial of human faculties—the creative instinct—and operated insensibly to prepare the English mind for a literature celebrating these uniquely human attributes in the African.

Just as the community created its own meaning in the practical terms of survival, so Sancho, Cugoano, and Equiano (as well as those talented African figures described in this chapter) transfigured those terms into a literary and intellectual expression that would present Black life wholly and truthfully. The elevation of the Black experience to the level of art lent credibility to the image of the Black as creator. It furthered the debate over the moral and intellectual equality of the African race, thereby calling more firmly into question the legality of slavery itself.

But the Black response, while it was born of impulses towards racial autonomy and of circumstances peculiar to African life in Britain, neither developed independently of, nor was likely to succeed isolated from, the broader currents that circulated in the mainstream of eighteenth-century intellectual life. . . .

Notes

1. *The Works of Tacitus,* The Oxford Translation, rev. ed., (London, 1884), 2:355.

2. J[oel] A. Rogers, *Sex and Race* (1944; reprint, New York: H. M. Rogers, 1967), 1:55.

3. See Kenneth Little, *Negroes in Britain* (London: Routledge & Kegan Paul, 1972), 187; and Paul

Edwards and James Walvin, "Africans in Britain, 1500-1800," in the *The African Diaspora,* ed. Martin Kilson and Robert Rotberg (Cambridge: Harvard University Press, 1976). These sources do not consider the Roman evidence sufficient to support the African claim.

4. *Scriptores Historiae Augustae,* trans. David Magie (Cambridge: Harvard University Press, 1960-61), 1:424-27.

5. For a full analysis and description of the evidence, see Roger Warwick, "Skeletal Remains," in *The Romano-British Cemetery at Trentholme Drive, York,* ed. Leslie P. Wenham (London: Her Majesty's Stationery Office, 1968), 146-57.

6. Edward Scobie, *Black Britannia* (Chicago: Johnson Publishing Company, 1972), 5-11. Chapter 1 of this book gives a lively account of the social impact of Blacks in England.

7. Edwards and Walvin, "Africans in Britain," 177.

8. *Acts of the Privy Council of England, 1542-1568,* n. s. 1596-97, ed. John Roche Dasent (London: Eyre and Spottiswoode, 1902), 26:16-21.

9. James Walvin, *Black and White* (London: Allen Lane, 1973), 36-37.

10. *Diary of Samuel Pepys,* ed. Robert C. Latham, 11 vols. (Berkeley: University of California Press, 1970), 3:95, 9:510.

11. Folarin O. Shyllon, *Black Slaves in Britain* (London: Oxford University Press, 1974), 3-5.

12. James Sutherland, *Background for Queen Anne,* quoted in Wylie Sypher, *Guinea's Captive Kings* (Chapel Hill: University of North Carolina Press, 1942), 3.

13. Scobie, *Black Britannia,* 12-13.

14. Michael Craton, James Walvin, and David Wright, *Slavery, Abolition and Emancipation* (New York: Longmans, 1976), 72. Although slavery was illegal in England, the sale of Black slaves was carried on quite openly. A street in Liverpool was nicknamed "Negro Row" to announce this commerce.

15. In this classification, I am following the categories described by J. Jean Hecht in "Continental and Colonial Servants in Eighteenth-Century England," *Smith College Studies in History* 40 (1954): 1-61. This is the most extensive account of Blacks in domestic service in England during the period. See also Hecht, *The Domestic Servant Class in Eighteenth-Century England* (London: Routledge & Kegan Paul, 1956), and Dorothy Marshall, "The Domestic Servants of the Eighteenth Century," *Economica* 9 (April 1929): 15-40.

16. J. J. Crooks, "Negroes in England in the Eighteenth Century," *Notes and Queries* 154 (1928): 173-74.

17. Craton, Walvin, Wright, *Slavery,* 172. See also Hecht, "Continental and Colonial Servants," 37.

18. The records of the Royal African Company, the African Committee, and philanthropic bodies like the Society for the Propagation of the Gospel provide circumstantial details about these scholars and the arrangements made for their studies in England. J. J. Crooks ("Negroes in England") documents the expenses of two other native youths who visited England from 1753 to 1755.

19. M. Dorothy George, *London Life in the Eighteenth Century* (1925; reprint, London: Kegan Paul, 1951), 219-22.

20. Philip Curtin, ed., *Africa Remembered* (Madison: University of Wisconsin Press, 1967), 15.

21. James Boswell, *Life of Johnson,* 3rd ed. (New York: Oxford University Press, 1933), 160.

22. Scobie, *Black Britannia,* 24-25; Walvin, *Black and White,* 70-72.

23. Sir Jonah Barrington, *Personal Sketches and Recollections of His Own Times* (Glasgow and London: Cameron and Ferguson, 1876), 367.

24. In addition, Hogarth's pictures, like those of Zoffany, Sir Joshua Reynolds, and Gainsborough, reflect the ever widening spheres of Black involvement in English social life. Both Scobie (*Black Britannia*) and Walvin (*Black and White*) reproduce a good selection of representative prints.

25. Carl Bernhard Wadstrom, *An Essay on Colonization* (1794; reprint, New York: A. M. Kelley, 1986), 695. See also Walvin, *Black and White,* 59.

26. Walvin, *Black and White,* 52-53.

27. The most thorough treatment of the displaced Loyalists' problems can be found in Ellen Gibson Wilson, *The Loyal Blacks* (New York: G. P. Putnam's Sons, 1976), 138-39.

28. *The Gentleman's Magazine* 34 (October 1764): 493.

29. Walvin, *Black and White,* 46-47.

30. Ignatius Sancho, *Letters of the Late Ignatius Sancho,* introd. Paul Edwards, 5th ed. (1830; reprint, London: Dawsons of Pall Mall, 1968). This is the most authoritative edition, from which all textual references in this study will be drawn. Sancho followed an invariable practice, perhaps out of his Shandean whimsy, of identifying his correspondents only by the initial letters of their surnames; but his first editor, Mrs. Crewe, has numbered the letters, and references throughout this study will follow her ordering.

31. See also Letters 13, 14, and 58.

32. Ottobah Cugoano, *Thoughts and Sentiments on the Evil of Slavery,* introd. Paul Edwards (1787; reprint, London: Dawsons of Pall Mall, 1969), hereafter cited as *Thoughts.*

33. Slaves, and even free Blacks, were commonly kidnapped by such agents for a price in England.

The practice was a gainful one for whites who were themselves often poor and needy.

34. Equiano's efforts were unsuccessful. Such incidents tested the true import of the landmark Mansfield decision (1722) in the case of James Somerset (see chap. 5) and were to continue well into the nineteenth century.

35. Olaudah Equiano, *The Life of Olaudah Equiano or Gustavus Vassa, the African,* introd. Paul Edwards, 2 vols. (1789; reprint, London: Dawsons of Pall Mall, 1969), hereafter cited as *Life.*

36. Walvin, *Black and White,* 57.

37. For further discussion of mixed attitudes to Blacks, see Philip Curtin, *The Image of Africa: British Ideas and Action, 1780-1850* (Madison: University of Wisconsin Press, 1964), 35; and J. Jean Hecht, "Continental and Colonial Servants," 43, especially for her discussion of the popularity and unpopularity of Black servants.

38. Edwards and Walvin, "Africans in Britain," 183; Sir John Fielding, *Extracts from the Penal Laws,* quoted in Shyllon, *Black People in Britain, 1553-1833* (London: Oxford University Press, 1977), 97.

39. Little, *Negroes in Britain,* 219-20.

40. George Birkbeck Hill, *Johnsonian Miscellany* (Oxford, 1817), 1:291.

41. Notwithstanding a hostile public posture, intimate black-white liaisons existed on the upper rungs of society. Hogarth's paintings mirrored several such relationships; gossip circles rang with the scandal of the duchess of Queensberry's relationship with her Black protégé, the incomparable and dashing Soubise. For further details, see Scobie, *Black Britannia,* 89-95, and Walvin, *Black and White,* 52-55.

42. Shyllon, *Black People in Britain,* 93.

43. *The London Chronicle* 16 (29 September-20 October 1764): 317.

44. Edward Long, *Candid Reflections,* quoted in Walvin, *Black and White,* 55.

45. "Spotted Negro Boy," *Notes and Queries,* n. s., 6 (1900): 55-56.

46. James Tobin, *Cursory Remarks* (London, 1785), 117, 188n.

47. Cedric Dover, *Hell in the Sunshine* (London: Secker & Warburg, 1942), 159.

48. Both Hecht ("Continental and Colonial Servants," 46) and Curtin (*Image of Africa,* 35) propose that the popular English attitude was one of moderate xenophobia rather than of racism as we know it today.

49. Sir John Fielding, quoted in Shyllon, *Black People in Britain,* 97. Similarly, as Fielding mentions, baptism and church membership were thought to render slaves free. See also Walvin, *Black and White,* 64-67.

50. *The London Chronicle* 31 (23 June 1772): 598c.

51. Shyllon, *Black People in Britain,* 81, 119.

52. Philip Thicknesse, quoted in Dover, *Hell in the Sunshine,* 159.

53. *The London Chronicle* 15 (18 Feb. 1764): 166c.

54. Aleyn Lyell Reade, *Johnsonian Gleanings* (London: Arden Press, 1912), 2:15.

55. Hecht, "Continental and Colonial Servants," 49.

56. *St. James' Evening Post,* quoted in Shyllon, *Black Slaves in Britain* (London: Oxford University Press, 1974), 81.

57. Shyllon, *Black People,* 81.

58. Scobie *Black Britannia,* 31. The most complete account of Latino's life and literary work is Valuarez Spratlin's *Juan Latino, Slave and Humanist* (New York: Spinner Press, 1938), on which I have drawn extensively. Short biographical notes on Latino can also be found in Jahnheinz Jahn's *Neo-African Literature* (New York: Grove Press, 1968), 31-34.

59. The best account of Amo's life is given in William E. Abraham's *The Mind of Africa* (Chicago: University of Chicago Press, 1962), 128-30, which is my chief source here. For purposes of comparison I have used Henri Gregoire's *Moral and Intellectual Faculties of Negroes* (1808; reprint, College Park, Maryland: McGrath Publishing Company, 1967), 173-76, a generally valuable text, which must be used with care, because Gregoire is not always scrupulously accurate, and his text is often vitiated by errors factual and technical. Both Scobie, *Black Britannia,* and Curtin, *Africa Remembered,* make brief notice of Amo.

60. The full title of Amo's Latin treatise is "Dissertatio inauguralis philosophica de humanae mentis ΑΠΑΘΕΙΑsuae sensionis ac facultates sentiendi in mente humana absenta et carum in corpore nostro organico ac vivo praesentia." There is now also a full modern English translation entitled *The ΑΠΑΘΕΙΑ of the Human Mind or the Absence of Sensation* (Halle and Wittenberg: Martin Luther University, 1968).

61. Except as otherwise indicated, the substantive facts of Capitein's career have been drawn from F. L. Bartels' "Jacobus Eliza Capitein, 1717-1747," *Transactions of the Historical Society of Ghana* 4, no. 1 (1959): 1-13.

62. Gregoire conjectures that Capitein may have been influenced by Dutch planters to take this proslavery position. See 204.

63. For the broad outlines of Williams's life, I have followed the memoir in Edward Long's *History of Jamaica* (London, 1774), 2:475-84. As Long's

expressed intention was to prove the inferiority of Blacks and assert the superiority of whites, his work is naturally biased. For a fairer assessment, see Gregoire, *Moral and Intellectual Faculties of Negroes,* 207-12, and Scobie, *Black Britannia,* 27-31.

64. None of Williams's biographers is any more precise about the date of his return.

65. T.H. MacDermot, "From a Jamaican Portfolio," *Journal of Negro History* 2 (1917): 147-59. This is an objective and refreshing critique of Williams.

66. MacDermot, "Jamaican Portfolio," 153.

67. All the sources cited above on Williams reprint this ode, as well as a selection of his other works.

68. Long, *History of Jamaica,* 484.

69. David Hume, "Essay on National Characters," in *Essays Moral Political and Literary* (1742; reprint, London: Longmans Green, 1875), 1:252n.

70. Quoted in Scobie, *Black Britannia,* 29.

71. James Ramsay, the author of *Essay on the Treatment and Coversion of Slaves in the British Sugar Colonies* (London, 1784), 238. Ramsay was an Anglican clergyman who lived in the West Indies for twenty years.

72. Ramsay, *Treatment and Conversion of Slaves,* 239.

73. Unless otherwise indicated, the biographical details on Phillis Wheatley have been taken from Vernon Loggins, *The Negro Author: His Development in America* (New York: Columbia University Press, 1931), and from William H. Robinson, *Phillis Wheatley in the Black American Beginnings* (Detroit: The Broadside Press, 1975), a brief but perceptive appreciation. A more comprehensive critical study is Merle A. Richmond's *Bid the Vassal Soar* (Washington, D.C.: Howard University Press, 1974).

74. The countess was patroness of two other eighteenth-century Blacks: James Albert Ukawsaw Gronniosaw, who dedicated his autobiography, *Narrative of the Most Remarkable Particulars . . . ,* to her; and John Morrant, an ex-slave from America, whose *Narrative* (1785) and *Journal* (1789) seemed to have been published at the countess' encouragement. See Loggins, *Negro Author,* 31-33.

75. See Richmond, *Bid the Vassal Soar,* 33.

76. William Legge (1731-1801), earl of Dartmouth, became secretary of state for North America in 1772. He was also president of the British Board of Trade and a steadfast proslavery advocate. Phillis Wheatley dedicated a poem to him.

77. Gronniosaw's *Narrative* is often dated 1770, but this is dubious; 1774 is thought to be a more reliable date.

78. The elegy had seen over ten editions in Boston, Newport, and Philadelphia, and two editions in London. At least four poems from the 1773 volume had been printed previously. An early version of the poem "On Recollection" appeared in March 1772.

79. For a useful review of critical notices about Phillis Wheatley's poetry, see Julian D. Mason, ed., *The Poems of Phillis Wheatley* (Chapel Hill: University of North Carolina Press, 1966), xxxvi-xlviii.

80. See Letter 58.

81. Quoted in Shyllon, *Black People in Britain,* 197.

82. Thomas Clarkson, *An Essay on the Slavery and Commerce of the Human Species, particularly the African* (Philadelphia, 1786), 110-12.

83. Quoted in Mason, *Poems of Phillis Wheatley,* xxxix. According to Mason, the *Christian Examiner* was a critical journal of high caliber, perhaps the most important in America between 1830 and 1835.

84. Thomas Jefferson, *Notes on Virginia,* ed. William Peden (Chapel Hill: University of North Carolina Press, 1955), 140.

85. Quoted in Robinson, *Phillis Wheatley,* 28.

86. Robinson, *Phillis Wheatley,* 28.

87. Robinson adduces evidence based on Phillis' own revisions and changes made by editors and censors to show that she was not as benign as many critics believe. He finds a fairly clear racial consciousness covertly conveyed through biblical allusions and moral themes (see *Phillis Wheatley,* 57-62). He finds greater self-assertivemess in her London poems, especially the poem addressed to Lord Dartmouth. Finally, he recognizes realistically that if Phillis had been any more explicit, the colonial press would have rejected her work (see 30-38).

88. I base my descriptive details for this group on Shyllon, *Black People in Britain,* 45-66.

89. The first group of such students were twenty Congolese princes who arrived in Portugal in 1516.

90. Cf. Shyllon. *Black People,* 45-46. The most famous of these cases was that of the young Prince Annamaboe. He was entrusted to a slaving captain and sent to be educated in England; but the captain sold him. The captain's treachery reached official circles, and the British government ransomed the prince.

91. Biographical details of Quaque follow those in Bartels, "Philip Quaque 1741-1816," *Transactions of the Historical Society of Ghana* 1, part 5 (1955): 153-77.

92. Those youths were sent to Liverpool whose fathers desired them to acquire a practical education in trade and business matters.

93. Shyllon, *Black People in Britain,* 58.

94. My account of Job's life derives mainly from the biographical sketch in Curtin, *Africa Remembered,* 17-59. Curtin's source, the earliest and most

comprehensive record of Job's enslavement and travels, is Thomas Bluett's *Some Memoirs of the Life of Job, the Son of Solomon, the High Priest of Boonda in Africa* (London, 1734).

95. Oglethorpe was later to become the first governor of Georgia. He was a reformer and philanthropist and had initially refused to permit slavery in the colony.

96. Bluett, quoted in Douglas Grant, *The Fortunate Slave* (London: Oxford University Press, 1968), 90. This is the most complete modern biography of Job and a highly valuable source on other related matters.

97. Grant, *Fortunate Slave,* 94.

98. Grant, *Fortunate Slave,* 99-101.

99. Grant, *Fortunate Slave,* 94.

100. Grant, *Fortunate Slave,* 108.

Jesús Benito and Ana Manzanas (essay date 1999)

SOURCE: "The (De)Construction of the 'Other' in *The Interesting Narrative of the Life of Olaudah Equiano,*" in *Black Imagination and the Middle Passage,* edited by Maria Diedrich, Henry Louis Gates, Jr., and Carl Pedersen, Oxford University Press, 1999, pp. 47-56.

[*In the following essay, Benito and Manzanas examine the concept of the "other" in Olaudah Equiano's* Narrative, *pointing out that Equiano viewed the white man as the "other" against whom he struggled, while at the same time he sought to adopt white culture. According to the critics, this "crisscrossing of identities" creates an "uneasy balance in the authorial voice" of the work.*]

Throughout the seventeenth and eighteenth centuries, European travelers in remote regions of the world easily found new subjects for the position of "the other," that elusive and mobile entity that constitutes the opposite of self. "The other" becomes a discursive concept upon which the so-called "civilized" imagination projects its fantasies and anxieties. Nowhere did travelers blend fact and fiction in their accounts as much as in their description of Africa. The tradition went back to classical historians such as Herodotus and Pliny, who had already peopled Africa with monstrous wonders such as beings without heads and with mouth and eyes in their breasts.[1] These monstrous "others," along with Acridophagi (insect eaters), Ichthyophagi (fish eaters), Ilophagi (wood eaters), Spermatophagi (seed eaters), and the common Anthropophagi as described by classical writers, were to fertilize the Elizabethan imagination, thirsty as it was for the details of savage life, which the Elizabethans located in the newly opened world overseas.[2]

Travel literature in the eighteenth century confirms and refutes the previous accounts with facts and supposed eyewitness reports. Discussions about the monstrous "other"

who inhabited Africa heightened in the debate about the legitimacy of slavery. New explorations reached the most unknown parts of Africa in search for the "Noble Negro" and therefore offered new material for antislavery writings like John Atkins's *Voyage to Guinea* (1735). Other accounts, such as William Snelgrave's *New Account of Guinea* (1734), provided the familiar description of the Africans as lascivious, anthropophagous pagans given to the worship of snakes.

Deeply influenced by the works of antislavery writers such as Benezet and his *Some Historical Account of Guinea* (1770), which Equiano credits in two footnotes,[3] Equiano creates in his *Narrative* an account that contrasts African primitivism with the barbarity of Western civilization. His autobiography can be considered a peculiar kind of travel literature that works as an ironic counterpoint as it subverts the categories the Europeans established in their encounters with the unenlightened or uncivilized. For Equiano, as an accidental tourist or traveler taken into a world of wonders, the white man is "the other."

Slavery, as we read in the *Narrative,* was already known and practiced in Africa. There were "orthodox" ways of obtaining slaves, who were "prisoners of wars,"[4] and "unorthodox" ways through abduction. But these slaves within Africa do not seem to fit the category of "the other," of the opposite of the self, which Equiano presents in his descriptions of the whites. The line that separated a slave from a free man was indeed very tenuous, and any African could become a slave to the rest of the community if he committed a serious crime. In Africa, slavery would imply moral corruption and a state of degeneracy. The slaves caught in wars would approximate the concept of "otherness" since, as Jordan explains, "warfare was usually waged against another people"[5] and captives were usually foreigners or strangers to the community. But in any case, a slave's situation in Africa was radically different from his condition in the West Indies. Equiano explains that "they do no more work than other members of the community" and that "some of these slaves have even slaves under them, as their own property, and for their own use" (19). As described by Equiano, slavery in Africa seems to represent a relationship of service rather than one based on power. Slavery refers to a social status but does not deprive the slave of his status as a human being. Loss of freedom was not viewed as loss of humanity. The term "slave" was therefore rather circumstantial and did not seem to qualify the bearer as "the other" in African society.

Equiano's first intuition of whiteness (as associated with otherness) is a brief reference in chapter 1 mentioning light-colored children within his community who were seen as deformed.[6] Equiano's view of white complexions as a sign of deformity confirms the impressions of an English traveler, Sir John Mandeville, who in the fourteenth century already noted that the people of Egypt "are black in color, and they consider that a great beauty, and the blacker they are the fairer they seem to each other. And they say that if they were to paint an angel and a devil, they would paint the angel black and the devil white."[7] The category of "the other" as the ontologically different appears when Equiano first encounters the white crew of a slave ship in chapter 2. When Equiano sees the white crew, he does not think of the Europeans as "deformed men"; they are not only not human but spirits with evil tendencies. Tossed and handled by the crew, Equiano is persuaded he had "got into a world of bad spirits" (33). The features Equiano emphasizes render the Europeans as a homogeneous, indistinguishable "other," deprived of individual qualities. Interestingly enough, like the Europeans when they came into contact with Africans, Equiano uses color, together with the whites' long hair, to categorize them. Subtly, Equiano reminds the reader that, for the African, the white man is "the other." The white man automatically embodies in Equiano's imagination savage tendencies, as he confirms when he "saw a large furnace or copper boiling and a multitude of black people" (33), a clear indication for Equiano that he was going to be eaten by these white spirits.

Clearly, Equiano demonstrates his limited comprehension of his new situation as a slave. The narrator can give a subjective account of his perceptions but knows nothing of causality.[8] Equiano's naïveté and his lack of knowledge of the workings of the slave trade are, at the same time, a subtle deconstruction of one of the key tenets of proslavery theoreticians such as William Snelgrave: that Africans had degenerated into cannibalism. In fact, the image of Africans as anthropophagi occurred frequently in the accounts of classical historians such as Pliny. The association of slaves and the anthropophagi is clear in the revealing title of G. Fitzhugh's *Cannibals All! or Slaves without Masters.* Fitzhugh's book reminds the reader of the Africans' natural tendencies and the necessity to keep them under slavery. Perhaps aware of numerous eyewitness reports and proslavery literature, which maintained that Africans eat each other, either alive or dead, with the same casualness with which Europeans eat beef or mutton,[9] Equiano subverts one of the practices that in the Europeans' eyes made Africans Wild Men. In Equiano's eyes, "those white men with horrible looks, red faces, and long hair" (33) are the degenerate and wild "other," the feared anthropophagi.[10]

Gradually, Equiano forges the image of the white man as "the other," the obverse of the travel books' idea of the Negro as "the other." Like an accidental and involuntary traveler, Equiano notes the "irrationality" that rules the world of the white "spirits." Equiano observes how "the white men had some spell or magic they put in the water, when they liked, in order to stop the vessel" (35). Astonished at the vision of whites on horseback, Equiano claims "these people [were] full of nothing but magical arts" (37). The naive and uninitiated voice of the young slave wonders at the so-called "civilized" ways of the whites but also subtly reminds the reader that only the eye of the beholder determines what is magic or irrational and what is perfectly logical and rational. Equiano subverts the com-

mon belief that Africans were all inveterate conjurers given to the study of black magic, as they appear in Herodotus's account,[11] and projects it onto "the other," thus implying that the European travelers who emphasized the irrationality of the Africans revealed only their own misconceptions and their own ignorance about the ways of "the other." In Equiano's *Narrative,* the accounts that presented the ultimate "otherness" of the Africans undergo Bakhtinian "dialogization" as they are relativized and parodied. As Equiano writes his own travel book, the subjectivity and the relativism implicit in the authoritative discourse peculiar to proslavery travel tales are laid bare.[12]

Yet Equiano starts to deconstruct his initial image of the whites on his way to England and after he is purchased by a new master, Henry Pascal. If the people to be "othered" are always homogenized, the individuation of one of them paves the way for the dissolution of the category of "the other." In the *Narrative* an individual, Richard Baker, appears in whom, we read, Equiano finds a faithful companion and friend. Moreover, Equiano seems to forget that whiteness for the African equates "otherness" and harbors, at least unconsciously, the desire to become white: "I therefore tried oftentimes myself if I could not by washing make my face of the same colour as my little play-mate, Mary, but it was all in vain; and I then began to be mortified at the difference in our complexions" (44). This anecdote, situated in the *Narrative* at a moment when Equiano is about to convert to cultural whiteness, appears quite symbolic. Convinced of the impossibility of "washing an Ethiop white," Equiano seems to realize that his Africanness and blackness are there to stay. Three years after he was taken to England, Equiano completed the deconstruction of his previous vision of whites as spirits. Whites are not strangers anymore, as Equiano explains: "I no longer looked upon them as spirits, but as men superior to us; and therefore I had the strongest desire to resemble them" (51-52). Equiano can turn into the perfect mimic man[13] as he imitates the English customs and mores. However, as he is unable to erase his blackness, his identification with the English, with the colonizer and slave holder, will never be complete.

White spirits turn into men, thus erasing the insurmountable difference—of kind—between white (spirits) and black (men). The only difference Equiano now perceives is a difference of degree, a quantitative differentiation because white men are superior. This new perception of what used to be "the other" as superior involves a new perception of the self as inferior or incomplete. Disturbing as this new category—superior/inferior—may sound, it reveals how Equiano, perhaps conditioned by the fluid barriers in African slavery, views the border between free men and slaves as tenuous, permeable enough to disappear in three years or, more astonishing, in a few pages. It seems on the one hand that Equiano feels the need to soften his ways and his perceptions of Englishmen once he is living among them. On the other hand, Equiano's fascination with European culture and morality reveals more than blind imitation. His admiration for English culture works as a critique of the uses and abuses it was put to by a majority of Europeans who, as we see throughout the *Narrative,* failed to live up to their own standards. Further, Equiano's understanding and admiration for the ways of the Europeans only confirm his qualities as a perceptive traveler on a foreign ground who is well trained in cultural relativism. Unlike some of the travelers who ventured into Africa and looked at Africans from a "literary" distance—as established by their predecessors' accounts—Equiano illustrates the notion that once one immerses oneself in the ways of "the other," barriers are removed. That might be one reason why Equiano finds that whites, contrary to his first intuition, were not spirits; neither did they live in a world of magic. Away from the horrific scenes he witnessed in the slave ship during the Middle Passage, Equiano seems to "convert" to whiteness. The barrier between the self and "the other" is therefore "blurred." Equiano has absorbed the principles and the language of "the other" and describes himself in the terms set by the English. In just two chapters Equiano has constructed and deconstructed a myth of whiteness, thus creating two contrasting voices that will blend in the remainder of the *Narrative.*

But this deconstruction of "the other" is far from definite in Equiano's *Narrative.* The alleged superiority of the whites is compromised when, against Equiano's expectations, his "benign" master, Henry Farmer, sells him to Captain Doran. At that moment and during his crossing of the Atlantic on his way to the West Indies, Equiano finds out that even though he had been baptized and "by the laws of the land" no man had a right to sell him, he was still will-less merchandise in the eyes of the whites. Even though Equiano considers himself an Englishman, Englishmen "proper" do not consider him an Englishman. If heathenism were a fundamental "defect" that set Africans—and Equiano—apart from Englishmen, the conversion of Africans to Christianity did not imply they had become civilized and were the same kind of men. Being a Christian, as Jordan explains, "was not merely a matter of subscribing to certain doctrines; it was a quality inherent in oneself and in one's society" (24), a quality intimately related to racial issues. Although a Christian, Equiano finds out that he does not participate in the "unity of man" and the continuity of mankind the Christian faith postulated. Despite being a Christian, he was still "the other" in white society. Equiano's conversion does not eradicate the difference that separated him from the whites. Equiano realizes that, even though he has traveled "transatlantic distances" to convert to the Christian faith, he is not fully accepted as a Christian. Further, as he states in the *Narrative,* he finds that "otherness" is a mobile category that encompasses other peoples like the Indians and changes according to the interests of the white majority, always including Negroes. What remains stable and fixed is that insuperable barrier or difference that separated slaves and masters and gives, in Equiano's words, "one man a dominion over his fellows which God could never intend" (80).[14] Instead of erasing differences, slave masters intensify and perpetuate them by denying the slave access to education, thus fixing him as irreversibly other, as Equiano denounces. Equi-

ano's *Narrative* advocates the removal of racial and religious barriers in the inscription on the title page of the abolitionist slogan: "Am I not a Man and a brother."

Sailing back to the West Indies with his new master implies his return to the "land of bondage" and, accordingly, his reconstruction of whites as the deceitful, uncivilized "other." Even though Equiano is bought by another benign master, Mr King, who does not treat him "as a common slave" (71), Equiano always maintains a detached and ambivalent position toward whites, as Paul Edwards has demonstrated.[15] As the *Narrative* progresses, Equiano still fixes whites in the category of "the other," but as he learns their ways and their language, his discourse becomes visibly influenced by the white perspective. This double position is illustrated in Equiano's indirect participation in the economics of slavery, as an overseer on Dr. Irving's estate who managed to keep Negroes cheerful and healthy (76) and as an assistant on slave ships in numerous Middle Passages: "After we had discharged our cargo there, we took in a live cargo, as we call a cargo of slaves" (98). Perhaps one of the most disturbing aspects of this kind of statement (which appears repeatedly, pp. 90, 107) is the inclusion of Equiano within the "we." Striking as well is Equiano's detachment when he refers to "a cargo of slaves" as "live cargo" without further comment. Equiano is clarifying his position, which is closer to the whites—to whom he is linked through the inclusive "we"—and remains more distant from his fellow slaves, who are referred to in the third person. In addition, the references to slaves (not to "Africans") are followed by completely different subjects, as if Equiano intended to delete from his narration further engagement with other slaves and at the same time emphasize his perfect knowledge of the workings of slavery. It seems that when Equiano accepts the language and roles of the more "civilized" culture, he frequently runs the risk of adopting the distorting stereotypes inherent in that language.

The *Narrative* keeps an uneasy balance between Equiano's desire for personal freedom and his forced passivity when he witnesses the abuses committed against other Negroes during many Middle Passages. On such occasions Equiano carries out a superb exercise in negotiation between his silence and his role as critical witness to the sexual abuses perpetrated against female slaves. His silence and passivity are compensated for years later by his exposure of the atrocities of slavery in his *Narrative.* Equiano's African name—meaning "one favoured, and having a loud voice and well spoken" (20)—endows him with a natural gift for eloquence. His mastery of words proves decisive in negotiating between his "two souls" as a European and as an African and between his indirect acquiescence to a dominant ideology—as exemplified in the economic and religious voice that predominates in the *Narrative*—and his larger commitment to the abolition of slavery and his race. It seems that Equiano has to incorporate "the other" as part of the self if he wants to preserve that very self. This double perspective is noticeable from the opening of the autobiography in Equiano's dedication, when he first ponders his predicament since his abduction from Africa and finally justifies the horrors of slavery by his initiation into the Christian doctrine. In a way, both Equiano and Wheatley (among other writers such as Jupiter Hammon) echo the alleged positive effects of slavery vaunted by slavery supporters such as William Grayson, John C. Calhoun, or Howell Cobb, among many others. Although Africa remains in Equiano's mind and he is linked to it through "tender connections," Equiano distances himself from the characters in African American folktales for whom Africa is the paradise away from the white man.

As a slave planning to escape from the West Indies, Equiano never thinks of Africa as his final destination but chooses to return to England. Although his decision sounds paradoxical, it may imply that for Equiano, as for Martin Luther King many years later, a man's return to Africa would imply avoiding a problem. For King, as for Equiano, the fight against slavery first, and segregation later, demanded a courageous decision to claim full American or—in Equiano's case—English citizenship. When Equiano intends to return to Africa, he does so in the capacity of a missionary of the Church of England and later as a commissary on the Sierra Leone expedition. In both attempts he tried not to recover his Africanness or the simplicity of his old African religion but to convert his countrymen to the Gospel faith. When he decides to return to Africa, he is not planning to return merely as an African but as an African European committed both to the Negro cause and to the spreading of the culture of the West. Equiano clearly measures the power of such disruptive forces as Christianity and imperialist economics and sees no radical escape to a primitive and undisrupted African past. He is conscious that this "past" (the Africa he evoked in the first two chapters of his *Narrative*) is no longer there after the African encounter with the white man. Consequently, he adopts the role of a knowledgeable mediator. He seems aware that the clash between African and European value systems and religious beliefs is more dramatic when it emanates from different ethnic and racial groups, but rather less significant when it comes from individuals within the same ethnic group, as he acknowledges in his letter to the Lord Bishop of London.

Equiano's dual identity as an African and a European is clear as well in his encounters with the Musquito Indians. Although there are common ties between Equiano and the Indians (both were part of the category of "the other" in the Caribbean colonies), Equiano adopts the position of the mediator who introduces the Indians to the Holy Word. Unlike the figure of the colonizer, who would impose the new religion on the savage, Equiano is willing to acknowledge the moral superiority and religious fervor of the Indians. Equiano finds in the natural religion of the Musquito Indians echoes of his own African religion (neither has places for worship or is acquainted with swearing), and he considers these unenlightened Indians more enlightened than many Christians. However, in his fluid role as intermediary, he crisscrosses the line between both religious practices as he personally transcended the barriers separating the white man and the black other. He tries to bring the Indians to the Holy Word, but his attitude is not that of imposition as much as of persuasion. Even if Equiano is instrumental in the conversion of the pagan and unenlightened to the Christian faith, his suspicions about the so-called Christians are present throughout the *Narrative*. Very characteristic of his style is the ironic usage of "christian" when he wants to emphasize a master's special cruelty. He finds as well that there are Christians, like the Assembly of Barbadoes, who rather deserve the appellation of "savages and brutes." Also ironic, Equiano—a convert—takes the liberty of teaching or reminding old Christians of some excerpts from the Bible they frequently forget: "I told him [Mr. D—] that the Christian doctrine taught us 'to do unto others as we would that others should do unto us'" (74-75).[16]

Equiano's commitment and questioning—"dialogization"—of white ideology and culture "from within" is present as well in the economic voice with which he closes the *Narrative*. As Houston Baker has demonstrated in his analysis of Equiano's *Narrative* in *Blues, Ideology, and Afro-American Literature,* Equiano appropriates the mercantile and calculating voice of the white man, the same voice that quantified and translated the African's life into economic terms. Although Equiano denounces a system that establishes the value of the African in purely economic terms, as stated by the Assembly of Barbadoes, he is fully aware that he needs to master the economic mechanisms of slavery in order to ameliorate and alter his status as property.[17] When he records his initial commercial transactions with the diligence of a trader's secular diary in chapter 7, Equiano is not passively mirroring or imitating white mercantilism but subverting the economics of slavery to effect the "ironic transformation of property by property into humanity."[18] Equiano's economic voice disrupts the economic mechanisms and the language of slavery from within, through the knowledge he has acquired as marketable property. Once Equiano manages to buy his freedom from Dr. King, his mastery of mercantilism is finally stated in the theory of trade that would replace the slave trade with "a commercial intercourse with Africa." Fully aware of British economic interests and at the same time devoted to the abolitionist cause, Equiano transforms African slaves into African customers, who would "insensibly adopt the British fashions, manners, customs, &c." (176) and therefore perpetuate their condition as dependents or colonial subjects. Equiano's margin of negotiation when he makes this abolitionist appeal is indeed very narrow. He seems aware of the impossibility that Africans aspire to absolute freedom and, very cautiously, suggests a compromise for both Europeans and Africans.

Equiano's crisscrossing of the Atlantic takes him to a crisscrossing of identities. Equiano oscillates between his Africanness, with his vision of whites as "the other," and his desire to become part of that other and convert his countrymen to the superior white culture and religion. This crisscrossing of identities constitutes Equiano's "double consciousness," to use Du Bois's words. Equiano manifests his peculiar "twoness," "two souls, two thoughts,"[19] but his strivings are intricately interwoven and reconciled in his *Narrative.* "The other" crisscrosses the self and the self crisscrosses "the other" to create a difficult and uneasy balance in the authorial voice. Equiano's ultimate exercise of negotiation, the utopian commercial imperialism, which runs parallel to his Christian utopia that he advocates in the conclusion of the *Narrative,* stands as his ultimate compromise. This utopian commercialism would indeed end slavery—and therefore show the fruitful results of Equiano's infiltration in the world of "the other"—but would perpetuate the infiltration of "the other" in Africa, for it would also make the African settle for a new kind of servitude, and thus satisfy "the other" in him.

Notes

1. Pliny, quoted in Eldred D. Jones, *The Elizabethan Image of Africa* (Amherst: Folger Books, 1971), p. 5.

2. See Winthrop Jordan, *White over Black: American Attitudes toward the Negro, 1550-1812* (New York: Norton, 1977), p. 25.

3. For a detailed comparative analysis of Benezet's *Some Historical Account of Guinea* and Equiano's *Narrative,* see Angelo Costanzo, *Surprizing Narrative: Olaudah Equiano and the Beginnings of Black Autobiography* (New York: Greenwood Press, 1987).

4. Olaudah Equiano, *The Interesting Narrative of the Life of Olaudah Equiano, or Gustavus Vassa, the African,* in Henry Louis Gates, ed., *The Classic Slave Narratives* (New York: New American Library, 1987), p. 17. All subsequent references to this edition appear parenthesized in the text.

5. See Jordan, *White over Black,* p. 55.

6. Deformity as a quality associated with whiteness appears clearly in Chinua Achebe, *Things Fall Apart* (New York: Fawcett Crest, 1959).

7. Sir John Mandeville, *The Travels of Sir John Mandeville* (Harmondsworth, England: Penguin, 1983), p. 64.

8. Susan Willis, "Crushed Geraniums: Juan Francisco Manzano and the Language of Slavery," in Charles T. Davis and Henry Louis Gates, Jr., eds., *The Slave's Narrative* (New York: Oxford University Press, 1985), p. 202.

9. See Jordan, *White over Black,* p. 25.

10. For the captive Allmuseri in Johnson's *Middle Passage* (New York: Plume Book, 1991), white men were "barbarians shipping them to America to be eaten." The Allmuseri, like Equiano, saw the white men as "savages," p. 65.

11. See Jones, *Elizabethan Image,* p. 4. In Shakespeare's *Othello,* Brabantio accuses Othello of having corrupted his daughter "By spells and medicines bought of mountebanks," I.iii.v, 61.

12. See M. M. Bakhtin, *The Dialogic Imagination* (Austin: University of Texas Press, 1981), pp. 342-343, 412-414.

13. See Homi K. Bhabha, *The Location of Culture* (London: Routledge, 1994), pp. 85-92, for the importance of "mimicry" in colonial discourse.

14. Perpetuity is indeed a very characteristic aspect of slavery in America. See Jordan, *White over Black,* pp. 52-53.

15. Paul Edwards, "The West African Writers of the 1780s," in Davis and Gates, eds., *Slave's Narrative,* pp. 187-195.

16. See Katalin Orban, "Dominant and Submerged Discourses in *The Life of Olaudah Equiano* (or Gustavus Vassa?)," *African-American Review* 27 (1993): 655-664.

17. Houston A. Baker, Jr., *Blues, Ideology, and Afro-American Literature: A Vernacular Theory* (Chicago: University of Chicago Press, 1984), pp. 34-35.

18. Baker, *Blues,* p. 36.

19. W. E. B. Du Bois, *The Souls of Black Folk* (New York: Bantam Books, 1989), p. 3.

FURTHER READING

Criticism

Conolly, L. W. "English Drama and the Slave Trade." *English Studies in Canada* 4 (1978): 393-412.
Survey of English plays about slavery in the 1700s and the early 1800s.

Diedrich, Maria, Henry Louis Gates, Jr., and Carl Pederson, eds.. *Black Imagination and the Middle Passage.* Oxford: Oxford University Press, 1999, 320 p.
Collection of essays examining the forced dispossession of Africans caused by slavery and the slave trade; analyzes the texts, religious rites, economic exchanges, dance, and music of the transatlantic journey and on the American continent.

Ebbatson, J. R. "Some 'Forgotten Scribblers' on the Slave Trade." *Ariel: A Review of International English Literature* 4, No. 4 (1973): 3-18.
Discusses the work of lesser-known eighteenth-century British writers who contributed to the slavery debate, such as Richard Mant, Elizabeth Berger, and William Dodd.

Ellis, Markman. "Sentimentalism and the Problem of Slavery." In *The Politics of Sensibility,* pp. 49-86. Cambridge: Cambridge University Press, 1996.

Discusses the references to and "theme" of slavery in eighteenth-century British sentimental literature by Laurence Sterne and compares it to the treatment of slavery in the works by ex-slave Ignatius Sancho. Ellis concludes that the sentimental approach, despite its humanitarian and benevolent intentions, failed to move beyond the depiction of its theme to a critique of the theme's subject—the actual existence of slavery and its effect on enslaved peoples.

Gardner, Jared. *Master Plots: Race and the Founding of an American Literature, 1787-1845.* Baltimore: The Johns Hopkins University Press, 1998, 238 p.

Examination of the intersection of racial and national discourses in the founding of a national literature in the United States. Includes a chapter on Royall Tyler's *The Algerian Captive.*

Gwilliam, Tassie. "'Scenes of Horror,' Scenes of Sensibility: Sentimentality and Slavery in John Gabriel Stedman's *Narrative of a Five Years Expedition against the Revolted Negroes of Surinam.*" *ELH* 65, No. 3 (1998): 653-73.

Argues that John Gabriel Stedman's *Narrative* (1790) demonstrates that slavery and colonialism can serve to illuminate the contradictions and internal pressures endemic to sentimental love plots and the problematic process of creating sentimentality itself.

Hudson, Nicholas. "From 'Nation' to 'Race': The Origin of Racial Classification in Eighteenth-Century Thought." *Eighteenth-Century Studies* 29, No. 3 (1996): 247-64

Discussion of the central development in the history of racial classification—the changing meaning of the term "race," along with the associated terms "nation" and "tribe," from the Renaissance to the Enlightenment.

Morrison, Anthea. "Samuel Taylor Coleridge's Greek Prize Ode on the Slave Trade." In *An Infinite Complexity: Essays in Romanticism,* edited by J. R. Watson. Edinburgh: Edinburgh University Press, 1983, 248 p.

Critical examination of Coleridge's "Ode on the Slave Trade."

Pederson, Carl. "Middle Passages: Representations of the Slave Trade in Caribbean and African-American Literature." *Massachusetts Review* 34, No. 2 (Summer 1993): 225-38.

Explores the works of five authors, from the 1700s to the 1990s, who have written about the Middle Passage from Africa to the Americas. Includes a discussion of the work of Olaudah Equiano.

Plasa, Carl and Betty J. Ring. *The Discourse of Slavery: Aphra Behn to Toni Morrison.* London: Routledge, 1994, 226 p.

Collection of essays that address the problematic of slavery within the literary, cultural, and political discourses of Britain and the United States from the seventeenth century to the late twentieth century.

Potkay, Adam and Sandra Burr, eds. *Black Atlantic Writers of the 18th Century: Living the Exodus in England and the Americas.* New York: St Martin's Press, 1995, 268 p.

Collection focusing on the works of Ukawsaw Gronniosaw, John Marrant, Ottobah Cugoano, and Olaudah Equiano that seeks to uncover the various contexts necessary for understanding the stories of the writers' lives.

Ransom, Stanley Austin, Jr., ed. *America's First Negro Poet: The Complete Works of Jupitor Hammon of Long Island.* Port Washington, N. Y.: Kennikat Press, 1970, 122 p.

Includes a biographical sketch of Hammon, a bibliography of his works, and commentary on his poetry and prose.

Rees, Christine. "Utopia Overseas." In *Utopian Imagination and Eighteenth-Century Fiction,* pp. 76-94. London: Longman Group, 1996.

Discusses the attitudes towards slavery of Daniel Defoe's protagonist in *Robinson Crusoe* and considers whether the character Friday was a slave not only by modern standards but according to theories posited by thinkers from Aristotle to John Locke.

Sandiford, Keith A. *Measuring the Moment: Strategies of Protest in Eighteenth-Century Afro-English Writing.* London: Associated University Presses, 1988, 181 p.

Examination of the significant impact of the African writers Ottobah Cugoano, Ignatius Sancho, and Olaudah Equiano on public conscience and the anti-slavery movement England.

Seeber, Edward D. "Anti-Slavery Opinion in the Poems of Some Early French Followers of James Thomson." *Modern Language Notes* 50, No. 7 (November 1935): 427-34.

Reviews the works of several French poets who were influenced by British poet James Thomson, who protested against slavery, and who contributed to the growth of abolitionist sentiment.

Spengemann, William C. "The Earliest American Novel: Aphra Behn's *Oronooko.*" *Nineteenth-Century Fiction* 38, No. 4 (March 1984): 384-414.

Contends that *Oronooko* should be considered an early American novel and that it has not been because of the novel's setting.

Sypher, Wylie. *Guinea's Captive Kings: British Anti-Slavery Literature of the XVIIIth Century.* Chapel Hill: The University of North Carolina Press, 1942, 340 p.

Important early study of slavery and English literature. Sypher argues that representations of slavery in the early seventeenth and eighteenth centuries were not primarily interested in the condition of chattel slavery.

Thomas, Hugh. *The Slave Trade: The Story of the Atlantic Slave Trade, 1440-1870.* New York: Simon and Schuster, 1997, 908 p.

Comprehensive historical study of the Atlantic slave trade told largely from the perspective of white participants, from the time of the first Portugese slaving expeditions to the era after the Emancipation Proclamation. Includes brief discussions of the literature of the era.

Tokson, Elliot H. *The Popular Image of the Black Man in English Drama, 1550-1668.* Boston: G. K. Hall, 1982, 178 p.

Studies the ways that English creative writers of the sixteenth and seventeenth centuries treated the black Africans who had been introduced into their culture in the 1550s.

Wheeler, Roxann. "'My Savage,' 'My Man': Racial Multiplicity in *Robinson Crusoe*." *ELH* 62, No. 4 (1995): 821-61.

Examines the representation of race in *Robinson Crusoe* and maintains that the difficulty of situating the character Friday in any stable category of cannibal or slave is central to analyzing the novel and reflects the cultural uncertainty about the significance of racial difference in the eighteenth century.

————. "The Complexion of Desire: Racial Ideology and Mid-Eighteenth-Century British Novels." *Eighteenth-Century Studies* 32, No. 3 (1999): 309-32.

Explores the understanding of difference and desire in eighteenth-century novels that feature racial intermarriage.

How to Use This Index

Literary Criticism Series
Cumulative Author Index

See also CLR 6; DA3; MAICYA; SATA 100; YABC 1

Anderson, C. Farley
See Mencken, H(enry) L(ouis); Nathan, George Jean

Anderson, Jessica (Margaret) Queale 1916-
.... **CLC 37**
See also CA 9-12R; CANR 4, 62

Anderson, Jon (Victor) 1940- . **CLC 9; DAM POET**
See also CA 25-28R; CANR 20

Anderson, Lindsay (Gordon) 1923-1994
.... **CLC 20**
See also CA 125; 128; 146; CANR 77

Anderson, Maxwell 1888-1959 ...... **TCLC 2; DAM DRAM**
See also CA 105; 152; DLB 7; MTCW 2

Anderson, Poul (William) 1926- ..... **CLC 15**
See also AAYA 5, 34; CA 1-4R, 181; CAAE 181; CAAS 2; CANR 2, 15, 34, 64; CLR 58; DLB 8; INT CANR-15; MTCW 1, 2; SATA 90; SATA-Brief 39; SATA-Essay 106

Anderson, Robert (Woodruff) 1917-
.... **CLC 23; DAM DRAM**
See also AITN 1; CA 21-24R; CANR 32; DLB 7

Anderson, Sherwood 1876-1941 .... **TCLC 1, 10, 24; DA; DAB; DAC; DAM MST, NOV; SSC 1; WLC**
See also AAYA 30; CA 104; 121; CANR 61; CDALB 1917-1929; DA3; DLB 4, 9, 86; DLBD 1; MTCW 1, 2

Andier, Pierre
See Desnos, Robert

Andouard
See Giraudoux, (Hippolyte) Jean

Andrade, Carlos Drummond de ..... **CLC 18**
See also Drummond de Andrade, Carlos

Andrade, Mario de 1893-1945 ...... **TCLC 43**

Andreae, Johann V(alentin) 1586-1654
.... **LC 32**
See also DLB 164

Andreas-Salome, Lou 1861-1937 .. **TCLC 56**
See also CA 178; DLB 66

Andress, Lesley
See Sanders, Lawrence

Andrewes, Lancelot 1555-1626 .... **LC 5**
See also DLB 151, 172

Andrews, Cicily Fairfield
See West, Rebecca

Andrews, Elton V.
See Pohl, Frederik

Andreyev, Leonid (Nikolaevich) 1871-1919
.... **TCLC 3**
See also CA 104; 185

Andric, Ivo 1892-1975 .... **CLC 8; SSC 36**
See also CA 81-84; 57-60; CANR 43, 60; DLB 147; MTCW 1

Androvar
See Prado (Calvo), Pedro

Angelique, Pierre
See Bataille, Georges

Angell, Roger 1920- .... **CLC 26**
See also CA 57-60; CANR 13, 44, 70; DLB 171, 185

Angelou, Maya 1928- ... **CLC 12, 35, 64, 77; BLC 1; DA; DAB; DAC; DAM MST, MULT, POET, POP; WLCS**
See also AAYA 7, 20; BW 2, 3; CA 65-68; CANR 19, 42, 65; CDALBS; CLR 53; DA3; DLB 38; MTCW 1, 2; SATA 49

Anna Comnena 1083-1153 .... **CMLC 25**

Annensky, Innokenty (Fyodorovich) 1856-1909 .... **TCLC 14**
See also CA 110; 155

Annunzio, Gabriele d'
See D'Annunzio, Gabriele

Anodos
See Coleridge, Mary E(lizabeth)

Anon, Charles Robert
See Pessoa, Fernando (Antonio Nogueira)

Anouilh, Jean (Marie Lucien Pierre) 1910-1987 .... **CLC 1, 3, 8, 13, 40, 50; DAM DRAM; DC 8**
See also CA 17-20R; 123; CANR 32; MTCW 1, 2

Anthony, Florence
See Ai

Anthony, John
See Ciardi, John (Anthony)

Anthony, Peter
See Shaffer, Anthony (Joshua); Shaffer, Peter (Levin)

Anthony, Piers 1934- ... **CLC 35; DAM POP**
See also AAYA 11; CA 21-24R; CANR 28, 56, 73; DLB 8; MTCW 1, 2; SAAS 22; SATA 84

Anthony, Susan B(rownell) 1916-1991
.... **TCLC 84**
See also CA 89-92; 134

Antoine, Marc
See Proust, (Valentin-Louis-George-Eugene-) Marcel

Antoninus, Brother
See Everson, William (Oliver)

Antonioni, Michelangelo 1912- .... **CLC 20**
See also CA 73-76; CANR 45, 77

Antschel, Paul 1920-1970
See Celan, Paul
See also CA 85-88; CANR 33, 61; MTCW 1

Anwar, Chairil 1922-1949 .... **TCLC 22**
See also CA 121

Anzaldua, Gloria 1942-
See also CA 175; DLB 122; HLCS 1

Apess, William 1798-1839(?) .... **NCLC 73; DAM MULT**
See also DLB 175; NNAL

Apollinaire, Guillaume 1880-1918 . **TCLC 3, 8, 51; DAM POET; PC 7**
See also Kostrowitzki, Wilhelm Apollinaris de
See also CA 152; MTCW 1

Appelfeld, Aharon 1932- .... **CLC 23, 47**
See also CA 112; 133; CANR 86

Apple, Max (Isaac) 1941- .... **CLC 9, 33**
See also CA 81-84; CANR 19, 54; DLB 130

Appleman, Philip (Dean) 1926- .... **CLC 51**
See also CA 13-16R; CAAS 18; CANR 6, 29, 56

Appleton, Lawrence
See Lovecraft, H(oward) P(hillips)

Apteryx
See Eliot, T(homas) S(tearns)

Apuleius, (Lucius Madaurensis) 125(?)-175(?) .... **CMLC 1**
See also DLB 211

Aquin, Hubert 1929-1977 .... **CLC 15**
See also CA 105; DLB 53

Aquinas, Thomas 1224(?)-1274 ... **CMLC 33**
See also DLB 115

Aragon, Louis 1897-1982 . **CLC 3, 22; DAM NOV, POET**
See also CA 69-72; 108; CANR 28, 71; DLB 72; MTCW 1, 2

Arany, Janos 1817-1882 .... **NCLC 34**

Aranyos, Kakay
See Mikszath, Kalman

Arbuthnot, John 1667-1735 .... **LC 1**
See also DLB 101

Archer, Herbert Winslow
See Mencken, H(enry) L(ouis)

Archer, Jeffrey (Howard) 1940- ..... **CLC 28; DAM POP**

See also AAYA 16; BEST 89:3; CA 77-80; CANR 22, 52; DA3; INT CANR-22

Archer, Jules 1915- .... **CLC 12**
See also CA 9-12R; CANR 6, 69; SAAS 5; SATA 4, 85

Archer, Lee
See Ellison, Harlan (Jay)

Arden, John 1930- ..... **CLC 6, 13, 15; DAM DRAM**
See also CA 13-16R; CAAS 4; CANR 31, 65, 67; DLB 13; MTCW 1

Arenas, Reinaldo 1943-1990 . **CLC 41; DAM MULT; HLC 1**
See also CA 124; 128; 133; CANR 73; DLB 145; HW 1; MTCW 1

Arendt, Hannah 1906-1975 .... **CLC 66, 98**
See also CA 17-20R; 61-64; CANR 26, 60; MTCW 1, 2

Aretino, Pietro 1492-1556 .... **LC 12**

Arghezi, Tudor 1880-1967 .... **CLC 80**
See also Theodorescu, Ion N.
See also CA 167

Arguedas, Jose Maria 1911-1969 ... **CLC 10, 18; HLCS 1**
See also CA 89-92; CANR 73; DLB 113; HW 1

Argueta, Manlio 1936- .... **CLC 31**
See also CA 131; CANR 73; DLB 145; HW 1

Arias, Ron(ald Francis) 1941-
See also CA 131; CANR 81; DAM MULT; DLB 82; HLC 1; HW 1, 2; MTCW 2

Ariosto, Ludovico 1474-1533 .... **LC 6**

Aristides
See Epstein, Joseph

Aristophanes 450B.C.-385B.C. ..... **CMLC 4; DA; DAB; DAC; DAM DRAM, MST; DC 2; WLCS**
See also DA3; DLB 176

Aristotle 384B.C.-322B.C. ... **CMLC 31; DA; DAB; DAC; DAM MST; WLCS**
See also DA3; DLB 176

Arlt, Roberto (Godofredo Christophersen) 1900-1942 ..... **TCLC 29; DAM MULT; HLC 1**
See also CA 123; 131; CANR 67; HW 1, 2

Armah, Ayi Kwei 1939- . **CLC 5, 33; BLC 1; DAM MULT, POET**
See also BW 1; CA 61-64; CANR 21, 64; DLB 117; MTCW 1

Armatrading, Joan 1950- .... **CLC 17**
See also CA 114; 186

Arnette, Robert
See Silverberg, Robert

Arnim, Achim von (Ludwig Joachim von Arnim) 1781-1831 .... **NCLC 5; SSC 29**
See also DLB 90

Arnim, Bettina von 1785-1859 ..... **NCLC 38**
See also DLB 90

Arnold, Matthew 1822-1888 ... **NCLC 6, 29; DA; DAB; DAC; DAM MST, POET; PC 5; WLC**
See also CDBLB 1832-1890; DLB 32, 57

Arnold, Thomas 1795-1842 .... **NCLC 18**
See also DLB 55

Arnow, Harriette (Louisa) Simpson 1908-1986 .... **CLC 2, 7, 18**
See also CA 9-12R; 118; CANR 14; DLB 6; MTCW 1, 2; SATA 42; SATA-Obit 47

Arouet, Francois-Marie
See Voltaire

Arp, Hans
See Arp, Jean

Arp, Jean 1887-1966 .... **CLC 5**
See also CA 81-84; 25-28R; CANR 42, 77

Arrabal
See Arrabal, Fernando

Arrabal, Fernando 1932- .. **CLC 2, 9, 18, 58**
See also CA 9-12R; CANR 15

See also CA 128; 113
Bakshi, Ralph 1938(?)- .... **CLC 26**
  See also CA 112; 138
Bakunin, Mikhail (Alexandrovich)
  1814-1876 .... **NCLC 25, 58**
Baldwin, James (Arthur) 1924-1987 . **CLC 1,**
  2, 3, 4, 5, 8, 13, 15, 17, 42, 50, 67, 90,
  127; BLC 1; DA; DAB; DAC; DAM
  MST, MULT, NOV, POP; DC 1; SSC
  10, 33; WLC
    See also AAYA 4, 34; BW 1; CA 1-4R; 124;
    CABS 1; CANR 3, 24; CDALB 1941-
    1968; DA3; DLB 2, 7, 33; DLBY 87;
    MTCW 1, 2; SATA 9; SATA-Obit 54
Ballard, J(ames) G(raham) 1930- .... **CLC 3,**
  6, 14, 36; DAM NOV, POP; SSC 1
    See also AAYA 3; CA 5-8R; CANR 15, 39,
    65; DA3; DLB 14, 207; MTCW 1, 2;
    SATA 93
Balmont, Konstantin (Dmitriyevich)
  1867-1943 .... **TCLC 11**
  See also CA 109; 155
Baltausis, Vincas
  See Mikszath, Kalman
Balzac, Honore de 1799-1850 .. **NCLC 5, 35,**
  53; DA; DAB; DAC; DAM MST, NOV;
  SSC 5; WLC
  See also DA3; DLB 119
Bambara, Toni Cade 1939-1995 ..... **CLC 19,**
  88; BLC 1; DA; DAC; DAM MST,
  MULT; SSC 35; WLCS
    See also AAYA 5; BW 2, 3; CA 29-32R;
    150; CANR 24, 49, 81; CDALBS; DA3;
    DLB 38; MTCW 1, 2; SATA 112
Bamdad, A.
  See Shamlu, Ahmad
Banat, D. R.
  See Bradbury, Ray (Douglas)
Bancroft, Laura
  See Baum, L(yman) Frank
Banim, John 1798-1842 .... **NCLC 13**
  See also DLB 116, 158, 159
Banim, Michael 1796-1874 .... **NCLC 13**
  See also DLB 158, 159
Banjo, The
  See Paterson, A(ndrew) B(arton)
Banks, Iain
  See Banks, Iain M(enzies)
Banks, Iain M(enzies) 1954- .... **CLC 34**
  See also CA 123; 128; CANR 61; DLB 194;
  INT 128
Banks, Lynne Reid .... **CLC 23**
  See also Reid Banks, Lynne
  See also AAYA 6
Banks, Russell 1940- .... **CLC 37, 72**
  See also CA 65-68; CAAS 15; CANR 19,
  52, 73; DLB 130
Banville, John 1945- .... **CLC 46, 118**
  See also CA 117; 128; DLB 14; INT 128
Banville, Theodore (Faullain) de 1832-1891
  .... **NCLC 9**
Baraka, Amiri 1934- . **CLC 1, 2, 3, 5, 10, 14,**
  33, 115; BLC 1; DA; DAC; DAM MST,
  MULT, POET, POP; DC 6; PC 4;
  WLCS
    See also BW 2, 3; CA 21-24R; CABS 3;
    CANR 27, 38, 61; CDALB 1941-1968;
    DA3; DLB 5, 7, 16, 38; DLBD 8; MTCW
    1, 2
Barbauld, Anna Laetitia 1743-1825
  .... **NCLC 50**
  See also DLB 107, 109, 142, 158
Barbellion, W. N. P. .... **TCLC 24**
  See also Cummings, Bruce F(rederick)
Barbera, Jack (Vincent) 1945- .... **CLC 44**
  See also CA 110; CANR 45
Barbey d'Aurevilly, Jules Amedee 1808-1889
  .... **NCLC 1; SSC 17**

See also DLB 119
Barbour, John c. 1316-1395 .... **CMLC 33**
  See also DLB 146
Barbusse, Henri 1873-1935 .... **TCLC 5**
  See also CA 105; 154; DLB 65
Barclay, Bill
  See Moorcock, Michael (John)
Barclay, William Ewert
  See Moorcock, Michael (John)
Barea, Arturo 1897-1957 .... **TCLC 14**
  See also CA 111
Barfoot, Joan 1946- .... **CLC 18**
  See also CA 105
Barham, Richard Harris 1788-1845
  .... **NCLC 77**
  See also DLB 159
Baring, Maurice 1874-1945 .... **TCLC 8**
  See also CA 105; 168; DLB 34
Baring-Gould, Sabine 1834-1924 . **TCLC 88**
  See also DLB 156, 190
Barker, Clive 1952- ..... **CLC 52; DAM POP**
    See also AAYA 10; BEST 90:3; CA 121;
    129; CANR 71; DA3; INT 129; MTCW
    1, 2
Barker, George Granville 1913-1991
  .... **CLC 8, 48; DAM POET**
    See also CA 9-12R; 135; CANR 7, 38; DLB
    20; MTCW 1
Barker, Harley Granville
  See Granville-Barker, Harley
  See also DLB 10
Barker, Howard 1946- .... **CLC 37**
  See also CA 102; DLB 13
Barker, Jane 1652-1732 .... **LC 42**
Barker, Pat(ricia) 1943- .... **CLC 32, 94**
  See also CA 117; 122; CANR 50; INT 122
Barlach, Ernst (Heinrich) 1870-1938
  .... **TCLC 84**
  See also CA 178; DLB 56, 118
Barlow, Joel 1754-1812 .... **NCLC 23**
  See also DLB 37
Barnard, Mary (Ethel) 1909- .... **CLC 48**
  See also CA 21-22; CAP 2
Barnes, Djuna 1892-1982 ... **CLC 3, 4, 8, 11,**
  29, 127; SSC 3
    See also CA 9-12R; 107; CANR 16, 55;
    DLB 4, 9, 45; MTCW 1, 2
Barnes, Julian (Patrick) 1946- .... **CLC 42;**
  DAB
    See also CA 102; CANR 19, 54; DLB 194;
    DLBY 93; MTCW 1
Barnes, Peter 1931- .... **CLC 5, 56**
    See also CA 65-68; CAAS 12; CANR 33,
    34, 64; DLB 13; MTCW 1
Barnes, William 1801-1886 .... **NCLC 75**
  See also DLB 32
Baroja (y Nessi), Pio 1872-1956 .... **TCLC 8;**
  HLC 1
  See also CA 104
Baron, David
  See Pinter, Harold
Baron Corvo
  See Rolfe, Frederick (William Serafino Aus-
  tin Lewis Mary)
Barondess, Sue K(aufman) 1926-1977
  .... **CLC 8**
  See also Kaufman, Sue
  See also CA 1-4R; 69-72; CANR 1
Baron de Teive
  See Pessoa, Fernando (Antonio Nogueira)
Baroness Von S.
  See Zangwill, Israel
Barres, (Auguste-) Maurice 1862-1923
  .... **TCLC 47**
  See also CA 164; DLB 123
Barreto, Afonso Henrique de Lima
  See Lima Barreto, Afonso Henrique de
Barrett, (Roger) Syd 1946- .... **CLC 35**

Barrett, William (Christopher) 1913-1992
  .... **CLC 27**
    See also CA 13-16R; 139; CANR 11, 67;
    INT CANR-11
Barrie, J(ames) M(atthew) 1860-1937
  .... **TCLC 2; DAB; DAM DRAM**
    See also CA 104; 136; CANR 77; CDBLB
    1890-1914; CLR 16; DA3; DLB 10, 141,
    156; MAICYA; MTCW 1; SATA 100;
    YABC 1
Barrington, Michael
  See Moorcock, Michael (John)
Barrol, Grady
  See Bograd, Larry
Barry, Mike
  See Malzberg, Barry N(athaniel)
Barry, Philip 1896-1949 .... **TCLC 11**
  See also CA 109; DLB 7
Bart, Andre Schwarz
  See Schwarz-Bart, Andre
Barth, John (Simmons) 1930- .. **CLC 1, 2, 3,**
  5, 7, 9, 10, 14, 27, 51, 89; DAM NOV;
  SSC 10
    See also AITN 1, 2; CA 1-4R; CABS 1;
    CANR 5, 23, 49, 64; DLB 2; MTCW 1
Barthelme, Donald 1931-1989 . **CLC 1, 2, 3,**
  5, 6, 8, 13, 23, 46, 59, 115; DAM NOV;
  SSC 2
    See also CA 21-24R; 129; CANR 20, 58;
    DA3; DLB 2; DLBY 80, 89; MTCW 1, 2;
    SATA 7; SATA-Obit 62
Barthelme, Frederick 1943- .... **CLC 36, 117**
    See also CA 114; 122; CANR 77; DLBY
    85; INT 122
Barthes, Roland (Gerard) 1915-1980
  .... **CLC 24, 83**
    See also CA 130; 97-100; CANR 66;
    MTCW 1, 2
Barzun, Jacques (Martin) 1907- ..... **CLC 51**
  See also CA 61-64; CANR 22
Bashevis, Isaac
  See Singer, Isaac Bashevis
Bashkirtseff, Marie 1859-1884 ..... **NCLC 27**
Basho
  See Matsuo Basho
Basil of Caesaria c. 330-379 .... **CMLC 35**
Bass, Kingsley B., Jr.
  See Bullins, Ed
Bass, Rick 1958- .... **CLC 79**
  See also CA 126; CANR 53; DLB 212
Bassani, Giorgio 1916- .... **CLC 9**
  See also CA 65-68; CANR 33; DLB 128,
  177; MTCW 1
Bastos, Augusto (Antonio) Roa
  See Roa Bastos, Augusto (Antonio)
Bataille, Georges 1897-1962 .... **CLC 29**
  See also CA 101; 89-92
Bates, H(erbert) E(rnest) 1905-1974
  ..... **CLC 46; DAB; DAM POP; SSC 10**
    See also CA 93-96; 45-48; CANR 34; DA3;
    DLB 162, 191; MTCW 1, 2
Bauchart
  See Camus, Albert
Baudelaire, Charles 1821-1867 ...... **NCLC 6,**
  29, 55; DA; DAB; DAC; DAM MST,
  POET; PC 1; SSC 18; WLC
  See also DA3
Baudrillard, Jean 1929- .... **CLC 60**
Baum, L(yman) Frank 1856-1919 .. **TCLC 7**
    See also CA 108; 133; CLR 15; DLB 22;
    JRDA; MAICYA; MTCW 1, 2; SATA 18,
    100
Baum, Louis F.
  See Baum, L(yman) Frank
Baumbach, Jonathan 1933- .... **CLC 6, 23**
    See also CA 13-16R; CAAS 5; CANR 12,
    66; DLBY 80; INT CANR-12; MTCW 1
Bausch, Richard (Carl) 1945- .... **CLC 51**

Bennett, Elizabeth
See Mitchell, Margaret (Munnerlyn)
Bennett, George Harold 1930-
See Bennett, Hal
See also BW 1; CA 97-100; CANR 87
Bennett, Hal .... **CLC 5**
See also Bennett, George Harold
See also DLB 33
Bennett, Jay 1912- .... **CLC 35**
See also AAYA 10; CA 69-72; CANR 11,
42, 79; JRDA; SAAS 4; SATA 41, 87;
SATA-Brief 27
Bennett, Louise (Simone) 1919- ..... **CLC 28;
BLC 1; DAM MULT**
See also BW 2, 3; CA 151; DLB 117
Benson, E(dward) F(rederic) 1867-1940
.... **TCLC 27**
See also CA 114; 157; DLB 135, 153
Benson, Jackson J. 1930- .... **CLC 34**
See also CA 25-28R; DLB 111
Benson, Sally 1900-1972 .... **CLC 17**
See also CA 19-20; 37-40R; CAP 1; SATA
1, 35; SATA-Obit 27
Benson, Stella 1892-1933 .... **TCLC 17**
See also CA 117; 155; DLB 36, 162
Bentham, Jeremy 1748-1832 .... **NCLC 38**
See also DLB 107, 158
Bentley, E(dmund) C(lerihew) 1875-1956
.... **TCLC 12**
See also CA 108; DLB 70
Bentley, Eric (Russell) 1916- .... **CLC 24**
See also CA 5-8R; CANR 6, 67; INT
CANR-6
Beranger, Pierre Jean de 1780-1857
.... **NCLC 34**
Berdyaev, Nicolas
See Berdyaev, Nikolai (Aleksandrovich)
Berdyaev, Nikolai (Aleksandrovich)
1874-1948 .... **TCLC 67**
See also CA 120; 157
Berdyayev, Nikolai (Aleksandrovich)
See Berdyaev, Nikolai (Aleksandrovich)
Berendt, John (Lawrence) 1939- .... **CLC 86**
See also CA 146; CANR 75; DA3; MTCW
1
Beresford, J(ohn) D(avys) 1873-1947
.... **TCLC 81**
See also CA 112; 155; DLB 162, 178, 197
Bergelson, David 1884-1952 .... **TCLC 81**
Berger, Colonel
See Malraux, (Georges-)Andre
Berger, John (Peter) 1926- .... **CLC 2, 19**
See also CA 81-84; CANR 51, 78; DLB 14,
207
Berger, Melvin H. 1927- .... **CLC 12**
See also CA 5-8R; CANR 4; CLR 32;
SAAS 2; SATA 5, 88
Berger, Thomas (Louis) 1924- . **CLC 3, 5, 8,
11, 18, 38; DAM NOV**
See also CA 1-4R; CANR 5, 28, 51; DLB
2; DLBY 80; INT CANR-28; MTCW 1, 2
Bergman, (Ernst) Ingmar 1918- .... **CLC 16,
72**
See also CA 81-84; CANR 33, 70; MTCW
2
Bergson, Henri(-Louis) 1859-1941 . **TCLC 32**
See also CA 164
Bergstein, Eleanor 1938- .... **CLC 4**
See also CA 53-56; CANR 5
Berkoff, Steven 1937- .... **CLC 56**
See also CA 104; CANR 72
Bermant, Chaim (Icyk) 1929- .... **CLC 40**
See also CA 57-60; CANR 6, 31, 57
Bern, Victoria
See Fisher, M(ary) F(rances) K(ennedy)
Bernanos, (Paul Louis) Georges 1888-1948
.... **TCLC 3**
See also CA 104; 130; DLB 72

Bernard, April 1956- .... **CLC 59**
See also CA 131
Berne, Victoria
See Fisher, M(ary) F(rances) K(ennedy)
Bernhard, Thomas 1931-1989 .... **CLC 3, 32,
61**
See also CA 85-88; 127; CANR 32, 57;
DLB 85, 124; MTCW 1
Bernhardt, Sarah (Henriette Rosine)
1844-1923 .... **TCLC 75**
See also CA 157
Berriault, Gina 1926-1999 ...... **CLC 54, 109;
SSC 30**
See also CA 116; 129; 185; CANR 66; DLB
130
Berrigan, Daniel 1921- .... **CLC 4**
See also CA 33-36R; CAAS 1; CANR 11,
43, 78; DLB 5
Berrigan, Edmund Joseph Michael, Jr.
1934-1983
See Berrigan, Ted
See also CA 61-64; 110; CANR 14
Berrigan, Ted .... **CLC 37**
See also Berrigan, Edmund Joseph Michael,
Jr.
See also DLB 5, 169
Berry, Charles Edward Anderson 1931-
See Berry, Chuck
See also CA 115
Berry, Chuck .... **CLC 17**
See also Berry, Charles Edward Anderson
Berry, Jonas
See Ashbery, John (Lawrence)
Berry, Wendell (Erdman) 1934- .. **CLC 4, 6,
8, 27, 46; DAM POET; PC 28**
See also AITN 1; CA 73-76; CANR 50, 73;
DLB 5, 6; MTCW 1
Berryman, John 1914-1972 . **CLC 1, 2, 3, 4,
6, 8, 10, 13, 25, 62; DAM POET**
See also CA 13-16; 33-36R; CABS 2;
CANR 35; CAP 1; CDALB 1941-1968;
DLB 48; MTCW 1, 2
Bertolucci, Bernardo 1940- .... **CLC 16**
See also CA 106
Berton, Pierre (Francis Demarigny) 1920-
.... **CLC 104**
See also CA 1-4R; CANR 2, 56; DLB 68;
SATA 99
Bertrand, Aloysius 1807-1841 .... **NCLC 31**
Bertran de Born c. 1140-1215 .... **CMLC 5**
Besant, Annie (Wood) 1847-1933 ... **TCLC 9**
See also CA 105; 185
Bessie, Alvah 1904-1985 .... **CLC 23**
See also CA 5-8R; 116; CANR 2, 80; DLB
26
Bethlen, T. D.
See Silverberg, Robert
Beti, Mongo . **CLC 27; BLC 1; DAM MULT**
See also Biyidi, Alexandre
See also CANR 79
Betjeman, John 1906-1984 ..... **CLC 2, 6, 10,
34, 43; DAB; DAM MST, POET**
See also CA 9-12R; 112; CANR 33, 56;
CDBLB 1945-1960; DA3; DLB 20;
DLBY 84; MTCW 1, 2
Bettelheim, Bruno 1903-1990 .... **CLC 79**
See also CA 81-84; 131; CANR 23, 61;
DA3; MTCW 1, 2
Betti, Ugo 1892-1953 .... **TCLC 5**
See also CA 104; 155
Betts, Doris (Waugh) 1932- ..... **CLC 3, 6, 28**
See also CA 13-16R; CANR 9, 66, 77;
DLBY 82; INT CANR-9
Bevan, Alistair
See Roberts, Keith (John Kingston)
Bey, Pilaff
See Douglas, (George) Norman
Bialik, Chaim Nachman 1873-1934
.... **TCLC 25**

See also CA 170
Bickerstaff, Isaac
See Swift, Jonathan
Bidart, Frank 1939- .... **CLC 33**
See also CA 140
Bienek, Horst 1930- .... **CLC 7, 11**
See also CA 73-76; DLB 75
Bierce, Ambrose (Gwinett) 1842-1914(?)
.... **TCLC 1, 7, 44; DA; DAC; DAM
MST; SSC 9; WLC**
See also CA 104; 139; CANR 78; CDALB
1865-1917; DA3; DLB 11, 12, 23, 71, 74,
186
Biggers, Earl Derr 1884-1933 .... **TCLC 65**
See also CA 108; 153
Billings, Josh
See Shaw, Henry Wheeler
Billington, (Lady) Rachel (Mary) 1942-
.... **CLC 43**
See also AITN 2; CA 33-36R; CANR 44
Binyon, T(imothy) J(ohn) 1936- ..... **CLC 34**
See also CA 111; CANR 28
Bion 335B.C.-245B.C. .... **CMLC 39**
Bioy Casares, Adolfo 1914-1999 .. **CLC 4, 8,
13, 88; DAM MULT; HLC 1; SSC 17**
See also CA 29-32R; 177; CANR 19, 43,
66; DLB 113; HW 1, 2; MTCW 1, 2
Bird, Cordwainer
See Ellison, Harlan (Jay)
Bird, Robert Montgomery 1806-1854
.... **NCLC 1**
See also DLB 202
Birkerts, Sven 1951- .... **CLC 116**
See also CA 128; 133; 176; CAAE 176;
CAAS 29; INT 133
Birney, (Alfred) Earle 1904-1995 . **CLC 1, 4,
6, 11; DAC; DAM MST, POET**
See also CA 1-4R; CANR 5, 20; DLB 88;
MTCW 1
Biruni, al 973-1048(?) .... **CMLC 28**
Bishop, Elizabeth 1911-1979 .... **CLC 1, 4, 9,
13, 15, 32; DA; DAC; DAM MST,
POET; PC 3**
See also CA 5-8R; 89-92; CABS 2; CANR
26, 61; CDALB 1968-1988; DA3; DLB
5, 169; MTCW 1, 2; SATA-Obit 24
Bishop, John 1935- .... **CLC 10**
See also CA 105
Bissett, Bill 1939- .... **CLC 18; PC 14**
See also CA 69-72; CAAS 19; CANR 15;
DLB 53; MTCW 1
Bissoondath, Neil (Devindra) 1955-
.... **CLC 120; DAC**
See also CA 136
Bitov, Andrei (Georgievich) 1937- .. **CLC 57**
See also CA 142
Biyidi, Alexandre 1932-
See Beti, Mongo
See also BW 1, 3; CA 114; 124; CANR 81;
DA3; MTCW 1, 2
Bjarme, Brynjolf
See Ibsen, Henrik (Johan)
Bjoernson, Bjoernstjerne (Martinius)
1832-1910 .... **TCLC 7, 37**
See also CA 104
Black, Robert
See Holdstock, Robert P.
Blackburn, Paul 1926-1971 .... **CLC 9, 43**
See also CA 81-84; 33-36R; CANR 34;
DLB 16; DLBY 81
Black Elk 1863-1950 .... **TCLC 33; DAM
MULT**
See also CA 144; MTCW 1; NNAL
Black Hobart
See Sanders, (James) Ed(ward)
Blacklin, Malcolm
See Chambers, Aidan

15, 22, 40, 62, 81, 94; DAB
See also Wilson, John (Anthony) Burgess
See also AAYA 25; AITN 1; CDBLB 1960
to Present; DLB 14, 194; DLBY 98;
MTCW 1

Burke, Edmund 1729(?)-1797 .... **LC 7, 36;
DA; DAB; DAC; DAM MST; WLC**
See also DA3; DLB 104

Burke, Kenneth (Duva) 1897-1993 .. **CLC 2,
24**
See also CA 5-8R; 143; CANR 39, 74; DLB
45, 63; MTCW 1, 2

Burke, Leda
See Garnett, David

Burke, Ralph
See Silverberg, Robert

Burke, Thomas 1886-1945 .... **TCLC 63**
See also CA 113; 155; DLB 197

Burney, Fanny 1752-1840 . **NCLC 12, 54, 81**
See also DLB 39

Burns, Robert 1759-1796 . **LC 3, 29, 40; DA;
DAB; DAC; DAM MST, POET; PC 6;
WLC**
See also CDBLB 1789-1832; DA3; DLB
109

Burns, Tex
See L'Amour, Louis (Dearborn)

Burnshaw, Stanley 1906- .... **CLC 3, 13, 44**
See also CA 9-12R; DLB 48; DLBY 97

Burr, Anne 1937- .... **CLC 6**
See also CA 25-28R

Burroughs, Edgar Rice 1875-1950 . **TCLC 2,
32; DAM NOV**
See also AAYA 11; CA 104; 132; DA3;
DLB 8; MTCW 1, 2; SATA 41

Burroughs, William S(eward) 1914-1997
... **CLC 1, 2, 5, 15, 22, 42, 75, 109; DA;
DAB; DAC; DAM MST, NOV, POP;
WLC**
See also AITN 2; CA 9-12R; 160; CANR
20, 52; DA3; DLB 2, 8, 16, 152; DLBY
81, 97; MTCW 1, 2

Burton, SirRichard F(rancis) 1821-1890
.... **NCLC 42**
See also DLB 55, 166, 184

Busch, Frederick 1941- ... **CLC 7, 10, 18, 47**
See also CA 33-36R; CAAS 1; CANR 45,
73; DLB 6

Bush, Ronald 1946- .... **CLC 34**
See also CA 136

Bustos, F(rancisco)
See Borges, Jorge Luis

Bustos Domecq, H(onorio)
See Bioy Casares, Adolfo; Borges, Jorge
Luis

Butler, Octavia E(stelle) 1947- .... **CLC 38,
121; BLCS; DAM MULT, POP**
See also AAYA 18; BW 2, 3; CA 73-76;
CANR 12, 24, 38, 73; CLR 65; DA3;
DLB 33; MTCW 1, 2; SATA 84

Butler, Robert Olen (Jr.) 1945- ...... **CLC 81;
DAM POP**
See also CA 112; CANR 66; DLB 173; INT
112; MTCW 1

Butler, Samuel 1612-1680 .... **LC 16, 43**
See also DLB 101, 126

Butler, Samuel 1835-1902 . **TCLC 1, 33; DA;
DAB; DAC; DAM MST, NOV; WLC**
See also CA 143; CDBLB 1890-1914; DA3;
DLB 18, 57, 174

Butler, Walter C.
See Faust, Frederick (Schiller)

Butor, Michel (Marie Francois) 1926-
.... **CLC 1, 3, 8, 11, 15**
See also CA 9-12R; CANR 33, 66; DLB
83; MTCW 1, 2

Butts, Mary 1892(?)-1937 .... **TCLC 77**
See also CA 148

Buzo, Alexander (John) 1944- .... **CLC 61**

See also CA 97-100; CANR 17, 39, 69

Buzzati, Dino 1906-1972 .... **CLC 36**
See also CA 160; 33-36R; DLB 177

Byars, Betsy (Cromer) 1928- .... **CLC 35**
See also AAYA 19; CA 33-36R, 183; CAAE
183; CANR 18, 36, 57; CLR 1, 16; DLB
52; INT CANR-18; JRDA; MAICYA;
MTCW 1; SAAS 1; SATA 4, 46, 80;
SATA-Essay 108

Byatt, A(ntonia) S(usan Drabble) 1936-
.... **CLC 19, 65; DAM NOV, POP**
See also CA 13-16R; CANR 13, 33, 50, 75;
DA3; DLB 14, 194; MTCW 1, 2

Byrne, David 1952- .... **CLC 26**
See also CA 127

Byrne, John Keyes 1926-
See Leonard, Hugh
See also CA 102; CANR 78; INT 102

Byron, George Gordon (Noel) 1788-1824
.. **NCLC 2, 12; DA; DAB; DAC; DAM
MST, POET; PC 16; WLC**
See also CDBLB 1789-1832; DA3; DLB
96, 110

Byron, Robert 1905-1941 .... **TCLC 67**
See also CA 160; DLB 195

C. 3. 3.
See Wilde, Oscar (Fingal O'Flahertie Wills)

Caballero, Fernan 1796-1877 .... **NCLC 10**

Cabell, Branch
See Cabell, James Branch

Cabell, James Branch 1879-1958 ... **TCLC 6**
See also CA 105; 152; DLB 9, 78; MTCW
1

Cable, George Washington 1844-1925
.... **TCLC 4; SSC 4**
See also CA 104; 155; DLB 12, 74; DLBD
13

Cabral de Melo Neto, Joao 1920- . **CLC 76;
DAM MULT**
See also CA 151

Cabrera Infante, G(uillermo) 1929- . **CLC 5,
25, 45, 120; DAM MULT; HLC 1; SSC
39**
See also CA 85-88; CANR 29, 65; DA3;
DLB 113; HW 1, 2; MTCW 1, 2

Cade, Toni
See Bambara, Toni Cade

Cadmus and Harmonia
See Buchan, John

Caedmon fl. 658-680 .... **CMLC 7**
See also DLB 146

Caeiro, Alberto
See Pessoa, Fernando (Antonio Nogueira)

Cage, John (Milton, Jr.) 1912-1992 . **CLC 41**
See also CA 13-16R; 169; CANR 9, 78;
DLB 193; INT CANR-9

Cahan, Abraham 1860-1951 .... **TCLC 71**
See also CA 108; 154; DLB 9, 25, 28

Cain, G.
See Cabrera Infante, G(uillermo)

Cain, Guillermo
See Cabrera Infante, G(uillermo)

Cain, James M(allahan) 1892-1977 . **CLC 3,
11, 28**
See also AITN 1; CA 17-20R; 73-76;
CANR 8, 34, 61; MTCW 1

Caine, Hall 1853-1931 .... **TCLC 97**

Caine, Mark
See Raphael, Frederic (Michael)

Calasso, Roberto 1941- .... **CLC 81**
See also CA 143; CANR 89

Calderon de la Barca, Pedro 1600-1681
.... **LC 23; DC 3; HLCS 1**

Caldwell, Erskine (Preston) 1903-1987
. **CLC 1, 8, 14, 50, 60; DAM NOV; SSC
19**
See also AITN 1; CA 1-4R; 121; CAAS 1;
CANR 2, 33; DA3; DLB 9, 86; MTCW
1, 2

Caldwell, (Janet Miriam) Taylor (Holland)
1900-1985 . **CLC 2, 28, 39; DAM NOV,
POP**
See also CA 5-8R; 116; CANR 5; DA3;
DLBD 17

Calhoun, John Caldwell 1782-1850
.... **NCLC 15**
See also DLB 3

Calisher, Hortense 1911- .... **CLC 2, 4, 8, 38;
DAM NOV; SSC 15**
See also CA 1-4R; CANR 1, 22, 67; DA3;
DLB 2; INT CANR-22; MTCW 1, 2

Callaghan, Morley Edward 1903-1990
.. **CLC 3, 14, 41, 65; DAC; DAM MST**
See also CA 9-12R; 132; CANR 33, 73;
DLB 68; MTCW 1, 2

Callimachus c. 305B.C.-c. 240B.C.
.... **CMLC 18**
See also DLB 176

Calvin, John 1509-1564 .... **LC 37**

Calvino, Italo 1923-1985 .. **CLC 5, 8, 11, 22,
33, 39, 73; DAM NOV; SSC 3**
See also CA 85-88; 116; CANR 23, 61;
DLB 196; MTCW 1, 2

Cameron, Carey 1952- .... **CLC 59**
See also CA 135

Cameron, Peter 1959- .... **CLC 44**
See also CA 125; CANR 50

Camoens, Luis Vaz de 1524(?)-1580
See also HLCS 1

Camoes, Luis de 1524(?)-1580
See also HLCS 1

Campana, Dino 1885-1932 .... **TCLC 20**
See also CA 117; DLB 114

Campanella, Tommaso 1568-1639 ..... **LC 32**

Campbell, John W(ood, Jr.) 1910-1971
.... **CLC 32**
See also CA 21-22; 29-32R; CANR 34;
CAP 2; DLB 8; MTCW 1

Campbell, Joseph 1904-1987 .... **CLC 69**
See also AAYA 3; BEST 89:2; CA 1-4R;
124; CANR 3, 28, 61; DA3; MTCW 1, 2

Campbell, Maria 1940- .... **CLC 85; DAC**
See also CA 102; CANR 54; NNAL

Campbell, (John) Ramsey 1946- ... **CLC 42;
SSC 19**
See also CA 57-60; CANR 7; INT CANR-7

Campbell, (Ignatius) Roy (Dunnachie)
1901-1957 .... **TCLC 5**
See also CA 104; 155; DLB 20; MTCW 2

Campbell, Thomas 1777-1844 ...... **NCLC 19**
See also DLB 93; 144

Campbell, Wilfred .... **TCLC 9**
See also Campbell, William

Campbell, William 1858(?)-1918
See Campbell, Wilfred
See also CA 106; DLB 92

Campion, Jane .... **CLC 95**
See also AAYA 33; CA 138; CANR 87

Camus, Albert 1913-1960 ..... **CLC 1, 2, 4, 9,
11, 14, 32, 63, 69, 124; DA; DAB; DAC;
DAM DRAM, MST, NOV; DC 2; SSC
9; WLC**
See also CA 89-92; DA3; DLB 72; MTCW
1, 2

Canby, Vincent 1924- .... **CLC 13**
See also CA 81-84

Cancale
See Desnos, Robert

Canetti, Elias 1905-1994 . **CLC 3, 14, 25, 75,
86**
See also CA 21-24R; 146; CANR 23, 61,
79; DA3; DLB 85, 124; MTCW 1, 2

Canfield, Dorothea F.
See Fisher, Dorothy (Frances) Canfield

Canfield, Dorothea Frances
See Fisher, Dorothy (Frances) Canfield

See also CA 104; 122; DAC; DAM MST, NOV; DA3

Chretien de Troyes c. 12th cent. - . **CMLC 10**
See also DLB 208

Christie
See Ichikawa, Kon

Christie, Agatha (Mary Clarissa) 1890-1976
.... **CLC 1, 6, 8, 12, 39, 48, 110; DAB;**
DAC; DAM NOV
See also AAYA 9; AITN 1, 2; CA 17-20R;
61-64; CANR 10, 37; CDBLB 1914-1945;
DA3; DLB 13, 77; MTCW 1, 2; SATA 36

Christie, (Ann) Philippa
See Pearce, Philippa
See also CA 5-8R; CANR 4

Christine de Pizan 1365(?)-1431(?) ...... **LC 9**
See also DLB 208

Chubb, Elmer
See Masters, Edgar Lee

Chulkov, Mikhail Dmitrievich 1743-1792
.... **LC 2**
See also DLB 150

Churchill, Caryl 1938- ... **CLC 31, 55; DC 5**
See also CA 102; CANR 22, 46; DLB 13;
MTCW 1

Churchill, Charles 1731-1764 .... **LC 3**
See also DLB 109

Chute, Carolyn 1947- .... **CLC 39**
See also CA 123

Ciardi, John (Anthony) 1916-1986 . **CLC 10,**
40, 44, 129; DAM POET
See also CA 5-8R; 118; CAAS 2; CANR 5,
33; CLR 19; DLB 5; DLBY 86; INT
CANR-5; MAICYA; MTCW 1, 2; SAAS
26; SATA 1, 65; SATA-Obit 46

Cicero, Marcus Tullius 106B.C.-43B.C.
.... **CMLC 3**
See also DLB 211

Cimino, Michael 1943- .... **CLC 16**
See also CA 105

Cioran, E(mil) M. 1911-1995 .... **CLC 64**
See also CA 25-28R; 149; CANR 91; DLB
220

Cisneros, Sandra 1954- . **CLC 69, 118; DAM**
MULT; HLC 1; SSC 32
See also AAYA 9; CA 131; CANR 64; DA3;
DLB 122, 152; HW 1, 2; MTCW 2

Cixous, Helene 1937- .... **CLC 92**
See also CA 126; CANR 55; DLB 83;
MTCW 1, 2

Clair, Rene .... **CLC 20**
See also Chomette, Rene Lucien

Clampitt, Amy 1920-1994 ... **CLC 32; PC 19**
See also CA 110; 146; CANR 29, 79; DLB
105

Clancy, Thomas L., Jr. 1947-
See Clancy, Tom
See also CA 125; 131; CANR 62; DA3;
INT 131; MTCW 1, 2

Clancy, Tom .... **CLC 45, 112; DAM NOV,**
POP
See also Clancy, Thomas L., Jr.
See also AAYA 9; BEST 89:1, 90:1; MTCW
2

Clare, John 1793-1864 .. **NCLC 9, 86; DAB;**
DAM POET; PC 23
See also DLB 55, 96

Clarin
See Alas (y Urena), Leopoldo (Enrique
Garcia)

Clark, Al C.
See Goines, Donald

Clark, (Robert) Brian 1932- .... **CLC 29**
See also CA 41-44R; CANR 67

Clark, Curt
See Westlake, Donald E(dwin)

Clark, Eleanor 1913-1996 .... **CLC 5, 19**
See also CA 9-12R; 151; CANR 41; DLB 6

Clark, J. P.
See Clark Bekedermo, J(ohnson) P(epper)
See also DLB 117

Clark, John Pepper
See Clark Bekedermo, J(ohnson) P(epper)

Clark, M. R.
See Clark, Mavis Thorpe

Clark, Mavis Thorpe 1909- .... **CLC 12**
See also CA 57-60; CANR 8, 37; CLR 30;
MAICYA; SAAS 5; SATA 8, 74

Clark, Walter Van Tilburg 1909-1971
.... **CLC 28**
See also CA 9-12R; 33-36R; CANR 63;
DLB 9, 206; SATA 8

Clark Bekedermo, J(ohnson) P(epper) 1935-
.... **CLC 38; BLC 1; DAM DRAM,**
MULT; DC 5
See also Clark, J. P.
See also BW 1; CA 65-68; CANR 16, 72;
MTCW 1

Clarke, Arthur C(harles) 1917- ... **CLC 1, 4,**
13, 18, 35; DAM POP; SSC 3
See also AAYA 4, 33; CA 1-4R; CANR 2,
28, 55, 74; DA3; JRDA; MAICYA;
MTCW 1, 2; SATA 13, 70, 115

Clarke, Austin 1896-1974 .. **CLC 6, 9; DAM**
POET
See also CA 29-32; 49-52; CAP 2; DLB 10,
20

Clarke, Austin C(hesterfield) 1934- . **CLC 8,**
53; BLC 1; DAC; DAM MULT
See also BW 1; CA 25-28R; CAAS 16;
CANR 14, 32, 68; DLB 53, 125

Clarke, Gillian 1937- .... **CLC 61**
See also CA 106; DLB 40

Clarke, Marcus (Andrew Hislop) 1846-1881
.... **NCLC 19**

Clarke, Shirley 1925- .... **CLC 16**

Clash, The
See Headon, (Nicky) Topper; Jones, Mick;
Simonon, Paul; Strummer, Joe

Claudel, Paul (Louis Charles Marie)
1868-1955 .... **TCLC 2, 10**
See also CA 104; 165; DLB 192

Claudius, Matthias 1740-1815 ...... **NCLC 75**
See also DLB 97

Clavell, James (duMaresq) 1925-1994
.... **CLC 6, 25, 87; DAM NOV, POP**
See also CA 25-28R; 146; CANR 26, 48;
DA3; MTCW 1, 2

Cleaver, (Leroy) Eldridge 1935-1998
..... **CLC 30, 119; BLC 1; DAM MULT**
See also BW 1, 3; CA 21-24R; 167; CANR
16, 75; DA3; MTCW 2

Cleese, John (Marwood) 1939- .... **CLC 21**
See also Monty Python
See also CA 112; 116; CANR 35; MTCW 1

Cleishbotham, Jebediah
See Scott, Walter

Cleland, John 1710-1789 .... **LC 2, 48**
See also DLB 39

Clemens, Samuel Langhorne 1835-1910
See Twain, Mark
See also CA 104; 135; CDALB 1865-1917;
DA; DAB; DAC; DAM MST, NOV; DA3;
DLB 11, 12, 23, 64, 74, 186, 189; JRDA;
MAICYA; SATA 100; YABC 2

Cleophil
See Congreve, William

Clerihew, E.
See Bentley, E(dmund) C(lerihew)

Clerk, N. W.
See Lewis, C(live) S(taples)

Cliff, Jimmy .... **CLC 21**
See also Chambers, James

Cliff, Michelle 1946- .... **CLC 120; BLCS**
See also BW 2; CA 116; CANR 39, 72;
DLB 157

Clifton, (Thelma) Lucille 1936- ...... **CLC 19,**

66; **BLC 1; DAM MULT, POET; PC 17**
See also BW 2, 3; CA 49-52; CANR 2, 24,
42, 76; CLR 5; DA3; DLB 5, 41; MAI-
CYA; MTCW 1, 2; SATA 20, 69

Clinton, Dirk
See Silverberg, Robert

Clough, Arthur Hugh 1819-1861 . **NCLC 27**
See also DLB 32

Clutha, Janet Paterson Frame 1924-
See Frame, Janet
See also CA 1-4R; CANR 2, 36, 76; MTCW
1, 2

Clyne, Terence
See Blatty, William Peter

Cobalt, Martin
See Mayne, William (James Carter)

Cobb, Irvin S(hrewsbury) 1876-1944
.... **TCLC 77**
See also CA 175; DLB 11, 25, 86

Cobbett, William 1763-1835 .... **NCLC 49**
See also DLB 43, 107, 158

Coburn, D(onald) L(ee) 1938- .... **CLC 10**
See also CA 89-92

Cocteau, Jean (Maurice Eugene Clement)
1889-1963 ... **CLC 1, 8, 15, 16, 43; DA;**
DAB; DAC; DAM DRAM, MST, NOV;
WLC
See also CA 25-28; CANR 40; CAP 2;
DA3; DLB 65; MTCW 1, 2

Codrescu, Andrei 1946- . **CLC 46, 121; DAM**
POET
See also CA 33-36R; CAAS 19; CANR 13,
34, 53, 76; DA3; MTCW 2

Coe, Max
See Bourne, Randolph S(illiman)

Coe, Tucker
See Westlake, Donald E(dwin)

Coen, Ethan 1958- .... **CLC 108**
See also CA 126; CANR 85

Coen, Joel 1955- .... **CLC 108**
See also CA 126

The Coen Brothers
See Coen, Ethan; Coen, Joel

Coetzee, J(ohn) M(ichael) 1940- .... **CLC 23,**
33, 66, 117; DAM NOV
See also CA 77-80; CANR 41, 54, 74; DA3;
MTCW 1, 2

Coffey, Brian
See Koontz, Dean R(ay)

Coffin, Robert P(eter) Tristram 1892-1955
.... **TCLC 95**
See also CA 123; 169; DLB 45

Cohan, George M(ichael) 1878-1942
.... **TCLC 60**
See also CA 157

Cohen, Arthur A(llen) 1928-1986 .... **CLC 7,**
31
See also CA 1-4R; 120; CANR 1, 17, 42;
DLB 28

Cohen, Leonard (Norman) 1934- .... **CLC 3,**
38; DAC; DAM MST
See also CA 21-24R; CANR 14, 69; DLB
53; MTCW 1

Cohen, Matt 1942- .... **CLC 19; DAC**
See also CA 61-64; CAAS 18; CANR 40;
DLB 53

Cohen-Solal, Annie 19(?)- .... **CLC 50**

Colegate, Isabel 1931- .... **CLC 36**
See also CA 17-20R; CANR 8, 22, 74; DLB
14; INT CANR-22; MTCW 1

Coleman, Emmett
See Reed, Ishmael

Coleridge, M. E.
See Coleridge, Mary E(lizabeth)

Coleridge, Mary E(lizabeth) 1861-1907
.... **TCLC 73**
See also CA 116; 166; DLB 19, 98

Coleridge, Samuel Taylor 1772-1834
.. **NCLC 9, 54; DA; DAB; DAC; DAM**

Delaney, Franey
See O'Hara, John (Henry)
Delaney, Shelagh 1939- .... **CLC 29; DAM DRAM**
See also CA 17-20R; CANR 30, 67; CD-BLB 1960 to Present; DLB 13; MTCW 1
Delany, Mary (Granville Pendarves) 1700-1788 .... **LC 12**
Delany, Samuel R(ay, Jr.) 1942- . **CLC 8, 14, 38; BLC 1; DAM MULT**
See also AAYA 24; BW 2, 3; CA 81-84; CANR 27, 43; DLB 8, 33; MTCW 1, 2
De La Ramee, (Marie) Louise 1839-1908
See Ouida
See also SATA 20
de la Roche, Mazo 1879-1961 .... **CLC 14**
See also CA 85-88; CANR 30; DLB 68; SATA 64
De La Salle, Innocent
See Hartmann, Sadakichi
Delbanco, Nicholas (Franklin) 1942-
.... **CLC 6, 13**
See also CA 17-20R; CAAS 2; CANR 29, 55; DLB 6
del Castillo, Michel 1933- .... **CLC 38**
See also CA 109; CANR 77
Deledda, Grazia (Cosima) 1875(?)-1936
.... **TCLC 23**
See also CA 123
Delgado, Abelardo (Lalo) B(arrientos) 1930-
See also CA 131; CAAS 15; CANR 90; DAM MST, MULT; DLB 82; HLC 1; HW 1, 2
Delibes, Miguel .... **CLC 8, 18**
See also Delibes Setien, Miguel
Delibes Setien, Miguel 1920-
See Delibes, Miguel
See also CA 45-48; CANR 1, 32; HW 1; MTCW 1
DeLillo, Don 1936- ... **CLC 8, 10, 13, 27, 39, 54, 76; DAM NOV, POP**
See also BEST 89:1; CA 81-84; CANR 21, 76; DA3; DLB 6, 173; MTCW 1, 2
de Lisser, H. G.
See De Lisser, H(erbert) G(eorge)
See also DLB 117
De Lisser, H(erbert) G(eorge) 1878-1944
.... **TCLC 12**
See also de Lisser, H. G.
See also BW 2; CA 109; 152
Deloney, Thomas 1560(?)-1600 .... **LC 41**
See also DLB 167
Deloria, Vine (Victor), Jr. 1933- ..... **CLC 21, 122; DAM MULT**
See also CA 53-56; CANR 5, 20, 48; DLB 175; MTCW 1; NNAL; SATA 21
Del Vecchio, John M(ichael) 1947- . **CLC 29**
See also CA 110; DLBD 9
de Man, Paul (Adolph Michel) 1919-1983
.... **CLC 55**
See also CA 128; 111; CANR 61; DLB 67; MTCW 1, 2
DeMarinis, Rick 1934- .... **CLC 54**
See also CA 57-60, 184; CAAE 184; CAAS 24; CANR 9, 25, 50
Dembry, R. Emmet
See Murfree, Mary Noailles
Demby, William 1922- ...... **CLC 53; BLC 1; DAM MULT**
See also BW 1, 3; CA 81-84; CANR 81; DLB 33
de Menton, Francisco
See Chin, Frank (Chew, Jr.)
Demetrius of Phalerum c. 307B.C.-
.... **CMLC 34**
Demijohn, Thom
See Disch, Thomas M(ichael)
de Molina, Tirso 1580-1648
See also HLCS 2

de Montherlant, Henry (Milon)
See Montherlant, Henry (Milon) de
Demosthenes 384B.C.-322B.C. ..... **CMLC 13**
See also DLB 176
de Natale, Francine
See Malzberg, Barry N(athaniel)
Denby, Edwin (Orr) 1903-1983 .... **CLC 48**
See also CA 138; 110
Denis, Julio
See Cortazar, Julio
Denmark, Harrison
See Zelazny, Roger (Joseph)
Dennis, John 1658-1734 .... **LC 11**
See also DLB 101
Dennis, Nigel (Forbes) 1912-1989 ..... **CLC 8**
See also CA 25-28R; 129; DLB 13, 15; MTCW 1
Dent, Lester 1904(?)-1959 .... **TCLC 72**
See also CA 112; 161
De Palma, Brian (Russell) 1940- ..... **CLC 20**
See also CA 109
De Quincey, Thomas 1785-1859 .... **NCLC 4, 87**
See also CDBLB 1789-1832; DLB 110; 144
Deren, Eleanora 1908(?)-1961
See Deren, Maya
See also CA 111
Deren, Maya 1917-1961 .... **CLC 16, 102**
See also Deren, Eleanora
Derleth, August (William) 1909-1971
.... **CLC 31**
See also CA 1-4R; 29-32R; CANR 4; DLB 9; DLBD 17; SATA 5
Der Nister 1884-1950 .... **TCLC 56**
de Routisie, Albert
See Aragon, Louis
Derrida, Jacques 1930- .... **CLC 24, 87**
See also CA 124; 127; CANR 76; MTCW 1
Derry Down Derry
See Lear, Edward
Dersonnes, Jacques
See Simenon, Georges (Jacques Christian)
Desai, Anita 1937- .... **CLC 19, 37, 97; DAB; DAM NOV**
See also CA 81-84; CANR 33, 53; DA3; MTCW 1, 2; SATA 63
Desai, Kiran 1971- .... **CLC 119**
See also CA 171
de Saint-Luc, Jean
See Glassco, John
de Saint Roman, Arnaud
See Aragon, Louis
Descartes, Rene 1596-1650 .... **LC 20, 35**
De Sica, Vittorio 1901(?)-1974 .... **CLC 20**
See also CA 117
Desnos, Robert 1900-1945 .... **TCLC 22**
See also CA 121; 151
Destouches, Louis-Ferdinand 1894-1961
.... **CLC 9, 15**
See also Celine, Louis-Ferdinand
See also CA 85-88; CANR 28; MTCW 1
de Tolignac, Gaston
See Griffith, D(avid Lewelyn) W(ark)
Deutsch, Babette 1895-1982 .... **CLC 18**
See also CA 1-4R; 108; CANR 4, 79; DLB 45; SATA 1; SATA-Obit 33
Devenant, William 1606-1649 .... **LC 13**
Devkota, Laxmiprasad 1909-1959 . **TCLC 23**
See also CA 123
De Voto, Bernard (Augustine) 1897-1955
.... **TCLC 29**
See also CA 113; 160; DLB 9
De Vries, Peter 1910-1993 .... **CLC 1, 2, 3, 7, 10, 28, 46; DAM NOV**
See also CA 17-20R; 142; CANR 41; DLB 6; DLBY 82; MTCW 1, 2
Dewey, John 1859-1952 .... **TCLC 95**
See also CA 114; 170

Dexter, John
See Bradley, Marion Zimmer
Dexter, Martin
See Faust, Frederick (Schiller)
Dexter, Pete 1943- . **CLC 34, 55; DAM POP**
See also BEST 89:2; CA 127; 131; INT 131; MTCW 1
Diamano, Silmang
See Senghor, Leopold Sedar
Diamond, Neil 1941- .... **CLC 30**
See also CA 108
Diaz del Castillo, Bernal 1496-1584 . **LC 31; HLCS 1**
di Bassetto, Corno
See Shaw, George Bernard
Dick, Philip K(indred) 1928-1982 .. **CLC 10, 30, 72; DAM NOV, POP**
See also AAYA 24; CA 49-52; 106; CANR 2, 16; DA3; DLB 8; MTCW 1, 2
Dickens, Charles (John Huffam) 1812-1870
...... **NCLC 3, 8, 18, 26, 37, 50, 86; DA; DAB; DAC; DAM MST, NOV; SSC 17; WLC**
See also AAYA 23; CDBLB 1832-1890; DA3; DLB 21, 55, 70, 159, 166; JRDA; MAICYA; SATA 15
Dickey, James (Lafayette) 1923-1997
.. **CLC 1, 2, 4, 7, 10, 15, 47, 109; DAM NOV, POET, POP**
See also AITN 1, 2; CA 9-12R; 156; CABS 2; CANR 10, 48, 61; CDALB 1968-1988; DA3; DLB 5, 193; DLBD 7; DLBY 82, 93, 96, 97, 98; INT CANR-10; MTCW 1, 2
Dickey, William 1928-1994 .... **CLC 3, 28**
See also CA 9-12R; 145; CANR 24, 79; DLB 5
Dickinson, Charles 1951- .... **CLC 49**
See also CA 128
Dickinson, Emily (Elizabeth) 1830-1886
. **NCLC 21, 77; DA; DAB; DAC; DAM MST, POET; PC 1; WLC**
See also AAYA 22; CDALB 1865-1917; DA3; DLB 1; SATA 29
Dickinson, Peter (Malcolm) 1927- . **CLC 12, 35**
See also AAYA 9; CA 41-44R; CANR 31, 58, 88; CLR 29; DLB 87, 161; JRDA; MAICYA; SATA 5, 62, 95
Dickson, Carr
See Carr, John Dickson
Dickson, Carter
See Carr, John Dickson
Diderot, Denis 1713-1784 .... **LC 26**
Didion, Joan 1934- . **CLC 1, 3, 8, 14, 32, 129; DAM NOV**
See also AITN 1; CA 5-8R; CANR 14, 52, 76; CDALB 1968-1988; DA3; DLB 2, 173, 185; DLBY 81, 86; MTCW 1, 2
Dietrich, Robert
See Hunt, E(verette) Howard, (Jr.)
Difusa, Pati
See Almodovar, Pedro
Dillard, Annie 1945- . **CLC 9, 60, 115; DAM NOV**
See also AAYA 6; CA 49-52; CANR 3, 43, 62, 90; DA3; DLBY 80; MTCW 1, 2; SATA 10
Dillard, R(ichard) H(enry) W(ilde) 1937-
.... **CLC 5**
See also CA 21-24R; CAAS 7; CANR 10; DLB 5
Dillon, Eilis 1920-1994 .... **CLC 17**
See also CA 9-12R; 182; 147; CAAE 182; CAAS 3; CANR 4, 38, 78; CLR 26; MAICYA; SATA 2, 74; SATA-Essay 105; SATA-Obit 83

Dimont, Penelope
  See Mortimer, Penelope (Ruth)
Dinesen, Isak .... **CLC 10, 29, 95; SSC 7**
  See also Blixen, Karen (Christentze Dinesen)
  See also MTCW 1
Ding Ling .... **CLC 68**
  See also Chiang, Pin-chin
Diphusa, Patty
  See Almodovar, Pedro
Disch, Thomas M(ichael) 1940- .. **CLC 7, 36**
  See also AAYA 17; CA 21-24R; CAAS 4; CANR 17, 36, 54, 89; CLR 18; DA3; DLB 8; MAICYA; MTCW 1, 2; SAAS 15; SATA 92
Disch, Tom
  See Disch, Thomas M(ichael)
d'Isly, Georges
  See Simenon, Georges (Jacques Christian)
Disraeli, Benjamin 1804-1881 . **NCLC 2, 39, 79**
  See also DLB 21, 55
Ditcum, Steve
  See Crumb, R(obert)
Dixon, Paige
  See Corcoran, Barbara
Dixon, Stephen 1936- .... **CLC 52; SSC 16**
  See also CA 89-92; CANR 17, 40, 54, 91; DLB 130
Doak, Annie
  See Dillard, Annie
Dobell, Sydney Thompson 1824-1874
  .... **NCLC 43**
  See also DLB 32
Doblin, Alfred .... **TCLC 13**
  See also Doeblin, Alfred
Dobrolyubov, Nikolai Alexandrovich 1836-1861 .... **NCLC 5**
Dobson, Austin 1840-1921 .... **TCLC 79**
  See also DLB 35; 144
Dobyns, Stephen 1941- .... **CLC 37**
  See also CA 45-48; CANR 2, 18
Doctorow, E(dgar) L(aurence) 1931-
  .... **CLC 6, 11, 15, 18, 37, 44, 65, 113; DAM NOV, POP**
  See also AAYA 22; AITN 2; BEST 89:3; CA 45-48; CANR 2, 33, 51, 76; CDALB 1968-1988; DA3; DLB 2, 28, 173; DLBY 80; MTCW 1, 2
Dodgson, Charles Lutwidge 1832-1898
  See Carroll, Lewis
  See also CLR 2; DA; DAB; DAC; DAM MST, NOV, POET; DA3; MAICYA; SATA 100; YABC 2
Dodson, Owen (Vincent) 1914-1983
  .... **CLC 79; BLC 1; DAM MULT**
  See also BW 1; CA 65-68; 110; CANR 24; DLB 76
Doeblin, Alfred 1878-1957 .... **TCLC 13**
  See also Doblin, Alfred
  See also CA 110; 141; DLB 66
Doerr, Harriet 1910- .... **CLC 34**
  See also CA 117; 122; CANR 47; INT 122
Domecq, H(onorio Bustos)
  See Bioy Casares, Adolfo
Domecq, H(onorio) Bustos
  See Bioy Casares, Adolfo; Borges, Jorge Luis
Domini, Rey
  See Lorde, Audre (Geraldine)
Dominique
  See Proust, (Valentin-Louis-George-Eugene-) Marcel
Don, A
  See Stephen, SirLeslie
Donaldson, Stephen R. 1947- .... **CLC 46; DAM POP**
  See also CA 89-92; CANR 13, 55; INT CANR-13

Donleavy, J(ames) P(atrick) 1926- ... **CLC 1, 4, 6, 10, 45**
  See also AITN 2; CA 9-12R; CANR 24, 49, 62, 80; DLB 6, 173; INT CANR-24; MTCW 1, 2
Donne, John 1572-1631 .... **LC 10, 24; DA; DAB; DAC; DAM MST, POET; PC 1; WLC**
  See also CDBLB Before 1660; DLB 121, 151
Donnell, David 1939(?)- .... **CLC 34**
Donoghue, P. S.
  See Hunt, E(verette) Howard, (Jr.)
Donoso (Yanez), Jose 1924-1996 .. **CLC 4, 8, 11, 32, 99; DAM MULT; HLC 1; SSC 34**
  See also CA 81-84; 155; CANR 32, 73; DLB 113; HW 1, 2; MTCW 1, 2
Donovan, John 1928-1992 .... **CLC 35**
  See also AAYA 20; CA 97-100; 137; CLR 3; MAICYA; SATA 72; SATA-Brief 29
Don Roberto
  See Cunninghame Graham, Robert (Gallnigad) Bontine
Doolittle, Hilda 1886-1961 ...... **CLC 3, 8, 14, 31, 34, 73; DA; DAC; DAM MST, POET; PC 5; WLC**
  See also H. D.
  See also CA 97-100; CANR 35; DLB 4, 45; MTCW 1, 2
Dorfman, Ariel 1942- ..... **CLC 48, 77; DAM MULT; HLC 1**
  See also CA 124; 130; CANR 67, 70; HW 1, 2; INT 130
Dorn, Edward (Merton) 1929- .. **CLC 10, 18**
  See also CA 93-96; CANR 42, 79; DLB 5; INT 93-96
Dorris, Michael (Anthony) 1945-1997
  .... **CLC 109; DAM MULT, NOV**
  See also AAYA 20; BEST 90:1; CA 102; 157; CANR 19, 46, 75; CLR 58; DA3; DLB 175; MTCW 2; NNAL; SATA 75; SATA-Obit 94
Dorris, Michael A.
  See Dorris, Michael (Anthony)
Dorsan, Luc
  See Simenon, Georges (Jacques Christian)
Dorsange, Jean
  See Simenon, Georges (Jacques Christian)
Dos Passos, John (Roderigo) 1896-1970
  ..... **CLC 1, 4, 8, 11, 15, 25, 34, 82; DA; DAB; DAC; DAM MST, NOV; WLC**
  See also CA 1-4R; 29-32R; CANR 3; CDALB 1929-1941; DA3; DLB 4, 9; DLBD 1, 15; DLBY 96; MTCW 1, 2
Dossage, Jean
  See Simenon, Georges (Jacques Christian)
Dostoevsky, Fedor Mikhailovich 1821-1881
  .... **NCLC 2, 7, 21, 33, 43; DA; DAB; DAC; DAM MST, NOV; SSC 2, 33; WLC**
  See also DA3
Doughty, Charles M(ontagu) 1843-1926
  .... **TCLC 27**
  See also CA 115; 178; DLB 19, 57, 174
Douglas, Ellen .... **CLC 73**
  See also Haxton, Josephine Ayres; Williamson, Ellen Douglas
Douglas, Gavin 1475(?)-1522 .... **LC 20**
  See also DLB 132
Douglas, George
  See Brown, George Douglas
Douglas, Keith (Castellain) 1920-1944
  .... **TCLC 40**
  See also CA 160; DLB 27
Douglas, Leonard
  See Bradbury, Ray (Douglas)
Douglas, Michael
  See Crichton, (John) Michael

Douglas, (George) Norman 1868-1952
  .... **TCLC 68**
  See also CA 119; 157; DLB 34, 195
Douglas, William
  See Brown, George Douglas
Douglass, Frederick 1817(?)-1895 . **NCLC 7, 55; BLC 1; DA; DAC; DAM MST, MULT; WLC**
  See also CDALB 1640-1865; DA3; DLB 1, 43, 50, 79; SATA 29
Dourado, (Waldomiro Freitas) Autran 1926-
  .... **CLC 23, 60**
  See also CA 25-28R; 179; CANR 34, 81; DLB 145; HW 2
Dourado, Waldomiro Autran 1926-
  See Dourado, (Waldomiro Freitas) Autran
  See also CA 179
Dove, Rita (Frances) 1952- ...... **CLC 50, 81; BLCS; DAM MULT, POET; PC 6**
  See also BW 2; CA 109; CAAS 19; CANR 27, 42, 68, 76; CDALBS; DA3; DLB 120; MTCW 1
Doveglion
  See Villa, Jose Garcia
Dowell, Coleman 1925-1985 .... **CLC 60**
  See also CA 25-28R; 117; CANR 10; DLB 130
Dowson, Ernest (Christopher) 1867-1900
  .... **TCLC 4**
  See also CA 105; 150; DLB 19, 135
Doyle, A. Conan
  See Doyle, Arthur Conan
Doyle, Arthur Conan 1859-1930 ... **TCLC 7; DA; DAB; DAC; DAM MST, NOV; SSC 12; WLC**
  See also AAYA 14; CA 104; 122; CDBLB 1890-1914; DA3; DLB 18, 70, 156, 178; MTCW 1, 2; SATA 24
Doyle, Conan
  See Doyle, Arthur Conan
Doyle, John
  See Graves, Robert (von Ranke)
Doyle, Roddy 1958(?)- .... **CLC 81**
  See also AAYA 14; CA 143; CANR 73; DA3; DLB 194
Doyle, Sir A. Conan
  See Doyle, Arthur Conan
Doyle, Sir Arthur Conan
  See Doyle, Arthur Conan
Dr. A
  See Asimov, Isaac; Silverstein, Alvin
Drabble, Margaret 1939- ..... **CLC 2, 3, 5, 8, 10, 22, 53, 129; DAB; DAC; DAM MST, NOV, POP**
  See also CA 13-16R; CANR 18, 35, 63; CDBLB 1960 to Present; DA3; DLB 14, 155; MTCW 1, 2; SATA 48
Drapier, M. B.
  See Swift, Jonathan
Drayham, James
  See Mencken, H(enry) L(ouis)
Drayton, Michael 1563-1631 .... **LC 8; DAM POET**
  See also DLB 121
Dreadstone, Carl
  See Campbell, (John) Ramsey
Dreiser, Theodore (Herman Albert) 1871-1945 ... **TCLC 10, 18, 35, 83; DA; DAC; DAM MST, NOV; SSC 30; WLC**
  See also CA 106; 132; CDALB 1865-1917; DA3; DLB 9, 12, 102, 137; DLBD 1; MTCW 1, 2
Drexler, Rosalyn 1926- .... **CLC 2, 6**
  See also CA 81-84; CANR 68
Dreyer, Carl Theodor 1889-1968 .... **CLC 16**
  See also CA 116
Drieu la Rochelle, Pierre(-Eugene) 1893-1945 .... **TCLC 21**
  See also CA 117; DLB 72

Felsen, Henry Gregor 1916-1995 .... **CLC 17**
See also CA 1-4R; 180; CANR 1; SAAS 2;
SATA 1

Fenno, Jack
See Calisher, Hortense

Fenollosa, Ernest (Francisco) 1853-1908
.... **TCLC 91**

Fenton, James Martin 1949- .... **CLC 32**
See also CA 102; DLB 40

Ferber, Edna 1887-1968 .... **CLC 18, 93**
See also AITN 1; CA 5-8R; 25-28R; CANR
68; DLB 9, 28, 86; MTCW 1, 2; SATA 7

Ferguson, Helen
See Kavan, Anna

Ferguson, Samuel 1810-1886 .... **NCLC 33**
See also DLB 32

Fergusson, Robert 1750-1774 .... **LC 29**
See also DLB 109

Ferling, Lawrence
See Ferlinghetti, Lawrence (Monsanto)

Ferlinghetti, Lawrence (Monsanto) 1919(?)-
.... **CLC 2, 6, 10, 27, 111; DAM POET;
PC 1**
See also CA 5-8R; CANR 3, 41, 73;
CDALB 1941-1968; DA3; DLB 5, 16;
MTCW 1, 2

Fern, Fanny 1811-1872
See Parton, Sara Payson Willis

Fernandez, Vicente Garcia Huidobro
See Huidobro Fernandez, Vicente Garcia

Ferre, Rosario 1942- .... **SSC 36; HLCS 1**
See also CA 131; CANR 55, 81; DLB 145;
HW 1, 2; MTCW 1

Ferrer, Gabriel (Francisco Victor) Miro
See Miro (Ferrer), Gabriel (Francisco
Victor)

Ferrier, Susan (Edmonstone) 1782-1854
.... **NCLC 8**
See also DLB 116

Ferrigno, Robert 1948(?)- .... **CLC 65**
See also CA 140

Ferron, Jacques 1921-1985 ... **CLC 94; DAC**
See also CA 117; 129; DLB 60

Feuchtwanger, Lion 1884-1958 .... **TCLC 3**
See also CA 104; DLB 66

Feuillet, Octave 1821-1890 .... **NCLC 45**
See also DLB 192

Feydeau, Georges (Leon Jules Marie)
1862-1921 ..... **TCLC 22; DAM DRAM**
See also CA 113; 152; CANR 84; DLB 192

Fichte, Johann Gottlieb 1762-1814
.... **NCLC 62**
See also DLB 90

Ficino, Marsilio 1433-1499 .... **LC 12**

Fiedeler, Hans
See Doeblin, Alfred

Fiedler, Leslie A(aron) 1917- . **CLC 4, 13, 24**
See also CA 9-12R; CANR 7, 63; DLB 28,
67; MTCW 1, 2

Field, Andrew 1938- .... **CLC 44**
See also CA 97-100; CANR 25

Field, Eugene 1850-1895 .... **NCLC 3**
See also DLB 23, 42, 140; DLBD 13; MAI-
CYA; SATA 16

Field, Gans T.
See Wellman, Manly Wade

Field, Michael 1915-1971 .... **TCLC 43**
See also CA 29-32R

Field, Peter
See Hobson, Laura Z(ametkin)

Fielding, Henry 1707-1754 ... **LC 1, 46; DA;
DAB; DAC; DAM DRAM, MST, NOV;
WLC**
See also CDBLB 1660-1789; DA3; DLB
39, 84, 101

Fielding, Sarah 1710-1768 .... **LC 1, 44**
See also DLB 39

Fields, W. C. 1880-1946 .... **TCLC 80**

See also DLB 44

Fierstein, Harvey (Forbes) 1954- ... **CLC 33;
DAM DRAM, POP**
See also CA 123; 129; DA3

Figes, Eva 1932- .... **CLC 31**
See also CA 53-56; CANR 4, 44, 83; DLB
14

Finch, Anne 1661-1720 .... **LC 3; PC 21**
See also DLB 95

Finch, Robert (Duer Claydon) 1900-
.... **CLC 18**
See also CA 57-60; CANR 9, 24, 49; DLB
88

Findley, Timothy 1930- . **CLC 27, 102; DAC;
DAM MST**
See also CA 25-28R; CANR 12, 42, 69;
DLB 53

Fink, William
See Mencken, H(enry) L(ouis)

Firbank, Louis 1942-
See Reed, Lou
See also CA 117

Firbank, (Arthur Annesley) Ronald
1886-1926 .... **TCLC 1**
See also CA 104; 177; DLB 36

Fisher, Dorothy (Frances) Canfield
1879-1958 .... **TCLC 87**
See also CA 114; 136; CANR 80; DLB 9,
102; MAICYA; YABC 1

Fisher, M(ary) F(rances) K(ennedy)
1908-1992 .... **CLC 76, 87**
See also CA 77-80; 138; CANR 44; MTCW
1

Fisher, Roy 1930- .... **CLC 25**
See also CA 81-84; CAAS 10; CANR 16;
DLB 40

Fisher, Rudolph 1897-1934 . **TCLC 11; BLC
2; DAM MULT; SSC 25**
See also BW 1, 3; CA 107; 124; CANR 80;
DLB 51, 102

Fisher, Vardis (Alvero) 1895-1968 .... **CLC 7**
See also CA 5-8R; 25-28R; CANR 68; DLB
9, 206

Fiske, Tarleton
See Bloch, Robert (Albert)

Fitch, Clarke
See Sinclair, Upton (Beall)

Fitch, John IV
See Cormier, Robert (Edmund)

Fitzgerald, Captain Hugh
See Baum, L(yman) Frank

FitzGerald, Edward 1809-1883 ...... **NCLC 9**
See also DLB 32

Fitzgerald, F(rancis) Scott (Key) 1896-1940
.... **TCLC 1, 6, 14, 28, 55; DA; DAB;
DAC; DAM MST, NOV; SSC 6, 31;
WLC**
See also AAYA 24; AITN 1; CA 110; 123;
CDALB 1917-1929; DA3; DLB 4, 9, 86;
DLBD 1, 15, 16; DLBY 81, 96; MTCW
1, 2

Fitzgerald, Penelope 1916-2000 ...... **CLC 19,
51, 61**
See also CA 85-88; CAAS 10; CANR 56,
86; DLB 14, 194; MTCW 2

Fitzgerald, Robert (Stuart) 1910-1985
.... **CLC 39**
See also CA 1-4R; 114; CANR 1; DLBY
80

FitzGerald, Robert D(avid) 1902-1987
.... **CLC 19**
See also CA 17-20R

Fitzgerald, Zelda (Sayre) 1900-1948
.... **TCLC 52**
See also CA 117; 126; DLBY 84

Flanagan, Thomas (James Bonner) 1923-
.... **CLC 25, 52**
See also CA 108; CANR 55; DLBY 80; INT
108; MTCW 1

Flaubert, Gustave 1821-1880 .. **NCLC 2, 10,
19, 62, 66; DA; DAB; DAC; DAM MST,
NOV; SSC 11; WLC**
See also DA3; DLB 119

Flecker, Herman Elroy
See Flecker, (Herman) James Elroy

Flecker, (Herman) James Elroy 1884-1915
.... **TCLC 43**
See also CA 109; 150; DLB 10, 19

Fleming, Ian (Lancaster) 1908-1964 . **CLC 3,
30; DAM POP**
See also AAYA 26; CA 5-8R; CANR 59;
CDBLB 1945-1960; DA3; DLB 87, 201;
MTCW 1, 2; SATA 9

Fleming, Thomas (James) 1927- ..... **CLC 37**
See also CA 5-8R; CANR 10; INT CANR-
10; SATA 8

Fletcher, John 1579-1625 .... **LC 33; DC 6**
See also CDBLB Before 1660; DLB 58

Fletcher, John Gould 1886-1950 .. **TCLC 35**
See also CA 107; 167; DLB 4, 45

Fleur, Paul
See Pohl, Frederik

Flooglebuckle, Al
See Spiegelman, Art

Flying Officer X
See Bates, H(erbert) E(rnest)

Fo, Dario 1926- .... **CLC 32, 109; DAM
DRAM; DC 10**
See also CA 116; 128; CANR 68; DA3;
DLBY 97; MTCW 1, 2

Fogarty, Jonathan Titulescu Esq.
See Farrell, James T(homas)

Follett, Ken(neth Martin) 1949- .... **CLC 18;
DAM NOV, POP**
See also AAYA 6; BEST 89:4; CA 81-84;
CANR 13, 33, 54; DA3; DLB 87; DLBY
81; INT CANR-33; MTCW 1

Fontane, Theodor 1819-1898 .... **NCLC 26**
See also DLB 129

Foote, Horton 1916- .... **CLC 51, 91; DAM
DRAM**
See also CA 73-76; CANR 34, 51; DA3;
DLB 26; INT CANR-34

Foote, Shelby 1916- ... **CLC 75; DAM NOV,
POP**
See also CA 5-8R; CANR 3, 45, 74; DA3;
DLB 2, 17; MTCW 2

Forbes, Esther 1891-1967 .... **CLC 12**
See also AAYA 17; CA 13-14; 25-28R; CAP
1; CLR 27; DLB 22; JRDA; MAICYA;
SATA 2, 100

Forche, Carolyn (Louise) 1950- ..... **CLC 25,
83, 86; DAM POET; PC 10**
See also CA 109; 117; CANR 50, 74; DA3;
DLB 5, 193; INT 117; MTCW 1

Ford, Elbur
See Hibbert, Eleanor Alice Burford

Ford, Ford Madox 1873-1939 . **TCLC 1, 15,
39, 57; DAM NOV**
See also CA 104; 132; CANR 74; CDBLB
1914-1945; DA3; DLB 162; MTCW 1, 2

Ford, Henry 1863-1947 .... **TCLC 73**
See also CA 115; 148

Ford, John 1586-(?) .... **DC 8**
See also CDBLB Before 1660; DAM
DRAM; DA3; DLB 58

Ford, John 1895-1973 .... **CLC 16**
See also CA 45-48

Ford, Richard 1944- .... **CLC 46, 99**
See also CA 69-72; CANR 11, 47, 86;
MTCW 1

Ford, Webster
See Masters, Edgar Lee

Foreman, Richard 1937- .... **CLC 50**
See also CA 65-68; CANR 32, 63

Forester, C(ecil) S(cott) 1899-1966 . **CLC 35**
See also CA 73-76; 25-28R; CANR 83;
DLB 191; SATA 13

Fuller, Margaret .... **NCLC 5, 50**
See also Fuller, Sarah Margaret

Fuller, Roy (Broadbent) 1912-1991 . **CLC 4, 28**
See also CA 5-8R; 135; CAAS 10; CANR 53, 83; DLB 15, 20; SATA 87

Fuller, Sarah Margaret 1810-1850
See Fuller, Margaret
See also CDALB 1640-1865; DLB 1, 59, 73, 83, 223

Fulton, Alice 1952- .... **CLC 52**
See also CA 116; CANR 57, 88; DLB 193

Furphy, Joseph 1843-1912 .... **TCLC 25**
See also CA 163

Fussell, Paul 1924- .... **CLC 74**
See also BEST 90:1; CA 17-20R; CANR 8, 21, 35, 69; INT CANR-21; MTCW 1, 2

Futabatei, Shimei 1864-1909 .... **TCLC 44**
See also CA 162; DLB 180

Futrelle, Jacques 1875-1912 .... **TCLC 19**
See also CA 113; 155

Gaboriau, Emile 1835-1873 .... **NCLC 14**

Gadda, Carlo Emilio 1893-1973 ...... **CLC 11**
See also CA 89-92; DLB 177

Gaddis, William 1922-1998 .. **CLC 1, 3, 6, 8, 10, 19, 43, 86**
See also CA 17-20R; 172; CANR 21, 48; DLB 2; MTCW 1, 2

Gage, Walter
See Inge, William (Motter)

Gaines, Ernest J(ames) 1933- ..... **CLC 3, 11, 18, 86; BLC 2; DAM MULT**
See also AAYA 18; AITN 1; BW 2, 3; CA 9-12R; CANR 6, 24, 42, 75; CDALB 1968-1988; CLR 62; DA3; DLB 2, 33, 152; DLBY 80; MTCW 1, 2; SATA 86

Gaitskill, Mary 1954- .... **CLC 69**
See also CA 128; CANR 61

Galdos, Benito Perez
See Perez Galdos, Benito

Gale, Zona 1874-1938 .... **TCLC 7; DAM DRAM**
See also CA 105; 153; CANR 84; DLB 9, 78

Galeano, Eduardo (Hughes) 1940- . **CLC 72; HLCS 1**
See also CA 29-32R; CANR 13, 32; HW 1

Galiano, Juan Valera y Alcala
See Valera y Alcala-Galiano, Juan

Galilei, Galileo 1546-1642 .... **LC 45**

Gallagher, Tess 1943- ..... **CLC 18, 63; DAM POET; PC 9**
See also CA 106; DLB 212

Gallant, Mavis 1922- . **CLC 7, 18, 38; DAC; DAM MST; SSC 5**
See also CA 69-72; CANR 29, 69; DLB 53; MTCW 1, 2

Gallant, Roy A(rthur) 1924- .... **CLC 17**
See also CA 5-8R; CANR 4, 29, 54; CLR 30; MAICYA; SATA 4, 68, 110

Gallico, Paul (William) 1897-1976 .... **CLC 2**
See also AITN 1; CA 5-8R; 69-72; CANR 23; DLB 9, 171; MAICYA; SATA 13

Gallo, Max Louis 1932- .... **CLC 95**
See also CA 85-88

Gallois, Lucien
See Desnos, Robert

Gallup, Ralph
See Whitemore, Hugh (John)

Galsworthy, John 1867-1933 ... **TCLC 1, 45; DA; DAB; DAC; DAM DRAM, MST, NOV; SSC 22; WLC**
See also CA 104; 141; CANR 75; CDBLB 1890-1914; DA3; DLB 10, 34, 98, 162; DLBD 16; MTCW 1

Galt, John 1779-1839 .... **NCLC 1**
See also DLB 99, 116, 159

Galvin, James 1951- .... **CLC 38**
See also CA 108; CANR 26

Gamboa, Federico 1864-1939 .... **TCLC 36**
See also CA 167; HW 2

Gandhi, M. K.
See Gandhi, Mohandas Karamchand

Gandhi, Mahatma
See Gandhi, Mohandas Karamchand

Gandhi, Mohandas Karamchand 1869-1948
.... **TCLC 59; DAM MULT**
See also CA 121; 132; DA3; MTCW 1, 2

Gann, Ernest Kellogg 1910-1991 .... **CLC 23**
See also AITN 1; CA 1-4R; 136; CANR 1, 83

Garber, Eric 1943(?)-
See Holleran, Andrew
See also CANR 89

Garcia, Cristina 1958- .... **CLC 76**
See also CA 141; CANR 73; HW 2

Garcia Lorca, Federico 1898-1936 . **TCLC 1, 7, 49; DA; DAB; DAC; DAM DRAM, MST, MULT, POET; DC 2; HLC 2; PC 3; WLC**
See also Lorca, Federico Garcia
See also CA 104; 131; CANR 81; DA3; DLB 108; HW 1, 2; MTCW 1, 2

Garcia Marquez, Gabriel (Jose) 1928-
.... **CLC 2, 3, 8, 10, 15, 27, 47, 55, 68; DA; DAB; DAC; DAM MST, MULT, NOV, POP; HLC 1; SSC 8; WLC**
See also Marquez, Gabriel (Jose) Garcia
See also AAYA 3, 33; BEST 89:1, 90:4; CA 33-36R; CANR 10, 28, 50, 75, 82; DA3; DLB 113; HW 1, 2; MTCW 1, 2

Garcilaso de la Vega, El Inca 1503-1536
See also HLCS 1

Gard, Janice
See Latham, Jean Lee

Gard, Roger Martin du
See Martin du Gard, Roger

Gardam, Jane 1928- .... **CLC 43**
See also CA 49-52; CANR 2, 18, 33, 54; CLR 12; DLB 14, 161; MAICYA; MTCW 1; SAAS 9; SATA 39, 76; SATA-Brief 28

Gardner, Herb(ert) 1934- .... **CLC 44**
See also CA 149

Gardner, John (Champlin), Jr. 1933-1982
. **CLC 2, 3, 5, 7, 8, 10, 18, 28, 34; DAM NOV, POP; SSC 7**
See also AITN 1; CA 65-68; 107; CANR 33, 73; CDALBS; DA3; DLB 2; DLBY 82; MTCW 1; SATA 40; SATA-Obit 31

Gardner, John (Edmund) 1926- .... **CLC 30; DAM POP**
See also CA 103; CANR 15, 69; MTCW 1

Gardner, Miriam
See Bradley, Marion Zimmer

Gardner, Noel
See Kuttner, Henry

Gardons, S. S.
See Snodgrass, W(illiam) D(e Witt)

Garfield, Leon 1921-1996 .... **CLC 12**
See also AAYA 8; CA 17-20R; 152; CANR 38, 41, 78; CLR 21; DLB 161; JRDA; MAICYA; SATA 1, 32, 76; SATA-Obit 90

Garland, (Hannibal) Hamlin 1860-1940
.... **TCLC 3; SSC 18**
See also CA 104; DLB 12, 71, 78, 186

Garneau, (Hector de) Saint-Denys 1912-1943
.... **TCLC 13**
See also CA 111; DLB 88

Garner, Alan 1934- .... **CLC 17; DAB; DAM POP**
See also AAYA 18; CA 73-76, 178; CAAE 178; CANR 15, 64; CLR 20; DLB 161; MAICYA; MTCW 1, 2; SATA 18, 69; SATA-Essay 108

Garner, Hugh 1913-1979 .... **CLC 13**
See also CA 69-72; CANR 31; DLB 68

Garnett, David 1892-1981 .... **CLC 3**

See also CA 5-8R; 103; CANR 17, 79; DLB 34; MTCW 2

Garos, Stephanie
See Katz, Steve

Garrett, George (Palmer) 1929- . **CLC 3, 11, 51; SSC 30**
See also CA 1-4R; CAAS 5; CANR 1, 42, 67; DLB 2, 5, 130, 152; DLBY 83

Garrick, David 1717-1779 ...... **LC 15; DAM DRAM**
See also DLB 84

Garrigue, Jean 1914-1972 .... **CLC 2, 8**
See also CA 5-8R; 37-40R; CANR 20

Garrison, Frederick
See Sinclair, Upton (Beall)

Garro, Elena 1920(?)-1998
See also CA 131; 169; DLB 145; HLCS 1; HW 1

Garth, Will
See Hamilton, Edmond; Kuttner, Henry

Garvey, Marcus (Moziah, Jr.) 1887-1940
.... **TCLC 41; BLC 2; DAM MULT**
See also BW 1; CA 120; 124; CANR 79

Gary, Romain .... **CLC 25**
See also Kacew, Romain
See also DLB 83

Gascar, Pierre .... **CLC 11**
See also Fournier, Pierre

Gascoyne, David (Emery) 1916- ..... **CLC 45**
See also CA 65-68; CANR 10, 28, 54; DLB 20; MTCW 1

Gaskell, Elizabeth Cleghorn 1810-1865
.. **NCLC 70; DAB; DAM MST; SSC 25**
See also CDBLB 1832-1890; DLB 21, 144, 159

Gass, William H(oward) 1924- . **CLC 1, 2, 8, 11, 15, 39, 132; SSC 12**
See also CA 17-20R; CANR 30, 71; DLB 2; MTCW 1, 2

Gassendi, Pierre 1592-1655 .... **LC 54**

Gasset, Jose Ortega y
See Ortega y Gasset, Jose

Gates, Henry Louis, Jr. 1950- .... **CLC 65; BLCS; DAM MULT**
See also BW 2, 3; CA 109; CANR 25, 53, 75; DA3; DLB 67; MTCW 1

Gautier, Theophile 1811-1872 . **NCLC 1, 59; DAM POET; PC 18; SSC 20**
See also DLB 119

Gawsworth, John
See Bates, H(erbert) E(rnest)

Gay, John 1685-1732 . **LC 49; DAM DRAM**
See also DLB 84, 95

Gay, Oliver
See Gogarty, Oliver St. John

Gaye, Marvin (Penze) 1939-1984 .... **CLC 26**
See also CA 112

Gebler, Carlo (Ernest) 1954- .... **CLC 39**
See also CA 119; 133

Gee, Maggie (Mary) 1948- .... **CLC 57**
See also CA 130; DLB 207

Gee, Maurice (Gough) 1931- .... **CLC 29**
See also CA 97-100; CANR 67; CLR 56; SATA 46, 101

Gelbart, Larry (Simon) 1923- ... **CLC 21, 61**
See also CA 73-76; CANR 45

Gelber, Jack 1932- .... **CLC 1, 6, 14, 79**
See also CA 1-4R; CANR 2; DLB 7

Gellhorn, Martha (Ellis) 1908-1998
.... **CLC 14, 60**
See also CA 77-80; 164; CANR 44; DLBY 82, 98

Genet, Jean 1910-1986 . **CLC 1, 2, 5, 10, 14, 44, 46; DAM DRAM**
See also CA 13-16R; CANR 18; DA3; DLB 72; DLBY 86; MTCW 1, 2

Gent, Peter 1942- .... **CLC 29**
See also AITN 1; CA 89-92; DLBY 82

See also CA 53-56; CANR 6, 40; DLB 120

Goldberg, Anatol 1910-1982 .... **CLC 34**
See also CA 131; 117

Goldemberg, Isaac 1945- .... **CLC 52**
See also CA 69-72; CAAS 12; CANR 11, 32; HW 1

Golding, William (Gerald) 1911-1993
. **CLC 1, 2, 3, 8, 10, 17, 27, 58, 81; DA; DAB; DAC; DAM MST, NOV; WLC**
See also AAYA 5; CA 5-8R; 141; CANR 13, 33, 54; CDBLB 1945-1960; DA3; DLB 15, 100; MTCW 1, 2

Goldman, Emma 1869-1940 .... **TCLC 13**
See also CA 110; 150; DLB 221

Goldman, Francisco 1954- .... **CLC 76**
See also CA 162

Goldman, William (W.) 1931- ..... **CLC 1, 48**
See also CA 9-12R; CANR 29, 69; DLB 44

Goldmann, Lucien 1913-1970 .... **CLC 24**
See also CA 25-28; CAP 2

Goldoni, Carlo 1707-1793 .... **LC 4; DAM DRAM**

Goldsberry, Steven 1949- .... **CLC 34**
See also CA 131

Goldsmith, Oliver 1728-1774 . **LC 2, 48; DA; DAB; DAC; DAM DRAM, MST, NOV, POET; DC 8; WLC**
See also CDBLB 1660-1789; DLB 39, 89, 104, 109, 142; SATA 26

Goldsmith, Peter
See Priestley, J(ohn) B(oynton)

Gombrowicz, Witold 1904-1969 ... **CLC 4, 7, 11, 49; DAM DRAM**
See also CA 19-20; 25-28R; CAP 2

Gomez de la Serna, Ramon 1888-1963
.... **CLC 9**
See also CA 153; 116; CANR 79; HW 1, 2

Goncharov, Ivan Alexandrovich 1812-1891
.... **NCLC 1, 63**

Goncourt, Edmond (Louis Antoine Huot) de 1822-1896 .... **NCLC 7**
See also DLB 123

Goncourt, Jules (Alfred Huot) de 1830-1870
.... **NCLC 7**
See also DLB 123

Gontier, Fernande 19(?)- .... **CLC 50**

Gonzalez Martinez, Enrique 1871-1952
.... **TCLC 72**
See also CA 166; CANR 81; HW 1

Goodman, Paul 1911-1972 .... **CLC 1, 2, 4, 7**
See also CA 19-20; 37-40R; CANR 34; CAP 2; DLB 130; MTCW 1

Gordimer, Nadine 1923- .... **CLC 3, 5, 7, 10, 18, 33, 51, 70; DA; DAB; DAC; DAM MST, NOV; SSC 17; WLCS**
See also CA 5-8R; CANR 3, 28, 56, 88; DA3; INT CANR-28; MTCW 1, 2

Gordon, Adam Lindsay 1833-1870
.... **NCLC 21**

Gordon, Caroline 1895-1981 ...... **CLC 6, 13, 29, 83; SSC 15**
See also CA 11-12; 103; CANR 36; CAP 1; DLB 4, 9, 102; DLBD 17; DLBY 81; MTCW 1, 2

Gordon, Charles William 1860-1937
See Connor, Ralph
See also CA 109

Gordon, Mary (Catherine) 1949- .. **CLC 13, 22, 128**
See also CA 102; CANR 44; DLB 6; DLBY 81; INT 102; MTCW 1

Gordon, N. J.
See Bosman, Herman Charles

Gordon, Sol 1923- .... **CLC 26**
See also CA 53-56; CANR 4; SATA 11

Gordone, Charles 1925-1995 .... **CLC 1, 4; DAM DRAM; DC 8**

See also BW 1, 3; CA 93-96; 180; 150; CAAE 180; CANR 55; DLB 7; INT 93-96; MTCW 1

Gore, Catherine 1800-1861 .... **NCLC 65**
See also DLB 116

Gorenko, Anna Andreevna
See Akhmatova, Anna

Gorky, Maxim 1868-1936 ... **TCLC 8; DAB; SSC 28; WLC**
See Peshkov, Alexei Maximovich
See also MTCW 2

Goryan, Sirak
See Saroyan, William

Gosse, Edmund (William) 1849-1928
.... **TCLC 28**
See also CA 117; DLB 57, 144, 184

Gotlieb, Phyllis Fay (Bloom) 1926- . **CLC 18**
See also CA 13-16R; CANR 7; DLB 88

Gottesman, S. D.
See Kornbluth, C(yril) M.; Pohl, Frederik

Gottfried von Strassburg fl. c. 1210-
.... **CMLC 10**
See also DLB 138

Gould, Lois .... **CLC 4, 10**
See also CA 77-80; CANR 29; MTCW 1

Gourmont, Remy (-Marie-Charles) de 1858-1915 .... **TCLC 17**
See also CA 109; 150; MTCW 2

Govier, Katherine 1948- .... **CLC 51**
See also CA 101; CANR 18, 40

Goyen, (Charles) William 1915-1983
.... **CLC 5, 8, 14, 40**
See also AITN 2; CA 5-8R; 110; CANR 6, 71; DLB 2; DLBY 83; INT CANR-6

Goytisolo, Juan 1931- . **CLC 5, 10, 23; DAM MULT; HLC 1**
See also CA 85-88; CANR 32, 61; HW 1, 2; MTCW 1, 2

Gozzano, Guido 1883-1916 .... **PC 10**
See also CA 154; DLB 114

Gozzi, (Conte) Carlo 1720-1806 ... **NCLC 23**

Grabbe, Christian Dietrich 1801-1836
.... **NCLC 2**
See also DLB 133

Grace, Patricia Frances 1937- .... **CLC 56**
See also CA 176

Gracian y Morales, Baltasar 1601-1658
.... **LC 15**

Gracq, Julien .... **CLC 11, 48**
See Poirier, Louis
See also DLB 83

Grade, Chaim 1910-1982 .... **CLC 10**
See also CA 93-96; 107

Graduate of Oxford, A
See Ruskin, John

Grafton, Garth
See Duncan, Sara Jeannette

Graham, John
See Phillips, David Graham

Graham, Jorie 1951- .... **CLC 48, 118**
See also CA 111; CANR 63; DLB 120

Graham, R(obert) B(ontine) Cunninghame
See Cunninghame Graham, Robert (Gallnigad) Bontine
See also DLB 98, 135, 174

Graham, Robert
See Haldeman, Joe (William)

Graham, Tom
See Lewis, (Harry) Sinclair

Graham, W(illiam) S(ydney) 1918-1986
.... **CLC 29**
See also CA 73-76; 118; DLB 20

Graham, Winston (Mawdsley) 1910-
.... **CLC 23**
See also CA 49-52; CANR 2, 22, 45, 66; DLB 77

Grahame, Kenneth 1859-1932 ..... **TCLC 64; DAB**

See also CA 108; 136; CANR 80; CLR 5; DA3; DLB 34, 141, 178; MAICYA; MTCW 2; SATA 100; YABC 1

Granovsky, Timofei Nikolaevich 1813-1855
.... **NCLC 75**
See also DLB 198

Grant, Skeeter
See Spiegelman, Art

Granville-Barker, Harley 1877-1946
.... **TCLC 2; DAM DRAM**
See also Barker, Harley Granville
See also CA 104

Grass, Guenter (Wilhelm) 1927- . **CLC 1, 2, 4, 6, 11, 15, 22, 32, 49, 88; DA; DAB; DAC; DAM MST, NOV; WLC**
See also CA 13-16R; CANR 20, 75; DA3; DLB 75, 124; MTCW 1, 2

Gratton, Thomas
See Hulme, T(homas) E(rnest)

Grau, Shirley Ann 1929- . **CLC 4, 9; SSC 15**
See also CA 89-92; CANR 22, 69; DLB 2; INT CANR-22; MTCW 1

Gravel, Fern
See Hall, James Norman

Graver, Elizabeth 1964- .... **CLC 70**
See also CA 135; CANR 71

Graves, Richard Perceval 1945- ..... **CLC 44**
See also CA 65-68; CANR 9, 26, 51

Graves, Robert (von Ranke) 1895-1985
.... **CLC 1, 2, 6, 11, 39, 44, 45; DAB; DAC; DAM MST, POET; PC 6**
See also CA 5-8R; 117; CANR 5, 36; CDBLB 1914-1945; DA3; DLB 20, 100, 191; DLBD 18; DLBY 85; MTCW 1, 2; SATA 45

Graves, Valerie
See Bradley, Marion Zimmer

Gray, Alasdair (James) 1934- .... **CLC 41**
See also CA 126; CANR 47, 69; DLB 194; INT 126; MTCW 1, 2

Gray, Amlin 1946- .... **CLC 29**
See also CA 138

Gray, Francine du Plessix 1930- ... **CLC 22; DAM NOV**
See also BEST 90:3; CA 61-64; CAAS 2; CANR 11, 33, 75, 81; INT CANR-11; MTCW 1, 2

Gray, John (Henry) 1866-1934 ..... **TCLC 19**
See also CA 119; 162

Gray, Simon (James Holliday) 1936-
.... **CLC 9, 14, 36**
See also AITN 1; CA 21-24R; CAAS 3; CANR 32, 69; DLB 13; MTCW 1

Gray, Spalding 1941- ... **CLC 49, 112; DAM POP; DC 7**
See also CA 128; CANR 74; MTCW 2

Gray, Thomas 1716-1771 ...... **LC 4, 40; DA; DAB; DAC; DAM MST; PC 2; WLC**
See also CDBLB 1660-1789; DA3; DLB 109

Grayson, David
See Baker, Ray Stannard

Grayson, Richard (A.) 1951- .... **CLC 38**
See also CA 85-88; CANR 14, 31, 57

Greeley, Andrew M(oran) 1928- .... **CLC 28; DAM POP**
See also CA 5-8R; CAAS 7; CANR 7, 43, 69; DA3; MTCW 1, 2

Green, Anna Katharine 1846-1935
.... **TCLC 63**
See also CA 112; 159; DLB 202, 221

Green, Brian
See Card, Orson Scott

Green, Hannah
See Greenberg, Joanne (Goldenberg)

Green, Hannah 1927(?)-1996 .... **CLC 3**
See also CA 73-76; CANR 59

Green, Henry 1905-1973 .... **CLC 2, 13, 97**
See also Yorke, Henry Vincent

See also CA 175; DLB 15
Green, Julian (Hartridge) 1900-1998
  See Green, Julien
  See also CA 21-24R; 169; CANR 33, 87;
  DLB 4, 72; MTCW 1
Green, Julien .... **CLC 3, 11, 77**
  See also Green, Julian (Hartridge)
  See also MTCW 2
Green, Paul (Eliot) 1894-1981 .... **CLC 25;**
  DAM DRAM
  See also AITN 1; CA 5-8R; 103; CANR 3;
  DLB 7, 9; DLBY 81
Greenberg, Ivan 1908-1973
  See Rahv, Philip
  See also CA 85-88
Greenberg, Joanne (Goldenberg) 1932-
  .... **CLC 7, 30**
  See also AAYA 12; CA 5-8R; CANR 14,
  32, 69; SATA 25
Greenberg, Richard 1959(?)- .... **CLC 57**
  See also CA 138
Greene, Bette 1934- .... **CLC 30**
  See also AAYA 7; CA 53-56; CANR 4; CLR
  2; JRDA; MAICYA; SAAS 16; SATA 8,
  102
Greene, Gael .... **CLC 8**
  See also CA 13-16R; CANR 10
Greene, Graham (Henry) 1904-1991
  ... **CLC 1, 3, 6, 9, 14, 18, 27, 37, 70, 72,**
  125; DA; DAB; DAC; DAM MST, NOV;
  SSC 29; WLC
  See also AITN 2; CA 13-16R; 133; CANR
  35, 61; CDBLB 1945-1960; DA3; DLB
  13, 15, 77, 100, 162, 201, 204; DLBY 91;
  MTCW 1, 2; SATA 20
Greene, Robert 1558-1592 .... **LC 41**
  See also DLB 62, 167
Greer, Germaine 1939- .... **CLC 131**
  See also AITN 1; CA 81-84; CANR 33, 70;
  MTCW 1, 2
Greer, Richard
  See Silverberg, Robert
Gregor, Arthur 1923- .... **CLC 9**
  See also CA 25-28R; CAAS 10; CANR 11;
  SATA 36
Gregor, Lee
  See Pohl, Frederik
Gregory, Isabella Augusta (Persse)
  1852-1932 .... **TCLC 1**
  See also CA 104; 184; DLB 10
Gregory, J. Dennis
  See Williams, John A(lfred)
Grendon, Stephen
  See Derleth, August (William)
Grenville, Kate 1950- .... **CLC 61**
  See also CA 118; CANR 53
Grenville, Pelham
  See Wodehouse, P(elham) G(renville)
Greve, Felix Paul (Berthold Friedrich)
  1879-1948
  See Grove, Frederick Philip
  See also CA 104; 141; 175; CANR 79;
  DAC; DAM MST
Grey, Zane 1872-1939 . **TCLC 6; DAM POP**
  See also CA 104; 132; DA3; DLB 212;
  MTCW 1, 2
Grieg, (Johan) Nordahl (Brun) 1902-1943
  .... **TCLC 10**
  See also CA 107
Grieve, C(hristopher) M(urray) 1892-1978
  .... **CLC 11, 19; DAM POET**
  See also MacDiarmid, Hugh; Pteleon
  See also CA 5-8R; 85-88; CANR 33;
  MTCW 1
Griffin, Gerald 1803-1840 .... **NCLC 7**
  See also DLB 159
Griffin, John Howard 1920-1980 .... **CLC 68**
  See also AITN 1; CA 1-4R; 101; CANR 2
Griffin, Peter 1942- .... **CLC 39**

See also CA 136
Griffith, D(avid Lewelyn) W(ark)
  1875(?)-1948 .... **TCLC 68**
  See also CA 119; 150; CANR 80
Griffith, Lawrence
  See Griffith, D(avid Lewelyn) W(ark)
Griffiths, Trevor 1935- .... **CLC 13, 52**
  See also CA 97-100; CANR 45; DLB 13
Griggs, Sutton (Elbert) 1872-1930 . **TCLC 77**
  See also CA 123; 186; DLB 50
Grigson, Geoffrey (Edward Harvey)
  1905-1985 .... **CLC 7, 39**
  See also CA 25-28R; 118; CANR 20, 33;
  DLB 27; MTCW 1, 2
Grillparzer, Franz 1791-1872 .... **NCLC 1;**
  SSC 37
  See also DLB 133
Grimble, Reverend Charles James
  See Eliot, T(homas) S(tearns)
Grimke, Charlotte L(ottie) Forten
  1837(?)-1914
  See Forten, Charlotte L.
  See also BW 1; CA 117; 124; DAM MULT,
  POET
Grimm, Jacob Ludwig Karl 1785-1863
  .... **NCLC 3, 77; SSC 36**
  See also DLB 90; MAICYA; SATA 22
Grimm, Wilhelm Karl 1786-1859 . **NCLC 3,**
  77; SSC 36
  See also DLB 90; MAICYA; SATA 22
Grimmelshausen, Johann Jakob Christoffel
  von 1621-1676 .... **LC 6**
  See also DLB 168
Grindel, Eugene 1895-1952
  See Eluard, Paul
  See also CA 104
Grisham, John 1955- .. **CLC 84; DAM POP**
  See also AAYA 14; CA 138; CANR 47, 69;
  DA3; MTCW 2
Grossman, David 1954- .... **CLC 67**
  See also CA 138
Grossman, Vasily (Semenovich) 1905-1964
  .... **CLC 41**
  See also CA 124; 130; MTCW 1
Grove, Frederick Philip .... **TCLC 4**
  See also Greve, Felix Paul (Berthold
  Friedrich)
  See also DLB 92
Grubb
  See Crumb, R(obert)
Grumbach, Doris (Isaac) 1918- ...... **CLC 13,**
  22, 64
  See also CA 5-8R; CAAS 2; CANR 9, 42,
  70; INT CANR-9; MTCW 2
Grundtvig, Nicolai Frederik Severin
  1783-1872 .... **NCLC 1**
Grunge
  See Crumb, R(obert)
Grunwald, Lisa 1959- .... **CLC 44**
  See also CA 120
Guare, John 1938- . **CLC 8, 14, 29, 67; DAM**
  DRAM
  See also CA 73-76; CANR 21, 69; DLB 7;
  MTCW 1, 2
Gudjonsson, Halldor Kiljan 1902-1998
  See Laxness, Halldor
  See also CA 103; 164
Guenter, Erich
  See Eich, Guenter
Guest, Barbara 1920- .... **CLC 34**
  See also CA 25-28R; CANR 11, 44, 84;
  DLB 5, 193
Guest, Edgar A(lbert) 1881-1959 . **TCLC 95**
  See also CA 112; 168
Guest, Judith (Ann) 1936- .... **CLC 8, 30;**
  DAM NOV, POP
  See also AAYA 7; CA 77-80; CANR 15,
  75; DA3; INT CANR-15; MTCW 1, 2
Guevara, Che .... **CLC 87; HLC 1**

See also Guevara (Serna), Ernesto
Guevara (Serna), Ernesto 1928-1967
  .... **CLC 87; DAM MULT; HLC 1**
  See also Guevara, Che
  See also CA 127; 111; CANR 56; HW 1
Guicciardini, Francesco 1483-1540 ... **LC 49**
Guild, Nicholas M. 1944- .... **CLC 33**
  See also CA 93-96
Guillemin, Jacques
  See Sartre, Jean-Paul
Guillen, Jorge 1893-1984 ..... **CLC 11; DAM**
  MULT, POET; HLCS 1
  See also CA 89-92; 112; DLB 108; HW 1
Guillen, Nicolas (Cristobal) 1902-1989
  .... **CLC 48, 79; BLC 2; DAM MST,**
  MULT, POET; HLC 1; PC 23
  See also BW 2; CA 116; 125; 129; CANR
  84; HW 1
Guillevic, (Eugene) 1907- .... **CLC 33**
  See also CA 93-96
Guillois
  See Desnos, Robert
Guillois, Valentin
  See Desnos, Robert
Guimaraes Rosa, Joao 1908-1967
  See also CA 175; HLCS 2
Guiney, Louise Imogen 1861-1920 . **TCLC 41**
  See also CA 160; DLB 54
Guiraldes, Ricardo (Guillermo) 1886-1927
  .... **TCLC 39**
  See also CA 131; HW 1; MTCW 1
Gumilev, Nikolai (Stepanovich) 1886-1921
  .... **TCLC 60**
  See also CA 165
Gunesekera, Romesh 1954- .... **CLC 91**
  See also CA 159
Gunn, Bill .... **CLC 5**
  See also Gunn, William Harrison
  See also DLB 38
Gunn, Thom(son William) 1929- . **CLC 3, 6,**
  18, 32, 81; DAM POET; PC 26
  See also CA 17-20R; CANR 9, 33; CDBLB
  1960 to Present; DLB 27; INT CANR-33;
  MTCW 1
Gunn, William Harrison 1934(?)-1989
  See Gunn, Bill
  See also AITN 1; BW 1, 3; CA 13-16R;
  128; CANR 12, 25, 76
Gunnars, Kristjana 1948- .... **CLC 69**
  See also CA 113; DLB 60
Gurdjieff, G(eorgei) I(vanovich)
  1877(?)-1949 .... **TCLC 71**
  See also CA 157
Gurganus, Allan 1947- . **CLC 70; DAM POP**
  See also BEST 90:1; CA 135
Gurney, A(lbert) R(amsdell), Jr. 1930-
  .... **CLC 32, 50, 54; DAM DRAM**
  See also CA 77-80; CANR 32, 64
Gurney, Ivor (Bertie) 1890-1937 .. **TCLC 33**
  See also CA 167
Gurney, Peter
  See Gurney, A(lbert) R(amsdell), Jr.
Guro, Elena 1877-1913 .... **TCLC 56**
Gustafson, James M(oody) 1925- . **CLC 100**
  See also CA 25-28R; CANR 37
Gustafson, Ralph (Barker) 1909- ... **CLC 36**
  See also CA 21-24R; CANR 8, 45, 84; DLB
  88
Gut, Gom
  See Simenon, Georges (Jacques Christian)
Guterson, David 1956- .... **CLC 91**
  See also CA 132; CANR 73; MTCW 2
Guthrie, A(lfred) B(ertram), Jr. 1901-1991
  .... **CLC 23**
  See also CA 57-60; 134; CANR 24; DLB
  212; SATA 62; SATA-Obit 67
Guthrie, Isobel
  See Grieve, C(hristopher) M(urray)

See also CA 77-80; 126; CANR 58; DLB 87; SATA 14; SATA-Obit 59

Housman, A(lfred) E(dward) 1859-1936
... **TCLC 1, 10; DA; DAB; DAC; DAM MST, POET; PC 2; WLCS**
See also CA 104; 125; DA3; DLB 19; MTCW 1, 2

Housman, Laurence 1865-1959 ...... **TCLC 7**
See also CA 106; 155; DLB 10; SATA 25

Howard, Elizabeth Jane 1923- .... **CLC 7, 29**
See also CA 5-8R; CANR 8, 62

Howard, Maureen 1930- .... **CLC 5, 14, 46**
See also CA 53-56; CANR 31, 75; DLBY 83; INT CANR-31; MTCW 1, 2

Howard, Richard 1929- .... **CLC 7, 10, 47**
See also AITN 1; CA 85-88; CANR 25, 80; DLB 5; INT CANR-25

Howard, Robert E(rvin) 1906-1936 . **TCLC 8**
See also CA 105; 157

Howard, Warren F.
See Pohl, Frederik

Howe, Fanny (Quincy) 1940- .... **CLC 47**
See also CA 117; CAAS 27; CANR 70; SATA-Brief 52

Howe, Irving 1920-1993 .... **CLC 85**
See also CA 9-12R; 141; CANR 21, 50; DLB 67; MTCW 1, 2

Howe, Julia Ward 1819-1910 .... **TCLC 21**
See also CA 117; DLB 1, 189

Howe, Susan 1937- .... **CLC 72**
See also CA 160; DLB 120

Howe, Tina 1937- .... **CLC 48**
See also CA 109

Howell, James 1594(?)-1666 .... **LC 13**
See also DLB 151

Howells, W. D.
See Howells, William Dean

Howells, William D.
See Howells, William Dean

Howells, William Dean 1837-1920 . **TCLC 7, 17, 41; SSC 36**
See also CA 104; 134; CDALB 1865-1917; DLB 12, 64, 74, 79, 189; MTCW 2

Howes, Barbara 1914-1996 .... **CLC 15**
See also CA 9-12R; 151; CAAS 3; CANR 53; SATA 5

Hrabal, Bohumil 1914-1997 ...... **CLC 13, 67**
See also CA 106; 156; CAAS 12; CANR 57

Hroswitha of Gandersheim c. 935-c. 1002
.... **CMLC 29**
See also DLB 148

Hsun, Lu
See Lu Hsun

Hubbard, L(afayette) Ron(ald) 1911-1986
.... **CLC 43; DAM POP**
See also CA 77-80; 118; CANR 52; DA3; MTCW 2

Huch, Ricarda (Octavia) 1864-1947
.... **TCLC 13**
See also CA 111; DLB 66

Huddle, David 1942- .... **CLC 49**
See also CA 57-60; CAAS 20; CANR 89; DLB 130

Hudson, Jeffrey
See Crichton, (John) Michael

Hudson, W(illiam) H(enry) 1841-1922
.... **TCLC 29**
See also CA 115; DLB 98, 153, 174; SATA 35

Hueffer, Ford Madox
See Ford, Ford Madox

Hughart, Barry 1934- .... **CLC 39**
See also CA 137

Hughes, Colin
See Creasey, John

Hughes, David (John) 1930- .... **CLC 48**
See also CA 116; 129; DLB 14

Hughes, Edward James
See Hughes, Ted
See also DAM MST, POET; DA3

Hughes, (James) Langston 1902-1967
. **CLC 1, 5, 10, 15, 35, 44, 108; BLC 2; DA; DAB; DAC; DAM DRAM, MST, MULT, POET; DC 3; PC 1; SSC 6; WLC**
See also AAYA 12; BW 1, 3; CA 1-4R; 25-28R; CANR 1, 34, 82; CDALB 1929-1941; CLR 17; DA3; DLB 4, 7, 48, 51, 86; JRDA; MAICYA; MTCW 1, 2; SATA 4, 33

Hughes, Richard (Arthur Warren)
1900-1976 .... **CLC 1, 11; DAM NOV**
See also CA 5-8R; 65-68; CANR 4; DLB 15, 161; MTCW 1; SATA 8; SATA-Obit 25

Hughes, Ted 1930-1998 . **CLC 2, 4, 9, 14, 37, 119; DAB; DAC; PC 7**
See also Hughes, Edward James
See also CA 1-4R; 171; CANR 1, 33, 66; CLR 3; DLB 40, 161; MAICYA; MTCW 1, 2; SATA 49; SATA-Brief 27; SATA-Obit 107

Hugo, Richard F(ranklin) 1923-1982
.... **CLC 6, 18, 32; DAM POET**
See also CA 49-52; 108; CANR 3; DLB 5, 206

Hugo, Victor (Marie) 1802-1885 ... **NCLC 3, 10, 21; DA; DAB; DAC; DAM DRAM, MST, NOV, POET; PC 17; WLC**
See also AAYA 28; DA3; DLB 119, 192; SATA 47

Huidobro, Vicente
See Huidobro Fernandez, Vicente Garcia

Huidobro Fernandez, Vicente Garcia
1893-1948 .... **TCLC 31**
See also CA 131; HW 1

Hulme, Keri 1947- .... **CLC 39, 130**
See also CA 125; CANR 69; INT 125

Hulme, T(homas) E(rnest) 1883-1917
.... **TCLC 21**
See also CA 117; DLB 19

Hume, David 1711-1776 .... **LC 7, 56**
See also DLB 104

Humphrey, William 1924-1997 .... **CLC 45**
See also CA 77-80; 160; CANR 68; DLB 212

Humphreys, Emyr Owen 1919- ...... **CLC 47**
See also CA 5-8R; CANR 3, 24; DLB 15

Humphreys, Josephine 1945- .... **CLC 34, 57**
See also CA 121; 127; INT 127

Huneker, James Gibbons 1857-1921
.... **TCLC 65**
See also DLB 71

Hungerford, Pixie
See Brinsmead, H(esba) F(ay)

Hunt, E(verette) Howard, (Jr.) 1918- . **CLC 3**
See also AITN 1; CA 45-48; CANR 2, 47

Hunt, Francesca
See Holland, Isabelle

Hunt, Kyle
See Creasey, John

Hunt, (James Henry) Leigh 1784-1859
.... **NCLC 1, 70; DAM POET**
See also DLB 96, 110, 144

Hunt, Marsha 1946- .... **CLC 70**
See also BW 2, 3; CA 143; CANR 79

Hunt, Violet 1866(?)-1942 .... **TCLC 53**
See also CA 184; DLB 162, 197

Hunter, E. Waldo
See Sturgeon, Theodore (Hamilton)

Hunter, Evan 1926- .... **CLC 11, 31; DAM POP**
See also CA 5-8R; CANR 5, 38, 62; DLBY 82; INT CANR-5; MTCW 1; SATA 25

Hunter, Kristin (Eggleston) 1931- .. **CLC 35**

See also AITN 1; BW 1; CA 13-16R; CANR 13; CLR 3; DLB 33; INT CANR-13; MAICYA; SAAS 10; SATA 12

Hunter, Mary
See Austin, Mary (Hunter)

Hunter, Mollie 1922- .... **CLC 21**
See also McIlwraith, Maureen Mollie Hunter
See also AAYA 13; CANR 37, 78; CLR 25; DLB 161; JRDA; MAICYA; SAAS 7; SATA 54, 106

Hunter, Robert (?)-1734 .... **LC 7**

Hurston, Zora Neale 1903-1960 . **CLC 7, 30, 61; BLC 2; DA; DAC; DAM MST, MULT, NOV; DC 12; SSC 4; WLCS**
See also AAYA 15; BW 1, 3; CA 85-88; CANR 61; CDALBS; DA3; DLB 51, 86; MTCW 1, 2

Huston, John (Marcellus) 1906-1987
.... **CLC 20**
See also CA 73-76; 123; CANR 34; DLB 26

Hustvedt, Siri 1955- .... **CLC 76**
See also CA 137

Hutten, Ulrich von 1488-1523 .... **LC 16**
See also DLB 179

Huxley, Aldous (Leonard) 1894-1963
... **CLC 1, 3, 4, 5, 8, 11, 18, 35, 79; DA; DAB; DAC; DAM MST, NOV; SSC 39; WLC**
See also AAYA 11; CA 85-88; CANR 44; CDBLB 1914-1945; DA3; DLB 36, 100, 162, 195; MTCW 1, 2; SATA 63

Huxley, T(homas) H(enry) 1825-1895
.... **NCLC 67**
See also DLB 57

Huysmans, Joris-Karl 1848-1907 .. **TCLC 7, 69**
See also CA 104; 165; DLB 123

Hwang, David Henry 1957- . **CLC 55; DAM DRAM; DC 4**
See also CA 127; 132; CANR 76; DA3; DLB 212; INT 132; MTCW 2

Hyde, Anthony 1946- .... **CLC 42**
See also CA 136

Hyde, Margaret O(ldroyd) 1917- .... **CLC 21**
See also CA 1-4R; CANR 1, 36; CLR 23; JRDA; MAICYA; SAAS 8; SATA 1, 42, 76

Hynes, James 1956(?)- .... **CLC 65**
See also CA 164

Hypatia c. 370-415 .... **CMLC 35**

Ian, Janis 1951- .... **CLC 21**
See also CA 105

Ibanez, Vicente Blasco
See Blasco Ibanez, Vicente

Ibarbourou, Juana de 1895-1979
See also HLCS 2; HW 1

Ibarguengoitia, Jorge 1928-1983 ..... **CLC 37**
See also CA 124; 113; HW 1

Ibsen, Henrik (Johan) 1828-1906 .. **TCLC 2, 8, 16, 37, 52; DA; DAB; DAC; DAM DRAM, MST; DC 2; WLC**
See also CA 104; 141; DA3

Ibuse, Masuji 1898-1993 .... **CLC 22**
See also CA 127; 141; DLB 180

Ichikawa, Kon 1915- .... **CLC 20**
See also CA 121

Idle, Eric 1943- .... **CLC 21**
See also Monty Python
See also CA 116; CANR 35, 91

Ignatow, David 1914-1997 . **CLC 4, 7, 14, 40**
See also CA 9-12R; 162; CAAS 3; CANR 31, 57; DLB 5

Ignotus
See Strachey, (Giles) Lytton

Ihimaera, Witi 1944- .... **CLC 46**
See also CA 77-80

Ilf, Ilya .... **TCLC 21**

Kerry, Lois
See Duncan, Lois

Kesey, Ken (Elton) 1935- ... **CLC 1, 3, 6, 11, 46, 64; DA; DAB; DAC; DAM MST, NOV, POP; WLC**
See also AAYA 25; CA 1-4R; CANR 22, 38, 66; CDALB 1968-1988; DA3; DLB 2, 16, 206; MTCW 1, 2; SATA 66

Kesselring, Joseph (Otto) 1902-1967
.... **CLC 45; DAM DRAM, MST**
See also CA 150

Kessler, Jascha (Frederick) 1929- ..... **CLC 4**
See also CA 17-20R; CANR 8, 48

Kettelkamp, Larry (Dale) 1933- ..... **CLC 12**
See also CA 29-32R; CANR 16; SAAS 3; SATA 2

Key, Ellen 1849-1926 .... **TCLC 65**

Keyber, Conny
See Fielding, Henry

Keyes, Daniel 1927- ..... **CLC 80; DA; DAC; DAM MST, NOV**
See also AAYA 23; CA 17-20R, 181; CAAE 181; CANR 10, 26, 54, 74; DA3; MTCW 2; SATA 37

Keynes, John Maynard 1883-1946
.... **TCLC 64**
See also CA 114; 162, 163; DLBD 10; MTCW 2

Khanshendel, Chiron
See Rose, Wendy

Khayyam, Omar 1048-1131 .... **CMLC 11; DAM POET; PC 8**
See also DA3

Kherdian, David 1931- .... **CLC 6, 9**
See also CA 21-24R; CAAS 2; CANR 39, 78; CLR 24; JRDA; MAICYA; SATA 16, 74

Khlebnikov, Velimir .... **TCLC 20**
See also Khlebnikov, Viktor Vladimirovich

Khlebnikov, Viktor Vladimirovich 1885-1922
See Khlebnikov, Velimir
See also CA 117

Khodasevich, Vladislav (Felitsianovich) 1886-1939 .... **TCLC 15**
See also CA 115

Kielland, Alexander Lange 1849-1906
.... **TCLC 5**
See also CA 104

Kiely, Benedict 1919- .... **CLC 23, 43**
See also CA 1-4R; CANR 2, 84; DLB 15

Kienzle, William X(avier) 1928- .... **CLC 25; DAM POP**
See also CA 93-96; CAAS 1; CANR 9, 31, 59; DA3; INT CANR-31; MTCW 1, 2

Kierkegaard, Soren 1813-1855 .... **NCLC 34, 78**

Kieslowski, Krzysztof 1941-1996 .. **CLC 120**
See also CA 147; 151

Killens, John Oliver 1916-1987 .... **CLC 10**
See also BW 2; CA 77-80; 123; CAAS 2; CANR 26; DLB 33

Killigrew, Anne 1660-1685 .... **LC 4**
See also DLB 131

Killigrew, Thomas 1612-1683 .... **LC 57**
See also DLB 58

Kim
See Simenon, Georges (Jacques Christian)

Kincaid, Jamaica 1949- .. **CLC 43, 68; BLC 2; DAM MULT, NOV**
See also AAYA 13; BW 2, 3; CA 125; CANR 47, 59; CDALBS; CLR 63; DA3; DLB 157; MTCW 2

King, Francis (Henry) 1923- ...... **CLC 8, 53; DAM NOV**
See also CA 1-4R; CANR 1, 33, 86; DLB 15, 139; MTCW 1

King, Kennedy
See Brown, George Douglas

King, Martin Luther, Jr. 1929-1968
...... **CLC 83; BLC 2; DA; DAB; DAC; DAM MST, MULT; WLCS**
See also BW 2, 3; CA 25-28; CANR 27, 44; CAP 2; DA3; MTCW 1, 2; SATA 14

King, Stephen (Edwin) 1947- ... **CLC 12, 26, 37, 61, 113; DAM NOV, POP; SSC 17**
See also AAYA 1, 17; BEST 90:1; CA 61-64; CANR 1, 30, 52, 76; DA3; DLB 143; DLBY 80; JRDA; MTCW 1, 2; SATA 9, 55

King, Steve
See King, Stephen (Edwin)

King, Thomas 1943- .. **CLC 89; DAC; DAM MULT**
See also CA 144; DLB 175; NNAL; SATA 96

Kingman, Lee .... **CLC 17**
See also Natti, (Mary) Lee
See also SAAS 3; SATA 1, 67

Kingsley, Charles 1819-1875 .... **NCLC 35**
See also DLB 21, 32, 163, 190; YABC 2

Kingsley, Sidney 1906-1995 .... **CLC 44**
See also CA 85-88; 147; DLB 7

Kingsolver, Barbara 1955- .... **CLC 55, 81, 130; DAM POP**
See also AAYA 15; CA 129; 134; CANR 60; CDALBS; DA3; DLB 206; INT 134; MTCW 2

Kingston, Maxine (Ting Ting) Hong 1940-
...... **CLC 12, 19, 58, 121; DAM MULT, NOV; WLCS**
See also AAYA 8; CA 69-72; CANR 13, 38, 74, 87; CDALBS; DA3; DLB 173, 212; DLBY 80; INT CANR-13; MTCW 1, 2; SATA 53

Kinnell, Galway 1927- ... **CLC 1, 2, 3, 5, 13, 29, 129; PC 26**
See also CA 9-12R; CANR 10, 34, 66; DLB 5; DLBY 87; INT CANR-34; MTCW 1, 2

Kinsella, Thomas 1928- .... **CLC 4, 19**
See also CA 17-20R; CANR 15; DLB 27; MTCW 1, 2

Kinsella, W(illiam) P(atrick) 1935- . **CLC 27, 43; DAC; DAM NOV, POP**
See also AAYA 7; CA 97-100; CAAS 7; CANR 21, 35, 66, 75; INT CANR-21; MTCW 1, 2

Kinsey, Alfred C(harles) 1894-1956
.... **TCLC 91**
See also CA 115; 170; MTCW 2

Kipling, (Joseph) Rudyard 1865-1936
... **TCLC 8, 17; DA; DAB; DAC; DAM MST, POET; PC 3; SSC 5; WLC**
See also AAYA 32; CA 105; 120; CANR 33; CDBLB 1890-1914; CLR 39, 65; DA3; DLB 19, 34, 141, 156; MAICYA; MTCW 1, 2; SATA 100; YABC 2

Kirkland, Caroline M. 1801-1864 . **NCLC 85**
See also DLB 3, 73, 74; DLBD 13

Kirkup, James 1918- .... **CLC 1**
See also CA 1-4R; CAAS 4; CANR 2; DLB 27; SATA 12

Kirkwood, James 1930(?)-1989 .... **CLC 9**
See also AITN 2; CA 1-4R; 128; CANR 6, 40

Kirshner, Sidney
See Kingsley, Sidney

Kis, Danilo 1935-1989 .... **CLC 57**
See also CA 109; 118; 129; CANR 61; DLB 181; MTCW 1

Kivi, Aleksis 1834-1872 .... **NCLC 30**

Kizer, Carolyn (Ashley) 1925- . **CLC 15, 39, 80; DAM POET**
See also CA 65-68; CAAS 5; CANR 24, 70; DLB 5, 169; MTCW 2

Klabund 1890-1928 .... **TCLC 44**
See also CA 162; DLB 66

Klappert, Peter 1942- .... **CLC 57**

See also CA 33-36R; DLB 5

Klein, A(braham) M(oses) 1909-1972
.... **CLC 19; DAB; DAC; DAM MST**
See also CA 101; 37-40R; DLB 68

Klein, Norma 1938-1989 .... **CLC 30**
See also AAYA 2; CA 41-44R; 128; CANR 15, 37; CLR 2, 19; INT CANR-15; JRDA; MAICYA; SAAS 1; SATA 7, 57

Klein, T(heodore) E(ibon) D(onald) 1947-
.... **CLC 34**
See also CA 119; CANR 44, 75

Kleist, Heinrich von 1777-1811 ..... **NCLC 2, 37; DAM DRAM; SSC 22**
See also DLB 90

Klima, Ivan 1931- .... **CLC 56; DAM NOV**
See also CA 25-28R; CANR 17, 50, 91

Klimentov, Andrei Platonovich 1899-1951
See Platonov, Andrei
See also CA 108

Klinger, Friedrich Maximilian von 1752-1831 .... **NCLC 1**
See also DLB 94

Klingsor the Magician
See Hartmann, Sadakichi

Klopstock, Friedrich Gottlieb 1724-1803
.... **NCLC 11**
See also DLB 97

Knapp, Caroline 1959- .... **CLC 99**
See also CA 154

Knebel, Fletcher 1911-1993 .... **CLC 14**
See also AITN 1; CA 1-4R; 140; CAAS 3; CANR 1, 36; SATA 36; SATA-Obit 75

Knickerbocker, Diedrich
See Irving, Washington

Knight, Etheridge 1931-1991 . **CLC 40; BLC 2; DAM POET; PC 14**
See also BW 1, 3; CA 21-24R; 133; CANR 23, 82; DLB 41; MTCW 2

Knight, Sarah Kemble 1666-1727 .... **LC 7**
See also DLB 24, 200

Knister, Raymond 1899-1932 .... **TCLC 56**
See also CA 186; DLB 68

Knowles, John 1926- . **CLC 1, 4, 10, 26; DA; DAC; DAM MST, NOV**
See also AAYA 10; CA 17-20R; CANR 40, 74, 76; CDALB 1968-1988; DLB 6; MTCW 1, 2; SATA 8, 89

Knox, Calvin M.
See Silverberg, Robert

Knox, John c. 1505-1572 .... **LC 37**
See also DLB 132

Knye, Cassandra
See Disch, Thomas M(ichael)

Koch, C(hristopher) J(ohn) 1932- .. **CLC 42**
See also CA 127; CANR 84

Koch, Christopher
See Koch, C(hristopher) J(ohn)

Koch, Kenneth 1925- ... **CLC 5, 8, 44; DAM POET**
See also CA 1-4R; CANR 6, 36, 57; DLB 5; INT CANR-36; MTCW 2; SATA 65

Kochanowski, Jan 1530-1584 .... **LC 10**

Kock, Charles Paul de 1794-1871 . **NCLC 16**

Koda Rohan 1867-
See Koda Shigeyuki

Koda Shigeyuki 1867-1947 .... **TCLC 22**
See also CA 121; 183; DLB 180

Koestler, Arthur 1905-1983 . **CLC 1, 3, 6, 8, 15, 33**
See also CA 1-4R; 109; CANR 1, 33; CDBLB 1945-1960; DLBY 83; MTCW 1, 2

Kogawa, Joy Nozomi 1935- ... **CLC 78, 129; DAC; DAM MST, MULT**
See also CA 101; CANR 19, 62; MTCW 2; SATA 99

Kohout, Pavel 1928- .... **CLC 13**
See also CA 45-48; CANR 3

See also BW 1; CA 125; CANR 83; DLB 51

Lee, (Nelle) Harper 1926- . **CLC 12, 60; DA; DAB; DAC; DAM MST, NOV; WLC**
See also AAYA 13; CA 13-16R; CANR 51; CDALB 1941-1968; DA3; DLB 6; MTCW 1, 2; SATA 11

Lee, Helen Elaine 1959(?)- .... **CLC 86**
See also CA 148

Lee, Julian
See Latham, Jean Lee

Lee, Larry
See Lee, Lawrence

Lee, Laurie 1914-1997 .... **CLC 90; DAB; DAM POP**
See also CA 77-80; 158; CANR 33, 73; DLB 27; MTCW 1

Lee, Lawrence 1941-1990 .... **CLC 34**
See also CA 131; CANR 43

Lee, Li-Young 1957- .... **PC 24**
See also CA 153; DLB 165

Lee, Manfred B(ennington) 1905-1971
.... **CLC 11**
See also Queen, Ellery
See also CA 1-4R; 29-32R; CANR 2; DLB 137

Lee, Shelton Jackson 1957(?)- ..... **CLC 105; BLCS; DAM MULT**
See also Lee, Spike
See also BW 2, 3; CA 125; CANR 42

Lee, Spike
See Lee, Shelton Jackson
See also AAYA 4, 29

Lee, Stan 1922- .... **CLC 17**
See also AAYA 5; CA 108; 111; INT 111

Lee, Tanith 1947- .... **CLC 46**
See also AAYA 15; CA 37-40R; CANR 53; SATA 8, 88

Lee, Vernon .... **TCLC 5; SSC 33**
See also Paget, Violet
See also DLB 57, 153, 156, 174, 178

Lee, William
See Burroughs, William S(eward)

Lee, Willy
See Burroughs, William S(eward)

Lee-Hamilton, Eugene (Jacob) 1845-1907
.... **TCLC 22**
See also CA 117

Leet, Judith 1935- .... **CLC 11**

Le Fanu, Joseph Sheridan 1814-1873
.... **NCLC 9, 58; DAM POP; SSC 14**
See also DA3; DLB 21, 70, 159, 178

Leffland, Ella 1931- .... **CLC 19**
See also CA 29-32R; CANR 35, 78, 82; DLBY 84; INT CANR-35; SATA 65

Leger, Alexis
See Leger, (Marie-Rene Auguste) Alexis Saint-Leger

Leger, (Marie-Rene Auguste) Alexis Saint-Leger 1887-1975 . **CLC 4, 11, 46; DAM POET; PC 23**
See also CA 13-16R; 61-64; CANR 43; MTCW 1

Leger, Saintleger
See Leger, (Marie-Rene Auguste) Alexis Saint-Leger

Le Guin, Ursula K(roeber) 1929- .... **CLC 8, 13, 22, 45, 71; DAB; DAC; DAM MST, POP; SSC 12**
See also AAYA 9, 27; AITN 1; CA 21-24R; CANR 9, 32, 52, 74; CDALB 1968-1988; CLR 3, 28; DA3; DLB 8, 52; INT CANR-32; JRDA; MAICYA; MTCW 1, 2; SATA 4, 52, 99

Lehmann, Rosamond (Nina) 1901-1990
.... **CLC 5**
See also CA 77-80; 131; CANR 8, 73; DLB 15; MTCW 2

Leiber, Fritz (Reuter, Jr.) 1910-1992
.... **CLC 25**
See also CA 45-48; 139; CANR 2, 40, 86; DLB 8; MTCW 1, 2; SATA 45; SATA-Obit 73

Leibniz, Gottfried Wilhelm von 1646-1716
.... **LC 35**
See also DLB 168

Leimbach, Martha 1963-
See Leimbach, Marti
See also CA 130

Leimbach, Marti .... **CLC 65**
See also Leimbach, Martha

Leino, Eino .... **TCLC 24**
See also Loennbohm, Armas Eino Leopold

Leiris, Michel (Julien) 1901-1990 ... **CLC 61**
See also CA 119; 128; 132

Leithauser, Brad 1953- .... **CLC 27**
See also CA 107; CANR 27, 81; DLB 120

Lelchuk, Alan 1938- .... **CLC 5**
See also CA 45-48; CAAS 20; CANR 1, 70

Lem, Stanislaw 1921- .... **CLC 8, 15, 40**
See also CA 105; CAAS 1; CANR 32; MTCW 1

Lemann, Nancy 1956- .... **CLC 39**
See also CA 118; 136

Lemonnier, (Antoine Louis) Camille 1844-1913 .... **TCLC 22**
See also CA 121

Lenau, Nikolaus 1802-1850 .... **NCLC 16**

L'Engle, Madeleine (Camp Franklin) 1918-
.... **CLC 12; DAM POP**
See also AAYA 28; AITN 2; CA 1-4R; CANR 3, 21, 39, 66; CLR 1, 14, 57; DA3; DLB 52; JRDA; MAICYA; MTCW 1, 2; SAAS 15; SATA 1, 27, 75

Lengyel, Jozsef 1896-1975 .... **CLC 7**
See also CA 85-88; 57-60; CANR 71

Lenin 1870-1924
See Lenin, V. I.
See also CA 121; 168

Lenin, V. I. .... **TCLC 67**
See also Lenin

Lennon, John (Ono) 1940-1980 . **CLC 12, 35**
See also CA 102; SATA 114

Lennox, Charlotte Ramsay 1729(?)-1804
.... **NCLC 23**
See also DLB 39

Lentricchia, Frank (Jr.) 1940- .... **CLC 34**
See also CA 25-28R; CANR 19

Lenz, Siegfried 1926- .... **CLC 27; SSC 33**
See also CA 89-92; CANR 80; DLB 75

Leonard, Elmore (John, Jr.) 1925- . **CLC 28, 34, 71, 120; DAM POP**
See also AAYA 22; AITN 1; BEST 89:1, 90:4; CA 81-84; CANR 12, 28, 53, 76; DA3; DLB 173; INT CANR-28; MTCW 1, 2

Leonard, Hugh .... **CLC 19**
See also Byrne, John Keyes
See also DLB 13

Leonov, Leonid (Maximovich) 1899-1994
.... **CLC 92; DAM NOV**
See also CA 129; CANR 74, 76; MTCW 1, 2

Leopardi, (Conte) Giacomo 1798-1837
.... **NCLC 22**

Le Reveler
See Artaud, Antonin (Marie Joseph)

Lerman, Eleanor 1952- .... **CLC 9**
See also CA 85-88; CANR 69

Lerman, Rhoda 1936- .... **CLC 56**
See also CA 49-52; CANR 70

Lermontov, Mikhail Yuryevich 1814-1841
.... **NCLC 47; PC 18**
See also DLB 205

Leroux, Gaston 1868-1927 .... **TCLC 25**
See also CA 108; 136; CANR 69; SATA 65

Lesage, Alain-Rene 1668-1747 .... **LC 2, 28**

Leskov, Nikolai (Semyonovich) 1831-1895
.... **NCLC 25; SSC 34**

Lessing, Doris (May) 1919- . **CLC 1, 2, 3, 6, 10, 15, 22, 40, 94; DA; DAB; DAC; DAM MST, NOV; SSC 6; WLCS**
See also CA 9-12R; CAAS 14; CANR 33, 54, 76; CDBLB 1960 to Present; DA3; DLB 15, 139; DLBY 85; MTCW 1, 2

Lessing, Gotthold Ephraim 1729-1781 . **LC 8**
See also DLB 97

Lester, Richard 1932- .... **CLC 20**

Lever, Charles (James) 1806-1872 . **NCLC 23**
See also DLB 21

Leverson, Ada 1865(?)-1936(?) ..... **TCLC 18**
See also Elaine
See also CA 117; DLB 153

Levertov, Denise 1923-1997 . **CLC 1, 2, 3, 5, 8, 15, 28, 66; DAM POET; PC 11**
See also CA 1-4R; 178; 163; CAAE 178; CAAS 19; CANR 3, 29, 50; CDALBS; DLB 5, 165; INT CANR-29; MTCW 1, 2

Levi, Jonathan .... **CLC 76**

Levi, Peter (Chad Tigar) 1931- .... **CLC 41**
See also CA 5-8R; CANR 34, 80; DLB 40

Levi, Primo 1919-1987 ..... **CLC 37, 50; SSC 12**
See also CA 13-16R; 122; CANR 12, 33, 61, 70; DLB 177; MTCW 1, 2

Levin, Ira 1929- .... **CLC 3, 6; DAM POP**
See also CA 21-24R; CANR 17, 44, 74; DA3; MTCW 1, 2; SATA 66

Levin, Meyer 1905-1981 . **CLC 7; DAM POP**
See also AITN 1; CA 9-12R; 104; CANR 15; DLB 9, 28; DLBY 81; SATA 21; SATA-Obit 27

Levine, Norman 1924- .... **CLC 54**
See also CA 73-76; CAAS 23; CANR 14, 70; DLB 88

Levine, Philip 1928- . **CLC 2, 4, 5, 9, 14, 33, 118; DAM POET; PC 22**
See also CA 9-12R; CANR 9, 37, 52; DLB 5

Levinson, Deirdre 1931- .... **CLC 49**
See also CA 73-76; CANR 70

Levi-Strauss, Claude 1908- .... **CLC 38**
See also CA 1-4R; CANR 6, 32, 57; MTCW 1, 2

Levitin, Sonia (Wolff) 1934- .... **CLC 17**
See also AAYA 13; CA 29-32R; CANR 14, 32, 79; CLR 53; JRDA; MAICYA; SAAS 2; SATA 4, 68

Levon, O. U.
See Kesey, Ken (Elton)

Levy, Amy 1861-1889 .... **NCLC 59**
See also DLB 156

Lewes, George Henry 1817-1878 . **NCLC 25**
See also DLB 55, 144

Lewis, Alun 1915-1944 ..... **TCLC 3; SSC 40**
See also CA 104; DLB 20, 162

Lewis, C. Day
See Day Lewis, C(ecil)

Lewis, C(live) S(taples) 1898-1963 ... **CLC 1, 3, 6, 14, 27, 124; DA; DAB; DAC; DAM MST, NOV, POP; WLC**
See also AAYA 3; CA 81-84; CANR 33, 71; CDBLB 1945-1960; CLR 3, 27; DA3; DLB 15, 100, 160; JRDA; MAICYA; MTCW 1, 2; SATA 13, 100

Lewis, Janet 1899-1998 .... **CLC 41**
See also Winters, Janet Lewis
See also CA 9-12R; 172; CANR 29, 63; CAP 1; DLBY 87

Lewis, Matthew Gregory 1775-1818
.... **NCLC 11, 62**
See also DLB 39, 158, 178

Lewis, (Harry) Sinclair 1885-1951 . **TCLC 4, 13, 23, 39; DA; DAB; DAC; DAM MST, NOV; WLC**

Loris
    See Hofmannsthal, Hugo von
Loti, Pierre .... **TCLC 11**
    See also Viaud, (Louis Marie) Julien
    See also DLB 123
Lou, Henri
    See Andreas-Salome, Lou
Louie, David Wong 1954- .... **CLC 70**
    See also CA 139
Louis, Father M.
    See Merton, Thomas
Lovecraft, H(oward) P(hillips) 1890-1937
    .... **TCLC 4, 22; DAM POP; SSC 3**
    See also AAYA 14; CA 104; 133; DA3;
    MTCW 1, 2
Lovelace, Earl 1935- .... **CLC 51**
    See also BW 2; CA 77-80; CANR 41, 72;
    DLB 125; MTCW 1
Lovelace, Richard 1618-1657 .... **LC 24**
    See also DLB 131
Lowell, Amy 1874-1925 ... **TCLC 1, 8; DAM POET; PC 13**
    See also CA 104; 151; DLB 54, 140;
    MTCW 2
Lowell, James Russell 1819-1891 ... **NCLC 2**
    See also CDALB 1640-1865; DLB 1, 11,
    64, 79, 189
Lowell, Robert (Traill Spence, Jr.)
    1917-1977 ... **CLC 1, 2, 3, 4, 5, 8, 9, 11,
    15, 37, 124; DA; DAB; DAC; DAM
    MST, NOV; PC 3; WLC**
    See also CA 9-12R; 73-76; CABS 2; CANR
    26, 60; CDALBS; DA3; DLB 5, 169;
    MTCW 1, 2
Lowenthal, Michael (Francis) 1969-
    .... **CLC 119**
    See also CA 150
Lowndes, Marie Adelaide (Belloc) 1868-1947
    .... **TCLC 12**
    See also CA 107; DLB 70
Lowry, (Clarence) Malcolm 1909-1957
    .... **TCLC 6, 40; SSC 31**
    See also CA 105; 131; CANR 62; CDBLB
    1945-1960; DLB 15; MTCW 1, 2
Lowry, Mina Gertrude 1882-1966
    See Loy, Mina
    See also CA 113
Loxsmith, John
    See Brunner, John (Kilian Houston)
Loy, Mina ..... **CLC 28; DAM POET; PC 16**
    See also Lowry, Mina Gertrude
    See also DLB 4, 54
Loyson-Bridet
    See Schwob, Marcel (Mayer Andre)
Lucan 39-65 .... **CMLC 33**
    See also DLB 211
Lucas, Craig 1951- .... **CLC 64**
    See also CA 137; CANR 71
Lucas, E(dward) V(errall) 1868-1938
    .... **TCLC 73**
    See also CA 176; DLB 98, 149, 153; SATA
    20
Lucas, George 1944- .... **CLC 16**
    See also AAYA 1, 23; CA 77-80; CANR
    30; SATA 56
Lucas, Hans
    See Godard, Jean-Luc
Lucas, Victoria
    See Plath, Sylvia
Lucian c. 120-c. 180 .... **CMLC 32**
    See also DLB 176
Ludlam, Charles 1943-1987 ...... **CLC 46, 50**
    See also CA 85-88; 122; CANR 72, 86
Ludlum, Robert 1927- ... **CLC 22, 43; DAM
    NOV, POP**
    See also AAYA 10; BEST 89:1, 90:3; CA
    33-36R; CANR 25, 41, 68; DA3; DLBY
    82; MTCW 1, 2
Ludwig, Ken .... **CLC 60**

Ludwig, Otto 1813-1865 .... **NCLC 4**
    See also DLB 129
Lugones, Leopoldo 1874-1938 ..... **TCLC 15;
    HLCS 2**
    See also CA 116; 131; HW 1
Lu Hsun 1881-1936 .... **TCLC 3; SSC 20**
    See also Shu-Jen, Chou
Lukacs, George .... **CLC 24**
    See also Lukacs, Gyorgy (Szegeny von)
Lukacs, Gyorgy (Szegeny von) 1885-1971
    See Lukacs, George
    See also CA 101; 29-32R; CANR 62;
    MTCW 2
Luke, Peter (Ambrose Cyprian) 1919-1995
    .... **CLC 38**
    See also CA 81-84; 147; CANR 72; DLB
    13
Lunar, Dennis
    See Mungo, Raymond
Lurie, Alison 1926- .... **CLC 4, 5, 18, 39**
    See also CA 1-4R; CANR 2, 17, 50, 88;
    DLB 2; MTCW 1; SATA 46, 112
Lustig, Arnost 1926- .... **CLC 56**
    See also AAYA 3; CA 69-72; CANR 47;
    SATA 56
Luther, Martin 1483-1546 .... **LC 9, 37**
    See also DLB 179
Luxemburg, Rosa 1870(?)-1919 .... **TCLC 63**
    See also CA 118
Luzi, Mario 1914- .... **CLC 13**
    See also CA 61-64; CANR 9, 70; DLB 128
Lyly, John 1554(?)-1606 .... **LC 41; DAM
    DRAM; DC 7**
    See also DLB 62, 167
L'Ymagier
    See Gourmont, Remy (-Marie-Charles) de
Lynch, B. Suarez
    See Bioy Casares, Adolfo; Borges, Jorge
    Luis
Lynch, B. Suarez
    See Bioy Casares, Adolfo
Lynch, David (K.) 1946- .... **CLC 66**
    See also CA 124; 129
Lynch, James
    See Andreyev, Leonid (Nikolaevich)
Lynch Davis, B.
    See Bioy Casares, Adolfo; Borges, Jorge
    Luis
Lyndsay, Sir David 1490-1555 .... **LC 20**
Lynn, Kenneth S(chuyler) 1923- ..... **CLC 50**
    See also CA 1-4R; CANR 3, 27, 65
Lynx
    See West, Rebecca
Lyons, Marcus
    See Blish, James (Benjamin)
Lyre, Pinchbeck
    See Sassoon, Siegfried (Lorraine)
Lytle, Andrew (Nelson) 1902-1995 .. **CLC 22**
    See also CA 9-12R; 150; CANR 70; DLB
    6; DLBY 95
Lyttelton, George 1709-1773 .... **LC 10**
Maas, Peter 1929- .... **CLC 29**
    See also CA 93-96; INT 93-96; MTCW 2
Macaulay, Rose 1881-1958 .... **TCLC 7, 44**
    See also CA 104; DLB 36
Macaulay, Thomas Babington 1800-1859
    .... **NCLC 42**
    See also CDBLB 1832-1890; DLB 32, 55
MacBeth, George (Mann) 1932-1992
    .... **CLC 2, 5, 9**
    See also CA 25-28R; 136; CANR 61, 66;
    DLB 40; MTCW 1; SATA 4; SATA-Obit
    70
MacCaig, Norman (Alexander) 1910-
    .... **CLC 36; DAB; DAM POET**
    See also CA 9-12R; CANR 3, 34; DLB 27
MacCarthy, Sir(Charles Otto) Desmond
    1877-1952 .... **TCLC 36**

See also CA 167
MacDiarmid, Hugh .... **CLC 2, 4, 11, 19, 63;
    PC 9**
    See also Grieve, C(hristopher) M(urray)
    See also CDBLB 1945-1960; DLB 20
MacDonald, Anson
    See Heinlein, Robert A(nson)
Macdonald, Cynthia 1928- .... **CLC 13, 19**
    See also CA 49-52; CANR 4, 44; DLB 105
MacDonald, George 1824-1905 ...... **TCLC 9**
    See also CA 106; 137; CANR 80; DLB 18,
    163, 178; MAICYA; SATA 33, 100
Macdonald, John
    See Millar, Kenneth
MacDonald, John D(ann) 1916-1986
    .... **CLC 3, 27, 44; DAM NOV, POP**
    See also CA 1-4R; 121; CANR 1, 19, 60;
    DLB 8; DLBY 86; MTCW 1, 2
Macdonald, John Ross
    See Millar, Kenneth
Macdonald, Ross ..... **CLC 1, 2, 3, 14, 34, 41**
    See also Millar, Kenneth
    See also DLBD 6
MacDougal, John
    See Blish, James (Benjamin)
MacDougal, John
    See Blish, James (Benjamin)
MacEwen, Gwendolyn (Margaret)
    1941-1987 .... **CLC 13, 55**
    See also CA 9-12R; 124; CANR 7, 22; DLB
    53; SATA 50; SATA-Obit 55
Macha, Karel Hynek 1810-1846 .. **NCLC 46**
Machado (y Ruiz), Antonio 1875-1939
    .... **TCLC 3**
    See also CA 104; 174; DLB 108; HW 2
Machado de Assis, Joaquim Maria
    1839-1908 .... **TCLC 10; BLC 2; HLCS
    2; SSC 24**
    See also CA 107; 153; CANR 91
Machen, Arthur .... **TCLC 4; SSC 20**
    See also Jones, Arthur Llewellyn
    See also CA 179; DLB 36, 156, 178
Machiavelli, Niccolo 1469-1527 .... **LC 8, 36;
    DA; DAB; DAC; DAM MST; WLCS**
MacInnes, Colin 1914-1976 .... **CLC 4, 23**
    See also CA 69-72; 65-68; CANR 21; DLB
    14; MTCW 1, 2
MacInnes, Helen (Clark) 1907-1985
    .... **CLC 27, 39; DAM POP**
    See also CA 1-4R; 117; CANR 1, 28, 58;
    DLB 87; MTCW 1, 2; SATA 22; SATA-
    Obit 44
Mackenzie, Compton (Edward Montague)
    1883-1972 .... **CLC 18**
    See also CA 21-22; 37-40R; CAP 2; DLB
    34, 100
Mackenzie, Henry 1745-1831 .... **NCLC 41**
    See also DLB 39
Mackintosh, Elizabeth 1896(?)-1952
    See Tey, Josephine
    See also CA 110
MacLaren, James
    See Grieve, C(hristopher) M(urray)
Mac Laverty, Bernard 1942- .... **CLC 31**
    See also CA 116; 118; CANR 43, 88; INT
    118
MacLean, Alistair (Stuart) 1922(?)-1987
    .... **CLC 3, 13, 50, 63; DAM POP**
    See also CA 57-60; 121; CANR 28, 61;
    MTCW 1; SATA 23; SATA-Obit 50
Maclean, Norman (Fitzroy) 1902-1990
    .... **CLC 78; DAM POP; SSC 13**
    See also CA 102; 132; CANR 49; DLB 206
MacLeish, Archibald 1892-1982 .. **CLC 3, 8,
    14, 68; DAM POET**
    See also CA 9-12R; 106; CANR 33, 63;
    CDALBS; DLB 4, 7, 45; DLBY 82;
    MTCW 1, 2

MacLennan, (John) Hugh 1907-1990
.... **CLC 2, 14, 92; DAC; DAM MST**
See also CA 5-8R; 142; CANR 33; DLB
68; MTCW 1, 2

MacLeod, Alistair 1936- ...... **CLC 56; DAC;
DAM MST**
See also CA 123; DLB 60; MTCW 2

Macleod, Fiona
See Sharp, William

MacNeice, (Frederick) Louis 1907-1963
.. **CLC 1, 4, 10, 53; DAB; DAM POET**
See also CA 85-88; CANR 61; DLB 10, 20;
MTCW 1, 2

MacNeill, Dand
See Fraser, George MacDonald

Macpherson, James 1736-1796 .... **LC 29**
See also Ossian
See also DLB 109

Macpherson, (Jean) Jay 1931- .... **CLC 14**
See also CA 5-8R; CANR 90; DLB 53

MacShane, Frank 1927-1999 .... **CLC 39**
See also CA 9-12R; 186; CANR 3, 33; DLB
111

Macumber, Mari
See Sandoz, Mari(e Susette)

Madach, Imre 1823-1864 .... **NCLC 19**

Madden, (Jerry) David 1933- ..... **CLC 5, 15**
See also CA 1-4R; CAAS 3; CANR 4, 45;
DLB 6; MTCW 1

Maddern, Al(an)
See Ellison, Harlan (Jay)

Madhubuti, Haki R. 1942- . **CLC 6, 73; BLC
2; DAM MULT, POET; PC 5**
See also Lee, Don L.
See also BW 2, 3; CA 73-76; CANR 24,
51, 73; DLB 5, 41; DLBD 8; MTCW 2

Maepenn, Hugh
See Kuttner, Henry

Maepenn, K. H.
See Kuttner, Henry

Maeterlinck, Maurice 1862-1949 .. **TCLC 3;
DAM DRAM**
See also CA 104; 136; CANR 80; DLB 192;
SATA 66

Maginn, William 1794-1842 .... **NCLC 8**
See also DLB 110, 159

Mahapatra, Jayanta 1928- .. **CLC 33; DAM
MULT**
See also CA 73-76; CAAS 9; CANR 15,
33, 66, 87

Mahfouz, Naguib (Abdel Aziz Al-Sabilgi)
1911(?)-
See Mahfuz, Najib
See also BEST 89:2; CA 128; CANR 55;
DAM NOV; DA3; MTCW 1, 2

Mahfuz, Najib .... **CLC 52, 55**
See also Mahfouz, Naguib (Abdel Aziz Al-
Sabilgi)
See also DLBY 88

Mahon, Derek 1941- .... **CLC 27**
See also CA 113; 128; CANR 88; DLB 40

Mailer, Norman 1923- . **CLC 1, 2, 3, 4, 5, 8,
11, 14, 28, 39, 74, 111; DA; DAB; DAC;
DAM MST, NOV, POP**
See also AAYA 31; AITN 2; CA 9-12R;
CABS 1; CANR 28, 74, 77; CDALB
1968-1988; DA3; DLB 2, 16, 28, 185;
DLBD 3; DLBY 80, 83; MTCW 1, 2

Maillet, Antonine 1929- . **CLC 54, 118; DAC**
See also CA 115; 120; CANR 46, 74, 77;
DLB 60; INT 120; MTCW 2

Mais, Roger 1905-1955 .... **TCLC 8**
See also BW 1, 3; CA 105; 124; CANR 82;
DLB 125; MTCW 1

Maistre, Joseph de 1753-1821 ...... **NCLC 37**

Maitland, Frederic 1850-1906 ...... **TCLC 65**

Maitland, Sara (Louise) 1950- .... **CLC 49**
See also CA 69-72; CANR 13, 59

Major, Clarence 1936- . **CLC 3, 19, 48; BLC
2; DAM MULT**
See also BW 2, 3; CA 21-24R; CAAS 6;
CANR 13, 25, 53, 82; DLB 33

Major, Kevin (Gerald) 1949- . **CLC 26; DAC**
See also AAYA 16; CA 97-100; CANR 21,
38; CLR 11; DLB 60; INT CANR-21;
JRDA; MAICYA; SATA 32, 82

Maki, James
See Ozu, Yasujiro

Malabaila, Damiano
See Levi, Primo

Malamud, Bernard 1914-1986 . **CLC 1, 2, 3,
5, 8, 9, 11, 18, 27, 44, 78, 85; DA; DAB;
DAC; DAM MST, NOV, POP; SSC 15;
WLC**
See also AAYA 16; CA 5-8R; 118; CABS
1; CANR 28, 62; CDALB 1941-1968;
DA3; DLB 2, 28, 152; DLBY 80, 86;
MTCW 1, 2

Malan, Herman
See Bosman, Herman Charles; Bosman,
Herman Charles

Malaparte, Curzio 1898-1957 .... **TCLC 52**

Malcolm, Dan
See Silverberg, Robert

Malcolm X .... **CLC 82, 117; BLC 2; WLCS**
See also Little, Malcolm

Malherbe, Francois de 1555-1628 .... **LC 5**

Mallarme, Stephane 1842-1898 ..... **NCLC 4,
41; DAM POET; PC 4**

Mallet-Joris, Francoise 1930- .... **CLC 11**
See also CA 65-68; CANR 17; DLB 83

Malley, Ern
See McAuley, James Phillip

Mallowan, Agatha Christie
See Christie, Agatha (Mary Clarissa)

Maloff, Saul 1922- .... **CLC 5**
See also CA 33-36R

Malone, Louis
See MacNeice, (Frederick) Louis

Malone, Michael (Christopher) 1942-
.... **CLC 43**
See also CA 77-80; CANR 14, 32, 57

Malory, (Sir) Thomas 1410(?)-1471(?)
.. **LC 11; DA; DAB; DAC; DAM MST;
WLCS**
See also CDBLB Before 1660; DLB 146;
SATA 59; SATA-Brief 33

Malouf, (George Joseph) David 1934-
.... **CLC 28, 86**
See also CA 124; CANR 50, 76; MTCW 2

Malraux, (Georges-)Andre 1901-1976
..... **CLC 1, 4, 9, 13, 15, 57; DAM NOV**
See also CA 21-22; 69-72; CANR 34, 58;
CAP 2; DA3; DLB 72; MTCW 1, 2

Malzberg, Barry N(athaniel) 1939- .. **CLC 7**
See also CA 61-64; CAAS 4; CANR 16;
DLB 8

Mamet, David (Alan) 1947- . **CLC 9, 15, 34,
46, 91; DAM DRAM; DC 4**
See also AAYA 3; CA 81-84; CABS 3;
CANR 15, 41, 67, 72; DA3; DLB 7;
MTCW 1, 2

Mamoulian, Rouben (Zachary) 1897-1987
.... **CLC 16**
See also CA 25-28R; 124; CANR 85

Mandelstam, Osip (Emilievich)
1891(?)-1938(?) .... **TCLC 2, 6; PC 14**
See also CA 104; 150; MTCW 2

Mander, (Mary) Jane 1877-1949 .. **TCLC 31**
See also CA 162

Mandeville, John fl. 1350- .... **CMLC 19**
See also DLB 146

Mandiargues, Andre Pieyre de .... **CLC 41**
See also Pieyre de Mandiargues, Andre
See also DLB 83

Mandrake, Ethel Belle
See Thurman, Wallace (Henry)

Mangan, James Clarence 1803-1849
.... **NCLC 27**

Maniere, J.-E.
See Giraudoux, (Hippolyte) Jean

Mankiewicz, Herman (Jacob) 1897-1953
.... **TCLC 85**
See also CA 120; 169; DLB 26

Manley, (Mary) Delariviere 1672(?)-1724
.... **LC 1, 42**
See also DLB 39, 80

Mann, Abel
See Creasey, John

Mann, Emily 1952- .... **DC 7**
See also CA 130; CANR 55

Mann, (Luiz) Heinrich 1871-1950 .. **TCLC 9**
See also CA 106; 164, 181; DLB 66, 118

Mann, (Paul) Thomas 1875-1955 .. **TCLC 2,
8, 14, 21, 35, 44, 60; DA; DAB; DAC;
DAM MST, NOV; SSC 5; WLC**
See also CA 104; 128; DA3; DLB 66;
MTCW 1, 2

Mannheim, Karl 1893-1947 .... **TCLC 65**

Manning, David
See Faust, Frederick (Schiller)

Manning, Frederic 1887(?)-1935 .. **TCLC 25**
See also CA 124

Manning, Olivia 1915-1980 .... **CLC 5, 19**
See also CA 5-8R; 101; CANR 29; MTCW
1

Mano, D. Keith 1942- .... **CLC 2, 10**
See also CA 25-28R; CAAS 6; CANR 26,
57; DLB 6

Mansfield, Katherine . **TCLC 2, 8, 39; DAB;
SSC 9, 23, 38; WLC**
See also Beauchamp, Kathleen Mansfield
See also DLB 162

Manso, Peter 1940- .... **CLC 39**
See also CA 29-32R; CANR 44

Mantecon, Juan Jimenez
See Jimenez (Mantecon), Juan Ramon

Manton, Peter
See Creasey, John

Man Without a Spleen, A
See Chekhov, Anton (Pavlovich)

Manzoni, Alessandro 1785-1873 ... **NCLC 29**

Map, Walter 1140-1209 .... **CMLC 32**

Mapu, Abraham (ben Jekutiel) 1808-1867
.... **NCLC 18**

Mara, Sally
See Queneau, Raymond

Marat, Jean Paul 1743-1793 .... **LC 10**

Marcel, Gabriel Honore 1889-1973 . **CLC 15**
See also CA 102; 45-48; MTCW 1, 2

March, William 1893-1954 .... **TCLC 96**

Marchbanks, Samuel
See Davies, (William) Robertson

Marchi, Giacomo
See Bassani, Giorgio

Margulies, Donald .... **CLC 76**

Marie de France c. 12th cent. - .... **CMLC 8;
PC 22**
See also DLB 208

Marie de l'Incarnation 1599-1672 ..... **LC 10**

Marier, Captain Victor
See Griffith, D(avid Lewelyn) W(ark)

Mariner, Scott
See Pohl, Frederik

Marinetti, Filippo Tommaso 1876-1944
.... **TCLC 10**
See also CA 107; DLB 114

Marivaux, Pierre Carlet de Chamblain de
1688-1763 .... **LC 4; DC 7**

Markandaya, Kamala .... **CLC 8, 38**
See also Taylor, Kamala (Purnaiya)

Markfield, Wallace 1926- .... **CLC 8**
See also CA 69-72; CAAS 3; DLB 2, 28

Markham, Edwin 1852-1940 .... **TCLC 47**
See also CA 160; DLB 54, 186

Markham, Robert
 See Amis, Kingsley (William)
Marks, J
 See Highwater, Jamake (Mamake)
Marks-Highwater, J
 See Highwater, Jamake (Mamake)
Markson, David M(errill) 1927- ..... **CLC 67**
 See also CA 49-52; CANR 1, 91
Marley, Bob .... **CLC 17**
 See also Marley, Robert Nesta
Marley, Robert Nesta 1945-1981
 See Marley, Bob
 See also CA 107; 103
Marlowe, Christopher 1564-1593 ..... **LC 22,**
 47; DA; DAB; DAC; DAM DRAM,
 MST; DC 1; WLC
 See also CDBLB Before 1660; DA3; DLB
 62
Marlowe, Stephen 1928-
 See Queen, Ellery
 See also CA 13-16R; CANR 6, 55
Marmontel, Jean-Francois 1723-1799 . **LC 2**
Marquand, John P(hillips) 1893-1960
 .... **CLC 2, 10**
 See also CA 85-88; CANR 73; DLB 9, 102;
 MTCW 2
Marques, Rene 1919-1979 ... **CLC 96; DAM**
 MULT; HLC 2
 See also CA 97-100; 85-88; CANR 78;
 DLB 113; HW 1, 2
Marquez, Gabriel (Jose) Garcia
 See Garcia Marquez, Gabriel (Jose)
Marquis, Don(ald Robert Perry) 1878-1937
 .... **TCLC 7**
 See also CA 104; 166; DLB 11, 25
Marric, J. J.
 See Creasey, John
Marryat, Frederick 1792-1848 .... **NCLC 3**
 See also DLB 21, 163
Marsden, James
 See Creasey, John
Marsh, (Edith) Ngaio 1899-1982 ...... **CLC 7,**
 53; DAM POP
 See also CA 9-12R; CANR 6, 58; DLB 77;
 MTCW 1, 2
Marshall, Garry 1934- .... **CLC 17**
 See also AAYA 3; CA 111; SATA 60
Marshall, Paule 1929- . **CLC 27, 72; BLC 3;**
 DAM MULT; SSC 3
 See also BW 2, 3; CA 77-80; CANR 25,
 73; DA3; DLB 157; MTCW 1, 2
Marshallik
 See Zangwill, Israel
Marsten, Richard
 See Hunter, Evan
Marston, John 1576-1634 .... **LC 33; DAM**
 DRAM
 See also DLB 58, 172
Martha, Henry
 See Harris, Mark
Marti (y Perez), Jose (Julian) 1853-1895
 .... **NCLC 63; DAM MULT; HLC 2**
 See also HW 2
Martial c. 40-c. 104 .... **CMLC 35; PC 10**
 See also DLB 211
Martin, Ken
 See Hubbard, L(afayette) Ron(ald)
Martin, Richard
 See Creasey, John
Martin, Steve 1945- .... **CLC 30**
 See also CA 97-100; CANR 30; MTCW 1
Martin, Valerie 1948- .... **CLC 89**
 See also BEST 90:2; CA 85-88; CANR 49,
 89
Martin, Violet Florence 1862-1915
 .... **TCLC 51**
Martin, Webber
 See Silverberg, Robert

Martindale, Patrick Victor
 See White, Patrick (Victor Martindale)
Martin du Gard, Roger 1881-1958
 .... **TCLC 24**
 See also CA 118; DLB 65
Martineau, Harriet 1802-1876 ..... **NCLC 26**
 See also DLB 21, 55, 159, 163, 166, 190;
 YABC 2
Martines, Julia
 See O'Faolain, Julia
Martinez, Enrique Gonzalez
 See Gonzalez Martinez, Enrique
Martinez, Jacinto Benavente y
 See Benavente (y Martinez), Jacinto
Martinez Ruiz, Jose 1873-1967
 See Azorin; Ruiz, Jose Martinez
 See also CA 93-96; HW 1
Martinez Sierra, Gregorio 1881-1947
 .... **TCLC 6**
 See also CA 115
Martinez Sierra, Maria (de la O'LeJarraga)
 1874-1974 .... **TCLC 6**
 See also CA 115
Martinsen, Martin
 See Follett, Ken(neth Martin)
Martinson, Harry (Edmund) 1904-1978
 .... **CLC 14**
 See also CA 77-80; CANR 34
Marut, Ret
 See Traven, B.
Marut, Robert
 See Traven, B.
Marvell, Andrew 1621-1678 . **LC 4, 43; DA;**
 DAB; DAC; DAM MST, POET; PC 10;
 WLC
 See also CDBLB 1660-1789; DLB 131
Marx, Karl (Heinrich) 1818-1883 . **NCLC 17**
 See also DLB 129
Masaoka Shiki .... **TCLC 18**
 See also Masaoka Tsunenori
Masaoka Tsunenori 1867-1902
 See Masaoka Shiki
 See also CA 117
Masefield, John (Edward) 1878-1967
 .... **CLC 11, 47; DAM POET**
 See also CA 19-20; 25-28R; CANR 33;
 CAP 2; CDBLB 1890-1914; DLB 10, 19,
 153, 160; MTCW 1, 2; SATA 19
Maso, Carole 19(?)- .... **CLC 44**
 See also CA 170
Mason, Bobbie Ann 1940- . **CLC 28, 43, 82;**
 SSC 4
 See also AAYA 5; CA 53-56; CANR 11, 31,
 58, 83; CDALBS; DA3; DLB 173; DLBY
 87; INT CANR-31; MTCW 1, 2
Mason, Ernst
 See Pohl, Frederik
Mason, Lee W.
 See Malzberg, Barry N(athaniel)
Mason, Nick 1945- .... **CLC 35**
Mason, Tally
 See Derleth, August (William)
Mass, William
 See Gibson, William
Master Lao
 See Lao Tzu
Masters, Edgar Lee 1868-1950 ...... **TCLC 2,**
 25; DA; DAC; DAM MST, POET; PC
 1; WLCS
 See also CA 104; 133; CDALB 1865-1917;
 DLB 54; MTCW 1, 2
Masters, Hilary 1928- .... **CLC 48**
 See also CA 25-28R; CANR 13, 47
Mastrosimone, William 19(?)- .... **CLC 36**
 See also CA 186
Mathe, Albert
 See Camus, Albert
Mather, Cotton 1663-1728 .... **LC 38**

 See also CDALB 1640-1865; DLB 24, 30,
 140
Mather, Increase 1639-1723 .... **LC 38**
 See also DLB 24
Matheson, Richard Burton 1926- ... **CLC 37**
 See also AAYA 31; CA 97-100; CANR 88;
 DLB 8, 44; INT 97-100
Mathews, Harry 1930- .... **CLC 6, 52**
 See also CA 21-24R; CAAS 6; CANR 18,
 40
Mathews, John Joseph 1894-1979 . **CLC 84;**
 DAM MULT
 See also CA 19-20; 142; CANR 45; CAP 2;
 DLB 175; NNAL
Mathias, Roland (Glyn) 1915- .... **CLC 45**
 See also CA 97-100; CANR 19, 41; DLB
 27
Matsuo Basho 1644-1694 .... **PC 3**
 See also DAM POET
Mattheson, Rodney
 See Creasey, John
Matthews, (James) Brander 1852-1929
 .... **TCLC 95**
 See also DLB 71, 78; DLBD 13
Matthews, Greg 1949- .... **CLC 45**
 See also CA 135
Matthews, William (Procter, III) 1942-1997
 .... **CLC 40**
 See also CA 29-32R; 162; CAAS 18; CANR
 12, 57; DLB 5
Matthias, John (Edward) 1941- .... **CLC 9**
 See also CA 33-36R; CANR 56
Matthiessen, Peter 1927- .. **CLC 5, 7, 11, 32,**
 64; DAM NOV
 See also AAYA 6; BEST 90:4; CA 9-12R;
 CANR 21, 50, 73; DA3; DLB 6, 173;
 MTCW 1, 2; SATA 27
Maturin, Charles Robert 1780(?)-1824
 .... **NCLC 6**
 See also DLB 178
Matute (Ausejo), Ana Maria 1925- . **CLC 11**
 See also CA 89-92; MTCW 1
Maugham, W. S.
 See Maugham, W(illiam) Somerset
Maugham, W(illiam) Somerset 1874-1965
 .... **CLC 1, 11, 15, 67, 93; DA; DAB;**
 DAC; DAM DRAM, MST, NOV; SSC
 8; WLC
 See also CA 5-8R; 25-28R; CANR 40; CD-
 BLB 1914-1945; DA3; DLB 10, 36, 77,
 100, 162, 195; MTCW 1, 2; SATA 54
Maugham, William Somerset
 See Maugham, W(illiam) Somerset
Maupassant, (Henri Rene Albert) Guy de
 1850-1893 . **NCLC 1, 42, 83; DA; DAB;**
 DAC; DAM MST; SSC 1; WLC
 See also DA3; DLB 123
Maupin, Armistead 1944- .... **CLC 95; DAM**
 POP
 See also CA 125; 130; CANR 58; DA3;
 INT 130; MTCW 2
Maurhut, Richard
 See Traven, B.
Mauriac, Claude 1914-1996 .... **CLC 9**
 See also CA 89-92; 152; DLB 83
Mauriac, Francois (Charles) 1885-1970
 .... **CLC 4, 9, 56; SSC 24**
 See also CA 25-28; CAP 2; DLB 65;
 MTCW 1, 2
Mavor, Osborne Henry 1888-1951
 See Bridie, James
 See also CA 104
Maxwell, William (Keepers, Jr.) 1908-
 .... **CLC 19**
 See also CA 93-96; CANR 54; DLBY 80;
 INT 93-96
May, Elaine 1932- .... **CLC 16**
 See also CA 124; 142; DLB 44

Mayakovski, Vladimir (Vladimirovich)
1893-1930 .... **TCLC 4, 18**
See also CA 104; 158; MTCW 2

Mayhew, Henry 1812-1887 .... **NCLC 31**
See also DLB 18, 55, 190

Mayle, Peter 1939(?)- .... **CLC 89**
See also CA 139; CANR 64

Maynard, Joyce 1953- .... **CLC 23**
See also CA 111; 129; CANR 64

Mayne, William (James Carter) 1928-
.... **CLC 12**
See also AAYA 20; CA 9-12R; CANR 37,
80; CLR 25; JRDA; MAICYA; SAAS 11;
SATA 6, 68

Mayo, Jim
See L'Amour, Louis (Dearborn)

Maysles, Albert 1926- .... **CLC 16**
See also CA 29-32R

Maysles, David 1932- .... **CLC 16**

Mazer, Norma Fox 1931- .... **CLC 26**
See also AAYA 5; CA 69-72; CANR 12,
32, 66; CLR 23; JRDA; MAICYA; SAAS
1; SATA 24, 67, 105

Mazzini, Guiseppe 1805-1872 .... **NCLC 34**

McAlmon, Robert (Menzies) 1895-1956
.... **TCLC 97**
See also CA 107; 168; DLB 4, 45; DLBD
15

McAuley, James Phillip 1917-1976 . **CLC 45**
See also CA 97-100

McBain, Ed
See Hunter, Evan

McBrien, William (Augustine) 1930-
.... **CLC 44**
See also CA 107; CANR 90

McCaffrey, Anne (Inez) 1926- .... **CLC 17;
DAM NOV, POP**
See also AAYA 6, 34; AITN 2; BEST 89:2;
CA 25-28R; CANR 15, 35, 55; CLR 49;
DA3; DLB 8; JRDA; MAICYA; MTCW
1, 2; SAAS 11; SATA 8, 70, 116

McCall, Nathan 1955(?)- .... **CLC 86**
See also BW 3; CA 146; CANR 88

McCann, Arthur
See Campbell, John W(ood, Jr.)

McCann, Edson
See Pohl, Frederik

McCarthy, Charles, Jr. 1933-
See McCarthy, Cormac
See also CANR 42, 69; DAM POP; DA3;
MTCW 2

McCarthy, Cormac 1933- .... **CLC 4, 57, 59,
101**
See also McCarthy, Charles, Jr.
See also DLB 6, 143; MTCW 2

McCarthy, Mary (Therese) 1912-1989
..... **CLC 1, 3, 5, 14, 24, 39, 59; SSC 24**
See also CA 5-8R; 129; CANR 16, 50, 64;
DA3; DLB 2; DLBY 81; INT CANR-16;
MTCW 1, 2

McCartney, (James) Paul 1942- ..... **CLC 12,
35**
See also CA 146

McCauley, Stephen (D.) 1955- .... **CLC 50**
See also CA 141

McClure, Michael (Thomas) 1932- .. **CLC 6,
10**
See also CA 21-24R; CANR 17, 46, 77;
DLB 16

McCorkle, Jill (Collins) 1958- .... **CLC 51**
See also CA 121; DLBY 87

McCourt, Frank 1930- .... **CLC 109**
See also CA 157

McCourt, James 1941- .... **CLC 5**
See also CA 57-60

McCourt, Malachy 1932- .... **CLC 119**

McCoy, Horace (Stanley) 1897-1955
.... **TCLC 28**
See also CA 108; 155; DLB 9

McCrae, John 1872-1918 .... **TCLC 12**
See also CA 109; DLB 92

McCreigh, James
See Pohl, Frederik

McCullers, (Lula) Carson (Smith) 1917-1967
.. **CLC 1, 4, 10, 12, 48, 100; DA; DAB;
DAC; DAM MST, NOV; SSC 9, 24;
WLC**
See also AAYA 21; CA 5-8R; 25-28R;
CABS 1, 3; CANR 18; CDALB 1941-
1968; DA3; DLB 2, 7, 173; MTCW 1, 2;
SATA 27

McCulloch, John Tyler
See Burroughs, Edgar Rice

McCullough, Colleen 1938(?)- .... **CLC 27,
107; DAM NOV, POP**
See also CA 81-84; CANR 17, 46, 67; DA3;
MTCW 1, 2

McDermott, Alice 1953- .... **CLC 90**
See also CA 109; CANR 40, 90

McElroy, Joseph 1930- .... **CLC 5, 47**
See also CA 17-20R

McEwan, Ian (Russell) 1948- .. **CLC 13, 66;
DAM NOV**
See also BEST 90:4; CA 61-64; CANR 14,
41, 69, 87; DLB 14, 194; MTCW 1, 2

McFadden, David 1940- .... **CLC 48**
See also CA 104; DLB 60; INT 104

McFarland, Dennis 1950- .... **CLC 65**
See also CA 165

McGahern, John 1934- .. **CLC 5, 9, 48; SSC
17**
See also CA 17-20R; CANR 29, 68; DLB
14; MTCW 1

McGinley, Patrick (Anthony) 1937- . **CLC 41**
See also CA 120; 127; CANR 56; INT 127

McGinley, Phyllis 1905-1978 .... **CLC 14**
See also CA 9-12R; 77-80; CANR 19; DLB
11, 48; SATA 2, 44; SATA-Obit 24

McGinniss, Joe 1942- .... **CLC 32**
See also AITN 2; BEST 89:2; CA 25-28R;
CANR 26, 70; DLB 185; INT CANR-26

McGivern, Maureen Daly
See Daly, Maureen

McGrath, Patrick 1950- .... **CLC 55**
See also CA 136; CANR 65

McGrath, Thomas (Matthew) 1916-1990
.... **CLC 28, 59; DAM POET**
See also CA 9-12R; 132; CANR 6, 33;
MTCW 1; SATA 41; SATA-Obit 66

McGuane, Thomas (Francis III) 1939-
.... **CLC 3, 7, 18, 45, 127**
See also AITN 2; CA 49-52; CANR 5, 24,
49; DLB 2, 212; DLBY 80; INT CANR-
24; MTCW 1

McGuckian, Medbh 1950- ... **CLC 48; DAM
POET; PC 27**
See also CA 143; DLB 40

McHale, Tom 1942(?)-1982 .... **CLC 3, 5**
See also AITN 1; CA 77-80; 106

McIlvanney, William 1936- .... **CLC 42**
See also CA 25-28R; CANR 61; DLB 14,
207

McIlwraith, Maureen Mollie Hunter
See Hunter, Mollie
See also SATA 2

McInerney, Jay 1955- .. **CLC 34, 112; DAM
POP**
See also AAYA 18; CA 116; 123; CANR
45, 68; DA3; INT 123; MTCW 2

McIntyre, Vonda N(eel) 1948- .... **CLC 18**
See also CA 81-84; CANR 17, 34, 69;
MTCW 1

McKay, Claude . **TCLC 7, 41; BLC 3; DAB;
PC 2**
See also McKay, Festus Claudius
See also DLB 4, 45, 51, 117

McKay, Festus Claudius 1889-1948
See McKay, Claude

McKuen, Rod 1933- .... **CLC 1, 3**
See also AITN 1; CA 41-44R; CANR 40

McLoughlin, R. B.
See Mencken, H(enry) L(ouis)

McLuhan, (Herbert) Marshall 1911-1980
.... **CLC 37, 83**
See also CA 9-12R; 102; CANR 12, 34, 61;
DLB 88; INT CANR-12; MTCW 1, 2

McMillan, Terry (L.) 1951- ...... **CLC 50, 61,
112; BLCS; DAM MULT, NOV, POP**
See also AAYA 21; BW 2, 3; CA 140;
CANR 60; DA3; MTCW 2

McMurtry, Larry (Jeff) 1936- . **CLC 2, 3, 7,
11, 27, 44, 127; DAM NOV, POP**
See also AAYA 15; AITN 1; BEST 89:2;
CA 5-8R; CANR 19, 43, 64; CDALB
1968-1988; DA3; DLB 2, 143; DLBY 80,
87; MTCW 1, 2

McNally, T. M. 1961- .... **CLC 82**

McNally, Terrence 1939- .. **CLC 4, 7, 41, 91;
DAM DRAM**
See also CA 45-48; CANR 2, 56; DA3;
DLB 7; MTCW 2

McNamer, Deirdre 1950- .... **CLC 70**

McNeal, Tom .... **CLC 119**

McNeile, Herman Cyril 1888-1937
See Sapper
See also CA 184; DLB 77

McNickle, (William) D'Arcy 1904-1977
.... **CLC 89; DAM MULT**
See also CA 9-12R; 85-88; CANR 5, 45;
DLB 175, 212; NNAL; SATA-Obit 22

McPhee, John (Angus) 1931- .... **CLC 36**
See also BEST 90:1; CA 65-68; CANR 20,
46, 64, 69; DLB 185; MTCW 1, 2

McPherson, James Alan 1943- . **CLC 19, 77;
BLCS**
See also BW 1, 3; CA 25-28R; CAAS 17;
CANR 24, 74; DLB 38; MTCW 1, 2

McPherson, William (Alexander) 1933-
.... **CLC 34**
See also CA 69-72; CANR 28; INT
CANR-28

Mead, George Herbert 1873-1958 . **TCLC 89**

Mead, Margaret 1901-1978 .... **CLC 37**
See also AITN 1; CA 1-4R; 81-84; CANR
4; DA3; MTCW 1, 2; SATA-Obit 20

Meaker, Marijane (Agnes) 1927-
See Kerr, M. E.
See also CA 107; CANR 37, 63; INT 107;
JRDA; MAICYA; MTCW 1; SATA 20,
61, 99; SATA-Essay 111

Medoff, Mark (Howard) 1940- .. **CLC 6, 23;
DAM DRAM**
See also AITN 1; CA 53-56; CANR 5; DLB
7; INT CANR-5

Medvedev, P. N.
See Bakhtin, Mikhail Mikhailovich

Meged, Aharon
See Megged, Aharon

Meged, Aron
See Megged, Aharon

Megged, Aharon 1920- .... **CLC 9**
See also CA 49-52; CAAS 13; CANR 1

Mehta, Ved (Parkash) 1934- .... **CLC 37**
See also CA 1-4R; CANR 2, 23, 69; MTCW
1

Melanter
See Blackmore, R(ichard) D(oddridge)

Melies, Georges 1861-1938 .... **TCLC 81**

Melikow, Loris
See Hofmannsthal, Hugo von

Melmoth, Sebastian
See Wilde, Oscar (Fingal O'Flahertie Wills)

Meltzer, Milton 1915- .... **CLC 26**

See also AAYA 8; CA 13-16R; CANR 38; CLR 13; DLB 61; JRDA; MAICYA; SAAS 1; SATA 1, 50, 80

Melville, Herman 1819-1891 ... **NCLC 3, 12, 29, 45, 49; DA; DAB; DAC; DAM MST, NOV; SSC 1, 17; WLC**
See also AAYA 25; CDALB 1640-1865; DA3; DLB 3, 74; SATA 59

Menander c. 342B.C.-c. 292B.C. .. **CMLC 9; DAM DRAM; DC 3**
See also DLB 176

Menchu, Rigoberta 1959-
See also HLCS 2

Menchu, Rigoberta 1959-
See also CA 175; HLCS 2

Mencken, H(enry) L(ouis) 1880-1956
.... **TCLC 13**
See also CA 105; 125; CDALB 1917-1929; DLB 11, 29, 63, 137; MTCW 1, 2

Mendelsohn, Jane 1965(?)- .... **CLC 99**
See also CA 154

Mercer, David 1928-1980 .... **CLC 5; DAM DRAM**
See also CA 9-12R; 102; CANR 23; DLB 13; MTCW 1

Merchant, Paul
See Ellison, Harlan (Jay)

Meredith, George 1828-1909 . **TCLC 17, 43; DAM POET**
See also CA 117; 153; CANR 80; CDBLB 1832-1890; DLB 18, 35, 57, 159

Meredith, William (Morris) 1919- ... **CLC 4, 13, 22, 55; DAM POET; PC 28**
See also CA 9-12R; CAAS 14; CANR 6, 40; DLB 5

Merezhkovsky, Dmitry Sergeyevich 1865-1941 .... **TCLC 29**
See also CA 169

Merimee, Prosper 1803-1870 .. **NCLC 6, 65; SSC 7**
See also DLB 119, 192

Merkin, Daphne 1954- .... **CLC 44**
See also CA 123

Merlin, Arthur
See Blish, James (Benjamin)

Merrill, James (Ingram) 1926-1995 . **CLC 2, 3, 6, 8, 13, 18, 34, 91; DAM POET; PC 28**
See also CA 13-16R; 147; CANR 10, 49, 63; DA3; DLB 5, 165; DLBY 85; INT CANR-10; MTCW 1, 2

Merriman, Alex
See Silverberg, Robert

Merriman, Brian 1747-1805 .... **NCLC 70**

Merritt, E. B.
See Waddington, Miriam

Merton, Thomas 1915-1968 ... **CLC 1, 3, 11, 34, 83; PC 10**
See also CA 5-8R; 25-28R; CANR 22, 53; DA3; DLB 48; DLBY 81; MTCW 1, 2

Merwin, W(illiam) S(tanley) 1927- .. **CLC 1, 2, 3, 5, 8, 13, 18, 45, 88; DAM POET**
See also CA 13-16R; CANR 15, 51; DA3; DLB 5, 169; INT CANR-15; MTCW 1, 2

Metcalf, John 1938- .... **CLC 37**
See also CA 113; DLB 60

Metcalf, Suzanne
See Baum, L(yman) Frank

Mew, Charlotte (Mary) 1870-1928 . **TCLC 8**
See also CA 105; DLB 19, 135

Mewshaw, Michael 1943- .... **CLC 9**
See also CA 53-56; CANR 7, 47; DLBY 80

Meyer, Conrad Ferdinand 1825-1905
.... **NCLC 81**
See also DLB 129

Meyer, June
See Jordan, June

Meyer, Lynn
See Slavitt, David R(ytman)

Meyer-Meyrink, Gustav 1868-1932
See Meyrink, Gustav
See also CA 117

Meyers, Jeffrey 1939- .... **CLC 39**
See also CA 73-76; CAAE 186; CANR 54; DLB 111

Meynell, Alice (Christina Gertrude Thompson) 1847-1922 .... **TCLC 6**
See also CA 104; 177; DLB 19, 98

Meyrink, Gustav .... **TCLC 21**
See also Meyer-Meyrink, Gustav
See also DLB 81

Michaels, Leonard 1933- ... **CLC 6, 25; SSC 16**
See also CA 61-64; CANR 21, 62; DLB 130; MTCW 1

Michaux, Henri 1899-1984 .... **CLC 8, 19**
See also CA 85-88; 114

Micheaux, Oscar (Devereaux) 1884-1951
.... **TCLC 76**
See also BW 3; CA 174; DLB 50

Michelangelo 1475-1564 .... **LC 12**

Michelet, Jules 1798-1874 .... **NCLC 31**

Michels, Robert 1876-1936 .... **TCLC 88**

Michener, James A(lbert) 1907(?)-1997 . **CLC 1, 5, 11, 29, 60, 109; DAM NOV, POP**
See also AAYA 27; AITN 1; BEST 90:1; CA 5-8R; 161; CANR 21, 45, 68; DA3; DLB 6; MTCW 1, 2

Mickiewicz, Adam 1798-1855 .... **NCLC 3**

Middleton, Christopher 1926- .... **CLC 13**
See also CA 13-16R; CANR 29, 54; DLB 40

Middleton, Richard (Barham) 1882-1911
.... **TCLC 56**
See also DLB 156

Middleton, Stanley 1919- .... **CLC 7, 38**
See also CA 25-28R; CAAS 23; CANR 21, 46, 81; DLB 14

Middleton, Thomas 1580-1627 .... **LC 33; DAM DRAM, MST; DC 5**
See also DLB 58

Migueis, Jose Rodrigues 1901- .... **CLC 10**

Mikszath, Kalman 1847-1910 .... **TCLC 31**
See also CA 170

Miles, Jack .... **CLC 100**

Miles, Josephine (Louise) 1911-1985 . **CLC 1, 2, 14, 34, 39; DAM POET**
See also CA 1-4R; 116; CANR 2, 55; DLB 48

Militant
See Sandburg, Carl (August)

Mill, John Stuart 1806-1873 ... **NCLC 11, 58**
See also CDBLB 1832-1890; DLB 55, 190

Millar, Kenneth 1915-1983 .. **CLC 14; DAM POP**
See also Macdonald, Ross
See also CA 9-12R; 110; CANR 16, 63; DA3; DLB 2; DLBD 6; DLBY 83; MTCW 1, 2

Millay, E. Vincent
See Millay, Edna St. Vincent

Millay, Edna St. Vincent 1892-1950 ... **TCLC 4, 49; DA; DAB; DAC; DAM MST, POET; PC 6; WLCS**
See also CA 104; 130; CDALB 1917-1929; DA3; DLB 45; MTCW 1, 2

Miller, Arthur 1915- ..... **CLC 1, 2, 6, 10, 15, 26, 47, 78; DA; DAB; DAC; DAM DRAM, MST; DC 1; WLC**
See also AAYA 15; AITN 1; CA 1-4R; CABS 3; CANR 2, 30, 54, 76; CDALB 1941-1968; DA3; DLB 7; MTCW 1, 2

Miller, Henry (Valentine) 1891-1980 . **CLC 1, 2, 4, 9, 14, 43, 84; DA; DAB; DAC; DAM MST, NOV; WLC**

See also CA 9-12R; 97-100; CANR 33, 64; CDALB 1929-1941; DA3; DLB 4, 9; DLBY 80; MTCW 1, 2

Miller, Jason 1939(?)- .... **CLC 2**
See also AITN 1; CA 73-76; DLB 7

Miller, Sue 1943- .... **CLC 44; DAM POP**
See also BEST 90:3; CA 139; CANR 59, 91; DA3; DLB 143

Miller, Walter M(ichael, Jr.) 1923- .. **CLC 4, 30**
See also CA 85-88; DLB 8

Millett, Kate 1934- .... **CLC 67**
See also AITN 1; CA 73-76; CANR 32, 53, 76; DA3; MTCW 1, 2

Millhauser, Steven (Lewis) 1943- ... **CLC 21, 54, 109**
See also CA 110; 111; CANR 63; DA3; DLB 2; INT 111; MTCW 2

Millin, Sarah Gertrude 1889-1968 . **CLC 49**
See also CA 102; 93-96

Milne, A(lan) A(lexander) 1882-1956 . **TCLC 6, 88; DAB; DAC; DAM MST**
See also CA 104; 133; CLR 1, 26; DA3; DLB 10, 77, 100, 160; MAICYA; MTCW 1, 2; SATA 100; YABC 1

Milner, Ron(ald) 1938- ..... **CLC 56; BLC 3; DAM MULT**
See also AITN 1; BW 1; CA 73-76; CANR 24, 81; DLB 38; MTCW 1

Milnes, Richard Monckton 1809-1885
.... **NCLC 61**
See also DLB 32, 184

Milosz, Czeslaw 1911- .... **CLC 5, 11, 22, 31, 56, 82; DAM MST, POET; PC 8; WLCS**
See also CA 81-84; CANR 23, 51, 91; DA3; MTCW 1, 2

Milton, John 1608-1674 .... **LC 9, 43; DA; DAB; DAC; DAM MST, POET; PC 19, 29; WLC**
See also CDBLB 1660-1789; DA3; DLB 131, 151

Min, Anchee 1957- .... **CLC 86**
See also CA 146

Minehaha, Cornelius
See Wedekind, (Benjamin) Frank(lin)

Miner, Valerie 1947- .... **CLC 40**
See also CA 97-100; CANR 59

Minimo, Duca
See D'Annunzio, Gabriele

Minot, Susan 1956- .... **CLC 44**
See also CA 134

Minus, Ed 1938- .... **CLC 39**
See also CA 185

Miranda, Javier
See Bioy Casares, Adolfo

Miranda, Javier
See Bioy Casares, Adolfo

Mirbeau, Octave 1848-1917 .... **TCLC 55**
See also DLB 123, 192

Miro (Ferrer), Gabriel (Francisco Victor) 1879-1930 .... **TCLC 5**
See also CA 104; 185

Mishima, Yukio 1925-1970 .. **CLC 2, 4, 6, 9, 27; DC 1; SSC 4**
See also Hiraoka, Kimitake
See also DLB 182; MTCW 2

Mistral, Frederic 1830-1914 .... **TCLC 51**
See also CA 122

Mistral, Gabriela .... **TCLC 2; HLC 2**
See also Godoy Alcayaga, Lucila
See also MTCW 2

Mistry, Rohinton 1952- .... **CLC 71; DAC**
See also CA 141; CANR 86

Mitchell, Clyde
See Ellison, Harlan (Jay); Silverberg, Robert

Mitchell, James Leslie 1901-1935
See Gibbon, Lewis Grassic
See also CA 104; DLB 15

See also De La Ramee, (Marie) Louise
See also DLB 18, 156

Ousmane, Sembene 1923- .. **CLC 66; BLC 3**
See also BW 1, 3; CA 117; 125; CANR 81;
MTCW 1

Ovid 43B.C.-17 . **CMLC 7; DAM POET; PC
2**
See also DA3; DLB 211

Owen, Hugh
See Faust, Frederick (Schiller)

Owen, Wilfred (Edward Salter) 1893-1918
... **TCLC 5, 27; DA; DAB; DAC; DAM
MST, POET; PC 19; WLC**
See also CA 104; 141; CDBLB 1914-1945;
DLB 20; MTCW 2

Owens, Rochelle 1936- .... **CLC 8**
See also CA 17-20R; CAAS 2; CANR 39

Oz, Amos 1939- .... **CLC 5, 8, 11, 27, 33, 54;
DAM NOV**
See also CA 53-56; CANR 27, 47, 65;
MTCW 1, 2

Ozick, Cynthia 1928- .... **CLC 3, 7, 28, 62;
DAM NOV, POP; SSC 15**
See also BEST 90:1; CA 17-20R; CANR
23, 58; DA3; DLB 28, 152; DLBY 82;
INT CANR-23; MTCW 1, 2

Ozu, Yasujiro 1903-1963 .... **CLC 16**
See also CA 112

Pacheco, C.
See Pessoa, Fernando (Antonio Nogueira)

Pacheco, Jose Emilio 1939-
See also CA 111; 131; CANR 65; DAM
MULT; HLC 2; HW 1, 2

Pa Chin .... **CLC 18**
See also Li Fei-kan

Pack, Robert 1929- .... **CLC 13**
See also CA 1-4R; CANR 3, 44, 82; DLB 5

Padgett, Lewis
See Kuttner, Henry

Padilla (Lorenzo), Heberto 1932- ... **CLC 38**
See also AITN 1; CA 123; 131; HW 1

Page, Jimmy 1944- .... **CLC 12**

Page, Louise 1955- .... **CLC 40**
See also CA 140; CANR 76

Page, P(atricia) K(athleen) 1916- .... **CLC 7,
18; DAC; DAM MST; PC 12**
See also CA 53-56; CANR 4, 22, 65; DLB
68; MTCW 1

Page, Thomas Nelson 1853-1922 ...... **SSC 23**
See also CA 118; 177; DLB 12, 78; DLBD
13

Pagels, Elaine Hiesey 1943- .... **CLC 104**
See also CA 45-48; CANR 2, 24, 51

Paget, Violet 1856-1935
See Lee, Vernon
See also CA 104; 166

Paget-Lowe, Henry
See Lovecraft, H(oward) P(hillips)

Paglia, Camille (Anna) 1947- .... **CLC 68**
See also CA 140; CANR 72; MTCW 2

Paige, Richard
See Koontz, Dean R(ay)

Paine, Thomas 1737-1809 .... **NCLC 62**
See also CDALB 1640-1865; DLB 31, 43,
73, 158

Pakenham, Antonia
See Fraser, (Lady) Antonia (Pakenham)

Palamas, Kostes 1859-1943 .... **TCLC 5**
See also CA 105

Palazzeschi, Aldo 1885-1974 .... **CLC 11**
See also CA 89-92; 53-56; DLB 114

Pales Matos, Luis 1898-1959
See also HLCS 2; HW 1

Paley, Grace 1922- .... **CLC 4, 6, 37; DAM
POP; SSC 8**
See also CA 25-28R; CANR 13, 46, 74;
DA3; DLB 28; INT CANR-13; MTCW 1,
2

Palin, Michael (Edward) 1943- .... **CLC 21**
See also Monty Python
See also CA 107; CANR 35; SATA 67

Palliser, Charles 1947- .... **CLC 65**
See also CA 136; CANR 76

Palma, Ricardo 1833-1919 .... **TCLC 29**
See also CA 168

Pancake, Breece Dexter 1952-1979
See Pancake, Breece D'J
See also CA 123; 109

Pancake, Breece D'J .... **CLC 29**
See also Pancake, Breece Dexter
See also DLB 130

Panko, Rudy
See Gogol, Nikolai (Vasilyevich)

Papadiamantis, Alexandros 1851-1911
.... **TCLC 29**
See also CA 168

Papadiamantopoulos, Johannes 1856-1910
See Moreas, Jean
See also CA 117

Papini, Giovanni 1881-1956 .... **TCLC 22**
See also CA 121; 180

Paracelsus 1493-1541 .... **LC 14**
See also DLB 179

Parasol, Peter
See Stevens, Wallace

Pardo Bazan, Emilia 1851-1921 .... **SSC 30**

Pareto, Vilfredo 1848-1923 .... **TCLC 69**
See also CA 175

Parfenie, Maria
See Codrescu, Andrei

Parini, Jay (Lee) 1948- .... **CLC 54**
See also CA 97-100; CAAS 16; CANR 32,
87

Park, Jordan
See Kornbluth, C(yril) M.; Pohl, Frederik

Park, Robert E(zra) 1864-1944 .... **TCLC 73**
See also CA 122; 165

Parker, Bert
See Ellison, Harlan (Jay)

Parker, Dorothy (Rothschild) 1893-1967
. **CLC 15, 68; DAM POET; PC 28; SSC
2**
See also CA 19-20; 25-28R; CAP 2; DA3;
DLB 11, 45, 86; MTCW 1, 2

Parker, Robert B(rown) 1932- .... **CLC 27;
DAM NOV, POP**
See also AAYA 28; BEST 89:4; CA 49-52;
CANR 1, 26, 52, 89; INT CANR-26;
MTCW 1

Parkin, Frank 1940- .... **CLC 43**
See also CA 147

Parkman, Francis Jr., Jr. 1823-1893
.... **NCLC 12**
See also DLB 1, 30, 186

Parks, Gordon (Alexander Buchanan) 1912-
.... **CLC 1, 16; BLC 3; DAM MULT**
See also AITN 2; BW 2, 3; CA 41-44R;
CANR 26, 66; DA3; DLB 33; MTCW 2;
SATA 8, 108

Parmenides c. 515B.C.-c. 450B.C. . **CMLC 22**
See also DLB 176

Parnell, Thomas 1679-1718 .... **LC 3**
See also DLB 94

Parra, Nicanor 1914- ..... **CLC 2, 102; DAM
MULT; HLC 2**
See also CA 85-88; CANR 32; HW 1;
MTCW 1

Parra Sanojo, Ana Teresa de la 1890-1936
See also HLCS 2

Parrish, Mary Frances
See Fisher, M(ary) F(rances) K(ennedy)

Parson
See Coleridge, Samuel Taylor

Parson Lot
See Kingsley, Charles

Parton, Sara Payson Willis 1811-1872
.... **NCLC 86**
See also DLB 43, 74

Partridge, Anthony
See Oppenheim, E(dward) Phillips

Pascal, Blaise 1623-1662 .... **LC 35**

Pascoli, Giovanni 1855-1912 .... **TCLC 45**
See also CA 170

Pasolini, Pier Paolo 1922-1975 . **CLC 20, 37,
106; PC 17**
See also CA 93-96; 61-64; CANR 63; DLB
128, 177; MTCW 1

Pasquini
See Silone, Ignazio

Pastan, Linda (Olenik) 1932- .... **CLC 27;
DAM POET**
See also CA 61-64; CANR 18, 40, 61; DLB
5

Pasternak, Boris (Leonidovich) 1890-1960
... **CLC 7, 10, 18, 63; DA; DAB; DAC;
DAM MST, NOV, POET; PC 6; SSC 31;
WLC**
See also CA 127; 116; DA3; MTCW 1, 2

Patchen, Kenneth 1911-1972 . **CLC 1, 2, 18;
DAM POET**
See also CA 1-4R; 33-36R; CANR 3, 35;
DLB 16, 48; MTCW 1

Pater, Walter (Horatio) 1839-1894 . **NCLC 7**
See also CDBLB 1832-1890; DLB 57, 156

Paterson, A(ndrew) B(arton) 1864-1941
.... **TCLC 32**
See also CA 155; SATA 97

Paterson, Katherine (Womeldorf) 1932-
.... **CLC 12, 30**
See also AAYA 1, 31; CA 21-24R; CANR
28, 59; CLR 7, 50; DLB 52; JRDA; MAI-
CYA; MTCW 1; SATA 13, 53, 92

Patmore, Coventry Kersey Dighton
1823-1896 .... **NCLC 9**
See also DLB 35, 98

Paton, Alan (Stewart) 1903-1988 ..... **CLC 4,
10, 25, 55, 106; DA; DAB; DAC; DAM
MST, NOV; WLC**
See also AAYA 26; CA 13-16; 125; CANR
22; CAP 1; DA3; DLBD 17; MTCW 1, 2;
SATA 11; SATA-Obit 56

Paton Walsh, Gillian 1937-
See Walsh, Jill Paton
See also AAYA 11; CANR 38, 83; DLB
161; JRDA; MAICYA; SAAS 3; SATA 4,
72, 109

Patton, George S. 1885-1945 .... **TCLC 79**

Paulding, James Kirke 1778-1860 . **NCLC 2**
See also DLB 3, 59, 74

Paulin, Thomas Neilson 1949-
See Paulin, Tom
See also CA 123; 128

Paulin, Tom .... **CLC 37**
See also Paulin, Thomas Neilson
See also DLB 40

Pausanias c. 1st cent. - .... **CMLC 36**

Paustovsky, Konstantin (Georgievich)
1892-1968 .... **CLC 40**
See also CA 93-96; 25-28R

Pavese, Cesare 1908-1950 . **TCLC 3; PC 13;
SSC 19**
See also CA 104; 169; DLB 128, 177

Pavic, Milorad 1929- .... **CLC 60**
See also CA 136; DLB 181

Pavlov, Ivan Petrovich 1849-1936 . **TCLC 91**
See also CA 118; 180

Payne, Alan
See Jakes, John (William)

Paz, Gil
See Lugones, Leopoldo

Paz, Octavio 1914-1998 . **CLC 3, 4, 6, 10, 19,
51, 65, 119; DA; DAB; DAC; DAM
MST, MULT, POET; HLC 2; PC 1;
WLC**

See also CA 73-76; 165; CANR 32, 65;
DA3; DLBY 90, 98; HW 1, 2; MTCW 1,
2

p'Bitek, Okot 1931-1982 ... **CLC 96; BLC 3;
DAM MULT**
See also BW 2, 3; CA 124; 107; CANR 82;
DLB 125; MTCW 1, 2

Peacock, Molly 1947- .... **CLC 60**
See also CA 103; CAAS 21; CANR 52, 84;
DLB 120

Peacock, Thomas Love 1785-1866 . **NCLC 22**
See also DLB 96, 116

Peake, Mervyn 1911-1968 .... **CLC 7, 54**
See also CA 5-8R; 25-28R; CANR 3; DLB
15, 160; MTCW 1; SATA 23

Pearce, Philippa .... **CLC 21**
See also Christie, (Ann) Philippa
See also CLR 9; DLB 161; MAICYA;
SATA 1, 67

Pearl, Eric
See Elman, Richard (Martin)

Pearson, T(homas) R(eid) 1956- ... **CLC 39**
See also CA 120; 130; INT 130

Peck, Dale 1967- .... **CLC 81**
See also CA 146; CANR 72

Peck, John 1941- .... **CLC 3**
See also CA 49-52; CANR 3

Peck, Richard (Wayne) 1934- .... **CLC 21**
See also AAYA 1, 24; CA 85-88; CANR
19, 38; CLR 15; INT CANR-19; JRDA;
MAICYA; SAAS 2; SATA 18, 55, 97;
SATA-Essay 110

Peck, Robert Newton 1928- ... **CLC 17; DA;
DAC; DAM MST**
See also AAYA 3; CA 81-84, 182; CAAE
182; CANR 31, 63; CLR 45; JRDA; MAI-
CYA; SAAS 1; SATA 21, 62, 111; SATA-
Essay 108

Peckinpah, (David) Sam(uel) 1925-1984
.... **CLC 20**
See also CA 109; 114; CANR 82

Pedersen, Knut 1859-1952
See Hamsun, Knut
See also CA 104; 119; CANR 63; MTCW
1, 2

Peeslake, Gaffer
See Durrell, Lawrence (George)

Peguy, Charles Pierre 1873-1914 . **TCLC 10**
See also CA 107

Peirce, Charles Sanders 1839-1914
.... **TCLC 81**

Pellicer, Carlos 1900(?)-1977
See also CA 153; 69-72; HLCS 2; HW 1

Pena, Ramon del Valle y
See Valle-Inclan, Ramon (Maria) del

Pendennis, Arthur Esquir
See Thackeray, William Makepeace

Penn, William 1644-1718 .... **LC 25**
See also DLB 24

PEPECE
See Prado (Calvo), Pedro

Pepys, Samuel 1633-1703 .... **LC 11, 58; DA;
DAB; DAC; DAM MST; WLC**
See also CDBLB 1660-1789; DA3; DLB
101

Percy, Walker 1916-1990 ..... **CLC 2, 3, 6, 8,
14, 18, 47, 65; DAM NOV, POP**
See also CA 1-4R; 131; CANR 1, 23, 64;
DA3; DLB 2; DLBY 80, 90; MTCW 1, 2

Percy, William Alexander 1885-1942
.... **TCLC 84**
See also CA 163; MTCW 2

Perec, Georges 1936-1982 .... **CLC 56, 116**
See also CA 141; DLB 83

**Pereda (y Sanchez de Porrua), Jose Maria
de** 1833-1906 .... **TCLC 16**
See also CA 117

Pereda y Porrua, Jose Maria de
See Pereda (y Sanchez de Porrua), Jose
Maria de

Peregoy, George Weems
See Mencken, H(enry) L(ouis)

Perelman, S(idney) J(oseph) 1904-1979
.... **CLC 3, 5, 9, 15, 23, 44, 49; DAM
DRAM; SSC 32**
See also AITN 1, 2; CA 73-76; 89-92;
CANR 18; DLB 11, 44; MTCW 1, 2

Peret, Benjamin 1899-1959 .... **TCLC 20**
See also CA 117; 186

Peretz, Isaac Loeb 1851(?)-1915 . **TCLC 16;
SSC 26**
See also CA 109

Peretz, Yitzkhok Leibush
See Peretz, Isaac Loeb

Perez Galdos, Benito 1843-1920 . **TCLC 27;
HLCS 2**
See also CA 125; 153; HW 1

Peri Rossi, Cristina 1941-
See also CA 131; CANR 59, 81; DLB 145;
HLCS 2; HW 1, 2

Perlata
See Peret, Benjamin

Perrault, Charles 1628-1703 .. **LC 3, 52; DC
12**
See also MAICYA; SATA 25

Perry, Anne 1938- .... **CLC 126**
See also CA 101; CANR 22, 50, 84

Perry, Brighton
See Sherwood, Robert E(mmet)

Perse, St.-John
See Leger, (Marie-Rene Auguste) Alexis
Saint-Leger

Perutz, Leo(pold) 1882-1957 .... **TCLC 60**
See also CA 147; DLB 81

Peseenz, Tulio F.
See Lopez y Fuentes, Gregorio

Pesetsky, Bette 1932- .... **CLC 28**
See also CA 133; DLB 130

Peshkov, Alexei Maximovich 1868-1936
See Gorky, Maxim
See also CA 105; 141; CANR 83; DA;
DAC; DAM DRAM, MST, NOV; MTCW
2

Pessoa, Fernando (Antonio Nogueira)
1888-1935 ...... **TCLC 27; DAM MULT;
HLC 2; PC 20**
See also CA 125; 183

Peterkin, Julia Mood 1880-1961 ..... **CLC 31**
See also CA 102; DLB 9

Peters, Joan K(aren) 1945- .... **CLC 39**
See also CA 158

Peters, Robert L(ouis) 1924- .... **CLC 7**
See also CA 13-16R; CAAS 8; DLB 105

Petofi, Sandor 1823-1849 .... **NCLC 21**

Petrakis, Harry Mark 1923- .... **CLC 3**
See also CA 9-12R; CANR 4, 30, 85

Petrarch 1304-1374 .... **CMLC 20; DAM
POET; PC 8**
See also DA3

Petronius c. 20-66 .... **CMLC 34**
See also DLB 211

Petrov, Evgeny .... **TCLC 21**
See also Kataev, Evgeny Petrovich

Petry, Ann (Lane) 1908-1997 .. **CLC 1, 7, 18**
See also BW 1, 3; CA 5-8R; 157; CAAS 6;
CANR 4, 46; CLR 12; DLB 76; JRDA;
MAICYA; MTCW 1; SATA 5; SATA-Obit
94

Petursson, Halligrimur 1614-1674 .... **LC 8**

Peychinovich
See Vazov, Ivan (Minchov)

Phaedrus c. 18B.C.-c. 50 .... **CMLC 25**
See also DLB 211

Philips, Katherine 1632-1664 .... **LC 30**
See also DLB 131

Philipson, Morris H. 1926- .... **CLC 53**
See also CA 1-4R; CANR 4

Phillips, Caryl 1958- . **CLC 96; BLCS; DAM
MULT**
See also BW 2; CA 141; CANR 63; DA3;
DLB 157; MTCW 2

Phillips, David Graham 1867-1911
.... **TCLC 44**
See also CA 108; 176; DLB 9, 12

Phillips, Jack
See Sandburg, Carl (August)

Phillips, Jayne Anne 1952- .... **CLC 15, 33;
SSC 16**
See also CA 101; CANR 24, 50; DLBY 80;
INT CANR-24; MTCW 1, 2

Phillips, Richard
See Dick, Philip K(indred)

Phillips, Robert (Schaeffer) 1938- ... **CLC 28**
See also CA 17-20R; CAAS 13; CANR 8;
DLB 105

Phillips, Ward
See Lovecraft, H(oward) P(hillips)

Piccolo, Lucio 1901-1969 .... **CLC 13**
See also CA 97-100; DLB 114

Pickthall, Marjorie L(owry) C(hristie)
1883-1922 .... **TCLC 21**
See also CA 107; DLB 92

Pico della Mirandola, Giovanni 1463-1494
.... **LC 15**

Piercy, Marge 1936- ... **CLC 3, 6, 14, 18, 27,
62, 128; PC 29**
See also CA 21-24R; CAAS 1; CANR 13,
43, 66; DLB 120; MTCW 1, 2

Piers, Robert
See Anthony, Piers

Pieyre de Mandiargues, Andre 1909-1991
See Mandiargues, Andre Pieyre de
See also CA 103; 136; CANR 22, 82

Pilnyak, Boris .... **TCLC 23**
See also Vogau, Boris Andreyevich

Pincherle, Alberto 1907-1990 ... **CLC 11, 18;
DAM NOV**
See also Moravia, Alberto
See also CA 25-28R; 132; CANR 33, 63;
MTCW 1

Pinckney, Darryl 1953- .... **CLC 76**
See also BW 2, 3; CA 143; CANR 79

Pindar 518B.C.-446B.C. .. **CMLC 12; PC 19**
See also DLB 176

Pineda, Cecile 1942- .... **CLC 39**
See also CA 118

Pinero, Arthur Wing 1855-1934 .. **TCLC 32;
DAM DRAM**
See also CA 110; 153; DLB 10

Pinero, Miguel (Antonio Gomez) 1946-1988
.... **CLC 4, 55**
See also CA 61-64; 125; CANR 29, 90; HW
1

Pinget, Robert 1919-1997 ...... **CLC 7, 13, 37**
See also CA 85-88; 160; DLB 83

Pink Floyd
See Barrett, (Roger) Syd; Gilmour, David;
Mason, Nick; Waters, Roger; Wright, Rick

Pinkney, Edward 1802-1828 .... **NCLC 31**

Pinkwater, Daniel Manus 1941- ...... **CLC 35**
See also Pinkwater, Manus
See also AAYA 1; CA 29-32R; CANR 12,
38, 89; CLR 4; JRDA; MAICYA; SAAS
3; SATA 46, 76, 114

Pinkwater, Manus
See Pinkwater, Daniel Manus
See also SATA 8

Pinsky, Robert 1940- ...... **CLC 9, 19, 38, 94,
121; DAM POET; PC 27**
See also CA 29-32R; CAAS 4; CANR 58;
DA3; DLBY 82, 98; MTCW 2

Pinta, Harold
See Pinter, Harold

Pinter, Harold 1930- . **CLC 1, 3, 6, 9, 11, 15,**

27, 58, 73; DA; DAB; DAC; DAM DRAM, MST; WLC
See also CA 5-8R; CANR 33, 65; CDBLB 1960 to Present; DA3; DLB 13; MTCW 1, 2

Piozzi, Hester Lynch (Thrale) 1741-1821
.... **NCLC 57**
See also DLB 104, 142

Pirandello, Luigi 1867-1936 .... **TCLC 4, 29; DA; DAB; DAC; DAM DRAM, MST; DC 5; SSC 22; WLC**
See also CA 104; 153; DA3; MTCW 2

Pirsig, Robert M(aynard) 1928- .. **CLC 4, 6, 73; DAM POP**
See also CA 53-56; CANR 42, 74; DA3; MTCW 1, 2; SATA 39

Pisarev, Dmitry Ivanovich 1840-1868
.... **NCLC 25**

Pix, Mary (Griffith) 1666-1709 .... **LC 8**
See also DLB 80

Pixerecourt, (Rene Charles) Guilbert de 1773-1844 .... **NCLC 39**
See also DLB 192

Plaatje, Sol(omon) T(shekisho) 1876-1932
.... **TCLC 73; BLCS**
See also BW 2, 3; CA 141; CANR 79

Plaidy, Jean
See Hibbert, Eleanor Alice Burford

Planche, James Robinson 1796-1880
.... **NCLC 42**

Plant, Robert 1948- .... **CLC 12**

Plante, David (Robert) 1940- ..... **CLC 7, 23, 38; DAM NOV**
See also CA 37-40R; CANR 12, 36, 58, 82; DLBY 83; INT CANR-12; MTCW 1

Plath, Sylvia 1932-1963 .... **CLC 1, 2, 3, 5, 9, 11, 14, 17, 50, 51, 62, 111; DA; DAB; DAC; DAM MST, POET; PC 1; WLC**
See also AAYA 13; CA 19-20; CANR 34; CAP 2; CDALB 1941-1968; DA3; DLB 5, 6, 152; MTCW 1, 2; SATA 96

Plato 428(?)B.C.-348(?)B.C. .. **CMLC 8; DA; DAB; DAC; DAM MST; WLCS**
See also DA3; DLB 176

Platonov, Andrei .... **TCLC 14; SSC 38**
See also Klimentov, Andrei Platonovich

Platt, Kin 1911- .... **CLC 26**
See also AAYA 11; CA 17-20R; CANR 11; JRDA; SAAS 17; SATA 21, 86

Plautus c. 251B.C.-184B.C. .. **CMLC 24; DC 6**
See also DLB 211

Plick et Plock
See Simenon, Georges (Jacques Christian)

Plimpton, George (Ames) 1927- ...... **CLC 36**
See also AITN 1; CA 21-24R; CANR 32, 70; DLB 185; MTCW 1, 2; SATA 10

Pliny the Elder c. 23-79 .... **CMLC 23**
See also DLB 211

Plomer, William Charles Franklin 1903-1973
.... **CLC 4, 8**
See also CA 21-22; CANR 34; CAP 2; DLB 20, 162, 191; MTCW 1; SATA 24

Plowman, Piers
See Kavanagh, Patrick (Joseph)

Plum, J.
See Wodehouse, P(elham) G(renville)

Plumly, Stanley (Ross) 1939- .... **CLC 33**
See also CA 108; 110; DLB 5, 193; INT 110

Plumpe, Friedrich Wilhelm 1888-1931
.... **TCLC 53**
See also CA 112

Po Chu-i 772-846 .... **CMLC 24**

Poe, Edgar Allan 1809-1849 .... **NCLC 1, 16, 55, 78; DA; DAB; DAC; DAM MST, POET; PC 1; SSC 34; WLC**
See also AAYA 14; CDALB 1640-1865; DA3; DLB 3, 59, 73, 74; SATA 23

Poet of Titchfield Street, The
See Pound, Ezra (Weston Loomis)

Pohl, Frederik 1919- .... **CLC 18; SSC 25**
See also AAYA 24; CA 61-64; CAAS 1; CANR 11, 37, 81; DLB 8; INT CANR-11; MTCW 1, 2; SATA 24

Poirier, Louis 1910-
See Gracq, Julien
See also CA 122; 126

Poitier, Sidney 1927- .... **CLC 26**
See also BW 1; CA 117

Polanski, Roman 1933- .... **CLC 16**
See also CA 77-80

Poliakoff, Stephen 1952- .... **CLC 38**
See also CA 106; DLB 13

Police, The
See Copeland, Stewart (Armstrong); Summers, Andrew James; Sumner, Gordon Matthew

Polidori, John William 1795-1821 . **NCLC 51**
See also DLB 116

Pollitt, Katha 1949- .... **CLC 28, 122**
See also CA 120; 122; CANR 66; MTCW 1, 2

Pollock, (Mary) Sharon 1936- .... **CLC 50; DAC; DAM DRAM, MST**
See also CA 141; DLB 60

Polo, Marco 1254-1324 .... **CMLC 15**

Polonsky, Abraham (Lincoln) 1910-
.... **CLC 92**
See also CA 104; DLB 26; INT 104

Polybius c. 200B.C.-c. 118B.C. ..... **CMLC 17**
See also DLB 176

Pomerance, Bernard 1940- .. **CLC 13; DAM DRAM**
See also CA 101; CANR 49

Ponge, Francis 1899-1988 . **CLC 6, 18; DAM POET**
See also CA 85-88; 126; CANR 40, 86

Poniatowska, Elena 1933-
See also CA 101; CANR 32, 66; DAM MULT; DLB 113; HLC 2; HW 1, 2

Pontoppidan, Henrik 1857-1943 ... **TCLC 29**
See also CA 170

Poole, Josephine .... **CLC 17**
See also Helyar, Jane Penelope Josephine
See also SAAS 2; SATA 5

Popa, Vasko 1922-1991 .... **CLC 19**
See also CA 112; 148; DLB 181

Pope, Alexander 1688-1744 .. **LC 3, 58; DA; DAB; DAC; DAM MST, POET; PC 26; WLC**
See also CDBLB 1660-1789; DA3; DLB 95, 101

Porter, Connie (Rose) 1959(?)- .... **CLC 70**
See also BW 2, 3; CA 142; CANR 90; SATA 81

Porter, Gene(va Grace) Stratton 1863(?)-1924 .... **TCLC 21**
See also CA 112

Porter, Katherine Anne 1890-1980 .. **CLC 1, 3, 7, 10, 13, 15, 27, 101; DA; DAB; DAC; DAM MST, NOV; SSC 4, 31**
See also AITN 2; CA 1-4R; 101; CANR 1, 65; CDALBS; DA3; DLB 4, 9, 102; DLBD 12; DLBY 80; MTCW 1, 2; SATA 39; SATA-Obit 23

Porter, Peter (Neville Frederick) 1929-
.... **CLC 5, 13, 33**
See also CA 85-88; DLB 40

Porter, William Sydney 1862-1910
See Henry, O.
See also CA 104; 131; CDALB 1865-1917; DA; DAB; DAC; DAM MST; DA3; DLB 12, 78, 79; MTCW 1, 2; YABC 2

Portillo (y Pacheco), Jose Lopez
See Lopez Portillo (y Pacheco), Jose

Portillo Trambley, Estela 1927-1998
See also CANR 32; DAM MULT; DLB 209; HLC 2; HW 1

Post, Melville Davisson 1869-1930 . **TCLC 39**
See also CA 110

Potok, Chaim 1929- . **CLC 2, 7, 14, 26, 112; DAM NOV**
See also AAYA 15; AITN 1, 2; CA 17-20R; CANR 19, 35, 64; DA3; DLB 28, 152; INT CANR-19; MTCW 1, 2; SATA 33, 106

Potter, Dennis (Christopher George) 1935-1994 .... **CLC 58, 86**
See also CA 107; 145; CANR 33, 61; MTCW 1

Pound, Ezra (Weston Loomis) 1885-1972
. **CLC 1, 2, 3, 4, 5, 7, 10, 13, 18, 34, 48, 50, 112; DA; DAB; DAC; DAM MST, POET; PC 4; WLC**
See also CA 5-8R; 37-40R; CANR 40; CDALB 1917-1929; DA3; DLB 4, 45, 63; DLB 15; MTCW 1, 2

Povod, Reinaldo 1959-1994 .... **CLC 44**
See also CA 136; 146; CANR 83

Powell, Adam Clayton, Jr. 1908-1972
.... **CLC 89; BLC 3; DAM MULT**
See also BW 1, 3; CA 102; 33-36R; CANR 86

Powell, Anthony (Dymoke) 1905- . **CLC 1, 3, 7, 9, 10, 31**
See also CA 1-4R; CANR 1, 32, 62; CDBLB 1945-1960; DLB 15; MTCW 1, 2

Powell, Dawn 1897-1965 .... **CLC 66**
See also CA 5-8R; DLBY 97

Powell, Padgett 1952- .... **CLC 34**
See also CA 126; CANR 63

Power, Susan 1961- .... **CLC 91**
See also CA 145

Powers, J(ames) F(arl) 1917-1999 ... **CLC 1, 4, 8, 57; SSC 4**
See also CA 1-4R; 181; CANR 2, 61; DLB 130; MTCW 1

Powers, John J(ames) 1945-
See Powers, John R.
See also CA 69-72

Powers, John R. .... **CLC 66**
See also Powers, John J(ames)

Powers, Richard (S.) 1957- .... **CLC 93**
See also CA 148; CANR 80

Pownall, David 1938- .... **CLC 10**
See also CA 89-92; 180; CAAS 18; CANR 49; DLB 14

Powys, John Cowper 1872-1963 .. **CLC 7, 9, 15, 46, 125**
See also CA 85-88; DLB 15; MTCW 1, 2

Powys, T(heodore) F(rancis) 1875-1953
.... **TCLC 9**
See also CA 106; DLB 36, 162

Prado (Calvo), Pedro 1886-1952 .. **TCLC 75**
See also CA 131; HW 1

Prager, Emily 1952- .... **CLC 56**

Pratt, E(dwin) J(ohn) 1883(?)-1964
.... **CLC 19; DAC; DAM POET**
See also CA 141; 93-96; CANR 77; DLB 92

Premchand .... **TCLC 21**
See also Srivastava, Dhanpat Rai

Preussler, Otfried 1923- .... **CLC 17**
See also CA 77-80; SATA 24

Prevert, Jacques (Henri Marie) 1900-1977
.... **CLC 15**
See also CA 77-80; 69-72; CANR 29, 61; MTCW 1; SATA-Obit 30

Prevost, Abbe (Antoine Francois) 1697-1763
.... **LC 1**

Price, (Edward) Reynolds 1933- .. **CLC 3, 6, 13, 43, 50, 63; DAM NOV; SSC 22**
See also CA 1-4R; CANR 1, 37, 57, 87; DLB 2; INT CANR-37

Price, Richard 1949- .... **CLC 6, 12**
See also CA 49-52; CANR 3; DLBY 81

Prichard, Katharine Susannah 1883-1969
.... **CLC 46**
See also CA 11-12; CANR 33; CAP 1;
MTCW 1; SATA 66

Priestley, J(ohn) B(oynton) 1894-1984
... **CLC 2, 5, 9, 34; DAM DRAM, NOV**
See also CA 9-12R; 113; CANR 33; CD-
BLB 1914-1945; DA3; DLB 10, 34, 77,
100, 139; DLBY 84; MTCW 1, 2

Prince 1958(?)- .... **CLC 35**

Prince, F(rank) T(empleton) 1912- . **CLC 22**
See also CA 101; CANR 43, 79; DLB 20

Prince Kropotkin
See Kropotkin, Peter (Aleksieevich)

Prior, Matthew 1664-1721 .... **LC 4**
See also DLB 95

Prishvin, Mikhail 1873-1954 .... **TCLC 75**

Pritchard, William H(arrison) 1932-
.... **CLC 34**
See also CA 65-68; CANR 23; DLB 111

Pritchett, V(ictor) S(awdon) 1900-1997
.... **CLC 5, 13, 15, 41; DAM NOV; SSC**
14
See also CA 61-64; 157; CANR 31, 63;
DA3; DLB 15, 139; MTCW 1, 2

Private 19022
See Manning, Frederic

Probst, Mark 1925- .... **CLC 59**
See also CA 130

Prokosch, Frederic 1908-1989 ..... **CLC 4, 48**
See also CA 73-76; 128; CANR 82; DLB
48; MTCW 2

Propertius, Sextus c. 50B.C.-c. 16B.C.
.... **CMLC 32**
See also DLB 211

Prophet, The
See Dreiser, Theodore (Herman Albert)

Prose, Francine 1947- .... **CLC 45**
See also CA 109; 112; CANR 46; SATA
101

Proudhon
See Cunha, Euclides (Rodrigues Pimenta)
da

Proulx, Annie
See Proulx, E(dna) Annie

Proulx, E(dna) Annie 1935- . **CLC 81; DAM**
POP
See also CA 145; CANR 65; DA3; MTCW
2

Proust, (Valentin-Louis-George-Eugene-)
Marcel 1871-1922 ...... **TCLC 7, 13, 33;**
DA; DAB; DAC; DAM MST, NOV;
WLC
See also CA 104; 120; DA3; DLB 65;
MTCW 1, 2

Prowler, Harley
See Masters, Edgar Lee

Prus, Boleslaw 1845-1912 .... **TCLC 48**

Pryor, Richard (Franklin Lenox Thomas)
1940- .... **CLC 26**
See also CA 122; 152

Przybyszewski, Stanislaw 1868-1927
.... **TCLC 36**
See also CA 160; DLB 66

Pteleon
See Grieve, C(hristopher) M(urray)
See also DAM POET

Puckett, Lute
See Masters, Edgar Lee

Puig, Manuel 1932-1990 ... **CLC 3, 5, 10, 28,**
65; DAM MULT; HLC 2
See also CA 45-48; CANR 2, 32, 63; DA3;
DLB 113; HW 1, 2; MTCW 1, 2

Pulitzer, Joseph 1847-1911 .... **TCLC 76**
See also CA 114; DLB 23

Purdy, A(lfred) W(ellington) 1918- .. **CLC 3,**
6, 14, 50; DAC; DAM MST, POET

See also CA 81-84; CAAS 17; CANR 42,
66; DLB 88

Purdy, James (Amos) 1923- ... **CLC 2, 4, 10,**
28, 52
See also CA 33-36R; CAAS 1; CANR 19,
51; DLB 2; INT CANR-19; MTCW 1

Pure, Simon
See Swinnerton, Frank Arthur

Pushkin, Alexander (Sergeyevich) 1799-1837
.... **NCLC 3, 27, 83; DA; DAB; DAC;**
DAM DRAM, MST, POET; PC 10; SSC
27; WLC
See also DA3; DLB 205; SATA 61

P'u Sung-ling 1640-1715 ...... **LC 49; SSC 31**

Putnam, Arthur Lee
See Alger, Horatio Jr., Jr.

Puzo, Mario 1920-1999 ...... **CLC 1, 2, 6, 36,**
107; DAM NOV, POP
See also CA 65-68; 185; CANR 4, 42, 65;
DA3; DLB 6; MTCW 1, 2

Pygge, Edward
See Barnes, Julian (Patrick)

Pyle, Ernest Taylor 1900-1945
See Pyle, Ernie
See also CA 115; 160

Pyle, Ernie 1900-1945 .... **TCLC 75**
See also Pyle, Ernest Taylor
See also DLB 29; MTCW 2

Pyle, Howard 1853-1911 .... **TCLC 81**
See also CA 109; 137; CLR 22; DLB 42,
188; DLBD 13; MAICYA; SATA 16, 100

Pym, Barbara (Mary Crampton) 1913-1980
.... **CLC 13, 19, 37, 111**
See also CA 13-14; 97-100; CANR 13, 34;
CAP 1; DLB 14, 207; DLBY 87; MTCW
1, 2

Pynchon, Thomas (Ruggles, Jr.) 1937-
. **CLC 2, 3, 6, 9, 11, 18, 33, 62, 72; DA;**
DAB; DAC; DAM MST, NOV, POP;
SSC 14; WLC
See also BEST 90:2; CA 17-20R; CANR
22, 46, 73; DA3; DLB 2, 173; MTCW 1,
2

Pythagoras c. 570B.C.-c. 500B.C. . **CMLC 22**
See also DLB 176

Q
See Quiller-Couch, SirArthur (Thomas)

Qian Zhongshu
See Ch'ien Chung-shu

Qroll
See Dagerman, Stig (Halvard)

Quarrington, Paul (Lewis) 1953- .... **CLC 65**
See also CA 129; CANR 62

Quasimodo, Salvatore 1901-1968 .... **CLC 10**
See also CA 13-16; 25-28R; CAP 1; DLB
114; MTCW 1

Quay, Stephen 1947- .... **CLC 95**

Quay, Timothy 1947- .... **CLC 95**

Queen, Ellery .... **CLC 3, 11**
See also Dannay, Frederic; Davidson,
Avram (James); Lee, Manfred
B(ennington); Marlowe, Stephen; Stur-
geon, Theodore (Hamilton); Vance, John
Holbrook

Queen, Ellery, Jr.
See Dannay, Frederic; Lee, Manfred
B(ennington)

Queneau, Raymond 1903-1976 .... **CLC 2, 5,**
10, 42
See also CA 77-80; 69-72; CANR 32; DLB
72; MTCW 1, 2

Quevedo, Francisco de 1580-1645 ..... **LC 23**

Quiller-Couch, SirArthur (Thomas)
1863-1944 .... **TCLC 53**
See also CA 118; 166; DLB 135, 153, 190

Quin, Ann (Marie) 1936-1973 .... **CLC 6**
See also CA 9-12R; 45-48; DLB 14

Quinn, Martin
See Smith, Martin Cruz

Quinn, Peter 1947- .... **CLC 91**

Quinn, Simon
See Smith, Martin Cruz

Quintana, Leroy V. 1944-
See also CA 131; CANR 65; DAM MULT;
DLB 82; HLC 2; HW 1, 2

Quiroga, Horacio (Sylvestre) 1878-1937
.... **TCLC 20; DAM MULT; HLC 2**
See also CA 117; 131; HW 1; MTCW 1

Quoirez, Francoise 1935- .... **CLC 9**
See also Sagan, Francoise
See also CA 49-52; CANR 6, 39, 73;
MTCW 1, 2

Raabe, Wilhelm (Karl) 1831-1910 . **TCLC 45**
See also CA 167; DLB 129

Rabe, David (William) 1940- . **CLC 4, 8, 33;**
DAM DRAM
See also CA 85-88; CABS 3; CANR 59;
DLB 7

Rabelais, Francois 1483-1553 ..... **LC 5; DA;**
DAB; DAC; DAM MST; WLC

Rabinovitch, Sholem 1859-1916
See Aleichem, Sholom
See also CA 104

Rabinyan, Dorit 1972- .... **CLC 119**
See also CA 170

Rachilde
See Vallette, Marguerite Eymery

Racine, Jean 1639-1699 . **LC 28; DAB; DAM**
MST
See also DA3

Radcliffe, Ann (Ward) 1764-1823 . **NCLC 6,**
55
See also DLB 39, 178

Radiguet, Raymond 1903-1923 ..... **TCLC 29**
See also CA 162; DLB 65

Radnoti, Miklos 1909-1944 .... **TCLC 16**
See also CA 118

Rado, James 1939- .... **CLC 17**
See also CA 105

Radvanyi, Netty 1900-1983
See Seghers, Anna
See also CA 85-88; 110; CANR 82

Rae, Ben
See Griffiths, Trevor

Raeburn, John (Hay) 1941- .... **CLC 34**
See also CA 57-60

Ragni, Gerome 1942-1991 .... **CLC 17**
See also CA 105; 134

Rahv, Philip 1908-1973 .... **CLC 24**
See also Greenberg, Ivan
See also DLB 137

Raimund, Ferdinand Jakob 1790-1836
.... **NCLC 69**
See also DLB 90

Raine, Craig 1944- .... **CLC 32, 103**
See also CA 108; CANR 29, 51; DLB 40

Raine, Kathleen (Jessie) 1908- ... **CLC 7, 45**
See also CA 85-88; CANR 46; DLB 20;
MTCW 1

Rainis, Janis 1865-1929 .... **TCLC 29**
See also CA 170; DLB 220

Rakosi, Carl 1903- .... **CLC 47**
See also Rawley, Callman
See also CAAS 5; DLB 193

Raleigh, Richard
See Lovecraft, H(oward) P(hillips)

Raleigh, Sir Walter 1554(?)-1618 . **LC 31, 39**
See also CDBLB Before 1660; DLB 172

Rallentando, H. P.
See Sayers, Dorothy L(eigh)

Ramal, Walter
See de la Mare, Walter (John)

Ramana Maharshi 1879-1950 .... **TCLC 84**

Ramoacn y Cajal, Santiago 1852-1934
.... **TCLC 93**

Ramon, Juan
See Jimenez (Mantecon), Juan Ramon
Ramos, Graciliano 1892-1953 .... **TCLC 32**
See also CA 167; HW 2
Rampersad, Arnold 1941- .... **CLC 44**
See also BW 2, 3; CA 127; 133; CANR 81;
DLB 111; INT 133
Rampling, Anne
See Rice, Anne
Ramsay, Allan 1684(?)-1758 .... **LC 29**
See also DLB 95
Ramuz, Charles-Ferdinand 1878-1947
.... **TCLC 33**
See also CA 165
Rand, Ayn 1905-1982 ..... **CLC 3, 30, 44, 79;
DA; DAC; DAM MST, NOV, POP;
WLC**
See also AAYA 10; CA 13-16R; 105; CANR
27, 73; CDALBS; DA3; MTCW 1, 2
Randall, Dudley (Felker) 1914- .... **CLC 1;
BLC 3; DAM MULT**
See also BW 1, 3; CA 25-28R; CANR 23,
82; DLB 41
Randall, Robert
See Silverberg, Robert
Ranger, Ken
See Creasey, John
Ransom, John Crowe 1888-1974 . **CLC 2, 4,
5, 11, 24; DAM POET**
See also CA 5-8R; 49-52; CANR 6, 34;
CDALBS; DA3; DLB 45, 63; MTCW 1,
2
Rao, Raja 1909- .... **CLC 25, 56; DAM NOV**
See also CA 73-76; CANR 51; MTCW 1, 2
Raphael, Frederic (Michael) 1931- .. **CLC 2,
14**
See also CA 1-4R; CANR 1, 86; DLB 14
Ratcliffe, James P.
See Mencken, H(enry) L(ouis)
Rathbone, Julian 1935- .... **CLC 41**
See also CA 101; CANR 34, 73
Rattigan, Terence (Mervyn) 1911-1977
.... **CLC 7; DAM DRAM**
See also CA 85-88; 73-76; CDBLB 1945-
1960; DLB 13; MTCW 1, 2
Ratushinskaya, Irina 1954- .... **CLC 54**
See also CA 129; CANR 68
Raven, Simon (Arthur Noel) 1927- . **CLC 14**
See also CA 81-84; CANR 86
Ravenna, Michael
See Welty, Eudora
Rawley, Callman 1903-
See Rakosi, Carl
See also CA 21-24R; CANR 12, 32, 91
Rawlings, Marjorie Kinnan 1896-1953
.... **TCLC 4**
See also AAYA 20; CA 104; 137; CANR
74; CLR 63; DLB 9, 22, 102; DLBD 17;
JRDA; MAICYA; MTCW 2; SATA 100;
YABC 1
Ray, Satyajit 1921-1992 . **CLC 16, 76; DAM
MULT**
See also CA 114; 137
Read, Herbert Edward 1893-1968 .... **CLC 4**
See also CA 85-88; 25-28R; DLB 20, 149
Read, Piers Paul 1941- .... **CLC 4, 10, 25**
See also CA 21-24R; CANR 38, 86; DLB
14; SATA 21
Reade, Charles 1814-1884 .... **NCLC 2, 74**
See also DLB 21
Reade, Hamish
See Gray, Simon (James Holliday)
Reading, Peter 1946- .... **CLC 47**
See also CA 103; CANR 46; DLB 40
Reaney, James 1926- . **CLC 13; DAC; DAM
MST**
See also CA 41-44R; CAAS 15; CANR 42;
DLB 68; SATA 43
Rebreanu, Liviu 1885-1944 .... **TCLC 28**

See also CA 165; DLB 220
Rechy, John (Francisco) 1934- ..... **CLC 1, 7,
14, 18, 107; DAM MULT; HLC 2**
See also CA 5-8R; CAAS 4; CANR 6, 32,
64; DLB 122; DLBY 82; HW 1, 2; INT
CANR-6
Redcam, Tom 1870-1933 .... **TCLC 25**
Reddin, Keith .... **CLC 67**
Redgrove, Peter (William) 1932- . **CLC 6, 41**
See also CA 1-4R; CANR 3, 39, 77; DLB
40
Redmon, Anne .... **CLC 22**
See also Nightingale, Anne Redmon
See also DLBY 86
Reed, Eliot
See Ambler, Eric
Reed, Ishmael 1938- . **CLC 2, 3, 5, 6, 13, 32,
60; BLC 3; DAM MULT**
See also BW 2, 3; CA 21-24R; CANR 25,
48, 74; DA3; DLB 2, 5, 33, 169; DLBD
8; MTCW 1, 2
Reed, John (Silas) 1887-1920 .... **TCLC 9**
See also CA 106
Reed, Lou .... **CLC 21**
See also Firbank, Louis
Reese, Lizette Woodworth 1856-1935 . **PC 29**
See also CA 180; DLB 54
Reeve, Clara 1729-1807 .... **NCLC 19**
See also DLB 39
Reich, Wilhelm 1897-1957 .... **TCLC 57**
Reid, Christopher (John) 1949- ...... **CLC 33**
See also CA 140; CANR 89; DLB 40
Reid, Desmond
See Moorcock, Michael (John)
Reid Banks, Lynne 1929-
See Banks, Lynne Reid
See also CA 1-4R; CANR 6, 22, 38, 87;
CLR 24; JRDA; MAICYA; SATA 22, 75,
111
Reilly, William K.
See Creasey, John
Reiner, Max
See Caldwell, (Janet Miriam) Taylor
(Holland)
Reis, Ricardo
See Pessoa, Fernando (Antonio Nogueira)
Remarque, Erich Maria 1898-1970
. **CLC 21; DA; DAB; DAC; DAM MST,
NOV**
See also AAYA 27; CA 77-80; 29-32R;
DA3; DLB 56; MTCW 1, 2
Remington, Frederic 1861-1909 ... **TCLC 89**
See also CA 108; 169; DLB 12, 186, 188;
SATA 41
Remizov, A.
See Remizov, Aleksei (Mikhailovich)
Remizov, A. M.
See Remizov, Aleksei (Mikhailovich)
Remizov, Aleksei (Mikhailovich) 1877-1957
.... **TCLC 27**
See also CA 125; 133
Renan, Joseph Ernest 1823-1892 . **NCLC 26**
Renard, Jules 1864-1910 .... **TCLC 17**
See also CA 117
Renault, Mary .... **CLC 3, 11, 17**
See also Challans, Mary
See also DLBY 83; MTCW 2
Rendell, Ruth (Barbara) 1930- ...... **CLC 28,
48; DAM POP**
See also Vine, Barbara
See also CA 109; CANR 32, 52, 74; DLB
87; INT CANR-32; MTCW 1, 2
Renoir, Jean 1894-1979 .... **CLC 20**
See also CA 129; 85-88
Resnais, Alain 1922- .... **CLC 16**
Reverdy, Pierre 1889-1960 .... **CLC 53**
See also CA 97-100; 89-92
Rexroth, Kenneth 1905-1982 ... **CLC 1, 2, 6,**

11, 22, 49, 112; DAM POET; PC 20
See also CA 5-8R; 107; CANR 14, 34, 63;
CDALB 1941-1968; DLB 16, 48, 165,
212; DLBY 82; INT CANR-14; MTCW
1, 2
Reyes, Alfonso 1889-1959 . **TCLC 33; HLCS
2**
See also CA 131; HW 1
Reyes y Basoalto, Ricardo Eliecer Neftali
See Neruda, Pablo
Reymont, Wladyslaw (Stanislaw)
1868(?)-1925 .... **TCLC 5**
See also CA 104
Reynolds, Jonathan 1942- .... **CLC 6, 38**
See also CA 65-68; CANR 28
Reynolds, Joshua 1723-1792 .... **LC 15**
See also DLB 104
Reynolds, Michael S(hane) 1937- ... **CLC 44**
See also CA 65-68; CANR 9, 89
Reznikoff, Charles 1894-1976 .... **CLC 9**
See also CA 33-36; 61-64; CAP 2; DLB 28,
45
Rezzori (d'Arezzo), Gregor von 1914-1998
.... **CLC 25**
See also CA 122; 136; 167
Rhine, Richard
See Silverstein, Alvin
Rhodes, Eugene Manlove 1869-1934
.... **TCLC 53**
Rhodius, Apollonius c. 3rd cent. B.C.-
.... **CMLC 28**
See also DLB 176
R'hoone
See Balzac, Honore de
Rhys, Jean 1890(?)-1979 .... **CLC 2, 4, 6, 14,
19, 51, 124; DAM NOV; SSC 21**
See also CA 25-28R; 85-88; CANR 35, 62;
CDBLB 1945-1960; DA3; DLB 36, 117,
162; MTCW 1, 2
Ribeiro, Darcy 1922-1997 .... **CLC 34**
See also CA 33-36R; 156
Ribeiro, Joao Ubaldo (Osorio Pimentel)
1941- .... **CLC 10, 67**
See also CA 81-84
Ribman, Ronald (Burt) 1932- .... **CLC 7**
See also CA 21-24R; CANR 46, 80
Ricci, Nino 1959- .... **CLC 70**
See also CA 137
Rice, Anne 1941- . **CLC 41, 128; DAM POP**
See also AAYA 9; BEST 89:2; CA 65-68;
CANR 12, 36, 53, 74; DA3; MTCW 2
Rice, Elmer (Leopold) 1892-1967 .... **CLC 7,
49; DAM DRAM**
See also CA 21-22; 25-28R; CAP 2; DLB
4, 7; MTCW 1, 2
Rice, Tim(othy Miles Bindon) 1944-
.... **CLC 21**
See also CA 103; CANR 46
Rich, Adrienne (Cecile) 1929- .. **CLC 3, 6, 7,
11, 18, 36, 73, 76, 125; DAM POET; PC
5**
See also CA 9-12R; CANR 20, 53, 74;
CDALBS; DA3; DLB 5, 67; MTCW 1, 2
Rich, Barbara
See Graves, Robert (von Ranke)
Rich, Robert
See Trumbo, Dalton
Richard, Keith .... **CLC 17**
See also Richards, Keith
Richards, David Adams 1950- .... **CLC 59;
DAC**
See also CA 93-96; CANR 60; DLB 53
Richards, I(vor) A(rmstrong) 1893-1979
.... **CLC 14, 24**
See also CA 41-44R; 89-92; CANR 34, 74;
DLB 27; MTCW 2
Richards, Keith 1943-
See Richard, Keith
See also CA 107; CANR 77

See also DLB 146

Rolvaag, O(le) E(dvart)
  See Roelvaag, O(le) E(dvart)

Romain Arnaud, Saint
  See Aragon, Louis

Romains, Jules 1885-1972 .... **CLC 7**
  See also CA 85-88; CANR 34; DLB 65;
  MTCW 1

Romero, Jose Ruben 1890-1952 ... **TCLC 14**
  See also CA 114; 131; HW 1

Ronsard, Pierre de 1524-1585 ...... **LC 6, 54;**
  PC 11

Rooke, Leon 1934- . **CLC 25, 34; DAM POP**
  See also CA 25-28R; CANR 23, 53

Roosevelt, Franklin Delano 1882-1945
  .... **TCLC 93**
  See also CA 116; 173

Roosevelt, Theodore 1858-1919 .... **TCLC 69**
  See also CA 115; 170; DLB 47, 186

Roper, William 1498-1578 .... **LC 10**

Roquelaure, A. N.
  See Rice, Anne

Rosa, Joao Guimaraes 1908-1967 . **CLC 23;**
  HLCS 1
  See also CA 89-92; DLB 113

Rose, Wendy 1948- . **CLC 85; DAM MULT;**
  PC 13
  See also CA 53-56; CANR 5, 51; DLB 175;
  NNAL; SATA 12

Rosen, R. D.
  See Rosen, Richard (Dean)

Rosen, Richard (Dean) 1949- .... **CLC 39**
  See also CA 77-80; CANR 62; INT
  CANR-30

Rosenberg, Isaac 1890-1918 .... **TCLC 12**
  See also CA 107; DLB 20

Rosenblatt, Joe .... **CLC 15**
  See also Rosenblatt, Joseph

Rosenblatt, Joseph 1933-
  See Rosenblatt, Joe
  See also CA 89-92; INT 89-92

Rosenfeld, Samuel
  See Tzara, Tristan

Rosenstock, Sami
  See Tzara, Tristan

Rosenstock, Samuel
  See Tzara, Tristan

Rosenthal, M(acha) L(ouis) 1917-1996
  .... **CLC 28**
  See also CA 1-4R; 152; CAAS 6; CANR 4,
  51; DLB 5; SATA 59

Ross, Barnaby
  See Dannay, Frederic

Ross, Bernard L.
  See Follett, Ken(neth Martin)

Ross, J. H.
  See Lawrence, T(homas) E(dward)

Ross, John Hume
  See Lawrence, T(homas) E(dward)

Ross, Martin
  See Martin, Violet Florence
  See also DLB 135

Ross, (James) Sinclair 1908-1996 .. **CLC 13;**
  DAC; DAM MST; SSC 24
  See also CA 73-76; CANR 81; DLB 88

Rossetti, Christina (Georgina) 1830-1894
  .... **NCLC 2, 50, 66; DA; DAB; DAC;**
  DAM MST, POET; PC 7; WLC
  See also DA3; DLB 35, 163; MAICYA;
  SATA 20

Rossetti, Dante Gabriel 1828-1882 . **NCLC 4,**
  77; DA; DAB; DAC; DAM MST,
  POET; WLC
  See also CDBLB 1832-1890; DLB 35

Rossner, Judith (Perelman) 1935- .... **CLC 6,**
  9, 29

See also AITN 2; BEST 90:3; CA 17-20R;
  CANR 18, 51, 73; DLB 6; INT CANR-
  18; MTCW 1, 2

Rostand, Edmond (Eugene Alexis)
  1868-1918 ...... **TCLC 6, 37; DA; DAB;**
  DAC; DAM DRAM, MST; DC 10
  See also CA 104; 126; DA3; DLB 192;
  MTCW 1

Roth, Henry 1906-1995 ... **CLC 2, 6, 11, 104**
  See also CA 11-12; 149; CANR 38, 63;
  CAP 1; DA3; DLB 28; MTCW 1, 2

Roth, Philip (Milton) 1933- . **CLC 1, 2, 3, 4,**
  6, 9, 15, 22, 31, 47, 66, 86, 119; DA;
  DAB; DAC; DAM MST, NOV, POP;
  SSC 26; WLC
  See also BEST 90:3; CA 1-4R; CANR 1,
  22, 36, 55, 89; CDALB 1968-1988; DA3;
  DLB 2, 28, 173; DLBY 82; MTCW 1, 2

Rothenberg, Jerome 1931- .... **CLC 6, 57**
  See also CA 45-48; CANR 1; DLB 5, 193

Roumain, Jacques (Jean Baptiste) 1907-1944
  .... **TCLC 19; BLC 3; DAM MULT**
  See also BW 1; CA 117; 125

Rourke, Constance (Mayfield) 1885-1941
  .... **TCLC 12**
  See also CA 107; YABC 1

Rousseau, Jean-Baptiste 1671-1741 ..... **LC 9**

Rousseau, Jean-Jacques 1712-1778 .. **LC 14,**
  36; DA; DAB; DAC; DAM MST; WLC
  See also DA3

Roussel, Raymond 1877-1933 .... **TCLC 20**
  See also CA 117

Rovit, Earl (Herbert) 1927- .... **CLC 7**
  See also CA 5-8R; CANR 12

Rowe, Elizabeth Singer 1674-1737 .... **LC 44**
  See also DLB 39, 95

Rowe, Nicholas 1674-1718 .... **LC 8**
  See also DLB 84

Rowley, Ames Dorrance
  See Lovecraft, H(oward) P(hillips)

Rowson, Susanna Haswell 1762(?)-1824
  .... **NCLC 5, 69**
  See also DLB 37, 200

Roy, Arundhati 1960(?)- .... **CLC 109**
  See also CA 163; CANR 90; DLBY 97

Roy, Gabrielle 1909-1983 .... **CLC 10, 14;**
  DAB; DAC; DAM MST
  See also CA 53-56; 110; CANR 5, 61; DLB
  68; MTCW 1; SATA 104

Royko, Mike 1932-1997 .... **CLC 109**
  See also CA 89-92; 157; CANR 26

Rozewicz, Tadeusz 1921- . **CLC 9, 23; DAM**
  POET
  See also CA 108; CANR 36, 66; DA3;
  MTCW 1, 2

Ruark, Gibbons 1941- .... **CLC 3**
  See also CA 33-36R; CAAS 23; CANR 14,
  31, 57; DLB 120

Rubens, Bernice (Ruth) 1923- .. **CLC 19, 31**
  See also CA 25-28R; CANR 33, 65; DLB
  14, 207; MTCW 1

Rubin, Harold
  See Robbins, Harold

Rudkin, (James) David 1936- .... **CLC 14**
  See also CA 89-92; DLB 13

Rudnik, Raphael 1933- .... **CLC 7**
  See also CA 29-32R

Ruffian, M.
  See Hasek, Jaroslav (Matej Frantisek)

Ruiz, Jose Martinez .... **CLC 11**
  See also Martinez Ruiz, Jose

Rukeyser, Muriel 1913-1980 . **CLC 6, 10, 15,**
  27; DAM POET; PC 12
  See also CA 5-8R; 93-96; CANR 26, 60;
  DA3; DLB 48; MTCW 1, 2; SATA-Obit
  22

Rule, Jane (Vance) 1931- .... **CLC 27**
  See also CA 25-28R; CAAS 18; CANR 12,
  87; DLB 60

Rulfo, Juan 1918-1986 ..... **CLC 8, 80; DAM**
  MULT; HLC 2; SSC 25
  See also CA 85-88; 118; CANR 26; DLB
  113; HW 1, 2; MTCW 1, 2

Rumi, Jalal al-Din 1297-1373 ...... **CMLC 20**

Runeberg, Johan 1804-1877 .... **NCLC 41**

Runyon, (Alfred) Damon 1884(?)-1946
  .... **TCLC 10**
  See also CA 107; 165; DLB 11, 86, 171;
  MTCW 2

Rush, Norman 1933- .... **CLC 44**
  See also CA 121; 126; INT 126

Rushdie, (Ahmed) Salman 1947- ... **CLC 23,**
  31, 55, 100; DAB; DAC; DAM MST,
  NOV, POP; WLCS
  See also BEST 89:3; CA 108; 111; CANR
  33, 56; DA3; DLB 194; INT 111; MTCW
  1, 2

Rushforth, Peter (Scott) 1945- .... **CLC 19**
  See also CA 101

Ruskin, John 1819-1900 .... **TCLC 63**
  See also CA 114; 129; CDBLB 1832-1890;
  DLB 55, 163, 190; SATA 24

Russ, Joanna 1937- .... **CLC 15**
  See also CA 5-28R; CANR 11, 31, 65; DLB
  8; MTCW 1

Russell, George William 1867-1935
  See Baker, Jean H.
  See also CA 104; 153; CDBLB 1890-1914;
  DAM POET

Russell, (Henry) Ken(neth Alfred) 1927-
  .... **CLC 16**
  See also CA 105

Russell, William Martin 1947- .... **CLC 60**
  See also CA 164

Rutherford, Mark .... **TCLC 25**
  See also White, William Hale
  See also DLB 18

Ruyslinck, Ward 1929- .... **CLC 14**
  See also Belser, Reimond Karel Maria de

Ryan, Cornelius (John) 1920-1974 ... **CLC 7**
  See also CA 69-72; 53-56; CANR 38

Ryan, Michael 1946- .... **CLC 65**
  See also CA 49-52; DLBY 82

Ryan, Tim
  See Dent, Lester

Rybakov, Anatoli (Naumovich) 1911-1998
  .... **CLC 23, 53**
  See also CA 126; 135; 172; SATA 79;
  SATA-Obit 108

Ryder, Jonathan
  See Ludlum, Robert

Ryga, George 1932-1987 ...... **CLC 14; DAC;**
  DAM MST
  See also CA 101; 124; CANR 43, 90; DLB
  60

S. H.
  See Hartmann, Sadakichi

S. S.
  See Sassoon, Siegfried (Lorraine)

Saba, Umberto 1883-1957 .... **TCLC 33**
  See also CA 144; CANR 79; DLB 114

Sabatini, Rafael 1875-1950 .... **TCLC 47**
  See also CA 162

Sabato, Ernesto (R.) 1911- .... **CLC 10, 23;**
  DAM MULT; HLC 2
  See also CA 97-100; CANR 32, 65; DLB
  145; HW 1, 2; MTCW 1, 2

Sa-Carniero, Mario de 1890-1916 . **TCLC 83**

Sacastru, Martin
  See Bioy Casares, Adolfo

Sacastru, Martin
  See Bioy Casares, Adolfo

Sacher-Masoch, Leopold von 1836(?)-1895
  .... **NCLC 31**

Sachs, Marilyn (Stickle) 1927- .... **CLC 35**

See also AAYA 2; CA 17-20R; CANR 13, 47; CLR 2; JRDA; MAICYA; SAAS 2; SATA 3, 68; SATA-Essay 110

Sachs, Nelly 1891-1970 .... **CLC 14, 98**
See also CA 17-18; 25-28R; CANR 87; CAP 2; MTCW 2

Sackler, Howard (Oliver) 1929-1982
.... **CLC 14**
See also CA 61-64; 108; CANR 30; DLB 7

Sacks, Oliver (Wolf) 1933- .... **CLC 67**
See also CA 53-56; CANR 28, 50, 76; DA3; INT CANR-28; MTCW 1, 2

Sadakichi
See Hartmann, Sadakichi

Sade, Donatien Alphonse Francois, Comte de 1740-1814 .... **NCLC 47**

Sadoff, Ira 1945- .... **CLC 9**
See also CA 53-56; CANR 5, 21; DLB 120

Saetone
See Camus, Albert

Safire, William 1929- .... **CLC 10**
See also CA 17-20R; CANR 31, 54, 91

Sagan, Carl (Edward) 1934-1996 .. **CLC 30, 112**
See also AAYA 2; CA 25-28R; 155; CANR 11, 36, 74; DA3; MTCW 1, 2; SATA 58; SATA-Obit 94

Sagan, Francoise .... **CLC 3, 6, 9, 17, 36**
See also Quoirez, Francoise
See also DLB 83; MTCW 2

Sahgal, Nayantara (Pandit) 1927- .. **CLC 41**
See also CA 9-12R; CANR 11, 88

Saint, H(arry) F. 1941- .... **CLC 50**
See also CA 127

St. Aubin de Teran, Lisa 1953-
See Teran, Lisa St. Aubin de
See also CA 118; 126; INT 126

Saint Birgitta of Sweden c. 1303-1373
.... **CMLC 24**

Sainte-Beuve, Charles Augustin 1804-1869
.... **NCLC 5**

Saint-Exupery, Antoine (Jean Baptiste Marie Roger) de 1900-1944 .. **TCLC 2, 56; DAM NOV; WLC**
See also CA 108; 132; CLR 10; DA3; DLB 72; MAICYA; MTCW 1, 2; SATA 20

St. John, David
See Hunt, E(verette) Howard, (Jr.)

Saint-John Perse
See Leger, (Marie-Rene Auguste) Alexis Saint-Leger

Saintsbury, George (Edward Bateman) 1845-1933 .... **TCLC 31**
See also CA 160; DLB 57, 149

Sait Faik .... **TCLC 23**
See also Abasiyanik, Sait Faik

Saki .... **TCLC 3; SSC 12**
See also Munro, H(ector) H(ugh)
See also MTCW 2

Sala, George Augustus .... **NCLC 46**

Saladin 1138-1193 .... **CMLC 38**

Salama, Hannu 1936- .... **CLC 18**

Salamanca, J(ack) R(ichard) 1922- . **CLC 4, 15**
See also CA 25-28R

Salas, Floyd Francis 1931-
See also CA 119; CAAS 27; CANR 44, 75; DAM MULT; DLB 82; HLC 2; HW 1, 2; MTCW 2

Sale, J. Kirkpatrick
See Sale, Kirkpatrick

Sale, Kirkpatrick 1937- .... **CLC 68**
See also CA 13-16R; CANR 10

Salinas, Luis Omar 1937- .... **CLC 90; DAM MULT; HLC 2**
See also CA 131; CANR 81; DLB 82; HW 1, 2

Salinas (y Serrano), Pedro 1891(?)-1951
.... **TCLC 17**
See also CA 117; DLB 134

Salinger, J(erome) D(avid) 1919- . **CLC 1, 3, 8, 12, 55, 56; DA; DAB; DAC; DAM MST, NOV, POP; SSC 2, 28; WLC**
See also AAYA 2; CA 5-8R; CANR 39; CDALB 1941-1968; CLR 18; DA3; DLB 2, 102, 173; MAICYA; MTCW 1, 2; SATA 67

Salisbury, John
See Caute, (John) David

Salter, James 1925- .... **CLC 7, 52, 59**
See also CA 73-76; DLB 130

Saltus, Edgar (Everton) 1855-1921 . **TCLC 8**
See also CA 105; DLB 202

Saltykov, Mikhail Evgrafovich 1826-1889
.... **NCLC 16**

Samarakis, Antonis 1919- .... **CLC 5**
See also CA 25-28R; CAAS 16; CANR 36

Sanchez, Florencio 1875-1910 .... **TCLC 37**
See also CA 153; HW 1

Sanchez, Luis Rafael 1936- .... **CLC 23**
See also CA 128; DLB 145; HW 1

Sanchez, Sonia 1934- .. **CLC 5, 116; BLC 3; DAM MULT; PC 9**
See also BW 2, 3; CA 33-36R; CANR 24, 49, 74; CLR 18; DA3; DLB 41; DLBD 8; MAICYA; MTCW 1, 2; SATA 22

Sand, George 1804-1876 ... **NCLC 2, 42, 57; DA; DAB; DAC; DAM MST, NOV; WLC**
See also DA3; DLB 119, 192

Sandburg, Carl (August) 1878-1967 . **CLC 1, 4, 10, 15, 35; DA; DAB; DAC; DAM MST, POET; PC 2; WLC**
See also AAYA 24; CA 5-8R; 25-28R; CANR 35; CDALB 1865-1917; DA3; DLB 17, 54; MAICYA; MTCW 1, 2; SATA 8

Sandburg, Charles
See Sandburg, Carl (August)

Sandburg, Charles A.
See Sandburg, Carl (August)

Sanders, (James) Ed(ward) 1939- . **CLC 53; DAM POET**
See also CA 13-16R; CAAS 21; CANR 13, 44, 78; DLB 16

Sanders, Lawrence 1920-1998 .... **CLC 41; DAM POP**
See also BEST 89:4; CA 81-84; 165; CANR 33, 62; DA3; MTCW 1

Sanders, Noah
See Blount, Roy (Alton), Jr.

Sanders, Winston P.
See Anderson, Poul (William)

Sandoz, Mari(e Susette) 1896-1966 . **CLC 28**
See also CA 1-4R; 25-28R; CANR 17, 64; DLB 9, 212; MTCW 1, 2; SATA 5

Saner, Reg(inald Anthony) 1931- ...... **CLC 9**
See also CA 65-68

Sankara 788-820 .... **CMLC 32**

Sannazaro, Jacopo 1456(?)-1530 ...... **LC 8**

Sansom, William 1912-1976 .... **CLC 2, 6; DAM NOV; SSC 21**
See also CA 5-8R; 65-68; CANR 42; DLB 139; MTCW 1

Santayana, George 1863-1952 ...... **TCLC 40**
See also CA 115; DLB 54, 71; DLBD 13

Santiago, Danny .... **CLC 33**
See also James, Daniel (Lewis)
See also DLB 122

Santmyer, Helen Hoover 1895-1986 . **CLC 33**
See also CA 1-4R; 118; CANR 15, 33; DLBY 84; MTCW 1

Santoka, Taneda 1882-1940 .... **TCLC 72**

Santos, Bienvenido N(uqui) 1911-1996
.... **CLC 22; DAM MULT**
See also CA 101; 151; CANR 19, 46

Sapper .... **TCLC 44**
See also McNeile, Herman Cyril

Sapphire
See Sapphire, Brenda

Sapphire, Brenda 1950- .... **CLC 99**

Sappho fl. 6th cent. B.C.- .... **CMLC 3; DAM POET; PC 5**
See also DA3; DLB 176

Saramago, Jose 1922- .... **CLC 119; HLCS 1**
See also CA 153

Sarduy, Severo 1937-1993 .... **CLC 6, 97; HLCS 1**
See also CA 89-92; 142; CANR 58, 81; DLB 113; HW 1, 2

Sargeson, Frank 1903-1982 .... **CLC 31**
See also CA 25-28R; 106; CANR 38, 79

Sarmiento, Domingo Faustino 1811-1888
See also HLCS 2

Sarmiento, Felix Ruben Garcia
See Dario, Ruben

Saro-Wiwa, Ken(ule Beeson) 1941-1995
.... **CLC 114**
See also BW 2; CA 142; 150; CANR 60; DLB 157

Saroyan, William 1908-1981 .. **CLC 1, 8, 10, 29, 34, 56; DA; DAB; DAC; DAM DRAM, MST, NOV; SSC 21; WLC**
See also CA 5-8R; 103; CANR 30; CDALBS; DA3; DLB 7, 9, 86; DLBY 81; MTCW 1, 2; SATA 23; SATA-Obit 24

Sarraute, Nathalie 1900- .. **CLC 1, 2, 4, 8, 10, 31, 80**
See also CA 9-12R; CANR 23, 66; DLB 83; MTCW 1, 2

Sarton, (Eleanor) May 1912-1995 .... **CLC 4, 14, 49, 91; DAM POET**
See also CA 1-4R; 149; CANR 1, 34, 55; DLB 48; DLBY 81; INT CANR-34; MTCW 1, 2; SATA 36; SATA-Obit 86

Sartre, Jean-Paul 1905-1980 .... **CLC 1, 4, 7, 9, 13, 18, 24, 44, 50, 52; DA; DAB; DAC; DAM DRAM, MST, NOV; DC 3; SSC 32; WLC**
See also CA 9-12R; 97-100; CANR 21; DA3; DLB 72; MTCW 1, 2

Sassoon, Siegfried (Lorraine) 1886-1967
. **CLC 36, 130; DAB; DAM MST, NOV, POET; PC 12**
See also CA 104; 25-28R; CANR 36; DLB 20, 191; DLBD 18; MTCW 1, 2

Satterfield, Charles
See Pohl, Frederik

Satyremont
See Peret, Benjamin

Saul, John (W. III) 1942- ..... **CLC 46; DAM NOV, POP**
See also AAYA 10; BEST 90:4; CA 81-84; CANR 16, 40, 81; SATA 98

Saunders, Caleb
See Heinlein, Robert A(nson)

Saura (Atares), Carlos 1932- .... **CLC 20**
See also CA 114; 131; CANR 79; HW 1

Sauser-Hall, Frederic 1887-1961 ..... **CLC 18**
See also Cendrars, Blaise
See also CA 102; 93-96; CANR 36, 62; MTCW 1

Saussure, Ferdinand de 1857-1913
.... **TCLC 49**

Savage, Catharine
See Brosman, Catharine Savage

Savage, Thomas 1915- .... **CLC 40**
See also CA 126; 132; CAAS 15; INT 132

Savan, Glenn 19(?)- .... **CLC 50**

Sayers, Dorothy L(eigh) 1893-1957
.... **TCLC 2, 15; DAM POP**
See also CA 104; 119; CANR 60; CDBLB 1914-1945; DLB 10, 36, 77, 100; MTCW 1, 2

Sayers, Valerie 1952- .... **CLC 50, 122**

See also DLB 119

Stael-Holstein, Anne Louise Germaine Necker Baronn 1766-1817 ...... **NCLC 3**
See also Stael, Germaine de
See also DLB 192

Stafford, Jean 1915-1979 . **CLC 4, 7, 19, 68; SSC 26**
See also CA 1-4R; 85-88; CANR 3, 65; DLB 2, 173; MTCW 1, 2; SATA-Obit 22

Stafford, William (Edgar) 1914-1993
.... **CLC 4, 7, 29; DAM POET**
See also CA 5-8R; 142; CAAS 3; CANR 5, 22; DLB 5, 206; INT CANR-22

Stagnelius, Eric Johan 1793-1823 . **NCLC 61**

Staines, Trevor
See Brunner, John (Kilian Houston)

Stairs, Gordon
See Austin, Mary (Hunter)

Stairs, Gordon
See Austin, Mary (Hunter)

Stalin, Joseph 1879-1953 .... **TCLC 92**

Stannard, Martin 1947- .... **CLC 44**
See also CA 142; DLB 155

Stanton, Elizabeth Cady 1815-1902
.... **TCLC 73**
See also CA 171; DLB 79

Stanton, Maura 1946- .... **CLC 9**
See also CA 89-92; CANR 15; DLB 120

Stanton, Schuyler
See Baum, L(yman) Frank

Stapledon, (William) Olaf 1886-1950
.... **TCLC 22**
See also CA 111; 162; DLB 15

Starbuck, George (Edwin) 1931-1996
.... **CLC 53; DAM POET**
See also CA 21-24R; 153; CANR 23

Stark, Richard
See Westlake, Donald E(dwin)

Staunton, Schuyler
See Baum, L(yman) Frank

Stead, Christina (Ellen) 1902-1983 .. **CLC 2, 5, 8, 32, 80**
See also CA 13-16R; 109; CANR 33, 40; MTCW 1, 2

Stead, William Thomas 1849-1912
.... **TCLC 48**
See also CA 167

Steele, Richard 1672-1729 .... **LC 18**
See also CDBLB 1660-1789; DLB 84, 101

Steele, Timothy (Reid) 1948- .... **CLC 45**
See also CA 93-96; CANR 16, 50; DLB 120

Steffens, (Joseph) Lincoln 1866-1936
.... **TCLC 20**
See also CA 117

Stegner, Wallace (Earle) 1909-1993 . **CLC 9, 49, 81; DAM NOV; SSC 27**
See also AITN 1; BEST 90:3; CA 1-4R; 141; CAAS 9; CANR 1, 21, 46; DLB 9, 206; DLBY 93; MTCW 1, 2

Stein, Gertrude 1874-1946 .. **TCLC 1, 6, 28, 48; DA; DAB; DAC; DAM MST, NOV, POET; PC 18; WLC**
See also CA 104; 132; CDALB 1917-1929; DA3; DLB 4, 54, 86; DLBD 15; MTCW 1, 2

Steinbeck, John (Ernst) 1902-1968 .. **CLC 1, 5, 9, 13, 21, 34, 45, 75, 124; DA; DAB; DAC; DAM DRAM, MST, NOV; SSC 11, 37; WLC**
See also AAYA 12; CA 1-4R; 25-28R; CANR 1, 35; CDALB 1929-1941; DA3; DLB 7, 9, 212; DLBD 2; MTCW 1, 2; SATA 9

Steinem, Gloria 1934- .... **CLC 63**
See also CA 53-56; CANR 28, 51; MTCW 1, 2

Steiner, George 1929- . **CLC 24; DAM NOV**

See also CA 73-76; CANR 31, 67; DLB 67; MTCW 1, 2; SATA 62

Steiner, K. Leslie
See Delany, Samuel R(ay, Jr.)

Steiner, Rudolf 1861-1925 .... **TCLC 13**
See also CA 107

Stendhal 1783-1842 .... **NCLC 23, 46; DA; DAB; DAC; DAM MST, NOV; SSC 27; WLC**
See also DA3; DLB 119

Stephen, Adeline Virginia
See Woolf, (Adeline) Virginia

Stephen, SirLeslie 1832-1904 .... **TCLC 23**
See also CA 123; DLB 57, 144, 190

Stephen, Sir Leslie
See Stephen, SirLeslie

Stephen, Virginia
See Woolf, (Adeline) Virginia

Stephens, James 1882(?)-1950 .... **TCLC 4**
See also CA 104; DLB 19, 153, 162

Stephens, Reed
See Donaldson, Stephen R.

Steptoe, Lydia
See Barnes, Djuna

Sterchi, Beat 1949- .... **CLC 65**

Sterling, Brett
See Bradbury, Ray (Douglas); Hamilton, Edmond

Sterling, Bruce 1954- .... **CLC 72**
See also CA 119; CANR 44

Sterling, George 1869-1926 .... **TCLC 20**
See also CA 117; 165; DLB 54

Stern, Gerald 1925- .... **CLC 40, 100**
See also CA 81-84; CANR 28; DLB 105

Stern, Richard (Gustave) 1928- .. **CLC 4, 39**
See also CA 1-4R; CANR 1, 25, 52; DLBY 87; INT CANR-25

Sternberg, Josef von 1894-1969 ...... **CLC 20**
See also CA 81-84

Sterne, Laurence 1713-1768 . **LC 2, 48; DA; DAB; DAC; DAM MST, NOV; WLC**
See also CDBLB 1660-1789; DLB 39

Sternheim, (William Adolf) Carl 1878-1942
.... **TCLC 8**
See also CA 105; DLB 56, 118

Stevens, Mark 1951- .... **CLC 34**
See also CA 122

Stevens, Wallace 1879-1955 ..... **TCLC 3, 12, 45; DA; DAB; DAC; DAM MST, POET; PC 6; WLC**
See also CA 104; 124; CDALB 1929-1941; DA3; DLB 54; MTCW 1, 2

Stevenson, Anne (Katharine) 1933- . **CLC 7, 33**
See also CA 17-20R; CAAS 9; CANR 9, 33; DLB 40; MTCW 1

Stevenson, Robert Louis (Balfour) 1850-1894 . **NCLC 5, 14, 63; DA; DAB; DAC; DAM MST, NOV; SSC 11; WLC**
See also AAYA 24; CDBLB 1890-1914; CLR 10, 11; DA3; DLB 18, 57, 141, 156, 174; DLBD 13; JRDA; MAICYA; SATA 100; YABC 2

Stewart, J(ohn) I(nnes) M(ackintosh) 1906-1994 .... **CLC 7, 14, 32**
See also CA 85-88; 147; CAAS 3; CANR 47; MTCW 1, 2

Stewart, Mary (Florence Elinor) 1916-
.... **CLC 7, 35, 117; DAB**
See also AAYA 29; CA 1-4R; CANR 1, 59; SATA 12

Stewart, Mary Rainbow
See Stewart, Mary (Florence Elinor)

Stifle, June
See Campbell, Maria

Stifter, Adalbert 1805-1868 . **NCLC 41; SSC 28**
See also DLB 133

Still, James 1906- .... **CLC 49**
See also CA 65-68; CAAS 17; CANR 10, 26; DLB 9; SATA 29

Sting 1951-
See Sumner, Gordon Matthew
See also CA 167

Stirling, Arthur
See Sinclair, Upton (Beall)

Stitt, Milan 1941- .... **CLC 29**
See also CA 69-72

Stockton, Francis Richard 1834-1902
See Stockton, Frank R.
See also CA 108; 137; MAICYA; SATA 44

Stockton, Frank R. .... **TCLC 47**
See also Stockton, Francis Richard
See also DLB 42, 74; DLBD 13; SATA-Brief 32

Stoddard, Charles
See Kuttner, Henry

Stoker, Abraham 1847-1912
See Stoker, Bram
See also CA 105; 150; DA; DAC; DAM MST, NOV; DA3; SATA 29

Stoker, Bram 1847-1912 ...... **TCLC 8; DAB; WLC**
See also Stoker, Abraham
See also AAYA 23; CDBLB 1890-1914; DLB 36, 70, 178

Stolz, Mary (Slattery) 1920- .... **CLC 12**
See also AAYA 8; AITN 1; CA 5-8R; CANR 13, 41; JRDA; MAICYA; SAAS 3; SATA 10, 71

Stone, Irving 1903-1989 . **CLC 7; DAM POP**
See also AITN 1; CA 1-4R; 129; CAAS 3; CANR 1, 23; DA3; INT CANR-23; MTCW 1, 2; SATA 3; SATA-Obit 64

Stone, Oliver (William) 1946- .... **CLC 73**
See also AAYA 15; CA 110; CANR 55

Stone, Robert (Anthony) 1937- .. **CLC 5, 23, 42**
See also CA 85-88; CANR 23, 66; DLB 152; INT CANR-23; MTCW 1

Stone, Zachary
See Follett, Ken(neth Martin)

Stoppard, Tom 1937- . **CLC 1, 3, 4, 5, 8, 15, 29, 34, 63, 91; DA; DAB; DAC; DAM DRAM, MST; DC 6; WLC**
See also CA 81-84; CANR 39, 67; CDBLB 1960 to Present; DA3; DLB 13; DLBY 85; MTCW 1, 2

Storey, David (Malcolm) 1933- . **CLC 2, 4, 5, 8; DAM DRAM**
See also CA 81-84; CANR 36; DLB 13, 14, 207; MTCW 1

Storm, Hyemeyohsts 1935- .... **CLC 3; DAM MULT**
See also CA 81-84; CANR 45; NNAL

Storm, Theodor 1817-1888 .... **SSC 27**

Storm, (Hans) Theodor (Woldsen) 1817-1888
.... **NCLC 1; SSC 27**
See also DLB 129

Storni, Alfonsina 1892-1938 . **TCLC 5; DAM MULT; HLC 2**
See also CA 104; 131; HW 1

Stoughton, William 1631-1701 .... **LC 38**
See also DLB 24

Stout, Rex (Todhunter) 1886-1975 .... **CLC 3**
See also AITN 2; CA 61-64; CANR 71

Stow, (Julian) Randolph 1935- . **CLC 23, 48**
See also CA 13-16R; CANR 33; MTCW 1

Stowe, Harriet (Elizabeth) Beecher 1811-1896 ...... **NCLC 3, 50; DA; DAB; DAC; DAM MST, NOV; WLC**
See also CDALB 1865-1917; DA3; DLB 1, 12, 42, 74, 189; JRDA; MAICYA; YABC 1

Strabo c. 64B.C.-c. 25 .... **CMLC 37**
See also DLB 176

Tarantino, Quentin (Jerome) 1963-
.... CLC 125
See also CA 171
Tarassoff, Lev
See Troyat, Henri
Tarbell, Ida M(inerva) 1857-1944 . TCLC 40
See also CA 122; 181; DLB 47
Tarkington, (Newton) Booth 1869-1946
.... TCLC 9
See also CA 110; 143; DLB 9, 102; MTCW
2; SATA 17
Tarkovsky, Andrei (Arsenyevich) 1932-1986
.... CLC 75
See also CA 127
Tartt, Donna 1964(?)- .... CLC 76
See also CA 142
Tasso, Torquato 1544-1595 .... LC 5
Tate, (John Orley) Allen 1899-1979 . CLC 2,
4, 6, 9, 11, 14, 24
See also CA 5-8R; 85-88; CANR 32; DLB
4, 45, 63; DLBD 17; MTCW 1, 2
Tate, Ellalice
See Hibbert, Eleanor Alice Burford
Tate, James (Vincent) 1943- .... CLC 2, 6, 25
See also CA 21-24R; CANR 29, 57; DLB
5, 169
Tauler, Johannes c. 1300-1361 ..... CMLC 37
See also DLB 179
Tavel, Ronald 1940- .... CLC 6
See also CA 21-24R; CANR 33
Taylor, C(ecil) P(hilip) 1929-1981 ... CLC 27
See also CA 25-28R; 105; CANR 47
Taylor, Edward 1642(?)-1729 .... LC 11; DA;
DAB; DAC; DAM MST, POET
See also DLB 24
Taylor, Eleanor Ross 1920- .... CLC 5
See also CA 81-84; CANR 70
Taylor, Elizabeth 1912-1975 .... CLC 2, 4, 29
See also CA 13-16R; CANR 9, 70; DLB
139; MTCW 1; SATA 13
Taylor, Frederick Winslow 1856-1915
.... TCLC 76
Taylor, Henry (Splawn) 1942- .... CLC 44
See also CA 33-36R; CAAS 7; CANR 31;
DLB 5
Taylor, Kamala (Purnaiya) 1924-
See Markandaya, Kamala
See also CA 77-80
Taylor, Mildred D. .... CLC 21
See also AAYA 10; BW 1; CA 85-88;
CANR 25; CLR 9, 59; DLB 52; JRDA;
MAICYA; SAAS 5; SATA 15, 70
Taylor, Peter (Hillsman) 1917-1994 . CLC 1,
4, 18, 37, 44, 50, 71; SSC 10
See also CA 13-16R; 147; CANR 9, 50;
DLBY 81, 94; INT CANR-9; MTCW 1, 2
Taylor, Robert Lewis 1912-1998 ..... CLC 14
See also CA 1-4R; 170; CANR 3, 64; SATA
10
Tchekhov, Anton
See Chekhov, Anton (Pavlovich)
Tchicaya, Gerald Felix 1931-1988 . CLC 101
See also CA 129; 125; CANR 81
Tchicaya U Tam'si
See Tchicaya, Gerald Felix
Teasdale, Sara 1884-1933 .... TCLC 4
See also CA 104; 163; DLB 45; SATA 32
Tegner, Esaias 1782-1846 .... NCLC 2
Teilhard de Chardin, (Marie Joseph) Pierre
1881-1955 .... TCLC 9
See also CA 105
Temple, Ann
See Mortimer, Penelope (Ruth)
Tennant, Emma (Christina) 1937- . CLC 13,
52
See also CA 65-68; CAAS 9; CANR 10,
38, 59, 88; DLB 14

Tenneshaw, S. M.
See Silverberg, Robert
Tennyson, Alfred 1809-1892 .. NCLC 30, 65;
DA; DAB; DAC; DAM MST, POET;
PC 6; WLC
See also CDBLB 1832-1890; DA3; DLB
32
Teran, Lisa St. Aubin de .... CLC 36
See also St. Aubin de Teran, Lisa
Terence c. 184B.C.-c. 159B.C. .... CMLC 14;
DC 7
See also DLB 211
Teresa de Jesus, St. 1515-1582 .... LC 18
Terkel, Louis 1912-
See Terkel, Studs
See also CA 57-60; CANR 18, 45, 67; DA3;
MTCW 1, 2
Terkel, Studs .... CLC 38
See Terkel, Louis
See also AAYA 32; AITN 1; MTCW 2
Terry, C. V.
See Slaughter, Frank G(ill)
Terry, Megan 1932- .... CLC 19
See also CA 77-80; CABS 3; CANR 43;
DLB 7
Tertullian c. 155-c. 245 .... CMLC 29
Tertz, Abram
See Sinyavsky, Andrei (Donatevich)
Tesich, Steve 1943(?)-1996 .... CLC 40, 69
See also CA 105; 152; DLBY 83
Tesla, Nikola 1856-1943 .... TCLC 88
Teternikov, Fyodor Kuzmich 1863-1927
See Sologub, Fyodor
See also CA 104
Tevis, Walter 1928-1984 .... CLC 42
See also CA 113
Tey, Josephine .... TCLC 14
See also Mackintosh, Elizabeth
See also DLB 77
Thackeray, William Makepeace 1811-1863
. NCLC 5, 14, 22, 43; DA; DAB; DAC;
DAM MST, NOV; WLC
See also CDBLB 1832-1890; DA3; DLB
21, 55, 159, 163; SATA 23
Thakura, Ravindranatha
See Tagore, Rabindranath
Tharoor, Shashi 1956- .... CLC 70
See also CA 141; CANR 91
Thelwell, Michael Miles 1939- .... CLC 22
See also BW 2; CA 101
Theobald, Lewis, Jr.
See Lovecraft, H(oward) P(hillips)
Theodorescu, Ion N. 1880-1967
See Arghezi, Tudor
See also CA 116; DLB 220
Theriault, Yves 1915-1983 ... CLC 79; DAC;
DAM MST
See also CA 102; DLB 88
Theroux, Alexander (Louis) 1939- ... CLC 2,
25
See also CA 85-88; CANR 20, 63
Theroux, Paul (Edward) 1941- .... CLC 5, 8,
11, 15, 28, 46; DAM POP
See also AAYA 28; BEST 89:4; CA 33-36R;
CANR 20, 45, 74; CDALBS; DA3; DLB
2; MTCW 1, 2; SATA 44, 109
Thesen, Sharon 1946- .... CLC 56
See also CA 163
Thevenin, Denis
See Duhamel, Georges
Thibault, Jacques Anatole Francois
1844-1924
See France, Anatole
See also CA 106; 127; DAM NOV; DA3;
MTCW 1, 2
Thiele, Colin (Milton) 1920- .... CLC 17
See also CA 29-32R; CANR 12, 28, 53;
CLR 27; MAICYA; SAAS 2; SATA 14,
72

Thomas, Audrey (Callahan) 1935- .. CLC 7,
13, 37, 107; SSC 20
See also AITN 2; CA 21-24R; CAAS 19;
CANR 36, 58; DLB 60; MTCW 1
Thomas, Augustus 1857-1934 .... TCLC 97
Thomas, D(onald) M(ichael) 1935- . CLC 13,
22, 31, 132
See also CA 61-64; CAAS 11; CANR 17,
45, 75; CDBLB 1960 to Present; DA3;
DLB 40, 207; INT CANR-17; MTCW 1,
2
Thomas, Dylan (Marlais) 1914-1953
.... TCLC 1, 8, 45; DA; DAB; DAC;
DAM DRAM, MST, POET; PC 2; SSC
3; WLC
See also CA 104; 120; CANR 65; CDBLB
1945-1960; DA3; DLB 13, 20, 139;
MTCW 1, 2; SATA 60
Thomas, (Philip) Edward 1878-1917
.... TCLC 10; DAM POET
See also CA 106; 153; DLB 98
Thomas, Joyce Carol 1938- .... CLC 35
See also AAYA 12; BW 2, 3; CA 113; 116;
CANR 48; CLR 19; DLB 33; INT 116;
JRDA; MAICYA; MTCW 1, 2; SAAS 7;
SATA 40, 78
Thomas, Lewis 1913-1993 .... CLC 35
See also CA 85-88; 143; CANR 38, 60;
MTCW 1, 2
Thomas, M. Carey 1857-1935 ...... TCLC 89
Thomas, Paul
See Mann, (Paul) Thomas
Thomas, Piri 1928- .... CLC 17; HLCS 2
See also CA 73-76; HW 1
Thomas, R(onald) S(tuart) 1913- ..... CLC 6,
13, 48; DAB; DAM POET
See also CA 89-92; CAAS 4; CANR 30;
CDBLB 1960 to Present; DLB 27; MTCW
1
Thomas, Ross (Elmore) 1926-1995 . CLC 39
See also CA 33-36R; 150; CANR 22, 63
Thompson, Francis Clegg
See Mencken, H(enry) L(ouis)
Thompson, Francis Joseph 1859-1907
.... TCLC 4
See also CA 104; CDBLB 1890-1914; DLB
19
Thompson, Hunter S(tockton) 1939-
.... CLC 9, 17, 40, 104; DAM POP
See also BEST 89:1; CA 17-20R; CANR
23, 46, 74, 77; DA3; DLB 185; MTCW
1, 2
Thompson, James Myers
See Thompson, Jim (Myers)
Thompson, Jim (Myers) 1906-1977(?)
.... CLC 69
See also CA 140
Thompson, Judith .... CLC 39
Thomson, James 1700-1748 .. LC 16, 29, 40;
DAM POET
See also DLB 95
Thomson, James 1834-1882 .... NCLC 18;
DAM POET
See also DLB 35
Thoreau, Henry David 1817-1862 . NCLC 7,
21, 61; DA; DAB; DAC; DAM MST;
PC 30; WLC
See also CDALB 1640-1865; DA3; DLB 1,
223
Thornton, Hall
See Silverberg, Robert
Thucydides c. 455B.C.-399B.C. ... CMLC 17
See also DLB 176
Thumboo, Edwin 1933- .... PC 30
Thurber, James (Grover) 1894-1961 . CLC 5,
11, 25, 125; DA; DAB; DAC; DAM
DRAM, MST, NOV; SSC 1

Tuck, Lily 1938- .... **CLC 70**
See also CA 139; CANR 90

Tu Fu 712-770 .... **PC 9**
See also DAM MULT

Tunis, John R(oberts) 1889-1975 .... **CLC 12**
See also CA 61-64; CANR 62; DLB 22,
171; JRDA; MAICYA; SATA 37; SATA-
Brief 30

Tuohy, Frank .... **CLC 37**
See also Tuohy, John Francis
See also DLB 14, 139

Tuohy, John Francis 1925-1999
See Tuohy, Frank
See also CA 5-8R; 178; CANR 3, 47

Turco, Lewis (Putnam) 1934- .... **CLC 11, 63**
See also CA 13-16R; CAAS 22; CANR 24,
51; DLBY 84

Turgenev, Ivan 1818-1883 ... **NCLC 21; DA;
DAB; DAC; DAM MST, NOV; DC 7;
SSC 7; WLC**

Turgot, Anne-Robert-Jacques 1727-1781
.... **LC 26**

Turner, Frederick 1943- .... **CLC 48**
See also CA 73-76; CAAS 10; CANR 12,
30, 56; DLB 40

Tutu, Desmond M(pilo) 1931- .... **CLC 80;
BLC 3; DAM MULT**
See also BW 1, 3; CA 125; CANR 67, 81

Tutuola, Amos 1920-1997 ..... **CLC 5, 14, 29;
BLC 3; DAM MULT**
See also BW 2, 3; CA 9-12R; 159; CANR
27, 66; DA3; DLB 125; MTCW 1, 2

Twain, Mark .... **TCLC 6, 12, 19, 36, 48, 59;
SSC 34; WLC**
See also Clemens, Samuel Langhorne
See also AAYA 20; CLR 58, 60; DLB 11,
12, 23, 64, 74

Tyler, Anne 1941- . **CLC 7, 11, 18, 28, 44, 59,
103; DAM NOV, POP**
See also AAYA 18; BEST 89:1; CA 9-12R;
CANR 11, 33, 53; CDALBS; DLB 6, 143;
DLBY 82; MTCW 1, 2; SATA 7, 90

Tyler, Royall 1757-1826 .... **NCLC 3**
See also DLB 37

Tynan, Katharine 1861-1931 .... **TCLC 3**
See also CA 104; 167; DLB 153

Tyutchev, Fyodor 1803-1873 .... **NCLC 34**

Tzara, Tristan 1896-1963 ..... **CLC 47; DAM
POET; PC 27**
See also CA 153; 89-92; MTCW 2

Uhry, Alfred 1936- . **CLC 55; DAM DRAM,
POP**
See also CA 127; 133; DA3; INT 133

Ulf, Haerved
See Strindberg, (Johan) August

Ulf, Harved
See Strindberg, (Johan) August

Ulibarri, Sabine R(eyes) 1919- .... **CLC 83;
DAM MULT; HLCS 2**
See also CA 131; CANR 81; DLB 82; HW
1, 2

Unamuno (y Jugo), Miguel de 1864-1936
. **TCLC 2, 9; DAM MULT, NOV; HLC
2; SSC 11**
See also CA 104; 131; CANR 81; DLB 108;
HW 1, 2; MTCW 1, 2

Undercliffe, Errol
See Campbell, (John) Ramsey

Underwood, Miles
See Glassco, John

Undset, Sigrid 1882-1949 .... **TCLC 3; DA;
DAB; DAC; DAM MST, NOV; WLC**
See also CA 104; 129; DA3; MTCW 1, 2

Ungaretti, Giuseppe 1888-1970 .. **CLC 7, 11,
15**
See also CA 19-20; 25-28R; CAP 2; DLB
114

Unger, Douglas 1952- .... **CLC 34**
See also CA 130

Unsworth, Barry (Forster) 1930- ... **CLC 76,
127**
See also CA 25-28R; CANR 30, 54; DLB
194

Updike, John (Hoyer) 1932- . **CLC 1, 2, 3, 5,
7, 9, 13, 15, 23, 34, 43, 70; DA; DAB;
DAC; DAM MST, NOV, POET, POP;
SSC 13, 27; WLC**
See also CA 1-4R; CABS 1; CANR 4, 33,
51; CDALB 1968-1988; DA3; DLB 2, 5,
143; DLBD 3; DLBY 80, 82, 97; MTCW
1, 2

Upshaw, Margaret Mitchell
See Mitchell, Margaret (Munnerlyn)

Upton, Mark
See Sanders, Lawrence

Upward, Allen 1863-1926 .... **TCLC 85**
See also CA 117; DLB 36

Urdang, Constance (Henriette) 1922-
.... **CLC 47**
See also CA 21-24R; CANR 9, 24

Uriel, Henry
See Faust, Frederick (Schiller)

Uris, Leon (Marcus) 1924- .... **CLC 7, 32;
DAM NOV, POP**
See also AITN 1, 2; BEST 89:2; CA 1-4R;
CANR 1, 40, 65; DA3; MTCW 1, 2;
SATA 49

Urista, Alberto H. 1947-
See Alurista
See also CA 45-48, 182; CANR 2, 32;
HLCS 1; HW 1

Urmuz
See Codrescu, Andrei

Urquhart, Guy
See McAlmon, Robert (Menzies)

Urquhart, Jane 1949- .... **CLC 90; DAC**
See also CA 113; CANR 32, 68

Usigli, Rodolfo 1905-1979
See also CA 131; HLCS 1; HW 1

Ustinov, Peter (Alexander) 1921- ...... **CLC 1**
See also AITN 1; CA 13-16R; CANR 25,
51; DLB 13; MTCW 2

U Tam'si, Gerald Felix Tchicaya
See Tchicaya, Gerald Felix

U Tam'si, Tchicaya
See Tchicaya, Gerald Felix

Vachss, Andrew (Henry) 1942- ..... **CLC 106**
See also CA 118; CANR 44

Vachss, Andrew H.
See Vachss, Andrew (Henry)

Vaculik, Ludvik 1926- .... **CLC 7**
See also CA 53-56; CANR 72

Vaihinger, Hans 1852-1933 .... **TCLC 71**
See also CA 116; 166

Valdez, Luis (Miguel) 1940- . **CLC 84; DAM
MULT; DC 10; HLC 2**
See also CA 101; CANR 32, 81; DLB 122;
HW 1

Valenzuela, Luisa 1938- .... **CLC 31, 104;
DAM MULT; HLCS 2; SSC 14**
See also CA 101; CANR 32, 65; DLB 113;
HW 1, 2

Valera y Alcala-Galiano, Juan 1824-1905
.... **TCLC 10**
See also CA 106

Valery, (Ambroise) Paul (Toussaint Jules)
1871-1945 .. **TCLC 4, 15; DAM POET;
PC 9**
See also CA 104; 122; DA3; MTCW 1, 2

Valle-Inclan, Ramon (Maria) del 1866-1936
.... **TCLC 5; DAM MULT; HLC 2**
See also CA 106; 153; CANR 80; DLB 134;
HW 2

Vallejo, Antonio Buero
See Buero Vallejo, Antonio

Vallejo, Cesar (Abraham) 1892-1938
...... **TCLC 3, 56; DAM MULT; HLC 2**
See also CA 105; 153; HW 1

Valles, Jules 1832-1885 .... **NCLC 71**
See also DLB 123

Vallette, Marguerite Eymery 1860-1953
.... **TCLC 67**
See also CA 182; DLB 123, 192

Valle Y Pena, Ramon del
See Valle-Inclan, Ramon (Maria) del

Van Ash, Cay 1918- .... **CLC 34**

Vanbrugh, Sir John 1664-1726 .... **LC 21;
DAM DRAM**
See also DLB 80

Van Campen, Karl
See Campbell, John W(ood, Jr.)

Vance, Gerald
See Silverberg, Robert

Vance, Jack .... **CLC 35**
See also Vance, John Holbrook
See also DLB 8

Vance, John Holbrook 1916-
See Queen, Ellery; Vance, Jack
See also CA 29-32R; CANR 17, 65; MTCW
1

**Van Den Bogarde, Derek Jules Gaspard
Ulric Niven** 1921-1999 .... **CLC 14**
See also CA 77-80; 179; DLB 19

Vandenburgh, Jane .... **CLC 59**
See also CA 168

Vanderhaeghe, Guy 1951- .... **CLC 41**
See also CA 113; CANR 72

van der Post, Laurens (Jan) 1906-1996
.... **CLC 5**
See also CA 5-8R; 155; CANR 35; DLB
204

van de Wetering, Janwillem 1931- . **CLC 47**
See also CA 49-52; CANR 4, 62, 90

Van Dine, S. S. .... **TCLC 23**
See also Wright, Willard Huntington

Van Doren, Carl (Clinton) 1885-1950
.... **TCLC 18**
See also CA 111; 168

Van Doren, Mark 1894-1972 .... **CLC 6, 10**
See also CA 1-4R; 37-40R; CANR 3; DLB
45; MTCW 1, 2

Van Druten, John (William) 1901-1957
.... **TCLC 2**
See also CA 104; 161; DLB 10

Van Duyn, Mona (Jane) 1921- ..... **CLC 3, 7,
63, 116; DAM POET**
See also CA 9-12R; CANR 7, 38, 60; DLB
5

Van Dyne, Edith
See Baum, L(yman) Frank

van Itallie, Jean-Claude 1936- .... **CLC 3**
See also CA 45-48; CAAS 2; CANR 1, 48;
DLB 7

van Ostaijen, Paul 1896-1928 .... **TCLC 33**
See also CA 163

Van Peebles, Melvin 1932- .... **CLC 2, 20;
DAM MULT**
See also BW 2, 3; CA 85-88; CANR 27,
67, 82

Vansittart, Peter 1920- .... **CLC 42**
See also CA 1-4R; CANR 3, 49, 90

Van Vechten, Carl 1880-1964 .... **CLC 33**
See also CA 183; 89-92; DLB 4, 9, 51

Van Vogt, A(lfred) E(lton) 1912- .... **CLC 1**
See also CA 21-24R; CANR 28; DLB 8;
SATA 14

Varda, Agnes 1928- .... **CLC 16**
See also CA 116; 122

Vargas Llosa, (Jorge) Mario (Pedro) 1936-
...... **CLC 3, 6, 9, 10, 15, 31, 42, 85; DA;
DAB; DAC; DAM MST, MULT, NOV;
HLC 2**
See also CA 73-76; CANR 18, 32, 42, 67;
DA3; DLB 145; HW 1, 2; MTCW 1, 2

Vasiliu, Gheorghe 1881-1957
See Bacovia, George
See also CA 123; DLB 220

Author Index

Literary Criticism Series
Cumulative Topic Index

This index lists all topic entries in Gale's *Classical and Medieval Literature Criticism, Contemporary Literary Criticism, Literature Criticism from 1400 to 1800, Nineteenth-Century Literature Criticism,* and *Twentieth-Century Literary Criticism.*

Topic Index

LC Cumulative Nationality Index

AFGHAN

Babur **18**

AMERICAN

Bradstreet, Anne **4, 30**
Edwards, Jonathan **7, 54**
Eliot, John **5**
Franklin, Benjamin **25**
Hathorne, John **38**
Hopkinson, Francis **25**
Knight, Sarah Kemble **7**
Mather, Cotton **38**
Mather, Increase **38**
Munford, Robert **5**
Penn, William **25**
Sewall, Samuel **38**
Stoughton, William **38**
Taylor, Edward **11**
Washington, George **25**
Wheatley (Peters), Phillis **3, 50**
Winthrop, John

BENINESE

Equiano, Olaudah **16**

CANADIAN

Marie de l'Incarnation **10**

CHINESE

Lo Kuan-chung **12**
P'u Sung-ling **3, 49**
Ts'ao Hsueh-ch'in **1**
Wu Ch'eng-en **7**
Wu Ching-tzu **2**

DANISH

Holberg, Ludvig **6**
Wessel, Johan Herman **7**

DUTCH

Erasmus, Desiderius **16**
Lipsius, Justus **16**
Spinoza, Benedictus de **9, 58**

ENGLISH

Addison, Joseph **18**
Amory, Thomas **48**
Andrewes, Lancelot **5**
Arbuthnot, John **1**
Aubin, Penelope **9**
Bacon, Francis **18, 32**
Barker, Jane **42**
Beaumont, Francis **33**
Behn, Aphra **1, 30, 42**
Boswell, James **4, 50**
Bradstreet, Anne **4, 30**
Brooke, Frances **6, 48**
Bunyan, John **4**
Burke, Edmund **7, 36**
Butler, Samuel **16, 43**

Carew, Thomas **13**
Cary, Elizabeth, Lady Falkland **30**
Cavendish, Margaret Lucas **30**
Caxton, William **17**
Chapman, George **22**
Charles I **13**
Chatterton, Thomas **3, 54**
Chaucer, Geoffrey **17, 56**
Churchill, Charles **3**
Cleland, John **2, 48**
Collier, Jeremy **6**
Collins, William **4, 40**
Congreve, William **5, 21**
Coventry, Francis **46**
Crashaw, Richard **24**
Daniel, Samuel **24**
Davenant, William **13**
Davys, Mary **1, 46**
Day, Thomas **1**
Dee, John **20**
Defoe, Daniel **1, 42**
Dekker, Thomas **22**
Delany, Mary (Granville Pendarves) **12**
Deloney, Thomas **41**
Dennis, John **11**
Devenant, William **13**
Donne, John **10, 24**
Drayton, Michael **8**
Dryden, John **3, 21**
Elyot, Sir Thomas **11**
Equiano, Olaudah **16**
Fanshawe, Ann **11**
Farquhar, George **21**
Fielding, Henry **1, 46**
Fielding, Sarah **1, 44**
Fletcher, John **33**
Foxe, John **14**
Garrick, David **15**
Gay, John **49**
Gray, Thomas **4, 40**
Greene, Robert **41**
Hakluyt, Richard **31**
Hawes, Stephen **17**
Haywood, Eliza (Fowler) **1, 44**
Henry VIII **10**
Herbert, George **24**
Herrick, Robert **13**
Hobbes, Thomas **36**
Howell, James **13**
Hunter, Robert **7**
Johnson, Samuel **15, 52**
Jonson, Ben(jamin) **6, 33**
Julian of Norwich **6, 52**
Kempe, Margery **6, 56**
Killigrew, Anne **4**
Killigrew, Thomas **57**
Kyd, Thomas **22**
Langland, William **19**
Lanyer, Aemilia **10, 30**
Lilly, William **27**
Locke, John **7, 35**
Lodge, Thomas **41**
Lovelace, Richard **24**

Lyly, John **41**
Lyttelton, George **10**
Malory, (Sir) Thomas **11**
Manley, (Mary) Delariviere **1, 42**
Marlowe, Christopher **22, 47**
Marston, John **33**
Marvell, Andrew **4, 43**
Middleton, Thomas **33**
Milton, John **9, 43**
Montagu, Mary (Pierrepont) Wortley **9, 57**
More, Henry **9**
More, Sir Thomas **10, 32**
Newton, Isaac **35, 52**
Parnell, Thomas **3**
Pepys, Samuel **11, 58**
Philips, Katherine **30**
Pix, Mary (Griffith) **8**
Pope, Alexander **3, 58**
Prior, Matthew **4**
Raleigh, Sir Walter
Reynolds, Joshua **15**
Richardson, Samuel **1, 44**
Roper, William **10**
Rowe, Nicholas **8**
Sheridan, Frances **7**
Sidney, Mary **19, 39**
Sidney, Sir Philip **19, 39**
Smart, Christopher **3**
Smith, John **9**
Spenser, Edmund **5, 39**
Steele, Richard **18**
Swift, Jonathan **1, 42**
Trotter (Cockburn), Catharine **8**
Vanbrugh, Sir John **21**
Vaughan, Henry **27**
Walpole, Horace **2, 49**
Warton, Thomas **15**
Webster, John **33**
Winstanley, Gerrard **52**
Winthrop, John
Wollstonecraft, Mary **5, 50**
Wroth, Mary **30**
Wycherley, William **8, 21**
Young, Edward **3, 40**

FRENCH

Boileau-Despreaux, Nicolas **3**
Calvin, John **37**
Christine de Pizan **9**
Condillac, Etienne Bonnot de **26**
Corneille, Pierre **28**
Crebillon, Claude Prosper Jolyot de (fils) **1, 28**
Descartes, Rene **20, 35**
Diderot, Denis **26**
Duclos, Charles Pinot **1**
Gassendi, Pierre **54**
Helvetius, Claude-Adrien **26**
Holbach, Paul Henri Thiry Baron **14**
La Bruyere, Jean de **17**
La Fayette, Marie (Madelaine Pioche de la Vergne Comtes) **2**
La Fontaine, Jean de **50**